The Editors

JOEL PORTE was Ernest I. White Professor of American Studies and Humane Letters at Cornell University. He was previously Ernest Bernbaum Professor of Literature at Harvard University. He is the author of *In Respect to Egotism: Studies in American Romantic Writing; Representative Man: Ralph Waldo Emerson in His Time; The Romance in America: Studies in Cooper, Poe, Hawthorne, Melville, and James;* and *Emerson and Thoreau: Transcendentalists in Conflict.* He is editor, with Saundra Morris, of *The Cambridge Companion to Ralph Waldo Emerson.*

SAUNDRA MORRIS is Associate Professor of English and Senior Fellow of the Social Justice College at Bucknell University, where she has taught since 1995. She is editor, with Joel Porte, of *The Cambridge Companion to Ralph Waldo Emerson* and author of articles on various topics in American literature.

W. W. NORTON & COMPANY, INC.
Also Publishes

THE NORTON ANTHOLOGY OF AFRICAN AMERICAN LITERATURE
edited by Henry Louis Gates Jr. and Nellie Y. McKay et al.

THE NORTON ANTHOLOGY OF AMERICAN LITERATURE
edited by Nina Baym et al.

THE NORTON ANTHOLOGY OF CONTEMPORARY FICTION
edited by R. V. Cassill and Joyce Carol Oates

THE NORTON ANTHOLOGY OF ENGLISH LITERATURE
edited by M. H. Abrams and Stephen Greenblatt et al.

THE NORTON ANTHOLOGY OF LITERATURE BY WOMEN
edited by Sandra M. Gilbert and Susan Gubar

THE NORTON ANTHOLOGY OF MODERN POETRY
edited by Richard Ellmann and Robert O'Clair

THE NORTON ANTHOLOGY OF POETRY
edited by Margaret Ferguson, Mary Jo Salter, and Jon Stallworthy

THE NORTON ANTHOLOGY OF SHORT FICTION
edited by R. V. Cassill and Richard Bausch

THE NORTON ANTHOLOGY OF THEORY AND CRITICISM
edited by Vincent B. Leitch et al.

THE NORTON ANTHOLOGY OF WORLD LITERATURE
edited by Sarah Lawall et al.

THE NORTON FACSIMILE OF THE FIRST FOLIO OF SHAKESPEARE
prepared by Charlton Hinman

THE NORTON INTRODUCTION TO LITERATURE
edited by Jerome Beaty, Alison Booth, J. Paul Hunter, and Kelly J. Mays

THE NORTON INTRODUCTION TO THE SHORT NOVEL
edited by Jerome Beaty

THE NORTON READER
edited by Linda H. Peterson, John C. Brereton, and Joan E. Hartman

THE NORTON SAMPLER
edited by Thomas Cooley

THE NORTON SHAKESPEARE, BASED ON THE OXFORD EDITION
edited by Stephen Greenblatt et al.

For a complete list of Norton Critical Editions, visit
www.wwnorton.com/college/english/nce.welcome.htm

A NORTON CRITICAL EDITION

EMERSON'S PROSE AND POETRY

AUTHORITATIVE TEXTS
CONTEXTS
CRITICISM

Selected and Edited by

JOEL PORTE

LATE OF CORNELL UNIVERSITY

SAUNDRA MORRIS

BUCKNELL UNIVERSITY

W • W • NORTON & COMPANY • *New York* • *London*

Copyright © 2001 by W. W. Norton & Company, Inc.

All rights reserved.
Printed in the United States of America.
First Edition.

The text of this book is composed in Electra
with the display set in Bernhard Modern.
Composition by Publishing Synthesis Ltd., New York.
Manufacturing by Courier Companies.
Book design by Antonina Krass.

Library of Congress Cataloging-in-Publication Data

Emerson, Ralph Waldo, 1803–1882.
[Selections. 2000. W.W. Norton]
Emerson's prose and poetry : authoritative texts, contexts, criticism /
selected and edited by Joel Porte, Saundra Morris.
p. cm.—(A Norton critical edition)

ISBN 0-393-96792-1 (pbk).

1. Emerson, Ralph Waldo, 1803–1882—Criticism and interpretation. I. Porte, Joel.
II. Morris, Saundra, 1956–   III. Title

PS1603.P67 2000
814'.3—dc21   00-056879

W. W. Norton & Company, Inc., 500 Fifth Avenue, New York, N.Y. 10110
www.wwnorton.com

W. W. Norton & Company Ltd., Castle House, 75/76 Wells Street, London W1T 3QT

4 5 6 7 8 9 0

Contents

Contexts

Criticism

Preface

As we approach the year 2003—the two hundredth anniversary of Emerson's birth—we are once again challenged to reassess and reimagine his crucial presence in American culture. Emerson has regularly been canonized, decanonized, jettisoned, and recovered, but he will not go away; he does not need, as they say, to be brought back, because he remains an ineluctable voice in American letters. His writings have helped shape literary study, philosophy, politics, social reform, and, indeed—directly or indirectly—how we live our lives almost two centuries after his birth. Emerson's work is particularly appropriate for a Norton Critical Edition, with its strong focus on classroom pedagogy. As our teacher and as one of our prime authors, he charges our schools and colleges to "set the hearts of their youth on flame."

Emerson is a manifestly multivocal author, and which tones of his we hear most clearly depends on who "we" are. Our America of the year 2000 and the readership within it are much different from Emerson's. The nation is heterogeneous and multicultural, and we have an understandable difficulty, especially in educational institutions, deciding which voices speak for "us." But Emerson himself helps us with this question, because his endurance can in part be explained by his paradoxical insistence on telling us not to listen to him—in his always returning us to ourselves. Walt Whitman, among Emerson's many readers and hearers, perhaps most fully absorbed that lesson, so that Emerson's influence led Whitman to sing the "Song of Myself" (which, in turn, he hopes each of us will sing for ourselves). Emerson's "antidisciples" have continued typically to be rebellious adherents—such as Emily Dickinson, who persisted in her "spasmodic" gait despite urgings to the contrary, and Henry Thoreau, who spent his night in jail to Emerson's chagrin, but who would echo Emerson in his own defense. Nonetheless, some scholars argue that Emerson's thought leads us down the dark path of capitalistic self-interest; others insist that the consequence of Emersonian self-reliance is ultimate submission. All these readers have continued to engage Emerson thoughtfully and persistently, whether in devotion or in defiance. And, in fact, Emerson also applied such scrutiny, and readiness to differ, to his own thought, often enacting his dictum that "a foolish consistency is the hobgoblin of little minds, adored by little statesmen and philosophers and divines. With consistency a great soul has simply nothing to do."

Emerson had plenty to do. He lectured, he wrote essays, he composed poetry, he led a full family life, he was an active citizen of Concord, and, increasingly, he played an important role in the social questions and debates of his time. One of the new emphases of Emerson studies that this volume seeks to represent involves how Emerson's imagination was reluctantly but inevitably shaped by current events—by the displacement of the Cherokees, by the slavery question, by myriad reform movements, by the call for greater social, political, and economic justice. Emerson was America's teacher; but he was also

receiving an education in shifting civic realities that we can usefully re-experi-
ence. All of this is to say that our relationship to Emerson can be a fruitfully
vexed—even an argumentative—one. As Irving Howe observes, "Simple Emersonians we can no longer be. We are descendants, through mixed blood, who
have left home after friendly quarrels." Yet, he continues, Emerson's voice "still
rings clear" as that of a "revolutionary of consciousness."

   This is what Emerson seems to have wanted. He insists in his journal, "I
will agitate others, being agitated myself." And agitated by Emerson we have
been. The Norton Critical Edition format is also appropriate for the study of
Emerson precisely because of the rich history of reader response to his work.
We have attempted to represent here what we believe to be the most suggestive
of the many reactions Emerson has provoked throughout the decades and generations. The appearance of this Norton Critical Edition almost one hundred
years after the centenary of Emerson's birth not only pays due homage to his
cultural significance but also acknowledges his continuing presence among
those who care seriously about the tradition of American letters and wish to
transmit that tradition to students and the general reader. The twentieth century, as we know, has been the scene of both great disasters and great developments in the arts and sciences. Emerson certainly would not recognize our
world as the plausible continuation of his own, nor would he have expected to
do so ("Life is a series of surprises, and would not be worth taking or keeping,
if it were not"). Perhaps he would be pleasantly surprised, then, to observe that
we have not left him behind. The second half of the twentieth century, in particular, has seen an impressive outpouring of essays and books on the American
sage. It has also been notable for the devoted work of Emerson scholars. We now
have comprehensive editions of Emerson's journals, of his letters, of his sermons, of his poetry notebooks, and of his topical notebooks. The re-editing of
his lectures and published works continues. Needless to say, this Norton Critical Edition has been able to make use of these one hundred years of labor in
the Emersonian vineyards, and we are happy to acknowledge our debt to the
large number of scholars whose work has made this edition possible. It is work
that challenges us to ask the perennial Emersonian questions: Where do we find
ourselves? and How shall I live?

                                                          JOEL PORTE
                                                          SAUNDRA MORRIS

Acknowledgments

We are grateful to Cornell and Bucknell Universities for providing research funding and released time that has enabled us to complete this project, and to the Houghton Library, Harvard University, for Saundra Morris's receipt of the Stanley J. Kahrl Fellowship in Literary Manuscripts, which provided crucial access to resources. We also thank student research assistants at Cornell, Bucknell, and the University of Nevada Las Vegas for their efforts in behalf of this project: Katey Kuhns Castellano, Diana Leech, Dawn Lonsinger, Molly O'Brien, Sabeth Ryan, and Stacey Waite at Bucknell; Sally Jacob and Janet Shmaryahu at Cornell; and Jeff Strasburg and Pam Cantrell at UNLV. We gratefully acknowledge the work of other Emerson scholars, especially Ronald A. Bosco, Len Gougeon, David W. Hill, Joel Myerson, and the editors of the *Poetry Notebooks*, *The Sermons*, *The Collected Works of Ralph Waldo Emerson*, *The Journals and Miscellaneous Notebooks of Ralph Waldo Emerson*, and the *Topical Notebooks*. We have also depended on the work of Edward Waldo Emerson, William Gilman, Stephen Whicher, Richard Poirier, Harold Bloom, Paul Kane, Nancy Craig Simmons, and Joseph Thomas. For their suggestions regarding the contents of this volume, we thank Albert von Frank, Joseph Thomas, Julie Ellison, Len Gougeon, Roger Gilbert, Paul Gilmore, Bryan Waterman, John Ronan, and our students in seminars at University of Nevada Las Vegas, Bucknell University, and Cornell University. We thank the Houghton Library, Harvard; the Concord Free Public Library, especially Leslie Perrin Wilson, Curator, Special Collections; and the Concord Museum, especially David Wood, Curator, for generous access to Emerson's books and manuscripts, for photographic services, and for permission to print the materials we have included from their archives. We also thank Carol Bemis, of W. W. Norton and Company, for her help and infinite patience. Candace Levy did a heroic job of copyediting our very complex manuscript. We owe particular gratitude to Kristen Hawley of Bucknell University and the Bucknell University Undergraduate Research Fellowship awards program for Kristen's considerable work on this text. We also thank Master Michael Shinagel, of Quincy House, Harvard, and his administrator, Suzanne Watts, for providing housing for Saundra Morris while she worked at the Houghton Library. For various kindnesses, we are indebted to M. H. Abrams, Margaret Emerson Bancroft, Naomi Blanks, William Holzberger, Cynthia Hogue, Robert Morgan, John Rickard, Edgar Rosenberg, Charles Sackrey, Myrna Treston, Stephanie Smith-Waterman, and Carol Wayne White. Finally, we thank our families, Helene, Susanna, and Paige, for their love and continuing support and for once again allowing the sage of Concord to be a member of our households.

A Note on the Texts

In the absence of a complete modern critical edition of Emerson's works, we have drawn our copytexts from a variety of sources and made emendations as we explain here. Emerson's sermons are reproduced from *The Complete Sermons of Ralph Waldo Emerson*, edited by Albert J. von Frank et al. (University of Missouri Press, 1989–92). We print the texts of *Nature* and selected early addresses and lectures from the 1849 volume *Nature; Addresses, and Lectures*. The texts of the essays from *Essays: First Series, Essays: Second Series*, and *Representative Men* are drawn from *The Collected Works of Ralph Waldo Emerson*, edited by Robert Spiller et al. (Harvard University Press, 1971–). For essays from *The Conduct of Life* we use first edition texts with corrections and emendations. The text of "Thoreau" is drawn from the "Biographical Sketch" in Thoreau's *Excursions* (1863), its first book publication and the only time Emerson himself included that piece in a book. The addresses "Abraham Lincoln" and "Historic Notes of Life and Letters in New England" are reprinted from *The Complete Works of Ralph Waldo Emerson*, edited by Edward Waldo Emerson (Centenary Edition, 1903–04). Essays from *The Dial* are printed from the original publication. The texts of "Letter to Martin Van Buren," "Address . . . on . . . the Emancipation of the Negroes in the British West Indies," and "Address to the Citizens of Concord on the Fugitive Slave Law" are drawn, with corrections, from Len Gougeon and Joel Myerson's *Emerson's Antislavery Writings* (Yale University Press, 1995). The selections from *Memoirs of Margaret Fuller Ossoli* are reprinted from the original edition (1852). We print Emerson's poems with texts prepared as explained in the headnote to the poetry. In the case of Emerson's two late compositions, "Poetry and Imagination" and "Quotation and Originality," editorial options are less than satisfactory. The latter piece, delivered as a lecture in 1859 and published in *The North American Review* in 1868, has been known for almost a hundred years in the Centenary version Edward Waldo Emerson prepared for the volume *Letters and Social Aims*. The same is true of "Poetry and Imagination," which was not published previously in a periodical and has a more complex history. It first appeared, along with "Quotation and Originality," in the 1876 Riverside Edition of *Letters and Social Aims* mainly prepared by Ellen Emerson and James Elliot Cabot but, it seems, without the extensive intervention by Emerson characteristic of *Selected Poems* of 1876 (see headnote to "Selected Poetry"). Because the 1876 Riverside Edition texts bear questionable authority, contain errors, and lack the cultural currency enjoyed by Edward Waldo Emerson's Centenary Edition versions, we reproduce the latter, which will presumably be superseded by modern critical texts produced in forthcoming volumes of the Harvard *Collected Works*. Emerson's journal entries are printed from *Journals and Miscellaneous Notebooks of Ralph Waldo Emerson*, edited by William Gilman et al. (Harvard University Press, 1961–82), with corrections. Emerson's letters are drawn, with corrections, from Ralph L. Rusk and Eleanor M. Tilton's *The Letters of Ralph Waldo Emerson* (Columbia University Press, 1939—95) as well as from Joseph Slater's *Correspondence of Emerson and Carlyle* (Columbia University Press, 1964).

Abbreviations

CS   *Complete Sermons of Ralph Waldo Emerson.* Edited by Albert J. von Frank et al. 4 vols. Columbia: U of Missouri P, 1989–92.

CW   *The Collected Works of Ralph Waldo Emerson.* Edited by Robert Spiller, et al. 5 vols. to date. Cambridge, Mass.: Belknap P of Harvard UP, 1971–.

EAW   *Emerson's Antislavery Writings.* Edited by Len Gougeon and Joel Myerson. New Haven, Conn.: Yale UP, 1995.

EJ   *Emerson in His Journals.* Edited by Joel Porte. Cambridge, Mass.: Belknap P of Harvard UP, 1982.

EL   *The Early Lectures of Ralph Waldo Emerson.* Edited by Stephen Whicher et al. 3 vols. Cambridge, Mass.: Belknap P of Harvard UP, 1960–72.

JMN   *The Journals and Miscellaneous Notebooks of Ralph Waldo Emerson.* Edited by William Gilman et al. 16 vols. Cambridge, Mass.: Belknap P of Harvard UP, 1960–82.

L   *The Letters of Ralph Waldo Emerson.* Edited by Ralph L. Rusk and Eleanor M. Tilton. 10 vols. New York: Columbia UP, 1939–95.

PN   *The Poetry Notebooks of Ralph Waldo Emerson.* Edited by Ralph H. Orth et al. Columbia: U of Missouri P, 1986.

RE   *Poems.* Vol. 9. Riverside ed. Boston: Houghton Mifflin, 1884.

SP   *Selected Poems.* New and rev. ed. Boston: James R. Osgood & Co., 1876.

W   *The Complete Works of Ralph Waldo Emerson.* Edited by Edward Waldo Emerson. 12 vols. Centenary ed. Boston: Houghton Mifflin, 1903–04.

The Texts of
EMERSON'S PROSE
AND POETRY

Sermons[†]

I

Pray without ceasing.[1]

I THESSALONIANS 5:17

It is the duty of men to judge men only by their actions. Our faculties furnish us with no means of arriving at the motive, the character, the secret self. We call the tree good from its fruits, and the man, from his works. Since we have no power, we have no right, to assign for the actions of our neighbor any other than those motives which ought in similar circumstances to guide our own. But because *we* are not able to discern the processes of thought, to see the soul — it were very ridiculous to doubt or deny that any beings can. It is not incredible, that, the thoughts of the mind are the subjects of perception to some beings, as properly, as the sounds of the voice, or the motions of the hand are to us. Indeed, every man's feeling may be appealed to on this question, whether the idea, that other beings can read his thoughts, has not appeared so natural and probable, that he has checked sometimes a train of thoughts that seemed too daring or indecent, for any unknown beholders to be trusted with.

It ought to be distinctly felt by us that we stand in the midst of two worlds, the world of matter and the world of spirit. Our bodies belong to one; our thoughts to the other. It has been one of the best uses of the Christian religion to teach, that the world of spirits is more certain and stable than the material universe. Every thoughtful man has felt, that there was a more awful reality to thought and feeling, than to the infinite panorama of nature around him. The world he has found indeed consistent and uniform enough throughout the mixed sensations of thirty or forty years, but it seems to him at times, when the intellect is invigorated, to ebb from him, like a sea, and to leave nothing permanent but thought. Nevertheless it is a truth not easily nor early acquired, and the prejudice that assigns greater fixture and certainty to the material world is a source of great practical error. I need hardly remind you of the great points of this error. I need not ask you if the objects that every day are the cause of the greatest number of steps taken, of the greatest industry of the hands and the feet, the heart and the head, are the perishable things of sense, or the imperishable things of the soul; whether all this stir from day to day, from hour to hour of all this mighty multitude, is to ascertain some question dear to the understanding

† Reprinted by permission of the Ralph Waldo Emerson Memorial Association.
1. Completed and dated July 25, 1826. Preached fourteen times between 1826 and 1828. We have incorporated some annotation from CS. We have not in every case annotated Emerson's copious allusions, especially his many biblical echoes. We also do not typically note the minor ways in which Emerson's citations (presumably from memory, and in many cases from secondary sources) differ from the originals, as they often do. The biblical text appears in a letter of advice by Paul (5?–67? C.E.), Christian apostle to the Gentiles, written to the early church at Thessalonica, a city in what is now Greece.

3

concerning the nature of God, the true Constitution and destination of the human soul, the proper balance of the faculties and the proper office of each; or (what of immortal thought comes nearer to practical value) whether all men are eagerly intent to study the best systems of education for themselves and their children? Is it not rather the great wonder of all who think enough to wonder that almost all that sits near the heart, all that colours the countenance, and engrosses conversation at the family board are these humble things of mortal date, and in the history of the universe absolutely insignificant? Is it not outside shews, the pleasures of appetite, or at best of pride; is it not bread and wine and dress, and our houses, and our furniture, that give the law to the great mass of actions and words? This is the great error which the strong feeling of the reality of things unseen must correct. It is time greater force should be given to the statement of this doctrine; it is time men should be instructed that their inward is more valuable than their outward estate; that thoughts and passions, even those to which no language is ever given, are not fugitive undefined shadows, born in a moment, and in a moment blotted from the soul, but are so many parts of the imperishable universe of morals; they should be taught that they do not think *alone*; that when they retreat from the public eye and hide themselves to conceal in solitude guilty recollections or guilty wishes, the great congregation of moral natures, the spirits of just men made perfect; angels and arch-angels; the Son of God, and the Father everlasting, open their eyes upon them and speculate on these clandestine meditations.

I. The necessary inference from these reflexions, is the fact which gives them all their importance, and is the doctrine I am chiefly anxious to inculcate. It is not only when we audibly and in form, address our petitions to the Deity, that we pray. We pray without ceasing. Every secret wish is a prayer. Every house is a church, the corner of every street is a closet of devotion. There is no rhetoric, let none deceive himself; there is no rhetoric in this. There *is* delusion of the most miserable kind, in that fiction on which the understanding pleads to itself its own excuse, when it knows not God and is thoughtless of him. I mean that outward respect, that is paid to the name and worship of God, whilst the thoughts and the actions are enlisted in the service of sin. 'I will not swear by God's name,' says the wary delinquent; 'I will not ask him to lend his aid to my fraud, to my lewdness, to my revenge; nor will I even give discountenance to the laws I do not myself observe. I will not unmask my villany to the world, that I should stand in the way of others, more scrupulous, nay, better than I.'

And is it by this paltry counterfeit of ignorance that you would disguise from yourselves the truth? And will you really endeavour to persuade yourself, that, God is such an one as you yourself, and will be amused by professions, and may, by fraudulent language, be kept out of the truth? Is it possible, that men of discretion in common affairs, can think so grossly? Do you not know that the knowledge of God is perfect and immense; that it breaks down the fences of presumption, and the arts of hypocrisy; that night, and artifice, and time, and the grave, are naked before it; that the deep gives up its dead, that the gulfs of Chaos are disembowelled before him; that the minds of men are not so much independent existences, as they are ideas present to the mind of God; that he is not so much the observer of your actions, as he is the potent principle by which they are bound together; not so much the reader of your thoughts, as the active Creator by whom they are aided into being; and, casting away the deceptive subterfuges of language, and speaking with strict philosophical truth, that every faculty is but a mode of his action; that your reason is God, your virtue is God, and nothing but your liberty, can you call securely and absolutely your own?

Since, then, we are thus, by the inevitable law of our being, surrendered unreservedly to the unsleeping observation of the Divinity, we cannot shut our eyes to the conclusion, that, *every desire of the human mind, is a prayer uttered to God and registered in heaven.*

II. The next fact of sovereign importance in this connexion is, that *our prayers are granted.* Upon the account I have given of prayer, this ulterior fact is a faithful consequence. What then! if I pray that fire shall fall from heaven to consume mine enemies, will the lightning come down? If I pray that the wealth of India may be piled in my coffers, shall I straightway become rich? If I covet my neighbor's beauty, or wit, or honourable celebrity,—will these desirable advantages be at once transferred from being the sources of his happiness, to become the sources of mine? It is plain there is a sense in which this is not true. But it is equally undeniable that in the sense in which I have explained the nature of prayer, and which seems the only proper sense, the position is universally true. For those are not prayers, which begin with the ordinary appellatives of the Deity and end with his son's name, and a ceremonial word—those are not prayers, if they utter no one wish of our hearts, no one real and earnest affection, but are formal repetitions of sentiments taken at second hand, in words the supple memory has learned of fashion; O my friends, these are not prayers, but mockeries of prayers. But the true prayers are the daily, hourly, momentary desires, that come without impediment, without fear, into the soul, and bear testimony at each instant to its shifting character. And these prayers are granted.

For is it not clear that what we strongly and earnestly desire we shall make every effort to obtain; and has not God so furnished us with powers of body and of mind that we can acquire whatsoever we seriously and unceasingly strive after?

For it is the very root and rudiment of the relation of man to this world, that we are in a condition of wants which have their appropriate gratifications *within our reach*; and that we have faculties which can bring us to our ends; that we are full of capacities that are near neighbors to their objects, and our free agency consists in this, that we are able to reach those sources of gratification, on which our election falls. And if this be so, will not he who thinks lightly of all other things in comparison with riches; who thinks little of the poor man's virtue, or the slave's misery as they cross his path in life, because his observant eye is fixed on the rich man's manners and is searching in the lines of his countenance, with a sort of covetousness, the tokens of a pleased contemplation of the goods he has in store, and the consideration that, on this account, is conceded to him in society; will not such an one, if his thoughts daily point towards this single hope, if no exertion is grateful to him which has not this for its aim; if the bread is bitter to him that removes his riches one day farther from his hand, and the friends barren of comfort to him that are not aiding to this dishonourable ambition;—will not such an one arrive at the goal, such as it is, of his expectation and find, sooner or later, a way to the heaven where he has garnered up his heart? Assuredly he will.

And will not the votary of other lusts, the lover of animal delight, who is profuse of the joys of sense, who loveth meats and drinks, soft raiment and the wine when it moveth itself aright, and giveth its colour in the cup; or the more offensive libertine who has no relish left for any sweet in moral life, but only waits opportunity to surrender himself over to the last damning debauchery; will not these petitioners who have knocked so loudly at heaven's doors, receive what they have so importunately desired? Assuredly they will. There is a commission to nature, there is a charge to the elements made out in the name of the Author of events, whereby they shall help the purposes of man, a pre-existent harmony between thoughts and things whereby prayers shall become effects, and these warm imaginations settle down into events.

And if there be, in this scene of things, any spirit of a different complexion, who has felt, in the recesses of his soul, "how awful goodness is, and virtue in her own shape how lovely,"[2] who has admired the excellence of others, and set himself by precepts of the wise, and by imitation, which, a wise man said, is 'a globe of precepts,'[3] to assimilate himself to the model, or to surpass the uncertain limit of human virtue, and found no model in the Universe, beneath God, level with his venerated idea of virtue; who looks with scorn at the cheap admiration of crowds, and loves the applause of good men, but values more his own; and has so far outstripped humanity, that he can appreciate the love of the Supreme; if he aspire to do signal service to mankind, by the rich gift of a good example, and by unceasing and sober efforts to instruct and benefit men; will this man wholly fail, and waste his requests on the wind? Assuredly he will not. His prayers, in a certain sense, are like the will of the Supreme Being:

> "His word leaps forth to its effect at once,
> He calls for things that are not, and they come."[4]

His prayers are granted; all prayers are granted. Unceasing endeavours always attend true prayers, and, by the law of the Universe, unceasing endeavours do not fail of their end.

Let me not be misunderstood as thinking lightly of the positive duty of stated seasons of prayer. That solemn service of man to his maker is a duty of too high authority and too manifest importance to excuse any indifference to its claims. It is because that privilege is abused, because men in making prayers forget the purpose of prayer, forget that praying is to make them leave off sinning, that I urge it in its larger extent when it enters into daily life.

I have attempted to establish two simple positions, that, we are always praying, and that it is the order of Providence in the world, that our prayers should be granted. If exceptions can be quoted to me out of the book of common life, to the universality of either of these doctrines, I shall admit them in their full force, nor shall I now detain you by any inquiry into the abstract metaphysical nature of that happiness human beings are permitted to derive from what are called possessions, and how far it belongs to the imagination. I shall content myself, at present, with having stated the general doctrine and with adverting to its value as a practical principle.

And certainly, my friends, it is not a small thing that we have learned. If we have distinctly apprehended the fact which I have attempted to set in its true

---

2. From *Paradise Lost* 4.8.47–48, by John Milton (1608–1674), English poet, essayist, and scholar who is best known for the epic poem *Paradise Lost* (1667), an account of humanity's fall from grace.
3. From "Of Great Place," an essay by Francis Bacon (1561–1626), English philosopher, essayist, scientist, and politician.
4. Quoted without attribution in *Inquiry into the Relation of Cause and Effect*, a treatise by Thomas Brown (1778–1820), Scottish philosopher.

light, it cannot fail to elevate very much our conception of our relations and our duties. Weep no more for human frailty, weep no more, for what there may be of sorrow in the past or of despondency in the present hour. Spend no more unavailing regrets for the goods of which God in his Providence has deprived you. Cast away this sickly despair that eats into the soul debarred from high events and noble gratification. Beware of easy assent to false opinion, to low employment, to small vices, out of a reptile reverence to men of consideration in society. Beware, (if it teach nothing else let it teach this) beware of indolence, the suicide of the soul, that lets the immortal faculties, each in their orbit of light, wax dim and feeble, and star by star expire. — These considerations let our doctrine enforce. Weep not for man's frailty—for if the might of Omnipotence has made the elements obedient to the fervency of his daily prayers, he is no puny sufferer tottering, ill at ease, in the Universe, but a being of giant energies, architect of his fortunes, master of his eternity. Weep not for the past; for this is duration over which the secret virtue of prayer is powerless, over which the Omnipotence of God is powerless; send no voice of unprofitable wailing back into the depths of time; for prayer can reverse in the future the events of the past. Weep not for your wasted possessions, for the immeasurable future is before you and the wealth of the Universe invites your industry. Nor despair that your present daily lot is lowly, nor succumb to the shallow understanding or ill example of men whose worldly lot is higher. Be not deceived; for what is the Past? It is nothing worth. Its value, except as means of wisdom, is, in the nature of things actually nothing. And what is the imposing present? what are the great men and great things that surround you? All that they can do for you is dust, and less than dust to what you can do for yourself. They are like you stretching forward to an infinite hope, the citizens in trust of a future world. They think little of the present; though they seem satisfied, they are not satisfied but repine and endeavour after greater good. They, like you, are born to live when the sun has gone down in darkness and the moon is turned to blood.

My friends, in the remarks that have just been made I have already in part anticipated the third great branch of our subject, which is that *our prayers are written in Heaven.*

III. The great moral doctrines we have attempted to teach would be of limited worth if there were no farther consideration in this series of thought. You are pleased with the acquisition of property; you pray without ceasing to become rich. You lay no tax of conscience on the means. You desire to become rich by dint of virtue or of vice; of force or of fraud. And in virtue of the order of things that prevails in the world, as I have stated, you come to your ends. Is this all? Is the design of Providence complete? Is there no conclusion to this train of events, thus far conducted?

The wicked has flourished up to his hope. He has ground the faces of the poor. He has the tears of the widow and the curse of the fatherless but they lie light on his habitation; for he has builded his house where these cannot come, in the midst of his broad lands, on a pleasant countryside, sheltered by deep ornamental woods, and the voices of the harp and the viol tinkle in his saloons; the gay and the grave, the rich and the fair swarm to him in crowds and though they salute him and smile often upon him they do not utter one syllable of reproach nor repeat one imprecation of the poor. But far away, too far to be any impediment to his enjoyment, the wretches he has cruelly stripped of their last decent comforts, and the well-saved means with which sinking poverty yet strives to bear up, and make a respectable appearance in society,—are now, in small unaccommodated tenements, eating a morsel of bread, and uttering in unvisited, unremembered solitude, the name of the oppressor. And have we seen all, my friends, and is poor struggling worth to be rewarded only with worth, and be poor and vile besides, and is Vice to go triumphing on to the grave? Aye; to the grave. Hitherto, shalt thou go, and no farther, and here shall thy proud waves be staid.[5] My friends, there is another world. After death there is life. After death in another state, revives your capacity of pleasure and of pain, the evil memory of evil actions, revives yourself, the man within the breast, the gratified petitioner in the exact condition to which his fulfilled desires have, by the inevitable force of things, contracted or expanded his character. There is another world; a world of remuneration; a world to which you and I are going and which it deeply behoves us to survey and scrutinize as faithfully as we can, as it lies before us, "though shadows, clouds, and darkness rest upon it." It is plain that *as* we die in this world, we shall be born into that. It is plain, that, it is, if it be any thing, a world of spirits; that body, and the pleasures and pains appertaining to body can have no exercise, no mansion there; that it can be the appropriate home only of high thought and noble virtue. Hence it must happen, that, if a soul can have access to that ethereal society, fleshed over with bodily appetites, in which no love has grown up of thought and moral beauty, and no sympathy and worship of virtue, but in their place gnawing lusts have coiled themselves with a serpent's trail into the place of every noble affection that God set up in the recesses of the soul when he balanced the parts and modulated the harmony of the whole. And these pampered appetites that grew in the soil of this world, find no aliment for them in heaven, no gaudy vanities of dress, no riotous excitement of song and dances, no filthy gluttony of meats and drinks, no unclean enjoyments, finding none of all this, it must happen, that these appetites will turn upon their master, in the shape of direst tormentors; and if the economy of the universe provide no natural issue, whereby these mortal impurities can be purged with fire out of the texture of the soul, they must continue from hour to hour, from age to age, to arm the principles of his nature against the happiness of man.

Of this mysterious eternity, about to open upon us, of the nature of its employments and our relation to it, we know little. But of one thing be certain, that if the analogies of time can teach aught of eternity, if the moral laws taking place in this world, have relation to those of the next, and even the forecasting sagacity of the Pagan philosopher taught him that the Laws below were sisters of the Laws above,—then the riches of the future are dealt out on a system of compensations.[6] That great class of human beings who in every age turned aside from temptation to pursue the bent of moral nature shall now have *their* interests consulted. They have cast their bread on the waters, (for the choice lay often between virtue and their bread), trusting that after many days a solemn retribution of good should be rendered to them in the face of the world. Insult and sorrow, rags and beggary they have borne; they have kept the faith though they dwelled in the dust, and now, the pledge of God that supported them in the trial

5. Job 38.11.
6. *Compensation* remained an important term and concept for Emerson; cf. his essay "Compensation" (p. 137) in his first series of essays. *Pagan philosopher:* Socrates (470?–399 B.C.E.), Greek philosopher who initiated a question and answer method of teaching as a means of achieving self-knowledge. His theories of virtue and justice have survived through the writings of Plato, his most important pupil. Socrates was tried for corrupting the minds of Athenian youth and subsequently put to death.

must be redeemed, and shall be, to the wonder of themselves, through the furthest periods of their undying existence.

Their joy and triumph is that revelation of the gospel which is most emphatically enforced by images borrowed from whatever was most grand and splendid in the imaginations of men; but crowns and thrones of judgment, and purple robes are but poor shadows of that moral magnificence, with which in the company of souls disembodied, Virtue asserts its majesty, and becomes the home and fountain of unlimited happiness.

Nothing remains but the obligation there is on each of us to make what use we can of this momentous doctrine. Is it to another condition than yours, to some removed mode of life, to the vices of some other class of society that this preaching, with strict propriety, belongs? No, my friends, if you are of the great household of God; if you are distinguishers of good and evil; if you believe in your own eternity; if you are tempted by what you feel to be evil attractions; if you are mortal,—it belongs to you. If you have ever felt a desire for what Conscience, God's vicegerent, enthroned within you, condemned; if impelled by that desire, and wilfully deaf to that condemnation, you swerved towards the gratification, and obtained the object, and stifled the monitor—then it is you, and not another; then you have uttered these unseemly prayers; the prayer is granted and is written in heaven; and at this moment, though men are not privy to all the passages of your life, and will salute you respectfully, and though it may be your own violated memory has ceased to treasure heedfully the number of your offences—yet every individual transgression has stamped its impress on your character, and moral beings in all the wide tracts of God's dominion and God over all fasten their undeceived eyes on this spectacle of moral ruin. To you therefore it belongs, to every one who now hears me, to look anxiously to his ways; to look less at his outward demeanour, his general plausible action, but *to cleanse his thoughts.* The heart, the heart is pure or impure, and out of it, are the issues of life and of DEATH.

XXXIX

*The day is thine, the night also is thine: thou hast prepared the
light, and the sun. Thou hast set all the borders of the earth,
thou hast made summer.*

PSALMS 74:16–17[1]

In this grateful season, the most careless eye is caught by the beauty of the external world. The most devoted of the sons of gain cannot help feeling that there is pleasure in the blowing of the southwest wind; that the green tree with its redundant foliage and its fragrant blossoms shows fairer than it did a few weeks since when its arms were naked and its trunk was sapless. The inhabitants of cities pay a high tax for their social advantages, their increased civilization, in their exclusion from the sight of the unlimited glory of the earth. Imprisoned in

1. Manuscript dated June 13, 1829. Preached three times between 1829 and 1837. Emerson drew heavily on a few sermons for later compositions. This particular work is closely related to his most famous sermon/address, the summer of 1838 "Address" to the Harvard Divinity School graduating class (p. 69), which begins "In this refulgent summer, it has been a luxury to draw the breath of life."

streets of brick and stone, in tainted air and hot and dusty corners they only get glimpses of the glorious sun, of the ever changing glory of the clouds, of the firmament, and of the face of the green pastoral earth which the great Father of all is now adorning with matchless beauty as one wide garden. Still something of the mighty process of vegetation forces itself on every human eye. The grass springs up between the pavements at our feet and the poplar and the elm send out as vigorous and as graceful branches to shade and to fan the town as in their native forest.

Those who yield themselves to these pleasant influences behold in the activity of vegetation a new expression from moment to moment of the Divine power and goodness. They know that this excellent order did not come of itself, that this organized creation of every new year indicates the presence of God.

We are confident children, confident in God's goodness. Though we all of us know that the year's subsistence to us depends on the fidelity with which rain and sun shall act on the seed, we never doubt the permanence of the Order. We do not refer our own subsistence, especially in cities, to the rain and the sun and the soil. We do not refer the loaf in our basket, or the meats that smoke on our board to the last harvest. And when we do, we fail often to derive from the changes of nature that lesson which to a pious, to a Christian, mind, they ought to convey.

My brethren, all nature is a book on which one lesson is written, and blessed are the eyes that can read it. On the glorious sky it is writ in characters of fire; on earth it is writ in the majesty of the green ocean; it is writ on the volcanoes of the south, and the icebergs of the polar sea; on the storm, in winter; in summer on every trembling leaf; on man in the motion of the limbs, and the changing expression of the face, in all his dealings, in all his language it is seen, and may be read and pondered and practised in all. This lesson is the omnipresence of God—the presence of a love that is tender and boundless. Yet man shuts his eyes to this sovereign goodness, thinks little of the evidence that comes from nature, and looks upon the great system of the world only in parcels as its order happens to affect his petty interest. In the seasons he thinks only whether a rain or sunshine will suit his convenience. In the regions of the world he thinks only of his farm or his town. Let us lift up our eyes to a more generous and thankful view of the earth and the Seasons.

Do they not come from Heaven and go like Angels round the globe scattering hope and pleasant toil and recompense and rest? Each righting the seeming disorders, supplying the defects which the former left; converting its refuse into commodity and drawing out of the ancient earth new treasures to swell the capital of human comfort. Each fulfils the errand on which it was sent. The faintness and despondence of a spring that never opened into summer; the languor of a constant summer; the satiety of an unceasing harvest; the torpor or the terror of a fourfold winter are not only prevented by the ordination of Providence, but they are not feared; and emotions of an opposite character are called forth as we hail the annual visits of these friendly changes at once too familiar to surprize and too distinct and distant to weary us. It is in these as they come and go, that we may recognize the steps of our heavenly Father. We may accustom our minds to discern his power and benevolence in the profusion and the beauty of his common gifts, as the wheat and the vine. Nor do these seem sufficiently appreciated. We look at the works of human art—a pyramid, a stately church, and do not conceal our pleasure and surprise at the skill and force of men to lift such masses and to create such magnificent forms, which skill after all does but remove, combine, and shape the works of God. For the granite, and the marble, and the hands that hewed them from the quarry, are his work. But after they are builded, and the scaffolding is thrown down, and they stand in strength and beauty, there is more exquisite art goes to the formation of a strawberry than is in the costliest palace that human pride has ever reared. In the constitution of that small fruit is an art that eagle eyed science cannot explore, but sits down baffled. It cannot detect how the odour is formed and lodged in these minute vessels, or where the delicate life of the fruit resides.

Our patient science explores, as it can, every process, opens its microscopes upon every fibre, and hunts every globule of sap that ascends in the stem, but it never has detected the secret it seeks. It cannot restore the vegetable it has dissected and analyzed. Where should we go for an ear of corn if the earth refused her increase? With all our botany how should we transform a seed into an ear, or make from the grain of one stalk the green promise and the full harvest that covers acres with its sheaves. The frequency of occurrence makes it expected that a little kernel, properly sowed, will become at harvest time a great number of kernels. Because we have observed the same result on many trials, this multiplication is expected. But explain to me, man of learning! any part of this productiveness. There is no tale of metamorphosis in poetry, no fabulous transformation that children read in the Arabian Tales[2] more unaccountable, none so benevolent, as this constant natural process which is going on at this moment in every garden, in every foot of vacant land in three zones of the globe.

Go out into a garden and examine a seed; examine the same plant in the bud and in the fruit, and you must confess the whole process a miracle, a perpetual miracle. Take it at any period, make yourself as familiar with all the facts as you can, at each period, and in each explanation, there will be some step or appearance to be referred directly to the great Creator; something not the effect of the sower's deposit, nor of the waterer's hope. It is not the loam, nor the gravel, it is not the furrow of the ploughshare nor the glare of the sun that calls greenness from the dust, it is the present power of Him who said 'Seedtime and harvest shall not fail.'[3] Needs there, my brethren, any other book than this returning summer that reminds us of the first creation to suggest the presence of God? Shall we indulge our querulous temper in this earth where nature is fragrant with healthful odours and glowing with every pleasant colour? Man marks with emphatic pleasure or complaint the pleasant and the unpleasant days, as if he forgot the uses of the storm, the masses of vapour it collects and scatters over thirsty soils and the plants that were hardened or moistened by the rough weather, forgot the ships that were borne homeward by the breeze that chills him, or in short, as if he forgot that our Father is in Heaven, and the winds and the seas obey him.

We have been looking at nature as an exhibition of God's benevolence. It will be felt the more to be so when it is considered that *the same results might have been brought about without this beauty*. The earth contains abundant materials for the nourishment of the human stomach, but they do not exist there in a state proper for our use. Now the tree, the vegetable, may be properly considered as a machine by which the nutritious matter is separated from other el-

---

2. *Arabian Nights Entertainments* or *The Thousand and One Nights*, collection of Indian, Persian, and Arabic folk tales (dating from ca. 1450) told by the fictive Scheherazade.
3. Genesis 8.22; part of God's postdiluvian covenant with Noah.

ements, is taken up out of chalk, and clay, and manures, and prepared as by a culinary process into grateful forms and delicious flavours for the pleasure of our taste and for our sustenance. The little seed of the apple does not contain the large tree that shall spring from it; it is merely an assimilating engine which has the power to take from the ground whatever particles of water or manure it needs, and turn them to its own substance and give them its own arrangement.

For the nourishment of animal life this process goes on, and to such incomputable activity and extent, not in one spot, not in one land, but on the whole surface of the globe. Each soil is finishing its own, and each a different fruit. Not only on the hard soil of New England, the oak, the potato and the corn are swelling their fruit, but on the shores of the Red Sea[4] the coffee tree is ripening its berries; on the hills of France and Spain the grape is gathering sweetness. The West Indies are covered with the green canes and the East with spices—and the mulberries for the silk worm. The cotton plant is bursting its pod in the warm plantations of the south, and the orange and the fig bloom in the mediterranean islands.

But all this food might have been prepared as well without this glorious show. To what end this unmeasured magnificence? It is for the soul of man. For his eye the harvest waves, for him the landscape wears this glorious show. For to what end else can it be! Can the wheat admire its own tasselled top? or the oak in autumn its crimson foliage, or the rose and the lily their embroidery? If there were no mind in the Universe, to what purpose this profusion of design? It is adapted to give pleasure to us. I cannot behold the cheering beauty of a country landscape at this season without believing that it was intended that I should derive from it this pleasure. It is for the same reason as the rainbow is beautiful and the sun is bright.

But there is more in nature than beauty; there is more to be seen than the outward eye perceives; there is more to be heard than the pleasant rustle of the corn. There is the language of its everlasting analogies by which it seems to be the prophet and the monitor of the race of man. The Scripture is always appealing to the tree and the flower and the grass as the emblems[5] of our mortal estate. It was the history of man in the beginning, and it is the history of man now. Man is like the flower of the field. In the morning he is like grass that groweth up; in the Evening he is cut down and withereth.[6] There is nothing in external nature but is an emblem, a hieroglyphic of some thing in us. Youth is the Spring, and manhood the Summer, and age the Autumn, and Death the Winter of Man. My brethren, do you say these things are old and trite? that is their very value and warning; so is the harvest old—the apple that hangs on your tree, six thousand times has shown its white bloom, its green germ, and its ripening yellow since our period of the world begins. And this day, as the fruit is as fresh, so is its moral as fresh and significant to us as it was to Adam in the garden.

I have spoken of the great system of external nature as exciting in our minds the perception of the benevolence of God by the wonderful contrivance their fruits exhibit; by the food they furnish us, and by the beauty that is added to them; and now, of the admonition they seem intended to convey of our short life.

4. Located between northeast Africa and the Arabian Peninsula.
5. Emerson's use of *emblems* here and throughout his writings suggests Renaissance emblem books, in which an allegorical picture was followed by an epigraph and a short poem of elaboration.
6. Psalm 90.5–6.

But there is yet a louder and more solemn admonition which they convey to my mind as they do from year to year their appointed work. They speak to man as a moral being, and reproach his lassitude by their brute fidelity. Here we sit waiting the growing of the grain, with an undoubting reliance. If it is blasted in one field, we are sure it will thrive in another. Yet we know that if one harvest of the earth fails, the race must perish from the face of the earth. We have an expectation always of the proper performance of the vegetable functions that would not be increased if one rose from the dead.

Well, now, whilst thus directly we depend on this process on the punctuality of the sun, on the timely action of saps and seed vessels, and rivers and rains, *are we as punctual to our orbit?* Are we as trustworthy as the weed at our feet? Yet is that a poor machine—and I, besides the animal machinery that is given me, have been entrusted with a portion of the spirit that governs the material Creation, that made and directs the machinery.—Are ye not much better than they?

Shall we to whom the light of the Almighty has been given, shall we who have been raised in the scale of the Creation to the power of self government, not govern ourselves? shall the flower of the field reprove us and make it clear that it had been better for us to have wanted than to have received intelligence?

My friends, let us accustom ourselves thus to look at the fruits of the earth and the seasons of the year. Let all that we see without, only turn our attention with stricter scrutiny on all that is within us. In the beautiful order of the world, shall man alone, the highly endowed inhabitant, present a spectacle of disorder, the misrule of the passions, and rebellion against the laws of his Maker? Let us learn also the lesson they are appointed to teach of trust in God; that he will provide for us if we do his will; remembering the words of the Lord Jesus, who said—"If God so clothe the grass of the field, which today is and tomorrow is cast into the oven, will he not much more care for you, o ye of little faith!"[7]

XC

For what is a man profited, if he gain the whole world and lose his own soul?[1]

MATTHEW 16:26

All the instructions which religion addresses to man imply a supposition of the utmost importance, which is, that every human mind is capable of receiving and acting upon these sublime principles. That which is made for an immortal life must be of an infinite nature. That which is taught that its daily duty lies in overcoming the pleasures of sense, and in being superior to all the shows and powers of this world, must indeed have something real and noble in its own possessions. And that which can sustain such relations to God as will justify the uniform language of the Scripture in speaking of good men must have costly and

7. Cf. Matthew 6.30 and Luke 12.28; Jesus to his disciples.
1. Delivered four times, as both sermon and lecture, between October 1830 and November 1837; precursor of Emerson's 1841 essay "Self-Reliance" (p. 120). The biblical text is a question posed rhetorically by Jesus to his disciples.

venerable attributes. It is no small trust to have the keeping of a soul. And compared with their capacity men are not such as they ought to be.

It is the effect of religion to produce a higher self-respect, a greater confidence in what God has done for each of our minds than is commonly felt among men. It seems to me, brethren, that a great calamity with which men are contending after all the preaching of Christianity is their distrust of themselves. They do not know, because they have not tried, the spiritual force that belongs to them. If a man has a soul, he has an infinite spiritual estate, he has a responsibility that is tremendous, simply in the view of the duration of its being; but far more so in the view of its nature and connexions.

If God has made us with such intention as revelation discloses, then it must be that there are in each of us all the elements of moral and intellectual excellence, that is to say, if you act out yourself, you will attain and exhibit a perfect character. Our Saviour, in the confidence of all the worth which his instructions supposed in human nature, says to his disciples, What is a man profited though he gain the whole world, and lose his own soul? The lesson that may be gathered from this scripture, is, to value our own souls, to have them in such estimation as never to offend them, and this is the theme of the present discourse. I wish to enforce the doctrine that a man should trust himself; should have a perfect confidence that there is no defect or inferiority in his nature; that when he discovers in himself different powers, or opinions, or manners, from others whom he loves and respects, he should not think himself in that degree inferior, but only different; and that for every defect there is probably some compensation[2] provided in his system, and that wherever there is manifest imperfection in his character, it springs from his own neglect to cultivate some part of his mind. I am afraid of this great tendency to uniformity of action and conversation among men. I am afraid of the great evil done to so sacred a property as a man's own soul by an imitation arising out of an unthinking admiration of others. I believe God gave to every man the germ of a peculiar character.

The ends of action are the same, but the means and the manner are infinitely various. As every man occupies a position in some respects singular, every man has probably thoughts that never entered the mind of any other man. Cast your thoughts round upon your different acquaintances, and see if any two present the same character to your imagination. And the more finished the character the more striking is its individuality. And the better is the state of the world, the more unlike will be men's characters, and the more similar their purposes. If you name over men that have the most decided greatness you will find that they present very dissimilar ideas to your thought. Abraham, Moses, Socrates, Milton, Fenelon,[3] these are all eminently good men yet how wholly unlike.

But instead of society's exhibiting this striking variety of mind there may be noticed everywhere a tame resemblance of one man's thoughts and conversation to another's. The gardeners say that the reason why vines were thought to fail in this country, was that they tried to get out of one soil the flavor that belonged to another soil, would raise Madeira grape in America when often the fruit is very different that grows on either side of the same fence, and much more

2. See n. 6, p. 8.
3. François Fénelon (1651–1715), French political figure and author. Socrates, see n. 6, p. 8. Milton, see n. 2, p. 6.

in different latitudes and continents. But cultivate in every soil the grape of that soil. In like manner, men fail in neglecting the intimations of their own inborn intelligence out of an unlimited deference to other characters. Let them on the contrary have greater confidence in the plan yet to them unknown which the moral Architect has traced for them. If he has appointed to it some present defect or less measure than he has given another, as will doubtless be true, he has also given it its own excellences. Explore the mine and make it yield such ores as are in it. Be sure that nothing therein was made in vain. It is not uncommon to hear a man express with great interest his regret that he possesses some particular manner of intellectual superiority or some quickness of feeling which, though reckoned advantages, he thinks rather stand in the way of greatness. It seems to me this self-condemnation is ungrateful and injurious. He thinks this quality is not good, because others who are great do not have it. Let him rather trust the wisdom of God and extort from these faculties all their treasury of good. When I look at the vegetable world, I admire a tree, a flower, and see that each oak and each lily is perfect in its kind though different in its proportions and number and arrangement of branches and leaves from every other oak and lily in the field. And shall I not believe as much of every mind; that it has its own beauty and character and was never meant to resemble any other one, and that God pronounced it good after its own kind? Every man has his own voice, manner, eloquence, and, just as much, his own sort of love, and grief, and imagination, and action. He has some power over other men that arises to him from his peculiar education and the cast of his circumstances and the complexion of his mind, and it were the extreme of folly if he forbears to use it, because he has never seen it used by anybody else. Let him scorn to *imitate* any being. Let him scorn to be a secondary man. Let him fully trust his own share of God's goodness, that if used to the uttermost, it will lead him on to a perfection which has no type[4] yet in the Universe save only in the Divine Mind.

One measure of a man's character is his effect upon his fellow-men. And any one who will steadily observe his own experience will I think become convinced, that every false word he has uttered, that is to say, every departure from his own convictions, out of deference to others has been a sacrifice of a certain amount of his power over other men. For every man knows whether he has been accustomed to receive truth or falsehood,—valuable opinions or foolish talking,—from his brother, and this knowledge must inevitably determine his respect.

Now what is it to speak from one's own convictions, to trust yourself,— what is it but to keep one's mind ever awake, to use the senses and the reason, to rely on your birthright of powers which God bestowed? But how little of this virtue enters into conversation. Men speak not from themselves but from the floating parlance of the time; they think—what is expected to be said?—What have others said?—what is safest to be said?—instead of what they hold to be true. Is it not wonderful that they do not see the infinite advantage that he must possess who always listens only to himself? I think this cannot be illustrated better than by comparing the looseness of men's discourse upon those questions

4. Loosely, a symbol; however, Emerson uses this term and related ones (such as *typical*) with conflated typological and Platonic connotations. Typology is an elaborate interpretive system that reads persons and events in the Hebrew Bible as foreshadowings, or types, later fulfilled by their corresponding New Testament antitypes. A type for the Greek philosopher Plato (427?–347 B.C.E.) was an "archetype," or original idea, represented by its imperfect image in the world. Plato's writings were crucial to Emerson; see, e.g., Emerson's essays in *Representative Men*, "Plato, or the Philosopher" and "Plato: New Readings."

most deeply interesting to our nature with the cogency of their talk in common affairs. How clear and strong is the language of a man speaking the truth in things concerning his ordinary business, that a commodity sold for so much, that a stage runs on such a road, the wind blows from such a quarter, or such were the numbers of a contested vote. No ingenuity, no sophism that the learning or eloquence of a man would intrude in such a conversation could be any match to the force of their speech. It would be ridiculous weakness. For when men converse on their pressing affairs *they* do not so much seem to speak as to become mere organs through which facts themselves speak.

Now that is precisely the way in which God seems to justify those who withdraw their eyes from every thing else, and fix them on their own thoughts only. They become, as it were, passive, and are merely the voice of things. If a man would always as exclusively consult his own thoughts as men do in these things, he would always speak with the same force, a force which would be felt to be far greater than belonged to him or to any mortal, but was proper to immortal truth.

It is important to observe that this self-reliance which grows out of the Scripture doctrine of the value of the soul is not inconsistent either with our duties to our fellow men or to God. Some will say, to press on a man the necessity of guiding himself only by the unaided light of his own understanding, and to shun as dangerous the imitation of other men seems inconsistent with the Scripture commandments that enjoin self abasement and unlimited love to others, and also with our natural relations to other men who are older and wiser and better than we are. Certainly it is our duty to prefer another's good always to our own, and gratefully to borrow all the light of his understanding as far as it agrees with ours, but the duty is quite as plain, the moment our own convictions of duty contradict another's, we ought to forsake his leading, let him be of what wisdom or condition he will, and without fear to follow our own. Brethren, I beg each of you to remember, whether, when you have in any instance forsaken your first impression of a book, or a character, or a question of duty, and adopted new ones from complaisance, you have not by and by been compelled to receive your own again, with the mortification of being overcome by your own weapons. Certainly other men, especially good men, are entitled from a good man to all respect. I honour the modesty and benevolence which is respectful to men of worth and thinks there is soundness in all their opinions. But I honour more this image of God in human nature which has placed a standard of character in every human breast which is above the highest copy of living excellence. Every man has an idea of a greatness that was never realized. Take the history of a great and good man, of Newton, or Franklin,[5] or Washington, and explain all its details to the most obscure and ignorant wretch that wears the human form, and you shall find that whilst he understands all its elevation he will be able to put his finger upon imperfections in that life. Which shows that in his heart there is a greater man than any that has lived in the world.

Nor, on the other hand, let it be thought that there is in this self-reliance any thing of presumption, anything inconsistent with a spirit of dependence and piety toward God. In listening more intently to our own soul we are not becoming in the ordinary sense more selfish, but are departing farther from what

---

5. Benjamin Franklin (1706–1790), American political figure, author, and scientist. Sir Isaac Newton (1642–1727), English mathematician, philosopher, and scientist.

is low and falling back upon truth and upon God. For the whole value of the soul depends on the fact that it contains a divine principle, that it is a house of God, and the voice of the eternal inhabitant may always be heard within it.

A good man, says Solomon,[6] is satisfied from himself. An original mind is not an eccentric mind. To be wholly independent of other men's judgments does not mean to come under their censure by any extravagance of action. But it is only those who are so that can bear the severest scrutiny of other men's judgments. It is by following other men's opinions that we are misled and depraved. It is those who have steadily listened to their own who have found out the great truths of religion which are the salvation of the human soul. My friends, let me beseech you to remember that it is only by looking inward that the outward means of knowledge can be made of any avail. The soul, the soul is full of truth. The bible is a sealed book to him who has not first heard its laws from his soul. The drunkard and the voluptuary might as well read it in an unknown language as in their mother tongue. And it is this fact that gives such immense meaning to the precept Know Thyself.[7] To him who has reached this wisdom how ridiculous is Caesar and Bonaparte[8] wandering from one extreme of civilization to the other to conquer men,—himself, the while, unconquered, unexplored, almost wholly unsuspected to himself. Yet Europe and Asia are not so broad and deep, have nothing so splendid, so durable, as the possessions of this empire. What shall it profit a man though he gain the whole world and lose his own soul?

My friends, the deep religious interest of this question is apparent to you. The body we inhabit shall shortly be laid in the dust, but the soul assures us, with the voice of God to confirm it, that it will not die. Let this strange and awful being that we possess have that reverence that is due from us. Let us leave this immoderate regard to meats and drinks, to dress and pleasure and to unfounded praise, and let us go alone and converse with ourselves, and the word of God in us. What that bids us do, let us do with unshaken firmness, and what it bids us forbear, let us forbear. Let us love and respect each other as those who can assist us in understanding ourselves. And let us hear the distinct voice of Scripture which has taught us to forsake the world and its vanities and deceptions, and seek God who is to be worshipped in our hearts.

CLXII

The kingdom of God is not meat and drink; but righteousness and peace and joy in the holy ghost.[1]

ROMANS 14:17

In the history of the Church no subject has been more fruitful of controversy than the Lord's Supper. There never has been any unanimity in the under-

---

6. King of Israel (tenth century B.C.E.), son of King David, known for his wisdom and for building the Temple in Jerusalem; presumed author of the Book of Proverbs; cf. Proverbs 14.14.
7. Attributed to Solon (638?–559? B.C.E.), Athenian legislator.
8. Napoleon Bonaparte (1769–1821), French emperor. Gaius Julius Caesar (100–44 B.C.E.), Roman general and emperor.
1. This sermon, known as "The Lord's Supper" sermon, is Emerson's most famous. He preached it at the Second Church in Boston on September 9, 1832, to explain his resignation from his pastoral duties there; the resignation was accepted on October 28, 1832. With this message, the only regular sermon of his to

standing of its nature nor any uniformity in the mode of celebrating it. Without considering the frivolous questions which have been hotly debated as to the posture in which men should partake or whether mixed or unmixed wine should be served, whether leavened or unleavened bread should be broken, the questions have been settled differently in every church, who should be admitted to partake, and how often it should be prepared. In the Catholic Church once infants were permitted and then forbidden to partake. Since the ninth Century, bread only is given to the laity and the cup is reserved to the priesthood. So as to the time. In the fourth Lateran Council it was decreed that every believer should communicate[2] once in a year at Easter. Afterwards three times—But more important have been the controversies respecting its nature. The great question of the Real Presence[3] was the main controversy between the Church of England and the Church of Rome. The doctrine of the Consubstantiation maintained by Luther was denied by Calvin.[4] In the Church of England Archbishops Laud and Wake maintained that it was a Eucharist or sacrifice of thanksgiving to God, Cudworth and Warburton that it was not a sacrifice but a feast after a sacrifice, and Bishop Hoadly[5] that it was a simple commemoration.

If there seem to you an agreement in this last opinion among our churches it is only but of yesterday and within narrow limits.

And finally it is now near 200 years since the society of Quakers[6] denied the authority of the supper altogether and gave good reasons for disusing it.

I allude to these facts only to show that so far from the Supper being a tradition in which all are fully agreed, there has always been the widest room for difference of opinion upon this particular.

Having recently paid particular attention to this subject, I was led to the conclusion that Jesus did not intend to establish an institution for perpetual observance when he ate the passover[7] with his disciples; and further to the opinion that it is not expedient to celebrate it as we do. I shall now endeavour to state distinctly my reasons for these two opinions.

An account of the last Supper of Christ with his disciples is given by the four Evangelists, Matthew, Mark, Luke and John.[8]

---

be published in his lifetime, Emerson effectively broke his official connection with the Unitarian Church and ended his service as a settled cleric. The version printed here from CS is edited from the original manuscript and differs slightly from the one Emerson edited for early publication. The biblical text comes from a letter of the apostle Paul (see n. 1, p. 3) to the early church at Rome. The Lord's Supper, or Holy Communion, is the Christian Eucharist.

2. Participate in the Lord's Supper. *Fourth Lateran Council*: A legislative session of the Roman Catholic Church held at Rome in 1215.

3. Transubstantiation, the Roman Catholic belief that the elements are actually transformed into the body and blood of Jesus, as opposed to the Protestant belief of consubstantiation (mentioned below), the doctrine that the body and blood of Jesus exist symbolically with the actual bread and wine in the Eucharist.

4. John Calvin (1509–1564), French-born Swiss Protestant theologian whose doctrines formed the basis of Presbyterianism. Martin Luther (1483–1546), German theologian and leader of the Protestant Reformation.

5. William Laud (1573–1645), and William Wake (1657–1737), archbishops of Canterbury. Ralph Cudworth (1617–1688), Cambridge Platonist philosopher; William Warburton (1698–1779), bishop of Gloucester; and Benjamin Hoadley (1676–1761), bishop of Bangor, Hereford, Salisbury, and Winchester, wrote treatises on the Lord's Supper.

6. Or Society of Friends, a Christian pacifist denomination founded in mid-seventeenth-century England that is opposed to sacraments, formal creeds, and a priesthood. The term *quake* derives from their admonition that one should tremble at the word of the Lord.

7. Pesach (from the Hebrew), a holiday commemorating the exodus of the Jews from Egypt. Emerson refers to the seder (or order of service) and the meal that accompanies it.

8. Authors of the Gospels, accounts of the life of Christ that constitute the first four books of the New Testament of the Bible.

In St. Matthew's Gospel (26:26) are recorded the words of Jesus in giving bread and wine on that occasion to his disciples but no expression occurs intimating that this feast was hereafter to be commemorated.

In St. Mark the same words are recorded and still with no intimation that the occasion was to be remembered (14:22).

St. Luke, after relating the breaking of the bread, has these words: "This do in remembrance of me' (22:15).[9]

In St. John, although other occurrences of the same evening are related, this whole transaction is passed over without notice.

Now observe the facts. Two of the evangelists (namely, Matthew and John) were of the twelve disciples and were present on that occasion. Neither of them drops the slightest intimation of any intention on the part of Jesus to set up any thing permanent. John especially, the beloved disciple, who has recorded with minuteness the conversation and the transactions of that memorable evening, has quite omitted such a notice.

Neither did it come to the knowledge of St. Mark, who relates the other facts. It is found in Luke alone, who was not present. There is no reason, however, that we know for rejecting the account of Luke. I doubt not that the expression was used by Jesus. I shall presently consider its meaning. I have only brought these accounts together that you may judge whether it is likely that a solemn institution to be continued to the end of time, by all mankind, as they should come, nation after nation, within the influence of the Christian religion, was to be established in this slight manner, in a manner so slight that the intention of remembering it should not have caught the ear or dwelt in the mind of the only two among the twelve, who wrote down what happened!

Still we must suppose that this expression—This do in remembrance of me—had come to the ear of Luke from some disciple present. What did it really signify? It is a prophetic and an affectionate expression. Jesus is a Jew sitting with his countrymen celebrating their national feast. He thinks of his own impending death and wishes the minds of his disciples to be prepared for it and says to them, "When hereafter you shall keep the passover it will have an altered aspect in your eyes. It is now a historical covenant of God with the Jewish nation. Hereafter it will remind you of a new covenant sealed with my blood. In years to come, as long as your people shall come up to Jerusalem to keep this feast (forty years) the connexion which has subsisted between us will give a new meaning in your eyes to the national festival as the anniversary of my death." — I see natural feeling and beauty in the use of such language from Jesus, a friend to his friends. I can readily imagine that he was willing and desirous that when his disciples met, his memory should hallow their intercourse, but I cannot bring myself to believe that he looked beyond the living generation, beyond the abolition of the festival he was celebrating and the scattering of the nation, and meant to impose a memorial feast upon the whole world.

But though the words *Do this in remembrance*,[1] to which so much meaning has been given, do not occur in Matthew, Mark, or John, yet many persons are apt to imagine that the very striking and formal manner in which this eating and drinking is described intimates a striking and formal purpose to found a festival. This opinion would easily occur to any one reading only the New Tes-

---

9. Actually Luke 22.19.
1. In most Christian orders of worship, the words said by the minister when the Eucharist is administered.

tament, but the impression is removed by reading any narrative of the mode in which the ancient or the modern Jews kept the passover. It is then perceived at once that the leading circumstances in the gospel are only a faithful account of that ceremony. Jesus did not celebrate the passover and afterwards the supper, but the supper *was* the passover. He did with his disciples exactly what every master of a family in Jerusalem was doing at the same hour with his household. It appears that the Jews ate the lamb and the unleavened bread and drank wine after a prescribed manner. It was the custom for the Lord or master of the feast to break the bread and to bless it, using this formula, which the Talmudists[2] have preserved to us, 'Blessed be thou O Lord who givest us the fruits of the earth,' and to give it to every one at the table. It was the custom for the master of the family to take the cup which contained the wine and to bless it saying, 'Blessed be thou O Lord who givest us the fruit of the vine,' and then to give the cup to all. Among the modern Jews, a hymn is sung after this ceremony, specifying the twelve great works done by God for the deliverance of their fathers out of Egypt.[3] And Jesus did the same thing.

But why did he use expressions so extraordinary and emphatic as these: This is my body which is broken for you. Take, Eat. This is my blood which is shed for you. Drink it. They are not extraordinary expressions from him. They were familiar in his mouth. He always taught by parables and symbols. It was the national way of teaching and was largely used by him. Remember the readiness which he always showed to spiritualize every occurrence. He stooped and wrote on the sand. He admonished his disciples respecting the leaven of the Pharisees.[4] He instructed the woman of Samaria[5] respecting living water. He permitted himself to be anointed, declaring it was for interment. He washed the feet of his disciples. These are admitted to be symbolical actions and expressions. Here in like manner he calls the bread his body and bids the disciples eat. He had used the same expression repeatedly before. The reason why St. John does not repeat the words here, seems to be that he had narrated a similar discourse of Jesus to the people of Capernaum[6] more at length already (John 6:27). He there tells the Jews—'Except ye eat the flesh of the Son of Man and drink his blood ye have no life in you.'[7]

And when the Jews on that occasion complained that they did not comprehend what he meant, he added for their better understanding, and as if for our understanding, that we might not think that his body was to be actually eaten, that he only meant we should live by his commandment. He closed his discourse with these explanatory expressions: "The flesh profiteth nothing;—the *words* that I speak to you, they are spirit and they are life."[8]

Whilst I am upon this topic I cannot help remarking that it is very singular we should have preserved this rite and insisted upon perpetuating one symbolical act of Christ whilst we have totally neglected others, particularly one other which had at least an equal claim to our observance. Jesus washed the feet

---

2. Scholars of the Talmud, ancient rabbinical writings consisting of the Mishnah and the Gemara, foundation of religious authority in Orthodox Judaism.
3. Emerson alludes to a hymn found in the Haggadah, a compilation that contains the ritual of the Passover seder as well as stories, songs, and prayers.
4. Members of an ancient Jewish sect who emphasized strict adherence to written and oral Mosaic law.
5. Ancient Palestinian city. Cf. John 4.7–15.
6. City in ancient Palestine that was Jesus' home for much of his life.
7. Cf. John 6.53.
8. Cf. John 6.63.

of his disciples and told them that 'As he had washed their feet, they ought to wash one another's feet, for he had given them an example that they should do as he had done to them.'[9] I ask any person who believes the Supper to have been designed by Jesus to be commemorated forever, to go and read the account of it in the other gospels, and then compare with it the account of this transaction in St. John and tell me if it is not much more explicitly authorized than the supper. It only differs in this, that we have found the Supper used in New England and the washing of the feet not. It we had found this rite established, it would be much more difficult to show its defective authority. That rite is used by the Church of Rome and the Sandemanians.[1] It has been very properly dropped by other Christians. Why? 1. Because it was a local custom and unsuitable in western countries, and 2. because it was typical and all understand that humility is the thing signified. But the passover was local too and does not concern us; and its bread and wine were typical[2] and do not help us to understand the love which they signified.

These views of the original account of the Lord's Supper lead me to esteem it an occasion full of solemn and prophetic interest but never intended by Jesus to be the foundation of a perpetual institution.

It appears however from Paul's Epistle to the Corinthians[3] that the disciples had very early taken advantage of these impressive words of Christ to hold religious meetings where they broke bread and drank wine as symbols.

I look upon this fact as very natural in the circumstances of the Church. The disciples lived together; they threw all their property into a common stock; they were bound together by the memory of Christ and nothing could be more natural than that this eventful evening should be affectionately remembered by them; that they, Jews like Jesus, should adopt his expression and his type, and furthermore that what was done with peculiar propriety by them, by his personal friends, should come to be extended to their companions also. In this way religious feasts grew up among the early Christians. They were readily adopted by the Jewish converts who were familiar with religious feasts, and also by the Pagan converts whose idolatrous worship had been made up of sacred festivals and who very readily abused these to gross riot as appears from the censures of St. Paul. Many persons consider this fact, the observance of such a memorial feast by the early disciples, decisive of the question whether it ought to be observed by us. For my part I see nothing to wonder at in its originating there; all that is surprizing is that it should exist amongst us. It had great propriety for his personal friends to remember their friend and repeat his words. It was but too probable that among the half-converted Pagans and Jews any rite, any form would be cherished whilst yet unable to comprehend the spiritual character of Christianity.

The circumstance however that St. Paul favors these views has seemed to many persons conclusive in favor of the institution. I am of opinion that it is wholly on this passage and not upon the gospels that the ordinance stands. A careful examination of that passage will not I think make that evidence so weighty as it seems. That passage, the eleventh chapter I Corinthians, appears

9. Cf. John 13.14–15.
1. Originally Glasites, members of a primitivistic Christian sect founded in early eighteenth-century Scotland by John Glas (1695–1773), a Presbyterian minister, and later led by his son-in-law Robert Sandeman (1718–1771).
2. See n. 4, p. 15.
3. Early Christians in the church at Corinth, a city in ancient Greece.

to be a reproof to the Corinthian converts of certain gross abuses that had grown up among them, offending against decency not less than against Christianity: accusing their contentiousness; the fanaticism of certain of their women; and the intemperance into which they had fallen at the Lord's supper. The end he has in view, in that Chapter, and this is observable, is not to enjoin upon them to observe the supper, but to censure their abuse of it. We quote the passage nowadays as if it enjoined attendance on the supper, but he wrote it merely to chide them for drunkenness. To make their enormity plainer he goes back to the origin of this religious feast to show what that feast was out of which this their riot came and so relates the transactions of the Lord's supper. *I have received of the Lord*, he says. By this expression it is often thought that a miraculous communication is implied, but certainly without good reason if it is remembered that St. Paul was living in the lifetime of all the apostles who could give him an account of the transaction, and it is contrary to all experience to suppose that God should work a miracle to convey information that might be so easily got by natural means. So that the import of the expression is that he had got the account of the Evangelists, which we also possess.

But the material circumstance which diminishes our confidence in the correctness of the apostle's view is the observation that his mind had not escaped the prevalent error of the primitive Church, the belief namely that the second coming of Christ[4] would shortly occur, until which time, he tells them, this feast was to be kept. At that time the world would be burnt with fire, and a new government established in which the Saints[5] would sit on thrones; so slow were the disciples during the life and after the ascension of Christ to receive the idea which we receive that his Second Coming was a spiritual kingdom, the domination of his religion in the hearts of men to be extended gradually over the whole world.

In this manner I think we may see clearly enough how this ancient ordinance got its footing among the early Christians and this single expectation of a speedy reappearance of a temporal messiah upon earth, which kept its influence even over so spiritual a man as St. Paul, would naturally tend to preserve the use of the rite when once established.

We arrive then at this conclusion: 1. That it does not appear from a careful examination of the account of the Last Supper in the Evangelists that it was designed by Jesus to be perpetual. 2. It does not appear that the opinion of St. Paul, all things considered, ought to alter our opinion derived from the Evangelists.

I have not attempted to ascertain precisely the purpose in the mind of Jesus. But you will see that many opinions may be entertained of his intention all consistent with the opinion that he did not design the ordinance to be perpetual. He may have foreseen that his disciples would meet together to remember him and seen good in it. It may have crossed his mind that this would be easily continued a hundred or a thousand years, as men more easily transmit a form than a virtue, and yet have been altogether out of his purpose to fasten it upon men in all times and all countries.

Admitting that the disciples kept it and admitting Paul's feeling of its perpetuity, that does not settle the question for us. I think it was good for them. I think it is not suited to this day. We do not take them for guides in other things.

---

4. Christian belief that Christ will return and establish his kingdom on earth.
5. Those deemed by God worthy of salvation on Judgment Day, at the second coming.

They were, as we know, obstinately attached to their Jewish prejudices. All the intercourse with the most persuasive of teachers seems to have done very little to enlarge their views. On every subject we have learned to think differently, and why shall not we form a judgment upon this, more in accordance with the spirit of Christianity than was the practice of the early ages?

But it is said, Admit that the rite was not designed to be perpetual. What harm doth it? Here it stands generally accepted under some form by the Christian world, the undoubted occasion of much good; is it not better it should remain? This is the question of Expediency.

I proceed to notice a few objections that in my judgment lie against its use in its present form.

1. If the view which I have taken of the history of the institution be correct, then the claim of authority should be dropped in administering it. You say, every time you celebrate the rite, that Jesus enjoined it, and the whole language you use conveys that impression. But if you read the New Testament as I do, you do not believe he did.

2. It has seemed to me (yet I make the objection with diffidence) that the use of this ordinance tends to produce confusion in our views of the relation of the soul to God. It is the old objection to the doctrine of the Trinity that the true worship was transferred from God to Christ or that such confusion was introduced into the soul that an undivided worship was given nowhere. Is not that the effect of the Lord's Supper? I appeal now to the convictions of communicants and ask such persons whether they have not been occasionally conscious of a painful confusion of thought between the worship due to God and the commemoration due to Christ. For the service does not stand upon the basis of a voluntary act, but is imposed by authority. It is an expression of gratitude to him enjoined by him. There is an endeavour to keep Jesus in mind whilst yet the prayers are addressed to God. I fear it is the effect of this ordinance to clothe Jesus with an authority which he never claimed and which distracts the mind of the worshipper. I know our opinions differ much respecting the nature and offices of Christ and the degree of veneration to which he is entitled. I am so much a Unitarian[6] as this, that I believe the human mind cannot admit but one God, and that every effort to pay religious homage to more than one being goes to take away all right ideas. I appeal, brethren, to your individual experience. In the moment when you make the least petition to God, though it be but a silent wish that he may approve you, or add one moment to your life — do you not — in the very act — necessarily exclude all other beings from your thought? In that act the soul stands alone with God, and Jesus is no more present to the mind than your brother or your child.

But is not Jesus called in Scripture the Mediator? He is the Mediator in that only sense in which possibly any being can mediate between God and man, that is an Instructer of man. He teaches us how to become like God. And a true disciple of Jesus will receive the light he gives most thankfully, but the thanks he offers and which an exalted being will accept are not compliments, commemorations — but the use of that instruction.

3. To pass by other objections, I come to this: that the *use of the elements*,[7] however suitable to the people and the modes of thought in the East where it

6. Now Unitarian Universalist, a member of the Christian denomination originally established in opposition to Trinitarianism.
7. The bread and wine of the Eucharist.

originated, is foreign and unsuited to affect us. Whatever long usage and strong association may have done in some individuals to deaden this repulsion I apprehend that their use is rather tolerated than loved by any of us. We are not accustomed to express our thoughts or emotions by symbolical actions. Most men find the bread and wine no aid to devotion and to some persons it is an impediment. To eat bread is one thing; to love the precepts of Christ and resolve to obey them is quite another. It is of the greatest importance that whatever forms we use should be animated by our feelings; that our religion through all its acts should be living and operative.

The statement of this objection leads me to say that I think this difficulty, wherever it is felt, to be entitled to the greatest weight. It is alone a sufficient objection to the ordinance. It is my own objection. This mode of commemorating Christ is not suitable to me. That is reason enough why I should abandon it. If I believed that it was enjoined by Jesus on his disciples, and that he even contemplated to make permanent this mode of commemoration every way agreeable to an Eastern mind, and yet on trial it was disagreeable to my own feelings, I should not adopt it. I should choose other ways which he would approve more. For what could he wish to be commemorated for? Only that men might be filled with his spirit. I find that other modes comport with my education and habits of thought. For I chuse[8] that my remembrances of him should be pleasing, affecting, religious. I will love him as a glorified friend after the free way of friendship and not pay him a stiff sign of respect as men do to those whom they fear. A passage read from his discourses, the provoking each other to works like his, any act or meeting which tends to awaken a pure thought, a glow of love, an original design of virtue I call a worthy, a true commemoration.

4. In the last place the importance ascribed to this particular ordinance is not consistent with the spirit of Christianity. The general object and effect of this ordinance is unexceptionable. It has been and is, I doubt not, the occasion of indefinite good, but an importance is given by the friends of the rite to it which never can belong to any form. My friends, the kingdom of God is not meat and drink. Forms are as essential as bodies. It would be foolish to declaim against them, but to adhere to one form a moment after it is outgrown is foolish. That form only is good and Christian which answers its end. Jesus came to take the load of ceremonies from the shoulders of men and substitute principles. If I understand the distinction of Christianity, the reason why it is to be preferred over all other systems and is divine is this, that it is a moral system; that it presents men with truths which are their own reason, and enjoins practices that are their own justification; that if miracles may be said to have been its evidence to the first Christians they are not its evidence to us, but the doctrines themselves; that every practice is Christian which praises itself and every practice unchristian which condemns itself. I am not engaged to Christianity by decent forms; it is not saving ordinances, it is not usage, it is not what I do not understand that engages me to it—let these be the sandy foundation of falsehoods. What I revere and obey in it is its reality, its boundless charity, its deep interior life, the rest it gives to my mind, the echo it returns to my thoughts, the perfect accord it makes with my reason, the persuasion and courage that come out of it to lead me upward and onward.

---

8. Choose.

Freedom is the essence of Christianity. It has for its object simply to make men good and wise. Its institutions should be as flexible as the wants of men. That form out of which the life and suitableness have departed should be as worthless in its eyes as the dead leaves that are falling around us.

And therefore, though for the satisfaction of others I have labored to show by the history that it was not intended to be perpetual, though I have gone back to weigh the expressions of Paul, I feel that here is the true way of viewing it. In the midst of considerations as to what Paul thought and why he so thought, I cannot help feeling that it is labor misspent to argue to or from his convictions or those of Luke or John respecting any form. I seem to lose the substance in seeking the shadow. That for which Paul lived and died so gloriously; that for which Jesus was crucified; the end that animated the thousand martyrs and heroes that have followed him, was to redeem us from a formal religion, and teach us to seek our wellbeing in the reformation of the soul. The whole world was full of idols and ordinances. The Jewish was a religion of forms; the Pagan was a religion of forms; it was all body, it had no life,—and the Almighty God was pleased to qualify and send forth a man to teach men that they must serve him with the heart; that only that life was religious which was thoroughly good, that sacrifice was smoke and forms were shadows, and this man lived and died true to this purpose, and now, with his blessed words and life before us, Christians must contend that it is a matter of vital importance, really a duty, to commemorate him by a certain form, whether that form be agreeable to their understandings or not.

Is not this to make vain the gift of God? Is not this to turn back the hand on the dial? Is not this to make men, to make ourselves, forget that not forms but duties, not names but righteousness and love are enjoined and that in the eye of God there is no other measure of the value of any one form than the measure of its use?

There remain some practical objections to the ordinance which I need not state. There is one on which I had intended to say a few words, the unfavorable relation in which it puts those persons who abstain from it merely from disinclination to that rite.

Influenced by these considerations, I have proposed to the brethren of the church to drop the use of the elements and the claim of authority in the administration of this ordinance, and have suggested a mode in which a meeting for the same purpose might be held, free of objection.

They have considered my views with patience and candor, and have recommended unanimously an adherence to the present form. I have therefore been compelled to consider whether it becomes me to administer it. I am clearly of opinion that I ought not. This discourse has already been so far extended that I can only say that the reason of my determination is shortly this— It is my desire, in the office of a Christian minister, to do nothing which I cannot do with my whole heart. Having said this, I have said all. I have no hostility to this institution. I am only stating my want of sympathy with it. Neither should I ever have obtruded this opinion upon other people, had I not been called by my office to administer it. That is the end of my opposition, that I am not interested in it. I am content that it stand to the end of the world if it please men and please heaven, and shall rejoice in all the good it produces.

As it is the prevailing opinion and feeling in our religious community that it is an indispensable part of the pastoral office to administer this ordinance, I am about to resign into your hands that office which you have confided to me. It has many duties for which I am feebly qualified. It has some which it will always be my delight to discharge according to my ability wherever I exist. And whilst the thought of its claims oppresses me with a sense of my unworthiness, I am consoled by the hope that no time and no change can deprive me of the satisfaction of pursuing and exercising its highest functions.

Nature

A subtle chain of countless rings
The next unto the farthest brings;
The eye reads omens where it goes,
And speaks all languages the rose;
And, striving to be man, the worm
Mounts through all the spires of form.[1]

Introduction

Our age is retrospective.[2] It builds the sepulchres of the fathers.[3] It writes biographies, histories, and criticism. The foregoing generations beheld God and nature face to face;[4] we, through their eyes. Why should not we also enjoy an original relation to the universe? Why should not we have a poetry and philosophy of insight and not of tradition, and a religion by revelation to us, and not the history of theirs? Embosomed for a season in nature, whose floods of life stream around and through us, and invite us by the powers they supply, to action proportioned to nature, why should we grope among the dry bones of the past,[5] or put the living generation into masquerade out of its faded wardrobe? The sun shines to-day also. There is more wool and flax in the fields. There are new lands, new men, new thoughts. Let us demand our own works and laws and worship.

Undoubtedly we have no questions to ask which are unanswerable. We must trust the perfection of the creation so far, as to believe that whatever curiosity the order of things has awakened in our minds, the order of things can satisfy. Every man's condition is a solution in hieroglyphic to those inquiries he would put. He acts it as life, before he apprehends it as truth. In like manner, nature is already, in its forms and tendencies, describing its own design. Let us interrogate the great apparition, that shines so peacefully around us. Let us inquire, to what end is nature?

All science has one aim, namely, to find a theory of nature. We have theories of races and of functions, but scarely yet a remote approach to an idea of creation. We are now so far from the road to truth, that religious teachers dispute and hate each other, and speculative men are esteemed unsound and frivolous. But to a sound judgment, the most abstract truth is the most practical. Whenever a true theory appears, it will be its own evidence. Its test is, that it will

---

1. For the 1849 *Nature; Addresses, and Lectures*, Emerson replaced the original epigraph to *Nature* with these lines of his own composition. The 1836 motto reads "Nature is but an image or imitation of wisdom, the last thing of the soul; nature being a thing which doth only do, but not know." It is attributed to Plotinus (205–270), Roman neo-Platonic philosopher born in Egypt. From 1844, Emerson increasingly used his own poetry for essay epigraphs.
2. Contrast the title of the last chapter of *Nature*, "Prospects" (p. 51), and the first and last sentences of its last paragraph (pp. 54–55).
3. Cf. Luke 11.47.
4. Cf. I Corinthians 13.12.
5. Cf. Ezekiel 37.2–5.

explain all phenomena. Now many are thought not only unexplained but inexplicable; as language, sleep, madness, dreams, beasts, sex.

Philosophically considered, the universe is composed of Nature and the
Soul. Strictly speaking, therefore, all that is separate from us, all which Philosophy distinguishes as the NOT ME,[6] that is, both nature and art, all other men
and my own body, must be ranked under this name, NATURE. In enumerating
the values of nature and casting up their sum, I shall use the word in both
senses;—in its common and in its philosophical import. In inquiries so general
as our present one, the inaccuracy is not material; no confusion of thought will
occur. Nature, in the common sense, refers to essences unchanged by man;
space, the air, the river, the leaf. Art is applied to the mixture of his will with the
same things, as in a house, a canal, a statue, a picture. But his operations taken
together are so insignificant, a little chipping, baking, patching, and washing,
that in an impression so grand as that of the world on the human mind, they do
not vary the result.

Chapter I. Nature

To go into solitude, a man needs to retire as much from his chamber as from
society. I am not solitary whilst I read and write, though nobody is with me. But
if a man would be alone, let him look at the stars. The rays that come from those
heavenly worlds, will separate between him and what he touches. One might
think the atmosphere was made transparent with this design, to give man, in the
heavenly bodies, the perpetual presence of the sublime. Seen in the streets of
cities, how great they are! If the stars should appear one night in a thousand
years, how would men believe and adore; and preserve for many generations
the remembrance of the city of God which had been shown! But every night
come out these envoys of beauty, and light the universe with their admonishing
smile.

The stars awaken a certain reverence, because though always present, they
are inaccessible; but all natural objects make a kindred impression, when the
mind is open to their influence. Nature never wears a mean appearance. Neither does the wisest man extort her secret, and lose his curiosity by finding out
all her perfection. Nature never became a toy to a wise spirit. The flowers, the
animals, the mountains, reflected the wisdom of his best hour, as much as they
had delighted the simplicity of his childhood.

When we speak of nature in this manner, we have a distinct but most poetical sense in the mind. We mean the integrity[7] of impression made by manifold natural objects. It is this which distinguishes the stick of timber of the
wood-cutter, from the tree of the poet. The charming landscape which I saw
this morning, is indubitably made up of some twenty or thirty farms. Miller
owns this field, Locke that, and Manning the woodland beyond.[8] But none of
them owns the landscape. There is a property in the horizon which no man has
but he whose eye can integrate all the parts, that is, the poet. This is the best
part of these men's farms, yet to this their warranty-deeds give no title.

---

6. Emerson's friend and correspondent Thomas Carlyle (1795–1881), Scottish author, uses the German
philosophical terms ME and NOT ME in his Sartor Resartus (The tailor retailored, 1833–34), a burlesque philosophical treatise first published in book form in Boston (1836) with an introduction by Emerson.
7. Unity.
8. I.e., various people. The names are commonplace.

To speak truly, few adult persons can see nature. Most persons do not see the sun. At least they have a very superficial seeing. The sun illuminates only the eye of the man, but shines into the eye and the heart of the child. The lover of nature is he whose inward and outward senses are still truly adjusted to each other; who has retained the spirit of infancy even into the era of manhood. His intercourse with heaven and earth, becomes part of his daily food. In the presence of nature, a wild delight runs through the man, in spite of real sorrows. Nature says, — he is my creature, and maugre[9] all his impertinent griefs, he shall be glad with me. Not the sun or the summer alone, but every hour and season yields its tribute of delight; for every hour and change corresponds to and authorizes a different state of the mind, from breathless noon to grimmest midnight. Nature is a setting that fits equally well a comic or a mourning piece. In good health, the air is a cordial of incredible virtue. Crossing a bare common, in snow puddles, at twilight, under a clouded sky, without having in my thoughts any occurrence of special good fortune, I have enjoyed a perfect exhilaration. I am glad to the brink of fear.[1] In the woods too, a man casts off his years, as the snake his slough, and at what period soever of life, is always a child. In the woods, is perpetual youth. Within these plantations of God,[2] a decorum and sanctity reign, a perennial festival is dressed, and the guest sees not how he should tire of them in a thousand years. In the woods, we return to reason and faith. There I feel that nothing can befall me in life, — no disgrace, no calamity, (leaving me my eyes,) which nature cannot repair. Standing on the bare ground, — my head bathed by the blithe air, and uplifted into infinite space, — all mean egotism vanishes. I become a transparent eye-ball;[3] I am nothing; I see all; the currents of the Universal Being circulate through me; I am part or particle of God. The name of the nearest friend sounds then foreign and accidental: to be brothers, to be acquaintances, — master or servant, is then a trifle and a disturbance. I am the lover of uncontained and immortal beauty. In the wilderness, I find something more dear and connate than in streets or villages. In the tranquil landscape, and especially in the distant line of the horizon, man beholds somewhat as beautiful as his own nature.

The greatest delight which the fields and woods minister, is the suggestion of an occult[4] relation between man and the vegetable. I am not alone and unacknowledged. They nod to me, and I to them. The waving of the boughs in the storm, is new to me and old. It takes me by surprise, and yet is not unknown. Its effect is like that of a higher thought or a better emotion coming over me, when I deemed I was thinking justly or doing right.

Yet it is certain that the power to produce this delight, does not reside in nature, but in man, or in a harmony of both. It is necessary to use these pleasures with great temperance. For, nature is not always tricked in holiday attire, but the same scene which yesterday breathed perfume and glittered as for the frolic of the nymphs, is overspread with melancholy today. Nature always wears the colors of the spirit. To a man laboring under calamity, the heat of his own fire hath sadness in it. Then, there is a kind of contempt of the landscape felt

---

9. Notwithstanding, in spite of (archaic).
1. In 1836, Emerson wrote, "Almost I fear to think how glad I am."
2. Perhaps a pun on nature as the plantation of God, in contrast to ungodly human plantations worked by slaves.
3. For a contemporary parody of this famous passage, see Christopher Cranch's Emerson caricatures (p. 584).
4. Hidden, inscrutable.

by him who has just lost by death a dear friend. The sky is less grand as it shuts down over less worth in the population.

Chapter II. Commodity

Whoever considers the final cause of the world, will discern a multitude of uses that enter as parts into that result. They all admit of being thrown into one of the following classes; Commodity; Beauty; Language; and Discipline.

Under the general name of Commodity, I rank all those advantages which our senses owe to nature. This, of course, is a benefit which is temporary and mediate, not ultimate, like its service to the soul. Yet although low, it is perfect in its kind, and is the only use of nature which all men apprehend. The misery of man appears like childish petulance, when we explore the steady and prodigal[5] provision that has been made for his support and delight on this green ball which floats him through the heavens. What angels invented these splendid ornaments, these rich conveniences, this ocean of air above, this ocean of water beneath, this firmament of earth between? this zodiac of lights, this tent of dropping clouds, this striped coat of climates, this fourfold year? Beasts, fire, water, stones, and corn serve him. The field is at once his floor, his work-yard, his playground, his garden, and his bed.

> "More servants wait on man
> Than he'll take notice of." —— [6]

Nature, in its ministry to man, is not only the material, but is also the process and the result. All the parts incessantly work into each other's hands for the profit of man. The wind sows the seed; the sun evaporates the sea; the wind blows the vapor to the field; the ice, on the other side of the planet, condenses rain on this; the rain feeds the plant; the plant feeds the animal; and thus the endless circulations of the divine charity nourish man.

The useful arts are reproductions or new combinations by the wit of man, of the same natural benefactors. He no longer waits for favoring gales, but by means of steam, he realizes the fable of Æolus's bag,[7] and carries the two and thirty winds in the boiler of his boat. To diminish friction, he paves the road with iron bars, and, mounting a coach with a ship-load of men, animals, and merchandise behind him, he darts through the country, from town to town, like an eagle or a swallow through the air.[8] By the aggregate of these aids, how is the face of the world changed, from the era of Noah to that of Napoleon![9] The private poor man hath cities, ships, canals, bridges, built for him. He goes to the post-office, and the human race run on his errands; to the book-shop, and the human race read and write of all that happens, for him; to the court-house, and nations repair his wrongs. He sets his house upon the road, and the human race go forth every morning, and shovel out the snow, and cut a path for him.

---

5. Extravagant or lavish, but perhaps also an allusion to Jesus' parable of the errant prodigal son who was welcomed back home by his father (Luke 15.11–32).
6. From "Man," by George Herbert (1593–1633), English Metaphysical poet, author of *The Temple* (1633). See also chapter 8 (p. 51).
7. Aeolus, Greek god of the winds, gave Odysseus a bag containing adverse breezes that his curious fellow sailors open in the *Odyssey* (book 10), Homer's epic poem about the wanderings of Odysseus after the fall of Troy. *Realizes:* makes real.
8. I.e., modern people use nature to build a railroad.
9. See n. 8, p. 17.

But there is no need of specifying particulars in this class of uses. The catalogue is endless, and the examples so obvious, that I shall leave them to the reader's reflection, with the general remark, that this mercenary benefit is one which has respect to a farther good. A man is fed, not that he may be fed, but that he may work.

Chapter III. Beauty

A nobler want of man is served by nature, namely, the love of Beauty.

The ancient Greeks called the world κόσμος,[1] beauty. Such is the constitution of all things, or such the plastic[2] power of the human eye, that the primary forms, as the sky, the mountain, the tree, the animal, give us a delight *in and for themselves*; a pleasure arising from outline, color, motion, and grouping. This seems partly owing to the eye itself. The eye is the best of artists. By the mutual action of its structure and of the laws of light, perspective is produced, which integrates every mass of objects, of what character soever, into a well colored and shaded globe, so that where the particular objects are mean and unaffecting, the landscape which they compose, is round and symmetrical. And as the eye is the best composer,[3] so light is the first of painters. There is no object so foul that intense light will not make beautiful. And the stimulus it affords to the sense, and a sort of infinitude which it hath, like space and time, make all matter gay. Even the corpse has its own beauty. But besides this general grace diffused over nature, almost all the individual forms are agreeable to the eye, as is proved by our endless imitations of some of them, as the acorn, the grape, the pine-cone, the wheat-ear, the egg, the wings and forms of most birds, the lion's claw, the serpent, the butterfly, sea-shells, flames, clouds, buds, leaves, and the forms of many trees, as the palm.

For better consideration, we may distribute the aspects of Beauty in a threefold manner.

I. First, the simple perception of natural forms is a delight. The influence of the forms and actions in nature, is so needful to man, that, in its lowest functions, it seems to lie on the confines of commodity and beauty. To the body and mind which have been cramped by noxious work or company, nature is medicinal and restores their tone. The tradesman, the attorney comes out of the din and craft of the street, and sees the sky and the woods, and is a man again. In their eternal calm, he finds himself. The health of the eye seems to demand a horizon. We are never tired, so long as we can see far enough.

But in other hours, Nature satisfies by its loveliness, and without any mixture of corporeal benefit. I see the spectacle of morning from the hill-top over against my house, from day-break to sun-rise, with emotions which an angel might share. The long slender bars of cloud float like fishes in the sea of crimson light. From the earth, as a shore, I look out into the silent sea. I seem to partake its rapid transformations: the active enchantment reaches my dust, and I dilate and conspire with the morning wind. How does Nature deify us with a few and cheap elements! Give me health and a day, and I will make the pomp

---

1. *Cosmos*, which means both "order" and "beauty."
2. In biology, capable of building tissue, formative. Emerson may also have been thinking of Samuel Taylor Coleridge's phrase, in his biographical and philosophical *Biographia Literaria* (1814; chapter 13), "escmplastic power" — a coinage that defines the imagination as a force that shapes things into a unified whole. Coleridge (1772–1834), English Romantic poet and theorist.
3. In painting, arranger.

of emperors ridiculous. The dawn is my Assyria; the sun-set and moon-rise my Paphos, and unimaginable realms of faerie; broad noon shall be my England of the senses and the understanding; the night shall be my Germany of mystic philosophy and dreams.[4]

Not less excellent, except for our less susceptibility in the afternoon, was the charm, last evening, of a January sunset. The western clouds divided and subdivided themselves into pink flakes modulated with tints of unspeakable softness; and the air had so much life and sweetness, that it was a pain to come within doors. What was it that nature would say? Was there no meaning in the live repose of the valley behind the mill, and which Homer or Shakspeare[5] could not re-form for me in words? The leafless trees become spires of flame in the sunset, with the blue east for their back-ground, and the stars of the dead calices[6] of flowers, and every withered stem and stubble rimed with frost, contribute something to the mute music.

The inhabitants of cities suppose that the country landscape is pleasant only half the year. I please myself with the graces of the winter scenery, and believe that we are as much touched by it as by the genial influences of summer. To the attentive eye, each moment of the year has its own beauty, and in the same field, it beholds, every hour, a picture which was never seen before, and which shall never be seen again. The heavens change every moment, and reflect their glory or gloom on the plains beneath. The state of the crop in the surrounding farms alters the expression of the earth from week to week. The succession of native plants in the pastures and roadsides, which makes the silent clock by which time tells the summer hours, will make even the divisions of the day sensible to a keen observer. The tribes of birds and insects, like the plants punctual to their time, follow each other, and the year has room for all. By water-courses, the variety is greater. In July, the blue pontederia or pickerel-weed blooms in large beds in the shallow parts of our pleasant river, and swarms with yellow butterflies in continual motion. Art cannot rival this pomp of purple and gold. Indeed the river is a perpetual gala, and boasts each month a new ornament.

But this beauty of Nature which is seen and felt as beauty, is the least part. The shows of day, the dewy morning, the rainbow, mountains, orchards in blossom, stars, moonlight, shadows in still water, and the like, if too eagerly hunted, become shows merely, and mock us with their unreality. Go out of the house to see the moon, and 't is mere tinsel; it will not please as when its light shines upon your necessary journey. The beauty that shimmers in the yellow afternoons of October, who ever could clutch it? Go forth to find it, and it is gone: 't is only a mirage as you look from the windows of diligence.[7]

2. The presence of a higher, namely, of the spiritual element is essential to its perfection. The high and divine beauty which can be loved without effeminacy, is that which is found in combination with the human will. Beauty is the mark God sets upon virtue. Every natural action is graceful. Every heroic

---

4. Emerson's fanciful cultural geography uses Assyria (an ancient west Asian empire) to stand for the birth of civilization, Paphos (city on Cyprus, ancient center of Venus worship) to stand for the romantic moon-struck adolescence of culture, modern England (e.g., seventeenth-century British empirical philosophy) to stand for culture's sensible adulthood, and contemporary German post-Kantian "mystical" subjectivism to stand for the darkening maturity of culture.
5. Emerson's usual spelling for Shakespeare.
6. Plural of calix, a chalice; cup of a flower.
7. Presumably the archaic English term based on the French *diligence* (industry, haste; also, stagecoach).

act is also decent, and causes the place and the bystanders to shine. We are taught by great actions that the universe is the property of every individual in it. Every rational creature has all nature for his dowry and estate. It is his, if he will. He may divest himself of it; he may creep into a corner, and abdicate his kingdom, as most men do, but he is entitled to the world by his constitution. In proportion to the energy of his thought and will, he takes up the world into himself. "All those things for which men plough, build, or sail, obey virtue;" said Sallust.[8] "The winds and waves," said Gibbon, "are always on the side of the ablest navigators."[9] So are the sun and moon and all the stars of heaven. When a noble act is done,—perchance in a scene of great natural beauty; when Leonidas and his three hundred martyrs consume one day in dying, and the sun and moon come each and look at them once in the steep defile of Thermopylæ; when Arnold Winkelried,[1] in the high Alps, under the shadow of the avalanche, gathers in his side a sheaf of Austrian spears to break the line for his comrades; are not these heroes entitled to add the beauty of the scene to the beauty of the deed? When the bark of Columbus nears the shore of America;—before it, the beach lined with savages, fleeing out of all their huts of cane; the sea behind; and the purple mountains of the Indian Archipelago around, can we separate the man from the living picture? Does not the New World clothe his form with her palm-groves and savannahs as fit drapery? Ever does natural beauty steal in like air, and envelope great actions. When Sir Harry Vane was dragged up the Tower-hill, sitting on a sled, to suffer death, as the champion of the English laws, one of the multitude cried out to him, "You never sate on so glorious a seat." Charles II., to intimidate the citizens of London, caused the patriot Lord Russel[2] to be drawn in an open coach, through the principal streets of the city, on his way to the scaffold. "But," his biographer says, "the multitude imagined they saw liberty and virtue sitting by his side." In private places, among sordid objects, an act of truth or heroism seems at once to draw to itself the sky as its temple, the sun as its candle. Nature stretcheth out her arms to embrace man, only let his thoughts be of equal greatness. Willingly does she follow his steps with the rose and the violet, and bend her lines of grandeur and grace to the decoration of her darling child. Only let his thoughts be of equal scope, and the frame will suit the picture. A virtuous man is in unison with her works, and makes the central figure of the visible sphere. Homer, Pindar, Socrates, Phocion,[3] associate themselves fitly in our memory with the geography and climate of Greece. The visible heavens and earth sympathize with Jesus. And in common life, whosoever has seen a person of powerful character and happy genius,

---

8. Gaius Sallustius Crispus (86–34 B.C.E.), Roman historian and politician. On Emerson's use of allusion and quotation, see n. 1, p. 3.
9. From *The History of the Decline and Fall of the Roman Empire* (1776–88), massive study of Roman history from the second century to the 1453 fall of Constantinople, by Edward Gibbon (1737–1794), English historian.
1. Arnold von Winkelried, Swiss knight who sacrificed himself in his army's defeat of Austria at the Battle of Sempach, July 9, 1386. Leonidas, king of Sparta, killed along with most of his army at Thermopylae, a narrow pass in east-central Greece, in 480 B.C.E. as they fought the invading Persians. *Defile:* here, a narrow gorge or pass that restricts lateral movement, especially that of an army.
2. Vane (1613–1662), English-appointed governor of Massachusetts (1636–37) and Puritan leader during the English Civil War, and William Russell (1639–1683), Whig parliamentarian, were among those executed by order of Charles II (1630–1685), king of England, Scotland, and Ireland (r. 1660–85), for opposing the Restoration of the Crown.
3. Athenian general (ca. 402–318 B.C.E.). Pindar (522?–443? B.C.E.), Greek lyric poet. Socrates, see n. 6, p. 8.

will have remarked how easily he took all things along with him,—the persons, the opinions, and the day, and nature became ancillary to a man.

3. There is still another aspect under which the beauty of the world may be viewed, namely, as it becomes an object of the intellect. Beside the relation of things to virtue, they have a relation to thought. The intellect searches out the absolute order of things as they stand in the mind of God, and without the colors of affection. The intellectual and the active powers seem to succeed each other, and the exclusive activity of the one, generates the exclusive activity of the other. There is something unfriendly in each to the other, but they are like the alternate periods of feeding and working in animals; each prepares and will be followed by the other. Therefore does beauty, which, in relation to actions, as we have seen, comes unsought, and comes because it is unsought, remain for the apprehension and pursuit of the intellect; and then again, in its turn, of the active power. Nothing divine dies. All good is eternally reproductive. The beauty of nature reforms itself in the mind, and not for barren contemplation, but for new creation.

All men are in some degree impressed by the face of the world; some men even to delight. This love of beauty is Taste. Others have the same love in such excess, that, not content with admiring, they seek to embody it in new forms. The creation of beauty is Art.

The production of a work of art throws a light upon the mystery of humanity. A work of art is an abstract or epitome of the world. It is the result or expression of nature, in miniature. For, although the works of nature are innumerable and all different, the result or the expression of them all is similar and single. Nature is a sea of forms radically alike and even unique. A leaf, a sun-beam, a landscape, the ocean, make an analogous impression on the mind. What is common to them all,—that perfectness and harmony, is beauty. The standard of beauty is the entire circuit of natural forms,—the totality of nature; which the Italians expressed by defining beauty "il piu nell' uno."[4] Nothing is quite beautiful alone: nothing but is beautiful in the whole. A single object is only so far beautiful as it suggests this universal grace. The poet, the painter, the sculptor, the musician, the architect, seek each to concentrate this radiance of the world on one point, and each in his several work to satisfy the love of beauty which stimulates him to produce. Thus is Art, a nature passed through the alembic of man. Thus in art, does nature work through the will of a man filled with the beauty of her first works.

The world thus exists to the soul to satisfy the desire of beauty. This element I call an ultimate end. No reason can be asked or given why the soul seeks beauty. Beauty, in its largest and profoundest sense, is one expression for the universe. God is the all-fair. Truth, and goodness, and beauty, are but different faces of the same All. But beauty in nature is not ultimate. It is the herald of inward and eternal beauty, and is not alone a solid and satisfactory good. It must stand as a part, and not as yet the last or highest expression of the final cause of Nature.

---

4. The many in the one (Italian). Recurrent Emerson motif; see, e.g., the poem "Each and All" (p. 432).

Chapter IV. Language

Language is a third use which Nature subserves to man. Nature is the vehicle of thought, and in a simple, double, and threefold degree.

1. Words are signs of natural facts.
2. Particular natural facts are symbols of particular spiritual facts.
3. Nature is the symbol of spirit.

1. Words are signs of natural facts. The use of natural history is to give us aid in supernatural history: the use of the outer creation, to give us language for the beings and changes of the inward creation. Every word which is used to express a moral or intellectual fact, if traced to its root, is found to be borrowed from some material appearance. *Right* means *straight*; *wrong* means *twisted*. *Spirit* primarily means *wind*; *transgression*, the crossing of a *line*; *supercilious*, the *raising of the eyebrow*. We say the *heart* to express emotion, the *head* to denote thought; and *thought* and *emotion* are words borrowed from sensible things, and now appropriated to spiritual nature. Most of the process by which this transformation is made, is hidden from us in the remote time when language was framed; but the same tendency may be daily observed in children. Children and savages use only nouns or names of things, which they convert into verbs, and apply to analogous mental acts.

2. But this origin of all words that convey a spiritual import,—so conspicuous a fact in the history of language,—is our least debt to nature. It is not words only that are emblematic; it is things which are emblematic.[5] Every natural fact is a symbol of some spiritual fact. Every appearance in nature corresponds[6] to some state of the mind, and that state of the mind can only be described by presenting that natural appearance as its picture. An enraged man is a lion, a cunning man is a fox, a firm man is a rock, a learned man is a torch. A lamb is innocence; a snake is subtle spite; flowers express to us the delicate affections. Light and darkness are our familiar expression for knowledge and ignorance; and heat for love. Visible distance behind and before us, is respectively our image of memory and hope.

Who looks upon a river in a meditative hour, and is not reminded of the flux of all things? Throw a stone into the stream, and the circles that propagate themselves are the beautiful type[7] of all influence. Man is conscious of a universal soul within or behind his individual life, wherein, as in a firmament, the natures of Justice, Truth, Love, Freedom, arise and shine. This universal soul, he calls Reason:[8] it is not mine, or thine, or his, but we are its; we are its property and men. And the blue sky in which the private earth is buried, the sky with its eternal calm, and full of everlasting orbs, is the type of Reason. That which, intellectually considered, we call Reason, considered in relation to nature, we

---

5. See n. 5, p. 12.
6. Emerson was influenced by the doctrine of "correspondence" developed by Emanuel Swedenborg (1668–1772), Swedish scientist and theologian whose visions and writings inspired his followers to establish the Church of the New Jerusalem after his death. Emerson includes a chapter on him ("Swedenborg, or the Mystic") in *Representative Men*.
7. See n. 4, p. 15. Emerson uses the word frequently in this and other works.
8. Emerson uses the term here, and later in contrast to *Understanding*, partly in the sense of Coleridge in the *Biographia Literaria*. For Coleridge, the Understanding classifies and perceives superficial likenesses, whereas the Reason, the highest imaginative function, creates organic syntheses. Emerson's capitalization here also suggests an allusion to the German nouns employed by the philosopher Immanuel Kant (1724–1804)—*Vernunft* and *Verstand* ("Reason" and "Understanding").

call Spirit. Spirit is the Creator. Spirit hath life in itself. And man in all ages and countries, embodies it in his language, as the FATHER.

It is easily seen that there is nothing lucky or capricious in these analogies, but that they are constant, and pervade nature. These are not the dreams of a few poets, here and there, but man is an analogist, and studies relations in all objects. He is placed in the centre of beings, and a ray of relation passes from every other being to him. And neither can man be understood without these objects, nor these objects without man. All the facts in natural history taken by themselves, have no value, but are barren, like a single sex. But marry it to human history, and it is full of life. Whole Floras, all Linnæus' and Buffon's[9] volumes, are dry catalogues of facts; but the most trivial of these facts, the habit of a plant, the organs, or work, or noise of an insect, applied to the illustration of a fact in intellectual philosophy, or, in any way associated to human nature, affects us in the most lively and agreeable manner. The seed of a plant,—to what affecting analogies in the nature of man, is that little fruit made use of, in all discourse, up to the voice of Paul, who calls the human corpse a seed,—"It is sown a natural body; it is raised a spiritual body."[1] The motion of the earth round its axis, and round the sun, makes the day, and the year. These are certain amounts of brute light and heat. But is there no intent of an analogy between man's life and the seasons? And do the seasons gain no grandeur or pathos from that analogy? The instincts of the ant are very unimportant, considered as the ant's; but the moment a ray of relation is seen to extend from it to man, and the little drudge is seen to be a monitor, a little body with a mighty heart, then all its habits, even that said to be recently observed, that it never sleeps,[2] become sublime.

Because of this radical correspondence between visible things and human thoughts, savages, who have only what is necessary, converse in figures. As we go back in history, language becomes more picturesque, until its infancy, when it is all poetry; or all spiritual facts are represented by natural symbols. The same symbols are found to make the original elements of all languages. It has moreover been observed, that the idioms of all languages approach each other in passages of the greatest eloquence and power. And as this is the first language, so is it the last. This immediate dependence of language upon nature, this conversion of an outward phenomenon into a type of somewhat in human life, never loses its power to affect us. It is this which gives that piquancy to the conversation of a strong-natured farmer or back-woodsman, which all men relish.

A man's power to connect his thought with its proper symbol, and so to utter it, depends on the simplicity of his character, that is, upon his love of truth, and his desire to communicate it without loss. The corruption of man is followed by the corruption of language. When simplicity of character and the sovereignty of ideas is broken up by the prevalence of secondary desires, the desire of riches, of pleasure, of power, and of praise,—and duplicity and falsehood take place of simplicity and truth, the power over nature as an interpreter of the will, is in a degree lost; new imagery ceases to be created, and old words are perverted

---

9. George Louis Leclerc, comte de Buffon (1707–1788), French naturalist, author of *Histoire naturelle* (1749–88). *Floras:* books that systematically describe plants in particular regions. Carolus Linnaeus (1707–1778), Swedish scientist, founder of the modern scientific classification system.
1. 1 Corinthians 15.44. Paul, see n. 1, p. 3.
2. Actually, modern research suggests that many, perhaps most, insects exhibit clear circadian cycles of rest and activity that appear to be analogous to sleep and arousal in mammals.

to stand for things which are not; a paper currency is employed, when there is no bullion in the vaults. In due time, the fraud is manifest, and words lose all power to stimulate the understanding or the affections. Hundreds of writers may be found in every long-civilized nation, who for a short time believe, and make others believe, that they see and utter truths, who do not of themselves clothe one thought in its natural garment, but who feed unconsciously on the language created by the primary writers of the country, those, namely, who hold primarily on nature.

But wise men pierce this rotten diction and fasten words again to visible things; so that picturesque language is at once a commanding certificate that he who employs it, is a man in alliance with truth and God. The moment our discourse rises above the ground line of familiar facts, and is inflamed with passion or exalted by thought, it clothes itself in images. A man conversing in earnest, if he watch his intellectual processes, will find that a material image, more or less luminous, arises in his mind, cotemporaneous with every thought, which furnishes the vestment of the thought. Hence, good writing and brilliant discourse are perpetual allegories. This imagery is spontaneous. It is the blending of experience with the present action of the mind. It is proper creation. It is the working of the Original Cause through the instruments he has already made.

These facts may suggest the advantage which the country-life possesses for a powerful mind, over the artificial and curtailed life of cities. We know more from nature than we can at will communicate. Its light flows into the mind evermore, and we forget its presence. The poet, the orator, bred in the woods, whose senses have been nourished by their fair and appeasing changes, year after year, without design and without heed,—shall not lose their lesson altogether, in the roar of cities or the broil of politics. Long hereafter, amidst agitation and terror in national councils,—in the hour of revolution,—these solemn images shall reappear in their morning lustre, as fit symbols and words of the thoughts which the passing events shall awaken. At the call of a noble sentiment, again the woods wave, the pines murmur, the river rolls and shines, and the cattle low upon the mountains, as he saw and heard them in his infancy. And with these forms, the spells of persuasion, the keys of power are put into his hands.

3. We are thus assisted by natural objects in the expression of particular meanings. But how great a language to convey such pepper-corn[3] informations! Did it need such noble races of creatures, this profusion of forms, this host of orbs in heaven, to furnish man with the dictionary and grammar of his municipal speech? Whilst we use this grand cipher to expedite the affairs of our pot and kettle, we feel that we have not yet put it to its use, neither are able. We are like travellers using the cinders of a volcano to roast their eggs. Whilst we see that it always stands ready to clothe what we would say, we cannot avoid the question, whether the characters are not significant of themselves. Have mountains, and waves, and skies, no significance but what we consciously give them, when we employ them as emblems of our thoughts? The world is emblematic. Parts of speech are metaphors, because the whole of nature is a metaphor of the human mind. The laws of moral nature answer to those of matter as face to face in a glass. "The visible world and the relation of its parts, is the dial plate of the

3. Trivial, small.

invisible."[4] The axioms of physics translate the laws of ethics. Thus, "the whole is greater than its part;" "reaction is equal to action;" "the smallest weight may be made to lift the greatest, the difference of weight being compensated by time;" and many the like propositions, which have an ethical as well as physical sense. These propositions have a much more extensive and universal sense when applied to human life, than when confined to technical use.

In like manner, the memorable words of history, and the proverbs of nations, consist usually of a natural fact, selected as a picture or parable of a moral truth. Thus; A rolling stone gathers no moss; A bird in the hand is worth two in the bush; A cripple in the right way, will beat a racer in the wrong; Make hay while the sun shines; 'T is hard to carry a full cup even; Vinegar is the son of wine; The last ounce broke the camel's back; Long-lived trees make roots first;—and the like. In their primary sense these are trivial facts, but we repeat them for the value of their analogical import. What is true of proverbs, is true of all fables, parables, and allegories.

This relation between the mind and matter is not fancied by some poet, but stands in the will of God, and so is free to be known by all men. It appears to men, or it does not appear. When in fortunate hours we ponder this miracle, the wise man doubts, if, at all other times, he is not blind and deaf;

> ——"Can these things be,
> And overcome us like a summer's cloud,
> Without our special wonder?"[5]

for the universe becomes transparent, and the light of higher laws than its own, shines through it. It is the standing problem which has exercised the wonder and the study of every fine genius since the world began; from the era of the Egyptians and the Brahmins, to that of Pythagoras, of Plato, of Bacon, of Leibnitz,[6] of Swedenborg. There sits the Sphinx[7] at the road-side, and from age to age, as each prophet comes by, he tries his fortune at reading her riddle. There seems to be a necessity in spirit to manifest itself in material forms; and day and night, river and storm, beast and bird, acid and alkali, preëxist in necessary Ideas in the mind of God, and are what they are by virtue of preceding affections, in the world of spirit.[8] A fact is the end or last issue of spirit. The visible creation is the terminus or the circumference of the invisible world. "Material objects," said a French philosopher, "are necessarily kinds of scoriæ of the substantial

---

4. Swedenborg, quoted in the *New Jerusalem Magazine* 5 (July 1832), a publication of the American Swedenborgian society that Emerson read enthusiastically. The phrase also provides the title for *The Dial*, the Transcendentalist periodical edited by Emerson and his close friend and associate the author Margaret Fuller (1810–1850). Excerpts from *The Dial* and from Emerson's comments on Fuller appear later in this volume.
5. Shakespeare, *Macbeth* 3.4.110–12.
6. Baron Gottfried Wilhelm von Leibnitz (1646–1716), German philosopher and mathematician. *Brahmins*: members of the highest Hindu caste, originally also priests; responsible for officiating at religious rites and studying and teaching the Vedas. Pythagoras (fl. sixth century B.C.E.), Greek philosopher and mathematician. Bacon, see n. 3, p. 6.
7. Figure in Egyptian myth having the body of a lion and the head of a man, ram, or hawk; often stands before pyramids as a guardian, most famously before the Great Pyramids at Giza. In Greek myth, winged creature having the head of a woman and the body of a lion, who sat on a pinnacle at the gate of Thebes posing questions to travelers, who were killed when they could not answer its riddle. The riddle was answered by Oedipus, who slew the Sphinx. See Emerson's poem "The Sphinx" (p. 429) and the essay by Saundra Morris (p. 777).
8. These concepts and terms are Platonic (see n. 4, p. 15).

thoughts of the Creator, which must always preserve an exact relation to their first origin; in other words, visible nature must have a spiritual and moral side."[9] This doctrine is abstruse, and though the images of "garment," "scoriæ," "mirror," &c., may stimulate the fancy, we must summon the aid of subtler and more vital expositors to make it plain. "Every scripture is to be interpreted by the same spirit which gave it forth," — is the fundamental law of criticism.[1] A life in harmony with nature, the love of truth and of virtue, will purge the eyes to understand her text. By degrees we may come to know the primitive sense of the permanent objects of nature, so that the world shall be to us an open book, and every form significant of its hidden life and final cause.

A new interest surprises us, whilst, under the view now suggested, we contemplate the fearful extent and multitude of objects; since "every object rightly seen, unlocks a new faculty of the soul."[2] That which was unconscious truth, becomes, when interpreted and defined in an object, a part of the domain of knowledge—a new weapon in the magazine of power.

Chapter V. Discipline

In view of the significance of nature, we arrive at once at a new fact, that nature is a discipline. This use of the world includes the preceding uses, as parts of itself.

Space, time, society, labor, climate, food, locomotion, the animals, the mechanical forces, give us sincerest lessons, day by day, whose meaning is unlimited. They educate both the Understanding and the Reason.[3] Every property of matter is a school for the understanding, — its solidity or resistance, its inertia, its extension, its figure, its divisibility. The understanding adds, divides, combines, measures, and finds nutriment and room for its activity in this worthy scene. Meantime, Reason transfers all these lessons into its own world of thought, by perceiving the analogy that marries Matter and Mind.

1. Nature is a discipline of the understanding in intellectual truths. Our dealing with sensible[4] objects is a constant exercise in the necessary lessons of difference, of likeness, of order, of being and seeming, of progressive arrangement; of ascent from particular to general; of combination to one end of manifold forces. Proportioned to the importance of the organ to be formed, is the extreme care with which its tuition is provided, — a care pretermitted in no single case. What tedious training, day after day, year after year, never ending, to form the common sense; what continual reproduction of annoyances, inconveniences, dilemmas; what rejoicing over us of little men; what disputing of prices, what reckonings of interest, — and all to form the Hand of the mind; — to instruct us that "good thoughts are no better than good dreams, unless they be executed!"[5]

The same good office is performed by Property and its filial systems of debt and credit. Debt, grinding debt, whose iron face the widow, the orphan, and the

9. From G. Oegger, *The True Messiah; or the Old and New Testaments, Examined According to the Principles of Language and Nature*, trans. Elizabeth Peabody (1842). *Scoriæ*: skor, excrement (Greek); cinderlike fragments of dark lava or refuse of smelted metal; slag.
1. George Fox (1624–1691), English founder of the Society of Friends, quoted in William Sewel's *History of the Rise, Increase, and Progress of the Christian People Called Quakers* (1823). See also n. 6, p. 18.
2. Quoted from Coleridge's *Aids to Reflection*, a religious and philosophical treatise.
3. See n. 8, p. 35.
4. Able to be perceived by the senses.
5. From the essay "Of Great Place" by Francis Bacon.

sons of genius fear and hate;—debt, which consumes so much time, which so cripples and disheartens a great spirit with cares that seem so base, is a preceptor whose lessons cannot be forgone, and is needed most by those who suffer from it most. Moreover, property, which has been well compared to snow,—"if it fall level to-day, it will be blown into drifts to-morrow,"—is the surface action of internal machinery, like the index on the face of a clock. Whilst now it is the gymnastics of the understanding, it is hiving[6] in the foresight of the spirit, experience in profounder laws.

The whole character and fortune of the individual are affected by the least inequalities in the culture of the understanding; for example, in the perception of differences. Therefore is Space, and therefore Time, that man may know that things are not huddled and lumped, but sundered and individual. A bell and a plough have each their use, and neither can do the office of the other. Water is good to drink, coal to burn, wool to wear; but wool cannot be drunk, nor water spun, nor coal eaten. The wise man shows his wisdom in separation, in gradation, and his scale of creatures and of merits is as wide as nature. The foolish have no range in their scale, but suppose every man is as every other man. What is not good they call the worst, and what is not hateful, they call the best.

In like manner, what good heed, nature forms in us! She pardons no mistakes. Her yea is yea, and her nay, nay.[7]

The first steps in Agriculture, Astronomy, Zoölogy, (those first steps which the farmer, the hunter, and the sailor take,) teach that nature's dice are always loaded; that in her heaps and rubbish are concealed sure and useful results.

How calmly and genially the mind apprehends one after another the laws of physics! What noble emotions dilate the mortal as he enters into the counsels of the creation, and feels by knowledge the privilege to BE! His insight refines him. The beauty of nature shines in his own breast. Man is greater that he can see this, and the universe less, because Time and Space relations vanish as laws are known.

Here again we are impressed and even daunted by the immense Universe to be explored. "What we know, is a point to what we do not know."[8] Open any recent journal of science, and weigh the problems suggested concerning Light, Heat, Electricity, Magnetism, Physiology, Geology, and judge whether the interest of natural science is likely to be soon exhausted.

Passing by many particulars of the discipline of nature, we must not omit to specify two.

The exercise of the Will or the lesson of power is taught in every event. From the child's successive possession of his several senses up to the hour when he saith, "Thy will be done!"[9] he is learning the secret, that he can reduce under his will, not only particular events, but great classes, nay the whole series of events, and so conform all facts to his character. Nature is thoroughly mediate. It is made to serve. It receives the dominion of man as meekly as the ass on which the Saviour rode. It offers all its kingdoms to man as the raw material which he may mould into what is useful. Man is never weary of working it up. He forges the subtile and delicate air into wise and melodious words, and gives them wing as angels of persuasion and command. One after another, his victo-

6. Storing up, accumulating, as bees do honey.
7. Cf. Matthew 5.37.
8. Ascribed to Joseph Butler (1692–1752), bishop of Bristol and Durham. Cf. EL 2.358.
9. Cf. Matthew 6.10 and 26.42.

rious thought comes up with and reduces all things, until the world becomes, at last, only a realized will,—the double of the man.

2. Sensible objects conform to the premonitions of Reason and reflect the conscience. All things are moral; and in their boundless changes have an unceasing reference to spiritual nature. Therefore is nature glorious with form, color, and motion, that every globe in the remotest heaven; every chemical change from the rudest crystal up to the laws of life; every change of vegetation from the first principle of growth in the eye of a leaf, to the tropical forest and antediluvian coal-mine; every animal function from the sponge up to Hercules,[1] shall hint or thunder to man the laws of right and wrong, and echo the Ten Commandments. Therefore is nature ever the ally of Religion: lends all her pomp and riches to the religious sentiment. Prophet and priest, David, Isaiah,[2] Jesus, have drawn deeply from this source. This ethical character so penetrates the bone and marrow of nature, as to seem the end for which it was made. Whatever private purpose is answered by any member or part, this is its public and universal function, and is never omitted. Nothing in nature is exhausted in its first use. When a thing has served an end to the uttermost, it is wholly new for an ulterior service. In God, every end is converted into a new means. Thus the use of commodity, regarded by itself, is mean and squalid. But it is to the mind an education in the doctrine of Use, namely, that a thing is good only so far as it serves; that a conspiring of parts and efforts to the production of an end, is essential to any being. The first and gross manifestation of this truth, is our inevitable and hated training in values and wants, in corn and meat.

It has already been illustrated, that every natural process is a version of a moral sentence. The moral law lies at the centre of nature and radiates to the circumference. It is the pith and marrow of every substance, every relation, and every process. All things with which we deal, preach to us. What is a farm but a mute gospel? The chaff and the wheat, weeds and plants, blight, rain, insects, sun,—it is a sacred emblem from the first furrow of spring to the last stack which the snow of winter overtakes in the fields. But the sailor, the shepherd, the miner, the merchant, in their several resorts, have each an experience precisely parallel, and leading to the same conclusion: because all organizations are radically alike. Nor can it be doubted that this moral sentiment which thus scents the air, grows in the grain, and impregnates the waters of the world, is caught by man and sinks into his soul. The moral influence of nature upon every individual is that amount of truth which it illustrates to him. Who can estimate this? Who can guess how much firmness the sea-beaten rock has taught the fisherman? how much tranquillity has been reflected to man from the azure sky, over whose unspotted deeps the winds forevermore drive flocks of stormy clouds, and leave no wrinkle or stain? how much industry and providence and affection we have caught from the pantomime of brutes? What a searching preacher of self-command is the varying phenomenon of Health!

Herein is especially apprehended the unity of Nature—the unity in variety—which meets us everywhere. All the endless variety of things make an iden-

---

1. Son of Zeus and Alcmene, known for his extraordinary strength.
2. Hebrew prophet (eighth century b.c.e.). David (d. ca. 962 b.c.e.), second king of Judah and Israel; said as a youth to have slain Philistine giant Goliath and later to have authored many of the biblical Psalms.

tical impression. Xenophanes[3] complained in his old age, that, look where he
would, all things hastened back to Unity. He was weary of seeing the same entity in the tedious variety of forms. The fable of Proteus[4] has a cordial truth. A
leaf, a drop, a crystal, a moment of time is related to the whole, and partakes of
the perfection of the whole. Each particle is a microcosm, and faithfully renders the likeness of the world.

Not only resemblances exist in things whose analogy is obvious, as when
we detect the type of the human hand in the flipper of the fossil saurus,[5] but
also in objects wherein there is great superficial unlikeness. Thus architecture
is called "frozen music," by De Stael and Goethe. Vitruvius thought an architect should be a musician. "A Gothic church," said Coleridge, "is a petrified religion." Michael Angelo maintained, that, to an architect, a knowledge of
anatomy is essential. In Haydn's[6] oratorios, the notes present to the imagination
not only motions, as, of the snake, the stag, and the elephant, but colors also; as
the green grass. The law of harmonic sounds reappears in the harmonic colors.
The granite is differenced in its laws only by the more or less of heat, from the
river that wears it away. The river, as it flows, resembles the air that flows over
it; the air resembles the light which traverses it with more subtile currents; the
light resembles the heat which rides with it through Space. Each creature is
only a modification of the other; the likeness in them is more than the difference, and their radical law is one and the same. A rule of one art, or a law of one
organization, holds true throughout nature. So intimate is this Unity, it is easily seen, it lies under the undermost garment of nature, and betrays its source
in Universal Spirit. For, it pervades Thought also. Every universal truth which
we express in words, implies or supposes every other truth. *Omne verum vero
consonat.*[7] It is like a great circle on a sphere, comprising all possible circles;
which, however, may be drawn, and comprise it, in like manner. Every such
truth is the absolute Ens[8] seen from one side. But it has innumerable sides.

The central Unity is still more conspicuous in actions. Words are finite organs of the infinite mind. They cannot cover the dimensions of what is in truth.
They break, chop, and impoverish it. An action is the perfection and publication of thought. A right action seems to fill the eye, and to be related to all nature. "The wise man, in doing one thing, does all; or, in the one thing he does
rightly, he sees the likeness of all which is done rightly."[9]

Words and actions are not the attributes of brute nature. They introduce
us to the human form, of which all other organizations appear to be degradations. When this appears among so many that surround it, the spirit prefers it
to all others. It says, 'From such as this, have I drawn joy and knowledge; in
such as this, have I found and beheld myself; I will speak to it; it can speak

3. Greek philosopher-poet (560?–478? B.C.E.), Cf. Emerson's poem "Xenophanes."
4. In Greek mythology, an old man and a prophet who was capable of assuming various forms to avoid
   soothsaying but who took his own shape and revealed truths when caught and bound.
5. Dinosaur.
6. Franz Joseph Haydn (1732–1809), Austrian composer. Madame de Staël, Baronne Anne Louise Germaine Necker de Staël-Holstein (1766–1817), French author and salon personality; for selections from
   her *On Germany* (1813) see p. 573. Johann Wolfgang von Goethe (1749–1832), German Romantic author, scientist, and philosopher crucial for Emerson and his circle. Marcus Vitruvius Pollio (first century
   B.C.E.), Roman architect and writer. Michelangelo Buonarroti (1475–1564), Italian sculptor, poet,
   painter, and architect.
7. All truth is consonant with truth (Latin).
8. Philosophical term for being in itself (Latin).
9. From Goethe's *Wilhelm Meister's Travels* (1822), part of a four-volume *Bildungsroman*, or novel of development, translated by Carlyle (1827).

again; it can yield me thought already formed and alive.' In fact, the eye,—the mind,—is always accompanied by these forms, male and female; and these are incomparably the richest informations of the power and order that lie at the heart of things. Unfortunately, every one of them bears the marks as of some injury; is marred and superficially defective. Nevertheless, far different from the deaf and dumb nature around them, these all rest like fountain-pipes on the unfathomed sea of thought and virtue where-to they alone, of all organizations, are the entrances.

It were a pleasant inquiry to follow into detail their ministry to our education, but where would it stop? We are associated in adolescent and adult life with some friends, who, like skies and waters, are coextensive with our idea; who, answering each to a certain affection of the soul, satisfy our desire on that side; whom we lack power to put at such focal distance from us, that we can mend or even analyze them. We cannot choose but love them. When much intercourse with a friend has supplied us with a standard of excellence, and has increased our respect for the resources of God who thus sends a real person to outgo our ideal; when he has, moreover, become an object of thought, and, whilst his character retains all its unconscious effect, is converted in the mind into solid and sweet wisdom,—it is a sign to us that his office is closing, and he is commonly withdrawn from our sight in a short time.

Chapter VI. Idealism[1]

Thus is the unspeakable but intelligible and practicable meaning of the world conveyed to man, the immortal pupil,[2] in every object of sense. To this one end of Discipline, all parts of nature conspire.

A noble doubt perpetually suggests itself, whether this end be not the Final Cause of the Universe; and whether nature outwardly exists. It is a sufficient account of that Appearance we call the World, that God will teach a human mind, and so makes it the receiver of a certain number of congruent sensations, which we call sun and moon, man and woman, house and trade. In my utter impotence to test the authenticity of the report of my senses, to know whether the impressions they make on me correspond with outlying objects, what difference does it make, whether Orion[3] is up there in heaven, or some god paints the image in the firmament of the soul? The relations of parts and the end of the whole remaining the same, what is the difference, whether land and sea interact, and worlds revolve and intermingle without number or end,—deep yawning under deep, and galaxy balancing galaxy, throughout absolute space,—or, whether, without relations of time and space, the same appearances are inscribed in the constant faith of man? Whether nature enjoy a substantial existence without, or is only in the apocalypse of the mind, it is alike useful and alike venerable to me. Be it what it may, it is ideal to me, so long as I cannot try the accuracy of my senses.

---

1. Emerson refers to the term in its various philosophical senses, from the Platonic notion of the ultimate reality of the noumenal (ideal) world as opposed to the phenomenal; to the "Ideal theory" ("to be is to be perceived") of George Berkeley (1685–1753), Irish prelate and philosopher; to the belief (characteristic of German Romantic philosophers, especially Kant and his followers) that the mind, or cognition, plays a key role in the constitution of our knowledge of reality.
2. Cf. the "transparent eye-ball" in chapter 1 (p. 29), and note Emerson's intentional pun.
3. Constellation in the celestial equator near Gemini and Taurus named for the mythological Greek hunter; it contains the stars Betelgeuse and Rigel.

The frivolous make themselves merry with the Ideal theory, as if its consequences were burlesque; as if it affected the stability of nature. It surely does
not. God never jests with us, and will not compromise the end of nature, by permitting any inconsequence in its procession. Any distrust of the permanence of
laws, would paralyze the faculties of man. Their permanence is sacredly respected, and his faith therein is perfect. The wheels and springs of man are all
set to the hypothesis of the permanence of nature. We are not built like a ship
to be tossed, but like a house to stand. It is a natural consequence of this structure, that, so long as the active powers predominate over the reflective, we resist with indignation any hint that nature is more short-lived or mutable than
spirit. The broker, the wheelwright, the carpenter, the tollman, are much dis-
pleased at the intimation.

But whilst we acquiesce entirely in the permanence of natural laws, the
question of the absolute existence of nature still remains open. It is the uniform
effect of culture on the human mind, not to shake our faith in the stability of
particular phenomena, as of heat, water, azote;[4] but to lead us to regard nature
as a phenomenon, not a substance; to attribute necessary existence to spirit; to
esteem nature as an accident and an effect.

To the senses and the unrenewed understanding, belongs a sort of instinctive belief in the absolute existence of nature. In their view, man and nature are indissolubly joined. Things are ultimates, and they never look beyond
their sphere. The presence of Reason mars this faith. The first effort of thought
tends to relax this despotism of the senses, which binds us to nature as if we were
a part of it, and shows us nature aloof, and, as it were, afloat. Until this higher
agency intervened, the animal eye sees, with wonderful accuracy, sharp outlines and colored surfaces. When the eye of Reason opens, to outline and surface are at once added, grace and expression. These proceed from imagination
and affection, and abate somewhat of the angular distinctness of objects. If the
Reason be stimulated to more earnest vision, outlines and surfaces become
transparent, and are no longer seen; causes and spirits are seen through them.
The best moments of life are these delicious awakenings of the higher powers,
and the reverential withdrawing of nature before its God.

Let us proceed to indicate the effects of culture. I. Our first institution in
the Ideal philosophy is a hint from nature herself.

Nature is made to conspire with spirit to emancipate us. Certain mechanical changes, a small alteration in our local position apprizes us of a dualism. We are strangely affected by seeing the shore from a moving ship, from a
balloon, or through the tints of an unusual sky. The least change in our point
of view, gives the whole world a pictorial air. A man who seldom rides, needs
only to get into a coach and traverse his own town, to turn the street into a pup-
pet-show. The men, the women,—talking, running, bartering, fighting,—the
earnest mechanic, the lounger, the beggar, the boys, the dogs, are unrealized at
once, or, at least, wholly detached from all relation to the observer, and seen as
apparent, not substantial beings. What new thoughts are suggested by seeing a
face of country quite familiar, in the rapid movement of the rail-road car! Nay,
the most wonted objects, (make a very slight change in the point of vision,)
please us most. In a camera obscura, the butcher's cart, and the figure of one of
our own family amuse us. So a portrait of a well-known face gratifies us. Turn

4. Nitrogen (archaic).

the eyes upside down, by looking at the landscape through your legs, and how agreeable is the picture, though you have seen it any time these twenty years!

In these cases, by mechanical means, is suggested the difference between the observer and the spectacle,—between man and nature. Hence arises a pleasure mixed with awe; I may say, a low degree of the sublime[5] is felt from the fact, probably, that man is hereby apprized, that, whilst the world is a spectacle, something in himself is stable.

2. In a higher manner, the poet communicates the same pleasure. By a few strokes he delineates, as on air, the sun, the mountain, the camp, the city, the hero, the maiden, not different from what we know them, but only lifted from the ground and afloat before the eye. He unfixes the land and the sea, makes them revolve around the axis of his primary thought, and disposes them anew. Possessed himself by a heroic passion, he uses matter as symbols of it. The sensual man[6] conforms thoughts to things; the poet conforms things to his thoughts. The one esteems nature as rooted and fast; the other, as fluid, and impresses his being thereon. To him, the refractory world is ductile and flexible; he invests dust and stones with humanity, and makes them the words of the Reason. The Imagination may be defined to be, the use which the Reason makes of the material world. Shakspeare possesses the power of subordinating nature for the purposes of expression, beyond all poets. His imperial muse tosses the creation like a bauble from hand to hand, and uses it to embody any caprice of thought that is upper-most in his mind. The remotest spaces of nature are visited, and the farthest sundered things are brought together, by a subtle spiritual connection. We are made aware that magnitude of material things is relative, and all objects shrink and expand to serve the passion of the poet. Thus, in his sonnets, the lays of birds, the scents and dyes of flowers, he finds to be the *shadow*[7] of his beloved; time, which keeps her from him, is his *chest*; the suspicion she has awakened, is her *ornament*;

> The ornament of beauty is Suspect,
> A crow which flies in heaven's sweetest air.[8]

His passion is not the fruit of chance; it swells, as he speaks, to a city, or a state.

> No, it was builded far from accident;
> It suffers not in smiling pomp, nor falls
> Under the brow of thralling discontent;
> It fears not policy, that heretic,
> That works on leases of short numbered hours,
> But all alone stands hugely politic.[9]

---

5. Here and elsewhere, Emerson uses the term in its general and technical senses. In aesthetics, cf. Longinus (fl. first century C.E.), Greek philosopher, whose *On the Sublime* identifies as sublime something that provokes a spark of connection between reader and writer. Later, Edmund Burke (1729–1797), Irish-born English philosopher and politician, makes the distinction between "sublime," being magnificently awe inspiring, and "beautiful," having more finite and less overwhelming appeal (*A Philosophical Inquiry into the Origin of our Ideas of the Sublime and the Beautiful*, 1756).
6. One who grounds reality in the world as perceived by the senses, as opposed to the idealist, who emphasizes the world as idea.
7. The dim reflection of an ideal. In Plato, a thing in the world is a shadow of its image in the ideal world of Forms; in typology, types are mere shadows of their fulfillments, their antitypes (see n. 4, p. 15).
8. From Shakespeare, Sonnet 70.
9. From Shakespeare, Sonnet 124.

In the strength of his constancy, the Pyramids seem to him recent and transitory. The freshness of youth and love dazzles him with its resemblance to morning.

> Take those lips away
> Which so sweetly were forsworn;
> And those eyes,—the break of day,
> Lights that do mislead the morn![1]

The wild beauty of this hyperbole, I may say, in passing, it would not be easy to match in literature.

This transfiguration which all material objects undergo through the passion of the poet,—this power which he exerts to dwarf the great, to magnify the small,—might be illustrated by a thousand examples from his Plays. I have before me the Tempest, and will cite only these few lines.

> ARIEL. The strong based promontory
> Have I made shake, and by the spurs plucked up
> The pine and cedar.

Prospero calls for music to soothe the frantic Alonzo, and his companions;

> A solemn air, and the best comforter
> To an unsettled fancy, cure thy brains
> Now useless, boiled within thy skull.

Again;

> The charm dissolves apace,
> And, as the morning steals upon the night,
> Melting the darkness, so their rising senses
> Begin to chase the ignorant fumes that mantle
> Their clearer reason.
> Their understanding
> Begins to swell: and the approaching tide
> Will shortly fill the reasonable shores
> That now lie foul and muddy.[2]

The perception of real affinities between events, (that is to say, of *ideal* affinities, for those only are real,) enables the poet thus to make free with the most imposing forms and phenomena of the world, and to assert the predominance of the soul.

3. Whilst thus the poet animates nature with his own thoughts, he differs from the philosopher only herein, that the one proposes Beauty as his main end; the other Truth. But the philosopher, not less than the poet, postpones the apparent order and relations of things to the empire of thought. "The problem of

---

1. Shakespeare, *Measure for Measure* 4.1.1–4.
2. Shakespeare, *The Tempest* 5.1.45ff. Actually, all lines are spoken by Prospero, magician, ruler of the enchanted island, and deposed duke of Milan, as Emerson correctly notes in his 1835 lecture on Shakespeare (see *EL* 1.292–93).

philosophy," according to Plato, "is, for all that exists conditionally, to find a ground unconditioned and absolute."[3] It proceeds on the faith that a law determines all phenomena, which being known, the phenomena can be predicted. That law, when in the mind, is an idea. Its beauty is infinite. The true philosopher and the true poet are one, and a beauty, which is truth, and a truth, which is beauty, is the aim of both. Is not the charm of one of Plato's or Aristotle's definitions, strictly like that of the Antigone of Sophocles?[4] It is, in both cases, that a spiritual life has been imparted to nature; that the solid seeming block of matter has been pervaded and dissolved by a thought; that this feeble human being has penetrated the vast masses of nature with an informing soul, and recognised itself in their harmony, that is, seized their law. In physics, when this is attained, the memory disburthens itself of its cumbrous catalogues of particulars, and carries centuries of observation in a single formula.

Thus even in physics, the material is degraded before the spiritual. The astronomer, the geometer, rely on their irrefragable analysis, and disdain the results of observation. The sublime remark of Euler on his law of arches, "This will be found contrary to all experience, yet is true;"[5] had already transferred nature into the mind, and left matter like an outcast corpse.

4. Intellectual science has been observed to beget invariably a doubt of the existence of matter. Turgot[6] said, "He that has never doubted the existence of matter, may be assured he has no aptitude for metaphysical inquiries." It fastens the attention upon immortal necessary uncreated natures, that is, upon Ideas; and in their presence, we feel that the outward circumstance is a dream and a shade. Whilst we wait in this Olympus[7] of gods, we think of nature as an appendix to the soul. We ascend into their region, and know that these are the thoughts of the Supreme Being. "These are they who were set up from everlasting, from the beginning, or ever the earth was. When he prepared the heavens, they were there; when he established the clouds above, when he strengthened the fountains of the deep. Then they were by him, as one brought up with him. Of them took he counsel."[8]

Their influence is proportionate. As objects of science, they are accessible to few men. Yet all men are capable of being raised by piety or by passion, into their region. And no man touches these divine natures, without becoming, in some degree, himself divine. Like a new soul, they renew the body. We become physically nimble and lightsome; we tread on air; life is no longer irksome, and we think it will never be so. No man fears age or misfortune or death, in their serene company, for he is transported out of the district of change. Whilst we behold unveiled the nature of Justice and Truth, we learn the difference between the absolute and the conditional or relative. We apprehend the absolute. As it were, for the first time, *we exist*. We become immortal, for we learn that time and space are relations of matter; that, with a perception of truth, or a virtuous will, they have no affinity.

---

3. Cited in *The Friend* (1809–10), a weekly periodical edited and mostly written by Coleridge.
4. Greek dramatist (496?–406 B.C.E.), whose play *Antigone* is about the daughter of Oedipus (Antigone), who is sentenced to death for burying her brother, Polyneices, after he was killed attacking Thebes. Aristotle (384–322 B.C.E.), Greek philosopher, pupil of Plato.
5. Leonhard Euler (1707–1783), Swiss mathematician, philosopher, and physicist, cited by Coleridge in *Aids to Reflection*.
6. Anne Robert Jacques Turgot, baron de l'Aulne (1727–1781), French politician, economist, and reformer.
7. Mount Olympus, in Greece, is the mythological home of the Greek gods.
8. Cf. Proverbs 8.23ff.

5. Finally, religion and ethics, which may be fitly called,—the practice of ideas, or the introduction of ideas into life,—have an analogous effect with all lower culture, in degrading nature and suggesting its dependence on spirit. Ethics and religion differ herein; that the one is the system of human duties commencing from man; the other, from God. Religion includes the personality of God; Ethics does not. They are one to our present design. They both put nature under foot. The first and last lesson of religion is, "The things that are seen, are temporal; the things that are unseen, are eternal."[9] It puts an affront upon nature. It does that for the unschooled, which philosophy does for Berkeley and Viasa.[1] The uniform language that may be heard in the churches of the most ignorant sects, is,—"Contemn the unsubstantial shows of the world; they are vanities, dreams, shadows, unrealities; seek the realities of religion." The devotee flouts nature. Some theosophists have arrived at a certain hostility and indignation towards matter, as the Manichean[2] and Plotinus. They distrusted in themselves any looking back to these flesh-pots of Egypt.[3] Plotinus was ashamed of his body. In short, they might all say of matter, what Michael Angelo said of external beauty, "it is the frail and weary weed, in which God dresses the soul, which he has called into time."[4]

It appears that motion, poetry, physical and intellectual science, and religion, all tend to affect our convictions of the reality of the external world. But I own there is something ungrateful in expanding too curiously the particulars of the general proposition, that all culture tends to imbue us with idealism. I have no hostility to nature, but a child's love to it. I expand and live in the warm day like corn and melons. Let us speak her fair. I do not wish to fling stones at my beautiful mother, nor soil my gentle nest. I only wish to indicate the true position of nature in regard to man, wherein to establish man, all right education tends; as the ground which to attain is the object of human life, that is, of man's connection with nature. Culture inverts the vulgar views of nature, and brings the mind to call that apparent, which it uses to call real, and that real, which it uses to call visionary. Children, it is true, believe in the external world. The belief that it appears only, is an afterthought, but with culture, this faith will as surely arise on the mind as did the first.

The advantage of the ideal theory over the popular faith, is this, that it presents the world in precisely that view which is most desirable to the mind. It is, in fact, the view which Reason, both speculative and practical, that is, philosophy and virtue, take. For, seen in the light of thought, the world always is phenomenal; and virtue subordinates it to the mind. Idealism sees the world in God. It beholds the whole circle of persons and things, of actions and events, of country and religion, not as painfully accumulated, atom after atom, act after act, in an aged creeping Past, but as one vast picture, which God paints on the instant eternity, for the contemplation of the soul. Therefore the soul holds itself off from a too trivial and microscopic study of the universal tablet. It respects the end too much, to immerse itself in the means. It sees something more important in Christianity, than the scandals of ecclesiastical history, or the niceties

---

9. Cf. 2 Corinthians 4.18.
1. Or Vyasa, proverbial author or arranger of the Vedas, ancient sacred writings of Hinduism.
2. Follower of Manes, or Mani (third century), Persian mystic who believed that there is a perpetual conflict in the world between the forces of light and dark.
3. Cf. Exodus 16.2–3.
4. Cf. Michaelangelo, Sonnet 51.

of criticism; and, very incurious concerning persons or miracles, and not at all disturbed by chasms of historical evidence, it accepts from God the phenomenon, as it finds it, as the pure and awful[5] form of religion in the world. It is not hot and passionate at the appearance of what it calls its own good or bad fortune, at the union or opposition of other persons. No man is its enemy. It accepts whatsoever befalls, as part of its lesson. It is a watcher more than a doer, and it is a doer, only that it may the better watch.

Chapter VII. Spirit

It is essential to a true theory of nature and of man, that it should contain somewhat progressive. Uses that are exhausted or that may be, and facts that end in the statement, cannot be all that is true of this brave lodging wherein man is harbored, and wherein all his faculties find appropriate and endless exercise. And all the uses of nature admit of being summed in one, which yields the activity of man an infinite scope. Through all its kingdoms, to the suburbs and outskirts of things, it is faithful to the cause whence it had its origin. It always speaks of Spirit. It suggests the absolute. It is a perpetual effect. It is a great shadow pointing always to the sun behind us.[6]

The aspect of nature is devout. Like the figure of Jesus, she stands with bended head, and hands folded upon the breast. The happiest man is he who learns from nature the lesson of worship.

Of that ineffable essence which we call Spirit, he that thinks most, will say least. We can foresee God in the coarse, and, as it were, distant phenomena of matter; but when we try to define and describe himself, both language and thought desert us, and we are as helpless as fools and savages. That essence refuses to be recorded in propositions, but when man has worshipped him intellectually, the noblest ministry of nature is to stand as the apparition of God. It is the organ through which the universal spirit speaks to the individual, and strives to lead back the individual to it.

When we consider Spirit, we see that the views already presented do not include the whole circumference of man. We must add some related thoughts.

Three problems are put by nature to the mind; What is matter? Whence is it? and Whereto? The first of these questions only, the ideal theory answers. Idealism saith: matter is a phenomenon, not a substance. Idealism acquaints us with the total disparity between the evidence of our own being, and the evidence of the world's being. The one is perfect; the other, incapable of any assurance; the mind is a part of the nature of things; the world is a divine dream, from which we may presently awake to the glories and certainties of day. Idealism is a hypothesis to account for nature by other principles than those of carpentry and chemistry. Yet, if it only deny the existence of matter, it does not satisfy the demands of the spirit. It leaves God out of me. It leaves me in the splendid labyrinth of my perceptions, to wander without end. Then the heart resists it, because it balks the affections in denying substantive being to men and women. Nature is so pervaded with human life, that there is something of hu-

---

5. Inspiring awe.
6. Emerson alludes to Plato's Allegory of the Cave (in *The Republic*, book 7) in which the unenlightened person is represented as chained in a cave and mistaking shadows of the world reflected on the wall for reality.

manity in all, and in every particular. But this theory makes nature foreign to me, and does not account for that consanguinity which we acknowledge to it.

Let it stand, then, in the present state of our knowledge, merely as a useful introductory hypothesis, serving to apprize us of the eternal distinction between the soul and the world.

But when, following the invisible steps of thought, we come to inquire, Whence is matter? and Whereto? many truths arise to us out of the recesses of consciousness. We learn that the highest is present to the soul of man, that the dread universal essence, which is not wisdom, or love, or beauty, or power, but all in one, and each entirely, is that for which all things exist, and that by which they are; that spirit creates; that behind nature, throughout nature, spirit is present; one and not compound, it does not act upon us from without, that is, in space and time, but spiritually, or through ourselves: therefore, that spirit, that is, the Supreme Being, does not build up nature around us, but puts it forth through us, as the life of the tree puts forth new branches and leaves through the pores of the old. As a plant upon the earth, so a man rests upon the bosom of God; he is nourished by unfailing fountains, and draws, at his need, inexhaustible power. Who can set bounds to the possibilities of man? Once inhale the upper air, being admitted to behold the absolute natures of justice and truth, and we learn that man has access to the entire mind of the Creator, is himself the creator in the finite. This view, which admonishes me where the sources of wisdom and power lie, and points to virtue as to

"The golden key
Which opes the palace of eternity,"[7]

carries upon its face the highest certificate of truth, because it animates me to create my own world through the purification of my soul.

The world proceeds from the same spirit as the body of man. It is a remoter and inferior incarnation of God, a projection of God in the unconscious. But it differs from the body in one important respect. It is not, like that, now subjected to the human will. Its serene order is inviolable by us. It is, therefore, to us, the present expositor of the divine mind. It is a fixed point whereby we may measure our departure. As we degenerate, the contrast between us and our house is more evident. We are as much strangers in nature, as we are aliens from God. We do not understand the notes of birds. The fox and the deer run away from us; the bear and tiger rend us. We do not know the uses of more than a few plants, as corn and the apple, the potato and the vine. Is not the landscape, every glimpse of which hath a grandeur, a face of him? Yet this may show us what discord is between man and nature, for you cannot freely admire a noble landscape, if laborers are digging in the field hard by. The poet finds something ridiculous in his delight, until he is out of the sight of men.

7. Cf. Milton (see n. 2, p. 6) in the masque *Comus*, lines 13–14. Published in 1637, *Comus* is a verse drama about the capture of a lady by Comus, Milton's invented son of Bacchus (or Dionysus), Greek god of wine and revelry, and Circe, Greek sorceress who turned men into swine.

Chapter VIII. Prospects[8]

In inquiries respecting the laws of the world and the frame of things, the highest reason is always the truest. That which seems faintly possible—it is so refined, is often faint and dim because it is deepest seated in the mind among the eternal verities. Empirical science is apt to cloud the sight, and, by the very knowledge of functions and processes, to bereave the student of the manly contemplation of the whole. The savant becomes unpoetic. But the best read naturalist who lends an entire and devout attention to truth, will see that there remains much to learn of his relation to the world, and that it is not to be learned by any addition or subtraction or other comparison of known quantities, but is arrived at by untaught sallies of the spirit, by a continual self-recovery, and by entire humility. He will perceive that there are far more excellent qualities in the student than preciseness and infallibility; that a guess is often more fruitful than an indisputable affirmation, and that a dream may let us deeper into the secret of nature than a hundred concerted experiments.

For, the problems to be solved are precisely those which the physiologist and the naturalist omit to state. It is not so pertinent to man to know all the individuals of the animal kingdom, as it is to know whence and whereto is this tyrannizing unity in his constitution, which evermore separates and classifies things, endeavoring to reduce the most diverse to one form. When I behold a rich landscape, it is less to my purpose to recite correctly the order and superposition of the strata, than to know why all thought of multitude is lost in a tranquil sense of unity. I cannot greatly honor minuteness in details, so long as there is no hint to explain the relation between things and thoughts; no ray upon the *metaphysics* of conchology, of botany, of the arts, to show the relation of the forms of flowers, shells, animals, architecture, to the mind, and build science upon ideas. In a cabinet of natural history, we become sensible of a certain occult recognition and sympathy in regard to the most unwieldy and eccentric forms of beast, fish, and insect. The American who has been confined, in his own country, to the sight of buildings designed after foreign models, is surprised on entering York Minster or St. Peter's at Rome, by the feeling that these structures are imitations also,—faint copies of an invisible archetype.[9] Nor has science sufficient humanity, so long as the naturalist overlooks that wonderful congruity which subsists between man and the world; of which he is lord, not because he is the most subtile inhabitant, but because he is its head and heart, and finds something of himself in every great and small thing, in every mountain stratum, in every new law of color, fact of astronomy, or atmospheric influence which observation or analysis lay open. A perception of this mystery inspires the muse of George Herbert, the beautiful psalmist of the seventeenth century. The following lines are part of his little poem on Man.

> "Man is all symmetry,
> Full of proportions, one limb to another,
> And to all the world besides.
> Each part may call the farthest, brother;
> For head with foot hath private amity,
> And both with moons and tides.

8. See n. 2, p. 27.
9. Emerson's terminology here is Platonic. York Minster is a Norman cathedral in York, England. St. Peter's is the Roman Catholic church at the Vatican.

"Nothing hath got so far
But man hath caught and kept it as his prey;
  His eyes dismount the highest star;
  He is in little all the sphere.
Herbs gladly cure our flesh, because that they
  Find their acquaintance there.

"For us, the winds do blow,
The earth doth rest, heaven move, and fountains flow;
  Nothing we see, but means our good,
  As our delight, or as our treasure;
The whole is either our cupboard of food,
  Or cabinet of pleasure.

"The stars have us to bed:
Night draws the curtain; which the sun withdraws.
  Music and light attend our head.
  All things unto our flesh are kind,
In their descent and being; to our mind,
  In their ascent and cause.

"More servants wait on man
Than he'll take notice of. In every path,
  He treads down that which doth befriend him
  When sickness makes him pale and wan.
Oh mighty love! Man is one world, and hath
  Another to attend him."[1]

The perception of this class of truths makes the attraction which draws men to science, but the end is lost sight of in attention to the means. In view of this half-sight of science, we accept the sentence of Plato,[2] that, "poetry comes nearer to vital truth than history." Every surmise and vaticination of the mind is entitled to a certain respect, and we learn to prefer imperfect theories, and sentences, which contain glimpses of truth, to digested systems which have no one valuable suggestion. A wise writer will feel that the ends of study and composition are best answered by announcing undiscovered regions of thought, and so communicating, through hope, new activity to the torpid spirit.

I shall therefore conclude this essay with some traditions of man and nature, which a certain poet[3] sang to me; and which, as they have always been in the world, and perhaps reappear to every bard, may be both history and prophecy.

The foundations of man are not in matter, but in spirit. But the element of spirit is eternity. To it, therefore, the longest series of events, the oldest chronologies are young and recent. In the cycle of the universal man, from whom the known individuals proceed, centuries are points, and all history is but the epoch of one degradation.

1. These are selected and modernized stanzas.
2. Actually Aristotle, in *Poetics*, his treatise on literature and aesthetics.
3. Although sometimes identified as A. Bronson Alcott (1799–1888), philosopher, friend of Emerson, and father of author Louisa May Alcott (1832–1888), the voice is best read as an externalization of Emerson's own most hyperbolically poetic mood. See also "The Poet," p. 190.

'We distrust and deny inwardly our sympathy with nature. We own and disown our relation to it, by turns. We are, like Nebuchadnezzar,[4] dethroned, bereft of reason, and eating grass like an ox. But who can set limits to the remedial[5] force of spirit?

'A man is a god in ruins. When men are innocent, life shall be longer, and shall pass into the immortal, as gently as we awake from dreams. Now, the world would be insane and rabid, if these disorganizations should last for hundreds of years. It is kept in check by death and infancy. Infancy is the perpetual Messiah, which comes into the arms of fallen men, and pleads with them to return to paradise.

'Man is the dwarf of himself. Once he was permeated and dissolved by spirit. He filled nature with his overflowing currents. Out from him sprang the sun and moon; from man, the sun; from woman, the moon. The laws of his mind, the periods of his actions externized themselves into day and night, into the year and the seasons. But, having made for himself this huge shell, his waters retired; he no longer fills the veins and veinlets; he is shrunk to a drop. He sees, that the structure still fits him, but fits him colossally. Say, rather, once it fitted him, now it corresponds to him from far and on high. He adores timidly his own work. Now is man the follower of the sun, and woman the follower of the moon. Yet sometimes he starts in his slumber, and wonders at himself and his house, and muses strangely at the resemblance betwixt him and it. He perceives that if his law is still paramount, if still he have elemental power, "if his word is sterling yet in nature,"[6] it is not conscious power, it is not inferior but superior to his will. It is Instinct.' Thus my Orphic[7] poet sang.

At present, man applies to nature but half his force. He works on the world with his understanding alone. He lives in it, and masters it by a penny-wisdom;[8] and he that works most in it, is but a half-man, and whilst his arms are strong and his digestion good, his mind is imbruted, and he is a selfish savage. His relation to nature, his power over it, is through the understanding; as by manure; the economic use of fire, wind, water, and the mariner's needle; steam, coal, chemical agriculture; the repairs of the human body by the dentist and the surgeon. This is such a resumption of power, as if a banished king should buy his territories inch by inch, instead of vaulting at once into his throne. Meantime, in the thick darkness, there are not wanting gleams of a better light, — occasional examples of the action of man upon nature with his entire force, — with reason as well as understanding. Such examples are; the traditions of miracles in the earliest antiquity of all nations; the history of Jesus Christ; the achievements of a principle, as in religious and political revolutions, and in the abolition of the Slave-trade; the miracles of enthusiasm, as those reported of Swedenborg, Hohenlohe, and the Shakers; many obscure and yet contested facts, now arranged under the name of Animal Magnetism;[9] prayer; eloquence;

4. Nebuchadnezzar II (630?–562 B.C.E.), king of Babylonia (r. 605–562) who destroyed Jerusalem and carried the Israelites into captivity. Cf. Daniel 4.25ff.
5. Remedy-producing.
6. Cf. Shakespeare, *Richard II* 4.1.264, the defeated Richard speaking to Northumberland, follower of his rival, Bolingbroke, duke of Hereford, who succeeds Richard as Henry IV.
7. From Orpheus, legendary Thracian poet-musician whose songs could animate vegetation, cause wild creatures to follow him, and soothe monsters and humans. A mystical Orphic religion evolved from his legendary descent to and return from the underworld.
8. Cf. the proverb Pennywise and pound foolish.
9. Hypnotism or mesmerism; a pseudo-science based on the theories of Franz Anton Mesmer (1734–1815), Austrian physician, that was a craze in the nineteenth century. Prince Alexander Leopold of Hohenlohe-

self-healing; and the wisdom of children. These are examples of Reason's momentary grasp of the sceptre; the exertions of a power which exists not in time or space, but an instantaneous in-streaming causing power. The difference between the actual and the ideal force of man is happily figured by the schoolmen, in saying, that the knowledge of man is an evening knowledge, *vespertina cognitio*, but that of God is a morning knowledge, *matutina cognitio*.[1]

The problem of restoring to the world original and eternal beauty, is solved by the redemption of the soul. The ruin or the blank, that we see when we look at nature, is in our own eye. The axis of vision is not coincident with the axis of things, and so they appear not transparent but opake. The reason why the world lacks unity, and lies broken and in heaps, is, because man is disunited with himself. He cannot be a naturalist, until he satisfies all the demands of the spirit. Love is as much its demand, as perception. Indeed, neither can be perfect without the other. In the uttermost meaning of the words, thought is devout, and devotion is thought. Deep calls unto deep.[2] But in actual life, the marriage is not celebrated. There are innocent men who worship God after the tradition of their fathers, but their sense of duty has not yet extended to the use of all their faculties. And there are patient naturalists, but they freeze their subject under the wintry light of the understanding. Is not prayer also a study of truth,—a sally of the soul into the unfound infinite? No man ever prayed heartily, without learning something. But when a faithful thinker, resolute to detach every object from personal relations, and see it in the light of thought, shall, at the same time, kindle science with the fire of the holiest affections, then will God go forth anew into the creation.

It will not need, when the mind is prepared for study, to search for objects. The invariable mark of wisdom is to see the miraculous in the common. What is a day? What is a year? What is summer? What is woman? What is a child? What is sleep? To our blindness, these things seem unaffecting, We make fables to hide the baldness of the fact and conform it, as we say, to the higher law of the mind. But when the fact is seen under the light of an idea, the gaudy fable fades and shrivels. We behold the real higher law. To the wise, therefore, a fact is true poetry, and the most beautiful of fables. These wonders are brought to our own door. You also are a man. Man and woman, and their social life, poverty, labor, sleep, fear, fortune, are known to you. Learn that none of these things is superficial, but that each phenomenon has its roots in the faculties and affections of the mind. Whilst the abstract question occupies your intellect, nature brings it in the concrete to be solved by your hands. It were a wise inquiry for the closet, to compare, point by point, especially at remarkable crises in life, our daily history, with the rise and progress of ideas in the mind.

So shall we come to look at the world with new eyes.[3] It shall answer the endless inquiry of the intellect,—What is truth? and of the affections,—What is good? by yielding itself passive to the educated Will. Then shall come to pass what my poet said; 'Nature is not fixed but fluid. Spirit alters, moulds, makes it. The immobility or bruteness of nature, is the absence of spirit; to pure spirit, it

---

Waldenberg-Schillingsfürst (1794–1849), German Roman Catholic cleric and author. *Shakers:* millenarian, celibate religious sect that originated in England in 1747. They moved to Watervliet, New York, in 1776 under the guidance of Ann Lee.
1. Differentiation in scholastic philosophy between humanity's partial knowledge (evening knowledge), and God's perfect knowledge (morning, or mature, knowledge).
2. Cf. Psalm 42.7.
3. See n. 2, p. 27.

is fluid, it is volatile, it is obedient. Every spirit builds itself a house; and beyond its house a world; and beyond its world, a heaven. Know then, that the world exists for you. For you is the phenomenon perfect. What we are, that only can we see. All that Adam had, all that Cæsar could, you have and can do. Adam called his house, heaven and earth; Cæsar called his house, Rome; you perhaps call yours, a cobler's trade; a hundred acres of ploughed land; or a scholar's garret. Yet line for line and point for point, your dominion is a great as theirs, though without fine names. Build, therefore, your own world. As fast as you conform your life to the pure idea in your mind, that will unfold its great proportions. A correspondent revolution in things will attend the influx of the spirit. So fast will disagreeable appearances, swine, spiders, snakes, pests, madhouses, prisons, enemies, vanish; they are temporary and shall be no more seen. The sordor[4] and filths of nature, the sun shall dry up, and the wind exhale. As when the summer comes from the south; the snow-banks melt, and the face of the earth becomes green before it, so shall the advancing spirit create its ornaments along its path, and carry with it the beauty it visits, and the song which enchants it; it shall draw beautiful faces, warm hearts, wise discourse, and heroic acts, around its way, until evil is no more seen. The kingdom of man over nature, which cometh not with observation,[5] — a dominion such as now is beyond his dream of God, — he shall enter without more wonder than the blind man feels who is gradually restored to perfect sight.'

---

4. Dirt, with connotations of moral degradation (cf. sordid).
5. Cf. Luke 17.20–21.

Selected Early Addresses and Lectures

The American Scholar

An Oration delivered before the Phi Beta Kappa Society,[1] at
Cambridge, August 31, 1837

Mr. President and Gentlemen,

I greet you on the re-commencement[2] of our literary year. Our anniversary is one of hope, and perhaps, not enough of labor. We do not meet for games of strength or skill, for the recitation of histories, tragedies, and odes, like the ancient Greeks; for parliaments of love and poesy, like the Troubadours;[3] nor for the advancement of science, like our contemporaries in the British and European capitals. Thus far, our holiday has been simply a friendly sign of the survival of the love of letters amongst a people too busy to give to letters any more. As such, it is precious as the sign of an indestructible instinct. Perhaps the time is already come, when it ought to be, and will be, something else; when the sluggard intellect of this continent will look from under its iron lids, and fill the postponed expectation of the world with something better than the exertions of mechanical skill. Our day of dependence,[4] our long apprenticeship to the learning of other lands, draws to a close. The millions, that around us are rushing into life, cannot always be fed on the sere remains of foreign harvests. Events, actions arise, that must be sung, that will sing themselves. Who can doubt, that poetry will revive and lead in a new age, as the star in the constellation Harp, which now flames in our zenith, astronomers announce, shall one day be the pole-star[5] for a thousand years?

In this hope, I accept the topic which not only usage, but the nature of our association, seem to prescribe to this day,—the AMERICAN SCHOLAR.[6] Year by year, we come up hither to read one more chapter of his biography. Let us inquire what light new days and events have thrown on his character, and his hopes.

---

1. Collegiate academic honor society founded at William and Mary College in 1776. The Greek letters stand for "philosophy the guide of life."
2. The address was delivered at the Harvard commencement in the summer of 1837.
3. Twelfth- and thirteenth-century wandering poet-singers of courtly love in Provence, northern Italy, and northern Spain.
4. Emerson's early biographer Oliver Wendell Holmes has called this address America's "intellectual Declaration of Independence."
5. The North Star, a star of the second magnitude at the end of the handle of the Little Dipper and almost at the north celestial pole. Emerson's prediction does not appear to be justified. Harp: the constellation Lyra, legendarily created from the lyre of Orpheus (see n. 7, p. 53), hence Emerson's association of it with poetry.
6. It was traditional for the speaker at the Harvard Phi Beta Kappa meeting to discourse on this subject. The official journal of the national society is, in fact, called *The American Scholar*.

56

It is one of those fables, which, out of an unknown antiquity, convey an un-looked-for wisdom, that the gods, in the beginning, divided Man into men, that he might be more helpful to himself; just as the hand was divided into fingers, the better to answer its end.[7] The old fable covers a doctrine ever new and sublime; that there is One Man, — present to all particular men only partially, or through one faculty; and that you must take the whole society to find the whole man. Man is not a farmer, or a professor, or an engineer, but he is all. Man is priest, and scholar, and states-man, and producer, and soldier. In the *divided* or social state, these functions are parcelled out to individuals, each of whom aims to do his stint of the joint work, whilst each other performs his. The fable implies, that the individual, to possess himself, must sometimes return from his own labor to embrace all the other laborers. But unfortunately, this original unit, this fountain of power, has been so distributed to multitudes, has been so minutely subdivided and peddled out, that it is spilled into drops, and cannot be gathered. The state of society is one in which the members have suffered amputation from the trunk, and strut about so many walking monsters, — a good finger, a neck, a stomach, an elbow, but never a man.

Man is thus metamorphosed into a thing, into many things. The planter, who is Man sent out into the field to gather food, is seldom cheered by any idea of the true dignity of his ministry. He sees his bushel and his cart, and nothing beyond, and sinks into the farmer, instead of Man on the farm. The tradesman scarcely ever gives an ideal worth to his work, but is ridden by the routine of his craft, and the soul is subject to dollars. The priest becomes a form; the attorney, a statute-book; the mechanic, a machine; the sailor, a rope of a ship.

In this distribution of functions, the scholar is the delegated intellect. In the right state, he is, *Man Thinking*. In the degenerate state, when the victim of society, he tends to become a mere thinker, or, still worse, the parrot of other men's thinking.

In this view of him, as Man Thinking, the theory of his office is contained. Him nature solicits with all her placid, all her monitory pictures; him the past instructs; him the future invites. Is not, indeed, every man a student, and do not all things exist for the student's behoof? And, finally, is not the true scholar the only true master? But the old oracle said, 'All things have two handles: beware of the wrong one.' In life, too often, the scholar errs with mankind and forfeits his privilege. Let us see him in his school, and consider him in reference to the main influences he receives.

I. The first in time and the first in importance of the influences upon the mind is that of nature. Every day, the sun; and, after sunset, night and her stars. Ever the winds blow; ever the grass grows. Every day, men and women, con-versing, beholding and beholden.[8] The scholar is he of all men whom this spec-tacle most engages. He must settle its value in his mind. What is nature to him? There is never a beginning, there is never an end, to the inexplicable continu-ity of this web of God, but always circular[9] power returning into itself. Therein

---

7. Told in Plato's (see n. 4, p. 15) *Symposium* and mentioned in the *Moralia* of Plutarch. Plutarch (46?–120?), Greek biographer and philosopher who wrote *Parallel Lives*, a collection of biographies that Shakespeare used in preparing his Roman plays.
8. Both being watched and being indebted.
9. A central Emerson theme; cf. the poem "Uriel" (p. 436) and the essay "Circles" (p. 174).

it resembles his own spirit, whose beginning, whose ending, he never can find,—so entire, so boundless. Far, too, as her splendors shine, system on system shooting like rays, upward, downward, without centre, without circumference,—in the mass and in the particle, nature hastens to render account of herself to the mind. Classification begins. To the young mind, every thing is individual, stands by itself. By and by, it finds how to join two things, and see in them one nature; then three, then three thousand; and so, tyrannized over by its own unifying instinct, it goes on tying things together, diminishing anomalies, discovering roots running under ground, whereby contrary and remote things cohere, and flower out from one stem. It presently learns, that, since the dawn of history, there has been a constant accumulation and classifying of facts. But what is classification but the perceiving that these objects are not chaotic, and are not foreign, but have a law which is also a law of the human mind? The astronomer discovers that geometry, a pure abstraction of the human mind, is the measure of planetary motion. The chemist finds proportions and intelligible method throughout matter; and science is nothing but the finding of analogy, identity, in the most remote parts. The ambitious soul sits down before each refractory fact; one after another, reduces all strange constitutions, all new powers, to their class and their law, and goes on for ever to animate the last fibre of organization, the outskirts of nature, by insight.

Thus to him, to this school-boy under the bending dome of day, is suggested, that he and it proceed form one root; one is leaf and one is flower; relation, sympathy, stirring in every vein. And what is that Root? Is not that the soul of his soul?—A thought too bold,—a dream too wild. Yet when this spiritual light shall have revealed the law of more earthly natures,—when he has learned to worship the soul, and to see that the natural philosophy[1] that now is, is only the first gropings of its gigantic hand, he shall look forward to an ever expanding knowledge as to a becoming creator. He shall see, that nature is the opposite of the soul, answering to it part for part. One is seal, and one is print. Its beauty is the beauty of his own mind. Its laws are the laws of his own mind. Nature then becomes to him the measure of his attainments. So much of nature as he is ignorant of, so much of his own mind does he not yet possess. And, in fine, the ancient precept, "Know thyself,"[2] and the modern precept, "Study nature," become at last one maxim.

II. The next great influence into the spirit of the scholar, is, the mind of the Past,—in whatever form, whether of literature, of art, of institutions, that mind is inscribed. Books are the best type[3] of the influence of the past, and perhaps we shall get at the truth,—learn the amount of this influence more conveniently,—by considering their value alone.

The theory of books is noble. The scholar of the first age received into him the world around; brooded thereon;[4] gave it the new arrangement of his own mind, and uttered it again. It came into him, life; it went out from him, truth. It came to him, short-lived actions; it went out from him, immortal thoughts. It came to him, business; it went from him, poetry. It was dead fact; now, it is quick

---

1. The then current term for what we now call science.
2. The Greek words γνωθι σεαυτον were inscribed above the temple of Apollo at Delphi.
3. See n. 4, p. 15; Emerson's pun is resonant.
4. Cf. *Paradise Lost* 1.19–22, the invocation to the Heavenly Muse who "from the first / [Was] present, and, with mighty wings outspread, / Dove-like [sat] brooding on the vast Abyss, / And [made] it pregnant."

thought. It can stand, and it can go. It now endures, it now flies, it now inspires. Precisely in proportion to the depth of mind from which it issued, so high does it soar, so long does it sing.

Or, I might say, it depends on how far the process had gone, of transmuting life into truth.[5] In proportion to the completeness of the distillation, so will the purity and imperishableness of the product be. But none is quite perfect. As no air-pump can by any means make a perfect vacuum, so neither can any artist entirely exclude the conventional, the local, the perishable from his book, or write a book of pure thought, that shall be as efficient, in all respects, to a remote posterity, as to cotemporaries, or rather to the second age. Each age, it is found, must write its own books; or rather, each generation for the next succeeding. The books of an older period will not fit this.

Yet hence arises a grave mischief. The sacredness which attaches to the act of creation,—the act of thought,—is transferred to the record. The poet chanting, was felt to be a divine man: henceforth the chant is divine also. The writer was a just and wise spirit: henceforward it is settled, the book is perfect; as love of the hero corrupts into worship of his statue. Instantly, the book becomes noxious: the guide is a tyrant. The sluggish and perverted mind of the multitude, slow to open to the incursions of Reason,[6] having once so opened, having once received this book, stands upon it, and makes an outcry, if it is disparaged. Colleges are built on it. Books are written on it by thinkers, not by Man Thinking; by men of talent, that is, who start wrong, who set out from accepted dogmas, not from their own sight of principles. Meek young men grow up in libraries, believing it their duty to accept the views, which Cicero, which Locke, which Bacon,[7] have given, forgetful that Cicero, Locke, and Bacon were only young men in libraries, when they wrote these books.

Hence, instead of Man Thinking, we have the bookworm. Hence, the book-learned class, who value books, as such; not as related to nature and the human constitution, but as making a sort of Third Estate with the world and the soul. Hence, the restorers of readings, the emendators, the bibliomaniacs of all degrees.

Books are the best of things, well used; abused, among the worst. What is the right use? What is the one end, which all means go to effect? They are for nothing but to inspire. I had better never see a book, than to be warped by its attraction clean out of my own orbit, and made a satellite instead of a system. The one thing in the world, of value, is the active soul. This every man is entitled to; this every man contains within him, although, in almost all men, obstructed, and as yet unborn. The soul active sees absolute truth; and utters truth, or creates. In this action, it is genius;[8] not the privilege of here and there a favorite, but the sound estate of every man. In its essence, it is progressive. The book, the college, the school of art, the institution of any kind, stop with some past utterance of genius. This is good, say they,—let us hold by this. They pin me down. They look backward and not forward. But genius looks forward: the eyes of man are set in his forehead, not in his hindhead: man hopes: genius creates. Whatever talents may be, if the man create not, the pure efflux of the Deity

5. Cf. the Divinity School "Address" (p. 76).
6. In Coleridge's sense of higher understanding (see n. 2, p. 31).
7. See n. 3, p. 6. Marcus Tullius Cicero (106–43 B.C.E.), Roman statesman and orator. John Locke (1632–1704), English empiricist philosopher, author of An Essay Concerning Human Understanding (1690) and Two Treatises on Government (1690).
8. Cf. the Latin genius, "procreative divinity"; from generare, "to beget."

is not his;—cinders and smoke there may be, but not yet flame. There are creative manners, there are creative actions, and creative words; manners, actions, words, that is, indicative of no custom or authority, but springing spontaneous from the mind's own sense of good and fair.

On the other part, instead of being its own seer, let it receive from another mind its truth, though it were in torrents of light, without periods of solitude, inquest, and self-recovery, and a fatal disservice is done. Genius is always sufficiently the enemy of genius by over-influence. The literature of every nation bear me witness. The English dramatic poets have Shakspearized now for two hundred years.

Undoubtedly there is a right way of reading, so it be sternly subordinated. Man Thinking must not be subdued by his instruments. Books are for the scholar's idle times. When he can read God directly, the hour is too precious to be wasted in other men's transcripts of their readings. But when the intervals of darkness come, as come they must,—when the sun is hid, and the stars withdraw their shining,—we repair to the lamps which were kindled by their ray, to guide our steps to the East again, where the dawn is. We hear, that we may speak. The Arabian proverb says, "A fig tree, looking on a fig tree, becometh fruitful."

It is remarkable, the character of the pleasure we derive from the best books. They impress us with the conviction, that one nature wrote and the same reads. We read the verses of one of the great English poets, of Chaucer, of Marvell, of Dryden,[9] with the most modern joy,—with a pleasure, I mean, which is in great part caused by the abstraction of all *time* from their verses. There is some awe mixed with the joy of our surprise, when this poet, who lived in some past world, two or three hundred years ago, says that which lies close to my own soul, that which I also had wellnigh thought and said. But for the evidence thence afforded to the philosophical doctrine of the identity of all minds, we should suppose some preëstablished harmony, some foresight of souls that were to be, and some preparation of stores for their future wants, like the fact observed in insects, who lay up food before death for the young grub they shall never see.

I would not be hurried by any love of system, by any exaggeration of instincts, to underrate the Book. We all know, that, as the human body can be nourished on any food, though it were boiled grass and the broth of shoes, so the human mind can be fed by any knowledge. And great and heroic men have existed, who had almost no other information than by the printed page. I only would say, that it needs a strong head to bear that diet. One must be an inventor to read well. As the proverb says, "He that would bring home the wealth of the Indies, must carry out the wealth of the Indies." There is then creative reading as well as creative writing. When the mind is braced by labor and invention, the page of whatever book we read becomes luminous with manifold allusion. Every sentence is doubly significant, and the sense of our author is as broad as the world. We then see, what is always true, that, as the seer's hour of vision is short and rare among heavy days and months, so is its record, perchance, the

---

9. John Dryden (1631–1700), English writer and poet laureate (after 1668). The outstanding literary figure of the Restoration, he wrote critical essays, poems, such as *Absalom and Achitophel* (1681), and dramas, including *All for Love* (1678). Geoffrey Chaucer (1340?–1400), English poet regarded as the greatest literary figure of medieval England. His works include *The Book of the Duchess* (1369), *Troilus and Criseyde* (ca. 1385), and his masterwork, *The Canterbury Tales* (1387–1400). Andrew Marvell (1621–1678), English Metaphysical poet.

least part of his volume. The discerning will read, in his Plato or Shakspeare, only that least part,—only the authentic utterances of the oracle;—all the rest he rejects, were it never so many times Plato's and Shakspeare's.

Of course, there is a portion of reading quite indispensable to a wise man. History and exact science he must learn by laborious reading. Colleges, in like manner, have their indispensable office,—to teach elements. But they can only highly serve us, when they aim not to drill, but to create; when they gather from far every ray of various genius to their hospitable halls, and, by the concentrated fires, set the hearts of their youth on flame. Thought and knowledge are natures in which apparatus and pretension avail nothing. Gowns, and pecuniary foundations, though of towns of gold, can never counter-vail the least sentence or syllable of wit. Forget this, and our American colleges will recede in their public importance, whilst they grow richer every year.

III. There goes in the world a notion, that the scholar should be a recluse, a valetudinarian,—as unfit for any handiwork or public labor, as a penknife for an axe. The so-called 'practical men' sneer at speculative men, as if, because they speculate or see,[1] they could do nothing. I have heard it said that the clergy,—who are always, more universally than any other class, the scholars of their day,—are addressed as women; that the rough, spontaneous conversation of men they do not hear, but only a mincing and diluted speech. They are often virtually disfranchised; and, indeed, there are advocates for their celibacy. As far as this is true of the studious classes, it is not just and wise. Action is with the scholar subordinate, but it is essential. Without it, he is not yet man. Without it, thought can never ripen into truth. Whilst the world hangs before the eye as a cloud of beauty, we cannot even see its beauty. Inaction is cowardice, but there can be no scholar without the heroic mind. The preamble of thought, the transition through which it passes from the unconscious to the conscious, is action. Only so much do I know, as I have lived. Instantly we know whose words are loaded with life, and whose not.

The world,—this shadow of the soul, or *other me*,[2] lies wide around. Its attractions are the keys which unlock my thoughts and make me acquainted with myself. I run eagerly into this resounding tumult. I grasp the hands of those next me, and take my place in the ring to suffer and to work, taught by an instinct, that so shall the dumb abyss be vocal with speech. I pierce its order; I dissipate its fear; I dispose of it within the circuit of my expanding life. So much only of life as I know by experience, so much of the wilderness have I vanquished and planted, or so far have I extended my being, my dominion. I do not see how any man can afford, for the sake of his nerves and his nap, to spare any action in which he can partake. It is pearls and rubies to his discourse. Drudgery, calamity, exasperation, want, are instructers in eloquence and wisdom. The true scholar grudges every opportunity of action past by, as a loss of power.

It is the raw material out of which the intellect moulds her splendid products. A strange process too, this, by which experience is converted into thought, as a mulberry leaf is converted into satin. The manufacture goes forward at all hours.

---

1. "Speculate or *see*" illustrates Emerson's characteristic sensitivity to Latin word roots.
2. Cf. Nature's "NOT ME" (n. 6, p. 28).

The actions and events of our childhood and youth, are now matters of calmest observation. They lie like fair pictures in the air. Not so with our recent actions,—with the business which we now have in hand. On this we are quite unable to speculate. Our affections as yet circulate through it. We no more feel or know it, than we feel the feet, or the hand, or the brain of our body. The new deed is yet a part of life,—remains for a time immersed in our unconscious life. In some contemplative hour, it detaches itself from the life like a ripe fruit, to become a thought of the mind. Instantly, it is raised, transfigured; the corruptible has put on incorruption. Henceforth it is an object of beauty, however base its origin and neighborhood. Observe, too, the impossibility of antedating this act. In its grub state, it cannot fly, it cannot shine, it is a dull grub. But suddenly, without observation, the selfsame thing unfurls beautiful wings, and is an angel of wisdom. So is there no fact, no event, in our private history, which shall not, sooner or later, lose its adhesive, inert form, and astonish us by soaring from our body into the empyrean. Cradle and infancy, school and playground, the fear of boys, and dogs, and ferules, the love of little maids and berries, and many another fact that once filled the whole sky, are gone already; friend and relative, profession and party, town and country, nation and world, must also soar and sing.

Of course, he who has put forth his total strength in fit actions, has the richest return of wisdom. I will not shut myself out of this globe of action, and transplant an oak into a flower-pot, there to hunger and pine; nor trust the revenue of some single faculty, and exhaust one vein of thought, much like those Savoyards,[3] who, getting their livelihood by carving shepherds, shepherdesses, and smoking Dutchmen, for all Europe, went out one day to the mountain to find stock, and discovered that they had whittled up the last of their pine-trees. Authors we have, in numbers, who have written out their vein, and who, moved by a commendable prudence, sail for Greece or Palestine, follow the trapper into the prairie, or ramble round Algiers, to replenish their merchantable stock.

If it were only for a vocabulary, the scholar would be covetous of action. Life is our dictionary. Years are well spent in country labors; in town,—in the insight into trades and manufactures; in frank intercourse with many men and women; in science; in art; to the one end of mastering in all their facts a language by which to illustrate and embody our perceptions. I learn immediately from any speaker how much he has already lived, through the poverty or the splendor of his speech. Life lies behind us as the quarry from whence we get tiles and copestones for the masonry of to-day. This is the way to learn grammar. Colleges and books only copy the language which the field and the work-yard made.

But the final value of action, like that of books, and better than books, is, that it is a resource. That great principle of Undulation in nature, that shows itself in the inspiring and expiring of the breath; in desire and satiety; in the ebb and flow of the sea; in day and night; in heat and cold; and as yet more deeply ingrained in every atom and every fluid, is known to us under the name of Polarity,—these "fits of easy transmission and reflection," as Newton[4] called them, are the law of nature because they are the law of spirit.

The mind now thinks; now acts; and each fit reproduces the other. When the artist has exhausted his materials, when the fancy no longer paints, when

---

3. Inhabitants of the Savoy region in the French Alps.
4. See n. 5, p. 16.

thoughts are no longer apprehended, and books are a weariness, — he has always the resource *to live*. Character is higher than intellect. Thinking is the function. Living is the functionary. The stream retreats to its source. A great soul will be strong to live, as well as strong to think. Does he lack organ or medium to impart his truths? He can still fall back on this elemental force of living them. This is a total act. Thinking is a partial act. Let the grandeur of justice shine in his affairs. Let the beauty of affection cheer his lowly roof. Those 'far from fame,' who dwell and act with him, will feel the force of his constitution in the doings and passages of the day better than it can be measured by any public and designed display. Time shall teach him, that the scholar loses no hour which the man lives. Herein he unfolds the sacred germ of his instinct, screened from influence. What is lost in seemliness is gained in strength. Not out of those, on whom systems of education have exhausted their culture, comes the helpful giant to destroy the old or to build the new, but out of unhandselled savage nature, out of terrible Druids and Berserkirs, come at last Alfred[5] and Shakspeare.

I hear therefore with joy whatever is beginning to be said of the dignity and necessity of labor to every citizen. There is virtue yet in the hoe and the spade, for learned as well as for unlearned hands. And labor is everywhere welcome; always we are invited to work; only be this limitation observed, that a man shall not for the sake of wider activity sacrifice any opinion to the popular judgments and modes of action.

I have now spoken of the education of the scholar by nature, by books, and by action. It remains to say somewhat of his duties.

They are such as become Man Thinking. They may all be comprised in self-trust. The office of the scholar is to cheer, to raise, and to guide men by showing them facts amidst appearances. He plies the slow, unhonored, and unpaid task of observation. Flamsteed and Herschel,[6] in their glazed observatories, may catalogue the stars with the praise of all men, and, the results being splendid and useful, honor is sure. But he, in his private observatory, cataloguing obscure and nebulous stars of the human mind, which as yet no man has thought of as such, — watching days and months, sometimes, for a few facts; correcting still his old records; — must relinquish display and immediate fame. In the long period of his preparation, he must betray often an ignorance and shiftlessness in popular arts, incurring the disdain of the able who shoulder him aside. Long he must stammer in his speech; often forego the living for the dead. Worse yet, he must accept, — how often! poverty and solitude. For the ease and pleasure of treading the old road, accepting the fashions, the education, the religion of society, he takes the cross of making his own, and, of course, the self-accusation, the faint heart, the frequent uncertainty and loss of time, which are the nettles and tangling vines in the way of the self-relying[7] and self-directed; and the state of virtual hostility in which he seems to stand to society, and especially to edu-

---

5. Alfred the Great (849–899), king of Wessex, translator, reformer; stabilized England and its language. *Unhandselled:* not made auspicious through ceremony; rough and unpolished. *Druids:* priestly order in ancient Gaul and Britain; they appear in legends of Wales and Ireland as prophets and magicians. *Berserkirs:* or Berserkers, those who fight with abandon and rage; formerly ancient Scandinavian warriors who fought wildly and without armor; hence the modern word *berserk.*
6. John Flamsteed (1646–1719), English astronomer. Sir William Herschel (1738–1822), English astronomer, who discovered Uranus (1781), was astronomer to George III, and cataloged more than eight hundred double stars and twenty-five hundred nebulae.
7. Cf. Emerson's essay "Self-Reliance" (p. 120).

cated society. For all this loss and scorn, what offset? He is to find consolation in exercising the highest functions of human nature. He is one, who raises himself from private considerations, and breathes and lives on public and illustrious thoughts. He is the world's eye. He is the world's heart. He is to resist the vulgar prosperity that retrogrades ever to barbarism, by preserving and communicating heroic sentiments, noble biographies, melodious verse, and the conclusions of history. Whatsoever oracles the human heart, in all emergencies, in all solemn hours, has uttered as its commentary on the world of actions,—these he shall receive and impart. And whatsoever new verdict Reason from her inviolable seat pronounces on the passing men and events of to-day,—this he shall hear and promulgate.

These being his functions, it becomes him to feel all confidence in himself, and to defer never to the popular cry. He and he only knows the world. The world of any moment is the merest appearance. Some great decorum, some fetish of a government, some ephemeral trade, or war, or man, is cried up by half mankind and cried down by the other half, as if all depended on this particular up or down. The odds are that the whole question is not worth the poorest thought which the scholar has lost in listening to the controversy. Let him not quit his belief that a popgun is a popgun, though the ancient and honorable of the earth affirm it to be the crack of doom. In silence, in steadiness, in severe abstraction, let him hold by himself; add observation to observation, patient of neglect, patient of reproach; and bide his own time,—happy enough, if he can satisfy himself alone, that this day he has seen something truly. Success treads on every right step. For the instinct is sure, that prompts him to tell his brother what he thinks. He then learns, that in going down into the secrets of his own mind, he has descended into the secrets of all minds. He learns that he who has mastered any law in his private thoughts, is master to that extent of all men whose language he speaks, and of all into whose language his own can be translated. The poet, in utter solitude remembering his spontaneous thoughts and recording them, is found to have recorded that, which men in crowded cities find true for them also. The orator distrusts at first the fitness of his frank confessions,—his want of knowledge of the persons he addresses,—until he finds that he is the complement of his hearers;—that they drink his words because he fulfils for them their own nature; the deeper he dives into his privatest, secretest presentiment, to his wonder he finds, this is the most acceptable, most public, and universally true. The people delight in it; the better part of every man feels, This is my music; this is myself.

In self-trust, all the virtues are comprehended. Free should the scholar be,—free and brave. Free even to the definition of freedom, "without any hindrance that does not arise out of his own constitution." Brave; for fear is a thing, which a scholar by his very function puts behind him. Fear always springs from ignorance. It is a shame to him if his tranquility, amid dangerous times, arise from the presumption, that, like children and women, his is a protected class; or if he seek a temporary peace by the diversion of his thoughts from politics or vexed questions, hiding his head like an ostrich in the flowering bushes, peeping into microscopes, and turning rhymes, as a boy whistles to keep his courage up. So is the danger a danger still; so is the fear worse. Manlike let him turn and face it. Let him look into its eye and search its nature, inspect its origin,—see the whelping of this lion,—which lies no great way back; he will then find in himself a perfect comprehension of its nature and extent; he will have made his hands meet on the other side, and can henceforth defy it, and pass on superior. The world is his, who can see through its pretension. What deafness, what stone-blind custom, what overgrown error you behold, is there only by sufferance,—by your sufferance. See it to be a lie, and you have already dealt it its mortal blow.

Yes, we are the cowed,—we the trustless. It is a mischievous notion that we are come late into nature; that the world was finished a long time ago. As the world was plastic[8] and fluid in the hands of God, so it is ever to so much of his attributes as we bring to it. To ignorance and sin, it is flint. They adapt themselves to it as they may; but in proportion as a man has any thing in him divine, the firmament flows before him and takes his signet and form. Not he is great who can alter matter, but he who can alter my state of mind. They are the kings of the world who give the color of their present thought to all nature and all art, and persuade men by the cheerful serenity of their carrying the matter, that this thing which they do, is the apple which the ages have desired to pluck, now at last ripe, and inviting nations to the harvest. The great man makes the great thing. Wherever Macdonald sits, there is the head of the table.[9] Linnæus makes botany the most alluring of studies, and wins it from the farmer and the herbwoman; Davy, chemistry; and Cuvier,[1] fossils. The day is always his, who works in it with serenity and great aims. The unstable estimates of men crowd to him whose mind is filled with a truth, as the heaped waves of the Atlantic follow the moon.

For this self-trust, the reason is deeper than can be fathomed,—darker than can be enlightened. I might not carry with me the feeling of my audience in stating my own belief. But I have already shown the ground of my hope, in adverting to the doctrine that man is one. I believe man has been wronged; he has wronged himself. He has almost lost the light, that can lead him back to his prerogatives. Men are become of no account. Men in history, men in the world of to-day are bugs, are spawn, and are called 'the mass' and 'the herd.' In a century, in a millennium, one or two men; that is to say,—one or two approximations to the right state of every man. All the rest behold in the hero or the poet their own green and crude being,—ripened; yes, and are content to be less, so *that* may attain to its full stature. What a testimony,—full of grandeur, full of pity, is borne to the demands of his own nature, by the poor clansman, the poor partisan, who rejoices in the glory of his chief. The poor and the low find some amends to their immense moral capacity, for their acquiescence in a political and social inferiority. They are content to be brushed like flies from the path of a great person, so that justice shall be done by him to that common nature which it is the dearest desire of all to see enlarged and glorified. They sun themselves in the great man's light, and feel it to be their own element. They cast the dignity of man from their downtrod selves upon the shoulders of a hero, and will perish to add one drop of blood to make the great heart beat, those giant sinews combat and conquer. He lives for us, and we live in him.

Men such as they are, very naturally seek money or power; and power because it is as good as money,—the "spoils," so called, "of office." And why not?

8. Malleable.
9. Popularly, "Where Macgregor sits . . . table," attributed to Rob Roy (Robert) Macgregor (1671–1734), Scottish Jacobite hero. Cf. Scottish author Walter Scott's (1771–1832) novel *Rob Roy* (1817).
1. Georges Léopold Chrétien Frédéric Dagobert, Baron Cuvier (1769–1832), French anatomist and paleontologist. Linnaeus, see n. 9, p. 36. Sir Humphry Davy (1778–1829), English chemist.

for they aspire to the highest, and this, in their sleep-walking, they dream is highest. Wake them, and they shall quit the false good, and leap to the true, and leave governments to clerks and desks. This revolution is to be wrought by the gradual domestication of the idea of Culture. The main enterprise of the world for splendor, for extent, is the upbuilding of a man. Here are the materials strown along the ground. The private life of one man shall be a more illustrious monarchy, — more formidable to its enemy, more sweet and serene in its influence to its friend, than any kingdom in history. For a man, rightly viewed, comprehendeth the particular natures of all men. Each philosopher, each bard, each actor, has only done for me, as by a delegate, what one day I can do for myself. The books which once we valued more than the apple of the eye, we have quite exhausted. What is that but saying, that we have come up with the point of view which the universal mind took through the eyes of one scribe; we have been that man, and have passed on. First, one; then, another; we drain all cisterns, and, waxing greater by all these supplies, we crave a better and more abundant food. The man has never lived that can feed us ever. The human mind cannot be enshrined in a person, who shall set a barrier on any one side to this unbounded, unboundable empire. It is one central fire, which, flaming now out of the lips of Etna, lightens the capes of Sicily; and, now out of the throat of Vesuvius,[2] illuminates the towers and vineyards of Naples. It is one light which beams out of a thousand stars. It is one soul which animates all men.

But I have dwelt perhaps tediously upon this abstraction of the Scholar. I ought not to delay longer to add what I have to say, of nearer reference to the time and to this country.

Historically, there is thought to be a difference in the ideas which predominate over successive epochs, and there are data for marking the genius of the Classic, of the Romantic, and now of the Reflective or Philosophical age.[3] With the views I have intimated of the oneness or the identity of the mind through all individuals, I do not much dwell on these differences. In fact, I believe each individual passes through all three. The boy is a Greek; the youth, romantic; the adult, reflective. I deny not, however, that a revolution in the leading idea may be distinctly enough traced.

Our age is bewailed as the age of Introversion. Must that needs be evil? We, it seems, are critical; we are embarrassed with second thoughts; we cannot enjoy any thing for hankering to know whereof the pleasure consists; we are lined with eyes; we see with our feet; the time is infected with Hamlet's unhappiness, —

"Sicklied o'er with the pale cast of thought."[4]

Is it so bad then? Sight is the last thing to be pitied. Would we be blind? Do we fear lest we should outsee nature and God, and drink truth dry? I look upon the discontent of the literary class, as a mere announcement of the fact, that they find themselves not in the state of mind of their fathers, and regret the coming

2. Active volcano in western Italy. Mount Etna (or Aetna), in eastern Sicily, is the highest active volcano in Europe.
3. Cf. n. 4, p. 32. Classic refers to ancient Greece and Rome; Romantic, to late-eighteenth- and early-nineteenth-century Europe; and Reflective or Philosophical, to Emerson's own age.
4. Shakespeare, *Hamlet* 3.1.87, near the end of the famous "To be or not to be" soliloquy.

state as untried; as a boy dreads the water before he has learned that he can swim. If there is any period one would desire to be born in, —is it not the age of Revolution; when the old and the new stand side by side, and admit of being compared; when the energies of all men are searched by fear and by hope; when the historic glories of the old, can be compensated by the rich possibilities of the new era? This time, like all times, is a very good one, if we but know what to do with it.

I read with joy some of the auspicious signs of the coming days, as they glimmer already through poetry and art, through philosophy and science, through church and state.

One of these signs is the fact, that the same movement which effected the elevation of what was called the lowest class in the state, assumed in literature a very marked and as benign an aspect. Instead of the sublime and beautiful; the near, the low, the common, was explored and poetized.[5] That, which had been negligently trodden under foot by those who were harnessing and provisioning themselves for long journeys into far countries, is suddenly found to be richer than all foreign parts. The literature of the poor, the feelings of the child, the philosophy of the street, the meaning of household life, are the topics of the time. It is a great stride. It is a sign, —is it not? of new vigor, when the extremities are made active, when currents of warm life run into the hands and the feet. I ask not for the great, the remote, the romantic; what is doing in Italy or Arabia; what is Greek art, or Provençal minstrelsy;[6] I embrace the common, I explore and sit at the feet of the familiar, the low. Give me insight into to-day, and you may have the antique and future worlds. What would we really know the meaning of? The meal in the firkin; the milk in the pan; the ballad in the street; the news of the boat; the glance of the eye; the form and the gait of the body; — show me the ultimate reason of these matters; show me the sublime presence of the highest spiritual cause lurking, as always it does lurk, in these suburbs and extremities of nature; let me see every trifle bristling with the polarity that ranges it instantly on an eternal law; and the shop, the plough, and the leger, referred to the like cause by which light undulates and poets sing; —and the world lies no longer a dull miscellany and lumber-room,[7] but has form and order; there is no trifle; there is no puzzle; but one design unites and animates the farthest pinnacle and the lowest trench.

This idea has inspired the genius of Goldsmith, Burns, Cowper, and, in a newer time, of Goethe, Wordsworth, and Carlyle.[8] This idea they have differently followed and with various success. In contrast with their writing, the style of Pope, of Johnson, of Gibbon,[9] looks cold and pedantic. This writing is blood-warm. Man is surprised to find that things near are not less beautiful and won-

---

5. The "elevation" of "the low, the common" was advocated by Wordsworth in his Preface to the second edition of *Lyrical Ballads*. William Wordsworth (1770–1850), English Romantic poet and friend of Coleridge, who collaborated with Wordsworth in the composition of *Lyrical Ballads* (first edition, 1798). *Sublime and beautiful*: see n. 3, p. 45.
6. See n. 3, p. 56.
7. Storage room for miscellaneous unused items.
8. See n. 6, p. 28. Oliver Goldsmith (1730?–1774), English poet, dramatist, and novelist. Robert Burns (1759–1796), Scottish Romantic lyric poet. William Cowper (1731–1800), English pre-Romantic poet. Goethe, see n. 6, p. 42.
9. See n. 9, p. 33. Alexander Pope (1688–1744), English neo-classic poet and theorist best remembered for his satirical mock-epic poems *The Rape of the Lock* (1712) and *The Dunciad* (1728). Samuel Johnson (1709–1784), known as "Dr. Johnson," British writer and lexicographer. One of the leading literary figures in eighteenth-century England, he compiled a *Dictionary of the English Language* (1755) and wrote *Lives of the Poets* (1779–81).

drous than things remote. The near explains the far. The drop is a small ocean. A man is related to all nature. This perception of the worth of the vulgar[1] is fruitful in discoveries. Goethe, in this very thing the most modern of the moderns, has shown us, as none ever did, the genius of the ancients.

There is one man of genius, who has done much for this philosophy of life, whose literary value has never yet been rightly estimated;—I mean Emanuel Swedenborg.[2] The most imaginative of men, yet writing with the precision of a mathematician, he endeavored to engraft a purely philosophical Ethics on the popular Christianity of his time. Such an attempt, of course, must have difficulty, which no genius could surmount. But he saw and showed the connection between nature and the affections of the soul. He pierced the emblematic[3] or spiritual character of the visible, audible, tangible world. Especially did his shade-loving muse hover over and interpret the lower parts of nature; he showed the mysterious bond that allies moral evil to the foul material forms, and has given in epical parables a theory of insanity, of beasts, of unclean and fearful things.

Another sign of our times, also marked by an analogous political movement, is, the new importance given to the single person. Every thing that tends to insulate the individual,—to surround him with barriers of natural respect, so that each man shall feel the world is his, and man shall treat with man as a sovereign state with a sovereign state;—tends to true union as well as greatness. "I learned," said the melancholy Pestalozzi,[4] "that no man in God's wide earth is either willing or able to help any other man." Help must come from the bosom alone. The scholar is that man who must take up into himself all the ability of the time, all the contributions of the past, all the hopes of the future. He must be an university of knowledges. If there be one lesson more than another, which should pierce his ear, it is, The world is nothing, the man is all; in yourself is the law of all nature, and you know not yet how a globule of sap ascends; in yourself slumbers the whole of Reason; it is for you to know all, it is for you to dare all. Mr. President and Gentlemen, this confidence in the unsearched might of man belongs, by all motives, by all prophecy, by all preparation, to the American Scholar. We have listened too long to the courtly muses of Europe. The spirit of the American freeman is already suspected to be timid, imitative, tame. Public and private avarice make the air we breathe thick and fat. The scholar is decent, indolent, complaisant. See already the tragic consequence. The mind of this country, taught to aim at low objects, eats upon itself. There is no work for any but the decorous and the complaisant. Young men of the fairest promise, who begin life upon our shores, inflated by the mountain winds, shined upon by all the stars of God, find the earth below not in unison with these,—but are hindered from action by the disgust which the principles on which business is managed inspire, and turn drudges, or die of disgust,—some of them suicides. What is the remedy? They did not yet see, and thousands of young men as hopeful now crowding to the barriers for the career, do not yet see, that, if the single man plant himself indomitably on his instincts, and there abide, the huge world will come round to him. Patience,—patience;—with the shades of all the good

---

1. Commonplace.
2. See n. 6, p. 35.
3. See n. 5, p. 12.
4. Johann Heinrich Pestalozzi (1746–1827), Swiss educational reformer and philanthropist; particularly influential for Emerson's associates Bronson Alcott and Elizabeth Peabody.

and great for company; and for solace, the perspective of your own infinite life; and for work, the study and the communication of principles, the making those instincts prevalent, the conversion of the world.[5] Is it not the chief disgrace in the world, not to be an unit;—not to be reckoned one character;—not to yield that peculiar fruit which each man was created to bear, but to be reckoned in the gross, in the hundred, or the thousand, of the party, the section, to which we belong; and our opinion predicted geographically, as the north, or the south? Not so, brothers and friends,—please God, ours shall not be so. We will walk on our own feet; we will work with our own hands; we will speak our own minds. The study of letters shall be no longer a name for pity, for doubt, and for sensual indulgence. The dread of man and the love of man shall be a wall of defence and a wreath of joy around all. A nation of men will for the first time exist, because each believes himself inspired by the Divine Soul which also inspires all men.

An Address

Delivered before the Senior Class in Divinity College, Cambridge,
Sunday Evening, July 15, 1838[1]

In this refulgent summer, it has been a luxury to draw the breath of life. The grass grows, the buds burst, the meadow is spotted with fire and gold in the tint of flowers. The air is full of birds, and sweet with the breath of the pine, the balm-of-Gilead,[2] and the new hay. Night brings no gloom to the heart with its welcome shade. Through the transparent darkness the stars pour their almost spiritual rays. Man under them seems a young child, and his huge globe a toy. The cool night bathes the world as with a river, and prepares his eyes again for the crimson dawn.[3] The mystery of nature was never displayed more happily. The corn and the wine[4] have been freely dealt to all creatures, and the never-broken silence with which the old bounty goes forward, has not yielded yet one word of explanation. One is constrained to respect the perfection of this world, in which our senses converse. How wide; how rich; what invitation from every property it gives to every faculty of man! In its fruitful soils; in its navigable sea; in its mountains of metal and stone; in its forests of all woods; in its animals; in its chemical ingredients; in the powers and path of light, heat, attraction, and life, it is well worth the pith and heart of great men to subdue and enjoy it. The

---

5. Emerson puns here on the idea of religious conversion and the desire of some churches to effect the conversion of the world to their particular belief.
1. Emerson so enraged the faculty with this address that a controversy was spawned in the popular press (see Perry Miller, *The Transcendentalists*, 192–246, for documents from the debate), and Emerson was not invited to speak again at Harvard for many years, though now his name graces the philosophy building, Emerson Hall.
2. A poplar tree with large, fragrant, heart-shaped leaves, common in and around Concord in Emerson's time. Emerson's cousin, George B. Emerson, describes the balm of Gilead in his *Report on the Trees and Shrubs Growing Naturally in the Forests of Massachusetts* (1846). The tree is mentioned in the opening of the poem "May-Day" (p. 463). Cf. Jeremiah 8.22.
3. Emerson's language throughout this passage locates the sacramental within nature, as opposed to the institutional church, by drawing on biblical and theological discourse. The doctrine of preparation, for example, was a crucial part of Calvinistic theology whereby sinners invited God's grace by "preparing" their souls.
4. *Corn* is used here, as frequently in the nineteenth century, to mean grain in general; thus the phrase suggests the Eucharistic bread and wine.

planters, the mechanics, the inventors, the astronomers, the builders of cities, and the captains, history delights to honor.

But when the mind opens, and reveals the laws which traverse the universe, and make things what they are, then shrinks the great world at once into a mere illustration and fable of this mind. What am I? and What is? asks the human spirit with a curiosity new-kindled, but never to be quenched. Behold these outrunning laws, which our imperfect apprehension can see tend this way and that, but not come full circle. Behold these infinite relations, so like, so unlike; many, yet one. I would study, I would know, I would admire forever. These works of thought have been the entertainments of the human spirit in all ages.

A more secret, sweet, and overpowering beauty appears to man when his heart and mind open to the sentiment of virtue. Then he is instructed in what is above him. He learns that his being is without bound; that, to the good, to the perfect, he is born, low as he now lies in evil and weakness. That which he venerates is still his own, though he has not realized it yet. *He ought.* He knows the sense of that grand word, though his analysis fails entirely to render account of it. When in innocency, or when by intellectual perception, he attains to say,— 'I love the Right; Truth is beautiful within and without, forevermore. Virtue, I am thine: save me: use me: thee will I serve, day and night, in great, in small, that I may be not virtuous, but virtue;'—then is the end of the creation answered, and God is well pleased.[5]

The sentiment of virtue is a reverence and delight in the presence of certain divine laws. It perceives that this homely game of life we play, covers, under what seem foolish details, principles that astonish. The child amidst his baubles, is learning the action of light, motion, gravity, muscular force; and in the game of human life, love, fear, justice, appetite, man, and God, interact. These laws refuse to be adequately stated. They will not be written out on paper, or spoken by the tongue. They elude our persevering thought; yet we read them hourly in each other's faces, in each other's actions, in our own remorse. The moral traits which are all globed into every virtuous act and thought,—in speech, we must sever, and describe or suggest by painful enumeration of many particulars. Yet, as this sentiment is the essence of all religion, let me guide your eye to the precise objects of the sentiment, by an enumeration of some of those classes of facts in which this element is conspicuous.

The intuition of the moral sentiment is an insight of the perfection of the laws of the soul. These laws execute themselves. They are out of time, out of space, and not subject to circumstance. Thus; in the soul of man there is a justice whose retributions are instant and entire. He who does a good deed, is instantly ennobled. He who does a mean deed, is by the action itself contracted. He who puts off impurity, thereby puts on purity. If a man is at heart just, then in so far is he God; the safety of God, the immortality of God, the majesty of God do enter into that man with justice. If a man dissemble, deceive, he deceives himself, and goes out of acquaintance with his own being. A man in the view of absolute goodness, adores, with total humility. Every step so downward, is a step upward. The man who renounces himself, comes to himself.

See how this rapid intrinsic energy worketh everywhere, righting wrongs, correcting appearances, and bringing up facts to a harmony with thoughts. Its operation in life, though slow to the senses, is, at last, as sure as in the soul. By

5. Cf. Matthew 3.17.

it, a man is made the Providence to himself, dispensing good to his goodness, and evil to his sin. Character is always known. Thefts never enrich; alms never impoverish; murder will speak out of stone walls. The least admixture of a lie, — for example, the taint of vanity, the least attempt to make a good impression, a favorable appearance, — will instantly vitiate the effect. But speak the truth, and all nature and all spirits help you with unexpected furtherance. Speak the truth, and all things alive or brute are vouchers, and the very roots of the grass underground there, do seem to stir and move to bear you witness. See again the perfection of the Law as it applies itself to the affections, and becomes the law of society. As we are, so we associate. The good, by affinity, seek the good; the vile, by affinity, the vile. Thus of their own volition, souls proceed into heaven, into hell.

These facts have always suggested to man the sublime creed, that the world is not the product of manifold power, but of one will, of one mind; and that one mind is everywhere active, in each ray of the star, in each wavelet of the pool; and whatever opposes that will, is everywhere balked and baffled, because things are made so, and not otherwise. Good is positive. Evil is merely privative,[6] not absolute; it is like cold, which is the privation of heat. All evil is so much death or nonentity. Benevolence is absolute and real. So much benevolence as a man hath, so much life hath he. For all things proceed out of this same spirit, which is differently named love, justice, temperance, in its different applications, just as the ocean receives different names on the several shores which it washes. All things proceed out of the same spirit, and all things conspire with it. Whilst a man seeks good ends, he is strong by the whole strength of nature. In so far as he roves from these ends, he bereaves himself of power, of auxiliaries; his being shrinks out of all remote channels, he becomes less and less, a mote, a point, until absolute badness is absolute death.

The perception of this law of laws awakens in the mind a sentiment which we call the religious sentiment, and which makes our highest happiness. Wonderful is its power to charm and to command. It is a mountain air. It is the embalmer of the world. It is myrrh and storax, and chlorine and rosemary. It makes the sky and the hills sublime, and the silent song of the stars is it. By it, is the universe made safe and habitable, not by science or power. Thought may work cold and intransitive in things, and find no end or unity; but the dawn of the sentiment of virtue on the heart, gives and is the assurance that Law is sovereign over all natures; and the worlds, time, space, eternity, do seem to break out into joy.

This sentiment is divine and deifying. It is the beatitude of man. It makes him illimitable. Through it, the soul first knows itself. It corrects the capital mistake of the infant man, who seeks to be great by following the great, and hopes to derive advantages *from another*, — by showing the fountain of all good to be in himself, and that he, equally with every man, is an inlet into the deeps of Reason.[7] When he says, "I ought;" when love warms him; when he chooses, warned from on high, the good and great deed; then, deep melodies wander through his soul from Supreme Wisdom. Then he can worship, and be enlarged by his

---

6. Augustinian, as opposed to Manichean (see n. 2, p. 48); i.e., the Manicheans believed that evil is an active force, equal and opposite to good.
7. See n. 8, p. 35.

worship; for he can never go behind this sentiment. In the sublimest flights of the soul, rectitude is never surmounted, love is never outgrown.

This sentiment lies at the foundation of society, and successively creates all forms of worship. The principle of veneration never dies out. Man fallen into superstition, into sensuality, is never quite without the visions of the moral sentiment. In like manner, all the expressions of this sentiment are sacred and permanent in proportion to their purity. The expressions of this sentiment affect us more than all other compositions. The sentences of the oldest time, which ejaculate[8] this piety, are still fresh and fragrant. This thought dwelled always deepest in the minds of men in the devout and contemplative East; not alone in Palestine, where it reached its purest expression, but in Egypt, in Persia, in India, in China. Europe has always owed to oriental genius, its divine impulses. What these holy bards said, all sane men found agreeable and true. And the unique impression of Jesus upon mankind, whose name is not so much written as ploughed into the history of this world, is proof of the subtle virtue of this infusion.

Meantime, whilst the doors of the temple stand open, night and day, before every man, and the oracles of this truth cease never, it is guarded by one stern condition; this, namely; it is an intuition. It cannot be received at second hand. Truly speaking, it is not instruction, but provocation, that I can receive from another soul. What he announces, I must find true in me, or wholly reject; and on his word, or as his second, be he who he may, I can accept nothing. On the contrary, the absence of this primary faith is the presence of degradation. As is the flood so is the ebb. Let this faith depart, and the very words it spake, and the things it made, become false and hurtful. Then falls the church, the state, art, letters, life. The doctrine of the divine nature being forgotten, a sickness infects and dwarfs the construction. Once man was all; now he is an appendage, a nuisance. And because the indwelling Supreme Spirit cannot wholly be got rid of, the doctrine of it suffers this perversion, that the divine nature is attributed to one or two persons, and denied to all the rest, and denied with fury. The doctrine of inspiration is lost; the base doctrine of the majority of voices, usurps the place of the doctrine of the soul. Miracles, prophecy, poetry; the ideal life, the holy life, exist as ancient history merely; they are not in the belief, nor in the aspiration of society; but, when suggested, seem ridiculous. Life is comic or pitiful, as soon as the high ends of being fade out of sight, and man becomes nearsighted, and can only attend to what addresses the senses.

These general views, which, whilst they are general, none will contest, find abundant illustration in the history of religion, and especially in the history of the Christian church. In that, all of us have had our birth and nurture. The truth contained in that, you, my young friends, are now setting forth to teach. As the Cultus,[9] or established worship of the civilized world, it has great historical interest for us. Of its blessed words, which have been the consolation of humanity, you need not that I should speak. I shall endeavor to discharge my duty to you, on this occasion, by pointing out two errors in its administration, which daily appear more gross from the point of view we have just now taken.

Jesus Christ belonged to the true race of prophets. He saw with open eye the mystery of the soul. Drawn by its severe harmony, ravished with its beauty,

---

8. To utter suddenly and passionately; exclaim.
9. Worship (Latin).

he lived in it, and had his being there. Alone in all history, he estimated the greatness of man. One man was true to what is in you and me. He saw that God incarnates himself in man, and evermore goes forth anew to take possession of his world. He said, in this jubilee of sublime emotion, 'I am divine. Through me, God acts; through me, speaks. Would you see God, see me; or, see thee, when thou also thinkest as I now think.' But what a distortion did his doctrine and memory suffer in the same, in the next, and the following ages! There is no doctrine of the Reason which will bear to be taught by the Understanding. The understanding caught this high chant from the poet's lips, and said, in the next age, 'This was Jehovah come down out of heaven. I will kill you, if you say he was a man.' The idioms of his language, and the figures of his rhetoric, have usurped the place of his truth; and churches are not built on his principles, but on his tropes.[1] Christianity became a Mythus,[2] as the poetic teaching of Greece and of Egypt, before. He spoke of miracles; for he felt that man's life was a miracle, and all that man doth, and he knew that this daily miracle shines, as the character ascends. But the word Miracle, as pronounced by Christian churches, gives a false impression; it is Monster. It is not one with the blowing clover and the falling rain.

He felt respect for Moses and the prophets; but no unfit tenderness at postponing their initial revelations, to the hour and the man that now is; to the eternal revelation in the heart. Thus was he a true man. Having seen that the law in us is commanding, he would not suffer it to be commanded. Boldly, with hand, and heart, and life, he declared it was God. Thus is he, as I think, the only soul in history who has appreciated the worth of a man.

1. In this point of view we become very sensible of the first defect of historical Christianity. Historical Christianity has fallen into the error that corrupts all attempts to communicate religion. As it appears to us, and as it has appeared for ages, it is not the doctrine of the soul, but an exaggeration of the personal, the positive, the ritual. It has dwelt, it dwells, with noxious exaggeration about the *person* of Jesus. The soul knows no persons. It invites every man to expand to the full circle of the universe, and will have no preferences but those of spontaneous love. But by this eastern monarchy of a Christianity, which indolence and fear have built, the friend of man is made the injurer of man.[3] The manner in which his name is surrounded with expressions, which were once sallies of admiration and love, but are now petrified into official titles, kills all generous sympathy and liking. All who hear me, feel, that the language that describes Christ to Europe and America, is not the style of friendship and enthusiasm to a good and noble heart, but is appropriated and formal, —paints a demigod, as the Orientals or the Greeks would describe Osiris or Apollo.[4] Accept the injurious impositions of our early catachetical instruction, and even honesty and self-denial were but splendid sins, if they did not wear the Christian name. One would rather be

'A pagan, suckled in a creed outworn,'[5]

---

1. On Christ's poetic use of language.
2. *Muthos* (Greek), a traditional story dealing with supernatural beings.
3. I.e., through extreme veneration of the personality of Christ.
4. Phoebus Apollo, Greek god of prophecy, music, medicine, and poetry, often associated with the sun. Osiris, supreme god of ancient Egypt whose annual death and resurrection represented nature's rebirth and fertility.
5. From Wordsworth's sonnet "The world is too much with us . . ."

than to be defrauded of his manly right in coming into nature, and finding not names and places, not land and professions, but even virtue and truth foreclosed and monopolized. You shall not be a man even. You shall not own the world; you shall not dare, and live after the infinite Law that is in you, and in company with the infinite Beauty which heaven and earth reflect to you in all lovely forms; but you must subordinate your nature to Christ's nature; you must accept our interpretations; and take his portrait as the vulgar draw it.

That is always best which gives me to myself. The sublime is excited in me by the great stoical doctrine, Obey thyself. That which shows God in me, fortifies me. That which shows God out of me, makes me a wart and a wen. There is no longer a necessary reason for my being. Already the long shadows of untimely oblivion creep over me, and I shall decease forever.

The divine bards are the friends of my virtue, of my intellect, of my strength. They admonish me, that the gleams which flash across my mind, are not mine, but God's; that they had the like, and were not disobedient to the heavenly vision.[6] So I love them. Noble provocations go out from them, inviting me to resist evil; to subdue the world; and to Be. And thus by his holy thoughts, Jesus serves us, and thus only. To aim to convert a man by miracles, is a profanation of the soul. A true conversion, a true Christ, is now, as always, to be made, by the reception of beautiful sentiments. It is true that a great and rich soul, like his, falling among the simple, does so preponderate, that, as his did, it names the world. The world seems to them to exist for him, and they have not yet drunk so deeply of his sense, as to see that only by coming again to themselves, or to God in themselves, can they grow forevermore. It is a low benefit to give me something; it is a high benefit to enable me to do somewhat of myself. The time is coming when all men will see, that the gift of God to the soul is not a vaunting, overpowering, excluding sanctity, but a sweet, natural goodness, a goodness like thine and mine, and that so invites thine and mine to be and to grow.

The injustice of the vulgar[7] tone of preaching is not less flagrant to Jesus, than to the souls which it profanes. The preachers do not see that they make his gospel not glad, and shear him of the locks of beauty and the attributes of heaven. When I see a majestic Epaminondas,[8] or Washington; when I see among my contemporaries, a true orator, an upright judge, a dear friend; when I vibrate to the melody and fancy of a poem; I see beauty that is to be desired. And so lovely, and with yet more entire consent of my human being, sounds in my ear the severe music of the bards that have sung of the true God in all ages. Now do not degrade the life and dialogues of Christ out of the circle of this charm, by insulation and peculiarity. Let them lie as they befel, alive and warm, part of human life, and of the landscape, and of the cheerful day.

2. The second defect of the traditional and limited way of using the mind of Christ is a consequence of the first; this, namely; that the Moral Nature, that Law of laws, whose revelations introduce greatness,—yea, God himself, into the open soul, is not explored as the fountain of the established teaching in society. Men have come to speak of the revelation as somewhat long ago given and

---

6. Cf. Acts 26.19.
7. Common; usual.
8. Theban general (418?–362 B.C.E.).

done, as if God were dead. The injury to faith throttles the preacher; and the goodliest of institutions becomes an uncertain and inarticulate voice.

It is very certain that it is the effect of conversation with the beauty of the soul, to beget a desire and need to impart to others the same knowledge and love. If utterance is denied, the thought lies like a burden on the man. Always the seer is a sayer. Somehow his dream is told: somehow he publishes it with solemn joy: sometimes with pencil on canvas; sometimes with chisel on stone; sometimes in towers and aisles of granite, his soul's worship is builded; sometimes in anthems of indefinite music; but clearest and most permanent, in words.

The man enamored of this excellency, becomes its priest or poet. The office is coeval with the world. But observe the condition, the spiritual limitation of the office. The spirit only can teach. Not any profane man, not any sensual, not any liar, not any slave can teach, but only he can give, who has; he only can create, who is. The man on whom the soul descends, through whom the soul speaks, alone can teach. Courage, piety, love, wisdom, can teach; and every man can open his door to these angels, and they shall bring him the gift of tongues. But the man who aims to speak as books enable, as synods use, as the fashion guides, and as interest commands, babbles. Let him hush.

To this holy office, you propose to devote yourselves. I wish you may feel your call in throbs of desire and hope. The office is the first in the world. It is of that reality, that it cannot suffer the deduction of any falsehood. And it is my duty to say to you, that the need was never greater of new revelation than now. From the views I have already expressed, you will infer the sad conviction, which I share, I believe, with numbers, of the universal decay and now almost death of faith in society. The soul is not preached. The Church seems to totter to its fall, almost all life extinct. On this occasion, any complaisance would be criminal, which told you, whose hope and commission it is to preach the faith of Christ, that the faith of Christ is preached.

It is time that this ill-suppressed murmur of all thoughtful men against the famine of our churches; this moaning of the heart because it is bereaved of the consolation, the hope, the grandeur, that come alone out of the culture of the moral nature; should be heard through the sleep of indolence, and over the din of routine. This great and perpetual office of the preacher is not discharged. Preaching is the expression of the moral sentiment in application to the duties of life. In how many churches, by how many prophets, tell me, is man made sensible that he is an infinite Soul; that the earth and heavens are passing into his mind; that he is drinking forever the soul of God? Where now sounds the persuasion, that by its very melody imparadises[9] my heart, and so affirms its own origin in heaven? Where shall I hear words such as in elder ages drew men to leave all and follow,—father and mother, house and land, wife and child? Where shall I hear these august laws of moral being so pronounced, as to fill my ear, and I feel ennobled by the offer of my uttermost action and passion? The test of the true faith, certainly, should be its power to charm and command the soul, as the laws of nature control the activity of the hands,—so commanding that we find pleasure and honor in obeying. The faith should blend with the light of rising and of setting suns, with the flying cloud, the singing bird, and the breath of flowers. But now the priest's Sabbath has lost the splendor of na-

9. Puts into or makes into paradise.

ture; it is unlovely; we are glad when it is done; we can make, we do make, even sitting in our pews, a far better, holier, sweeter, for ourselves.

Whenever the pulpit is usurped by a formalist,[1] then is the worshipper defrauded and disconsolate. We shrink as soon as the prayers begin, which do not uplift, but smite and offend us. We are fain to wrap our cloaks about us, and secure, as best we can, a solitude that hears not. I once heard a preacher who sorely tempted me to say, I would go to church no more. Men go, thought I, where they are wont to go, else had no soul entered the temple in the afternoon. A snow storm was falling around us. The snow storm was real; the preacher merely spectral; and the eye felt the sad contrast in looking at him, and then out of the window behind him, into the beautiful meteor of the snow.[2] He had lived in vain. He had no one word intimating that he had laughed or wept, was married or in love, had been commended, or cheated, or chagrined. If he had ever lived and acted, we were none the wiser for it. The capital secret of his profession, namely, to convert life into truth, he had not learned. Not one fact in all his experience, had he yet imported into his doctrine. This man had ploughed, and planted, and talked, and bought, and sold; he had read books; he had eaten and drunken; his head aches; his heart throbs; he smiles and suffers; yet was there not a surmise, a hint, in all the discourse, that he had ever lived at all. Not a line did he draw out of real history. The true preacher can be known by this, that he deals out to the people his life, — life passed through the fire of thought. But of the bad preacher, it could not be told from his sermon, what age of the world he fell in; whether he had a father or a child; whether he was a freeholder[3] or a pauper; whether he was a citizen or a countryman; or any other fact of his biography. It seemed strange that the people should come to church. It seemed as if their houses were very unentertaining, that they should prefer this thoughtless clamor. It shows that there is a commanding attraction in the moral sentiment, that can lend a faint tint of light to dulness and ignorance, coming in its name and place. The good hearer is sure he has been touched sometimes; is sure there is somewhat to be reached, and some word that can reach it. When he listens to these vain words, he comforts himself by their relation to his remembrance of better hours, and so they clatter and echo unchallenged.

I am not ignorant that when we preach unworthily, it is not always quite in vain. There is a good ear, in some men, that draws supplies to virtue out of very indifferent nutriment. There is poetic truth concealed in all the commonplaces of prayer and of sermons, and though foolishly spoken, they may be wisely heard; for, each is some select expression that broke out in a moment of piety from some stricken or jubilant soul, and its excellency made it remembered. The prayers and even the dogmas of our church, are like the zodiac of Denderah,[4] and the astronomical monuments of the Hindoos, wholly insulated from anything now extant in the life and business of the people. They mark the height to which the waters once rose. But this docility is a check upon the mischief from the good and devout. In a large portion of the community, the religious service gives rise to quite other thoughts and emotions. We need not chide the negligent servant. We are struck with pity, rather, at the swift retribution of

---

1. One who adheres rigidly to the forms, or rules and rites, of an established group.
2. Emerson is implicitly punning on the name of the junior pastor at his step-grandfather's church in Concord. Barzillai Frost was not known for the warmth of his preaching.
3. Term from feudalism for one who holds an estate in fee or for life.
4. Egyptian temple in the town of that name whose ceiling is decorated with the signs of the zodiac.

his sloth. Alas for the unhappy man that is called to stand in the pulpit, and *not* give bread of life. Everything that befalls, accuses him. Would he ask contributions for the missions, foreign or domestic? Instantly his face is suffused with shame, to propose to his parish, that they should send money a hundred or a thousand miles, to furnish such poor fare as they have at home, and would do well to go the hundred or the thousand miles to escape. Would he urge people to a godly way of living;—and can he ask a fellow-creature to come to Sabbath meetings, when he and they all know what is the poor uttermost they can hope for therein? Will he invite them privately to the Lord's Supper?[5] He dares not. If no heart warm this rite, the hollow, dry, creaking formality is too plain, than that he can face a man of wit and energy, and put the invitation without terror. In the street, what has he to say to the bold village blasphemer? The village blasphemer sees fear in the face, form, and gait of the minister.

Let me not taint the sincerity of this plea by any oversight of the claims of good men. I know and honor the purity and strict conscience of numbers of the clergy. What life the public worship retains, it owes to the scattered company of pious men, who minister here and there in the churches, and who, sometimes accepting with too great tenderness the tenet of the elders, have not accepted from others, but from their own heart, the genuine impulses of virtue, and so still command our love and awe, to the sanctity of character. Moreover, the exceptions are not so much to be found in a few eminent preachers, as in the better hours, the truer inspirations of all,—nay, in the sincere moments of every man. But with whatever exception, it is still true, that tradition characterizes the preaching of this country; that it comes out of the memory, and not out of the soul; that it aims at what is usual, and not at what is necessary and eternal; that thus, historical Christianity destroys the power of preaching, by withdrawing it from the exploration of the moral nature of man, where the sublime is, where are the resources of astonishment and power. What a cruel injustice it is to that Law, the joy of the whole earth, which alone can make thought dear and rich; that Law whose fatal sureness the astronomical orbits poorly emulate, that it is travestied and depreciated, that it is behooted and behowled, and not a trait, not a word of it articulated. The pulpit in losing sight of this Law, loses its reason, and gropes after it knows not what. And for want of this culture, the soul of the community is sick and faithless. It wants nothing so much as a stern, high, stoical, Christian discipline, to make it know itself and the divinity that speaks through it. Now man is ashamed of himself; he skulks and sneaks through the world, to be tolerated, to be pitied, and scarcely in a thousand years does any man dare to be wise and good, and so draw after him the tears and blessings of his kind.

Certainly there have been periods when, from the inactivity of the intellect on certain truths, a greater faith was possible in names and persons. The Puritans in England and America, found in the Christ of the Catholic Church, and in the dogmas inherited from Rome, scope for their austere piety, and their longings for civil freedom. But their creed is passing away, and none arises in its room. I think no man can go with his thoughts about him, into one of our churches, without feeling, that what hold the public worship had on men is gone, or going. It has lost its grasp on the affection of the good, and the fear of the bad. In the country, neighborhoods, half parishes are *signing off,*—to use

---

5. See n. 1, p. 17.

the local term. It is already beginning to indicate character and religion to with-draw from the religious meetings. I have heard a devout person,[6] who prized the Sabbath, say in bitterness of heart, "On Sundays, it seems wicked to go to church." And the motive, that holds the best there, is now only a hope and a waiting. What was once a mere circumstance, that the best and the worst men in the parish, the poor and the rich, the learned and the ignorant, young and old, should meet one day as fellows in one house, in sign of an equal right in the soul, — has come to be a paramount motive for going thither.

My friends, in these two errors, I think, I find the causes of a decaying church and a wasting unbelief. And what greater calamity can fall upon a na-tion, than the loss of worship? Then all things go to decay. Genius leaves the temple, to haunt the senate, or the market. Literature becomes frivolous. Sci-ence is cold. The eye of youth is not lighted by the hope of other worlds, and age is without honor. Society lives to trifles, and when men die, we do not men-tion them.

And now, my brothers, you will ask, What in these desponding days can be done by us? The remedy is already declared in the ground of our complaint of the Church. We have contrasted the Church with the Soul. In the soul, then, let the redemption be sought. Wherever a man comes, there comes revolution. The old is for slaves. When a man comes, all books are legible, all things trans-parent, all religions are forms. He is religious. Man is the wonderworker. He is seen amid miracles. All men bless and curse. He saith yea and nay, only.[7] The stationariness of religion; the assumption that the age of inspiration is past, that the Bible is closed; the fear of degrading the character of Jesus by representing him as a man; indicate with sufficient clearness the falsehood of our theology. It is the office of a true teacher to show us that God is, not was; that He speaketh, not spake. The true Christianity, — a faith like Christ's in the infinitude of man, — is lost. None believeth in the soul of man, but only in some man or per-son old and departed. Ah me! no man goeth alone. All men go in flocks to this saint or that poet, avoiding the God who seeth in secret.[8] They cannot see in se-cret; they love to be blind in public. They think society wiser than their soul, and know not that one soul, and their soul, is wiser than the whole world. See how nations and races flit by on the sea of time, and leave no ripple to tell where they floated or sunk, and one good soul shall make the name of Moses, or of Zeno, or of Zoroaster,[9] reverend forever. None assayeth the stern ambition to be the Self of the nation, and of nature, but each would be an easy secondary to some Christian scheme, or sectarian connection, or some eminent man. Once leave your own knowledge of God, your own sentiment, and take sec-ondary knowledge, as St. Paul's, or George Fox's, or Swedenborg's,[1] and you get wide from God with every year this secondary form lasts, and if, as now, for cen-turies, — the chasm yawns to that breadth, that men can scarcely be convinced there is in them anything divine.

6. Probably Emerson's wife Lidian; see *JMN* 5.442 (December 3, 1837).
7. Cf. 2 Corinthians 1.17–19.
8. Cf. Matthew 6.4 and 6.18.
9. Or Zarathustra, Persian philosopher and mystic, founder of Zoroastrianism ca. 1000 B.C.E. Either Zeno of Elea (fl. 460 B.C.E.), logician famous for propounding "Zeno's paradox," or Zeno of Citium (ca. 362–ca. 264 B.C.E.), Greek philosopher, founder of Stoicism, school of philosophy believing that human beings should be free from passion and should calmly accept all occurrences as the unavoidable result of divine will or of the natural order.
1. See n. 6, p. 35. St. Paul, see n. 1, p. 3. Fox, see n. 1, p. 39.

Let me admonish you, first of all, to go alone; to refuse the good models, even those which are sacred in the imagination of men, and dare to love God without mediator or veil. Friends enough you shall find who will hold up to your emulation Wesleys and Oberlins,[2] Saints and Prophets. Thank God for these good men, but say, 'I also am a man.' Imitation cannot go above its model. The imitator dooms himself to hopeless mediocrity. The inventor did it, because it was natural to him, and so in him it has a charm. In the imitator, something else is natural, and he bereaves himself of his own beauty, to come short of another man's.

Yourself a newborn bard of the Holy Ghost,—cast behind you all conformity, and acquaint men at first hand with Deity. Look to it first and only, that fashion, custom, authority, pleasure, and money, are nothing to you,—are not bandages over your eyes, that you cannot see,—but live with the privilege of the immeasurable mind. Not too anxious to visit periodically all families and each family in your parish connection,—when you meet one of these men or women, be to them a divine man; be to them thought and virtue; let their timid aspirations find in you a friend; let their trampled instincts be genially tempted[3] out in your atmosphere; let their doubts know that you have doubted, and their wonder feel that you have wondered. By trusting your own heart, you shall gain more confidence in other men. For all our penny-wisdom,[4] for all our soul-destroying slavery to habit, it is not to be doubted, that all men have sublime thoughts; that all men value the few real hours of life; they love to be heard; they love to be caught up into the vision of principles. We mark with light in the memory the few interviews we have had, in the dreary years of routine and of sin, with souls that made our souls wiser; that spoke what we thought; that told us what we knew; that gave us leave to be what we inly were. Discharge to men the priestly office, and, present or absent, you shall be followed with their love as by an angel.

And, to this end, let us not aim at common degrees of merit. Can we not leave, to such as love it, the virtue that glitters for the commendation of society, and ourselves pierce the deep solitudes of absolute ability and worth? We easily come up to the standard of goodness in society. Society's praise can be cheaply secured, and almost all men are content with those easy merits; but the instant effect of conversing with God, will be, to put them away. There are persons who are not actors, not speakers, but influences; persons too great for fame, for display; who disdain eloquence; to whom all we call art and artist, seems too nearly allied to show and byends, to the exaggeration of the finite and selfish, and loss of the universal. The orators, the poets, the commanders encroach on us only as fair women do, by our allowance and homage. Slight them by preoccupation of mind, slight them, as you can well afford to do, by high and universal aims, and they instantly feel that you have right, and that it is in lower places that they must shine. They also feel your right; for they with you are open to the influx of the all-knowing Spirit, which annihilates before its broad noon

---

2. Jean Frédéric Oberlin (1740–1826), Alsatian Protestant cleric, reformer, and philanthropist, after whom Oberlin College is named. John Wesley (1703–1791), English cleric; with his brother Charles founded Methodism, a Protestant religion.
3. This "genial" tempting is opposed to that of the preacher, who "sorely tempted me to say, I would go to church no more"; see p. 76.
4. See n. 8, p. 53.

the little shades and gradations of intelligence in the compositions we call wiser and wisest.

In such high communion, let us study the grand strokes of rectitude: a bold benevolence, an independence of friends, so that not the unjust wishes of those who love us, shall impair our freedom, but we shall resist for truth's sake the freest flow of kindness, and appeal to sympathies far in advance; and,—what is the highest form in which we know this beautiful element,—a certain solidity of merit, that has nothing to do with opinion, and which is so essentially and manifestly virtue, that it is taken for granted, that the right, the brave, the generous step will be taken by it, and nobody thinks of commending it. You would compliment a coxcomb[5] doing a good act, but you would not praise an angel. The silence that accepts merit as the most natural thing in the world, is the highest applause. Such souls, when they appear, are the Imperial Guard of Virtue, the perpetual reserve, the dictators of fortune. One needs not praise their courage,—they are the heart and soul of nature. O my friends, there are resources in us on which we have not drawn. There are men who rise refreshed on hearing a threat; men to whom a crisis which intimidates and paralyzes the majority,—demanding not the faculties of prudence and thrift, but comprehension, immovableness, the readiness of sacrifice,—comes graceful and beloved as a bride. Napoleon said of Massena,[6] that he was not himself until the battle began to go against him; then, when the dead began to fall in ranks around him, awoke his powers of combination, and he put on terror and victory as a robe. So it is in rugged crises, in unweariable endurance, and in aims which put sympathy out of question, that the angel is shown. But these are heights that we can scarce remember and look up to, without contrition and shame. Let us thank God that such things exist.

And now let us do what we can to rekindle the smouldering, nigh quenched fire on the altar. The evils of the church that now is are manifest. The question returns, What shall we do? I confess, all attempts to project and establish a Cultus with new rites and forms, seem to me vain. Faith makes us, and not we it, and faith makes its own forms. All attempts to contrive a system are as cold as the new worship introduced by the French to the goddess of Reason[7]—to-day, pasteboard and fillagree, and ending to-morrow in madness and murder. Rather let the breath of new life[8] be breathed by you through the forms already existing. For, if once you are alive, you shall find they shall become plastic[9] and new. The remedy to their deformity is, first, soul, and second, soul, and evermore, soul. A whole popedom of forms, one pulsation of virtue can uplift and vivify. Two inestimable advantages Christianity has given us; first; the Sabbath, the jubilee of the whole world; whose light dawns welcome alike into the closet of the philosopher, into the garret of toil, and into prison cells, and everywhere suggests, even to the vile, the dignity of spiritual being. Let it stand forevermore, a temple, which new love, new faith, new sight shall restore to more than its first splendor to mankind. And secondly, the institution of preaching,—the speech of man to men,—essentially the most flexible of all organs, of all forms. What

---

5. A conceited dandy; a fop.
6. André Masséna (1758–1817), one of Napoleon's (see n. 8, p. 17) field marshals.
7. During the French Revolution, Christianity was proscribed and statues of the "goddess of Reason" were set up in some churches.
8. Cf. the opening sentence (p. 69) and Genesis 2.7.
9. Malleable.

hinders that now, everywhere, in pulpits, in lecture-rooms, in houses, in fields, wherever the invitation of men or your own occasions lead you, you speak the very truth, as your life and conscience teach it, and cheer the waiting, fainting hearts of men with new hope and new revelation?

I look for the hour when that supreme Beauty, which ravished the souls of those eastern men, and chiefly of those Hebrews, and through their lips spoke oracles to all time, shall speak in the West also. The Hebrew and Greek Scriptures contain immortal sentences, that have been bread of life to millions. But they have no epical[1] integrity; are fragmentary; are not shown in their order to the intellect. I look for the new Teacher, that shall follow so far those shining laws, that he shall see them come full circle; shall see their rounding complete grace; shall see the world to be the mirror of the soul; shall see the identity of the law of gravitation with purity of heart;[2] and shall show that the Ought, that Duty, is one thing with Science, with Beauty, and with Joy.

The Method of Nature

An Oration delivered before the Society of the Adelphi in Waterville
College, Maine, August 11, 1841

Gentlemen,

Let us exchange congratulations on the enjoyments and the promises of this literary anniversary. The land we live in has no interest so dear, if it knew its want, as the fit consecration of days of reason and thought. Where there is no vision, the people perish.[1] The scholars are the priests of that thought which establishes the foundations of the earth. No matter what is their special work or profession, they stand for the spiritual interest of the world, and it is a common calamity if they neglect their post in a country where the material interest is so predominant as it is in America. We hear something too much of the results of machinery, commerce, and the useful arts. We are a puny and a fickle folk. Avarice, hesitation, and following, are our diseases. The rapid wealth which hundreds in the community acquire in trade, or by the incessant expansions of our population and arts, enchants the eyes of all the rest; the luck of one is the hope of thousands, and the bribe acts like the neighborhood of a gold mine to impoverish the farm, the school, the church, the house, and the very body and feature of man.

I do not wish to look with sour aspect at the industrious manufacturing village, or the mart of commerce. I love the music of the water-wheel; I value the railway; I feel the pride which the sight of a ship inspires; I look on trade and every mechanical craft as education also. But let me discriminate what is precious herein. There is in each of these works an act of invention, an intellectual step, or short series of steps taken; that act or step is the spiritual act; all the rest is mere repetition of the same a thousand times. And I will not be deceived into admiring the routine of handicrafts and mechanics, how splendid soever the result, any more than I admire the routine of the scholars or clerical class. That

1. As in a well-composed epic; or perhaps Emerson means artistic (from the Greek *epos*, "song" or "word").
2. Cf. Matthew 5.8.
1. Proverbs 29.18.

splendid results ensue from the labors of stupid men, is the fruit of higher laws than their will, and the routine is not to be praised for it. I would not have the laborer sacrificed to the result,—I would not have the laborer sacrificed to my convenience and pride, nor to that of a great class of such as me. Let there be worse cotton and better men. The weaver should not be bereaved of his superiority to his work, and his knowledge that the product or the skill is of no value, except so far as it embodies his spiritual prerogatives. If I see nothing to admire in the unit, shall I admire a million units? Men stand in awe of the city, but do not honor any individual citizen; and are continually yielding to this dazzling result of numbers, that which they would never yield to the solitary example of any one.

Whilst the multitude of men degrade each other, and give currency to desponding doctrines, the scholar must be a bringer of hope, and must reinforce man against himself. I sometimes believe that our literary anniversaries will presently assume a greater importance, as the eyes of men open to their capabilities. Here, a new set of distinctions, a new order of ideas, prevail. Here, we set a bound to the respectability of wealth, and a bound to the pretensions of the law and the church. The bigot must cease to be a bigot to-day. Into our charmed circle, power cannot enter; and the sturdiest defender of existing institutions feels the terrific inflammability of this air which condenses heat in every corner that may restore to the elements the fabrics of ages. Nothing solid is secure; every thing tilts and rocks. Even the scholar is not safe; he too is searched and revised. Is his learning dead? Is he living in his memory? The power of mind is not mortification, but life. But come forth, thou curious child! hither, thou loving, all-hoping poet! hither, thou tender, doubting heart, who hast not yet found any place in the world's market fit for thee; any wares which thou couldst buy or sell,—so large is thy love and ambition,—thine and not theirs is the hour. Smooth thy brow, and hope and love on, for the kind heaven justifies thee, and the whole world feels that thou art in the right.

We ought to celebrate this hour by expressions of manly joy. Not thanks, not prayer seem quite the highest or truest name for our communication with the infinite,—but glad and conspiring reception,—reception that becomes giving in its turn, as the receiver is only the All-Giver in part and in infancy. I cannot,—nor can any man,—speak precisely of things so sublime, but it seems to me, the wit of man, his strength, his grace, his tendency, his art, is the grace and the presence of God. It is beyond explanation. When all is said and done, the rapt saint is found the only logician. Not exhortation, not argument becomes our lips, but pæans of joy and praise. But not of adulation: we are too nearly related in the deep of the mind to that we honor. It is God in us which checks the language of petition by a grander thought. In the bottom of the heart, it is said; 'I am, and by me, O child! this fair body and world of thine stands and grows. I am; all things are mine: and all mine are thine.'

The festival of the intellect, and the return to its source, cast a strong light on the always interesting topics of Man and Nature. We are forcibly reminded of the old want. There is no man; there hath never been. The Intellect still asks that a man may be born. The flame of life flickers feebly in human breasts. We demand of men a richness and universality we do not find. Great men do not content us. It is their solitude, not their force, that makes them conspicuous. There is somewhat indigent and tedious about them. They are poorly tied to one thought. If they are prophets, they are egotists; if polite and various, they are shallow. How tardily men arrive at any result! how tardily they pass from it to another! The crystal sphere of thought is as concentrical as the geological structure of the globe. As our soils and rocks lie in strata, concentric strata, so do all men's thinkings run laterally, never vertically. Here comes by a great inquisitor with auger and plumb-line, and will bore an Artesian well[2] through our conventions and theories, and pierce to the core of things. But as soon as he probes the crust, behold gimlet, plumb-line, and philosopher take a lateral direction, in spite of all resistance, as if some strong wind took everything off its feet, and if you come month after month to see what progress our reformer has made, —not an inch has he pierced, —you still find him with new words in the old place, floating about in new parts of the same old vein or crust. The new book says, 'I will give you the key to nature,' and we expect to go like a thunderbolt to the centre. But the thunder is a surface phenomenon, makes a skin-deep cut, and so does the sage. The wedge turns out to be a rocket. Thus a man lasts but a very little while for his monomania becomes insupportably tedious in a few months. It is so with every book and person: and yet—and yet—we do not take up a new book, or meet a new man, without a pulse-beat of expectation. And this invincible hope of a more adequate interpreter is the sure prediction of his advent.

In the absence of man, we turn to nature, which stands next. In the divine order, intellect is primary; nature, secondary; it is the memory of the mind. That which once existed in intellect as pure law, has now taken body as Nature. It existed already in the mind in solution; now, it has been precipitated, and the bright sediment is the world. We can never be quite strangers or inferiors in nature. It is flesh of our flesh, and bone of our bone. But we no longer hold it by the hand; we have lost our miraculous power; our arm is no more as strong as the frost; nor our will equivalent to gravity and the elective attractions. Yet we can use nature as a convenient standard, and the meter of our rise and fall. It has this advantage as a witness, it cannot be debauched. When man curses, nature still testifies to truth and love. We may, therefore, safely study the mind in nature, because we cannot steadily gaze on it in mind; as we explore the face of the sun in a pool, when our eyes cannot brook his direct splendors.

It seems to me, therefore, that it were some suitable pæan, if we should piously celebrate this hour by exploring the *method of nature*. Let us see *that*, as nearly as we can, and try how far it is transferable to the literary life. Every earnest glance we give to the realities around us, with intent to learn, proceeds from a holy impulse, and is really songs of praise. What difference can it make whether it take the shape of exhortation, or of passionate exclamation, or of scientific statement? These are forms merely. Through them we express, at last, the fact, that God has done thus or thus.

In treating a subject so large, in which we must necessarily appeal to the intuition, and aim much more to suggest, than to describe, I know it is not easy to speak with the precision attainable on topics of less scope. I do not wish in attempting to paint a man, to describe an air-fed, unimpassioned, impossible ghost. My eyes and ears are revolted by any neglect of the physical facts, the limitations of man. And yet one, who conceives the true order of nature, and beholds the visible as proceeding from the invisible, cannot state his thought, without seeming to those who study the physical laws, to do them some injus-

2. A deep well in which water rises to the surface by internal hydrostatic pressure.

tice. There is an intrinsic defect in the organ. Language overstates. Statements of the infinite are usually felt to be unjust to the finite, and blasphemous. Empedocles undoubtedly spoke a truth of thought, when he said, "I am God;" but the moment it was out of his mouth, it became a lie to the ear; and the world revenged itself for the seeming arrogance, by the good story about his shoe.[3] How can I hope for better hap in my attempts to enunciate spiritual facts? Yet let us hope, that as far as we receive the truth, so far shall we be felt by every true person to say what is just.

The method of nature: who could ever analyze it? That rushing stream will not stop to be observed. We can never surprise nature in a corner; never find the end of a thread; never tell where to set the first stone. The bird hastens to lay her egg: the egg hastens to be a bird. The wholeness we admire in the order of the world, is the result of infinite distribution. Its smoothness is the smoothness of the pitch of the cataract. Its permanence is a perpetual inchoation. Every natural fact is an emanation,[4] and that from which it emanates is an emanation also, and from every emanation is a new emanation. If anything could stand still, it would be crushed and dissipated by the torrent it resisted, and if it were a mind, would be crazed; as insane persons are those who hold fast to one thought, and do not flow with the course of nature. Not the cause, but an ever novel effect, nature descends always from above. It is unbroken obedience. The beauty of these fair objects is imported into them from a metaphysical and eternal spring. In all animal and vegetable forms, the physiologist concedes that no chemistry, no mechanics, can account for the facts, but a mysterious principle of life must be assumed, which not only inhabits the organ, but makes the organ.

How silent, how spacious, what room for all, yet without place to insert an atom,—in graceful succession, in equal fulness, in balanced beauty, the dance of the hours goes forward still. Like an odor of incense, like a strain of music, like a sleep, it is inexact and boundless. It will not be dissected, nor unravelled, nor shown. Away profane philosopher! seekest thou in nature the cause? This refers to that, and that to the next, and the next to the third, and everything refers. Thou must ask in another mood, thou must feel it and love it, thou must behold it in a spirit as grand as that by which it exists, ere thou canst know the law. Known it will not be, but gladly beloved and enjoyed.

The simultaneous life throughout the whole body, the equal serving of innumerable ends without the least emphasis or preference to any, but the steady degradation of each to the success of all, allows the understanding no place to work. Nature can only be conceived as existing to a universal and not to a particular end, to a universe of ends, and not to one,—a work of *ecstasy*, to be represented by a circular movement, as intention might be signified by a straight line of definite length. Each effect strengthens every other. There is no revolt in all the kingdoms from the commonweal: no detachment of an individual. Hence the catholic character which makes every leaf an exponent of the world. When we behold the landscape in a poetic spirit, we do not reckon individuals. Nature knows neither palm nor oak, but only vegetable life, which sprouts into forests, and festoons the globe with a garland of grasses and vines.

---

3. According to Greek tradition, Empedocles (fl. 444 B.C.E.) threw himself into the crater of Mount Aetna as a demonstration of his divine nature. He did not emerge from the crater, but his shoe was expelled.
4. Something that issues from a source; an emission.

That no single end may be selected, and nature judged thereby, appears from this, that if man himself be considered as the end, and it be assumed that the final cause of the world is to make holy or wise or beautiful men, we see that it has not succeeded. Read alternately in natural and in civil history, a treatise of astronomy, for example, with a volume of French *Memoires pour servir*.[5] When we have spent our wonder in computing this wasteful hospitality with which boon nature turns off new firmaments without end into her wide common, as fast as the madrepores make coral,—suns and planets hospitable to souls,—and then shorten the sight to look into this court of Louis Quatorze,[6] and see the game that is played there,—duke and marshal, abbé and madame, —a gambling table where each is laying traps for the other, where the end is ever by some lie or fetch to outwit your rival and ruin him with this solemn fop in wig and stars,—the king; one can hardly help asking if this planet is a fair specimen of the so generous astronomy, and if so, whether the experiment have not failed, and whether it be quite worth while to make more, and glut the innocent space with so poor an article.

I think we feel not much otherwise if, instead of beholding foolish nations, we take the great and wise men, the eminent souls, and narrowly inspect their biography. None of them seen by himself—and his performance compared with his promise or idea, will justify the cost of that enormous apparatus of means by which this spotted and defective person was at last procured.

To questions of this sort, nature replies, 'I grow.' All is nascent, infant. When we are dizzied with the arithmetic of the savant toiling to compute the length of her line, the return of her curve, we are steadied by the perception that a great deal is doing; that all seems just begun; remote aims are in active accomplishment. We can point nowhere to anything final; but tendency appears on all hands: planet, system, constellation, total nature is growing like a field of maize in July; is becoming somewhat else; is in rapid metamorphosis. The embryo does not more strive to be man, than yonder burr of light we call a nebula tends to be a ring, a comet, a globe, and parent of new stars. Why should not then these messieurs of Versailles[7] strut and plot for tabourets and ribbons, for a season, without prejudice to their faculty to run on better errands by and by?

But nature seems further to reply, 'I have ventured so great a stake as my success, in no single creature. I have not yet arrived at any end. The gardener aims to produce a fine peach or pear, but my aim is the health of the whole tree,—root, stem, leaf, flower, and seed,—and by no means the pampering of a monstrous pericarp[8] at the expense of all the other functions.'

In short, the spirit and peculiarity of that impression nature makes on us, is this, that it does not exist to any one or to any number of particular ends, but to numberless and endless benefit; that there is in it no private will, no rebel leaf or limb, but the whole is oppressed by one superincumbent tendency, obeys that redundancy or excess of life which in conscious beings we call *ecstasy*.

---

5. A collection of anecdotes or memoirs intended to be used later in the preparation of a formal biography.
6. Louis XIV (1643–1715), the Sun King, grand monarch of France, known for his extravagance and his lavish patronage of the arts.
7. A city of north-central France west-southwest of Paris. It is best known for its magnificent palace, built by Louis XIV in the mid-seventeenth century.
8. The ripened and variously modified walls of a plant ovary that form the substance of a fruit and enclose the seeds.

With this conception of the genius or method of nature, let us go back to man. It is true, he pretends to give account of himself to himself, but, at last, what has he to recite but the fact that there is a Life not to be described or known otherwise than by possession? What account can he give of his essence more than *so it was to be*? The *royal* reason, the Grace of God seems the only description of our multiform but ever identical fact. There is virtue, there is genius, there is success, or there is not. There is the incoming or the receding of God: that is all we can affirm; and we can show neither how nor why. Self-accusation, remorse, and the didactic morals of self-denial and strife with sin, is a view we are constrained by our constitution to take of the fact seen from the platform of action; but seen from the platform of intellection, there is nothing for us but praise and wonder.

The termination of the world in a man, appears to be the last victory of intelligence. The universal does not attract us until housed in an individual. Who heeds the waste abyss of possibility? The ocean is everywhere the same, but it has no character until seen with the shore or the ship. Who would value any number of miles of Atlantic brine bounded by lines of latitude and longitude? Confine it by granite rocks, let it wash a shore where wise men dwell, and it is filled with expression; and the point of greatest interest is where the land and water meet. So must we admire in man, the form of the formless, the concentration of the vast, the house of reason, the cave of memory. See the play of thoughts! what nimble gigantic creatures are these! what saurians, what palaiotheria[9] shall be named with these agile movers? The great Pan[1] of old, who was clothed in a leopard skin to signify the beautiful variety of things, and the firmament, his coat of stars, —was but the representative of thee, O rich and various Man! thou palace of sight and sound, carrying in thy senses the morning and the night and the unfathomable galaxy; in thy brain, the geometry of the City of God,[2] in thy heart, the bower of love and the realms of right and wrong. An individual man is a fruit which it cost all the foregoing ages to form and ripen. The history of the genesis or the old mythology repeats itself in the experience of every child. He too is a demon or god thrown into a particular chaos, where he strives ever to lead things from disorder into order. Each individual soul is such, in virtue of its being a power to translate the world into some particular language of its own; if not into a picture, a statue, or a dance, —why, then, into a trade, an art, a science, a mode of living, a conversation, a character, an influence. You admire pictures, but it is as impossible for you to paint a right picture, as for grass to bear apples. But when the genius comes, it makes fingers: it is pliancy, and the power of transferring the affair in the street into oils and colors. Raphael must be born, and Salvator[3] must be born.

There is no attractiveness like that of a new man. The sleepy nations are occupied with their political routine. England, France and America read Parliamentary Debates, which no high genius now enlivens; and nobody will read them who trusts his own eye: only they who are deceived by the popular repe-

9. Ancient beasts (Greek); extinct animals, such as dinosaurs. *Saurians:* from the Greek *sauros*, "lizard." Any of various reptiles of the suborder Sauria, which includes the lizards and in older classifications the crocodiles and dinosaurs.
1. In Greek mythology, the god of woods, fields, and flocks, having a human torso and head with a goat's legs, horns, and ears. See also "The Poet" (p. 197).
2. *Civitas dei* (Latin); Augustinian term for the body of Christians belonging to the church.
3. Salvator Rosa (1615–1673), Italian painter noted for his moody and dramatic treatment of nature. Raphael (1483–1520), Italian painter and architect, whose works, including religious subjects, portraits, and frescoes, exemplify the ideals of the High Renaissance.

tition of distinguished names. But when Napoleon[4] unrolls his map the eye is commanded by original power. When Chatham[5] leads the debate, men may well listen, because they must listen. A man, a personal ascendency is the only great phenomenon. When nature has work to be done, she creates a genius to do it. Follow the great man, and you shall see what the world has at heart in these ages. There is no omen like that.

But what strikes us in the fine genius is that which belongs of right to every one. A man should know himself for a necessary actor. A link was wanting between two craving parts of nature, and he was hurled into being as the bridge over that yawning need, the mediator betwixt two else unmarriageable facts. His two parents held each of one of the wants, and the union of foreign constitutions in him enables him to do gladly and gracefully what the assembled human race could not have sufficed to do. He knows his materials; he applies himself to his work; he cannot read, or think, or look, but he unites the hitherto separated strands into a perfect cord. The thoughts he delights to utter are the reason of his incarnation. Is it for him to account himself cheap and superfluous, or to linger by the wayside for opportunities? Did he not come into being because something must be done which he and no other is and does? If only he *sees*, the world will be visible enough. He need not study where to stand, nor to put things in favorable lights; in him is the light, from him all things are illuminated, to their centre. What patron shall he ask for employment and reward? Hereto was he born, to deliver the thought of his heart from the universe to the universe, to do an office which nature could not forego, nor he be discharged from rendering, and then immerge again into the holy silence and eternity out of which as a man he arose. God is rich, and many more men than one he harbors in his bosom, biding their time and the needs and the beauty of all. Is not this the theory of every man's genius or faculty? Why then goest thou as some Boswell[6] or listening worshipper to this saint or to that? That is the only lese-majesty. Here art thou with whom so long the universe travailed in labor; darest thou think meanly of thyself whom the stalwart Fate brought forth to unite his ragged sides, to shoot the gulf, to reconcile the irreconcilable?

Whilst a necessity so great caused the man to exist, his health and erectness consist in the fidelity with which he transmits influences from the vast and universal to the point on which his genius can act. The ends are momentary: they are vents for the current of inward life which increases as it is spent. A man's wisdom is to know that all ends are momentary, that the best end must be superseded by a better. But there is a mischievous tendency in him to transfer his thought from the life to the ends, to quit his agency and rest in his acts: the tools run away with the workman, the human with the divine. I conceive a man as always spoken to from behind and unable to turn his head and see the speaker. In all the millions who have heard the voice, none ever saw the face. As children in their play run behind each other, and seize one by the ears and make him walk before them, so is the spirit our unseen pilot. That well-known voice speaks in all languages, governs all men, and none ever caught a glimpse of its form. If the man will exactly obey it, it will adopt him, so that he shall not any

4. See n. 8, p. 17.
5. William Pitt, first earl of Chatham (1708–1778), a popular and powerful British politician and orator who was called "the Great Commoner."
6. James Boswell (1740–1795), Scottish lawyer, diarist, and writer, renowned as the biographer of Samuel Johnson, to whom he devoted the better part of his life.

longer separate it from himself in his thought, he shall seem to be it, he shall be it. If he listen with insatiable ears, richer and greater wisdom is taught him, the sound swells to a ravishing music, he is borne away as with a flood, he becomes careless of his food and of his house, he is the fool of ideas,[7] and leads a heavenly life. But if his eye is set on the things to be done, and not on the truth that is still taught, and for the sake of which the things are to be done, then the voice grows faint, and at last is but a humming in his ears. His health and greatness consist in his being the channel through which heaven flows to earth, in short, in the fullness in which an ecstatical state takes place in him. It is pitiful to be an artist, when, by forbearing to be artists, we might be vessels filled with the divine overflowings, enriched by the circulations of omniscience and omnipresence. Are there not moments in the history of heaven when the human race was not counted by individuals, but was only the Influenced, was God in distribution, God rushing into multiform benefit? It is sublime to receive, sublime to love, but this lust of imparting as from *us*, this desire to be loved, the wish to be recognized as individuals, — is finite, comes of a lower strain.

Shall I say, then, that, as far as we can trace the natural history of the soul, its health consists in the fulness of its reception, — call it piety, call it veneration — in the fact, that enthusiasm is organized therein. What is best in any work of art, but that part which the work itself seems to require and do; that which the man cannot do again, that which flows from the hour and the occasion, like the eloquence of men in a tumultuous debate? It was always the theory of literature that the word of a poet was authoritative and final. He was supposed to be the mouth of a divine wisdom. We rather envied his circumstance than his talent. We too could have gladly prophesied standing in that place. We so quote our Scriptures; and the Greeks so quoted Homer, Theognis, Pindar,[8] and the rest. If the theory has receded out of modern criticism, it is because we have not had poets. Whenever they appear, they will redeem their own credit.

This ecstatical state seems to direct a regard to the whole and not to the parts; to the cause and not to the ends; to the tendency, and not to the act. It respects genius and not talent; hope, and not possession: the anticipation of all things by the intellect, and not the history itself; art, and not works of art; poetry, and not experiment; virtue, and not duties.

There is no office or function of man but is rightly discharged by this divine method, and nothing that is not noxious to him if detached from its universal relations. Is it his work in the world to study nature, or the laws of the world? Let him beware of proposing to himself any end. Is it for use? nature is debased, as if one looking at the ocean can remember only the price of fish. Or is it for pleasure? he is mocked: there is a certain infatuating air in woods and mountains which draws on the idler to want and misery. There is something social and intrusive in the nature of all things; they seek to penetrate and overpower, each the nature of every other creature, and itself alone in all modes and throughout space and spirit to prevail and possess. Every star in heaven is discontented and insatiable. Gravitation and chemistry cannot content them. Ever they woo and court the eye of every beholder. Every man who comes into the

---

7. Emerson noted that *fool* should read "prophet" in his wife's copy, but he changed the word to "drinker" for the 1870 edition.
8. See n. 3, p. 33. Homer (fl. 850 B.C.E.), Greek epic poet. Two of the greatest works in Western literature, the *Iliad* and the *Odyssey*, are attributed to him. Theognis (sixth century B.C.E.), Greek poet.

world they seek to fascinate and possess, to pass into his mind, for they desire to republish themselves in a more delicate world than that they occupy. It is not enough that they are Jove, Mars, Orion, and the North Star, in the gravitating firmament: they would have such poets as Newton, Herschel and Laplace,[9] that they may re-exist and re-appear in the finer world of rational souls, and fill that realm with their fame. So is it with all immaterial objects. These beautiful basilisks set their brute, glorious eyes on the eye of every child, and, if they can, cause their nature to pass through his wondering eyes into him, and so all things are mixed.

Therefore man must be on his guard against this cup of enchantments, and must look at nature with a supernatural eye. By piety alone, by conversing with the cause of nature, is he safe and commands it. And because all knowledge is assimilation to the object of knowledge, as the power or genius of nature is ec-static, so must its science or the description of it be. The poet must be a rhap-sodist: his inspiration a sort of bright casualty: his will in it only the surrender of will to the Universal Power, which will not be seen face to face, but must be re-ceived and sympathetically known. It is remarkable that we have out of the deeps of antiquity in the oracles ascribed to the half fabulous Zoroaster[1] a state-ment of this fact, which every lover and seeker of truth will recognize. "It is not proper," said Zoroaster, "to understand the Intelligible with vehemence, but if you incline your mind, you will apprehend it: not too earnestly, but bringing a pure and inquiring eye. You will not understand it as when understanding some particular thing, but with the flower of the mind. Things divine are not attain-able by mortals who understand sensual things, but only the light-armed arrive at the summit."[2]

And because ecstasy is the law and cause of nature, therefore you cannot in-terpret it in too high and deep a sense. Nature represents the best meaning of the wisest man. Does the sunset landscape seem to you the palace of Friendship, — those purple skies and lovely waters the amphitheatre dressed and garnished only for the exchange of thought and love of the purest souls? It is that. All other mean-ings which base men have put on it are conjectural and false. You cannot bathe twice in the same river, said Heraclitus;[3] and I add, a man never sees the same ob-ject twice: with his own enlargement the object acquires new aspects.

Does not the same law hold for virtue? It is vitiated by too much will. He who aims at progress, should aim at an infinite, not at a special benefit. The re-forms whose fame now fills the land with Temperance, Anti-Slavery, Non-Re-sistance,[4] No Government, Equal Labor, fair and generous as each appears, are poor bitter things when prosecuted for themselves as an end. To every reform,

9. Marquis Pierre Simon de La Place (1749–1827), French mathematician and astronomer noted for his theory of a nebular origin of the solar system and his investigations into gravity and the stability of plan-etary motion. Jove (or Jupiter), in Roman mythology, the supreme god, patron of the Roman state and brother and husband of Juno. Mars, in Roman mythology, the god of war. Orion, see n. 3, p. 43. *North Star:* see n. 5, p. 56. Sir Isaac Newton, see n. 5, p. 16. Herschel, family of British astronomers, including Sir William Herschel (see n. 6, p. 63). His sister Caroline Herschel (1750–1848) assisted in his work and published a star catalog. His son Sir John Frederick William Herschel (1792–1871) augmented William's work with the discovery of 525 nebulae and conducted notable research on light, photogra-phy, and astrophysics.
1. See n. 9, p. 78.
2. Edward Waldo Emerson suggests that this quotation was probably copied from Thomas Taylor's *Collec-tions of Chaldean Oracles* (1817–18).
3. Heraclitus (fl. 500 B.C.E.), Greek philosopher who maintained that strife and change are natural condi-tions of the universe.
4. The practice or principle of refusing to resort to force even in defense against violence. *Temperance:* re-straint in the use of, or abstinence from, alcoholic liquors.

in proportion to its energy, early disgusts are incident, so that the disciple is surprised at the very hour of his first triumphs, with chagrins, and sickness, and a general distrust: so that he shuns his associates, hates the enterprise which lately seemed so fair, and meditates to cast himself into the arms of that society and manner of life which he had newly abandoned with so much pride and hope. Is it that he attached the value of virtue to some particular practices, as, the denial of certain appetites in certain specified indulgences, and, afterward, found himself still as wicked and as far from happiness in that abstinence, as he had been in the abuse? But the soul can be appeased not by a deed but by a tendency. It is in a hope that she feels her wings. You shall love rectitude and not the disuse of money or the avoidance of trade: an unimpeded mind, and not a monkish diet; sympathy and usefulness, and not hoeing or coopering. Tell me not how great your project is, the civil liberation of the world, its conversion into a Christian church, the establishment of public education, cleaner diet, a new division of labor and of land, laws of love for laws of property;—I say to you plainly there is no end to which your practical faculty can aim, so sacred or so large, that, if pursued for itself, will not at last become carrion and an offence to the nostril. The imaginative faculty of the soul must be fed with objects immense and eternal. Your end should be one inapprehensible to the senses: then will it be a god always approached,—never touched; always giving health. A man adorns himself with prayer and love, as an aim adorns an action. What is strong but goodness, and what is energetic but the presence of a brave man? The doctrine in vegetable physiology of the *presence*, or the general influence of any substance over and above its chemical influence, as of an alkali or a living plant, is more predicable of man. You need not speak to me, I need not go where you are, that you should exert magnetism on me. Be you only whole and sufficient, and I shall feel you in every part of my life and fortune, and I can as easily dodge the gravitation of the globe as escape your influence.

But there are other examples of this total and supreme influence, besides Nature and the conscience. "From the poisonous tree, the world," say the Brahmins, "two species of fruit are produced, sweet as the waters of life, Love or the society of beautiful souls, and Poetry, whose taste is like the immortal juice of Vishnu."[5] What is Love, and why is it the chief good, but because it is an overpowering enthusiasm? Never self-possessed or prudent, it is all abandonment. Is it not a certain admirable wisdom, preferable to all other advantages, and whereof all others are only secondaries and indemnities, because this is that in which the individual is no longer his own foolish master, but inhales an odorous and celestial air, is wrapped round with awe of the object, blending for the time that object with the real and only good, and consults every omen in nature with tremulous interest. When we speak truly,—is not he only unhappy who is not in love? his fancied freedom and self-rule—is it not so much death? He who is in love is wise and is becoming wiser, sees newly every time he looks at the object beloved, drawing from it with his eyes and his mind those virtues which it possesses. Therefore if the object be not itself a living and expanding soul, he presently exhausts it. But the love remains in his mind, and the wisdom it brought him; and it craves a new and higher object. And the reason why all men honor love, is because it looks up and not down; aspires and not despairs.

---

5. One of the principal Hindu deities, worshiped as the protector and preserver of worlds. Vishnu is often conceived as a member of the triad including also Brahma and Shiva. *Brahmins:* see n. 6, p. 38.

And what is Genius but finer love, a love impersonal, a love of the flower and perfection of things, and a desire to draw a new picture or copy of the same? It looks to the cause and life: it proceeds from within outward, whilst Talent goes from without inward. Talent finds its models, methods, and ends, in society, exists for exhibition, and goes to the soul only for power to work. Genius is its own end, and draws its means and the style of its architecture from within, going abroad only for audience, and spectator, as we adapt our voice and phrase to the distance and character of the ear we speak to. All your learning of all literatures would never enable you to anticipate one of its thoughts or expressions, and yet each is natural and familiar as household words. Here about us coils forever the ancient enigma, so old and so unutterable. Behold! there is the sun, and the rain, and the rocks: the old sun, the old stones. How easy were it to describe all this fitly; yet no word can pass. Nature is a mute, and man, her articulate speaking brother, lo! he also is a mute. Yet when Genius arrives, its speech is like a river; it has no straining to describe, more than there is straining in nature to exist. When thought is best, there is most of it. Genius sheds wisdom like perfume, and advertises us that it flows out of a deeper source than the foregoing silence, that it knows so deeply and speaks so musically, because it is itself a mutation of the thing it describes. It is sun and moon and wave and fire in music, as astronomy is thought and harmony in masses of matter.

What is all history but the work of ideas, a record of the incomputable energy which his infinite aspirations infuse into man? Has any thing grand and lasting been done? Who did it? Plainly not any man, but all men: it was the prevalence and inundation of an idea. What brought the pilgrims here? One man says, civil liberty; another, the desire of founding a church; and a third, discovers that the motive force was plantation and trade. But if the Puritans[6] could rise from the dust, they could not answer. It is to be seen in what they were, and not in what they designed; it was the growth and expansion of the human race, and resembled herein the sequent Revolution, which was not begun in Concord, or Lexington, or Virginia,[7] but was the overflowing of the sense of natural right in every clear and active spirit of the period. Is a man boastful and knowing, and his own master? — we turn from him without hope: but let him be filled with awe and dread before the Vast and the Divine, which uses him glad to be used, and our eye is riveted to the chain of events. What a debt is ours to that old religion which, in the childhood of most of us, still dwelt like a sabbath morning in the country of New England, teaching privation, self-denial and sorrow! A man was born not for prosperity, but to suffer for the benefit of others, like the noble rock-maple which all around our villages bleeds for the service of man. Not praise, not men's acceptance of our doing, but the spirit's holy errand through us absorbed the thought. How dignified was this! How all that is called talents and success, in our noisy capitals, becomes buzz and din before this man-worthiness! How our friendships and the complaisances we use, shame us now! Shall we not quit our companions, as if they were thieves and pot-companions, and betake ourselves to some desert cliff of mount Katahdin,

6. English Protestants, followers of John Calvin, who left the Church of England and migrated to Massachusetts Bay in 1630 to establish their own Congregational churches. They advocated strict religious discipline along with simplification of the ceremonies and creeds of the Church of England.
7. Concord, a town of eastern Massachusetts on the Concord River west-northwest of Boston, where an early battle of the Revolutionary War was fought on April 19, 1775, as at Lexington, five miles east of Concord, earlier in the same day. Emerson's mention of Virginia is probably meant to stand for Thomas Jefferson and the drafting of the Declaration of Independence.

some unvisited recess in Moosehead Lake,[8] to bewail our innocency and to recover it, and with it the power to communicate again with these sharers of a
more sacred idea?

And what is to replace for us the piety of that race? We cannot have theirs:
it glides away from us day by day, but we also can bask in the great morning
which rises forever out of the eastern sea, and be ourselves the children of the
light. I stand here to say, Let us worship the mighty and transcendent Soul. It is
the office, I doubt not, of this age to annul that adulterous divorce which the superstition of many ages has effected between the intellect and holiness. The
lovers of goodness have been one class, the students of wisdom another, as if either could exist in any purity without the other. Truth is always holy, holiness
always wise. I will that we keep terms with sin, and a sinful literature and society, no longer, but live a life of discovery and performance. Accept the intellect,
and it will accept us. Be the lowly ministers of that pure omniscience, and deny
it not before men. It will burn up all profane literature, all base current opinions, all the false powers of the world, as in a moment of time. I draw from nature the lesson of an intimate divinity. Our health and reason as men needs our
respect to this fact, against the heedlessness and against the contradiction of society. The sanity of man needs the poise of this immanent force. His nobility
needs the assurance of this inexhaustible reserved power. How great soever have
been its bounties, they are a drop to the sea whence they flow. If you say, 'the
acceptance of the vision is also the act of God:'—I shall not seek to penetrate
the mystery, I admit the force of what you say. If you ask, 'How can any rules be
given for the attainment of gifts so sublime?" I shall only remark that the solicitations of this spirit, as long as there is life, are never forborne. Tenderly, tenderly, they woo and court us from every object in nature, from every fact in life,
from every thought in the mind. The one condition coupled with the gift of
truth is its use. That man shall be learned who reduceth his learning to practice. Emanuel Swedenborg[9] affirmed that it was opened to him, "that the spirits who knew truth in this life, but did it not, at death shall lose their knowledge."
"If knowledge," said Ali the Caliph,[1] "calleth unto practice, well; if not, it goeth
away." The only way unto nature is to enact our best insight. Instantly we are
higher poets, and can speak a deeper law. Do what you know, and perception
is converted into character, as islands and continents were built by invisible in-
fusories, or, as these forest leaves absorb light, electricity, and volatile gases, and
the gnarled oak to live a thousand years is the arrest and fixation of the most
volatile and ethereal currents. The doctrine of this Supreme Presence is a cry
of joy and exultation. Who shall dare think he has come late into nature, or has
missed anything excellent in the past, who seeth the admirable stars of possibility, and the yet untouched continent of hope glittering with all its mountains
in the vast West? I praise with wonder this great reality, which seems to drown
all things in the deluge of its light. What man seeing this, can lose it from his
thoughts, or entertain a meaner subject? The entrance of this into his mind
seems to be the birth of man. We cannot describe the natural history of the soul,
but we know that it is divine. I cannot tell if these wonderful qualities which

8. In west-central Maine north of Augusta, a wilderness area. Katahdin, a mountain (5,268 feet high) in
    north-central Maine.
9. See n. 6, p. 35.
1. Ali the Caliph (?600–661), Ali Ibn Abu Talib, who married the daughter of Mahomet and became caliph
    [Edward Waldo Emerson].

house to-day in this mortal frame, shall ever re-assemble in equal activity in a similar frame, or whether they have before had a natural history like that of this body you see before you; but this one thing I know, that these qualities did not now begin to exist, cannot be sick with my sickness, nor buried in any grave; but that they circulate through the Universe: before the world was, they were. Nothing can bar them out, or shut them in, but they penetrate the ocean and land, space and time, form and essence, and hold the key to universal nature. I draw from this faith courage and hope. All things are known to the soul. It is not to be surprised by any communication. Nothing can be greater than it. Let those fear and those fawn who will. The soul is in her native realm, and it is wider than space, older than time, wide as hope, rich as love. Pusillanimity and fear she refuses with a beautiful scorn: they are not for her who putteth on her coronation robes, and goes out through universal love to universal power.

The Transcendentalist

A Lecture read at the Masonic Temple, Boston, January, 1842[1]

The first thing we have to say respecting what are called *new views* here in New England, at the present time, is, that they are not new, but the very oldest of thoughts cast into the mould of these new times. The light is always identical in its composition, but it falls on a great variety of objects, and by so falling is first revealed to us, not in its own form, for it is formless, but in theirs; in like manner, thought only appears in the objects it classifies. What is popularly called Transcendentalism among us, is Idealism; Idealism as it appears in 1842. As thinkers, mankind have ever divided into two sects, Materialists and Idealists;[2] the first class founding on experience, the second on consciousness; the first class beginning to think from the data of the senses, the second class perceive that the senses are not final, and say, the senses give us representations of things, but what are the things themselves, they cannot tell. The materialist insists on facts, on history, on the force of circumstances, and the animal wants of man; the idealist on the power of Thought and of Will, on inspiration, on miracle, on individual culture. These two modes of thinking are both natural, but the idealist contends that his way of thinking is in higher nature. He concedes all that the other affirms, admits the impressions of sense, admits their coherency, their use and beauty, and then asks the materialist for his grounds of assurance that things are as his senses represent them. But I, he says, affirm facts not affected by the illusions of sense, facts which are of the same nature as the faculty which reports them, and not liable to doubt; facts which in their first ap-

---

1. This lecture was in fact first delivered on December 23, 1841, as the fourth in Emerson's series of lectures on "the times." The first edition printing dated it "January, 1841," with an erratum on the contents page changing the date to "January, 1842." Henry David Thoreau (1817–1862), Emerson's fellow-Transcendentalist and author of *Walden* (1854) and "Resistance to Civil Government" (or "Civil Disobedience," as it is now known) lived in the Emerson house when Emerson was working on this address; many of the statements seem made with him in mind. Though Emerson is often today, and was in his own time, considered the quintessential Transcendentalist, here he generally refers to such individuals in the third person, dissociating himself from "them." The Masonic Temple was a meeting-place for the local branch of the Freemasons, or Free and Accepted Masons, an international fraternal and charitable organization with secret rites and signs.
2. Emerson glosses the terms, but see n. 6, p. 45, on the difference between the "sensual" man and the idealist.

pearance to us assume a native superiority to material facts, degrading these into a language by which the first are to be spoken; facts which it only needs a retirement from the senses to discern. Every materialist will be an idealist; but an idealist can never go backward to be a materialist.

The idealist, in speaking of events, sees them as spirits. He does not deny the sensuous fact: by no means; but he will not see that alone. He does not deny the presence of this table, this chair, and the walls of this room, but he looks at these things as the reverse side of the tapestry, as the *other end*, each being a sequel or completion of a spiritual fact which nearly concerns him. This manner of looking at things, transfers every object in nature from an independent and anomalous position without there, into the consciousness. Even the materialist Condillac,[3] perhaps the most logical expounder of materialism, was constrained to say, "Though we should soar into the heavens, though we should sink into the abyss, we never go out of ourselves; it is always our own thought that we perceive." What more could an idealist say?

The materialist, secure in the certainty of sensation, mocks at fine-spun theories, at star-gazers and dreamers, and believes that his life is solid, that he at least takes nothing for granted, but knows where he stands, and what he does. Yet how easy it is to show him, that he also is a phantom walking and working amid phantoms, and that he need only ask a question or two beyond his daily questions, to find his solid universe growing dim and impalpable before his sense. The sturdy capitalist, no matter how deep and square on blocks of Quincy granite[4] he lays the foundations of his banking-house or Exchange, must set it, at last, not on a cube corresponding to the angles of his structure, but on a mass of unknown materials and solidity, red-hot or white-hot, perhaps at the core, which rounds off to an almost perfect sphericity, and lies floating in soft air, and goes spinning away, dragging bank and banker with it at a rate of thousands of miles the hour, he knows not whither, — a bit of bullet, now glimmering, now darkling through a small cubic space on the edge of an unimaginable pit of emptiness. And this wild balloon, in which his whole venture is embarked, is a just symbol of his whole state and faculty. One thing, at least, he says is certain, and does not give me the headache, that figures do not lie; the multiplication table has been hitherto found unimpeachable truth; and, moreover, if I put a gold eagle[5] in my safe, I find it again to-morrow; — but for these thoughts, I know not whence they are. They change and pass away. But ask him why he believes that an uniform experience will continue uniform, or on what grounds he founds his faith in his figures, and he will perceive that his mental fabric is built up on just as strange and quaking foundations as his proud edifice of stone.

In the order of thought, the materialist takes his departure from the external world, and esteems a man as one product of that. The idealist takes his departure from his consciousness, and reckons the world an appearance. The materialist respects sensible masses,[6] Society, Government, social art, and luxury, every establishment, every mass, whether majority of numbers, or extent of space, or amount of objects, every social action. The idealist has another mea-

3. Étienne Bonnot, abbé de Condillac (1715–1780), French sensationalist philosopher, follower of John Locke (see n. 7, p. 59).
4. Unusually hard stone quarried in Quincy, Massachusetts, and elsewhere.
5. U.S. $10 gold coin. This is an eagle that will not fly away.
6. Apparent to the senses; also, "masses" that make sense.

sure, which is metaphysical, namely, the *rank* which things themselves take in his consciousness; not at all, the size or appearance. Mind is the only reality, of which men and all other natures are better or worse reflectors. Nature, litera-ture, history, are only subjective phenomena. Although in his action overpow-ered by the laws of action, and so, warmly coöperating with men, even preferring them to himself, yet when he speaks scientifically, or after the order of thought, he is constrained to degrade persons into representatives of truths. He does not respect labor, or the products of labor, namely, property, otherwise than as a manifold symbol, illustrating with wonderful fidelity of details the laws of being; he does not respect government, except as far as it reiterates the law of his mind; nor the church; nor charities; nor arts, for themselves; but hears, as at a vast distance, what they say, as if his consciousness would speak to him through a pantomimic scene. His thought, — that is the Universe. His experi-ence inclines him to behold the procession of facts you call the world, as flow-ing perpetually outward from an invisible, unsounded centre in himself, centre alike of him and of them, and necessitating him to regard all things as having a subjective or relative existence, relative to that aforesaid Unknown Centre of him.

From this transfer of the world into the consciousness, this beholding of all things in the mind, follow easily his whole ethics. It is simpler to be self-de-pendent. The height, the deity of man is, to be self-sustained, to need no gift, no foreign force. Society is good when it does not violate me; but best when it is likest to solitude. Everything real is self-existent. Everything divine shares the self-existence of Deity. All that you call the world is the shadow[7] of that sub-stance which you are, the perpetual creation of the powers of thought, of those that are dependent and of those that are independent of your will. Do not cum-ber yourself with fruitless pains to mend and remedy remote effects; let the soul be erect, and all things will go well. You think me the child of my circum-stances: I make my circumstance. Let any thought or motive of mine be differ-ent from that they are, the difference will transform my condition and economy. I — this thought which is called I, — is the mould into which the world is poured like melted wax. The mould is invisible, but the world betrays the shape of the mould. You call it the power of circumstance, but it is the power of me. Am I in harmony with myself? my position will seem to you just and commanding. Am I vicious and insane? my fortunes will seem to you obscure and descend-ing. As I am, so shall I associate, and, so shall I act; Cæsar's history will paint out Cæsar.[8] Jesus acted so, because he thought so. I do not wish to overlook or to gainsay any reality; I say, I make my circumstance: but if you ask me, Whence am I? I feel like other men my relation to that Fact which cannot be spoken, or defined, nor even thought, but which exists, and will exist.

The Transcendentalist adopts the whole connection of spiritual doctrine. He believes in miracle, in the perpetual openness of the human mind to new influx of light and power; he believes in inspiration, and in ecstasy. He wishes that the spiritual principle should be suffered to demonstrate itself to the end, in all possible applications to the state of man, without the admission of any-thing unspiritual; that is, anything positive, dogmatic, personal. Thus, the spir-itual measure of inspiration is the depth of the thought, and never, who said it?

7. See n. 7, p. 45.
8. See n. 8, p. 17.

And so he resists all attempts to palm other rules and measures on the spirit than its own.

In action, he easily incurs the charge of antinomianism[9] by his avowal that he, who has the Lawgiver, may with safety not only neglect, but even contravene every written commandment. In the play of Othello, the expiring Desdemona absolves her husband of the murder, to her attendant Emilia. Afterwards, when Emilia charges him with the crime, Othello exclaims,

"You heard her say herself it was not I."

Emilia replies,

"The more angel she, and thou the blacker devil."[1]

Of this fine incident, Jacobi, the Transcendental moralist, makes use, with other parallel instances, in his reply to Fichte.[2] Jacobi, refusing all measure of right and wrong except the determinations of the private spirit, remarks that there is no crime but has sometimes been a virtue. "I," he says, "am that atheist, that godless person who, in opposition to an imaginary doctrine of calculation, would lie as the dying Desdemona lied; would lie and deceive, as Pylades when he personated Orestes; would assassinate like Timoleon; would perjure myself like Epaminondas, and John de Witt; I would resolve on suicide like Cato;[3] I would commit sacrilege with David; yea, and pluck ears of corn on the Sabbath, for no other reason than that I was fainting for lack of food. For, I have assurance in myself, that, in pardoning these faults according to the letter, man exerts the sovereign right which the majesty of his being confers on him; he sets the seal of his divine nature to the grace he accords."[4]

In like manner, if there is anything grand and daring in human thought or virtue, any reliance on the vast, the unknown; any presentiment; any extravagance of faith, the spiritualist adopts it as most in nature. The oriental mind has always tended to this largeness. Buddhism is an expression of it. The Buddhist who thanks no man, who says, "do not flatter your benefactors," but who, in his conviction that every good deed can by no possibility escape its reward, will not deceive the benefactor by pretending that he has done more than he should, is a Transcendentalist.

You will see by this sketch that there is no such thing as a Transcendental *party*; that there is no pure Transcendentalist; that we know of none but

9. Literally, "against-the-law-ism." Emerson may have been thinking of the famous seventeenth-century Antinomian Anne Hutchinson, who was tried, convicted, and banished from the Massachusetts Bay Colony in 1638 for her belief that anyone who experienced the indwelling of the Holy Spirit was free to abrogate church laws and duties.
1. Shakespeare, *Othello* 5.2.127 and 130.
2. Friedrich Heinrich Jacobi (1743–1819) and Johann Gottlieb Fichte (1762–1814), German philosophers, followers of Immanuel Kant (see n. 8, p. 35), although their "absolute idealism" differs from Kant's more nuanced interest in the mind's contribution to knowledge.
3. Coleridge (see n. 2, p. 31) quotes Jacobi's "Letter to Fichte" in his *The Friend*. In Greek legend, Pylades helped Orestes murder Clytemnestra (Orestes' mother) in revenge for her murder of Orestes' father, Agamemnon, leader of the Greeks at the siege of Troy. Timoleon (d. 337 B.C.E.), Greek politician and general who assassinated his brother, Timophanes, because of the latter's political ambitions. Epaminondas, see n. 8, p. 74. Johann de Witt (1625–1672), chief official of the Dutch Republic, fell into disrepute by granting concessions to Louis XIV (see n. 6, p. 85) to try to establish peace; murdered by a mob with his brother Cornelius. Cato the Younger (95–46 B.C.E.), Roman politician, committed suicide after his enemy, Caesar, defeated his ally Pompey and then conquered the army of the nobility in North Africa.
4. Coleridge's Translation. [Emerson]

prophets and heralds of such a philosophy; that all who by strong bias of nature have leaned to the spiritual side in doctrine, have stopped short of their goal. We have had many harbingers and forerunners; but of a purely spiritual life, history has afforded no example. I mean, we have yet no man who has leaned entirely on his character, and eaten angels' food; who, trusting to his sentiments, found life made of miracles; who, working for universal aims, found himself fed, he knew not how; clothed, sheltered, and weaponed, he knew not how, and yet it was done by his own hands. Only in the instinct of the lower animals, we find the suggestion of the methods of it, and something higher than our understanding. The squirrel hoards nuts, and the bee gathers honey, without knowing what they do, and they are thus provided for without selfishness or disgrace.

Shall we say, then, that Transcendentalism is the Saturnalia[5] or excess of Faith; the presentiment of a faith proper to man in his integrity, excessive only when his imperfect obedience hinders the satisfaction of his wish. Nature is transcendental, exists primarily, necessarily, ever works and advances, yet takes no thought for the morrow.[6] Man owns the dignity of the life which throbs around him in chemistry, and tree, and animal, and in the involuntary functions of his own body; yet he is balked when he tries to fling himself into this enchanted circle, where all is done without degradation. Yet genius and virtue predict in man the same absence of private ends, and of condescension to circumstances, united with every trait and talent of beauty and power.

This way of thinking, falling on Roman times, made Stoic philosophers; falling on despotic times, made patriot Catos and Brutuses;[7] falling on superstitious times, made prophets and apostles; on popish times, made protestants and ascetic monks, preachers of Faith against the preachers of Works; on prelatical times, made Puritans and Quakers;[8] and falling on Unitarian and commercial times, makes the peculiar shades of Idealism which we know.

It is well known to most of my audience, that the Idealism of the present day acquired the name of Transcendental, from the use of that term by Immanuel Kant, of Konigsberg, who replied to the skeptical philosophy of Locke, which insisted that there was nothing in the intellect which was not previously in the experience of the senses, by showing that there was a very important class of ideas, or imperative forms, which did not come by experience, but through which experience was acquired; that these were intuitions of the mind itself; and he denominated them *Transcendental* forms. The extraordinary profoundness and precision of that man's thinking have given vogue to his nomenclature, in Europe and America, to that extent, that whatever belongs to the class of intuitive thought, is popularly called at the present day *Transcendental*.[9]

---

5. The festival of Saturn in ancient Rome, usually associated with unrestrained disorder and licentiousness.
6. Cf. Matthew 6.34.
7. Marcus Junius Brutus (85?–42 B.C.E.), Roman politician and general who conspired to assassinate Julius Caesar. In the subsequent power struggle with Mark Antony and Octavian, Brutus was defeated at the Battle of Philippi and committed suicide. Stoic: see n. 9, p. 78.
8. See n. 6, p. 18.
9. Emerson here seems to conflate Kant's notions about the "transcendental" deduction of the forms and categories of knowledge (pure reason) with intuitive knowledge of the "transcendent"—i.e., things like knowledge of the divinity, which are beyond the range of cognition. Kant was normally skeptical about our ability to "know" such things. As Stephen Whicher points out, however, "though the term 'transcendental' was given vogue by Kant, it reached New England very indirectly" (*Selections from Ralph Waldo Emerson: An Organic Anthology*, pp. 487–88).

Although, as we have said, there is no pure Transcendentalist, yet the tendency to respect the intuitions, and to give them, at least in our creed, all authority over our experience, has deeply colored the conversation and poetry of the present day; and the history of genius and of religion in these times, though impure, and as yet not incarnated in any powerful individual, will be the history of this tendency.

It is a sign of our times, conspicuous to the coarsest observer, that many intelligent and religious persons withdraw themselves from the common labors and competitions of the market and the caucus, and betake themselves to a certain solitary and critical way of living, from which no solid fruit has yet appeared to justify their separation. They hold themselves aloof; they feel the disproportion between their faculties and the work offered them, and they prefer to ramble in the country and perish of ennui, to the degradation of such charities and such ambitions as the city can propose to them. They are striking work, and crying out for somewhat worthy to do! What they do, is done only because they are overpowered by the humanities that speak on all sides; and they consent to such labor as is open to them, though to their lofty dream the writing of Iliads or Hamlets, or the building of cities or empires seems drudgery.

Now every one must do after his kind, be he asp or angel, and these must. The question, which a wise man and a student of modern history will ask, is, what that kind is? And truly, as in ecclesiastical history we take so much pains to know what the Gnostics, what the Essenes, what the Manichees, and what the Reformers[1] believed, it would not misbecome us to inquire nearer home, what these companions and contemporaries of ours think and do, at least so far as these thoughts and actions appear to be not accidental and personal, but common to many, and the inevitable flower of the Tree of Time. Our American literature and spiritual history are, we confess, in the optative mood;[2] but whoso knows these seething brains, these admirable radicals, these unsocial worshippers, these talkers who talk the sun and moon away, will believe that this heresy cannot pass away without leaving its mark.

They are lonely; the spirit of their writing and conversation is lonely; they repel influences; they shun general society; they incline to shut themselves in their chamber in the house, to live in the country rather than in the town, and to find their tasks and amusements in solitude. Society, to be sure, does not like this very well; it saith, Whoso goes to walk alone, accuses the whole world; he declareth all to be unfit to be his companions; it is very uncivil, nay, insulting; Society will retaliate. Meantime, this retirement does not proceed from any whim on the part of these separators;[3] but if any one will take pains to talk with them, he will find that this part is chosen both from temperament and from principle; with some unwillingness, too, and as a choice of the less of two evils; for these persons are not by nature melancholy, sour, and unsocial,—they are not stockish or brute,—but joyous; susceptible, affectionate; they have even

---

1. Leaders of the Protestant Reformation (see also n. 4, p. 18). Gnostics were "knowers" as opposed to "believers" and constituted various sects in the first six centuries of the Christian era. They tried to blend Christianity with Greek and Eastern thought, teaching that knowledge, rather than faith, is the key to salvation. From the Greek *gnosis*, "knowledge." Essenes, an ancient Jewish sect that left behind the oldest existing texts of Hebrew scripture (starting ca. 200 B.C.E.; these manuscripts, discovered in 1947, are called the Dead Sea Scrolls). Manicheanism, see n. 2, p. 48.
2. In grammar, the verb mood used to express a wish.
3. Emerson's use of this term aligns these freethinkers with certain seventeenth-century Puritans, such as William Bradford and the other *Mayflower* Pilgrims, who had "separated" from the Church of England.

more than others a great wish to be loved. Like the young Mozart, they are rather ready to cry ten times a day, "But are you sure you love me?"[4] Nay, if they tell you their whole thought, they will own that love seems to them the last and highest gift of nature; that there are persons whom in their hearts they daily thank for existing,—persons whose faces are perhaps unknown to them, but whose fame and spirit have penetrated their solitude,—and for whose sake they wish to exist. To behold the beauty of another character, which inspires a new interest in our own; to behold the beauty lodged in a human being, with such vivacity of apprehension, that I am instantly forced home to inquire if I am not deformity itself: to behold in another the expression of a love so high that it as- sures itself,—assures itself also to me against every possible casualty except my unworthiness;—these are degrees on the scale of human happiness, to which they have ascended; and it is a fidelity to this sentiment which has made com- mon association distasteful to them. They wish a just and even fellowship, or none. They cannot gossip with you, and they do not wish, as they are sincere and religious, to gratify any mere curiosity which you may entertain. Like fairies, they do not wish to be spoken of. Love me, they say, but do not ask who is my cousin and my uncle. If you do not need to hear my thought, because you can read it in my face and behavior, then I will tell it you from sunrise to sun- set. If you cannot divine it, you would not understand what I say. I will not mo- lest myself for you. I do not wish to be profaned.

And yet, it seems as if this loneliness, and not this love, would prevail in their circumstances, because of the extravagant demand they make on human nature. That, indeed, constitutes a new feature in their portrait, that they are the most exacting and extortionate critics. Their quarrel with every man they meet, is not with his kind, but with his degree. There is not enough of him,—that is the only fault. They prolong their privilege of childhood in this wise, of doing nothing,—but making immense demands on all the gladiators in the lists of ac- tion and fame. They make us feel the strange disappointment which overcasts every human youth. So many promising youths, and never a finished man! The profound nature will have a savage rudeness; the delicate one will be shallow, or the victim of sensibility; the richly accomplished will have some capital ab- surdity; and so every piece has a crack. 'T is strange, but this masterpiece is a re- sult of such an extreme delicacy, that the most unobserved flaw in the boy will neutralize the most aspiring genius, and spoil the work. Talk with a seaman of the hazards to life in his profession, and he will ask you, "Where are the old sailors? do you not see that all are young men?" And we, on this sea of human thought, in like manner inquire, Where are the old idealists? where are they who represented to the last generation that extravagant hope, which a few happy aspirants suggest to ours? In looking at the class of counsel, and power, and wealth, and at the matronage of the land, amidst all the prudence and all the triviality, one asks, Where are they who represented genius, virtue, the invisible and heavenly world, to these? Are they dead,—taken in early ripeness to the gods,—as as ancient wisdom foretold their fate? Or did the high idea die out of them, and leave their unperfumed body as its tomb and tablet, announcing to all that the celestial inhabitant, who once gave them beauty, had departed? Will it be better with the new generation? We easily predict a fair future to each new candidate who enters the lists, but we are frivolous and volatile, and by low aims

4. See *The Dial* 2 (October 1841): 168.

and ill example do what we can to defeat this hope. Then these youths bring us a rough but effectual aid. By their unconcealed dissatisfaction, they expose our poverty, and the insignificance of man to man. A man is a poor limitary benefactor. He ought to be a shower of benefits—a great influence, which should never let his brother go, but should refresh old merits continually with new ones; so that, though absent, he should never be out of my mind, his name never far from my lips; but if the earth should open at my side, or my last hour were come, his name should be the prayer I should utter to the Universe. But in our experience, man is cheap, and friendship wants its deep sense. We affect to dwell with our friends in their absence, but we do not; when deed, word, or letter comes not, they let us go. These exacting children advertise us of our wants. There is no compliment, no smooth speech with them; they pay you only this one compliment, of insatiable expectation; they aspire, they severely exact, and if they only stand fast in this watchtower, and persist in demanding unto the end, and without end, then are they terrible friends, whereof poet and priest cannot choose but stand in awe; and what if they eat clouds, and drink wind,[5] they have not been without service to the race of man.

With this passion for what is great and extraordinary, it cannot be wondered at, that they are repelled by vulgarity and frivolity in people. They say to themselves, It is better to be alone than in bad company. And it is really a wish to be met,—the wish to find society for their hope and religion,—which prompts them to shun what is called society. They feel that they are never so fit for friendship, as when they have quitted mankind, and taken themselves to friend. A picture, a book, a favorite spot in the hills or the woods, which they can people with the fair and worthy creation of the fancy, can give them often forms so vivid, that these for the time shall seem real, and society the illusion.

But their solitary and fastidious manners not only withdraw them from the conversation, but from the labors of the world; they are not good citizens, not good members of society; unwillingly they bear their part of the public and private burdens; they do not willingly share in the public charities, in the public religious rites, in the enterprises of education, of missions foreign or domestic, in the abolition of the slave-trade, or in the temperance society. They do not even like to vote. The philanthropists inquire whether Transcendentalism does not mean sloth: they had as lief hear that their friend is dead, as that he is a Transcendentalist; for then is he paralyzed, and can never do anything for humanity. What right, cries the good world, has the man of genius to retreat from work, and indulge himself? The popular literary creed seems to be, 'I am a sublime genius; I ought not therefore to labor.' But genius is the power to labor better and more availably. Deserve thy genius: exalt it. The good, the illuminated, sit apart from the rest, censuring their dulness and vices, as if they thought that, by sitting very grand in their chairs, the very brokers, attorneys, and congressmen would see the error of their ways, and flock to them. But the good and wise must learn to act, and carry salvation to the combatants and demagogues in the dusty arena below.

On the part of these children, it is replied, that life and their faculty seem to them gifts too rich to be squandered on such trifles as you propose to them. What you call your fundamental institutions, your great and holy causes, seem

5. Cf. *Hamlet* 3.2.98: "I eat the air, promise-crammed."

to them great abuses, and, when nearly seen, paltry matters. Each 'Cause,' as it is called,—say Abolition, Temperance, say Calvinism, or Unitarianism,[6]—becomes speedily a little shop, where the article, let it have been at first never so subtle and ethereal, is now made up into portable and convenient cakes, and retailed in small quantities to suit purchasers. You make very free use of these words 'great' and 'holy,' but few things appear to them such. Few persons have any magnificence of nature to inspire enthusiasm, and the philanthropies and charities have a certain air of quackery. As to the general course of living, and the daily employments of men, they cannot see much virtue in these, since they are parts of this vicious circle; and, as no great ends are answered by the men, there is nothing noble in the arts by which they are maintained. Nay, they have made the experiment, and found that, from the liberal professions to the coarsest manual labor, and from the courtesies of the academy and the college to the conventions of the cotillon-room and the morning call, there is a spirit of cowardly compromise and seeming, which intimates a frightful skepticism, a life without love, and an activity without an aim.

Unless the action is necessary, unless it is adequate, I do not wish to perform it. I do not wish to do one thing but once. I do not love routine. Once possessed of the principle, it is equally easy to make four or forty thousand applications of it. A great man will be content to have indicated in any the slightest manner his perception of the reigning Idea of his time, and will leave to those who like it the multiplication of examples. When he has hit the white, the rest may shatter the target. Every thing admonishes us how needlessly long life is. Every moment of a hero so raises and cheers us, that a twelve-month is an age. All that the brave Xanthus brings home from his wars, is the recollection that, at the storming of Samos, "in the heat of the battle, Pericles smiled on me, and passed on to another detachment."[7] It is the quality of the moment, not the number of days, of events, or of actors, that imports.

New, we confess, and by no means happy, is our condition: if you want the aid of our labor, we ourselves stand in greater want of the labor. We are miserable with inaction. We perish of rest and rust: but we do not like your work.

'Then,' says the world, 'show me your own.'

'We have none.'

'What will you do, then?' cries the world.

'We will wait.'

'How long?'

'Until the Universe rises up and calls us to work.'

'But whilst you wait, you grow old and useless.'

'Be it so: I can sit in a corner and *perish*, (as you call it,) but I will not move until I have the highest command.[8] If no call should come for years, for centuries, then I know that the want of the Universe is the attestation of faith by my abstinence. Your virtuous projects, so called, do not cheer me. I know that which shall come will cheer me. If I cannot work, at least I need not lie. All that is clearly due to-day is not to lie. In other places, other men have encountered

---

6. See n. 6, p. 23. Temperance, see n. 4, p. 89.

7. Edward Waldo Emerson informs us that his father is quoting from Walter Savage Landor's *Pericles and Aspasia* (1836).

8. Emerson may be alluding to his disciple Thoreau's apparent idleness in the face of the world's call to work. Some scholars believe this passage inspired Herman Melville's story "Bartleby, the Scrivener," in which an impoverished copyist responds to all requests for his services with the sentence "I would prefer not to."

sharp trials, and have behaved themselves well. The martyrs were sawn asunder, or hung alive on meat-hooks. Cannot we screw our courage to patience and truth, and without complaint, or even with good-humor, await our turn of action in the Infinite Counsels?'

But, to come a little closer to the secret of these persons, we must say, that to them it seems a very easy matter to answer the objections of the man of the world, but not so easy to dispose of the doubts and objections that occur to themselves. They are exercised in their own spirit with queries, which acquaint them with all adversity, and with the trials of the bravest heroes. When I asked them concerning their private experience, they answered somewhat in this wise: It is not to be denied that there must be some wide difference between my faith and other faith; and mine is a certain brief experience, which surprised me in the highway or in the market, in some place, at some time, — whether in the body or out of the body, God knoweth, — and made me aware that I had played the fool with fools all this time, but that law existed for me and for all; that to me belonged trust, a child's trust and obedience, and the worship of ideas, and I should never be fool more. Well, in the space of an hour, probably, I was let down from this height; I was at my old tricks, the selfish member of a selfish society. My life is superficial, takes no root in the deep world; I ask, When shall I die, and be relieved of the responsibility of seeing an Universe which I do not use? I wish to exchange this flash-of-lightning faith for continuous daylight, this fever-glow for a benign climate.

These two states of thought diverge every moment, and stand in wild contrast. To him who looks at his life from these moments of illumination, it will seem that he skulks and plays a mean, shiftless, and subaltern part in the world. That is to be done which he has not skill to do, or to be said which others can say better, and he lies by, or occupies his hands with some plaything, until his hour comes again. Much of our reading, much of our labor, seems mere waiting: it was not that we were born for. Any other could do it as well, or better. So little skill enters into these works, so little do they mix with the divine life, that it really signifies little what we do, whether we turn a grindstone, or ride, or run, or make fortunes, or govern the state. The worst feature of this double consciousness is, that the two lives, of the understanding and of the soul, which we lead, really show very little relation to each other, never meet and measure each other: one prevails now, all buzz and din; and the other prevails then, all infinitude and paradise; and, with the progress of life, the two discover no greater disposition to reconcile themselves. Yet, what is my faith? What am I? What but a thought of serenity and independence, an abode in the deep blue sky? Presently the clouds shut down again; yet we retain the belief that this petty web we weave will at last be overshot and reticulated with veins of the blue, and that the moments will characterize the days. Patience, then, is for us, is it not? Patience, and still patience. When we pass, as presently we shall, into some new infinitude, out of this Iceland of negations, it will please us to reflect that, though we had few virtues or consolations, we bore with our indigence, nor once strove to repair it with hypocrisy or false heat of any kind.

But this class are not sufficiently characterized, if we omit to add that they are lovers and worshippers of Beauty. In the eternal trinity of Truth, Goodness, and Beauty,[9] each in its perfection including the three, they prefer to make Beauty the sign and head. Something of the same taste is observable in all the

9. Cf. "The Poet" (p. 184).

moral movements of the time, in the religious and benevolent enterprises. They have a liberal, even an æsthetic spirit. A reference to Beauty in action sounds, to be sure, a little hollow and ridiculous in the ears of the old church. In politics, it has often sufficed, when they treated of justice, if they kept the bounds of selfish calculation. If they granted restitution, it was prudence which granted it. But the justice which is now claimed for the black, and the pauper, and the drunkard is for Beauty, — is for a necessity to the soul of the agent, not of the beneficiary. I say, this is the tendency, not yet the realization. Our virtue totters and trips, does not yet walk firmly. Its representatives are austere; they preach and denounce; their rectitude is not yet a grace. They are still liable to that slight taint of burlesque which, in our strange world, attaches to the zealot. A saint should be as dear as the apple of the eye. Yet we are tempted to smile, and we flee from the working to the speculative reformer, to escape that same slight ridicule. Alas for these days of derision and criticism! We call the Beautiful the highest, because it appears to us the golden mean, escaping the dowdiness of the good, and the heartlessness of the true. — They are lovers of nature also, and find an indemnity in the inviolable order of the world for the violated order and grace of man.

There is, no doubt, a great deal of well-founded objection to be spoken or felt against the sayings and doings of this class, some of whose traits we have selected; no doubt, they will lay themselves open to criticism and to lampoons, and as ridiculous stories will be to be told of them as of any. There will be cant and pretension; there will be subtilty and moonshine. These persons are of unequal strength, and do not all prosper. They complain that everything around them must be denied; and if feeble, it takes all their strength to deny, before they can begin to lead their own life. Grave seniors insist on their respect to this institution, and that usage; to an obsolete history; to some vocation, or college, or etiquette, or beneficiary, or charity, or morning or evening call, which they resist, as what does not concern them. But it costs such sleepless nights, alienations and misgivings, — they have so many moods about it; — these old guardians never change *their* minds; they have but one mood on the subject, namely, that Antony is very perverse, — that it is quite as much as Antony can do, to assert his rights, abstain from what he thinks foolish, and keep his temper. He cannot help the reaction of this injustice in his own mind. He is braced-up and stilted; all freedom and flowing genius, all sallies of wit and frolic nature are quite out of the question; it is well if he can keep from lying, injustice, and suicide. This is no time for gaiety and grace. His strength and spirits are wasted in rejection. But the strong spirits overpower those around them without effort. Their thought and emotion comes in like a flood, quite withdraws them from all notice of these carping critics; they surrender themselves with glad heart to the heavenly guide, and only by implication reject the clamorous nonsense of the hour. Grave seniors talk to the deaf, — church and old book mumble and ritualize to an unheeding, preöccupied and advancing mind, and thus they by happiness of greater momentum lose no time, but take the right road at first.

But all these of whom I speak are not proficients; they are novices; they only show the road in which man should travel, when the soul has greater health and prowess. Yet let them feel the dignity of their charge, and deserve a larger power. Their heart is the ark in which the fire is concealed, which shall burn in a broader and universal flame. Let them obey the Genius[1] then most when his impulse is

1. See n. 8, p. 59.

wildest; then most when he seems to lead to uninhabitable desarts of thought and life; for the path which the hero travels alone is the highway of health and benefit to mankind. What is the privilege and nobility of our nature, but its persistency, through its power to attach itself to what is permanent?

Society also has its duties in reference to this class, and must behold them with what charity it can. Possibly some benefit may yet accrue from them to the state. In our Mechanics' Fair, there must be not only bridges, ploughs, carpenters' planes, and baking troughs, but also some few finer instruments,—rain-gauges, thermometers, and telescopes; and in society, besides farmers, sailors, and weavers, there must be a few persons of purer fire kept specially as gauges and meters of character; persons of a fine, detecting instinct, who betray the smallest accumulations of wit and feeling in the bystander. Perhaps too there might be room for the exciters and monitors; collectors of the heavenly spark with power to convey the electricity to others.[2] Or, as the storm-tossed vessel at sea speaks the frigate or 'line packet'[3] to learn its longitude, so it may not be without its advantage that we should now and then encounter rare and gifted men, to compare the points of our spiritual compass, and verify our bearings from superior chronometers.

Amidst the downward tendency and proneness of things, when every voice is raised for a new road or another statute, or a subscription of stock, for an improvement in dress, or in dentistry, for a new house or a larger business, for a political party, or the division of an estate,—will you not tolerate one or two solitary voices in the land, speaking for thoughts and principles not marketable or perishable? Soon these improvements and mechanical inventions will be superseded; these modes of living lost out of memory; these cities rotted, ruined by war, by new inventions, by new seats of trade, or the geologic changes:—all gone, like the shells which sprinkle the seabeach with a white colony to-day, forever renewed to be forever destroyed. But the thoughts which these few hermits strove to proclaim by silence, as well as by speech, not only by what they did, but by what they forbore to do, shall abide in beauty and strength, to reorganize themselves in nature, to invest themselves anew in other, perhaps higher endowed and happier mixed clay than ours, in fuller union with the surrounding system.

2. The editors of CW inform us that these are "technical terms from the science of static electricity."
3. According to CW, "originally a vessel employed by government to convey despatches or mails." *Speaks:* Communicates with.

From Essays: First Series

History

There is no great and no small
To the Soul that maketh all:
And where it cometh, all things are;
And it cometh everywhere.

I am owner of the sphere,
Of the seven stars and the solar year,
Of Cæsar's hand, and Plato's[1] brain,
Of Lord Christ's heart, and Shakspeare's strain.

There is one mind common to all individual men. Every man is an inlet to the same and to all of the same. He that is once admitted to the right of reason is made a freeman of the whole estate. What Plato has thought, he may think; what a saint has felt, he may feel; what at any time has befallen any man, he can understand. Who hath access to this universal mind, is a party to all that is or can be done, for this is the only and sovereign agent.

Of the works of this mind history is the record. Its genius is illustrated by the entire series of days. Man is explicable by nothing less than all his history. Without hurry, without rest, the human spirit goes forth from the beginning to embody every faculty, every thought, every emotion, which belongs to it in appropriate events. But the thought is always prior to the fact; all the facts of history preëxist in the mind as laws. Each law in turn is made by circumstances predominant, and the limits of nature give power to but one at a time. A man is the whole encyclopædia of facts. The creation of a thousand forests is in one acorn, and Egypt, Greece, Rome, Gaul,[2] Britain, America, lie folded already in the first man. Epoch after epoch, camp, kingdom, empire, republic, democracy, are the application of his manifold spirit to the manifold world.

This human mind wrote history and this must read it. The Sphinx[3] must solve her own riddle. If the whole of history is in one man, it is all to be explained from individual experience. There is a relation between the hours of our life and the centuries of time. As the air I breathe is drawn from the great repositories of nature, as the light on my book is yielded by a star a hundred millions of miles distant, as the poise of my body depends on the equilibrium of centrifugal and centripetal forces, so the hours should be instructed by the ages, and the ages explained by the hours. Of the universal mind each individual man is one more incarnation. All its properties consist in him. Each new fact in his

---

1. See n. 4, p. 15. Caesar, see n. 8, p. 17.
2. Ancient name for, roughly, modern France and Belgium.
3. See n. 7, p. 38.

105

private experience flashes a light on what great bodies of men have done, and the crises of his life refer to national crises. Every revolution was first a thought in one man's mind, and when the same thought occurs to another man, it is the key to that era. Every reform was once a private opinion, and when it shall be a private opinion again, it will solve the problem of the age. The fact narrated must correspond to something in me to be credible or intelligible. We as we read must become Greeks, Romans, Turks, priest and king, martyr and executioner, must fasten these images to some reality in our secret experience, or we shall learn nothing rightly. What befell Asdrubal or Cæsar Borgia,[4] is as much an illustration of the mind's powers and depravations as what has befallen us. Each new law and political movement has meaning for you. Stand before each of its tablets and say, 'Under this mask did my Proteus[5] nature hide itself.' This remedies the defect of our too great nearness to ourselves. This throws our actions into perspective: and as crabs, goats, scorpions, the balance and the waterpot, lose their meanness when hung as signs in the zodiack, so I can see my own vices without heat in the distant persons of Solomon, Alcibiades, and Catiline.[6]

It is the universal nature which gives worth to particular men and things. Human life as containing this is mysterious and inviolable, and we hedge it round with penalties and laws. All laws derive hence their ultimate reason; all express more or less distinctly some command of this supreme illimitable essence. Property also holds of the soul, covers great spiritual facts, and instinctively we at first hold to it with swords and laws, and wide and complex combinations. The obscure consciousness of this fact is the light of all our day, the claim of claims; the plea for education, for justice, for charity, the foundation of friendship and love, and of the heroism and grandeur which belong to acts of self-reliance.[7] It is remarkable that involuntarily we always read as superior beings. Universal history, the poets, the romancers, do not in their stateliest pictures—in the sacerdotal, the imperial palaces, in the triumphs of will, or of genius—anywhere lose our ear, anywhere make us feel that we intrude, that this is for better men; but rather is it true that in their grandest strokes we feel most at home. All that Shakspeare says of the king, yonder slip of a boy that reads in the corner, feels to be true of himself. We sympathize in the great moments of history, in the great discoveries, the great resistances, the great prosperities of men;—because there law was enacted, the sea was searched, the land was found, or the blow was struck *for us*, as we ourselves in that place would have done or applauded.

We have the same interest in condition and character. We honor the rich because they have externally the freedom, power and grace which we feel to be proper to man, proper to us. So all that is said of the wise man by stoic[8] or oriental or modern essayist, describes to each reader his own idea, describes his

---

4. Cesare Borgia (1475?–1507), Italian cardinal, general, and political leader, a model perhaps for Machiavelli's *The Prince*. Asdrubal, probably Hasdrubal, most likely the brother of Hannibal. He died bravely in his first major battle on Italian soil.
5. Changeable; see also n. 4, p. 42.
6. Lucius Sergius Catilina (d. 62 B.C.E.), Roman politician; conspired to overthrow the Roman government by force; spoken against by Cicero; died in battle. Solomon, see n. 6, p. 17. Alcibiades (450?–404 B.C.E.), Athenian general, headstrong and reckless, who led Athenian troops on a disastrous expedition to Sicily; exiled and assassinated.
7. Cf. Emerson's essay of that title (p. 120).
8. See n. 9, p. 78.

unattained but attainable self. All literature writes the character of the wise man. Books, monuments, pictures, conversation, are portraits in which he finds the lineaments he is forming. The silent and the eloquent praise him, and accost him, and he is stimulated wherever he moves as by personal allusions. A true aspirant, therefore, never needs look for allusions personal and laudatory in discourse. He hears the commendation, not of himself, but more sweet, of that character he seeks, in every word that is said concerning character, yea, further, in every fact and circumstance, — in the running river, and the rustling corn. Praise is looked, homage tendered, love flows from mute nature, from the mountains and the lights of the firmament.

These hints, dropped as it were from sleep and night, let us use in broad day. The student is to read history actively and not passively; to esteem his own life the text, and books the commentary. Thus compelled, the muse of history[9] will utter oracles, as never to those who do not respect themselves. I have no expectation that any man will read history aright, who thinks that what was done in a remote age, by men whose names have resounded far, has any deeper sense than what he is doing to-day.

The world exists for the education of each man. There is no age or state of society or mode of action in history, to which there is not somewhat corresponding in his life. Every thing tends in a wonderful manner to abbreviate itself and yield its own virtue to him. He should see that he can live all history in his own person. He must sit solidly at home, and not suffer himself to be bullied by kings or empires, but know that he is greater than all the geography and all the government of the world; he must transfer the point of view from which history is commonly read, from Rome and Athens and London to himself, and not deny his conviction that he is the Court, and if England or Egypt have any thing to say to him, he will try the case; if not, let them forever be silent. He must attain and maintain that lofty sight where facts yield their secret sense, and poetry and annals are alike. The instinct of the mind, the purpose of nature betrays itself in the use we make of the signal narrations of history. Time dissipates to shining ether the solid angularity of facts. No anchor, no cable, no fences avail to keep a fact a fact. Babylon, Troy, Tyre, Palestine,[1] and even early Rome, have passed or are passing into fiction. The Garden of Eden, the Sun standing still in Gibeon,[2] is poetry thenceforward to all nations. Who cares what the fact was, when we have made a constellation of it to hang in heaven an immortal sign? London and Paris and New York must go the same way. "What is History," said Napoleon,[3] "but a fable agreed upon?" This life of ours is stuck round with Egypt, Greece, Gaul, England, War, Colonization, Church, Court, and Commerce, as with so many flowers and wild ornaments grave and gay. I will not make more account of them. I believe in Eternity. I can find Greece, Asia, Italy, Spain, and the Is-

---

9. In Greek mythology, Clio; one of the nine sisters who were guardians of individual arts and sciences.
1. Region of southwest Asia between the east Mediterranean shore and the Jordan River; sometimes called "the Holy Land." Babylon, capital of the ancient Kingdom of Babylonia, was located about eighty kilometers south of present-day Baghdad. Troy, ancient city of northwest Asia Minor, sacked by the Greeks during the Trojan War. Tyre, ancient Phoenician capital city on the Mediterranean, in what is now southern Lebanon.
2. Town of ancient Palestine near Jerusalem whose population, according to the Hebrew Bible, was enslaved by Joshua and the Israelites. Joshua's making the sun stand still is recorded in Joshua 10.12–13.
3. See n. 8, p. 17.

lands,—the genius and creative principle of each and of all eras in my own mind.

We are always coming up with the emphatic facts of history in our private experience, and verifying them here. All history becomes subjective; in other words, there is properly no History; only Biography. Every mind must know the whole lesson for itself—must go over the whole ground. What it does not see, what it does not live, it will not know. What the former age has epitomized into a formula or rule for manipular convenience, it will lose all the good of verifying for itself, by means of the wall of that rule. Somewhere, sometime, it will demand and find compensation for that loss by doing the work itself. Ferguson[4] discovered many things in astronomy which had long been known. The better for him.

History must be this or it is nothing. Every law which the state enacts, indicates a fact in human nature; that is all. We must in ourselves see the necessary reason of every fact,—see how it could and must be. So stand before every public and private work; before an oration of Burke, before a victory of Napoleon, before a martyrdom of Sir Thomas More, of Sidney, of Marmaduke Robinson, before a French Reign of Terror, and a Salem hanging of witches, before a fanatic Revival, and the Animal Magnetism in Paris, or in Providence.[5] We assume that we under like influence should be alike affected, and should achieve the like; and we aim to master intellectually the steps, and reach the same height or the same degradation that our fellow, our proxy has done.

All inquiry into antiquity,—all curiosity respecting the pyramids, the excavated cities, Stonehenge, the Ohio Circles, Mexico, Memphis,[6]—is the desire to do away this wild, savage and preposterous There or Then, and introduce in its place the Here and the Now. Belzoni[7] digs and measures in the mummy-pits and pyramids of Thebes, until he can see the end of the difference between the monstrous work and himself. When he has satisfied himself, in general and in detail, that it was made by such a person as he, so armed and so motived, and to ends to which he himself should also have worked, the problem is solved; his thought lives along the whole line of temples and sphinxes and catacombs, passes through them all with satisfaction, and they live again to the mind, or are now.

A Gothic[8] cathedral affirms that it was done by us, and not done by us. Surely it was by man, but we find it not in our man. But we apply ourselves to the history of its production. We put ourselves into the place and state of the builder. We re-

---

4. James Ferguson (1710–1776), Scottish astronomer.
5. Burke, see n. 5, p. 45. Sir Thomas More (1478–1535), English politician, scholar, and author, most famously, of the political essay *Utopia* (1516), which imagines an ideal kingdom. He was executed by Henry VIII because of his loyalty to the pope. Sidney, probably Algernon Sidney (1622–1683), one of the anti-Restoration judges executed for treason by Charles II. Marmaduke Robinson, probably conflation of two Quakers executed on Boston Common by the Puritans in 1659, Marmaduke Stevenson and William Robinson. Reign of Terror (1793–94), a period of anarchy, bloodshed, and confiscation during the French Revolution. Salem Village, in Massachusetts, was the site of witch trials and executions in 1692. Animal magnetism, see n. 9, p. 53. Providence, Rhode Island, one of many nineteenth-century American cities where animal magnetism was a fad.
6. Ancient Egyptian city. Stonehenge, group of standing stones on the Salisbury Plain in southern England, dating to ca. 2000–1800 B.C.E. The arrangement of the stones suggests that Stonehenge was used as a religious center and also as an astronomical observatory. Emerson visited Stonehenge in 1833. Ohio Circles, ancient Native American circular earthworks in southern Ohio. Mexico, Emerson seems to be referring to the rediscovery of Aztec Civilization in central Mexico.
7. Giovanni Battista Belzoni (1778–1823), Italian traveler and archaeologist who excavated the necropolis at Thebes and discovered the central chamber of the second pyramid at Gizeh (from CW).
8. Of or relating to an architectural style prevalent in western Europe from the twelfth through the fifteenth centuries and characterized by pointed arches, rib vaulting, and flying buttresses.

member the forest dwellers, the first temples, the adherence to the first type, and the decoration of it as the wealth of the nation increased; the value which is given to wood by carving led to the carving over the whole mountain of stone of a cathedral. When we have gone through this process, and added thereto the Catholic Church, its cross, its music, its processions, its Saints' days and image-worship, we have, as it were, been the man that made the minster; we have seen how it could and must be. We have the sufficient reason.

The difference between men is in their principle of association. Some men classify objects by color and size and other accidents of appearance; others by intrinsic likeness, or by the relation of cause and effect. The progress of the intellect is to the clearer vision of causes, which neglects surface differences. To the poet, to the philosopher, to the saint, all things are friendly and sacred, all events profitable, all days holy, all men divine. For the eye is fastened on the life, and slights the circumstance. Every chemical substance, every plant, every animal in its growth, teaches the unity of cause, the variety of appearance.

Upborne and surrounded as we are by this all-creating nature, soft and fluid as a cloud or the air, why should we be such hard pedants, and magnify a few forms? Why should we make account of time, or of magnitude, or of figure? The soul knows them not, and genius, obeying its law, knows how to play with them as a young child plays with greybeards and in churches. Genius studies the causal thought, and far back in the womb of things, sees the rays parting from one orb, that diverge ere they fall by infinite diameters. Genius watches the monad through all his masks as he performs the metempsychosis[9] of nature. Genius detects through the fly, through the caterpillar, through the grub, through the egg, the constant individual; through countless individuals the fixed species; through many species the genus; through all genera the steadfast type; through all the kingdoms of organized life the eternal unity. Nature is a mutable cloud, which is always and never the same. She casts the same thought into troops of forms, as a poet makes twenty fables with one moral. Through the bruteness and toughness of matter, a subtle spirit bends all things to its own will. The adamant streams into soft but precise form before it, and, whilst I look at it, its outline and texture are changed again. Nothing is so fleeting as form; yet never does it quite deny itself. In man we still trace the remains or hints of all that we esteem badges of servitude in the lower races, yet in him they enhance his nobleness and grace; as Io, in Æschylus,[1] transformed to a cow, offends the imagination, but how changed when as Isis in Egypt she meets Osiris-Jove, a beautiful woman, with nothing of the metamorphosis left but the lunar horns as the splendid ornament of her brows.

The identity of history is equally intrinsic, the diversity equally obvious. There is at the surface infinite variety of things; at the centre there is simplicity of cause. How many are the acts of one man in which we recognize the same character. Observe the sources of our information in respect to the Greek genius. We have the *civil history* of that people, as Herodotus, Thucydides, Xenophon, and Plutarch[2] have given it — a very sufficient account of what man-

9. Reincarnation. *Monad:* a term employed in the philosophy of Leibnitz (see n. 6, p. 38) that Emerson uses to mean "unit" or "individual."
1. Greek tragic dramatist (525–456 B.C.E.), uses this story in his *Prometheus Bound.* Io, in Greek mythology, priestless of Hera, beloved of Zeus, who changed her into a heifer to hide her from his wife, then finally restored her to her original form as Isis.
2. See n. 7, p. 57. Herodotus (fifth century B.C.E.), Greek historian whose writings, chiefly concerning the Persian Wars, are the earliest known examples of narrative history. Thucydides (460?–400? B.C.E.), Greek

ner of persons they were, and what they did. We have the same national mind expressed for us again in their *literature*, in epic and lyric poems, drama, and philosophy; a very complete form. Then we have it once more in their *architecture*, a beauty as of temperance itself, limited to the straight line and the square,—a builded geometry. Then we have it once again in *sculpture*, the "tongue[3] on the balance of expression," a multitude of forms in the utmost freedom of action, and never transgressing the ideal serenity; like votaries performing some religious dance before the gods, and, though in convulsive pain or mortal combat, never daring to break the figure and decorum of their dance. Thus, of the genius of one remarkable people, we have a fourfold representation: and to the senses what more unlike than an ode of Pindar, a marble Centaur, the Peristyle of the Parthenon, and the last actions of Phocion?[4]

Every one must have observed faces and forms which, without any resembling feature, make a like impression on the beholder. A particular picture or copy of verses, if it do not awaken the same train of images, will yet superinduce the same sentiment as some wild mountain walk, although the resemblance is nowise obvious to the senses, but is occult and out of the reach of the understanding. Nature is an endless combination and repetition of a very few laws. She hums the old well known air through innumerable variations.

Nature is full of a sublime family likeness throughout her works; and delights in startling us with resemblances in the most unexpected quarters. I have seen the head of an old sachem of the forest, which at once reminded the eye of a bald mountain summit, and the furrows of the brow suggested the strata of the rock. There are men whose manners have the same essential splendor as the simple and awful sculpture on the friezes of the Parthenon, and the remains of the earliest Greek art. And there are compositions of the same strain to be found in the books of all ages. What is Guido's[5] Rospigliosi Aurora but a morning thought, as the horses in it are only a morning cloud. If any one will but take pains to observe the variety of actions to which he is equally inclined in certain moods of mind, and those to which he is averse, he will see how deep is the chain of affinity.

A painter told me that nobody could draw a tree without in some sort becoming a tree; or draw a child by studying the outlines of its form merely,—but, by watching for a time his motions and plays, the painter enters into his nature, and can then draw him at will in every attitude. So Roos[6] "entered into the inmost nature of a sheep." I knew a draughtsman employed in a public survey, who found that he could not sketch the rocks until their geological structure was first explained to him. In a certain state of thought is the common origin of very diverse works. It is the spirit and not the fact that is identical. By a deeper apprehension, and not primarily by a painful acquisition of many manual skills, the artist attains the power of awakening other souls to a given activity.

---

historian. Considered the greatest historian of antiquity, he wrote a critical history of the Peloponnesian War that contains the funeral oration of Pericles. Xenophon (430?–355? B.C.E.), Greek soldier and writer. A disciple of Socrates, he joined Cyrus the Younger in an attack on Persia. After the death of Cyrus, Xenophon led the Greek troops to the Black Sea, an ordeal he recounted in *Anabasis*.

3. Here, the index on a balance scale.
4. See n. 3, p. 33. Parthenon, the chief temple of the goddess Athena built on the acropolis at Athens between 447 and 432 B.C.E. and considered a supreme example of Doric architecture.
5. Guido Reni (1575–1642), Italian painter whose lyrical, idealistic works include the *Crucifixion of Saint Peter* and the Aurora fresco (1613–14). An engraving of the latter, a gift from Thomas Carlyle, still hangs in the parlor of the Emerson house in Concord.
6. Perhaps Philipp Peter Roos (1655–1706), known for his paintings and etchings of animals.

It has been said that "common souls pay with what they do; nobler souls with that which they are." And why? Because a profound nature awakens in us by its actions and words, by its very looks and manners, the same power and beauty that a gallery of sculpture, or of pictures, addresses.

Civil and natural history, the history of art and of literature, must be explained from individual history, or must remain words. There is nothing but is related to us, nothing that does not interest us—kingdom, college, tree, horse, or iron shoe, the roots of all things are in man. Santa Croce and the Dome of St. Peter's[7] are lame copies after a divine model. Strasburg Cathedral is a material counterpart of the soul of Erwin of Steinbach.[8] The true poem is the poet's mind; the true ship is the ship-builder. In the man, could we lay him open, we should see the reason for the last flourish and tendril of his work, as every spine and tint in the seashell preëxist in the secreting organs of the fish. The whole of heraldry and of chivalry is in courtesy. A man of fine manners shall pronounce your name with all the ornament that titles of nobility could ever add.

The trivial experience of every day is always verifying some old prediction to us, and converting into things the words and signs which we had heard and seen without heed. A lady, with whom I was riding in the forest, said to me, that the woods always seemed to her *to wait*, as if the genii who inhabit them suspended their deeds until the wayfarer has passed onward: a thought which poetry has celebrated in the dance of the fairies which breaks off on the approach of human feet. The man who has seen the rising moon break out of the clouds at midnight, has been present like an archangel at the creation of light and of the world. I remember one summer day, in the fields, my companion pointed out to me a broad cloud, which might extend a quarter of a mile parallel to the horizon, quite accurately in the form of a cherub as painted over churches,—a round block in the centre which it was easy to animate with eyes and mouth, supported on either side by wide-stretched symmetrical wings. What appears once in the atmosphere may appear often, and it was undoubtedly the archetype of that familiar ornament. I have seen in the sky a chain of summer lightning which at once showed to me that the Greeks drew from nature when they painted the thunderbolt in the hand of Jove.[9] I have seen a snow-drift along the sides of the stone wall which obviously gave the idea of the common architectural scroll to abut a tower.

By surrounding ourselves with the original circumstances, we invent anew the orders and the ornaments of architecture, as we see how each people merely decorated its primitive abodes. The Doric temple preserves the semblance of the wooden cabin in which the Dorian[1] dwelt. The Chinese pagoda is plainly a Tartar[2] tent. The Indian and Egyptian temples still betray the mounds and subterranean houses of their forefathers. "The custom of making houses and tombs in the living rock," (says Heeren,[3] in his Researches on the Ethiopians)

---

7. Michelangelo began erecting the dome of St. Peter's in 1547; cf. Emerson's "The Problem" (p. 433). Santa Croce, a church in Florence, Italy, that Emerson visited in 1833.
8. German architect (thirteenth century), who designed Strasbourg Cathedral in northeast France.
9. See n. 9, p. 89.
1. A pre-Classical people who invaded Greece in the twelfth century B.C.E. Doric: the simplest of the orders of architecture in ancient Greece.
2. Peoples of central Asia who invaded western Asia and eastern Europe in the Middle Ages; hence, a person regarded as ferocious or violent.
3. Arnold H. L. Heeren (1760–1842), German historian of antiquity, whose *Historical Researches* Emerson quotes from here and below (see CW 2.225).

"determined very naturally the principal character of the Nubian Egyptian architecture to the colossal form which it assumed. In these caverns already prepared by nature, the eye was accustomed to dwell on huge shapes and masses, so that when art came to the assistance of nature, it could not move on a small scale without degrading itself. What would statues of the usual size, or neat porches and wings have been, associated with those gigantic halls before which only Colossi could sit as watchmen, or lean on the pillars of the interior?"

The Gothic church plainly originated in a rude adaptation of the forest trees with all their boughs to a festal or solemn arcade, as the bands about the cleft pillars still indicate the green withes that tied them. No one can walk in a road cut through pine woods, without being struck with the architectural appearance of the grove, especially in winter, when the bareness of all other trees shows the low arch of the Saxons.[4] In the woods in a winter afternoon one will see as readily the origin of the stained glass window with which the Gothic cathedrals are adorned, in the colors of the western sky seen through the bare and crossing branches of the forest. Nor can any lover of nature enter the old piles of Oxford and the English cathedrals without feeling that the forest overpowered the mind of the builder, and that his chisel, his saw, and plane still reproduced its ferns, its spikes of flowers, its locust, elm, oak, pine, fir, and spruce.

The Gothic cathedral is a blossoming in stone subdued by the insatiable demand of harmony in man. The mountain of granite blooms into an eternal flower with the lightness and delicate finish as well as the aerial proportions and perspective of vegetable beauty.

In like manner all public facts are to be individualized, all private facts are to be generalized. Then at once History becomes fluid and true, and Biography deep and sublime. As the Persian imitated in the slender shafts and capitals of his architecture the stem and flower of the lotus and palm, so the Persian Court in its magnificent era never gave over the Nomadism of its barbarous tribes, but travelled from Ecbatana, where the spring was spent, to Susa[5] in summer, and to Babylon for the winter.

In the early history of Asia and Africa, Nomadism and Agriculture are the two antagonist facts. The geography of Asia and of Africa necessitated a nomadic life. But the nomads were the terror of all those whom the soil or the advantages of a market had induced to build towns. Agriculture therefore was a religious injunction because of the perils of the state from nomadism. And in these late and civil countries of England and America, these propensities still fight out the old battle in the nation and in the individual. The nomads of Africa were constrained to wander by the attacks of the gadfly, which drives the cattle mad, and so compels the tribe to emigrate in the rainy season and to drive off the cattle to the higher sandy regions. The nomads of Asia follow the pasturage from month to month. In America and Europe the nomadism is of trade and curiosity; a progress certainly from the gadfly of Astaboras to the Anglo and Italo-mania[6] of Boston Bay. Sacred cities, to which a periodical religious pil-

---

4. A west Germanic tribal group that inhabited northern Gemany and invaded Britain in the fifth and sixth centuries with the Angles and Jutes; a person of English or Lowland Scots birth or descent as distinguished from one of Irish, Welsh, or Highland Scots birth or descent.
5. A ruined city of southwest Iran south of Hamaden. It was the capital of the kingdom of Elam and of the Persian Empire under Cyrus the Great. Ecbatana, city of ancient Media on the site of present-day Hamadan in western Iran.
6. Excessive veneration of English and Italian things, which Emerson ascribes to the educated classes of Boston. Astaboras, or the Atbara, a river flowing into the Nile from Ethiopia.

grimage was enjoined, or stringent laws and customs, tending to invigorate the national bond, were the check on the old rovers; and the cumulative values of long residence are the restraints on the itineracy of the present day. The antagonism of the two tendencies is not less active in individuals, as the love of adventure or the love of repose happens to predominate. A man of rude health and flowing spirits has the faculty of rapid domestication, lives in his wagon, and roams through all latitudes as easily as a Calmuc.[7] At sea, or in the forest, or in the snow, he sleeps as warm, dines with as good appetite, and associates as happily, as beside his own chimneys. Or perhaps his facility is deeper seated, in the increased range of his faculties of observation, which yield him points of interest wherever fresh objects meet his eyes. The pastoral nations were needy and hungry to desperation; and this intellectual nomadism, in its excess, bankrupts the mind, through the dissipation of power on a miscellany of objects. The home-keeping wit, on the other hand, is that continence or content which finds all the elements of life in its own soil; and which has its own perils of monotony and deterioration, if not stimulated by foreign infusions.

Every thing the individual sees without him, corresponds to his states of mind, and every thing is in turn intelligible to him, as his onward thinking leads him into the truth to which that fact or series belongs.

The primeval world, — the Fore-World, as the Germans say, — I can dive to it in myself as well as grope for it with researching fingers in catacombs, libraries, and the broken reliefs and torsos of ruined villas.

What is the foundation of that interest all men feel in Greek history, letters, art and poetry, in all its periods, from the heroic or Homeric age, down to the domestic life of the Athenians and Spartans,[8] four or five centuries later? What but this, that every man passes personally through a Grecian period. The Grecian state is the era of the bodily nature, the perfection of the senses, — of the spiritual nature unfolded in strict unity with the body. In it existed those human forms which supplied the sculptor with his models of Hercules, Phœbus,[9] and Jove; not like the forms abounding in the streets of modern cities, wherein the face is a confused blur of features, but composed of incorrupt, sharply defined and symmetrical features, whose eye-sockets are so formed that it would be impossible for such eyes to squint, and take furtive glances on this side and on that, but they must turn the whole head. The manners of that period are plain and fierce. The reverence exhibited is for personal qualities, courage, address, self-command, justice, strength, swiftness, a loud voice, a broad chest. Luxury and elegance are not known. A sparse population and want make every man his own valet, cook, butcher, and soldier, and the habit of supplying his own needs educates the body to wonderful performances. Such are the Agamemnon and Diomed of Homer, and not far different is the picture Xenophon[1] gives of himself and his compatriots in the Retreat of the Ten Thousand. "After the army had crossed the river Teleboas in Armenia, there fell much snow, and the troops lay miserably on the ground covered with it. But Xenophon arose naked, and taking an axe, began to split wood; whereupon oth-

7. Or Kalmyk, a member of a Buddhist Mongol people now located primarily in Kalmyk.
8. The Athenians and the Spartans were traditional enemies, as evidenced by the Peloponnesian Wars (431–404 B.C.E.). Rigorously self-disciplined and frugal, the Spartans lived in an oligarchical, conservative state as opposed to the democratic, pleasure-loving Athenians.
9. See n. 4, p. 73. Hercules, see n. 1, p. 41.
1. From his Anabasis 4.11–12. Agamemnon, see n. 3, p. 96. Diomed, or Diomedes, Greek hero in the Trojan War. Homer, see n. 8, p. 88.

ers rose and did the like." Throughout his army exists a boundless liberty of speech. They quarrel for plunder, they wrangle with the generals on each new order, and Xenophon is as sharp-tongued as any, and sharper-tongued than most, and so gives as good as he gets. Who does not see that this is a gang of great boys with such a code of honor and such lax discipline as great boys have?

The costly charm of the ancient tragedy and indeed of all the old literature is, that the persons speak simply, — speak as persons who have great good sense without knowing it, before yet the reflective habit has become the predominant habit of the mind. Our admiration of the antique is not admiration of the old, but of the natural. The Greeks are not reflective, but perfect in their senses and in their health, with the finest physical organization in the world. Adults acted with the simplicity and grace of children. They made vases, tragedies, and statues such as healthy senses should—that is, in good taste. Such things have continued to be made in all ages, and are now, wherever a healthy physique exists; but, as a class, from their superior organization, they have surpassed all. They combine the energy of manhood with the engaging unconsciousness of childhood. The attraction of these manners is, that they belong to man, and are known to every man in virtue of his being once a child; besides that there are always individuals who retain these characteristics. A person of childlike genius and inborn energy is still a Greek, and revives our love of the muse of Hellas. I admire the love of nature in the Philoctetes.[2] In reading those fine apostrophes to sleep, to the stars, rocks, mountains, and waves, I feel time passing away as an ebbing sea. I feel the eternity of man, the identity of his thought. The Greek had, it seems, the same fellow beings as I. The sun and moon, water and fire, met his heart precisely as they meet mine. Then the vaunted distinction between Greek and English, between Classic and Romantic schools seems superficial and pedantic. When a thought of Plato becomes a thought to me, — when a truth that fired the soul of Pindar fires mine, time is no more. When I feel that we two meet in a perception, that our two souls are tinged with the same hue, and do, as it were, run into one, why should I measure degrees of latitude, why should I count Egyptian years?

The student interprets the age of chivalry by his own age of chivalry, and the days of maritime adventure and circumnavigation by quite parallel miniature experiences of his own. To the sacred history of the world, he has the same key. When the voice of a prophet out of the deeps of antiquity merely echoes to him a sentiment of his infancy, a prayer of his youth, he then pierces to the truth through all the confusion of tradition and the caricature of institutions.

Rare, extravagant spirits come by us at intervals, who disclose to us new facts in nature. I see that men of God have, from time to time, walked among men and made their commission felt in the heart and soul of the commonest hearer. Hence, evidently, the tripod, the priest, the priestess inspired by the divine afflatus.

Jesus astonishes and overpowers sensual people. They cannot unite him to history or reconcile him with themselves. As they come to revere their intuitions and aspire to live holily, their own piety explains every fact, every word.

---

2. Hero of the Trojan War, and the protagonist of Sophocles' play of that title.

How easily these old worships of Moses, of Zoroaster, of Menu, of Socrates,[3] domesticate themselves in the mind. I cannot find any antiquity in them. They are mine as much as theirs.

I have seen the first monks and anchorets[4] without crossing seas or centuries. More than once some individual has appeared to me with such negligence of labor and such commanding contemplation, a haughty beneficiary, begging in the name of God, as made good to the nineteenth century Simeon the Stylite, the Thebais, and the first Capuchins.[5]

The priestcraft of the East and West, of the Magian, Brahmin, Druid and Inca,[6] is expounded in the individual's private life. The cramping influence of a hard formalist on a young child in repressing his spirits and courage, paralyzing the understanding, and that without producing indignation, but only fear and obedience, and even much sympathy with the tyranny, — is a familiar fact explained to the child when he becomes a man, only by seeing that the oppressor of his youth is himself a child tyrannized over by those names and words and forms, of whose influence he was merely the organ to the youth. The fact teaches him how Belus was worshipped, and how the pyramids were built, better than the discovery by Champollion[7] of the names of all the workmen and the cost of every tile. He finds Assyria and the Mounds of Cholula[8] at his door, and himself has laid the courses.

Again, in that protest which each considerate person makes against the superstition of his times, he repeats step for step the part of old reformers, and in the search after truth finds like them new perils to virtue. He learns again what moral vigor is needed to supply the girdle of a superstition. A great licentiousness treads on the heels of a reformation. How many times in the history of the world has the Luther of the day had to lament the decay of piety in his own household. "Doctor," said his wife to Martin Luther[9] one day, "how is it that whilst subject to papacy, we prayed so often and with such fervor, whilst now we pray with the utmost coldness and very seldom?"

The advancing man discovers how deep a property he has in literature, — in all fable as well as in all history. He finds that the poet was no odd fellow who described strange and impossible situations, but that universal man wrote by his pen a confession true for one and true for all. His own secret biography he finds in lines wonderfully intelligible to him, dotted down before he was born. One after another he comes up in his private adventures with every fable of Æsop, of Homer, of Hafiz, of Ariosto, of Chaucer,[1] of Scott, and verifies them with his own head and hands.

---

3. See n. 6, p. 8. Zoroaster, see n. 9, p. 78. Menu, or Manu (ca. fifth century B.C.E.), son of Brahma. He is said to have codified Hindu law in his *Ordinances of Menu*.
4. Or anchorites, religious hermits.
5. The Order of Friars Minor Capuchin, an independent order of Franciscans founded in Italy in 1525–28 and dedicated to preaching and missionary work. Simeon Stylites (d. 596), Syrian monk who spent sixty-eight years living on various pillars. Thebais, the Latin name for a city on the upper Nile, near Karnak and Luxor, where the first Christian monastic communities were established.
6. Member of the group of Quechuan pre-Columbian peoples of highland Peru who established an empire from northern Ecuador to central Chile before the Spanish conquest. Magian, or magus, member of the Zoroastrian priestly caste of the Medes and Persians. Brahmin, see n. 6, p. 38. Druid, see n. 5, p. 63.
7. Jean François Champollion (1790–1832), French Egyptologist, whose study of the Rosetta Stone made possible the deciphering of ancient priestly hieroglyphics. Belus, presumably Emerson is referring to Bel, or Baal, a Babylonian god also worshiped in Egypt.
8. A town in east-central Mexico west of Puebla, site of an ancient Toltec center and a city sacred to the Aztecs that was destroyed by Hernando Cortés in 1519. Assyria, see n. 4, p. 32.
9. See n. 4, p. 18. For the source of the quotation, see CW 2.226.
1. See n. 9, p. 60. Aesop (sixth century B.C.E.), Greek fabulist traditionally considered the author of Aesop's Fables. Hafiz, pen name of Shams ud-din Muhammad (ca. 1300–1388), Persian lyric poet and theolo-

The beautiful fables of the Greeks, being proper creations of the Imagination and not of the Fancy,[2] are universal verities. What a range of meanings and what perpetual pertinence has the story of Prometheus![3] Beside its primary value as the first chapter of the history of Europe, (the mythology thinly veiling authentic facts, the invention of the mechanic arts, and the migration of colonies,) it gives the history of religion with some closeness to the faith of later ages. Prometheus is the Jesus of the old mythology. He is the friend of man; stands between the unjust 'justice' of the Eternal Father, and the race of mortals; and readily suffers all things on their account. But where it departs from the Calvinistic Christianity,[4] and exhibits him as the defier of Jove, it represents a state of mind which readily appears wherever the doctrine of Theism is taught in a crude, objective form, and which seems the self-defence of man against this untruth, namely, a discontent with the believed fact that a God exists, and a feeling that the obligation of reverence is onerous. It would steal, if it could, the fire of the Creator, and live apart from him, and independent of him. The Prometheus Vinctus is the romance of skepticism. Not less true to all time are the details of that stately apologue.[5] Apollo kept the flocks of Admetus,[6] said the poets. When the gods come among men, they are not known. Jesus was not; Socrates and Shakspeare were not. Antæus was suffocated by the gripe of Hercules,[7] but every time he touched his mother earth, his strength was renewed. Man is the broken giant, and in all his weakness, both his body and his mind are invigorated by habits of conversation with nature. The power of music, the power of poetry to unfix, and as it were, clap wings to solid nature, interprets the riddle of Orpheus.[8] The philosophical perception of identity through endless mutations of form, makes him know the Proteus. What else am I who laughed or wept yesterday, who slept last night like a corpse, and this morning stood and ran? And what see I on any side but the transmigrations of Proteus? I can symbolize my thought by using the name of any creature, of any fact, because every creature is man agent or patient.[9] Tantalus[1] is but a name for you and me. Tantalus means the impossibility of drinking the waters of thought which are always

gian. Ludovico Ariosto (1474–1533), Italian poet, author of *Orlando Furioso* (Roland mad), a long narrative poem about a knight of Charlemagne.

2. On Emerson's use of these terms, cf. Coleridge's *Biographia Literaria*, chapter 13:

> The Imagination . . . I consider either as primary, or secondary. The primary Imagination I hold to be the living power and prime agent of all human perception, and as a repetition in the finite mind of the eternal act of creation in the infinite I AM. The secondary Imagination I consider as an echo of the former, co-existing with the conscious will, yet still as identical with the primary in the *kind* of its agency, and differing only in *degree*, and in the *mode* of its operation. It dissolves, diffuses, dissipates, in order to re-create: or where this process is rendered impossible, yet still at all events it struggles to idealize and to unify. It is essentially *vital*, even as all objects (*as* objects) are essentially fixed and dead.
>
> FANCY, on the contrary, has no other counters to play with, but fixities and definites. The fancy is indeed no other than a mode of memory emancipated from the order of time and space; while it is blended with, and modified by that empirical phenomenon of the will, which we express by the word Choice.

3. Titan who stole fire from Olympus and gave it to humankind, whereby Zeus chained him to a rock and sent an eagle to peck at his liver, which grew back daily. The subject is treated both in Aeschylus' *Prometheus Bound* (*Prometheus Vinctus*) and in Shelley's *Prometheus Unbound* (1820).
4. See n. 4, p. 18.
5. A moral fable; a parable.
6. King of Thessaly and husband of Alcestis, who agreed to die in place of her husband and was later rescued from Hades by Hercules.
7. Antaeus, in Greek mythology, a giant who was invulnerable while in contact with his mother, earth; Hercules held him in the air and choked him to death.
8. See n. 7, p. 53.
9. From the Latin roots for *acting* and *suffering*.
1. Greek king who, for his crimes, was condemned in Hades to stand in water that receded when he tried to drink and to stand beneath fruit that was snatched away when he tried to reach for it.

gleaming and waving within sight of the soul. The transmigration of souls[2] is no fable. I would it were; but men and women are only half human. Every animal of the barn-yard, the field and the forest, of the earth and of the waters that are under the earth, has contrived to get a footing and to leave the print of its features and form in some one or other of these upright, heaven-facing speakers. Ah! brother, stop the ebb of thy soul—ebbing downward into the forms into whose habits thou hast now for many years slid. As near and proper to us is also that old fable of the Sphinx, who was said to sit in the roadside and put riddles to every passenger. If the man could not answer she swallowed him alive. If he could solve he riddle, the Sphinx was slain. What is our life but an endless flight of winged facts or events! In splendid variety these changes come, all putting questions to the human spirit. Those men who cannot answer by a superior wisdom these facts or questions of time, serve them. Facts encumber them, tyrannize over them, and make the men of routine, the men of *sense*, in whom a literal obedience to facts has extinguished every spark of that light by which man is truly man. But if the man is true to his better instincts or sentiments, and refuses the dominion of facts, as one that comes of a higher race, remains fast by the soul and sees the principle, then the facts fall aptly and supple into their places; they know their master, and the meanest of them glorifies him.

See in Goethe's Helena the same desire that every word should be a thing. These figures, he would say, these Chirons, Griffins, Phorkyas, Helen, and Leda,[3] are somewhat, and do exert a specific influence on the mind. So far then are they eternal entities, as real to-day as in the first Olympiad.[4] Much revolving them, he writes out freely his humor, and gives them body to his own imagination. And although that poem be as vague and fantastic as a dream, yet is it much more attractive than the more regular dramatic pieces of the same author, for the reason that it operates a wonderful relief to the mind from the routine of customary images, — awakens the reader's invention and fancy by the wild freedom of the design, and by the unceasing succession of brisk shocks of surprise.

The universal nature, too strong for the petty nature of the bard, sits on his neck and writes through his hand; so that when he seems to vent a mere caprice and wild romance, the issue is an exact allegory. Hence Plato said that "poets utter great and wise things which they do not themselves understand."[5] All the fictions of the Middle Age explain themselves as a masked or frolic expression of that which in grave earnest the mind of that period toiled to achieve. Magic, and all that is ascribed to it, is a deep presentiment of the powers of science. The shoes of swiftness, the sword of sharpness, the power of subduing the elements, of using the secret virtues of minerals, of understanding the voices of birds, are the obscure efforts of the mind in a right direction. The preternatural prowess of the hero, the gift of perpetual youth, and the like, are alike the endeavor of the human spirit "to bend the shows of things to the desires of the mind."[6]

---

2. Metempsychosis.
3. These figures from Greek myth appear in Goethe's *Faust* (see n. 6, p. 42). Chiron, a wise centaur who tutored Achilles, Hercules, and Asclepius. *Griffins:* beasts with heads and wings of eagles and bodies of lions. Phorkyas, sea god, sometimes said to be grandfather of the Eumenides. Helen, Greek daughter of Zeus and Leda and wife of Menelaus, who was known for her beauty; her abduction by Paris caused the Trojan War. Leda, queen of Sparta and mother, by Zeus in the form of a swan, of Helen and Pollux and, by her husband Tyndareus, of Castor and Clytemnestra.
4. The Olympic games.
5. From his *Apology*, 22.
6. This sentence appears in Bacon (see n. 3, p. 6), *Advancement of Learning*, Book 2, chapter 4.

In Perceforest and Amadis de Gaul,[7] a garland and a rose bloom on the head of her who is faithful, and fade on the brow of the inconstant. In the story of the Boy and the Mantle, even a mature reader may be surprised with a glow of virtuous pleasure at the triumph of the gentle Genelas; and indeed, all the postulates of elfin annals,—that the Fairies do not like to be named; that their gifts are capricious and not to be trusted; that who seeks a treasure must not speak; and the like,—I find true in Concord, however they might be in Cornwall or Bretagne.[8]

Is it otherwise in the newest romance? I read the Bride of Lammermoor.[9] Sir William Ashton is a mask for a vulgar temptation, Ravenswood Castle a fine name for proud poverty, and the foreign mission of state only a Bunyan disguise[1] for honest industry. We may all shoot a wild bull that would toss the good and beautiful, by fighting down the unjust and sensual. Lucy Ashton is another name for fidelity, which is always beautiful and always liable to calamity in this world.

But along with the civil and metaphysical history of man, another history goes daily forward—that of the external world,—in which he is not less strictly implicated. He is the compend of time: he is also the correlative of nature. His power consists in the multitude of his affinities, in the fact that his life is intertwined with the whole chain of organic and inorganic being. In old Rome the public roads beginning at the Forum proceeded north, south, east, west, to the centre of every province of the empire, making each market-town of Persia, Spain and Britain, pervious to the soldiers of the capital: so out of the human heart go, as it were, highways to the heart of every object in nature, to reduce it under the dominion of man. A man is a bundle of relations, a knot of roots, whose flower and fruitage is the world. His faculties refer to natures out of him, and predict the world he is to inhabit, as the fins of the fish foreshow that water exists, or the wings of an eagle in the egg presuppose air. He cannot live without a world. Put Napoleon in an island prison, let his faculties find no men to act on, no Alps to climb, no stake to play for, and he would beat the air and appear stupid. Transport him to large countries, dense population, complex interests, and antagonist power, and you shall see that the man Napoleon, bounded, that is, by such a profile and outline, is not the virtual Napoleon. This is but Talbot's shadow;

> "His substance is not here:
> For what you see is but the smallest part,
> And least proportion of humanity;
> But were the whole frame here,
> It is of such a spacious, lofty pitch,
> Your roof were not sufficient to contain it."
>   Henry VI.[2]

---

7. Illegitimate son of Periòn, king of Gaul (Wales), appears in a fourteenth-century romance. Perceforest, lengendary king of Britain, hero of an old romance.
8. Or Brittany, province of northwest France on a peninsula between the English channel and the Bay of Biscay. Genelas, character in the German fairy tale "The Short Mantle." Cornwall, a region in extreme southwest England on a peninsula bounded by the Atlantic Ocean and the English Channel.
9. Novel (1819) by Sir Walter Scott (see n. 9, p. 65). The following names are of characters in the novel.
1. Emerson means that the characters he names could be considered allegorical figures, as in Pilgrim's Progress, by John Bunyan (1628–1688).
2. Cf. Shakespeare, Henry VI, Part I, 2.3.50–56.

Columbus needs a planet to shape his course upon. Newton and Laplace need myriads of ages and thick-strown celestial areas. One may say a gravitating solar system is already prophesied in the nature of Newton's mind. Not less does the brain of Davy or of Gay-Lussac,[3] from childhood exploring the affinities and repulsions of particles, anticipate the laws of organization. Does not the eye of the human embryo predict the light? the ear of Handel[4] predict the witchcraft of harmonic sound? Do not the constructive fingers of Watt, Fulton, Whittemore, Arkwright[5] predict the fusible, hard, and temperable texture of metals, the properties of stone, water and wood? Do not the lovely attributes of the maiden child predict the refinements and decorations of civil society? Here also we are reminded of the action of man on man. A mind might ponder its thought for ages, and not gain so much self-knowledge as the passion of love shall teach it in a day. Who knows himself before he has been thrilled with indignation at an outrage, or has heard an eloquent tongue, or has shared the throb of thousands in a national exultation or alarm? No man can antedate his experience, or guess what faculty or feeling a new object shall unlock, any more than he can draw to-day the face of a person whom he shall see to-morrow for the first time.

I will not now go behind the general statement to explore the reason of this correspondency. Let it suffice that in the light of these two facts, namely, that the mind is One, and that nature is its correlative, history is to be read and written.

Thus in all ways does the soul concentrate and reproduce its treasures for each pupil. He, too, shall pass through the whole cycle of experience. He shall collect into a focus the rays of nature. History no longer shall be a dull book. It shall walk incarnate in every just and wise man. You shall not tell me by languages and titles a catalogue of the volumes you have read. You shall make me feel what periods you have lived. A man shall be the Temple of Fame.[6] He shall walk, as the poets have described that goddess, in a robe painted all over with wonderful events and experiences; — his own form and features by their exalted intelligence shall be that variegated vest. I shall find in him the Foreworld; in his childhood the Age of Gold; the Apples of Knowledge; the Argonautic Expedition; the calling of Abraham; the building of the Temple; the Advent of Christ; Dark Ages; the Revival of Letters; the Reformation;[7] the discovery of new lands, the opening of new sciences, and new regions in man. He shall be the priest of Pan,[8] and bring with him into humble cottages the blessing of the morning stars and all the recorded benefits of heaven and earth.

Is there somewhat overweening in this claim? Then I reject all I have written, for what is the use of pretending to know what we know not? But it is the fault of our rhetoric that we cannot strongly state one fact without seeming to belie some other. I hold our actual knowledge very cheap. Hear the rats in the wall, see the lizard on the fence, the fungus under foot, the lichen on the log.

3. Joseph-Louis Gay-Lussac (1778–1850), French chemist and physicist. Davy, see n. 1, p. 65.
4. George Frideric Handel (1685–1759), German composer long resident in England, renowned for his operas and oratorios.
5. Sir Richard Arkwright (1732–1792) English inventor who developed machinery important for the nascent textile industry. James Watt (1736–1819), British engineer and inventor. Robert Fulton (1765–1815), American engineer and inventor who developed the first commercially successful steamboat. Amos Whittemore (1759–1828), gunsmith and inventor from Cambridge, Massachusetts.
6. Or House of Fame, as in Chaucer's poem of that name.
7. Protestant Reformation of the sixteenth century (see n. 4, p. 18). *Argonautic Expedition*: in Greek mythology, Jason's journey in search of the Golden Fleece. Abraham, first biblical patriarch, father of the Hebrew peoples. *Building of Temple*: probably refers to Solomon's Temple, first erected in Jerusalem ca. 1006 B.C.E. *Revival of Letters*: the Renaissance, beginning ca. 1300.
8. See n. 1, p. 86. Cf. "The Poet," p. 197.

What do I know sympathetically, morally, of either of these worlds of life? As old as the Caucasian man,—perhaps older,—these creatures have kept their counsel beside him, and there is no record of any word or sign that has passed from one to the other. What connection do the books show between the fifty or sixty chemical elements, and the historical eras? Nay, what does history yet record of the metaphysical annals of man? What light does it shed on those mysteries which we hide under the names Death and Immortality? Yet every history should be written in a wisdom which divined the range of our affinities and looked at facts as symbols. I am ashamed to see what a shallow village tale our so-called History is. How many times we must say Rome, and Paris, and Constantinople.[9] What does Rome know of rat and lizard? What are Olympiads and Consulates[1] to these neighboring systems of being? Nay, what food or experience or succor have they for the Esquimaux seal-hunter, for the Kanàka[2] in his canoe, for the fisherman, the stevedore, the porter?

Broader and deeper we must write our annals—from an ethical reformation, from an influx of the ever new, ever sanative conscience, —if we would truelier express our central and wide-related nature, instead of this old chronology of selfishness and pride to which we have too long lent our eyes. Already that day exists for us, shines in on us at unawares, but the path of science and of letters is not the way into nature. The idiot, the Indian, the child, and unschooled farmer's boy, stand nearer to the light by which nature is to be read, than the dissector or the antiquary.

Self-Reliance

"Ne te quæsiveris extra."[1]

"Man is his own star; and the soul that can
Render an honest and a perfect man,
Commands all light, all influence, all fate;
Nothing to him falls early or too late.
Our acts our angels are, or good or ill,
Our fatal shadows that walk by us still."
                    EPILOGUE TO BEAUMONT AND FLETCHER'S
                            HONEST MAN'S FORTUNE.

Cast the bantling on the rocks,
Suckle him with the she-wolf's teat;
Wintered with the hawk and fox,
Power and speed be hands and feet.

I read the other day some verses written by an eminent painter[2] which were original and not conventional. The soul always hears an admonition in such lines, let the subject be what it may. The sentiment they instil is of more value

---

9. Former capital of the Eastern Roman Empire; now Istanbul, the largest city in Turkey; in ancient times, called Byzantium.
1. The two chief magistrates of the Roman Republic.
2. A South Sea Islander, especially one brought to Australia as a laborer in the nineteenth and early twentieth centuries.
1. Persius, *Satires* I.7, 'Do not seek yourself outside yourself."
2. Probably Washington Allston (1779–1843), American painter whose romantic works, such as *Elijah in the Desert* and *Jeremiah Dictating to the Scribe Baruch*, often depict religious subjects.

than any thought they may contain. To believe your own thought, to believe that what is true for you in your private heart, is true for all men, — that is genius. Speak your latent conviction and it shall be the universal sense; for the inmost in due time becomes the outmost, — and our first thought is rendered back to us by the trumpets of the Last Judgment. Familiar as the voice of the mind is to each, the highest merit we ascribe to Moses, Plato, and Milton,[3] is that they set at naught books and traditions, and spoke not what men but what they thought. A man should learn to detect and watch that gleam of light which flashes across his mind from within, more than the lustre of the firmament of bards and sages. Yet he dismisses without notice his thought, because it is his. In every work of genius we recognize our own rejected thoughts: they come back to us with a certain alienated majesty. Great works of art have no more affecting lesson for us than this. They teach us to abide by our spontaneous impression with good-humored inflexibility then most when the whole cry of voices is on the other side. Else, tomorrow a stranger will say with masterly good sense precisely what we have thought and felt all the time, and we shall be forced to take with shame our own opinion from another.

There is a time in every man's education when he arrives at the conviction that envy is ignorance; that imitation is suicide; that he must take himself for better, for worse, as his portion; that though the wide universe is full of good, no kernel of nourishing corn can come to him but through his toil bestowed on that plot of ground which is given to him to till. The power which resides in him is new in nature, and none but he knows what that is which he can do, nor does he know until he has tried. Not for nothing one face, one character, one fact makes much impression on him, and another none. This sculpture in the memory is not without preëstablished harmony. The eye was placed where one ray should fall, that it might testify of that particular ray. We but half express ourselves, and are ashamed of that divine idea which each of us represents. It may be safely trusted as proportionate and of good issues, so it be faithfully imparted, but God will not have his work made manifest by cowards. A man is relieved and gay when he has put his heart into his work and done his best; but what he has said or done otherwise, shall give him no peace. It is a deliverance which does not deliver. In the attempt his genius[4] deserts him; no muse befriends; no invention, no hope.

Trust thyself: every heart vibrates to that iron string. Accept the place the divine Providence has found for you; the society of your contemporaries, the connexion of events. Great men have always done so and confided themselves childlike to the genius of their age, betraying their perception that the absolutely trustworthy was seated at their heart, working through their hands, predominating in all their being. And we are now men, and must accept in the highest mind the same transcendent destiny; and not minors and invalids in a protected corner, not cowards fleeing before a revolution, but guides, redeemers, and benefactors, obeying the Almighty effort, and advancing on Chaos and the Dark.

What pretty oracles nature yields us on this text in the face and behavior of children, babes and even brutes. That divided and rebel mind, that distrust of a sentiment because our arithmetic has computed the strength and means opposed to our purpose, these have not. Their mind being whole, their eye is as

3. See n. 2, p. 6. Plato, see n. 4, p. 15.
4. See n. 8, p. 59.

yet unconquered, and when we look in their faces, we are disconcerted. Infancy conforms to nobody: all conform to it, so that one babe commonly makes four or five out of the adults who prattle and play to it. So God has armed youth and puberty and manhood no less with its own piquancy and charm, and made it enviable and gracious and its claims not to be put by, if it will stand by itself. Do not think the youth has no force because he cannot speak to you and me. Hark! in the next room his voice is sufficiently clear and emphatic. It seems he knows how to speak to his contemporaries. Bashful or bold, then, he will know how to make us seniors very unnecessary.

The nonchalance of boys who are sure of a dinner, and would disdain as much as a lord to do or say aught to conciliate one, is the healthy attitude of human nature. A boy is in the parlour what the pit is in the playhouse; independent, irresponsible, looking out from his corner on such people and facts as pass by, he tries and sentences them on their merits, in the swift summary way of boys, as good, bad, interesting, silly, eloquent, troublesome. He cumbers himself never about consequences, about interests: he gives an independent, genuine verdict. You must court him: he does not court you. But the man is, as it were, clapped into jail by his consciousness. As soon as he has once acted or spoken with eclat, he is a committed person, watched by the sympathy or the hatred of hundreds whose affections must now enter into his account. There is no Lethe[5] for this. Ah, that he could pass again into his neutrality! Who can thus avoid all pledges, and having observed, observe again from the same unaffected, unbiassed, unbribable, unaffrighted innocence, must always be formidable. He would utter opinions on all passing affairs, which being seen to be not private but necessary, would sink like darts into the ear of men, and put them in fear.

These are the voices which we hear in solitude, but they grow faint and inaudible as we enter into the world. Society everywhere is in conspiracy against the manhood of every one of its members. Society is a joint-stock company in which the members agree for the better securing of his bread to each shareholder, to surrender the liberty and culture of the eater. The virtue in most request is conformity. Self-reliance is its aversion. It loves not realities and creators, but names and customs.

Whoso would be a man must be a nonconformist.[6] He who would gather immortal palms must not be hindered by the name of goodness, but must explore if it be goodness. Nothing is at last sacred but the integrity of your own mind. Absolve you to yourself,[7] and you shall have the suffrage of the world. I remember an answer which when quite young I was prompted to make to a valued adviser who was wont to importune me with the dear old doctrines of the church. On my saying, What have I to do with the sacredness of traditions, if I live wholly from within? my friend suggested—"But these impulses may be from below, not from above." I replied, "They do not seem to me to be such; but if I am the Devil's child, I will live then from the Devil." No law can be sacred to me but that of my nature. Good and bad are but names very readily transferable to that or this; the only right is what is after my constitution, the only wrong what is against it. A man is to carry himself in the presence of all oppo-

---

5. In Greek mythology, one of the rivers of Hades. The souls of all the dead are obliged to taste its water, so they may forget their earthly lives. See also "Experience" (p. 198).
6. Hearkens back to the history of the English Puritan "nonconformists" or "dissenters" who refused to conform to the doctrines and practices of the Church of England.
7. Emerson may also be thinking of the familiar practice in the Catholic Church in which the sinner makes confession, does penance, and is absolved by the priest.

sition as if every thing were titular and ephemeral but he. I am ashamed to think how easily we capitulate to badges and names, to large societies and dead institutions. Every decent and well-spoken individual affects and sways me more than is right. I ought to go upright and vital, and speak the rude truth in all ways. If malice and vanity wear the coat of philanthropy, shall that pass? If an angry bigot assumes this bountiful cause of Abolition, and comes to me with his last news from Barbadoes,[8] why should I not say to him, 'Go love thy infant; love thy woodchopper: be good-natured and modest: have that grace; and never varnish your hard, uncharitable ambition with this incredible tenderness for black folk a thousand miles off. Thy love afar is spite at home.' Rough and graceless would be such greeting, but truth is handsomer than the affectation of love. Your goodness must have some edge to it—else it is none. The doctrine of hatred must be preached as the counteraction of the doctrine of love when that pules and whines. I shun father and mother and wife and brother, when my genius calls me. I would write on the lintels of the door-post, *Whim*.[9] I hope it is somewhat better than whim at last, but we cannot spend the day in explanation. Expect me not to show cause why I seek or why I exclude company. Then, again, do not tell me, as a good man did to-day, of my obligation to put all poor men in good situations. Are they *my* poor? I tell thee, thou foolish philanthropist, that I grudge the dollar, the dime, the cent I give to such men as do not belong to me and to whom I do not belong. There is a class of persons to whom by all spiritual affinity I am bought and sold; for them I will go to prison, if need be; but your miscellaneous popular charities; the education at college of fools; the building of meeting-houses to the vain end to which many now stand; alms to sots; and the thousandfold Relief Societies;—though I confess with shame I sometimes succumb and give the dollar, it is a wicked dollar which by and by I shall have the manhood to withhold.

Virtues are in the popular estimate rather the exception than the rule. There is the man *and* his virtues. Men do what is called a good action, as some piece of courage or charity, much as they would pay a fine in expiation of daily non-appearance on parade. Their works are done as an apology or extenuation of their living in the world,—as invalids and the insane pay a high board. Their virtues are penances. I do not wish to expiate, but to live. My life is for itself and not for a spectacle. I much prefer that it should be of a lower strain, so it be genuine and equal, than that it should be glittering and unsteady. I wish it to be sound and sweet, and not to need diet and bleeding.[1] I ask primary evidence that you are a man, and refuse this appeal from the man to his actions. I know that for myself it makes no difference whether I do or forbear those actions which are reckoned excellent. I cannot consent to pay for a privilege where I have intrinsic right. Few and mean as my gifts may be, I actually am, and do not need for my own assurance or the assurance of my fellows any secondary testimony.

What I must do, is all that concerns me, not what the people think. This rule, equally arduous in actual and in intellectual life, may serve for the whole distinction between greatness and meanness. It is the harder, because you will

---

8. In the British West Indies; slavery was abolished there in 1834. Despite his harsh-seeming words, Emerson was well on his way to becoming a committed abolitionist.
9. Cf. Matthew 10.37 and Exodus 12.23. The implication is that Emerson replaces sacred scripture and the blood of the lamb with his own inclination, or intuitions. Cf. Deuteronomy 6.9 and the Jewish practice of placing a *mezuzah* (Hebrew for "doorpost")—a small capsule containing texts from Deuteronomy—on the doorjamb of one's dwelling to invoke divine protection.
1. An allusion to the former medical practice of bleeding patients to relieve the symptoms of disease.

always find those who think they know what is your duty better than you know it. It is easy in the world to live after the world's opinion; it is easy in solitude to live after our own; but the great man is he who in the midst of the crowd keeps with perfect sweetness the independence of solitude.

The objection to conforming to usages that have become dead to you, is, that it scatters your force. It loses your time and blurs the impression of your character. If you maintain a dead church, contribute to a dead Bible-Society, vote with a great party either for the Government or against it, spread your table like base housekeepers,—under all these screens, I have difficulty to detect the precise man you are. And, of course, so much force is withdrawn from your proper life. But do your work,[2] and I shall know you. Do your work, and you shall reinforce yourself. A man must consider what a blindman's-buff is this game of conformity. If I know your sect, I anticipate your argument. I hear a preacher announce for his text and topic the expediency of one of the institutions of his church. Do I not know beforehand that not possibly can he say a new and spontaneous word? Do I not know that with all this ostentation of examining the grounds of the institution, he will do no such thing? Do I not know that he is pledged to himself not to look but at one side,—the permitted side, not as a man, but as a parish minister? He is a retained attorney, and these airs of the bench are the emptiest affectation. Well, most men have bound their eyes with one or another handkerchief, and attached themselves to some one of these communities of opinion. This conformity makes them not false in a few particulars, authors of a few lies, but false in all particulars. Their every truth is not quite true. Their two is not the real two, their four not the real four: so that every word they say chagrins us, and we know not where to begin to set them right. Meantime nature is not slow to equip us in the prison-uniform of the party to which we adhere. We come to wear one cut of face and figure, and acquire by degrees the gentlest asinine expression. There is a mortifying experience in particular which does not fail to wreak itself also in the general history; I mean "the foolish face of praise,"[3] the forced smile which we put on in company where we do not feel at ease in answer to conversation which does not interest us. The muscles, not spontaneously moved, but moved by a low usurping wilfulness, grow tight about the outline of the face with the most disagreeable sensation.

For nonconformity the world whips you with its displeasure. And therefore a man must know how to estimate a sour face. The bystanders look askance on him in the public street or in the friend's parlor. If this aversation had its origin in contempt and resistance like his own, he might well go home with a sad countenance; but the sour faces of the multitude, like their sweet faces, have no deep cause, but are put on and off as the wind blows, and a newspaper directs. Yet is the discontent of the multitude more formidable than that of the senate and the college. It is easy enough for a firm man who knows the world to brook the rage of the cultivated classes. Their rage is decorous and prudent, for they are timid as being very vulnerable themselves. But when to their feminine rage the indignation of the people is added, when the ignorant and the poor are aroused, when the unintelligent brute force that lies at the bottom of society is made to growl and mow, it needs the habit of magnanimity and religion to treat it godlike as a trifle of no concernment.

2. In the first edition text (1841), Emerson wrote: "But do your thing."
3. Alexander Pope (see n. 9, p. 67), *Epistle to Dr. Arbuthnot* 1.212.

The other terror that scares us from self-trust is our consistency; a reverence for our past act or word, because the eyes of others have no other data for computing our orbit than our past acts, and we are loath to disappoint them.

But why should you keep your head over your shoulder? Why drag about this corpse of your memory, lest you contradict somewhat you have stated in this or that public place? Suppose you should contradict yourself; what then? It seems to be a rule of wisdom never to rely on your memory alone, scarcely even in acts of pure memory, but to bring the past for judgment into the thousand-eyed present, and live ever in a new day. In your metaphysics you have denied personality to the Deity: yet when the devout motions of the soul come, yield to them heart and life, though they should clothe God with shape and color. Leave your theory as Joseph his coat in the hand of the harlot, and flee.[4]

A foolish consistency is the hobgoblin of little minds, adored by little statesmen and philosophers and divines. With consistency a great soul has simply nothing to do. He may as well concern himself with his shadow on the wall. Speak what you think now in hard words, and to-morrow speak what to-morrow thinks in hard words again, though it contradict every thing you said to-day.— 'Ah, so you shall be sure to be misunderstood.'—Is it so bad then to be misunderstood? Pythagoras was misunderstood, and Socrates, and Jesus, and Luther, and Copernicus, and Galileo, and Newton,[5] and every pure and wise spirit that ever took flesh. To be great is to be misunderstood.

I suppose no man can violate his nature. All the sallies of his will are rounded in by the law of his being as the inequalities of Andes and Himmaleh are insignificant in the curve of the sphere. Nor does it matter how you gauge and try him. A character is like an acrostic or Alexandrian stanza;—read it forward, backward, or across, it still spells the same thing.[6] In this pleasing contrite wood-life which God allows me, let me record day by day my honest thought without prospect or retrospect, and, I cannot doubt, it will be found symmetrical, though I mean it not, and see it not. My book should smell of pines and resound with the hum of insects. The swallow over my window should interweave that thread or straw he carries in his bill into my web also. We pass for what we are. Character teaches above our wills. Men imagine that they communicate their virtue or vice only by overt actions and do not see that virtue or vice emit a breath every moment.

There will be an agreement in whatever variety of actions, so they be each honest and natural in their hour. For of one will, the actions will be harmonious, however unlike they seem. These varieties are lost sight of at a little distance, at a little height of thought. One tendency unites them all. The voyage of the best ship is a zigzag line of a hundred tacks. See the line from a sufficient distance, and it straightens itself to the average tendency. Your genuine action will explain itself and will explain your other genuine actions. Your conformity explains nothing. Act singly, and what you have already done singly, will justify

---

4. Cf. Genesis 39.12.
5. See n. 5, p. 16. Pythagoras, see n. 6, p. 38. Socrates, see n. 6, p. 8. Luther, see n. 4, p. 18. Nicolaus Copernicus (1473–1543), Polish astronomer, who advanced the theory that the earth and other planets revolve around the sun, disrupting the Ptolemaic system of astronomy. Galileo Galilei (1564–1642), Italian astronomer and physicist; the first to use a telescope to study the stars (1610), he was an outspoken advocate of Copernicus's theory. Cf. "Experience" (p. 202).
6. According to the editors of CW (2.230), the Alexandrian school of poets (ca. 310 B.C.E.) did not write palindromes (sentences that read the same backwards and forwards). *Acrostic:* a poem or series of lines in which certain letters, usually the first in each line, form a name, motto, or message when read in sequence.

you now. Greatness appeals to the future. If I can be firm enough to-day to do right and scorn eyes, I must have done so much right before, as to defend me now. Be it how it will, do right now. Always scorn appearances, and you always may. The force of character is cumulative. All the foregone days of virtue work their health into this. What makes the majesty of the heroes of the senate and the field, which so fills the imagination? The consciousness of a train of great days and victories behind. They shed an united light on the advancing actor. He is attended as by a visible escort of angels. That is it which throws thunder into Chatham's voice, and dignity into Washington's port, and America into Adams's[7] eye. Honor is venerable to us because it is no ephemeris. It is always ancient virtue. We worship it to-day, because it is not of to-day. We love it and pay it homage, because it is not a trap for our love and homage, but is self-dependent, self-derived, and therefore of an old immaculate pedigree, even if shown in a young person.

I hope in these days we have heard the last of conformity and consistency. Let the words be gazetted[8] and ridiculous henceforward. Instead of the gong for dinner, let us hear a whistle from the Spartan fife. Let us never bow and apologize more. A great man is coming to eat at my house. I do not wish to please him: I wish that he should wish to please me. I will stand here for humanity, and though I would make it kind, I would make it true. Let us affront and reprimand the smooth mediocrity and squalid contentment of the times, and hurl in the face of custom, and trade, and office, the fact which is the upshot of all history, that there is a great responsible Thinker and Actor working wherever a man works; that a true man belongs to no other time or place, but is the centre of things. Where he is, there is nature. He measures you, and all men, and all events. Ordinarily every body in society reminds us of somewhat else or of some other person. Character, reality, reminds you of nothing else; it takes place of the whole creation. The man must be so much that he must make all circumstances indifferent. Every true man is a cause, a country, and an age; requires infinite spaces and numbers and time fully to accomplish his design;—and posterity seem to follow his steps as a train of clients. A man Cæsar[9] is born, and for ages after, we have a Roman Empire. Christ is born, and millions of minds so grow and cleave to his genius, that he is confounded with virtue and the possible of man. An institution is the lengthened shadow of one man; as, Monachism, of the Hermit Antony; the Reformation, of Luther; Quakerism, of Fox; Methodism, of Wesley; Abolition, of Clarkson.[1] Scipio, Milton[2] called "the height of Rome;" and all history resolves itself very easily into the biography of a few stout and earnest persons.

Let a man then know his worth, and keep things under his feet. Let him not peep or steal, or skulk up and down with the air of a charity-boy, a bastard, or an interloper, in the world which exists for him. But the man in the street finding no

---

7. Emerson may be referring to Samuel Adams (1722–1803), revolutionary leader; John Adams (1735–1826), second president of the United States; or John Quincy Adams (1767–1848), sixth president of the United States. Chatham, see n. 5, p. 87.
8. Retired from use.
9. See n. 8, p. 17.
1. Thomas Clarkson (1769–1846), British abolitionist, who wrote a prize essay against slavery while an undergraduate at Cambridge University in 1786. Emerson cites it in his address "Emancipation of the Negroes in the British West Indies" (p. 357). St. Anthony (third or fourth century C.E.), the first Christian monastic; he founded a fraternity of ascetics who lived in the deserts of Egypt. Quakerism, see n. 6, p. 18. Fox, see n. 1, p. 39. Wesley, see n. 2, p. 79.
2. In *Paradise Lost* 9.510.

worth in himself which corresponds to the force which built a tower or sculptured a marble god, feels poor when he looks on these. To him a palace, a statue, or a costly book have an alien and forbidding air, much like a gay equipage, and seem to say like that, 'Who are you, sir?' Yet they all are his, suitors for his notice, petitioners to his faculties that they will come out and take possession. The picture waits for my verdict: it is not to command me, but I am to settle its claims to praise. That popular fable of the sot who was picked up dead drunk in the street, carried to the duke's house, washed and dressed and laid in the duke's bed, and, on his waking, treated with all obsequious ceremony like the duke, and assured that he had been insane, owes its popularity to the fact, that it symbolizes so well the state of man, who is in the world a sort of sot, but now and then wakes up, exercises his reason, and finds himself a true prince.[3]

Our reading is mendicant and sycophantic. In history, our imagination plays us false. Kingdom and lordship, power and estate are a gaudier vocabulary than private John and Edward in a small house and common day's work: but the things of life are the same to both: the sum total of both is the same. Why all this deference to Alfred, and Scanderbeg, and Gustavus?[4] Suppose they were virtuous: did they wear out virtue? As great a stake depends on your private act to-day, as followed their public and renowned steps. When private men shall act with original views, the lustre will be transferred from the actions of kings to those of gentlemen.

The world has been instructed by its kings, who have so magnetized the eyes of nations. It has been taught by this colossal symbol the mutual reverence that is due from man to man. The joyful loyalty with which men have everywhere suffered the king, the noble, or the great proprietor to walk among them by a law of his own, make his own scale of men and things, and reverse theirs, pay for benefits not with money but with honor, and represent the Law in his person, was the hieroglyphic by which they obscurely signified their consciousness of their own right and comeliness, the right of every man.

The magnetism[5] which all original action exerts is explained when we inquire the reason of self-trust. Who is the Trustee? What is the aboriginal Self on which a universal reliance may be grounded? What is the nature and power of that science-baffling star, without parallax,[6] without calculable elements, which shoots a ray of beauty even into trivial and impure actions, if the least mark of independence appear? The inquiry leads us to that source, at once the essence of genius, of virtue, and of life, which we call Spontaneity or Instinct. We denote this primary wisdom as Intuition, whilst all later teachings are tuitions. In that deep force, the last fact behind which analysis cannot go, all things find their common origin. For the sense of being which in calm hours rises, we know not how, in the soul, is not diverse from things, from space, from light, from time, from man, but one with them, and proceeds obviously from the same

---

3. Cf. the Induction to Shakespeare, *The Taming of the Shrew*.
4. Gustavus Adolphus (Gustavus II; 1594–1632), king of Sweden (1611–32), supported the Protestant cause in the Thirty Years' War (1618–48). Alfred, see n. 5, p. 63. Scanderbeg, or Skanderbeg, originally George Kastrioti (1405–1468), Albanian military leader who repelled numerous Turkish invasions, maintaining Albanian independence until his death.
5. Here, both "to hypnotize" (see n. 9, p. 53) and "to attract."
6. The difference in direction of a celestial body as measured from two points on Earth or from opposite points on Earth's orbit. Emerson seems to be saying that this celestial body, the exemplar of "self-trust," moves unvaryingly in one direction no matter the vantage point. Perhaps he was thinking of Shakespeare's definition of true love in Sonnet 116: "it is an ever-fixed mark, / That looks on tempests and is never shaken; / It is the star to every wandering bark."

source whence their life and being also proceed. We first share the life by which things exist, and afterwards see them as appearances in nature, and forget that we have shared their cause. Here is the fountain of action and of thought. Here are the lungs of that inspiration which giveth man wisdom, and which cannot be denied without impiety and atheism. We lie in the lap of immense intelligence, which makes us receivers of its truth and organs of its activity. When we discern justice, when we discern truth, we do nothing of ourselves, but allow a passage to its beams. If we ask whence this comes, if we seek to pry into the soul that causes, all philosophy is at fault. Its presence or its absence is all we can affirm. Every man discriminates between the voluntary acts of his mind, and his involuntary perceptions, and knows that to his involuntary perceptions a perfect faith is due. He may err in the expression of them, but he knows that these things are so, like day and night, not to be disputed. My wilful actions and acquisitions are but roving;—the idlest reverie, the faintest native emotion, command my curiosity and respect. Thoughtless people contradict as readily the statement of perceptions as of opinions, or rather much more readily; for, they do not distinguish between perception and notion. They fancy that I choose to see this or that thing. But perception is not whimsical, but fatal. If I see a trait, my children will see it after me, and in course of time, all mankind,—although it may chance that no one has seen it before me. For my perception of it is as much a fact as the sun.

The relations of the soul to the divine spirit are so pure that it is profane to seek to interpose helps. It must be that when God speaketh, he should communicate not one thing, but all things; should fill the world with his voice; should scatter forth light, nature, time, souls, from the centre of the present thought; and new date and new create the whole. Whenever a mind is simple, and receives a divine wisdom, old things pass away,—means, teachers, texts, temples fall; it lives now and absorbs past and future into the present hour. All things are made sacred by relation to it,—one as much as another. All things are dissolved to their centre by their cause, and in the universal miracle petty and particular miracles disappear. If, therefore, a man claims to know and speak of God, and carries you backward to the phraseology of some old mouldered nation in another country, in another world, believe him not. Is the acorn better than the oak which is its fulness and completion? Is the parent better than the child into whom he has cast his ripened being? Whence then this worship of the past? The centuries are conspirators against the sanity and authority of the soul. Time and space are but physiological colors which the eye makes, but the soul is light; where it is, is day; where it was, is night; and history is an impertinence and an injury, if it be anything more than a cheerful apologue or parable of my being and becoming.

Man is timid and apologetic; he is no longer upright; he dares not say 'I think,' 'I am,'[7] but quotes some saint or sage. He is ashamed before the blade of grass or the blowing rose. These roses under my window make no reference to former roses or to better ones; they are for what they are; they exist with God today. There is no time to them. There is simply the rose; it is perfect in every moment of its existence. Before a leaf-bud has burst, its whole life acts; in the full-blown flower, there is no more; in the leafless root, there is no less. Its nature is satisfied, and it satisfies nature, in all moments alike. But man postpones

---

7. Cf. René Descartes (1596–1650): *Cogito, ergo sum* (I think, therefore I am).

or remembers; he does not live in the present, but with reverted eye laments the past, or, heedless of the riches that surround him, stands on tiptoe to foresee the future. He cannot be happy and strong until he too lives with nature in the present, above time.

This should be plain enough. Yet see what strong intellects dare not yet hear God himself, unless he speak the phraseology of I know not what David, or Jeremiah, or Paul.[8] We shall not always set so great a price on a few texts, on a few lives. We are like children who repeat by rote the sentences of grandames and tutors, and, as they grow older, of the men of talents and character they chance to see,—painfully recollecting the exact words they spoke; afterwards, when they come into the point of view which those had who uttered these sayings, they understand them, and are willing to let the words go; for, at any time, they can use words as good, when occasion comes. If we live truly, we shall see truly. It is as easy for the strong man to be strong, as it is for the weak to be weak. When we have new perception, we shall gladly disburden the memory of its hoarded treasures as old rubbish. When a man lives with God, his voice shall be as sweet as the murmur of the brook and the rustle of the corn.

And now at last the highest truth on this subject remains unsaid; probably, cannot be said; for all that we say is the far off remembering of the intuition. That thought, by what I can now nearest approach to say it, is this. When good is near you, when you have life in yourself, it is not by any known or accustomed way; you shall not discern the foot-prints of any other; you shall not see the face of man; you shall not hear any name;—the way, the thought, the good shall be wholly strange and new. It shall exclude example and experience. You take the way from man, not to man. All persons that ever existed are its forgotten ministers. Fear and hope are alike beneath it. There is somewhat low even in hope. In the hour of vision, there is nothing that can be called gratitude, nor properly joy. The soul raised over passion beholds identity and eternal causation, perceives the self-existence of Truth and Right, and calms itself with knowing that all things go well. Vast spaces of nature, the Atlantic Ocean, the South Sea,[9]— long intervals of time, years, centuries,—are of no account. This which I think and feel underlay every former state of life and circumstances, as it does underlie my present, and what is called life, and what is called death.

Life only avails, not the having lived. Power ceases in the instant of repose; it resides in the moment of transition from a past to a new state, in the shooting of the gulf, in the darting to an aim. This one fact the world hates, that the soul *becomes*; for, that forever degrades the past, turns all riches to poverty, all reputation to a shame, confounds the saint with the rogue, shoves Jesus and Judas equally aside. Why then do we prate of self-reliance? Inasmuch as the soul is present, there will be power not confident but agent.[1] To talk of reliance, is a poor external way of speaking. Speak rather of that which relies, because it works and is. Who has more obedience than I, masters me, though he should not raise his finger. Round him I must revolve by the gravitation of spirits. We fancy it rhetoric when we speak of eminent virtue. We do not yet see that virtue is Height, and that a man or a company of men plastic and permeable to prin-

8. See n. 1, p. 3. David see n. 2, p. 41. Jeremiah (seventh to sixth century B.C.E.), Hebrew prophet.
9. The oceans south of the equator, especially the southern Pacific Ocean. The term was originally used by Balboa for the entire Pacific Ocean.
1. Not trusting or believing in someone or something else, but acting for itself.

ciples, by the law of nature must overpower and ride all cities, nations, kings, rich men, poets, who are not.

This is the ultimate fact which we so quickly reach on this as on every topic, the resolution of all into the ever blessed One. Self-existence is the attribute of the Supreme Cause,[2] and it constitutes the measure of good by the degree in which it enters into all lower forms. All things real are so by so much virtue as they contain. Commerce, husbandry, hunting, whaling, war, eloquence, personal weight, are somewhat, and engage my respect as examples of its presence and impure action. I see the same law working in nature for conservation and growth. Power is in nature the essential measure of right. Nature suffers nothing to remain in her kingdoms which cannot help itself. The genesis and maturation of a planet, its poise and orbit, the bended tree recovering itself from the strong wind, the vital resources of every animal and vegetable, are demonstrations of the self-sufficing, and therefore self-relying soul.

Thus all concentrates; let us not rove; let us sit at home with the cause. Let us stun and astonish the intruding rabble of men and books and institutions by a simple declaration of the divine fact. Bid the invaders take the shoes from off their feet, for God is here within.[3] Let our simplicity judge them, and our docility to our own law demonstrate the poverty of nature and fortune beside our native riches.

But now we are a mob. Man does not stand in awe of man, nor is his genius admonished to stay at home, to put itself in communication with the internal ocean, but it goes abroad to beg a cup of water of the urns of other men. We must go alone. I like the silent church before the service begins, better than any preaching. How far off, how cool, how chaste the persons look, begirt each one with a precinct or sanctuary. So let us always sit. Why should we assume the faults of our friend, or wife, or father, or child, because they sit around our hearth, or are said to have the same blood? All men have my blood, and I have all men's. Not for that will I adopt their petulance or folly, even to the extent of being ashamed of it. But your isolation must not be mechanical, but spiritual, that is, must be elevation. At times the whole world seems to be in conspiracy to importune you with emphatic trifles. Friend, client, child, sickness, fear, want, charity, all knock at once at thy closet door and say, — 'Come out unto us.'[4] But keep thy state; come not into their confusion. The power men possess to annoy me, I give them by a weak curiosity. No man can come near me but through my act. "What we love that we have, but by desire we bereave ourselves of the love."[5]

If we cannot at once rise to the sanctities of obedience and faith, let us at least resist our temptations; let us enter into the state of war, and wake Thor and Woden, courage and constancy, in our Saxon breasts. This is to be done in our smooth times by speaking the truth. Check this lying hospitality and lying affection. Live no longer to the expectation of these deceived and deceiving people with whom we converse. Say to them, O father, O mother, O wife, O brother, O friend, I have lived with you after appearances hitherto. Henceforward I am the truth's. Be it known unto you that henceforward I obey no law

2. Cf. Exodus 3.14: "i am that i am."
3. Cf. Exodus 3.5.
4. Cf. Isaiah 36.16.
5. Attributed by Emerson in his journal to Johann Christoph Friedrich von Schiller (1759–1805), German dramatist, poet, and aesthetic theorist, author of *William Tell*. A leading romanticist, Schiller is well known for his historical plays, such as *Don Carlos* (1787) and *Wallenstein* (1798–99), and for his long, didactic poems.

less than the eternal law. I will have no covenants but proximities. I shall endeavor to nourish my parents, to support my family, to be the chaste husband of one wife,—but these relations I must fill after a new and unprecedented way. I appeal from your customs. I must be myself. I cannot break myself any longer for you, or you. If you can love me for what I am, we shall be the happier. If you cannot, I will still seek to deserve that you should. I will not hide my tastes or aversions. I will so trust that what is deep is holy, that I will do strongly before the sun and moon whatever inly rejoices me, and the heart appoints. If you are noble, I will love you; if you are not, I will not hurt you and myself by hypocritical attentions. If you are true, but not in the same truth with me, cleave to your companions; I will seek my own. I do this not selfishly, but humbly and truly. It is alike your interest and mine and all men's, however long we have dwelt in lies, to live in truth. Does this sound harsh to-day? You will soon love what is dictated by your nature as well as mine, and if we follow the truth, it will bring us out safe at last.—But so you may give these friends pain. Yes, but I cannot sell my liberty and my power, to save their sensibility. Besides, all persons have their moments of reason when they look out into the region of absolute truth; then will they justify me and do the same thing.

The populace think that your rejection of popular standards is a rejection of all standard, and mere antinomianism; and the bold sensualist[6] will use the name of philosophy to gild his crimes. But the law of consciousness abides. There are two confessionals, in one or the other of which we must be shriven. You may fulfil your round of duties by clearing yourself in the *direct*, or, in the *reflex* way. Consider whether you have satisfied your relations to father, mother, cousin, neighbor, town, cat, and dog; whether any of these can upbraid you. But I may also neglect this reflex standard, and absolve me to myself. I have my own stern claims and perfect circle. It denies the name of duty to many offices that are called duties. But if I can discharge its debts, it enables me to dispense with the popular code. If any one imagines that this law is lax, let him keep its commandment one day.

And truly it demands something godlike in him who has cast off the common motives of humanity, and has ventured to trust himself for a taskmaster. High be his heart, faithful his will, clear his sight, that he may in good earnest be doctrine, society, law to himself, that a simple purpose may be to him as strong as iron necessity is to others.

If any man consider the present aspects of what is called by distinction *society*, he will see the need of these ethics. The sinew and heart of man seem to be drawn out, and we are become timorous desponding whimperers. We are afraid of truth, afraid of fortune, afraid of death, and afraid of each other. Our age yields no great and perfect persons. We want men and women who shall renovate life and our social state, but we see that most natures are insolvent, cannot satisfy their own wants, have an ambition out of all proportion to their practical force, and do lean and beg day and night continually. Our housekeeping is mendicant, our arts, our occupations, our marriages, our religion we have not chosen, but society has chosen for us. We are parlor soldiers. We shun the rugged battle of fate, where strength is born.

If our young men miscarry in their first enterprizes, they lose all heart. If the young merchant fails, men say he is *ruined*. If the finest genius studies at

6. See n. 6, p. 45. *Antinomianism*: see n. 9, p. 96.

one of our colleges, and is not installed in an office within one year afterwards in the cities or suburbs of Boston or New York, it seems to his friends and to himself that he is right in being disheartened and in complaining the rest of his life. A sturdy lad from New Hampshire or Vermont, who in turn tries all the professions, who *teams it, farms it, peddles,* keeps a school, preaches, edits a newspaper, goes to Congress, buys a township, and so forth, in successive years, and always, like a cat, falls on his feet, is worth a hundred of these city dolls. He walks abreast with his days, and feels no shame in not 'studying a profession,' for he does not postpone his life, but lives already. He has not one chance, but a hundred chances. Let a Stoic[7] open the resources of man, and tell men they are not leaning willows, but can and must detach themselves; that with the exercise of self-trust, new powers shall appear; that a man is the word made flesh, born to shed healing to the nations,[8] that he should be ashamed of our compassion, and that the moment he acts from himself, tossing the laws, the books, idolatries, and customs out of the window, we pity him no more but thank and revere him,—and that teacher shall restore the life of man to splendor, and make his name dear to all History.

It is easy to see that a greater self-reliance must work a revolution in all the offices and relations of men; in their religion; in their education; in their pursuits; their modes of living; their association; in their property; in their speculative views.

1. In what prayers do men allow themselves! That which they call a holy office, is not so much as brave and manly. Prayer looks abroad and asks for some foreign addition to come through some foreign virtue, and loses itself in endless mazes of natural and supernatural, and mediatorial and miraculous. Prayer that craves a particular commodity,—any thing less than all good,—is vicious. Prayer is the contemplation of the facts of life from the highest point of view. It is the soliloquy of a beholding and jubilant soul. It is the spirit of God pronouncing his works good. But prayer as a means to effect a private end, is meanness and theft. It supposes dualism and not unity in nature and consciousness. As soon as the man is at one with God, he will not beg. He will then see prayer in all action. The prayer of the farmer kneeling in his field to weed it, the prayer of the rower kneeling with the stroke of his oar, are true prayers heard throughout nature, though for cheap ends. Caratach, in Fletcher's *Bonduca,* when admonished to inquire the mind of the god Audate,[9] replies,—

> "His hidden meaning lies in our endeavors,
> Our valors are our best gods."

Another sort of false prayers are our regrets. Discontent is the want of self-reliance: it is infirmity of will. Regret calamities, if you can thereby help the sufferer; if not, attend your own work, and already the evil begins to be repaired. Our sympathy is just as base. We come to them who weep foolishly, and sit down and cry for company, instead of imparting to them truth and health in rough

---

7. See n. 9, p. 78.
8. Cf. John 1.14 and Revelation 22.2.
9. According to the editors of *CW,* a "bloody war-god of the Britons." For the quotation, cf. Beaumont and Fletcher, *Bonduca* 3.1. Francis Beaumont (1584–1616), English poet and playwright. He wrote his major works, including *The Maid's Tragedy* (1611), *The Coxcomb* (1612), and *The Knight of Malta* (1619), with John Fletcher (1579–1625).

electric shocks, putting them once more in communication with their own reason. The secret of fortune is joy in our hands. Welcome evermore to gods and
men is the self-helping man. For him all doors are flung wide: him all tongues
greet, all honors crown, all eyes follow with desire. Our love goes out to him
and embraces him, because he did not need it. We solicitously and apologeti-
cally caress and celebrate him, because he held on his way and scorned our disapprobation. The gods love him because men hated him. "To the persevering
mortal," said Zoroaster,[1] "the blessed Immortals are swift."

As men's prayers are a disease of the will, so are their creeds a disease of the
intellect. They say with those foolish Israelites, 'Let not God speak to us, lest we
die. Speak thou, speak any man with us, and we will obey.'[2] Everywhere I am
hindered of meeting God in my brother, because he has shut his own temple
doors, and recites fables merely of his brother's, or his brother's brother's God.
Every new mind is a new classification. If it prove a mind of uncommon activity and power, a Locke, a Lavoisier, a Hutton, a Bentham, a Fourier,[3] it imposes
its classification on other men, and lo! a new system. In proportion to the depth
of the thought, and so to the number of the objects it touches and brings within
reach of the pupil, is his complacency. But chiefly is this apparent in creeds and
churches, which are also classifications of some powerful mind acting on the
elemental thought of Duty, and man's relation to the Highest. Such is Calvinism, Quakerism, Swedenborgianism.[4] The pupil takes the same delight in subordinating every thing to the new terminology, as a girl who has just learned
botany in seeing a new earth and new seasons thereby. It will happen for a time,
that the pupil will find his intellectual power has grown by the study of his master's mind. But in all unbalanced minds, the classification is idolized, passes for
the end, and not for a speedily exhaustible means, so that the walls of the system blend to their eye in the remote horizon with the walls of the universe; the
luminaries of heaven seem to them hung on the arch their master built. They
cannot imagine how you aliens have any right to see, — how you can see; 'It must
be somehow that you stole the light from us.' They do not yet perceive, that
light, unsystematic, indomitable, will break into any cabin, even into theirs. Let
them chirp awhile and call it their own. If they are honest and do well, presently
their neat new pinfold will be too strait and low, will crack, will lean, will rot
and vanish, and the immortal light, all young and joyful, million-orbed, mil-
lion-colored, will beam over the universe as on the first morning.

2. It is for want of self-culture that the superstition of Travelling, whose
idols are Italy, England, Egypt, retains its fascination for all educated Americans. They who made England, Italy, or Greece venerable in the imagination,
did so by sticking fast where they were, like an axis of the earth. In manly hours,
we feel that duty is our place. The soul is no traveller: the wise man stays at
home, and when his necessities, his duties, on any occasion call him from his
house, or into foreign lands, he is at home still, and shall make men sensible by
the expression of his countenance, that he goes the missionary of wisdom and

1. See n. 9, p. 78.
2. Cf. Exodus 20.19.
3. Charles Fourier (1772–1837), French social thinker and reformer much discussed in Emerson's time.
Locke, see n. 7, p. 59. Antoine Lavoisier (1743–94), French chemist guillotined during the revolution.
James Hutton (1726–1797), Scottish geologist. Jeremy Bentham (1748–1832), English philosopher of
the utilitarian school.
4. See n. 6, p. 35.

virtue, and visits cities and men like a sovereign, and not like an interloper or a valet.

I have no churlish objection to the circumnavigation of the globe, for the purposes of art, of study, and benevolence, so that the man is first domesticated, or does not go abroad with the hope of finding somewhat greater than he knows. He who travels to be amused, or to get somewhat which he does not carry, travels away from himself, and grows old even in youth among old things. In Thebes, in Palmyra,[5] his will and mind have become old and dilapidated as they. He carries ruins to ruins.

Travelling is a fool's paradise. Our first journeys discover to us the indifference of places. At home I dream that at Naples, at Rome, I can be intoxicated with beauty, and lose my sadness. I pack my trunk, embrace my friends, embark on the sea, and at last wake up in Naples, and there beside me is the stern Fact, the sad self, unrelenting, identical, that I fled from. I seek the Vatican, and the palaces. I affect to be intoxicated with sights and suggestions, but I am not intoxicated. My giant goes with me wherever I go.

3. But the rage of travelling is a symptom of a deeper unsoundness affecting the whole intellectual action. The intellect is vagabond, and our system of education fosters restlessness. Our minds travel when our bodies are forced to stay at home. We imitate; and what is imitation but the travelling of the mind? Our houses are built with foreign taste; our shelves are garnished with foreign ornaments; our opinions, our tastes, our faculties, lean, and follow the Past and the Distant. The soul created the arts wherever they have flourished. It was in his own mind that the artist sought his model. It was an application of his own thought to the thing to be done and the conditions to be observed. And why need we copy the Doric or the Gothic[6] model? Beauty, convenience, grandeur of thought, and quaint expression are as near to us as to any, and if the American artist will study with hope and love the precise thing to be done by him, considering the climate, the soil, the length of the day, the wants of the people, the habit and form of the government, he will create a house in which all these will find themselves fitted, and taste and sentiment will be satisfied also.

Insist on yourself; never imitate. Your own gift you can present every moment with the cumulative force of a whole life's cultivation; but of the adopted talent of another, you have only an extemporaneous, half possession. That which each can do best, none but his Maker can teach him. No man yet knows what it is, nor can, till that person has exhibited it. Where is the master who could have taught Shakspeare? Where is the master who could have instructed Franklin, or Washington, or Bacon, or Newton?[7] Every great man is a unique. The Scipionism of Scipio[8] is precisely that part he could not borrow. Shakspeare will never be made by the study of Shakspeare. Do that which is assigned you, and you cannot hope too much or dare too much. There is at this moment for you an utterance brave and grand as that of the colossal chisel of Phidias,[9] or trowel of the Egyptians, or the pen of Moses, or Dante, but different from all these. Not possibly will the soul all rich, all eloquent, with thousand-cloven

---

5. The biblical Tadmor, a city east of Syria. Thebes, either a city in Egypt also known as Thebais (see n. 5, p. 115) or the ancient city in east-central Greece.
6. See n. 8, p. 108. *Doric:* see n. 1, p. 111.
7. See n. 5, p. 16. Bacon, see n. 3, p. 6.
8. One of the greatest Roman soldiers (237–183 B.C.E.).
9. Greek sculptor (5th century B.C.E.) who supervised work on the Parthenon.

tongue,[1] deign to repeat itself; but if you can hear what these patriarchs say, surely you can reply to them in the same pitch of voice: for the ear and the tongue are two organs of one nature. Abide in the simple and noble regions of thy life, obey thy heart, and thou shalt reproduce the Foreworld again.

4. As our Religion, our Education, our Art look abroad, so does our spirit of society. All men plume themselves on the improvement of society, and no man improves.

Society never advances. It recedes as fast on one side as it gains on the other. It undergoes continual changes: it is barbarous, it is civilized, it is christianized, it is rich, it is scientific; but this change is not amelioration. For every thing that is given, something is taken. Society acquires new arts and loses old instincts. What a contrast between the well-clad, reading, writing, thinking American, with a watch, a pencil, and a bill of exchange in his pocket, and the naked New Zealander, whose property is a club, a spear, a mat, and an undivided twentieth of a shed to sleep under. But compare the health of the two men, and you shall see that the white man has lost his aboriginal strength. If the traveller tell us truly, strike the savage with a broad axe, and in a day or two the flesh shall unite and heal as if you struck the blow into soft pitch, and the same blow shall send the white to his grave.

The civilized man has built a coach, but has lost the use of his feet. He is supported on crutches, but lacks so much support of muscle. He has a fine Geneva watch, but he fails of the skill to tell the hour by the sun. A Greenwich nautical almanac he has, and so being sure of the information when he wants it, the man in the street does not know a star in the sky. The solstice he does not observe; the equinox he knows as little; and the whole bright calendar of the year is without a dial in his mind. His note-books impair his memory; his libraries overload his wit; the insurance office increases the number of accidents; and it may be a question whether machinery does not encumber; whether we have not lost by refinement some energy, by a Christianity entrenched in establishments and forms, some vigor of wild virtue. For every stoic was a stoic; but in Christendom where is the Christian?

There is no more deviation in the moral standard than in the standard of height or bulk. No greater men are now than ever were. A singular equality may be observed between the great men of the first and of the last ages; nor can all the science, art, religion and philosophy of the nineteenth century avail to educate greater men than Plutarch's heroes, three or four and twenty centuries ago. Not in time is the race progressive. Phocion, Socrates, Anaxagoras, Diogenes,[2] are great men, but they leave no class. He who is really of their class will not be called by their name, but will be his own man, and, in his turn the founder of a sect. The arts and inventions of each period are only its costume, and do not invigorate men. The harm of the improved machinery may compensate its good. Hudson and Behring accomplished so much in their fishing-boats, as to astonish Parry and Franklin,[3] whose equipment exhausted the

---

1. Cf. Acts 2.1–4.
2. Greek Cynic philosopher (ca. 412–323 B.C.E.), who is said to have lived in a tub and searched in daylight with a lantern for an honest man. Phocion, see n. 3, p. 33. Anaxagoras of Clazomenae (500?–428 B.C.E.), Greek philosopher and astronomer. who believed in a dualistic universe consisting of chaotic matter and ordering mind.
3. Sir William Edward Parry (1790–1855) and Sir John Franklin (1786–1847) were well-known explorers. Henry Hudson (d. ca. 1611) explored the river named after him. Vitus Bering (1681–1741) discovered the strait and sea named after him.

resources of science and art. Galileo, with an opera-glass, discovered a more splendid series of celestial phenomena than any one since. Columbus found the New World in an undecked boat. It is curious to see the periodical disuse and perishing of means and machinery which were introduced with loud laudation, a few years or centuries before. The great genius returns to essential man. We reckoned the improvements of the art of war among the triumphs of science, and yet Napoleon conquered Europe by the Bivouac, which consisted of falling back on naked valor, and disencumbering it of all aids. The Emperor held it impossible to make a perfect army, says Las Cases,[4] "without abolishing our arms, magazines, commissaries, and carriages, until in imitation of the Roman custom, the soldier should receive his supply of corn, grind it in his hand-mill, and bake his bread himself."

Society is a wave. The wave moves onward, but the water of which it is composed, does not. The same particle does not rise from the valley to the ridge. Its unity is only phenomenal.[5] The persons who make up a nation to-day, next year die, and their experience with them.

And so the reliance on Property, including the reliance on governments which protect it, is the want of self-reliance. Men have looked away from themselves and at things so long, that they have come to esteem the religious, learned, and civil institutions, as guards of property, and they deprecate assaults on these, because they feel them to be assaults on property. They measure their esteem of each other, by what each has, and not by what each is. But a cultivated man becomes ashamed of his property, out of new respect for his nature. Especially he hates what he has, if he see that it is accidental,—came to him by inheritance, or gift, or crime; then he feels that it is not having; it does not belong to him, has no root in him, and merely lies there, because no revolution or no robber takes it away. But that which a man is, does always by necessity acquire, and what the man acquires is living property, which does not wait the beck of rulers, or mobs, or revolutions, or fire, or storm, or bankruptcies, but perpetually renews itself wherever the man breathes. "Thy lot or portion of life," said the Caliph Ali,[6] "is seeking after thee; therefore be at rest from seeking after it." Our dependence on these foreign goods leads us to our slavish respect for numbers. The political parties meet in numerous conventions; the greater the concourse, and with each new uproar of announcement, The delegation from Essex! The Democrats from New Hampshire! The Whigs of Maine! the young patriot feels himself stronger than before by a new thousand of eyes and arms. In like manner the reformers summon conventions, and vote and resolve in multitude. Not so, O friends! will the God deign to enter and inhabit you, but by a method precisely the reverse. It is only as a man puts off all foreign support, and stands alone, that I see him to be strong and to prevail. He is weaker by every recruit to his banner. Is not a man better than a town? Ask nothing of men, and in the endless mutation, thou only firm column must presently appear the upholder of all that surrounds thee. He who knows that power is inborn, that he is weak because he has looked for good out of him and elsewhere, and so perceiving, throws himself unhesitatingly on his thought, instantly rights him-

---

4. Comte Emmanuel Las Casas (1766–1842), published *Journal of the Private Life and Conversations of the Emperor Napoleon at Saint Helena*. Napoleon, see n. 8, p. 17.
5. Only an appearance.
6. See n. 1, p. 92.

self, stands in the erect position, commands his limbs, works miracles; just as a man who stands on his feet is stronger than a man who stands on his head.

So use all that is called Fortune. Most men gamble with her, and gain all, and lose all, as her wheel rolls. But do thou leave as unlawful these winnings, and deal with Cause and Effect, the chancellors of God. In the Will work and acquire, and thou hast chained the wheel of Chance, and shalt sit hereafter out of fear from her rotations. A political victory, a rise of rents, the recovery of your sick, or the return of your absent friend, or some other favorable event, raises your spirits, and you think good days are preparing for you. Do not believe it. Nothing can bring you peace but yourself. Nothing can bring you peace but the triumph of principles.

Compensation

The wings of Time are black and white,
Pied with morning and with night.
Mountain tall and ocean deep
Trembling balance duly keep.
In changing moon, in tidal wave,
Glows the feud of Want and Have.
Gauge of more and less through space
Electric star and pencil plays.
The lonely Earth amid the balls
That hurry through the eternal halls,
A makeweight flying to the void,
Supplemental asteroid,
Or compensatory spark,
Shoots across the neutral Dark.

Man's the elm, and Wealth the vine;
Stanch and strong the tendrils twine:
Though the frail ringlets thee deceive,
None from its stock that vine can reave.
Fear not, then, thou child infirm,
There's no god dare wrong a worm.
Laurel crowns cleave to deserts,
And power to him who power exerts;
Hast not thy share? On winged feet,
Lo! it rushes thee to meet;
And all that Nature made thy own,
Floating in air or pent in stone,
Will rive the hills and swim the sea,
And, like thy shadow, follow thee.[1]

Ever since I was a boy, I have wished to write a discourse on Compensation: for, it seemed to me when very young, that, on this subject, Life was ahead of theology, and the people knew more than the preachers taught. The documents too, from which the doctrine is to be drawn, charmed my fancy by their endless variety, and lay always before me, even in sleep; for they are the tools in our hands, the bread in our basket, the transactions of the street, the farm, and the dwelling-house, greetings, relations, debts and credits, the influence of

---

1. These two poetic epigraphs, by Emerson, were added to the second edition of *Essays* (1847).

character, the nature and endowment of all men. It seemed to me also that in it might be shown men a ray of divinity, the present action of the Soul of this world, clean from all vestige of tradition, and so the heart of man might be bathed by an inundation of eternal love, conversing with that which he knows was always and always must be, because it really is now. It appeared, moreover, that if this doctrine could be stated in terms with any resemblance to those bright intuitions in which this truth is sometimes revealed to us, it would be a star in many dark hours and crooked passages in our journey that would not suffer us to lose our way.

I was lately confirmed in these desires by hearing a sermon at church. The preacher, a man esteemed for his orthodoxy, unfolded in the ordinary manner the doctrine of the Last Judgment. He assumed that judgment is not executed in this world; that the wicked are successful; that the good are miserable; and then urged from reason and from Scripture a compensation to be made to both parties in the next life. No offence appeared to be taken by the congregation at this doctrine. As far as I could observe, when the meeting broke up, they separated without remark on the sermon.

Yet what was the import of this teaching? What did the preacher mean by saying that the good are miserable in the present life? Was it that houses and lands, offices, wine, horses, dress, luxury, are had by unprincipled men, whilst the saints are poor and despised; and that a compensation is to be made to these last hereafter, by giving them the like gratifications another day, — bank-stock and doubloons, venison and champagne? This must be the compensation intended; for, what else? Is it that they are to have leave to pray and praise? to love and serve men? Why, that they can do now. The legitimate inference the disciple would draw was, — 'We are to have *such* a good time as the sinners have now;' — or, to push it to its extreme import, — 'You sin now; we shall sin by and by; we would sin now, if we could; not being successful, we expect our revenge tomorrow.'

The fallacy lay in the immense concession that the bad are successful; that justice is not done now. The blindness of the preacher consisted in deferring to the base estimate of the market of what constitutes a manly success, instead of confronting and convicting the world from the truth; announcing the Presence of the Soul; the omnipotence of the Will: and so establishing the standard of good and ill, of success and falsehood.

I find a similar base tone in the popular religious works of the day, and the same doctrines assumed by the literary men when occasionally they treat the related topics. I think that our popular theology has gained in decorum, and not in principle, over the superstitions it has displaced. But men are better than this theology. Their daily life gives it the lie. Every ingenuous and aspiring soul leaves the doctrine behind him in his own experience; and all men feel sometimes the falsehood which they cannot demonstrate. For men are wiser than they know. That which they hear in schools and pulpits without afterthought, if said in conversation, would probably be questioned in silence. If a man dogmatize in a mixed company on Providence and the divine laws, he is answered by a silence which conveys well enough to an observer the dissatisfaction of the hearer, but his incapacity to make his own statement.

I shall attempt in this and the following chapter to record some facts that indicate the path of the law of Compensation; happy beyond my expectation, if I shall truly draw the smallest arc of this circle.

Polarity, or action and reaction, we meet in every part of nature; in darkness and light; in heat and cold; in the ebb and flow of waters; in male and female; in the inspiration and expiration of plants and animals; in the equation of quantity and quality in the fluids of the animal body; in the systole and diastole of the heart; in the undulations of fluids, and of sound; in the centrifugal and centripetal gravity;[2] in electricity, galvanism, and chemical affinity.[3] Superinduce magnetism at one end of a needle; the opposite magnetism takes place at the other end. If the south attracts, the north repels. To empty here, you must condense there. An inevitable dualism bisects nature, so that each thing is a half, and suggests another thing to make it whole; as spirit, matter; man, woman; odd, even; subjective, objective; in, out; upper, under; motion, rest; yea, nay.

Whilst the world is thus dual, so is every one of its parts. The entire system of things gets represented in every particle. There is somewhat that resembles the ebb and flow of the sea, day and night, man and woman, in a single needle of the pine, in a kernel of corn, in each individual of every animal tribe. The reaction so grand in the elements, is repeated within these small boundaries. For example, in the animal kingdom, the physiologist has observed that no creatures are favorites, but a certain compensation balances every gift and every defect. A surplusage given to one part is paid out of a reduction from another part of the same creature. If the head and neck are enlarged, the trunk and extremities are cut short.

The theory of the mechanic forces is another example. What we gain in power is lost in time; and the converse. The periodic or compensating errors of the planets, is another instance. The influences of climate and soil in political history are another. The cold climate invigorates. The barren soil does not breed fevers, crocodiles, tigers, or scorpions.

The same dualism underlies the nature and condition of man. Every excess causes a defect; every defect an excess. Every sweet hath its sour; every evil its good. Every faculty which is a receiver of pleasure, has an equal penalty put on its abuse. It is to answer for its moderation with its life. For every grain of wit there is a grain of folly. For every thing you have missed, you have gained something else; and for every thing you gain, you lose something. If riches increase, they are increased that use them. If the gatherer gathers too much, nature takes out of the man what she puts into his chest; swells the estate, but kills the owner. Nature hates monopolies and exceptions. The waves of the sea do not more speedily seek a level from their loftiest tossing, than the varieties of condition tend to equalize themselves. There is always some levelling circumstance that puts down the overbearing, the strong, the rich, the fortunate, substantially on the same ground with all others. Is a man too strong and fierce for society, and by temper and position a bad citizen,—a morose ruffian with a dash of the pirate in him;—nature sends him a troop of pretty sons and daughters who are getting along in the dame's classes at the village school, and love and fear for them smooths his grim scowl to courtesy. Thus she contrives to intenerate the

2. Emerson means, of course, that the force that impels things outward and away from the earth owing to its rotation is balanced by the force of gravity.
3. Emerson seems to be referring here to the phenomenon of attraction/repulsion found in all three processes. As the editors of CW point out, "during the nineteenth century the word 'electricity' was sometimes used to mean electric current produced by frictional means and was distinguished from 'galvanism,' electrical current produced by chemical means, as in a battery."

granite and felspar,[4] takes the boar out and puts the lamb in, and keeps her balance true.

The farmer imagines power and place are fine things. But the President has paid dear for his White House. It has commonly cost him all his peace and the best of his manly attributes. To preserve for a short time so conspicuous an appearance before the world, he is content to eat dust before the real masters who stand erect behind the throne. Or, do men desire the more substantial and permanent grandeur of genius? Neither has this an immunity. He who by force of will or of thought is great, and overlooks thousands, has the charges of that eminence. With every influx of light, comes new danger. Has he light? he must bear witness to the light, and always outrun that sympathy which gives him such keen satisfaction, by his fidelity to new revelations of the incessant soul. He must hate father and mother, wife and child. Has he all that the world loves and admires and covets?—he must cast behind him their admiration, and afflict them by faithfulness to his truth, and become a byword and a hissing.

This Law writes the laws of cities and nations. It is in vain to build or plot or combine against it. Things refuse to be mismanaged long. *Res nolunt diu male administrari.*[5] Though no checks to a new evil appear, the checks exist and will appear. If the government is cruel, the governor's life is not safe. If you tax too high, the revenue will yield nothing. If you make the criminal code sanguinary, juries will not convict. If the law is too mild, private vengeance comes in. If the government is a terrific democracy, the pressure is resisted by an overcharge of energy in the citizen, and life glows with a fiercer flame. The true life and satisfactions of man seem to elude the utmost rigors or felicities of condition, and to establish themselves with great indifference under all varieties of circumstances. Under all governments the influence of character remains the same,—in Turkey and in New England about alike. Under the primeval despots of Egypt, history honestly confesses that man must have been as free as culture could make him.

These appearances indicate the fact that the universe is represented in every one of its particles. Every thing in nature contains all the powers of nature. Every thing is made of one hidden stuff; as the naturalist sees one type under every metamorphosis, and regards a horse as a running man, a fish as a swimming man, a bird as a flying man, a tree as a rooted man. Each new form repeats not only the main character of the type, but part for part all the details, all the aims, furtherances, hindrances, energies, and whole system of every other. Every occupation, trade, art, transaction, is a compend of the world, and a correlative of every other. Each one is an entire emblem of human life; of its good and ill, its trials, its enemies, its course and its end. And each one must somehow accommodate the whole man, and recite all his destiny.

The world globes itself in a drop of dew. The microscope cannot find the animalcule which is less perfect for being little. Eyes, ears, taste, smell, motion, resistance, appetite, and organs of reproduction that take hold on eternity,—all find room to consist in the small creature. So do we put our life into every act. The true doctrine of omnipresence is, that God re-appears with all his parts in every moss and cobweb. The value of the universe contrives to throw itself into

---

4. Or feldspar, a rock-forming mineral. *Intenerate:* to soften.
5. The gloss precedes this Latin proverb.

every point. If the good is there, so is the evil; if the affinity, so the repulsion; if the force, so the limitation.

Thus is the universe alive. All things are moral. That soul which within us is a sentiment, outside of us is a law. We feel its inspiration; out there in history we can see its fatal strength. "It is in the world and the world was made by it."[6] Justice is not postponed. A perfect equity adjusts its balance in all parts of life. Οἱ κύβοι Διὸς ἀεί εὐπίπτουσι,—The dice of God are always loaded.[7] The world looks like a multiplication-table or a mathematical equation, which, turn it how you will, balances itself. Take what figure you will, its exact value, nor more nor less, still returns to you. Every secret is told, every crime is punished, every virtue rewarded, every wrong redressed, in silence and certainty. What we call retribution, is the universal necessity by which the whole appears wherever a part appears. If you see smoke, there must be fire. If you see a hand or a limb, you know that the trunk to which it belongs, is there behind.

Every act rewards itself, or, in other words, integrates itself, in a twofold manner; first, in the thing, or, in real nature; and secondly, in the circumstance, or, in apparent nature. Men call the circumstance the retribution. The causal retribution is in the thing, and is seen by the soul. The retribution in the circumstance, is seen by the understanding; it is inseparable from the thing, but is often spread over a long time, and so does not become distinct until after many years. The specific stripes may follow late after the offence, but they follow because they accompany it. Crime and punishment grow out of one stem. Punishment is a fruit that unsuspected ripens within the flower of the pleasure which concealed it. Cause and effect, means and ends, seed and fruit, cannot be severed; for the effect already blooms in the cause, the end preëxists in the means, the fruit in the seed.

Whilst thus the world will be whole, and refuses to be disparted, we seek to act partially, to sunder, to appropriate; for example,—to gratify the senses, we sever the pleasure of the senses from the needs of the character. The ingenuity of man has always been dedicated to the solution of one problem,—how to detach the sensual sweet, the sensual strong, the sensual bright, &c. from the moral sweet, the moral deep, the moral fair; that is, again, to contrive to cut clean off this upper surface so thin as to leave it bottomless; to get a *one end*, without an *other end*. The soul says, Eat; the body would feast. The soul says, The man and woman shall be one flesh and one soul; the body would join the flesh only. The soul says, Have dominion over all things to the ends of virtue; the body would have the power over things to its own ends.

The soul strives amain to live and work through all things. It would be the only fact. All things shall be added unto it,[8]—power, pleasure, knowledge, beauty. The particular man aims to be somebody; to set up for himself; to truck and higgle for a private good; and, in particulars, to ride, that he may ride; to dress, that he may be dressed; to eat, that he may eat; and to govern that he may be seen. Men seek to be great; they would have offices, wealth, power and fame. They think that to be great is to possess one side of nature—the sweet, without the other side—the bitter.

---

6. Cf. John 1.10.
7. As the editors of CW point out, Emerson's translation of this Greek expression by Sophocles "is colloquial and presumably ironic." The notion that God is a dishonest gambler puts a definite twist on Sophocles' belief that things always fall out in God's favor.
8. Cf. Luke 12.31.

This dividing and detaching is steadily counteracted. Up to this day, it must be owned, no projector has had the smallest success. The parted water re-unites behind our hand. Pleasure is taken out of pleasant things, profit out of profitable things, power out of strong things, as soon as we seek to separate them from the whole. We can no more halve things and get the sensual good, by itself, than we can get an inside that shall have no outside, or a light without a shadow. "Drive out nature with a fork, she comes running back."[9]

Life invests itself with inevitable conditions, which the unwise seek to dodge, which one and another brags that he does not know; that they do not touch him;—but the brag is on his lips, the conditions are in his soul. If he escapes them in one part, they attack him in another more vital part. If he has escaped them in form, and in the appearance, it is because he has resisted his life, and fled from himself, and the retribution is so much death. So signal is the failure of all attempts to make this separation of the good from the tax, that the experiment would not be tried,—since to try it is to be mad,—but for the circumstance, that when the disease began in the will, of rebellion and separation, the intellect is at once infected, so that the man ceases to see God whole in each object, but is able to see the sensual allurement of an object, and not see the sensual hurt; he sees the mermaid's head, but not the dragon's tail; and thinks he can cut off that which he would have, from that which he would not have. "How secret art thou who dwellest in the highest heavens in silence, O thou only great God, sprinkling with an unwearied Providence certain penal blindnesses upon such as have unbridled desires!"[1]

The human soul is true to these facts in the painting of fable, of history, of law, of proverbs, of conversation. It finds a tongue in literature unawares. Thus the Greeks called Jupiter, Supreme Mind; but having traditionally ascribed to him many base actions, they involuntarily made amends to Reason, by tying up the hands of so bad a god. He is made as helpless as a king of England. Prometheus knows one secret, which Jove must bargain for; Minerva,[2] another. He cannot get his own thunders; Minerva keeps the key of them.

> "Of all the gods I only know the keys
> That ope the solid doors within whose vaults
> His thunders sleep."[3]

A plain confession of the in-working of the All, and of its moral aim. The Indian mythology ends in the same ethics; and it would seem impossible for any fable to be invented and get any currency which was not moral. Aurora forgot to ask youth for her lover, and though Tithonus[4] is immortal, he is old. Achilles is not quite invulnerable; the sacred waters did not wash the heel by which Thetis[5] held him. Siegfried,[6] in the Nibelungen, is not quite immortal, for a leaf fell on

---

9. Cf. Horace, *Epistles* 1.9.24.
1. St. Augustine, *Confessions*, B. I [Emerson].
2. In Roman mythology, the goddess of wisdom and patroness of the arts and trades. Prometheus, see n. 3, p. 116. Jove, see n. 9, p. 89.
3. From Aeschylus, *The Furies* 894–96.
4. In Greek legend, a beautiful Trojan who was beloved of Eos (Aurora), goddess of the dawn. She grants his wish for immortality but allows him to grow old, because he neglected to ask for eternal youth.
5. A sea-goddess, who bore Achilles, the hero of the *Iliad*; she tried to immortalize him by dipping him in the river Styx (one of the rivers in Hades, the underworld kingdom of the dead), but the heel by which she held him remained vulnerable. During battle, he was fatally wounded there by an arrow shot by the Trojan prince Paris.
6. The hero of the medieval German epic *The Niebelungenlied*.

his back whilst he was bathing in the Dragon's blood, and that spot which it covered is mortal. And so it must be. There is a crack in every thing God has made. It would seem, there is always this vindictive circumstance stealing in at unawares, even into the wild poesy in which the human fancy attempted to make bold holiday, and to shake itself free of the old laws, — this back-stroke, this kick of the gun, certifying that the law is fatal; that in Nature, nothing can be given, all things are sold.

This is that ancient doctrine of Nemesis,[7] who keeps watch in the Universe, and lets no offence go unchastised. The Furies,[8] they said, are attendants on Justice, and if the sun in heaven should transgress his path, they would punish him. The poets related that stone walls, and iron swords, and leathern thongs had an occult sympathy with the wrongs of their owners; that the belt which Ajax gave Hector[9] dragged the Trojan hero over the field at the wheels of the car of Achilles, and the sword which Hector gave Ajax was that on whose point Ajax fell. They recorded that when the Thasians erected a statue to Theogenes,[1] a victor in the games, one of his rivals went to it by night, and endeavored to throw it down by repeated blows, until at last he moved it from its pedestal and was crushed to death beneath its fall.

This voice of fable has in it somewhat divine. It came from thought above the will of the writer. That is the best part of each writer, which has nothing private in it; that which he does not know; that which flowed out of his constitution, and not from his too active invention; that which in the study of a single artist you might not easily find, but in the study of many, you would abstract as the spirit of them all. Phidias it is not, but the work of man in that early Hellenic world, that I would know. The name and circumstance of Phidias, however convenient for history, embarrass when we come to the highest criticism. We are to see that which man was tending to do in a given period, and was hindered, or, if you will, modified in doing, by the interfering volitions of Phidias,[2] of Dante, of Shakspeare, the organ whereby man at the moment wrought.

Still more striking is the expression of this fact in the proverbs of all nations, which are always the literature of Reason, or the statements of an absolute truth, without qualification. Proverbs, like the sacred books of each nation, are the sanctuary of the Intuitions. That which the droning world, chained to appearances, will not allow the realist to say in his own words, it will suffer him to say in proverbs without contradiction. And this law of laws which the pulpit, the senate and the college deny, is hourly preached in all markets and workshops by flights of proverbs, whose teaching is as true and as omnipresent as that of birds and flies.

All things are double, one against another. — Tit for tat; an eye for an eye; a tooth for a tooth; blood for blood; measure for measure; love for love. — Give and it shall be given you. — He that watereth shall be watered himself. — What

7. In Greek mythology, the goddess of retributive justice or vengeance.
8. Three terrible, winged goddesses with serpentine hair—Alecto, Megaera, and Tisiphone—who pursue and punish those guilty of unavenged crimes. Also called Erinyes, in later Greek mythology they are pacified and renamed (euphemistically) the Eumenides (the kindly ones).
9. A Trojan prince, the eldest son of Priam and Hecuba, who was killed by Achilles (who lashed him to his chariot and dragged the body in triumph three times around the walls of Troy). Ajax, king of Salamis (an island off the coast of Greece not far from Athens) and a warrior of great stature and prowess who fought against Troy.
1. A celebrated victor in the public games of Greece, who was from Thasos, an island in the Aegean Sea east of Thessalonika.
2. Phidias, see n. 9, p. 134.

will you have? quoth God; pay for it and take it.—Nothing venture, nothing have.—Thou shalt be paid exactly for what thou hast done, no more, no less.— Who doth not work shall not eat.—Harm watch, harm catch.—Curses always recoil on the head of him who imprecates them.—If you put a chain around the neck of a slave, the other end fastens itself around your own.—Bad counsel confounds the adviser.—The devil is an ass.[3]

It is thus written, because it is thus in life. Our action is overmastered and characterized above our will by the law of nature. We aim at a petty end quite aside from the public good, but our act arranges itself by irresistible magnetism in a line with the poles of the world.

A man cannot speak but he judges himself. With his will, or against his will, he draws his portrait to the eye of his companions by every word. Every opinion reacts on him who utters it. It is a thread-ball thrown at a mark, but the other end remains in the thrower's bag. Or, rather, it is a harpoon hurled at the whale, unwinding, as it flies, a coil of cord in the boat, and if the harpoon is not good, or not well thrown, it will go nigh to cut the steersman in twain, or to sink the boat.

You cannot do wrong without suffering wrong. "No man had ever a point of pride that was not injurious to him," said Burke.[4] The exclusive in fashionable life does not see that he excludes himself from enjoyment, in the attempt to appropriate it. The exclusionist in religion does not see that he shuts the door of heaven on himself, in striving to shut out others. Treat men as pawns and ninepins, and you shall suffer as well as they. If you leave out their heart, you shall lose your own. The senses would make things of all persons; of women, of children, of the poor. The vulgar proverb, "I will get it from his purse or get it from his skin," is sound philosophy.

All infractions of love and equity in our social relations are speedily punished. They are punished by Fear. Whilst I stand in simple relations to my fellow man, I have no displeasure in meeting him. We meet as water meets water, or as two currents of air mix, with perfect diffusion and interpenetration of nature. But as soon as there is any departure from simplicity, and attempt at halfness, or good for me that is not good for him, my neighbor feels the wrong; he shrinks from me as far as I have shrunk from him; his eyes no longer seek mine; there is war between us; there is hate in him and fear in me.

All the old abuses in society, universal and particular, all unjust accumulations of property and power, are avenged in the same manner. Fear is an instructer of great sagacity, and the herald of all revolutions. One thing he teaches, that there is rottenness where he appears. He is a carrion crow, and though you see not well what he hovers for, there is death somewhere. Our property is timid, our laws are timid, our cultivated classes are timid. Fear for ages has boded and mowed and gibbered over government and property. That obscene bird is not there for nothing. He indicates great wrongs which must be revised.

Of the like nature is that expectation of change which instantly follows the suspension of our voluntary activity. The terror of cloudless noon, the emerald of Polycrates,[5] the awe of prosperity, the instinct which leads every generous

---

3. Emerson was fond of collecting proverbs and using them in his work.
4. Burke (see n. 5, p. 45), famous for his oratory, pleaded the cause of the American colonists in Parliament.
5. Tyrant of the island of Samos (sixth century B.C.E.), who, fearing Nemesis because of his good fortune, threw an emerald into the sea; but it returned in the belly of a fish, and trouble followed.

soul to impose on itself tasks of a noble asceticism and vicarious virtue, are the tremblings of the balance of justice through the heart and mind of man.

Experienced men of the world know very well that it is best to pay scot and lot as they go along, and that a man often pays dear for a small frugality. The borrower runs in his own debt. Has a man gained any thing who has received a hundred favors and rendered none? Has he gained by borrowing, through indolence or cunning, his neighbor's wares, or horses, or money? There arises on the deed the instant acknowledgment of benefit on the one part, and of debt on the other; that is, of superiority and inferiority. The transaction remains in the memory of himself and his neighbor; and every new transaction alters, according to its nature, their relation to each other. He may soon come to see that he had better have broken his own bones than to have ridden in his neighbor's coach, and that "the highest price he can pay for a thing is to ask for it."[6]

A wise man will extend this lesson to all parts of life, and know that it is the part of prudence to face every claimant, and pay every just demand on your time, your talents, or your heart. Always pay; for, first or last, you must pay your entire debt. Persons and events may stand for a time between you and justice, but it is only a postponement. You must pay at last your own debt. If you are wise, you will dread a prosperity which only loads you with more. Benefit is the end of nature. But for every benefit which you receive, a tax is levied. He is great who confers the most benefits. He is base,—and that is the one base thing in the universe,—to receive favors and render none. In the order of nature we cannot render benefits to those from whom we receive them, or only seldom. But the benefit we receive must be rendered again, line for line, deed for deed, cent for cent, to somebody. Beware of too much good staying in your hand. It will fast corrupt and worm worms. Pay it away quickly in some sort.

Labor is watched over by the same pitiless laws. Cheapest, say the prudent, is the dearest labor. What we buy in a broom, a mat, a wagon, a knife, is some application of good sense to a common want. It is best to pay in your land a skilful gardener, or to buy good sense applied to gardening; in your sailor, good sense applied to navigation; in the house, good sense applied to cooking, sewing, serving; in your agent, good sense applied to accounts and affairs. So do you multiply your presence, or spread yourself throughout your estate. But because of the dual constitution of things, in labor as in life there can be no cheating. The thief steals from himself. The swindler swindles himself. For the real price of labor is knowledge and virtue, whereof wealth and credit are signs. These signs, like paper money, may be counterfeited or stolen, but that which they represent, namely, knowledge and virtue, cannot be counterfeited or stolen. These ends of labor cannot be answered but by real exertions of the mind, and in obedience to pure motives. The cheat, the defaulter, the gambler, cannot extort the knowledge of material and moral nature which his honest care and pains yield to the operative. The law of nature is, Do the thing, and you shall have the power: but they who do not the thing have not the power.

Human labor, through all its forms, from the sharpening of a stake to the construction of a city or an epic, is one immense illustration of the perfect compensation of the universe. The absolute balance of Give and Take, the doctrine that every thing has its price,—and if that price is not paid, not that thing but something else is obtained, and that it is impossible to get any thing without its

---

6. Edward Waldo Emerson reports that his father placed a good deal of stock in this maxim.

price,—is not less sublime in the columns of a leger than in the budgets of states, in the laws of light and darkness, in all the action and reaction of nature. I cannot doubt that the high laws which each man sees implicated in those processes with which he is conversant, the stern ethics which sparkle on his chisel-edge, which are measured out by his plumb and foot-rule, which stand as manifest in the footing of the shop-bill as in the history of a state,—do recommend to him his trade, and though seldom named, exalt his business to his imagination.

The league between virtue and nature engages all things to assume a hostile front to vice. The beautiful laws and substances of the world persecute and whip the traitor. He finds that things are arranged for truth and benefit, but there is no den in the wide world to hide a rogue. Commit a crime, and the earth is made of glass. Commit a crime, and it seems as if a coat of snow fell on the ground, such as reveals in the woods the track of every partridge and fox and squirrel and mole. You cannot recall the spoken word, you cannot wipe out the foot-track, you cannot draw up the ladder, so as to leave no inlet or clew. Some damning circumstance always transpires. The laws and substances of nature — water, snow, wind, gravitation—become penalties to the thief.

On the other hand, the law holds with equal sureness for all right action. Love, and you shall be loved. All love is mathematically just, as much as the two sides of an algebraic equation. The good man has absolute good, which like fire turns every thing to its own nature, so that you cannot do him any harm; but as the royal armies sent against Napoleon, when he approached, cast down their colors and from enemies became friends, so disasters of all kinds, as sickness, offence, poverty, prove benefactors:—

> "Winds blow and waters roll
> Strength to the brave, and power and deity,
> Yet in themselves are nothing."[7]

The good are befriended even by weakness and defect. As no man had ever a point of pride that was not injurious to him, so no man had ever a defect that was not somewhere made useful to him. The stag in the fable admired his horns and blamed his feet, but when the hunter came, his feet saved him, and afterwards, caught in the thicket, his horns destroyed him. Every man in his lifetime needs to thank his faults. As no man thoroughly understands a truth until he has contended against it, so no man has a thorough acquaintance with the hindrances or talents of men, until he has suffered from the one, and seen the triumph of the other over his own want of the same. Has he a defect of temper that unfits him to live in society? Thereby he is driven to entertain himself alone, and acquire habits of self-help; and thus, like the wounded oyster, he mends his shell with pearl.

Our strength grows out of our weakness. The indignation which arms itself with secret forces does not awaken until we are pricked and stung and sorely assailed. A great man is always willing to be little. Whilst he sits on the cushion of advantages, he goes to sleep. When he is pushed, tormented, defeated, he has a chance to learn something; he has been put on his wits, on his manhood; he has gained facts; learns his ignorance; is cured of the insanity of conceit; has

---

7. From Wordsworth's sonnet "September, 1802, near Dover."

got moderation and real skill. The wise man throws himself on the side of his assailants. It is more his interest than it is theirs to find his weak point. The wound cicatrizes and falls off from him, like a dead skin, and when they would triumph, lo! he has passed on invulnerable. Blame is safer than praise. I hate to be defended in a newspaper. As long as all that is said, is said against me, I feel a certain assurance of success. But as soon as honied words of praise are spoken for me, I feel as one that lies unprotected before his enemies. In general, every evil to which we do not succumb, is a benefactor. As the Sandwich Islander believes that the strength and valor of the enemy he kills, passes into himself, so we gain the strength of the temptation we resist.

The same guards which protect us from disaster, defect, and enmity, defend us, if we will, from selfishness and fraud. Bolts and bars are not the best of our institutions, nor is shrewdness in trade a mark of wisdom. Men suffer all their life long, under the foolish superstition that they can be cheated. But it is as impossible for a man to be cheated by any one but himself, as for a thing to be, and not to be, at the same time. There is a third silent party to all our bargains. The nature and soul of things takes on itself the guaranty of the fulfilment of every contract, so that honest service cannot come to loss. If you serve an ungrateful master, serve him the more. Put God in your debt. Every stroke shall be repaid. The longer the payment is withholden, the better for you; for compound interest on compound interest is the rate and usage of this exchequer.

The history of persecution is a history of endeavors to cheat nature, to make water run up hill, to twist a rope of sand. It makes no difference whether the actors be many or one, a tyrant or a mob. A mob is a society of bodies voluntarily bereaving themselves of reason and traversing its work. The mob is man voluntarily descending to the nature of the beast. Its fit hour of activity is night. Its actions are insane like its whole constitution. It persecutes a principle; it would whip a right; it would tar and feather justice, by inflicting fire and outrage upon the houses and persons of those who have these. It resembles the prank of boys who run with fire-engines to put out the ruddy aurora streaming to the stars. The inviolate spirit turns their spite against the wrongdoers. The martyr cannot be dishonored. Every lash inflicted is a tongue of fame; every prison a more illustrious abode; every burned book or house enlightens the world; every suppressed or expunged word reverberates through the earth from side to side. Hours of sanity and consideration are always arriving to communities, as to individuals, when the truth is seen, and the martyrs are justified.

Thus do all things preach the indifferency of circumstances. The man is all. Every thing has two sides, a good and an evil. Every advantage has its tax. I learn to be content. But the doctrine of compensation is not the doctrine of indifferency. The thoughtless say, on hearing these representations, — What boots it to do well? there is one event to good and evil; if I gain any good, I must pay for it; if I lose any good, I gain some other; all actions are indifferent.

There is a deeper fact in the soul than compensation, to wit, its own nature. The soul is not a compensation, but a life. The soul *is*. Under all this running sea of circumstance, whose waters ebb and flow with perfect balance, lies the aboriginal abyss of real Being. Essence, or God, is not a relation, or a part, but the whole. Being is the vast affirmative, excluding negation, self-balanced, and swallowing up all relations, parts and times, within itself. Nature, truth, virtue are the influx from thence. Vice is the absence or departure of the same.

Nothing, Falsehood, may indeed stand as the great Night or shade, on which, as a background, the living universe paints itself forth; but no fact is begotten by it; it cannot work; for it is not. It cannot work any good; it cannot work any harm. It is harm inasmuch as it is worse not to be than to be.

We feel defrauded of the retribution due to evil acts, because the criminal adheres to his vice and contumacy, and does not come to a crisis or judgment anywhere in visible nature. There is no stunning confutation of his nonsense before men and angels. Has he therefore outwitted the law? Inasmuch as he carries the malignity and the lie with him, he so far deceases from nature. In some manner there will be a demonstration of the wrong to the understanding also; but should we not see it, this deadly deduction makes square the eternal account.

Neither can it be said, on the other hand, that the gain of rectitude must be bought by any loss. There is no penalty to virtue; no penalty to wisdom; they are proper additions of being. In a virtuous action, I properly *am*; in a virtuous act, I add to the world; I plant into deserts conquered from Chaos and Nothing, and see the darkness receding on the limits of the horizon. There can be no excess to love; none to knowledge; none to beauty, when these attributes are considered in the purest sense. The soul refuses limits, and always affirms an Optimism, never a Pessimism.

Man's life is a progress, and not a station. His instinct is trust. Our instinct uses "more" and "less" in application to him, of the *presence of the soul*, and not of its absence; the brave man is greater than the coward; the true, the benevolent, the wise, is more a man and not less, than the fool and knave. There is no tax on the good of virtue; for, that is the incoming of God himself, or absolute existence, without any comparative. Material good has its tax, and if it came without desert or sweat, has no root in me and the next wind will blow it away. But all the good of nature is the soul's, and may be had, if paid for in nature's lawful coin, that is, by labor which the heart and the head allow. I no longer wish to meet a good I do not earn, for example, to find a pot of buried gold, knowing that it brings with it new burdens. I do not wish more external goods, — neither possessions, nor honors, nor powers, nor persons. The gain is apparent: the tax is certain. But there is no tax on the knowledge that the compensation exists, and that it is not desirable to dig up treasure. Herein I rejoice with a serene eternal peace. I contract the boundaries of possible mischief. I learn the wisdom of St. Bernard,[8] — "Nothing can work me damage except myself; the harm that I sustain, I carry about with me, and never am a real sufferer but by my own fault."

In the nature of the soul is the compensation for the inequalities of condition. The radical tragedy of nature seems to be the distinction of More and Less. How can Less not feel the pain; how not feel indignation or malevolence towards More? Look at those who have less faculty, and one feels sad, and knows not well what to make of it. He almost shuns their eye; he fears they will upbraid God. What should they do? It seems a great injustice. But see the facts nearly, and these mountainous inequalities vanish. Love reduces them, as the sun melts the iceberg in the sea. The heart and soul of all men being one, this bitterness of *His and Mine* ceases. His is mine. I am my brother, and my brother is me. If I feel overshadowed and outdone by great neighbors, I can yet love; I can still receive; and he that loveth, maketh his own the grandeur he loves. Thereby I make the discovery that my brother is my guardian, acting for me with

---

8. Bernard of Clairvaux (1090–1153), famed Cistercian monk and preacher.

the friendliest designs, and the estate I so admired and envied, is my own. It is the nature of the soul to appropriate all things. Jesus and Shakspeare are fragments of the soul, and by love I conquer and incorporate them in my own conscious domain. His virtue,—is not that mine? His wit,—if it cannot be made mine, it is not wit.

Such, also, is the natural history of calamity. The changes which break up at short intervals the prosperity of men, are advertisements of a nature whose law is growth. Every soul is by this intrinsic necessity quitting its whole system of things, its friends, and home, and laws, and faith, as the shell-fish crawls out of its beautiful but stony case, because it no longer admits of its growth, and slowly forms a new house. In proportion to the vigor of the individual, these revolutions are frequent, until in some happier mind they are incessant, and all worldly relations hang very loosely about him, becoming, as it were, a transparent fluid membrane through which the living form is seen, and not as in most men an indurated heterogeneous fabric of many dates, and of no settled character, in which the man is imprisoned. Then there can be enlargement, and the man of to-day scarcely recognizes the man of yesterday. And such should be the outward biography of man in time, a putting off of dead circumstances day by day, as he renews his raiment day by day. But to us, in our lapsed estate, resting, not advancing, resisting, not coöperating with the divine expansion, this growth comes by shocks.

We cannot part with our friends. We cannot let our angels go. We do not see that they only go out, that archangels may come in. We are idolaters of the old. We do not believe in the riches of the soul, in its proper eternity and omnipresence. We do not believe there is any force in to-day to rival or re-create that beautiful yesterday. We linger in the ruins of the old tent, where once we had bread and shelter and organs, nor believe that the spirit can feed, cover, and nerve us again. We cannot again find aught so dear, so sweet, so graceful. But we sit and weep in vain. The voice of the Almighty saith, 'Up and onward forevermore!' We cannot stay amid the ruins. Neither will we rely on the New; and so we walk ever with reverted eyes, like those monsters who look backwards.

And yet the compensations of calamity are made apparent to the understanding also, after long intervals of time. A fever, a mutilation, a cruel disappointment, a loss of wealth, a loss of friends seems at the moment unpaid loss, and unpayable. But the sure years reveal the deep remedial force that underlies all facts. The death of a dear friend, wife, brother, lover, which seemed nothing but privation, somewhat later assumes the aspect of a guide or genius; for it commonly operates revolutions in our way of life, terminates an epoch of infancy or of youth which was waiting to be closed, breaks up a wonted occupation, or a household, or style of living, and allows the formation of new ones more friendly to the growth of character. It permits or constrains the formation of new acquaintances, and the reception of new influences that prove of the first importance to the next years; and the man or woman who would have remained a sunny garden flower, with no room for its roots and too much sunshine for its head, by the falling of the walls and the neglect of the gardener, is made the banian[9] of the forest, yielding shade and fruit to wide neighborhoods of men.

---

9. Or banyan, a tropical fig tree having many aerial roots that descend from the branches and develop new trunks.

Spiritual Laws

> The living Heaven thy prayers respect,
> House at once and architect,
> Quarrying man's rejected hours,
> Builds therewith eternal towers;
> Sole and self-commanded works,
> Fears not undermining days,
> Grows by decays,
> And, by the famous might that lurks
> In reaction and recoil,
> Makes flame to freeze, and ice to boil;
> Forging, through swart arms of Offence,
> The silver seat of Innocence.[1]

When the act of reflection takes place in the mind, when we look at ourselves in the light of thought, we discover that our life is embosomed in beauty. Behind us, as we go, all things assume pleasing forms, as clouds do far off. Not only things familiar and stale, but even the tragic and terrible are comely, as they take their place in the pictures of memory. The river-bank, the weed at the water-side, the old house, the foolish person,—however neglected in the passing,—have a grace in the past. Even the corpse that has lain in the chambers has added a solemn ornament to the house. The soul will not know either deformity or pain. If in the hours of clear reason we should speak the severest truth, we should say, that we had never made a sacrifice. In these hours the mind seems so great, that nothing can be taken from us that seems much. All loss, all pain is particular: the universe remains to the heart unhurt. Neither vexations nor calamities abate our trust. No man ever stated his griefs as lightly as he might. Allow for exaggeration in the most patient and sorely ridden hack that ever was driven. For it is only the finite that has wrought and suffered; the infinite lies stretched in smiling repose.

The intellectual life may be kept clean and healthful, if man will live the life of nature, and not import into his mind difficulties which are none of his. No man need be perplexed in his speculations. Let him do and say what strictly belongs to him, and though very ignorant of books, his nature shall not yield him any intellectual obstructions and doubts. Our young people are diseased with the theological problems of original sin, origin of evil, predestination, and the like. These never presented a practical difficulty to any man,—never darkened across any man's road, who did not go out of his way to seek them. These are the soul's mumps and measles, and whooping-coughs, and those who have not caught them, cannot describe their health or prescribe the cure. A simple mind will not know these enemies. It is quite another thing that he should be able to give account of his faith, and expound to another the theory of his self-union and freedom. This requires rare gifts. Yet without this self-knowledge, there may be a sylvan strength and integrity in that which he is. "A few strong instincts and a few plain rules"[2] suffice us.

My will never gave the images in my mind the rank they now take. The regular course of studies, the years of academical and professional education have not yielded me better facts than some idle books under the bench at the

---

1. This epigraph, by Emerson, was added to the 1847 edition of *Essays*.
2. From Wordsworth's sonnet "Alas! What Boots the Long Laborious Quest."

Latin school. What we do not call education is more precious than that which we call so. We form no guess at the time of receiving a thought, of its comparative value. And education often wastes its effort in attempts to thwart and baulk this natural magnetism, which is sure to select what belongs to it.

In like manner, our moral nature is vitiated by any interference of our will. People represent virtue as a struggle, and take to themselves great airs upon their attainments, and the question is everywhere vexed, when a noble nature is commended, whether the man is not better who strives with temptation. But there is no merit in the matter. Either God is there, or he is not there. We love characters in proportion as they are impulsive and spontaneous. The less a man thinks or knows about his virtues, the better we like him. Timoleon's victories are the best victories; which ran and flowed like Homer's verses, Plutarch[3] said. When we see a soul whose acts are all regal, graceful and pleasant as roses, we must thank God that such things can be and are, and not turn sourly on the angel, and say, 'Crump is a better man with his grunting resistance to all his native devils.'

Not less conspicuous is the preponderance of nature over will in all practical life. There is less intention in history than we ascribe to it. We impute deep-laid, far-sighted plans to Cæsar and Napoleon; but the best of their power was in nature, not in them. Men of an extraordinary success, in their honest moments, have always sung, 'Not unto us, not unto us.'[4] According to the faith of their times, they have built altars to Fortune or to Destiny, or to St. Julian. Their success lay in their parallelism to the course of thought, which found in them an unobstructed channel; and the wonders of which they were the visible conductors, seemed to the eye their deed. Did the wires generate the galvanism? It is even true that there was less in them on which they could reflect, than in another; as the virtue of a pipe is to be smooth and hollow. That which externally seemed will and immovableness, was willingness and self-annihilation. Could Shakspeare give a theory of Shakspeare? Could ever a man of prodigious mathematical genius convey to others any insight into his methods? If he could communicate that secret, it would instantly lose its exaggerated value, blending with the daylight and the vital energy, the power to stand and to go.

The lesson is forcibly taught by these observations that our life might be much easier and simpler than we make it; that the world might be a happier place than it is; that there is no need of struggles, convulsions, and despairs, of the wringing of the hands and the gnashing of the teeth; that we miscreate our own evils. We interfere with the optimism of nature, for, whenever we get this vantage ground of the past, or of a wiser mind in the present, we are able to discern that we are begirt with laws which execute themselves.

The face of external nature teaches the same lesson. Nature will not have us fret and fume. She does not like our benevolence or our learning, much better than she likes our frauds and wars. When we come out of the caucus, or the bank, or the Abolition convention, or the Temperance meeting, or the Transcendental club, into the fields and woods, she says to us, 'So hot? my little Sir.'

We are full of mechanical actions. We must needs intermeddle, and have things in our own way, until the sacrifices and virtues of society are odious. Love should make joy; but our benevolence is unhappy. Our Sunday schools and

---

3. Plutarch (see n. 7, p. 57), *Life of Timoleon*.
4. Cf. Psalm 115.1.

churches and pauper-societies are yokes to the neck. We pain ourselves to please nobody. There are natural ways of arriving at the same ends at which these aim, but do not arrive. Why should all virtue work in one and the same way? Why should all give dollars? It is very inconvenient to us country folk, and we do not think any good will come of it. We have not dollars; merchants have; let them give them. Farmers will give corn; poets will sing; women will sew; laborers will lend a hand; the children will bring flowers. And why drag this dead weight of a Sunday school over the whole Christendom? It is natural and beautiful that childhood should inquire, and maturity should teach; but it is time enough to answer questions, when they are asked. Do not shut up the young people against their will in a pew, and force the children to ask them questions for an hour against their will.

If we look wider, things are all alike; laws, and letters, and creeds and modes of living, seem a travestie of truth. Our society is encumbered by ponderous machinery which resembles the endless aqueducts which the Romans built over hill and dale, and which are superseded by the discovery of the law that water rises to the level of its source. It is a Chinese wall which any nimble Tartar can leap over. It is a standing army, not so good as a peace. It is a graduated, titled, richly appointed Empire, quite superfluous when Town-meetings are found to answer just as well.

Let us draw a lesson from nature, which always works by short ways. When the fruit is ripe, it falls. When the fruit is despatched, the leaf falls. The circuit of the waters is mere falling. The walking of man and all animals is a falling forward. All our manual labor and works of strength, as prying, splitting, digging, rowing, and so forth, are done by dint of continual falling, and the globe, earth, moon, comet, sun, star, fall forever and ever.

The simplicity of the universe is very different from the simplicity of a machine. He who sees moral nature out and out, and thoroughly knows how knowledge is acquired and character formed, is a pedant. The simplicity of nature is not that which may easily be read, but is inexhaustible. The last analysis can no wise be made. We judge of a man's wisdom by his hope, knowing that the perception of the inexhaustibleness of nature is an immortal youth. The wild fertility of nature is felt in comparing our rigid names and reputations with our fluid consciousness. We pass in the world for sects and schools, for erudition and piety, and we are all the time jejune babes. One sees very well how Pyrrhonism[5] grew up. Every man sees that he is that middle point whereof every thing may be affirmed and denied with equal reason. He is old, he is young, he is very wise, he is altogether ignorant. He hears and feels what you say of the seraphim, and of the tin-pedlar. There is no permanent wise man, except in the figment of the stoics. We side with the hero, as we read or paint, against the coward and the robber; but we have been ourselves that coward and robber, and shall be again, not in the low circumstance, but in comparison with the grandeurs possible to the soul.

A little consideration of what takes place around us every day would show us, that a higher law than that of our will regulates events; that our painful labors are unnecessary, and fruitless; that only in our easy, simple, spontaneous action

5. Pyrrho (ca. 365–275 b.c.e.), Greek philosopher who founded the school of Pyrrhonism, believed "that the only condition worthy of a philosopher was that of suspended judgment. Virtuous imperturbability was the highest aim of life, but truth was unattainable" [Quoted by Edward Waldo Emerson from Appleton's *Encyclopedia*].

are we strong, and by contenting ourselves with obedience we become divine. Belief and love,—a believing love will relieve us of a vast load of care. O my brothers, God exists. There is a soul at the centre of nature, and over the will of every man, so that none of us can wrong the universe. It has so infused its strong enchantment into nature, that we prosper when we accept its advice, and when we struggle to wound its creatures, our hands are glued to our sides, or they beat our own breasts. The whole course of things goes to teach us faith. We need only obey. There is guidance for each of us, and by lowly listening we shall hear the right word. Why need you choose so painfully your place, and occupation, and associates, and modes of action, and of entertainment? Certainly there is a possible right for you that precludes the need of balance and wilful election. For you there is a reality, a fit place and congenial duties. Place yourself in the middle of the stream of power and wisdom which animates all whom it floats, and you are without effort impelled to truth, to right, and a perfect contentment. Then you put all gainsayers in the wrong. Then you are the world, the measure of right, of truth, of beauty. If we will not be mar-plots with our miserable interferences, the work, the society, letters, arts, science, religion of men, would go on far better than now, and the Heaven predicted from the beginning of the world, and still predicted from the bottom of the heart, would organize itself, as do now the rose and the air and the sun.

I say, *do not choose*; but that is a figure of speech by which I would distinguish what is commonly called *choice* among men, and which is a partial act, the choice of the hands, of the eyes, of the appetites, and not a whole act of the man. But that which I call right or goodness, is the choice of my constitution; and that which I call heaven, and inwardly aspire after, is the state or circumstance desirable to my constitution; and the action which I in all my years tend to do, is the work for my faculties. We must hold a man amenable to reason or the choice of his daily craft or profession. It is not an excuse any longer for his deeds that they are the custom of his trade. What business has he with an evil trade? Has he not a *calling* in his character.

Each man has his own vocation. The talent is the call. There is one direction in which all space is open to him. He has faculties silently inviting him thither to endless exertion. He is like a ship in a river; he runs against obstructions on every side but one; on that side, all obstruction is taken away, and he sweeps serenely over a deepening channel into an infinite sea. This talent and this call depend on his organization, or the mode in which the general soul incarnates itself in him. He inclines to do something which is easy to him, and good when it is done, but which no other man can do. He has no rival. For the more truly he consults his own powers, the more difference will his work exhibit from the work of any other. His ambition is exactly proportioned to his powers. The height of the pinnacle is determined by the breadth of the base. Every man has this call of the power to do somewhat unique, and no man has any other call. The pretence that he has another call, a summons by name and personal election and outward "signs that mark him extraordinary, and not in the roll of common men,"[6] is fanaticism, and betrays obtuseness to perceive that there is one mind in all the individuals, and no respect of persons therein.

By doing his work, he makes the need felt which he can supply, and creates the taste by which he is enjoyed. By doing his own work, he unfolds him-

---

6. The boast of Glendower to Hotspur, in Shakespeare, *I Henry IV* 3.1.41–43.

self. It is the vice of our public speaking, that it has not abandonment. Somewhere, not only every orator but every man should let out all the length of all the reins; should find or make a frank and hearty expression of what force and meaning is in him. The common experience is, that the man fits himself as well as he can to the customary details of that work or trade he falls into, and tends it as a dog turns a spit. Then is he a part of the machine he moves; the man is lost. Until he can manage to communicate himself to others in his full stature and proportion, he does not yet find his vocation. He must find in that an outlet for his character, so that he may justify his work to their eyes. If the labor is mean, let him by his thinking and character, make it liberal. Whatever he knows and thinks, whatever in his apprehension is worth doing, that let him communicate, or men will never know and honor him aright. Foolish, whenever you take the meanness and formality of that thing you do, instead of converting it into the obedient spiracle of your character and aims.

We like only such actions as have already long had the praise of men, and do not perceive that any thing man can do, may be divinely done. We think greatness entailed or organized in some places or duties, in certain offices or occasions, and do not see that Paganini can extract rapture from a catgut, and Eulenstein from a jews-harp, and a nimble-fingered lad out of shreds of paper with his scissors, and Landseer[7] out of swine, and the hero out of the pitiful habitation and company in which he was hidden. What we call obscure condition or vulgar society, is that condition and society whose poetry is not yet written, but which you shall presently make as enviable and renowned as any. In our estimates, let us take a lesson from kings. The parts of hospitality, the connection of families, the impressiveness of death, and a thousand other things, royalty makes its own estimate of, and a royal mind will. To make habitually a new estimate, — that is elevation.

What a man does, that he has. What has he to do with hope or fear? In himself is his might. Let him regard no good as solid, but that which is in his nature, and which must grow out of him as long as he exists. The goods of fortune may come and go like summer leaves; let him scatter them on every wind as the momentary signs of his infinite productiveness.

He may have his own. A man's genius, the quality that differences him from every other, the susceptibility to one class of influences, the selection of what is fit for him, the rejection of what is unfit, determines for him the character of the universe. A man is a method, a progressive arrangement; a selecting principle, gathering his like to him, wherever he goes. He takes only his own, out of the multiplicity that sweeps and circles round him. He is like one of those booms which are set out from the shore on rivers to catch drift-wood, or like the loadstone amongst splinters of steel.

Those facts, words, persons which dwell in his memory without his being able to say why, remain, because they have a relation to him not less real for being as yet unapprehended. They are symbols of value to him, as they can interpret parts of his consciousness which he would vainly seek words for in the conventional images of books and other minds. What attracts my attention shall have it, as I will go to the man who knocks at my door, whilst a thousand per-

7. Sir Edwin Henry Landseer (1802–1873), British painter known for his sentimental paintings of animals. Nicolò Paganini (1782–1840), Italian virtuoso violinist and composer. Charles Eulenstein (1802–1890), accomplished performer on the Jew's harp.

sons, as worthy, go by it, to whom I give no regard. It is enough that these particulars speak to me. A few anecdotes, a few traits of character, manners, face, a few incidents have an emphasis in your memory out of all proportion to their apparent significance, if you measure them by the ordinary standards. They relate to your gift. Let them have their weight, and do not reject them and cast about for illustration and facts more usual in literature. What your heart thinks great, is great. The soul's emphasis is always right.

Over all things that are agreeable to his nature and genius, the man has the highest right. Everywhere he may take what belongs to his spiritual estate, nor can he take any thing else, though all doors were open, nor can all the force of men hinder him from taking so much. It is vain to attempt to keep a secret from one who has a right to know it. It will tell itself. That mood into which a friend can bring us, is his dominion over us. To the thoughts of that state of mind, he has a right. All the secrets of that state of mind, he can compel. This is a law which statesmen use in practice. All the terrors of the French Republic, which held Austria in awe, were unable to command her diplomacy. But Napoleon sent to Vienna M. de Narbonne, one of the old noblesse, with the morals, manners and name of that interest, saying, that it was indispensable to send to the old aristocracy of Europe, men of the same connexion, which, in fact, constitutes a sort of free-masonry. M. de Narbonne, in less than a fortnight, penetrated all the secrets of the Imperial Cabinet.

Nothing seems so easy as to speak and to be understood. Yet a man may come to find *that* the strongest of defences and of ties,—that he has been understood; and he who has received an opinion, may come to find it the most inconvenient of bonds.

If a teacher have any opinion which he wishes to conceal, his pupils will become as fully indoctrinated into that as into any which he publishes. If you pour water into a vessel twisted into coils and angles, it is vain to say, I will pour it only into this or that;—it will find its level in all. Men feel and act the consequences of your doctrine, without being able to show how they follow. Show us an arc of the curve, and a good mathematician will find out the whole figure. We are always reasoning from the seen to the unseen. Hence the perfect intelligence that subsists between wise men of remote ages. A man cannot bury his meanings so deep in his book, but time and like-minded men will find them. Plato had a secret doctrine, had he? What secret can he conceal from the eyes of Bacon? of Montaigne? of Kant? Therefore, Aristotle[8] said of his works, "They are published and not published."

No man can learn what he has not preparation for learning, however near to his eyes is the object. A chemist may tell his most precious secrets to a carpenter, and he shall be never the wiser,—the secrets he would not utter to a chemist for an estate. God screens us evermore from premature ideas. Our eyes are holden that we cannot see[9] things that stare us in the face, until the hour arrives when the mind is ripened; then we behold them, and the time when we saw them not, is like a dream.

Not in nature but in man is all the beauty and worth he sees. The world is very empty, and is indebted to this gilding, exalting soul for all its pride. "Earth

---

8. See n. 4, p. 47. Plato, see n. 4, p. 15. Bacon, see n. 3, p. 6. Michel de Montaigne (1533–1592), French essayist; see also Emerson's essay "Montaigne" (p. 234). Kant, see n. 8, p. 35.
9. Cf. Luke 24.13–16.

fills her lap with splendors" *not her own*.[1] The vale of Tempe, Tivoli, and Rome are earth and water, rocks and sky. There are as good earth and water in a thousand places, yet how unaffecting!

People are not the better for the sun and moon, the horizon and the trees; as it is not observed that the keepers of Roman galleries, or the valets of painters have any elevation of thought, or that librarians are wiser men than others. There are graces in the demeanor of a polished and noble person, which are lost upon the eye of a churl. These are like the stars whose light has not yet reached us.

He may see what he maketh. Our dreams are the sequel of our waking knowledge. The visions of the night bear some proportion to the visions of the day. Hideous dreams are exaggerations of the sins of the day. We see our evil affections embodied in bad physiognomies. On the Alps, the traveller sometimes beholds his own shadow magnified to a giant, so that every gesture of his hand is terrific. "My children," said an old man to his boys scared by a figure in the dark entry, "my children, you will never see any thing worse than yourselves." As in dreams, so in the scarcely less fluid events of the world, every man sees himself in colossal, without knowing that it is himself. The good, compared to the evil which he sees, is as his own good to his own evil. Every quality of his mind is magnified in some one acquaintance, and every emotion of his heart in some one. He is like a quincunx[2] of trees, which counts five, east, west, north, or south; or, an initial, medial, and terminal acrostic. And why not? He cleaves to one person, and avoids another, according to their likeness or unlikeness to himself, truly seeking himself in his associates, and moreover in his trade, and habits, and gestures, and meats, and drinks; and comes at last to be faithfully represented by every view you take of his circumstances.

He may read what he writes. What can we see or acquire, but what we are? You have observed a skilful man reading Virgil.[3] Well, that author is a thousand books to a thousand persons. Take the book into your two hands, and read your eyes out; you will never find what I find. If any ingenious reader would have a monopoly of the wisdom or delight he gets, he is as secure now the book is Englished, as if it were imprisoned in the Pelews' tongue. It is with a good book as it is with good company. Introduce a base person among gentlemen: it is all to no purpose: he is not their fellow. Every society protects itself. The company is perfectly safe, and he is not one of them, though his body is in the room.

What avails it to fight with the eternal laws of mind, which adjust the relation of all persons to each other, by the mathematical measure of their havings and beings? Gertrude is enamored of Guy; how high, how aristocratic, how Roman his mien and manners! to live with him were life indeed: and no purchase is too great; and heaven and earth are moved to that end. Well, Gertrude has Guy: but what now avails how high, how aristocratic, how Roman his mien and manners, if his heart and aims are in the senate, in the theatre, and in the billiard room, and she has no aims, no conversation that can enchant her graceful lord?

He shall have his own society. We can love nothing but nature. The most wonderful talents, the most meritorious exertions really avail very little with us;

---

1. Cf. Wordsworth, "Ode: Intimations of Immortality," line 77.
2. A square marked by one point at each corner and a fifth at the center.
3. Roman poet (70–19 B.C.E.), whose greatest work is the epic poem *Aeneid*, which tells of the wanderings of Aeneas after the sack of Troy.

but nearness or likeness of nature,—how beautiful is the ease of its victory! Persons approach us famous for their beauty, for their accomplishments, worthy of all wonder for their charms and gifts: they dedicate their whole skill to the hour and the company, with very imperfect result. To be sure, it would be ungrateful in us not to praise them loudly. Then, when all is done, a person of related mind, a brother or sister by nature, comes to us so softly and easily, so nearly and intimately, as if it were the blood in our proper veins, that we feel as if some one was gone, instead of another having come: we are utterly relieved and refreshed: it is a sort of joyful solitude. We foolishly think, in our days of sin, that we must court friends by compliance to the customs of society, to its dress, its breeding and its estimates. But only that soul can be my friend, which I encounter on the line of my own march, that soul to which I do not decline, and which does not decline to me, but, native of the same celestial latitude, repeats in its own all my experience. The scholar forgets himself, and apes the customs and costumes of the man of the world, to deserve the smile of beauty, and follows some giddy girl, not yet taught by religious passion to know the noble woman with all that is serene, oracular and beautiful in her soul. Let him be great, and love shall follow him. Nothing is more deeply punished than the neglect of the affinities by which alone society should be formed, and the insane levity of choosing associates by others' eyes.

He may set his own rate. It is a maxim worthy of all acceptation, that a man may have that allowance he takes. Take the place and attitude which belong to you, and all men acquiesce. The world must be just. It leaves every man, with profound unconcern, to set his own rate. Hero or driveller, it meddles not in the matter. It will certainly accept your own measure of your doing and being, whether you sneak about and deny your own name, or, whether you see your work produced to the concave sphere of the heavens, one with the revolution of the stars.

The same reality pervades all teaching. The man may teach by doing, and not otherwise. If he can communicate himself, he can teach, but not by words. He teaches who gives, and he learns who receives. There is no teaching until the pupil is brought into the same state or principle in which you are; a transfusion takes place: he is you, and you are he; then is a teaching, and by no unfriendly chance or bad company can he ever quite lose the benefit. But your propositions run out of one ear as they ran in at the other. We see it advertised that Mr. Grand will deliver an oration on the Fourth of July, and Mr. Hand before the Mechanics' Association, and we do not go thither, because we know that these gentlemen will not communicate their own character and experience to the company. If we had reason to expect such a confidence, we should go through all inconvenience and opposition. The sick would be carried in litters. But a public oration is an escapade, a non-committal, an apology, a gag, and not a communication, not a speech, not a man.

A like Nemesis[4] presides over all intellectual works. We have yet to learn, that the thing uttered in words is not therefore affirmed. It must affirm itself, or no forms of logic or of oath can give it evidence. The sentence must also contain its own apology for being spoken.

The effect of any writing on the public mind is mathematically measurable by its depth of thought. How much water does it draw? If it awaken you to think, if it lift you from your feet with the great voice of eloquence, then the effect is to

4. See n. 7, p. 143.

be wide, slow, permanent, over the minds of men; if the pages instruct you not, they will die like flies in the hour. The way to speak and write what shall not go out of fashion, is, to speak and write sincerely. The argument which has not power to reach my own practice, I may well doubt, will fail to reach yours. But take Sidney's maxim: — "Look in thy heart, and write."[5] He that writes to himself, writes to an eternal public. That statement only is fit to be made public which you have come at in attempting to satisfy your own curiosity. The writer who takes his subject from his ear and not from his heart, should know that he has lost as much as he seems to have gained, and when the empty book has gathered all its praise, and half the people say, 'What poetry! what genius!' it still needs fuel to make fire. That only profits which is profitable. Life alone can impart life; and though we should burst, we can only be valued as we make ourselves valuable. There is no luck in literary reputation. They who make up the final verdict upon every book, are not the partial and noisy readers of the hour when it appears; but a court as of angels, a public not to be bribed, not to be entreated, and not to be overawed, decides upon every man's title to fame. Only those books come down which deserve to last. Gilt edges, vellum, and morocco, and presentation-copies to all the libraries will not preserve a book in circulation beyond its intrinsic date. It must go with all Walpole's[6] Noble and Royal Authors to its fate. Blackmore, Kotzebue, or Pollok[7] may endure for a night, but Moses and Homer stand forever. There are not in the world at any time more than a dozen persons who read and understand Plato: — never enough to pay for an edition of his works; yet to every generation these come duly down, for the sake of those few persons, as if God brought them in his hand. "No book," said Bentley,[8] "was ever written down by any but itself." The permanence of all books is fixed by no effort friendly or hostile, but by their own specific gravity, or the intrinsic importance of their contents to the constant mind of man. "Do not trouble yourself too much about the light on your statue," said Michel Angelo[9] to the young sculptor; "the light of the public square will test its value."

In like manner the effect of every action is measured by the depth of the sentiment from which it proceeds. The great man knew not that he was great. It took a century or two, for that fact to appear. What he did, he did because he must; it was the most natural thing in the world, and grew out of the circumstances of the moment. But now, every thing he did, even to the lifting of his finger, or the eating of bread, looks large, all-related, and is called an institution.

These are the demonstrations in a few particulars of the genius of nature: they show the direction of the stream. But the stream is blood: every drop is alive. Truth has not single victories: all things are its organs, — not only dust and stones, but errors and lies. The laws of disease, physicians say, are as beautiful as the laws of health. Our philosophy is affirmative, and readily accepts the tes-

5. Sir Philip Sidney (1554–1586), English poet, soldier, and politician. His most important works are the sonnet sequence *Astrophel and Stella* and the collection of pastoral idylls *Arcadia*. Emerson quotes here from *Astrophel and Stella* 1.14.
6. Horace Walpole, fourth earl of Oxford (1717–1797), compiled *A Catalogue of the Royal and Noble Authors of England*.
7. Robert Pollok (1798–1827), author of the long poem *The Course of Time*, which was once very popular. Sir Richard Blackmore (ca. 1650–1729), author of the 350-page philosophical poem *Creation* (1712). August von Kotzebue (1761–1819), German dramatist noted for his ridicule of romanticism and his more than two hundred plays.
8. Richard Bentley (1662–1742), English cleric and classical scholar noted for his *Letter to Dr. John Mill* (1691) and *Dissertation upon the Epistles of Phalaris* (1699).
9. Michelangelo, see n. 6, p. 42.

timony of negative facts, as every shadow points to the sun. By a divine necessity, every fact in nature is constrained to offer its testimony.

Human character evermore publishes itself. The most fugitive deed and word, the mere air of doing a thing, the intimated purpose, expresses character. If you act, you show character; if you sit still, if you sleep, you show it. You think because you have spoken nothing, when others spoke, and have given no opinion on the times, on the church, on slavery, on marriage, on socialism, on secret societies, on the college, on parties and persons, that your verdict is still expected with curiosity as a reserved wisdom. Far otherwise; your silence answers very loud. You have no oracle to utter, and your fellow men have learned that you cannot help them; for, oracles speak. Doth not wisdom cry, and understanding put forth her voice?[1]

Dreadful limits are set in nature to the powers of dissimulation. Truth tyrannizes over the unwilling members of the body. Faces never lie, it is said. No man need be deceived, who will study the changes of expression. When a man speaks the truth in the spirit of truth, his eye is as clear as the heavens. When he has base ends, and speaks falsely, the eye is muddy and sometimes asquint.

I have heard an experienced counsellor say, that he never feared the effect upon a jury, of a lawyer who does not believe in his heart that his client ought to have a verdict. If he does not believe it, his unbelief will appear to the jury, despite all his protestations, and will become their unbelief. This is that law whereby a work of art, of whatever kind, sets us in the same state of mind wherein the artist was, when he made it. That which we do not believe, we cannot adequately say, though we may repeat the words never so often. It was this conviction which Swedenborg[2] expressed, when he described a group of persons in the spiritual world endeavoring in vain to articulate a proposition which they did not believe: but they could not, though they twisted and folded their lips even to indignation.

A man passes for that he is worth. Very idle is all curiosity concerning other people's estimate of us, and all fear of remaining unknown is not less so. If a man know that he can do any thing, — that he can do it better than any one else, — he has a pledge of the acknowledgment of that fact by all persons. The world is full of judgment days, and into every assembly that a man enters, in every action he attempts, he is gauged and stamped. In every troop of boys that whoop and run in each yard and square, a new comer is as well and accurately weighed in the course of a few days, and stamped with his right number, as if he had undergone a formal trial of his strength, speed, and temper. A stranger comes from a distant school, with better dress, with trinkets in his pockets, with airs and pretensions: an older boy says to himself, 'It's of no use: we shall find him out tomorrow.' 'What has he done?' is the divine question which searches men, and transpierces every false reputation. A fop may sit in any chair of the world, nor be distinguished for his hour from Homer and Washington; but there need never by any doubt concerning the respective ability of human beings. Pretension may sit still, but cannot act. Pretension never feigned an act of real greatness. Pretension never wrote an Iliad, nor drove back Xerxes[3] nor christianized the world, nor abolished slavery.

---

1. Proverbs 8.1.
2. See n. 6, p. 35.
3. Xerxes I (519?–465 B.C.E.), king of Persia (486–465 B.C.E.), who organized a vast army that defeated the Greeks at Thermopylae and destroyed Athens (480 B.C.E.). After the defeat of his navy at Salamis (480 B.C.E.) and of his army at Plataea (479 B.C.E.), he retreated to Persia, where he was later assassinated.

As much virtue as there is, so much appears; as much goodness as there is, so much reverence it commands. All the devils respect virtue. The high, the generous, the self-devoted sect will always instruct and command mankind. Never was a sincere word utterly lost. Never a magnanimity fell to the ground, but there is some heart to greet and accept it unexpectedly. A man passes for that he is worth. What he is, engraves itself on his face, on his form, on his fortunes, in letters of light. Concealment avails him nothing; boasting, nothing. There is confession in the glances of our eyes; in our smiles; in salutations; and the grasp of hands. His sin bedaubs him, mars all his good impression. Men know not why they do not trust him; but they do not trust him. His vice glasses his eye, cuts lines of mean expression in his cheek, pinches the nose, sets the mark of the beast on the back of the head,[4] and writes O fool! fool! on the forehead of a king.

If you would not be known to do any thing, never do it. A man may play the fool in the drifts of a desert, but every grain of sand shall seem to see. He may be a solitary eater, but he cannot keep his foolish counsel. A broken complexion, a swinish look, ungenerous acts, and the want of due knowledge, — all blab. Can a cook, a Chiffinch, an Iachimo be mistaken for Zeno or Paul? Confucius[5] exclaimed, — "How can a man be concealed! How can a man be concealed!"

On the other hand, the hero fears not, that if he withhold the avowal of a just and brave act, it will go unwitnessed and unloved. One knows it, — himself, — and is pledged by it to sweetness of peace, and to nobleness of aim, which will prove in the end a better proclamation of it than the relating of the incident. Virtue is the adherence in action to the nature of things, and the nature of things makes it prevalent. It consists in a perpetual substitution of being for seeming, and with sublime propriety God is described as saying, I AM.[6]

The lesson which these observations convey is, Be, and not seem. Let us acquiesce. Let us take our bloated nothingness out of the path of the divine circuits. Let us unlearn our wisdom of the world. Let us lie low in the Lord's power, and learn that truth alone makes rich and great.

If you visit your friend, why need you apologize for not having visited him, and waste his time and deface your own act? Visit him now. Let him feel that the highest love has come to see him, in thee its lowest organ. Or why need you torment yourself and friend by secret self-reproaches that you have not assisted him or complimented him with gifts and salutations heretofore? Be a gift and a benediction. Shine with real light, and not with the borrowed reflection of gifts. Common men are apologies for men; they bow the head, excuse themselves with prolix reasons, and accumulate appearances, because the substance is not.

We are full of these superstitions of sense, the worship of magnitude. We call the poet inactive, because he is not a president, a merchant, or a porter. We adore an institution, and do not see that it is founded on a thought which we have. But real action is in silent moments. The epochs of our life are not in the visible facts of our choice of a calling, our marriage, our acquisition of an office, and the like, but in a silent thought by the way-side as we walk; in a thought

---

4. Cf. Revelation 13.15–16.
5. Chinese philosopher (ca. 551–497 B.C.E.), whose *Analects* contain a collection of his sayings and dialogues compiled by disciples after his death. Chiffinch and Iachimo are rascally characters in, respectively, Scott's *Peveril of the Peak* and Shakespeare's *Cymbeline*. Zeno, see n. 9, p. 78. Paul, see n. 1, p. 3.
6. See n. 2, p. 130.

which revises our entire manner of life, and says, — 'Thus hast thou done, but it were better thus.' And all our after years, like menials, serve and wait on this, and, according to their ability, execute its will. This revisal or correction is a constant force, which, as a tendency, reaches through our lifetime. The object of the man, the aim of these moments is to make daylight shine through him, to suffer the law to traverse his whole being without obstruction, so that, on what point soever of his doing your eye falls, it shall report truly of his character, whether it be his diet, his house, his religious forms, his society, his mirth, his vote, his opposition. Now he is not homogeneous, but heterogeneous, and the ray does not traverse; there are no thorough lights:[7] but the eye of the beholder is puzzled, detecting many unlike tendencies, and a life not yet at one.

Why should we make it a point with our false modesty to disparage that man we are, and that form of being assigned to us? A good man is contented. I love and honor Epaminondas, but I do not wish to be Epaminondas. I hold it more just to love the world of this hour, than the world of his hour. Nor can you, if I am true, excite me to the least uneasiness by saying, 'he acted, and thou sittest still.' I see action to be good, when the need is, and sitting still to be also good. Epaminondas,[8] if he was the man I take him for, would have sat still with joy and peace, if his lot had been mine. Heaven is large, and affords space for all modes of love and fortitude. Why should we be busy-bodies and superserviceable? Action and inaction are alike to the true. One piece of the tree is cut for a weathercock, and one for the sleeper[9] of a bridge; the virtue of the wood is apparent in both.

I desire not to disgrace the soul. The fact that I am here, certainly shows me that the soul had need of an organ here. Shall I not assume the post? Shall I skulk and dodge and duck with my unseasonable apologies and vain modesty, and imagine my being here impertinent? less pertinent than Epaminondas or Homer being there? and that the soul did not know its own needs? Besides, without any reasoning on the matter, I have no discontent. The good soul nourishes me, and unlocks new magazines of power and enjoyment to me every day. I will not meanly decline the immensity of good, because I have heard that it has come to others in another shape.

Besides, why should we be cowed by the name of Action? 'T is a trick of the senses, — no more. We know that the ancestor of every action is a thought. The poor mind does not seem to itself to be any thing, unless it have an outside badge, — some Gentoo[1] diet, or Quaker coat, or Calvinistic prayer-meeting, or philanthropic society, or a great donation, or a high office, or, any how, some wild contrasting action to testify that it is somewhat. The rich mind lies in the sun and sleeps, and is Nature. To think is to act.

Let us, if we must have great actions, make our own so. All action is of an infinite elasticity, and the least admits of being inflated with the celestial air until it eclipses the sun and moon. Let us seek *one* peace by fidelity. Let me heed my duties. Why need I go gadding into the scenes and philosophy of Greek and Italian history, before I have justified myself to my benefactors? How dare I read Washington's campaigns, when I have not answered the letters of

7. Windows positioned to allow sunlight to enter a room.
8. See n. 8, p. 74.
9. A horizontal support beam.
1. Hindu. Here, Emerson's coupling of the term with *diet* suggests a vegetarian health regime such as many American reformers supported in the 1830s and 1840s. See the essay "Experience," p. 205.

my own correspondents? Is not that a just objection to much of our reading? It is a pusillanimous desertion of our work to gaze after our neighbors. It is peeping. Byron says of Jack Bunting,—

> "He knew not what to say, and so, he swore."[2]

I may say it of our preposterous use of books,—He knew not what to do, and so, *he read.* I can think of nothing to fill my time with, and I find the Life of Brant. It is a very extravagant compliment to pay to Brant, or to General Schuyler,[3] or to General Washington. My time should be as good as their time,—my facts, my net of relations as good as theirs, or either of theirs. Rather let me do my work so well that other idlers, if they choose, may compare my texture with the texture of these and find it identical with the best.

This over-estimate of the possibilities of Paul and Pericles, this under-estimate of our own, comes from a neglect of the fact of an identical nature. Bonaparte knew but one Merit, and rewarded in one and the same way the good soldier, the good astronomer, the good poet, the good player. The poet uses the names of Cæsar, of Tamerlane, of Bonduca, of Belisarius;[4] the painter uses the conventional story of the Virgin Mary, of Paul, of Peter. He does not, therefore, defer to the nature of these accidental men, of these stock heroes. If the poet write a true drama, then he is Cæsar, and not the player of Cæsar; then the self-same strain of thought, emotion as pure, wit as subtle, motions as swift, mounting, extravagant, and a heart as great, self-sufficing, dauntless, which on the waves of its love and hope can uplift all that is reckoned solid and precious in the world,—palaces, gardens, money, navies, kingdoms,—marking its own incomparable worth by the slight it casts on these gauds of men,—these all are his, and by the power of these he rouses the nations. Let a man believe in God, and not in names and places and persons. Let the great soul incarnated in some woman's form, poor and sad and single, in some Dolly or Joan, go out to service, and sweep chambers and scour floors, and its effulgent daybeams cannot be muffled or hid, but to sweep and scour will instantly appear supreme and beautiful actions, the top and radiance of human life, and all people will get mops and brooms; until, lo, suddenly the great soul has enshrined itself in some other form, and done some other deed, and that is now the flower and head of all living nature.

We are the photometers, we the irritable goldleaf and tinfoil that measure the accumulations of the subtle element.[5] We know the authentic effects of the true fire through every one of its million disguises.

---

2. Cf. Byron's *The Island* 3.5.12. George Gordon, Lord Byron (1788–1824), British poet acclaimed as one of the leading figures of the Romantic movement. The Byronic hero—lonely, rebellious, and brooding—first appeared in *Manfred* (1817).
3. Philip John Schuyler (1733–1804), Revolutionary War general of Colonial forces in New York State who was relieved of his command after the British capture of Fort Ticonderoga (1777). He later served as a U.S. senator from New York (1789–91 and 1797–98). Joseph Brant (1742–1807), Mohawk leader who supported the British in the French and Indian War and the American Revolution. His *Life* was written by William Stone (1838).
4. Byzantine general (505?–565) under Emperor Justinian I who led campaigns against the barbarians in North Africa and Italy. Caesar, see n. 8, p. 17. Tamerlane (1336–1405), Mongol conqueror, protagonist of *Tamburlaine the Great*, a drama in blank verse by Christopher Marlowe (1564–1593). *Bonduca*, see n. 9, p. 132.
5. According to *CW* (2.242–43), "in the middle 1840's either goldleaf or tinfoil was an essential element in an electrometer."

The Over-Soul

"But souls that of his own good life partake,
He loves as his own self; dear as his eye
They are to Him: He'll never them forsake:
When they shall die, then God himself shall die:
They live, they live in blest eternity."

HENRY MORE.[1]

Space is ample, east and west,
But two cannot go abreast,
Cannot travel in it two:
Yonder masterful cuckoo
Crowds every egg out of the nest,
Quick or dead, except its own;
A spell is laid on sod and stone,
Night and Day were tampered with,
Every quality and pith
Surcharged and sultry with a power
That works its will on age and hour.[2]

There is a difference between one and another hour of life, in their authority and subsequent effect. Our faith comes in moments; our vice is habitual. Yet there is a depth in those brief moments, which constrains us to ascribe more reality to them than to all other experiences. For this reason, the argument, which is always forthcoming to silence those who conceive extraordinary hopes of man, namely, the appeal to experience, is forever invalid and vain. We give up the past to the objector, and yet we hope. He must explain this hope. We grant that human life is mean; but how did we find out that it was mean? What is the ground of this uneasiness of ours; of this old discontent? What is the universal sense of want and ignorance, but the fine innuendo by which the soul makes its enormous claim? Why do men feel that the natural history of man has never been written, but he is always leaving behind what you have said of him, and it becomes old, and books of metaphysics worthless? The philosophy of six thousand years has not searched the chambers and magazines of the soul. In its experiments there has always remained, in the last analysis, a residuum it could not resolve. Man is a stream whose source is hidden. Our being is descending into us from we know not whence. The most exact calculator has no prescience that somewhat incalculable may not baulk the very next moment. I am constrained every moment to acknowledge a higher origin for events than the will I call mine.

As with events, so is it with thoughts. When I watch that flowing river, which, out of regions I see not, pours for a season its streams into me, I see that I am a pensioner; not a cause, but a surprised spectator of this ethereal water; that I desire and look up, and put myself in the attitude of reception, but from some alien energy the visions come.

The Supreme Critic on the errors of the past and the present, and the only prophet of that which must be, is that great nature in which we rest, as the earth lies in the soft arms of the atmosphere; that Unity, that Over-Soul, within which every man's particular being is contained and made one with all other; that

---

1. Henry More (1614–1687), "Psychozoia, or, the life of the Soul," in *Philosophical Poems* (1647) 2.19.
2. Emerson added this epigraph to the 1847 edition of *Essays.* The version printed here is from 1870.

common heart, of which all sincere conversation is the worship, to which all
right action is submission; that overpowering reality which confutes our tricks
and talents, and constrains every one to pass for what he is, and to speak from
his character and not from his tongue, and which evermore tends and aims to
pass into our thought and hand, and become wisdom, and virtue, and power,
and beauty. We live in succession, in division, in parts, in particles. Meantime
within man is the soul of the whole; the wise silence; the universal beauty, to
which every part and particle is equally related; the eternal ONE. And this deep
power in which we exist, and whose beatitude is all accessible to us, is not only
self-sufficing and perfect in every hour, but the act of seeing and the thing seen,
the seer and the spectacle, the subject and the object, are one. We see the world
piece by piece, as the sun, the moon, the animal, the tree; but the whole, of
which these are the shining parts, is the soul. Only by the vision of that Wisdom
can the horoscope of the ages be read, and by falling back on our better
thoughts, by yielding to the spirit of prophecy which is innate in every man, we
can know what it saith. Every man's words, who speaks from that life, must
sound vain to those who do not dwell in the same thought on their own part. I
dare not speak for it. My words do not carry its august sense; they fall short and
cold. Only itself can inspire whom it will, and behold! their speech shall be lyrical, and sweet, and universal as the rising of the wind. Yet I desire, even by profane words, if I may not use sacred, to indicate the heaven of this deity, and to
report what hints I have collected of the transcendent simplicity and energy of
the Highest Law.

If we consider what happens in conversation, in reveries, in remorse, in
times of passion, in surprises, in the instructions of dreams wherein often we see
ourselves in masquerade, — the droll disguises only magnifying and enhancing
a real element, and forcing it on our distinct notice, — we shall catch many hints
that will broaden and lighten into knowledge of the secret of nature. All goes to
show that the soul in man is not an organ, but animates and exercises all the organs; is not a function, like the power of memory, of calculation, of comparison, but uses these as hands and feet; is not a faculty, but a light; is not the
intellect or the will, but the master of the intellect and the will; is the background of our being, in which they lie, — an immensity not possessed and that
cannot be possessed. From within or from behind, a light shines through us
upon things, and makes us aware that we are nothing, but the light is all. A man
is the façade of a temple wherein all wisdom and all good abide. What we commonly call man, the eating, drinking, planting, counting man, does not, as we
know him, represent himself, but misrepresents himself. Him we do not respect, but the soul, whose organ he is, would he let it appear through his action,
would make our knees bend. When it breathes through his intellect, it is genius; when it breathes through his will, it is virtue; when it flows through his affection, it is love. And the blindness of the intellect begins, when it would be
something of itself. The weakness of the will begins when the individual would
be something of himself. All reform aims, in some one particular, to let the soul
have its way through us; in other words, to engage us to obey.

Of this pure nature every man is at some time sensible. Language cannot
paint it with his colors. It is too subtle. It is undefinable, unmeasurable, but we
know that it pervades and contains us. We know that all spiritual being is in
man. A wise old proverb says, "God comes to see us without bell:" that is, as
there is no screen or ceiling between our heads and the infinite heavens, so is

there no bar or wall in the soul where man, the effect, ceases, and God, the cause, begins. The walls are taken away. We lie open on one side to the deeps of spiritual nature, to all the attributes of God. Justice we see and know, Love, Freedom, Power. These natures no man ever got above, but they tower over us, and most in the moment when our interests tempt us to wound them.

The sovereignty of this nature whereof we speak, is made known by its independency of those limitations which circumscribe us on every hand. The soul circumscribes all things. As I have said, it contradicts all experience. In like manner it abolishes time and space. The influence of the senses has, in most men, overpowered the mind to that degree, that the walls of time and space have come to look real and insurmountable; and to speak with levity of these limits, is, in the world, the sign of insanity. Yet time and space are but inverse measures of the force of the soul. The spirit sports with time—

> "Can crowd eternity into an hour,
> Or stretch an hour to eternity."[3]

We are often made to feel that there is another youth and age than that which is measured from the year of our natural birth. Some thoughts always find us young and keep us so. Such a thought is the love of the universal and eternal beauty. Every man parts from that contemplation with the feeling that it rather belongs to ages than to mortal life. The least activity of the intellectual powers redeems us in a degree from the conditions of time. In sickness, in languor, give us a strain of poetry or a profound sentence, and we are refreshed; or produce a volume of Plato, or Shakspeare, or remind us of their names, and instantly we come into a feeling of longevity. See how the deep, divine thought reduces centuries, and millenniums, and makes itself present through all ages. Is the teaching of Christ less effective now than it was when first his mouth was opened? The emphasis of facts and persons in my thought has nothing to do with time. And so, always, the soul's scale is one; the scale of the senses and the understanding is another. Before the revelations of the soul, Time, Space and Nature shrink away. In common speech, we refer all things to time, as we habitually refer the immensely sundered stars to one concave sphere. And so we say that the Judgment is distant or near, that the Millennium approaches, that a day of certain political, moral, social reforms is at hand, and the like, when we mean, that in the nature of things, one of the facts we contemplate is external and fugitive, and the other is permanent and connate with the soul. The things we now esteem fixed, shall, one by one, detach themselves, like ripe fruit, from our experience, and fall. The wind shall blow them none knows whither.[4] The landscape, the figures, Boston, London, are facts as fugitive as any institution past, or any whiff of mist or smoke, and so is society, and so is the world. The soul looketh steadily forwards, creating a world before her, leaving worlds behind her. She has no dates, nor rites, nor persons, nor specialties, nor men. The soul knows only the soul; the web of events is the flowing robe in which she is clothed.

After its own law and not by arithmetic is the rate of its progress to be computed. The soul's advances are not made by gradation, such as can be repre-

---

3. Byron (see n. 2, p. 162), *Cain* 1.1.536–37.
4. Cf. Isaiah 41.16 and John 3.8.

sented by motion in a straight line; but rather by ascension of state, such as can be represented by metamorphosis,—from the egg to the worm, from the worm to the fly. The growths of genius are of a certain *total* character, that does not advance the elect individual first over John, then Adam, then Richard, and give to each the pain of discovered inferiority, but by every throe of growth, the man expands there where he works, passing, at each pulsation, classes, populations of men. With each divine impulse the mind rends the thin rinds of the visible and finite, and comes out into eternity, and inspires and expires its air. It converses with truths that have always been spoken in the world, and becomes conscious of a closer sympathy with Zeno and Arrian,[5] than with persons in the house.

This is the law of moral and of mental gain. The simple rise as by specific levity, not into a particular virtue, but into the region of all the virtues. They are in the spirit which contains them all. The soul requires purity, but purity is not it; requires justice, but justice is not that; requires beneficence, but is somewhat better: so that there is a kind of descent and accommodation felt when we leave speaking of moral nature, to urge a virtue which it enjoins. To the well-born child, all the virtues are natural, and not painfully acquired. Speak to his heart, and the man becomes suddenly virtuous.

Within the same sentiment is the germ of intellectual growth, which obeys the same law. Those who are capable of humility, of justice, of love, of aspiration, stand already on a platform that commands the sciences and arts, speech and poetry, action and grace. For whoso dwells in this moral beatitude already anticipates those special powers which men prize so highly. The lover has no talent, no skill, which passes for quite nothing with his enamored maiden, however little she may possess of related faculty; and the heart which abandons itself to the Supreme Mind finds itself related to all its works and will travel a royal road to particular knowledges and powers. In ascending to this primary and aboriginal sentiment, we have come from our remote station on the circumference instantaneously to the centre of the world, where, as in the closet of God, we see causes, and anticipate the universe, which is but a slow effect.

One mode of the divine teaching is the incarnation of the spirit in a form,—in forms, like my own. I live in society; with persons who answer to thoughts in my own mind, or express a certain obedience to the great instincts to which I live. I see its presence to them. I am certified of a common nature; and these other souls, these separated selves, draw me as nothing else can. They stir in me the new emotions we call passion; of love, hatred, fear, admiration, pity; thence comes conversation, competition, persuasion, cities, and war. Persons are supplementary to the primary teaching of the soul. In youth we are mad for persons. Childhood and youth see all the world in them. But the larger experience of man discovers the identical nature appearing through them all. Persons themselves acquaint us with the impersonal. In all conversation between two persons, tacit reference is made as to a third party, to a common nature. That third party or common nature is not social; it is impersonal; is God. And so in groups where debate is earnest, and especially on high questions, the company become aware that the thought rises to an equal level in all bosoms, that all have a spiritual property in what was said, as well as the sayer. They all be-

5. A disciple of Epictetus (fl. 100 c.e.), a Greek Stoic philosopher. Zeno, see n. 9, p. 78.

come wiser than they were. It arches over them like a temple, this unity of thought, in which every heart beats with nobler sense of power and duty, and thinks and acts with unusual solemnity. All are conscious of attaining to a higher self-possession. It shines for all. There is a certain wisdom of humanity which is common to the greatest men with the lowest, and which our ordinary education often labors to silence and obstruct. The mind is one, and the best minds who love truth for its own sake, think much less of property in truth. They accept it thankfully everywhere, and do not label or stamp it with any man's name, for it is theirs long beforehand, and from eternity. The learned and the studious of thought have no monopoly of wisdom. Their violence of direction in some degree disqualifies them to think truly. We owe many valuable observations to people who are not very acute or profound, and who say the thing without effort, which we want and have long been hunting in vain. The action of the soul is oftener in that which is felt and left unsaid, than in that which is said in any conversation. It broods over every society, and they unconsciously seek for it in each other. We know better than we do. We do not yet possess ourselves, and we know at the same time that we are much more. I feel the same truth how often in my trivial conversation with my neighbors, that somewhat higher in each of us overlooks this by-play, and Jove nods to Jove from behind each of us.

Men descend to meet. In their habitual and mean service to the world, for which they forsake their native nobleness, they resemble those Arabian Sheikhs, who dwell in mean houses and affect an external poverty, to escape the rapacity of the Pacha, and reserve all their display of wealth for their interior and guarded retirements.

As it is present in all persons, so it is in every period of life. It is adult already in the infant man. In my dealing with my child, my Latin and Greek, my accomplishments and my money, stead me nothing; but as much soul as I have avails. If I am wilful, he sets his will against mine, one for one, and leaves me, if I please, the degradation of beating him by my superiority of strength. But if I renounce my will, and act for the soul, setting that up as umpire between us two, out of his young eyes looks the same soul; he reveres and loves with me.

The soul is the perceiver and revealer of truth. We know truth when we see it, let skeptic and scoffer say what they choose. Foolish people ask you, when you have spoken what they do not wish to hear, 'How do you know it is truth, and not an error of your own?' We know truth when we see it, from opinion, as we know when we are awake that we are awake. It was a grand sentence of Emanuel Swedenborg,[6] which would alone indicate the greatness of that man's perception,—"It is no proof of a man's understanding to be able to confirm whatever he pleases; but to be able to discern that what is true is true, and that what is false is false, this is the mark and character of intelligence." In the book I read, the good thought returns to me, as every truth will, the image of the whole soul. To the bad thought which I find in it, the same soul becomes a discerning, separating sword and lops it away. We are wiser than we know. If we will not interfere with our thought, but will act entirely, or see how the thing stands in God, we know the particular thing, and every thing, and every man. For, the Maker of all things and all persons, stands behind us, and casts his dread omniscience through us over things.

6. See n. 6, p. 35.

But beyond this recognition of its own in particular passages of the individual's experience, it also reveals truth. And here we should seek to reinforce ourselves by its very presence, and to speak with a worthier, loftier strain of that advent. For the soul's communication of truth is the highest event in nature, since it then does not give somewhat from itself, but it gives itself, or passes into and becomes that man whom it enlightens; or in proportion to that truth he receives, it takes him to itself.

We distinguish the announcements of the soul, its manifestations of its own nature, by the term *Revelation*. These are always attended by the emotion of the sublime. For this communication is an influx of the Divine mind into our mind. It is an ebb of the individual rivulet before the flowing surges of the sea of life. Every distinct apprehension of this central commandment agitates men with awe and delight. A thrill passes through all men at the reception of new truth, or at the performance of a great action, which comes out of the heart of nature. In these communications, the power to see, is not separated from the will to do, but the insight proceeds from obedience, and the obedience proceeds from a joyful perception. Every moment when the individual feels himself invaded by it, is memorable. By the necessity of our constitution, a certain enthusiasm attends the individual's consciousness of that divine presence. The character and duration of this enthusiasm varies with the state of the individual, from an extasy and trance and prophetic inspiration,—which is its rarer appearance,—to the faintest glow of virtuous emotion, in which form it warms, like our household fires, all the families and associations of men, and makes society possible. A certain tendency to insanity has always attended the opening of the religious sense in men, as if they had been "blasted with excess of light."[7] The trances of Socrates, the "union" of Plotinus, the vision of Porphyry, the conversion of Paul, the aurora of Behmen, the convulsions of George Fox and his Quakers,[8] the illumination of Swedenborg, are of this kind. What was in the case of these remarkable persons a ravishment, has, in innumerable instances in common life, been exhibited in less striking manner. Everywhere the history of religion betrays a tendency to enthusiasm. The rapture of the Moravian and Quietist; the opening of the internal sense of the World, in the language of the New Jerusalem Church; the *revival* of the Calvinistic churches; the *experiences* of the Methodists,[9] are varying forms of that shudder of awe and delight with which the individual soul always mingles with the universal soul.

The nature of these revelations is the same; they are perceptions of the absolute law. They are solutions of the soul's own questions. They do not answer the questions which the understanding asks. The soul answers never by words, but by the thing itself that is inquired after.

---

7. In this line from "The Progress of Poesy," the poet Thomas Gray (1716–1771) refers to John Milton, whose blindness is seen as the result of his ecstatic "sublime" vision.
8. See n. 6, p. 18. Fox, see n. 1, p. 39. Plotinus (see n. 1, p. 27) and his disciple Porphyry (233–ca. 301) believed they had been united with God. Jakob Böhme or Boehme (1575–1624), sometimes called the "mystical shoemaker," published his *Aurora, or the Rising Dawn*, in 1612.
9. Originally members of an English Protestant sect who followed John Wesley and his brother Charles (see n. 2, p. 79). The Moravian Brotherhood, a pietistic sect based on the teachings of the fifteenth-century Bohemian reformer John Hus, was revived in Silesia in the early eighteenth century. Many members of the group emigrated to America shortly after and settled in Pennsylvania. The Quietists, followers of the Spanish mystic Miguel Molinos (1640–1696), believed in a direct relationship between the soul and God. New Jerusalem Church, see n. 6, p. 35.

Revelation is the disclosure of the soul. The popular notion of a revelation, is, that it is a telling of fortunes. In past oracles of the soul, the understanding seeks to find answers to sensual questions, and undertakes to tell from God how long men shall exist, what their hands shall do, and who shall be their company, adding names, and dates, and places. But we must pick no locks. We must check this low curiosity. An answer in words is delusive; it is really no answer to the questions you ask. Do not require a description of the countries towards which you sail. The description does not describe them to you, and to-morrow you arrive there, and know them by inhabiting them. Men ask concerning the immortality of the soul, the employments of heaven, the state of the sinner, and so forth. They even dream that Jesus has left replies to precisely these interrogatories. Never a moment did that sublime spirit speak in their *patois*. To truth, justice, love, the attributes of the soul, the idea of immutableness is essentially associated. Jesus, living in these moral sentiments, heedless of sensual fortunes, heeding only the manifestations of these, never made the separation of the idea of duration from the essence of these attributes, nor uttered a syllable concerning the duration of the soul. It was left to his disciples to sever duration from the moral elements and to teach the immortality of the soul as a doctrine, and maintain it by evidences. The moment the doctrine of the immortality is separately taught, man is already fallen. In the flowing of love, in the adoration of humility, there is no question of continuance. No inspired man ever asks this question, or condescends to these evidences. For the soul is true to itself, and the man in whom it is shed abroad, cannot wander from the present, which is infinite, to a future, which would be finite.

These questions which we lust to ask about the future, are a confession of sin. God has no answer for them. No answer in words can reply to a question of things. It is not in an arbitrary "decree of God," but in the nature of man that a veil shuts down on the facts of to-morrow: for the soul will not have us read any other cipher than that of cause and effect. By this veil, which curtains events, it instructs the children of men to live in to-day. The only mode of obtaining an answer to these questions of the senses, is, to forego all low curiosity, and, accepting the tide of being which floats us into the secret of nature, work and live, work and live, and all unawares, the advancing soul has built and forged for itself a new condition, and the question and the answer are one.

By the same fire, vital, consecrating, celestial, which burns until it shall dissolve all things into the waves and surges of an ocean of light, we see and know each other, and what spirit each is of. Who can tell the grounds of his knowledge of the character of the several individuals in his circle of friends? No man. Yet their acts and words do not disappoint him. In that man, though he knew no ill of him, he put no trust. In that other, though they had seldom met, authentic signs had yet passed, to signify that he might be trusted as one who had an interest in his own character. We know each other very well,—which of us has been just to himself, and whether that which we teach or behold, is only an aspiration, or is our honest effort also.

We are all discerners of spirits. That diagnosis lies aloft in our life or unconscious power. The intercourse of society,—its trade, its religion, its friendships, its quarrels,—is one wide, judicial investigation of character. In full court, or in small committee, or confronted face to face, accuser and accused, men offer themselves to be judged. Against their will they exhibit those decisive trifles by which character is read. But who judges? and what? Not our understanding. We do not read them by learning or craft. No; the wisdom of the wise man consists herein, that he does not judge them; he lets them judge themselves, and merely reads and records their own verdict.

By virtue of this inevitable nature, private will is overpowered, and, maugre[1] our efforts, or our imperfections, your genius will speak from you, and mine from me. That which we are, we shall teach, not voluntarily, but involuntarily. Thoughts come into our minds by avenues which we never left open, and thoughts go out of our minds through avenues which we never voluntarily opened. Character teaches over our head. The infallible index of true progress is found in the tone the man takes. Neither his age, nor his breeding, nor company, nor books, nor actions, nor talents, nor all together, can hinder him from being deferential to a higher spirit than his own. If he have not found his home in God, his manners, his forms of speech, the turn of his sentences, the build, shall I say, of all his opinions will involuntarily confess it, let him brave it out how he will. If he have found his centre, the Deity will shine through him, through all the disguises of ignorance, of ungenial temperament, of unfavorable circumstance. The tone of seeking, is one, and the tone of having is another.

The great distinction between teachers sacred or literary, — between poets like Herbert, and poets like Pope, — between philosophers like Spinoza, Kant, and Coleridge, and philosophers like Locke, Paley, Mackintosh, and Stewart,[2] — between men of the world, who are reckoned accomplished talkers, and here and there a fervent mystic, prophesying, half-insane under the infinitude of his thought, — is, that one class speak *from within*, or from experience, as parties and possessors of the fact; and the other class, *from without*, as spectators merely, or perhaps as acquainted with the fact, on the evidence of third persons. It is of no use to preach to me from without. I can do that too easily myself. Jesus speaks always from within, and in a degree that transcends all others. In that, is the miracle. I believe beforehand that it ought so to be. All men stand continually in the expectation of the appearance of such a teacher. But if a man do not speak from within the veil, where the word is one with that it tells of, let him lowly confess it.

The same Omniscience flows into the intellect, and makes what we call genius. Much of the wisdom of the world is not wisdom, and the most illuminated class of men are no doubt superior to literary fame, and are not writers. Among the multitude of scholars and authors, we feel no hallowing presence; we are sensible of a knack and skill rather than of inspiration; they have a light, and know not whence it comes, and call it their own; their talent is some exaggerated faculty, some overgrown member, so that their strength is a disease. In these instances, the intellectual gifts do not make the impression of virtue, but almost of vice; and we feel that a man's talents stand in the way of his advancement in truth. But genius is religious. It is a larger imbibing of the common heart. It is not anomalous, but more like, and not less like other men. There is in all great poets, a wisdom of humanity, which is superior to any talents they exercise. The author, the wit, the partisan, the fine gentleman, does not take

---

1. See n. 9, p. 29.
2. Sir James Mackintosh (1765–1832) and Dugald Stewart (1753–1828), Scottish rationalist philosophers. Herbert, see n. 6, p. 30. Pope, see n. 9, p. 67. Baruch Spinoza (1632–1677), Dutch philosopher generally regarded as a Pantheist, hardly qualifies as a "fervent mystic," since his *Ethics* (1677) is geometrical in its rationality and offers the "intellectual love of God" as the highest good. Kant, see n. 8, p. 35. Coleridge, see n. 2, p. 31. Locke, see n. 7, p. 59. William Paley (1743–1805), a Deist who became famous for comparing God to a clockmaker.

place of the man. Humanity shines in Homer, in Chaucer, in Spenser, in Shak-speare, in Milton.[3] They are content with truth. They use the positive degree. They seem frigid and phlegmatic to those who have been spiced with the fran-tic passion and violent coloring of inferior, but popular writers. For, they are poets by the free course which they allow to the informing soul, which through their eyes beholds again, and blesses the things which it hath made. The soul is superior to its knowledge; wiser than any of its works. The great poet makes us feel our own wealth, and then we think less of his compositions. His best communication to our mind, is, to teach us to despise all he has done. Shaks-peare carries us to such a lofty strain of intelligent activity, as to suggest a wealth which beggars his own; and we then feel that the splendid works which he has created, and which in other hours, we extol as a sort of self-existent poetry, take no stronger hold of real nature than the shadow of a passing traveller on the rock. The inspiration which uttered itself in Hamlet and Lear, could utter things as good from day to day, forever. Why then should I make account of Hamlet and Lear, as if we had not the soul from which they fell as syllables from the tongue?

This energy does not descend into individual life, on any other condition than entire possession. It comes to the lowly and simple; it comes to whomso-ever will put off what is foreign and proud; it comes as insight; it comes as seren-ity and grandeur. When we see those whom it inhabits, we are apprized of new degrees of greatness. From that inspiration the man comes back with a changed tone. He does not talk with men, with an eye to their opinion. He tries them. It requires of us to be plain and true. The vain traveller attempts to embellish his life by quoting my Lord, and the Prince, and the Countess, who thus said or did to *him*. The ambitious vulgar, show you their spoons, and brooches, and rings, and preserve their cards and compliments. The more cultivated, in their ac-count of their own experience, cull out the pleasing poetic circumstance, — the visit to Rome, the man of genius they saw, the brilliant friend they know; still further on, perhaps, the gorgeous landscape, the mountain lights, the moun-tain thoughts, they enjoyed yesterday, — and so seek to throw a romantic color over their life. But the soul that ascends to worship the great God, is plain and true; has no rose-color, no fine friends, no chivalry, no adventures; does not want admiration; dwells in the hour that now is, in the earnest experience of the common day, — by reason of the present moment and the mere trifle having be-come porous to thought, and bibulous of the sea of light.

Converse with a mind that is grandly simple, and literature looks like word-catching. The simplest utterances are worthiest to be written, yet are they so cheap, and so things of course, that in the infinite riches of the soul, it is like gathering a few pebbles off the ground, or bottling a little air in a phial, when the whole earth, and the whole atmosphere are ours. Nothing can pass there, or make you one of the circle, but the casting aside your trappings, and dealing man to man in naked truth, plain confession and omniscient affirmation.

Souls, such as these, treat you as gods would; walk as gods in the earth, ac-cepting without any admiration, your wit, your bounty, your virtue even, — say rather your act of duty, for your virtue they own as their proper blood, royal as

3. See n. 2, p. 6. Homer, see n. 8, p. 88. Chaucer, see n. 9, p. 60. Edmund Spenser (1552?–1599), English poet known chiefly for his allegorical epic romance *The Faerie Queene* (1590–96). His other works in-clude the pastoral *Shepeardes Calendar* (1579) and the lyrical marriage poem *Epithalamion* (1595). See also "Shakspeare" (p. 247).

themselves, and over-royal, and the father of the gods. But what rebuke their plain fraternal bearing casts on the mutual flattery with which authors solace each other, and wound themselves! These flatter not. I do not wonder that these men go to see Cromwell, and Christina, and Charles II., and James I., and the Grand Turk.[4] For they are in their own elevation, the fellows of kings, and must feel the servile tone of conversation in the world. They must always be a godsend to princes, for they confront them, a king to a king, without ducking or concession, and give a high nature the refreshment and satisfaction of resistance, of plain humanity, of even companionship, and of new ideas. They leave them wiser and superior men. Souls like these make us feel that sincerity is more excellent than flattery. Deal so plainly with man and woman, as to constrain the utmost sincerity, and destroy all hope of trifling with you. It is the highest compliment you can pay. Their "highest praising," said Milton, "is not flattery, and their plainest advice is a kind of praising."[5]

Ineffable is the union of man and God in every act of the soul. The simplest person, who in his integrity worships God, becomes God; yet forever and ever the influx of this better and universal self is new and unsearchable. It inspires awe and astonishment. How dear, how soothing to man, arises the idea of God, peopling the lonely place, effacing the scars of our mistakes and disappointments! When we have broken our god of tradition, and ceased from our god of rhetoric, then may God fire the heart with his presence. It is the doubling of the heart itself, nay, the infinite enlargement of the heart with a power of growth to a new infinity on every side. It inspires in man an infallible trust. He has not the conviction, but the sight that the best is the true, and may in that thought easily dismiss all particular uncertainties and fears, and adjourn to the sure revelation of time, the solution of his private riddles. He is sure that his welfare is dear to the heart of being. In the presence of law to his mind, he is overflowed with a reliance so universal, that it sweeps away all cherished hopes and the most stable projects of mortal condition in its flood. He believes that he cannot escape from his good. The things that are really for thee, gravitate to thee. You are running to seek your friend. Let your feet run, but your mind need not. If you do not find him, will you not acquiesce that it is best you should not find him? for there is a power, which, as it is in you, is in him also, and could therefore very well bring you together, if it were for the best. You are preparing with eagerness to go and render a service to which your talent and your taste invite you, the love of men, and the hope of fame. Has it not occurred to you, that you have no right to go, unless you are equally willing to be prevented from going? O believe, as thou livest, that every sound that is spoken over the round world, which thou oughtest to hear, will vibrate on thine ear. Every proverb, every book, every by-word that belongs to thee for aid or comfort, shall surely come home through open or winding passages. Every friend whom not thy fantastic will, but the great and tender heart in thee craveth, shall lock

---

4. Probably Suleiman the Magnificent, who reigned from 1520 to 1566. Oliver Cromwell (1599–1658) displaced the monarchy and established a Puritan Commonwealth in England, serving as the dictatorial lord protector (1653–58). His son Richard (1626–1712) succeeded him briefly as lord protector (1658–59) but was dismissed in 1659. Christina (1626–1689), queen of Sweden (r. 1632–54), patron of learning and the arts, who unexpectedly abdicated her throne, embraced Roman Catholicism, and spent much of the rest of her life in Rome. Charles II, see n. 2, p. 33. James I (1566–1625), king of England (1603–25) and of Scotland as James VI (1568–1625). The son of Mary Queen of Scots, he succeeded the heirless Elizabeth I as the first Stuart king of England. His belief in the divine right of kings and his attempts to keep peace with Spain created resentment in Parliament that led to the English Civil War. He sponsored the King James Bible.
5. Cf. Milton *Areopagitica*, paragraph 4.

thee in his embrace. And this, because the heart in thee is the heart of all; not a valve, not a wall, not an intersection is there anywhere in nature, but one blood rolls uninterruptedly, an endless circulation through all men, as the water of the globe is all one sea, and, truly seen, its tide is one.

Let man then learn the revelation of all nature, and all thought to his heart; this, namely; that the Highest dwells with him; that the sources of nature are in his own mind, if the sentiment of duty is there. But if he would know what the great God speaketh, he must 'go into his closet and shut the door,'[6] as Jesus said. God will not make himself manifest to cowards. He must greatly listen to himself, withdrawing himself from all the accents of other men's devotion. Even their prayers are hurtful to him, until he have made his own. Our religion vulgarly stands on numbers of believers. Whenever the appeal is made,—no matter how indirectly,—to numbers, proclamation is then and there made, that religion is not. He that finds God a sweet, enveloping thought to him, never counts his company. When I sit in that presence, who shall dare to come in? When I rest in perfect humility, when I burn with pure love,—what can Calvin or Swedenborg say?

It makes no difference whether the appeal is to numbers or to one. The faith that stands on authority is not faith. The reliance on authority, measures the decline of religion, the withdrawal of the soul. The position men have given to Jesus, now for many centuries of history, is a position of authority. It characterizes themselves. It cannot alter the eternal facts. Great is the soul, and plain. It is no flatterer, it is no follower; it never appeals from itself. It believes in itself. Before the immense possibilities of man, all mere experience, all past biography, however spotless and sainted, shrinks away. Before that heaven which our presentiments foreshow us, we cannot easily praise any form of life we have seen or read of. We not only affirm that we have few great men, but absolutely speaking, that we have none; that we have no history, no record of any character or mode of living, that entirely contents us. The saints and demigods whom history worships, we are constrained to accept with a grain of allowance. Though in our lonely hours, we draw a new strength out of their memory, yet pressed on our attention, as they are by the thoughtless and customary, they fatigue and invade. The soul gives itself alone, original, and pure, to the Lonely, Original and Pure, who, on that condition, gladly inhabits, leads, and speaks through it. Then is it glad, young, and nimble. It is not wise, but it sees through all things. It is not called religious, but it is innocent. It calls the light its own, and feels that the grass grows, and the stone falls by a law inferior to, and dependent on its nature. Behold, it saith, I am born into the great, the universal mind. I the imperfect, adore my own Perfect. I am somehow receptive of the great soul, and thereby I do overlook the sun and the stars, and feel them to be the fair accidents and effects which change and pass. More and more the surges of everlasting nature enter into me, and I become public and human in my regards and actions. So come I to live in thoughts, and act with energies which are immortal. Thus revering the soul, and learning, as the ancient said, that "its beauty is immense,"[7] man will come to see that the world is the perennial miracle which the soul worketh, and be less astonished at particular wonders; he will learn that there is no profane history; that all history is sacred; that the universe

6. Cf. Matthew 6.6.
7. From Plotinus.

is represented in an atom, in a moment of time. He will weave no longer a spotted life of shreds and patches,[8] but he will live with a divine unity. He will cease from what is base and frivolous in his life, and be content with all places and with any service he can render. He will calmly front the morrow in the negligency of that trust which carries God with it, and so hath already the whole future in the bottom of the heart.

Circles

> Nature centres into balls,
> And her proud ephemerals,
> Fast to surface and outside,
> Scan the profile of the sphere;
> Knew they what that signified,
> A new genesis were here.[1]

The eye is the first circle; the horizon which it forms is the second; and throughout nature this primary figure is repeated without end. It is the highest emblem in the cipher[2] of the world. St. Augustine described the nature of God as a circle whose centre was everywhere, and its circumference nowhere.[3] We are all our lifetime reading the copious sense of this first of forms. One moral we have already deduced in considering the circular or compensatory[4] character of every human action. Another analogy we shall now trace; that every action admits of being outdone. Our life is an apprenticeship to the truth, that around every circle another can be drawn; that there is no end in nature, but every end is a beginning; that there is always another dawn risen on mid-noon, and under every deep a lower deep opens.[5]

This fact, as far as it symbolizes the moral fact of the Unattainable, the flying Perfect, around which the hands of man can never meet, at once the inspirer and the condemner of every success, may conveniently serve us to connect many illustrations of human power in every department.

There are no fixtures in nature. The universe is fluid and volatile. Permanence is but a word of degrees. Our globe seen by God, is a transparent law, not a mass of facts. The law dissolves the fact and holds it fluid. Our culture is the predominance of an idea which draws after it this train of cities and institutions. Let us rise into another idea: they will disappear. The Greek sculpture is all melted away, as if it had been statues of ice: here and there a solitary figure or fragment remaining, as we see flecks and scraps of snow left in cold dells and mountain clefts, in June and July. For, the genius that created it, creates now somewhat else. The Greek letters last a little longer, but are already passing under the same sentence, and tumbling into the inevitable pit which the cre-

---

8. Cf. *Hamlet* 3.4.102.
1. The epigraph, Emerson's own composition, was added in the 1847 version of *Essays*. As Stephen Whicher points out, "proud ephemerals" refers to human beings ("proud," though creatures of a day).
2. Here both "circle" (as in cipher, or zero) and "puzzle" (as in a code that must be broken). Emblem, see n. 5, p. 12.
3. As the editors of CW point out (2.253–54), the phrase has not been located in St. Augustine's writings, though various other authors Emerson read use similar language. St. Augustine, bishop of Hippo (345–430).
4. Cf. Emerson's essay "Compensation" (p. 137).
5. Cf. Milton, *Paradise Lost* 5.310–11.

ation of new thought opens for all that is old. The new continents are built out of the ruins of an old planet: the new races fed out of the decomposition of the foregoing. New arts destroy the old. See the investment of capital in aqueducts, made useless by hydraulics; fortifications, by gunpowder; roads and canals, by railways; sails, by steam; steam by electricity.

You admire this tower of granite, weathering the hurts of so many ages. Yet a little waving hand built this huge wall, and that which builds, is better than that which is built. The hand that built, can topple it down much faster. Better than the hand, and nimbler, was the invisible thought which wrought through it, and thus ever behind the coarse effect, is a fine cause, which, being narrowly seen, is itself the effect of a finer cause. Every thing looks permanent until its secret is known. A rich estate appears to women a firm and lasting fact; to a merchant, one easily created out of any materials, and easily lost. An orchard, good tillage, good grounds, seem a fixture, like a gold mine, or a river, to a citizen; but to a large farmer, not much more fixed than the state of the crop. Nature looks provokingly stable and secular,[6] but it has a cause like all the rest; and when once I comprehend that, will these fields stretch so immovably wide, these leaves hang so individually considerable? Permanence is a word of degrees. Every thing is medial. Moons are no more bounds to spiritual power than bat-balls.

The key to every man is his thought. Sturdy and defying though he look, he has a helm which he obeys, which is, the idea after which all his facts are classified. He can only be reformed by showing him a new idea which commands his own. The life of man is a self-evolving circle, which, from a ring imperceptibly small, rushes on all sides outwards to new and larger circles, and that without end. The extent to which this generation of circles, wheel without wheel will go, depends on the force or truth of the individual soul. For, it is the inert effort of each thought having formed itself into a circular wave of circumstance,—as, for instance, an empire, rules of an art, a local usage, a religious rite,—to heap itself on that ridge, and to solidify, and hem in the life. But if the soul is quick and strong, it bursts over that boundary on all sides, and expands another orbit on the great deep, which also runs up into a high wave, with attempt again to stop and to bind. But the heart refuses to be imprisoned; in its first and narrowest pulses, it already tends outward with a vast force, and to immense and innumerable expansions.

Every ultimate fact is only the first of a new series. Every general law only a particular fact of some more general law presently to disclose itself. There is no outside, no enclosing wall, no circumference to us. The man finishes his story,—how good! how final! how it puts a new face on all things! He fills the sky. Lo! on the other side rises also a man, and draws a circle around the circle we had just pronounced the outline of the sphere. Then already is our first speaker, not man, but only a first speaker. His only redress is forthwith to draw a circle outside of his antagonist. And so men do by themselves. The result of to-day which haunts the mind and cannot be escaped, will presently be abridged into a word, and the principle that seemed to explain nature, will itself be included as one example of a bolder generalization. In the thought of to-morrow there is a power to upheave all thy creed, all the creeds, all the literatures of the nations, and marshal thee to a heaven which no epic dream

6. Lasting throughout centuries.

has yet depicted. Every man is not so much a workman in the world, as he is a suggestion of that he should be. Men walk as prophecies of the next age.

Step by step we scale this mysterious ladder: the steps are actions; the new prospect is power. Every several result is threatened and judged by that which follows. Every one seems to be contradicted by the new; it is only limited by the new. The new statement is always hated by the old, and, to those dwelling in the old, comes like an abyss of skepticism. But the eye soon gets wonted to it, for the eye and it are effects of one cause; then its innocency and benefit appear, and, presently, all its energy spent, it pales and dwindles before the revelation of the new hour.

Fear not the new generalization. Does the fact look crass and material, threatening to degrade thy theory of spirit? Resist it not; it goes to refine and raise thy theory of matter just as much.

There are no fixtures to men, if we appeal to consciousness. Every man supposes himself not to be fully understood; and if there is any truth in him, if he rests at last on the divine soul, I see not how it can be otherwise. The last chamber, the last closet, he must feel, was never opened; there is always a residuum unknown, unanalyzable. That is, every man believes that he has a greater possibility.

Our moods do not believe in each other. To-day, I am full of thoughts, and can write what I please. I see no reason why I should not have the same thought, the same power of expression to-morrow. What I write, whilst I write it, seems the most natural thing in the world: but, yesterday, I saw a dreary vacuity in this direction in which now I see so much; and a month hence, I doubt not, I shall wonder who he was that wrote so many continuous pages. Alas for this infirm faith, this will not strenuous, this vast ebb of a vast flow! I am God in nature; I am a weed by the wall.

The continual effort to raise himself above himself, to work a pitch above his last height, betrays itself in a man's relations. We thirst for approbation, yet cannot forgive the approver. The sweet of nature is love; yet if I have a friend, I am tormented by my imperfections. The love of me accuses the other party. If he were high enough to slight me, then could I love him, and rise by my affection to new heights. A man's growth is seen in the successive choirs of his friends. For every friend whom he loses for truth, he gains a better. I thought, as I walked in the woods and mused on my friends, why should I play with them this game of idolatry? I know and see too well, when not voluntarily blind, the speedy limits of persons called high and worthy. Rich, noble, and great they are by the liberality of our speech, but truth is sad. O blessed Spirit, whom I forsake for these, they are not thou! Every personal consideration that we allow, costs us heavenly state. We sell the thrones of angels for a short and turbulent pleasure.

How often must we learn this lesson? Men cease to interest us when we find their limitations. The only sin is limitation. As soon as you once come up with a man's limitations, it is all over with him. Has he talents? has he enterprises? has he knowledge? it boots not. Infinitely alluring and attractive was he to you yesterday, a great hope, a sea to swim in; now, you have found his shores, found it a pond, and you care not if you never see it again.

Each new step we take in thought reconciles twenty seemingly discordant facts, as expressions of one law. Aristotle and Plato[7] are reckoned the respective

---

7. See n. 4, p. 15. Aristotle (see n. 4, p. 47) was in fact a student of Plato.

heads of two schools. A wise man will see that Aristotle Platonizes. By going one step farther back in thought, discordant opinions are reconciled, by being seen to be two extremes of one principle, and we can never go so far back as to preclude a still higher vision.

Beware when the great God lets loose a thinker on this planet. Then all things are at risk. It is as when a conflagration has broken out in a great city, and no man knows what is safe, or where it will end. There is not a piece of science, but its flank may be turned to-morrow; there is not any literary reputation, not the so-called eternal names of fame, that may not be revised and condemned. The very hopes of man, the thoughts of his heart, the religion of nations, the manners and morals of mankind, are all at the mercy of a new generalization. Generalization is always a new influx of the divinity into the mind. Hence the thrill that attends it.

Valor consists in the power of self-recovery, so that a man cannot have his flank turned, cannot be outgeneralled, but put him where you will, he stands. This can only be by his preferring truth to his past apprehension of truth; and his alert acceptance of it from whatever quarter; the intrepid conviction that his laws, his relations to society, his Christianity, his world, may at any time be superseded and decease.

There are degrees in idealism. We learn first to play with it academically, as the magnet was once a toy. Then we see in the heyday of youth and poetry that it may be true, that it is true in gleams and fragments. Then, its countenance waxes stern and grand, and we see that it must be true. It now shows itself ethical and practical. We learn that God IS; that he is in me; and that all things are shadows of him. The idealism of Berkeley[8] is only a crude statement of the idealism of Jesus, and that, again, is a crude statement of the fact that all nature is the rapid efflux of goodness executing and organizing itself. Much more obviously is history and the state of the world at any one time, directly dependent on the intellectual classification then existing in the minds of men. The things which are dear to men at this hour, are so on account of the ideas which have emerged on their mental horizon, and which cause the present order of things as a tree bears its apple. A new degree of culture would instantly revolutionize the entire system of human pursuits.

Conversation is a game of circles. In conversation we pluck up the *termini* which bound the common of silence on every side. The parties are not to be judged by the spirit they partake and even express under this Pentecost.[9] To-morrow they will have receded from this high-water mark. To-morrow you shall find them stooping under the old packsaddles. Yet let us enjoy the cloven flame[1] whilst it glows on our walls. When each new speaker strikes a new light, emancipates us from the oppression of the last speaker, to oppress us with the greatness and exclusiveness of his own thought, then yields us to another redeemer, we seem to recover our rights, to become men. O what truths profound and executable only in ages and orbs, are supposed in the announcement of every truth! In common hours, society sits cold and statuesque. We all stand waiting, empty,—knowing, possibly, that we can be full, surrounded by mighty symbols

8. See n. 1, p. 43.
9. The descent of the Holy Spirit; used loosely here to refer to the spirit that moves individuals in conversation.
1. See n. 1, p. 135.

which are not symbols to us, but prose and trivial toys. Then cometh the god, and converts the statues into fiery men, and by a flash of his eye burns up the veil[2] which shrouded all things, and the meaning of the very furniture, of cup and saucer, of chair and clock and tester, is manifest. The facts which loomed so large in the fogs of yesterday,—property, climate, breeding, personal beauty, and the like, have strangely changed their proportions. All that we reckoned settled, shakes and rattles; and literatures, cities, climates, religions, leave their foundations, and dance before our eyes. And yet here again see the swift circumscription. Good as is discourse, silence is better, and shames it. The length of the discourse indicates the distance of thought betwixt the speaker and the hearer. If they were at a perfect understanding in any part, no words would be necessary thereon. If at one in all parts, no words would be suffered.

Literature is a point outside of our hodiernal[3] circle, through which a new one may be described. The use of literature is to afford us a platform whence we may command a view of our present life, a purchase[4] by which we may move it. We fill ourselves with ancient learning; install ourselves the best we can in Greek, in Punic,[5] in Roman houses, only that we may wiselier see French, English, and American houses and modes of living. In like manner, we see literature best from the midst of wild nature, or from the din of affairs, or from a high religion. The field cannot be well seen from within the field. The astronomer must have his diameter of the earth's orbit as a base to find the parallax[6] of any star.

Therefore, we value the poet. All the argument, and all the wisdom, is not in the encyclopedia, or the treatise on metaphysics, or the Body of Divinity, but in the sonnet or the play. In my daily work I incline to repeat my old steps, and do not believe in remedial force, in the power of change and reform. But some Petrarch or Ariosto,[7] filled with the new wine of his imagination, writes me an ode, or a brisk romance, full of daring thought and action. He smites and arouses me with his shrill tones, breaks up my whole chain of habits, and I open my eye on my own possibilities. He claps wings to the sides of all the solid old lumber of the world, and I am capable once more of choosing a straight path in theory and practice.

We have the same need to command a view of the religion of the world. We can never see Christianity from the catechism:—from the pastures, from a boat in the pond, from amidst the songs of wood-birds, we possibly may. Cleansed by the elemental light and wind, steeped in the sea of beautiful forms which the field offers us, we may chance to cast a right glance back upon biography. Christianity is rightly dear to the best of mankind; yet was there never a young philosopher whose breeding had fallen into the Christian church, by whom that brave text of Paul's, was not specially prized:—"Then shall also the Son be subject unto Him who put all things under him, that God may be all in all."[8] Let the claims and virtues of persons be never so great and welcome, the

---

2. Emerson punningly suggests that the burning up of the "veil" provides a new revelation (literally, the removal of the veil).
3. Daily.
4. Device, such as a tackle or lever, used to obtain mechanical advantage. Emerson is building here on Archimedes' famous sentence, "Give me a place to stand and I will move the world."
5. Of or relating to ancient Carthage, its inhabitants, or their language.
6. See n. 6, p. 127.
7. See n. 1, p. 116. Francesco Petrarch (1304–1374), Italian poet, scholar, and humanist who was a towering figure in the early Renaissance.
8. Cf. 1 Corinthians 15.28.

instinct of man presses eagerly onward to the impersonal and illimitable, and gladly arms itself against the dogmatism of bigots with this generous word, out of the book itself.

The natural world may be conceived of as a system of concentric circles, and we now and then detect in nature slight dislocations, which apprize us that this surface on which we now stand, is not fixed, but sliding. These manifold tenacious qualities, this chemistry and vegetation, these metals and animals, which seem to stand there for their own sake, are means and methods only, — are words of God, and as fugitive as other words. Has the naturalist or chemist learned his craft, who has explored the gravity of atoms and the elective affinities,[9] who has not yet discerned the deeper law whereof this is only a partial or approximate statement, namely, that like draws to like; and that the goods which belong to you, gravitate to you, and need not be pursued with pains and cost? Yet is that statement approximate also, and not final. Omnipresence is a higher fact. Not through subtle, subterranean channels, need friend and fact be drawn to their counterpart, but, rightly considered, these things proceed from the eternal generation of the soul. Cause and effect are two sides of one fact.

The same law of eternal procession ranges all that we call the virtues, and extinguishes each in the light of a better. The great man will not be prudent in the popular sense; all his prudence will be so much deduction from his grandeur. But it behoves each to see when he sacrifices prudence, to what god he devotes it; if to ease and pleasure, he had better be prudent still: if to a great trust, he can well spare his mule and panniers, who has a winged chariot instead. Geoffrey draws on his boots to go through the woods, that his feet may be safer from the bite of snakes; Aaron never thinks of such a peril. In many years, neither is harmed by such an accident. Yet it seems to me that with every precaution you take against such an evil, you put yourself into the power of the evil. I suppose that the highest prudence is the lowest prudence. Is this too sudden a rushing from the centre to the verge of our orbit? Think how many times we shall fall back into pitiful calculations, before we take up our rest in the great sentiment, or make the verge of to-day the new centre. Besides, your bravest sentiment is familiar to the humblest men. The poor and the low have their way of expressing the last facts of philosophy as well as you. "Blessed be nothing," and "the worse things are, the better they are," are proverbs which express the transcendentalism of common life.

One man's justice is another's injustice; one man's beauty, another's ugliness; one man's wisdom, another's folly; as one beholds the same objects from a higher point. One man thinks justice consists in paying debts, and has no measure in his abhorrence of another who is very remiss in this duty, and makes the creditor wait tediously. But that second man has his own way of looking at things; asks himself, which debt must I pay first, the debt to the rich, or the debt to the poor? the debt of money, or the debt of thought to mankind, of genius to nature? For you, O broker, there is no other principle but arithmetic. For me, commerce is of trivial import; love, faith, truth of character, the aspiration of man, these are sacred: nor can I detach one duty, like you, from all other duties, and concentrate my forces mechanically on the payment of moneys. Let

---

9. A term from chemistry referring to the fact that when certain compounds are mixed, their component elements change partners, so to speak. Emerson would have been familiar with the concept from Goethe's (see n. 6, p. 42) use of the term as a title for his 1809 novel.

me live onward: you shall find that, though slower, the progress of my character will liquidate all these debts without injustice to higher claims. If a man
should dedicate himself to the payment of notes, would not this be injustice?
Does he owe no debt but money? And are all claims on him to be postponed to
a landlord's or a banker's?

There is no virtue which is final; all are initial. The virtues of society are
vices of the saint. The terror of reform is the discovery that we must cast away
our virtues, or what we have always esteemed such, into the same pit that has
consumed our grosser vices.

> "Forgive his crimes, forgive his virtues too,
> Those smaller faults, half converts to the right."[1]

It is the highest power of divine moments that they abolish our contritions
also. I accuse myself of sloth and unprofitableness, day by day; but when these
waves of God flow into me, I no longer reckon lost time. I no longer poorly compute my possible achievement by what remains to me of the month or the year;
for these moments confer a sort of omnipresence and omnipotence, which asks
nothing of duration, but sees that the energy of the mind is commensurate with
the work to be done, without time.

And thus, O circular philosopher, I hear some reader exclaim, you have
arrived at a fine pyrrhonism,[2] at an equivalence and indifferency of all actions,
and would fain teach us, that, *if we are true,* forsooth, our crimes may be lively
stones out of which we shall construct the temple of the true God.[3]

I am not careful to justify myself. I own I am gladdened by seeing the predominance of the saccharine principle throughout vegetable nature, and not less
by beholding in morals that unrestrained inundation of the principle of good into
every chink and hole that selfishness has left open, yea, into selfishness and sin itself; so that no evil is pure, nor hell itself without its extreme satisfactions. But lest
I should mislead any when I have my own head, and obey my whims, let me remind the reader that I am only an experimenter. Do not set the least value on what
I do, or the least discredit on what I do not, as if I pretended to settle anything as
true or false. I unsettle all things. No facts are to me sacred; none are profane; I
simply experiment, an endless seeker, with no Past at my back.

Yet this incessant movement and progression, which all things partake,
could never become sensible[4] to us, but by contrast to some principle of fixture
or stability in the soul. Whilst the eternal generation of circles proceeds, the
eternal generator abides. That central life is somewhat superior to creation, superior to knowledge and thought, and contains all its circles. Forever it labors
to create a life and thought as large and excellent as itself, suggesting to our
thought a certain development, as if that which is made, instructs how to make
a better.

Thus there is no sleep, no pause, no preservation, but all things renew, ger-
minate, and spring. Why should we import rags and relics into the new hour?
Nature abhors the old, and old age seems the only disease: all others run into

---

1. Cf. Edward Young, *The Complaint; or, Night Thoughts* (1742–46), 9.2316–17. Young (1683–1765), a
   cleric, poet, and critic, is usually linked with the graveyard school of eighteenth-century writers.
2. See n. 5, p. 152.
3. Cf. 1 Peter 2.5.
4. Able to be sensed.

this one. We call it by many names,—fever, intemperance, insanity, stupidity, and crime: they are all forms of old age: they are rest, conservatism, appropriation, inertia, not newness, not the way onward. We grizzle every day. I see no need of it. Whilst we converse with what is above us, we do not grow old, but grow young. Infancy, youth, receptive, aspiring, with religious eye looking upward, counts itself nothing, and abandons itself to the instruction flowing from all sides. But the man and woman of seventy assume to know all, they have outlived their hope, they renounce aspiration, accept the actual for the necessary, and talk down to the young. Let them then become organs of the Holy Ghost; let them be lovers; let them behold truth; and their eyes are uplifted, their wrinkles smoothed, they are perfumed again with hope and power. This old age ought not to creep on a human mind. In nature, every moment is new; the past is always swallowed and forgotten; the coming only is sacred. Nothing is secure but life, transition, the energizing spirit. No love can be bound by oath or covenant to secure it against a higher love. No truth so sublime but it may be trivial tomorrow in the light of new thoughts. People wish to be settled: only as far as they are unsettled, is there any hope for them.

Life is a series of surprises. We do not guess to-day the mood, the pleasure, the power of to-morrow, when we are building up our being. Of lower states,—of acts of routine and sense,—we can tell somewhat; but the masterpieces of God, the total growths and universal movements of the soul, he hideth; they are incalculable. I can know that truth is divine and helpful, but how it shall help me, I can have no guess, for, *so to be* is the sole inlet of *so to know*. The new position of the advancing man has all the powers of the old, yet has them all new. It carries in its bosom all the energies of the past, yet is itself an exhalation of the morning. I cast away in this new moment all my once hoarded knowledge, as vacant and vain. Now, for the first time, seem I to know any thing rightly. The simplest words,—we do not know what they mean, except when we love and aspire.

The difference between talents and character is adroitness to keep the old and trodden round, and power and courage to make a new road to new and better goals. Character makes an over-powering present, a cheerful, determined hour, which fortifies all the company, by making them see that much is possible and excellent, that was not thought of. Character dulls the impression of particular events. When we see the conqueror, we do not think much of any one battle or success. We see that we had exaggerated the difficulty. It was easy to him. The great man is not convulsible or tormentable; events pass over him without much impression. People say sometimes, 'See what I have overcome; see how cheerful I am; see how completely I have triumphed over these black events.' Not if they still remind me of the black event. True conquest is the causing the calamity to fade and disappear as an early cloud of insignificant result in a history so large and advancing.

The one thing which we seek with insatiable desire, is to forget ourselves, to be surprised out of our propriety, to lose our sempiternal[5] memory, and to do something without knowing how or why; in short, to draw a new circle. Nothing great was ever achieved without enthusiasm.[6] The way of life is wonderful: it is by abandonment. The great moments of history are the facilities of perfor-

---

5. Never-ending.
6. Emerson takes this sentence from Coleridge's *The Statesman's Manual*, paragraph 18. Coleridge goes on to say: "For what is enthusiasm but the oblivion and swallowing up of self in an object dearer than self, or in an idea more vivid." See CW 2.255.

mance through the strength of ideas, as the works of genius and religion. "A man," said Oliver Cromwell,[7] "never rises so high as when he knows not whither he is going." Dreams and drunkenness, the use of opium and alcohol are the semblance and counterfeit of this oracular genius, and hence their dangerous attraction for men. For the like reason, they ask the aid of wild passions, as in gaming and war, to ape in some manner these flames and generosities of the heart.

7. See n. 4, p. 172.

From Essays: Second Series

The Poet[1]

A moody child and wildly wise,
Pursued the game with joyful eyes,
Which chose, like meteors, their way,
And rived the dark with private ray:
They overleapt the horizon's edge,
Searched with Apollo's privilege;
Through man, and woman, and sea, and star,
Saw the dance of nature forward far;
Through worlds, and races, and terms, and times,
Saw musical order, and pairing rhymes.

Olympian bards who sung
  Divine ideas below,
Which always find us young,
  And always keep us so.

Those who are esteemed umpires of taste, are often persons who have acquired some knowledge of admired pictures or sculptures, and have an inclination for whatever is elegant; but if you inquire whether they are beautiful souls, and whether their own acts are like fair pictures, you learn that they are selfish and sensual. Their cultivation is local, as if you should rub a log of dry wood in one spot to produce fire, all the rest remaining cold. Their knowledge of the fine arts is some study of rules and particulars, or some limited judgment of color or form, which is exercised for amusement or for show. It is a proof of the shallowness of the doctrine of beauty, as it lies in the minds of our amateurs, that men seem to have lost the perception of the instant dependence of form upon soul. There is no doctrine of forms in our philosophy. We were put into our bodies, as fire is put into a pan, to be carried about; but there is no accurate adjustment between the spirit and the organ, much less is the latter the germination of the former. So in regard to other forms, the intellectual men do not believe in any essential dependence of the material world on thought and volition. Theologians think it a pretty air-castle to talk of the spiritual meaning of a ship or a cloud, of a city or a contract, but they prefer to come again to the solid ground of historical evidence; and even the poets are contented with a civil and conformed manner of living, and to write poems from the fancy,[2] at a safe distance from their own experience. But the highest minds of the world have never ceased to explore the double meaning, or, shall I say, the quadruple, or the centuple, or much more manifold mean-

---

1. This essay is best read as a companion piece to "Experience," which follows it in *Essays: Second Series.* The essay is from a lecture Emerson delivered, but Emerson substantially recast the lecture as he was writing "Experience" after the sudden death of his firstborn son, Waldo, of scarlatina at age five. See also "Threnody," p. 455.
2. See n. 2, p. 116.

ing, of every sensuous fact: Orpheus, Empedocles, Heraclitus, Plato, Plutarch, Dante, Swedenborg,[3] and the masters of sculpture, picture, and poetry. For we are not pans and barrows, nor even porters of the fire and torch-bearers, but children of the fire,[4] made of it, and only the same divinity transmuted, and at two or three removes when we know least about it. And this hidden truth, that the fountains whence all this river of Time, and its creatures, floweth, are intrinsically ideal and beautiful, draws us to the consideration of the nature and functions of the Poet, or the man of Beauty, to the means and materials he uses, and to the general aspect of the art in the present time.

The breadth of the problem is great, for the poet is representative. He stands among partial men for the complete man, and apprises us not of his wealth, but of the commonwealth. The young man reveres men of genius, because, to speak truly, they are more himself than he is. They receive of the soul as he also receives, but they more. Nature enhances her beauty to the eye of loving men, from their belief that the poet is beholding her shows at the same time. He is isolated among his contemporaries, by truth and by his art, but with this consolation in his pursuits, that they will draw all men sooner or later. For all men live by truth, and stand in need of expression. In love, in art, in avarice, in politics, in labor, in games, we study to utter our painful secret. The man is only half himself, the other half is his expression.

Notwithstanding this necessity to be published, adequate expression is rare. I know not how it is that we need an interpreter; but the great majority of men seem to be minors, who have not yet come into possession of their own, or mutes, who cannot report the conversation they have had with nature. There is no man who does not anticipate a supersensual utility in the sun, and stars, earth, and water. These stand and wait to render him a peculiar service.[5] But there is some obstruction, or some excess of phlegm[6] in our constitution, which does not suffer them to yield the due effect. Too feeble fall the impressions of nature on us to make us artists. Every touch should thrill. Every man should be so much an artist, that he could report in conversation what had befallen him. Yet, in our experience, the rays or appulses have sufficient force to arrive at the senses, but not enough to reach the quick, and compel the reproduction of themselves in speech. The poet is the person in whom these powers are in balance, the man without impediment, who sees and handles that which others dream of, traverses the whole scale of experience, and is representative of man, in virtue of being the largest power to receive and to impart.

For the Universe has three children, born at one time, which reappear, under different names, in every system of thought, whether they be called cause, operation, and effect; or, more poetically, Jove, Pluto, Neptune; or, theologically, the Father, the Spirit, and the Son; but which we will call here, the Knower, the Doer, and the Sayer.[7] These stand respectively for the love of truth, for the love

3. See n. 6, p. 35. Orpheus, see n. 7, p. 53. Empedocles, see n. 3, p. 84. Heraclitus, see n. 3, p. 89. Plato, see n. 4, p. 15. Plutarch, see n. 7, p. 57. Dante Alighieri (1265–1321), greatest of Italian poets, author of the *Divine Comedy*.
4. The doctrine of the immanence of spirit—the universal mind—imaged in the doctrine of Heracleitus that Fire is the ultimate ground of the world. [Edward Waldo Emerson's note].
5. Cf. Milton, sonnet 19.14: "They also serve who only stand and wait."
6. In the old theory of the four humors, the hot and wet humor that causes people to be "phlegmatic." The other humors are blood, choler (bile), and black bile (causing "melancholy"). See the opening of "Experience," p. 198.
7. Emerson's formulation here is clarified by a passage from the Cambridge Platonist Ralph Cudworth (1617–1688) in his *True Intellectual System of the Universe*: "Jupiter, who, together with Neptune and

of good, and for the love of beauty. These three are equal. Each is that which he is essentially, so that he cannot be surmounted or analyzed, and each of these three has the power of the others latent in him, and his own patent.[8]

The poet is the sayer, the namer, and represents beauty. He is a sovereign, and stands on the centre. For the world is not painted, or adorned, but is from the beginning beautiful; and God has not made some beautiful things, but Beauty is the creator of the universe. Therefore the poet is not any permissive potentate, but is emperor in his own right. Criticism is infested with a cant of materialism, which assumes that manual skill and activity is the first merit of all men, and disparages such as say and do not, overlooking the fact, that some men, namely, poets, are natural sayers, sent into the world to the end of expression, and confounds them with those whose province is action, but who quit it to imitate the sayers. But Homer's words are as costly and admirable to Homer, as Agamemnon's victories are to Agamemnon. The poet does not wait for the hero or the sage, but, as they act and think primarily, so he writes primarily what will and must be spoken, reckoning the others, though primaries also, yet, in respect to him, secondaries and servants; as sitters or models in the studio of a painter, or as assistants who bring building materials to an architect.

For poetry was all written before time was, and whenever we are so finely organized that we can penetrate into that region where the air is music, we hear those primal warblings, and attempt to write them down, but we lose ever and anon a word, or a verse, and substitute something of our own, and thus miswrite the poem. The men of more delicate ear write down these cadences more faithfully, and these transcripts, though imperfect, become the songs of the nations. For nature is as truly beautiful as it is good, or as it is reasonable, and must as much appear, as it must be done, or be known. Words and deeds are quite different[9] modes of the divine energy. Words are also actions, and actions are a kind of words.

The sign and credentials of the poet are, that he announces that which no man foretold. He is the true and only doctor;[1] he knows and tells; he is the only teller of news, for he was present and privy to the appearance which he describes. He is a beholder of ideas, and an utterer of the necessary and causal. For we do not speak now of men of poetical talents, or of industry and skill in metre, but of the true poet. I took part in a conversation the other day, concerning a recent writer of lyrics, a man of subtle mind, whose head appeared to be a music-box of delicate tunes and rhythms, and whose skill, and command of language, we could not sufficiently praise. But when the question arose, whether he was not only a lyrist, but a poet, we were obliged to confess that he is plainly a contemporary, not an eternal man. He does not stand out of our low limitations, like a Chimborazo[2] under the line, running up from the torrid base through all the climates of the globe, with belts of the herbage of every latitude on its high and mottled sides; but this genius is the landscape-garden of a modern house, adorned with fountains and statues, with well-bred men and women standing and sitting in the walks and terraces. We hear, through all the varied music, the ground-tone

---

Pluto, is said to have been the son of Saturn, was not the supreme Deity . . . but only the Aether [ether], as Neptune was the sea, and Pluto the earth. . . . These three . . . were not really three distinct substantial beings, but only so many names for the Supreme God." See CW 3.172. Cf. "The Transcendentalist," p. 102.

8. Exposed to sight.
9. Not different.
1. In the Latin sense, a teacher. Also alludes to Apollo (see n. 4, p. 73).
2. The highest mountain in Ecuador, located just south of the Equator (*under the line*).

of conventional life. Our poets are men of talents who sing, and not the children of music. The argument is secondary, the finish of the verses is primary.

For it is not metres, but a metre-making argument, that makes a poem,— a thought so passionate and alive, that, like the spirit of a plant or an animal, it has an architecture of its own, and adorns nature with a new thing. The thought and the form are equal in the order of time, but in the order of genesis the thought is prior to the form. The poet has a new thought: he has a whole new experience to unfold; he will tell us how it was with him, and all men will be the richer in his fortune. For, the experience of each new age requires a new confession, and the world seems always waiting for its poet. I remember, when I was young, how much I was moved one morning by tidings that genius had appeared in a youth who sat near me at table. He had left his work, and gone rambling none knew whither, and had written hundreds of lines, but could not tell whether that which was in him was therein told: he could tell nothing but that all was changed,—man, beast, heaven, earth, and sea. How gladly we listened! how credulous! Society seemed to be compromised. We sat in the aurora of a sunrise which was to put out all the stars. Boston seemed to be at twice the distance it had the night before, or was much farther than that. Rome,—what was Rome? Plutarch and Shakspeare were in the yellow leaf,[3] and Homer no more should be heard of. It is much to know that poetry has been written this very day, under this very roof, by your side. What! that wonderful spirit has not expired! these stony moments are still sparkling and animated! I had fancied that the oracles were all silent, and nature had spent her fires, and behold! all night, from every pore, these fine auroras[4] have been streaming. Every one has some interest in the advent of the poet, and no one knows how much it may concern him. We know that the secret of the world is profound, but who or what shall be our interpreter, we know not. A mountain ramble, a new style of face, a new person, may put the key into our hands. Of course, the value of genius to us is in the veracity of its report. Talent may frolic and juggle; genius realizes and adds. Mankind, in good earnest, have arrived so far in understanding themselves and their work, that the foremost watchman on the peak announces his news. It is the truest word ever spoken, and the phrase will be the fittest, most musical, and the unerring voice of the world for that time.

All that we call sacred history attests that the birth of a poet is the principal event in chronology. Man, never so often deceived, still watches for the arrival of a brother who can hold him steady to a truth, until he has made it his own. With what joy I begin to read a poem, which I confide in as an inspiration! And now my chains are to be broken; I shall mount above these clouds and opaque airs in which I live,—opaque, though they seem transparent,—and from the heaven of truth I shall see and comprehend my relations. That will reconcile me to life, and renovate nature, to see trifles animated by a tendency, and to know what I am doing. Life will no more be a noise; now I shall see men and women, and know the signs by which they may be discerned from fools and satans. This day shall be better than my birthday: then I became an animal: now I am invited into the science of the real. Such is the hope, but the fruition is postponed. Oftener it falls, that this winged man, who will carry me into the heaven, whirls me into mists, then leaps and frisks about with me as it were from cloud to cloud, still affirming

3. Cf. Shakespeare, *Macbeth* 5.3.23.
4. Northern lights.

that he is bound heavenward; and I, being myself a novice, am slow in perceiving that he does not know the way into the heavens, and is merely bent that I should admire his skill to rise, like a fowl or a flying fish, a little way from the ground or the water; but the all-piercing, all-feeding, and ocular air of heaven, that man shall never inhabit. I tumble down again soon into my old nooks, and lead the life of exaggerations as before, and have lost some faith in the possibility of any guide who can lead me thither where I would be.

But leaving these victims of vanity, let us, with new hope, observe how nature, by worthier impulses, has ensured the poet's fidelity to his office of announcement and affirming, namely, by the beauty of things, which becomes a new, and higher beauty, when expressed. Nature offers all her creatures to him as a picture-language. Being used as a type,[5] a second wonderful value appears in the object, far better than its old value, as the carpenter's stretched cord, if you hold your ear close enough, is musical in the breeze. "Things more excellent than every image," says Jamblichus,[6] "are expressed through images." Things admit of being used as symbols, because nature is a symbol, in the whole, and in every part. Every line we can draw in the sand, has expression; and there is no body without its spirit or genius. All form is an effect of character; all condition, of the quality of the life; all harmony, of health; (and, for this reason, a perception of beauty should be sympathetic, or proper only to the good.) The beautiful rests on the foundations of the necessary. The soul makes the body, as the wise Spenser teaches: —

> "So every spirit, as it is most pure,
> And hath in it the more of heavenly light,
> So it the fairer body doth procure
> To habit in, and it more fairly dight,
> With cheerful grace and amiable sight.
> For, of the soul, the body form doth take,
> For soul is form, and doth the body make."[7]

Here we find ourselves, suddenly, not in a critical speculation, but in a holy place, and should go very warily and reverently. We stand before the secret of the world, there where Being passes into Appearance, and Unity into Variety.

The Universe is the externization of the soul. Wherever the life is, that bursts into appearance around it. Our science is sensual, and therefore superficial. The earth, and the heavenly bodies, physics, and chemistry, we sensually treat, as if they were self-existent; but these are the retinue of that Being we have. "The mighty heaven," said Proclus, "exhibits, in its transfigurations, clear images of the splendor of intellectual perceptions; being moved in conjunction with the unapparent periods of intellectual natures." Therefore, science always goes abreast with the just elevation of the man, keeping step with religion and metaphysics; or, the state of science is an index of our self-knowledge. Since everything in nature answers to a moral power, if any phenomenon remains brute and dark, it is because the corresponding faculty in the observer is not yet active.

---

5. See n. 4, p. 15.
6. Or Iamblichus (ca. fourth century B.C.E.), a pupil of Porphyry (see n. 8, p. 168) and the teacher of Greek Neoplatonic philosopher Proclus (ca. 410–485). The sentence has not been located in Iamblichus's writings.
7. Spenser (see n. 3, p. 171), "An Hymne in Honour of Beautie," lines 127–33.

No wonder, then, if these waters be so deep, that we hover over them with a religious regard. The beauty of the fable proves the importance of the sense; to the poet, and to all others; or, if you please, every man is so far a poet as to be susceptible of these enchantments of nature: for all men have the thoughts whereof the universe is the celebration. I find that the fascination resides in the symbol. Who loves nature? Who does not? Is it only poets, and men of leisure and cultivation, who live with her? No; but also hunters, farmers, grooms, and butchers, though they express their affection in their choice of life, and not in their choice of words. The writer wonders what the coachman or the hunter values in riding, in horses, and dogs. It is not superficial qualities. When you talk with him, he holds these at as slight a rate as you. His worship is sympathetic; he has no definitions, but he is commanded in nature, by the living power which he feels to be there present. No imitation, or playing of these things, would content him; he loves the earnest of the north wind, of rain, of stone, and wood, and iron. A beauty not explicable, is dearer than a beauty which we can see to the end of. It is nature the symbol, nature certifying the supernatural, body overflowed by life, which he worships, with coarse, but sincere rites.

The inwardness, and mystery, of this attachment, drive men of every class to the use of emblems. The schools of poets, and philosophers, are not more intoxicated with their symbols, than the populace with theirs. In our political parties, compute the power of badges and emblems. See the huge wooden ball[8] rolled by successive ardent crowds from Baltimore to Bunker hill! In the political processions, Lowell goes in a loom, and Lynn in a shoe, and Salem in a ship.[9] Witness the cider-barrel, the log-cabin, the hickory-stick, the palmetto,[1] and all the cognizances of party. See the power of national emblems. Some stars, lilies, leopards, a crescent, a lion, an eagle, or other figure, which came into credit God knows how, on an old rag of bunting, blowing in the wind, on a fort, at the ends of the earth, shall make the blood tingle under the rudest, or the most conventional exterior. The people fancy they hate poetry, and they are all poets and mystics!

Beyond this universality of the symbolic language, we are apprised of the divineness of this superior use of things, whereby the world is a temple, whose walls are covered with emblems, pictures, and commandments of the Deity, in this, that there is no fact in nature which does not carry the whole sense of nature; and the distinctions which we make in events, and in affairs, of low and high, honest and base, disappear when nature is used as a symbol. Thought makes everything fit for use. The vocabulary of an omniscient man would embrace words and images excluded from polite conversation. What would be base, or even obscene, to the obscene, becomes illustrious, spoken in a new connexion of thought. The piety of the Hebrew prophets purges their grossness. The circumcision is an example of the power of poetry to raise the low and offensive. Small and mean things serve as well as great symbols. The meaner the type by which a law is expressed, the more pungent it is, and the more lasting in the memories of men: just as we choose the smallest box, or case, in which any needful utensil can be carried. Bare lists of words are found suggestive, to an imaginative and excited mind; as it is related of Lord Chatham,[2] that he was accustomed to read in Bailey's Dic-

8. Emerson saw the "great ball" in Concord in 1840 as the Whigs pushed the candidacy of William Henry Harrison.
9. These three Massachusetts towns symbolized their chief industries, as Emerson indicates.
1. A tree; refers to South Carolina. The *cider barrel* and *log cabin* were associated with the Harrison campaign. *Hickory-stick*: symbolizes Andrew Jackson.
2. See n. 5, p. 87.

tionary, when he was preparing to speak in Parliament. The poorest experience is rich enough for all the purposes of expressing thought. Why covet a knowledge of new facts? Day and night, house and garden, a few books, a few actions, serve us as well as would all trades and all spectacles. We are far from having exhausted the significance of the few symbols we use. We can come to use them yet with a terrible simplicity. It does not need that a poem should be long. Every word was once a poem. Every new relation is a new word. Also, we use defects and deformities to a sacred purpose, so expressing our sense that the evils of the world are such only to the evil eye. In the old mythology, mythologists observe, defects are ascribed to divine natures, as lameness to Vulcan, blindness to Cupid,[3] and the like, to signify exuberances.

For, as it is dislocation and detachment from the life of God, that makes things ugly, the poet, who re-attaches things to nature and the Whole, — re-attaching even artificial things, and violations of nature, to nature, by a deeper insight, — disposes very easily of the most disagreeable facts. Readers of poetry see the factory-village, and the railway, and fancy that the poetry of the landscape is broken up by these; for these works of art are not yet consecrated in their reading; but the poet sees them fall within the great Order not less than the bee-hive, or the spider's geometrical web. Nature adopts them very fast into her vital circles, and the gliding train of cars she loves like her own. Besides, in a centred mind, it signifies nothing how many mechanical inventions you exhibit. Though you add millions, and never so surprising, the fact remains unalterable, by many or by few particulars; as no mountain is of any appreciable height to break the curve of the sphere. A shrewd country-boy goes to the city for the first time, and the complacent citizen is not satisfied with his little wonder. It is not that he does not see all the fine houses, and know that he never saw such before, but he disposes of them as easily as the poet finds place for the railway. The chief value of the new fact, is to enhance the great and constant fact of Life, which can dwarf any and every circumstance, and to which the belt of wampum, and the commerce of America, are alike.

The world being thus put under the mind for verb and noun, the poet is he who can articulate it. For, though life is great, and fascinates, and absorbs, — and though all men are intelligent of the symbols through which it is named, — yet they cannot originally use them. We are symbols, and inhabit symbols; workmen, work, and tools, words and things, birth and death, all are emblems; but we sympathize with the symbols, and, being infatuated with the economical uses of things, we do not know that they are thoughts. The poet, by an ulterior intellectual perception, gives them a power which makes their old use forgotten, and puts eyes, and a tongue, into every dumb and inanimate object. He perceives the thought's independence of the symbol, the stability of the thought, the accidency and fugacity of the symbol. As the eyes of Lyncæus[4] were said to see through the earth, so the poet turns the world to glass, and shows us all things in their right series and procession. For, through that better perception, he stands one step nearer to things, and sees the flowing or metamorphosis; perceives that thought is multiform; that within the form of every creature

---

3. In Roman mythology son of Venus, the god of love, is famously depicted as being blind. Vulcan, in Roman mythology, son of Jupiter and Juno, god of fire and metalworking; he is depicted as being lame, perhaps because he was identified with the Greek god Hephaestus, whose mother, Hera, threw him out of heaven, permanently laming him in the process.
4. In Greek mythology, one of the Argonauts who traveled with Jason in search of the Golden Fleece; he was said to be so sharp-sighted that he could see through the earth.

is a force impelling it to ascend into a higher form; and, following with his eyes the life, uses the forms which express that life, and so his speech flows with the flowing of nature. All the facts of the animal economy,—sex, nutriment, gestation, birth, growth—are symbols of the passage of the world into the soul of man, to suffer there a change, and reappear a new and higher fact. He uses forms according to the life, and not according to the form. This is true science. The poet alone knows astronomy, chemistry, vegetation, and animation, for he does not stop at these facts, but employs them as signs. He knows why the plain, or meadow of space, was strown with these flowers we call suns, and moons, and stars; why the great deep is adorned with animals, with men, and gods; for, in every word he speaks he rides on them as the horses of thought.

By virtue of this science the poet is the Namer, or Language-maker, naming things sometimes after their appearance, sometimes after their essence, and giving to every one its own name and not another's, thereby rejoicing the intellect, which delights in detachment or boundary. The poets made all the words, and therefore language is the archives of history, and, if we must say it, a sort of tomb of the muses. For, though the origin of most of our words is forgotten, each word was at first a stroke of genius, and obtained currency, because for the moment it symbolized the world to the first speaker and to the hearer. The etymologist finds the deadest word to have been once a brilliant picture. Language is fossil poetry. As the limestone of the continent consists of infinite masses of the shells of animalcules, so language is made up of images, or tropes, which now, in their secondary use, have long ceased to remind us of their poetic origin. But the poet names the thing because he sees it, or comes one step nearer to it than any other. This expression, or naming, is not art, but a second nature, grown out of the first, as a leaf out of a tree. What we call nature, is a certain self-regulated motion, or change; and nature does all things by her own hands, and does not leave another to baptize her, but baptizes herself; and this through the metamorphosis again. I remember that a certain poet described it to me thus:

Genius is the activity which repairs the decays of things, whether wholly or partly of a material and finite kind. Nature, through all her kingdoms, insures herself. Nobody cares for planting the poor fungus: so she shakes down from the gills of one agaric countless spores, any one of which, being preserved, transmits new billions of spores to-morrow or next day. The new agaric[5] of this hour has a chance which the old one had not. This atom of seed is thrown into a new place, not subject to the accidents which destroyed its parent two rods off. She makes a man; and having brought him to ripe age, she will no longer run the risk of losing this wonder at a blow, but she detaches from him a new self, that the kind may be safe from accidents to which the individual is exposed. So when the soul of the poet has come to ripeness of thought, she detaches and sends away from it its poems or songs,—a fearless, sleepless, deathless progeny, which is not exposed to the accidents of the weary kingdom of time: a fearless, vivacious offspring, clad with wings (such was the virtue of the soul out of which they came), which carry them fast and far, and infix them irrecoverably into the hearts of men. These wings are the beauty of the poet's soul. The songs, thus flying immortal from their mortal parent, are pursued by clamorous flights of censures, which swarm in far greater numbers, and threaten to devour them; but these last are not winged. At the end

5. *Agaricus campestris*, the Latin nomenclature for the common meadow mushroom, or champignon.

of a very short leap they fall plump down, and rot, having received from the souls out of which they came no beautiful wings. But the melodies of the poet ascend, and leap, and pierce into the deeps of infinite time.

So far the bard taught me, using his freer speech. But nature has a higher end, in the production of new individuals, than security, namely, *ascension*, or, the passage of the soul into higher forms. I knew, in my younger days, the sculptor who made the statue of the youth which stands in the public garden. He was, as I remember, unable to tell, directly, what made him happy, or unhappy, but by wonderful indirections he could tell. He rose one day, according to his habit, before the dawn, and saw the morning break, grand as the eternity out of which it came, and, for many days after, he strove to express this tranquillity, and, lo! his chisel had fashioned out of marble the form of a beautiful youth, Phosphor,[6] whose aspect is such, that, it is said, all persons who look on it become silent. The poet also resigns himself to his mood, and that thought which agitated him is expressed, but *alter idem*,[7] in a manner totally new. The expression is organic, or, the new type which things themselves take when liberated. As, in the sun, objects paint their images on the retina of the eye, so they, sharing the aspiration of the whole universe, tend to paint a far more delicate copy of their essence in his mind. Like the metamorphosis of things into higher organic forms, is their change into melodies. Over everything stands its dæmon, or soul, and, as the form of the thing is reflected by the eye, so the soul of the thing is reflected by a melody. The sea, the mountain-ridge, Niagara, and every flower-bed, pre-exist, or super-exist, in pre-cantations, which sail like odors in the air, and when any man goes by with an ear sufficiently fine, he overhears them, and endeavors to write down the notes, without diluting or depraving them. And herein is the legitimation of criticism, in the mind's faith, that the poems are a corrupt version of some text in nature, with which they ought to be made to tally. A rhyme in one of our sonnets should not be less pleasing than the iterated nodes of a sea-shell, or the resembling difference of a group of flowers. The pairing of the birds is an idyl, not tedious as our idyls are; a tempest is a rough ode without falsehood or rant; a summer, with its harvest sown, reaped, and stored, is an epic song, subordinating how many admirably executed parts. Why should not the symmetry and truth that modulate these, glide into our spirits, and we participate the invention of nature?

This insight, which expresses itself by what is called Imagination,[8] is a very high sort of seeing, which does not come by study, but by the intellect being where and what it sees, by sharing the path, or circuit of things through forms, and so making them translucid to others. The path of things is silent. Will they suffer a speaker to go with them? A spy they will not suffer; a lover, a poet, is the transcendency of their own nature, — him they will suffer. The condition of true naming, on the poet's part, is his resigning himself to the divine *aura* which breathes through forms, and accompanying that.

It is a secret which every intellectual man quickly learns, that, beyond the energy of his possessed and conscious intellect, he is capable of a new energy (as of an intellect doubled on itself), by abandonment to the nature of things;

6. Or Lucifer, "bearer of light," sometimes identified with the morning star.
7. Another yet the same (Latin).
8. For the Coleridgean definition see n. 2, p. 116.

that, beside his privacy of power as an individual man, there is a great public power, on which he can draw, by unlocking, at all risks, his human doors, and suffering the ethereal tides to roll and circulate through him: then he is caught up into the life of the Universe, his speech is thunder, his thought is law, and his words are universally intelligible as the plants and animals. The poet knows that he speaks adequately, then only when he speaks somewhat wildly, or, "with the flower of the mind;"[9] not with the intellect, used as an organ, but with the intellect released from all service, and suffered to take its direction from its celestial life; or, as the ancients were wont to express themselves, not with intellect alone, but with the intellect inebriated by nectar.[1] As the traveller who has lost his way, throws his reins on his horse's neck, and trusts to the instinct of the animal to find his road, so must we do with the divine animal who carries us through this world. For if in any manner we can stimulate this instinct, new passages are opened for us into nature, the mind flows into and through things hardest and highest, and the metamorphosis is possible.

This is the reason why bards love wine, mead, narcotics, coffee, tea, opium, the fumes of sandal-wood and tobacco, or whatever other procurers of animal exhilaration. All men avail themselves of such means as they can, to add this extraordinary power to their normal powers; and to this end they prize conversation, music, pictures, sculpture, dancing, theatres, travelling, war, mobs, fires, gaming, politics, or love, or science, or animal intoxication, which are several coarser or finer quasi-mechanical substitutes for the true nectar, which is the ravishment of the intellect by coming nearer to the fact. These are auxiliaries to the centrifugal tendency of a man, to his passage out into free space, and they help him to escape the custody of that body in which he is pent up, and of that jail-yard of individual relations in which he is enclosed. Hence a great number of such as were professionally expressors of Beauty, as painters, poets, musicians, and actors, have been more than others wont to lead a life of pleasure and indulgence; all but the few who received the true nectar; and, as it was a spurious mode of attaining freedom, as it was an emancipation not into the heavens, but into the freedom of baser places, they were punished for that advantage they won, by a dissipation and deterioration. But never can any advantage be taken of nature by a trick. The spirit of the world, the great calm presence of the creator, comes not forth to the sorceries of opium or of wine. The sublime vision comes to the pure and simple soul in a clean and chaste body. That is not an inspiration which we owe to narcotics, but some counterfeit excitement and fury. Milton says, that the lyric poet may drink wine and live generously, but the epic poet, he who shall sing of the gods, and their descent unto men, must drink water out of a wooden bowl. For poetry is not 'Devil's wine,' but God's wine.[2] It is with this as it is with toys. We fill the hands and nurseries of our children with all manner of dolls, drums, and horses, withdrawing their eyes from the plain face and sufficing objects of nature, the sun, and moon, the animals, the water, and stones, which should be their toys. So the poet's habit of living should be set on a key so low, that the common influences should delight him. His cheerfulness should be the gift of the sunlight; the air should suffice for his inspiration, and he should be tipsy with water.[3] That

---

9. The phrase is associated with Zoroaster (see n. 9, p. 78). There is an explanation in CW 3.176.
1. In Greek and Roman mythology, the drink of the gods. See also Emerson's poem "Bacchus," p. 452.
2. The whole passage from John Milton's Latin Sixth Elegy is given in translation by Edward Waldo Emerson.
3. This phrase is the likely inspiration for Emily Dickinson's "Inebriate of Air—am I— / And Debauchee of Dew—" (Poem #214).

spirit which suffices quiet hearts, which seems to come forth to such from every dry knoll of sere grass, from every pine-stump, and half-imbedded stone, on which the dull March sun shines, comes forth to the poor and hungry, and such as are of simple taste. If thou fill thy brain with Boston and New York, with fashion and covetousness, and wilt stimulate thy jaded senses with wine and French coffee, thou shalt find no radiance of wisdom in the lonely waste of the pinewoods.

If the imagination intoxicates the poet, it is not inactive in other men. The metamorphosis excites in the beholder an emotion of joy. The use of symbols has a certain power of emancipation and exhilaration for all men. We seem to be touched by a wand, which makes us dance and run about happily, like children. We are like persons who come out of a cave or cellar into the open air. This is the effect on us of tropes, fables, oracles, and all poetic forms. Poets are thus liberating gods. Men have really got a new sense, and found within their world, another world, or nest of worlds; for, the metamorphosis once seen, we divine that it does not stop. I will not now consider how much this makes the charm of algebra and the mathematics, which also have their tropes, but it is felt in every definition; as, when Aristotle defines *space* to be an immovable vessel, in which things are contained; — or, when Plato defines a *line* to be a flowing point; or, *figure* to be a bound of solid; and many the like. What a joyful sense of freedom we have, when Vitruvius[4] announces the old opinion of artists, that no architect can build any house well, who does not know something of anatomy. When Socrates, in Charmides,[5] tells us that the soul is cured of its maladies by certain incantations, and that these incantations are beautiful reasons, from which temperance is generated in souls; when Plato calls the world an animal; and Timæus affirms that the plants also are animals; or affirms a man to be a heavenly tree, growing with his root, which is his head, upward; and, as George Chapman,[6] following him, writes, —

> "So in our tree of man, whose nervie root
> Springs in his top;"

when Orpheus speaks of hoariness as "that white flower which marks extreme old age;" when Proclus calls the universe the statue of the intellect; when Chaucer,[7] in his praise of 'Gentilesse,' compares good blood in mean condition to fire, which, though carried to the darkest house betwixt this and the mount of Caucasus, will yet hold its natural office, and burn as bright as if twenty thousand men did it behold; when John[8] saw, in the apocalypse, the ruin of the world through evil, and the stars fall from heaven, as the figtree casteth her untimely fruit; when Æsop[9] reports the whole catalogue of common daily relations through the masquerade of birds and beasts; — we take the cheerful hint of the

---

4. See n. 6, p. 42.
5. Socrates is the principal figure in Plato's early dialogue *Charmides*.
6. English dramatist and writer (1559?–1634), noted for his translations of Homer's *Iliad* (1598–1611) and *Odyssey* (1616). Emerson quotes lines 132–33 of the "Epistle Dedicatory" to Chapman's *Iliad*. Stephen Whicher quotes as follows from *Timaeus* 90: "We declare that God has given to each of us, as his daemon, that kind of soul which is housed in the top of our body and which raises us — seeing that we are not an earthly but a heavenly plant — up from earth towards our kindred in the heaven. And herein we speak most truly; for it is by suspending our head and root from that region whence the substance of our soul first came that the Divine Power keeps upright our whole body."
7. See n. 9, p. 60. For his "praise of 'Gentilesse,'" cf. "The Wife of Bath's Tale," lines 1132–45.
8. See Revelation 6.13.
9. See n. 1, p. 115.

immortality of our essence, and its versatile habit and escapes, as when the gypsies say of themselves, "it is in vain to hang them, they cannot die."

The poets are thus liberating gods. The ancient British bards had for the title of their order, "Those who are free throughout the world." They are free, and they make free. An imaginative book renders us much more service at first, by stimulating us through its tropes, than afterward, when we arrive at the precise sense of the author. I think nothing is of any value in books, excepting the transcendental and extraordinary. If a man is inflamed and carried away by his thought, to that degree that he forgets the authors and the public, and heeds only this one dream, which holds him like an insanity, let me read his paper, and you may have all the arguments and histories and criticism. All the value which attaches to Pythagoras, Paracelsus, Cornelius Agrippa, Cardan, Kepler, Swedenborg, Schelling, Oken,[1] or any other who introduces questionable facts into his cosmogony, as angels, devils, magic, astrology, palmistry, mesmerism, and so on, is the certificate we have of departure from routine, and that here is a new witness. That also is the best success in conversation, the magic of liberty, which puts the world, like a ball, in our hands. How cheap even the liberty then seems; how mean to study, when an emotion communicates to the intellect the power to sap and upheave nature: how great the perspective! nations, times, systems, enter and disappear, like threads in tapestry of large figure and many colors; dream delivers us to dream, and, while the drunkenness lasts, we will sell our bed, our philosophy, our religion, in our opulence.

There is good reason why we should prize this liberation. The fate of the poor shepherd, who, blinded and lost in the snowstorm, perishes in a drift within a few feet of his cottage door, is an emblem of the state of man. On the brink of the waters of life and truth, we are miserably dying. The inaccessibleness of every thought but that we are in, is wonderful. What if you come near to it, — you are as remote, when you are nearest, as when you are farthest. Every thought is also a prison; every heaven is also a prison. Therefore we love the poet, the inventor, who in any form, whether in an ode, or in an action, or in looks and behavior, has yielded us a new thought. He unlocks our chains, and admits us to a new scene.

This emancipation is dear to all men, and the power to impart it, as it must come from greater depth and scope of thought, is a measure of intellect. Therefore all books of the imagination endure, all which ascend to that truth, that the writer sees nature beneath him, and uses it as his exponent. Every verse or sentence, possessing this virtue, will take care of its own immortality. The religions of the world are the ejaculations[2] of a few imaginative men.

But the quality of the imagination is to flow, and not to freeze. The poet did not stop at the color, or the form, but read their meaning; neither may he rest in this meaning, but he makes the same objects exponents of his new thought. Here is the difference betwixt the poet and the mystic, that the last

---

1. Lorenz Oken (1779–1851), "a follower of Schelling and a founder of what was once called 'transcendental anatomy'" (CW 3.179), nourished various occult beliefs. Pythagoras, see n. 6, p. 38. Paracelsus (1493–1541), German-Swiss alchemist and physician who introduced the concept of disease to medicine. Cornelius Heinrich Agrippa (1486–1535), German thinker whose "dog had a devil tied to his collar"; CW 3.179. Jerome Cardan, Girolamo Cardano (1501–1576), Italian philosopher and mathematician, who "gives much information concerning invisible devils." Cf. Emerson's remarks on p. 338. Johannes Kepler (1571–1630), German astronomer and mathematician, who — according to Robert Burton (1577–1640) as quoted by Emerson — "believed Saturn and Jupiter to be inhabited by superhuman beings." Considered the founder of modern astronomy, he formulated three laws to clarify the theory that the planets revolve around the sun. Swedenborg (see n. 6, p. 35) was given to all sorts of visions. Friedrich Wilhelm Joseph von Schelling (1775–1854), German Romantic philosopher, apparently went through a period of mysticism.
2. See n. 8, p. 72.

nails a symbol to one sense, which was a true sense for a moment, but soon becomes old and false. For all symbols are fluxional;[3] all language is vehicular and transitive, and is good, as ferries and horses are, for conveyance, not as farms and houses are, for homestead. Mysticism consists in the mistake of an accidental and individual symbol for an universal one. The morning-redness happens to be the favorite meteor to the eyes of Jacob Behmen,[4] and comes to stand to him for truth and faith; and he believes should stand for the same realities to every reader. But the first reader prefers as naturally the symbol of a mother and child, or a gardener and his bulb, or a jeweller polishing a gem. Either of these, or of a myriad more, are equally good to the person to whom they are significant. Only they must be held lightly, and be very willingly translated into the equivalent terms which others use. And the mystic must be steadily told,—All that you say is just as true without the tedious use of that symbol as with it. Let us have a little algebra, instead of this trite rhetoric,—universal signs, instead of these village symbols,—and we shall both be gainers. The history of hierarchies seems to show, that all religious error consisted in making the symbol too stark and solid, and, at last, nothing but an excess of the organ of language.

Swedenborg, of all men in the recent ages, stands eminently for the translator of nature into thought. I do not know the man in history to whom things stood so uniformly for words. Before him the metamorphosis continually plays. Everything on which his eye rests, obeys the impulses of moral nature. The figs become grapes whilst he eats them. When some of his angels affirmed a truth, the laurel twig which they held blossomed in their hands. The noise which, at a distance, appeared like gnashing and thumping, on coming nearer was found to be the voice of disputants. The men, in one of his visions, seen in heavenly light, appeared like dragons, and seemed in darkness; but, to each other, they appeared as men, and, when the light from heaven shone into their cabin, they complained of the darkness, and were compelled to shut the window that they might see.

There was this perception in him, which makes the poet or seer an object of awe and terror, namely, that the same man, or society of men, may wear one aspect to themselves and their companions, and a different aspect to higher intelligences. Certain priests, whom he describes as conversing very learnedly together, appeared to the children, who were at some distance, like dead horses; and many the like misappearances. And instantly the mind inquires, whether these fishes under the bridge, yonder oxen in the pasture, those dogs in the yard, are immutably fishes, oxen, and dogs, or only so appear to me, and perchance to themselves appear upright men; and whether I appear as a man to all eyes. The Bramins and Pythagoras[5] propounded the same question, and if any poet has witnessed the transformation, he doubtless found it in harmony with various experiences. We have all seen changes as considerable in wheat and caterpillars. He is the poet, and shall draw us with love and terror, who sees, through the flowing vest, the firm nature, and can declare it.

I look in vain for the poet whom I describe. We do not, with sufficient plainness, or sufficient profoundness, address ourselves to life, nor dare we chaunt our own times and social circumstance. If we filled the day with bravery, we should not shrink from celebrating it. Time and nature yield us many gifts, but not yet

3. Continually changing.
4. See n. 8, p. 168.
5. Emerson alludes to what he understood was the Hindu and Pythagorean belief in metempsychosis or reincarnation.

the timely man, the new religion, the reconciler, whom all things await. Dante's praise is, that he dared to write his autobiography in colossal cipher, or into universality. We have yet had no genius in America, with tyrannous eye, which knew the value of our incomparable materials, and saw, in the barbarism and materialism of the times, another carnival of the same gods whose picture he so much admires in Homer; then in the middle age; then in Calvinism. Banks and tariffs, the newspaper and caucus, methodism and unitarianism, are flat and dull to dull people, but rest on the same foundations of wonder as the town of Troy, and the temple of Delphi, and are as swiftly passing away. Our logrolling, our stumps and their politics, our fisheries, our Negroes, and Indians, our boasts, and our repudiations,[6] the wrath of rogues, and the pusillanimity of honest men, the northern trade, the southern planting, the western clearing, Oregon, and Texas, are yet unsung. Yet America is a poem in our eyes; its ample geography dazzles the imagination, and it will not wait long for metres. If I have not found that excellent combination of gifts in my countrymen which I seek, neither could I aid myself to fix the idea of the poet by reading now and then in Chalmers's[7] collection of five centuries of English poets. These are wits, more than poets, though there have been poets among them. But when we adhere to the ideal of the poet, we have our difficulties even with Milton and Homer. Milton is too literary, and Homer too literal and historical.

But I am not wise enough for a national criticism, and must use the old largeness a little longer, to discharge my errand from the muse to the poet concerning his art.

Art is the path of the creator to his work. The paths, or methods, are ideal and eternal, though few men ever see them, not the artist himself for years, or for a lifetime, unless he come into the conditions. The painter, the sculptor, the composer, the epic rhapsodist, the orator, all partake one desire, namely, to express themselves symmetrically and abundantly, not dwarfishly and fragmentarily. They found or put themselves in certain conditions, as, the painter and sculptor before some impressive human figures; the orator, into the assembly of the people; and the others, in such scenes as each has found exciting to his intellect; and each presently feels the new desire. He hears a voice, he sees a beckoning. Then he is apprised, with wonder, what herds of demons hem him in. He can no more rest; he says, with the old painter, "By God, it is in me, and must go forth of me." He pursues a beauty, half seen, which flies before him. The poet pours out verses in every solitude. Most of the things he says are conventional, no doubt; but by and by he says something which is original and beautiful. That charms him. He would say nothing else but such things. In our way of talking, we say, 'That is yours, this is mine;' but the poet knows well that it is not his; that it is as strange and beautiful to him as to you; he would fain hear the like eloquence at length. Once having tasted this immortal ichor, he cannot have enough of it, and, as an admirable creative power exists in these intellections, it is of the last importance that these things get spoken. What a little of all we know is said! What drops of all the sea of our science are baled up! and by what accident it is that these are exposed, when so many secrets sleep in

6. The practice adopted by some states of repudiating their public debt was also well known, particularly among angry foreign investors, a number of whom—such as Thomas Carlyle—were Emerson's friends. *Boasts:* American boasts, especially in the developing tradition of southwestern humor, were becoming proverbial.

7. Alexander Chalmers (1759–1834), editor of the multivolume collection *The Works of the English Poets, from Chaucer to Cowper* (1810). In this paragraph Emerson seems almost to call for Whitman.

nature! Hence the necessity of speech and song; hence these throbs and heart-beatings in the orator, at the door of the assembly, to the end, namely, that thought may be ejaculated as Logos, or Word.[8]

Doubt not, O poet, but persist. Say, 'It is in me, and shall out.' Stand there, baulked and dumb, stuttering and stammering, hissed and hooted, stand and strive, until, at last, rage draw out of thee that *dream*-power which every night shows thee is thine own; a power transcending all limit and privacy, and by virtue of which a man is the conductor of the whole river of electricity. Nothing walks, or creeps, or grows, or exists, which must not in turn arise and walk before him as exponent of his meaning. Comes he to that power, his genius is no longer exhaustible. All the creatures, by pairs and by tribes, pour into his mind as into a Noah's[9] ark, to come forth again to people a new world. This is like the stock of air for our respiration, or for the combustion of our fireplace, not a measure of gallons, but the entire atmosphere if wanted, And therefore the rich poets, as Homer, Chaucer, Shakspeare, and Raphael,[1] have obviously no limits to their works, except the limits of their lifetime, and resemble a mirror carried through the street, ready to render an image of every created thing.

O poet! a new nobility is conferred in groves and pastures, and not in castles, or by the sword-blade, any longer. The conditions are hard, but equal. Thou shalt leave the world, and know the muse only. Thou shalt not know any longer the times, customs, graces, politics, or opinions of men, but shalt take all from the muse. For the time of towns is tolled from the world by funereal chimes, but in nature the universal hours are counted by succeeding tribes of animals and plants, and by growth of joy on joy. God wills also that thou abdicate a duplex and manifold life, and that thou be content that others speak for thee. Others shall be thy gentlemen, and shall represent all courtesy and worldly life for thee; others shall do the great and resounding actions also. Thou shalt lie close hid with nature, and canst not be afforded to the Capitol or the Exchange.[2] The world is full of renunciations and apprenticeships, and this is thine; thou must pass for a fool and a churl for a long season. This is the screen and sheath in which Pan[3] has protected his well-beloved flower, and thou shalt be known only to thine own, and they shall console thee with tenderest love. And thou shalt not be able to rehearse the names of thy friends in thy verse, for an old shame before the holy ideal. And this is the reward: that the ideal shall be real to thee, and the impressions of the actual world shall fall like summer rain, copious, but not troublesome, to thy invulnerable essence. Thou shalt have the whole land for thy park and manor, the sea for thy bath and navigation, without tax and without envy; the woods and the rivers thou shalt own; and thou shalt possess that wherein others are only tenants and boarders. Thou true land-lord! sea-lord! air-lord! Wherever snow falls, or water flows, or birds fly, wherever day and night meet in twilight, wherever the blue heaven is hung by clouds, or sown with stars, wherever are forms with transparent boundaries, wherever are outlets into celestial space, wherever is danger, and awe, and love, there is Beauty, plenteous as rain, shed for thee, and though

---

8. Cf. John 1.1. The beginning of this sentence in the journal source reads, "hence the oestrum of speech." See *JMN* 9.72.
9. In the Book of Genesis, the patriarch who was chosen by God to build an ark, in which he, his family, and a pair of every animal were saved from the Flood.
1. See n. 3, p. 86.
2. The stock exchange.
3. See n. 1, p. 86. He sometimes is credited with creating "panic" when he appears. This may account for Emerson's associating the poet, Pan's "well-beloved flower," with "awe and terror."

thou shouldst walk the world over, thou shalt not be able to find a condition inopportune or ignoble.

Experience[1]

The lords of life, the lords of life, —
I saw them pass,
In their own guise,
Like and unlike,
Portly and grim,
Use and Surprise,
Surface and Dream,
Succession swift, and spectral Wrong,
Temperament without a tongue,
And the inventor of the game
Omnipresent without name; —
Some to see, some to be guessed,
They marched from east to west:
Little man, least of all,
Among the legs of his guardians tall,
Walked about with puzzled look: —
Him by the hand dear nature took;
Dearest nature, strong and kind,
Whispered, 'Darling, never mind!
Tomorrow they will wear another face,
The founder thou! these are thy race!'

Where do we find ourselves? In a series, of which we do not know the extremes, and believe that it has none. We wake and find ourselves on a stair: there are stairs below us, which we seem to have ascended; there are stairs above us, many a one, which go upward and out of sight. But the Genius[2] which, according to the old belief, stands at the door by which we enter, and gives us the lethe[3] to drink, that we may tell no tales, mixed the cup too strongly, and we cannot shake off the lethargy now at noonday. Sleep lingers all our lifetime about our eyes, as night hovers all day in the boughs of the fir-tree. All things swim and glimmer. Our life is not so much threatened as our perception. Ghostlike we glide through nature, and should not know our place again. Did our birth fall in some fit of indigence and frugality in nature, that she was so sparing of her fire and so liberal of her earth, that it appears to us that we lack the affirmative principle, and though we have health and reason, yet we have no superfluity of spirit for new creation? We have enough to live and bring the year about, but not an ounce to impart or to invest. Ah that our Genius were a little more of a genius! We are like millers on the lower levels of a stream, when the factories above them have exhausted the water. We too fancy that the upper people must have raised their dams.

If any of us knew what we were doing, or where we are going, then when we think we best know! We do not know today whether we are busy or idle. In times when we thought ourselves indolent, we have afterwards discovered, that much was accomplished, and much was begun in us. All our days are so unprofitable

1. See n. 1, p. 183.
2. Presiding spirit.
3. See n. 5, p. 122.

while they pass, that 'tis wonderful where or when we ever got anything of this which we call wisdom, poetry, virtue. We never got it on any dated calendar day. Some heavenly days must have been intercalated somewhere, like those that Hermes won with dice of the Moon, that Osiris might be born.[4] It is said, all martyrdoms looked mean when they were suffered. Every ship is a romantic object, except that we sail in. Embark, and the romance quits our vessel, and hangs on every other sail in the horizon. Our life looks trivial, and we shun to record it. Men seem to have learned of the horizon the art of perpetual retreating and reference. 'Yonder uplands are rich pasturage, and my neighbor has fertile meadow, but my field,' says the querulous farmer, 'only holds the world together.' I quote another man's saying; unluckily, that other withdraws himself in the same way, and quotes me. 'Tis the trick of nature thus to degrade today; a good deal of buzz, and somewhere a result slipped magically in. Every roof is agreeable to the eye, until it is lifted; then we find tragedy and moaning women, and hard-eyed husbands, and deluges of lethe, and the men ask, 'What's the news?' as if the old were so bad. How many individuals can we count in society? how many actions? how many opinions? So much of our time is preparation, so much is routine, and so much retrospect, that the pith of each man's genius contracts itself to a very few hours. The history of literature—take the net result of Tiraboschi, Warton, or Schlegel,[5]—is a sum of very few ideas, and of very few original tales,—all the rest being variation of these. So in this great society wide lying around us, a critical analysis would find very few spontaneous actions. It is almost all custom and gross sense. There are even few opinions, and these seem organic in the speakers, and do not disturb the universal necessity.

What opium is instilled into all disaster! It shows formidable as we approach it, but there is at last no rough rasping friction, but the most slippery sliding surfaces: we fall soft on a thought: *Ate Dea* is gentle,

> "Over men's heads walking aloft,
> With tender feet treading so soft."[6]

People grieve and bemoan themselves, but it is not half so bad with them as they say. There are moods in which we court suffering, in the hope that here, at least, we shall find reality, sharp peaks and edges of truth. But it turns out to be scene-painting and counterfeit. The only thing grief has taught me, is to know how shallow it is. That, like all the rest, plays about the surface, and never introduces me into the reality, for contact with which, we would even pay the costly price of sons and lovers. Was it Boscovich[7] who found out that bodies never come in contact? Well, souls never touch their objects. An innavigable sea washes with

---

4. The editors of CW (3.181) explain as follows: "Plutarch, in 'Of Isis and Osiris,' wrote that the Sun, having discovered Rhea's infidelity with Saturn, 'pronounced a solemn Curse against her . . . that she should not be delivered in any Month or Year.' Hermes, also Rhea's lover, cast dice with the Moon and won 'five new Days' which became the birthdays of the Egyptian gods. On 'the first of these they say *Osiris* was born.'" In Greek mythology, Hermes is the messenger of the gods. Rhea, one of the Titans, is wife and sister of Cronos and mother of Zeus and other Olympians. Osiris, see n. 4, p. 73.

5. August Wilhelm von Schlegel (1767–1845), German scholar who wrote influential criticism, translated several Shakespearean works, and composed poetry. He also edited a literary magazine with his brother Friedrich (1772–1829), a philosopher, poet, and critic whose essays formed the intellectual basis of German Romanticism. Girolamo Tiraboschi (1731–1794) published a thirteen-volume history of Italian literature. Thomas Warton (1728–1790), the author of *History of English Poetry*.

6. Emerson quotes these lines about Homer's fierce goddess from English author Robert Burton's (1577–1640) *Anatomy of Melancholy*.

7. Ruggiero Boscovich (1711–1787), Italian mathematician and physicist, who defined matter as composed of individual and mutually repulsive atoms.

silent waves between us and the things we aim at and converse with. Grief too will make us idealists. In the death of my son, now more than two years ago, I seem to have lost a beautiful estate,—no more. I cannot get it nearer to me.[8] If tomorrow I should be informed of the bankruptcy of my principal debtors, the loss of my property would be a great inconvenience to me, perhaps, for many years; but it would leave me as it found me,—neither better nor worse. So is it with this calamity: it does not touch me: something which I fancied was a part of me, which could not be torn away without tearing me, nor enlarged without enriching me, falls off from me, and leaves no scar. It was caducous. I grieve that grief can teach me nothing, nor carry me one step into real nature. The Indian who was laid under a curse, that the wind should not blow on him, nor water flow to him, nor fire burn him, is a type of us all.[9] The dearest events are summer-rain, and we the Para coats[1] that shed every drop. Nothing is left us now but death. We look to that with a grim satisfaction, saying, there at least is reality that will not dodge us.

I take this evanescence and lubricity of all objects, which lets them slip through our fingers then when we clutch hardest, to be the most unhandsome part of our condition. Nature does not like to be observed, and likes that we should be her fools and playmates. We may have the sphere for our cricket-ball, but not a berry for our philosophy. Direct strokes she never gave us power to make; all our blows glance, all our hits are accidents. Our relations to each other are oblique and casual.

Dream delivers us to dream, and there is no end to illusion.[2] Life is a train of moods like a string of beads, and, as we pass through them, they prove to be many-colored lenses which paint the world their own hue, and each shows only what lies in its focus. From the mountain you see the mountain. We animate what we can, and we see only what we animate. Nature and books belong to the eyes that see them. It depends on the mood of the man, whether he shall see the sunset or the fine poem. There are always sunsets, and there is always genius; but only a few hours so serene that we can relish nature or criticism. The more or less depends on structure or temperament. Temperament is the iron wire on which the beads are strung. Of what use is fortune or talent to a cold and defective nature? Who cares what sensibility or discrimination a man has at some time shown, if he falls asleep in his chair? or if he laugh and giggle? or if he apologize? or is infected with egotism? or thinks of his dollar? or cannot pass by food? or has gotten a child in his boyhood? Of what use is genius, if the organ is too convex or too concave, and cannot find a focal distance within the actual horizon of human life? Of what use, if the brain is too cold or too hot, and the man does not care enough for results, to stimulate him to experiment, and hold him up in it? or if the web is too finely woven, too irritable by pleasure and pain, so that life stagnates from too much reception, without due outlet? Of what use to make heroic vows of amendment, if the same old law-breaker is to keep them? What cheer can the religious sentiment yield, when that is suspected to be secretly dependent on the seasons of the year, and the state of the

---

8. Emerson was actually devastated by the death of his five-year-old son Waldo Emerson on January 28, 1842. Two months later he wrote in his journal: "I comprehend nothing of this fact but its bitterness."
9. Emerson took this story from Robert Southey's *The Curse of Kehama* (1810). See CW 3.183.
1. Raincoats made from Brazilian rubber.
2. Cf. "The Poet," p. 194.

blood? I knew a witty physician who found the creed in the biliary duct, and used to affirm that if there was disease in the liver, the man became a Calvinist, and if that organ was sound, he became a Unitarian.[3] Very mortifying is the reluctant experience that some unfriendly excess or imbecility neutralizes the promise of genius. We see young men who owe us a new world, so readily and lavishly they promise, but they never acquit the debt; they die young and dodge the account: or if they live, they lose themselves in the crowd.

Temperament also enters fully into the system of illusions, and shuts us in a prison of glass which we cannot see. There is an optical illusion about every person we meet. In truth, they are all creatures of given temperament, which will appear in a given character, whose boundaries they will never pass: but we look at them, they seem alive, and we presume there is impulse in them. In the moment, it seems impulse; in the year, in the lifetime, it turns out to be a certain uniform tune which the revolving barrel of the music-box must play. Men resist the conclusion in the morning, but adopt it as the evening wears on, that temper prevails over everything of time, place, and condition, and is inconsumable in the flames of religion. Some modifications the moral sentiment avails to impose, but the individual texture holds its dominion, if not to bias the moral judgments, yet to fix the measure of activity and of enjoyment.

I thus express the law as it is read from the platform of ordinary life, but must not leave it without noticing the capital exception. For temperament is a power which no man willingly hears any one praise but himself. On the platform of physics, we cannot resist the contracting influences of so-called science. Temperament puts all divinity to rout. I know the mental proclivity of physicians. I hear the chuckle of the phrenologists.[4] Theoretic kidnappers and slave-drivers, they esteem each man the victim of another, who winds him round his finger by knowing the law of his being, and by such cheap signboards as the color of his beard, or the slope of his occiput, reads the inventory of his fortunes and character. The grosset ignorance does not disgust like this impudent knowingness. The physicians say, they are not materialists;[5] but they are: — Spirit is matter reduced to an extreme thinness: O *so* thin! — But the definition of *spiritual* should be, *that which is its own evidence.*[6] What notions do they attach to love! what to religion! One would not willingly pronounce these words in their hearing, and give them the occasion to profane them. I saw a gracious gentleman who adapts his conversation to the form of the head of the man he talks with! I had fancied that the value of life lay in its inscrutable possibilities; in the fact that I never know, in addressing myself to a new individual, what may befall me. I carry the keys of my castle in my hand, ready to throw them at the feet of my lord, whenever and in what disguise soever he shall appear. I know he is in the neighborhood, hidden among vagabonds. Shall I preclude my future, by taking a high seat, and kindly adapting my conversation to the shape of heads? When I come to that, the doctors shall buy me for a cent. — 'But, sir, medical history; the report to the Institute; the proven facts!' — I distrust the facts and the inferences. Temperament is the veto or limitation-power in the constitution,

---

3. Emerson humorously blames the stern Calvinism of his Puritan forebears on biliousness, as opposed to the presumably healthy and optimistic liberalism of contemporary Unitarianism.
4. Practitioners of phrenology, the study of the shape and protuberances of the skull, based on the now-discredited belief, which was popular in Emerson's time, that they reveal character and mental capacity.
5. Believers in materialism, the theory that physical matter is the only reality and that everything, including thought, feeling, mind, and will, can be explained in terms of matter and physical phenomena.
6. Stephen Whicher suggests that Emerson is here paraphrasing Coleridge's *The Statesman's Manual.*

very justly applied to restrain an opposite excess in the constitution, but absurdly offered as a bar to original equity. When virtue is in presence, all subordinate powers sleep. On its own level, or in view of nature, temperament is final. I see not, if one be once caught in this trap of so-called sciences, any escape for the man from the links of the chain of physical necessity. Given such an embryo, such a history must follow. On this platform, one lives in a sty of sensualism, and would soon come to suicide. But it is impossible that the creative power should exclude itself. Into every intelligence there is a door which is never closed, through which the creator passes. The intellect, seeker of absolute truth, or the heart, lover of absolute good, intervenes for our succor, and at one whisper of these high powers, we awake from ineffectual struggles with this nightmare. We hurl it into its own hell, and cannot again contract ourselves to so base a state.

The secret of the illusoriness is in the necessity of a succession of moods or objects. Gladly we would anchor, but the anchorage is quicksand. This onward trick of nature is too strong for us: *Pero si muove.*[7] When, at night, I look at the moon and stars, I seem stationary, and they to hurry. Our love of the real draws us to permanence, but health of body consists in circulation, and sanity of mind in variety or facility of association. We need change of objects. Dedication to one thought is quickly odious. We house with the insane, and must humor them; then conversation dies out. Once I took such delight in Montaigne, that I thought I should not need any other book; before that, in Shakspeare; then in Plutarch; then in Plotinus; at one time in Bacon; afterwards in Goethe; even in Bettine;[8] but now I turn the pages of either of them languidly, whilst I still cherish their genius. So with pictures; each will bear an emphasis of attention once, which it cannot retain, though we fain would continue to be pleased in that manner. How strongly I have felt of pictures, that when you have seen one well, you must take your leave of it; you shall never see it again. I have had good lessons from pictures, which I have since seen without emotion or remark. A deduction must be made from the opinion, which even the wise express of a new book or occurrence. Their opinion gives me tidings of their mood, and some vague guess at the new fact, but is nowise to be trusted as the lasting relation between that intellect and that thing. The child asks, 'Mamma, why don't I like the story as well as when you told it me yesterday?' Alas, child, it is even so with the oldest cherubim of knowledge. But will it answer thy question to say, Because thou wert born to a whole, and this story is a particular? The reason of the pain this discovery causes us (and we make it late in respect to works of art and intellect), is the plaint of tragedy which murmurs from it in regard to persons, to friendship and love.

That immobility and absence of elasticity which we find in the arts, we find with more pain in the artist. There is no power of expansion in men. Our friends early appear to us as representatives of certain ideas, which they never pass or exceed. They stand on the brink of the ocean of thought and power, but they never take the single step that would bring them there. A man is like a bit of Labrador

---

7. Facing ecclesiastical persecution, Galileo (see n. 5, p. 125) recanted on his observation that the earth turns round the sun, but then added: "And yet it does move."
8. Elizabeth (Brentano) von Arnim (1785–1859) found a ready audience in Emerson's circle, where her imaginary letters to Goethe (*Correspondence with a Child*) were enthusiastically received. Montaigne, see n. 8, p. 155. Plutarch, see n. 7, p. 57. Plotinus, see n. 1, p. 27. Bacon, see n. 3, p. 6. Goethe, see n. 6, p. 42.

spar,[9] which has no lustre as you turn it in your hand, until you come to a particular angle; then it shows deep and beautiful colors. There is no adaptation or universal applicability in men, but each has his special talent, and the mastery of
successful men consists in adroitly keeping themselves where and when that turn
shall be oftenest to be practised. We do what we must, and call it by the best names
we can, and would fain have the praise of having intended the result which en-
sues. I cannot recall any form of man who is not superfluous sometimes. But is
not this pitiful? Life is not worth the taking, to do tricks in.

Of course, it needs the whole society, to give the symmetry we seek. The
parti-colored wheel must revolve very fast to appear white. Something is learned
too by conversing with so much folly and defect. In fine, whoever loses, we are
always of the gaining party. Divinity is behind our failures and follies also. The
plays of children are nonsense, but very educative nonsense. So is it with the
largest and solemnest things, with commerce, government, church, marriage,
and so with the history of every man's bread, and the ways by which he is to
come by it. Like a bird which alights nowhere, but hops perpetually from bough
to bough, is the Power which abides in no man and in no woman, but for a moment speaks from this one, and for another moment from that one.

But what help from these fineries or pedantries? What help from thought?
Life is not dialectics. We, I think, in these times, have had lessons enough of the
futility of criticism. Our young people have thought and written much on labor
and reform, and for all that they have written, neither the world nor themselves
have got on a step. Intellectual tasting of life will not supersede muscular activity. If a man should consider the nicety of the passage of a piece of bread down
his throat, he would starve. At Education-Farm,[1] the noblest theory of life sat
on the noblest figures of young men and maidens, quite powerless and melancholy. It would not rake or pitch a ton of hay; it would not rub down a horse;
and the men and maidens it left pale and hungry. A political orator wittily compared our party promises to western roads, which opened stately enough, with
planted trees on either side, to tempt the traveller, but soon became narrow and
narrower, and ended in a squirrel-track, and ran up a tree. So does culture with
us; it ends in headache. Unspeakably sad and barren does life look to those, who
a few months ago were dazzled with the splendor of the promise of the times.
"There is now no longer any right course of action, nor any self-devotion left
among the Iranis."[2] Objections and criticism we have had our fill of. There are
objections to every course of life and action, and the practical wisdom infers an
indifference, from the omnipresence of objection. The whole frame of things
preaches indifference. Do not craze yourself with thinking, but go about your
business anywhere. Life is not intellectual or critical, but sturdy. Its chief good
is for well-mixed people who can enjoy what they find, without question. Nature hates peeping, and our mothers speak her very sense when they say, "Children, eat your victuals, and say no more of it." To fill the hour,—that is
happiness; to fill the hour, and leave no crevice for a repentance or an approval.

---

9. A kind of feldspar (see n. 4, p. 140) with brilliantly variegated colors.
1. Emerson is undoubtedly alluding to Brook Farm, a utopian community in West Roxbury, Massachus-
   setts, founded by George Ripley and others in 1841. Ripley (1802–1880), Massachusetts religious
   thinker, writer, and reformer. See Emerson's journal entry for Oct. 17, 1840 (p. 505).
2. Emerson's quote comes from the *Desatir, or Sacred Writings of the ancient Persian Prophets*. For the complicated story of this publication see CW 3.185–87.

We live amid surfaces, and the true art of life is to skate well on them. Under the oldest mouldiest conventions, a man of native force prospers just as well as in the newest world, and that by skill of handling and treatment. He can take hold anywhere. Life itself is a mixture of power and form, and will not bear the least excess of either. To finish the moment, to find the journey's end in every step of the road, to live the greatest number of good hours, is wisdom. It is not the part of men, but of fanatics, or of mathematicians, if you will, to say, that, the shortness of life considered, it is not worth caring whether for so short a duration we were sprawling in want, or sitting high. Since our office is with moments, let us husband them. Five minutes of today are worth as much to me, as five minutes in the next millennium. Let us be poised, and wise, and our own, today. Let us treat the men and women well: treat them as if they were real: perhaps they are. Men live in their fancy, like drunkards whose hands are too soft and tremulous for successful labor. It is a tempest of fancies, and the only ballast I know, is a respect to the present hour. Without any shadow of doubt, amidst this vertigo of shows and politics, I settle myself ever the firmer in the creed, that we should not postpone and refer and wish, but do broad justice where we are, by whomsoever we deal with, accepting our actual companions and circumstances, however humble or odious, as the mystic officials to whom the universe has delegated its whole pleasure for us. If these are mean and malignant, their contentment, which is the last victory of justice, is a more satisfying echo to the heart, than the voice of poets and the casual sympathy of admirable persons. I think that however a thoughtful man may suffer from the defects and absurdities of his company, he cannot without affectation deny to any set of men and women, a sensibility to extraordinary merit. The coarse and frivolous have an instinct of superiority, if they have not a sympathy, and honor it in their blind capricious way with sincere homage.

The fine young people despise life, but in me, and in such as with me are free from dyspepsia, and to whom a day is a sound and solid good, it is a great excess of politeness to look scornful and to cry for company. I am grown by sympathy a little eager and sentimental, but leave me alone, and I should relish every hour and what it brought me, the potluck of the day, as heartily as the oldest gossip in the bar-room. I am thankful for small mercies. I compared notes with one of my friends who expects everything of the universe, and is disappointed when anything is less than the best, and I found that I begin at the other extreme, expecting nothing, and am always full of thanks for moderate goods. I accept the clangor and jangle of contrary tendencies. I find my account in sots and bores also. They give a reality to the circumjacent[3] picture, which such a vanishing meteorous appearance can ill spare. In the morning I awake, and find the old world, wife, babes, and mother, Concord and Boston, the dear old spiritual world, and even the dear old devil not far off. If we will take the good we find, asking no questions, we shall have heaping measures. The great gifts are not got by analysis. Everything good is on the highway. The middle region of our being is the temperate zone. We may climb into the thin and cold realm of pure geometry and lifeless science, or sink into that of sensation. Between these extremes is the equator of life, of thought, of spirit, of poetry,—a narrow belt. Moreover, in popular experience, everything good is on the highway. A collector peeps into all the picture-shops of Europe, for a landscape of Poussin, a

3. Surrounding.

crayon-sketch of Salvator; but the Transfiguration, the Last Judgment, the Communion of St. Jerome,[4] and what are as transcendent as these, are on the walls of the Vatican, the Uffizi, or the Louvre, where every footman may see them; to say nothing of nature's pictures in every street, of sunsets and sunrises every day, and the sculpture of the human body never absent. A collector recently bought at public auction, in London, for one hundred and fifty-seven guineas, an autograph of Shakspeare: but for nothing a school-boy can read Hamlet, and can detect secrets of highest concernment yet unpublished therein. I think I will never read any but the commonest books, — the Bible, Homer, Dante, Shakspeare, and Milton. Then we are impatient of so public a life and planet, and run hither and thither for nooks and secrets. The imagination delights in the wood-craft of Indians, trappers, and bee-hunters. We fancy that we are strangers, and not so intimately domesticated in the planet as the wild man, and the wild beast and bird. But the exclusion reaches them also; reaches the climbing, flying, gliding, feathered and four-footed man. Fox and woodchuck, hawk and snipe, and bittern, when nearly seen, have no more root in the deep world than man, and are just such superficial tenants of the globe. Then the new molecular philosophy shows astronomical interspaces betwixt atom and atom, shows that the world is all outside: it has no inside.[5]

The mid-world is best. Nature, as we know her, is no saint. The lights of the church, the ascetics, Gentoos and corn-eaters,[6] she does not distinguish by any favor. She comes eating and drinking and sinning. Her darlings, the great, the strong, the beautiful, are not children of our law, do not come out of the Sunday School, nor weigh their food, nor punctually keep the commandments. If we will be strong with her strength, we must not harbor such disconsolate consciences, borrowed too from the consciences of other nations. We must set up the strong present tense against all the rumors of wrath, past or to come. So many things are unsettled which it is of the first importance to settle, — and, pending their settlement, we will do as we do. Whilst the debate goes forward on the equity of commerce, and will not be closed for a century or two, New and Old England may keep shop. Law of copyright and international copyright is to be discussed, and, in the interim, we will sell our books for the most we can. Expediency of literature, reason of literature, lawfulness of writing down a thought, is questioned; much is to say on both sides, and, while the fight waxes hot, thou, dearest scholar, stick to thy foolish task, add a line every hour, and between whiles add a line. Right to hold land, right of property, is disputed, and the conventions convene, and before the vote is taken, dig away in your garden, and spend your earnings as a waif or godsend to all serene and beautiful purposes. Life itself is a bubble and a skepticism, and a sleep within a sleep. Grant it, and as much more as they will, — but thou, God's darling! heed thy private dream: thou wilt not be missed in the scorning and skepticism: there are enough of them: stay there in thy closet, and toil, until the rest are agreed what to do about it. Thy sickness, they say, and thy puny habit, require that thou do this or avoid that, but know that thy life is a flitting state, a tent for a night, and do thou,

---

4. Domenichino, Domenico Zampieri (1581–1641) painted the *Last Communion of St. Jerome* in 1614. Nicholas Poussin (1594–1665), French painter, master of the classical school. Salvator, see n. 3, p. 86. Raphael's (see n. 3, p. 86) *The Transfiguration of Christ* is in the Vatican. Michelangelo's (see n. 6, p. 42) *Last Judgment* is in the Sistine Chapel, also in the Vatican.
5. Stephen Whicher believes this refers to Dalton's Atomic Theory.
6. Or Grahamites, followers of Sylvester Graham (1794–1851), a popular writer and lecturer on health issues. *Gentoos:* see n. 1, p. 161.

sick or well, finish that stint. Thou art sick, but shalt not be worse, and the universe, which holds thee dear, shall be the better.

Human life is made up of the two elements, power and form, and the proportion must be invariably kept, if we would have it sweet and sound. Each of these elements in excess makes a mischief as hurtful as its defect. Everything runs to excess: every good quality is noxious, if unmixed, and, to carry the danger to the edge of ruin, nature causes each man's peculiarity to superabound. Here, among the farms, we adduce the scholars as examples of this treachery. They are nature's victims of expression. You who see the artist, the orator, the poet, too near, and find their life no more excellent than that of mechanics or farmers, and themselves victims of partiality, very hollow and haggard, and pronounce them failures,—not heroes, but quacks,—conclude very reasonably, that these arts are not for man, but are disease. Yet nature will not bear you out. Irresistible nature made men such, and makes legions more of such, every day. You love the boy reading in a book, gazing at a drawing, or a cast: yet what are these millions who read and behold, but incipient writers and sculptors? Add a little more of that quality which now reads and sees, and they will seize the pen and chisel. And if one remembers how innocently he began to be an artist, he perceives that nature joined with his enemy. A man is a golden impossibility. The line he must walk is a hair's breadth. The wise through excess of wisdom is made a fool.

How easily, if fate would suffer it, we might keep forever these beautiful limits, and adjust ourselves, once for all, to the perfect calculation of the kingdom of known cause and effect. In the street and in the newspapers, life appears so plain a business, that manly resolution and adherence to the multiplication-table through all weathers, will insure success. But ah! presently comes a day—or is it only a half-hour, with its angel-whispering—which discomfits the conclusions of nations and of years! Tomorrow again, everything looks real and angular, the habitual standards are reinstated, common sense is as rare as genius,—is the basis of genius, and experience is hands and feet to every enterprise;—and yet, he who should do his business on this understanding, would be quickly bankrupt. Power keeps quite another road than the turnpikes of choice and will, namely, the subterranean and invisible tunnels and channels of life. It is ridiculous that we are diplomatists, and doctors, and considerate people: there are no dupes like these. Life is a series of surprises, and would not be worth taking or keeping, if it were not. God delights to isolate us every day, and hide from us the past and the future. We would look about us, but with grand politeness he draws down before us an impenetrable screen of purest sky, and another behind us of purest sky. 'You will not remember,' he seems to say, 'and you will not expect.' All good conversation, manners, and action, come from a spontaneity which forgets usages, and makes the moment great. Nature hates calculators; her methods are saltatory and impulsive. Man lives by pulses; our organic movements are such; and the chemical and ethereal agents are undulatory and alternate; and the mind goes antagonizing on, and never prospers but by fits. We thrive by casualties.[7] Our chief experiences have been casual. The most attractive class of people are those who are powerful obliquely, and not by the direct stroke: men of genius, but not yet accredited: one gets the cheer of their light, without paying too great a tax. Theirs is

---

7. In the Latin sense of "chance events."

the beauty of the bird, or the morning light, and not of art. In the thought of genius there is always a surprise; and the moral sentiment is well called "the newness," for it is never other; as new to the oldest intelligence as to the young child, — "the kingdom that cometh without observation."[8] In like manner, for practical success, there must not be too much design. A man will not be observed in doing that which he can do best. There is a certain magic about his properest action, which stupefies your powers of observation, so that though it is done before you, you wist not of it. The art of life has pudency,[9] and will not be exposed. Every man is an impossibility, until he is born; every thing impossible, until we see a success. The ardors of piety agree at last with the coldest skepticism, — that nothing is of us or our works, — that all is of God. Nature will not spare us the smallest leaf of laurel. All writing comes by the grace of God, and all doing and having. I would gladly be moral, and keep due metes and bounds, which I dearly love, and allow the most to the will of man, but I have set my heart on honesty in this chapter, and I can see nothing at last, in success or failure, than more or less of vital force supplied from the Eternal. The results of life are uncalculated and uncalculable. The years teach much which the days never know. The persons who compose our company, converse, and come and go, and design and execute many things, and somewhat comes of it all, but an unlooked-for result. The individual is always mistaken. He designed many things, and drew in other persons as coadjutors, quarrelled with some or all, blundered much, and something is done; all are a little advanced, but the individual is always mistaken. It turns out somewhat new, and very unlike what he promised himself.

The ancients, struck with this irreducibleness of the elements of human life to calculation, exalted Chance[1] into a divinity, but that is to stay too long at the spark, — which glitters truly at one point, — but the universe is warm with the latency of the same fire. The miracle of life which will not be expounded, but will remain a miracle, introduces a new element. In the growth of the embryo, Sir Everard Home,[2] I think, noticed that the evolution was not from one central point, but coactive from three or more points. Life has no memory. That which proceeds in succession might be remembered, but that which is coexistent, or ejaculated from a deeper cause, as yet far from being conscious, knows not its own tendency. So is it with us, now skeptical, or without unity, because immersed in forms and effects all seeming to be of equal yet hostile value, and now religious, whilst in the reception of spiritual law. Bear with these distractions, with this coetaneous[3] growth of the parts: they will one day be *members*, and obey one will. On that one will, on that secret cause, they nail our attention and hope. Life is hereby melted into an expectation or a religion. Underneath the inharmonious and trivial particulars, is a musical perfection, the Ideal journeying always with us, the heaven without rent or seam. Do but observe the mode of our illumination. When I converse with a profound mind, or if at any time being alone I have good thoughts, I do not at once arrive at satisfactions, as when, being thirsty, I drink water, or go to the fire, being cold: no! but I am at first apprised of my vicinity to a new and excellent region of life. By persisting to read or to think, this re-

8. Cf. Luke 17.20 as well as the last sentence of *Nature* (p. 55).
9. Modesty or shame in Latin (cf. *pudenda*).
1. Fortuna among the Romans.
2. Surgeon and student of comparative anatomy (1756–1832).
3. Occurring at the same time.

gion gives further sign of itself, as it were in flashes of light, in sudden discoveries of its profound beauty and repose, as if the clouds that covered it parted at intervals, and showed the approaching traveller the inland mountains, with the tranquil eternal meadows spread at their base, whereon flocks graze, and shepherds pipe and dance. But every insight from this realm of thought is felt as initial, and promises a sequel. I do not make it; I arrive there, and behold what was there already. I make! O no! I clap my hands in infantine joy and amazement, before the first opening to me of this august magnificence, old with the love and homage of innumerable ages, young with the life of life, the sunbright Mecca of the desert. And what a future it opens! I feel a new heart beating with the love of the new beauty. I am ready to die out of nature, and be born again into this new yet unapproachable America I have found in the West.

> "Since neither now nor yesterday began
> These thoughts, which have been ever, nor yet can
> A man be found who their first entrance knew."[4]

If I have described life as a flux of moods, I must now add, that there is that in us which changes not, and which ranks all sensations and states of mind. The consciousness in each man is a sliding scale, which identifies him now with the First Cause, and now with the flesh of his body; life above life, in infinite degrees. The sentiment from which it sprung determines the dignity of any deed, and the question ever is, not, what you have done or forborne, but, at whose command you have done or forborne it.

Fortune, Minerva, Muse, Holy Ghost, — these are quaint names, too narrow to cover this unbounded substance. The baffled intellect must still kneel before this cause, which refuses to be named, — ineffable cause, which every fine genius has essayed to represent by some emphatic symbol, as, Thales by water, Anaximenes by air, Anaxagoras by (Noûs) thought, Zoroaster[5] by fire, Jesus and the moderns by love: and the metaphor of each has become a national religion. The Chinese Mencius[6] has not been the least successful in his generalization. "I fully understand language," he said, "and nourish well my vast-flowing vigor." — "I beg to ask what you call vast-flowing vigor?" said his companion. "The explanation," replied Mencius, "is difficult. This vigor is supremely great, and in the highest degree unbending. Nourish it correctly, and do it no injury, and it will fill up the vacancy between heaven and earth. This vigor accords with and assists justice and reason, and leaves no hunger." In our more correct writing, we give to this generalization the name of Being, and thereby confess that we have arrived as far as we can go. Suffice it for the joy of the universe, that we have not arrived at a wall, but at interminable oceans. Our life seems not present, so much as prospective; not for the affairs on which it is wasted, but as a hint of this vast-flowing vigor. Most of life seems to be mere advertisement of faculty: information is given us not to sell ourselves cheap; that we are very great. So, in particulars, our greatness is always in a tendency or direction, not in an action. It is for us to believe in the rule, not in the exception. The noble are thus known from the igno-

---

4. From Sophocles, *Antigone*, lines 455–57.
5. See n. 9, p. 78. Thales (ca. 624–ca. 526 B.C.E.), considered one of the "seven wise men" of ancient Greece. Anaximenes (fl. 525 B.C.E.), member of the Milesian school along with Thales. Anaxagoras, see n. 2, p. 135.
6. Mencius (372–289 B.C.E.), follower of Confucius (see n. 5, p. 160).

ble. So in accepting the leading of the sentiments, it is not what we believe concerning the immortality of the soul, or the like, but *the universal impulse to believe*,[7] that is the material circumstance, and is the principal fact in the history of the globe. Shall we describe this cause as that which works directly? The spirit is not helpless or needful of mediate organs. It has plentiful powers and direct effects. I am explained without explaining, I am felt without acting, and where I am not. Therefore all just persons are satisfied with their own praise. They refuse to explain themselves, and are content that new actions should do them that office. They believe that we communicate without speech, and above speech, and that no right action of ours is quite unaffecting to our friends, at whatever distance; for the influence of action is not to be measured by miles. Why should I fret myself, because a circumstance has occurred, which hinders my presence where I was expected? If I am not at the meeting, my presence where I am should be as useful to the commonwealth of friendship and wisdom, as would be my presence in that place. I exert the same quality of power in all places. Thus journeys the mighty Ideal before us; it never was known to fall into the rear. No man ever came to an experience which was satiating, but his good is tidings of a better. Onward and onward! In liberated moments, we know that a new picture of life and duty is already possible; the elements already exist in many minds around you, of a doctrine of life which shall transcend any written record we have. The new statement will comprise the skepticisms, as well as the faiths of society, and out of unbeliefs a creed shall be formed. For, skepticisms are not gratuitous or lawless, but are limitations of the affirmative statement, and the new philosophy must take them in, and make affirmations outside of them, just as much as it must include the oldest beliefs.

It is very unhappy, but too late to be helped, the discovery we have made, that we exist. That discovery is called the Fall of Man.[8] Ever afterwards, we suspect our instruments. We have learned that we do not see directly, but mediately, and that we have no means of correcting these colored and distorting lenses which we are, or of computing the amount of their errors. Perhaps these subject-lenses have a creative power; perhaps there are no objects. Once we lived in what we saw; now, the rapaciousness of this new power, which threatens to absorb all things, engages us. Nature, art, persons, letters, religions, — objects, successively tumble in, and God is but one of its ideas. Nature and literature are subjective phenomena; every evil and every good thing is a shadow which we cast. The street is full of humiliations to the proud. As the fop contrived to dress his bailiffs in his livery, and make them wait on his guests at table, so the chagrins which the bad heart gives off as bubbles, at once take form as ladies and gentlemen in the street, shopmen or barkeepers in hotels, and threaten or insult whatever is threatenable and insultable in us. 'Tis the same with our idolatries. People forget that it is the eye which makes the horizon, and the rounding mind's eye which makes this or that man a type or representative of humanity with the name of hero or saint. Jesus the "providential man," is a good man on whom many people are agreed that these optical laws shall take effect. By love on one part, and by forbearance to press objection on the other part, it is for a time settled, that we will look at him in the centre of the horizon, and ascribe to him the properties that will attach to any man so seen. But the

7. The American philosopher William James (1842–1910), an appreciative reader of Emerson, would appropriate this concept for the title of his book *The Will to Believe* (1897).
8. Emerson here redefines this familiar Judeo-Christian notion in existential and epistemological terms.

longest love or aversion has a speedy term. The great and crescive self, rooted in absolute nature, supplants all relative existence, and ruins the kingdom of mortal friendship and love. Marriage (in what is called the spiritual world) is impossible, because of the inequality between every subject and every object. The subject is the receiver of Godhead, and at every comparison must feel his being enhanced by that cryptic might. Though not in energy, yet by presence, this magazine of substance cannot be otherwise than felt: nor can any force of intellect attribute to the object the proper deity which sleeps or wakes forever in every subject. Never can love make consciousness and ascription equal in force. There will be the same gulf between every me and thee, as between the original and the picture. The universe is the bride of the soul. All private sympathy is partial. Two human beings are like globes, which can touch only in a point, and, whilst they remain in contact, all other points of each of the spheres are inert; their turn must also come, and the longer a particular union lasts, the more energy of appetency the parts not in union acquire.

Life will be imaged, but cannot be divided nor doubled. Any invasion of its unity would be chaos. The soul is not twin-born, but the only begotten, and though revealing itself as child in time, child in appearance, is of a fatal and universal power, admitting no co-life. Every day, every act betrays the ill-concealed deity. We believe in ourselves, as we do not believe in others. We permit all things to ourselves, and that which we call sin in others, is experiment for us. It is an instance of our faith in ourselves, that men never speak of crime as lightly as they think: or, every man thinks a latitude safe for himself, which is nowise to be indulged to another. The act looks very differently on the inside, and on the outside; in its quality, and in its consequences. Murder in the murderer is no such ruinous thought as poets and romancers will have it; it does not unsettle him, or fright him from his ordinary notice of trifles: it is an act quite easy to be contemplated, but in its sequel, it turns out to be a horrible jangle and confounding of all relations. Especially the crimes that spring from love, seem right and fair from the actor's point of view, but, when acted, are found destructive of society. No man at last believes that he can be lost, nor that the crime in him is as black as in the felon. Because the intellect qualifies in our own case the moral judgments. For there is no crime to the intellect. That is antinomian or hypernomian,[9] and judges law as well as fact. "It is worse than a crime, it is a blunder," said Napoleon, speaking the language of the intellect. To it, the world is a problem in mathematics or the science of quantity, and it leaves out praise and blame, and all weak emotions. All stealing is comparative. If you come to absolutes, pray who does not steal? Saints are sad, because they behold sin, (even when they speculate,) from the point of view of the conscience, and not of the intellect; a confusion of thought. Sin seen from the thought, is a diminution or *less*: seen from the conscience or will, it is pravity or *bad*. The intellect names it shade, absence of light, and no essence. The conscience must feel it as essence, essential evil. This it is not: it has an objective existence, but no subjective.

Thus inevitably does the universe wear our color, and every object fall successively into the subject itself. The subject exists, the subject enlarges; all things sooner or later fall into place. As I am, so I see; use what language we will, we can never say anything but what we are; Hermes, Cadmus,[1] Columbus, Newton,

---

9. See n. 9, p. 96.
1. In Greek mythology, the founder of Thebes and ancestor of Oedipus. Hermes, see n. 4, p. 199.

Bonaparte, are the mind's ministers. Instead of feeling a poverty when we encounter a great man, let us treat the new comer like a travelling geologist, who
passes through our estate, and shows us good slate, or limestone, or anthracite, in
our brush pasture. The partial action of each strong mind in one direction, is a
telescope for the objects on which it is pointed. But every other part of knowledge
is to be pushed to the same extravagance, ere the soul attains her due sphericity.
Do you see that kitten chasing so prettily her own tail? If you could look with her
eyes, you might see her surrounded with hundreds of figures performing complex
dramas, with tragic and comic issues, long conversations, many characters, many
ups and downs of fate,—and meantime it is only puss and her tail. How long before our masquerade will end its noise of tambourines, laughter, and shouting,
and we shall find it was a solitary performance?—A subject and an object,—it
takes so much to make the galvanic circuit complete, but magnitude adds nothing. What imports it whether it is Kepler[2] and the sphere; Columbus and America; a reader and his book; or puss with her tail?

It is true that all the muses and love and religion hate these developments,
and will find a way to punish the chemist, who publishes in the parlor the secrets
of the laboratory. And we cannot say too little of our constitutional necessity of
seeing things under private aspects, or saturated with our humors. And yet is the
God the native of these bleak rocks. That need makes in morals the capital virtue
of self-trust. We must hold hard to this poverty, however scandalous, and by more
vigorous self-recoveries, after the sallies of action, possess our axis more firmly.
The life of truth is cold, and so far mournful; but it is not the slave of tears, contritions, and perturbations. It does not attempt another's work, nor adopt another's facts. It is a main lesson of wisdom to know your own from another's. I have
learned that I cannot dispose of other people's facts; but I possess such a key to my
own, as persuades me against all their denials, that they also have a key to theirs.
A sympathetic person is placed in the dilemma of a swimmer among drowning
men, who all catch at him, and if he give so much as a leg or a finger, they will
drown him. They wish to be saved from the mischiefs of their vices, but not from
their vices. Charity would be wasted on this poor waiting on the symptoms. A wise
and hardy physician will say, *Come out of that*, as the first condition of advice.

In this our talking America, we are ruined by our good nature and listening on all sides. This compliance takes away the power of being greatly useful.
A man should not be able to look other than directly and forthright. A preoccupied attention is the only answer to the importunate frivolity of other people:
an attention, and to an aim which makes their wants frivolous. This is a divine
answer, and leaves no appeal, and no hard thoughts. In Flaxman's drawing of
the Eumenides of Æschylus, Orestes supplicates Apollo, whilst the Furies[3]
sleep on the threshold. The face of the god expresses a shade of regret and compassion, but [is] calm with the conviction of the irreconcilableness of the two
spheres. He is born into other politics, into the eternal and beautiful. The man
at his feet asks for his interest in turmoils of the earth, into which his nature cannot enter. And the Eumenides there lying express pictorially this disparity. The
god is surcharged with his divine destiny.

2. See n. 1, p. 194.
3. See n. 8, p. 143. John Flaxman (1755–1826) illustrated Aeschylus' (see n. 1, p. 109) *Eumenides*. Apollo,
   see n. 4, p. 73. Orestes see n. 3, p. 96.

Illusion, Temperament, Succession, Surface, Surprise, Reality, Subjective-ness,—these are threads on the loom of time, these are the lords of life. I dare not assume to give their order, but I name them as I find them in my way. I know bet-ter than to claim any completeness for my picture. I am a fragment, and this is a fragment of me. I can very confidently announce one or another law, which throws itself into relief and form, but I am too young yet by some ages to compile a code. I gossip for my hour concerning the eternal politics. I have seen many fair pictures not in vain. A wonderful time I have lived in. I am not the novice I was fourteen, nor yet seven years ago. Let who will ask, where is the fruit? I find a pri-vate fruit sufficient. This is a fruit,—that I should not ask for a rash effect from meditations, counsels, and the hiving[4] of truths. I should feel it pitiful to demand a result on this town and county, an overt effect on the instant month and year. The effect is deep and secular[5] as the cause. It works on periods in which mortal lifetime is lost. All I know is reception; I am and I have: but I do not get, and when I have fancied I had gotten anything, I found I did not. I worship with wonder the great Fortune. My reception has been so large, that I am not annoyed by receiv-ing this or that superabundantly. I say to the Genius, if he will pardon the proverb, *In for a mill, in for a million.* When I receive a new gift, I do not macerate my body to make the account square, for, if I should die, I could not make the account square. The benefit overran the merit the first day, and has overran the merit ever since. The merit itself, so-called, I reckon part of the receiving.

Also, that hankering after an overt or practical effect seems to me an apos-tasy. In good earnest, I am willing to spare this most unnecessary deal of doing. Life wears to me a visionary face. Hardest, roughest action is visionary also. It is but a choice between soft and turbulent dreams. People disparage knowing and the intellectual life, and urge doing. I am very content with knowing, if only I could know. That is an august entertainment, and would suffice me a great while. To know a little, would be worth the expense of this world. I hear always the law of Adrastia,[6] "that every soul which had acquired any truth, should be safe from harm until another period."

I know that the world I converse with in the city and in the farms, is not the world I *think*. I observe that difference, and shall observe it. One day, I shall know the value and law of this discrepance. But I have not found that much was gained by manipular attempts to realize the world of thought. Many eager per-sons successively make an experiment in this way, and make themselves ridicu-lous. They acquire democratic manners, they foam at the mouth, they hate and deny. Worse, I observe, that, in the history of mankind, there is never a solitary example of success,—taking their own tests of success. I say this polemically, or in reply to the inquiry, why not realize your world? But far be from me the de-spair which prejudges the law by a paltry empiricism,—since there never was a right endeavor, but it succeeded. Patience and patience, we shall win at the last. We must be very suspicious of the deceptions of the element of time. It takes a good deal of time to eat or to sleep, or to earn a hundred dollars, and a very lit-tle time to entertain a hope and an insight which becomes the light of our life. We dress our garden, eat our dinners, discuss the household with our wives, and these things make no impression, are forgotten next week; but in the solitude to which every man is always returning, he has a sanity and revelations, which

4. Storing.
5. See n. 6, p. 175.
6. Goddess of justice or retribution. Cf. Plato, *Phaedrus*, 248c.

in his passage into new worlds he will carry with him. Never mind the ridicule, never mind the defeat: up again, old heart![7] — it seems to say, — there is victory yet for all justice; and the true romance which the world exists to realize, will be the transformation of genius into practical power.

Politics

Gold and iron are good
To buy iron and gold;
All earth's fleece and food
For their like are sold.
Hinted Merlin[1] wise,
Proved Napoleon great, —
Nor kind nor coinage buys
Aught above its rate.
Fear, Craft, and Avarice
Cannot rear a State.
Out of dust to build
What is more than dust, —
Walls Amphion[2] piled
Phœbus stablish must.
When the Muses nine
With the Virtues meet,
Find to their design
An Atlantic seat,
By green orchard boughs
Fended from the heat,
Where the statesman ploughs
Furrow for the wheat;
When the Church is social worth,
When the state-house is the hearth,
Then the perfect State is come,
The republican at home.

In dealing with the State, we ought to remember that its institutions are not aboriginal, though they existed before we were born: that they are not superior to the citizen: that every one of them was once the act of a single man: every law and usage was a man's expedient to meet a particular case: that they all are imitable, all alterable; we may make as good; we may make better. Society is an illusion to the young citizen. It lies before him in rigid repose, with certain names, men, and institutions, rooted like oak-trees to the centre, round which all arrange themselves the best they can. But the old statesman knows that society is fluid; there are no such roots and centres; but any particle may suddenly become the centre of the movement, and compel the system to gyrate round it, as every man of strong will, like Pisistratus, or Cromwell,[3] does for a time, and every man of truth, like Plato, or Paul, does forever. But politics rest

7. Emerson here echoes the Latin mass (*sursum corda*, lift up your hearts). Cf. his poem "Sursum Corda."
1. In Arthurian legend, a magician and prophet who served as counselor to King Arthur.
2. In Greek legend, son of Zeus. He shared the throne of Thebes with his brother, Zethus; together they built the city walls. It is said that Amphion completed his part of the task by playing such ravishing music that the stones moved into place on their own. Emerson's sense seems to be that the archaic, magical powers of Amphion must give way to the "establishing" arts and crafts, represented by Apollo.
3. See n. 4, p. 172. Pisistratus (d. 527 B.C.E.), Athenian tyrant (560–27) remembered for encouraging athletic contests and literary efforts. He left a prosperous and stable state to his sons, but they could not maintain the power they inherited.

on necessary foundations, and cannot be treated with levity. Republics abound in young civilians, who believe that the laws make the city, that grave modifications of the policy and modes of living, and employments of the population, that commerce, education, and religion, may be voted in or out; and that any measure, though it were absurd, may be imposed on a people, if only you can get sufficient voices to make it a law. But the wise know that foolish legislation is a rope of sand, which perishes in the twisting; that the State must follow, and not lead the character and progress of the citizen; the strongest usurper is quickly got rid of; and they only who build on Ideas, build for eternity; and that the form of government which prevails, is the expression of what cultivation exists in the population which permits it. The law is only a memorandum. We are superstitious, and esteem the statute somewhat: so much life as it has in the character of living men, is its force. The statute stands there to say, yesterday we agreed so and so, but how feel ye this article today? Our statute is a currency, which we stamp with our own portrait: it soon becomes unrecognizable, and in process of time will return to the mint. Nature is not democratic, nor limited-monarchical, but despotic, and will not be fooled or abated of any jot of her authority, by the pertest of her sons: and as fast as the public mind is opened to more intelligence, the code is seen to be brute and stammering. It speaks not articulately, and must be made to. Meantime the education of the general mind never stops. The reveries of the true and simple are prophetic. What the tender poetic youth dreams, and prays, and paints today, but shuns the ridicule of saying aloud, shall presently be the resolutions of public bodies, then shall be carried as grievance and bill of rights through conflict and war, and then shall be triumphant law and establishment for a hundred years, until it gives place, in turn, to new prayers and pictures. The history of the State sketches in coarse outline the progress of thought, and follows at a distance the delicacy of culture and of aspiration.

The theory of politics, which has possessed the mind of men, and which they have expressed the best they could in their laws and in their revolutions, considers persons and property as the two objects for whose protection government exists. Of persons, all have equal rights, in virtue of being identical in nature. This interest, of course, with its whole power demands a democracy. Whilst the rights of all as persons are equal, in virtue of their access to reason, their rights in property are very unequal. One man owns his clothes, and another owns a county. This accident, depending, primarily, on the skill and virtue of the parties, of which there is every degree, and, secondarily, on patrimony, falls unequally, and its rights, of course, are unequal. Personal rights, universally the same, demand a government framed on the ratio of the census: property demands a government framed on the ratio of owners and of owning. Laban, who has flocks and herds, wishes them looked after by an officer on the frontiers, lest the Midianites shall drive them off, and pays a tax to that end. Jacob has no flocks or herds, and no fear of the Midianites, and pays no tax to the officer. It seemed fit that Laban and Jacob should have equal rights to elect the officer, who is to defend their persons, but that Laban, and not Jacob, should elect the officer who is to guard the sheep and cattle.[4] And, if question arise whether additional officers or watch-towers should be provided, must not Laban and Isaac, and those who must sell part of their herds to buy protection for the rest, judge

---

4. Cf. Genesis 28–31. Emerson is rather free with the story as told in the Bible.

better of this, and with more right, than Jacob, who, because he is a youth and a traveller, eats their bread and not his own?

In the earliest society the proprietors made their own wealth, and so long as it comes to the owners in the direct way, no other opinion would arise in any equitable community, than that property should make the law for property, and persons the law for persons.

But property passes through donation or inheritance to those who do not create it. Gift, in one case, makes it as really the new owner's, as labor made it the first owner's: in the other case, of patrimony, the law makes an ownership, which will be valid in each man's view according to the estimate which he sets on the public tranquility.

It was not, however, found easy to embody the readily admitted principle, that property should make law for property, and persons for persons: since persons and property mixed themselves in every transaction. At last it seemed settled, that the rightful distinction was, that the proprietors should have more elective franchise than non-proprietors, on the Spartan principle of "calling that which is just, equal; not that which is equal, just."[5]

That principle no longer looks so self-evident[6] as it appeared in former times, partly, because doubts have arisen whether too much weight had not been allowed in the laws, to property, and such a structure given to our usages, as allowed the rich to encroach on the poor, and to keep them poor; but mainly, because there is an instinctive sense, however obscure and yet inarticulate, that the whole constitution of property, on its present tenures, is injurious, and its influence on persons deteriorating and degrading; that truly, the only interest for the consideration of the State, is persons: that property will always follow persons; that the highest end of government is the culture of men: and if men can be educated, the institutions will share their improvement, and the moral sentiment will write the law of the land.

If it be not easy to settle the equity of this question, the peril is less when we take note of our natural defences. We are kept by better guards than the vigilance of such magistrates as we commonly elect. Society always consists, in greatest part, of young and foolish persons. The old, who have seen through the hypocrisy of courts and statesmen, die, and leave no wisdom to their sons. These believe their own newspaper, as their fathers did at their age. With such an ignorant and deceivable majority, States would soon run to ruin, but that there are limitations, beyond which the folly and ambition of governors cannot go. Things have their laws, as well as men; and things refuse to be trifled with.[7] Property will be protected. Corn will not grow, unless it is planted and manured; but the farmer will not plant or hoe it, unless the chances are a hundred to one, that he will cut and harvest it. Under any forms, persons and property must and will have their just sway. They exert their power, as steadily as matter its attraction. Cover up a pound of earth never so cunningly, divide and subdivide it; melt it to liquid, convert it to gas; it will always weigh a pound: it will always attract and resist other matter, by the full virtue of one pound weight;—and the attributes of a person, his wit and his moral energy, will exercise, under any law or extinguishing tyranny, their proper force,—if not overtly, then covertly; if not

5. From Plutarch's *Moralia*.
6. This is perhaps a subtle allusion to the "self-evident" truths confidently asserted in the opening of the Declaration of Independence.
7. Emerson offers a slightly different version of this Latin proverb in "Compensation," p. 140.

for the law, then against it; if not wholesomely, then poisonously; with right, or by might.

The boundaries of personal influence it is impossible to fix, as persons are organs of moral or supernatural force. Under the dominion of an idea, which possesses the minds of multitudes, as civil freedom, or the religious sentiment, the powers of persons are no longer subjects of calculation. A nation of men unanimously bent on freedom, or conquest, can easily confound the arithmetic of statists,[8] and achieve extravagant actions, out of all proportion to their means; as, the Greeks, the Saracens, the Swiss, the Americans, and the French have done.

In like manner, to every particle of property belongs its own attraction.[9] A cent is the representative of a certain quantity of corn or other commodity. Its value is in the necessities of the animal man. It is so much warmth, so much bread, so much water, so much land. The law may do what it will with the owner of property, its just power will still attach to the cent. The law may in a mad freak say, that all shall have power except the owners of property: they shall have no vote. Nevertheless, by a higher law, the property will, year after year, write every statute that respects property. The non-proprietor will be the scribe of the proprietor. What the owners wish to do, the whole power of property will do, either through the law, or else in defiance of it. Of course, I speak of all the property, not merely of the great estates. When the rich are outvoted, as frequently happens, it is the joint treasury of the poor which exceeds their accumulations. Every man owns something, if it is only a cow, or a wheelbarrow, or his arms, and so has that property to dispose of.

The same necessity which secures the rights of person and property against the malignity or folly of the magistrate, determines the form and methods of governing, which are proper to each nation, and to its habit of thought, and nowise transferable to other states of society. In this country, we are very vain of our political institutions, which are singular in this, that they sprung, within the memory of living men, from the character and condition of the people, which they still express with sufficient fidelity,—and we ostentatiously prefer them to any other in history. They are not better, but only fitter for us. We may be wise in asserting the advantage in modern times of the democratic form, but to other states of society, in which religion consecrated the monarchical, that and not this was expedient. Democracy is better for us, because the religious sentiment of the present time accords better with it. Born democrats, we are nowise qualified to judge of monarchy, which, to our fathers living in the monarchical idea, was also relatively right. But our institutions, though in coincidence with the spirit of the age, have not any exemption from the practical defects which have discredited other forms. Every actual State is corrupt. Good men must not obey the laws too well. What satire on government can equal the severity of censure conveyed in the word *politic*, which now for ages has signified *cunning*, intimating that the State is a trick?

The same benign necessity and the same practical abuse appear in the parties into which each State divides itself, of opponents and defenders of the administration of the government. Parties are also founded on instincts, and have better guides to their own humble aims than the sagacity of their leaders. They have nothing perverse in their origin, but rudely mark some real and lasting re-

8. Statisticians.
9. Note Emerson's appropriation of the language of physics for political purposes.

lation. We might as wisely reprove the east wind, or the frost, as a political party, whose members, for the most part, could give no account of their position, but stand for the defence of those interests in which they find themselves. Our quarrel with them begins, when they quit this deep natural ground at the bidding of some leader, and, obeying personal considerations, throw themselves into the maintenance and defence of points, nowise belonging to their system. A party is perpetually corrupted by personality. Whilst we absolve the association from dishonesty, we cannot extend the same charity to their leaders. They reap the rewards of the docility and zeal of the masses which they direct. Ordinarily, our parties are parties of circumstance, and not of principle; as, the planting interest in conflict with the commercial; the party of capitalists, and that of operatives; parties which are identical in their moral character, and which can easily change ground with each other, in the support of many of their measures. Parties of principle, as, religious sects, or the party of free-trade, of universal suffrage, of abolition of slavery, of abolition of capital punishment, degenerate into personalities, or would inspire enthusiasm. The vice of our leading parties in this country (which may be cited as a fair specimen of these societies of opinion) is, that they do not plant themselves on the deep and necessary grounds to which they are respectively entitled, but lash themselves to fury in the carrying of some local and momentary measure, nowise useful to the commonwealth. Of the two great parties, which, at this hour, almost share the nation between them, I should say, that, one has the best cause, and the other contains the best men.[1] The philosopher, the poet, or the religious man, will, of course, wish to cast his vote with the democrat, for free-trade, for wide suffrage, for the abolition of legal cruelties in the penal code, and for facilitating in every manner the access of the young and the poor to the sources of wealth and power. But he can rarely accept the persons whom the so-called popular party propose to him as representatives of these liberalities. They have not at heart the ends which give to the name of democracy what hope and virtue are in it. The spirit of our American radicalism is destructive and aimless: it is not loving; it has no ulterior and divine ends; but is destructive only out of hatred and selfishness. On the other side, the conservative party, composed of the most moderate, able, and cultivated part of the population, is timid, and merely defensive of property. It vindicates no right, it aspires to no real good, it brands no crime, it proposes no generous policy, it does not build, nor write, nor cherish the arts, nor foster religion, nor establish schools, nor encourage science, nor emancipate the slave, nor befriend the poor, or the Indian, or the immigrant. From neither party, when in power, has the world any benefit to expect in science, art, or humanity, at all commensurate with the resources of the nation.

I do not for these defects despair of our republic. We are not at the mercy of any waves of chance. In the strife of ferocious parties, human nature always finds itself cherished, as the children of the convicts at Botany Bay[2] are found to have as healthy a moral sentiment as other children. Citizens of feudal states are alarmed at our democratic institutions lapsing into anarchy; and the older and more cautious among ourselves are learning from Europeans to look with some terror at our turbulent freedom. It is said that in our license of construing the Constitution, and in the despotism of public opinion, we have no anchor; and

1. Emerson was fond of saying that the Democrats had the best principles and the Whigs the best men.
2. Charles Wilkes reported in his *Narrative of the United States Exploring Expedition* (1844) that the children of transported criminals at Botany Bay, New South Wales, seemed to be healthy and happy.

one foreign observer[3] thinks he has found the safeguard in the sanctity of Marriage among us; and another thinks he has found it in our Calvinism. Fisher Ames[4] expressed the popular security more wisely, when he compared a monarchy and a republic, saying, "that a monarchy is a merchantman, which sails well, but will sometimes strike on a rock, and go to the bottom; whilst a republic is a raft, which would never sink, but then your feet are always in water." No forms can have any dangerous importance, whilst we are befriended by the laws of things. It makes no difference how many tons weight of atmosphere presses on our heads, so long as the same pressure resists it within the lungs. Augment the mass a thousand fold, it cannot begin to crush us, as long as reaction is equal to action. The fact of two poles, of two forces, centripetal and centrifugal, is universal, and each force by its own activity develops the other. Wild liberty develops iron conscience. Want of liberty, by strengthening law and decorum, stupefies conscience. 'Lynch-law' prevails only where there is greater hardihood and self-subsistency in the leaders. A mob cannot be a permanency: everybody's interest requires that it should not exist, and only justice satisfies all.

We must trust infinitely to the beneficent necessity which shines through all laws. Human nature expresses itself in them as characteristically as in statues, or songs, or railroads, and an abstract of the codes of nations would be a transcript of the common conscience. Governments have their origin in the moral identity of men. Reason for one is seen to be reason for another, and for every other. There is a middle measure which satisfies all parties, be they never so many, or so resolute for their own. Every man finds a sanction for his simplest claims and deeds in decisions of his own mind, which he calls Truth and Holiness. In these decisions all the citizens find a perfect agreement, and only in these; not in what is good to eat, good to wear, good use of time, or what amount of land, or of public aid, each is entitled to claim. This truth and justice men presently endeavor to make application of, to the measuring of land, the apportionment of service, the protection of life and property. Their first endeavors, no doubt, are very awkward. Yet absolute right is the first governor; or, every government is an impure theocracy. The idea, after which each community is aiming to make and mend its law, is, the will of the wise man. The wise man, it cannot find in nature, and it makes awkward but earnest efforts to secure his government by contrivance; as, by causing the entire people to give their voices on every measure; or, by a double choice to get the representation of the whole; or, by a selection of the best citizens; or, to secure the advantages of efficiency and internal peace, by confiding the government to one, who may himself select his agents. All forms of government symbolize an immortal government, common to all dynasties and independent of numbers, perfect where two men exist, perfect where there is only one man.

Every man's nature is a sufficient advertisement to him of the character of his fellows. My right and my wrong, is their right and their wrong. Whilst I do what is fit for me, and abstain from what is unfit, my neighbor and I shall often agree in our means, and work together for a time to one end. But whenever I find my dominion over myself not sufficient for me, and undertake the direction of him also, I overstep the truth, and come into false relations to him. I may have so much more skill or strength than he, that he cannot express adequately his sense of

---

3. The editors of CW (3.219) suggest that the likeliest "foreign observer" was Alexis de Tocqueville in his *Democracy in America* (1836–40), who believed that "turbulent freedom" in America was mitigated by the institutions of religion and marriage.
4. Federalist lawyer and congressional representative, known for his wit (1758–1808).

wrong, but it is a lie, and hurts like a lie both him and me. Love and nature cannot maintain the assumption: it must be executed by a practical lie, namely, by force. This undertaking for another, is the blunder which stands in colossal ugliness in the governments of the world. It is the same thing in numbers, as in a pair, only not quite so intelligible. I can see well enough a great difference between my setting myself down to a self-control, and my going to make somebody else act after my views: but when a quarter of the human race assume to tell me what I must do, I may be too much disturbed by the circumstances to see so clearly the absurdity of their command. Therefore, all public ends look vague and quixotic beside private ones. For, any laws but those which men make for themselves, are laughable. If I put myself in the place of my child, and we stand in one thought, and see that things are thus or thus, that perception is law for him and me. We are both there, both act. But if, without carrying him into the thought, I look over into his plot, and, guessing how it is with him, ordain this or that, he will never obey me. This is the history of governments, — one man does something which is to bind another. A man who cannot be acquainted with me, taxes me; looking from afar at me, ordains that a part of my labor shall go to this or that whimsical end, not as I, but as he happens to fancy. Behold the consequence. Of all debts, men are least willing to pay the taxes. What a satire is this on government! Everywhere they think they get their money's worth, except for these.

Hence, the less government we have, the better, — the fewer laws, and the less confided power. The antidote to this abuse of formal Government, is, the influence of private character, the growth of the Individual; the appearance of the principal to supersede the proxy; the appearance of the wise man, of whom the existing government, is, it must be owned, but a shabby imitation. That which all things tend to educe, which freedom, cultivation, intercourse, revolutions, go to form and deliver, is character; that is the end of nature, to reach unto this coronation of her king. To educate the wise man, the State exists; and with the appearance of the wise man, the State expires. The appearance of character makes the State unnecessary. The wise man is the State. He needs no army, fort, or navy, — he loves men too well; no bribe, or feast, or palace, to draw friends to him; no vantage ground, no favorable circumstance. He needs no library, for he has not done thinking; no church, for he is a prophet; no statute book, for he has the lawgiver; no money, for he is value; no road, for he is at home where he is; no experience, for the life of the creator shoots through him, and looks from his eyes. He has no personal friends, for he who has the spell to draw the prayer and piety of all men unto him, needs not husband and educate a few, to share with him a select and poetic life. His relation to men is angelic; his memory is myrrh to them; his presence, frankincense and flowers.

We think our civilization near its meridian, but we are yet only at the cockcrowing and the morning star. In our barbarous society the influence of character is in its infancy. As a political power, as the rightful lord who is to tumble all rulers from their chairs, its presence is hardly yet suspected. Malthus and Ricardo quite omit it; the Annual Register is silent; in the Conversations' Lexicon,[5] it is not set down; the President's Message, the Queen's Speech, have not mentioned it; and yet it is never nothing. Every thought which genius and piety throw into the world, alters the world. The gladiators in the lists of power feel, through

---

5. The *Annual Register* and *Conversations' Lexicon* were summaries of current events and civic matters. Thomas Robert Malthus (1766–1834) and David Ricardo (1772–1823), English political economists.

all their frocks of force and simulation, the presence of worth. I think the very strife of trade and ambition are confession of this divinity; and successes in those fields are the poor amends, the fig-leaf with which the shamed soul attempts to hide its nakedness. I find the like unwilling homage in all quarters. It is because we know how much is due from us, that we are impatient to show some petty talent as a substitute for worth. We are haunted by a conscience of this right to grandeur of character, and are false to it. But each of us has some talent, can do somewhat useful, or graceful, or formidable, or amusing, or lucrative. That we do, as an apology to others and to ourselves, for not reaching the mark of a good and equal life. But it does not satisfy *us*, whilst we thrust it on the notice of our companions. It may throw dust in their eyes, but does not smooth our own brow, or give us the tranquillity of the strong when we walk abroad. We do penance as we go. Our talent is a sort of expiation, and we are constrained to reflect on our splendid moment, with a certain humiliation, as somewhat too fine, and not as one act of many acts, a fair expression of our permanent energy. Most persons of ability meet in society with a kind of tacit appeal. Each seems to say, 'I am not all here.' Senators and presidents have climbed so high with pain enough, not because they think the place specially agreeable, but as an apology for real worth, and to vindicate their manhood in our eyes. This conspicuous chair is their compensation to themselves for being of a poor, cold, hard nature. They must do what they can. Like one class of forest animals, they have nothing but a prehensile tail: climb they must, or crawl. If a man found himself so rich-natured that he could enter into strict relations with the best persons, and make life serene around him by the dignity and sweetness of his behavior, could he afford to circumvent the favor of the caucus and the press, and covet relations so hollow and pompous, as those of a politician? Surely nobody would be a charlatan, who could afford to be sincere.

The tendencies of the times favor the idea of self-government, and leave the individual, for all code, to the rewards and penalties of his own constitution, which work with more energy than we believe, whilst we depend on artificial restraints. The movement in this direction has been very marked in modern history. Much has been blind and discreditable, but the nature of the revolution is not affected by the vices of the revolters; for this is a purely moral force. It was never adopted by any party in history, neither can be. It separates the individual from all party, and unites him, at the same time, to the race. It promises a recognition of higher rights than those of personal freedom, or the security of property. A man has a right to be employed, to be trusted, to be loved, to be revered. The power of love, as the basis of a State, has never been tried. We must not imagine that all things are lapsing into confusion, if every tender protestant be not compelled to bear his part in certain social conventions: nor doubt that roads can be built, letters carried, and the fruit of labor secured, when the government of force is at an end. Are our methods now so excellent that all competition is hopeless? Could not a nation of friends even devise better ways? On the other hand, let not the most conservative and timid fear anything from a premature surrender of the bayonet, and the system of force. For, according to the order of nature, which is quite superior to our will, it stands thus; there will always be a government of force, where men are selfish; and when they are pure enough to abjure the code of force, they will be wise enough to see how these public ends of the post-office, of the highway, of commerce, and the exchange of property, of museums and libraries, of institutions of art and science, can be answered.

We live in a very low state of the world, and pay unwilling tribute to governments founded on force. There is not, among the most religious and instructed men of the most religious and civil nations, a reliance on the moral sentiment, and a sufficient belief in the unity of things to persuade them that society can be maintained without artificial restraints, as well as the solar system; or that the private citizen might be reasonable, and a good neighbor, without the hint of a jail or a confiscation. What is strange too, there never was in any man sufficient faith in the power of rectitude, to inspire him with the broad design of renovating the State on the principle of right and love. All those who have pretended this design, have been partial reformers, and have admitted in some manner the supremacy of the bad State. I do not call to mind a single human being who has steadily denied the authority of the laws, on the simple ground of his own moral nature. Such designs, full of genius and full of fate as they are, are not entertained except avowedly as air-pictures. If the individual who exhibits them, dare to think them practicable, he disgusts scholars and churchmen; and men of talent, and women of superior sentiments, cannot hide their contempt. Not the less does nature continue to fill the heart of youth with suggestions of this enthusiasm, and there are now men, — if indeed I can speak in the plural number, — more exactly, I will say, I have just been conversing with one man, to whom no weight of adverse experience will make it for a moment appear impossible, that thousands of human beings might share and obey each with the other the grandest and truest sentiments, as well as a knot of friends, or a pair of lovers.

New England Reformers

A Lecture Read before the Society in Amory Hall,[1] on Sunday, 3 March, 1844.

> In the suburb, in the town,
> On the railway, in the square,
> Came a beam of goodness down
> Doubling daylight everywhere:
> Peace now each for malice takes,
> Beauty for his sinful weeds,
> For the angel Hope aye makes
> Him an angel whom she leads.[2]

Whoever has had opportunity of acquaintance with society in New England, during the last twenty-five years, with those middle and with those leading sections that may constitute any just representation of the character and aim of the community, will have been struck with the great activity of thought and experimenting. His attention must be commanded by the signs that the Church, or religious party, is falling from the church nominal, and is appearing in temperance and non-resistance societies, in movements of abolitionists and of socialists,

---

1. The "Society" at Amory Hall, Boston, has recently been identified as a loosely connected group of reformers associated with various causes who arranged a lecture series to substitute addresses related to radical social action for traditional Sunday church services. In his oration Emerson was thus, as Linck C. Johnson explains, bent on "Reforming the Reformers." Among other participants in the series were William Lloyd Garrison (1807–1879), journalist and founder of the American Anti-Slavery Society; Wendell Phillips (1811–1884), American abolitionist and reformer known for his eloquence; and — probably owing to Emerson's instigation — Thoreau (see n. 1, p. 93).
2. This motto, by Emerson, was added in the 1850 edition of *Essays: Second Series.*

and in very significant assemblies, called Sabbath and Bible Conventions,—composed of ultraists, of seekers, of all the soul of the soldiery of dissent, and meeting to call in question the authority of the Sabbath, of the priesthood, and of the church. In these movements, nothing was more remarkable than the discontent they begot in the movers. The spirit of protest and of detachment, drove the members of these Conventions to bear testimony against the church, and immediately afterward, to declare their discontent with these Conventions, their independence of their colleagues, and their impatience of the methods whereby they were working. They defied each other, like a congress of kings, each of whom had a realm to rule, and a way of his own that made concert unprofitable. What a fertility of projects for the salvation of the world! One apostle thought all men should go to farming; and another, that no man should buy or sell: that the use of money was the cardinal evil; another, that the mischief was in our diet, that we eat and drink damnation. These made unleavened bread, and were foes to the death to fermentation. It was in vain urged by the housewife, that God made yeast, as well as dough, and loves fermentation just as dearly as he loves vegetation; that fermentation develops the saccharine element in the grain, and makes it more palatable and more digestible. No; they wish the pure wheat, and will die but it shall not ferment. Stop, dear nature, these incessant advances of thine; let us scotch these ever-rolling wheels! Others attacked the system of agriculture, the use of animal manures in farming; and the tyranny of man over brute nature; these abuses polluted his food. The ox must be taken from the plough, and the horse from the cart, the hundred acres of the farm must be spaded, and the man must walk wherever boats and locomotives will not carry him. Even the insect world was to be defended,—that had been too long neglected, and a society for the protection of ground-worms, slugs, and mosquitos was to be incorporated without delay. With these appeared the adepts of homœopathy, of hydropathy, of mesmerism, of phrenology,[3] and their wonderful theories of the Christian miracles! Others assailed particular vocations, as that of the lawyer, that of the merchant, of the manufacturer, of the clergyman, of the scholar. Others attacked the institution of marriage, as the fountain of social evils. Others devoted themselves to the worrying of churches and meetings for public worship; and the fertile forms of antinomianism[4] among the elder puritans, seemed to have their match in the plenty of the new harvest of reform.

With this din of opinion and debate, there was a keener scrutiny of institutions and domestic life than any we had known, there was sincere protesting against existing evils, and there were changes of employment dictated by conscience. No doubt, there was plentiful vaporing, and cases of backsliding might occur. But in each of these movements emerged a good result, a tendency to the adoption of simpler methods, and an assertion of the sufficiency of the private man. Thus it was directly in the spirit and genius of the age, what happened in one instance, when a church censured and threatened to excommunicate one of its members, on account of the somewhat hostile part to the church, which his conscience led him to take in the anti-slavery business; the threatened individual immediately excommunicated the church in a public and formal process. This has been several times repeated: it was excellent when it was done the first time,

---

3. Emerson singles out some current fads. *Homeopathy:* a system for treating disease that prescribes small doses of drugs that in larger doses produce the symptoms of the disease. *Hydropathy:* called "the water cure." *Mesmerism:* see n. 9, p. 53. *Phrenology:* see n. 4, p. 201.

4. See n. 9, p. 96.

but, of course, loses all value when it is copied. Every project in the history of re-form, no matter how violent and surprising, is good, when it is the dictate of a man's genius and constitution, but very dull and suspicious when adopted from another. It is right and beautiful in any man to say, 'I will take this coat, or this book, or this measure of corn of yours,'—in whom we see the act to be original, and to flow from the whole spirit and faith of him; for then that taking will have a giving as free and divine: but we are very easily disposed to resist the same gen-erosity of speech, when we miss originality and truth to character in it.

There was in all the practical activities of New England, for the last quar-ter of a century, a gradual withdrawal of tender consciences from the social or-ganizations. There is observable throughout, the contest between mechanical and spiritual methods, but with a steady tendency of the thoughtful and virtu-ous to a deeper belief and reliance on spiritual facts.

In politics, for example, it is easy to see the progress of dissent. The country is full of rebellion; the country is full of kings. Hands off! let there be no control and no interference in the administration of the affairs of this kingdom of me. Hence the growth of the doctrine and of the party of Free Trade, and the willing-ness to try that experiment, in the face of what appear incontestable facts. I con-fess, the motto of the Globe newspaper is so attractive to me, that I can seldom find much appetite to read what is below it in its columns, "The world is governed too much." So the country is frequently affording solitary examples of resistance to the government, solitary nullifiers, who throw themselves on their reserved rights; nay, who have reserved all their rights; who reply to the assessor, and to the clerk of court, that they do not know the State; and embarrass the courts of law, by non-juring, and the commander-in-chief of the militia, by non-resistance.

The same disposition to scrutiny and dissent appeared in civil, festive, neighborly, and domestic society. A restless, prying, conscientious criticism broke out in unexpected quarters. Who gave me the money with which I bought my coat? Why should professional labor and that of the counting-house be paid so disproportionately to the labor of the porter, and woodsawyer? This whole business of Trade gives me to pause and think, as it constitutes false re-lations between men; inasmuch as I am prone to count myself relieved of any responsibility to behave well and nobly to that person whom I pay with money, whereas if I had not that commodity, I should be put on my good behavior in all companies, and man would be a benefactor to man, as being himself his only certificate that he had a right to those aids and services which each asked of the other. Am I not too protected a person? is there not a wide disparity between the lot of me and the lot of thee, my poor brother, my poor sister? Am I not de-frauded of my best culture in the loss of those gymnastics which manual labor and the emergencies of poverty constitute? I find nothing healthful or exalting in the smooth conventions of society; I do not like the close air of saloons.[5] I begin to suspect myself to be a prisoner, though treated with all this courtesy and luxury. I pay a destructive tax in my conformity.

The same insatiable criticism may be traced in the efforts for the reform of Education. The popular education has been taxed with a want of truth and na-ture. It was complained that an education to things was not given. We are students of words: we are shut up in schools, and colleges, and recitation-rooms, for ten or fifteen years, and come out at last with a bag of wind, a memory of words, and do

5. Used here to mean drawing rooms or ballrooms; salons.

not know a thing. We cannot use our hands, or our legs, or our eyes, or our arms. We do not know an edible root in the woods, we cannot tell our course by the stars, nor the hour of the day by the sun. It is well if we can swim and skate. We are afraid of a horse, of a cow, of a dog, of a snake, of a spider. The Roman rule was, to teach a boy nothing that he could not learn standing. The old English rule was, 'All summer in the field, and all winter in the study.' And it seems as if a man should learn to plant, or to fish, or to hunt, that he might secure his subsistence at all events, and not be painful to his friends and fellow men. The lessons of science should be experimental also. The sight of the planet through a telescope, is worth all the course on astronomy; the shock of the electric spark in the elbow, outvalues all the theories; the taste of the nitrous oxide, the firing of an artificial volcano,[6] are better than volumes of chemistry.

One of the traits of the new spirit, is the inquisition it fixed on our scholastic devotion to the dead languages. The ancient languages, with great beauty of structure, contain wonderful remains of genius, which draw, and always will draw, certain likeminded men, — Greek men, and Roman men, in all countries, to their study; but by a wonderful drowsiness of usage, they had exacted the study of *all* men. Once (say two centuries ago), Latin and Greek had a strict relation to all the science and culture there was in Europe, and the Mathematics had a momentary importance at some era of activity in physical science. These things became stereotyped as *education*, as the manner of men is. But the Good Spirit never cared for the colleges, and though all men and boys were now drilled in Latin, Greek, and Mathematics, it had quite left these shells high and dry on the beach, and was now creating and feeding other matters at other ends of the world. But in a hundred high schools and colleges, this warfare against common sense still goes on. Four, or six, or ten years, the pupil is parsing Greek and Latin, and as soon as he leaves the University, as it is ludicrously styled, he shuts those books for the last time. Some thousands of young men are graduated at our colleges in this country every year, and the persons who, at forty years, still read Greek, can all be counted on your hand. I never met with ten. Four or five persons I have seen who read Plato.[7]

But is not this absurd, that the whole liberal talent of this country should be directed in its best years on studies which lead to nothing? What was the consequence? Some intelligent persons said or thought: 'Is that Greek and Latin some spell to conjure with, and not words of reason? If the physician, the lawyer, the divine, never use it to come at their ends, I need never learn it to come at mine. Conjuring is gone out of fashion, and I will omit this conjugating, and go straight to affairs.' So they jumped the Greek and Latin, and read law, medicine, or sermons, without it. To the astonishment of all, the self-made men took even ground at once with the oldest of the regular graduates, and in a few months the most conservative circles of Boston and New York had quite forgotten who of their gownsmen was college-bred, and who was not.

One tendency appears alike in the philosophical speculation, and in the rudest democratical movements, through all the petulance and all the puerility, the wish, namely, to cast aside the superfluous, arrive at short methods, urged, as I suppose, by an intuition that the human spirit is equal to all emergencies, alone, and that man is more often injured than helped by the means he uses.

6. A sputtering firework. *Nitrous oxide:* laughing gas; Emerson observed his brother-in-law, Dr. Charles T. Jackson, use it as an anesthetic.
7. For the long debate in America about the value of a classical education see CW 3.221.

I conceive this gradual casting off of material aids, and the indication of growing trust in the private, self-supplied powers of the individual, to be the affirmative principle of the recent philosophy: and that it is feeling its own profound truth, and is reaching forward at this very hour to the happiest conclusions. I readily concede that in this, as in every period of intellectual activity, there has been a noise of denial and protest; much was to be resisted, much was to be got rid of by those who were reared in the old, before they could begin to affirm and to construct. Many a reformer perishes in his removal of rubbish, — and that makes the offensiveness of the class. They are partial; they are not equal to the work they pretend. They lose their way; in the assault on the kingdom of darkness, they expend all their energy on some accidental evil, and lose their sanity and power of benefit. It is of little moment that one or two, or twenty errors of our social system be corrected, but of much that the man be in his senses.

The criticism and attack on institutions which we have witnessed, has made one thing plain, that society gains nothing whilst a man, not himself renovated, attempts to renovate things around him: he has become tediously good in some particular, but negligent or narrow in the rest; and hypocrisy and vanity are often the disgusting result.

It is handsomer to remain in the establishment better than the establishment, and conduct that in the best manner, than to make a sally against evil by some single improvement, without supporting it by a total regeneration. Do not be so vain of your one objection. Do you think there is only one? Alas! my good friend, there is no part of society or of life better than any other part. All our things are right and wrong together. The wave of evil washes all our institutions alike. Do you complain of our Marriage? Our marriage is no worse than our education, our diet, our trade, our social customs. Do you complain of the laws of Property? It is a pedantry to give such importance to them. Can we not play the game of life with these counters, as well as with those; in the institution of property, as well as out of it. Let into it the new and renewing principle of love, and property[8] will be universality. No one gives the impression of superiority to the institution, which he must give who will reform it. It makes no difference what you say: you must make me feel that you are aloof from it; by your natural and supernatural advantages, do easily see to the end of it, — do see how man can do without it. Now all men are on one side. No man deserves to be heard against property. Only Love, only an Idea, is against property, as we hold it.

I cannot afford to be irritable and captious, nor to waste all my time in attacks. If I should go out of church whenever I hear a false sentiment, I could never stay there five minutes. But why come out?[9] the street is as false as the church, and when I get to my house, or to my manners, or to my speech, I have not got away from the lie. When we see an eager assailant of one of these wrongs, a special reformer, we feel like asking him. What right have you, sir, to your one virtue? Is virtue piecemeal? This is a jewel amidst the rags of a beggar.

In another way the right will be vindicated. In the midst of abuses, in the heart of cities, in the aisles of false churches, alike in one place and in another, — wherever, namely, a just and heroic soul finds itself, there it will do what is next at hand, and by the new quality of character it shall put forth, it shall abrogate that old condition, law or school in which it stands, before the law of its own mind.

8. In the Latin sense of *proprius*: "that which belongs to oneself."
9. In New England, *come-outer* had developed the meaning of "a dissenter, a religious radical." Cf. 2 Corinthians 6.17.

If partiality was one fault of the movement party, the other defect was their reliance on Association. Doubts such as those I have intimated, drove many good persons to agitate the questions of social reform. But the revolt against the spirit of commerce, the spirit of aristocracy, and the inveterate abuses of cities, did not appear possible to individuals; and to do battle against numbers, they armed themselves with numbers, and against concert, they relied on new concert.

Following, or advancing beyond the ideas of St. Simon, of Fourier, and of Owen, three communities have already been formed in Massachusetts on kindred plans, and many more in the country at large.[1] They aim to give every member a share in the manual labor, to give an equal reward to labor and to talent, and to unite a liberal culture with an education to labor. The scheme offers, by the economies of associated labor and expense, to make every member rich, on the same amount of property, that, in separate families, would leave every member poor. These new associations are composed of men and women of superior talents and sentiments: yet it may easily be questioned, whether such a community will draw, except in its beginnings, the able and the good; whether those who have energy, will not prefer their chance of superiority and power in the world, to the humble certainties of the association; whether such a retreat does not promise to become an asylum to those who have tried and failed, rather than a field to the strong; and whether the members will not necessarily be fractions of men, because each finds that he cannot enter it, without some compromise. Friendship and association are very fine things, and a grand phalanx of the best of the human race, banded for some catholic object: yes, excellent; but remember that no society can ever be so large as one man. He in his friendship, in his natural and momentary associations, doubles or multiplies himself; but in the hour in which he mortgages himself to two or ten or twenty, he dwarfs himself below the stature of one.

But the men of less faith could not thus believe, and to such, concert appears the sole specific of strength. I have failed, and you have failed, but perhaps together we shall not fail. Our housekeeping is not satisfactory to us, but perhaps a phalanx, a community, might be. Many of us have differed in opinion, and we could find no man who could make the truth plain, but possibly a college, or an ecclesiastical council might. I have not been able either to persuade my brother or to prevail on myself, to disuse the traffic or the potation of brandy, but perhaps a pledge of total abstinence might effectually restrain us. The candidate my party votes for is not to be trusted with a dollar, but he will be honest in the Senate, for we can bring public opinion to bear on him. Thus concert was the specific in all cases. But concert is neither better nor worse, neither more nor less potent than individual force. All the men in the world cannot make a statue walk and speak, cannot make a drop of blood, or blade of grass, any more than one man can. But let there be one man, let there be truth in two men, in ten men, then is concert for the first time possible, because the force which moves the world is a new quality, and can never be furnished by adding whatever quantities of a different kind. What is the use of the concert of the false and the disunited?

1. In 1841 Emerson made the painful decision not to join George Ripley, Margaret Fuller, and others, in forming the Brook Farm Institute of Agriculture and Education in West Roxbury, Massachusetts (see p. 203). Influenced by Fourierism, the group changed its name to the Brook Farm Phalanx in 1846. *Phalanx*, originally a military term, was Fourier's name for a commune of fifteen hundred to two thousand people. Claude Henri de Rouvroy, comte de Saint Simon (1760–1825), French philosopher and social reformer. Fourier, see n. 3, p. 133. Robert Owen (1771–1858), Welsh-born English manufacturer and pioneer of British socialism. In 1825 he re-established the New Harmony Community in southern Indiana.

There can be no concert in two, where there is no concert in one. When the individual is not *individual*, but is dual; when his thoughts look one way, and his actions another; when his faith is traversed by his habits; when his will, enlightened by reason, is warped by his sense; when with one hand he rows, and with the other backs water, what concert can be?

I do not wonder at the interest these projects inspire. The world is awaking to the idea of union, and these experiments show what it is thinking of. It is and will be magic. Men will live and communicate, and plough, and reap, and govern, as by added ethereal power, when once they are united; as in a celebrated experiment, by expiration and respiration exactly together, four persons lift a heavy man from the ground by the little finger only, and without sense of weight. But this union must be inward, and not one of covenants, and is to be reached by a reverse of the methods they use. The union is only perfect, when all the uniters are isolated. It is the union of friends who live in different streets or towns. Each man, if he attempts to join himself to others, is on all sides cramped and diminished of his proportion; and the stricter the union, the smaller and the more pitiful he is. But leave him alone, to recognize in every hour and place the secret soul, he will go up and down doing the works of a true member, and, to the astonishment of all, the work will be done with concert, though no man spoke. Government will be adamantine[2] without any governor. The union must be ideal in actual individualism.

I pass to the indication in some particulars of that faith in man, which the heart is preaching to us in these days, and which engages the more regard, from the consideration, that the speculations of one generation are the history of the next following.

In alluding just now to our system of education, I spoke of the deadness of its details. But it is open to graver criticism than the palsy of its members: it is a system of despair. The disease with which the human mind now labors, is want of faith. Men do not believe in a power of education. We do not think we can speak to divine sentiments in man, and we do not try. We renounce all high aims. We believe that the defects of so many perverse and so many frivolous people, who make up society, are organic, and society is a hospital of incurables. A man of good sense but of little faith, whose compassion seemed to lead him to church as often as he went there, said to me, "that he liked to have concerts, and fairs, and churches, and other public amusements go on." I am afraid the remark is too honest, and comes from the same origin as the maxim of the tyrant, "If you would rule the world quietly, you must keep it amused." I notice too, that the ground on which eminent public servants urge the claims of popular education is fear: 'This country is filling up with thousands and millions of voters, and you must educate them to keep them from our throats.' We do not believe that any education, any system of philosophy, any influence of genius, will ever give depth of insight to a superficial mind. Having settled ourselves into this infidelity, our skill is expended to procure alleviations, diversion, opiates. We adorn the victim with manual skill, his tongue with languages, his body with inoffensive and comely manners. So have we cunningly hid the tragedy of limitation and inner death we cannot avert. Is it strange that society should be devoured by a secret melancholy, which breaks through all its smiles, and all its gayety and games?

---

2. Emerson seems to mean something like "unyielding"—i.e., the government will be strong though no one governs.

But even one step farther our infidelity has gone. It appears that some doubt is felt by good and wise men, whether really the happiness and probity of men is increased by the culture of the mind in those disciplines to which we give the name of education. Unhappily, too, the doubt comes from scholars, from persons who have tried these methods. In their experience, the scholar was not raised by the sacred thoughts amongst which he dwelt, but used them to selfish ends. He was a profane person, and became a showman, turning his gifts to a marketable use, and not to his own sustenance and growth. It was found that the intellect could be independently developed, that is, in separation from the man, as any single organ can be invigorated, and the result was monstrous. A canine appetite for knowledge was generated, which must still be fed, but was never satisfied, and this knowledge not being directed on action, never took the character of substantial, humane truth, blessing those whom it entered. It gave the scholar certain powers of expression, the power of speech, the power of poetry, of literary art, but it did not bring him to peace, or to beneficence.

When the literary class betray a destitution of faith, it is not strange that society should be disheartened and sensualized by unbelief. What remedy? Life must be lived on a higher plane. We must go up to a higher platform, to which we are always invited to ascend; there, the whole aspect of things changes. I resist the skepticism of our education, and of our educated men. I do not believe that the differences of opinion and character in men are organic. I do not recognize, beside the class of the good and the wise, a permanent class of skeptics, or a class of conservatives, or of malignants, or of materialists. I do not believe in two classes. You remember the story of the poor woman who importuned King Philip of Macedon to grant her justice, which Philip refused: the woman exclaimed, "I appeal": the king, astonished, asked to whom she appealed: the woman replied, "from Philip drunk to Philip sober." The text will suit me very well. I believe not in two classes of men, but in man in two moods, in Philip drunk and Philip sober. I think, according to the good-hearted word of Plato, "Unwillingly the soul is deprived of truth." Iron conservative, miser, or thief, no man is, but by a supposed necessity, which he tolerates by shortness or torpidity of sight. The soul lets no man go without some visitations and holydays of a diviner presence. It would be easy to show, by a narrow scanning of any man's biography, that we are not so wedded to our paltry performances of every kind, but that every man has at intervals the grace to scorn his performances, in comparing them with his belief of what he should do, that he puts himself on the side of his enemies, listening gladly to what they say of him, and accusing himself of the same things.

What is it men love in Genius, but its infinite hope, which degrades all it has done? Genius counts all its miracles poor and short. Its own idea it never executed. The Iliad, the Hamlet, the Doric column, the Roman arch, the Gothic minster, the German anthem, when they are ended, the master casts behind him. How sinks the song in the waves of melody which the universe pours over his soul! Before that gracious Infinite, out of which he drew these few strokes, how mean they look, though the praises of the world attend them. From the triumphs of his art, he turns with desire to this greater defeat. Let those admire who will. With silent joy he sees himself to be capable of a beauty that eclipses all which his hands have done, all which human hands have ever done.

Well, we are all the children of genius, the children of virtue,—and feel their inspirations in our happier hours. Is not every man sometimes a radical in politics? Men are conservatives when they are least vigorous, or when they are most luxurious. They are conservatives after dinner, or before taking their rest; when they are sick, or aged: in the morning, or when their intellect or their conscience has been aroused, when they hear music, or when they read poetry, they are radicals. In the circle of the rankest tories that could be collected in England, Old or New, let a powerful and stimulating intellect, a man of great heart and mind, act on them, and very quickly these frozen conservators will yield to the friendly influence, these hopeless will begin to hope, these haters will begin to love, these immovable statues will begin to spin and revolve. I cannot help recalling the fine anecdote which Warton relates of Bishop Berkeley,[3] when he was preparing to leave England, with his plan of planting the gospel among the American savages. "Lord Bathurst told me, that the members of the Scriblerus club, being met at his house at dinner, they agreed to rally Berkeley, who was also his guest, on his scheme at Bermudas. Berkeley, having listened to the many lively things they had to say, begged to be heard in his turn, and displayed his plan with such an astonishing and animating force of eloquence and enthusiasm, that they were struck dumb, and, after some pause, rose up all together with earnestness, exclaiming, 'Let us set out with him immediately.'" Men in all ways are better than they seem. They like flattery for the moment, but they know the truth for their own. It is a foolish cowardice which keeps us from trusting them, and speaking to them rude truth. They resent your honesty for an instant, they will thank you for it always. What is it we heartily wish of each other? Is it to be pleased and flattered? No, but to be convicted and exposed, to be shamed out of our nonsense of all kinds, and made men of, instead of ghosts and phantoms. We are weary of gliding ghostlike through the world, which is itself so slight and unreal. We crave a sense of reality, though it come in strokes of pain. I explain so,—by this manlike love of truth,—those excesses and errors into which souls of great vigor, but not equal insight, often fall. They feel the poverty at the bottom of all the seeming affluence of the world. They know the speed with which they come straight through the thin masquerade, and conceive a disgust at the indigence of nature: Rousseau, Mirabeau, Charles Fox, Napoleon, Byron,[4]—and I could easily add names nearer home, of raging riders, who drive their steeds so hard, in the violence of living to forget its illusion: they would know the worst, and tread the floors of hell. The heroes of ancient and modern fame, Cimon, Themistocles, Alcibiades, Alexander, Cæsar,[5] have treated life and fortune as a game to be well and skilfully played, but the stake not to be so valued, but that any time, it could be held as a trifle light as air, and thrown up. Cæsar, just before the battle of Pharsalia,[6] discourses with the Egyptian priest, concerning the fountains of the Nile, and offers to quit the army, the empire, and Cleopatra, if he will show him those mysterious sources.

3. Berkeley (see n. 1, p. 43) was enthusiastic about the promise of the New World and lived in Rhode Island from 1728 to 1732. His poem "On the Prospect of Planting Arts and Learning in America" contains the famous line, "Westward the course of empire takes its way." Joseph Warton (1722–1800), English writer and critic.
4. See n. 2, p. 162. Jean Jacques Rousseau (1712–1778), French philosopher and writer who held that humanity is essentially good but corrupted by society. His written works include *The Social Contract* and the novel *Emile* (both 1762) as well as *Confessions* (1766–70). Honoré Gabriel Victor Riqueti, comte de Mirabeau (1749–1791), French orator and revolutionary leader. Charles James Fox (1749–1806), celebrated English politician and orator, favored reconciliation with the American colonies, urged the abolition of slavery, and supported the French Revolution. Napoleon, see n. 8, p. 17.
5. See n. 8, p. 17. Cimon (fifth century B.C.E.), Athenian general who succeeded in expelling the Persians from Greece. Themistocles (ca. 528–ca. 462 B.C.E.), Athenian political leader and general whose genius helped ensure Athens's great victory at Salamis (480 B.C.E.). Alcibiades, see n. 6, p. 106. Alexander the Great (356–323 B.C.E.), celebrated king of Macedon and conquerer of empires.
6. For Caesar and the battle of Pharsalia, see CW 3.234.

The same magnanimity shows itself in our social relations, in the preference, namely, which each man gives to the society of superiors over that of his equals. All that a man has, will he give for right relations with his mates. All that he has, will he give for an erect demeanor in every company and on each occasion. He aims at such things as his neighbors prize, and gives his days and nights, his talents and his heart, to strike a good stroke, to acquit himself in all men's sight as a man. The consideration of an eminent citizen, of a noted merchant, of a man of mark in his profession; naval and military honor, a general's commission, a marshal's baton, a ducal coronet, the laurel of poets, and, anyhow procured, the acknowledgment of eminent merit, have this lustre for each candidate, that they enable him to walk erect and unashamed, in the presence of some persons, before whom he felt himself inferior. Having raised himself to this rank, having established his equality with class after class, of those with whom he would live well, he still finds certain others, before whom he cannot possess himself, because they have somewhat fairer, somewhat grander, somewhat purer, which extorts homage of him. Is his ambition pure? then, will his laurels and his possessions seem worthless: instead of avoiding these men who make his fine gold dim,[7] he will cast all behind him, and seek their society only, woo and embrace this his humiliation and mortification, until he shall know why his eye sinks, his voice is husky, and his brilliant talents are paralyzed in this presence. He is sure that the soul which gives the lie to all things, will tell none. His constitution will not mislead him. If it cannot carry itself as it ought, high and unmatchable in the presence of any man, if the secret oracles whose whisper makes the sweetness and dignity of his life, do here withdraw and accompany him no longer, it is time to undervalue what he has valued, to dispossess himself of what he has acquired, and with Cæsar to take in his hand the army, the empire, and Cleopatra, and say, "All these will I relinquish, if you will show me the fountains of the Nile." Dear to us are those who love us, the swift moments we spend with them are a compensation for a great deal of misery; they enlarge our life; — but dearer are those who reject us as unworthy, for they add another life: they build a heaven before us, whereof we had not dreamed, and thereby supply to us new powers out of the recesses of the spirit, and urge us to new and unattempted performances.

As every man at heart wishes the best and not inferior society, wishes to be convicted of his error, and to come to himself, so he wishes that the same healing should not stop in his thought, but should penetrate his will or active power. The selfish man suffers more from his selfishness, than he from whom that selfishness withholds some important benefit. What he most wishes is to be lifted to some higher platform, that he may see beyond his present fear the transalpine good, so that his fear, his coldness, his custom may be broken up like fragments of ice, melted and carried away in the great stream of good will. Do you ask my aid? I also wish to be a benefactor. I wish more to be a benefactor and servant, than you wish to be served by me, and surely the greatest good fortune that could befall me, is precisely to be so moved by you that I should say, 'Take me and all mine, and use me and mine freely to your ends!' for, I could not say it, otherwise than because a great enlargement had come to my heart and mind, which made me superior to my fortunes. Here we are paralyzed with fear; we hold on to our little properties, house and land, office and money, for the bread which they have in our experience yielded us, although we confess, that our

---

7. Cf. Lamentations 4.1.

being does not flow through them. We desire to be made great, we desire to be touched with that fire which shall command this ice to stream, and make our existence a benefit. If therefore we start objections to your project, O friend of the slave, or friend of the poor, or of the race, understand well, that it is because we wish to drive you to drive us into your measures. We wish to hear ourselves confuted. We are haunted with a belief that you have a secret, which it would highliest advantage us to learn, and we would force you to impart it to us, though it should bring us to prison, or to worse extremity.

Nothing shall warp me from the belief, that every man is a lover of truth. There is no pure lie, no pure malignity in nature. The entertainment of the proposition of depravity is the last profligacy and profanation. There is no skepticism, no atheism but that. Could it be received into common belief, suicide would unpeople the planet. It has had a name to live in some dogmatic theology, but each man's innocence and his real liking of his neighbor, have kept it a dead letter. I remember standing at the polls one day, when the anger of the political contest gave a certain grimness to the faces of the independent electors, and a good man at my side looking on the people, remarked, "I am satisfied that the largest part of these men, on either side, mean to vote right." I suppose, considerate observers looking at the masses of men, in their blameless, and in their equivocal actions, will assent, that in spite of selfishness and frivolity, the general purpose in the great number of persons is fidelity. The reason why any one refuses his assent to your opinion, or his aid to your benevolent design, is in you: he refuses to accept you as a bringer of truth, because, though you think you have it, he feels that you have it not. You have not given him the authentic sign.

If it were worth while to run into details this general doctrine of the latent but ever soliciting Spirit, it would be easy to adduce illustration in particulars of a man's equality to the church, of his equality to the state, and of his equality to every other man. It is yet in all men's memory, that, a few years ago, the liberal churches complained, that the Calvinistic church denied to them the name of Christian. I think the complaint was confession: a religious church would not complain. A religious man like Behmen, Fox, or Swedenborg,[8] is not irritated by wanting the sanction of the church, but the church feels the accusation of his presence and belief.

It only needs, that a just man should walk in our streets, to make it appear how pitiful and inartificial[9] a contrivance is our legislation. The man whose part is taken, and who does not wait for society in anything, has a power which society cannot choose but feel. The familiar experiment, called the hydrostatic paradox, in which a capillary column of water balances the ocean, is a symbol of the relation of one man to the whole family of men. The wise Dandamis,[1] on hearing the lives of Socrates, Pythagoras, and Diogenes read, "judged them to be great men every way, excepting, that they were too much subjected to the reverence of the laws, which to second and authorize, true virtue must abate very much of its original vigor."

And as a man is equal to the church, and equal to the state, so he is equal to every other man. The disparities of power in men are superficial; and all frank and searching conversation, in which a man lays himself open to his brother, apprizes each of their radical unity. When two persons sit and converse in a thor-

8. See n. 6, p. 35. Behmen, n. 8, p. 168. Fox, see n. 1, p. 39.
9. Lacking in art or skill.
1. An Indian sage. Emerson got this anecdote from Montaigne; see CW 3.235.

oughly good understanding, the remark is sure to be made, See how we have disputed about words! Let a clear, apprehensive mind, such as every man knows among his friends, converse with the most commanding poetic genius, I think, it would appear that there was no inequality such as men fancy between them; that a perfect understanding, a like receiving, a like perceiving, abolished differences, and the poet would confess, that his creative imagination gave him no deep advantage, but only the superficial one, that he could express himself, and the other could not; that his advantage was a knack, which might impose on indolent men, but could not impose on lovers of truth; for they know the tax of talent, or, what a price of greatness the power of expression too often pays. I believe it is the conviction of the purest men, that the net amount of man and man does not much vary. Each is incomparably superior to his companion in some faculty. His want of skill in other directions, has added to his fitness for his own work. Each seems to have some compensation yielded to him by his infirmity, and every hindrance operates as a concentration of his force.

These and the like experiences intimate, that man stands in strict connexion with a higher fact never yet manifested. There is power over and behind us, and we are the channels of its communications. We seek to say thus and so, and over our head some spirit sits, which contradicts what we say. We would persuade our fellow to this or that; another self within our eyes dissuades him. That which we keep back, this reveals. In vain we compose our faces and our words; it holds uncontrollable communication with the enemy, and he answers civilly to us, but believes the spirit. We exclaim, 'There's a traitor in the house!' but at last it appears that he is the true man, and I am the traitor. This open channel to the highest life is the first and last reality, so subtle, so quiet, yet so tenacious, that although I have never expressed the truth, and although I have never heard the expression of it from any other, I know that the whole truth is here for me. What if I cannot answer your questions? I am not pained that I cannot frame a reply to the question, What is the operation we call Providence? There lies the unspoken thing, present, omnipresent. Every time we converse, we seek to translate it into speech, but whether we hit, or whether we miss, we have the fact. Every discourse is an approximate answer: but it is of small consequence, that we do not get it into verbs and nouns, whilst it abides for contemplation forever.

If the auguries of the prophesying heart shall make themselves good in time, the man who shall be born, whose advent men and events prepare and foreshow, is one who shall enjoy his connexion with a higher life, with the man within man; shall destroy distrust by his trust, shall use his native but forgotten methods, shall not take counsel of flesh and blood, but shall rely on the Law alive and beautiful, which works over our heads and under our feet. Pitiless, it avails itself of our success, when we obey it, and of our ruin, when we contravene it. Men are all secret believers in it, else, the word justice would have no meaning: they believe that the best is the true; that right is done at last; or chaos would come. It rewards actions after their nature, and not after the design of the agent. 'Work,' it saith to man, 'in every hour, paid or unpaid, see only that thou work, and thou canst not escape the reward: whether thy work be fine or coarse, planting corn, or writing epics, so only it be honest work, done to thine own approbation, it shall earn a reward to the senses as well as to the thought: no matter, how often defeated, you are born to victory. The reward of a thing well done, is to have done it.'

As soon as a man is wonted to look beyond surfaces, and to see how this high will prevails without an exception or an interval, he settles himself into serenity. He can already rely on the laws of gravity, that every stone will fall where it is due; the good globe is faithful, and carries us securely through the celestial spaces, anxious or resigned: we need not interfere to help it on, and he will learn, one day, the mild lesson they teach, that our own orbit is all our task, and we need not assist the administration of the universe. Do not be so impatient to set the town right concerning the unfounded pretensions and the false reputation of certain men of standing. They are laboring harder to set the town right concerning themselves, and will certainly succeed. Suppress for a few days your criticism on the insufficiency of this or that teacher or experimenter, and he will have demonstrated his insufficiency to all men's eyes. In like manner, let a man fall into the divine circuits, and he is enlarged. Obedience to his genius is the only liberating influence. We wish to escape from subjection, and a sense of inferiority,—and we make self-denying ordinances, we drink water, we eat grass, we refuse the laws, we go to jail: it is all in vain; only by obedience to his genius; only by the freest activity in the way constitutional to him, does an angel seem to arise before a man, and lead him by the hand out of all the wards of the prison.

That which befits us, embosomed in beauty and wonder as we are, is cheerfulness and courage, and the endeavor to realize our aspirations. The life of man is the true romance, which, when it is valiantly conducted, will yield the imagination a higher joy than any fiction. All around us, what powers are wrapped up under the coarse mattings of custom, and all wonder prevented. It is so wonderful to our neurologists that a man can see without his eyes, that it does not occur to them, that it is just as wonderful, that he should see with them; and that is ever the difference between the wise and the unwise: the latter wonders at what is unusual, the wise man wonders at the usual. Shall not the heart which has received so much, trust the Power by which it lives? May it not quit other leadings, and listen to the Soul that has guided it so gently, and taught it so much, secure that the future will be worthy of the past?

From Representative Men

Montaigne, or the Skeptic[1]

Every fact is related on one side to sensation, and, on the other, to morals. The game of thought is, on the appearance of one of these two sides, to find the other: given the upper, to find the under side. Nothing so thin, but has these two faces, and, when the observer has seen the obverse, he turns it over to see the reverse. Life is a pitching of this penny, — heads or tails. We never tire of the game, because there is still a slight shudder of astonishment at the exhibition of the other face, at the contrast of the two faces. A man is flushed with success, and bethinks himself what this good luck signifies. He drives his bargain in the street, but it occurs, that he also is bought and sold. He sees the beauty of a human face, and searches the cause of that beauty, which must be more beautiful. He builds his fortunes, maintains the laws, cherishes his children, but he asks himself, Why? and Whereto? This head and this tail are called in the language of philosophy, Infinite and Finite; Relative and Absolute; Apparent and Real; and many fine names beside.

Each man is born with a predisposition to one or the other of these sides of nature, and, it will easily happen that men will be found devoted to one or the other. One class has the perception of Differences, and is conversant with facts and surfaces; cities and persons; and the bringing certain things to pass; — the men of talent and action. Another class have the perception of Identity, and are men of faith and philosophy, men of genius.

Each of these riders drives too fast. Plotinus believes only in philosophers; Fénelon, in saints; Pindar and Byron,[2] in poets. Read the haughty language in which Plato[3] and the Platonists speak of all men who are not devoted to their own shining abstractions: Other men are rats and mice. The literary class is usually proud and exclusive. The correspondence of Pope and Swift describes mankind around them as monsters; and that of Goethe and Schiller,[4] in our own time, is scarcely more kind.

It is easy to see how this arrogance comes. The genius is a genius by the first look he casts on any object. Is his eye creative? Does he not rest in angles and colours, but beholds the design; he will presently undervalue the actual object. In powerful moments, his thought has dissolved the works of art and nature into their causes, so that the works appear heavy and faulty. He has a conception of beauty, which the sculptor cannot embody. Picture, statue, temple,

---

1. Michel Eyquem de Montaigne (1533–1592) was one of Emerson's favorite authors. His *Essays* (1580, 1588) are very personal and pithy.
2. See n. 2, p. 162. Fénelon, see n. 3, p. 14. Plotinus, see n. 1, p. 27. Pindar, see n. 3, p. 33.
3. See n. 4, p. 15.
4. See n. 5, p. 130. Pope, see n. 9, p. 67. Jonathan Swift (1667–1745), Irish-born English writer known for his satirical works, including *Gulliver's Travels* (1726) and *A Modest Proposal* (1729). Goethe, see n. 6, p. 42.

railroad, steamengine, existed first in an artist's mind, without flaw, mistake, or friction, which impair the executed models. So did the church, the state, college, court, social circle, and all the institutions. It is not strange that these men, remembering what they have seen and hoped of ideas, should affirm disdainfully the superiority of ideas. Having at some time seen that the happy soul will carry all the arts in power, they say, Why cumber ourselves with superfluous realizations? And, like dreaming beggars, they assume to speak and act as if these values were already substantiated.

On the other part, the men of toil and trade and luxury, the animal world, including the animal in the philosopher and poet also,—and the practical world, including the painful drudgeries which are never excused to philosopher or poet any more than to the rest, weigh heavily on the other side. The trade in our streets believes in no metaphysical causes, thinks nothing of the force which necessitated traders and a trading planet to exist; no, but sticks to cotton, sugar, wool, and salt. The ward-meetings on election-days are not softened by any misgiving of the value of these ballotings. Hot life is streaming in a single direction. To the men of this world, to the animal strength and spirits, to the men of practical power whilst immersed in it, the man of ideas appears out of his reason. They alone have reason.

Things always bring their own philosophy with them, that is, prudence. No man acquires property without acquiring with it a little arithmetic also. In England, the richest country that ever existed, property stands for more compared with personal ability, than in any other. After dinner, a man believes less, denies more: verities have lost some charm. After dinner, arithmetic is the only science: Ideas are disturbing, incendiary, follies of young men, repudiated by the solid portion of society: and a man comes to be valued by his athletic and animal qualities. Spence relates, that Mr Pope was with Sir Godfrey Kneller,[5] one day, when his nephew, a Guinea trader, came in. "Nephew," said Sir Godfrey, "you have the honour of seeing the two greatest men in the world." — "I don't know how great men you may be," said the Guinea man,[6] "but I don't like your looks. I have often bought a man much better than both of you, all muscles and bones, for ten guineas." Thus the men of the senses revenge themselves on the professors, and repay scorn for scorn. The first had leaped to conclusions not yet ripe, and say more than is true; the others make themselves merry with the philosopher, and weigh man by the pound. They believe that mustard bites the tongue, that pepper is hot, friction-matches are incendiary, revolvers to be avoided, and suspenders hold up pantaloons; that there is much sentiment in a chest of tea; and a man will be eloquent if you give him good wine. Are you tender and scrupulous, you must eat more mince-pie. They hold that Luther had milk in him when he said,

Wer nicht liebt Wein, Weib, und Gesang,
Der bleibt ein Narr sein Leben lang,[7]

---

5. German-born English portrait painter (1646?–1723) whose subjects included English royalty, aristocrats, and scholars; a friend of Pope.
6. Guinea, a country in western Africa on the Atlantic Ocean, was once a French colony (1898–1958). A *Guinea man* was a slave trader.
7. He who doesn't love wine, women and song / Remains a fool his whole life long (German).

and when he advised a young scholar perplexed with foreordination and free-will, to get well drunk. "The nerves," says Cabanis,[8] "they are the man." My neighbor, a jolly farmer in the tavern bar-room, thinks that the use of money is sure and speedy spending. "For his part," he says, "he puts his down his neck, and gets the good of it."

The inconvenience of this way of thinking is that it runs into indifferentism, and then into disgust. Life is eating us up. We shall be fables presently. Keep cool: It will be all one a hundred years hence. Why should we fret and drudge? Our meat will taste tomorrow as it did yesterday, and we may at last have had enough of it. "Ah," said my languid gentleman at Oxford, "there's nothing new, or true, — and no matter."

With a little more bitterness the cynic moans, Our life is like an ass led to market by a bundle of hay being carried before him; he sees nothing but the bundle of hay. "There is so much trouble in coming into the world," said Lord Bolingbroke,[9] "and so much more, as well as meanness, in going out of it, that 'tis hardly worth while to be here at all." I knew a philosopher of this kidney who was accustomed briefly to sum up his experience of human nature, in saying, "Mankind is a damned rascal."[1] And the natural corollary is pretty sure to follow, 'The world lives by humbug, and so will I.'

The abstractionist and the materialist thus mutually exasperating each other, and the scoffer expressing the worst of materialism, there arises a third party to occupy the middle ground between these two, the skeptic, namely. He finds both wrong by being in extremes. He labours to plant his feet, to be the beam of the balance. He will not go beyond his card. He sees the onesidedness of these men of the street; he will not be a Gibeonite;[2] he stands for the intellectual faculties, a cool head, and whatever serves to keep it cool: no unadvised industry, no unrewarded self-devotion, no loss of the brains in toil. Am I an ox or a dray? — You are both in extremes, he says. You who will have all solid, and a world of piglead, deceive yourselves grossly. You believe yourselves rooted and grounded on adamant, and yet if we uncover the last facts of our knowledge, you are spinning like bubbles in a river, you know not whither or whence, and you are bottomed and capped and wrapped in delusions.

Neither will he be betrayed to a book, and wrapped in a gown. The studious class are their own victims: they are thin and pale, their feet are cold, their heads are hot, the night is without sleep, the day a fear of interruption, pallor, squalor, hunger, and egotism. If you come near them, and see what conceits they entertain, — they are abstractionists, and spend their days and nights in dreaming some dream; in expecting the homage of society to some precious scheme built on a truth, but destitute of proportion in its presentment, of justness in its application, and of all energy of will in the schemer to embody and vitalize it.

But I see plainly, he says, that I cannot see. I know that human strength is not in extremes, but in avoiding extremes. I, at least, will shun the weakness of philosophizing beyond my depth. What is the use of pretending to powers we have not? What is the use of pretending to assurances we have not, respecting

---

8. Pierre Cabanis (1757–1808), French physiologist and philosopher.
9. Henry St. John, first Viscount Bolingbroke (1678–1751), English politician, orator, and writer; a friend of Alexander Pope.
1. One of Emerson's neighbors made this remark.
2. Inhabitants of Gibeon (see n. 2, p. 107).

the other life? Why exaggerate the power of virtue? Why be an angel before your time? These strings wound up too high will snap. If there is a wish for immortality, and no evidence, why not say just that? If there are conflicting evidences, why not state them? If there is not ground for a candid thinker to make up his mind, yea or nay,—why not suspend the judgment? I weary of these dogmatizers. I tire of these hacks of routine, who deny the dogmas. I neither affirm nor deny. I stand here to try the case. I am here to consider, σκέπτειν,[3] to consider how it is. I will try to keep the balance true. Of what use to take the chair, and glibly rattle off theories of society, religion, and nature, when I know that practical objections lie in the way insurmountable by me and by my mates? Why so talkative in public, when each of my neighbors can pin me to my seat by arguments I cannot refute? Why pretend that life is so simple a game, when we know how subtle and elusive the Proteus[4] is? Why think to shut up all things in your narrow coop, when we know there are not one or two only, but ten, twenty, a thousand things, and unlike. Why fancy that you have all the truth in your keeping? There is much to say on all sides.

Who shall forbid a wise skepticism, seeing that there is no practical question on which anything more than an approximate solution can be had. Is not marriage an open question, when it is alleged, from the beginning of the world, that such as are in the institution wish to get out; and such as are out, wish to get in? And the reply of Socrates[5] to him who asked whether he should choose a wife, still remains reasonable, "That, whether he should choose one or not, he would repent it." Is not the State a question? All society is divided in opinion on the subject of the State. Nobody loves it, great numbers dislike it, and suffer conscientious scruples to allegiance. And the only defence set up, is, the fear of doing worse in disorganizing. Is it otherwise with the Church? Or to put any of the questions which touch mankind nearest, Shall the young man aim at a leading part in law, in politics, in trade? It will not be pretended that a success in either of these kinds is quite coincident with what is best and inmost in his mind. Shall he, then, cutting the stays that hold him fast to the social state, put out to sea with no guidance but his genius? There is much to say on both sides. Remember the open question between the present order of "competition," and the friends of "attractive and associated Labour." The generous minds embrace the proposition of labour shared by all; it is the only honesty; nothing else is safe. It is from the poor man's hut alone, that strength and virtue come: and yet, on the other side, it is alleged, that labour impairs the form and breaks the spirit of man, and the labourers cry unanimously, 'We have no thoughts.' Culture, how indispensable! I cannot forgive you the want of accomplishments: and yet culture will instantly impair that chiefest beauty of spontaneousness. Excellent is culture for a savage; but once let him read in the book, and he is no longer able not to think of Plutarch's[6] heroes. In short, since true fortitude of understanding consists "in not letting what we know be embarrassed by what we do not know," we ought to secure those advantages which we can command, and not risk them by clutching after the airy and unattainable. Come, no chimæras![7] Let us go abroad, let us mix in affairs, let us learn, and get, and have,

3. To consider (Greek).
4. See n. 4, p. 42.
5. See n. 6, p. 8.
6. See n. 7, p. 57.
7. In Greek mythology, fire-breathing she-monsters usually represented as a composite of a lion, goat, and serpent.

and climb. "Men are a sort of moving plants, and, like trees, receive a great part of their nourishment from the air. If they keep too much at home, they pine." Let us have a robust manly life, let us know what we know for certain. What we have, let it be solid, and seasonable, and our own. A world in the hand is worth two in the bush. Let us have to do with real men and women, and not with skipping ghosts.

This, then, is the right ground of the skeptic, this of consideration, of self-containing, not at all of unbelief, not at all of universal denying, nor of universal doubting, doubting even that he doubts; least of all, of scoffing, and profligate jeering at all that is stable and good. These are no more his moods, than are those of religion and philosophy. He is the Considerer, the prudent, taking in sail, counting stock, husbanding his means, believing that a man has too many enemies, than that he can afford to be his own foe; that we cannot give ourselves too many advantages, in this unequal conflict, with powers so vast and unweariable ranged on one side, and this little conceited vulnerable popinjay that a man is, bobbing up and down into every danger, on the other. It is a position taken up for better defence, as of more safety, and one that can be maintained, and it is one of more opportunity and range; as, when we build a house, the rule is, to set it not too high nor too low, under the wind, but out of the dirt.

The philosophy we want is one of fluxions and mobility. The Spartan and Stoic[8] schemes are too stark and stiff for our occasion. A theory of Saint John, and of nonresistance, seems, on the other hand, too thin and aerial. We want some coat woven of elastic steel, stout as the first, and limber as the second. We want a *ship*, in these billows we inhabit. An angular dogmatic house would be rent to chips and splinters, in this storm of many elements. No, it must be tight, and fit to the form of man, to live at all; as a shell must dictate the architecture of a house founded on the sea. The soul of man must be the type of our scheme, just as the body of man is the type after which a dwellinghouse is built. Adaptiveness is the peculiarity of human nature. We are golden averages, volitant stabilities, compensated or periodic errours, houses founded on the sea.

The wise skeptic wishes to have a near view of the best game, and the chief players, what is best in the planet, art and nature, places and events, but mainly men. Every thing that is excellent in mankind, a form of grace, an arm of iron, lips of persuasion, a brain of resources, every one skilful to play and win, he will see and judge.

The terms of admission to this spectacle, are, that he have a certain solid and intelligible way of living of his own, some method of answering the inevitable needs of human life; proof that he has played with skill and success: that he has evinced the temper, stoutness, and the range of qualities which, among his contemporaries and countrymen, entitle him to fellowship and trust. For, the secrets of life are not shown except to sympathy and likeness. Men do not confide themselves to boys, or coxcombs, or pedants, but to their peers. Some wise limitation, as the modern phrase is; some condition between the extremes, and having itself a positive quality, some stark and sufficient man, who is not salt or sugar, but sufficiently related to the world to do justice to Paris and London, and, at the same time, a vigorous and original thinker, whom cities

---

8. See n. 9, p. 78. Sparta was the ancient capital of Laconia in Greece, whose people were known for their courage, endurance, and frugality (even in speech: cf. *laconic*).

cannot overawe, but who uses them, — is the fit person to occupy this ground of speculation. These qualities meet in the character of Montaigne. And yet, since the personal regard which I entertain for Montaigne may be unduly great, I will, under the shield of this prince of egotists, offer as an apology for electing him as the representative of Skepticism, a word or two to explain how my love began and grew for this admirable gossip.

A single odd volume of Cotton's[9] translation of the Essays remained to me from my father's library, when a boy. It lay long neglected, until, after many years, when I was newly escaped from college, I read the book, and procured the remaining volumes. I remember the delight and wonder in which I lived with it. It seemed to me as if I had myself written the book in some former life, so sincerely it spoke to my thought and experience. It happened, when in Paris, in 1833, that, in the Cemetery of Père Lachaise, I came to a tomb of Auguste Collignon, who died in 1830, aged sixty-eight years, and who, said the monument, "lived to do right, and had formed himself to virtue on the Essays of Montaigne." Some years later, I became acquainted with an accomplished English poet, John Sterling,[1] and, in prosecuting my correspondence, I found that, from a love of Montaigne, he had made a pilgrimage to his chateau, still standing near Castellan, in Périgord, and, after two hundred and fifty years, had copied from the walls of his library the inscriptions which Montaigne had written there. That Journal of Mr Sterling's, published in the (London) Westminster Review, Hazlitt[2] has reprinted in the Prolegomena to his edition of the Essays. I heard with pleasure that one of the newly discovered autographs of William Shakspeare was in a copy of Florio's[3] translation of Montaigne. It is the only book which we certainly know to have been in the poet's library. And oddly enough, the duplicate copy of Florio which the British Museum purchased with a view of protecting the Shakspeare autograph, (as I was informed in the Museum,) turned out to have the autograph of Ben Jonson in the flyleaf. Leigh Hunt[4] relates of Lord Byron, that Montaigne was the only great writer of past times whom he read with avowed satisfaction. Other coincidences not needful to be mentioned here, concurred to make this old Gascon still new and immortal for me.

In 1571, on the death of his father, Montaigne, then thirty-eight years old, retired from the practice of law at Bordeaux,[5] and settled himself on his estate. Though he had been a man of pleasure, and sometimes a courtier, his studious habits now grew on him, and he loved the compass, staidness, and independence, of the country gentleman's life. He took up his economy in good earnest, and made his farms yield the most. Downright and plaindealing, and abhorring to be deceived or to deceive, he was esteemed in the country for his sense and probity. In the civil wars of the League,[6] which converted every house into a

9. Charles Cotton (1630–1687), English poet and translator, known for his poems on country life as well as his translation (1685) of Montaigne's *Essays*.
1. English essayist and poet (1806–1844); a friend of Thomas Carlyle (see n. 6, p. 28), who introduced him to Emerson; they corresponded but never met (Sterling died four years before Emerson's second trip to England).
2. William Hazlitt (1811–1893), editor of *The Complete Works of Montaigne* (1842) and son of William Hazlitt, critic, essayist, and friend of Coleridge and Wordsworth.
3. John Florio's translation of Montaigne's *Essays* was published in 1603.
4. Leigh Hunt (1784–1859), English poet, essayist, and political radical, was a sometime friend of Byron and wrote about him.
5. A city of southwest France on the Garonne River. It was under English rule from 1154 to 1453.
6. The Holy League, formed in 1576, united Catholics against Protestants in a series of wars that ended with the victory of Henry IV (Henry of Navarre) in 1594.

fort, Montaigne kept his gates open, and his house without defence. All parties freely came and went, his courage and honour being universally esteemed. The neighboring lords and gentry brought jewels and papers to him for safe-keeping. Gibbon[7] reckons in these bigoted times but two men of liberality in France, Henry IV and Montaigne.

Montaigne is the frankest and honestest of all writers. His French freedom runs into grossness, but he has anticipated all censure by the bounty of his own confessions. In his times, books were written to one sex only, and almost all were written in Latin; so that, in a humourist, a certain nakedness of statement was permitted, which our manners of a literature addressed equally to both sexes, do not allow. But, though a biblical plainness coupled with a most uncanonical levity, may shut his pages to many sensitive readers, yet the offence is superficial. He parades it: he makes the most of it: nobody can think or say worse of him, than he does. He pretends to most of the vices, and, if there be any virtue in him, he says, it got in by stealth. There is no man, in his opinion, who has not deserved hanging five or six times; and he pretends no exception in his own behalf. "Five or six as ridiculous stories," too, he says, "can be told of me, as of any man living." But, with all this really superfluous frankness, the opinion of an invincible probity grows into every reader's mind.

"When I the most strictly and religiously confess myself, I find that the best virtue I have has in it some tincture of vice; and I am afraid that Plato, in his purest virtue, (I, who am as sincere and perfect a lover of virtue of that stamp as any other whatever,) if he had listened, and laid his ear close to himself, would have heard some jarring sound of human mixture; but faint and remote, and only to be perceived by himself."

Here is an impatience and fastidiousness about colour or pretence of any kind. He has been in courts so long as to have conceived a furious disgust at appearances, he will indulge himself with a little cursing and swearing, he will talk with sailors and gipsies, use flash and streetballads: he has stayed in doors, till he is deadly sick; he will to the open air, though it rain bullets. He has seen too much of Gentlemen of the long robe, until he wishes for cannibals; and is so nervous by factitious life, that he thinks the more barbarous man is, the better he is. He likes his saddle. You may read theology and grammar and metaphysics elsewhere. Whatever you get here, shall smack of the earth and of real life, sweet or smart or stinging. He makes no hesitation to entertain you with the records of his disease; and his journey to Italy is quite full of that matter. He took and kept this position of equilibrium. Over his name, he drew an emblematic pair of scales, and wrote *Que sçais je?*[8] under it. As I look at his effigy opposite the title page, I seem to hear him say, You may play Old Poz,[9] if you will; you may rail and exaggerate. I stand here for truth, and will not, for all the states and churches and revenues and personal reputations of Europe, overstate the dry fact, as I see it; I will rather mumble and prose about what I certainly know; my house and barns; my father, my wife and my tenants; my old lean bald pate; my knives and forks; what meats I eat; and what drinks I prefer; and a hundred straws, just as ridiculous; than I will write with a fine crowquill a fine romance. I like gray days and autumn and winter weather. I am gray and

---

7. See n. 9, p. 33.
8. What do I know? (French).
9. A character in the writing of Irish novelist Maria Edgeworth (1767–1849) who is always sure of his knowledge.

autumnal myself, and think an undress, and old shoes that do not pinch my feet, and old friends who do not constrain me, and plain topics where I do not need to strain myself and pump my brains, the most suitable. Our condition as men is risky and ticklish enough. One cannot be sure of himself and his fortune an hour, but he may be whisked off into some pitiable or ridiculous plight. Why should I vapour and play the philosopher, instead of ballasting the best I can this dancing balloon. So, at least, I live within compass, keep myself ready for action, and can shoot the gulf, at last, with decency. If there be anything farcical in such a life, the blame is not mine: let it lie at Fate's and nature's door.

The Essays, therefore, are an entertaining soliloquy on every random topic that comes into his head, treating everything without ceremony, yet with masculine sense. There have been men with deeper insight, but, one would say, never a man with such abundance of thoughts. He is never dull, never insincere, and has the genius to make the reader care for all that he cares for.

The sincerity and marrow of the man reaches to his sentences. I know not anywhere the book that seems less written. It is the language of conversation transferred to a book. Cut these words, and they would bleed; they are vascular and alive. One has the same pleasure in it that we have in listening to the necessary speech of men about their work, when any unusual circumstance gives momentary importance to the dialogue. For blacksmiths and teamsters do not trip in their speech; it is a shower of bullets; it is Cambridge men who correct themselves, and begin again at every half sentence, and moreover will pun, and refine too much, and swerve from the matter to the expression. Montaigne talks with shrewdness, knows the world, and books, and himself, and uses the positive degree: never shrieks, or protests, or prays; no weakness, no convulsion, no superlative: does not wish to jump out of his skin, or play any antics, or annihilate space or time, but is stout and solid; tastes every moment of the day; likes pain, because it makes him feel himself, and realize things; as we pinch ourselves to know that we are awake. He keeps the plain; he rarely mounts or sinks; likes to feel solid ground, and the stones underneath. His writing has no enthusiasms, no aspiration; contented, selfrespecting, and keeping the middle of the road. There is but one exception,—in his love for Socrates. In speaking of him, for once his cheek flushes, and his style rises to passion.

Montaigne died of a quinsy, at the age of sixty, in 1592. When he came to die, he caused the mass to be celebrated in his chamber. At the age of thirty-three, he had been married. "But," he says, "might I have had my own will, I would not have married Wisdom herself, if she would have had me: but 'tis to much purpose to evade it, the common custom and use of life will have it so. Most of my actions are guided by example, not choice." In the hour of death he gave the same weight to custom. *Que sçais je?* What do I know?

This book of Montaigne the world has endorsed, by translating it into all tongues, and printing seventy-five editions of it in Europe: and that, too, a circulation somewhat chosen, namely, among courtiers, soldiers, princes, men of the world, and men of wit and generosity.

Shall we say that Montaigne has spoken wisely, and given the right and permanent expression of the human mind on the conduct of life?

We are natural believers. Truth or the connection of cause and effect alone interests us. We are persuaded that a thread runs through all things: all worlds are strung on it as beads: and men and events and life come to us only because of that thread: they pass and repass only that we may know the direction and continuity of that line. A book or statement which goes to show that there is no line, but random and chaos; a calamity out of nothing, a prosperity and no account of it, a hero born from a fool, a fool from a hero,—dispirits us. Seen or unseen, we believe the tie exists. Talent makes counterfeit ties; Genius finds the real ones. We hearken to the man of science, because we anticipate the sequence in natural phenomena which he uncovers. We love whatever affirms, connects, preserves, and dislike what scatters or pulls down. One man appears whose nature is to all men's eyes conserving and constructive: His presence supposes a well-ordered society, agriculture, trade, large institutions, and empire. If these did not exist, they would begin to exist through his endeavours. Therefore he cheers and comforts men, who feel all this in him very readily. The nonconformist and the rebel say all manner of unanswerable things against the existing republic, but discover to our sense no plan of house or state of their own. Therefore, though the town and state and way of living which our counsellor contemplated, might be a very modest or musty prosperity, yet men rightly go for him, and reject the Reformer, so long as he comes only with axe and crowbar.

But though we are natural conservers and causationists, and reject a sour dumpish unbelief, the skeptical class which Montaigne represents, have reason, and every man, at some time, belongs to it. Every superior mind will pass through this domain of equilibration,—I should rather say, will know how to avail himself of the checks and balances in nature, as a natural weapon against the exaggeration and formalism of bigots and blockheads.

Skepticism is the attitude assumed by the student in relation to the particulars which society adores, but which he sees to be reverend only in their tendency and spirit. The ground occupied by the skeptic is the vestibule of the temple. Society does not like to have any breath of question blown on the existing order. But the interrogation of custom at all points is an inevitable stage in the growth of every superior mind, and is the evidence of its perception of the flowing power which remains itself in all changes.

The superior mind will find itself equally at odds with the evils of society, and with the projects that are offered to relieve them. The wise skeptic is a bad citizen; no conservative; he sees the selfishness of property and the drowsiness of institutions. But neither is he fit to work with any democratic party that ever was constituted; for parties wish every one committed, and he penetrates the popular patriotism. His politics are those of the "Soul's Errand" of Sir Walter Raleigh; or of Krishna, in the Bhagavat,[1] "There is none who is worthy of my love or hatred;" whilst he sentences law, physic, divinity, commerce, and custom. He is a Reformer; yet he is no better member of the philanthropic association. It turns out that he is not the champion of the operative, the pauper, the prisoner, the slave. It stands in his mind, that our life in this world is not of quite so easy interpretation as churches and schoolbooks say. He does not wish to take ground against these benevolences, to play the part of devil's attorney, and blazon every doubt and sneer that darkens the sun for him. But he says, There are doubts.

---

1. *Bhagavad-Gita, or Dialogues of Kreeshna and Arjoon*, a Hindu scripture crucial to Emerson's thought (see, e.g., "Brahma," p. 464). Krishna, in Hinduism the eighth and principal avator of Vishnu (see n. 5, p. 90). Sir Walter Raleigh (1552?–1618), English courtier, navigator, colonizer, and writer. His literary works include poetry, memoirs, and a world history. "Soul's Errand" is now commonly known as "The Lie."

I mean to use the occasion and celebrate the calendar-day of our Saint Michel de Montaigne, by counting and describing these doubts or negations. I wish to ferret them out of their holes, and sun them a little. We must do with them as the police do with old rogues, who are shown up to the public at the Marshal's office. They will never be so formidable, when once they have been identified and registered. But I mean honestly by them, that justice shall be done to their terrors. I shall not take Sunday objections, made up on purpose to be put down. I shall take the worst I can find, whether I can dispose of them, or they of me.

I do not press the skepticism of the materialist. I know, the quadruped opinion will not prevail. 'Tis of no importance what bats and oxen think. The first dangerous symptom I report is the levity of intellect, as if it were fatal to earnestness to know much. Knowledge is the knowing that we cannot know. The dull pray; the geniuses are light mockers. How respectable is earnestness on every platform! but intellect kills it. Nay, San Carlo, my subtle and admirable friend, one of the most penetrating of men, finds that all direct ascension, even of lofty piety, leads to this ghastly insight and sends back the votary orphaned. My astonishing San Carlo thought the lawgivers and saints infected. They found the ark empty, saw and would not tell; and tried to choke off their approaching followers, by saying, 'Action, action, my dear fellows, is for you!' Bad as was to me this detection by San Carlo,[2] this frost in July, this blow from a bride, there was still a worse, namely, the cloy or satiety of the saints. In the mount of vision, ere they have yet risen from their knees, they say, We discover that this our homage and beatitude is partial and deformed. We must fly for relief to the suspected and reviled Intellect, to the Understanding, the Mephistopheles,[3] to the gymnastics of talent.

This is Hobgoblin the first, and though it has been the subject of much elegy in our nineteenth century from Byron, Goethe, and other poets of less fame, not to mention many distinguished private observers, I confess, it is not very affecting to my imagination. For it seems to concern the shattering of babyhouses and crockery shops. What flutters the Church of Rome or of England or of Geneva or of Boston, may yet be very far from touching any principle of faith. I think that the intellect and moral sentiment are unanimous; and that though philosophy extirpates bugbears, yet it supplies the natural checks of vice, and polarity to the soul. I think that the wiser a man is, the more stupendous he finds the natural and moral economy, and lifts himself to a more absolute reliance.

There is the power of moods, each setting at nought all but its own tissue of facts and beliefs. There is the power of complexions—obviously modifying the dispositions and sentiments. The beliefs and unbeliefs appear to be structural, and, as soon as each man attains the poise and vivacity which allow the whole machinery to play, he will not need extreme examples, but will rapidly alternate all opinions in his own life. Our life is March weather, savage and serene in one hour. We go forth austere, dedicated, believing in the iron links of Destiny, and will not turn on our heel to save our life: but a book, or a bust, or only the sound of a name, shoots a spark through the nerves, and we suddenly believe in will; my finger-ring shall be the seal of Solomon; Fate is for imbe-

2. Emerson's humorous sobriquet for Charles K. Newcomb, a minor Transcendentalist known for his mystical tendencies and gentle nature.
3. In the Faust legend, the devil to whom Faust sold his soul. Faust (or Faustus; ca. 1488–1541) is said to have been a wandering magician who traded his soul for youth and power.

ciles. All is possible to the resolved mind. Presently, a new experience gives a new turn to our thoughts; commonsense resumes its tyranny. We say, 'Well, the army, after all, is the gate to fame, manners, and poetry: and, look you, on the whole selfishness plants best, prunes best, makes the best commerce, and the best citizen.' Are the opinions of a man on right and wrong, on fate and causation, at the mercy of a broken sleep, or an indigestion? Is his belief in God and Duty no deeper than a stomach evidence? And what guaranty for the permanence of his opinions? I like not the French celerity, a new church and state once a week. This is the second negation; and I shall let it pass for what it will. As far as it asserts rotation of states of mind, I suppose it suggests its own remedy, namely, in the record of larger periods. What is the mean of many states; of all the states? Does the general voice of ages affirm any principle, or is no community of sentiment discoverable in distant times and places? And when it shows the power of selfinterest, I accept that as part of the divine law and must reconcile it with aspiration the best I can.

The word Fate or Destiny expresses the sense of mankind in all ages that the laws of the world do not always befriend, but often hurt and crush us. Fate in the shape of *Kinde*[4] or Nature, grows over us like grass. We paint Time with a scythe; Love and Fortune blind; and Destiny, deaf. We have too little power of resistance against this ferocity which champs us up. What front can we make against these unavoidable, victorious, maleficent forces? What can I do against the influence of *Race* in my history? What can I do against hereditary and constitutional habits, against scrofula, lymph, impotence? against climate, against barbarism, in my country? I can reason down or deny everything except this perpetual Belly: feed he must and will, and I cannot make him respectable.

But the main resistance which the affirmative impulse finds and one including all others is in the doctrine of the Illusionists. There is a painful rumour in circulation that we have been practised upon in all the principal performances of life, and free agency is the emptiest name. We have been sopped and drugged with the air, with food, with woman, with children, with customs, with sciences, with events; which leave us exactly where they found us. The mathematics, 'tis complained, leave the mind where they find it: so do all sciences, and so do all events and actions. I find a man who has passed through all the sciences the churl he was, and through all the offices, learned, civil, social, I can detect the child. We are not the less necessitated to dedicate life to them. In fact we may come to accept it as the fixed rule and theory of our state of education that God is a substance, and his method is illusion. The eastern sages owned the Goddess Yoganidra, the great illusory energy of Vishnu by whom as utter ignorance the whole world is beguiled.

Or, shall I state it thus? The astonishment of life, is, the absence of any appearance of reconciliation between the theory and practice of life. Reason, the prized reality, the Law, is apprehended now and then for a serene and profound moment amidst the hubbub of cares and works which have no direct bearing on it;—is then lost, for months or years, and again found, for an interval, to be lost again. If we compute it in time, we may, in fifty years, have half a dozen reasonable hours. But what are these cares and works the better? A method in the world we do not see, but this parallelism of great and little, which never react

4. Nature (Old English).

on each other, nor discover the smallest tendency to converge. Experiences, fortunes, governings, readings, writings, are nothing to the purpose; as when a man comes into the room, it does not appear whether he has been fed on yams or buffalo,—he has contrived to get so much bone and fibre as he wants, out of rice or out of snow. So vast is the disproportion between the sky of law and the pismire of performance under it, that, whether he is a man of worth or a sot, is not so great a matter as we say. Shall I add, as one juggle of this enchantment, the stunning non-intercourse law which makes cooperation impossible. The young spirit pants to enter society. But all the ways of culture and greatness lead to solitary imprisonment. He had been often balked. He did not expect a sympathy with his thought from the village, but he went with it to the chosen and intelligent, and found no entertainment for it, but mere misapprehension, distaste, and scoffing. Men are strangely mistimed and misapplied, and the excellence of each is an inflamed individualism which separates him more.

There are these and more than these diseases of thought, which our ordinary teachers do not attempt to remove. Now shall we, because a good nature inclines us to Virtue's side, say, There are no doubts,—and lie for the right? Is life to be led in a brave, or in a cowardly manner? and is not the satisfaction of the doubts essential to all manliness? Is the name of Virtue to be a barrier to that which is Virtue? Can you not believe that a man of earnest and burly habit may find small good in tea, essays, and catechism, and want a rougher instruction, want men, labour, trade, farming, war, hunger, plenty, love, hatred, doubt, and terror, to make things plain to him, and has he not a right to insist on being convinced in his own way? When he is convinced, he will be worth the pains.

Belief consists in accepting the affirmations of the soul; Unbelief, in denying them. Some minds are incapable of skepticism. The doubts they profess to entertain are rather a civility or accommodation to the common discourse of their company. They may well give themselves leave to speculate, for they are secure of a return. Once admitted to the heaven of thought, they see no relapse into night, but infinite invitation on the other side. Heaven is within heaven, and sky over sky, and they are encompassed with divinities. Others there are, to whom the heaven is brass, and it shuts down to the surface of the earth. It is a question of temperament, or of more or less immersion in nature. The last class must needs have a reflex or parasitic faith; not a sight of realities, but an instinctive reliance on the seers and believers of realities. The manners and thoughts of believers astonish them and convince them that these have seen something which is hid from themselves. But their sensual habit would fix the believer to his last position, whilst he as inevitably advances: and presently the unbeliever for love of belief burns the believer.

Great believers are always reckoned infidels, impracticable, fantastic, atheistic, and really men of no account. The spiritualist finds himself driven to express his faith by a series of skepticisms. Charitable souls come with their projects, and ask his cooperation. How can he hesitate? It is the rule of mere comity and courtesy, to agree where you can, and to turn your sentence with something auspicious and not sneering and sinister. But he is forced to say, 'O these things will be as they must be; what can you do? These particular griefs and crimes are the foliage and fruit of such trees as we see growing. It is vain to complain of the leaf or the berry: cut it off, it will bear another just as bad. You must begin your cure lower down.' The generosities of the day prove an intractable element for him. The people's questions are not his; their methods are not his; and against all the dictates of good nature, he is driven to say, he has no pleasure in them.

Even the doctrines dear to the hope of man, of the divine Providence and of the immortality of the Soul, his neighbours cannot put the statement so, that he shall affirm it. But he denies out of more faith, and not less. He denies out of honesty. He had rather stand charged with the imbecility of skepticism, than with untruth. I believe, he says, in the moral design of the universe; it exists hospitably for the weal of souls; but your dogmas seem to me caricatures. Why should I make believe them? — Will any say this is cold and infidel? The wise and magnanimous will not say so. They will exult in his farsighted goodwill, that can abandon to the adversary all the ground of tradition and common belief, without losing a jot of strength. It sees to the end of all transgression. George Fox[5] saw that there was "an ocean of darkness and death but withal an infinite ocean of light and love which flowed over that of darkness."

The final solution in which Skepticism is lost, is, in the moral sentiment, which never forfeits its supremacy. All moods may be safely tried, and their weight allowed to all objections: the moral sentiment as easily outweighs them all, as any one. This is the drop which balances the sea. I play with the miscellany of facts and take those superficial views which we call Skepticism but I know that they will presently appear to me in that order which makes Skepticism impossible. A man of thought must feel the thought that is parent of the universe: that the masses of nature do undulate and flow.

This faith avails to the whole emergency of life and objects. The world is saturated with deity and with law. He is content with just and unjust, with sots and fools, with the triumph of folly and fraud. He can behold with serenity, the yawning gulf between the ambition of man and his power of performance, between the demand and supply of power which makes the tragedy of all souls.

Charles Fourier[6] announced that "the attractions of man are proportioned to his destinies," in other words, that every desire predicts its own satisfaction. Yet all experience exhibits the reverse of this; the incompetency of power is the universal grief of young and ardent minds. They accuse the divine Providence of a certain parsimony. It has shown the heaven and earth to every child, and filled him with a desire for the whole; a desire raging, infinite, a hunger as of space to be filled with planets; a cry of famine as of devils for souls. Then for the satisfaction; — to each man is administered a single drop, a bead of dew of vital power, *per day*, — a cup as large as space, and one drop of the water of life in it. Each man woke in the morning with an appetite that could eat the solar system like a cake; a spirit for action and passion without bounds; he could lay his hand on the morningstar; he could try conclusions with gravitation or chemistry; but on the first motion to prove his strength, hands, feet, senses, gave way, and would not serve him. He was an emperor deserted by his states, and left to whistle by himself or thrust into a mob of emperors all whistling: and still the sirens sung, "The attractions are proportioned to the destinies." In every house, in the heart of each maiden and of each boy, in the soul of the soaring saint, this chasm is found, — between the largest promise of ideal power, and the shabby experience.

5. See n. 1, p. 39.
6. See n. 3, p. 133.

The expansive nature of truth comes to our succour, elastic, not to be surrounded. Man helps himself by larger generalizations. The lesson of life is practically to generalize, to believe what the years and the centuries say against the hours; to resist the usurpation of particulars; to penetrate to their catholic sense. Things seem to say one thing, and say the reverse. The appearance is immoral; the result is moral. Things seem to tend downward, to justify despondency, to promote rogues, to defeat the just; and by knaves, as by martyrs, the just cause is carried forward. Although knaves win in every political struggle, although society seems to be delivered over from the hands of one set of criminals into the hands of another set of criminals, as fast as the government is changed, and the march of civilization is a train of felonies, yet, general ends are somehow answered. We see now, events forced on, which seem to retard or retrograde the civility of ages. But the world spirit is a good swimmer, and storms and waves cannot drown him. He snaps his finger at laws: and so, throughout history, heaven seems to affect low and poor means. (The needles are nothing; the magnetism is all.) Through the years and the centuries, through evil agents, through toys and atoms, a great and beneficent tendency irresistibly streams.

Let a man learn to look for the permanent in the mutable and fleeting; let him learn to bear the disappearance of things he was wont to reverence, without losing his reverence; let him learn that he is here not to work, but to be worked upon, and, that, though abyss open under abyss, and opinion displace opinion, all are at last contained in the eternal Cause.

"If my bark sink, 'tis to another sea."[7]

Shakspeare,[1] or the Poet

Great men are more distinguished by range and extent, than by originality. If we require the originality which consists in weaving like a spider their web from their own bowels, in finding clay, and making bricks, and building the house, no great men are original. Nor does valuable originality consist in unlikeness to other men. The hero is in the press of knights, and the thick of events, and, seeing what men want, and sharing their desire, he adds the needful length of sight and of arm to come at the desired point. The greatest genius is the most indebted man. A poet is no rattlebrain saying what comes uppermost, and, because he says everything, saying, at last, something good; but a heart in unison with his time and country. There is nothing whimsical and fantastic in his production, but sweet and sad earnest, freighted with the weightiest convictions and pointed with the most determined aim which any man or class knows of in his times.

The genius of our life is jealous of individuals, and will not have any individual great, except through the general. There is no choice to genius. A great man does not wake up on some fine morning, and say, I am full of life, I will go to sea, and find an Antarctic continent: today, I will square the circle: I will ran-

---

7. This is the last line of "A Poet's Hope," by Emerson's friend and neighbor William Ellery Channing "The Younger" (1817–1901). Channing, called "Ellery" by his friends, was the nephew of the great Unitarian theologian whose name he bore.
1. Emerson's preferred spelling.

sack botany, and find a new food for man: I have a new architecture in my mind: I foresee a new mechanic power: no; but he finds himself in the river of the thoughts and events, forced onward by the ideas and necessities of his contemporaries. He stands where all the eyes of men look one way, and their hands all point in the direction in which he should go. The Church has reared him amidst rites and pomps, and he carries out the advice which her music gave him, and builds a cathedral needed by her chants and processions. He finds a war ranging; it educates him by trumpet in barracks, and he betters the instruction. He finds two counties groping to bring coal, or flour, or fish, from the place of production to the place of consumption, and he hits on a railroad. Every master has found his materials collected, and his power lay in his sympathy with his people, and in his love of the materials he wrought in. What an economy of power! and what a compensation for the shortness of life! All is done to his hand. The world has brought him thus far on his way. The human race has gone out before him, sunk the hills, filled the hollows, and bridged the rivers. Men, nations, poets, artisans, women, all have worked for him, and he enters into their labours. Choose any other thing, out of the line of tendency, out of the national feeling and history, and he would have all to do for himself: his powers would be expended in the first preparations. Great genial power, one would almost say, consists in not being original at all; in being altogether receptive; in letting the world do all, and suffering the spirit of the hour to pass unobstructed through the mind.

Shakspeare's youth fell in a time when the English people were importunate for dramatic entertainments. The court took offence easily at political allusions, and attempted to suppress them. The Puritans,[2] a growing and energetic party, and the religious within the Anglican Church would suppress them. But the people wanted them. Innyards, houses without roofs, or extemporaneous enclosures at country fairs, were the ready theatres of strolling players. The people had tasted this new joy, and, as we could not hope to suppress newspapers now, no, not by the strongest party, neither then, could king, prelate, or puritan, alone or united, suppress an organ, which was ballad, epic, newspaper, caucus, lecture, Punch,[3] and library, at the same time. Probably king, prelate, and puritan, all found their own account in it. It had become by all causes a national interest, — by no means conspicuous, so that some great scholar would have thought of treating it in an English history, — but not a whit less considerable because it was cheap, and of no account, like a baker's shop. The best proof of its vitality is the crowd of writers which suddenly broke into this field; Kyd, Marlow, Greene, Jonson, Chapman, Dekker, Webster, Heywood, Middleton, Peele, Ford, Massinger, Beaumont, and Fletcher.[4]

---

2. See n. 6, p. 91.
3. Emerson probably uses the term here to stand for humorous entertainment generally.
4. See n. 9, p. 132. Thomas Kyd (1558–1594), English dramatist who wrote *The Spanish Tragedy* (1592), thought to have contributed to Shakespeare's *Titus Andronicus* and *Henry VI* and may have written a version of *Hamlet*. Christopher Marlowe (1564–1593), English playwright and poet whose development of blank verse influenced Shakespeare. His plays include *Tamburlaine the Great* (1587), *The Jew of Malta* (1589), and *Edward II* (1593). Robert Greene (1558?–1592), English writer noted for his plays, such as *Friar Bacon and Friar Bungay* (ca. 1589). Ben Jonson (1572?–1637), English actor and writer. Among his major plays are *Every Man in His Humour* (1598) and *Volpone* (1606). Chapman, see n. 6, p. 193. Thomas Dekker (1572–1632), English playwright whose comedy *The Shoemaker's Holiday* (1600) is notable for its vivid portrayal of daily life in London. John Webster (1580?–1625?), English playwright whose works include *The White Devil* (published 1612) and *The Duchess of Malfi* (ca. 1613). Thomas Heywood (1574?–1641), English playwright noted for his works concerning domestic life, especially *A Woman Killed with Kindness* (1603). Thomas Middleton (1570?–1627), English playwright whose come-

The secure possession by the stage of the public mind is of the first importance to the poet who works for it. He loses no time in idle experiments. Here is audience and expectation prepared. In the case of Shakspeare, there is much more. At the time when he left Stratford,[5] and went up to London, a great body of stage plays of all dates and writers existed in manuscript, and were in turn produced on the boards. Here is the Tale of Troy, which the audience will bear hearing some part of, every week: the Death of Julius Cæsar, and other stories out of Plutarch, which they never tire of: a shelf full of English history, from the Chronicles of Brut and Arthur,[6] down to the royal Henries, which men hear eagerly: and a string of doleful tragedies, merry Italian tales, and Spanish voyages, which all the London prentices know. All the mass has been treated with more or less skill by every playwright, and the prompter has the soiled and tattered manuscripts. It is now no longer possible to say who wrote them first. They have been the property of the Theatre so long, and so many rising geniuses have enlarged or altered them, inserting a speech, or a whole scene, or adding a song, that no man can any longer claim copyright in this work of numbers. Happily, no man wishes to. They are not yet desired in that way. We have few readers, many spectators and hearers. They had best lie where they are.

Shakspeare, in common with his comrades, esteemed the mass of old plays waste stock, in which any experiment could be freely tried. Had the *prestige* which hedges about a modern tragedy existed, nothing could have been done. The rude warm blood of the living England circulated in the play, as in street ballads, and gave body which he wanted to his airy and majestic fancy. The poet needs a ground in popular tradition on which he may work, and which, again, may restrain his art within the due temperance. It holds him to the people, supplies a foundation for his edifice, and in furnishing so much work done to his hand, leaves him at leisure, and in full strength for the audacities of his imagination. In short, the poet owes to his legend, what Sculpture owed to the temple. Sculpture in Egypt, and in Greece, grew up in subordination to architecture. It was the ornament of the temple wall: at first, a rude relief carved on pediments, then the relief became bolder, and a head or arm was projected from the wall, the groups being still arranged with reference to the building, which serves also as a frame to hold the figures, and when, at last, the greatest freedom of style and treatment was reached, the prevailing genius of architecture still enforced a certain calmness and continence in the statue. As soon as the statue was begun for itself, and with no reference to the temple or palace, the art began to decline: freak, extravagance, and exhibition, took the place of the old temperance. This balance-wheel which the sculptor found in architecture, the perilous irritability of poetic talent found in the accumulated dramatic materials to which the people were al-

---

dies, written between 1604 and 1611, include *A Trick to Catch the Old One* and *A Chaste Maid in Cheapside*. George Peele (1556?–1596), English playwright. Among his works are *The Arraignment of Paris* (1594) and *The Battle of Alcazar* (1591). John Ford (1586–1639), English playwright whose works include *'Tis Pity She's a Whore* (1633) and collaborative efforts, notably with Dekker and Webster. Philip Massinger (1583–1640), English playwright known for his satirical comedies, most notably *A New Way to Pay Old Debts* (ca. 1625).

5. Stratford-upon-Avon, a municipal borough of central England south-southeast of Birmingham. Shakespeare was born and died in the borough, which has long been a popular tourist center.

6. A legendary British hero, said to have been king of the Britons in the sixth century C.E. and to have held court at Camelot. Caesar, see n. 8, p. 261. Plutarch, see n. 7, p. 57. Brut, or Brutus, great-grandson of Aeneas, said to have founded Britain in the tenth century B.C.E. Both Arthur and Brut figure in Geoffrey of Monmouth's *History of the Kings of Britain* (1136).

ready wonted, and which had a certain excellence, which no single genius, however extraordinary, could hope to create.

In point of fact it appears that Shakspeare did owe debts in all directions, and was able to use whatever he found; and the amount of indebtedness may be inferred from Malone's laborious computations in regard to the second and third parts of Henry VI,[7] in which, "out of 6043 lines, 1771 were written by some author preceding Shakspeare; 2373 by him on the foundation laid by his predecessors, and 1899 were entirely his own." And the proceeding investigation hardly leaves a single drama of his absolute invention. Malone's sentence is an important piece of external history. In Henry VIII,[8] I think I see plainly the cropping out of the original rock on which his own finer stratum was laid. The first play was written by a superior thoughtful man, with a vicious ear. I can mark his lines, and know well their cadence. See Wolsey's soliloquy and the following scene with Cromwell,[9] where, instead of the metre of Shakspeare, whose secret is, that the thought constructs the tune, so that reading for the sense will best bring out the rhythm, here the lines are constructed on a given tune, and the verse has even a trace of pulpit eloquence. But the play contains through all its length unmistakeable traits of Shakspeare's hand, and some passages, as the account of the Coronation, are like autographs. What is odd, the compliment to Queen Elizabeth[1] is in the bad rhythm.

Shakspeare knew that tradition supplies a better fable than any invention can. If he lost any credit of design, he augmented his resources, and, at that day, our petulant demand for originality was not so much pressed. There was no literature for the million. The universal reading, the cheap press, were unknown. A great poet who appears in illiterate times, absorbs into his sphere all the light which is anywhere radiating. Every intellectual jewel, every flower of sentiment, it is his fine office to bring to his people; and he comes to value his memory, equally with his invention. He is therefore little solicitous whence his thoughts have been derived, whether through translation, whether through tradition, whether by travel in distant countries, whether by inspiration: from whatever source, they are equally welcome to his uncritical audience. Nay, he borrows very near home. Other men say wise things as well as he; only they say a good many foolish things, and do not know when they have spoken wisely. He knows the sparkle of the true stone, and puts it in high place, wherever he finds it.

Such is the happy position of Homer, perhaps; of Chaucer, of Saadi.[2] They felt that all wit was their wit. And they are librarians and historiographers as well as poets. Each romancer was heir and dispenser of all the hundred tales of the world,—

7. King of England (1421–1471; r. 1422–61 and 1470–71), subject of a Shakespearean historical trilogy of plays. Edmund Malone (1741–1812), British scholar and literary critic noted for his chronology of Shakespeare's plays and his editions of Shakespeare (1790) and Dryden (1800). His "laborious computations" have since been challenged.
8. King of England (1491–1547; r. 1509–47); the play about him was probably written by Shakespeare and John Fletcher together.
9. The *soliloquy* and the *scene with Cromwell* are in *Henry VIII* 3.3.350ff. Thomas Wolsey (1475?–1530), English prelate and politician. The influential chief adviser to Henry VIII, he fell from favor after failing to secure papal approval of Henry's divorce from Catherine of Aragon (1529). Thomas Cromwell, earl of Essex (1485?–1540), secretary to Cardinal Wolsey and subsequently to Henry VIII.
1. *Henry VIII*, 4.1.
2. Or Sa'di, the pen name of Musharrif-uddin (ca. 1184–1291), perhaps the greatest Persian poet of all time. Emerson particularly delighted in Sa'di's *Gulistan* (Rose garden) and wrote a long poem of his own, "Saadi" (published in *The Dial* in October 1842), which clearly demonstrates Emerson's identification with the Persian poet. Homer, see n. 8, p. 88. Chaucer, see n. 9, p. 60.

"Presenting Thebes' and Pelops' line,
And the tale of Troy divine."[3]

The influence of Chaucer is conspicuous in all our early literature: and, more recently, not only Pope and Dryden[4] have been beholden to him, but in the whole society of English writers a large unacknowledged debt is easily traced. One is charmed with the opulence which feeds so many pensioners. But Chaucer is a huge borrower. Chaucer, it seems, drew continually through Lydgate and Caxton, from Guido di Colonna, whose Latin romance of the Trojan War was in turn a compilation from Dares Phrygius, Ovid, and Statius. Then Petrarch, Boccaccio, and the Provençal poets are his benefactors: the Romaunt of the Rose is only judicious translation from William of Lorris and John of Meun: Troilus and Creseide, from Lollius of Urbino: The Cock and the Fox, from the *Lais* of Marie: The House of Fame, from the French or Italian: and poor Gower he uses, as if he were only a brickkiln or stonequarry, out of which to build his house. He steals by this apology, that what he takes has no worth where he finds it, and the greatest where he leaves it. It has come to be practically a sort of rule in literature, that a man having once shown himself capable of original writing, is entitled thenceforth to steal from the writings of others at discretion. Thought is the property of him who can entertain it; and of him who can adequately place it. A certain aukwardness marks the use of borrowed thoughts; but as soon as we have learned what to do with them, they become our own.[5]

Thus all originality is relative. Every thinker is retrospective. The learned member of the legislature at Westminster or at Washington, speaks and votes for thousands. Show us the constituency, and the now invisible channels by which the senator is made aware of their wishes, the crowd of practical and knowing men, who, by correspondence or conversation, are feeding him with evidence, anecdotes, and estimates, and it will bereave his fine attitude and resistance of something of their impressiveness. As Sir Robert Peel and Mr Webster vote, so Locke and Rousseau think for thousands; and so there were fountains all around Homer, Menu, Saadi, or Milton,[6] from which they drew; friends, lovers, books, traditions, proverbs, — all perished, — which, if seen, would go to reduce the wonder. Did the bard speak with authority? did he feel himself overmatched by any companion? The appeal is to the consciousness of the writer. Is there at last in his breast a Delphi[7] whereof to ask concerning any thought or thing, whether it be

---

3. Emerson slightly misquotes from John Milton's "Il Penseroso" (1631?) lines 99–100: "Presenting Thebes, or Pelops' line, / Or the tale of Troy divine."
4. See n. 9, p. 60. Pope, see n. 9, p. 67.
5. Emerson's somewhat breezy trot through literary history is incorrect in many particulars, mainly because (as the editors of the Harvard edition of *Representative Men* point out) he was depending on misinformation gleaned from Thomas Warton's *History of English Poetry* (1824). For guidance through this thicket of references, see CW 4.220–21. The editors conclude by noting that Emerson was justified in saying that Chaucer was a "huge borrower" but not in claiming that the material Chaucer borrowed "has no worth where he finds it." The passage may perhaps best be taken as Emerson's covert justification for his own method.
6. See n. 2, p. 6. Peel (1788–1850), British politician. As home secretary (1822–27 and 1828–30) he established the London police force (1829) and helped pass the Catholic Emancipation Act (1829). He later served as prime minister (1834–35 and 1841–46). Daniel Webster (1782–1852), American politician; a U.S. representative from New Hampshire (1813–17) and later a representative (1823–27) and senator (1827–41 and 1845–50) from Massachusetts. He was a noted orator dedicated, above all, to the preservation of the Union. He twice served as secretary of state (1841–43 and 1850–52). Locke, see n. 7, p. 59. Menu, see n. 3, p. 115.
7. An ancient town of central Greece near Mount Parnassus. Dating to at least the seventh century B.C.E., it was the seat of a famous oracle of Apollo.

verily so, yea or nay? and to have answer, and to rely on that? All the debts which such a man could contract to other wit, would never disturb his consciousness of originality: for the ministrations of books and of other minds are a whiff of smoke to that most private reality with which he has conversed.

It is easy to see that what is best written or done by genius in the world was no man's work, but came by wide social labour, when a thousand wrought like one, sharing the same impulse. Our English Bible[8] is a wonderful specimen of the strength and music of the English language. But it was not made by one man or at one time; but centuries and churches brought it to perfection. There never was a time when there was not some translation existing. The Liturgy, admired for its energy and pathos, is an anthology of the piety of ages and nations, a translation of the prayers and forms of the Catholic Church, — these selected, too, in long periods, from the prayers and meditations of every saint and sacred writer, all over the world. Grotius[9] makes the like remark in respect to the Lord's Prayer, that the single clauses of which it is composed, were already in use, in the time of Christ, in the Rabbinical forms. He picked out the grains of gold. The nervous language of the Common Law,[1] the impressive forms of our courts, and the precision and substantial truth of the legal distinctions, are the contribution of all the sharp-sighted strongminded men who have lived in the countries where these laws govern. The translation of Plutarch gets its excellence by being translation on translation.[2] There never was a time when there was none. All the truly idiomatic and national phrases are kept, and all others successively picked out and thrown away. Something like the same process had gone on long before with the originals of these books. The world takes liberties with world-books. Vedas, Æsop's Fables, Pilpay, Arabian Nights, Cid, Iliad, Robin Hood, Scottish Minstrelsy,[3] are not the work of single men. In the composition of such works, the time thinks, the market thinks, the mason, the carpenter, the merchant, the farmer, the fop, all think for us. Every book supplies its time with one good word; every municipal law, every trade, every folly of the day; and the generic catholic genius, who is not afraid or ashamed to owe his originality to the originality of all, stands with the next age as the recorder and embodiment of his own.

We have to thank the researches of antiquaries and the Shakspeare Society, for ascertaining the steps of the English Drama, from the Mysteries celebrated in churches and by churchmen, and the final detachment from the church, and the completion of secular plays, from Ferrex and Porrex, and Gammer Gurton's Needle,[4] down to the possession of the stage by the very pieces

8. The King James Bible (1611).
9. Hugo Grotius (1583–1645), Dutch jurist, politician, and theologian. Emerson seems to be referring to Grotius's commentary on the gospel of Matthew.
1. The system of laws originated and developed in England and based on court decisions, on the doctrines implicit in those decisions, and on customs and usages rather than on codified written laws.
2. Emerson observes that not all the translations were from the original Greek.
3. Probably refers to Sir Walter Scott's *Minstrelsy of the Scottish Border* (1802–03). Vedas, any of the oldest Hindu sacred texts, composed in Sanskrit and gathered into four collections. Aesop, see n. 1, p. 115. *Pilpay*, or *Bidpai* (ca. 750), a collection of Indian fables variously circulated in Persian, Arabic, and English over the years. *Bidpai* means "court scholar"; the tales are told as an old man's advice to a young Indian prince. Arabian Nights, see n. 2, p. 11. Cid (1043?–1099), Spanish soldier and national hero whose military exploits, including the capture of Valencia (1094), are recounted in several literary works. Robin Hood (twelfth century), a legendary English outlaw, famous for his courage, chivalry, and practice of robbing the rich to aid the poor.
4. An English comedy first performed at Cambridge in 1566 and attributed variously to John Still (1543?–1607) and William Stevenson (d. 1575?). *Ferrex and Porrex:* characters in *Gorboduc* (1561–65), a tragedy in verse by Thomas Sackville and Thomas Norton based on material from Geoffrey of Monmouth.

which Shakspeare altered, remodelled, and finally made his own. Elated with success, and piqued by the growing interest of the problem, they have left no bookstall unsearched, no chest in a garret unopened, no file of old yellow accounts to decompose in damp and worms, so keen was the hope to discover whether the boy Shakspeare poached or not, whether he held horses at the theatre door, whether he kept school, and why he left in his will only his second best bed to Ann Hathaway his wife.[5]

There is somewhat touching in the madness with which the passing age mischooses the object on which all candles shine, and all eyes are turned; the care with which it registers every trifle touching Queen Elizabeth and King James and the Essexes, Leicesters, Burleighs, and Buckinghams, and lets pass without a single valuable note the founder of another dynasty, which alone will cause the Tudor dynasty to be remembered,—the man who carries the Saxon[6] race in him by the inspiration which feeds him, and on whose thoughts the foremost people of the world are now for some ages to be nourished, and minds to receive this, and not another bias. A popular player, nobody suspected he was the poet of the human race: and the secret was kept as faithfully from poets and intellectual men, as from courtiers and frivolous people. Bacon,[7] who took the inventory of the human understanding for his times, never mentioned his name. Ben Jonson, though we have strained his few words of regard and panegyric,[8] had no suspicion of the elastic fame whose first vibrations he was attempting. He, no doubt, thought the praise he has conceded to him generous, and esteemed himself, out of all question, the better poet of the two.

If it need wit to know wit, according to the proverb, Shakspeare's time should be capable of recognizing it. Sir Henry Wotton was born four years after Shakspeare, and died twenty-three years after him, and I find among his correspondents and acquaintances, the following persons: Theodore Beza, Isaac Casaubon, Sir Philip Sidney, Earl of Essex, Lord Bacon, Sir Walter Raleigh, John Milton, Sir Henry Vane, Isaak Walton, Dr Donne, Abraham Cowley, Bellarmine, Charles Cotton, John Pym, John Hales, Kepler, Vieta, Albericus Gentilis, Paul Sarpi, Arminius;[9] with all of whom exists some token of his having

---

5. Hathaway (1556?–1623) married Shakespeare in 1582.
6. See n. 4, p. 112. Elizabeth I (1533–1603), queen of England and Ireland (1558–1603) who succeeded the Catholic Mary I and re-established Protestantism in England. Her reign was marked by several plots to overthrow her, the execution of Mary, Queen of Scots (1587), the defeat of the Spanish Armada (1588), and domestic prosperity and literary achievement. James, see n. 4, p. 172. Essexes, Leicesters, Burleighs, and Buckinghams were English noble families, members of which were active in politics and the court during the reigns of Elizabeth and James. *Tudor dynasty*: English ruling dynasty (1485–1603), including Henry VII and his descendants, Henry VIII, Edward VI, Mary I, and Elizabeth I.
7. See n. 3, p. 6.
8. A formal eulogistic composition intended as a public compliment; elaborate praise or laudation; an encomium. Jonson dedicated two such poems to Shakespeare.
9. Jacobus Arminius (1560–1609), Dutch theologian and founder of Arminianism, which opposed the absolute predestinarianism of John Calvin and was influential throughout Europe. Sir Henry Wotton (1568–1639), English diplomat and writer. Most of his poetry and prose works are contained in *Reliquiae Wottonianae*, published posthumously in 1651. Beza (1519–1605), French theologian associated with John Calvin. Casaubon (1559–1614), French Classical Scholar, who lived in England from 1610 until his death. Sidney, see n. 5, p. 158. Robert Devereux, second earl of Essex (1566–1601), English nobleman and favorite of Elizabeth I. He was executed for treason after taking part in an uprising of the people of London. Raleigh, see n. 1, p. 242. Vane, see n. 2, p. 33. Izaak Walton (1593–1683), English writer primarily known for *The Compleat Angler* (1653), a philosophical treatise on fishing. John Donne (1572–1631), English Metaphysical poet and divine who served as chaplain to James I and dean of St. Paul's Cathedral (after 1621); his works include *Divine Poems* (1607). Abraham Cowley (1618–1667), English Metaphysical poet whose works include *Davideis* (1656), an epic on the life of King David. Robert Bellarmine (1542–1621), Italian Jesuit theologian. Cotton, see n. 9, p. 239. John Pym (1584–1643), English Parliamentarian who moved for the impeachment of the advisers to Charles I. The king's effort to arrest Pym in the House of Commons (1642) precipitated the English Civil War.

communicated, without enumerating many others whom doubtless he saw,—Shakspeare, Spenser, Jonson, Beaumont, Massinger, two Herberts, Marlow, Chapman,[1] and the rest. Since the constellation of great men who appeared in Greece, in the time of Pericles,[2] there was never any such society;—yet their genius failed them to find out the best head in the universe. Our poet's mask was impenetrable. You cannot see the mountain near. It took a century to make it suspected; and not until two centuries had passed, after his death, did any criticism which we think adequate begin to appear. It was not possible to write the history of Shakspeare till now; for he is the father of German literature: it was on the introduction of Shakspeare into German, by Lessing, and the translation of his works by Wieland and Schlegel,[3] that the rapid burst of German literature was most intimately connected. It was not until the nineteenth century, whose speculative genius is a sort of living Hamlet,[4] that the tragedy of Hamlet could find such wondering readers. Now, literature, philosophy, and thought are Shakspearized. His mind is the horizon beyond which at present we do not see. Our ears are educated to music by his rhythm. Coleridge and Goethe[5] are the only critics who have expressed our convictions with any adequate fidelity; but there is in all cultivated minds a silent appreciation of his superlative power and beauty, which, like Christianity, qualifies the period.

The Shakspeare Society have inquired in all directions, advertised the missing facts, offered money for any information that will lead to proof;—and with what result? Beside some important illustration of the history of the English stage to which I adverted, they have gleaned a few facts touching the property and dealings in regard to property of the Poet. It appears that from year to year he owned a larger share in the Blackfriars Theatre: its wardrobe and other appurtenances were his; that he bought an estate in his native village with his earnings as writer and shareholder; that he lived in the best house in Stratford; was intrusted by his neighbours with their commissions in London, as of borrowing money, and the like; that he was a veritable farmer. About the time when he was writing Macbeth,[6] he sues Philip Rogers, in the borough-court of Stratford, for thirty-five shillings, tenpence, for corn delivered to him at different times; and, in all respects, appears as a good husband, with no reputation for eccentricity or excess. He was a goodnatured sort of man, an actor and shareholder in the theatre, not in any striking manner distinguished from other actors and managers. I admit the importance of this information. It was well worth the pains that have been taken to procure it.

But whatever scraps of information concerning his condition these researches may have rescued, they can shed no light upon that infinite invention

---

Hales (1584–1656), English Scholar and divine. Kepler, see n. 1, p. 194. François Vieta (1540–1603), French mathematician, founder of algebra. Alberto Gentili (1552–1608), Italian-born legal scholar. Paolo Sarpi (1552–1623), Venetian friar, theologian, and historian; he wrote *History of the Council of Trent* (1610–18).

1. See n. 6, p. 193. Spenser, see n. 3, p. 171. Beaumont, see n. 9, p. 132. George Herbert (see n. 6, p. 30) and his brother Edward, Lord Herbert of Cherbury (1583–1648), a soldier, diplomat and philosopher.
2. Athenian leader (d. 429 B.C.E.), noted for advancing democracy in Athens and for ordering the construction of the Parthenon.
3. See n. 5, p. 199. Gotthold Ephraim Lessing (1729–1781), German playwright and critic. A leader of the Enlightenment, he wrote the plays *Minna von Barnheim* (1763) and *Nathan the Wise* (1779). Christoph Martin Wieland (1733–1813), German writer and translator whose works include ornate poetry, novels, such as the satire *Republic of Fools* (1774), and translations of many Shakespearean plays.
4. The brooding and indecisive hero of Shakespeare's longest play, *Hamlet*.
5. See n. 6, p. 42. Coleridge, see n. 2, p. 31.
6. King of Scotland (r. 1040–57), who ascended the throne after killing his cousin King Duncan (d. 1040) in battle. Legends of his rise to power and reign are the basis of Shakespeare's tragedy *Macbeth*.

which is the concealed magnet of his attraction for us. We are very clumsy writers of history. We tell the chronicle of parentage, birth, birthplace, schooling, schoolmates, earning of money, marriage, publication of books, celebrity, death, and when we have come to an end of this gossip, no ray of relation appears between it and the goddess-born; and it seems as if, had we dipped at random into the "Modern Plutarch," and read any other life there, it would have fitted the poems as well. It is the essence of poetry to spring like the rainbow daughter of Wonder from the invisible, to abolish the past, and refuse all history. Malone, Warburton, Dyce, and Collier[7] have wasted their oil. The famed theatres Covent Garden,[8] Drury Lane, the Park, and Tremont, have vainly assisted. Betterton, Garrick, Kemble, Kean, and Macready[9] dedicate their lives to this genius; him they crown, elucidate, obey, and express. The Genius knows them not. The recitation begins; one golden word leaps out immortal from all this painted pedantry, and sweetly torments us with invitations to its own inaccessible homes. I remember I went once to see the Hamlet of a famed performer, the pride of the English stage, and all I then heard and all I now remember of the tragedian, was that in which the tragedian had no part, simply Hamlet's question to the ghost, —

> "What may this mean,
> That thou, dead corse, again in complete steel
> Revisit'st thus the glimpses of the moon?"[1]

That imagination which dilates the closet he writes in to the world's dimension, crowds it with agents in rank and order, as quickly reduces the big reality to be the glimpses of the moon. These tricks of his magic spoil for us the illusions of the green room. Can any biography shed light on the localities into which the Midsummer Night's Dream[2] admits me? Did Shakspeare confide to any notary or parish Recorder, sacristan, or surrogate in Stratford, the genesis of that delicate creation? The forest of Arden, the nimble air of Scone Castle, the moonlight of Portia's villa, "the antres vast and desarts idle" of Othello's captivity,—where is the third cousin or grandnephew, the chancellor's file of accounts, or private letter, that has kept one word of those transcendant secrets? In fine, in this drama, as in all great works of art,—in the Cyclopæan architecture of Egypt and India; in the Phidian sculpture; the Gothic minsters;[3] the Ital-

---

7. John Payne Collier, director of the Shakespeare Society of London in the 1840s. Emerson was familiar with his *Works of William Shakespeare* (1842–44). Warburton, see n. 5, p. 18. Alexander Dyce (1798–1869), Scottish-born critic who edited the works of James Shirley (1833) and Christopher Marlowe (1850) and is best known for his edition of Shakespeare (1857).
8. An area in London long noted for its produce market (established in 1671) and its royal theater (first built in 1731–32).
9. William Charles Macready (1793–1873), British actor particularly noted for his Shakespearean roles and his contributions to modern stagecraft. Thomas Betterton (1635?–1710), renowned Shakespearean actor during the Restoration. David Garrick (1717–1779), British actor and theater manager who was considered the foremost Shakespearean player of his time. John Philip Kemble (1757–1823), British actor who managed the Drury Lane (1788–1803) and Covent Garden (1803–17) theaters in London and was an acclaimed tragedian. His niece Frances Anne Kemble (1809–1893), known as "Fanny," was a celebrated Shakespearean actress in Great Britain and the United States. Edmund Kean (1787–1833), British actor known for his portrayals of Shakespeare's great tragic characters.
1. *Hamlet* 1.4.51–53.
2. *A Midsummer Night's Dream* is set, not very realistically, in a forest near Athens. Emerson goes on to invoke the settings of other Shakespearean plays: the forest of Arden in *As You Like It*, Scotland in *Macbeth*, Portia's villa in *The Merchant of Venice*, and Othello's experiences in "antres vast and desarts idle" (*Othello* 1.3.140).
3. Emerson is referring to medieval monastery churches in Britain. *Cyclopaean:* or cyclopean, a primitive style of masonry, characterized by the use of massive stones of irregular shape and size, found in ancient ruins in Greece, Asia Minor, and Italy. Phidias, see n. 9, p. 134.

ian painting; the Ballads of Spain and Scotland;—the Genius draws up the ladder after him, when the creative age goes up to heaven, and gives way to a new,
which sees the works, and asks in vain for a history.

Shakspeare is the only biographer of Shakspeare, and even he can tell
nothing except to the Shakspeare in us, that is, to our most apprehensive and
sympathetic hour. He cannot step from off his tripod, and give us anecdotes of
his inspirations. Read the antique documents extricated, analyzed, and compared, by the assiduous Dyce and Collier; and now read one of those skiey sentences,—aerolites,—which seem to have fallen out of heaven, and which, not
your experience, but the man within the breast has accepted as words of fate,
and tell me if they match: if the former account in any manner for the latter, or
which gives the most historical insight into the man.

Hence, though our external history is so meagre, yet with Shakspeare for
biographer, instead of Aubrey and Rowe,[4] we have really the information which
is material, that which describes character and fortune, that which, if we were
about to meet the man and deal with him, would most import us to know. We
have his recorded convictions on those questions which knock for answer at
every heart, on life and death, on love, on wealth, and poverty, on the prizes of
life, and the ways whereby we come at them, on the characters of men, and the
influences occult and open which affect their fortunes, and on those mysterious and demoniacal powers which defy our science, and which yet interweave
their malice and their gift in our brightest hours. Who ever read the volume of
the "Sonnets,"[5] without finding that the Poet had there revealed, under masks
that are no masks to the intelligent, the lore of friendship and of love; the confusion of sentiments in the most susceptible, and, at the same time, the most intellectual of men? What trait of his private mind has he hidden in his dramas?
One can discern in his ample pictures of the gentleman and the king, what
forms and humanities pleased him; his delight in troops of friends, in large hospitality, in cheerful giving. Let Timon, let Warwick, let Antonio[6] the merchant,
answer for his great heart. So far from Shakspeare's being the least known, he is
the one person in all modern history known to us. What point of morals, of manners, of economy, of philosophy, of religion, of taste, of the conduct of life, has
he not settled? What mystery has he not signified his knowledge of? What office or function or district of man's work has he not remembered? What king
has he not taught state, as Talma taught Napoleon?[7] What maiden has not
found him finer than her delicacy? What lover has he not outloved? What sage
has he not outseen? What gentleman has he not instructed in the rudeness of
his behaviour?

Some able and appreciating critics think no criticism on Shakspeare valuable that does not rest purely on the dramatic merit; that he is falsely judged as
poet and philosopher. I think as highly as these critics of his dramatic merit, but
still think it secondary. He was a full man who liked to talk; a brain exhaling
thoughts and images which seeking vent, found the drama next at hand. Had

---

4. Nicholas Rowe (1674–1718), English writer whose works include drama, poetry, and an edition of
   Shakespeare. He was appointed poet laureate in 1715. John Aubrey (1626–1697), English antiquarian
   and writer whose *Brief Lives*, first published in 1813, contains anecdotes and sketches of seventeenth-
   century writers.
5. Shakespeare's *Sonnets* (1609) contains 154 poems, all in the same fourteen-line format (three quatrains
   and a rhyming couplet) now known as the Shakespearean sonnet.
6. All characters in Shakespeare's plays.
7. See n. 8, p. 17. François Joseph Talma (1763–1826), celebrated actor during the French Revolution, a
   close friend of Napoleon.

he been less, we should have had to consider how well he filled his place, how good a dramatist he was, and he is the best in the world. But it turns out, that what he has to say is of that weight, as to withdraw some attention from the vehicle; and he is like some saint whose history is to be rendered into all languages, into verse and prose, into songs and pictures, and cut up into proverbs, so that the occasion which gave the saint's meaning the form of a conversation or of a prayer or of a code of laws is immaterial, compared with the universality of its application. So it fares with the wise Shakspeare and his book of life. He wrote the airs for all our modern music. He wrote the text of modern life; the text of manners: he drew the man of England and Europe; the father of the man in America: he drew the man, and described the day, and what is done in it: he read the hearts of men and women, their probity, and their second thought and wiles; the wiles of innocence, and the transitions by which virtues and vices slide into their contraries: he could divide the mother's part from the father's part in the face of the child, or draw the fine demarcations of freedom and of fate: he knew the laws of repression, which make the police of nature: and all the sweets and all the terrors of human lot lay in his mind as truly but as softly as the landscape lies on the eye. And the importance of this wisdom of life sinks the form, as of Drama or Epic, out of notice. 'Tis like making a question concerning the paper on which a king's message is written.

Shakspeare is as much out of the category of eminent authors, as he is out of the crowd. He is inconceivably wise, the others conceivably. A good reader can in a sort nestle into Plato's brain, and think from thence, but not into Shakspeare's. We are still out of doors. For executive faculty, for creation, Shakspeare is unique. No man can imagine it better. He was the farthest reach of subtlety compatible with an individual self,—the subtilest of authors, and only just within the possibility of authorship. With this wisdom of life, is the equal endowment of imaginative and of lyric power. He clothed the creatures of his legend with form and sentiments, as if they were people who had lived under his roof, and few real men have left such distinct characters as these fictions. And they spoke in language as sweet as it was fit. Yet his talents never seduced him into an ostentation, nor did he harp on one string. An omnipresent humanity coordinates all his faculties. Give a man of talents a story to tell, and his partiality will presently appear. He has certain observations, opinions, topics, which have some accidental prominence, and which he disposes all to exhibit. He crams this part, and starves that other part, consulting not the fitness of the thing, but his fitness and strength. But Shakspeare has no peculiarity, no importunate topic, but all is duly given; no veins, no curiosities; no cowpainter, no birdfancier, no mannerist is he: he has no discoverable egotism: the great he tells greatly, the small subordinately. He is wise without emphasis or assertion; he is strong as nature is strong, who lifts the land into mountain slopes without effort, and by the same rule as she floats a bubble in the air, and likes as well to do the one as the other. This makes that equality of power in farce, tragedy, narrative, and lovesongs; a merit so incessant, that each reader is incredulous of the perception of other readers.

This power of expression, or of transferring the inmost truth of things into music and verse, makes him the type of the poet, and has added a new problem to metaphysics. This is that which throws him into natural history as a main production of the globe, and as announcing new eras and ameliorations. Things were mirrored in his poetry without loss or blur; he could paint the fine with precision, the great with compass; the tragic and the comic indifferently, and without any distortion or favour. He carried his powerful execution into minute details to a hair point; finishes an eyelash or a dimple as firmly as he draws a mountain; and yet these, like nature's, will bear the scrutiny of the solar microscope. In short, he is the chief example to prove that more or less of production, more or fewer pictures is a thing indifferent. He had the power to make one picture. Daguerre[8] learned how to let one flower etch its image on his plate of iodine; and then proceeds at leisure to etch a million. There are always objects; but there was never representation. Here is perfect representation, at last, and now let the world of figures sit for their portraits. No recipe can be given for the making of a Shakspeare; but the possibility of the translation of things into song, is demonstrated.

His lyric power lies in the genius of the piece. The sonnets, though their excellence is lost in the splendour of the dramas, are as inimitable as they: and it is not a merit of lines, but a total merit of the piece; like the tone of voice of some incomparable person, so is this a speech of poetic beings, and any clause as unproducible now, as a whole poem. Though the speeches in the plays, and single lines have a beauty which tempts the ear to pause on them for their euphuism, yet the sentence is so loaded with meaning, and so linked with its foregoers and followers, that the logician is satisfied. His means are as admirable as his ends; every subordinate invention by which he helps himself to connect some irreconcileable opposites, is a poem too. He is not reduced to dismount and walk, because his horses are running off with him in some distant direction: he always rides.

The finest poetry was first experience: but the thought has suffered a transformation since it was an experience. Cultivated men often attain a good degree of skill in writing verses, but it is easy to read through their poems their personal history: any one acquainted with parties, can name every figure: this is Andrew, and that is Rachel. The sense thus remains prosaic. It is a caterpillar with wings, and not yet a butterfly. In the poet's mind, the fact has gone quite over into the new element of thought, and has lost all that is exuvial. This generosity abides with Shakspeare. We say, from the truth and closeness of his pictures, that he knows the lesson by heart. Yet there is not a trace of egotism.

One more royal trait properly belongs to the Poet, I mean his cheerfulness, without which no man can be a poet, for beauty is his aim. He loves virtue, not for its obligation, but for its grace: he delights in the world, in man, in woman, for the lovely light which sparkles from them. Beauty, the spirit of joy and hilarity, he sheds over the universe. Epicurus[9] says that poetry hath such charms that a lover might forsake his mistress to partake of them. And the true bards have been noted for their firm and cheerful temper. Homer lies in sunshine, Chaucer is glad and erect; and Saadi says, "it was rumoured abroad that I was penitent, but what had I to do with repentance?" Not less sovereign and cheerful,—much more sovereign and cheerful is the tone of Shakspeare. His name suggests joy and emancipation to the heart of men. If he should appear in any

8. Louis Jacques Mandé Daguerre (1789–1851), French artist and inventor of the daguerreotype process for obtaining positive photographic prints on glass plates. Introduced into the United States in 1839, daguerreotypy became very popular, and Emerson had daguerreotypes taken of himself and other members of his family.
9. Greek philosopher (341?–270 B.C.E.), who founded his influential school of Epicureanism in Athens ca. 306 B.C.E., emphasized pleasure as the highest good.

company of human souls, who would not march in his troop? He touches nothing that does not borrow health and longevity from his festal style.

And now how stands the account of man with this bard and benefactor, when in solitude, shutting our ears to the reverberations of his fame, we seek to strike the balance? Solitude has austere lessons, it can teach us to spare both heroes and poets; and it weighs Shakspeare also, and finds him to share the halfness and imperfection of humanity.

Shakspeare, Homer, Dante,[1] Chaucer, saw the splendour of meaning that plays over the visible world; knew that a tree had another use than for apples, and corn another than for meal, and the ball of the earth than for tillage and roads: that these things bore a second and finer harvest to the mind, being emblems of its thoughts, and conveying in all their natural history a certain mute commentary on human life. Shakspeare employed them as colours to compose his picture. He rested in their beauty; and never took the step which seemed inevitable to such genius, namely, to explore the virtue which resides in these symbols, and imparts this power, —What is that which they themselves say? He converted the elements which waited on his command, into entertainments. He was master of the revels to mankind. Is it not as if one should have, through majestic powers of science, the comets given into his hand or the planets and their moons, and should draw them from their orbits to glare with the municipal fireworks on a holiday night, and advertise in all towns *very superior pyrotechny this evening?* Are the agents of nature and the power to understand them, worth no more than a street serenade or the breath of a cigar? One remembers again the trumpet text in the Koran, — "The Heavens and the earth and all that is between them, think ye we have created them in jest?" As long as the question is of talent and mental power, the world of men has not his equal to show. But when the question is to life, and its materials, and its auxiliaries, how does he profit me? What does it signify? It is but a Twelfth night, or Midsummer's night's dream, or a Winter evening's tale: What signifies another picture more or less? The Egyptian verdict of the Shakspeare Societies comes to mind, that he was a jovial actor and manager. I cannot marry this fact to his verse: Other admirable men have led lives in some sort of keeping with their thought, but this man in wide contrast. Had he been less, had he reached only the common measure of great authors, of Bacon, Milton, Tasso, Cervantes,[2] we might leave the fact in the twilight of human fate; but that this man of men, he who gave to the science of mind a new and larger subject than had ever existed, and planted the standard of humanity some furlongs forward into Chaos, —that he should not be wise for himself, —it must even go into the world's history, that the best poet led an obscure and profane life, using his genius for the public amusement.

Well, other men, priest and prophet, Israelite, German, and Swede, beheld the same objects: they also saw through them that which was contained. And to what purpose? The beauty straightway vanished, they read commandments, all-excluding mountainous duty; an obligation, a sadness, as of piled mountains fell on them, and life became ghastly, joyless, a pilgrim's progress, a

---

1. See n. 3, p. 184.
2. Miguel de Cervantes Saavedra (1547–1616), author of *Don Quixote* (1605, 1615). Torquato Tasso (1544–1595), Italian poet who wrote the epic *Jerusalem Delivered* (1581), an account of the capture of the city during the First Crusade.

probation, beleaguered round with doleful histories of Adam's fall and curse, behind us; with Doomsdays and purgatorial and penal fires before us; and the heart of the seer and the heart of the listener sunk in them.

It must be conceded that these are halfviews of halfmen. The world still wants its poet-priest, a reconciler who shall not trifle, with Shakspeare the player, nor shall grope in graves, with Swedenborg[3] the mourner, but who shall see, speak, and act, with equal inspiration. For knowledge will brighten the sunshine; right is more beautiful than private affection, and love is compatible with universal wisdom.

3. See n. 6, p. 35.

From The Conduct of Life

Fate[1]

Delicate omens traced in air
To the lone bard true witness bare;
Birds with auguries on their wings
Chanted undeceiving things
Him to beckon, him to warn;
Well might then the poet scorn
To learn of scribe or courier
Hints writ in vaster character;
And on his mind, at dawn of day,
Soft shadows of the evening lay.
For the prevision is allied
Unto the thing so signified;
Or say, the foresight that awaits
Is the same Genius that creates.

It chanced during one winter, a few years ago, that our cities were bent on discussing the theory of the Age. By an odd coincidence, four or five noted men were each reading a discourse to the citizens of Boston or New York, on the Spirit of the Times. It so happened that the subject had the same prominence in some remarkable pamphlets and journals issued in London in the same season. To me, however, the question of the times resolved itself into a practical question of the conduct of life. How shall I live? We are incompetent to solve the times. Our geometry cannot span the huge orbits of the prevailing ideas, behold their return, and reconcile their opposition. We can only obey our own polarity. 'Tis fine for us to speculate and elect our course, if we must accept an irresistible dictation.

In our first steps to gain our wishes, we come upon immovable limitations. We are fired with the hope to reform men. After many experiments, we find that we must begin earlier,—at school. But the boys and girls are not docile;[2] we can make nothing of them. We decide that they are not of good stock. We must begin our reform earlier still,—at generation: that is to say, there is Fate, or laws of the world.

But if there be irresistible dictation, this dictation understands itself. If we must accept Fate, we are not less compelled to affirm liberty, the significance of the individual, the grandeur of duty, the power of character. This is true, and that other is true. But our geometry cannot span these extreme points, and reconcile them. What to do? By obeying each thought frankly, by harping, or, if you will, pounding on each string, we learn at last its power. By the same obedience to other thoughts, we learn theirs, and then comes some reasonable hope of har-

---

1. This essay is a companion to "Power," which follows (p. 279).
2. I.e., susceptible to being taught.

monizing them. We are sure, that, though we know not how, necessity does comport with liberty, the individual with the world, my polarity with the spirit of the times. The riddle of the age has for each a private solution. If one would study his own time, it must be by this method of taking up in turn each of the leading topics which belong to our scheme of human life, and, by firmly stating all that is agreeable to experience on one, and doing the same justice to the opposing facts in the others, the true limitations will appear. Any excess of emphasis, on one part, would be corrected, and a just balance would be made.

But let us honestly state the facts. Our America has a bad name for superficialness. Great men, great nations, have not been boasters and buffoons, but perceivers of the terror of life, and have manned themselves to face it. The Spartan, embodying his religion in his country, dies before its majesty without a question. The Turk, who believes his doom is written on the iron leaf in the moment when he entered the world, rushes on the enemy's sabre with undivided will. The Turk, the Arab, the Persian, accepts the foreordained fate.

> "On two days, it steads not to run from thy grave,
>   The appointed, and the unappointed day;
> On the first, neither balm nor physician can save,
>   Nor thee, on the second, the Universe slay."[3]

The Hindoo, under the wheel,[4] is as firm. Our Calvinists, in the last generation, had something of the same dignity. They felt that the weight of the Universe held them down to their place. What could *they* do? Wise men feel that there is something which cannot be talked or voted away, —a strap or belt which girds the world.

> "The Destiny, minister general,
> That executeth in the world o'er all,
> The purveyance which God hath seen beforne,
> So strong it is, that tho' the world had sworn
> The contrary of a thing by yea or nay,
> Yet sometime it shall fallen on a day
> That falleth not oft in a thousand year;
> For, certainly, our appetités here,
> Be it of war, or peace, or hate, or love,
> All this is ruled by the sight above."
>   CHAUCER: *The Knighte's Tale.*

The Greek Tragedy expressed the same sense: "Whatever is fated, that will take place. The great immense mind of Jove is not to be transgressed."[5]

Savages cling to a local god of one tribe or town. The broad ethics of Jesus were quickly narrowed to village theologies, which preach an election or favoritism. And, now and then, an amiable parson, like Jung Stilling,[6] or Robert

---

3. Edward Waldo Emerson informs us that this quatrain is his father's translation, from the German of von Hammer Purgstall, of a poem by Ali ben Abu Talib (see n. 1, p. 92). In Emerson's *May-Day and Other Pieces* (1867) it is attributed to Omar Chiam.
4. Probably a reference to the belief that during the festival of Juggernaut (or Jagannath—one of the titles of the Hindu deity Krishna) in Puri, east India, some devotees would throw themselves under the wheels of the temple-replica that carried the god's image through the streets.
5. Cf. Aeschylus (see n. 1, p. 109), *The Suppliant Women,* lines 1047–49.
6. Johann Henrich Jung-Stilling (1740–1817), a German mystic and theosophist, an acquaintance interesting to Goethe, who describes his character in his *Autobiography.* [Edward Waldo Emerson]

Huntington, believes in a pistareen[7]-Providence, which, whenever the good man wants a dinner, makes that somebody shall knock at his door, and leave a half-dollar. But Nature is no sentimentalist,—does not cosset or pamper us. We must see that the world is rough and surly, and will not mind drowning a man or a woman; but swallows your ship like a grain of dust. The cold, inconsiderate of persons, tingles your blood, benumbs your feet, freezes a man like an apple. The diseases, the elements, fortune, gravity, lightning, respect no persons. The way of Providence is a little rude. The habit of snake and spider, the snap of the tiger and other leapers and bloody jumpers, the crackle of the bones of his prey in the coil of the anaconda,—these are in the system, and our habits are like theirs. You have just dined, and, however scrupulously the slaughter-house is concealed in the graceful distance of miles, there is complicity,—expensive races,—race living at the expense of race. The planet is liable to shocks from comets, perturbations from planets, rendings from earthquake and volcano, alterations of climate, precessions of equinoxes. Rivers dry up by opening of the forest. The sea changes its bed. Towns and counties fall into it. At Lisbon, an earthquake killed men like flies. At Naples, three years ago, ten thousand persons were crushed in a few minutes. The scurvy at sea; the sword of the climate in the west of Africa, at Cayenne, at Panama, at New Orleans, cut off men like a massacre. Our western prairie shakes with fever and ague. The cholera, the small-pox, have proved as mortal to some tribes, as a frost to the crickets, which, having filled the summer with noise, are silenced by a fall of the temperature of one night. Without uncovering what does not concern us, or counting how many species of parasites hang on a bombyx; or groping after intestinal parasites, or infusory biters, or the obscurities of alternate generation;—the forms of the shark, the *labrus*, the jaw of the sea-wolf paved with crushing teeth, the weapons of the grampus,[8] and other warriors hidden in the sea,—are hints of ferocity in the interiors of nature. Let us not deny it up and down. Providence has a wild, rough, incalculable road to its end, and it is of no use to try to whitewash its huge, mixed instrumentalities, or to dress up that terrific benefactor in a clean shirt and white neckcloth of a student in divinity.

Will you say, the disasters which threaten mankind are exceptional, and one need not lay his account for cataclysms every day? Aye, but what happens once, may happen again, and so long as these strokes are not to be parried by us, they must be feared.

But these shocks and ruins are less destructive to us, than the stealthy power of other laws which act on us daily. An expense of ends to means is fate;—organization tyrannizing over character. The menagerie, or forms and powers of the spine, is a book of fate: the bill of the bird, the skull of the snake, determines tyrannically its limits. So is the scale of races, of temperaments; so is sex; so is climate; so is the reaction of talents imprisoning the vital power in certain directions. Every spirit makes its house; but afterwards the house confines the spirit.

The gross lines are legible to the dull: the cabman is phrenologist[9] so far: he looks in your face to see if his shilling is sure. A dome of brow denotes one thing;

---

7. A Spanish silver coin of small value. Robert Huntington, Edward Emerson tells us, is probably a mistake for *William* Huntington, a popular and unorthodox eighteenth-century English preacher.
8. Usually refers to the killer whale. *Bombyx*: silkworm (from the Latin *bombyx*, "silk"). *Infusory biters*: probably a reference to infusorians, any of a heterogeneous group of minute organisms found especially in decomposing infusions of organic matter. *Alternate generation*: or alternation of generation; the successive occurrence of two or more different forms in the life cycle of a plant or animal, especially the alternation of a sexual generation with an asexual one. *Labrus*: a predatory fish with strong mandibles.
9. See n. 4, p. 201.

a pot-belly another; a squint, a pug-nose, mats of hair, the pigment of the epidermis, betray character. People seem sheathed in their tough organization. Ask Spurzheim, ask the doctors, ask Quetelet,[1] if temperaments decide nothing? or if there be anything they do not decide? Read the description in medical books of the four temperaments,[2] and you will think you are reading your own thoughts which you had not yet told. Find the part which black eyes, and which blue eyes, play severally in the company. How shall a man escape from his ancestors, or draw off from his veins the black drop which he drew from his father's or his mother's life? It often appears in a family, as if all the qualities of the progenitors were potted in several jars, — some ruling quality in each son or daughter of the house, — and sometimes the unmixed temperament, the rank unmitigated elixir, the family vice, is drawn off in a separate individual, and the others are proportionally relieved. We sometimes see a change of expression in our companion, and say, his father, or his mother, comes to the windows of his eyes, and sometimes a remote relative. In different hours, a man represents each of several of his ancestors, as if there were seven or eight of us rolled up in each man's skin, — seven or eight ancestors at least, — and they constitute the variety of notes for that new piece of music which his life is. At the corner of the street, you read the possibility of each passenger, in the facial angle, in the complexion, in the depth of his eye. His parentage determines it. Men are what their mothers made them. You may as well ask a loom which weaves huckaback, why it does not make cashmere, as expect poetry from this engineer, or a chemical discovery from that jobber. Ask the digger in the ditch to explain Newton's laws: the fine organs of his brain have been pinched by overwork and squalid poverty from father to son, for a hundred years. When each comes forth from his mother's womb, the gate of gifts closes behind him. Let him value his hands and feet, he has but one pair. So he has but one future, and that is already predetermined in his lobes, and described in that little fatty face, pig-eye, and squat form. All the privilege and all the legislation of the world cannot meddle or help to make a poet or a prince of him.

Jesus said, "When he looketh on her, he hath committed adultery."[3] But he is an adulterer before he has yet looked on the woman, by the superfluity of animal, and the defect of thought, in his constitution. Who meets him, or who meets her, in the street, sees that they are ripe to be each other's victim.

In certain men, digestion and sex absorb the vital force, and the stronger these are, the individual is so much weaker. The more of these drones perish, the better for the hive. If, later, they give birth to some superior individual, with force enough to add to this animal a new aim, and a complete apparatus to work it out, all the ancestors are gladly forgotten. Most men and most women are merely one couple more. Now and then, one has a new cell or camarilla opened in his brain, — an architectural, a musical, or a philological knack, some stray taste or talent for flowers, or chemistry, or pigments, or story-telling, a good hand for drawing, a good foot for dancing, an athletic frame for wide journeying, &c. — which skill nowise alters rank in the scale of nature, but serves to pass the

---

1. Lambert Adolphe Jacques Quételet (1796–1874), Belgian astronomer, statistician, and researcher in the field of probability theory who investigated the "average man." In May 1849 Emerson wrote in his journal: "One must study Quetelet to know the limits of freedom." More recently, science fiction writer Isaac Asimov summed up Quételet's achievement as follows: "Randomness invaded the human realm, and in one more way life (and humanity in particular) was shown to follow the same laws that govern the inanimate universe." Johann Gaspar Spurzheim (1776–1832), German phrenologist who lectured in Boston in 1832, where Emerson probably heard him.
2. Or four humors (see n. 6, p. 184).
3. Cf. Matthew 5.28.

time, the life of sensation going on as before. At last, these hints and tendencies are fixed in one, or in a succession. Each absorbs so much food and force, as to become itself a new centre. The new talent draws off so rapidly the vital force, that not enough remains for the animal functions, hardly enough for health; so that, in the second generation, if the like genius appear, the health is visibly deteriorated, and the generative force impaired.

People are born with the moral or with the material bias;—uterine brothers with this diverging destination: and I suppose, with high magnifiers, Mr. Frauenhofer or Dr. Carpenter might come to distinguish in the embryo at the fourth day, this is a Whig, and that a Free-soiler.[4]

It was a poetic attempt to lift this mountain of Fate, to reconcile this despotism of race with liberty, which led the Hindoos to say, "Fate is nothing but the deeds committed in a prior state of existence." I find the coincidence of the extremes of eastern and western speculation in the daring statement of Schelling,[5] "there is in every man a certain feeling, that he has been what he is from all eternity, and by no means became such in time." To say it less sublimely,—in the history of the individual is always an account of his condition, and he knows himself to be a party to his present estate.

A good deal of our politics is physiological. Now and then, a man of wealth in the heyday of youth adopts the tenet of broadest freedom. In England, there is always some man of wealth and large connection planting himself, during all his years of health, on the side of progress, who, as soon as he begins to die, checks his forward play, calls in his troops, and becomes conservative. All conservatives are such from personal defects. They have been effeminated by position or nature, born halt and blind, through luxury of their parents, and can only, like invalids, act on the defensive. But strong natures, backwoodsmen, New Hampshire giants, Napoleons, Burkes, Broughams, Websters, Kossuths,[6] are inevitable patriots, until their life ebbs, and their defects and gout, palsy and money, warp them.

The strongest idea incarnates itself in majorities and nations, in the healthiest and strongest. Probably, the election goes by avoirdupois weight, and, if you could weigh bodily the tonnage of any hundred of the Whig and the Democratic party in a town, on the Dearborn balance,[7] as they passed the hayscales, you could predict with certainty which party would carry it. On the whole, it would be rather the speediest way of deciding the vote, to put the selectmen or the mayor and aldermen at the hayscales.

In science, we have to consider two things: power and circumstance. All we know of the egg, from each successive discovery, is, *another vesicle*; and if, after five hundred years, you get a better observer, or a better glass, he finds within the last observed another. In vegetable and animal tissue, it is just alike, and all that the primary power or spasm operates, is, still, vesicles, vesicles. Yes,—but the tyrannical Circumstance! A vesicle in new circumstances, a vesicle lodged in darkness, Oken[8] thought, became animal; in light, a plant.

---

4. Member of the Free-Soil Party, formed in 1848 to oppose the extension of slavery. Joseph von Frauenhofer, or Fraunhofer (1787–1826), German physicist and optician who discovered "Fraunhofer lines" (dark lines in the solar spectrum caused by the passage of light through gas in the atmosphere). Dr. William B. Carpenter (1813–1885), author of *The Microscope, Its Revelations and Uses*.
5. Schelling, see n. 1, p. 194.
6. Lajos Kossuth (1802–1894), Hungarian patriot and revolutionary leader. Napoleon, see n. 8, p. 17. Burke, see n. 5, p. 45. Henry Peter, Baron Brougham and Vaux (1778–1868), Scottish jurist after whom a horse-drawn carriage was named. Webster, see n. 6, p. 251.
7. A scale.
8. Oken (see n. 1, p. 194) believed that all organisms originated in vesicles, or cells.

Lodged in the parent animal, it suffers changes, which end in unsheathing miraculous capability in the unaltered vesicle, and it unlocks itself to fish, bird, or quadruped, head and foot, eye and claw. The Circumstance is Nature. Nature is, what you may do. There is much you may not. We have two things,— the circumstance, and the life. Once we thought, positive power was all. Now we learn, that negative power, or circumstance, is half. Nature is the tyrannous circumstance, the thick skull, the sheathed snake, the ponderous, rock-like jaw; necessitated activity; violent direction; the conditions of a tool, like the locomotive, strong enough on its track, but which can do nothing but mischief off of it; or skates, which are wings on the ice, but fetters on the ground.

The book of Nature is the book of Fate. She turns the gigantic pages,—leaf after leaf,—never re-turning one. One leaf she lays down, a floor of granite; then a thousand ages, and a bed of slate; a thousand ages, and a measure of coal; a thousand ages, and a layer of marl and mud: vegetable forms appear; her first misshapen animals, zoophyte, trilobium,[9] fish; then, saurians,—rude forms, in which she has only blocked her future statue, concealing under these unwieldy monsters the fine type of her coming king. The face of the planet cools and dries, the races meliorate, and man is born. But when a race has lived its term, it comes no more again.

The population of the world is a conditional population; not the best, but the best that could live now; and the scale of tribes, and the steadiness with which victory adheres to one tribe, and defeat to another, is as uniform as the superposition of strata. We know in history what weight belongs to race. We see the English, French, and Germans planting themselves on every shore and market of America and Australia, and monopolizing the commerce of these countries. We like the nervous and victorious habit of our own branch of the family. We follow the step of the Jew, of the Indian, of the Negro. We see how much will has been expended to extinguish the Jew, in vain. Look at the unpalatable conclusions of Knox,[1] in his "Fragment of Races,"—a rash and unsatisfactory writer, but charged with pungent and unforget[t]able truths. "Nature respects race, and not hybrids." "Every race has its own *habitat*." "Detach a colony from the race, and it deteriorates to the crab." See the shades of the picture. The German and Irish millions, like the Negro, have a great deal of guano[2] in their destiny. They are ferried over the Atlantic, and carted over America, to ditch and to drudge, to make corn cheap, and then to lie down prematurely to make a spot of green grass on the prairie.

One more fagot[3] of these adamantine bandages, is, the new science of Statistics. It is a rule, that the most casual and extraordinary events—if the basis of population is broad enough—become matter of fixed calculation. It would not be safe to say when a captain like Bonaparte, a singer like Jenny Lind, or a navigator like Bowditch,[4] would be born in Boston: but, on a population of twenty or two hundred millions, something like accuracy may be had.[5]

---

9. Or trilobite, an extinct three-lobed marine arthropod of the Paleozoic Era. *Zoophyte:* any of various invertebrate animals, such as a sea anemone or sponge, that attach to surfaces and superficially resemble plants.
1. Robert Knox (1791–1862), Scottish anatomist.
2. The dung of sea birds or bats, used as fertilizer.
3. Stick used to make secure bindings.
4. Nathaniel Bowditch (1773–1838), American mathematician and astronomer, author of *The New American Practical Navigator* (1802). Jenny Lind (1820–1887), known as "the Swedish Nightingale," a soprano who toured the United States (1850–52) under the management of P. T. Barnum.
5. "Everything which pertains to the human species, considered as a whole, belongs to the order of physical facts. The greater the number of individuals, the more does the influence of the individual will dis-

'Tis frivolous to fix pedantically the date of particular inventions. They have all been invented over and over fifty times. Man is the arch machine, of which all these shifts drawn from himself are toy models. He helps himself on each emergency by copying or duplicating his own structure, just so far as the need is. 'Tis hard to find the right Homer, Zoroaster, or Menu; harder still to find the Tubal Cain, or Vulcan, or Cadmus, or Copernicus, or Fust, or Fulton,[6] the indisputable inventor. There are scores and centuries of them. "The air is full of men." This kind of talent so abounds, this constructive tool-making efficiency, as if it adhered to the chemic atoms, as if the air he breathes were made of Vaucansons, Franklins, and Watts.[7]

Doubtless, in every million there will be an astronomer, a mathematician, a comic poet, a mystic. No one can read the history of astronomy, without perceiving that Copernicus, Newton, Laplace, are not new men, or a new kind of men, but that Thales, Anaximenes, Hipparchus, Empedocles, Aristarchus, Pythagoras, Œnopides,[8] had anticipated them; each had the same tense geometrical brain, apt for the same vigorous computation and logic, a mind parallel to the movement of the world. The Roman mile probably rested on a measure of a degree of the meridian. Mahometan and Chinese know what we know of leap-year, of the Gregorian calendar, and of the precession of the equinoxes. As, in every barrel of cowries, brought to New Bedford, there shall be one *orangia*,[9] so there will, in a dozen millions of Malays and Mahometans, be one or two astronomical skulls. In a large city, the most casual things, and things whose beauty lies in their casualty, are produced as punctually and to order as the baker's muffin for breakfast. Punch[1] makes exactly one capital joke a week; and the journals contrive to furnish one good piece of news every day.

And not less work the laws of repression, the penalties of violated functions. Famine, typhus, frost, war, suicide, and effete races, must be reckoned calculable parts of the system of the world.

These are pebbles from the mountain, hints of the terms by which our life is walled up, and which show a kind of mechanical exactness, as of a loom or mill, in what we call casual or fortuitous events.

The force with which we resist these torrents of tendency looks so ridiculously inadequate, that it amounts to little more than a criticism or a protest made by a minority of one, under compulsion of millions. I seemed, in the height of a tempest, to see men overboard struggling in the waves, and driven about here and there. They glanced intelligently at each other, but 'twas little they could do for one another; 'twas much if each could keep afloat alone. Well, they had a right to their eye-beams, and all the rest was Fate.

appear, leaving predominance to a series of general facts dependent on causes by which society exists, and is preserved"—Quetelet. [Emerson]

6. See n. 5, p. 119. Homer, see n. 8, p. 88. Zoroaster, see n. 9, p. 78. Menu, see n. 3, p. 115. Tubal-Cain, third son of Lamech and Zillah and the first smith, "an instructor of every artificer in brass and iron" (see Genesis 4.22). Vulcan, see n. 3, p. 189. Cadmus, see n. 1, p. 210. Copernicus, see n. 5, p. 125. Johann Fust (1400?–1466), German printer who was the financial partner (1450?–55) and successor of Gutenberg.
7. See n. 5, p. 119. Jacques de Vaucanson (1709–1782), French inventor and mathematician. Franklin, see n. 5, p. 16.
8. Oenopides of Chios (fifth century B.C.E.), astronomer and mathematician. Newton, see n. 5, p. 16. Laplace, see n. 9, p. 89. Thales and Anaximemes, see n. 5, p. 208. Hipparchus (second century B.C.E.), Greek astronomer. Empedocles, see n. 3, p. 84. Aristarchus (fl. 156 B.C.E.), the greatest critic of antiquity and head of the Alexandrian library. Pythagoras, see n. 6, p.38.
9. Orange cowry, a shell used for adornment or financial exchange in the South Pacific.
1. English magazine known for its humor and cartoons.

We cannot trifle with this reality, this cropping-out in our planted gardens of the core of the world. No picture of life can have any veracity that does not admit the odious facts. A man's power is hooped in by a necessity, which, by many experiments, he touches on every side, until he learns its arc.

The element running through entire nature, which we popularly call Fate, is known to us as limitation. Whatever limits us, we call Fate. If we are brute and barbarous, the fate takes a brute and dreadful shape. As we refine, our checks become finer. If we rise to spiritual culture, the antagonism takes a spiritual form. In the Hindoo fables, Vishnu follows Maya[2] through all her ascending changes, from insect and crawfish up to elephant; whatever form she took, he took the male form of that kind, until she became at last woman and goddess, and he a man and a god. The limitations refine as the soul purifies, but the ring of necessity is always perched at the top.

When the gods in the Norse heaven were unable to bind the Fenris Wolf[3] with steel or with weight of mountains, — the one he snapped and the other he spurned with his heel, — they put round his foot a limp band softer than silk or cobweb, and this held him: the more he spurned it, the stiffer it drew. So soft and so stanch is the ring of Fate. Neither brandy, nor nectar, nor sulphuric ether,[4] nor hell-fire, nor ichor, nor poetry, nor genius, can get rid of this limp band. For if we give it the high sense in which the poets use it, even thought itself is not above Fate: that too must act according to eternal laws, and all that is wilful and fantastic in it is in opposition to its fundamental essence.

And, last of all, high over thought, in the world of morals, Fate appears as vindicator, levelling the high, lifting the low, requiring justice in man, and always striking soon or late, when justice is not done. What is useful will last; what is hurtful will sink. "The doer must suffer," said the Greeks: "you would soothe a Deity not to be soothed." "God himself cannot procure good for the wicked," said the Welsh triad. "God may consent, but only for a time," said the bard of Spain. The limitation is impassable by any insight of man. In its last and loftiest ascensions, insight itself, and the freedom of the will, is one of its obedient members. But we must not run into generalizations too large, but show the natural bounds or essential distinctions, and seek to do justice to the other elements as well.

Thus we trace Fate, in matter, mind, and morals, — in race, in retardations of strata, and in thought and character as well. It is everywhere bound or limitation. But Fate has its lord; limitation its limits; is different seen from above and from below; from within and from without. For, though Fate is immense, so is power, which is the other fact in the dual world, immense. If Fate follows and limits power, power attends and antagonizes Fate. We must respect Fate as natural history, but there is more than natural history. For who and what is this criticism that pries into the matter? Man is not order of nature, sack and sack, belly and members, link in a chain, nor any ignominious baggage, but a stupendous antagonism, a dragging together of the poles of the Universe. He betrays his relation to what is below him, — thick-skulled, small-brained, fishy, quadru-

---

2. In Hinduism, the transitory, manifold appearance of the sensible world, which obscures the undifferentiated spiritual reality from which it originates. See Emerson's essay "Illusions," p. 292. Vishnu, see n. 5, p. 90.
3. In Norse mythology, the wolf of Loki and the brother of Hel, typifying the goading of a guilty conscience. Odin sought vainly to chain him, but the wolf was expected to swallow Odin on the day of doom.
4. Emerson might mean what is now called ether ($C_2H_5OC_2H_5$), obtained by the distillation of alcohol with sulfuric acid and used as a reagent, solvent, and anesthetic.

manous,[5] — quadruped ill-disguised, hardly escaped into biped, and has paid for the new powers by loss of some of the old ones. But the lightning which explodes and fashions planets, maker of planets and suns, is in him. On one side, elemental order, sandstone and granite, rock-ledges, peat-bog, forest, sea and shore; and, on the other part, thought, the spirit which composes and decomposes nature, — here they are, side by side, god and devil, mind and matter, king and conspirator, belt and spasm, riding peacefully together in the eye and brain of every man.

Nor can he blink[6] the freewill. To hazard the contradiction, — freedom is necessary. If you please to plant yourself on the side of Fate, and say, Fate is all; then we say, a part of Fate is the freedom of man. Forever wells up the impulse of choosing and acting in the soul. Intellect annuls Fate. So far as a man thinks, he is free. And though nothing is more disgusting than the crowing about liberty by slaves, as most men are, and the flippant mistaking for freedom of some paper preamble like a "Declaration of Independence," or the statute right to vote, by those who have never dared to think or to act, yet it is wholesome to man to look not at Fate, but the other way: the practical view is the other. His sound relation to these facts is to use and command, not to cringe to them. "Look not on nature, for her name is fatal," said the oracle.[7] The too much contemplation of these limits induces meanness. They who talk much of destiny, their birth-star, &c., are in a lower dangerous plane, and invite the evils they fear.

I cited the instinctive and heroic races as proud believers in Destiny. They conspire with it; a loving resignation is with the event. But the dogma makes a different impression, when it is held by the weak and lazy. 'Tis weak and vicious people who cast the blame on Fate. The right use of Fate is to bring up our conduct to the loftiness of nature. Rude and invincible except by themselves are the elements. So let man be. Let him empty his breast of his windy conceits, and show his lordship by manners and deeds on the scale of nature. Let him hold his purpose as with the tug of gravitation. No power, no persuasion, no bribe shall make him give up his point. A man ought to compare advantageously with a river, an oak, or a mountain. He shall have not less the flow, the expansion, and the resistance of these.

'Tis the best use of Fate to teach a fatal courage. Go face the fire at sea, or the cholera in your friend's house, or the burglar in your own, or what danger lies in the way of duty, knowing you are guarded by the cherubim of Destiny. If you believe in Fate to your harm, believe it, at least, for your good.

For, if Fate is so prevailing, man also is part of it, and can confront fate with fate. If the Universe have these savage accidents, our atoms are as savage in resistance. We should be crushed by the atmosphere, but for the reaction of the air within the body. A tube made of a film of glass can resist the shock of the ocean, if filled with the same water. If there be omnipotence in the stroke, there is omnipotence of recoil.

1. But Fate against Fate is only parrying and defence: there are, also, the noble creative forces. The revelation of Thought takes man out of servitude into freedom. We rightly say of ourselves, we were born, and afterward we were born again, and many times. We have successive experiences so important, that the

---

5. Having four hands.
6. Intentionally overlook or ignore.
7. Edward Waldo Emerson states that this is one of the "Chaldean oracles" ascribed to Zoroaster.

new forgets the old, and hence the mythology of the seven or the nine heavens.[8]
The day of days, the great day of the feast of life, is that in which the inward eye
opens to the Unity in things, to the omnipresence of law; — sees that what is must
be, and ought to be, or is the best. This beatitude dips from on high down on us,
and we see. It is not in us so much as we are in it. If the air come to our lungs, we
breathe and live; if not, we die. If the light come to our eyes, we see; else not. And
if truth come to our mind, we suddenly expand to its dimensions, as if we grew to
worlds. We are as lawgivers; we speak for Nature; we prophesy and divine.

This insight throws us on the party and interest of the Universe, against all
and sundry; against ourselves, as much as others. A man speaking from insight affirms of himself what is true of the mind: seeing its immortality, he says, I am immortal; seeing its invincibility, he says, I am strong. It is not in us, but we are in it.
It is of the maker, not of what is made. All things are touched and changed by it.
This uses, and is not used. It distances those who share it, from those who share it
not. Those who share it not are flocks and herds. It dates from itself; — not from
former men or better men, — gospel, or constitution, or college, or custom.
Where it shines, Nature is no longer intrusive, but all things make a musical or
pictorial impression. The world of men show like a comedy without laughter: —
populations, interests, government, history; — 'tis all toy figures in a toy house. It
does not overvalue particular truths. We hear eagerly every thought and word
quoted from an intellectual man. But, in his presence, our own mind is roused to
activity, and we forget very fast what he says, much more interested in the new
play of our own thought, than in any thought of his. 'Tis the majesty into which
we have suddenly mounted, the impersonality, the scorn of egotisms, the sphere
of laws, that engage us. Once we were stepping a little this way, and a little that
way; now, we are as men in a balloon, and do not think so much of the point we
have left, or the point we would make, as of the liberty and glory of the way.

Just as much intellect as you add, so much organic power. He who sees
through the design, presides over it, and must will that which must be. We sit and
rule, and, though we sleep, our dream will come to pass. Our thought, though it
were only an hour old, affirms an oldest necessity, not to be separated from
thought, and not to be separated from will. They must always have coëxisted. It
apprises us of its sovereignty and godhead, which refuse to be severed from it. It is
not mine or thine, but the will of all mind. It is poured into the souls of all men,
as the soul itself which constitutes them men. I know not whether there be, as is
alleged, in the upper region of our atmosphere, a permanent westerly current,
which carries with it all atoms which rise to that height, but I see, that when souls
reach a certain clearness of perception, they accept a knowledge and motive
above selfishness. A breath of will blows eternally through the universe of souls in
the direction of the Right and Necessary. It is the air which all intellects inhale
and exhale, and it is the wind which blows the worlds into order and orbit.

Thought dissolves the material universe, by carrying the mind up into a
sphere where all is plastic.[9] Of two men, each obeying his own thought, he
whose thought is deepest will be the strongest character. Always one man more
than another represents the will of Divine Providence to the period.

---

8. According to Muslim and Cabalist lore, there are seven heavens, the seventh being the highest. In the
early Ptolemaic system there are nine spheres—those of the Moon, Mercury, Venus, the Sun, Mars,
Jupiter, Saturn, the Firmament, and the Crystalline Sphere.
9. Malleable.

2. If thought makes free, so does the moral sentiment. The mixtures of spiritual chemistry refuse to be analyzed. Yet we can see that with the perception of truth is joined the desire that it shall prevail. That affection is essential to will. Moreover, when a strong will appears, it usually results from a certain unity of organization, as if the whole energy of body and mind flowed in one direction. All great force is real and elemental. There is no manufacturing a strong will. There must be a pound to balance a pound. Where power is shown in will, it must rest on the universal force. Alaric[1] and Bonaparte must believe they rest on a truth, or their will can be bought or bent. There is a bribe possible for any finite will. But the pure sympathy with universal ends is an infinite force, and cannot be bribed or bent. Whoever has had experience of the moral sentiment cannot choose but believe in unlimited power. Each pulse from that heart is an oath from the Most High. I know not what the word *sublime* means, if it be not the intimations in this infant of a terrific force. A text of heroism, a name and anecdote of courage, are not arguments, but sallies of freedom. One of these is the verse of the Persian Hafiz,[2] "'Tis written on the gate of Heaven, 'Woe unto him who suffers himself to be betrayed by Fate!'" Does the reading of history make us fatalists? What courage does not the opposite opinion show! A little whim of will to be free gallantly contending against the universe of chemistry.

But insight is not will, nor is affection will. Perception is cold, and goodness dies in wishes; as Voltaire[3] said, 'tis the misfortune of worthy people that they are cowards; "*un des plus grands malheurs des honnêtes gens c'est qu'ils sont des lâches.*" There must be a fusion of these two to generate the energy of will. There can be no driving force, except through the conversion of the man into his will, making him the will, and the will him. And one may say boldly, that no man has a right perception of any truth, who has not been reacted on by it, so as to be ready to be its martyr.

The one serious and formidable thing in nature is a will. Society is servile from want of will, and therefore the world wants saviours and religions. One way is right to go: the hero sees it, and moves on that aim, and has the world under him for root and support. He is to others as the world. His approbation is honor; his dissent, infamy. The glance of his eye has the force of sunbeams. A personal influence towers up in memory only worthy, and we gladly forget numbers, money, climate, gravitation, and the rest of Fate.

We can afford to allow the limitation, if we know it is the meter[4] of the growing man. We stand against Fate, as children stand up against the wall in their father's house, and notch their height from year to year. But when the boy grows to man, and is master of the house, he pulls down that wall, and builds a new and bigger. 'Tis only a question of time. Every brave youth is in training to ride and rule this dragon. His science is to make weapons and wings of these passions and retarding forces. Now whether, seeing these two things, fate and power, we are permitted to believe in unity? The bulk of mankind believe in two gods. They are under one dominion here in the house, as friend and parent, in social circles, in letters, in art, in love, in religion: but in mechanics, in

---

1. Alaric (370?–410), king of the Visigoths, who invaded Greece in 395 and attacked Italy, conquering Rome in 410.
2. See n. 1, p. 115.
3. Pen name of François Marie Arouet (1694–1778), French philosopher, satirist, historian, dramatist and poet, known for his enmity to organized religion and to fanaticism, intolerance, and superstition.
4. Measure.

dealing with steam and climate, in trade, in politics, they think they come under another; and that it would be a practical blunder to transfer the method and way of working of one sphere, into the other. What good, honest, generous men at home, will be wolves and foxes on change![5] What pious men in the parlor will vote for what reprobates at the polls! To a certain point, they believe themselves the care of a Providence. But, in a steamboat, in an epidemic, in war, they believe a malignant energy rules.

But relation and connection are not somewhere and sometimes, but everywhere and always. The divine order does not stop where their sight stops. The friendly power works on the same rules, in the next farm, and the next planet. But, where they have not experience, they run against it, and hurt themselves. Fate, then, is a name for facts not yet passed under the fire of thought;—for causes which are unpenetrated.

But every jet of chaos which threatens to exterminate us, is convertible by intellect into wholesome force. Fate is unpenetrated causes. The water drowns ship and sailor, like a grain of dust. But learn to swim, trim your bark, and the wave which drowned it, will be cloven by it, and carry it, like its own foam, a plume and a power. The cold is inconsiderate of persons, tingles your blood, freezes a man like a dew-drop. But learn to skate, and the ice will give you a graceful, sweet, and poetic motion. The cold will brace your limbs and brain to genius, and make you foremost men of time. Cold and sea will train an imperial Saxon race, which nature cannot bear to lose, and, after cooping it up for a thousand years in yonder England, gives a hundred Englands, a hundred Mexicos. All the bloods it shall absorb and domineer: and more than Mexicos,—the secrets of water and steam, the spasms of electricity, the ductility of metals, the chariot of the air, the ruddered balloon are awaiting you.

The annual slaughter from typhus far exceeds that of war; but right drainage destroys typhus. The plague in the sea-service from scurvy is healed by lemon juice and other diets portable or procurable: the depopulation by cholera and small-pox is ended by drainage and vaccination; and every other pest is not less in the chain of cause and effect, and may be fought off. And, whilst art draws out the venom, it commonly extorts some benefit from the vanquished enemy. The mischievous torrent is taught to drudge for man: the wild beasts he makes useful for food, or dress, or labor; the chemic explosions are controlled like his watch. These are now the steeds on which he rides. Man moves in all modes, by legs of horses, by wings of wind, by steam, by gas of balloon, by electricity, and stands on tiptoe threatening to hunt the eagle in his own element. There's nothing he will not make his carrier.

Steam was, till the other day, the devil which we dreaded. Every pot made by any human potter or brazier had a hole in its cover, to let off the enemy, lest he should lift pot and roof, and carry the house away. But the Marquis of Worcester,[6] Watt, and Fulton bethought themselves, that, where was power, was not devil, but was God; that it must be availed of, and not by any means let off and wasted. Could he lift pots and roofs and houses so handily? he was the workman they were in search of. He could be used to lift away, chain, and compel other devils, far more reluctant and dangerous, namely, cubic miles of earth,

---

5. I.e., in the stock exchange.
6. Edward Somerset, Marquis of Worcester (1601–67), the devoted adherent of Charles I. and lord of Raglan Castle, was a remarkable experimenter, and wrote an account of his "Century of Inventions," among which was the use of the power of steam. [Edward Waldo Emerson]

mountains, weight or resistance of water, machinery, and the labors of all men in the world; and time he shall lengthen, and shorten space.

It has not fared much otherwise with higher kinds of steam. The opinion of the million was the terror of the world, and it was attempted, either to dissipate it, by amusing nations, or to pile it over with strata of society,—a layer of soldiers; over that, a layer of lords; and a king on the top; with clamps and hoops of castles, garrisons, and police. But, sometimes, the religious principle would get in, and burst the hoops, and rive every mountain laid on top of it. The Fultons and Watts of politics, believing in unity, saw that it was a power, and, by satisfying it, (as justice satisfies everybody,) through a different disposition of society,—grouping it on a level, instead of piling it into a mountain,—they have contrived to make of this terror the most harmless and energetic form of a State.

Very odious, I confess, are the lessons of Fate. Who likes to have a dapper phrenologist pronouncing on his fortunes? Who likes to believe that he has hidden in his skull, spine, and pelvis, all the vices of a Saxon or Celtic race, which will be sure to pull him down,—with what grandeur of hope and resolve he is fired,—into a selfish, huckstering, servile, dodging animal? A learned physician tells us, the fact is invariable with the Neapolitan, that, when mature, he assumes the forms of the unmistakable scoundrel. That is a little overstated.—but may pass.

But these are magazines and arsenals. A man must thank his defects, and stand in some terror of his talents. A transcendent talent draws so largely on his forces, as to lame him; a defect pays him revenues on the other side. The sufferance, which is the badge of the Jew, has made him, in these days, the ruler of the rulers of the earth. If Fate is ore and quarry, if evil is good in the making, if limitation is power that shall be, if calamities, oppositions, and weights are wings and means,—we are reconciled.

Fate involves the melioration. No statement of the Universe can have any soundness, which does not admit its ascending effort. The direction of the whole, and of the parts, is toward benefit, and in proportion to the health. Behind every individual, closes organization: before him, opens liberty,—the Better, the Best. The first and worst races are dead. The second and imperfect races are dying out, or remain for the maturing of higher. In the latest race, in man, every generosity, every new perception, the love and praise he extorts from his fellows, are certificates of advance out of fate into freedom. Liberation of the will from the sheaths and clogs of organization which he has outgrown, is the end and aim of this world. Every calamity is a spur and valuable hint; and where his endeavors do not yet fully avail, they tell as tendency. The whole circle of animal life,—tooth against tooth,—devouring war, war for food, a yelp of pain and a grunt of triumph, until, at last, the whole menagerie, the whole chemical mass is mellowed and refined for higher use,—pleases at a sufficient perspective.

But to see how fate slides into freedom, and freedom into fate, observe how far the roots of every creature run, or find, if you can, a point where there is no thread of connection. Our life is consentaneous[7] and far-related. This knot of nature is so well tied, that nobody was ever cunning enough to find the two ends. Nature is intricate, overlapped, interweaved, and endless. Christopher Wren[8] said of the beautiful King's College chapel, that "if anybody would tell

---

7. Achieved through agreement.
8. Sir Christopher Wren (1632–1723), English architect, known especially for his design of St. Paul's Cathedral in London as well as for Trinity College library at Cambridge University.

him where to lay the first stone, he would build such another." But where shall we find the first atom in this house of man, which is all consent, inosculation, and balance of parts?

The web of relation is shown in *habitat*, shown in hybernation. When hybernation was observed, it was found, that, whilst some animals became torpid in winter, others were torpid in summer: hybernation then was a false name. The *long sleep* is not an effect of cold, but is regulated by the supply of food proper to the animal. It becomes torpid when the fruit or prey it lives on is not in season, and regains its activity when its food is ready.

Eyes are found in light; ears in auricular air; feet on land; fins in water; wings in air; and, each creature where it was meant to be, with a mutual fitness. Every zone has its own *Fauna*. There is adjustment between the animal and its food, its parasite, its enemy. Balances are kept. It is not allowed to diminish in numbers, nor to exceed. The like adjustments exist for man. His food is cooked, when he arrives; his coal in the pit; the house ventilated; the mud of the deluge dried; his companions arrived at the same hour, and awaiting him with love, concert, laughter, and tears. These are coarse adjustments, but the invisible are not less. There are more belongings to every creature than his air and his food. His instincts must be met, and he has predisposing power that bends and fits what is near him to his use. He is not possible until the invisible things are right for him, as well as the visible. Of what changes, then, in sky and earth, and in finer skies and earths, does the appearance of some Dante or Columbus apprise us!

How is this effected? Nature is no spendthrift, but takes the shortest way to her ends. As the general says to his soldiers, "if you want a fort, build a fort," so nature makes every creature do its own work and get its living, — is it planet, animal, or tree. The planet makes itself. The animal cell makes itself; — then, what it wants. Every creature, — wren or dragon, — shall make its own lair. As soon as there is life, there is self-direction, and absorbing and using of material. Life is freedom, — life in the direct ratio of its amount. You may be sure, the new-born man is not inert. Life works both voluntarily and supernaturally in its neighborhood. Do you suppose, he can be estimated by his weight in pounds, or, that he is contained in his skin, — this reaching, radiating, jaculating fellow? The smallest candle fills a mile with its rays, and the papillæ[9] of a man run out to every star.

When there is something to be done, the world knows how to get it done. The vegetable eye makes leaf, pericarp, root, bark, or thorn, as the need is; the first cell converts itself into stomach, mouth, nose, or nail, according to the want: the world throws its life into a hero or a shepherd; and puts him where he is wanted. Dante and Columbus were Italians, in their time: they would be Russians or Americans to-day. Things ripen, new men come. The adaptation is not capricious. The ulterior aim, the purpose beyond itself, the correlation by which planets subside and crystallize, then animate beasts and men, will not stop, but will work into finer particulars, and from finer to finest.

The secret of the world is, the tie between person and event. Person makes event, and event person. The "times," "the age," what is that, but a few profound persons and a few active persons who epitomize the times? — Goethe, Hegel, Metternich, Adams, Calhoun, Guizot, Peel, Cobden, Kossuth, Rothschild,

9. Nipple (Latin); a small nipplelike projection, such as a protuberance on the skin, at the root of a hair or feather, or at the base of a developing tooth; one of the small, round or cone-shaped protuberances on the top of the tongue that contain taste buds.

Astor, Brunel,[1] and the rest. The same fitness must be presumed between a man and the time and event, as between the sexes, or between a race of animals and the food it eats, or the inferior races it uses. He thinks his fate alien, because the copula[2] is hidden. But the soul contains the event that shall befall it, for the event is only the actualization of its thoughts; and what we pray to ourselves for is always granted. The event is the print of your form. It fits you like your skin. What each does is proper to him. Events are the children of his body and mind. We learn that the soul of Fate is the soul of us, as Hafiz sings,

> Alas! till now I had not known,
> My guide and fortune's guide are one.

All the toys that infatuate men, and which they play for,—houses, land, money, luxury, power, fame, are the selfsame thing, with a new gauze or two of illusion overlaid. And of all the drums and rattles by which men are made willing to have their heads broke, and are led out solemnly every morning to parade,— the most admirable is this by which we are brought to believe that events are arbitrary, and independent of actions. At the conjuror's, we detect the hair by which he moves his puppet, but we have not eyes sharp enough to descry the thread that ties cause and effect.

Nature magically suits the man to his fortunes, by making these the fruit of his character. Ducks take to the water, eagles to the sky, waders to the sea margin, hunters to the forest, clerks to counting-rooms, soldiers to the frontier. Thus events grow on the same stem with persons; are sub-persons. The pleasure of life is according to the man that lives it, and not according to the work or the place. Life is an ecstasy. We know what madness belongs to love,—what power to paint a vile object in hues of heaven. As insane persons are indifferent to their dress, diet, and other accommodations, and, as we do in dreams, with equanimity, the most absurd acts, so, a drop more of wine in our cup of life will reconcile us to strange company and work. Each creature puts forth from itself its own condition and sphere, as the slug sweats out its slimy house on the pear-leaf, and the woolly aphides on the apple perspire their own bed, and the fish its shell. In youth, we clothe ourselves with rainbows, and go as brave as the zodiac. In age, we put out another sort of perspiration, —gout, fever, rheumatism, caprice, doubt, fretting, and avarice.

A man's fortunes are the fruit of his character. A man's friends are his magnetisms. We go to Herodotus and Plutarch[3] for examples of Fate; but we are ex-

---

1. Sir Marc Isambard Brunel (1769–1849), French-born British engineer who invented a tunneling shield and successfully used it in his construction of the Thames Tunnel (1825–43). His son Isambard Kingdom Brunel (1806–1859) designed the first transatlantic steamship, the *Great Western* (1838). Goethe, see n. 6, p. 42. Georg Wilhelm Hegel (1770–1831), one of the greatest German philosophers. Klemens von Metternich (1773–1859), Austrian politician. Adams, see n. 7, p. 126. John C. Calhoun (1782–1850), vice president of the United States (1825–32) under John Quincy Adams and Andrew Jackson and senator from South Carolina. In his political philosophy, he maintained that the states had the right to nullify federal legislation that they deemed unconstitutional. François Pierre Guillaume Guizot (1787–1874), French historian and politician who advocated a constitutional monarchy. Peel, see n. 6, p. 251. Richard Cobden (1804–1865), British politician, a leading supporter of free trade and an opponent of protectionism. Rothschild, German-Jewish family of bankers, including Mayer Amschal (1743–1812), who founded a bank at Frankfurt am Main. His sons, most notably Solomon (1774–1855) and Nathan Mayer (1777–1836), established branches of the bank throughout Europe. John Jacob Astor (1763–1848), German-born American fur trader and capitalist who became the wealthiest man of his time in the United States.
2. In grammar, a verb, such as a form of be or seem, that identifies the predicate of a sentence with the subject; also called linking verb.
3. See n. 7, p. 57. Herodotus, see n. 2, p. 109.

amples. *"Quisque suos patimur manes."*[4] The tendency of every man to enact all that is in his constitution is expressed in the old belief, that the efforts which we make to escape from our destiny only serve to lead us into it: and I have noticed, a man likes better to be complimented on his position, as the proof of the last or total excellence, than on his merits.

A man will see his character emitted in the events that seem to meet, but which exude from and accompany him. Events expand with the character. As once he found himself among toys, so now he plays a part in colossal systems, and his growth is declared in his ambition, his companions, and his performance. He looks like a piece of luck, but is a piece of causation;—the mosaic, angulated and ground to fit into the gap he fills. Hence in each town there is some man who is, in his brain and performance, an explanation of the tillage, production, factories, banks, churches, ways of living, and society, of that town. If you do not chance to meet him, all that you see will leave you a little puzzled: if you see him, it will become plain. We know in Massachusetts who built New Bedford, who built Lynn, Lowell, Lawrence, Clinton, Fitchburg, Holyoke, Portland, and many another noisy mart. Each of these men, if they were transparent, would seem to you not so much men, as walking cities, and, wherever you put them, they would build one.

History is the action and reaction of these two,—Nature and Thought;—two boys pushing each other on the curbstone of the pavement. Everything is pusher or pushed: and matter and mind are in perpetual tilt and balance, so. Whilst the man is weak, the earth takes up him. He plants his brain and affections. By and by he will take up the earth, and have his gardens and vineyards in the beautiful order and productiveness of his thought. Every solid in the universe is ready to become fluid on the approach of the mind, and the power to flux it is the measure of the mind. If the wall remain adamant, it accuses the want of thought. To a subtler force, it will stream into new forms, expressive of the character of the mind. What is the city in which we sit here, but an aggregate of incongruous materials, which have obeyed the will of some man? The granite was reluctant, but his hands were stronger, and it came. Iron was deep in the ground, and well combined with stone; but could not hide from his fires. Wood, lime, stuffs, fruits, gums, were dispersed over the earth and sea, in vain. Here they are, within reach of every man's day-labor,—what he wants of them. The whole world is the flux of matter over the wires of thought to the poles or points where it would build. The races of men rise out of the ground preoccupied with a thought which rules them, and divided into parties ready armed and angry to fight for this metaphysical abstraction. The quality of the thought differences the Egyptian and the Roman, the Austrian and the American. The men who come on the stage at one period are all found to be related to each other. Certain ideas are in the air. We are all impressionable, for we are made of them; all impressionable, but some more than others, and these first express them. This explains the curious contemporaneousness of inventions and discoveries. The truth is in the air, and the most impressionable brain will announce it first, but all will announce it a few minutes later. So

---

4. *Aeneid* 6.743: "The spirits who haunt us are ourselves." Robert Spiller suggests that the last four lines of Emerson's poem "Nemesis" constitute a gloss on Virgil's line:

> In spite of Virtue and the Muse,
> Nemesis will have her dues,
> And all our struggles and our toils
> Tighter wind the giant coils.

women, as most susceptible, are the best index of the coming hour. So the great man, that is, the man most imbued with the spirit of the time, is the impression-able man,—of a fibre irritable and delicate, like iodine to light. He feels the in-finitesimal attractions. His mind is righter than others, because he yields to a current so feeble as can be felt only by a needle delicately poised.

The correlation is shown in defects. Möller,[5] in his Essay on Architecture, taught that the building which was fitted accurately to answer its end, would turn out to be beautiful, though beauty had not been intended. I find the like unity in human structures rather virulent and pervasive; that a crudity in the blood will appear in the argument; a hump in the shoulder will appear in the speech and handiwork. If his mind could be seen, the hump would be seen. If a man has a seesaw in his voice, it will run into his sentences, into his poem, into the structure of his fable, into his speculation, into his charity. And, as every man is hunted by his own dæmon, vexed by his own disease, this checks all his activity.

So each man, like each plant, has his parasites. A strong, astringent, bilious nature has more truculent enemies than the slugs and moths that fret my leaves. Such an one has curculios, borers, knife-worms: a swindler ate him first, then a client, then a quack, then smooth, plausible gentlemen, bitter and selfish as Moloch.[6]

This correlation really existing can be divined. If the threads are there, thought can follow and show them. Especially when a soul is quick and docile; as Chaucer sings,

> "Or if the soul of proper kind
> Be so perfect as men find,
> That it wot what is to come,
> And that he warneth all and some
> Of every of their aventures,
> By previsions or figures;
> But that our flesh hath not might
> It to understand aright
> For it is warned too darkly." —[7]

Some people are made up of rhyme, coincidence, omen, periodicity, and presage: they meet the person they seek; what their companion prepares to say to them, they first say to him; and a hundred signs apprise them of what is about to befall.

Wonderful intricacy in the web, wonderful constancy in the design this vagabond life admits. We wonder how the fly finds its mate, and yet year after year we find two men, two women, without legal or carnal tie, spend a great part of their best time within a few feet of each other. And the moral is, that what we seek we shall find; what we flee from flees from us; as Goethe said, "what we wish for in youth, comes in heaps on us in old age,"[8] too often cursed with the granting of our prayer: and hence the high caution, that, since we are sure of having what we wish, we beware to ask only for high things.

---

5. Georg Möller (1784–1852), German architect.
6. In the Hebrew Bible, the god of the Ammonites and Phoenicians to whom first-born children were sac-rificed.
7. From Chaucer, *House of Fame* (ca. 1380).
8. From Goethe's autobiography, *Poetry and Truth* (1811–33).

One key, one solution to the mysteries of human condition, one solution to the old knots of fate, freedom, and foreknowledge, exists, the propounding, namely, of the double consciousness.[9] A man must ride alternately on the horses of his private and his public nature, as the equestrians in the circus throw themselves nimbly from horse to horse, or plant one foot on the back of one, and the other foot on the back of the other. So when a man is the victim of his fate, has sciatica in his loins, and cramp in his mind; a club-foot and a club in his wit; a sour face, and a selfish temper; a strut in his gait, and a conceit in his affection; or is ground to powder by the vice of his race; he is to rally on his relation to the Universe, which his ruin benefits. Leaving the dæmon who suffers, he is to take sides with the Deity who secures universal benefit by his pain.

To offset the drag of temperament and race, which pulls down, learn this lesson, namely, that by the cunning co-presence of two elements, which is throughout nature, whatever lames or paralyzes you, draws in with it the divinity, in some form, to repay. A good intention clothes itself with sudden power. When a god wishes to ride, any chip or pebble will bud and shoot out winged feet, and serve him for a horse.

Let us build altars to the Blessed Unity which holds nature and souls in perfect solution, and compels every atom to serve an universal end. I do not wonder at a snow-flake, a shell, a summer landscape, or the glory of the stars; but at the necessity of beauty under which the universe lies; that all is and must be pictorial; that the rainbow, and the curve of the horizon, and the arch of the blue vault are only results from the organism of the eye. There is no need for foolish amateurs to fetch me to admire a garden of flowers, or a sun-gilt cloud, or a waterfall, when I cannot look without seeing splendor and grace. How idle to choose a random sparkle here or there, when the indwelling necessity plants the rose of beauty on the brow of chaos, and discloses the central intention of Nature to be harmony and joy.

Let us build altars to the Beautiful Necessity. If we thought men were free in the sense, that, in a single exception one fantastical will could prevail over the law of things, it were all one as if a child's hand could pull down the sun. If, in the least particular, one could derange the order of nature,—who would accept the gift of life?

Let us build altars to the Beautiful Necessity, which secures that all is made of one piece; that plaintiff and defendant, friend and enemy, animal and planet, food and eater, are of one kind. In astronomy, is vast space, but no foreign system; in geology, vast time, but the same laws as to-day. Why should we be afraid of Nature, which is no other than "philosophy and theology embodied"? Why should we fear to be crushed by savage elements, we who are made up of the same elements? Let us build to the Beautiful Necessity, which makes man brave in believing that he cannot shun a danger that is appointed, nor incur one that is not; to the Necessity which rudely or softly educates him to the perception that there are no contingencies; that Law rules throughout existence, a Law which is not intelligent but intelligence,—not personal nor impersonal,—it disdains words and passes understanding; it dissolves persons; it vivifies nature; yet solicits the pure in heart[1] to draw on all its omnipotence.

---

9. Cf. "The Transcendentalist," p. 102.
1. Cf. Matthew 5.3ff.

Power

His tongue was framed to music,
And his hand was armed with skill,
His face was the mould of beauty,
And his heart the throne of will.

There is not yet any inventory of a man's faculties, any more than a bible of his opinions. Who shall set a limit to the influence of a human being? There are men, who, by their sympathetic attractions, carry nations with them, and lead the activity of the human race. And if there be such a tie, that, wherever the mind of man goes, nature will accompany him, perhaps there are men whose magnetisms are of that force to draw material and elemental powers, and, where they appear, immense instrumentalities organize around them. Life is a search after power; and this is an element with which the world is so saturated, — there is no chink or crevice in which it is not lodged, — that no honest seeking goes unrewarded. A man should prize events and possessions as the ore in which this fine mineral is found; and he can well afford to let events and possessions, and the breath of the body go, if their value has been added to him in the shape of power. If he have secured the elixir, he can spare the wide gardens from which it was distilled. A cultivated man, wise to know and bold to perform, is the end to which nature works, and the education of the will is the flowering and result of all this geology and astronomy.

All successful men have agreed in one thing, — they were *causationists*. They believed that things went not by luck, but by law; that there was not a weak or a cracked link in the chain that joins the first and last of things. A belief in causality, or strict connection between every trifle and the principle of being, and, in consequence, belief in compensation, or, that nothing is got for nothing, — characterizes all valuable minds, and must control every effort that is made by an industrious one. The most valiant men are the best believers in the tension of the laws. "All the great captains," said Bonaparte, "have performed vast achievements by conforming with the rules of the art, — by adjusting efforts to obstacles."

The key to the age may be this, or that, or the other, as the young orators describe; — the key to all ages is — Imbecility; imbecility in the vast majority of men, at all times, and, even in heroes, in all but certain eminent moments; victims of gravity, custom, and fear. This gives force to the strong, — that the multitude have no habit of self-reliance or original action.

We must reckon success a constitutional trait. Courage, — the old physicians taught, (and their meaning holds, if their physiology is a little mythical,) — courage, or the degree of life, is as the degree of circulation of the blood in the arteries. "During passion, anger, fury, trials of strength, wrestling, fighting, a large amount of blood is collected in the arteries, the maintenance of bodily strength requiring it, and but little is sent into the veins. This condition is constant with intrepid persons."[1] Where the arteries hold their blood, is courage and adventure possible. Where they pour it unrestrained into the veins, the spirit is low and feeble. For performance of great mark, it needs extraordinary health. If Eric is in robust health, and has slept well, and is at the top of his condition, and thirty years

---

1. From Swedenborg (see n. 6, p. 35). Emerson, who devoted a whole chapter of *Representative Men* to Swedenborg, was especially interested in Swedenborg's linking of the "animal economy" to man's moral and spiritual nature.

old, at his departure from Greenland, he will steer west, and his ships will reach Newfoundland. But take out Eric, and put in a stronger and bolder man, — Biorn, or Thorfin,[2] — and the ships will, with just as much ease, sail six hundred, one thousand, fifteen hundred miles further, and reach Labrador and New England. There is no chance in results. With adults, as with children, one class enter cordially into the game, and whirl with the whirling world; the others have cold hands, and remain bystanders; or are only dragged in by the humor and vivacity of those who can carry a dead weight. The first wealth is health. Sickness is poor-spirited, and cannot serve any one: it must husband its resources to live. But health or fulness answers its own ends, and has to spare, runs over, and inundates the neighborhoods and creeks of other men's necessities.

All power is of one kind, a sharing of the nature of the world. The mind that is parallel with the laws of nature will be in the current of events, and strong with their strength. One man is made of the same stuff of which events are made; is in sympathy with the course of things; can predict it. Whatever befalls, befalls him first; so that he is equal to whatever shall happen. A man who knows men, can talk well on politics, trade, law, war, religion. For, everywhere, men are led in the same manners.

The advantage of a strong pulse is not to be supplied by any labor, art, or concert. It is like the climate, which easily rears a crop, which no glass, or irrigation, or tillage, or manures, can elsewhere rival. It is like the opportunity of a city like New York, or Constantinople, which needs no diplomacy to force capital or genius or labor to it. They come of themselves, as the waters flow to it. So a broad, healthy, massive understanding seems to lie on the shore of unseen rivers, of unseen oceans, which are covered with barks, that, night and day, are drifted to this point. That is poured into its lap, which other men lie plotting for. It is in everybody's secret; anticipates everybody's discovery; and if it do not command every fact of the genius and the scholar, it is because it is large and sluggish, and does not think them worth the exertion which you do.

This affirmative force is in one, and is not in another, as one horse has the spring in him, and another in the whip. "On the neck of the young man," said Hafiz,[3] "sparkles no gem so gracious as enterprise." Import into any stationary district, as into an old Dutch population in New York or Pennsylvania, or among the planters of Virginia, a colony of hardy Yankees, with seething brains, heads full of steam-hammer, pulley, crank, and toothed wheel, — and everything begins to shine with values. What enhancement to all the water and land in England, is the arrival of James Watt or Brunel![4] In every company, there is not only the active and passive sex, but, in both men and women, a deeper and more important *sex of mind*, namely, the inventive or creative class of both men and women, and the uninventive or accepting class. Each *plus* man represents his set, and, if he have the accidental advantage of personal ascendency, — which implies neither more nor less of talent, but merely the temperamental or taming eye of a soldier or a schoolmaster, (which one has, and one has not, as one has a black moustache and one a blond,) then quite easily and without envy or resistance, all his coadjutors and feeders will admit his right to absorb them. The merchant works by book-

2. These names of Norwegian explorers are meant to stand generally for Norse exploration in the New World ca. 1000 C.E. It is traditionally believed that Eric's son, Leif, may have been the one who reached "Vinland" (variously, Labrador, Newfoundland, or even New England).
3. Hafiz, see n. 1, p. 115. Another version of these lines may be found in the "Translations" section of Emerson's *May-Day and Other Pieces* (1867).
4. See n. 1, p. 275. Watt, see n. 5, p. 119.

keeper and cashier; the lawyer's authorities are hunted up by clerks; the geologist reports the surveys of his subalterns; Commander Wilkes appropriates the results of all the naturalists attached to the Expedition; Thorwaldsen's statue is finished by stone-cutters; Dumas[5] has journeymen; and Shakspeare was theatre-manager, and used the labor of many young men, as well as the playbooks.

There is always room for a man of force, and he makes room for many. Society is a troop of thinkers, and the best heads among them take the best places. A feeble man can see the farms that are fenced and tilled, the houses that are built. The strong man sees the possible houses and farms. His eye makes estates, as fast as the sun breeds clouds.

When a new boy comes into school, when a man travels, and encounters strangers every day, or, when into any old club a new comer is domesticated, that happens which befalls, when a strange ox is driven into a pen or pasture where cattle are kept; there is at once a trial of strength between the best pair of horns and the new comer, and it is settled thenceforth which is the leader. So now, there is a measuring of strength, very courteous, but decisive, and an acquiescence thenceforward when these two meet. Each reads his fate in the other's eyes. The weaker party finds, that none of his information or wit quite fits the occasion. He thought he knew this or that: he finds that he omitted to learn the end of it. Nothing that he knows will quite hit the mark, whilst all the rival's arrows are good, and well thrown. But if he knew all the facts in the encyclopædia, it would not help him: for this is an affair of presence of mind, of attitude, of aplomb: the opponent has the sun and wind, and, in every cast, the choice of weapon and mark; and, when he himself is matched with some other antagonist, his own shafts fly well and hit. 'Tis a question of stomach and constitution. The second man is as good as the first, — perhaps better; but has not stoutness or stomach, as the first has, and so his wit seems over-fine or under-fine.

Health is good, — power, life, that resists disease, poison, and all enemies, and is conservative, as well as creative. Here is question, every spring, whether to graft with wax, or whether with clay; whether to whitewash or to potash, or to prune; but the one point is the thrifty tree. A good tree, that agrees with the soil, will grow in spite of blight, or bug, or pruning, or neglect, by night and by day, in all weathers and all treatments. Vivacity, leadership, must be had, and we are not allowed to be nice in choosing. We must fetch the pump with dirty water, if clean cannot be had. If we will make bread, we must have contagion, yeast, emptyings, or what not, to induce fermentation into the dough: as the torpid artist seeks inspiration at any cost, by virtue or by vice, by friend or by fiend, by prayer or by wine. And we have a certain instinct, that where is great amount of life, though gross and peccant, it has its own checks and purifications, and will be found at last in harmony with moral laws.

We watch in children with pathetic interest, the degree in which they possess recuperative force. When they are hurt by us, or by each other, or go to the bottom of the class, or miss the annual prizes, or are beaten in the game, — if they lose heart, and remember the mischance in their chamber at home, they have a serious check. But if they have the buoyancy and resistance that preoc-

5. Alexandre Dumas (1802–1870), known as "Dumas père," French writer of swashbuckling historical romances, such as *The Count of Monte Cristo* and *The Three Musketeers* (both 1844). He employed a team of collaborators—called "his factory"—who pored through the works of other authors to find material for him. Wilkes, see n. 2, p. 217. Bertel Thorwaldsen (1770–1844), Danish sculptor. The practice of a sculptor's having apprentices or assistants working with him in his studio is, of course, age-old.

cupies them with new interest in the new moment,—the wounds cicatrize,[6] and the fibre is the tougher for the hurt.

One comes to value this *plus* health, when he sees that all difficulties vanish before it. A timid man listening to the alarmists in Congress, and in the newspapers, and observing the profligacy of party,—sectional interests urged with a fury which shuts its eyes to consequences, with a mind made up to desperate extremities, ballot in one hand, and rifle in the other,—might easily believe that he and his country have seen their best days, and he hardens himself the best he can against the coming ruin. But, after this has been foretold with equal confidence fifty times, and government six per cents have not declined a quarter of a mill,[7] he discovers that the enormous elements of strength which are here in play, make our politics unimportant. Personal power, freedom, and the resources of nature strain every faculty of every citizen. We prosper with such vigor, that, like thrifty trees, which grow in spite of ice, lice, mice, and borers, so we do not suffer from the profligate swarms that fatten on the national treasury. The huge animals nourish huge parasites, and the rancor of the disease attests the strength of the constitution. The same energy in the Greek *Demos*[8] drew the remark, that the evils of popular government appear greater than they are; there is compensation for them in the spirit and energy it awakens. The rough and ready style which belongs to a people of sailors, foresters, farmers, and mechanics, has its advantages. Power educates the potentate. As long as our people quote English standards they dwarf their own proportions. A Western lawyer of eminence said to me he wished it were a penal offence to bring an English law-book into a court in this country, so pernicious had he found in his experience our deference to English precedent. The very word 'commerce' has only an English meaning, and is pinched to the cramp exigencies of English experience. The commerce of rivers, the commerce of railroads, and who knows but the commerce of air-balloons, must add an American extension to the pondhole of admiralty.[9] As long as our people quote English standards, they will miss the sovereignty of power; but let these rough riders,—legislators in shirtsleeves,—Hoosier, Sucker, Wolverine, Badger,[1]—or whatever hard head Arkansas, Oregon, or Utah sends, half orator, half assassin, to represent its wrath and cupidity at Washington,—let these drive as they may; and the disposition of territories and public lands, the necessity of balancing and keeping at bay the snarling majorities of German, Irish, and of native millions, will bestow promptness, address, and reason, at last, on our buffalo-hunter, and authority and majesty of manners. The instinct of the people is right. Men expect from good whigs, put into office by the respectability of the country, much less skill to deal with Mexico, Spain, Britain, or with our own malcontent members, than from some strong transgressor, like Jefferson, or Jackson, who first conquers his own government, and then uses the same genius to conquer the foreigner. The senators who dissented from Mr. Polk's Mexican war, were not those who knew better, but those who, from political position, could afford it; not Webster, but Benton and Calhoun.[2]

---

6. To heal or become healed by the formation of scar tissue.
7. I.e., government bonds at 6 percent interest have not lost one quarter of a mill (one thousandth of a dollar) of value.
8. The common people.
9. Maritime law (British).
1. Nicknames for natives of Indiana, Illinois, Michigan, and Wisconsin, respectively.
2. See n. 1, p. 275. James Knox Polk (1795–1849), eleventh president of the United States (1845–49), who led the country into a war with Mexico (1846–48). Webster, see n. 6, p. 251. Thomas Hart Benton (1782–1858), U.S. senator from Missouri (1821–51).

This power, to be sure, is not clothed in satin. 'Tis the power of Lynch law, of soldiers and pirates; and it bullies the peaceable and loyal. But it brings its own antidote; and here is my point, — that all kinds of power usually emerge at the same time; good energy, and bad; power of mind, with physical health; the ecstasies of devotion, with the exasperations of debauchery. The same elements are always present, only sometimes these conspicuous, and sometimes those; what was yesterday foreground, being to-day background, — what was surface, playing now a not less effective part as basis. The longer the drought lasts, the more is the atmosphere surcharged with water. The faster the ball falls to the sun, the force to fly off is by so much augmented. And, in morals, wild liberty breeds iron conscience; natures with great impulses have great resources, and return from far. In politics, the sons of democrats will be whigs; whilst red republicanism, in the father, is a spasm of nature to engender an intolerable tyrant in the next age. On the other hand, conservatism, ever more timorous and narrow, disgusts the children, and drives them for a mouthful of fresh air into radicalism.

Those who have most of this coarse energy, — the 'bruisers,' who have run the gauntlet of caucus and tavern through the county or the state, have their own vices, but they have the good nature of strength and courage. Fierce and unscrupulous, they are usually frank and direct, and above falsehood. Our politics fall into bad hands, and churchmen and men of refinement, it seems agreed, are not fit persons to send to Congress. Politics is a deleterious profession, like some poisonous handicrafts. Men in power have no opinions, but may be had cheap for any opinion, for any purpose, — and if it be only a question between the most civil and the most forcible, I lean to the last. These Hoosiers and Suckers are really better than the snivelling opposition. Their wrath is at least of a bold and manly cast. They see, against the unanimous declarations of the people, how much crime the people will bear; they proceed from step to step, and they have calculated but too justly upon their Excellencies, the New England governors, and upon their Honors, the New England legislators. The messages of the governors and the resolutions of the legislatures, are a proverb for expressing a sham virtuous indignation, which, in the course of events, is sure to be belied.

In trade, also, this energy usually carries a trace of ferocity. Philanthropic and religious bodies do not commonly make their executive officers out of saints. The communities hitherto founded by Socialists, — the Jesuits, the Port-Royalists, the American communities at New Harmony, at Brook Farm, at Zoar,[3] are only possible, by installing Judas as steward. The rest of the offices may be filled by good burgesses. The pious and charitable proprietor has a foreman not quite so pious and charitable. The most amiable of country gentlemen has a certain pleasure in the teeth of the bull-dog which guards his orchard. Of the Shaker[4] society, it was formerly a sort of proverb in the country, that they always sent the devil to market. And in representations of the Deity, painting, poetry, and popular religion have ever drawn the wrath from Hell. It is an esoteric doctrine of society,

3. In 1819, a group of German separatists founded a community at Zoar, Ohio. It is not clear why Emerson calls the Jesuits—the Society or Company of Jesus, founded by St. Ignatius Loyola in 1534—"Socialists," except that they led a communal life without private property, as usually understood. *Port-Royalists:* members of Port-Royal, a French Cistercian convent near Versailles, that also led a communal life. In the seventeenth century it became the center of Jansenism (a movement opposed to the Jesuits that adopted a theory of personal salvation resembling that found in Calvinism). *New Harmony:* a collectivist community in Indiana taken over by Robert Owen (see n. 1, p. 226) in 1825; it failed in 1828. *Brook Farm:* see n. 1, p. 203.
4. See n. 9, p. 54.

that a little wickedness is good to make muscle; as if conscience were not good for hands and legs, as if poor decayed formalists of law and order cannot run like wild goats, wolves, and conies; that, as there is a use in medicine for poisons, so the world cannot move without rogues; that public spirit and the ready hand are as well found among the malignants. 'Tis not very rare, the coincidence of sharp private and political practice, with public spirit, and good neighborhood.

I knew a burly Boniface[5] who for many years kept a public-house in one of our rural capitals. He was a knave whom the town could ill spare. He was a social, vascular creature, grasping and selfish. There was no crime which he did not or could not commit. But he made good friends of the selectmen, served them with his best chop, when they supped at his house, and also with his honor the Judge, he was very cordial, grasping his hand. He introduced all the friends, male and female, into the town, and united in his person the functions of bully, incendiary, swindler, barkeeper, and burglar. He girdled the trees, and cut off the horses' tails of the temperance people, in the night. He led the 'rummies' and radicals in town-meeting with a speech. Meantime, he was civil, fat, and easy, in his house, and precisely the most public-spirited citizen. He was active in getting the roads repaired and planted with shade-trees; he subscribed for the fountains, the gas, and the telegraph; he introduced the new horse-rake, the new scraper, the baby-jumper, and what not, that Connecticut sends to the admiring citizens.[6] He did this the easier, that the peddler stopped at his house, and paid his keeping, by setting up his new trap on the landlord's premises.

Whilst thus the energy for originating and executing work, deforms itself by excess, and so our axe chops off our own fingers,—this evil is not without remedy. All the elements whose aid man calls in, will sometimes become his masters, especially those of most subtle force. Shall he, then, renounce steam, fire, and electricity, or, shall he learn to deal with them? The rule for this whole class of agencies is,—all *plus* is good; only put it in the right place.

Men of this surcharge of arterial blood cannot live on nuts, herb-tea, and elegies; cannot read novels, and play whist; cannot satisfy all their wants at the Thursday Lecture, or the Boston Athenæum.[7] They pine for adventure, and must go to Pike's Peak; had rather die by the hatchet of a Pawnee, than sit all day and every day at a counting-room desk. They are made for war, for the sea, for mining, hunting, and clearing; for hair-breadth adventures, huge risks, and the joy of eventful living. Some men cannot endure an hour of calm at sea. I remember a poor Malay cook, on board a Liverpool packet, who, when the wind blew a gale, could not contain his joy; "Blow!" he cried, "me do tell you, blow!" Their friends and governors must see that some vent for their explosive complexion is provided. The roisters who are destined for infamy at home, if sent to Mexico, will "cover you with glory," and come back heroes and generals. There are Oregons, Californias, and Exploring Expeditions enough appertaining to America, to find them in files to gnaw, and in crocodiles to eat. The young English are fine animals, full of blood, and when they have no wars to breathe their riotous valors in, they seek for travels as dangerous as war, diving into Maelstroms; swimming Hellesponts; wading up the snowy Himmaleh; hunting lion, rhinoceros, ele-

---

5. The proprietor of an inn or tavern, named after a character in George Farquhar's play *The Beaux' Stratagem* (1707). Edward Waldo Emerson tells us that his father had the keeper of a Concord public house in mind.
6. Connecticut Yankees were at one time famous for their itinerant peddling of gadgets and knickknacks.
7. Formerly, an art collection and reading room for cultured Bostonians.

phant, in South Africa; gypsying with Borrow in Spain and Algiers; riding alligators in South America with Waterton; utilizing Bedouin, Sheik, and Pacha, with Layard; yachting among the icebergs of Lancaster Sound; peeping into craters on the equator; or running on the creases[8] of Malays in Borneo.

The excess of virility has the same importance in general history, as in private and industrial life. Strong race or strong individual rests at last on natural forces, which are best in the savage, who, like the beasts around him, is still in reception of the milk from the teats of Nature. Cut off the connection between any of our works, and this aboriginal source, and the work is shallow. The people lean on this, and the mob is not quite so bad an argument as we sometimes say, for it has this good side. "March without the people," said a French deputy from the tribune, "and you march into night: their instincts are a finger-pointing of Providence, always turned toward real benefit. But when you espouse an Orleans party, or a Bourbon, or a Montalembert party, or any other but an organic party, though you mean well, you have a personality instead of a principle, which will inevitably drag you into a corner."

The best anecdotes of this force are to be had from savage life, in explorers, soldiers, and buccaneers. But who cares for fallings-out of assassins, and fights of bears, or grindings of icebergs? Physical force has no value, where there is nothing else. Snow in snow-banks, fire in volcanoes and solfataras is cheap. The luxury of ice is in tropical countries, and midsummer days. The luxury of fire is, to have a little on our hearth: and of electricity, not volleys of the charged cloud, but the manageable stream on the battery-wires. So of spirit, or energy; the rests or remains of it in the civil and moral man, are worth all the cannibals in the Pacific.

In history, the great moment is, when the savage is just ceasing to be a savage, with all his hairy Pelasgic strength directed on his opening sense of beauty:—and you have Pericles and Phidias,—not yet passed over into the Corinthian[9] civility. Everything good in nature and the world is in that moment of transition, when the swarthy juices still flow plentifully from nature, but their astringency or acridity is got out by ethics and humanity.

The triumphs of peace have been in some proximity to war. Whilst the hand was still familiar with the sword-hilt, whilst the habits of the camp were still visible in the port and complexion of the gentleman, his intellectual power culminated: the compression and tension of these stern conditions is a training for the finest and softest arts, and can rarely be compensated in tranquil times, except by some analogous vigor drawn from occupations as hardy as war.

We say that success is constitutional; depends on a *plus* condition of mind and body, on power of work, on courage; that it is of main efficacy in carrying on the world, and, though rarely found in the right state for an article of commerce, but oftener in the supersaturate or excess, which makes it dangerous and destructive, yet it cannot be spared, and must be had in that form, and absorbents provided to take off its edge.

The affirmative class monopolize the homage of mankind. They originate and execute all the great feats. What a force was coiled up in the skull of

8. Or kris, a Malaysian or Indonesian dagger. George Henry Borrow (1803–1881), English traveler, philologist and writer, noted for his works on gypsies. Charles Waterton (1782–1865), British naturalist and traveler. Sir Austin Henry Layard (1817–1894), English archaeologist.
9. From ancient Greek city of Corinth, known for its high culture. The Corinthian order of architecture is the lightest and most ornate among the three Greek orders. *Pelasgic*: from Pelasgian, a member of a people living in the region of the Aegean Sea before the coming of the Greeks. Pericles, see n. 2, p. 254. Phidias, see n. 9, p. 134.

Napoleon! Of the sixty thousand men making his army at Eylau, it seems some thirty thousand were thieves and burglars. The men whom, in peaceful communities, we hold if we can, with iron at their legs, in prisons, under the muskets of sentinels, this man dealt with, hand to hand, dragged them to their duty, and won his victories by their bayonets.

This aboriginal might gives a surprising pleasure when it appears under conditions of supreme refinement, as in the proficients in high art. When Michel Angelo was forced to paint the Sistine Chapel in fresco,[1] of which art he knew nothing, he went down into the Pope's gardens behind the Vatican, and with a shovel dug out ochres, red and yellow, mixed them with glue and water with his own hands, and having, after many trials, at last suited himself, climbed his ladders, and painted away, week after week, month after month, the sibyls and prophets. He surpassed his successors in rough vigor, as much as in purity of intellect and refinement. He was not crushed by his one picture left unfinished at last. Michel was wont to draw his figures first in skeleton, then to clothe them with flesh, and lastly to drape them. "Ah!" said a brave painter to me, thinking on these things, "if a man has failed, you will find he has dreamed instead of working. There is no way to success in our art, but to take off your coat, grind paint, and work like a digger on the railroad, all day and every day."

Success goes thus invariably with a certain *plus* or positive power: an ounce of power must balance an ounce of weight. And, though a man cannot return into his mother's womb, and be born with new amounts of vivacity,[2] yet there are two economies, which are the best *succedanea*[3] which the case admits. The first is, the stopping off decisively our miscellaneous activity, and concentrating our force on one or a few points; as the gardener, by severe pruning, forces the sap of the tree into one or two vigorous limbs, instead of suffering it to spindle into a sheaf of twigs.

Enlarge not thy destiny," said the oracle: "endeavor not to do more than is given thee in charge."[4] The one prudence in life is concentration; the one evil is dissipation: and it makes no difference whether our dissipations are coarse or fine; property and its cares, friends, and a social habit, or politics, or music, or feasting. Everything is good which takes away one plaything and delusion more, and drives us home to add one stroke of faithful work. Friends, books, pictures, lower duties, talents, flatteries, hopes,—all are distractions which cause oscillations in our giddy balloon, and make a good poise and a straight course impossible. You must elect your work; you shall take what your brain can, and drop all the rest. Only so, can that amount of vital force accumulate, which can make the step from knowing to doing. No matter how much faculty of idle seeing a man has, the step from knowing to doing is rarely taken. 'Tis a step out of a chalk circle of imbecility into fruitfulness. Many an artist lacking this, lacks all: he sees the masculine Angelo or Cellini[5] with despair. He, too, is up to Nature and the First Cause in his thought. But the spasm to collect and swing his whole being

---

1. The art of painting on fresh, moist plaster with pigments dissolved in water. Michaelangelo, see n. 6, p. 42.
2. Cf. Nicodemus in John 3.4: "How can a man be born when he is old? can he enter the second time into his mother's womb, and be born?"
3. Substitute.
4. Edward Waldo Emerson identifies this quote as one of the Chaldean Oracles of Zoroaster. The editors of CW inform us that Emerson got the sentence from Thomas Stanley's *History of the Chaldaick Philosophy* (1701).
5. Benvenuto Cellini (1500–1571), Florentine goldsmith, sculptor, and author of one of the world's great autobiographies.

into one act, he has not. The poet Campbell[6] said, that "a man accustomed to work was equal to any achievement he resolved on, and, that, for himself, necessity not inspiration was the prompter of his muse."

Concentration is the secret of strength in politics, in war, in trade, in short, in all management of human affairs. One of the high anecdotes of the world is the reply of Newton to the inquiry, "how he had been able to achieve his discoveries?" — "By always intending my mind." Or if you will have a text from politics, take this from Plutarch: "There was, in the whole city, but one street in which Pericles was ever seen, the street which led to the market-place and the council house. He declined all invitations to banquets, and all gay assemblies and company. During the whole period of his administration, he never dined at the table of a friend." Or if we seek an example from trade, — "I hope," said a good man to Rothschild,[7] "your children are not too fond of money and business: I am sure you would not wish that." — "I am sure I should wish that: I wish them to give mind, soul, heart, and body to business, — that is the way to be happy. It requires a great deal of boldness and a great deal of caution, to make a great fortune, and when you have got it, it requires ten times as much wit to keep it. If I were to listen to all the projects proposed to me, I should ruin myself very soon. Stick to one business, young man. Stick to your brewery, (he said this to young Buxton,) and you will be the great brewer of London. Be brewer, and banker, and merchant, and manufacturer, and you will soon be in the Gazette."

Many men are knowing, many are apprehensive and tenacious, but they do not rush to a decision. But in our flowing affairs a decision must be made, — the best, if you can; but any is better than none. There are twenty ways of going to a point, and one is the shortest; but set out at once on one. A man who has that presence of mind which can bring to him on the instant all he knows, is worth for action a dozen men who know as much, but can only bring it to light slowly. The good Speaker in the House is not the man who knows the theory of parliamentary tactics, but the man who decides off-hand. The good judge is not he who does hair-splitting justice to every allegation, but who, aiming at substantial justice, rules something intelligible for the guidance of suitors. The good lawyer is not the man who has an eye to every side and angle of contingency, and qualifies all his qualifications, but who throws himself on your part so heartily, that he can get you out of a scrape. Dr. Johnson[8] said, in one of his flowing sentences, "Miserable beyond all names of wretchedness is that unhappy pair, who are doomed to reduce beforehand to the principles of abstract reason all the details of each domestic day. There are cases where little can be said, and much must be done."

The second substitute for temperament is drill, the power of use and routine. The hack is a better roadster than the Arab barb.[9] In chemistry, the galvanic stream, slow, but continuous, is equal in power to the electric spark, and is, in our arts, a better agent. So in human action, against the spasm of energy, we offset the continuity of drill. We spread the same amount of force over much time, instead of condensing it into a moment. 'Tis the same ounce of gold here in a ball, and there in a leaf. At West Point, Col. Buford, the chief engineer, pounded with a hammer on the trunnions of a cannon, until he broke them off. He fired a piece of ordnance some hundred times in swift succession, until it burst. Now which

---

6. Thomas Campbell (1777–1844), Scottish poet and editor.
7. Rothschild, see n. 1, p. 275.
8. See n. 9, p. 67. See also, n. 6, p. 87.
9. A barbary steed.

stroke broke the trunnion? Every stroke. Which blast burst the piece? Every blast. "*Diligence passe sens,*" Henry VIII. was wont to say, or, great is drill. John Kemble[1] said, that the worst provincial company of actors would go through a play better than the best amateur company. Basil Hall[2] likes to show that the worst regular troops will beat the best volunteers. Practice is nine tenths. A course of mobs is good practice for orators. All the great speakers were bad speakers at first. Stumping it through England for seven years, made Cobden[3] a consummate debater. Stumping it through New England for twice seven, trained Wendell Phillips.[4] The way to learn German, is, to read the same dozen pages over and over a hundred times, till you know every word and particle in them, and can pronounce and repeat them by heart. No genius can recite a ballad at first reading, so well as mediocrity can at the fifteenth or twentieth reading. The rule for hospitality and Irish 'help,' is, to have the same dinner every day throughout the year. At last, Mrs. O'Shaughnessy learns to cook it to a nicety, the host learns to carve it, and the guests are well served. A humorous friend of mine thinks, that the reason why Nature is so perfect in her art, and gets up such inconceivably fine sunsets, is, that she has learned how, at last, by dint of doing the same thing so very often. Cannot one converse better on a topic on which he has experience, than on one which is new? Men whose opinion is valued on 'Change, are only such as have a special experience, and off that ground their opinion is not valuable. "More are made good by exercitation, than by nature," said Democritus.[5] The friction in nature is so enormous that we cannot spare any power. It is not question to express our thought, to elect our way, but to overcome resistances of the medium and material in everything we do. Hence the use of drill, and the worthlessness of amateurs to cope with practitioners. Six hours every day at the piano, only to give facility of touch; six hours a day at painting, only to give command of the odious materials, oil, ochres, and brushes. The masters say, that they know a master in music, only by seeing the pose of the hands on the keys; — so difficult and vital an act is the command of the instrument. To have learned the use of the tools, by thousands of manipulations; to have learned the arts of reckoning, by endless adding and dividing, is the power of the mechanic and the clerk.

I remarked in England, in confirmation of a frequent experience at home, that, in literary circles, the men of trust and consideration, bookmakers, editors, university deans and professors, bishops, too, were by no means men of the largest literary talent, but usually of a low and ordinary intellectuality, with a sort of mercantile activity and working talent. Indifferent hacks and mediocrities tower, by pushing their forces to a lucrative point, or by working power, over multitudes of superior men, in Old as in New England.

I have not forgotten that there are sublime considerations which limit the value of talent and superficial success. We can easily overpraise the vulgar hero. There are sources on which we have not drawn. I know what I abstain from. I adjourn what I have to say on this topic to the chapters on Culture and Worship.[6] But this force or spirit, being the means relied on by Nature for bringing

1. See n. 9, p. 255.
2. Basil Hall (1788–1844) was bred in the British Navy, in which he rose to the command of a vessel, and afterwards wrote many books, mostly on his travels. [Edward Waldo Emerson]
3. See n. 1, p. 275.
4. See n. 1, p. 221.
5. Known as "the Laughing Philosopher" (460?–370? B.C.E.), Greek philosopher who developed an atomist theory of the universe and espoused the doctrine that pleasure, along with self-control, is the goal of human life.
6. Chapters that follow in *The Conduct of Life*.

the work of the day about,—as far as we attach importance to household life, and the prizes of the world, we must respect that. And I hold, that an economy may be applied to it; it is as much a subject of exact law and arithmetic as fluids and gases are; it may be husbanded, or wasted; every man is efficient only as he is a container or vessel of this force, and never was any signal act or achievement in history, but by this expenditure. This is not gold, but the gold-maker; not the fame, but the exploit.

If these forces and this husbandry are within reach of our will, and the laws of them can be read, we infer that all success, and all conceivable benefit for man, is also, first or last, within his reach, and has its own sublime economies by which it may be attained. The world is mathematical, and has no casualty,[7] in all its vast and flowing curve. Success has no more eccentricity, than the gingham and muslin we weave in our mills. I know no more affecting lesson to our busy, plotting New England brains, than to go into one of the factories with which we have lined all the watercourses in the States. A man hardly knows how much he is a machine, until he begins to make telegraph, loom, press, and locomotive, in his own image. But in these, he is forced to leave out his follies and hindrances, so that when we go to the mill, the machine is more moral than we. Let a man dare go to a loom, and see if he be equal to it. Let machine confront machine, and see how they come out. The world-mill is more complex than the calico-mill, and the architect stooped less. In the gingham-mill, a broken thread or a shred spoils the web through a piece of a hundred yards, and is traced back to the girl that wove it, and lessens her wages. The stockholder, on being shown this, rubs his hands with delight. Are you so cunning, Mr. Profit-loss, and do you expect to swindle your master and employer, in the web you weave? A day is a more magnificent cloth than any muslin, the mechanism that makes it is infinitely cunninger, and you shall not conceal the sleezy, fraudulent, rotten hours you have slipped into the piece, nor fear that any honest thread, or straighter steel, or more inflexible shaft, will not testify in the web.

Illusions

FLOW, flow the waves hated,
Accursed, adored,
The waves of mutation:
No anchorage is.
Sleep is not, death is not;
Who seem to die live.
House you were born in,
Friends of your spring-time,
Old man and young maid,
Day's toil and its guerdon,
They are all vanishing,
Fleeing to fables,
Cannot be moored.
See the stars through them,
Through treacherous marbles.
Know, the stars yonder,
The stars everlasting,
Are fugitive also,

7. See n. 7, p. 206.

And emulate, vaulted,
The lambent heat-lightning,
And fire-fly's flight.

When thou dost return
On the wave's circulation,
Beholding the shimmer,
The wild dissipation,
And, out of endeavor
To change and to flow,
The gas become solid,
And phantoms and nothings
Return to be things,
And endless imbroglio
Is law and the world, —
Then first shalt thou know,
That in the wild turmoil,
Horsed on the Proteus,
Thou ridest to power,
And to endurance.[1]

Some years ago, in company with an agreeable party, I spent a long summer day in exploring the Mammoth Cave in Kentucky. We traversed, through spacious galleries affording a solid masonry foundation for the town and county overhead, the six or eight black miles from the mouth of the cavern to the innermost recess which tourists visit, —a niche or grotto made of one seamless stalactite,[2] and called, I believe, Serena's Bower. I lost the light of one day. I saw high domes, and bottomless pits; heard the voice of unseen waterfalls; paddled three quarters of a mile in the deep Echo River, whose waters are peopled with the blind fish; crossed the streams "Lethe" and "Styx;"[3] plied with music and guns the echoes in these alarming galleries; saw every form of stalagmite[4] and stalactite in the sculptured and fretted chambers, —icicle, orange-flower, acanthus, grapes, and snowball. We shot Bengal lights into the vaults and groins of the sparry[5] cathedrals, and examined all the masterpieces which the four combined engineers, water, limestone, gravitation, and time, could make in the dark.

The mysteries and scenery of the cave had the same dignity that belongs to all natural objects, and which shames the fine things to which we foppishly compare them. I remarked, especially, the mimetic habit, with which Nature, on new instruments, hums her old tunes, making night to mimic day, and chemistry to ape vegetation. But I then took notice, and still chiefly remember, that the best thing which the cave had to offer was an illusion. On arriving at what is called the "Star-Chamber," our lamps were taken from us by the guide, and extinguished or put aside, and, on looking upwards, I saw or seemed to see the night heaven thick with stars glimmering more or less brightly over our heads, and even what seemed a comet flaming among them. All the party were touched with astonishment and pleasure. Our musical friends sung with much feeling a pretty song, "The stars are in the quiet sky," &c., and I sat down on the rocky floor to enjoy the serene picture. Some crystal specks in the black ceiling

1. This epigraph is one of Emerson's best when considered as an independent poem.
2. An icicle-shaped mineral deposit hanging from the roof of a cavern.
3. See n. 5, p. 142. Lethe, see n. 5, p. 122.
4. A conical mineral deposit built up from the floor of a cavern.
5. From *spar*, jagged mineral formations. *Bengal lights:* torches or a kind of fireworks producing a steady blue light.

high overhead, reflecting the light of a half-hid lamp, yielded this magnificent effect.

I own, I did not like the cave so well for eking out its sublimities with this theatrical trick. But I have had many experiences like it, before and since; and we must be content to be pleased without too curiously analyzing the occasions. Our conversation with Nature is not just what it seems. The cloud-rack, the sunrise and sunset glories, rainbows, and northern lights are not quite so spheral as our childhood thought them; and the part our organization plays in them is too large. The senses interfere everywhere, and mix their own structure with all they report of. Once, we fancied the earth a plane, and stationary. In admiring the sunset, we do not yet deduct the rounding, coördinating, pictorial powers of the eye.

The same interference from our organization creates the most of our pleasure and pain. Our first mistake is the belief that the circumstance gives the joy which we give to the circumstance. Life is an ecstasy. Life is sweet as nitrous oxide;[6] and the fisherman dripping all day over a cold pond, the switchman at the railway intersection, the farmer in the field, the negro in the rice-swamp, the fop in the street, the hunter in the woods, the barrister with the jury, the belle at the ball, all ascribe a certain pleasure to their employment, which they themselves give it. Health and appetite impart the sweetness to sugar, bread, and meat. We fancy that our civilization has got on far, but we still come back to our primers.

We live by our imaginations, by our admirations, by our sentiments. The child walks amid heaps of illusions, which he does not like to have disturbed. The boy, how sweet to him is his fancy! how dear the story of barons and battles! What a hero he is, whilst he feeds on his heroes! What a debt is his to imaginative books! He has no better friend or influence, than Scott, Shakspeare, Plutarch, and Homer. The man lives to other objects, but who dare affirm that they are more real? Even the prose of the streets is full of refractions. In the life of the dreariest alderman, fancy enters into all details, and colors them with rosy hue. He imitates the air and actions of people whom he admires, and is raised in his own eyes. He pays a debt quicker to a rich man than to a poor man. He wishes the bow and compliment of some leader in the state, or in society; weighs what he says; perhaps he never comes nearer to him for that, but dies at last better contented for this amusement of his eyes and his fancy.

The world rolls, the din of life is never hushed. In London, in Paris, in Boston, in San Francisco, the carnival, the masquerade is at its height. Nobody drops his domino.[7] The unities, the fictions of the piece it would be an impertinence to break. The chapter of fascinations is very long. Great is paint; nay, God is the painter; and we rightly accuse the critic who destroys too many illusions. Society does not love its unmaskers. It was wittily, if somewhat bitterly, said by D'Alembert, *"qu'un état de vapeur était un état très fâcheux, parcequ'il nous faisait voir les choses comme elles sont."*[8] I find men victims of illusion in all parts of life. Children, youths, adults, and old men, all are led by one bawble or another. Yoganidra, the goddess of illusion, Proteus, or Momus, or Gylfi's

---

6. See 6, p. 224.
7. A hooded robe worn with an eyemask at a masquerade.
8. Jean le Rond d'Alembert (1717–1783), French mathematician and skeptical philosopher. His epigram depends, for its wit, on a play on words. It seems to mean that "a vaporous state [or an attack of the "vapors"—i.e., a depressive state] is very painful because it makes us see things as they are [i.e., vague and insubstantial; cf. the Latin *vapidus*]."

Mocking,[9]—for the Power has many names,—is stronger than the Titans, stronger than Apollo.[1] Few have overheard the gods, or surprised their secret. Life is a succession of lessons which must be lived to be understood. All is riddle, and the key to a riddle is another riddle. There are as many pillows of illusion as flakes in a snow-storm. We wake from one dream into another dream.[2] The toys, to be sure, are various, and are graduated in refinement to the quality of the dupe. The intellectual man requires a fine bait; the sots are easily amused. But everybody is drugged with his own frenzy, and the pageant marches at all hours, with music and banner and badge.

Amid the joyous troop who give in to the charivari,[3] comes now and then a sad-eyed boy, whose eyes lack the requisite refractions to clothe the show in due glory, and who is afflicted with a tendency to trace home the glittering miscellany of fruits and flowers to one root. Science is a search after identity, and the scientific whim is lurking in all corners. At the State Fair, a friend of mine complained that all the varities of fancy pears in our orchards seem to have been selected by somebody who had a whim for a particular kind of pear, and only cultivated such as had that perfume; they were all alike. And I remember the quarrel of another youth with the confectioners, that, when he racked his wit to choose the best comfits in the shops, in all the endless varieties of sweetmeat he could only find three flavors, or two. What then? Pears and cakes are good for something; and because you, unluckily, have an eye or nose too keen, why need you spoil the comfort which the rest of us find in them? I knew a humorist, who, in a good deal of rattle, had a grain or two of sense. He shocked the company by maintaining that the attributes of God were two,—power and risibility; and that it was the duty of every pious man to keep up the comedy. And I have known gentlemen of great stake in the community, but whose sympathies were cold,—presidents of colleges, and governors, and senators,—who held themselves bound to sign every temperance pledge, and act with Bible societies, and missions, and peace-makers, and cry *Hist-a-boy!* to every good dog. We must not carry comity too far, but we all have kind impulses in this direction. When the boys come into my yard for leave to gather horse-chestnuts, I own I enter into Nature's game, and affect to grant the permission reluctantly, fearing that any moment they will find out the imposture of that showy chaff. But this tenderness is quite unnecessary; the enchantments are laid on very thick. Their young

9. Yoganidra is in the Hindoo Mythology the personification of illusion, also called Maya or Mahamaya. The allusion to the Greek fable of Proteus changing from one alarming, disconcerting or slippery form to another, to escape the mortal who would learn truth from his wisdom, is more readily understood than that to Momus, the God of Folly and Laughter. But Momus mocked at all the Gods save Venus, and was sometimes represented with malign features, yet holding the mask of a beautiful youth. In the Younger Edda of Snorri Sturleson is the story, better rendered the Delusion of Gylfi than "the Mocking." He was a wise king of Sweden, who, wondering what was the wisdom of the Æsir (gods), whereby all that they did was well, went to Asgard to find out, disguised as an ancient man. But the Æsir knew of his journey ere he came, and received him with illusions. A stranger received him courteously and showed him into a vast and wondrous hall, opening into other halls, where were people variously employed, and many things which seemed to him incredible. Here also were three gods in the likeness of great chieftains sitting on their thrones. Gylfi asked his guide if there were among them a sagacious man, and was told that if, in talk with them, he did not hold his own, it would be the worse for him. The questions and answers form a theme of the Younger Edda. [Edward Waldo Emerson]
1. See n. 4, p. 73. In Greek mythology the Titans, offspring of Uranos amd Ge (heaven and earth), were pre-Hellenic nature deities supplanted by the Olympian gods and goddesses.
2. Cf. "The Poet," p. 194 and "Experience," p. 200.
3. Shivaree is the most common American regional form of *charivari*, a French word meaning "a noisy mock serenade for newlyweds" and probably deriving in turn from a Late Latin word meaning "headache." The term, most likely borrowed from French traders and settlers along the Mississippi River, was well established in the United States by 1805.

life is thatched with them. Bare and grim to tears is the lot of the children in the hovel I saw yesterday; yet not the less they hung it round with frippery romance, like the children of the happiest fortune, and talked of "the dear cottage where so many joyful hours had flown." Well, this thatching of hovels is the custom of the country. Women, more than all, are the element and kingdom of illusion. Being fascinated, they fascinate. They see through Claude-Lorraines.[4] And how dare any one, if he could, pluck away the *coulisses*,[5] stage effects, and ceremonies, by which they live? Too pathetic, too pitiable, is the region of affection, and its atmosphere always liable to *mirage*.

We are not very much to blame for our bad marriages. We live amid hallucinations; and this especial trap is laid to trip up our feet with, and all are tripped up first or last. But the mighty Mother who had been so sly with us, as if she felt that she owed us some indemnity, insinuates into the Pandora-box[6] of marriage some deep and serious benefits, and some great joys. We find a delight in the beauty and happiness of children, that makes the heart too big for the body. In the worst-assorted connections there is ever some mixture of true marriage. Teague and his jade get some just relations of mutual respect, kindly observation, and fostering of each other, learn something, and would carry themselves wiselier, if they were now to begin.

'Tis fine for us to point at one or another fine madman, as if there were any exempts. The scholar in his library is none. I, who have all my life heard any number of orations and debates, read poems and miscellaneous books, conversed with many geniuses, am still the victim of any new page; and, if Marmaduke, or Hugh, or Moosehead, or any other, invent a new style or mythology, I fancy that the world will be all brave and right, if dressed in these colors, which I had not thought of. Then at once I will daub with this new paint; but it will not stick. 'Tis like the cement which the peddler sells at the door; he makes broken crockery hold with it, but you can never buy of him a bit of the cement which will make it hold when he is gone.

Men who make themselves felt in the world avail themselves of a certain fate in their constitution, which they know how to use. But they never deeply interest us, unless they lift a corner of the curtain, or betray never so slightly their penetration of what is behind it. 'Tis the charm of practical men, that outside of their practicality are a certain poetry and play, as if they led the good horse Power by the bridle, and preferred to walk, though they can ride so fiercely. Bonaparte is intellectual, as well as Cæsar; and the best soldiers, sea-captains, and railway men have a gentleness, when off duty; a good-natured admission that there are illusions, and who shall say that he is not their sport? We stigmatize the cast-iron fellows, who cannot so detach themselves, as "dragon-ridden," "thunder-stricken," and fools of fate, with whatever powers endowed.

Since our tuition is through emblems and indirections, 'tis well to know that there is method in it, a fixed scale, and rank above rank in the phantasms. We begin low with coarse masks, and rise to the most subtle and beautiful. The red men told Columbus, "they had an herb which took away fatigue;" but he found the illusion of "arriving from the east at the Indies" more composing to

---

4. Colored optical devices used to view the landscape, named after Claude Lorrain (1600–1682), a French painter whose scenes of nature are often suffused with a golden light.
5. Wings of a stage; painted backdrops.
6. Named after the first woman in Greek mythology; has come to mean a present that seems valuable but is in reality a source of trouble.

his lofty spirit than any tobacco. Is not our faith in the impenetrability of matter more sedative than narcotics? You play with jackstraws, balls, bowls, horse and gun, estates and politics; but there are finer games before you. Is not time a pretty toy? Life will show you masks that are worth all your carnivals. Yonder mountain must migrate into your mind. The fine star-dust and nebulous blur in Orion, "the portentous year of Mizar and Alcor,"[7] must come down and be dealt with in your household thought. What if you shall come to discern that the play and playground of all this pompous history are radiations from yourself, and that the sun borrows his beams? What terrible questions we are learning to ask! The former men believed in magic, by which temples, cities, and men were swallowed up, and all trace of them gone. We are coming on the secret of a magic which sweeps out of men's minds all vestige of theism and beliefs which they and their fathers held and were framed upon.

There are deceptions of the senses, deceptions of the passions, and the structural, beneficent illusions of sentiment and of the intellect. There is the illusion of love, which attributes to the beloved person all which that person shares with his or her family, sex, age, or condition, nay, with the human mind itself. 'Tis these which the lover loves, and Anna Matilda gets the credit of them. As if one shut up always in a tower, with one window, through which the face of heaven and earth could be seen, should fancy that all the marvels he beheld belonged to that window. There is the illusion of time, which is very deep; who has disposed of it? or come to the conviction that what seems the *succession* of thought is only the distribution of wholes into causal series? The intellect sees that every atom carries the whole of Nature; that the mind opens to omnipotence; that, in the endless striving and ascents, the metamorphosis is entire, so that the soul doth not know itself in its own act, when that act is perfected. There is illusion that shall deceive even the elect. There is illusion that shall deceive even the performer of the miracle. Though he make his body, he denies that he makes it. Though the world exist from thought, thought is daunted in presence of the world. One after the other we accept the mental laws, still resisting those which follow, which however must be accepted. But all our concessions only compel us to new profusion. And what avails it that science has come to treat space and time as simply forms of thought, and the material world as hypothetical, and withal our pretension of *property* and even of self-hood are fading with the rest, if, at last, even our thoughts are not finalities; but the incessant flowing and ascension reach these also, and each thought which yesterday was a finality, to-day is yielding to a larger generalization?

With such volatile elements to work in, 'tis no wonder if our estimates are loose and floating. We must work and affirm, but we have no guess of the value of what we say or do. The cloud is now as big as your hand, and now it covers a county. That story of Thor, who was set to drain the drinking-horn in Asgard, and to wrestle with the old woman, and to run with the runner Lok,[8] and presently found that he had been drinking up the sea, and wrestling with Time, and racing with Thought, describes us who are contending, amid these seeming trifles, with the supreme energies of Nature. We fancy we have fallen into bad company and squalid condition, low debts, shoe-bills, broken glass to pay for, pots to buy,

7. Mizar and Alcor are twin stars in the middle of the handle of the Big Dipper. Orion, see n. 3, p. 43.
8. Or Loki, the satanic Aesir (god) of strife and evil. Thor, in Norse mythology, the Aesir of thunder, second in importance to his father, Odin. Asgard, the celestial dwelling place of the Norse gods, equivalent to the Olympus of Greek mythology.

butcher's meat, sugar, milk, and coal. 'Set me some great task, ye gods! and I will show my spirit.' 'Not so,' says the good Heaven; 'plod and plough, vamp your old coats and hats, weave a shoestring; great affairs and the best wine by and by.' Well, 'tis all phantasm; and if we weave a yard of tape in all humility, and as well as we can, long hereafter we shall see it was no cotton tape at all, but some galaxy which we braided, and that the threads were Time and Nature.

We cannot write the order of the variable winds. How can we penetrate the law of our shifting moods and susceptibility? Yet they differ as all and nothing. Instead of the firmament of yesterday, which our eyes require, it is to-day an eggshell which coops us in; we cannot even see what or where our stars of destiny are. From day to day, the capital facts of human life are hidden from our eyes. Suddenly the mist rolls up, and reveals them, and we think how much good time is gone, that might have been saved, had any hint of these things been shown. A sudden rise in the road shows us the system of mountains, and all the summits, which have been just as near us all the year, but quite out of mind. But these alternations are not without their order, and we are parties to our various fortune. If life seem a succession of dreams, yet poetic justice is done in dreams also. The visions of good men are good; it is the undisciplined will that is whipped with bad thoughts and bad fortunes. When we break the laws, we lose our hold on the central reality. Like sick men in hospitals, we change only from bed to bed, from one folly to another; and it cannot signify much what becomes of such castaways,—wailing, stupid, comatose creatures,—lifted from bed to bed, from the nothing of life to the nothing of death.

In this kingdom of illusions we grope eagerly for stays and foundations. There is none but a strict and faithful dealing at home, and a severe barring out of all duplicity or illusion there. Whatever games are played with us, we must play no games with ourselves, but deal in our privacy with the last honesty and truth. I look upon the simple and childish virtues of veracity and honesty as the root of all that is sublime in character. Speak as you think, be what you are, pay your debts of all kinds. I prefer to be owned as sound and solvent, and my word as good as my bond, and to be what cannot be skipped, or dissipated, or undermined, to all the *éclat*[9] in the universe. This reality is the foundation of friendship, religion, poetry, and art. At the top or at the bottom of all illusions, I set the cheat which still leads us to work and live for appearances, in spite of our conviction, in all sane hours, that it is what we really are that avails with friends, with strangers, and with fate or fortune.

One would think from the talk of men, that riches and poverty were a great matter; and our civilization mainly respects it. But the Indians say, that they do not think the white man with his brow of care, always toiling, afraid of heat and cold, and keeping within doors, has any advantage of them. The permanent interest of every man is, never to be in a false position, but to have the weight of Nature to back him in all that he does. Riches and poverty are a thick or thin costume; and our life—the life of all of us—identical. For we transcend the circumstance continually, and taste the real quality of existence; as in our employments, which only differ in the manipulations, but express the same laws; or in our thoughts, which wear no silks, and taste no ice-creams. We see God face to face every hour, and know the savor of Nature.[1]

9. Great brilliance, as of performance or achievement; conspicuous success; great acclamation or applause.
1. Cf. the opening of *Nature* (p. 27).

The early Greek philosophers Heraclitus and Xenophanes measured their force on this problem of identity. Diogenes[2] of Apollonia said, that unless the atoms were made of one stuff, they could never blend and act with one another. But the Hindoos, in their sacred writings, express the liveliest feeling, both of the essential identity, and of that illusion which they conceive variety to be. "The notions, '*I am*,' and '*This is mine*,' which influence mankind, are but delusions of the mother of the world. Dispel, O Lord of all creatures! the conceit of knowledge which proceeds from ignorance,"[3] And the beatitude of man they hold to lie in being freed from fascination.

The intellect is stimulated by the statement of truth in a trope, and the will by clothing the laws of life in illusions. But the unities of Truth and of Right are not broken by the disguise. There need never be any confusion in these. In a crowded life of many parts and performers, on a stage of nations, or in the obscurest hamlet in Maine or California, the same elements offer the same choices to each new comer, and, according to his election, he fixes his fortune in absolute Nature. It would be hard to put more mental and moral philosophy than the Persians have thrown into a sentence: —

> "Fooled thou must be, though wisest of the wise:
> Then be the fool of virtue, not of vice."

There is no chance, and no anarchy, in the universe. All is system and gradation. Every god is there sitting in his sphere. The young mortal enters the hall of the firmament: there is he alone with them alone, they pouring on him benedictions and gifts, and beckoning him up to their thrones. On the instant, and incessantly, fall snow-storms of illusions. He fancies himself in a vast crowd which sways this way and that, and whose movement and doings he must obey: he fancies himself poor, orphaned, insignificant. The mad crowd drives hither and thither, now furiously commanding this thing to be done, now that. What is he that he should resist their will, and think or act for himself? Every moment, new changes, and new showers of deceptions, to baffle and distract him. And when, by and by, for an instant, the air clears, and the cloud lifts a little, there are the gods still sitting around him on their thrones, — they alone with him alone.

---

2. See n. 2, p. 135. Edward Waldo Emerson says that Diogenes "taught that the one original element, air, was the source of life and the essence of bodies. Intelligence was an attribute of air." Heraclitus, see n. 3, p. 89. Xenophanes, see n. 3, p. 42.

3. Emerson is quoting from *The Vishnu Purana*, a Sanskrit work written around 500 B.C.E. and serving as a secondary scripture of Hinduism. Edward Waldo Emerson gives the whole passage as follows: "Thou art all bodies. This thy illusion beguiles all who are ignorant of the true nature, the fools who imagine soul to be in that which is not spirit. The notions that 'I am—this is mine,' which influence mankind, are but delusions of the mother of the world, originating in thy active agency. Those men who, attentive to their spiritual duties, worship thee, traverse all this illusion and obtain spiritual freedom. . . . It is the sport of thy fascinations that induces men to glorify thee to obtain the continuance of their race or the annihilation of their enemies instead of eternal liberation. Dispel, O Lord of all creatures, the conceit of knowledge which proceeds from ignorance."

From Letters and Social Aims

From Poetry and Imagination[1]

But over all his crowning grace,
Wherefor thanks God his daily praise,
Is the purging of his eye
To see the people of the sky:
From blue mount and headland dim
Friendly hands stretch forth to him,
Him they beckon, him advise
Of heavenlier prosperities
And a more excelling grace
And a truer bosom-glow
Than the wine-fed feasters know.
They turn his heart from lovely maids,
And make the darlings of the earth
Swainish, coarse and nothing worth:
Teach him gladly to postpone
Pleasures to another stage
Beyond the scope of human age,
Freely as task at eve undone
Waits unblamed to-morrow's sun.

For Fancy's gift
Can mountains lift;
The Muse can knit
What is past, what is done,
With the web that's just begun;
Making free with time and size,
Dwindles here, there magnifies,
Swells a rain-drop to a tun;
So to repeat
No word or feat
Crowds in a day the sum of ages,
And blushing Love outwits the sages.

* * *

Poetry.—The primary use of a fact is low; the secondary use, as it is a figure or illustration of my thought, is the real worth. First the fact; second its impression, or what I think of it. Hence Nature was called "a kind of adulterated reason." Seas, forests, metals, diamonds and fossils interest the eye, but 't is only with some preparatory or predicting charm. Their value to the intellect appears

---

1. This essay was assembled by James Elliot Cabot and Ellen Emerson from several previous lectures, especially the 1854 "Poetry and English Poetry." The poetic epigraph was added by Edward in W. The lines appear in "Fragments on the Poet and the Poetic Gift" in the Riverside and Centenary *Poems*.

only when I hear their meaning made plain in the spiritual truth they cover. The mind, penetrated with its sentiment or its thought, projects it outward on whatever it beholds. The lover sees reminders of his mistress in every beautiful object; the saint, an argument for devotion in every natural process; and the facility with which Nature lends itself to the thoughts of man, the aptness with which a river, a flower, a bird, fire, day or night, can express his fortunes, is as if the world were only a disguised man, and, with a change of form, rendered to him all his experience. We cannot utter a sentence in sprightly conversation without a similitude. Note our incessant use of the word *like*,—like fire, like a rock, like thunder, like a bee, "like a year without a spring." Conversation is not permitted without tropes; nothing but great weight in things can afford a quite literal speech. It is ever enlivened by inversion and trope. God himself does not speak prose, but communicates with us by hints, omens, inference and dark resemblances in objects lying all around us.

Nothing so marks a man as imaginative expressions. A figurative statement arrests attention, and is remembered and repeated. How often has a phrase of this kind made a reputation. Pythagoras's Golden Sayings were such, and Socrates's; and Mirabeau's, and Burke's, and Bonaparte's. Genius thus makes the transfer from one part of Nature to a remote part, and betrays the rhymes and echoes that pole makes with pole. Imaginative minds cling to their images, and do not wish them rashly rendered into prose reality, as children resent your showing them that their doll Cinderella is nothing but pine wood and rags; and my young scholar does not wish to know what the leopard, the wolf, or Lucia, signify in Dante's Inferno, but prefers to keep their veils on. Mark the delight of an audience in an image. When some familiar truth or fact appears in a new dress, mounted as on a fine horse, equipped with a grand pair of ballooning wings, we cannot enough testify our surprise and pleasure. It is like the new virtue shown in some unprized old property, as when a boy finds that his pocket-knife will attract steel filings and take up a needle; or when the old horse-block in the yard is found to be a Torso Hercules of the Phidian age. Vivacity of expression may indicate this high gift, even when the thought is of no great scope, as when Michel Angelo, praising the *terra cottas*, said, "If this earth were to become marble, woe to the antiques!"[2] A happy symbol is a sort of evidence that your thought is just. I had rather have a good symbol of my thought, or a good analogy, than the suffrage of Kant or Plato. If you agree with me, or if Locke or Montesquieu agree, I may yet be wrong; but if the elm-tree thinks the same thing, if running water, if burning coal, if crystals, if alkalies, in their several fashions say what I say, it must be true. Thus a good symbol is the best argument, and is a missionary to persuade thousands. The Vedas, the Edda,[3] the Koran, are each remembered by their happiest figure. There is no more welcome gift to men than a new symbol. That satiates, transports, converts them. They assimilate themselves to it, deal with it in all ways, and it will last a hundred years. Then comes a new genius, and brings another. Thus the Greek mythology called the sea "the tear of Saturn." The return of the soul to God was described as "a flask of water broken in the sea." Saint John gave us the Christian figure of "souls washed in the blood of Christ." The aged Michel Angelo in-

---

2. The sense of this anecdote seems to be that if the earth were marble, antiquities would be at a discount.
3. Name given to a collection of Old Norse poems as well as to a poetic manual written by Snorri Sturluson (1178–1241). See also n. 9, p. 292. Vedas, see n. 3, p. 252.

dicates his perpetual study as in boyhood,—"I carry my satchel still."[4] Machiavel[5] described the papacy as "a stone inserted in the body of Italy to keep the wound open." To the Parliament debating how to tax America, Burke[6] exclaimed, "Shear the wolf." Our Kentuckian orator said of his dissent from his companion, "I showed him the back of my hand." And our proverb of the courteous soldier reads: "An iron hand in a velvet glove."

This belief that the higher use of the material world is to furnish us types or pictures to express the thoughts of the mind, is carried to its logical extreme by the Hindoos, who, following Buddha, have made it the central doctrine of their religion that what we call Nature, the external world, has no real existence,—is only phenomenal. Youth, age, property, condition, events, persons,—self, even,—are successive *maias* (deceptions) through which Vishnu mocks and instructs the soul. I think Hindoo books the best gymnastics for the mind, as showing treatment. All European libraries might almost be read without the swing of this gigantic arm being suspected. But these Orientals deal with worlds and pebbles freely.

For the value of a trope is that the hearer is one: and indeed Nature itself is a vast trope, and all particular natures are tropes. As the bird alights on the bough, then plunges into the air again, so the thoughts of God pause but for a moment in any form. All thinking is analogizing, and it is the use of life to learn metonymy. The endless passing of one element into new forms, the incessant metamorphosis, explains the rank which the imagination holds in our catalogue of mental powers. The imagination is the reader of these forms. The poet accounts all productions and changes of Nature as the nouns of language, uses them representatively, too well pleased with their ulterior to value much their primary meaning. Every new object so seen gives a shock of agreeable surprise. The impressions on the imagination make the great days of life: the book, the landscape or the personality which did not stay on the surface of the eye or ear but penetrated to the inward sense, agitates us, and is not forgotten. Walking, working or talking, the sole question is how many strokes vibrate on this mystic string,—how many diameters are drawn quite through from matter to spirit; for whenever you enunciate a natural law you discover that you have enunciated a law of the mind. Chemistry, geology, hydraulics, are secondary science. The atomic theory is only an interior process *produced*, as geometers say, or the effect of a foregone metaphysical theory. Swedenborg saw gravity to be only an external of the irresistible attractions of affection and faith. Mountains and oceans we think we understand;—yes, so long as they are contented to be such, and are safe with the geologist,—but when they are melted in Promethean alembics and come out men, and then, melted again, come out words, without any abatement, but with an exaltation of power!

In poetry we say we require the miracle. The bee flies among the flowers, and gets mint and marjoram, and generates a new product, which is not mint and marjoram, but honey; the chemist mixes hydrogen and oxygen to yield a new product, which is not these, but water; and the poet listens to conversation

---

4. Emerson was fond of this presumed motto of Michaelangelo (see n. 6, p. 42) and cites it in an early lecture on the artist (*EL* 1.102–03). He also copied it into his journal for February–March, 1847: "Ancora imparo—I carry my satchel [i.e., schoolbag] still." See *EJ* 365.
5. Niccolò Machiavelli (1469–1527), author of *The Prince*.
6. See n. 5, p. 45.

and beholds all objects in Nature, to give back, not them, but a new and transcendent whole.

Poetry is the perpetual endeavor to express the spirit of the thing, to pass
the brute body and search the life and reason which causes it to exist;—to see
that the object is always flowing away, whilst the spirit or necessity which causes
it subsists. Its essential mark is that it betrays in every word instant activity of
mind, shown in new uses of every fact and image, in preternatural quickness or
perception of relations. All its words are poems. It is a presence of mind that
gives a miraculous command of all means of uttering the thought and feeling
of the moment. The poet squanders on the hour an amount of life that would
more than furnish the seventy years of the man that stands next him.

The term "genius," when used with emphasis, implies imagination; use of
symbols, figurative speech. A deep insight will always, like Nature, ultimate its
thought in a thing. As soon as a man masters a principle and sees his facts in relation to it, fields, waters, skies, offer to clothe his thoughts in images. Then all
men understand him; Parthian, Mede, Chinese, Spaniard and Indian hear their
own tongue. For he can now find symbols of universal significance, which are
readily rendered into any dialect; as a painter, a sculptor, a musician, can in
their several ways express the same sentiment of anger, or love, or religion.

The thoughts are few, the forms many; the large vocabulary or many-colored coat of the indigent unity. The *savans* are chatty and vain, but hold them
hard to principle and definition, and they become mute and near-sighted. What
is motion? what is beauty? what is matter? what is life? what is force? Push them
hard and they will not be loquacious. They will come to Plato, Proclus and Swedenborg.[7] The invisible and imponderable is the sole fact. "Why changes not
the violet earth into musk?" What is the term of the ever-flowing metamorphosis? I do not know what are the stoppages, but I see that a devouring unity
changes all into that which changes not.

The act of imagination is ever attended by pure delight. It infuses a certain
volatility and intoxication into all Nature. It has a flute which sets the atoms of
our frame in a dance. Our indeterminate size is a delicious secret which it reveals to us. The mountains begin to dislimn, and float in the air. In the presence and conversation of a true poet, teeming with images to express his
enlarging thought, his person, his form, grows larger to our fascinated eyes. And
thus begins that deification which all nations have made of their heroes in every
kind,—saints, poets, lawgivers and warriors.

Imagination.—Whilst common sense looks at things or visible Nature as
real and final facts, poetry, or the imagination which dictates it, is a second sight,
looking through these, and using them as types or words for thoughts which
they signify. Or is this belief a metaphysical whim of modern times, and quite
too refined? On the contrary, it is as old as the human mind. Our best definition of poetry is one of the oldest sentences, and claims to come down to us from
the Chaldæan Zoroaster,[8] who wrote it thus: "Poets are standing transporters,
whose employment consists in speaking to the Father and to matter; in producing apparent imitations of unapparent natures, and inscribing things unapparent in the apparent fabrication of the world;" in other words, the world exists

7. See n. 6, p. 35. Plato, see n. 4, p. 15. Proclus, see n. 6, p. 187.
8. See n. 9, p. 78.

for thought: it is to make appear things which hide: mountains, crystals, plants, animals, are seen; that which makes them is not seen: these, then, are "apparent copies of unapparent natures." Bacon[9] expressed the same sense in his definition, "Poetry accommodates the shows of things to the desires of the mind;" and Swedenborg, when he said, "There is nothing existing in human thought, even though relating to the most mysterious tenet of faith, but has combined with it a natural and sensuous image." And again: "Names, countries, nations, and the like are not at all known to those who are in heaven; they have no idea of such things, but of the realities signified thereby." A symbol always stimulates the intellect; therefore is poetry ever the best reading. The very design of imagination is to domesticate us in another, in a celestial nature.

This power is in the image because this power is in Nature. It so affects, because it so is. All that is wondrous in Swedenborg is not his invention, but his extraordinary perception;—that he was necessitated so to see. The world realizes the mind. Better than images is seen through them. The selection of the image is no more arbitrary than the power and significance of the image. The selection must follow fate. Poetry, if perfected, is the only verity; is the speech of man after the real, and not after the apparent.

Or shall we say that the imagination exists by sharing the ethereal currents? The poet contemplates the central identity, sees it undulate and roll this way and that, with divine flowings, through remotest things; and, following it, can detect essential resemblances in natures never before compared. He can class them so audaciously because he is sensible of the sweep of the celestial stream, from which nothing is exempt. His own body is a fleeing apparition,—his personality as fugitive as the trope he employs. In certain hours we can almost pass our hand through our own body. I think the use or value of poetry to be the suggestion it affords of the flux or fugaciousness of the poet. The mind delights in measuring itself thus with matter, with history, and flouting both. A thought, any thought, pressed, followed, opened, dwarfs matter, custom, and all but itself. But this second sight does not necessarily impair the primary or common sense. Pindar, and Dante[1] yes, and the gray and timeworn sentences of Zoroaster, may all be parsed, though we do not parse them. The poet has a logic, though it be subtle. He observes higher laws than he transgresses. "Poetry must first be good sense, though it is something better."

This union of first and second sight reads Nature to the end of delight and of moral use. Men are imaginative, but not overpowered by it to the extent of confounding its suggestions with external facts. We live in both spheres, and must not mix them. Genius certifies its entire possession of its thought, by translating it into a fact which perfectly represents it, and is hereby education. Charles James Fox[2] thought "Poetry the great refreshment of the human mind,—the only thing, after all; that men first found out they had minds, by making and tasting poetry."

Man runs about restless and in pain when his condition or the objects about him do not fully match his thought. He wishes to be rich, to be old, to be young, that things may obey him. In the ocean, in fire, in the sky, in the forest, he finds facts adequate and as large as he. As his thoughts are deeper than he can fathom, so also are these. It is easier to read Sanscrit, to decipher the arrowhead character, than to interpret these familiar sights. It is even much to name

9. See n. 3, p. 6.
1. See n. 3, p. 184. Pindar, see n. 3, p. 33.
2. See n. 4, p. 229.

them. Thus Thomson's[3] Seasons and the best parts of many old and many new poets are simply enumerations by a person who felt the beauty of the common sights and sounds, without any attempt to draw a moral or affix a meaning.

The poet discovers that what men value as substances have a higher value as symbols; that Nature is the immense shadow of man. A man's action is only a picture-book of his creed. He does after what he believes. Your condition, your employment, is the fable of *you*. The world is thoroughly anthropomorphized, as if it had passed through the body and mind of man, and taken his mould and form. Indeed, good poetry is always personification, and heightens every species of force in Nature by giving it a human volition. We are advertised that there is nothing to which man is not related; that every thing is convertible into every other. The staff in his hand is the *radius vector* of the sun. The chemistry of this is the chemistry of that. Whatever one act we do, whatever one thing we learn, we are doing and learning all things, — marching in the direction of universal power. Every healthy mind is a true Alexander or Sesostris,[4] building a universal monarchy.

The senses imprison us, and we help them with metres as limitary, — with a pair of scales and a foot-rule and a clock. How long it took to find out what a day was, or what this sun, that makes days! It cost thousands of years only to make the motion of the earth suspected. Slowly, by comparing thousands of observations, there dawned on some mind a theory of the sun, — and we found the astronomical fact. But the astronomy is in the mind: the senses affirm that the earth stands still and the sun moves. The senses collect the surface facts of matter. The intellect acts on these brute reports, and obtains from them results which are the essence or intellectual form of the experiences. It compares, distributes, generalizes and uplifts them into its own sphere. It knows that these transfigured results are not the brute experiences, just as souls in heaven are not the red bodies they once animated. Many transfigurations have befallen them. The atoms of the body were once nebulæ, then rock, then loam, then corn, then chyme, then chyle, then blood; and now the beholding and co-energizing mind sees the same refining and ascent to the third, the seventh or the tenth power of the daily accidents which the senses report, and which make the raw material of knowledge. It was sensation; when memory came, it was experience; when mind acted, it was knowledge; when mind acted on it as knowledge, it was thought.

This metonymy, or seeing the same sense in things so diverse, gives a pure pleasure. Every one of a million times we find a charm in the metamorphosis. It makes us dance and sing. All men are so far poets. When people tell me they do not relish poetry, and bring me Shelley, or Aikin's[5] Poets, or I know not what volumes of rhymed English, to show that it has no charm, I am quite of their mind. But this dislike of the books only proves their liking of poetry. For they relish Æsop, — cannot forget him, or not use him; bring them Homer's Iliad, and they like that; or the Cid, and that rings well; read to them from Chaucer, and they reckon him an honest fellow. Lear and Macbeth and Richard III. they know pretty well without guide. Give them Robin Hood's ballads or Griselda, or Sir Andrew Barton, or Sir Patrick Spens, or Chevy Chase, or Tam O'Shanter,[6] and they

3. James Thomson (1700–1748), Scottish author of a very popular long poem, *The Seasons.*
4. Name of one of several monarchs of ancient Egypt. Alexander, see n. 5, p. 229.
5. John Aikin (1747–1822), English author and critic.
6. Emerson's list here runs from traditional English ballads to Robert Burns. *Patient Griselda:* a stock figure who turns up in Chaucer and elsewhere.

like these well enough. They like to see statues; they like to name the stars; they like to talk and hear of Jove, Apollo, Minerva, Venus and the Nine. See how tenacious we are of the old names. They like poetry without knowing it as such. They like to go to the theatre and be made to weep; to Faneuil Hall, and be taught by Otis, Webster, or Kossuth, or Phillips,[7] what great hearts they have, what tears, what new possible enlargements to their narrow horizons. They like to see sunsets on the hills or on a lake shore. Now a cow does not gaze at the rainbow, or show or affect any interest in the landscape, or a peacock, or the song of thrushes.

Nature is the true idealist. When she serves us best, when, on rare days, she speaks to the imagination, we feel that the huge heaven and earth are but a web drawn around us, that the light, skies and mountains are but the painted vicissitudes of the soul. Who has heard our hymn in the churches without accepting the truth, —

> "As o'er our heads the seasons roll,
> And soothe with *change of bliss* the soul"?[8]

Of course, when we describe man as poet, and credit him with the triumphs of the art, we speak of the potential or ideal man, — not found now in any one person. You must go through a city or a nation, and find one faculty here, one there, to build the true poet withal. Yet all men know the portrait when it is drawn, and it is part of religion to believe its possible incarnation.

He is the healthy, the wise, the fundamental, the manly man, seer of the secret; against all the appearance he sees and reports the truth, namely that the soul generates matter. And poetry is the only verity, — the expression of a sound mind speaking after the ideal, and not after the apparent. As a power it is the perception of the symbolic character of things, and the treating them as representative: as a talent it is a magnetic tenaciousness of an image, and by the treatment demonstrating that this pigment of thought is as palpable and objective to the poet as is the ground on which he stands, or the walls of houses about him. And this power appears in Dante and Shakspeare. In some individuals this insight or second sight has an extraordinary reach which compels our wonder, as in Behmen, Swedenborg and William Blake[9] the painter.

William Blake, whose abnormal genius, Wordsworth said, interested him more than the conversation of Scott or of Byron, writes thus: "He who does not imagine in stronger and better lineaments and in stronger and better light than his perishing mortal eye can see, does not imagine at all. The painter of this work asserts that all his imaginations appear to him infinitely more perfect and more minutely organized than anything seen by his mortal eye. . . . I assert for myself that I do not behold the outward creation, and that to me it would be a hindrance, and not action. I question not my corporeal eye any more than I would question a window concerning a sight. I look through it, and not with it."[1]

It is a problem of metaphysics to define the province of Fancy and Imagination. The words are often used, and the things confounded. Imagination respects

---

7. See n. 1, p. 221. Faneuil Hall, famous political gathering place in Boston. James Otis (1725–1783), American Revolutionary politician. Webster, see n. 6, p. 251. Kossuth, see n. 6, p. 265.
8. Edward Waldo Emerson tells us that these lines are by the English author Helen Maria Williams (1762–1827).
9. English poet, painter, engraver, and visionary (1757–1827). Behmen, see n. 8, p. 168.
1. Edward Waldo Emerson compares this passage to some lines from Blake's *Songs of Innocence*. See W 8.365.

the cause. It is the vision of an inspired soul reading arguments and affirmations in all Nature of that which it is driven to say. But as soon as this soul is released a little from its passion, and at leisure plays with the resemblances and types, for amusement, and not for its moral end, we call its action Fancy. Lear, mad with his affliction, thinks every man who suffers must have the like cause with his own. "What, have his daughters brought him to this pass?"[2] But when, his attention being diverted, his mind rests from this thought, he becomes fanciful with Tom, playing with the superficial resemblances of objects. Bunyan, in pain for his soul, wrote Pilgrim's Progress; Quarles,[3] after he was quite cool, wrote Emblems.

Imagination is central; fancy, superficial. Fancy relates to surface, in which a great part of life lies. The lover is rightly said to fancy the hair, eyes, complexion of the maid. Fancy is a wilful, imagination a spontaneous act; fancy, a play as with dolls and puppets which we choose to call men and women; imagination, a perception and affirming of a real relation between a thought and some material fact. Fancy amuses; imagination expands and exalts us. Imagination uses an organic classification. Fancy joins by accidental resemblance, surprises and amuses the idle, but is silent in the presence of great passion and action. Fancy aggregates; imagination animates. Fancy is related to color; imagination, to form. Fancy paints; imagination sculptures.[4]

Veracity. —I do not wish, therefore, to find that my poet is not partaker of the feast he spreads, or that he would kindle or amuse me with that which does not kindle or amuse him. He must believe in his poetry. Homer, Milton, Hafiz, Herbert, Swedenborg, Wordsworth, are heartily enamoured of their sweet thoughts. Moreover, they know that this correspondence of things to thoughts is far deeper than they can penetrate, —defying adequate expression; that it is elemental, or in the core of things. Veracity therefore is that which we require in poets, —that they shall say how it was with them, and not what might be said. And the fault of our popular poetry is that it is not sincere.

"What news?" asks man of man everywhere. The only teller of news is the poet. When he sings, the world listens with the assurance that now a secret of God is to be spoken. The right poetic mood is or makes a more complete sensibility, piercing the outward fact to the meaning of the fact; shows a sharper insight: and the perception creates the strong expression of it as the man who sees his way walks in it.

It is a rule in eloquence, that the moment the orator loses command of his audience, the audience commands him. So in poetry, the master rushes to deliver his thought, and the words and images fly to him to express it; whilst colder moods are forced to respect the ways of saying it, and insinuate, or, as it were, muffle the fact to suit the poverty or caprice of their expression, so that they only hint the matter, or allude to it, being unable to fuse and mould their words and images to fluid obedience. See how Shakspeare grapples at once with the main problem of the tragedy, as in Lear and Macbeth, and the opening of the Merchant of Venice.

All writings must be in a degree exoteric, written to a human *should* or *would*, instead of to the fatal *is:* this holds even of the bravest and sincerest writ-

2. Cf. *King Lear* 3.4.49–50.
3. Francis Quarles (1592–1644), English poet, well known for his emblem poems (see n. 5, p. 12), was a particular favorite of Henry Thoreau and Emily Dickinson. Bunyan, see n. 1, p. 118.
4. The influence of Coleridge is notable here. On Fancy and Imagination, see n. 2, p. 116.

ers. Every writer is a skater, and must go partly where he would, and partly where the skates carry him; or a sailor, who can only land where sails can be blown. And yet it is to be added that high poetry exceeds the fact, or Nature itself, just as skates allow the good skater far more grace than his best walking would show, or sails more than riding. The poet writes from a real experience, the amateur feigns one. Of course one draws the bow with his fingers and the other with the strength of his body; one speaks with his lips and the other with a chest voice. Talent amuses, but if your verse has not a necessary and autobiographic basis, though under whatever gay poetic veils, it shall not waste my time.

For poetry is faith. To the poet the world is virgin soil; all is practicable; the men are ready for virtue; it is always time to do right. He is a true re-commencer, or Adam in the garden again. He affirms the applicability of the ideal law to this moment and the present knot of affairs. Parties, lawyers and men of the world will invariably dispute such an application, as romantic and dangerous: they admit the general truth, but they and their affair always constitute a case in bar of the statute. Free trade, they concede, is very well as a principle, but it is never quite the time for its adoption without prejudicing actual interests. Chastity, they admit, is very well,—but then think of Mirabeau's[5] passion and temperament! Eternal laws are very well, which admit no violation,—but so extreme were the times and manners of mankind, that you must admit miracles, for the times constituted a case. Of course, we know what you say, that legends are found in all tribes,—but this legend is different. And so throughout; the poet affirms the laws, prose busies itself with exceptions,—with the local and individual.

I require that the poem should impress me so that after I have shut the book it shall recall me to itself, or that passages should. And inestimable is the criticism of memory as a corrective to first impressions. We are dazzled at first by new words and brilliancy of color, which occupy the fancy and deceive the judgment. But all this is easily forgotten. Later, the thought, the happy image which expressed it and which was a true experience of the poet, recurs to mind, and sends me back in search of the book. And I wish that the poet should foresee this habit of readers, and omit all but the important passages. Shakspeare is made up of important passages, like Damascus steel made up of old nails. Homer has his own,—

"One omen is best, to fight for one's country;"[6]

and again,—

"They heal their griefs, for curable are the hearts of the
    noble."[7]

Write, that I may know you. Style betrays you, as your eyes do. We detect at once by it whether the writer has a firm grasp on his fact or thought,—exists at the moment for that alone, or whether he has one eye apologizing, deprecatory, turned on his reader. In proportion always to his possession of his thought is his defiance of his readers. There is no choice of words for him who clearly sees the truth. That provides him with the best word.

5. See n. 4, p. 229.
6. Homer, *Iliad* 12.243.
7. Homer, *Iliad* 13.115.

Great design belongs to a poem, and is better than any skill of execution,— but how rare! I find it in the poems of Wordsworth,—Laodamia, and the Ode to Dion, and the plan of the Recluse.[8] We want design, and do not forgive the bards if they have only the art of enamelling. We want an architect, and they bring us an upholsterer.

If your subject do not appear to you the flower of the world at this moment, you have not rightly chosen it. No matter what it is, grand or gay, national or private, if it has a natural prominence to you, work away until you come to the heart of it: then it will, though it were a sparrow or a spider-web, as fully represent the central law and draw all tragic or joyful illustration, as if it were the book of Genesis or the book of Doom. The subject—we must so often say it—is indifferent. Any word, every word in language, every circumstance, becomes poetic in the hands of a higher thought.

The test or measure of poetic genius is the power to read the poetry of affairs,—to fuse the circumstance of to-day; not to use Scott's antique superstitions, or Shakspeare's, but to convert those of the nineteenth century and of the existing nations into universal symbols. 'T is easy to repaint the mythology of the Greeks, or of the Catholic Church, the feudal castle, the crusade, the martyrdoms of mediæval Europe; but to point out where the same creative force is now working in our own houses and public assemblies; to convert the vivid energies acting at this hour in New York and Chicago and San Francisco, into universal symbols, requires a subtile and commanding thought. 'T is boyish in Swedenborg to cumber himself with the dead scurf of Hebrew antiquity, as if the Divine creative energy had fainted in his own century. American life storms about us daily, and is slow to find a tongue. This contemporary insight is transubstantiation, the conversion of daily bread into the holiest symbols; and every man would be a poet if his intellectual digestion were perfect. The test of the poet is the power to take the passing day, with its news, its cares, its fears, as he shares them, and hold it up to a divine reason, till he sees it to have a purpose and beauty, and to be related to astronomy and history and the eternal order of the world. Then the dry twig blossoms in his hand. He is calmed and elevated.

The use of "occasional poems" is to give leave to originality. Every one delights in the felicity frequently shown in our drawing-rooms. In a game-party or picnic poem each writer is released from the solemn rhythmic traditions which alarm and suffocate his fancy, and the result is that one of the partners offers a poem in a new style that hints at a new literature. Yet the writer holds it cheap, and could do the like all day. On the stage, the farce is commonly far better given than the tragedy, as the stock actors understand the farce, and do not understand the tragedy. The writer in the parlor has more presence of mind, more wit and fancy, more play of thought, on the incidents that occur at table or about the house, than in the politics of Germany or Rome. Many of the fine poems of Herrick, Jonson[9] and their contemporaries had this casual origin.

I know there is entertainment and room for talent in the artist's selection of ancient or remote subjects; as when the poet goes to India, or to Rome, or to Persia, for his fable. But I believe nobody knows better than he that herein he consults his ease rather than his strength or his desire. He is very well convinced that the great moments of life are those in which his own house, his own body,

8. For Emerson's interest in the "Prospectus" to Wordsworth's *Recluse*, see *EL* 2.273. Wordsworth's text is reprinted in this volume (see p. 575).
9. See n. 4, p. 248. Robert Herrick (1591–1674), English lyric poet.

the tritest and nearest ways and words and things have been illuminated into prophets and teachers. What else is it to be a poet? What are his garland and singing-robes? What but a sensibility so keen that the scent of an elder-blow, or the timber-yard and corporation-works of a nest of pismires is event enough for him,—all emblems and personal appeals to him. His wreath and robe is to do what he enjoys; emancipation from other men's questions, and glad study of his own; escape from the gossip and routine of society, and the allowed right and practice of making better. He does not give his hand, but in sign of giving his heart; he is not affable with all, but silent, uncommitted or in love, as his heart leads him. There is no subject that does not belong to him,—politics, economy, manufactures and stock-brokerage, as much as sunsets and souls; only, these things, placed in their true order, are poetry; displaced, or put in kitchen order, they are unpoetic. Malthus is the right organ of the English proprietors; but we shall never understand political economy until Burns or Béranger[1] or some poet shall teach it in songs, and he will not teach Malthusianism.

Poetry is the *gai science*. The trait and test of the poet is that he builds, adds and affirms. The critic destroys: the poet says nothing but what helps somebody; let others be distracted with cares, he is exempt. All their pleasures are tinged with pain. All his pains are edged with pleasure. The gladness he imparts he shares. As one of the old Minnesingers[2] sung,—

> "Oft have I heard, and now believe it true,
> Whom man delights in, God delights in too."

Poetry is the consolation of mortal men. They live cabined, cribbed, confined[3] in a narrow and trivial lot,—in wants, pains, anxieties and superstitions, in profligate politics, in personal animosities, in mean employments,—and victims of these; and the nobler powers untried, unknown. A poet comes who lifts the veil; gives them glimpses of the laws of the universe; shows them the circumstance as illusion; shows that Nature is only a language to express the laws, which are grand and beautiful;—and lets them, by his songs, into some of the realities. Socrates, the Indian teachers of the Maia, the Bibles of the nations, Shakspeare, Milton, Hafiz, Ossian, the Welsh Bards;[4]—these all deal with Nature and history as means and symbols, and not as ends. With such guides they begin to see that what they had called pictures are realities, and the mean life is pictures. And this is achieved by words; for it is a few oracles spoken by perceiving men that are the texts on which religions and states are founded. And this perception has at once its moral sequence. Ben Jonson said, "The principal end of poetry is to inform men in the just reason of living."

Creation.—But there is a third step which poetry takes, and which seems higher than the others, namely, creation, or ideas taking forms of their own,— when the poet invents the fable, and invents the language which his heroes speak. He reads in the word or action of the man its yet untold results. His in-

---

1. Pierre-Jean de Béranger (1780–1857), French poet. Malthus, see n. 5, p. 219. Burns, see n. 8, p. 67.
2. Edward Waldo Emerson identifies the Minnesinger (i.e., "love-singer," or troubadour) as Pons de Capdueil (twelfth century), a baron of Provence.
3. Cf. *Macbeth* 3.4.24.
4. Taliesin and Aneirin are two of the earliest Welsh bards associated with the court of Maelgwn Gwynedd (d. 547 C.E.). Maia, or Maya, see n. 2, p. 268. Milton, see n. 2, p. 6. Hafiz, see n. 1, p. 115. Ossian, a presumed Gaelic bard invented by Scottish poet James Macpherson (1736–1796).

spiration is power to carry out and complete the metamorphosis, which, in the imperfect kinds arrested for ages, in the perfecter proceeds rapidly in the same individual. For poetry is science, and the poet a truer logician. Men in the courts or in the street think themselves logical and the poet whimsical. Do they think there is chance or wilfulness in what he sees and tells? To be sure, we demand of him what he demands of himself,—veracity, first of all. But with that, he is the lawgiver, as being an exact reporter of the essential law. He knows that he did not make his thought,—no, his thought made him, and made the sun and the stars. Is the solar system good art and architecture? the same wise achievement is in the human brain also, can you only wile it from interference and marring. We cannot look at works of art but they teach us how near man is to creating. Michel Angelo is largely filled with the Creator that made and makes men. How much of the original craft remains in him, and he a mortal man! In him and the like perfecter brains the instinct is resistless, knows the right way, is melodious, and at all points divine. The reason we set so high a value on any poetry,—as often on a line or a phrase as on a poem,—is that it is a new work of Nature as a man is. It must be as new as foam and as old as the rock. But a new verse comes once in a hundred years; therefore Pindar, Hafiz, Dante, speak so proudly of what seems to the clown a jingle.

The writer, like the priest, must be exempted from secular labor. His work needs a frolic health; he must be at the top of his condition. In that prosperity he is sometimes caught up into a perception of means and materials, of feats and fine arts, of fairy machineries and funds of power hitherto utterly unknown to him, whereby he can transfer his visions to mortal canvas, or reduce them into iambic or trochaic, into lyric or heroic rhyme. These successes are not less admirable and astonishing to the poet than they are to his audience. He has seen something which all the mathematics and the best industry could never bring him unto. Now at this rare elevation above his usual sphere, he has come into new circulations, the marrow of the world is in his bones, the opulence of forms begins to pour into his intellect, and he is permitted to dip his brush into the old paint-pot with which birds, flowers, the human cheek, the living rock, the broad landscape, the ocean and the eternal sky were painted.

These fine fruits of judgment, poesy and sentiment, when once their hour is struck, and the world is ripe for them, know as well as coarser how to feed and replenish themselves, and maintain their stock alive, and multiply; for roses and violets renew their race like oaks, and flights of painted moths are as old as the Alleghanies. The balance of the world is kept, and dewdrop and haze and the pencil of light are as long-lived as chaos and darkness.

Our science is always abreast of our self-knowledge. Poetry begins, or all becomes poetry, when we look from the centre outward, and are using all as if the mind made it. That only can we see which we are, and which we make. The weaver sees gingham; the broker sees the stock-list; the politician, the ward and county votes; the poet sees the horizon, and the shores of matter lying on the sky, the interaction of the elements,—the large effect of laws which correspond to the inward laws which he knows, and so are but a kind of extension of himself. "The attractions are proportional to the destinies."[5] Events or things are only the fulfilment of the prediction of the faculties. Better men saw heavens

---

5. Edward Waldo Emerson tells us that this is the Second Axiom of Charles Fourier (see n. 3, p. 133). Cf. W 8.368–69.

and earths; saw noble instruments of noble souls. We see railroads, mills and banks, and we pity the poverty of these dreaming Buddhists. There was as much creative force then as now, but it made globes and astronomic heavens, instead of broadcloth and wine-glasses.

The poet is enamoured of thoughts and laws. These know their way, and, guided by them, he is ascending from an interest in visible things to an interest in that which they signify, and from the part of a spectator to the part of a maker. And as everything streams and advances, as every faculty and every desire is procreant, and every perception is a destiny, there is no limit to his hope. "Anything, child, that the mind covets, from the milk of a cocoa to the throne of the three worlds, thou mayest obtain, by keeping the law of thy members and the law of thy mind."[6] It suggests that there is higher poetry than we write or read.

Rightly, poetry is organic. We cannot know things by words and writing, but only by taking a central position in the universe and living in its forms. We sink to rise: —

> "None any work can frame,
> Unless himself become the same."

All the parts and forms of Nature are the expression or production of divine faculties, and the same are in us. And the fascination of genius for us is this awful nearness to Nature's creations.

I have heard that the Germans think the creator of Trim and Uncle Toby, though he never wrote a verse, a greater poet than Cowper, and that Goldsmith's title to the name is not from his Deserted Village, but derived from the Vicar of Wakefield.[7] Better examples are Shakspeare's Ariel, his Caliban[8] and his fairies in the Mid-summer Night's Dream. Barthold Niebuhr[9] said well, "There is little merit in inventing a happy idea or attractive situation, so long as it is only the author's voice which we hear. As a being whom we have called into life by magic arts, as soon as it has received existence acts independently of the master's impulse, so the poet creates his persons, and then watches and relates what they do and say. Such creation is poetry, in the literal sense of the term, and its possibility is an unfathomable enigma. The gushing fulness of speech belongs to the poet, and it flows from the lips of each of his magic beings in the thoughts and words peculiar to its nature."

This force of representation so plants his figures before him that he treats them as real; talks to them as if they were bodily there; puts words in their mouth such as they should have spoken, and is affected by them as by persons. Vast is the difference between writing clean verses for magazines, and creating these new persons and situations, — new language with emphasis and reality. The humor of Falstaff, the terror of Macbeth, have each their swarm of fit thoughts and images, as if Shakspeare had known and reported the men, instead of inventing them at his desk. This power appears not only in the outline or portrait of his actors, but also in the bearing and behavior and style of each individual.

---

6. From the *Vishnu Purana* (see n. 3, p. 296).
7. Goldsmith's (see n. 8, p. 67) "The Deserted Village" is a narrative poem and *The Vicar of Wakefield* is his equally popular novel. *Trim and Uncle Toby*: characters in the zany novel *Tristram Shandy* by Laurence Sterne (1713–1768). Cowper, see n. 8, p. 67.
8. Ariel and Caliban appear in *The Tempest*.
9. Barthold George Niebuhr (1776–1831), Danish historian, philologist, and diplomat. Emerson himself identifies the source of the quote as Niebuhr's *Letters* 3.196.

Ben Jonson told Drummond[1] that "Sidney did not keep a decorum in making every one speak as well as himself."

We all have one key to this miracle of the poet, and the dunce has experiences that may explain Shakspeare to him,—one key, namely, dreams. In dreams we are true poets; we create the persons of the drama; we give them appropriate figures, faces, costume; they are perfect in their organs, attitude, manners: moreover they speak after their own characters, not ours;—they speak to us, and we listen with surprise to what they say. Indeed, I doubt if the best poet has yet written any five-act play that can compare in thoroughness of invention with this unwritten play in fifty acts, composed by the dullest snorer on the floor of the watch-house.

Melody, Rhyme, Form.—Music and rhyme are among the earliest pleasures of the child, and, in the history of literature, poetry precedes prose. Every one may see, as he rides on the highway through an uninteresting landscape, how a little water instantly relieves the monotony: no matter what objects are near it,—a gray rock, a grass-patch, an alder-bush, or a stake,—they become beautiful by being reflected. It is rhyme to the eye, and explains the charm of rhyme to the ear. Shadows please us as still finer rhymes. Architecture gives the like pleasure by the repetition of equal parts in a colonnade, in a row of windows, or in wings; gardens by the symmetric contrasts of the beds and walks. In society you have this figure in a bridal company, where a choir of white-robed maidens give the charm of living statues; in a funeral procession, where all wear black; in a regiment of soldiers in uniform.

The universality of this taste is proved by our habit of casting our facts into rhyme to remember them better, as so many proverbs may show. Who would hold the order of the almanac so fast but for the ding-dong,—

"Thirty days hath September," etc.;—

or of the Zodiac, but for

"The Ram, the Bull, the heavenly Twins," etc.?

We are lovers of rhyme and return, period and musical reflection. The babe is lulled to sleep by the nurse's song. Sailors can work better for their *yo-heave-o*. Soldiers can march better and fight better for the drum and trumpet. Metre begins with pulse-beat, and the length of lines in songs and poems is determined by the inhalation and exhalation of the lungs. If you hum or whistle the rhythm of the common English metres,—of the decasyllabic quatrain, or the octosyllabic with alternate sexisyllabic, or other rhythms,—you can easily believe these metres to be organic, derived from the human pulse, and to be therefore not proper to one nation, but to mankind. I think you will also find a charm heroic, plaintive, pathetic, in these cadences, and be at once set on searching for the words that can rightly fill these vacant beats. Young people like rhyme, drum-beat, tune, things in pairs and alternatives; and, in higher degrees, we know the instant power of music upon our temperaments to change our mood, and give us its own; and human passion, seizing these constitutional tunes, aims to fill them with appropriate words, or marry music to thought, be-

---

1. William Drummond of Hawthornden (1585–1649), Scottish writer and poet.

lieving, as we believe of all marriage, that matches are made in heaven, and that for every thought its proper melody or rhyme exists, though the odds are immense against our finding it, and only genius can rightly say the banns.

Another form of rhyme is iterations of phrase,

"At her feet he bowed, he fell, he lay down: at her feet he bowed, he fell: where he bowed, there he fell down dead."[2]

The fact is made conspicuous, nay, colossal, by this simple rhetoric:—

"They shall perish, but thou shalt endure: yea, all of them shall wax old like a garment; as a vesture shalt thou change them, and they shall be changed: but thou art the same, and thy years shall have no end."[3]

Milton delights in these iterations:—

"Though fallen on evil days,
On evil days though fallen, and evil tongues."[4]

"Was I deceived, or did a sable cloud
Turn forth its silver lining on the night?
I did not err, there does a sable cloud
Turn forth its silver lining on the night."
Comus.[5]

"A little onward lend thy guiding hand,
To these dark steps a little farther on."
Samson.[6]

So in our songs and ballads the refrain skilfully used, and deriving some novelty or better sense in each of many verses:—

"Busk thee, busk thee, my bonny bonny bride,
Busk thee, busk thee, my winsome marrow."
HAMILTON.[7]

Of course rhyme soars and refines with the growth of the mind. The boy liked the drum, the people liked an overpowering jewsharp tune. Later they like to transfer that rhyme to life, and to detect a melody as prompt and perfect in their daily affairs. Omen and coincidence show the rhythmical structure of man; hence the taste for signs, sortilege, prophecy and fulfilment, anniversaries, etc. By and by, when they apprehend real rhymes, namely, the correspondence of parts in Nature,—acid and alkali, body and mind, man and maid, character and history, action and reaction,—they do not longer value rattles and ding-dongs, or barbaric word-jingle. Astronomy, Botany, Chemistry, Hydraulics and the elemental forces have their own periods and returns, their own grand strains of harmony not less exact, up to the primeval apothegm that "there is nothing on earth which is not in the heavens in a heavenly form, and nothing in the heavens which is not on the earth in an earthly form." They furnish the poet with grander pairs and alternations, and will require an equal expansion in his metres.

2. Judges 5.27.
3. Psalm 102.26–27.
4. *Paradise Lost* 7.25–26.
5. *Comus* 221–24.
6. *Samson Agonistes* 1–2.
7. William Hamilton (1704–1754), Scottish poet. The lines come from his well-known song "The Braes of Yarrow."

There is under the seeming poverty of metres an infinite variety, as every artist knows. A right ode (however nearly it may adopt conventional metre, as the Spenserian, or the heroic blank-verse,[8] or one of the fixed lyric metres) will by any sprightliness be at once lifted out of conventionality, and will modify the metre. Every good poem that I know I recall by its rhythm also. Rhyme is a pretty good measure of the latitude and opulence of a writer. If unskilful, he is at once detected by the poverty of his chimes. A small, well-worn, sprucely brushed vocabulary serves him. Now try Spenser, Marlowe, Chapman, and see how wide they fly for weapons, and how rich and lavish their profusion. In their rhythm is no manufacture, but a vortex, or musical tornado, which, falling on words and the experience of a learned mind, whirls these materials into the same grand order as planets and moons obey, and seasons, and monsoons.

There are also prose poets. Thomas Taylor,[9] the Platonist, for instance, is really a better man of imagination, a better poet, or perhaps I should say a better feeder to a poet, than any man between Milton and Wordsworth. Thomas Moore[1] had the magnanimity to say, "If Burke and Bacon were not poets (measured lines not being necessary to constitute one), he did not know what poetry meant." And every good reader will easily recall expressions or passages in works of pure science which have given him the same pleasure which he seeks in professed poets. Richard Owen,[2] the eminent paleontologist, said:—

> "All hitherto observed causes of extirpation point either to continuous slowly operating geologic changes, or to no greater sudden cause than the, so to speak, spectral appearance of mankind on a limited tract of land not before inhabited."

St. Augustine[3] complains to God of his friends offering him the books of the philosophers:—

> "And these were the dishes in which they brought to me, being hungry, the Sun and the Moon instead of Thee."

It would not be easy to refuse to Sir Thomas Browne's[4] Fragment on Mummies the claim of poetry:—

> "Of their living habitations they made little account, conceiving of them but as *hospitia*, or inns, while they adorned the sepulchres of the dead, and, planting thereon lasting bases, defied the crumbling touches of time, and the misty vaporousness of oblivion. Yet all were but Babel vanities. Time sadly overcometh all things, and is now dominant and sitteth upon a Sphinx, and looketh unto Memphis and old Thebes, while his sister Oblivion reclineth semi-somnous on a pyramid, gloriously triumphing, making puzzles of Titanian erections, and turning old glories into dreams. History sinketh beneath her cloud. The traveller as he paceth through those deserts asketh of her, Who builded them? and she mumbleth something, but what it is he heareth not."

---

8. Unrhymed iambic pentameter. *Spenserian:* a nine-line stanza rhyming *ababbcbcc*—all in iambic pentameter, except for the final line, which has six beats.
9. Cambridge Neoplatonist (1758–1835).
1. Irish poet (1779–1852), sometimes considered the prime national bard, he also wrote a history of Ireland.
2. Sir Richard Owen (1804–1892), comparative anatomist and physiologist.
3. See n. 3, p. 174. The quote is from his *Confessions.*
4. English physician and writer (1605–1682), best known for his *Religio Medici* (1642).

Rhyme, being a kind of music, shares this advantage with music, that it has a privilege of speaking truth which all Philistia[5] is unable to challenge. Music is the poor man's Parnassus.[6] With the first note of the flute or horn, or the first strain of a song, we quit the world of common sense and launch on the sea of ideas and emotions: we pour contempt on the prose you so magnify; yet the sturdiest Philistine is silent. The like allowance is the prescriptive right of poetry. You shall not speak ideal truth in prose uncontradicted: you may in verse. The best thoughts run into the best words; imaginative and affectionate thoughts into music and metre. We ask for food and fire, we talk of our work, our tools and material necessities, in prose; that is, without any elevation or aim at beauty; but when we rise into the world of thought, and think of these things only for what they signify, speech refines into order and harmony. I know what you say of mediæval barbarism and sleighbell rhyme, but we have not done with music, no, nor with rhyme, nor must console ourselves with prose poets so long as boys whistle and girls sing.

Let Poetry then pass, if it will, into music and rhyme. That is the form which itself puts on. We do not enclose watches in wooden, but in crystal cases, and rhyme is the transparent frame that allows almost the pure architecture of thought to become visible to the mental eye. Substance is much, but so are mode and form much. The poet, like a delighted boy, brings you heaps of rainbow-bubbles, opaline, air-borne, spherical as the world, instead of a few drops of soap and water. Victor Hugo[7] says well, "An idea steeped in verse becomes suddenly more incisive and more brilliant: the iron becomes steel." Lord Bacon, we are told, "loved not to see poesy go on other feet than poetical dactyls and spondees;" and Ben Jonson said that "Donne,[8] for not keeping of accent, deserved hanging."

Poetry being an attempt to express, not the common sense, — as the avoirdupois of the hero, or his structure in feet and inches, — but the beauty and soul in his aspect as it shines to fancy and feeling; and so of all other objects in Nature; runs into fable, personifies every fact: — "the clouds clapped their hands," — "the hills skipped," — "the sky spoke." This is the substance, and this treatment always attempts a metrical grace. Outside of the nursery the beginning of literature is the prayers of a people, and they are always hymns, poetic, — the mind allowing itself range, and therewith is ever a corresponding freedom in the style, which becomes lyrical. The prayers of nations are rhythmic, have iterations and alliterations like the marriage-service and burial-service in our liturgies.

Poetry will never be a simple means, as when history or philosophy is rhymed, or laureate odes on state occasions are written. Itself must be its own end, or it is nothing. The difference between poetry and stock poetry is this, that in the latter the rhythm is given and the sense adapted to it; while in the former the sense dictates the rhythm. I might even say that the rhyme is there in the theme, thought and image themselves. Ask the fact for the form. For a verse is not a vehicle to carry a sentence as a jewel is carried in a case: the verse must

5. In the Bible, the home of the inveterate enemies of the Israelites (cf. David and Goliath). In modern usage it refers to ignorant and uncultured persons.
6. Mountain in Greece regarded as the seat of poetry and music. Emerson's own anthology of favorite poems is titled *Parnassus.*
7. French poet, novelist, and dramatist (1802–1885), towering figure in the nineteenth century.
8. See n. 9, p. 253. He was thought by Jonson and, later, Coleridge to have sometimes employed rather rough versification. Bacon, see n. 3, p. 6. *Dactyl:* metrical foot used in Greek and Latin epic poetry, consisting of one long and two short syllables; it is difficult to reproduce in English verse because classical scansion depended on quantity, not stress. *Spondee:* foot consisting of two long syllables.

be alive, and inseparable from its contents, as the soul of man inspires and directs the body, and we measure the inspiration by the music. In reading prose, I am sensitive as soon as a sentence drags; but in poetry, as soon as one word drags. Ever as the thought mounts, the expression mounts. 'T is cumulative also; the poem is made up of lines each of which fills the ear of the poet in its turn, so that mere synthesis produces a work quite superhuman.

Indeed, the masters sometimes rise above themselves to strains which charm their readers, and which neither any competitor could outdo, nor the bard himself again equal. Try this strain of Beaumont and Fletcher:[9]—

> "Hence, all ye vain delights,
> As short as are the nights
> In which you spend your folly!
> There's naught in this life sweet,
> If men were wise to see't,
> But only melancholy.
> Oh! sweetest melancholy!
> Welcome, folded arms and fixed eyes,
> A sigh that piercing mortifies,
> A look that's fastened to the ground,
> A tongue chained up without a sound;
> Fountain-heads and pathless groves,
> Places which pale Passion loves,
> Midnight walks, when all the fowls
> Are warmly housed, save bats and owls;
> A midnight bell, a passing groan,
> These are the sounds we feed upon,
> Then stretch our bones in a still, gloomy valley.
> Nothing's so dainty sweet as lovely melancholy."

Keats[1] disclosed by certain lines in his Hyperion this inward skill; and Coleridge showed at least his love and appetency for it. It appears in Ben Jonson's songs, including certainly The Faery beam upon you, etc., Waller's Go, Lovely Rose! Herbert's Virtue and Easter, and Lovelace's lines To Althea and To Lucasta, and Collins's[2] Ode to Evening, all but the last verse, which is academical. Perhaps this dainty style of poetry is not producible to-day, any more than a right Gothic cathedral. It belonged to a time and taste which is not in the world.

As the imagination is not a talent of some men but is the health of every man, so also is this joy of musical expression. I know the pride of mathematicians and materialists, but they cannot conceal from me their capital want. The critic, the philosopher, is a failed poet. Gray avows that "he thinks even a bad verse as good a thing or better than the best observation that was ever made on it." I honor the naturalist; I honor the geometer, but he has before him higher power and happiness than he knows. Yet we will leave to the masters their own forms. Newton may be permitted to call Terence[3] a playbook, and to wonder at the frivolous taste for rhymers: he only predicts, one would say, a grander po-

9. See n. 9, p. 132. The quote is from their *The Nice Valour* 3.3.40–58.
1. John Keats (1795–1821), English Romantic poet known especially for his odes and sonnets, published *Hyperion* in 1820.
2. William Collins (1721–1759), English poet. Edmund Waller (1606–1687) and George Herbert (see n. 6, p. 30), English lyric and religious poets. Richard Lovelace (1618–1658), English Cavalier poet.
3. Roman comic poet (ca. 190–159 B.C.E.). Newton, see n. 5, p. 16.

etry: he only shows that he is not yet reached; that the poetry which satisfies more youthful souls is not such to a mind like his, accustomed to grander harmonies;—this being a child's whistle to his ear; that the music must rise to a loftier strain, up to Händel, up to Beethoven, up to the thorough-base of the seashore, up to the largeness of astronomy: at last that great heart will hear in the music beats like its own; the waves of melody will wash and float him also, and set him into concert and harmony.

* * *

Morals.—We are sometimes apprised that there is a mental power and creation more excellent than anything which is commonly called philosophy and literature; that the high poets, that Homer, Milton, Shakspeare, do not fully content us. How rarely they offer us the heavenly bread! The most they have done is to intoxicate us once and again with its taste. They have touched this heaven and retain afterwards some sparkle of it: they betray their belief that such discourse is possible. There is something—our brothers on this or that side of the sea do not know it or own it; the eminent scholars of England, historians and reviewers, romancers and poets included, might deny and blaspheme it,—which is setting us and them aside and the whole world also, and planting itself. To true poetry we shall sit down as the result and justification of the age in which it appears, and think lightly of histories and statutes. None of your parlor or piano verse, none of your carpet poets, who are content to amuse, will satisfy us. Power, new power, is the good which the soul seeks. The poetic gift we want, as the health and supremacy of man,—not rhymes and sonneteering, not bookmaking and bookselling; surely not cold spying and authorship.

Is not poetry the little chamber in the brain where is generated the explosive force which, by gentle shocks, sets in action the intellectual world? Bring us the bards who shall sing all our old ideas out of our heads, and new ones in; men-making poets; poetry which, like the verses inscribed on Balder's columns in Breidablik, is capable of restoring the dead to life;—poetry like that verse of Saadi,[4] which the angels testified "met the approbation of Allah in Heaven;"—poetry which finds its rhymes and cadences in the rhymes and iterations of Nature, and is the gift to men of new images and symbols, each the ensign and oracle of an age; that shall assimilate men to it, mould itself into religions and mythologies, and impart its quality to centuries;—poetry which tastes the world and reports of it, upbuilding the world again in the thought;—

> "Not with tickling rhymes,
> But high and noble matter, such as flies
> From brains entranced, and filled with ecstasies."[5]

Poetry must be affirmative. It is the piety of the intellect. "Thus saith the Lord," should begin the song. The poet who shall use Nature as his hieroglyphic must have an adequate message to convey thereby. Therefore when we speak of the Poet in any high sense, we are driven to such examples as Zoroaster and Plato, St. John and Menu,[6] with their moral burdens. The Muse shall be the counter-

---

4. See n. 2, p. 250. Balder, or Baldur, in Norse mythology the god of light, summer, innocence, and purity. The son of Odin and Frigga, he dwelt at Breidhablik, one of the mansions of Asgard.
5. From Jonson *The Forest*, 12, toward the end of "Epistle to the Countess of Rutland."
6. See n. 3, p. 115.

part of Nature, and equally rich. I find her not often in books. We know Nature
and figure her exuberant, tranquil, magnificent in her fertility, coherent; so that
every creation is omen of every other. She is not proud of the sea, of the stars, of
space or time, or man or woman. All her kinds share the attributes of the selectest
extremes. But in current literature I do not find her. Literature warps away from
life, though at first it seems to bind it. In the world of letters how few commanding oracles! Homer did what he could; Pindar, Æschylus, and the Greek Gnomic
poets[7] and the tragedians. Dante was faithful when not carried away by his fierce
hatreds. But in so many alcoves of English poetry I can count only nine or ten authors who are still inspirers and lawgivers to their race.

The supreme value of poetry is to educate us to a height beyond itself, or
which it rarely reaches;—the subduing mankind to order and virtue. He is the
true Orpheus who writes his ode, not with syllables, but men. "In poetry," said
Goethe,[8] "only the really great and pure advances us, and this exists as a second
nature, either elevating us to itself, or rejecting us." The poet must let Humanity sit with the Muse in his head, as the charioteer sits with the hero in the Iliad.
"Show me," said Sarona in the novel, "one wicked man who has written poetry,
and I will show you where his poetry is not poetry; or rather, I will show you in
his poetry no poetry at all."[9]

I have heard that there is a hope which precedes and must precede all science of the visible or the invisible world; and that science is the realization of that
hope in either region. I count the genius of Swedenborg and Wordsworth as the
agents of a reform in philosophy, the bringing poetry back to Nature,—to the
marrying of Nature and mind, undoing the old divorce in which poetry had been
famished and false, and Nature had been suspected and pagan. The philosophy
which a nation receives, rules its religion, poetry, politics, arts, trades and whole
history. A good poem—say Shakspeare's Macbeth, or Hamlet, or the Tempest—
goes about the world offering itself to reasonable men, who read it with joy and
carry it to their reasonable neighbors. Thus it draws to it the wise and generous
souls, confirming their secret thoughts, and, through their sympathy, really publishing itself. It affects the characters of its readers by formulating their opinions
and feelings, and inevitably prompting their daily action. If they build ships, they
write "Ariel" or "Prospero" or "Ophelia"[1] on the ship's stern, and impart a tenderness and mystery to matters of fact. The ballad and romance work on the
hearts of boys, who recite the rhymes to their hoops or their skates if alone, and
these heroic songs or lines are remembered and determine many practical
choices which they make later. Do you think Burns has had no influence on the
life of men and women in Scotland,—has opened no eyes and ears to the face of
Nature and the dignity of man and the charm and excellence of woman?

We are a little civil, it must be owned, to Homer and Æschylus, to Dante and
Shakspeare, and give them the benefit of the largest interpretation. We must be a
little strict also, and ask whether, if we sit down at home, and do not go to Hamlet, Hamlet will come to us? whether we shall find our tragedy written in his,—
our hopes, wants, pains, disgraces, described to the life,—and the way opened to
the paradise which ever in the best hour beckons us? But our overpraise and ide-

7. Poets of the sixth century B.C.E. whose writings contain maxims and aphorisms. Aeschylus, see n. 1, p.
109.
8. See n. 6, p. 42.
9. Miss Shepard's "Counterparts," Vol. I, p. 67. [Emerson]
1. Characters in Shakespeare's *The Tempest* and *Hamlet*.

alization of famous masters is not in its origin a poor Boswellism,[2] but an impatience of mediocrity. The praise we now give to our heroes we shall unsay when we make larger demands. How fast we outgrow the books of the nursery, — then those that satisfied our youth. What we once admired as poetry has long since come to be a sound of tin pans; and many of our later books we have outgrown. Perhaps Homer and Milton will be tin pans yet. Better not to be easily pleased. The poet should rejoice if he has taught us to despise his song; if he has so moved us as to lift us, — to open the eye of the intellect to see farther and better.

In proportion as a man's life comes into union with truth, his thoughts approach to a parallelism with the currents of natural laws, so that he easily expresses his meaning by natural symbols, or uses the ecstatic or poetic speech. By successive states of mind all the facts of Nature are for the first time interpreted. In proportion as his life departs from this simplicity, he uses circumlocution, — by many words hoping to suggest what he cannot say. Vexatious to find poets, who are by excellence the thinking and feeling of the world, deficient in truth of intellect and of affection. Then is conscience unfaithful, and thought unwise. To know the merit of Shakspeare, read Faust.[3] I find Faust a little too modern and intelligible. We can find such a fabric at several mills, though a little inferior. Faust abounds in the disagreeable. The vice is prurient, learned, Parisian. In the presence of Jove, Priapus[4] may be allowed as an offset, but here he is an equal hero. The egotism, the wit, is calculated. The book is undeniably written by a master, and stands unhappily related to the whole modern world; but it is a very disagreeable chapter of literature, and accuses the author as well as the times. Shakspeare could no doubt have been disagreeable, had he less genius, and if ugliness had attracted him. In short, our English nature and genius has made us the worst critics of Goethe, —

> "We, who speak the tongue
> That Shakspeare spake, the faith and manners hold
> Which Milton held."[5]

It is not style or rhymes, or a new image more or less that imports, but sanity; that life should not be mean; that life should be an image in every part beautiful; that the old forgotten splendors of the universe should glow again for us; — that we should lose our wit, but gain our reason. And when life is true to the poles of Nature, the streams of truth will roll through us in song.

Transcendency. — In a cotillon some persons dance and others await their turn when the music and the figure come to them. In the dance of God there is not one of the chorus but can and will begin to spin, monumental as he now looks, whenever the music and figure reach his place and duty. O celestial Bacchus![6] drive them mad, — this multitude of vagabonds, hungry for eloquence, hungry for poetry, starving for symbols, perishing for want of electricity to vital-

---

2. See n. 6, p. 87.
3. Goethe's *Faust* appeared in two parts (1808 and 1832). See also n. 3, p. 243. See Edward Waldo Emerson's citation from his father's journal in W 8.373.
4. In Greek mythology, the phallic god of reproduction and fertility, later considered lascivious and obscene. Jove, see n. 9, p. 89.
5. From Wordsworth's Sonnet 16 in part 1 of his *Poems Dedicated to National Independence and Liberty.* Emerson changes Wordsworth's "morals" to "manners."
6. See n. 7, p. 50. Cf. Emerson's poem, "Bacchus" (p. 452).

ize this too much pasture, and in the long delay indemnifying themselves with the false wine of alcohol, of politics or of money.

Every man may be, and at some time a man is, lifted to a platform whence he looks beyond sense to moral and spiritual truth, and in that mood deals sovereignly with matter, and strings worlds like beads upon his thought. The success with which this is done can alone determine how genuine is the inspiration. The poet is rare because he must be exquisitely vital and sympathetic, and, at the same time, immovably centred. In good society, nay, among the angels in heaven, is not everything spoken in fine parable, and not so servilely as it befell to the sense? All is symbolized. Facts are not foreign, as they seem, but related. Wait a little and we see the return of the remote hyperbolic curve. The solid men complain that the idealist leaves out the fundamental facts; the poet complains that the solid men leave out the sky. To every plant there are two powers; one shoots down as rootlet, and one upward as tree. You must have eyes of science to see in the seed its nodes; you must have the vivacity of the poet to perceive in the thought its futurities. The poet is representative,—whole man, diamond-merchant, symbolizer, emancipator; in him the world projects a scribe's hand and writes the adequate genesis. The nature of things is flowing, a metamorphosis. The free spirit sympathizes not only with the actual form, but with the power or possible forms; but for obvious municipal or parietal uses God has given us a bias or a rest on to-day's forms. Hence the shudder of joy with which in each clear moment we recognize the metamorphosis, because it is always a conquest, a surprise from the heart of things. One would say of the force in the works of Nature, all depends on the battery. If it give one shock, we shall get to the fish form, and stop; if two shocks, to the bird; if three, to the quadruped; if four, to the man. Power of generalizing differences men. The number of successive saltations the nimble thought can make, measures the difference between the highest and lowest of mankind. The habit of saliency, of not pausing but going on, is a sort of importation or domestication of the Divine effort in a man. After the largest circle has been drawn, a larger can be drawn around it. The problem of the poet is to unite freedom with precision; to give the pleasure of color, and be not less the most powerful of sculptors. Music seems to you sufficient, or the subtle and delicate scent of lavender; but Dante was free imagination,—all wings,—yet he wrote like Euclid. And mark the equality of Shakspeare to the comic, the tender and sweet, and to the grand and terrible. A little more or less skill in whistling is of no account. See those weary pentameter tales of Dryden and others. Turnpike is one thing and blue sky another. Let the poet, of all men, stop with his inspiration. The inexorable rule in the muses' court, *either inspiration or silence,* compels the bard to report only his supreme moments. It teaches the enormous force of a few words, and in proportion to the inspiration checks loquacity. Much that we call poetry is but polite verse. The high poetry which shall thrill and agitate mankind, restore youth and health, dissipate the dreams under which men reel and stagger, and bring in the new thoughts, the sanity and heroic aims of nations, is deeper hid and longer postponed than was America or Australia, or the finding of steam or of the galvanic battery. We must not conclude against poetry from the defects of poets. They are, in our experience, men of every degree of skill,—some of them only once or twice receivers of an inspiration, and presently falling back on a low life. The drop of *ichor* that tingles in their veins has not yet refined their blood and cannot lift the whole man to the digestion and function of ichor,—that is, to godlike nature. Time will be when ichor shall be their blood, when what are now glimpses and aspirations shall be the routine of the day. Yet even partial ascents to poetry and ideas are forerunners, and announce the dawn. In the mire of the sensual life, their religion, their poets, their admiration of heroes and benefactors, even their novel and newspaper, nay, their superstitions also, are hosts of ideals,—a cordage of ropes that hold them up out of the slough. Poetry is inestimable as a lonely faith, a lonely protest in the uproar of atheism.

But so many men are ill-born or ill-bred,—the brains are so marred, so imperfectly formed, unheroically, brains of the sons of fallen men, that the doctrine is imperfectly received. One man sees a spark or shimmer of the truth and reports it, and his saying becomes a legend or golden proverb for ages, and other men report as much, but none wholly and well. Poems!—we have no poem. Whenever that angel shall be organized and appear on earth, the Iliad will be reckoned a poor ballad-grinding. I doubt never the riches of Nature, the gifts of the future, the immense wealth of the mind. O yes, poets we shall have, mythology, symbols, religion, of our own. We too shall know how to take up all this industry and empire, this Western civilization, into thought, as easily as men did when arts were few; but not by holding it high, but by holding it low. The intellect uses and is not used,—uses London and Paris and Berlin, East and West, to its end. The only heart that can help us is one that draws, not from our society, but from itself, a counterpoise to society. What if we find partiality and meanness in us? The grandeur of our life exists in spite of us,—all over and under and within us, in what of us is inevitable and above our control. Men are facts as well as persons, and the involuntary part of their life is so much as to fill the mind and leave them no countenance to say aught of what is so trivial as their selfish thinking and doing. Sooner or later that which is now life shall be poetry, and every fair and manly trait shall add a richer strain to the song.

Quotation and Originality[1]

> Old and new put their stamp to everything in Nature. The snowflake that is now falling is marked by both. The present moment gives the motion and the color of the flake, Antiquity its form and properties. All things wear a lustre which is the gift of the present, and a tarnish of time.

> Every book is a quotation; and every house is a quotation out of all forests and mines and stone-quarries; and every man is a quotation from all his ancestors.

Whoever looks at the insect world, at flies, aphides, gnats and innumerable parasites, and even at the infant mammals, must have remarked the extreme content they take in suction, which constitutes the main business of their life. If we go into a library or newsroom, we see the same function on a higher plane, performed with like ardor, with equal impatience of interruption, indicating the sweetness of the act. In the highest civilization the book is still the highest delight. He who has once known its satisfactions is provided with a resource

---

1. This piece, originally an 1859 lecture, was first published in the *North American Review* in 1868. It was further edited for *Letters and Social Aims* (1876). The epigraphs were added by Edward Waldo Emerson for W.

against calamity. Like Plato's disciple who has perceived a truth, "he is preserved from harm until another period."[2] In every man's memory, with the hours when life culminated are usually associated certain books which met his views. Of a large and powerful class we might ask with confidence, What is the event they most desire? what gift? What but the book that shall come, which they have sought through all libraries, through all languages, that shall be to their mature eyes what many a tinsel-covered toy pamphlet was to their childhood, and shall speak to the imagination? Our high respect for a well-read man is praise enough of literature. If we encountered a man of rare intellect, we should ask him what books he read. We expect a great man to be a good reader; or in proportion to the spontaneous power should be the assimilating power. And though such are a more difficult and exacting class, they are not less eager. "He that borrows the aid of an equal understanding," said Burke,[3] "doubles his own; he that uses that of a superior elevates his own to the stature of that he contemplates."

We prize books, and they prize them most who are themselves wise. Our debt to tradition through reading and conversation is so massive, our protest or private addition so rare and insignificant,—and this commonly on the ground of other reading or hearing,—that, in a large sense, one would say there is no pure originality. All minds quote. Old and new make the warp and woof of every moment. There is no thread that is not a twist of these two strands. By necessity, by proclivity and by delight, we all quote. We quote not only books and proverbs, but arts, sciences, religion, customs and laws; nay, we quote temples and houses, tables and chairs by imitation. The Patent-Office Commissioner knows that all machines in use have been invented and re-invented over and over; that the mariner's compass, the boat, the pendulum, glass, movable types, the kaleidoscope, the railway, the power-loom, etc., have been many times found and lost, from Egypt, China and Pompeii down; and if we have arts which Rome wanted, so also Rome had arts which we have lost; that the invention of yesterday of making wood indestructible by means of vapor of coal-oil or paraffine was suggested by the Egyptian method which has preserved its mummy-cases four thousand years.

The highest statement of new philosophy complacently caps itself with some prophetic maxim from the oldest learning. There is something mortifying in this perpetual circle. This extreme economy argues a very small capital of invention. The stream of affection flows broad and strong; the practical activity is a river of supply; but the dearth of design accuses the penury of intellect. How few thoughts! In a hundred years, millions of men and not a hundred lines of poetry, not a theory of philosophy that offers a solution of the great problems, not an art of education that fulfils the conditions. In this delay and vacancy of thought we must make the best amends we can by seeking the wisdom of others to fill the time.

If we confine ourselves to literature, 'tis easy to see that the debt is immense to past thought. None escapes it. The originals are not original. There is imitation, model and suggestion, to the very archangels, if we knew their history. The first book tyrannizes over the second. Read Tasso, and you think of Virgil; read Virgil, and you think of Homer; and Milton[4] forces you to reflect how narrow are the limits of human invention. The Paradise Lost had never existed but for these

2. This sentence from Plato's (see n. 4, p. 15) *Phaedrus* is also used in "Experience," p. 212.
3. See n. 5, p. 45.
4. See n. 2, p. 6. Tasso, see n. 2, p. 259. Virgil, see n. 3, p. 156.

precursors; and if we find in India or Arabia a book out of our horizon of thought and tradition, we are soon taught by new researches in its native country to discover its foregoers, and its latent, but real connection with our own Bibles.

Read in Plato and you shall find Christian dogmas, and not only so, but stumble on our evangelical phrases. Hegel preëxists in Proclus, and, long before, in Heraclitus and Parmenides.[5] Whoso knows Plutarch, Lucian, Rabelais, Montaigne and Bayle[6] will have a key to many supposed originalities. Rabelais is the source of many a proverb, story and jest, derived from him into all modern languages; and if we knew Rabelais's reading we should see the rill of the Rabelais river. Swedenborg, Behmen, Spinoza,[7] will appear original to uninstructed and to thoughtless persons: their originality will disappear to such as are either well read or thoughtful; for scholars will recognize their dogmas as reappearing in men of a similar intellectual elevation throughout history. Albert, the "wonderful doctor," St. Buonaventura, the "seraphic doctor," Thomas Aquinas,[8] the "angelic doctor" of the thirteenth century, whose books made the sufficient culture of these ages, Dante absorbed, and he survives for us. Renard the Fox, a German poem of the thirteenth century, was long supposed to be the original work, until Grimm[9] found fragments of another original a century older. M. Le Grand showed that in the old Fabliaux were the originals of the tales of Molière, La Fontaine, Boccaccio, and of Voltaire.[1]

Mythology is no man's work; but, what we daily observe in regard to the *bon-mots* that circulate in society, — that every talker helps a story in repeating it, until, at last, from the slenderest filament of fact a good fable is constructed, — the same growth befalls mythology: the legend is tossed from believer to poet, from poet to believer, everybody adding a grace or dropping a fault or rounding the form, until it gets an ideal truth.

Religious literature, the psalms and liturgies of churches, are of course of this slow growth, — a fagot of selections gathered through ages, leaving the worse and saving the better, until it is at last the work of the whole communion of worshippers. The Bible itself is like an old Cremona;[2] it has been played upon by the devotion of thousands of years until every word and particle is public and tunable. And whatever undue reverence may have been claimed for it by the prestige of philonic inspiration,[3] the stronger tendency we are describing is likely to undo. What divines had assumed as the distinctive revelations of Christianity, theologic criticism has matched by exact parallelisms from the Stoics

---

5. Greek philosopher (fifth century B.C.E.), who appears in Plato's dialogue of the same name. Hegel, see n. 1, p. 275. Proclus, see n. 6, p. 187. Heraclitus, see n. 3, p. 89.
6. Pierre Bayle (1647–1706), French philosopher, author of *Historical and Critical Dictionary*. Plutarch, see n. 7, p. 57. Lucian (ca. 120–200), Greek satirist. François Rabelais (1494?–1533), French scholar, physician, and satirist, author of *Gargantua and Pantagruel*, a lusty and frank narrative (hence the adjective "rabelaisian"). Montaigne, see n. 8, p. 155.
7. See n. 2, p. 170. Swedenborg, see n. 6, p. 35. Behmen, see n. 8, p. 168.
8. St. Thomas Aquinas (ca. 1225–1274), Italian scholastic theologian and philosopher. Known as the "angelic doctor," he was a disciple of Albertus Magnus. Magnus (1206?–1280), German scholastic philosopher and cleric, considered one of the most learned men of his time. Giovanni di Fidanza (ca. 1221–1274), canonized as St. Bonaventura, patron saint of Lyons.
9. The brothers Grimm (Jacob, 1785–1863; Wilhelm, 1786–1859), German folklorists and philologists, authors of *Grimm's Fairy Tales*.
1. See n. 3, p. 271. Pierre Jean Baptiste Le Grand d'Aussy (1737–1800), French writer and critic. Jean Baptiste Poquelin, known as Molière (1622–1673), French comic dramatist. Jean de la Fontaine (1621–1695), French author, known for his *Fables*. Giovanni Boccaccio (1313–1375), Italian humanist, known for the *Decameron*.
2. I.e., like a fine old Italian violin.
3. Following Philo Judaeus (fl. first century C.E.), Alexandrian Jew and Platonist concerned with establishing the Mosaic basis of Greek philosophy.

and poets of Greece and Rome. Later, when Confucius and the Indian scriptures were made known, no claim to monopoly of ethical wisdom could be
thought of; and the surprising results of the new researches into the history of
Egypt have opened to us the deep debt of the churches of Rome and England
to the Egyptian hierology.

The borrowing is often honest enough, and comes of magnanimity and
stoutness. A great man quotes bravely, and will not draw on his invention when
his memory serves him with a word as good. What he quotes, he fills with his
own voice and humor, and the whole cyclopædia of his table-talk is presently
believed to be his own. Thirty years ago, when Mr. Webster[4] at the bar or in the
Senate filled the eyes and minds of young men, you might often hear cited as
Mr. Webster's three rules: first, never to do to-day what he could defer till to-
morrow; secondly, never to do himself what he could make another do for him;
and, thirdly, never to pay any debt to-day. Well, they are none the worse for
being already told, in the last generation, of Sheridan; and we find in Grimm's
Mémoires that Sheridan got them from the witty D'Argenson;[5] who, no doubt,
if we could consult him, could tell of whom he first heard them told. In our
own college days we remember hearing other pieces of Mr. Webster's advice to
students,—among others, this: that, when he opened a new book, he turned to
the table of contents, took a pen, and sketched a sheet of matters and topics,
what he knew and what he thought, before he read the book. But we find in
Southey's Commonplace Book this said of the Earl of Strafford: "I learned one
rule of him," says Sir G. Radcliffe,[6] "which I think worthy to be remembered.
When he met with a well-penned oration or tract upon any subject, he framed
a speech upon the same argument, inventing and disposing what seemed fit to
be said upon that subject, before he read the book; then, reading, compared his
own with the author's, and noted his own defects and the author's art and fulness; whereby he drew all that ran in the author more strictly, and might better
judge of his own wants to supply them." I remember to have heard Mr. Samuel
Rogers, in London, relate, among other anecdotes of the Duke of Wellington,[7]
that a lady having expressed in his presence a passionate wish to witness a great
victory, he replied: "Madam, there is nothing so dreadful as a great victory,—
excepting a great defeat." But this speech is also D'Argenson's, and is reported
by Grimm. So the sarcasm attributed to Baron Alderson upon Brougham,[8]
"What a wonderful versatile mind has Brougham! he knows politics, Greek, history, science; if he only knew a little of law, he would know a little of everything."
You may find the original of this gibe in Grimm, who says that Louis XVI., going
out of chapel after hearing a sermon from the Abbé Maury,[9] said, "Si l' Abbé
nous avait parlé un peu de religion, il nous aurait parlé de tout." A pleasantry
which ran through all the newspapers a few years since, taxing the eccentricities of a gifted family connection in New England, was only a theft of Lady Mary

---

4. See n. 6, p. 251.
5. Marc Antoine René de Paulmy d'Argenson (1722–1787), diplomat, member of the French Academy,
   critic and scholar. Richard Brinsley Sheridan (1751–1816), Irish dramatist and wit.
6. Sir George Radcliffe (1593–1657), colleague of Strafford. Robert Southey (1774–1843), English Romantic poet and dramatist. Sir Thomas Wentworth, first earl of Strafford (1593–1641), English politician
   and adviser to Charles I; executed.
7. Arthur Wellesley, first duke of Wellington (1769–1852), British soldier and statesman, defeated
   Napoleon at Waterloo in 1815. Samuel Rogers (1763–1855), English banker and poet.
8. See n. 6, p. 265.
9. Jean Siffrein Maury (1746–1817), archbishop of Paris. The quotation is translated as "if the Abbé had
   told us a little about religion, he would have told us about everything" (French).

Wortley Montagu's *mot* of a hundred years ago, that "the world was made up of men and women and Herveys."[1]

Many of the historical proverbs have a doubtful paternity. Columbus's egg is claimed for Brunelleschi.[2] Rabelais's dying words, "I am going to see the great Perhaps" (*le grand Peut-être*), only repeats the "IF" inscribed on the portal of the temple at Delphi.[3] Goethe's favorite phrase, "the open secret," translates Aristotle's answer to Alexander,[4] "These books are published and not published." Madame de Staël's "Architecture is frozen music" is borrowed from Goethe's "dumb music," which is Vitruvius's[5] rule, that "the architect must not only understand drawing, but music." Wordsworth's hero acting "on the plan which pleased his childish thought," is Schiller's "Tell him to reverence the dreams of his youth," and earlier, Bacon's "*Consilia juventutis plus divinitatis habent.*"[6]

In romantic literature examples of this vamping[7] abound. The fine verse in the old Scotch ballad of The Drowned Lovers —

> "Thou art roaring ower loud, Clyde water,
>   Thy streams are ower strang;
> Make me thy wrack when I come back,
>   But spare me when I gang" —[8]

is a translation of Martial's epigram on Hero and Leander, where the prayer of Leander is the same: —

> "Parcite dum propero, mergite dum redeo."[9]

Hafiz furnished Burns with the song of John Barleycorn, and furnished Moore[1] with the original of the piece, —

> "When in death I shall calm recline,
>   Oh, bear my heart to my mistress dear," etc.

There are many fables which, as they are found in every language, and betray no sign of being borrowed, are said to be agreeable to the human mind. Such are The Seven Sleepers, Gyges's Ring, The Travelling Cloak, The Wandering Jew, The Pied Piper, Jack and his Beanstalk, the Lady Diving in the Lake and Rising in the Cave, — whose omnipresence only indicates how easily a good story crosses all frontiers. The popular incident of Baron Munchausen,[2] who hung his bugle up by the kitchen fire and the frozen tune thawed out, is found

1. John Hervey, Baron Hervey of Ickworth (1696–1743), was a friend of Lady Mary, but she seems to be alluding here to his ambiguous sexual identity. Lady Mary Wortley Montagu (1689–1762), English woman of letters.
2. Filippo Brunelleschi (1377–1446), Italian architect and goldsmith, credited with inventing linear perspective. The egg that Columbus is said to have balanced on end may have been hard-boiled and slightly flattened.
3. Edward Waldo Emerson mentions that there is a chapter in Plutarch's *Morals* titled "Of the Word EI [IF] engraved over the Gate of Apollo's Temple at Delphi."
4. See n. 5, p. 229. Goethe see n. 6, p. 42. Aristotle, see n. 4, p. 47.
5. See n. 6, p. 42.
6. The urgings of one's youthful spirit have more of divinity in them (Latin). Schiller, see n. 5, p. 130. Bacon, see n. 3, p. 6.
7. I.e., literary vampirism.
8. Sometimes called "Clyde's Water." See *English and Scottish Popular Ballads*, ed. Helen Child Sargent and George Lyman Kittredge (1904).
9. Spare me as I go, drown me as I return (Latin). Martial, Marcus Valerius Martialis (first century C.E.), Latin epigrammatist.
1. See n. 1, p. 312. Hafiz, see n. 1, p. 115. Burns, see n. 8, p. 67.
2. Author (ca. 1720–1797) of fantastic stories, which can be found in *Narrative of his Marvelous Travels* (1785), ed. Rudoph Erich Raspe.

in Greece in Plato's time. Antiphanes, one of Plato's friends, laughingly compared his writings to a city where the words froze in the air as soon as they were pronounced, and the next summer, when they were warmed and melted by the sun, the people heard what had been spoken in the winter. It is only within this century that England and America discovered that their nursery-tales were old German and Scandinavian stories; and now it appears that they came from India, and are the property of all the nations descended from the Aryan race, and have been warbled and babbled between nurses and children for unknown thousands of years.

If we observe the tenacity with which nations cling to their first types of costume, of architecture, of tools and methods in tillage, and of decoration,— if we learn how old are the patterns of our shawls, the capitals of our columns, the fret, the beads, and other ornaments on our walls, the alternate lotus-bud and leaf-stem of our iron fences,—we shall think very well of the first men, or ill of the latest.

Now shall we say that only the first men were well alive, and the existing generation is invalided and degenerate? Is all literature eavesdropping, and all art Chinese imitation? our life a custom, and our body borrowed, like a beggar's dinner, from a hundred charities? A more subtle and severe criticism might suggest that some dislocation has befallen the race; that men are off their centre; that multitudes of men do not live with Nature, but behold it as exiles. People go out to look at sunrises and sunsets who do not recognize their own, quietly and happily, but know that it is foreign to them. As they do by books, so they *quote* the sunset and the star, and do not make them theirs. Worse yet, they live as foreigners in the world of truth, and quote thoughts, and thus disown them. Quotation confesses inferiority. In opening a new book we often discover, from the unguarded devotion with which the writer gives his motto or text, all we have to expect from him. If Lord Bacon[3] appears already in the preface, I go and read the Instauration instead of the new book.

The mischief is quickly punished in general and in particular. Admirable mimics have nothing of their own. In every kind of parasite, when Nature has finished an aphis, a teredo or a vampire bat,—an excellent sucking-pipe to tap another animal, or a mistletoe or dodder among plants,—the self-supplying organs wither and dwindle, as being superfluous. In common prudence there is an early limit to this leaning on an original. In literature, quotation is good only when the writer whom I follow goes my way, and, being better mounted than I, gives me a cast, as we say; but if I like the gay equipage so well as to go out of my road, I had better have gone afoot.

But it is necessary to remember there are certain considerations which go far to qualify a reproach too grave. This vast mental indebtedness has every variety that pecuniary debt has,—every variety of merit. The capitalist of either kind is as hungry to lend as the consumer to borrow; and the transaction no more indicates intellectual turpitude in the borrower than the simple fact of debt involves bankruptcy. On the contrary, in far the greater number of cases the transaction is honorable to both. Can we not help ourselves as discreetly by the force of two in literature? Certainly it only needs two well placed and well tempered for coöperation, to get somewhat far transcending any private enter-

---

3. Bacon published parts of his *Great Instauration* as *The Advancement of Learning* (1605) and *Novum Organum* (1620).

prise! Shall we converse as spies? Our very abstaining to repeat and credit the fine remark of our friend is thievish. Each man of thought is surrounded by wiser men than he, if they cannot write as well. Cannot he and they combine? Cannot they sink their jealousies in God's love, and call their poem Beaumont and Fletcher, or the Theban Phalanx's?[4] The city will for nine days or nine years make differences and sinister comparisons: there is a new and more excellent public that will bless the friends. Nay, it is an inevitable fruit of our social nature. The child quotes his father, and the man quotes his friend. Each man is a hero and an oracle to somebody, and to that person whatever he says has an enhanced value. Whatever we think and say is wonderfully better for our spirits and trust, in another mouth. There is none so eminent and wise but he knows minds whose opinion confirms or qualifies his own, and men of extraordinary genius acquire an almost absolute ascendant over their nearest companions. The Comte de Crillon said one day to M. d'Allonville, with French vivacity, "If the universe and I professed one opinion and M. Necker[5] expressed a contrary one, I should be at once convinced that the universe and I were mistaken."

Original power is usually accompanied with assimilating power, and we value in Coleridge his excellent knowledge and quotations perhaps as much, possibly more, than his original suggestions. If an author give us just distinctions, inspiring lessons, or imaginative poetry, it is not so important to us whose they are. If we are fired and guided by these, we know him as a benefactor, and shall return to him as long as he serves us so well. We may like well to know what is Plato's and what is Montesquieu's or Goethe's part, and what thought was always dear to the writer himself; but the worth of the sentences consists in their radiancy and equal aptitude to all intelligence. They fit all our facts like a charm. We respect ourselves the more that we know them.

Next to the originator of a good sentence is the first quoter of it.[6] Many will read the book before one thinks of quoting a passage. As soon as he has done this, that line will be quoted east and west. Then there are great ways of borrowing. Genius borrows nobly. When Shakspeare is charged with debts to his authors, Landor[7] replies: "Yet he was more original than his originals. He breathed upon dead bodies and brought them into life." And we must thank Karl Ottfried Müller[8] for the just remark, "Poesy, drawing within its circle all that is glorious and inspiring, gave itself but little concern as to where its flowers originally grew." So Voltaire usually imitated, but with such superiority that Dubuc said: "He is like the false Amphitryon;[9] although the stranger, it is al-

---

4. Emerson seems to use this phrase to stand for a consortium of Greek writers. Beaumont and Fletcher, see n. 9, p. 132.
5. Jacques Necker (1732–1804), Swiss-born banker and French minister of finance who was also the father of Madame de Staël; see selections from her *Germany* (p. 573). The comte de Crillon, probably François Félix Dorothée Les Balbes de Berton, comte (later duc) de Crillon (1748–1820), and d'Allonville, probably Armand-François, comte d'Allonville (1764–1853), French military men.
6. This well-known epigram may owe its origin to a sentence that Emerson had read many years before in an essay by his friend Frederick Henry Hedge (1805–1890), "Coleridge's Literary Character" (in *The Christian Examiner*, March 1833): "Next to the writer of a good book, he most deserves our gratitude, who in any way helps to increase its circulation." It is interesting to note that Emerson's appropriation of Hedge's sentence exemplifies the very principle embodied in his terse epigram. Hedge was a Unitarian minister and student of German philosophy.
7. Walter Savage Landor (1775–1864), well known for his *Imaginary Conversations of Literary Men and Women* (1824–1829), also wrote a book on Shakspeare.
8. Edward Waldo Emerson says that Müller "did important work in archaeology in the first half of the nineteenth century." See W 8.401.
9. In Greek legend, this king of Mycenae was cuckolded by Zeus, who assumed his identity and thus was the "false Amphitryon." The story has been used many times in plays by such authors as Plautus, Molière, and Dryden.

ways he who has the air of being master of the house." Wordsworth, as soon as he heard a good thing, caught it up, meditated upon it, and very soon reproduced it in his conversation and writing. If De Quincey[1] said, "That is what I told you," he replied, "No: that is mine,—mine, and not yours." On the whole, we like the valor of it. 'T is on Marmontel's[2] principle, "I pounce on what is mine, wherever I find it;" and on Bacon's broader rule, "I take all knowledge to be my province." It betrays the consciousness that truth is the property of no individual, but is the treasure of all men. And inasmuch as any writer has ascended to a just view of man's condition, he has adopted this tone. In so far as the receiver's aim is on life, and not on literature, will be his indifference to the source. The nobler the truth or sentiment, the less imports the question of authorship. It never troubles the simple seeker from whom he derived such or such a sentiment. Whoever expresses to us a just thought makes ridiculous the pains of the critic who should tell him where such a word had been said before. "It is no more according to Plato than according to me." Truth is always present: it only needs to lift the iron lids of the mind's eye to read its oracles. But the moment there is the purpose of display, the fraud is exposed. In fact, it is as difficult to appropriate the thoughts of others, as it is to invent. Always some steep transition, some sudden alteration of temperature, or of point of view, betrays the foreign interpolation.

There is, besides, a new charm in such intellectual works as, passing through long time, have had a multitude of authors and improvers. We admire that poetry which no man wrote,—no poet less than the genius of humanity itself,—which is to be read in a mythology, in the effect of a fixed or national style of pictures, of sculptures, or drama, or cities, or sciences, on us. Such a poem also is language. Every word in the language has once been used happily. The ear, caught by that felicity, retains it, and it is used again and again, as if the charm belonged to the word and not to the life of thought which so enforced it. These profane uses, of course, kill it, and it is avoided. But a quick wit can at any time reinforce it, and it comes into vogue again. Then people quote so differently: one finding only what is gaudy and popular; another, the heart of the author, the report of his select and happiest hour; and the reader sometimes giving more to the citation than he owes to it. Most of the classical citations you shall hear or read in the current journals or speeches were not drawn from the originals, but from previous quotations in English books; and you can easily pronounce, from the use and relevancy of the sentence, whether it had not done duty many times before,—whether your jewel was got from the mine or from an auctioneer. We are as much informed of a writer's genius by what he selects as by what he originates. We read the quotation with his eyes, and find a new and fervent sense; as a passage from one of the poets, well recited, borrows new interest from the rendering. As the journals say, "the italics are ours." The profit of books is according to the sensibility of the reader. The profoundest thought or passion sleeps as in a mine until an equal mind and heart finds and publishes it. The passages of Shakspeare that we most prize were never quoted until within this century; and Milton's prose, and Burke, even, have their best fame within it. Every one, too, remembers his friends by their favorite poetry or other reading.

1. Thomas De Quincey (1785–1859), English essayist and critic.
2. Jean François Marmontel (1723–1799), French critic, dramatist, and short-story writer.

Observe also that a writer appears to more advantage in the pages of another book than in his own. In his own he waits as a candidate for your approbation; in another's he is a lawgiver.

Then another's thoughts have a certain advantage with us simply because they are another's. There is an illusion in a new phrase. A man hears a fine sentence out of Swedenborg, and wonders at the wisdom, and is very merry at heart that he has now got so fine a thing. Translate it out of the new words into his own usual phrase, and he will wonder again at his own simplicity, such tricks do fine words play with us.

It is curious what new interest an old author acquires by official canonization in Tiraboschi, or Dr. Johnson, or Von Hammer-Purgstall, or Hallam,[3] or other historian of literature. Their registration of his book, or citation of a passage, carries the sentimental value of a college diploma. Hallam, though never profound, is a fair mind, able to appreciate poetry unless it becomes deep, being always blind and deaf to imaginative and analogy-loving souls, like the Platonists, like Giordano Bruno, like Donne, Herbert, Crashaw and Vaughan; and Hallam cites a sentence from Bacon or Sidney, and distinguishes a lyric of Edwards or Vaux, and straightway it commends itself to us as if it had received the Isthmian crown.[4]

It is a familiar expedient of brilliant writers, and not less of witty talkers, the device of ascribing their own sentence to an imaginary person, in order to give it weight, — as Cicero, Cowley, Swift, Landor and Carlyle have done. And Cardinal de Retz,[5] at a critical moment in the Parliament of Paris, described himself in an extemporary Latin sentence, which he pretended to quote from a classic author, and which told admirably well. It is a curious reflex effect of this enhancement of our thought by citing it from another, that many men can write better under a mask than for themselves; as Chatterton in archaic ballad, Le Sage in Spanish costume, Macpherson[6] as "Ossian"; and, I doubt not, many a young barrister in chambers in London, who forges good thunder for the Times, but never works as well under his own name. This is a sort of dramatizing talent; as it is not rare to find great powers of recitation, without the least original eloquence, — or people who copy drawings with admirable skill, but are incapable of any design.

In hours of high mental activity we sometimes do the book too much honor, reading out of it better things than the author wrote, — reading, as we say, between the lines. You have had the like experience in conversation: the wit was in what you heard, not in what the speakers said. Our best thought came from others. We heard in their words a deeper sense than the speakers put into them, and could express ourselves in other people's phrases to finer purpose than they knew. In Moore's Diary, Mr. Hallam is reported as mentioning at dinner one of

3. Henry Hallam (1777–1859), English historian of England and Europe. Tiraboschi, see n. 5, p. 199. Johnson, see n. 9 p. 67. "Joseph, Baron von Hammer Purgstall (1774–1856), one of the best authorities upon Oriental history and literature." [Edward Waldo Emerson]
4. Awarded by the ancient Greeks at games held in the Isthmus of Corinth. Bruno (1548–1600), Italian philosopher who was a mystical Neoplatonist and pantheist. Donne, see n. 9, p. 253. Herbert, see n. 6, p. 30. Richard Crashaw (1612/13–1649), English poet of mostly devotional work. Henry Vaughan (1622–1695), English lyrical and devotional poet. Edwards, probably Richard Edwards (1523?–1566), compiler of *Paradyse of Dainty Devises* (1576). Thomas Vaux, second Baron Vaux of Harrowden (1509–1556), contributor to *Tottel's Miscellany* and *Paradyse of Dainty Devises*.
5. Paul de Gondi, Cardinal de Retz (1613–1679), French cleric, who was well known for his *Memoirs*.
6. See n. 4, p. 307. Thomas Chatterton (1752–1770), writer and literary forger. Alain René Le Sage (1668–1747), French novelist, dramatist, and translator of works by Spanish authors.

his friends who had said, "I don't know how it is, a thing that falls flat from me seems quite an excellent joke when given at second hand by Sheridan. I never like my own *bon-mots* until he adopts them." Dumont was exalted by being used by Mirabeau, by Bentham and by Sir Philip Francis, who, again, was less than his own "Junius"; and James Hogg (except in his poems Kilmeny and The Witch of Fife) is but a third-rate author, owing his fame to his effigy colossalized through the lens of John Wilson,[7]—who, again, writes better under the domino of "Christopher North" than in his proper clothes. The bold theory of Delia Bacon,[8] that Shakspeare's plays were written by a society of wits,—by Sir Walter Raleigh, Lord Bacon and others around the Earl of Southampton,—had plainly for her the charm of the superior meaning they would acquire when read under this light; this idea of the authorship controlling our appreciation of the works themselves. We once knew a man overjoyed at the notice of his pamphlet in a leading newspaper. What range he gave his imagination! Who could have written it? Was it not Colonel Carbine, or Senator Tonitrus, or, at the least, Professor Maximilian? Yes, he could detect in the style that fine Roman hand. How it seemed the very voice of the refined and discerning public, inviting merit at last to consent to fame, and come up and take place in the reserved and authentic chairs! He carried the journal with haste to the sympathizing Cousin Matilda, who is so proud of all we do. But what dismay when the good Matilda, pleased with his pleasure, confessed she had written the criticism, and carried it with her own hands to the post-office! "Mr. Wordsworth," said Charles Lamb,[9] "allow me to introduce to you my only admirer."

Swedenborg threw a formidable theory into the world, that every soul existed in a society of souls, from which all its thoughts passed into it, as the blood of the mother circulates in her unborn child; and he noticed that, when in his bed, alternately sleeping and waking,—sleeping, he was surrounded by persons disputing and offering opinions on the one side and on the other side of a proposition; waking, the like suggestions occurred for and against the proposition as his own thoughts; sleeping again, he saw and heard the speakers as before: and this as often as he slept or waked. And if we expand the image, does it not look as if we men were thinking and talking out of an enormous antiquity, as if we stood, not in a coterie of prompters that filled a sitting-room, but in a circle of intelligences that reached through all thinkers, poets, inventors and wits, men and women, English, German, Celt, Aryan, Ninevite, Copt,—back to the first geometer, bard, mason, carpenter, planter, shepherd,—back to the first negro, who, with more health or better perception, gave a shriller sound or name for the thing he saw and dealt with? Our benefactors are as many as the children who invented speech, word by word. Language is a city to the building of which every human being brought a stone; yet he is no more to be credited with the grand result than the acaleph which adds a cell to the coral reef which is the basis of the continent.

7. John Wilson (1785–1854), Scottish writer and journalist, who wrote under the pen name of "Christopher North." Pierre Etienne Louis Dumont (1759–1829), Swiss-born writer who was secretary to Jeremy Bentham (see n. 3, p. 133). Mirabeau, see n. 4, p. 229. Sir Philip Francis (1740–1818), presumed author of the "Junius" letters (political invective written from the Whig point of view). James Hogg (1770–1835), Scottish poet, called the "Ettrick Shepherd," now known mainly for his novel *Private Memoirs and Confessions of a Justified Sinner* (1824), a Presbyterian fantasy; he was a friend of Wilson's.
8. Delia Bacon (1811–1859), though she did not invent the notion, spent her life trying to convince the world that Francis Bacon was the principal author of Shakespeare's works. Emerson came to believe that she was not entirely sane.
9. Charles Lamb (1775–1834), English essayist and critic.

Πάντα ῥεῖ: all things are in flux.[1] It is inevitable that you are indebted to the past. You are fed and formed by it. The old forest is decomposed for the composition of the new forest. The old animals have given their bodies to the earth to furnish through chemistry the forming race, and every individual is only a momentary fixation of what was yesterday another's, is today his and will belong to a third to-morrow. So it is in thought. Our knowledge is the amassed thought and experience of innumerable minds: our language, our science, our religion, our opinions, our fancies we inherited. Our country, customs, laws, our ambitions, and our notions of fit and fair, — all these we never made, we found them ready-made; we but quote them. Goethe frankly said, "What would remain to me if this art of appropriation were derogatory to genius? Every one of my writings has been furnished to me by a thousand different persons, a thousand things: wise and foolish have brought me, without suspecting it, the offering of their thoughts, faculties and experience. My work is an aggregation of beings taken from the whole of Nature; it bears the name of Goethe."

But there remains the indefeasible persistency of the individual to be himself. One leaf, one blade of grass, one meridian, does not resemble another. Every mind is different; and the more it is unfolded, the more pronounced is that difference. He must draw the elements into him for food, and, if they be granite and silex, will prefer them cooked by sun and rain, by time and art, to his hand. But, however received, these elements pass into the substance of his constitution, will be assimilated, and tend always to form, not a partisan, but a possessor of truth. To all that can be said of the preponderance of the Past, the single word Genius is a sufficient reply. The divine resides in the new. The divine never quotes, but is, and creates. The profound apprehension of the Present is Genius, which makes the Past forgotten. Genius believes its faintest presentiment against the testimony of all history; for it knows that facts are not ultimates, but that a state of mind is the ancestor of everything. And what is Originality? It is being, being one's self, and reporting accurately what we see and are. Genius is in the first instance, sensibility, the capacity of receiving just impressions from the external world, and the power of coördinating these after the laws of thought. It implies Will, or original force, for their right distribution and expression. If to this the sentiment of piety be added, if the thinker feels that the thought most strictly his own is not his own, and recognizes the perpetual suggestion of the Supreme Intellect, the oldest thoughts become new and fertile whilst he speaks them.

Originals never lose their value. There is always in them a style and weight of speech which the immanence of the oracle bestowed, and which cannot be counterfeited. Hence the permanence of the high poets. Plato, Cicero and Plutarch cite the poets in the manner in which Scripture is quoted in our churches. A phrase or a single word is adduced, with honoring emphasis, from Pindar, Hesiod or Euripides,[2] as precluding all argument, because thus had they said: importing that the bard spoke not his own, but the words of some god. True poets have always ascended to this lofty platform, and met this expectation. Shakspeare, Milton, Wordsworth, were very conscious of their responsibilities. When a man thinks happily, he finds no foot-track in the field he

1. The principal doctrine of Heraclitus.
2. Euripides (480–406 B.C.E.), along with Aeschylus and Sophocles one of the greatest Athenian dramatists of classical Greece. Pindar, see n. 3, p. 33. Hesiod (eighth century B.C.E.), Greek poet. His *Theogony* is an account of the origins of the world and the gods.

traverses. All spontaneous thought is irrespective of all else. Pindar uses this haughty defiance, as if it were impossible to find his sources: "There are many swift darts within my quiver, which have a voice for those with understanding; but to the crowd they need interpreters. He is gifted with genius who knoweth much by natural talent."

Our pleasure in seeing each mind take the subject to which it has a proper right is seen in mere fitness in time. He that comes second must needs quote him that comes first. The earliest describers of savage life, as Captain Cook's account of the Society Islands, or Alexander Henry's[3] travels among our Indian tribes, have a charm of truth and just point of view. Landsmen and sailors freshly come from the most civilized countries, and with no false expectation, no sentimentality yet about wild life, healthily receive and report what they saw, — seeing what they must, and using no choice; and no man suspects the superior merit of the description, until Châteaubriand, or Moore, or Campbell, or Byron,[4] or the artists, arrive, and mix so much art with their picture that the incomparable advantage of the first narrative appears. For the same reason we dislike that the poet should choose an antique or far-fetched subject for his muse, as if he avowed want of insight. The great deal always with the nearest. Only as braveries of too prodigal power can we pardon it, when the life of genius is so redundant that out of petulance it flings its fire into some old mummy, and, lo! it walks and blushes again here in the street.

We cannot overstate our debt to the Past, but the moment has the supreme claim. The Past is for us; but the sole terms on which it can become ours are its subordination to the Present. Only an inventor knows how to borrow, and every man is or should be an inventor. We must not tamper with the organic motion of the soul. 'T is certain that thought has its own proper motion, and the hints which flash from it, the words overheard at unawares by the free mind, are trustworthy and fertile when obeyed and not perverted to low and selfish account. This vast memory is only raw material. The divine gift is ever the instant life, which receives and uses and creates, and can well bury the old in the omnipotency with which Nature decomposes all her harvest for recomposition.

3. Alexander Henry (1739–1834), American fur trader and explorer. His *Travels and Adventures* was much prized by Thoreau, who cites it in his *Week on the Concord and Merrimack Rivers*. James Cook (1728–1779), celebrated English navigator and explorer of the South Pacific.
4. Byron (see n. 2, p. 162) set much of his poetry in foreign lands. François René de Chateaubriand (1768–1848), French writer and orator, wrote three novels set in North America based on his visit in 1791. Emerson heard him speak in the French Assembly in 1848. Campbell's (see n. 6, p. 287) *Gertrude of Wyoming* (1809) narrates the story of the destruction of a settlement at Wyoming, Pennsylvania, by American Indians under the command of Joseph Brant (see n. 3, p. 162) in 1778.

From The Dial

The Editors to the Reader[1]

We invite the attention of our countrymen to a new design. Probably not quite unexpected or unannounced will our Journal appear, though small pains have been taken to secure its welcome. Those, who have immediately acted in editing the present Number, cannot accuse themselves of any unbecoming forwardness in their undertaking, but rather of a backwardness, when they remember how often in many private circles the work was projected, how eagerly desired, and only postponed because no individual volunteered to combine and concentrate the free-will offerings of many coöperators. With some reluctance the present conductors of this work have yielded themselves to the wishes of their friends, finding something sacred and not to be withstood in the importunity which urged the production of a Journal in a new spirit.

As they have not proposed themselves to the work, neither can they lay any the least claim to an option or determination of the spirit in which it is conceived, or to what is peculiar in the design. In that respect, they have obeyed, though with great joy, the strong current of thought and feeling, which, for a few years past, has led many sincere persons in New England to make new demands on literature, and to reprobate that rigor of our conventions of religion and education which is turning us to stone, which renounces hope, which looks only backward, which asks only such a future as the past, which suspects improvement, and holds nothing so much in horror as new views and the dreams of youth.

With these terrors the conductors of the present Journal have nothing to do,—not even so much as a word of reproach to waste. They know that there is a portion of the youth and of the adult population of this country, who have not shared them; who have in secret or in public paid their vows to truth and freedom; who love reality too well to care for names, and who live by a Faith too earnest and profound to suffer them to doubt the eternity of its object, or to shake themselves free from its authority. Under the fictions and customs which occupied others, these have explored the Necessary, the Plain, the True, the Human,—and so gained a vantage ground, which commands the history of the past and the present.

No one can converse much with different classes of society in New England, without remarking the progress of a revolution. Those who share in it have no external organization, no badge, no creed, no name. They do not vote, or print, or even meet together. They do not know each other's faces or names. They are united only in a common love of truth, and love of its work. They are of all conditions and constitutions. Of these acolytes, if some are happily born and well bred, many are no doubt ill dressed, ill placed, ill made—with as many

---

1. Published in *The Dial* 1.1 (July 1840): 1–4. This Transcendentalist journal (1840–44) was edited first by Margaret Fuller and then by Emerson.

scars of hereditary vice as other men. Without pomp, without trumpet, in lonely and obscure places, in solitude, in servitude, in compunctions and privations, trudging beside the team in the dusty road, or drudging a hireling in other men's cornfields, schoolmasters, who teach a few children rudiments for a pittance, ministers of small parishes of the obscurer sects, lone women in dependent condition, matrons and young maidens, rich and poor, beautiful and hardfavored, without concert or proclamation of any kind, they have silently given in their several adherence to a new hope, and in all companies do signify a greater trust in the nature and resources of man, than the laws or the popular opinions will well allow.

This spirit of the time is felt by every individual with some difference,—to each one casting its light upon the objects nearest to his temper and habits of thought;—to one, coming in the shape of special reforms in the state; to another, in modifications of the various callings of men, and the customs of business; to a third, opening a new scope for literature and art; to a fourth, in philosophical insight; to a fifth, in the vast solitudes of prayer. It is in every form a protest against usage, and a search for principles. In all its movements, it is peaceable, and in the very lowest marked with a triumphant success. Of course, it rouses the opposition of all which it judges and condemns, but it is too confident in its tone to comprehend an objection, and so builds no outworks for possible defence against contingent enemies. It has the step of Fate, and goes on existing like an oak or a river, because it must.

In literature, this influence appears not yet in new books so much as in the higher tone of criticism. The antidote to all narrowness is the comparison of the record with nature, which at once shames the record and stimulates to new attempts. Whilst we look at this, we wonder how any book has been thought worthy to be preserved. There is somewhat in all life untranslatable into language. He who keeps his eye on that will write better than others, and think less of his writing, and of all writing. Every thought has a certain imprisoning as well as uplifting quality, and, in proportion to its energy on the will, refuses to become an object of intellectual contemplation. Thus what is great usually slips through our fingers, and it seems wonderful how a lifelike word ever comes to be written. If our Journal share the impulses of the time, it cannot now prescribe its own course. It cannot foretell in orderly propositions what it shall attempt. All criticism should be poetic; unpredictable; superseding, as every new thought does, all foregone thoughts, and making a new light on the whole world. Its brow is not wrinkled with circumspection, but serene, cheerful, adoring. It has all things to say, and no less than all the world for its final audience.

Our plan embraces much more than criticism; were it not so, our criticism would be naught. Everything noble is directed on life, and this is. We do not wish to say pretty or curious things, or to reiterate a few propositions in varied forms, but, if we can, to give expression to that spirit which lifts men to a higher platform, restores to them the religious sentiment, brings them worthy aims and pure pleasures, purges the inward eye, makes life less desultory, and, through raising man to the level of nature, takes away its melancholy from the landscape, and reconciles the practical with the speculative powers.

But perhaps we are telling our little story too gravely. There are always great arguments at hand for a true action, even for the writing of a few pages. There is nothing but seems near it and prompts it,—the sphere in the ecliptic, the sap in the apple tree,—every fact, every appearance seem to persuade to it.

Our means correspond with the ends we have indicated. As we wish not to multiply books, but to report life, our resources are therefore not so much the pens of practised writers, as the discourse of the living, and the portfolios which friendship has opened to us. From the beautiful recesses of private thought; from the experience and hope of spirits which are withdrawing from all old forms, and seeking in all that is new somewhat to meet their inappeasable longings; from the secret confession of genius afraid to trust itself to aught but sympathy; from the conversation of fervid and mystical pietists; from tear-stained diaries of sorrow and passion; from the manuscripts of young poets; and from the records of youthful taste commenting on old works of art; we hope to draw thoughts and feelings, which being alive can impart life.

And so with diligent hands and good intent we set down our Dial on the earth. We wish it may resemble that instrument in its celebrated happiness, that of measuring no hours but those of sunshine. Let it be one cheerful rational voice amidst the din of mourners and polemics. Or to abide by our chosen image, let it be such a Dial, not as the dead face of a clock, hardly even such as the Gnomon[2] in a garden, but rather such a Dial as is the Garden itself, in whose leaves and flowers and fruits the suddenly awakened sleeper is instantly apprised not what part of dead time, but what state of life and growth is now arrived and arriving.

Thoughts on Modern Literature[1]

There is no better illustration of the laws by which the world is governed than Literature. There is no luck in it. It proceeds by Fate. Every scripture is given by the inspiration of God. Every composition proceeds out of a greater or less depth of thought, and this is the measure of its effect. The highest class of books are those which express the moral element; the next, works of imagination; and the next, works of science;—all dealing in realities,—what ought to be, what is, and what appears. These, in proportion to the truth and beauty they involve, remain; the rest perish. They proceed out of the silent living mind to be heard again by the living mind. Of the best books it is hardest to write the history. Those books which are for all time are written indifferently at any time. For high genius is a day without night, a Caspian Ocean which hath no tides. And yet is literature in some sort a creature of time. Always the oracular soul is the source of thought, but always the occasion is administered by the low mediations of circumstance. Religion, Love, Ambition, War, some fierce antagonism, or it may be, some petty annoyance must break the round of perfect circulation, or no spark, no joy, no event can be. The poet rambling through the fields or the forest, absorbed in contemplation to that degree, that his walk is but a pretty dream, would never awake to precise thought, if the scream of an eagle, the cries of a crow or curlew near his head did not break the sweet continuity. Nay the finest lyrics of the poet come of this unequal parentage; the imps of matter beget such child on the soul, fair daughter of God. Nature mixes facts with thoughts to yield a poem. But the gift of immortality is of the mother's

2. The pointer on a sundial.
1. Published in *The Dial* 1.2 (Oct. 1840): 137–58.

side. In the spirit in which they are written is the date of their duration, and never in the magnitude of the facts. Everything lasts in proportion to its beauty. In proportion as it was not polluted by any wilfulness of the writer, but flowed from his mind after the divine order of cause and effect, it was not his but nature's and shared the sublimity of the sea and sky. That which is truly told, nature herself takes in charge against the whims and injustice of men. For ages, Herodotus was reckoned a credulous gossip in his descriptions of Africa, and now the sublime silent desert testifies through the mouths of Bruce, Lyons, Caillaud, Burckhardt, Belzoni,[2] to the truth of the calumniated historian.

And yet men imagine that books are dice, and have no merit in their fortune; that the trade and the favor of a few critics can get one book into circulation, and defeat another; and that in the production of these things the author has chosen and may choose to do thus and so. Society also wishes to assign subjects and methods to its writers. But neither reader nor author may intermeddle. You cannot reason at will in this and that other vein, but only as you must. You cannot make quaint combinations, and bring to the crucible and alembic of truth things far fetched or fantastic or popular, but your method and your subject are foreordained in all your nature, and in all nature, or ever the earth was, or it has no worth. All that gives currency still to any book, advertised in the morning's newspaper in London or Boston, is the remains of faith in the breast of men that not adroit book makers, but the inextinguishable soul of the universe reports of itself in articulate discourse to-day as of old. The ancients strongly expressed their sense of the unmanageableness of these words of the spirit by saying, that the God made his priest insane, took him hither and thither as leaves are whirled by the tempest. But we sing as we are bid. Our inspirations are very manageable and tame. Death and sin have whispered in the ear of the wild horse of Heaven, and he has become a dray and a hack. And step by step with the entrance of this era of ease and convenience, the belief in the proper Inspiration of man has departed.

Literary accomplishments, skill in grammar and rhetoric, knowledge of books, can never atone for the want of things which demand voice. Literature is a poor trick when it busies itself to make words pass for things. The most original book in the world is the Bible. This old collection of the ejaculations of love and dread, of the supreme desires and contritions of men proceeding out of the region of the grand and eternal, by whatsoever different mouths spoken, and through a wide extent of times and countries, seems, especially if you add to our canon the kindred sacred writings of the Hindoos, Persians, and Greeks, the alphabet of the nations,—and all posterior literature either the chronicle of facts under very inferior ideas, or, when it rises to sentiment, the combinations, analogies, or degradations of this. The elevation of this book may be measured by observing, how certainly all elevation of thought clothes itself in the words and forms of speech of that book. For the human mind is not now sufficiently erect to judge and correct that scripture. Whatever is majestically thought in a great moral element, instantly approaches this old Sanscrit. It is in the nature of things that the highest originality must be moral. The only person, who can be entirely independent of this fountain of literature and equal to it, must be a

---

2. See n. 7, p. 108. Herodotus, see n. 2, p. 109. Captain George Francis Lyon (1795–1832), Frédéric Caillaud (1787–1869), John Lewis Burckhardt (1784–1817), and Belzoni all published accounts of their travels in North Africa, to the Nile, and in the Near East.

prophet in his own proper person. Shakspeare, the first literary genius of the world, the highest in whom the moral is not the predominating element, leans on the Bible: his poetry supposes it. If we examine this brilliant influence— Shakspeare—as it lies in our minds, we shall find it reverent not only of the letter of this book, but of the whole frame of society which stood in Europe upon it, deeply indebted to the traditional morality, in short, compared with the tone of the Prophets, *secondary*. On the other hand, the Prophets do not imply the existence of Shakspeare or Homer,—advert to no books or arts, only to dread ideas and emotions. People imagine that the place, which the Bible holds in the world, it owes to miracles. It owes it simply to the fact that it came out of a profounder depth of thought than any other book, and the effect must be precisely proportionate. Gibbon[3] fancied that it was combinations of circumstances that gave Christianity its place in history. But in nature it takes an ounce to balance an ounce.

All just criticism will not only behold in literature the action of necessary laws, but must also oversee literature itself. The erect mind disparages all books. What are books? it saith: they can have no permanent value. How obviously initial they are to their authors. The books of the nations, the universal books, are long ago forgotten by those who wrote them, and one day we shall forget this primer learning. Literature is made up of a few ideas and a few fables. It is a heap of nouns and verbs enclosing an intuition or two. We must learn to judge books by absolute standards. When we are aroused to a life in ourselves, these traditional splendors of letters grow very pale and cold. Men seem to forget that all literature is ephemeral, and unwillingly entertain the supposition of its utter disappearance. They deem not only letters in general, but the best books in particular, parts of a preëstablished harmony, fatal, unalterable, and do not go behind Virgil and Dante, much less behind Moses, Ezekiel, and St. John. But no man can be a good critic of any book, who does not read it in a wisdom which transcends the instructions of any book, and treats the whole extant product of the human intellect as only one age revisable and reversible by him.

In our fidelity to the higher truth, we need not disown our debt in our actual state of culture, in the twilights of experience to these rude helpers. They keep alive the memory and the hope of a better day. When we flout all particular books as initial merely, we truly express the privilege of spiritual nature; but, alas, not the fact and fortune of this low Massachusetts and Boston, of these humble Junes and Decembers of mortal life. Our souls are not self-fed, but do eat and drink of chemical water and wheat. Let us not forget the genial miraculous force we have known to proceed from a book. We go musing into the vault of day and night; no constellation shines, no muse descends, the stars are white points, the roses brick-colored leaves, and frogs pipe, mice cheep, and wagons creak along the road. We return to the house and take up Plutarch or Augustine, and read a few sentences or pages, and lo! the air swarms with life; the front of heaven is full of fiery shapes; secrets of magnanimity and grandeur invite us on every hand; life is made up of them. Such is our debt to a book. Observe, moreover, that we ought to credit literature with much more than the bare word it gives us. I have just been reading poems which now in my memory shine with a certain steady, warm, autumnal light. That is not in their grammatical construction which they give me. If I analyze the sentences, it eludes me, but is the

3. See n. 9, p. 33.

genius and suggestion of the whole. Over every true poem lingers a certain wild beauty, immeasurable; a happiness lightsome and delicious fills the heart and brain,—as they say, every man walks environed by his proper atmosphere, extending to some distance around him. This beautiful result must be credited to literature also in casting its account.

In looking at the library of the Present Age we are first struck with the fact of the immense miscellany. It can hardly be characterized by any species of book, for every opinion old and new, every hope and fear, every whim and folly has an organ. It prints a vast carcass of tradition every year, with as much solemnity as a new revelation. Along with these it vents books that breathe of new morning, that seem to heave with the life of millions, books for which men and women peak and pine; books which take the rose out of the cheek of him that wrote them, and give him to the midnight a sad, solitary, diseased man; which leave no man where they found him, but make him better or worse; and which work dubiously on society, and seem to inoculate it with a venom before any healthy result appears.

In order to any complete view of the literature of the present age, an inquiry should include what it quotes, what it writes, and what it wishes to write. In our present attempt to enumerate some traits of the recent literature, we shall have somewhat to offer on each of these topics, but we cannot promise to set in very exact order what we have to say.

In the first place, it has all books. It reprints the wisdom of the world. How can the age be a bad one, which gives me Plato and Paul and Plutarch, St. Augustine, Spinoza, Chapman, Beaumont and Fletcher, Donne and Sir Thomas Browne,[4] beside its own riches? Our presses groan every year with new editions of all the select pieces of the first of mankind,—meditations, history, classifications, opinions, epics, lyrics, which the age adopts by quoting them. If we should designate favorite studies in which the age delights more than in the rest of this great mass of the permanent literature of the human race, one or two instances would be conspicuous. First; the prodigious growth and influence of the genius of Shakspeare, in the last one hundred and fifty years, is itself a fact of the first importance. It almost alone has called out the genius of the German nation into an activity, which spreading from the poetic into the scientific, religious, and philosophical domains, has made theirs now at last the paramount intellectual influence of the world, reacting with great energy on England and America. And thus, and not by mechanical diffusion, does an original genius work and spread himself. Society becomes an immense Shakspeare. Not otherwise could the poet be admired, nay, not even seen;—not until his living, conversing, and writing had diffused his spirit into the young and acquiring class, so that he had multiplied himself into a thousand sons, a thousand Shakspeares, and so understands himself.

Secondly; the history of freedom it studies with eagerness in civil, in religious, in philosophic history. It has explored every monument of Anglo-Saxon history and law, and mainly every scrap of printed or written paper remaining from the period of the English Commonwealth. It has, out of England, devoted much thought and pains to the history of philosophy. It has groped in all nations where was any literature for the early poetry not only the dramatic, but the

4. See n. 4, p. 312. Plato, see n. 4, p. 15. Paul, see n. 1, p. 3. Plutarch, see n. 7, p. 57. St. Augustine, see n. 3, p. 174. Spinoza, see n. 2, p. 170. Chapman, see n. 6, p. 193. Beaumont and Fletcher, see n. 9, p. 132. Donne, see n. 9, p. 253.

rudest lyric; for songs and ballads, the Nibelungen Lied, the poems of Hans Sachs and Henry of Alckmaer in Germany, for the Cid[5] in Spain, for the rough-cast verse of the interior nations of Europe, and in Britain for the ballads of Scotland and of Robinhood.

In its own books also, our age celebrates its wants, achievements, and hopes. A wide superficial cultivation, often a mere clearing and whitewashing, indicate the new taste in the hitherto neglected savage, whether of the cities or the fields, to know the arts and share the spiritual efforts of the refined. The time is marked by the multitude of writers. Soldiers, sailors, servants, nobles, princes, women, write books. The progress of trade and the facilities for locomotion have made the world nomadic again. Of course it is well informed. All facts are exposed. The age is not to be trifled with: it wishes to know who is who, and what is what. Let there be no ghost stories more. Send Humboldt and Bonpland[6] to explore Mexico, Guiana, and the Cordilleras. Let Captain Parry learn if there be a northwest passage to America, and Mr. Lander[7] learn the true course of the Niger. Pückler Muskau will go to Algiers, and Sir Francis Head[8] to the Pampas, to the Brünnens of Nassau, and to Canada. Then let us have charts true and Gazeteers correct. We will know where Babylon stood, and settle the topography of the Roman Forum. We will know whatever is to be known of Australasia, of Japan, of Persia, of Egypt, of Timbuctoo, of Palestine.

Thus Christendom has become a great reading-room; and its books have the convenient merits of the newspaper, its eminent propriety, and its superficial exactness of information. The age is well bred, knows the world, has no nonsense, and herein is well distinguished from the learned ages that preceded ours. That there is no fool like your learned fool, is a proverb plentifully illustrated in the history and writings of the English and European scholars for the half millenium that preceded the beginning of the eighteenth century. The best heads of their time build or occupy such card-house theories of religion, politics, and natural science, as a clever boy would now blow away. What stuff in Kepler, in Cardan, in Lord Bacon.[9] Montaigne,[1] with all his French wit and downright sense, is little better: a sophomore would wind him round his finger. Some of the Medical Remains of Lord Bacon in the book for his own use, "Of the Prolongation of Life," will move a smile in the unpoetical practitioner of the Medical College. They remind us of the drugs and practice of the leeches and enchanters of Eastern romance. Thus we find in his whimsical collection of astringents:

"A stomacher of scarlet cloth; whelps or young healthy boys applied to the stomach; hippocratic wines, so they be made of austere materials.

"8. To remember masticatories for the mouth.

"9. And orange flower water to be smelled or snuffed up.

---

5. See n. 3, p. 252. Nibelungen Lied, see n. 6, p. 142. Hans Sachs and Henry of Alckmaer, sixteenth-century German Meistersingers.
6. Baron Alexander von Humboldt (1769–1859), great German naturalist and botanist, traveled with Aimé Bonpland, a French botanist, throughout Latin America (1799–1804).
7. Richard L. Lander (1804–1834) and his brother John (1807–1839) traveled in Africa. Parry, see n. 3, p. 135.
8. Sir Francis Head (1793–1875), English soldier and traveler in South America and the Caribbean. Herman von Pückler-Muskau (1785–1871) also traveled in Africa.
9. See n. 3, p. 6. Kepler and Cardan, see n. 1, p. 194.
1. See n. 8, p. 155. See also Emerson's essay, p. 234.

"10. In the third hour after the sun is risen to take in air from some high and open place with a ventilation of *rosæ moschatæ* and fresh violets, and to stir the earth with infusion of wine and mint.

"17. To use once during supper time wine in which gold is quenched.

"26. Heroic desires.

"28. To provide always an apt breakfast.

"29. To do nothing against a man's genius."

To the substance of some of these specifics we have no objection. We think we should get no better at the Medical College to-day: and of all astringents we should reckon the best, "heroic desires," and "doing nothing against one's genius." Yet the principle of modern classification is different. In the same place, it is curious to find a good deal of pretty nonsense concerning the virtues of the ashes of a hedgehog, the heart of an ape, the moss that groweth upon the skull of a dead man unburied, and the comfort that proceeds to the system from wearing beads of amber, coral, and hartshorn;—or from rings of sea horse teeth worn for cramp;—to find all these masses of moonshine side by side with the gravest and most valuable observations.

The good Sir Thomas Browne recommends as empirical cures for the gout:

"To wear shoes made of a lion's skin.

"Try transplantation: Give poultices taken from the part to dogs.

"Try the magnified amulet of Muffetus, of spiders' legs worn in a deer's skin, or of tortoises' legs cut off from the living tortoise and wrapped up in the skin of a kid."

Burton's[2] Anatomy of Melancholy is an encyclopædia of authors and of opions, where one who should forage for exploded theories might easily load his panniers. In dæmonology, for example; "The air," he says, "is not so full of flies in summer as it is at all times of invisible devils. They counterfeit suns and moons, and sit on ships' masts. They cause whirlwinds on a sudden and tempestuous storms, which though our meteorologists generally refer to natural causes, yet I am of Bodine's[3] mind, they are more often caused by those aerial devils in their several quarters. Cardan gives much information concerning them. His father had one of them, an aerial devil, bound to him for eight and twenty years; as Aggrippa's[4] dog had a devil tied to his collar. Some think that Paracelsus[5] had one confined in his sword pommel. Others wear them in rings. At Hammel in Saxony, the devil in the likeness of a pied piper carried away 130 children that were never after seen."

All this sky-full of cobwebs is now forever swept clean away. Another race is born. Humboldt and Herschel, Davy and Arago, Malthus and Bentham[6] have arrived. If Robert Burton should be quoted to represent the army of scholars, who have furnished a contribution to his moody pages, Horace Walpole,[7] whose letters circulate in the libraries, might be taken with some fitness to represent the spirit of much recent literature. He has taste, common sense, love of facts, impatience of humbug, love of history, love of splendor, love of justice,

2. See n. 6, p. 199.
3. Jean Bodin (1530–1596), French jurist and natural philosopher.
4. See n. 1, p. 194.
5. See n. 1, p. 194.
6. See n. 3, p. 133. Herschel, see n. 6, p. 63. Davy, see n. 1, p. 65. François Dominique Arago (1786–1853), French scientist. Malthus, see n. 5, p. 219.
7. See n. 6, p. 158.

and the sentiment of honor among gentlemen; but no life whatever of the higher faculties, no faith, no hope, no aspiration, no question touching the secret of nature.

The favorable side of this research and love of facts is the bold and systematic criticism, which has appeared in every department of literature. From Wolf's[8] attack upon the authenticity of the Homeric Poems, dates a new epoch in learning. Ancient history has been found to be not yet settled. It is to be subjected to common sense. It is to be cross examined. It is to be seen, whether its traditions will consist not with universal belief, but with universal experience. Neibuhr has sifted Roman history by the like methods. Heeren has made good essays towards ascertaining the necessary facts in the Grecian, Persian, Assyrian, Egyptian, Ethiopic, Carthaginian nations. English history has been analyzed by Turner, Hallam, Brodie, Lingard, Palgrave.[9] Goethe[1] has gone the circuit of human knowledge, as Lord Bacon did before him, writing True or False on every article. Bentham has attempted the same scrutiny in reference to Civil Law. Pestalozzi[2] out of a deep love undertook the reform of education. The ambition of Coleridge in England embraced the whole problem of philosophy; to find, that is, a foundation in thought for everything that existed in fact. The German philosophers, Schelling, Kant, Fichte, have applied their analysis to nature and thought with an antique boldness. There can be no honest inquiry, which is not better than acquiescence. Inquiries, which once looked grave and vital no doubt, change their appearance very fast, and come to look frivolous beside the later queries to which they gave occasion.

This skeptical activity, at first directed on circumstances and historical views deemed of great importance, soon penetrated deeper than Rome or Egypt, than history or institutions, or the vocabulary of metaphysics, namely, into the thinker himself, and into every function he exercises. The poetry and the speculation of the age are marked by a certain philosophic turn, which discriminates them from the works of earlier times. The poet is not content to see how "fair hangs the apple from the rock," "what music a sunbeam awoke in the groves," nor of Hardiknute,[3] how "stately steppes he east the way, and stately steppes he west," but he now revolves, What is the apple to me? and what the birds to me? and what is Hardiknute to me? and what am I? And this is called *subjectiveness*, as the eye is withdrawn from the object and fixed on the subject or mind.

We can easily concede that a steadfast tendency of this sort appears in modern literature. It is the new consciousness of the one mind which predominates in criticism. It is the uprise of the soul and not the decline. It is founded on that insatiable demand for unity—the need to recognise one nature in all the variety of objects,—which always characterizes a genius of the first order. Accustomed always to behold the presence of the universe in every part, the soul will not condescend to look at any new part as a stranger, but saith,—"I know all already, and what art thou? Show me thy relations to me, to all, and I will entertain thee also."

<hr>

8. Friedrich August Wolf (1759–1824), German philologist and Homeric scholar.
9. All English historians. Sharon Turner (1768–1847). Hallam, see n. 3, p. 327. George Brodie (1786–1867). John Lingard (1771–1831). Sir Francis Palgrave (1788–1861).
1. See n. 6, p. 42.
2. See n. 4, p. 68.
3. Or Hardicanute, king of England (1040–42). The lines are from a ballad.

There is a pernicious ambiguity in the use of the term *subjective*. We say, in accordance with the general view I have stated, that the single soul feels its right to be no longer confounded with numbers, but itself to sit in judgment on history and literature, and to summon all facts and parties before its tribunal. And in this sense the age is subjective.

But, in all ages, and now more, the narrow-minded have no interest in anything but its relation to their personality. What will help them to be delivered from some burden, eased in some circumstance, flattered, or pardoned, or enriched, what will help to marry or to divorce them, to prolong or to sweeten life, is sure of their interest, and nothing else. Every form under the whole heaven they behold in this most partial light or darkness of intense selfishness, until we hate their being. And this habit of intellectual selfishness has acquired in our day the fine name of subjectiveness.

Nor is the distinction between these two habits to be found in the circumstance of using the first person singular, or reciting facts and feelings of personal history. A man may say *I*, and never refer to himself as an individual; and a man may recite passages of his life with no feeling of egotism. Nor need a man have a vicious subjectiveness because he deals in abstract propositions.

But the criterion, which discriminates these two habits in the poet's mind, is the tendency of his composition; namely, whether it leads us to nature, or to the person of the writer. The great always introduce us to facts; small men introduce us always to themselves. The great man, even whilst he relates a private fact personal to him, is really leading us away from him to an universal experience. His own affection is in nature, in *What is*, and, of course, all his communication leads outward to it, starting from whatsoever point. The great never with their own consent become a load on the minds they instruct. The more they draw us to them, the farther from them or more independent of them we are, because they have brought us to the knowledge of somewhat deeper than both them and us. The great never hinder us; for, as the Jews had a custom of laying their beds north and south, founded on an opinion that the path of God was east and west, and they would not desecrate by the infirmities of sleep the Divine circuits, so the activity of the good is coincident with the axle of the world, with the sun and moon, with the course of the rivers and of the winds, with the stream of laborers in the street, and with all the activity and well being of the race. The great lead us to nature, and, in our age, to metaphysical nature, to the invisible awful facts, to moral abstractions, which are not less nature than is a river or a coal mine; nay, they are far more nature, but its essence and soul.

But the weak and evil, led also to analyze, saw nothing in thought but luxury. Thought for the selfish became selfish. They invited us to contemplate nature, and showed us an abominable self. Would you know the genius of the writer? Do not enumerate his talents or his feats, but ask thyself, What spirit is he of? Do gladness and hope and fortitude flow from his page into thy heart? Has he led thee to nature because his own soul was too happy in beholding her power and love; or is his passion for the wilderness only the sensibility of the sick, the exhibition of a talent, which only shines whilst you praise it; which has no root in the character, and can thus minister to the vanity but not to the happiness of the possessor; and which derives all its eclat from our conventional education, but would not make itself intelligible to the wise man of another age or country? The water we wash with never speaks of itself, nor does fire, or wind, or tree. Neither does the noble natural man: he yields himself to your occasion and use; but his act expresses a reference to universal good.

Another element of the modern poetry akin to this subjective tendency, or rather the direction of that same on the question of resources, is, the Feeling of the Infinite. Of the perception now fast becoming a conscious fact,—that there is One Mind, and that all the powers and privileges which lie in any, lie in all; that I as a man may claim and appropriate whatever of true or fair or good or strong has anywhere been exhibited; that Moses and Confucius, Montaigne and Leibnitz are not so much individuals as they are parts of man and parts of me, and my intelligence proves them my own,—literature is far the best expression. It is true, this is not the only nor the obvious lesson it teaches. A selfish commerce and government have caught the eye and usurped the hand of the masses. It is not to be contested that selfishness and the senses write the laws under which we live, and that the street seems to be built, and the men and women in it moving not in reference to pure and grand ends, but rather to very short and sordid ones. Perhaps no considerable minority, perhaps no one man leads a quite clean and lofty life. What then? We concede in sadness the fact. But we say that these low customary ways are not all that survives in human beings. There is that in us which mutters, and that which groans, and that which triumphs, and that which aspires. There are facts on which men of the world superciliously smile, which are worth all their trade and politics, the impulses, namely, which drive young men into gardens and solitary places, and cause extravagant gestures, starts, distortions of the countenance, and passionate exclamations; sentiments, which find no aliment or language for themselves on the wharves, in court, or market, but which are soothed by silence, by darkness, by the pale stars, and the presence of nature. All over the modern world the educated and susceptible have betrayed their discontent with the limits of our municipal life, and with the poverty of our dogmas of religion and philosophy. They betray this impatience by fleeing for resource to a conversation with nature—which is courted in a certain moody and exploring spirit, as if they anticipated a more intimate union of man with the world than has been known in recent ages. Those who cannot tell what they desire or expect, still sigh and struggle with indefinite thoughts and vast wishes. The very child in the nursery prattles mysticism, and doubts and philosophizes. A wild striving to express a more inward and infinite sense characterizes the works of every art. The music of Beethoven is said by those who understand it, to labor with vaster conceptions and aspirations than music has attempted before. This Feeling of the Infinite has deeply colored the poetry of the period. This new love of the vast, always native in Germany, was imported into France by De Staël, appeared in England in Coleridge, Wordsworth, Byron, Shelley, Felicia Hemans, and finds a most genial climate in the American mind. Scott and Crabbe,[4] who formed themselves on the past, had none of this tendency; their poetry is objective. In Byron, on the other hand, it predominates; but in Byron it is blind, it sees not its true end—an infinite good, alive and beautiful, a life nourished on absolute beatitudes, descending into nature to behold itself reflected there. His will is

4. George Crabbe (1754–1832), English poet. Madame de Staël, see n. 6, p. 42; see also selections from her *Germany*, (p. 573). Coleridge, see n. 2, p. 31. Wordsworth, see n. 5, p. 67. Byron, see n. 2, p. 162. Felicia Hemans (1793–1835), popular English poet.

perverted, he worships the accidents of society, and his praise of nature is thieving and selfish.

Nothing certifies the prevalence of this taste in the people more than the circulation of the poems,—one would say, most incongruously united by some bookseller,—of Coleridge, Shelley, and Keats. The only unity is in the subjectiveness and the aspiration common to the three writers. Shelley, though a poetic mind, is never a poet. His muse is uniformly imitative; all his poems composite. A good English scholar he is, with ear, taste, and memory, much more, he is a character full of noble and prophetic traits; but imagination, the original, authentic fire of the bard, he has not. He is clearly modern, and shares with Richter, Chateaubriand, Manzoni,[5] and Wordsworth, the feeling of the infinite, which so labors for expression in their different genius. But all his lines are arbitrary, not necessary. When we read poetry, the mind asks,—Was this verse one of twenty which the author might have written as well; or is this what that man was created to say? But, whilst every line of the true poet will be genuine, he is in a boundless power and freedom to say a million things. And the reason why he can say one thing well, is because his vision extends to the sight of all things, and so he describes each as one who knows many and all.

The fame of Wordsworth is a leading fact in modern literature, when it is considered how hostile his genius at first seemed to the reigning taste, and with what feeble poetic talents his great and steadily growing dominion has been established. More than any other poet his success has been not his own, but that of the idea which he shared with his coevals, and which he has rarely succeeded in adequately expressing. The Excursion[6] awakened in every lover of nature the right feeling. We saw stars shine, we felt the awe of mountains, we heard the rustle of the wind in the grass, and knew again the ineffable secret of solitude. It was a great joy. It was nearer to nature than anything we had before. But the interest of the poem ended almost with the narrative of the influences of nature on the mind of the Boy, in the first book. Obviously for that passage the poem was written, and with the exception of this and of a few strains of the like character in the sequel, the whole poem was dull. Here was no poem, but here was poetry, and a sure index where the subtle muse was about to pitch her tent and find the argument of her song. It was the human soul in these last ages striving for a just publication of itself. Add to this, however, the great praise of Wordsworth, that more than any other contemporary bard he is pervaded with a reverence of somewhat higher than (conscious) thought. There is in him that property common to all great poets, a wisdom of humanity, which is superior to any talents which they exert. It is the wisest part of Shakspeare and of Milton. For they are poets by the free course which they allow to the informing soul, which through their eyes beholdeth again and blesseth the things which it hath made. The soul is superior to its knowledge, wiser than any of its works.

With the name of Wordsworth rises to our recollection the name of his contemporary and friend, Walter Savage Landor[7]—a man working in a very different and peculiar spirit, yet one whose genius and accomplishments deserve a wiser criticism than we have yet seen applied to them, and the rather that his

---

5. Alessandro Manzoni (1785–1873), best known for his great novel *I Promessi Sposi* (The betrothed; 1827). Jean Paul Friedrich Richter (1763–1825), known simply as Jean Paul, German novelist and aesthete given to sentimentality and ironic humor. Chateaubriand, see n. 4, p. 330.
6. A poem in nine books published by Wordsworth in 1814.
7. See n. 7, p. 325.

name does not readily associate itself with any school of writers. Of Thomas Carlyle, also we shall say nothing at this time, since the quality and the energy of his influence on the youth of this country will require at our hands ere long a distinct and faithful acknowledgment.

But of all men he, who has united in himself and that in the most extraordinary degree the tendencies of the era, is the German poet, naturalist, and philosopher, Goethe. Whatever the age inherited or invented, he made his own. He has owed to Commerce and to the victories of the Understanding, all their spoils. Such was his capacity, that the magazines of the world's ancient or modern wealth, which arts and intercourse and skepticism could command— he wanted them all. Had there been twice so much, he could have used it as well. Geologist, mechanic, merchant, chemist, king, radical, painter, composer,—all worked for him, and a thousand men seemed to look through his eyes. He learned as readily as other men breathe. Of all the men of this time, not one has seemed so much at home in it as he. He was not afraid to live. And in him this encyclopædia of facts, which it has been the boast of the age to compile, wrought an equal effect. He was knowing; he was brave; he was clean from all narrowness; he has a perfect propriety and taste,—a quality by no means common to the German writers. Nay, since the earth, as we said, had become a reading-room, the new opportunities seem to have aided him to be that resolute realist he is, and seconded his sturdy determination to see things for what they are. To look at him, one would say, there was never an observer before. What sagacity, what industry of observation! to read his record is a frugality of time, for you shall find no word that does not stand for a thing, and he is of that comprehension, which can see the value of truth. His love of nature has seemed to give a new meaning to that word. There was never man more domesticated in this world than he. And he is an apology for the analytic spirit of the period, because, of his analysis, always wholes were the result. All conventions, all traditions he rejected. And yet he felt his entire right and duty to stand before and try and judge every fact in nature. He thought it necessary to dot round with his own pen the entire sphere of knowables; and for many of his stories, this seems the only reason: Here is a piece of humanity I had hitherto omitted to sketch;— take this. He does not say so in syllables,—yet a sort of conscientious feeling he had to be *up* to the universe, is the best account and apology for many of them. He shared also the subjectiveness of the age, and that too in both the senses I have discriminated. With the sharpest eye for form, color, botany, engraving, medals, persons, and manners, he never stopped at surface, but pierced the purpose of a thing, and studied to reconcile that purpose with his own being. What he could so reconcile was good; what he could not, was false. Hence a certain greatness encircles every fact he treats; for to him it has a soul, an eternal reason why it was so, and not otherwise. This is the secret of that deep realism, which went about among all objects he beheld, to find the cause why they must be what they are. It was with him a favorite task to find a theory of every institution, custom, art, work of art, which he observes. Witness his explanation of the Italian mode of reckoning the hours of the day, as growing out of the Italian climate; of the obelisk of Egypt, as growing out of a common natural fracture in the granite parallelopiped in Upper Egypt; of the Doric architecture, and the Gothic; of the Venetian music of the gondolier originating in the habit of the fishers' wives of the Lido singing to their husbands on the sea; of the Amphitheatre, which is the enclosure of the natural cup of heads that arranges itself round every spectacle in the street; of the coloring of Titian and Paul Veronese,[8] which one may verify in the common daylight in Venice every afternoon; of the Carnival at Rome; of the domestic rural architecture in Italy; and many the like examples.

But also that other vicious subjectiveness, that vice of the time, infected him also. We are provoked with his Olympian self-complacency, the patronizing air with which he vouchsafes to tolerate the genius and performances of other mortals, "the good Hiller," "our excellent Kant," "the friendly Wieland," &c. &c. There is a good letter from Wieland to Merck,[9] in which Wieland relates that Goethe read to a select party his journal of a tour in Switzerland with the Grand Duke, and their passage through Valois and over the St. Gothard. "It was," says Wieland, "as good as Xenophon's Anabasis. The piece is one of his most masterly productions, and is thought and written with the greatness peculiar to him. The fair hearers were enthusiastic at the nature in this piece; I liked the sly art in the composition, whereof they saw nothing, still better. It is a true poem, so concealed is the art too. But what most remarkably in this as in all his other works distinguishes him from Homer and Shakspeare, is, that the Me, the *Ille ego*, everywhere glimmers through, although without any boasting and with an infinite fineness." This subtle element of egotism in Goethe certainly does not seem to deform his compositions, but to lower the moral influence of the man. He differs from all the great in the total want of frankness. Whoso saw Milton, whoso saw Shakspeare, saw them do their best, and utter their whole heart manlike among their brethren. No man was permitted to call Goethe brother. He hid himself, and worked always to astonish, which is an egotism, and therefore little.

If we try Goethe by the ordinary canons of criticism, we should say that his thinking is of great altitude, and all level;—not a succession of summits, but a high Asiatic table land. Dramatic power, the rarest talent in literature, he has very little. He has an eye constant to the fact of life, and that never pauses in its advance. But the great felicities, the miracles of poetry, he has never. It is all design with him, just thought and instructed expression, analogies, allusion, illustration, which knowledge and correct thinking supply; but of Shakspeare and the transcendant muse, no syllable. Yet in the court and law to which we ordinarily speak, and without adverting to absolute standards, we claim for him the praise of truth, of fidelity to his intellectual nature. He is the king of all scholars. In these days and in this country, where the scholars are few and idle, where men read easy books and sleep after dinner, it seems as if no book could so safely be put in the hands of young men as the letters of Goethe, which attest the incessant activity of this man to eighty years, in an endless variety of studies with uniform cheerfulness and greatness of mind. They cannot be read without shaming us into an emulating industry. Let him have the praise of the love of truth. We think, when we contemplate the stupendous glory of the world, that it were life enough for one man merely to lift his hands and cry with St. Augustine, "Wrangle who pleases, I will wonder." Well, this he did. Here was a man, who, in the feeling that the thing itself was so admirable as to leave all comment behind, went up and down from object to object, lifting the veil from

---

8. Veronese, Paolo Cagliari (1528–1588), Venetian painter. Titian, Tiziano Vecelli (ca. 1477–1576), great master of the Venetian school of painting.
9. Johann Heinrich Merck (1741–1791), German writer and friend of Wieland's (see n. 3, p. 254).

everyone, and did no more. What he said of Lavater, may trulier be said of him, that "it was fearful to stand in the presence of one, before whom all the boundaries within which nature has circumscribed our being were laid flat." His are the bright and terrible eyes, which meet the modern student in every sacred chapel of thought, in every public enclosure.

But now, that we may not seem to dodge the question which all men ask, nor pay a great man so ill a compliment as to praise him only in the conventional and comparative speech, let us honestly record our thought upon the total worth and influence of this genius. Does he represent not only the achievement of that age in which he lived, but that which it would be and is now becoming? And what shall we think of that absence of the moral sentiment, that singular equivalence to him of good and evil in action, which discredits his compositions to the pure? The spirit of his biography, of his poems, of his tales, is identical, and we may here set down by way of comment on his genius the impressions recently awakened in us by the story of Wilhelm Meister.[1]

All great men have written proudly, nor cared to explain. They knew that the intelligent reader would come at last, and would thank them. So did Dante, so did Machiavel. Goethe has done this in Meister. We can fancy him saying to himself;—There are poets enough of the ideal; let me paint the Actual, as, after years of dreams, it will still appear and reappear to wise men. That all shall right itself in the long Morrow, I may well allow, and my novel may easily wait for the same regeneration. The age, that can damn it as false and falsifying, will see that it is deeply one with the genius and history of all the centuries. I have given my characters a bias to error. Men have the same. I have let mischances befall instead of good fortune. They do so daily. And out of many vices and misfortunes, I have let a great success grow, as I had known in my own and many other examples. Fierce churchmen and effeminate aspirants will chide and hate my name, but every keen beholder of life will justify my truth, and will acquit me of prejudging the cause of humanity by painting it with this morose fidelity. To a profound soul is not austere truth the sweetest flattery?

Yes, O Goethe! but the ideal is truer than the actual. That is ephemeral, but this changes not. Moreover, because nature is moral, that mind only can see, in which the same order entirely obtains. An interchangeable Truth, Beauty, and Goodness, each wholly interfused in the other, must make the humors of that eye, which would see causes reaching to their last effect and reproducing the world forever. The least inequality of mixture, the excess of one element over the other, in that degree diminishes the transparency of things, makes the world opaque to the observer, and destroys so far the value of his experience. No particular gifts can countervail this defect. In reading Meister, I am charmed with the insight; to use a phrase of Ben Jonson's, "it is rammed with life." I find there actual men and women even too faithfully painted. I am, moreover, instructed in the possibility of a highly accomplished society, and taught to look for great talent and culture under a grey coat. But this is all. The limits of artificial society are never quite out of sight. The vicious conventions, which hem us in like prison walls, and which the poet should explode at his touch, stand for all they are worth in the newspaper. I am never lifted above myself. I am not transported out of the dominion of the senses, or cheered with an infinite tenderness, or armed with a grand trust.

---

1. Goethe's famous novel was translated by Thomas Carlyle as *Wilhelm Meister's Travels* (1827).

Goethe, then, must be set down as the poet of the Actual, not of the Ideal; the poet of limitation, not of possibility; of this world, and not of religion and hope; in short, if I may say so, the poet of prose, and not of poetry. He accepts the base doctrine of Fate, and gleans what straggling joys may yet remain out of its ban. He is like a banker or a weaver with a passion for the country, he steals out of the hot streets before sunrise, or after sunset, or on a rare holiday, to get a draught of sweet air, and a gaze at the magnificence of summer, but dares not break from his slavery and lead a man's life in a man's relation to nature. In that which should be his own place, he feels like a truant, and is scourged back presently to his task and his cell. Poetry is with Goethe thus external, the gilding of the chain, the mitigation of his fate; but the muse never essays those thunder-tones, which cause to vibrate the sun and the moon, which dissipate by dreadful melody all this iron network of circumstance, and abolish the old heavens and the old earth before the free-will or Godhead of man. That Goethe had not a moral perception proportionate to his other powers, is not then merely a circumstance, as we might relate of a man that he had or had not the sense of tune or an eye for colors; but it is the cardinal fact of health or disease; since, lacking this, he failed in the high sense to be a creator, and with divine endowments drops by irreversible decree into the common history of genius. He was content to fall into the track of vulgar poets, and spend on common aims his splendid endowments, and has declined the office proffered to now and then a man in many centuries in the power of his genius—of a Redeemer of the human mind. He has written better than other poets, only as his talent was subtler, but the ambition of creation he refused. Life for him is prettier, easier, wiser, decenter, has a gem or two more on its robe, but its old eternal burden is not relieved; no drop of healthier blood flows yet in its veins. Let him pass. Humanity must wait for its physician still at the side of the road, and confess as this man goes out that they have served it better, who assured it out of the innocent hope in their hearts that a Physician will come, than this majestic Artist, with all the treasuries of wit, of science, and of power at his command.

The criticism, which is not so much spoken as felt in reference to Goethe, instructs us directly in the hope of literature. We feel that a man gifted like him should not leave the world as he found it. It is true, though somewhat sad, that every fine genius teaches us how to blame himself. Being so much, we cannot forgive him for not being more. When one of these grand monads is incarnated, whom nature seems to design for eternal men and draw to her bosom, we think that the old wearinesses of Europe and Asia, the trivial forms of daily life will now end, and a new morning break on us all. What is Austria? What is England? What is our graduated and petrified social scale of ranks and employments? Shall not a poet redeem us from these idolatries, and pale their legendary lustre before the fires of the Divine Wisdom which burn in his heart? All that in our sovereign moments each of us has divined of the powers of thought, all the hints of omnipresence and energy which we have caught, this man should unfold and constitute facts.

And this is the insatiable craving which alternately saddens and gladdens men at this day. The Doctrine of the Life of Man established after the truth through all his faculties;—this is the thought which the literature of this hour meditates and labors to say. This is that which tunes the tongue and fires the eye and sits in the silence of the youth. Verily it will not long want articulate and melodious expression. There is nothing in the heart but comes presently to the lips. The very depth of the sentiment, which is the author of all the cutaneous life we see, is guarantee for the riches of science and of song in the age to come. He, who doubts whether this age or this country can yield any contribution to the literature of the world, only betrays his own blindness to the necessities of the human soul. Has the power of poetry ceased, or the need? Have the eyes ceased to see that which they would have, and which they have not? Have they ceased to see other eyes? Are there no lonely, anxious, wondering children, who must tell their tale? Are we not evermore whipped by thoughts;

> "In sorrow steeped and steeped in love
> Of thoughts not yet incarnated?"

The heart beats in this age as of old, and the passions are busy as ever. Nature has not lost one ringlet of her beauty, one impulse of resistance and valor. From the necessity of loving none are exempt, and he that loves must utter his desires. A charm as radiant as beauty ever beamed, a love that fainteth at the sight of its object, is new to-day.

> "The world does not run smoother than of old,
> There are sad haps that must be told."

Man is not so far lost but that he suffers ever the great Discontent, which is the elegy of his loss and the prediction of his recovery. In the gay saloon he laments that these figures are not what Raphael and Guercino[2] painted. Withered though he stand and trifler though he be, the august spirit of the world looks out from his eyes. In his heart he knows the ache of spiritual pain, and his thought can animate the sea and land. What then shall hinder the Genius of the time from speaking its thought? It cannot be silent, if it would. It will write in a higher spirit, and a wider knowledge, and with a grander practical aim, than ever yet guided the pen of poet. It will write the annals of a changed world, and record the descent of principles into practice, of love into Government, of love into Trade. It will describe the new heroic life of man, the now unbelieved possibility of simple living and of clean and noble relations with men. Religion will bind again these that were sometime frivolous, customary, enemies, skeptics, self-seekers, into a joyful reverence for the circumambient Whole, and that which was ecstasy shall become daily bread.

2. Gian Francesco Barbieri, known as Il Guercino (1591–1666), Italian painter. Raphael, see n. 3, p. 86.

Miscellanies on His Contemporaries and His Times

From An Address . . . on . . . the Emancipation of the
Negroes in the British West Indies[1]

1 August 1844

Friends and Fellow Citizens,

We are met to exchange congratulations on the anniversary of an event singular in the history of civilization; a day of reason; of the clear light; of that which makes us better than a flock of birds and beasts: a day, which gave the immense fortification of a fact, — of gross history, — to ethical abstractions. It was the settlement, as far as a great Empire was concerned, of a question on which almost every leading citizen in it had taken care to record his vote; one which for many years absorbed the attention of the best and most eminent of mankind. I might well hesitate, coming from other studies, and without the smallest claim to be a special laborer in this work of humanity, to undertake to set this matter before you; which ought rather to be done by a strict cooperation of many well-advised persons; but I shall not apologize for my weakness. In this cause, no man's weakness is any prejudice; it has a thousand sons; if one man cannot speak, ten others can; and whether by the wisdom of its friends, or by the folly of the adversaries; by speech and by silence; by doing and by omitting to do, it goes forward. Therefore I will speak, — or, not I, but the might of liberty in my weakness. The subject is said to have the property of making dull men eloquent.

It has been in all men's experience a marked effect of the enterprise in behalf of the African, to generate an overbearing and defying spirit. The institution of slavery seems to its opponent to have but one side, and he feels that none but a stupid or a malignant person can hesitate on a view of the facts. Under such an impulse, I was about to say, If any cannot speak, or cannot hear the words of freedom, let him go hence, — I had almost said, Creep into your grave, the universe has no need of you! But I have thought better: let him not go. When we consider what remains to be done for this interest, in this country, the dictates of humanity make us tender of such as are not yet persuaded. The hardest selfishness is to be borne with. Let us withhold every reproachful, and, if we can, every indignant remark. In this cause, we must renounce our temper, and the risings of pride. If there be any man who thinks the ruin of a race of men a small matter, compared with the last decoration and completions of his own comfort, — who would not so

---

1. Emerson was invited to give this address in Concord by the Women's Anti-Slavery Society. In addition to Emerson, who was "the orator of the day," Frederick Douglass, among others, delivered a lecture. Slavery had been partially abolished in the British West Indies in 1834; full emancipation came on August 1, 1838.

much as part with his ice-cream, to save them from rapine and manacles, I think, I must not hesitate to satisfy that man, that also his cream and vanilla are safer and cheaper, by placing the negro nation on a fair footing, than by robbing them. If the Virginian piques himself on the picturesque luxury of his vassalage, on the heavy Ethiopian manners of his house-servants, their silent obedience, their hue of bronze, their turbaned heads, and would not exchange them for the more intelligent but precarious hired-service of whites, I shall not refuse to show him, that when their free-papers are made out, it will still be their interest to remain on his estate, and that the oldest planters of Jamaica are convinced, that it is cheaper to pay wages, than to own the slave.

The history of mankind interests us only as it exhibits a steady gain of truth and right, in the incessant conflict which it records, between the material and the moral nature. From the earliest monuments, it appears, that one race was victim, and served the other races. In the oldest temples of Egypt, negro captives are painted on the tombs of kings, in such attitudes as to show that they are on the point of being executed; and Herodotus, our oldest historian, relates that the Troglodytes[2] hunted the Ethiopians in four-horse-chariots. From the earliest time, the negro has been an article of luxury to the commercial nations. So has it been, down to the day that has just dawned on the world. Language must be raked, the secrets of slaughter-houses and infamous holes that cannot front the day, must be ransacked, to tell what negro-slavery has been. These men, our benefactors, as they are producers of corn and wine, of coffee, of tobacco, of cotton, of sugar, of rum, and brandy, gentle and joyous themselves, and producers of comfort and luxury for the civilized world,—there seated in the finest climates of the globe, children of the sun,—I am heart-sick when I read how they came there, and how they are kept there. Their case was left out of the mind and out of the heart of their brothers. The prizes of society, the trumpet of fame, the privileges of learning, of culture, of religion, the decencies and joys of marriage, honor, obedience, personal authority, and a perpetual melioration into a finer civility, these were for all, but not for them. For the negro, was the slave-ship to begin with, in whose filthy hold he sat in irons, unable to lie down; bad food, and insufficiency of that; disfranchisement; no property in the rags that covered him; no marriage, no right in the poor black woman that cherished him in her bosom,—no right to the children of his body; no security from the humors, none from the crimes, none from the appetites of his master: toil, famine, insult, and flogging; and, when he sunk in the furrow, no wind of good fame blew over him, no priest of salvation visited him with glad tidings: but he went down to death, with dusky dreams of African shadow-catchers and Obeahs[3] hunting him. Very sad was the negro tradition, that the Great Spirit, in the beginning, offered the black man, whom he loved better than the buckra[4] or white, his choice of two boxes, a big and a little one. The black man was greedy, and chose the largest. "The buckra box was full up with pen, paper, and whip, and the negro box with hoe and bill; and hoe and bill for negro to this day."

But the crude element of good in human affairs must work and ripen, spite of whips, and plantation-laws, and West Indian interest. Conscience rolled on its pillow, and could not sleep. We sympathize very tenderly here with the poor ag-

2. The name given by Greeks to various primitive tribes known for crude and uncivilized behavior. Herodotus, see n. 2, p. 109.
3. Charms or fetishes, here used to mean "Obeah men," or witch doctors.
4. Disparaging term used by blacks for whites.

grieved planter, of whom so many unpleasant things are said; but if we saw the whip applied to old men, to tender women; and, undeniably, though I shrink to say so, — pregnant women set in the treadmill for refusing to work, when, not they, but the eternal law of animal nature refused to work; — if we saw men's backs flayed with cowhides, and "hot rum poured on, superinduced with brine or pickle, rubbed in with a cornhusk, in the scorching heat of the sun;" — if we saw the runaways hunted with blood-hounds into swamps and hills; and, in cases of passion, a planter throwing his negro into a copper of boiling cane-juice, — if we saw these things with eyes, we too should wince. They are not pleasant sights. The blood is moral: the blood is anti-slavery: it runs cold in the veins: the stomach rises with disgust, and curses slavery. Well, so it happened; a good man or woman, a country-boy or girl, it would so fall out, once in a while saw these injuries, and had the indiscretion to tell of them. The horrid story ran and flew; the winds blew it all over the world. They who heard it, asked their rich and great friends, if it was true, or only missionary lies. The richest and greatest, the prime minister of England, the king's privy council were obliged to say, that it was too true. It became plain to all men, the more this business was looked into, that the crimes and cruelties of the slave-traders and slave-owners could not be overstated. The more it was searched, the more shocking anecdotes came up, — things not to be spoken. Humane persons who were informed of the reports, insisted on proving them.

* * *

I may here express a general remark, which the history of slavery seems to justify, that it is not founded solely on the avarice of the planter. We sometimes say, the planter does not want slaves, he only wants the immunities and the luxuries which the slaves yield him; give him money, give him a machine that will yield him as much money as the slaves, and he will thankfully let them go. He has no love of slavery, he wants luxury, and he will pay even this price of crime and danger for it. But I think experience does not warrant this favorable distinction, but shows the existence, beside the covetousness, of a bitterer element, the love of power, the voluptuousness of holding a human being in his absolute control. We sometimes observe, that spoiled children contract a habit of annoying quite wantonly those who have charge of them, and seem to measure their own sense of well-being, not by what they do, but by the degree of reaction they can cause. It is vain to get rid of them by not minding them: if purring and humming is not noticed, they squeal and screech; then if you chide and console them, they find the experiment succeeds, and they begin again. The child will sit in your arms contented, provided you do nothing. If you take a book and read, he commences hostile operations. The planter is the spoiled child of his unnatural habits, and has contracted in his indolent and luxurious climate the need of excitement by irritating and tormenting his slave.

* * *

I said, this event is signal in the history of civilization. There are many styles of civilization, and not one only. Ours is full of barbarities. There are many faculties in man, each of which takes its turn of activity, and that faculty which is paramount in any period, and exerts itself through the strongest nation, determines the civility of that age; and each age thinks its own the perfection of reason. Our culture is very cheap and intelligible. Unroof any house, and you shall find it. The well-being consists in having a sufficiency of coffee and toast, with a daily newspaper; a well-glazed parlor, with marbles, mirrors and centre-table; and the excitement of a few parties and a few rides in a year. Such as one house, such are all. The owner of a New York manor imitates the mansion and equipage of the London nobleman; the Boston merchant rivals his brother of New York; and the villages copy Boston. There have been nations elevated by great sentiments. Such was the civility of Sparta and the Dorian[5] race, whilst it was defective in some of the chief elements of ours. That of Athens, again, lay in an intellect dedicated to beauty. That of Asia Minor in poetry, music, and arts; that of Palestine in piety; that of Rome in military arts and virtues, exalted by a prodigious magnanimity; that of China and Japan in the last exaggeration of decorum and etiquette. Our civility, England determines the style of, inasmuch as England is the strongest of the family of existing nations, and as we are the expansion of that people. It is that of a trading nation; it is a shopkeeping civility. The English lord is a retired shopkeeper, and has the prejudices and timidities of that profession. And we are shopkeepers, and have acquired the vices and virtues that belong to trade. We peddle, we truck, we sail, we row, we ride in cars, we creep in teams, we go in canals—to market, and for the sale of goods. The national aim and employment streams into our ways of thinking, our laws, our habits, and our manners. The customer is the immediate jewel of our souls. Him we flatter, him we feast, compliment, vote for, and will not contradict. It was or it seemed the dictate of trade, to keep the negro down. We had found a race who were less warlike, and less energetic shopkeepers than we; who had very little skill in trade. We found it very convenient to keep them at work, since, by the aid of a little whipping, we could get their work for nothing but their board and the cost of whips. What if it cost a few unpleasant scenes on the coast of Africa? That was a great way off; and the scenes could be endured by some sturdy, unscrupulous fellows, who could go for high wages and bring us the men, and need not trouble our ears with the disagreeable particulars. If any mention was made of homicide, madness, adultery, and intolerable tortures, we would let the church-bells ring louder, the church organ swell its peal, and drown the hideous sound. The sugar they raised was excellent: nobody tasted blood in it. The coffee was fragrant; the tobacco was incense; the brandy made nations happy; the cotton clothed the world. What! all raised by these men, and no wages? Excellent! What a convenience! They seemed created by providence to bear the heat and the whipping, and make these fine articles.

But unhappily, most unhappily, gentlemen, man is born with intellect, as well as with a love of sugar, and with a sense of justice, as well as a taste for strong drink. These ripened, as well as those. You could not educate him, you could not get any poetry, any wisdom, any beauty in woman, any strong and commanding character in a man, but these absurdities would still come flashing out,—these absurdities of a demand for justice, a generosity for the weak and oppressed. Unhappily too, for the planter, the laws of nature are in harmony with each other: that which the head and the heart demand, is found to be, in the long run, for what the grossest calculator calls his advantage. The moral sense is always supported by the permanent interest of the parties. Else, I know not how, in our world, any good would ever get done. It was shown to the planters that they, as well as the negroes, were slaves; that though they paid no wages, they got very poor work; that their estates were ruining them, under the finest climate; and that they needed the severest monopoly laws at home to keep them from bankruptcy. The oppression of the slave recoiled on them. They were full of vices; their children were lumps of pride, sloth, sensuality and rottenness. The position of woman was nearly as bad as it could be, and, like other robbers, they could not sleep in security. Many planters have said, since the emancipation, that, before that day, they were the greatest slaves on the estates. Slavery is no scholar, no improver; it does not love the whistle of the railroad; it does not love the newspaper, the mailbag, a college, a book, or a preacher who has the absurd whim of saying what he thinks; it does not increase the white population; it does not improve the soil; everything goes to decay. For these reasons, the islands proved bad customers to England. It was very easy for manufacturers less shrewd than those of Birmingham and Manchester[6] to see, that if the state of things in the islands was altered, if the slaves had wages, the slaves would be clothed, would build houses, would fill them with tools, with pottery, with crockery, with hardware; and negro women love fine clothes as well as white women. In every naked negro of those thousands, they saw a future customer. Meantime, they saw further, that the slave-trade, by keeping in barbarism the whole coast of eastern Africa, deprives them of countries and nations of customers, if once freedom and civility, and European manners could get a foothold there. But the trade could not be abolished, whilst this hungry West Indian market, with an appetite like the grave, cried, "More, more, bring me a hundred a day;" they could not expect any mitigation in the madness of the poor African warchiefs. These considerations opened the eyes of the dullest in Britain. More than this, the West Indian estate was owned or mortgaged in England, and the owner and the mortgagee had very plain intimations that the feeling of English liberty was gaining every hour new mass and velocity, and the hostility to such as resisted it, would be fatal. The House of Commons would destroy the protection of island produce, and interfere on English politics in the island legislation: so they hastened to make the best of their position, and accepted the bill.

These considerations, I doubt not, had their weight, the interest of trade, the interest of the revenue, and, moreover, the good fame of the action. It was inevitable that men should feel these motives. But they do not appear to have had an excessive or unreasonable weight. On reviewing this history, I think the whole transaction reflects infinite honor on the people and parliament of England. It was a stately spectacle, to see the cause of human rights argued with so much patience and generosity, and with such a mass of evidence before that powerful people. It is a creditable incident in the history, that when, in 1789, the first privy-council report of evidence on the trade, a bulky folio, (embodying all the facts which the London Committee had been engaged for years in collecting, and all the examinations before the council,) was presented to the House of Commons, a late day being named for the discussion, in order to give members time, — Mr. Wilberforce, Mr. Pitt, the prime minister, and other gentlemen, took advantage of the postponement, to retire into the country, to read the report. For months and years the bill was debated, with some consciousness of the extent of its relations by the first citizens of England, the foremost men

---

6. English cities that were important centers for the manufacture of cloth and, therefore, dependent on cheap Southern cotton.

of the earth; every argument was weighed, every particle of evidence was sifted, and laid in the scale; and, at last, the right triumphed, the poor man was vindicated, and the oppressor was flung out. I know that England has the advantage of trying the question at a wide distance from the spot where the nuisance exists: the planters are not, excepting in rare examples, members of the legislature. The extent of the empire, and the magnitude and number of other questions crowding into court, keep this one in balance, and prevent it from obtaining that ascendancy, and being urged with that intemperance, which a question of property tends to acquire. There are causes in the composition of the British legislature, and the relation of its leaders to the country and to Europe, which exclude much that is pitiful and injurious in other legislative assemblies. From these reasons, the question was discussed with a rare independence and magnanimity. It was not narrowed down to a paltry electioneering trap, and, I must say, a delight in justice, an honest tenderness for the poor negro, for man suffering these wrongs, combined with the national pride, which refused to give the support of English soil, or the protection of the English flag, to these disgusting violations of nature.

Forgive me, fellow citizens, if I own to you, that in the last few days that my attention has been occupied with this history, I have not been able to read a page of it, without the most painful comparisons. Whilst I have read of England, I have thought of New England. Whilst I have meditated in my solitary walks on the magnanimity of the English Bench and Senate, reaching out the benefit of the law to the most helpless citizen in her world-wide realm, I have found myself oppressed by other thoughts. As I have walked in the pastures and along the edge of woods, I could not keep my imagination on those agreeable figures, for other images that intruded on me. I could not see the great vision of the patriots and senators who have adopted the slave's cause:—they turned their backs on me. No: I see other pictures—of mean men: I see very poor, very ill-clothed, very ignorant men, not surrounded by happy friends,—to be plain,—poor black men of obscure employment as mariners, cooks, or stewards, in ships, yet citizens of this our Commonwealth of Massachusetts,—freeborn as we,—whom the slave-laws of the States of South Carolina, Georgia, and Louisiana, have arrested in the vessels in which they visited those ports, and shut up in jails so long as the vessel remained in port, with the stringent addition, that if the shipmaster fails to pay the costs of this official arrest, and the board in jail, these citizens are to be sold for slaves, to pay that expense. This man, these men, I see, and no law to save them. Fellow citizens, this crime will not be hushed up any longer. I have learned that a citizen of Nantucket, walking in New Orleans, found a freeborn citizen of Nantucket, a man, too, of great personal worth, and, as it happened, very dear to him, as having saved his own life, working chained in the streets of that city, kidnapped by such a process as this. In the sleep of the laws, the private interference of two excellent citizens of Boston has, I have ascertained, rescued several natives of this State from these southern prisons. Gentlemen, I thought the deck of a Massachusetts ship was as much the territory of Massachusetts, as the floor on which we stand. It should be as sacred as the temple of God. The poorest fishing-smack, that floats under the shadow of an iceberg in the northern seas, or hunts the whale in the southern ocean, should be encompassed by her laws with comfort and protection, as much as within the arms of Cape Ann and Cape Cod. And this kidnapping is suffered within our own land and federation, whilst the fourth article of the

Constitution of the United States ordains in terms, that, "The citizens of each State shall be entitled to all privileges and immunities of citizens in the several States." If such a damnable outrage can be committed on the person of a citizen with impunity, let the Governor break the broad seal of the State; he bears the sword in vain. The Governor of Massachusetts[7] is a trifler: the State-house in Boston is a play-house: the General Court is a dishonored body: if they make laws which they cannot execute. The great-hearted Puritans have left no posterity. The rich men may walk in State-street, but they walk without honor; and the farmers may brag their democracy in the country, but they are disgraced men. If the State has no power to defend its own people in its own shipping, because it has delegated that power to the Federal Government, has it no representation in the Federal Government? Are those men dumb? I am no lawyer, and cannot indicate the forms applicable to the case, but here is something which transcends all forms. Let the senators and representatives of the State, containing a population of a million freemen, go in a body before the Congress, and say, that they have a demand to make on them so imperative, that all functions of government must stop, until it is satisfied. If ordinary legislation cannot reach it, then extraordinary must be applied. The Congress should instruct the President to send to those ports of Charleston, Savannah, and New Orleans, such orders and such force, as should release, forthwith, all such citizens of Massachusetts as were holden in prison without the allegation of any crime, and should set on foot the strictest inquisition to discover where such persons, brought into slavery by these local laws, at any time heretofore, may now be. That first;—and then, let order be taken to indemnify all such as have been incarcerated. As for dangers to the Union, from such demands!—the Union is already at an end, when the first citizen of Massachusetts is thus outraged. Is it an union and covenant in which the State of Massachusetts agrees to be imprisoned, and the State of Carolina to imprison? Gentlemen, I am loath to say harsh things, and perhaps I know too little of politics for the smallest weight to attach to any censure of mine,—but I am at a loss how to characterize the tameness and silence of the two senators and the ten representatives of the State at Washington. To what purpose, have we clothed each of those representatives with the power of seventy thousand persons, and each senator with near half a million, if they are to sit dumb at their desks, and see their constituents captured and sold;—perhaps to gentlemen sitting by them in the hall? There is a scandalous rumor that has been swelling louder of late years,—perhaps it is wholly false,—that members are bullied into silence by southern gentlemen. It is so easy to omit to speak, or even to be absent when delicate things are to be handled. I may as well say what all men feel, that whilst our very amiable and very innocent representatives and senators at Washington, are accomplished lawyers and merchants, and very eloquent at dinners and at caucuses, there is a disastrous want of *men* from New England. I would gladly make exceptions, and you will not suffer me to forget one eloquent old man, in whose veins the blood of Massachusetts rolls, and who singly has defended the freedom of speech, and the rights of the free, against the usurpation of the slave-holder. But the reader of Congressional debates, in New England, is perplexed to see with what admirable sweetness and patience the majority of the free States, are schooled and ridden by the minority of slave-holders. What if we should send thither repre-

---

7. George N. Briggs (1796–1861) was governor from 1844 to 1851.

sentatives who were a particle less amiable and less innocent? I entreat you, sirs, let not this stain attach, let not this misery accumulate any longer. If the managers of our political parties are too prudent and too cold; — if, most unhappily, the ambitious class of young men and political men have found out, that these neglected victims are poor and without weight; that they have no graceful hospitalities to offer; no valuable business to throw into any man's hands, no strong vote to cast at the elections; and therefore may with impunity be left in their chains or to the chance of chains, then let the citizens in their primary capacity take up their cause on this very ground, and say to the government of the State, and of the Union, that government exists to defend the weak and the poor and the injured party; the rich and the strong can better take care of themselves. And as an omen and assurance of success, I point you to the bright example which England set you, on this day, ten years ago.

There are other comparisons and other imperative duties which come sadly to mind, — but I do not wish to darken the hours of this day by crimination; I turn gladly to the rightful theme, to the bright aspects of the occasion.

This event was a moral revolution. The history of it is before you. Here was no prodigy, no fabulous hero, no Trojan horse, no bloody war, but all was achieved by plain means of plain men, working not under a leader, but under a sentiment. Other revolutions have been the insurrection of the oppressed; this was the repentance of the tyrant. It was the masters revolting from their mastery. The slave-holder said, I will not hold slaves. The end was noble, and the means were pure. Hence, the elevation and pathos of this chapter of history. The lives of the advocates are pages of greatness, and the connexion of the eminent senators with this question, constitutes the immortalizing moments of those men's lives. The bare enunciation of the theses, at which the lawyers and legislators arrived, gives a glow to the heart of the reader. Lord Chancellor Northington[8] is the author of the famous sentence, "As soon as any man puts his foot on English ground, he becomes free." "I was a slave," said the counsel of Somerset, speaking for his client, "for I was in America: I am now in a country, where the common rights of mankind are known and regarded." Granville Sharp filled the ear of the judges with the sound principles, that had from time to time been affirmed by the legal authorities. "Derived power cannot be superior to the power from which it is derived." "The reasonableness of the law is the soul of the law." "It is better to suffer every evil, than to consent to any." Out it would come, the God's truth, out it came, like a bolt from a cloud, for all the mumbling of the lawyers. One feels very sensibly in all this history that a great heart and soul are behind there, superior to any man, and making use of each, in turn, and infinitely attractive to every person according to the degree of reason in his own mind, so that this cause has had the power to draw to it every particle of talent and of worth in England, from the beginning. All the great geniuses of the British senate, Fox, Pitt, Burke, Grenville, Sheridan, Grey, Canning, ranged themselves on its side; the poet Cowper[9] wrote for it: Franklin, Jefferson, Washington, in this country, all recorded their votes. All men remember the subtlety and the fire of indignation, which the Edinburgh Review[1] contributed to the

---

8. Robert Henley, first earl of Northington (1708–1772), made the remark in the British slave case *Shanley v. Harvey.*
9. See n. 8, p. 67. Fox (see n. 4, p. 229), Pitt (see n. 5, p. 87), Burke (see n. 5, p. 45), Richard Grenville (1776–1839), Sheridan (see n. 5, p. 322), Charles Grey (1764–1845), and George Canning (1770–1827) were all Members of Parliament who sought to abolish the slave trade and slavery.
1. British quarterly periodical published from 1802 to 1929.

cause; and every liberal mind, poet, preacher, moralist, statesman, has had the fortune to appear somewhere for this cause. On the other part, appeared the reign of pounds and shillings, and all manner of rage and stupidity; a resistance which drew from Mr. Huddlestone in Parliament the observation, "That a curse attended this trade even in the mode of defending it. By a certain fatality, none but the vilest arguments were brought forward, which corrupted the very persons who used them. Every one of these was built on the narrow ground of interest, of pecuniary profit, of sordid gain, in opposition to every motive that had reference to humanity, justice, and religion, or to that great principle which comprehended them all." — This moral force perpetually reinforces and dignifies the friends of this cause. It gave that tenacity to their point which has insured ultimate triumph; and it gave that superiority in reason, in imagery, in eloquence, which makes in all countries anti-slavery meetings so attractive to the people, and has made it a proverb in Massachusetts, that, "eloquence is dog-cheap at the anti-slavery chapel."

I will say further, that we are indebted mainly to this movement, and to the continuers of it, for the popular discussion of every point of practical ethics, and a reference of every question to the absolute standard. It is notorious, that the political, religious, and social schemes, with which the minds of men are now most occupied, have been matured, or at least broached, in the free and daring discussions of these assemblies. Men have become aware through the emancipation, and kindred events, of the presence of powers, which, in their days of darkness, they had overlooked. Virtuous men will not again rely on political agents. They have found out the deleterious effect of political association. Up to this day, we have allowed to statesmen a paramount social standing, and we bow low to them as to the great. We cannot extend this deference to them any longer. The secret cannot be kept, that the seats of power are filled by underlings, ignorant, timid, and selfish, to a degree to destroy all claim, excepting that on compassion, to the society of the just and generous. What happened notoriously to an American ambassador in England, that he found himself compelled to palter, and to disguise the fact that he was a slave-breeder, happens to men of state. Their vocation is a presumption against them, among well-meaning people. The superstition respecting power and office, is going to the ground. The stream of human affairs flows its own way, and is very little affected by the activity of legislators. What great masses of men wish done, will be done; and they do not wish it for a freak, but because it is their state and natural end. There are now other energies than force, other than political, which no man in future can allow himself to disregard. There is direct conversation and influence. A man is to make himself felt, by his proper force. The tendency of things runs steadily to this point, namely, to put every man on his merits, and to give him so much power as he naturally exerts — no more, no less. Of course, the timid and base persons, all who are conscious of no worth in themselves, and who owe all their place to the opportunities which the old order of things allowed them to deceive and defraud men, shudder at the change, and would fain silence every honest voice, and lock up every house where liberty and innovation can be pleaded for. They would raise mobs, for fear is very cruel. But the strong and healthy yeomen and husbands of the land, the self-sustaining class of inventive and industrious men, fear no competition or superiority. Come what will, their faculty cannot be spared.

The First of August marks the entrance of a new element into modern politics, namely, the civilization of the negro. A man is added to the human family. Not the least affecting part of this history of abolition, is, the annihilation of the old indecent nonsense about the nature of the negro. In the case of the ship Zong,[2] in 1781, whose master had thrown one hundred and thirty-two slaves alive into the sea, to cheat the underwriters, the first jury gave a verdict in favor of the master and owners: they had a right to do what they had done. Lord Mansfield is reported to have said on the bench, "The matter left to the jury is, — Was it from necessity? For they had no doubt, — though it shocks one very much, — that the case of slaves was the same as if horses had been thrown overboard. It is a very shocking case." But a more enlightened and humane opinion began to prevail. Mr. Clarkson, early in his career, made a collection of African productions and manufactures, as specimens of the arts and culture of the negro; comprising cloths and loom, weapons, polished stones and woods, leather, glass, dyes, ornaments, soap, pipe-bowls, and trinkets. These he showed to Mr. Pitt, who saw and handled them with extreme interest. "On sight of these," says Clarkson, "many sublime thoughts seemed to rush at once into his mind, some of which he expressed;" and hence appeared to arise a project which was always dear to him, of the civilization of Africa, — a dream which forever elevates his fame. In 1791, Mr. Wilberforce announced to the House of Commons, "We have already gained one victory: we have obtained for these poor creatures the recognition of their human nature, which, for a time, was most shamefully denied them." It was the sarcasm of Montesquieu, "it would not do to suppose that negroes were men, lest it should turn out that whites were not;" for, the white has, for ages, done what he could to keep the negro in that hoggish state. His laws have been furies. It now appears, that the negro race is, more than any other, susceptible of rapid civilization. The emancipation is observed, in the islands, to have wrought for the negro a benefit as sudden as when a thermometer is brought out of the shade into the sun. It has given him eyes and ears. If, before, he was taxed with such stupidity, or such defective vision, that he could not set a table square to the walls of an apartment, he is now the principal, if not the only mechanic, in the West Indies; and is, besides, an architect, a physician, a lawyer, a magistrate, an editor, and a valued and increasing political power. The recent testimonies of Sturge, of Thome and Kimball, of Gurney, of Phillippo,[3] are very explicit on this point, the capacity and the success of the colored and the black population in employments of skill, of profit, and of trust; and, best of all, is the testimony to their moderation. They receive hints and advances from the whites, that they will be gladly received as subscribers to the Exchange, as members of this or that committee of trust. They hold back, and say to each other, that "social position is not to be gained by pushing."

I have said that this event interests us because it came mainly from the concession of the whites; I add, that in part it is the earning of the blacks. They won the pity and respect which they have received, by their powers and native endowments. I think this a circumstance of the highest import. Their whole fu-

---

2. In this famous case 133 slaves who had grown ill were cast into the sea by Captain Luke Collingwood. Only one survived. The insurance arrangement provided that if the slaves died a natural death, the loss would fall on the owners of the ship and the captain, but if they were thrown alive into the sea, on any pretext of necessity for the safety of the ship, it would be the underwriters' loss. See F. O. Shyllon, *Black Slaves in Britain* (1974), 184–209.
3. The Reverend James Phillippo (1798–1879), British Baptist missionary to the West Indies, published *Jamaica: Its Past and Present State*, which was issued in a second edition in 1843. Joseph Sturge (1793–1859) published *The West Indies* (1837) to document the abuse of slaves and apprentices in the West Indies. Joseph John Gurney (1788–1847), Quaker philanthropist, wrote *Winter in the West Indies* (1840).

ture is in it. Our planet, before the age of written history, had its races of savages, like the generations of sour paste, or the animalcules that wriggle and bite in a drop of putrid water. Who cares for these or for their wars? We do not wish a world of bugs or of birds; neither afterward of Scythians, Caraibs, or Feejees.[4] The grand style of nature, her great periods, is all we observe in them. Who cares for oppressing whites, or oppressed blacks, twenty centuries ago, more than for bad dreams? Eaters and food are in the harmony of nature; and there too is the germ forever protected, unfolding gigantic leaf after leaf, a newer flower, a richer fruit, in every period, yet its next product is never to be guessed. It will only save what is worth saving; and it saves not by compassion, but by power. It appoints no police to guard the lion, but his teeth and claws; no fort or city for the bird, but his wings; no rescue for flies and mites, but their spawning numbers, which no ravages can overcome. It deals with men after the same manner. If they are rude and foolish, down they must go. When at last in a race, a new principle appears, an idea;—*that* conserves it; ideas only save races. If the black man is feeble, and not important to the existing races, not on a parity with the best race, the black man must serve, and be exterminated. But if the black man carries in his bosom an indispensable element of a new and coming civilization, for the sake of that element, no wrong, nor strength, nor circumstance, can hurt him: he will survive and play his part. So now, the arrival in the world of such men as Toussaint,[5] and the Haytian heroes, or of the leaders of their race in Barbadoes and Jamaica, outweighs in good omen all the English and American humanity. The anti-slavery of the whole world, is dust in the balance before this,—is a poor squeamishness and nervousness: the might and the right are here: here is the anti-slave: here is man: and if you have man, black or white is an insignificance. The intellect,—that is miraculous! Who has it, has the talisman: his skin and bones, though they were of the color of night, are transparent, and the everlasting stars shine through, with attractive beams. But a compassion for that which is not and cannot be useful or lovely, is degrading and futile. All the songs, and newspapers, and money-subscriptions, and vituperation of such as do not think with us, will avail nothing against a fact. I say to you, you must save yourself, black or white, man or woman; other help is none. I esteem the occasion of this jubilee to be the proud discovery, that the black race can contend with the white; that, in the great anthem which we call history, a piece of many parts and vast compass, after playing a long time a very low and subdued accompaniment, they perceive the time arrived when they can strike in with effect, and take a master's part in the music. The civility of the world has reached that pitch, that their more moral genius is becoming indispensable, and the quality of this race is to be honored for itself. For this, they have been preserved in sandy deserts, in rice-swamps, in kitchens and shoeshops, so long: now let them emerge, clothed and in their own form.

There remains the very elevated consideration which the subject opens, but which belongs to more abstract views than we are now taking, this namely, that the civility of no race can be perfect whilst another race is degraded. It is a doctrine alike of the oldest, and of the newest philosophy, that, man is one, and that you cannot injure any member, without a sympathetic injury to all the members. America is not civil, whilst Africa is barbarous.

---

4. Inhabitants of the Fiji Islands. *Scythians:* name applied by the Greeks to various nomadic tribes of southeastern Europe and Persia. *Caraibs:* or Caribs, original inhabitants of the Caribbean islands.
5. Pierre Dominique Toussaint L'Ouverture (1743–1803), soldier, statesman, and liberator of Haiti.

These considerations seem to leave no choice for the action of the intellect and the conscience of the country. There have been moments in this, as well as in every piece of moral history, when there seemed room for the infusions of a skeptical philosophy; when it seemed doubtful, whether brute force would not triumph in the eternal struggle. I doubt not, that sometimes a despairing negro, when jumping over the ship's sides to escape from the white devils who surrounded him, has believed there was no vindication of right; it is horrible to think of, but it seemed so. I doubt not, that sometimes the negro's friend, in the face of scornful and brutal hundreds of traders and drivers, has felt his heart sink. Especially, it seems to me, some degree of despondency is pardonable, when he observes the men of conscience and of intellect, his own natural allies and champions,—those whose attention should be nailed to the grand objects of this cause, so hotly offended by whatever incidental petulances or infirmities of indiscreet defenders of the negro, as to permit themselves to be ranged with the enemies of the human race; and names which should be the alarums of liberty and the watch-words of truth, are mixed up with all the rotten rabble of selfishness and tyranny. I assure myself that this coldness and blindness will pass away. A single noble wind of sentiment will scatter them forever. I am sure that the good and wise elders, the ardent and generous youth will not permit what is incidental and exceptional to withdraw their devotion from the essential and permanent characters of the question. There have been moments, I said, when men might be forgiven, who doubted. Those moments are past. Seen in masses, it cannot be disputed, there is progress in human society. There is a blessed necessity by which the interest of men is always driving them to the right; and, again, making all crime mean and ugly. The genius of the Saxon race, friendly to liberty; the enterprise, the very muscular vigor of this nation, are inconsistent with slavery. The Intellect, with blazing eye, looking through history from the beginning onward, gazes on this blot, and it disappears. The sentiment of Right, once very low and indistinct, but ever more articulate, because it is the voice of the universe, pronounces Freedom. The Power that built this fabric of things affirms it in the heart; and in the history of the First of August, has made a sign to the ages, of his will.

Address to the Citizens of Concord on the Fugitive Slave Law[1]

3 May 1851

Fellow Citizens,

I accepted your invitation to speak to you on the great question of these days, with very little consideration of what I might have to offer; for there seems

---

1. Emerson was invited to deliver this address by thirty-five of his fellow male citizens of Concord. In their letter of invitation (April 26, 1851), the subscribers indicate that they are "very desirous of hearing your opinions upon the Fugitive Slave Law, & upon the aspects of the times." Emerson first gave the speech on May 3, 1851 in Concord. The *Liberator* (May 9, 1851) later reported that it was well received and "is said to have been one of the ablest and most forcible of that distinguished gentleman's productions." Eventually Emerson was prevailed upon to repeat the speech on at least nine occasions throughout the Middlesex district in an effort to elect John Gorham Palfrey, a Free Soiler, to the U.S. Congress. Emerson notes in a letter to Theodore Parker (May 9, 1851) that he is to read the lecture in "Lexington, in Fitchburg, & it is asked for in Cambridge & in Waltham also . . . which . . . you see, is stumping Palfrey's district" (*L* 8.277).

to be no option. The last year has forced us all into politics, and made it a para-mount duty to seek what it is often a duty to shun.

We do not breathe well. There is infamy in the air. I have a new experi-ence. I wake in the morning with a painful sensation, which I carry about all day, and which, when traced home, is the odious remembrance of that ig-nominy which has fallen on Massachusetts, which robs the landscape of beauty, and takes the sunshine out of every hour. I have lived all my life in this State, and never had any experience of personal inconvenience from the laws, until now. They never came near me to my discomfort before. I find the like sensi-bility in my neighbors. And in that class who take no interest in the ordinary questions of party politics. There are men who are as sure indexes of the equity of legislation and of the sane state of public feeling, as the barometer is of the weight of the air; and it is a bad sign when these are discontented. For, though they snuff oppression and dishonor at a distance, it is because they are more im-pressionable: the whole population will in a short time be as painfully affected.

Every hour brings us from distant quarters of the Union the expression of mortification at the late events in Massachusetts, and at the behavior of Boston. The tameness was indeed shocking. Boston, of whose fame for spirit and char-acter we have all been so proud; Boston, whose citizens, intelligent people in England told me, they could always distinguish by their culture among Ameri-cans; the Boston of the American Revolution, which figures so proudly in "John Adams's Diary,"[2] which the whole country has been reading, Boston, spoiled by prosperity, must bow its ancient honor in the dust, and make us irretrievably ashamed. In Boston,—we have said with such lofty confidence,—no fugitive slave can be arrested;—and now, we must transfer our vaunt to the country, and say with a little less confidence,—no fugitive man can be arrested here;—at least we can brag thus until tomorrow, when the farmers also may be corrupted.

The tameness is indeed complete. It appears, the only haste in Boston, after the rescue of Shadrach[3] last February, was, who should first put his name on the list of volunteers in aid of the marshal. I met the smoothest of episcopal clergymen the other day, and allusion being made to Mr. Webster's[4] treachery, he blandly replied, "Why, do you know I think *that* the great action of his life." It looked as if, in the city, and the suburbs, all were involved in one hot haste of terror,—presidents of colleges and professors, saints and brokers, insurers, lawyers, importers, manufacturers;—not an unpleasing sentiment, not a liberal recollection, not so much as a snatch of an old song for freedom, dares intrude on their passive obedience. The panic has paralysed the journals, with the fewest exceptions, so that one cannot open a newspaper, without being dis-gusted by new records of shame. I cannot read longer even the local good news. When I look down the columns at the titles of paragraphs, "Education in Mass-achusetts," "Board of Trade," "Art Union," "Revival of Religion," what bitter mockeries! The very convenience of property, the house and land we occupy, have lost their best value, and a man looks gloomily on his children, and thinks 'What have I done, that you should begin life in dishonor?' Every liberal study is discredited: Literature, and science appear effeminate and the hiding of the

2. Publication of the ten-volume *Works of John Adams* (1850–56), ed. Charles Francis Adams, had just begun.
3. Or Frederic Jenkins, or Wilkins, an escaped slave who had been rescued from custody in Boston on Feb-ruary 15, 1851, an early attempt to prevent the implementation of the Fugitive Slave Law.
4. See n. 6, p. 251. For Emerson's views on Webster, see pp. 518–22.

head. The college, the churches, the schools, the very shops and factories are discredited; real estate, every kind of wealth, every branch of industry, every avenue to power, suffers injury, and the value of life is reduced. Just now a friend came into my house and said, "If this law shall be repealed, I shall be glad that I have lived; if not, I shall be sorry that I was born." What kind of law is that which extorts language like this from the heart of a free and civilized people?

One intellectual benefit we owe to the late disgraces. The crisis had the illuminating power of a sheet of lightning at midnight. It showed truth. It ended a good deal of nonsense we had been wont to hear and to repeat, on the 19th April, the 17th June,[5] and the 4th July. It showed the slightness and unreliableness of our social fabric; it showed what stuff reputations are made of; what straws we dignify by office and title, and how competent we are to give counsel and help in a day of trial. It showed the shallowness of leaders; the divergence of parties from their alleged grounds; showed that men would not stick to what they had said: that the resolutions of public bodies, or the pledges never so often given and put on record of public men, will not bind them. The fact comes out more plainly, that you cannot rely on any man for the defence of truth, who is not constitutionally, or by blood and temperament, on that side. A man of a greedy and unscrupulous selfishness may maintain morals when they are in fashion: but he will not stick. However close Mr. Wolf's nails have been pared, however neatly he has been shaved, and tailored, and set up on end, and taught to say "Virtue and Religion," he cannot be relied on at a pinch: he will say, morality means pricking a vein. The popular assumption that all men loved freedom, and believed in the Christian religion, was found hollow American brag. Only persons who were known and tried benefactors are found standing for freedom: the sentimentalists went down stream. I question the value of our civilization, when I see that the public mind had never less hold of the strongest of all truths. The sense of injustice is blunted,—a sure sign of the shallowness of our intellect. I cannot accept the railroad and telegraph in exchange for reason and charity. It is not skill in iron locomotives that marks so fine civility as the jealousy of liberty. I cannot think the most judicious tubing a compensation for metaphysical debility. What is the use of admirable law-forms and political forms, if a hurricane of party feeling and a combination of monied interests can beat them to the ground? What is the use of courts, if judges only quote authorities, and no judge exerts original jurisdiction, or recurs to first principles? What is the use of a Federal Bench, if its opinions are the political breath of the hour? And what is the use of constitutions, if all the guaranties provided by the jealousy of ages for the protection of liberty are made of no effect, when a bad act of Congress finds a willing commissioner?

The levity of the public mind has been shown in the past year by the most extravagant actions. Who could have believed it, if foretold, that a hundred guns would be fired in Boston on the passage of the Fugitive Slave bill?[6] Nothing proves the want of all thought, the absence of standard in men's minds more than the dominion of party. Here are humane people who have tears for misery, an open purse for want, who should have been the defenders of the poor man, are found his embittered enemies, rejoicing in his rendition,—merely

---

5. The battles of Lexington and Concord were fought on April 19, 1775; the Battle of Bunker Hill was waged in Boston on June 17, 1775. See "Concord Hymn," p. 462.
6. One hundred guns were fired on Boston Common to celebrate the bill's passage.

from party ties. I thought none that was not ready to go on all fours, would back this law. And yet here are upright men, *compotes mentis*,[7] husbands, fathers, trustees, friends, open, generous, brave, who can see nothing in this claim for bare humanity and the health and honor of their native state, but canting fanaticism, sedition, and "one idea." Because of this preoccupied mind, the whole wealth and power of Boston,—200,000 souls, and 180 millions of money,—are thrown into the scale of crime; and the poor black boy, whom the fame of Boston had reached in the recesses of a rice-swamp, or in the alleys of Savannah, on arriving here, finds all this force employed to catch him. The famous town of Boston is his master's hound. The learning of the Universities, the culture of elegant society, the acumen of lawyers, the majesty of the Bench, the eloquence of the Christian pulpit, the stoutness of Democracy, the respectability of the Whig party, are all combined to kidnap him.

The crisis is interesting as it shows the self-protecting nature of the world, and of the divine laws. It is the law of the world as much immorality as there is, so much misery. The greatest prosperity will in vain resist the greatest calamity. You borrow the succour of the devil, and he must have his fee. He was never known to abate a penny of his rents. In every nation all the immorality that exists breeds plagues. Out of the corrupt society that exists we have never been able to combine any pure prosperity. There is always something in the very advantages of a condition which hurts it. Africa has its malformation; England has its Ireland; Germany its hatred of classes; France its love of gunpowder; Italy, its Pope; and America, the most prosperous country in the universe, has the greatest calamity in the universe, negro slavery.

Let me remind you a little in detail how the natural retributions act in reference to the statute which Congress passed a year ago. For these few months have shown very conspicuously its nature and impracticability.

It is contravened,

1. By the sentiment of duty. An immoral law makes it a man's duty to break it, at every hazard. For virtue is the very self of every man. It is therefore a principle of law, that an immoral contract is void, and that an immoral statute is void, for, as laws do not make right, but are simply declaratory of a right which already existed, it is not to be presumed that they can so stultify themselves as to command injustice.

It is remarkable how rare in the history of tyrants is an immoral law. Some color, some indirection was always used. If you take up the volumes of the "Universal History," you will find it difficult searching. The precedents are few. It is not easy to parallel the wickedness of this American law. And that is the head and body of this discontent, that the law is immoral. Here is a statute which enacts the crime of kidnapping,—a crime on one footing with arson and murder. A man's right to liberty is as inalienable as his right to life.

Pains seem to have been taken to give us in this statute a wrong pure from any mixture of right. If our resistance to this law is not right, there is no right. This is not meddling with other people's affairs: this is hindering other people from meddling with us. This is not going crusading into Virginia and Georgia after slaves, who, it is alleged, are very comfortable where they are;—that amiable argument falls to the ground: but this is befriending in our own state, on our own farms, a man who has taken the risk of being shot, or burned alive, or

---

7. Of sound mind (Latin).

cast into the sea, or starved to death, or suffocated in a wooden box, to get away from his driver; and this man who has run the gauntlet of a thousand miles for his freedom, the statute says, you men of Massachusetts shall hunt, and catch, and send back again to the dog-hutch he fled from.

It is contrary to the primal sentiment of duty, and therefore all men that are born are, in proportion to their power of thought and their moral sensibility, found to be the natural enemies of this law. The resistance of all moral beings is secured to it. I had thought, I confess, what must come at last would come at first, a banding of all men against the authority of this statute. I thought it a point on which all sane men were agreed, that the law must respect the public morality. I thought that all men of all conditions had been made sharers of a certain experience, that in certain rare and retired moments they had been made to see how man is man, or what makes the essence of rational beings, namely, that, whilst animals have to do with eating the fruits of the ground, men have to do with rectitude, with benefit, with truth, with something which *is*, independent of appearances: and that this tie makes the substantiality of life, this, and not their ploughing or sailing, their trade or the breeding of families. I thought that every time a man goes back to his own thoughts, these angels receive him, talk with him, and, that, in the best hours, he is uplifted in virtue of this essence, into a peace and into a power which the material world cannot give: that these moments counterbalance the years of drudgery, and that this owning of a law, be it called morals, religion, or godhead, or what you will, constituted the explanation of life, the excuse and indemnity for the errors and calamities which sadden it. In long years consumed in trifles they remember these moments, and are consoled. I thought it was this fair mystery, whose foundations are hidden in eternity, which made the basis of human society, and of law; and that to pretend any thing else, as, that the acquisition of property was the end of living, was to confound all distinctions, to make the world a greasy hotel, and, instead of noble motives and inspirations, and a heaven of companions and angels around and before us, to leave us in a grimacing menagerie of monkeys and idiots. All arts, customs, societies, books, and laws, are good as they foster and concur with this spiritual element; all men are beloved as they raise us to it; all are hateful as they deny or resist it. The laws especially draw their obligation only from their concurrence with it.

I am surprised that lawyers can be so blind as to suffer the principles of law to be discredited. A few months ago, in my dismay at hearing that the Higher Law was reckoned a good joke in the courts, I took pains to look into a few law-books. I had often heard that the Bible constituted a part of every technical law-library, and that it was a principle in law that immoral laws are void. I found accordingly, that the great jurists, Cicero, Grotius, Coke, Blackstone, Burlamaqui, Montesquieu, Vattel, Burke, Mackintosh, Jefferson,[8] do all affirm this.

---

8. Thomas Jefferson (1743–1826) wrote the first draft of the Declaration of Independence. Cicero, see n. 7, p. 59. Grotius (see n. 9, p. 252) wrote on the rights and duties of states. Sir Edward Coke (1552–1634), English lawyer and attorney general. Sir William Blackstone (1723–1780), British jurist and educator who wrote *Commentaries on the Laws of England* (1765–69), the most comprehensive single treatment of the body of English law. Jean-Jacques Burlamaqui (1694–1748), Swiss jurist. Charles Louis de Secondat, baron de la Brede et de Montesquieu (1689–1755), French philosopher and jurist; an outstanding figure of the early French Enlightenment, he wrote *The Spirit of the Laws* (1748), a discourse on government. Emmerich de Vattel (1714–1767), Swiss jurist and author of *Law of Nations* (1758). Burke, see n. 5, p. 45. Mackintosh, see n. 2, p. 170.

I have no intention to recite these passages I had marked:—such citation indeed seems to be something cowardly, for no reasonable person needs a quotation from Blackstone to convince him that white cannot be legislated to be black, and shall content myself with reading a single passage.

Blackstone admits the sovereignty "antecedent to any positive precept of the law of nature" among whose principles are, "that we should live honestly, should hurt nobody, and should render unto every one his due," etc. "*No human laws are of any validity, if contrary to this.*" "Nay, if any human law should allow or enjoin us to commit a crime" (his instance is murder) "we are bound to transgress that human law; or else we must offend both the natural and divine."

Lord Coke held, that where an act of parliament is against common right and reason, the common law shall control it, and adjudge it to be void. Chief Justice Hobart, Chief Justice Holt, and Chief Justice Mansfield[9] held the same. Lord Mansfield in the case of the slave Somerset, wherein the dicta of Lords Talbot and Hardwicke had been cited to the effect of carrying back the slave to the West Indies, said, "I care not for the supposed *dicta* of judges, however eminent, if they be contrary to all principle. Even the Canon Law says, (in malis promissis non expedit servare fidem) "neither allegiance nor oath can bind to obey that which is wrong." Vattel is equally explicit. "No engagement (to a sovereign) can oblige or even authorize a man to violate the laws of nature." All authors who have any conscience or modesty, agree, that a person ought not to obey such commands as are evidently contrary to the laws of God. Those governors of places who bravely refused to execute the barbarous orders of Charles IX. to the famous St. Bartholomew's, have been universally praised; and the court did not dare to punish them, at least, openly. "Sire," said the brave Orte, governor of Bayonne, in his letter; "I have communicated your majesty's command to your faithful inhabitants and warriors in the garrison, and I have found there only good citizens, and brave soldiers; not one hangman: therefore, both they and I most humbly entreat your majesty, to be pleased to employ your arms and lives in things that are possible, however hazardous they may be, and we will exert ourselves to the last drop of our blood."[1]

The practitioners should guard this dogma well, as the palladium of the profession, as their anchor in the respect of mankind; against a principle like this, all the arguments of Mr. Webster are the spray of a child's squirt against a granite wall.

2. It is contravened by all the sentiments. How can a law be enforced that fines pity, and imprisons charity? As long as men have bowels, they will disobey. You know that the Act of Congress of September 18, 1850, is a law which every one of you will break on the earliest occasion. There is not a manly whig, or a manly democrat, of whom, if a slave were hidden in one of our houses from the

---

9. All English chief justices. Henry Hobart (d. 1625). John Holt (1642–1710). William Murray, earl of Mansfield (1705–1793).

1. In August 1572 Charles IX of France, in response to the St. Bartholomew's Day Massacre of up to ten thousand Huguenots in Paris, wrote to his provincial governors ordering them to put to death Huguenots who attempted any form of assembly. Several governors refused to obey this edict. There is no hard evidence to confirm the story of Viscount d'Orthe's response, as reported by Vattel, which may be apocryphal, though in fact no massacre took place in Bayonne (see Robert Kingdon, *Myths about the St. Bartholomew's Day Massacres, 1572–1576* [1988]; and Vattel, *The Law of Nations; or Principles of the Law of Nature*, 1820, 1.4.77). Vattel is given as the source of this story in the manuscript and, indeed, much of it was taken directly from the book, a copy of which is in Emerson's library.

hounds, we should not ask with confidence to lend his wagon in aid of his escape, and he would lend it. The man would be too strong for the partisan.

And here I may say that it is absurd, what I often hear, to accuse the friends of freedom in the north with being the occasion of the new stringency of the southern slave-laws. If you starve or beat the orphan, in my presence, and I accuse your cruelty, can I help it? In the words of Electra, in the Greek tragedy,

> "Tis you that say it, not I. You do the deeds,
> And your ungodly deeds find me the words."[2]

Will you blame the ball for rebounding from the floor; blame the air for rushing in where a vacuum is made or the boiler for exploding under pressure of steam? These facts are after the laws of the world, and so is it law, that, when justice is violated, anger begins. The very defence which the God of Nature has provided for the innocent against cruelty, is the sentiment of indignation and pity in the bosom of the beholder. Mr. Webster tells the President, that "he has been in the north, and he has found no man whose opinion is of any weight who is opposed to the law." Ah! Mr. President, trust not the information. The gravid old universe goes spawning on; the womb conceives and the breasts give suck to thousands and millions of hairy babes formed not in the image of your statute, but in the image of the universe; too many to be bought off; too many than that they can be rich, and therefore peaceable; and necessitated to express first or last every feeling of the heart. You can keep no secret, for, whatever is true, some of them will unseasonably say. You can commit no crime, for they are created in their sentiments conscious of and hostile to it; and, unless you can suppress the newspaper, pass a law against bookshops, gag the English tongue in America, all short of this is futile. This dreadful English speech is saturated with songs, proverbs, and speeches that flatly contradict and defy every line of Mr. Mason's[3] statute. Nay, unless you can draw a sponge over those seditious ten commandments which are the root of our European and American civilization; and over that eleventh commandment, "Do unto others as you would have others do to you," your labor is vain.[4]

3. It is contravened by the written laws themselves, because the sentiments, of course, write the statutes. Laws are merely declaratory of the natural sentiments of mankind and the language of all permanent laws will be in contradiction to any immoral enactment: And thus it happens here: statute fights against statute. By the law of Congress, March 2, 1807, it is piracy and murder punishable with death, to enslave a man on the coast of Africa.[5] By law of Congress, September 1850, it is a high crime and misdemeanor punishable with fine and imprisonment to resist the re-enslaving of a man on the coast of America. Off soundings, it is piracy and murder to enslave him. On soundings, it is fine and prison not to re-enslave. What kind of legislation is this? What kind of Constitution which covers it? And yet the crime which the second law ordains is greater that the crime which the first law forbids under penalty of the gibbet. For it is a greater crime to re-enslave a man who has shown himself fit for free-

---

2. Sophocles, *Electra*, lines 626–27.
3. James Mason (1798–1871), senator from Virginia, drafted the Fugitive Slave Law.
4. Cf. Matthew 7.12.
5. On March 2, 1807, Congress passed a law prohibiting the African slave trade and the importation of slaves into America after January 1, 1808.

dom, than to enslave him at first, when it might be pretended to be a mitigation of his lot as a captive in war.

4. It is contravened by the mischiefs it operates. A wicked law can not be executed by good men, and must be by bad. Flagitious men must be employed, and every act of theirs is a stab at the public peace. It cannot be executed at such a cost, and so it brings a bribe in its hand. This law comes with infamy in it, and out of it. It offers a bribe in its own clauses for the consummation of the crime. To serve it, low and mean people are found by the groping of the government. No government ever found it hard to pick up tools for base actions. If you cannot find them in the huts of the poor, you shall find them in the palaces of the rich. Vanity can buy some, ambition others, and money others. The first execution of the law, as was inevitable, was a little hesitating; the second was easier; and the glib officials became, in a few weeks, quite practiced and handy at stealing men.

But worse, not the officials alone are bribed, but the whole community is solicited. The scowl of the community is attempted to be averted by the mischievous whisper, "Tariff and southern market, if you will be quiet; no tariff and loss of southern market, if you dare to murmur." I wonder that our acute people who have learned that the cheapest police is dear schools, should not find out that an immoral law costs more than the loss of the custom of a southern city.

The humiliating scandal of great men warping right into wrong was followed up very fast by the cities. New York advertised in southern markets, that it would go for slavery, and posted the names of merchants who would not. Boston, alarmed, entered into the same design. Philadelphia, more fortunate, had no conscience at all, and, in this auction of the rights of mankind, rescinded all its legislation against slavery. And the "Boston Advertiser" and the "Courier," in these weeks, urge the same course on the people of Massachusetts.[6] Nothing remains in this race of roguery, but to coax Connecticut or Maine to out-bid us all by adopting slavery into its constitution.

Great is the mischief of a legal crime. Every person who touches this business is contaminated. There has not been in our lifetime another moment when public men were personally lowered by their political action. But here are gentlemen whose believed probity was the confidence and fortification of multitudes, who, by fear of public opinion, or, through the dangerous ascendancy of southern manners, have been drawn into the support of this foul business. We poor men in the country who might once have thought it an honor to shake hands with them, or to dine at their boards, would now shrink from their touch, nor could they enter our humblest doors. You have a law which no man can obey, or abet the obeying, without loss of self-respect and forfeiture of the name of a gentleman. What shall we say of the functionary by whom the recent rendition was made? If he has rightly defined his powers, and has no authority to try the case, but only to prove the prisoner's identity, and remand him, what office is this for a reputable citizen to hold? No man of honor can sit on that bench. It is the extension of the planter's whipping-post: and its incumbents must rank with a class from which the turnkey, the hangman, and the informer

---

6. Emerson is referring to such sympathetic editorials as "Fugitive Slave Agitation" from the *Boston Daily Advertiser* (March 20, 1851, p. 2):

> The senseless excitement which was raised at New Bedford on Sunday last, by the active circulation of a false report, shows how ready a portion of the public are to become the dupes of a few designing men. . . . This transaction is a most unfortunate one, from the impression which it must produce abroad of the character of our community and the fidelity of our people to the Constitution.

are taken,—necessary functionaries, it may be, in a state, but to whom the dislike and the ban of society universally attaches.

5. These resistances appear in the history of the statute, in the retributions which speak so loud in every part of this business, that I think a tragic poet will know how to make it a lesson for all ages.

Mr. Webster's measure was, he told us, final. It was a pacification, it was a suppression, a measure of conciliation and adjustment. These were his words at different times: "there was to be no parleying more"; it was "irrepealable." Does it look final now? His final settlement has dislocated the foundations. The statehouse shakes like a tent. His pacification has brought all the honesty in every house, all scrupulous and good-hearted men, all women, and all children, to accuse the law. It has brought United States' swords into the streets, and chains round the courthouse. "A measure of pacification and union." What is its effect? To make one sole subject for conversation and painful thought throughout the continent, namely, slavery. There is not a man of thought or of feeling, but is concentrating his mind on it. There is not a clerk but recites its statistics; not a politician, but is watching its incalculable energy in the elections; not a jurist but is hunting up precedents; not a moralist but is prying into its quality; not an economist but is computing its profit and loss; Mr. Webster can judge whether this sort of solar microscope brought to bear on his law is likely to make opposition less.

The only benefit that has accrued from the law is its service to the education. It has been like a university to the entire people. It has turned every dinner-table into a debating club, and made every citizen a student of natural law. When a moral quality comes into politics, when a right is invaded, the discussion draws on deeper sources; general principles are laid bare, which cast light on the whole frame of society. And it is cheering to behold what champions the emergency called to this poor black boy; what subtlety, what logic, what learning, what exposure of the mischief of the law, and, above all, with what earnestness and dignity the advocates of freedom were inspired. It was one of the best compensations of this calamity.

But the Nemesis[7] works underneath again. It is a power that makes noonday dark, and draws us on to our undoing; and its dismal way is to pillory the offender in the moment of his triumph. The hands that put the chain on the slave are in that moment manacled. Who has seen anything like that which is now done?

The words of John Randolph,[8] wiser than he knew, have been ringing ominously in all echoes for thirty years,—words spoken in the heat of the Missouri debate.[9] "We do not govern the people of the north by our black slaves, but by their own white slaves. We know what we are doing. We have conquered you once, and we can and will conquer you again. Aye, we will drive you to the wall, and when we have you there once more, we will keep you there, and nail you down like base money." These words resounding ever since from California to Oregon, from Cape Florida to Cape Cod, come down now like the cry of Fate,

---

7. See n. 7, p. 143.
8. Of Roanoke (1773–1833), American politician known for his brilliant oratory and eccentric behavior during his tenure as a U.S. representative (twelve terms between 1799 and 1829) and senator (1825–27) from Virginia.
9. Missouri Compromise, an act of Congress (1820) whereby Maine was admitted into the Union as a free state, and Missouri as a slave state; slavery was barred from the territory acquired in the Louisiana Purchase north of the line 36° 30′.

in the moment when they are fulfilled. By white slaves, by a white slave, are we beaten. Who looked for such ghastly fulfilment, or to see what we see? Hills and Hallets,[1] servile editors by the hundred, we could have spared. But him, our best and proudest, the first man of the north in the very moment of mounting the throne, irresistibly taking the bit in his mouth, and the collar on his neck, and harnessing himself to the chariot of the planters.

The fairest American fame ends in this filthy law. Mr. Webster cannot choose but regret his loss. He must learn that those who make fame accuse him with one voice; that those who have no points to carry that are not identical with public morals and generous civilization, that the obscure and private who have no voice and care for none, so long as things go well, but who feel the disgrace of the new legislation creeping like a miasma into their homes, and blotting the daylight,—those to whom his name was once dear and honored, as the manly statesman to whom the choicest gifts of nature had been accorded, disown him: that he who was their pride in the woods and mountains of New England, is now their mortification,—they have torn down his picture from the wall, they have thrust his speeches into the chimney. No roars of New York mobs can drown this voice in Mr. Webster's ear. It will outwhisper all the salvos of the "Union Committee's" cannon. But I have said too much on this painful topic. I will not pursue that bitter history.

But passing from the ethical to the political view, I wish to place this statute, and we must use the introducer and substantial author of the bill as an illustration of the history.

I have as much charity for Mr. Webster, I think, as any one has. I need not say how much I have enjoyed his fame. Who has not helped to praise him? Simply, he was the one eminent American of our time, whom we could produce as a finished work of nature. We delighted in his form and face, in his voice, in his eloquence, in his power of labor, in his concentration, in his large understanding, in his daylight statement, simple force; the facts lay like strata of a cloud, or like the layers of the crust of the globe. He saw things as they were, and he stated them so. He has been by his clear perception and statement, in all these years, the best head in Congress, and the champion of the interests of the northern seaboard.

But as the activity and growth of slavery began to be offensively felt by his constituents, the senator became less sensitive to these evils. They were not for him to deal with: he was the commercial representative. He indulged occasionally in excellent expression of the known feeling of the New England people: but, when expected and when pledged, he omitted to speak, and he omitted to throw himself into the movement in those critical moments when his leadership would have turned the scale. At last, at a fatal hour, this sluggishness accumulated to downright counteraction, and, very unexpectedly to the whole Union, on the 7th March, 1850, in opposition to his education, association, and to all his own most explicit language for thirty years, he crossed the line, and became the head of the slavery party in this country.

Mr. Webster perhaps is only following the laws of his blood and constitution. I suppose his pledges were not quite natural to him. Mr. Webster is a man who

---

1. Benjamin Franklin Hallet (1797–1862), editor of the *Boston Post*, who supported the slavery advocate Franklin Pierce for president in 1852 and was rewarded with the post of district attorney of Boston. Probably Isaac Hill (1789–1851), New Hampshire editor and politician who opposed the abolitionists.

lives by his memory, a man of the past, not a man of faith or of hope. He obeys his powerful animal nature;—and his finely developed understanding only works truly and with all its force, when it stands for animal good; that is, for property. He believes, in so many words, that government exists for the protection of property. He looks at the Union as an estate, a large farm, and is excellent in the completeness of his defence of it so far. He adheres to the letter. Happily, he was born late,—after the independence had been declared, the Union agreed to, and the Constitution settled. What he finds already written, he will defend. Lucky that so much had got well written when he came. For he has no faith in the power of self-government; none whatever in extemporising a government. Not the smallest municipal provision, if it were new, would receive his sanction. In Massachusetts, in 1776, he would, beyond all question, have been a refugee. He praises Adams and Jefferson, but it is a past Adams and Jefferson that his mind can entertain. A present Adams and Jefferson he would denounce. So with the eulogies of liberty in his writings,—they are sentimentalism and youthful rhetoric. He can celebrate it, but it means as much from him as from Metternich or Talleyrand.[2] This is all inevitable from his constitution. All the drops of his blood have eyes that look downward. It is neither praise nor blame to say that he has no moral perception, no moral sentiment, but, in that *region*, to use the phrase of the phrenologists,[3] a hole in the head. The scraps of morality to be gleaned from his speeches are reflections of the minds of others. He says what he hears said, but often makes signal blunders in their use.

The destiny of this country is great and liberal, and is to be greatly administered. It is to be administered according to what is, and is to be, and not according to what is dead and gone. The Union of this people is a real thing, an alliance of men of one stock, one language, one religion, one system of manners and ideas. I hold it to be a real and not a statute Union. The people cleave to the Union, because they see their advantage in it, the added power of each.

I suppose the Union can be left to take care of itself. As much real Union as there is, the statutes will be sure to express. As much disunion as there is, no statutes can long conceal. Under the Union I suppose the fact to be that there are really two nations, the north and the south. It is not slavery that severs them, it is climate and temperament. The south does not like the north, slavery or no slavery, and never did. The north likes the south well enough, for it knows its own advantages. I am willing to leave them to the facts. If they continue to have a binding interest, they will be pretty sure to find it out: if not, they will consult their peace in parting. But one thing appears certain to me, that, as soon as the Constitution ordains an immoral law, it ordains disunion. The law is suicidal, and cannot be obeyed. The Union is at an end as soon as an immoral law is enacted. And he who writes a crime into the statute-book digs under the foundations of the capitol to plant there a powder magazine, and lays a train.

Nothing seems to me more hypocritical than the bluster about the Union. A year ago we were all lovers of the Union, and valued so dearly what seemed the immense destinies of this country, that we reckoned an impiety any act that compromised them. But in the new attitude in which we find ourselves the personal dishonor which now rests on every family in Massachusetts, the sentiment is changed. No man can look his neighbor in the face. We sneak about with the

2. Charles-Maurice de Périgord-Talleyrand (1754–1838), French diplomat. Metternich, see n. 1, p. 275.
3. See n. 4, p. 201.

infamy of crime, and cowardly allowance of it on our parts, and frankly, once for all, the Union, such an Union, is intolerable. The flag is an insult to ourselves. The Union,—I give you the sentiment of every decent citizen—The Union! O yes, I prized that, other things being equal; but what is the Union to a man self-condemned, with all sense of self-respect and chance of fair fame cut off, with the names of conscience and religion become bitter ironies, and liberty the ghastly mockery which Mr. Webster means by that word. The worst mischiefs that could follow from secession and new combination of the smallest fragments of the wreck, were slight and medicable to the calamity your Union has brought us.

It did not at first appear, and it was incredible, that the passage of the law would so absolutely defeat its proposed objects: but from the day when it was attempted to be executed in Massachusetts, this result has become certain, that the Union is no longer desireable. Whose deed is that?

I pass to say a few words to the question, What shall we do?

1. What is our federal capacity in our relation to the nation?

2. And what as citizens of a state?

I am an Unionist as we all are, or nearly all, and I strongly share the hope of mankind in the power, and, therefore, in the duties of the Union; and I conceive it demonstrated,—the necessity of common sense and justice entering into the laws.

What shall we do? First, abrogate this law; then proceed to confine slavery to slave states, and help them effectually to make an end of it. Or shall we, as we are advised on all hands, lie by, and wait the progress of the census? But will Slavery lie by? I fear not. She is very industrious, gives herself no holidays. No proclamations will put her down. She got Texas, and now will have Cuba, and means to keep her majority. The experience of the past gives us no encouragement to lie by.

Shall we call a new convention, or will any expert statesman furnish us a plan for the summary or gradual winding up of slavery, so far as the Republic is its patron? Where is the South itself? Since it is agreed by all sane men of all parties (or was yesterday) that slavery is mischievous, why does the South itself never offer the smallest counsel of her own? I have never heard in twenty years any project except Mr. Clay's.[4] Let us hear any project with candor and respect. Is it impossible to speak of it with reason and good nature? It is really the project fit for this country to entertain and accomplish. Every thing invites to emancipation. The grandeur of the design; the vast stake we hold; the national domain; the new importance of Liberia;[5] the manifest interests of the slave states; the religious effort of the free states; the public opinion of the world;—all join to demand it. It is said, it will cost a thousand millions of dollars to buy the slaves,—which sounds like a fabulous price. But if a price were named in good faith,—with the other elements of a practicable treaty in readiness, and with the convictions of mankind on this mischief once well awake and conspiring, I do not think any amount that figures could tell, founded on an esti-

4. Henry Clay (1777–1852), known as "the Great Compromiser," American politician who pushed the Missouri Compromise through the U.S. House of Representatives (1820) in an effort to reconcile free and slave states. He was instrumental in preparing the legislation that included the Fugitive Slave Law.
5. The African nation founded in 1822 by blacks, funded by the American Colonization Society, and declared a republic in 1847. A number of reformers suggested black emigration to Liberia as a solution to the slavery crisis.

mate, would be quite unmanageable. Every man in the world might give a week's work to sweep this mountain of calamities out of the earth.

Nothing is impracticable to this nation, which it shall set itself to do. Were ever men so endowed, so placed, so weaponed? Their power of territory seconded by a genius equal to every work[?] By new arts the earth is subdued, roaded, tunneled, telegraphed, gas-lighted; vast amounts of old labor disused; the sinews of man being relieved by sinews of steam. We are on the brink of more wonders.

The sun paints: presently we shall organize the echo, as now we do the shadow. Chemistry is extorting new aids. The genius of this people, it is found, can do anything which can be done by men. These thirty nations[6] are equal to any work, and are every moment stronger. In twenty-five years, they will be fifty millions. Is it not time to do something besides ditching and draining, and making the earth mellow and friable? Let them confront this mountain of poison, — bore, blast, excavate, pulverize, and shovel it once for all, down into the bottomless Pit. A thousand millions were cheap.

But grant that the heart of financiers, accustomed to practical figures, shrinks within them at these colossal amounts, and the embarrassments which complicate the problem. Granting that these contingencies are too many to be spanned by any human geometry, and that these evils are to be relieved only by the wisdom of God working in ages, — and by what instruments, — whether Liberia, whether flax-cotton, whether the working out this race by Irish and Germans, none can tell, or by what scourges God has guarded his law; still the question recurs, What must we do? One thing is plain, we cannot answer for the Union, but we must keep Massachusetts true. It is of unspeakable importance that she play her honest part. She must follow no vicious examples. Massachusetts is a little State. Countries have been great by ideas. Europe is little, compared with Asia and Africa. Yet Asia and Africa are its ox and its ass. Europe, the least of all the continents, has almost monopolized for twenty centuries the genius and power of them all. Greece was the least part of Europe. Attica[7] a little part of that, — one tenth of the size of Massachusetts. Yet that district still rules the intellect of men. Judaea was a petty country. Yet these two, Greece and Judaea, furnish the mind and the heart by which the rest of the world is sustained. And Massachusetts is little, but, if true to itself, can be the brain which turns about the behemoth. I say Massachusetts, but I mean Massachusetts in all the quarters of her dispersion; Massachusetts, as she is the mother of all the New England states, and as she sees her progeny scattered over the face of the land, in the farthest south and the uttermost west.

The immense power of rectitude is apt to be forgotten in politics. But they who have brought this great wrong on the country have not forgotten it. They avail themselves of the known probity and honor of Massachusetts, to endorse the statute. The ancient maxim still holds that never was any injustice effected except by the help of justice. The great game of the government has been to win the sanction of Massachusetts to the crime. Hitherto they have succeeded only so far as to win Boston to a certain extent. The behaviour of Boston was the reverse of what it should have been: it was supple and officious, and it put itself into the base attitude of pander to the crime. It should have placed obstruction at every step. Let the attitude of the state be firm. Let us respect the Union to all honest ends. But

---

6. I. e., the thirty states that constituted the Union in 1851.
7. An ancient region of east-central Greece around Athens. According to Greek legend, the four Attic tribes were unified into a single state by the Athenian king Theseus.

also respect an older and wider union, the law of nature and rectitude. Massachusetts is as strong as the universe, when it does that. We will never intermeddle with your slavery, — but you can in no wise be suffered to bring it to Cape Cod and Berkshire. This law must be made inoperative. It must be abrogated and wiped out of the statute book; but, whilst it stands there, it must be disobeyed.

We must make a small State great, by making every man in it true. It was the praise of Athens, "she could not lead countless armies into the field, but she knew how with a little band to defeat those who could." Every Roman reckoned himself at least a match for a province. Every Dorian did. Every Englishman in Australia, in South Africa, in India, or in whatever barbarous country their forts and factories have been set up, — represents London, represents the art, power, and law of Europe. Every man educated at the northern schools carries the like advantages into the south. For it is confounding distinctions to speak of the geographic sections of this country as of equal civilization. Every nation and every man bows, in spite of himself, to a higher mental and moral existence; and the sting of the late disgraces is, that this royal position of Massachusetts was foully lost, that the well-known sentiment of her people was not expressed. Let us correct this error. In this one fastness, let truth be spoken, and right done. Here let there be no confusion in our ideas. Let us not lie, nor steal, nor help to steal; and let us not call stealing by any fine names, such as "union" or "patriotism." Let us know, that not by the public, but by ourselves, our safety must be bought. That is the secret of southern power, that they rest not in meetings, but in private heats and courages. It is very certain from the perfect guaranties in the Constitution, and the high arguments of the defenders of liberty, which the occasion called out, that there is sufficient margin in the statute and the law for the spirit of the magistrate to show itself, and one, two, three occasions have just now occurred and passed, in either of which, if one man had felt the spirit of Coke or Mansfield or Parsons,[8] and read the law with the eye of freedom, the dishonor of Massachusetts had been prevented, and a limit set to these encroachments forever.

From Memoirs of Margaret Fuller Ossoli[1]

Visits to Concord

I became acquainted with Margaret in 1835. Perhaps it was a year earlier that Henry Hedge, who had long been her friend, told me of her genius and studies, and loaned me her manuscript translation of Goethe's Tasso. I was afterwards still more interested in her, by the warm praises of Harriet Martineau,[2] who had become acquainted with her at Cambridge, and who, finding Margaret's fancy for seeing me, took a generous interest in bringing us together. I remember, during a week in the winter of 1835-6, in which Miss Martineau was

---

8. William Parsons (1570–1650), lord justice of Ireland.
1. This two-volume reminiscence of Margaret Fuller, prepared by William Henry Channing, James Freeman Clarke, and Emerson, was published in 1852. After her death, Emerson wrote: "I have lost in her my audience." See journal entry for July–Aug. 1850 (p. 516). Channing (1810–1884), Unitarian minister, Christian socialist, and member of the Transcendental Club. See Emerson's "Ode" (p. 443). Clarke (1810–1888), Unitarian minister and writer who edited *The Western Messenger* (in which Emerson published several poems in 1839).
2. Harriet Martineau (1802–1876), English author, best known in America for her unfavorable critiques, *Society in America* (1837) and *Retrospect of Western Travel* (1838).

my guest, she returned again and again to the topic of Margaret's excelling genius and conversation, and enjoined it on me to seek her acquaintance; which I willingly promised. I am not sure that it was not in Miss Martineau's company, a little earlier, that I first saw her. And I find a memorandum, in her own journal, of a visit, made by my brother Charles and myself, to Miss Martineau, at Mrs. Farrar's. It was not, however, till the next July, after a little diplomatizing in billets by the ladies, that her first visit to our house was arranged, and she came to spend a fortnight with my wife. I still remember the first half-hour of Margaret's conversation. She was then twenty-six years old. She had a face and frame that would indicate fulness and tenacity of life. She was rather under the middle height; her complexion was fair, with strong fair hair. She was then, as always, carefully and becomingly dressed, and of ladylike self-possession. For the rest, her appearance had nothing prepossessing. Her extreme plainness,— a trick of incessantly opening and shutting her eyelids,—the nasal tone of her voice,—all repelled; and I said to myself, we shall never get far. It is to be said, that Margaret made a disagreeable first impression on most persons, including those who became afterwards her best friends, to such an extreme that they did not wish to be in the same room with her. This was partly the effect of her manners, which expressed an overweening sense of power, and slight esteem of others, and partly the prejudice of her fame. She had a dangerous reputation for satire, in addition to her great scholarship. The men thought she carried too many guns, and the women did not like one who despised them. I believe I fancied her too much interested in personal history; and her talk was a comedy in which dramatic justice was done to everybody's foibles. I remember that she made me laugh more than I liked; for I was, at that time, an eager scholar of ethics, and had tasted the sweets of solitude and stoicism, and I found something profane in the hours of amusing gossip into which she drew me, and, when I returned to my library, had much to think of the crackling of thorns under a pot. Margaret, who had stuffed me out as a philosopher, in her own fancy, was too intent on establishing a good footing between us, to omit any art of winning. She studied my tastes, piqued and amused me, challenged frankness by frankness, and did not conceal the good opinion of me she brought with her, nor her wish to please. She was curious to know my opinions and experiences. Of course, it was impossible long to hold out against such urgent assault. She had an incredible variety of anecdotes, and the readiest wit to give an absurd turn to whatever passed; and the eyes, which were so plain at first, soon swam with fun and drolleries, and the very tides of joy and superabundant life.

This rumor was much spread abroad, that she was sneering, scoffing, critical, disdainful of humble people, and of all but the intellectual. I had heard it whenever she was named. It was a superficial judgment. Her satire was only the pastime and necessity of her talent, the play of superabundant animal spirits. And it will be seen, in the sequel, that her mind presently disclosed many moods and powers, in successive platforms or terraces, each above each, that quite effaced this first impression, in the opulence of the following pictures.

* * *

When she came to Concord, she was already rich in friends, rich in experiences, rich in culture. She was well read in French, Italian, and German literature. She had learned Latin and a little Greek. But her English reading was incomplete; and, while she knew Molière, and Rousseau, and any quantity of French letters, memoirs, and novels, and was a dear student of Dante and Petrarca, and knew German books more cordially than any other person, she was little read in Shakspeare; and I believe I had the pleasure of making her acquainted with Chaucer, with Ben Jonson, with Herbert, Chapman, Ford, Beaumont and Fletcher, with Bacon, and Sir Thomas Browne. I was seven years her senior, and had the habit of idle reading in old English books, and, though not much versed, yet quite enough to give me the right to lead her. She fancied that her sympathy and taste had led her to an exclusive culture of southern European books.

She had large experiences. She had been a precocious scholar at Dr. Park's school; good in mathematics and in languages. Her father, whom she had recently lost, had been proud of her, and petted her. She had drawn, at Cambridge, numbers of lively young men about her. She had had a circle of young women who were devoted to her, and who described her as "a wonder of intellect, who had yet no religion." She had drawn to her every superior young man or young woman she had met, and whole romances of life and love had been confided, counselled, thought, and lived through, in her cognizance and sympathy.

These histories are rapid, so that she had already beheld many times the youth, meridian, and old age of passion. She had, besides, selected, from so many, a few eminent companions, and already felt that she was not likely to see anything more beautiful than her beauties, anything more powerful and generous than her youths. She had found out her own secret by early comparison, and knew what power to draw confidence, what necessity to lead in every circle, belonged of right to her. Her powers were maturing, and nobler sentiments were subliming the first heats and rude experiments. She had outward calmness and dignity. She had come to the ambition to be filled with all nobleness.

Of the friends who surrounded her, at that period, it is neither easy to speak, nor not to speak. A life of Margaret is impossible without them, she mixed herself so inextricably with her company; and when this little book was first projected, it was proposed to entitle it "Margaret and her Friends," the subject persisting to offer itself in the plural number. But, on trial, that form proved impossible, and it only remained that the narrative, like a Greek tragedy, should suppose the chorus always on the stage, sympathizing and sympathized with by the queen of the scene.

Yet I remember these persons as a fair, commanding troop, every one of them adorned by some splendor of beauty, of grace, of talent, or of character, and comprising in their band persons who have since disclosed sterling worth and elevated aims in the conduct of life.

Three beautiful women, — either of whom would have been the fairest ornament of Papanti's[3] Assemblies, but for the presence of the other, — were her friends. One of these early became, and long remained, nearly the central figure in Margaret's brilliant circle, attracting to herself, by her grace and her singular natural eloquence, every feeling of affection, hope, and pride.

* * *

There was another lady, more late and reluctantly entering Margaret's circle, with a mind as high, and more mathematically exact, drawn by taste to

3. A dancing academy for fashionable Bostonians.

Greek, as Margaret to Italian genius, tempted to do homage to Margaret's flowing expressive energy, but still more inclined and secured to her side by the good sense and the heroism which Margaret disclosed, perhaps not a little by the sufferings which she addressed herself to alleviate, as long as Margaret lived. Margaret had a courage in her address which it was not easy to resist. She called all her friends by their Christian names. In their early intercourse I suppose this lady's billets were more punctiliously worded than Margaret liked; so she subscribed herself, in reply, "Your affectionate 'Miss Fuller.'" When the difficulties were at length surmounted, and the conditions ascertained on which two admirable persons could live together, the best understanding grew up, and subsisted during her life. . . .

None interested her more at that time, and for many years after, than a youth with whom she had been acquainted in Cambridge before he left the University, and the unfolding of whose powers she had watched with the warmest sympathy. He was an amateur, and, but for the exactions not to be resisted of an *American*, that is to say, of a commercial, career,—his acceptance of which she never ceased to regard as an apostasy,—himself a high artist. He was her companion, and, though much younger, her guide in the study of art. With him she examined, leaf by leaf, the designs of Raphael, of Michel Angelo, of Da Vinci, of Guercino, the architecture of the Greeks, the books of Palladio, the Ruins, and Prisons of Piranesi;[4] and long kept up a profuse correspondence on books and studies in which they had a mutual interest. And yet, as happened so often, these literary sympathies, though sincere, were only veils and occasions to beguile the time, so profound was her interest in the character and fortunes of her friend.

There was another youth, whom she found later, of invalid habit, which had infected in some degree the tone of his mind, but of a delicate and pervasive insight, and the highest appreciation for genius in letters, arts, and life. Margaret describes "his complexion as clear in its pallor, and his eye steady." His turn of mind, and his habits of life, had almost a monastic turn,—a jealousy of the common tendencies of literary men either to display or to philosophy. Margaret was struck with the singular fineness of his perceptions, and the pious tendency of his thoughts, and enjoyed with him his proud reception, not as from above, but almost on equal ground, of Homer and Æschylus, of Dante and Petrarch, of Montaigne, of Calderon, of Goethe. Margaret wished, also, to defend his privacy from the dangerous solicitations to premature authorship.

* * *

I have thus vaguely designated, among the numerous group of her friends, only those who were much in her company, in the early years of my acquaintance with her.

She wore this circle of friends, when I first knew her, as a necklace of diamonds about her neck. They were so much to each other, that Margaret seemed to represent them all, and, to know her, was to acquire a place with them. The confidences given her were their best, and she held them to them. She was an

4. Giovanni Battista Piranesi (1720–1778), Italian architect who published etchings of the ruins of classical Rome, most famous for his *Carceri d'Invenzione*, or *Dream Prisons* (1745). Raphael, see n. 3, p. 86. Michelangelo, see n. 6, p. 42. Leonardo Da Vinci (1452–1519), Italian poet, painter, sculptor, architect, inventor, engineer, and musician; one of the great geniuses of the Western tradition. Andrea Palladio (1508–1580), neo-Classicist Italian architect, author of *Four Books of Architecture* (1570).

active, inspiring companion and correspondent, and all the art, the thought, and the nobleness in New England, seemed, at that moment, related to her, and she to it. She was everywhere a welcome guest. The houses of her friends in town and country were open to her, and every hospitable attention eagerly offered. Her arrival was a holiday, and so was her abode. She stayed a few days, often a week, more seldom a month, and all tasks that could be suspended were put aside to catch the favorable hour, in walking, riding, or boating, to talk with this joyful guest, who brought wit, anecdotes, love-stories, tragedies, oracles with her, and, with her broad web of relations to so many fine friends, seemed like the queen of some parliament of love, who carried the key to all confidences, and to whom every question had been finally referred.

Persons were her game, specially, if marked by fortune, or character, or success; — to such was she sent. She addressed them with a hardihood, — almost a haughty assurance, — queen-like. Indeed, they fell in her way, where the access might have seemed difficult, by wonderful casualties; and the inveterate recluse, the coyest maid, the waywardest poet, made no resistance, but yielded at discretion, as if they had been waiting for her, all doors to this imperious dame. She disarmed the suspicion of recluse scholars by the absence of bookishness. The ease with which she entered into conversation made them forget all they had heard of her; and she was infinitely less interested in literature than in life. They saw she valued earnest persons, and Dante, Petrarch, and Goethe, because they thought as she did, and gratified her with high portraits, which she was everywhere seeking. She drew her companions to surprising confessions. She was the wedding-guest, to whom the long-pent story must be told; and they were not less struck, on reflection, at the suddenness of the friendship which had established, in one day, new and permanent covenants. She extorted the secret of life, which cannot be told without setting heart and mind in a glow; and thus had the best of those she saw. Whatever romance, whatever virtue, whatever impressive experience, — this came to her; and she lived in a superior circle; for they suppressed all their common-place in her presence.

She was perfectly true to this confidence. She never confounded relations, but kept a hundred fine threads in her hand, without crossing or entangling any. An entire intimacy, which seemed to make both sharers of the whole horizon of each others' and of all truth; did not yet make her false to any other friend; gave no title to the history that an equal trust of another friend had put in her keeping. In this reticence was no prudery and no effort. For, so rich her mind, that she never was tempted to treachery, by the desire of entertaining. The day was never long enough to exhaust her opulent memory; and I, who knew her intimately for ten years, — from July, 1836, till August, 1846, when she sailed for Europe, — never saw her without surprise at her new powers.

Of the conversations above alluded to, the substance was whatever was suggested by her passionate wish for equal companions, to the end of making life altogether noble. With the firmest tact she led the discourse into the midst of their daily living and working, recognizing the good-will and sincerity which each man has in his aims, and treating so playfully and intellectually all the points, that one seemed to see his life *en beau*, and was flattered by beholding what he had found so tedious in its workday weeds, shining in glorious costume. Each of his friends passed before him in the new light; hope seemed to spring under his feet, and life was worth living. The auditor jumped for joy, and thirsted for unlimited draughts. What! is this the dame, who, I heard, was sneering and critical? this the blue-stocking, of whom I stood in terror and dislike? this wondrous woman, full of counsel, full of tenderness, before whom every mean thing is ashamed, and hides itself; this new Corinne,[5] more variously gifted, wise, sportive, eloquent, who seems to have learned all languages, Heaven knows when or how,—I should think she was born to them,— magnificent, prophetic, reading my life at her will, and puzzling me with riddles like this, "Yours is an example of a destiny springing from character": and, again, "I see your destiny hovering before you, but it always escapes from you."

The test of this eloquence was its range. It told on children, and on old people; on men of the world, and on sainted maids. She could hold them all by her honeyed tongue. A lady of the best eminence, whom Margaret occasionally visited, in one of our cities of spindles, speaking one day of her neighbors, said, "I stand in a certain awe of the moneyed men, the manufacturers, and so on, knowing that they will have small interest in Plato, or in Biot;[6] but I saw them approach Margaret, with perfect security, for she could give them bread that they could eat." Some persons are thrown off their balance when in society; others are thrown on to balance; the excitement of company, and the observation of other characters, correct their biases. Margaret always appeared to unexpected advantage in conversation with a large circle. She had more sanity than any other; whilst, in private, her vision was often through colored lenses.

Her talents were so various, and her conversation so rich and entertaining, that one might talk with her many times, by the parlor fire, before he discovered the strength which served as foundation to so much accomplishment and eloquence. But, concealed under flowers and music, was the broadest good sense, very well able to dispose of all this pile of native and foreign ornaments, and quite able to work without them. She could always rally on this, in every circumstance, and in every company, and find herself on a firm footing of equality with any party whatever, and make herself useful, and, if need be, formidable.

The old Anaximenes;[7] seeking, I suppose, for a source sufficiently diffusive, said, that Mind must be *in the air*, which, when all men breathed, they were filled with one intelligence. And when men have larger measures of reason, as Æsop, Cervantes, Franklin, Scott, they gain in universality, or are no longer confined to a few associates, but are good company for all persons,— philosophers, women, men of fashion, tradesmen, and servants. Indeed, an older philosopher than Anaximenes, namely, language itself, had taught to distinguish superior or purer sense as *common sense*.

Margaret had, with certain limitations, or, must we say, *strictures*, these larger lungs, inhaling this universal element, and could speak to Jew and Greek, free and bond, to each in his own tongue. The Concord stage-coachman distinguished her by his respect, and the chambermaid was pretty sure to confide to her, on the second day, her homely romance.

I regret that it is not in my power to give any true report of Margaret's conversation. She soon became an established friend and frequent inmate of our house, and continued, thenceforward, for years, to come, once in three or four

5. Although Emerson could be referring to a literary figure from ancient Greece, it is much more likely that his reference is to the heroine of Madame de Staël's (see n. 6, p. 42) *Corinne; or, Italy* (1807), a book passionately admired by Emerson, Fuller, and others in their circle. Madame de Staël herself was one of Fuller's idols. See also *On Germany* (p. 573).
6. Probably Jean Baptiste Biot (1774–1862), celebrated French astronomer and physicist. Plato, see n. 4, p. 15.
7. Anaximenes, see n. 5, p. 208.

months, to spend a week or a fortnight with us. She adopted all the people and all the interests she found here. Your people shall be my people, and yonder darling boy I shall cherish as my own. Her ready sympathies endeared her to my wife and my mother, each of whom highly esteemed her good sense and sincerity. She suited each, and all. Yet, she was not a person to be suspected of complaisance, and her attachments, one might say, were chemical.

She had so many tasks of her own, that she was a very easy guest to entertain, as she could be left to herself, day after day, without apology. According to our usual habit, we seldom met in the forenoon. After dinner, we read something together, or walked, or rode. In the evening, she came to the library, and many and many a conversation was there held, whose details, if they could be preserved, would justify all encomiums. They interested me in every manner;—talent, memory, wit, stern introspection; poetic play, religion, the finest personal feeling, the aspects of the future, each followed each in full activity, and left me, I remember, enriched and sometimes astonished by the gifts of my guest. Her topics were numerous, but the cardinal points of poetry, love, and religion, were never far off. She was a student of art, and, though untravelled, knew, much better than most persons who had been abroad, the conventional reputation of each of the masters. She was familiar with all the field of elegant criticism in literature. Among the problems of the day, these two attracted her chiefly, Mythology and Demonology; then, also, French Socialism, especially as it concerned woman; the whole prolific family of reforms, and, of course, the genius and career of each remarkable person.

She had other friends, in this town, beside those in my house. A lady, already alluded to, lived in the village, who had known her longer than I, and whose prejudices Margaret had resolutely fought down, until she converted her into the firmest and most efficient of friends. In 1842, Nathaniel Hawthorne, already then known to the world by his Twice-Told Tales, came to live in Concord, in the "Old Manse," with his wife,[8] who was herself an artist. With these welcomed persons Margaret formed a strict and happy acquaintance. She liked their old house, and the taste which had filled it with new articles of beautiful form, yet harmonized with the antique furniture left by the former proprietors. She liked, too, the pleasing walks, and rides, and boatings, which that neighborhood commanded.

In 1842, William Ellery Channing,[9] whose wife was her sister, built a house in Concord, and this circumstance made a new tie and another home for Margaret.

ARCANA

It was soon evident that there was somewhat a little pagan about her; that she had some faith more or less distinct in a fate, and in a guardian genius; that her fancy, or her pride, had played with her religion. She had a taste for gems, ciphers, talismans, omens, coincidences, and birth-days. She had a special love for the planet Jupiter, and a belief that the month of September was inauspi-

---

8. Hawthorne's wife, née Sophia Peabody, was the sister of Emerson's close friend Elizabeth Peabody. For the latter's review of *Nature*, see p. 590. *Twice-Told Tales* was published in 1837. The *"Old Manse"*: built just before the Revolution by Emerson's grandfather William Emerson.
9. See n. 7, p. 247. A ne'er-do-well poet and flaneur, he did little to make life comfortable for his long-suffering wife.

cious to her. She never forgot that her name, Margarita, signified a pearl. "When I first met with the name Leila," she said, "I knew, from the very look and sound, it was mine; I knew that it meant night,—night, which brings out stars, as sorrow brings out truths." Sortilege she valued. She tried *sortes biblicæ*,[1] and her hits were memorable. I think each new book which interested her, she was disposed to put to this test, and know if it had somewhat personal to say to her. As happens to such persons, these guesses were justified by the event. She chose carbuncle for her own stone, and when a dear friend was to give her a gem, this was the one selected. She valued what she had somewhere read, that carbuncles are male and female. The female casts out light, the male has his within himself. "Mine," she said, "is the male." And she was wont to put on her carbuncle, a bracelet, or some selected gem, to write letters to certain friends. One of her friends she coupled with the onyx, another in a decided way with the amethyst. She learned that the ancients esteemed this gem a talisman to dispel intoxication, to give good thoughts and understanding.

* * *

DÆMONOLOGY

This catching at straws of coincidence, where all is geometrical, seems the necessity of certain natures. It is true, that, in every good work, the particulars are right, and, that every spot of light on the ground, under the trees, is a perfect image of the sun. Yet, for astronomical purposes, an observatory is better than an orchard; and in a universe which is nothing but generations, or an unbroken suite of cause and effect, to infer Providence, because a man happens to find a shilling on the pavement just when he wants one to spend, is puerile, and much as if each of us should date his letters and notes of hand from his own birthday, instead of from Christ's or the king's reign, or the current Congress. These, to be sure, are also, at first, petty and private beginnings, but, by the world of men, clothed with a social and cosmical character.

It will be seen, however, that this propensity Margaret held with certain tenets of fate, which always swayed her, and which Goethe, who had found room and fine names for all this in his system, had encouraged; and, I may add, which her own experiences, early and late, seemed strangely to justify.

* * *

TEMPERAMENT

I said that Margaret had a broad good sense, which brought her near to all people. I am to say that she had also a strong temperament, which is that counter force which makes individuality, by driving all the powers in the direction of the ruling thought or feeling, and, when it is allowed full sway, isolating them. These two tendencies were always invading each other; and now one and now the other carried the day. This alternation perplexes the biographer, as it did the observer. We contradict on the second page what we affirm on the first: and I remember how often I was compelled to correct my impressions of her character when living; for after I had settled it once for all that she wanted this

---

1. A method of telling one's fortune, or reading omens, by opening the Bible at random and reading whatever verse one's eye fell upon.

or that perception, at our next interview she would say with emphasis the very word.

I think, in her case, there was something abnormal in those obscure habits and necessities which we denote by the word Temperament. In the first day of our acquaintance, I felt her to be a foreigner,—that, with her, one would always be sensible of some barrier, as if in making up a friendship with a cultivated Spaniard or Turk. She had a strong constitution, and of course its reäctions were strong; and this is the reason why in all her life she has so much to say of her *fate*. She was in jubilant spirits in the morning, and ended the day with nervous headache, whose spasms, my wife told me, produced total prostration. She had great energy of speech and action, and seemed formed for high emergencies.

Her life concentrated itself on certain happy days, happy hours, happy moments. The rest was a void. She had read that a man of letters must lose many days, to work well in one. Much more must a Sappho[2] or a sibyl. The capacity of pleasure was balanced by the capacity of pain. . . .

When I found she lived at a rate so much faster than mine, and which was violent compared with mine, I foreboded rash and painful crises, and had a feeling as if a voice cried, *Stand from under!*—as if, a little further on, this destiny was threatened with jars and reverses, which no friendship could avert or console. This feeling partly wore off, on better acquaintance, but remained latent; and I had always an impression that her energy was too much a force of blood, and therefore never felt the security for her peace which belongs to more purely intellectual natures. She seemed more vulnerable. For the same reason, she remained inscrutable to me; her strength was not my strength,—her powers were a surprise. She passed into new states of great advance, but I understood these no better. It were long to tell her peculiarities. Her childhood was full of presentiments. She was then a somnambulist. She was subject to attacks of delirium, and later, perceived that she had spectral illusions. When she was twelve, she had a determination of blood to the head. "My parents," she said, "were much mortified to see the fineness of my complexion destroyed. My own vanity was for a time severely wounded; but I recovered, and made up my mind to be bright and ugly."

She was all her lifetime the victim of disease and pain. She read and wrote in bed, and believed that she could understand anything better when she was ill. Pain acted like a girdle, to give tension to her powers. A lady, who was with her one day during a terrible attack of nervous headache, which made Margaret totally helpless, assured me that Margaret was yet in the finest vein of humor, and kept those who were assisting her in a strange, painful excitement, between laughing and crying, by perpetual brilliant sallies. There were other peculiarities of habit and power. When she turned her head on one side, she alleged she had second sight, like St. Francis. These traits or predispositions made her a willing listener to all the uncertain science of mesmerism and its goblin brood, which have been rife in recent years.

She had a feeling that she ought to have been a man, and said of herself, "A man's ambition with a woman's heart, is an evil lot."

* * *

2. One of the most famous of ancient lyric poets (b. 612 B.C.E.), a native of Lesbos.

She had, indeed, a rude strength, which, if it could have been supported by an equal health, would have given her the efficiency of the strongest men. As it was, she had great power of work. The account of her reading in Groton is at a rate like Gibbon's,[3] and, later, that of her writing, considered with the fact that writing was not grateful to her, is incredible. She often proposed to her friends, in the progress of intimacy, to write every day. "I think less than a daily offering of thought and feeling would not content me, so much seems to pass unspoken." In Italy, she tells Madame Arconati, that she has "more than a hundred correspondents;" and it was her habit there to devote one day of every week to those distant friends. The facility with which she assumed stints of literary labor, which veteran feeders of the press would shrink from, — assumed and performed, — when her friends were to be served, I have often observed with wonder, and with fear, when I considered the near extremes of ill-health, and the manner in which her life heaped itself in high and happy moments, which were avenged by lassitude and pain.

"As each task comes," she said, "I borrow a readiness from its aspect, as I always do brightness from the face of a friend. Yet, as soon as the hour is past, I sink."

I think most of her friends will remember to have felt, at one time or another, some uneasiness, as if this athletic soul craved a larger atmosphere than it found; as if she were ill-timed and mis-mated, and felt in herself a tide of life, which compared with the slow circulation of others as a torrent with a rill. She found no full expression of it but in music. Beethoven's Symphony was the only right thing the city of the Puritans had for her.

* * *

SELF-ESTEEM

Margaret at first astonished and repelled us by a complacency that seemed the most assured since the days of Scaliger. She spoke, in the quietest manner, of the girls she had formed, the young men who owed everything to her, the fine companions she had long ago exhausted. In the coolest way, she said to her friends, "I now know all the people worth knowing in America, and I find no intellect comparable to my own." In vain, on one occasion, I professed my reverence for a youth of genius, and my curiosity in his future — O no, she was intimate with his mind, and I spoiled him, by overrating him. Meantime, we knew that she neither had seen, nor would see, his subtle superiorities.

I have heard, that from the beginning of her life, she idealized herself as a sovereign. She told —— she early saw herself to be intellectually superior to those around her, and that for years she dwelt upon the idea, until she believed that she was not her parents' child, but an European princess confided to their care. She remembered, that, when a little girl, she was walking one day under the apple trees with such an air and step, that her father pointed her out to her sister, saying, *Incedit regina*.[4]

* * *

---

3. Gibbon, see n. 9, p. 33.
4. She walks like a queen (Latin); sometimes said of goddesses in classical epics.

It is certain that Margaret occasionally let slip, with all the innocence imaginable, some phrase betraying the presence of a rather mountainous ME, in a way to surprise those who knew her good sense. She could say, as if she were stating a scientific fact, in enumerating the merits of somebody, "He appreciates *me*." There was something of hereditary organization in this, and something of unfavorable circumstance in the fact, that she had in early life no companion, and few afterwards, in her finer studies; but there was also an ebullient sense of power, which she felt to be in her, which as yet had found no right channels.

* * *

I have inquired diligently of those who saw her often, and in different companies, concerning her habitual tone, and something like this is the report:— In conversation, Margaret seldom, except as a special grace, admitted others upon an equal ground with herself. She was exceedingly tender, when she pleased to be, and most cherishing in her influence; but to elicit this tenderness, it was necessary to submit first to her personally. When a person was overwhelmed by her, and answered not a word, except, "Margaret, be merciful to me, a sinner," then her love and tenderness would come like a seraph's, and often an acknowledgment that she had been too harsh, and even a craving for pardon, with a humility,—which, perhaps, she had caught from the other. But her instinct was not humility,—that was always an afterthought.

This arrogant tone of her conversation, if it came to be the subject of comment, of course, she defended, and with such broad good nature, and on grounds of simple truth, as were not easy to set aside. She quoted from Manzoni's[5] *Carmagnola*, the lines:—

> "Tolga il ciel che alcuno
> Piu altamente di me pensi ch'io stesso."

"God forbid that any one should conceive more highly of me than I myself." Meantime, the tone of her journals is humble, tearful, religious, and rises easily into prayer.

I am obliged to an ingenious correspondent for the substance of the following account of this idiosyncrasy:—

Margaret was one of the few persons who looked upon life as an art, and every person not merely as an artist, but as a work of art. She looked upon herself as a living statue, which should always stand on a polished pedestal, with right accessories, and under the most fitting lights. She would have been glad to have everybody so live and act. She was annoyed when they did not, and when they did not regard her from the point of view which alone did justice to her. No one could be more lenient in her judgments of those whom she saw to be living in this light. Their faults were to be held as "the disproportions of the ungrown giant." But the faults of persons who were unjustified by this ideal, were odious. Unhappily, her constitutional self-esteem sometimes blinded the eyes that should have seen that an idea lay at the bottom of some lives which she did not quite so readily comprehend as beauty; that truth had other manifestations than those which engaged her natural sympathies; that sometimes the

5. See n. 5, p. 342. His tragedy *Il Conte di Carmagnola* was published in 1820.

soul illuminated only the smallest arc—of a circle so large that it was lost in the clouds of another world.

This apology reminds me of a little speech once made to her, at his own house, by Dr. Channing, who held her in the highest regard: "Miss Fuller, when I consider that you are and have all that Miss——has so long wished for, and that you scorn her, and that she still admires you,—I think her place in heaven will be very high."

But qualities of this kind can only be truly described by the impression they make on the bystander; and it is certain that her friends excused in her, because she had a right to it, a tone which they would have reckoned intolerable in any other.

* * *

BOOKS

She had been early remarked for her sense and sprightliness, and for her skill in school exercises. Now she had added wide reading, and of the books most grateful to her. She had read the Italian poets by herself, and from sympathy. I said, that, by the leading part she naturally took, she had identified herself with all the elegant culture in this country. Almost every person who had any distinction for wit, or art, or scholarship, was known to her; and she was familiar with the leading books and topics. There is a kind of undulation in the popularity of the great writers, even of the first rank. We have seen a recent importance given to Behmen and Swedenborg;[6] and Shakspeare has unquestionably gained with the present generation. It is distinctive, too, of the taste of the period,—the new vogue given to the genius of Dante. An edition of Cary's translation, reprinted in Boston, many years ago, was rapidly sold; and, for the last twenty years, all studious youths and maidens have been reading the Inferno. Margaret had very early found her way to Dante, and from a certain native preference which she felt or fancied for the Italian genius.

* * *

Dante, Petrarca, Tasso, were her friends among the old poets,—for to Ariosto she assigned a far lower place,—Alfieri[7] and Manzoni, among the new. But what was of still more import to her education, she had read German books, and, for the three years before I knew her, almost exclusively,—Lessing, Schiller, Richter, Tieck, Novalis, and, above all, GOETHE.[8] It was very obvious at the first intercourse with her, though her rich and busy mind never reproduced undigested reading, that the last writer,—food or poison,—the most powerful of all mental reagents,—the pivotal mind in modern literature,—for all before him are ancients, and all who have read him are moderns,—that this mind had been her teacher, and, of course, the place was filled, nor was there room for any other. She had that symptom which appears in all the students of Goethe,—an ill-dissembled contempt of all criticism on him which they hear

6. See n. 6, p. 35. Behmen, see n. 8, p. 168.
7. All of these writers were among Emerson's favorites also. Vittorio Alfieri (1749–1803), Italian dramatist and poet. Dante, see n. 3, p. 184. Petrarca, see n. 7, p. 178. Tasso, see n. 2, p. 259.
8. See n. 6, p. 42. Lessing, see n. 3, p. 254. Schiller, see n. 5, p. 130. Richter, see n. 5, p. 342. Ludwig Tieck (1773–1853), German writer known for his romantic irony. Novalis, pen name of Friedrich Leopold Frei-herr von Hardenberg (1772–1801), German poet and novelist with mystical leanings.

from others, as if it were totally irrelevant; and they are themselves always preparing to say the right word,—a *prestige* which is allowed, of course, until they do speak: when they have delivered their volley, they pass, like their fore-goers, to the rear.

The effect on Margaret was complete. She was perfectly timed to it. She found her moods met, her topics treated, the liberty of thought she loved, the same climate of mind. Of course, this book superseded all others, for the time, and tinged deeply all her thoughts. The religion, the science, the catholicism, the worship of art, the mysticism and dæmonology, and withal the clear recognition of moral distinctions as final and eternal, all charmed her; and Faust, and Tasso, and Mignon, and Makaria, and Iphigenia,[9] became irresistible names. It was one of those agreeable historical coincidences, perhaps invariable, though not yet registered, the simultaneous appearance of a teacher and of pupils, between whom exists a strict affinity. Nowhere did Goethe find a braver, more intelligent, or more sympathetic reader. About the time I knew her, she was meditating a biography of Goethe, and did set herself to the task in 1837. She spent much time on it, and has left heaps of manuscripts, which are notes, transcripts, and studies in that direction. But she wanted leisure and health to finish it, amid the multitude of projected works with which her brain teemed. She used great discretion on this point, and made no promises. In 1839, she published her translation of Eckermann,[1] a book which makes the basis of the translation of Eckermann since published in London, by Mr. Oxenford. In the Dial, in July, 1841, she wrote an article on Goethe, which is, on many accounts, her best paper.

* * *

NATURE

Margaret's love of beauty made her, of course, a votary of nature, but rather for pleasurable excitement than with a deep poetic feeling. Her imperfect vision and her bad health were serious impediments to intimacy with woods and rivers. She had never paid,—and it is a little remarkable,—any attention to natural sciences. She neither botanized, nor geologized, nor dissected. Still she delighted in short country rambles, in the varieties of landscape, in pastoral country, in mountain outlines, and, above all, in the sea-shore. At Nantasket Beach, and at Newport, she spent a month or two of many successive summers. She paid homage to rocks, woods, flowers, rivers, and the moon. She spent a good deal of time out of doors, sitting, perhaps, with a book in some sheltered recess commanding a landscape. She watched, by day and by night, the skies and the earth, and believed she knew all their expressions. She wrote in her journal, or in her correspondence,—a series of "moonlights," in which she seriously attempts to describe the light and scenery of successive nights of the summer moon. Of course, her raptures must appear sickly and superficial to an observer, who, with equal feeling, had better powers of observation.

Nothing is more rare than a talent to describe landscape, and, especially, skyscape, or cloudscape, although a vast number of letters, from correspondents between the ages of twenty and thirty, are filled with experiments in this kind.

9. All characters in Goethe's works.
1. Johann Eckermann, *Conversations with Goethe* (1836).

Margaret, in her turn, made many vain attempts, and, to a lover of nature, who knows that every day has new and inimitable lights and shades, one of these descriptions is as vapid as the raptures of a citizen arrived at his first meadow. Of course, he is charmed, but, of course, he cannot tell what he sees, or what pleases him. Yet Margaret often speaks with a certain tenderness and beauty of the impressions made upon her.

* * *

ART

There are persons to whom a gallery is everywhere a home. In this country, the antique is known only by plaster casts, and by drawings. The Boston Athenæum,—on whose sunny roof and beautiful chambers may the benediction of centuries of students rest with mine!—added to its library, in 1823, a small, but excellent museum of the antique sculpture, in plaster;—the selection being dictated, it is said, by no less an adviser than Canova.[2] The Apollo, the Laocoon, the Venuses, Diana, the head of the Phidian Jove, Bacchus, Antinous, the Torso Hercules, the Discobolus, the Gladiator Borghese, the Apollino,—all these, and more, the sumptuous gift of Augustus Thorndike. It is much that one man should have power to confer on so many, who never saw him, a benefit so pure and enduring.

To these were soon added a heroic line of antique busts, and, at last, by Horatio Greenough,[3] the Night and Day of Michel Angelo. Here was old Greece and old Italy brought bodily to New England, and a verification given to all our dreams and readings. It was easy to collect, from the drawing-rooms of the city, a respectable picture-gallery for a summer exhibition. This was also done, and a new pleasure was invented for the studious, and a new home for the solitary. The Brimmer donation, in 1838, added a costly series of engravings, chiefly of the French and Italian museums, and the drawings of Guercino, Salvator Rosa,[4] and other masters. The separate chamber in which these collections were at first contained, made a favorite place of meeting for Margaret and a few of her friends, who were lovers of these works.

First led perhaps by Goethe, afterwards by the love she herself conceived for them, she read everything that related to Michel Angelo and Raphael. She read, pen in hand, Quatremère de Quincy's[5] lives of those two painters, and I have her transcripts and commentary before me. She read Condivi, Vasari, Benvenuto Cellini, Duppa, Fuseli, and Von Waagen,[6]—great and small. Every design of Michel, the four volumes of Raphael's designs, were in the rich portfolios of her most intimate friend. "I have been very happy," she writes,

2. Antonio Canova (1757–1822), Italian sculptor and author much admired by Margaret Fuller and generally by cultured Bostonians, who frequently placed statuette-sized reproductions of his work on their mantlepieces. The plaster models of the classical works Emerson mentions would have to serve art-hungry Bostonians who had not made the Grand Tour until museums (such as the Museum of Fine Arts, established 1870) began to collect original art and sculpture.
3. Horatio Greenough (1805–1852), a friend of Emerson, reproduced Michelangelo's allegorical sculptures carved for the Medici tombs in Florence between 1520 and 1524.
4. See n. 3, p. 86. Guercino, see n. 2, p. 347.
5. M. Antoine Chrysostome Quatremère de Quincy (1755–1849) published a study of Raphael in 1830.
6. Gustav Friedrich von Waagen (1794–1868), Dutch art historian. Ascanio Condivi (b. ca. 1520), author of the *Vita di Michelangelo*. Giorgio Vasari (1511–1574), Italian painter and architect, famous for his *Lives of the Most Eminent Painters, Sculptors, and Architects* (1550). Cellini, see n. 5, p. 286. Richard Duppa (1770–1831), author of a life of Michelangelo. Henry Fuseli (1741–1825), Swiss-born artist who settled in London; known for his Romantic/Gothic paintings, intense and frequently fantastic; he was a good friend of poet and painter William Blake (see n. 9, p. 303).

"with four hundred and seventy designs of Raphael in my possession for a week."

These fine entertainments were shared with many admirers, and, as I now remember them, certain months about the years 1839, 1840, seem colored with the genius of these Italians. Our walls were hung with prints of the Sistine frescoes; we were all petty collectors; and prints of Correggio[7] and Guercino took the place, for the time, of epics and philosophy.

In the summer of 1839, Boston was still more rightfully adorned with the Allston Gallery; and the sculptures of our compatriots Greenough, and Crawford, and Powers,[8] were brought hither. . . .

Margaret's love of art, like that of most cultivated persons in this country, was not at all technical, but truly a sympathy with the artist, in the protest which his work pronounced on the deformity of our daily manners; her co-perception with him of the eloquence of form; her aspiration with him to a fairer life. As soon as her conversation ran into the mysteries of manipulation and artistic effect, it was less trustworthy. I remember that in the first times when I chanced to see pictures with her, I listened reverently to her opinions, and endeavored to see what she saw. But, on several occasions, finding myself unable to reach it, I came to suspect my guide, and to believe, at last, that her taste in works of art, though honest, was not on universal, but on idiosyncratic, grounds. As it has proved one of the most difficult problems of the practical astronomer to obtain an achromatic telescope, so an achromatic eye, one of the most needed, is also one of the rarest instruments of criticism.

She was very susceptible to pleasurable stimulus, took delight in details of form, color, and sound. Her fancy and imagination were easily stimulated to genial activity; and she erroneously thanked the artist for the pleasing emotions and thoughts that rose in her mind. So that, though capable of it, she did not always bring that highest tribunal to a work of art, namely, the calm presence of greatness, which only greatness in the object can satisfy. Yet the opinion was often well worth hearing on its own account, though it might be wide of the mark as criticism. Sometimes, too, she certainly brought to beautiful objects a fresh and appreciating love; and her written notes, especially on sculpture, I found always original and interesting.

* * *

LETTERS

I fear the remark already made on that susceptibility to details in art and nature which precluded the exercise of Margaret's sound catholic judgment, must be extended to more than her connoisseurship. She *had* a sound judgment, on which, in conversation, she could fall back, and anticipate and speak the best sense of the largest company. But, left to herself, and in her correspondence, she was much the victim of Lord Bacon's *idols of the cave*,[9] or self-deceived by her own phantasms. I have looked over volumes of her letters to me

---

7. Antonio Allegri Correggio (1489–1534), Italian painter. Michelangelo painted the frescoes in the Sistine Chapel (1508–12) for Pope Julius II.
8. Thomas Crawford (1813–1857) and Hiram Powers (1805–1873), well-known sculptors. Washington Allston (see n. 2, p. 120) was a familiar figure in Cambridge and Boston and was much admired by both Emerson and Fuller.
9. On Bacon's (see n. 3, p. 6) "idols of the cave," see Emerson's 1835 lecture (*EL* 1.331).

and others. They are full of probity, talent, wit, friendship, charity, and high aspiration. They are tainted with a mysticism, which to me appears so much an
affair of constitution, that it claims no more respect than the charity or patriotism of a man who has dined well, and feels better for it. One sometimes talks
with a genial *bon vivant*, who looks as if the omelet and turtle have got into his
eyes. In our noble Margaret, her personal feeling colors all her judgment of persons, of books, of pictures, and even of the laws of the world. This is easily felt
in ordinary women, and a large deduction is civilly made on the spot by whosoever replies to their remark. But when the speaker has such brilliant talent and
literature as Margaret, she gives so many fine names to these merely sensuous
and subjective phantasms, that the hearer is long imposed upon, and thinks so
precise and glittering nomenclature cannot be of mere *muscae volitantes*,
phœnixes of the fancy, but must be of some real ornithology, hitherto unknown
to him. This mere feeling exaggerates a host of trifles into a dazzling mythology. But when one goes to sift it, and find if there be a real meaning, it eludes
search. Whole sheets of warm, florid writing are here, in which the eye is caught
by "sapphire," "heliotrope," "dragon," "aloes," "Magna Dea," "limboes,"
"stars," and "purgatory," but can connect all this, or any part of it, with no universal experience.

In short, Margaret often loses herself in sentimentalism. That dangerous
vertigo nature in her case adopted, and was to make respectable. As it sometimes happens that a grandiose style, like that of the Alexandrian Platonists, or
like Macpherson's[1] Ossian, is more stimulating to the imagination of nations,
than the true Plato, or than the simple poet, so here was a head so creative of
new colors, of wonderful gleams, — so iridescent, that it piqued curiosity, and
stimulated thought, and communicated mental activity to all who approached
her; though her perceptions were not to be compared to her fancy, and she
made numerous mistakes. Her integrity was perfect, and she was led and followed by love, and was really bent on truth, but too indulgent to the meteors of
her fancy.

FRIENDSHIP

"Friends she must have, but in no one could find
A tally fitted to so large a mind."

It is certain that Margaret, though unattractive in person, and assuming in
manners, so that the girls complained that "she put upon them," or, with her
burly masculine existence, quite reduced them to satellites, yet inspired an enthusiastic attachment. I hear from one witness, as early as 1829, that "all the
girls raved about Margaret Fuller," and the same powerful magnetism wrought,
as she went on, from year to year, on all ingenuous natures. The loveliest and
the highest endowed women were eager to lay their beauty, their grace, the hospitalities of sumptuous homes, and their costly gifts, at her feet. When I expressed, one day, many years afterwards, to a lady who knew her well, some
surprise at the homage paid her by men in Italy, — offers of marriage having
there been made her by distinguished parties, — she replied: "There is nothing
extraordinary in it. Had she been a man, any one of those fine girls of sixteen,
who surrounded her here, would have married her: they were all in love with

1. See n. 4, p. 307.

her, she understood them so well." She had seen many persons, and had entire confidence in her own discrimination of characters. She saw and foresaw all in the first interview. She had certainly made her own selections with great precision, and had not been disappointed. . . . .

I am to add, that she gave herself to her friendships with an entireness not possible to any but a woman, with a depth possible to few women. Her friendships, as a girl with girls, as a woman with women, were not unmingled with passion, and had passages of romantic sacrifice and of ecstatic fusion, which I have heard with the ear, but could not trust my profane pen to report. There were, also, the ebbs and recoils from the other party,—the mortal unequal to converse with an immortal,—ingratitude, which was more truly incapacity, the collapse of overstrained affections and powers. At all events, it is clear that Margaret, later, grew more strict, and values herself with her friends on having the tie now "redeemed from all search after Eros." So much, however, of intellectual aim and activity mixed with her alliances, as to breathe a certain dignity and myrrh through them all. She and her friends are fellow-students with noblest moral aims. She is there for help and for counsel. "Be to the best thou knowest ever true!" is her language to one. And that was the effect of her presence. Whoever conversed with her felt challenged by the strongest personal influence to a bold and generous life.

* * *

With this great heart, and these attractions, it was easy to add daily to the number of her friends. With her practical talent, her counsel and energy, she was pretty sure to find clients and sufferers enough, who wished to be guided and supported. . . . She could not make a journey, or go to an evening party, without meeting a new person, who wished presently to impart his history to her. Very early, she had written to——, "My museum is so well furnished, that I grow lazy about collecting new specimens of human nature." She had soon enough examples of the historic development of rude intellect under the first rays of culture. But, in a thousand individuals, the process is much the same; and, like a professor too long pent in his college, she rejoiced in encountering persons of untutored grace and strength, and felt no wish to prolong the intercourse when culture began to have its effect.

* * *

Of course, she made large demands on her companions, and would soon come to sound their knowledge, and guess pretty nearly the range of their thoughts. There yet remained to command her constancy, what she valued more, the quality and affection proper to each. But she could rarely find natures sufficiently deep and magnetic. With her sleepless curiosity, her magnanimity, and her diamond-ring, like Annie of Lochroyan's,[2] to exchange for gold or for

2. Emerson is alluding to a Scottish ballad, "Fair Annie of Lochroyan," which he could have read in the collection of Robert Jamieson (1780–1844), *Popular Ballads* (1806). He quotes the relevant stanza a few pages later:

> O yours was gude, and gude enough,
> But aye the best was mine;
> For yours was o' the gude red gold,
> But mine o' the diamond fine.

pewter, she might be pardoned for her impatient questionings. To me, she was uniformly generous; but neither did I escape. Our moods were very different; and I remember, that, at the very time when I, slow and cold, had come fully to admire her genius, and was congratulating myself on the solid good understanding that subsisted between us, I was surprised with hearing it taxed by her with superficiality and halfness. She stigmatized our friendship as commercial. It seemed, her magnanimity was not met, but I prized her only for the thoughts and pictures she brought me;—so many thoughts, so many facts yesterday,—so many to-day;—when there was an end of things to tell, the game was up: that, I did not know, as a friend should know, to prize a silence as much as a discourse,—and hence a forlorn feeling was inevitable; a poor counting of thoughts, and a taking the census of virtues, was the unjust reception so much love found. On one occasion, her grief broke into words like these: "The religious nature remained unknown to you, because it could not proclaim itself, but claimed to be divined. The deepest soul that approached you was, in your eyes, nothing but a magic lantern, always bringing out pretty shows of life."

But as I did not understand the discontent then,—of course, I cannot now. It was a war of temperaments, and could not be reconciled by words; but, after each party had explained to the uttermost, it was necessary to fall back on those grounds of agreement which remained, and leave the differences henceforward in respectful silence. The recital may still serve to show to sympathetic persons the true lines and enlargements of her genius. It is certain that this incongruity never interrupted for a moment the intercourse, such as it was, that existed between us.

I ought to add here, that certain mental changes brought new questions into conversation. In the summer of 1840, she passed into certain religious states, which did not impress me as quite healthy, or likely to be permanent; and I said, "I do not understand your tone; it seems exaggerated. You are one who can afford to speak and to hear the truth. Let us hold hard to the common-sense, and let us speak in the positive degree."

And I find, in later letters from her, sometimes playful, sometimes grave allusions to this explanation.

Is——there? Does water meet water?—no need of wine, sugar, spice, or even a *soupçon* of lemon to remind of a tropical climate? I fear me not. Yet, dear positives, believe me superlatively yours, Margaret.

* * *

PROBLEMS OF LIFE

Already, too, at this time, each of the main problems of human life had been closely scanned and interrogated by her, and some of them had been much earlier settled. A worshipper of beauty, why could not she also have been beautiful?—of the most radiant sociality, why should not she have been so placed, and so decorated, as to have led the fairest and highest?

* * *

Practical questions in plenty the days and months brought her to settle,— questions requiring all her wisdom, and sometimes more than all. None recurs with more frequency, at one period, in her journals, than the debate with herself, whether she shall make literature a profession. Shall it be woman, or shall it be artist?

WOMAN, OR ARTIST?

Margaret resolved, again and again, to devote herself no more to these disappointing forms of men and women, but to the children of the muse. "The *dramatis personæ*," she said, "of my poems shall henceforth be chosen from the children of immortal Muse. I fix my affections no more on these frail forms." But it was vain; she rushed back again to persons, with a woman's devotion.

Her pen was a non-conductor. She always took it up with some disdain, thinking it a kind of impiety to attempt to report a life so warm and cordial, and wrote on the fly-leaf of her journal, —

"Scrivo sol per sfogar' l'interno."[3]

*   *   *

HEROISM

These practical problems Margaret had to entertain and to solve the best way she could. She says truly, "there was none to take up her burden whilst she slept." But she was formed for action, and addressed herself quite simply to her part. She was a woman, an orphan, without beauty, without money; and these negatives will suggest what difficulties were to be surmounted where the tasks dictated by her talents required the good-will of "good society," in the town where she was to teach and write. But she was even-tempered and erect, and, if her journals are sometimes mournful, her mind was made up, her countenance beamed courage and cheerfulness around her. Of personal influence, speaking strictly, — an efflux, that is, purely of mind and character, excluding all effects of power, wealth, fashion, beauty, or literary fame, — she had an extraordinary degree; I think more than any person I have known. An interview with her was a joyful event. Worthy men and women, who had conversed with her, could not forget her, but worked bravely on in the remembrance that this heroic approver had recognized their aims. She spoke so earnestly, that the depth of the sentiment prevailed, and not the accidental expression, which might chance to be common. Thus I learned, the other day, that, in a copy of Mrs. Jameson's Italian Painters, against a passage describing Correggio as a true servant of God in his art, above sordid ambition, devoted to truth, "one of those superior beings of whom there are so few;" Margaret wrote on the margin, "And yet all might be such." The book lay long on the table of the owner, in Florence, and chanced to be read there by a young artist of much talent. "These words," said he, months afterwards, "struck out a new strength in me. They revived resolutions long fallen away, and made me set my face like a flint."

But Margaret's courage was thoroughly sweet in its temper. She accused herself in her youth of unamiable traits, but, in all the later years of her life, it is difficult to recall a moment of malevolence. The friends whom her strength of mind drew to her, her good heart held fast; and few persons were ever the objects of more persevering kindness. Many hundreds of her letters remain, and they are alive with proofs of generous friendship given and received.

---

3. I write only to clear the fog from my inner being (Italian).

Among her early friends, Mrs. Farrar, of Cambridge, appears to have discovered, at a critical moment in her career, the extraordinary promise of the young girl, and some false social position into which her pride and petulance, and the mistakes of others, had combined to bring her, and she set herself, with equal kindness and address, to make a second home for Margaret in her own house, and to put her on the best footing in the agreeable society of Cambridge. She busied herself, also, as she could, in removing all superficial blemishes from the gem. In a well-chosen travelling party, made up by Mrs. Farrar, and which turned out to be the beginning of much happiness by the friendships then formed, Margaret visited, in the summer of 1835, Newport, New York, and Trenton Falls; and, in the autumn, made the acquaintance, at Mrs. F.'s house, of Miss Martineau, whose friendship, at that moment, was an important stimulus to her mind.

Mrs. Farrar performed for her, thenceforward, all the offices of an almost maternal friendship. She admired her genius, and wished that all should admire it. She counselled and encouraged her, brought to her side the else unsuppliable aid of a matron and a lady, sheltered her in sickness, forwarded her plans with tenderness and constancy, to the last. I read all this in the tone of uniform gratitude and love with which this lady is mentioned in Margaret's letters. Friendships like this praise both parties; and the security with which people of a noble disposition approached Margaret, indicated the quality of her own infinite tenderness. A very intelligent woman applied to her what Stilling said of Goethe: "Her heart, which few knew, was as great as her mind, which all knew;" and added, that, "in character, Margaret was, of all she had beheld, the largest woman, and not a woman who wished to be a man." Another lady added, "She never disappointed you. To any one whose confidence she had once drawn out, she was thereafter faithful. She could talk of persons, and never gossip; for she had a fine instinct that kept her from any reality, and from any effect of treachery." I was still more struck with the remark that followed. "Her life, since she went abroad, is wholly unknown to me; but I have an unshaken trust that what Margaret did she can defend."

She was a right brave and heroic woman. She shrunk from no duty, because of feeble nerves. Although, after her father died, the disappointment of not going to Europe with Miss Martineau and Mrs. Farrar was extreme, and her mother and sister wished her to take her portion of the estate and go; and, on her refusal, entreated the interference of friends to overcome her objections; Margaret would not hear of it, and devoted herself to the education of her brothers and sisters, and then to the making a home for the family. She was exact and punctual in money matters, and maintained herself, and made her full contribution to the support of her family, by the reward of her labors as a teacher, and in her conversation classes.

* * *

Every one of her friends knew assuredly that her sympathy and aid would not fail them when required. She went, from the most joyful of all bridals, to attend a near relative during a formidable surgical operation. She was here to help others. As one of her friends writes, "She helped whoever knew her." She adopted the interests of humble persons, within her circle, with heart-cheering warmth, and her ardor in the cause of suffering and degraded women, at Sing-

Sing, was as irresistible as her love of books. She had, many years afterwards, scope for the exercise of all her love and devotion, in Italy, but she came to it as if it had been her habit and her natural sphere. The friends who knew her in that country, relate, with much surprise, that she, who had all her lifetime drawn people by her wit, should recommend herself so highly, in Italy, by her tenderness and large affection. Yet the tenderness was only a face of the wit; as before, the wit was raised above all other wit by the affection behind it. And, truly, there was an ocean of tears always, in her atmosphere, ready to fall.

There was, at New York, a poor adventurer, half patriot, half author, a miserable man, always in such depths of distress, with such squadrons of enemies, that no charity could relieve, and no intervention save him. He believed Europe banded for his destruction, and America corrupted to connive at it. Margaret listened to these woes with such patience and mercy, that she drew five hundred dollars, which had been invested for her in a safe place, and put them in those hapless hands, where, of course, the money was only the prey of new rapacity, to be bewailed by new reproaches.

* * *

TRUTH

But Margaret crowned all her talents and virtues with a love of truth, and the power to speak it. In great and in small matters, she was a woman of her word, and gave those who conversed with her the unspeakable comfort that flows from plain dealing. Her nature was frank and transparent, and she had a right to say, as she says in her journal: —

> I have the satisfaction of knowing, that, in my counsels, I have given myself no air of being better than I am.

* * *

Even in trifles, one might find with her the advantage and the electricity of a little honesty. I have had from an eye-witness a note of a little scene that passed in Boston, at the Academy of Music. A party had gone early, and taken an excellent place to hear one of Beethoven's symphonies. Just behind them were soon seated a young lady and two gentlemen, who made an incessant buzzing, in spite of bitter looks cast on them by the whole neighborhood, and destroyed all the musical comfort. After all was over, Margaret leaned across one seat, and catching the eye of this girl, who was pretty and well-dressed, said, in her blandest, gentlest voice, "May I speak with you one moment?" "Certainly," said the young lady, with a fluttered, pleased look, bending forward. "I only wish to say," said Margaret, "that I trust, that, in the whole course of your life, you will not suffer so great a degree of annoyance as you have inflicted on a large party of lovers of music this evening." This was said with the sweetest air, as if to a little child, and it was as good as a play to see the change of countenance which the young lady exhibited, who had no replication to make to so Christian a blessing.

On graver occasions, the same habit was only more stimulated; and I cannot remember certain passages which called it into play, without new regrets at the costly loss which our community sustains in the loss of this brave and eloquent soul.

People do not speak the truth, not for the want of not knowing and preferring it, but because they have not the organ to speak it adequately. It requires a clear sight, and, still more, a high spirit, to deal with falsehood in the decisive way. I have known several honest persons who valued truth as much as Peter and John, but, when they tried to speak it, *they* grew red and black in the face instead of Ananias,[4] until, after a few attempts, they decided that aggressive truth was not their vocation, and confined themselves thenceforward to silent honesty, except on rare occasions, when either an extreme outrage, or a happier inspiration, loosened their tongue. But a soul is now and then incarnated, whom indulgent nature has not afflicted with any cramp or frost, but who can speak the right word at the right moment, qualify the selfish and hypocritical act with its real name, and, without any loss of serenity, hold up the offence to the purest daylight. Such a truth-speaker is worth more than the best police, and more than the laws or governors; for these do not always know their own side, but will back the crime for want of this very truth-speaker to expose them. That is the theory of the newspaper, — to supersede official by intellectual influence. But, though the apostles establish the journal, it usually happens that, by some strange oversight, Ananias slips into the editor's chair. If, then, we could be provided with a fair proportion of truth-speakers, we could very materially and usefully contract the legislative and the executive functions. Still, the main sphere for this nobleness is private society, where so many mischiefs go unwhipped, being out of the cognizance of law, and supposed to be nobody's business. And society is, at all times, suffering for want of judges and headsmen, who will mark and lop these malefactors.

Margaret suffered no vice to insult her presence, but called the offender to instant account, when the law of right or of beauty was violated. She needed not, of course, to go out of her way to find the offender, and she never did, but she had the courage and the skill to cut heads off which were not worn with honor in her presence. Others might abet a crime by silence, if they pleased; she chose to clear herself of all complicity, by calling the act by its name.

It was curious to see the mysterious provocation which the mere presence of insight exerts in its neighborhood. Like moths about a lamp, her victims voluntarily came to judgment: conscious persons, encumbered with egotism; vain persons, bent on concealing some mean vice; arrogant reformers, with some halting of their own; the compromisers, who wished to reconcile right and wrong; — all came and held out their palms to the wise woman, to read their fortunes, and they were truly told. Many anecdotes have come to my ear, which show how useful the glare of her lamp proved in private circles, and what dramatic situations it created. But these cannot be told. The valor for dragging the accused spirits among his acquaintance to the stake is not in the heart of the present writer. The reader must be content to learn that she knew how, without loss of temper, to speak with unmistakable plainness to any party, when she felt that the truth or the right was injured.

*   *   *

ECSTASY

I have alluded to the fact, that, in the summer of 1840, Margaret underwent some change in the tone and the direction of her thoughts, to which she

---

4. He was struck dead for lying to the Holy Spirit (see Acts 5.1ff).

attributed a high importance. I remember, at an earlier period, when in earnest conversation with her, she seemed to have that height and daring, that I saw she was ready to do whatever she thought; and I observed that, with her literary riches, her invention and wit, her boundless fun and drollery, her light satire, and the most entertaining conversation in America, consisted a certain pathos of sentiment, and a march of character, threatening to arrive presently at the shores and plunge into the sea of Buddhism and mystical trances. The literature of asceticism and rapturous piety was familiar to her. The conversation of certain mystics, who had appeared in Boston about this time, had interested her, but in no commanding degree. But in this year, 1840, in which events occurred which combined great happiness and pain for her affections, she remained for some time in a sort of ecstatic solitude. She made many attempts to describe her frame of mind to me, but did not inspire me with confidence that she had now come to any experiences that were profound or permanent. She was vexed at the want of sympathy on my part, and I again felt that this craving for sympathy did not prove the inspiration. There was a certain restlessness and fever, which I did not like should deceive a soul which was capable of greatness. But jets of magnanimity were always natural to her; and her aspiring mind, eager for a higher and still a higher ground, made her gradually familiar with the range of the mystics, and, though never herself laid in the chamber called Peace, never quite authentically and originally speaking from the absolute or prophetic mount, yet she borrowed from her frequent visits to its precincts an occasional enthusiasm, which gave a religious dignity to her thought.

* * *

CONVERSATION

I have separated and distributed as I could some of the parts which blended in the rich composite energy which Margaret exerted during the ten years over which my occasional interviews with her were scattered. It remains to say, that all these powers and accomplishments found their best and only adequate channel in her conversation;—a conversation which those who have heard it, unanimously, as far as I know, pronounced to be, in elegance, in range, in flexibility, and adroit transition, in depth, in cordiality, and in moral aim, altogether admirable; surprising and cheerful as a poem, and communicating its own civility and elevation like a charm to all hearers. She was here, among our anxious citizens, and frivolous fashionists, as if sent to refine and polish her countrymen, and announce a better day. She poured a stream of amber over the endless store of private anecdotes, of bosom histories, which her wonderful persuasion drew forth, and transfigured them into fine fables. Whilst she embellished the moment, her conversation had the merit of being solid and true. She put her whole character into it, and had the power to inspire. The companion was made a thinker, and went away quite other than he came. The circle of friends who sat with her were not allowed to remain spectators or players, but she converted them into heroes, if she could. The muse woke the muses, and the day grew bright and eventful. Of course, there must be, in a person of such sincerity, much variety of aspect, according to the character of her company. Only, in Margaret's case, there is almost an agreement in the testimony to an invariable power over the minds of all.

* * *

Conversations in Boston

In the year 1839, Margaret removed from Groton, and, with her mother and family, took a house at Jamaica Plain, five miles from Boston. In November of the next year the family removed to Cambridge, and rented a house there, near their old home. In 1841, Margaret took rooms for the winter in town, retaining still the house in Cambridge. And from the day of leaving Groton, until the autumn of 1844, when she removed to New York, she resided in Boston, or its immediate vicinity. Boston was her social centre. There were the libraries, galleries, and concerts which she loved; there were her pupils and her friends; and there were her tasks, and the openings of a new career.

I have vaguely designated some of the friends with whom she was on terms of intimacy at the time when I was first acquainted with her. But the range of her talents required an equal compass in her society; and she gradually added a multitude of names to the list. She knew already all the active minds at Cambridge; and has left a record of one good interview she had with Allston. She now became intimate with Doctor Channing, and interested him to that point in some of her studies, that, at his request, she undertook to render some selections of German philosophy into English for him. But I believe this attempt was soon abandoned. She found a valuable friend in the late Miss Mary Rotch, of New Bedford, a woman of great strength of mind, connected with the Quakers not less by temperament than by birth, and possessing the best lights of that once spiritual sect. At Newport, Margaret had made the acquaintance of an elegant scholar, in Mr. Calvert, of Maryland. In Providence, she had won, as by conquest, such a homage of attachment, from young and old, that her arrival there, one day, on her return from a visit to Bristol, was a kind of ovation. In Boston, she knew people of every class,—merchants, politicians, scholars, artists, women, the migratory genius, and the rooted capitalist,—and, amongst all, many excellent people, who were every day passing, by new opportunities, conversations, and kind offices, into the sacred circle of friends. The late Miss Susan Burley had many points of attraction for her, not only in her elegant studies, but also in the deep interest which that lady took in securing the highest culture for women. She was very well read, and, avoiding abstractions, knew how to help herself with examples and facts. A friendship that proved of great importance to the next years was that established with Mr. George Ripley; an accurate scholar, a man of character, and of eminent powers of conversation, and already then deeply engaged in plans of an expansive practical bearing, of which the first fruit was the little community which flourished for a few years at Brook Farm. Margaret presently became connected with him in literary labors, and, as long as she remained in this vicinity, kept up her habits of intimacy with the colonists of Brook Farm. At West-Roxbury, too, she knew and prized the heroic heart, the learning and wit of Theodore Parker, whose literary aid was, subsequently, of the first importance to her. She had an acquaintance, for many years,—subject, no doubt, to alternations of sun and shade,—with Mr. Alcott. There was much antagonism in their habitual views, but each learned to respect the genius of the other. She had more sympathy with Mr. Alcott's English friend, Charles Lane, an ingenious mystic, and bold experimenter in practical reforms, whose dexterity and temper in debate she frankly admired, whilst his asceticism engaged her reverence. Neither could some marked difference of temperament remove her from the beneficent influences of Miss Elizabeth Peabody, who, by her constitutional hospitality to excellence, whether mental or moral, has made her modest abode for so many years the inevitable resort of studious feet, and a private theatre for the exposition of every question of letters, of philosophy, of ethics, and of art.

The events in Margaret's life, up to the year 1840, were few, and not of that dramatic interest which readers love. Of the few events of her bright and blameless years, how many are private, and must remain so. In reciting the story of an affectionate and passionate woman, the voice lowers itself to a whisper, and becomes inaudible. A woman in our society finds her safety and happiness in exclusions and privacies. She congratulates herself when she is not called to the market, to the courts, to the polls, to the stage, or to the orchestra. Only the most extraordinary genius can make the career of an artist secure and agreeable to her. Prescriptions almost invincible the female lecturer or professor of any science must encounter; and, except on points where the charities which are left to women as their legitimate province interpose against the ferocity of laws, with us a female politician is unknown. Perhaps this fact, which so dangerously narrows the career of a woman, accuses the tardiness of our civility, and many signs show that a revolution is already on foot.

Margaret had no love of notoriety, or taste for eccentricity, to goad her, and no weak fear of either. Willingly she was confined to the usual circles and methods of female talent. She had no false shame. Any task that called out her powers was good and desirable. She wished to live by her strength. She could converse, and teach, and write. She took private classes of pupils at her own house. She organized, with great success, a school for young ladies at Providence, and gave four hours a day to it, during two years. She translated Eckermann's Conversations with Goethe, and published in 1839. In 1841, she translated the Letters of Gunderode and Bettine,[5] and published them as far as the sale warranted the work. In 1843, she made a tour to Lake Superior and to Michigan, and published an agreeable narrative of it, called "Summer on the Lakes."

Apparently a more pretending, but really also a private and friendly service, she edited the "Dial," a quarterly journal, for two years from its first publication in 1840. She was eagerly solicited to undertake the charge of this work, which, when it began, concentrated a good deal of hope and affection. It had its origin in a club of speculative students, who found the air in America getting a little close and stagnant; and the agitation had perhaps the fault of being too secondary or bookish in its origin, or caught not from primary instincts, but from English, and still more from German books. The journal was commenced with much hope, and liberal promises of many coöperators. But the workmen of sufficient culture for a poetical and philosophical magazine were too few; and, as the pages were filled by unpaid contributors, each of whom had, according to the usage and necessity of this country, some paying employment, the journal did not get his best work, but his second best. Its scattered writers had not digested their theories into a distinct dogma, still less into a practical measure which the public could grasp; and the magazine was so eclectic and miscellaneous, that each of its readers and writers valued only a small portion of it. For these reasons it

---

5. The fictitious letters from Bettina Brentano von Arnim (see n. 8, p. 202) to poet Karoline von Günderode (1780–1806) were translated by Fuller for her *Dial* article "Bettina Brentano and her friend Günderode" (1842, 2.313–57). An extract was published in the same year by Elizabeth Peabody.

never had a large circulation, and it was discontinued after four years. But the Dial betrayed, through all its juvenility, timidity, and conventional rubbish, some sparks of the true love and hope, and of the piety to spiritual law, which had moved its friends and founders, and it was received by its early subscribers with almost a religious welcome. Many years after it was brought to a close, Margaret was surprised in England by very warm testimony to its merits; and, in 1848, the writer of these pages found it holding the same affectionate place in many a private bookshelf in England and Scotland, which it had secured at home. Good or bad, it cost a good deal of precious labor from those who served it, and from Margaret most of all. As editor, she received a compensation for the first years, which was intended to be two hundred dollars *per annum*, but which, I fear, never reached even that amount.

But it made no difference to her exertion. She put so much heart into it that she bravely undertook to open, in the Dial, the subjects which most attracted her; and she treated, in turn, Goethe, and Beethoven, the Rhine and the Romaic Ballads, the Poems of John Sterling, and several pieces of sentiment, with a spirit which spared no labor; and, when the hard conditions of journalism held her to an inevitable day, she submitted to jeopardizing a long-cherished subject, by treating it in the crude and forced article for the month. I remember, after she had been compelled by ill health to relinquish the journal into my hands, my grateful wonder at the facility with which she assumed the preparation of laborious articles, that might have daunted the most practised scribe.

But in book or journal she found a very imperfect expression of herself, and it was the more vexatious, because she was accustomed to the clearest and fullest. When, therefore, she had to choose an employment that should pay money, she consulted her own genius, as well as the wishes of a multitude of friends, in opening a class for conversation.

* * *

This first series of conversations extended to thirteen, the class meeting once a week at noon, and remaining together for two hours. The class were happy, and the interest increased. A new series of thirteen more weeks followed, and the general subject of the new course was "the Fine Arts." A few fragmentary notes only of these hours have been shown me, but all those who bore any part in them testify to their entire success.

* * *

In her writing she was prone to spin her sentences without a sure guidance, and beyond the sympathy of her reader. But in discourse, she was quick, conscious of power, in perfect tune with her company, and would pause and turn the stream with grace and adroitness, and with so much spirit, that her face beamed, and the young people came away delighted, among other things, with "her beautiful looks." When she was intellectually excited, or in high animal spirits, as often happened, all deformity of features was dissolved in the power of the expression. So I interpret this repeated story of sumptuousness of dress, that this appearance, like her reported beauty, was simply an effect of a general impression of magnificence made by her genius, and mistakenly attributed to some external elegance; for I have been told by her most intimate friend, who knew every particular of her conduct at that time, that there was nothing of special expense or splendor in her toilette.

The effect of the winter's work was happiest. Margaret was made intimately known to many excellent persons. In this company of matrons and maids, many tender spirits had been set in ferment. A new day had dawned for them; new thoughts had opened; the secret of life was shown, or, at least, that life had a secret. They could not forget what they had heard, and what they had been surprised into saying. A true refinement had begun to work in many who had been slaves to trifles. They went home thoughtful and happy, since the steady elevation of Margaret's aim had infused a certain un-expected greatness of tone into the conversation. It was, I believe, only an expression of the feeling of the class, the remark made, perhaps at the next year's course, by a lady of eminent powers, previously by no means partial to Margaret, and who expressed her frank admiration on leaving the house:— "I never heard, read of, or imagined a conversation at all equal to this we have now heard."

The strongest wishes were expressed, on all sides, that the conversations should be renewed at the beginning of the following winter. Margaret will-ingly consented; but, as I have already intimated, in the summer and au-tumn of 1840, she had retreated to some interior shrine, and believed that she came into life and society with some advantage from this devotion.

Of this feeling the new discussion bore evident traces. Most of the last year's class returned, and new members gave in their names. The first meeting was holden on the twenty-second of November, 1840. By all accounts it was the best of all her days.

* * *

Thoreau[1]

Henry David Thoreau was the last male descendent of a French ancestor who came to this country from the Isle of Guernsey.[2] His character exhibited occasional traits drawn from this blood in singular combination with a very strong Saxon genius.

He was born in Concord, Massachusetts, on the 12th of July, 1817. He was graduated at Harvard College, in 1837, but without any literary distinction. An iconoclast in literature, he seldom thanked colleges for their service to him, holding them in small esteem, whilst yet his debt to them was important. After leaving the University, he joined his brother in teaching a private school, which

---

1. See n. 1, p. 93. Emerson's refractory disciple and younger friend died of complications from tuberculo-sis in early May 1862. Emerson delivered this eulogy at a funeral service held shortly after Thoreau's death. A sometime resident in the Emerson household in the 1840s, Thoreau built his cabin on Emer-son's woodlot near Walden Pond and lived there from 1845 to 1847. Thoreau published only two books during his lifetime, A Week on the Concord and Merrimack Rivers (1849) and Walden (1854). He also kept a voluminous journal, from which Emerson quotes toward the end of this piece. This address was first published in the Atlantic Monthly in August 1862, then printed in Thoreau's Excursions (1863) under the title "Biographical Sketch."
2. One of the Channel Islands; a possession of the British Crown, located in the Gulf of St. Malo off the coast of Normandy, France. Thoreau's father's family was of French Huguenot (Protestant) descent.

he soon renounced. His father was a manufacturer of lead-pencils, and Henry applied himself for a time to this craft, believing he could make a better pencil than was then in use. After completing his experiments, he exhibited his work to chemists and artists in Boston, and having obtained their certificates to its excellence and to its equality with the best London manufacture, he returned home contented. His friends congratulated him that he had now opened his way to fortune. But he replied, that he should never make another pencil. "Why should I? I would not do again what I have done once." He resumed his endless walks and miscellaneous studies, making every day some new acquaintance with Nature, though as yet never speaking of zoölogy or botany, since, though very studious of natural facts, he was incurious of technical and textual science.

At this time, a strong, healthy youth, fresh from college, whilst all his companions were choosing their profession, or eager to begin some lucrative employment, it was inevitable that his thoughts should be exercised on the same question, and it required rare decision to refuse all the accustomed paths, and keep his solitary freedom at the cost of disappointing the natural expectations of his family and friends: all the more difficult that he had a perfect probity, was exact in securing his own independence, and in holding every man to the like duty. But Thoreau never faltered. He was a born protestant. He declined to give up his large ambition of knowledge and action for any narrow craft or profession, aiming at a much more comprehensive calling, the art of living well. If he slighted and defied the opinions of others, it was only that he was more intent to reconcile his practice with his own belief. Never idle or self-indulgent, he preferred, when he wanted money, earning it by some piece of manual labor agreeable to him, as building a boat or a fence, planting, grafting, surveying, or other short work, to any long engagements. With his hardy habits and few wants, his skill in wood-craft, and his powerful arithmetic, he was very competent to live in any part of the world. It would cost him less time to supply his wants than another. He was therefore secure of his leisure.

A natural skill for mensuration, growing out of his mathematical knowledge, and his habit of ascertaining the measures and distances of objects which interested him, the size of trees, the depth and extent of ponds and rivers, the height of mountains, and the air-line distance of his favorite summits, — this, and his intimate knowledge of the territory about Concord, made him drift into the profession of land-surveyor. It had the advantage for him that it led him continually into new and secluded grounds, and helped his studies of Nature. His accuracy and skill in this work were readily appreciated, and he found all the employment he wanted.

He could easily solve the problems of the surveyor, but he was daily beset with graver questions, which he manfully confronted. He interrogated every custom, and wished to settle all his practice on an ideal foundation. He was a protestant à l'outrance,[3] and few lives contain so many renunciations. He was bred to no profession; he never married; he lived alone; he never went to church; he never voted; he refused to pay a tax to the State; he ate no flesh, he drank no wine, he never knew the use of tobacco; and, though a naturalist, he used neither trap nor gun. He chose, wisely, no doubt, for himself, to be the bachelor of thought and Nature. He had no talent for wealth, and knew how to be poor without the least hint of squalor or inelegance. Perhaps he fell into his

3. To the utmost degree (French).

way of living without forecasting it much, but approved it with later wisdom. "I am often reminded," he wrote in his journal, "that, if I had bestowed on me the wealth of Crœsus,[4] my aims must be still the same, and my means essentially the same." He had no temptations to fight against,—no appetites, no passions, no taste for elegant trifles. A fine house, dress, the manners and talk of highly cultivated people were all thrown away on him. He much preferred a good Indian, and considered these refinements as impediments to conversation, wishing to meet his companion on the simplest terms. He declined invitations to dinner-parties, because there each was in every one's way, and he could not meet the individuals to any purpose. "They make their pride," he said, "in making their dinner cost much; I make my pride in making my dinner cost little." When asked at table what dish he preferred, he answered, "The nearest." He did not like the taste of wine, and never had a vice in his life. He said,— "I have a faint recollection of pleasure derived from smoking dried lily-stems, before I was a man. I had commonly a supply of these. I have never smoked any thing more noxious."

He chose to be rich by making his wants few, and supplying them himself. In his travels, he used the railroad only to get over so much country as was unimportant to the present purpose, walking hundreds of miles, avoiding taverns, buying a lodging in farmers' and fishermen's houses, as cheaper, and more agreeable to him, and because there he could better find the men and the information he wanted.

There was somewhat military in his nature not to be subdued, always manly and able, but rarely tender, as if he did not feel himself except in opposition. He wanted a fallacy to expose, a blunder to pillory, I may say required a little sense of victory, a roll of the drum, to call his powers into full exercise. It cost him nothing to say No; indeed, he found it much easier than to say Yes. It seemed as if his first instinct on hearing a proposition was to controvert it, so impatient was he of the limitations of our daily thought. This habit, of course, is a little chilling to the social affections; and though the companion would in the end acquit him of any malice or untruth, yet it mars conversation. Hence, no equal companion stood in affectionate relations with one so pure and guileless. "I love Henry," said one of his friends, "but I cannot like him; and as for taking his arm, I should as soon think of taking the arm of an elm-tree."[5]

Yet, hermit and stoic as he was, he was really fond of sympathy, and threw himself heartily and childlike into the company of young people whom he loved, and whom he delighted to entertain, as he only could, with the varied and endless anecdotes of his experiences by field and river. And he was always ready to lead a huckleberry party or a search for chestnuts or grapes. Talking, one day, of a public discourse, Henry remarked, that whatever succeeded with the audience was bad. I said, "Who would not like to write something which all can read, like 'Robinson Crusoe'?[6] and who does not see with regret that his page is not solid with a right materialistic treatment, which delights everybody?" Henry objected, of course, and vaunted the better lectures which reached only a few persons. But, at supper, a young girl, understanding that he was to lecture

---

4. King of Lydia famous for his wealth (fl. 550 B.C.E.).
5. Emerson is here conflating two different journal entries of his own. In the spring of 1843 he quotes Elizabeth Hoar as saying "I love Henry, but do not like him," and in the summer of 1848 he himself makes the remark about Thoreau's arm. See *EJ* 304, 391.
6. Daniel Defoe (1660–1731) published *Robinson Crusoe* in 1720.

at the Lyceum,[7] sharply asked him, "whether his lecture would be a nice, interesting story, such as she wished to hear, or whether it was one of those old
philosophical things that she did not care about." Henry turned to her, and
bethought himself, and, I saw, was trying to believe that he had matter that
might fit her and her brother, who were to sit up and go to the lecture, if it was
a good one for them.

He was a speaker and actor of the truth,—born such,—and was ever running into dramatic situations from this cause. In any circumstance, it interested
all bystanders to know what part Henry would take, and what he would say; and
he did not disappoint expectation, but used an original judgment on each emergency. In 1845 he built himself a small framed house on the shores of Walden
Pond, and lived there two years alone, a life of labor and study. This action was
quite native and fit for him. No one who knew him would tax him with affectation. He was more unlike his neighbors in his thought than in his action. As
soon as he had exhausted the advantages of that solitude, he abandoned it. In
1847,[8] not approving some uses to which the public expenditure was applied,
he refused to pay his town tax, and was put in jail. A friend paid the tax for him,
and he was released. The like annoyance was threatened the next year. But, as
his friends paid the tax, notwithstanding his protest, I believe he ceased to resist. No opposition or ridicule had any weight with him. He coldly and fully
stated his opinion without affecting to believe that it was the opinion of the company. It was of no consequence, if every one present held the opposite opinion.
On one occasion he went to the University Library to procure some books. The
librarian refused to lend them. Mr. Thoreau repaired to the President, who
stated to him the rules and usages, which permitted the loan of books to resident graduates, to clergymen who were alumni, and to some others resident
within a circle of ten miles' radius from the College. Mr. Thoreau explained to
the President that the railroad had destroyed the old scale of distances,—that
the library was useless, yes, and President and College useless, on the terms of
his rules,—that the one benefit he owed to the College was its library,—that, at
this moment, not only his want of books was imperative, but he wanted a large
number of books, and assured him that he, Thoreau, and not the librarian, was
the proper custodian of these. In short, the President found the petitioner so formidable, and the rules getting to look so ridiculous, that he ended by giving him
a privilege which in his hands proved unlimited thereafter.

No truer American existed than Thoreau. His preference of his country
and condition was genuine, and his aversion from English and European
manners and tastes almost reached contempt. He listened impatiently to news
or *bon mots* gleaned from London circles; and though he tried to be civil, these
anecdotes fatigued him. The men were all imitating each other, and on a small
mould. Why can they not live as far apart as possible, and each be a man by
himself? What he sought was the most energetic nature; and he wished to go to
Oregon, not to London. "In every part of Great Britain," he wrote in his diary,
"are discovered traces of the Romans, their funereal urns, their camps, their
roads, their dwellings. But New England, at least, is not based on any Roman
ruins. We have not to lay the foundations of our houses on the ashes of a former
civilization."

7. A grove in Attica where Aristotle taught; used here as a general term for the lecture circuit.
8. Thoreau spent his night in jail in the summer of 1846.

But, idealist as he was, standing for abolition of slavery, abolition of tariffs, almost for abolition of government, it is needless to say he found himself not only unrepresented in actual politics, but almost equally opposed to every class of reformers. Yet he paid the tribute of his uniform respect to the Anti-Slavery Party. One man, whose personal acquaintance he had formed, he honored with exceptional regard. Before the first friendly word had been spoken for Captain John Brown, after the arrest, he sent notices to most houses in Concord, that he would speak in a public hall on the condition and character of John Brown,[9] on Sunday evening, and invited all people to come. The Republican Committee, the Abolitionist Committee, sent him word that it was premature and not advisable. He replied, — "I did not send to you for advice, but to announce that I am to speak." The hall was filled at an early hour by people of all parties, and his earnest eulogy of the hero was heard by all respectfully, by many with a sympathy that surprised themselves.

It was said of Plotinus[1] that he was ashamed of his body, and 'tis very likely he had good reason for it, — that his body was a bad servant, and he had not skill in dealing with the material world, as happens often to men of abstract intellect. But Mr. Thoreau was equipped with a most adapted and serviceable body. He was of short stature, firmly built, of light complexion, with strong, serious blue eyes, and a grave aspect, — his face covered in the late years with a becoming beard. His senses were acute, his frame well-knit and hardy, his hands strong and skilful in the use of tools. And there was a wonderful fitness of body and mind. He could pace sixteen rods more accurately than another man could measure them with rod and chain. He could find his path in the woods at night, he said, better by his feet than his eyes. He could estimate the measure of a tree very well by his eye; he could estimate the weight of a calf or a pig, like a dealer. From a box containing a bushel or more of loose pencils, he could take up with his hands fast enough just a dozen pencils at every grasp. He was a good swimmer, runner, skater, boatman, and would probably outwalk most countrymen in a day's journey. And the relation of body to mind was still finer than we have indicated. He said he wanted every stride his legs made. The length of his walk uniformly made the length of his writing. If shut up in the house, he did not write at all.

He had a strong common sense, like that which Rose Flammock, the weaver's daughter, in Scott's romance, commends in her father, as resembling a yardstick, which, whilst it measures dowlas[2] and diaper, can equally well measure tapestry and cloth of gold. He had always a new resource. When I was planting forest-trees, and had procured half a peck of acorns, he said that only a small portion of them would be sound, and proceeded to examine them, and select the sound ones. But finding this took time, he said, "I think, if you put them all into water, the good ones will sink;" which experiment we tried with success. He could plan a garden, or a house, or a barn; would have been competent to lead a "Pacific Exploring Expedition"; could give judicious counsel in the gravest private or public affairs.

9. Thoreau delivered "A Plea for Captain John Brown" on October 30, 1859. Brown (1800–1859), an uncompromising abolitionist, seized a federal arsenal and armory at Harpers Ferry, Virginia (now West Virginia) on October 16, 1859. He was arrested, convicted of treason, and hanged.
1. See n. 1, p. 27.
2. A kind of linen cloth. *Scott's romance: The Betrothed* (1825). See also n. 9, p. 65.

He lived for the day, not cumbered and mortified by his memory. If he brought you yesterday a new proposition, he would bring you to-day another not less revolutionary. A very industrious man, and setting, like all highly organized men, a high value on his time, he seemed the only man of leisure in town, always ready for any excursion that promised well, or for conversation prolonged into late hours. His trenchant sense was never stopped by his rules of daily prudence, but was always up to the new occasion. He liked and used the simplest food, yet, when some one urged a vegetable diet, Thoreau thought all diets a very small matter, saying, that "the man who shoots the buffalo lives better than the man who boards at the Graham[3] house." He said, — "You can sleep near the railroad, and never be disturbed: Nature knows very well what sounds are worth attending to, and has made up her mind not to hear the railroad-whistle. But things respect the devout mind, and a mental ecstasy was never interrupted." He noted what repeatedly befell him, that, after receiving from a distance a rare plant, he would presently find the same in his own haunts. And those pieces of luck which happen only to good players happened to him. One day, walking with a stranger, who inquired where Indian arrow-heads could be found, he replied, "Everywhere," and, stooping forward, picked one on the instant from the ground. At Mount Washington, in Tuckerman's Ravine, Thoreau had a bad fall, and sprained his foot. As he was in the act of getting up from his fall, he saw for the first time the leaves of the *Arnica mollis*.[4]

His robust common sense, armed with stout hands, keen perceptions, and strong will, cannot yet account for the superiority which shone in his simple and hidden life. I must add the cardinal fact, that there was an excellent wisdom in him, proper to a rare class of men, which showed him the material world as a means and symbol. This discovery, which sometimes yields to poets a certain casual and interrupted light, serving for the ornament of their writing, was in him an unsleeping insight; and whatever faults or obstructions of temperament might cloud it, he was not disobedient to the heavenly vision. In his youth, he said, one day, "The other world is all my art: my pencils will draw no other; my jack-knife will cut nothing else; I do not use it as a means." This was the muse and genius that ruled his opinions, conversation, studies, work, and course of life. This made him a searching judge of men. At first glance he measured his companion, and, though insensible to some fine traits of culture, could very well report his weight and calibre. And this made the impression of genius which his conversation often gave.

He understood the matter in hand at a glance, and saw the limitations and poverty of those he talked with, so that nothing seemed concealed from such terrible eyes. I have repeatedly known young men of sensibility converted in a moment to the belief that this was the man they were in search of, the man of men, who could tell them all they should do. His own dealing with them was never affectionate, but superior, didactic, — scorning their petty ways, — very slowly conceding, or not conceding at all, the promise of his society at their houses, or even at his own. "Would he not walk with them?" "He did not know. There was nothing so important to him as his walk; he had no walks to throw away on company." Visits were offered him from respectful parties, but he declined them. Admiring friends offered to carry him at their own cost to the

3. See n. 6, p. 205.
4. A tincture of dried arnica flowers was used as a medication.

Yellow-Stone River, — to the West Indies, — to South America. But though nothing could be more grave or considered than his refusals, they remind one in quite new relations of that fop Brummel's[5] reply to the gentleman who offered him his carriage in a shower, "But where will *you* ride, then?"—and what accusing silences, and what searching and irresistible speeches, battering down all defences, his companions can remember!

Mr. Thoreau dedicated his genius with such entire love to the fields, hills, and waters of his native town, that he made them known and interesting to all reading Americans, and to people over the sea. The river on whose banks he was born and died he knew from its springs to its confluence with the Merrimack.[6] He had made summer and winter observations on it for many years, and at every hour of the day and the night. The result of the recent survey of the Water Commissioners appointed by the State of Massachusetts he had reached by his private experiments, several years earlier. Every fact which occurs in the bed, on the banks, or in the air over it; the fishes, and their spawning and nests, their manners, their food; the shad-flies which fill the air on a certain evening once a year, and which are snapped at by the fishes so ravenously that many of these die of repletion; the conical heaps of small stones on the river-shallows, one of which heaps will sometimes overfill a cart, — these heaps the huge nests of small fishes; the birds which frequent the stream, heron, duck, sheldrake, loon, osprey; the snake, musk-rat, otter, woodchuck, and fox, on the banks; the turtle, frog, hyla, and cricket, which make the banks vocal, — were all known to him, and, as it were, townsmen and fellow-creatures; so that he felt an absurdity or violence in any narrative of one of these by itself apart, and still more of its dimensions on an inch-rule, or in the exhibition of its skeleton, or the specimen of a squirrel or a bird in brandy. He liked to speak of the manners of the river, as itself a lawful creature, yet with exactness, and always to an observed fact. As he knew the river, so the ponds in this region.

One of the weapons he used, more important than microscope or alcohol-receiver[7] to other investigators, was a whim which grew on him by indulgence, yet appeared in gravest statement, namely, of extolling his own town and neighborhood as the most favored centre for natural observation. He remarked that the Flora of Massachusetts embraced almost all the important plants of America, — most of the oaks, most of the willows, the best pines, the ash, the maple, the beech, the nuts. He returned Kane's[8] "Arctic Voyage" to a friend of whom he had borrowed it, with the remark, that "most of the phenomena noted might be observed in Concord." He seemed a little envious of the Pole, for the coincident sunrise and sunset, or five minutes' day after six months: a splendid fact which Annursnuc[9] had never afforded him. He found red snow in one of his walks, and told me that he expected to find yet the *Victoria regia*[1] in Concord. He was the attorney of the indigenous plants, and owned to a preference of the weeds to the imported plants, as of the Indian to the civilized man, — and noticed, with pleasure, that the willow bean-poles of his neighbor had grown more

---

5. Beau Brummell was the nickname of George Bryan Brummell (1778–1840), English dandy and witticist.
6. The Concord River meets the Merrimack at Lowell, Massachusetts. Henry and his brother John traveled down the Concord and up the Merrimack in 1839.
7. Either a dish filled with alcohol for the reception of specimens or a device used for distillation.
8. Elisha Kane (1820–1857), Arctic explorer, author of *Arctic Explorations* (1853–55). Actually, Thoreau was an avid reader of books of travel and exploration.
9. A hill in Concord.
1. South American water lily.

than his beans. "See these weeds," he said, "which have been hoed at by a million farmers all spring and summer, and yet have prevailed, and just now come out triumphant over all lanes, pastures, fields, and gardens, such is their vigor. We have insulted them with low names, too, — as Pigweed, Wormwood, Chickweed, Shad Blossom." He says, "They have brave names too, — Ambrosia, Stellaria, Amelanchier, Amaranth, etc."

I think his fancy for referring every thing to the meridian of Concord did not grow out of any ignorance or depreciation of other longitudes or latitudes, but was rather a playful expression of his conviction of the indifference of all places, and that the best place for each is where he stands. He expressed it once in this wise: — "I think nothing is to be hoped from you, if this bit of mould under your feet is not sweeter to you to eat, than any other in this world, or in any world."

The other weapon with which he conquered all obstacles in science was patience. He knew how to sit immovable, a part of the rock he rested on, until the bird, the reptile, the fish, which had retired from him, should come back, and resume its habits, nay, moved by curiosity, should come to him and watch him.

It was a pleasure and a privilege to walk with him. He knew the country like a fox or a bird, and passed through it as freely by paths of his own. He knew every track in the snow or on the ground, and what creature had taken this path before him. One must submit abjectly to such a guide, and the reward was great. Under his arm he carried an old music-book to press plants; in his pocket, his diary and pencil, a spy-glass for birds, microscope, jack-knife, and twine. He wore straw hat, stout shoes, strong gray trowsers, to brave shrub-oaks and smilax, and to climb a tree for a hawk's or a squirrel's nest. He waded into the pool for the water-plants, and his strong legs were no insignificant part of his armor. On the day I speak of he looked for the Menyanthes,[2] detected it across the wide pool, and, on examination of the florets, decided that it had been in flower five days. He drew out of his breast-pocket his diary, and read the names of all the plants that should bloom on this day, whereof he kept account as a banker when his notes fall due. The Cypripedium[3] not due till to-morrow. He thought, that, if waked up from a trance, in this swamp, he could tell by the plants what time of the year it was within two days. The redstart was flying about, and presently the fine grosbeaks, whose brilliant scarlet makes the rash gazer wipe his eye,[4] and whose fine clear note Thoreau compared to that of a tanager which has got rid of its hoarseness. Presently he heard a note which he called that of the night-warbler, a bird he had never identified, had been in search of twelve years, which always, when he saw it, was in the act of diving down into a tree or bush, and which it was vain to seek; the only bird that sings indifferently by night and by day. I told him he must beware of finding and booking it, lest life should have nothing more to show him. He said, "What you seek in vain for, half your life, one day you come full upon all the family at dinner. You seek it like a dream, and as soon as you find it you become its prey."

His interest in the flower or the bird lay very deep in his mind, was connected with Nature, — and the meaning of Nature was never attempted to be defined by

2. A buckbean.
3. The sandal of Venus, an orchid-like flower.
4. Emerson alludes here to George Herbert's poem "Virtue" ("Sweet rose, whose hue angry and brave / Bids the rash gazer wipe his eye"). But cf. "The Rhodora" (p. 439) lines 8–9 ("Here might the red-bird come his plumes to cool, / And court the flower that cheapens his array"); the rhodora is a swamp rose. Thoreau quotes the first stanza of Herbert's poem in the "Thursday" section of *A Week on the Concord and Merrimack Rivers.*

him. He would not offer a memoir of his observations to the Natural History Society. "Why should I? To detach the description from its connections in my mind would make it no longer true or valuable to me: and they do not wish what belongs to it." His power of observation seemed to indicate additional senses. He saw as with microscope, heard as with ear-trumpet, and his memory was a photographic register of all he saw and heard. And yet none knew better than he that it is not the fact that imports, but the impression or effect of the fact on your mind. Every fact lay in glory in his mind, a type of the order and beauty of the whole.

His determination on Natural History was organic. He confessed that he sometimes felt like a hound or a panther, and, if born among Indians, would have been a fell[5] hunter. But, restrained by his Massachusetts culture, he played out the game in this mild form of botany and ichthyology. His intimacy with animals suggested what Thomas Fuller[6] records of Butler the apiologist, that "either he had told the bees things or the bees had told him." Snakes coiled round his leg; the fishes swam into his hand, and he took them out of the water; he pulled the woodchuck out of its hole by the tail, and took the foxes under his protection from the hunters. Our naturalist had perfect magnanimity; he had no secrets: he would carry you to the heron's haunt, or even to his most prized botanical swamp,—possibly knowing that you could never find it again, yet willing to take his risks.

No college ever offered him a diploma,[7] or a professor's chair; no academy made him its corresponding secretary, its discoverer, or even its member. [Perhaps] these learned bodies feared the satire of his presence. Yet so much knowledge of Nature's secret and genius few others possessed, none in a more large and religious synthesis. For not a particle of respect had he to the opinions of any man or body of men, but homage solely to the truth itself; and as he discovered everywhere among doctors some leaning of courtesy, it discredited them.[8] He grew to be revered and admired by his townsmen, who had at first known him only as an oddity. The farmers who employed him as a surveyor soon discovered his rare accuracy and skill, his knowledge of their lands, of trees, of birds, of Indian remains, and the like, which enabled him to tell every farmer more than he knew before of his own farm; so that he began to feel as if Mr. Thoreau had better rights in his land than he. They felt, too, the superiority of character which addressed all men with a native authority.

Indian relics abound in Concord,—arrow-heads, stone chisels, pestles, and fragments of pottery; and on the river-bank, large heaps of clam-shells and ashes mark spots which the savages frequented. These, and every circumstance touching the Indian, were important in his eyes. His visits to Maine were chiefly for love of the Indian. He had the satisfaction of seeing the manufacture of the bark-canoe, as well as of trying his hand in its management on the rapids. He was inquisitive about the making of the stone arrow-head and in his last days charged a youth setting out for the Rocky Mountains to find an Indian who could tell him that: "It was well worth a visit to California to learn it." Occasionally, a small party of Penobscot Indians[9] would visit Concord, and pitch

---

5. Deadly.
6. Fuller (1608–1661) wrote *The History of the Worthies of England* (1662).
7. Since Thoreau had an A.B. from Harvard (1837), Emerson must mean that he was offered no honorary degrees.
8. Meaning, presumably, that the tendency of scholars to defer to one another out of professional courtesy discredited them in Thoreau's eyes.
9. Native American peoples inhabiting central Maine.

their tents for a few weeks in summer on the river-bank. He failed not to make acquaintance with the best of them; though he well knew that asking questions of Indians is like catechizing beavers and rabbits. In his last visit to Maine he had great satisfaction from Joseph Polis, an intelligent Indian of Oldtown, who was his guide for some weeks.

He was equally interested in every natural fact. The depth of his perception found likeness of law throughout Nature, and I know not any genius who so swiftly inferred universal law from the single fact. He was no pedant of a department. His eye was open to beauty, and his ear to music. He found these, not in rare conditions, but wheresoever he went. He thought the best of music was in single strains; and he found poetic suggestion in the humming of the telegraph-wire.

His poetry might be bad or good; he no doubt wanted a lyric facility and technical skill; but he had the source of poetry in his spiritual perception. He was a good reader and critic, and his judgment on poetry was to the ground of it. He could not be deceived as to the presence or absence of the poetic element in any composition, and his thirst for this made him negligent and perhaps scornful of superficial graces. He would pass by many delicate rhythms, but he would have detected every live stanza or line in a volume, and knew very well where to find an equal poetic charm in prose. He was so enamored of the spiritual beauty that he held all actual written poems in very light esteem in the comparison. He admired Æschylus and Pindar;[1] but, when some one was commending them, he said that "Æschylus and the Greeks, in describing Apollo and Orpheus, had given no song, or no good one. They ought not to have moved trees, but to have chanted to the gods such a hymn as would have sung all their old ideas out of their heads, and new ones in." His own verses are often rude and defective. The gold does not yet run pure, is drossy and crude. The thyme and marjoram are not yet honey. But if he want lyric fineness, and technical merits, if he have not the poetic temperament, he never lacks the causal thought, showing that his genius was better than his talent. He knew the worth of the Imagination for the uplifting and consolation of human life, and liked to throw every thought into a symbol. The fact you tell is of no value, but only the impression. For this reason his presence was poetic, always piqued the curiosity to know more deeply the secrets of his mind. He had many reserves, an unwillingness to exhibit to profane eyes what was still sacred in his own, and knew well how to throw a poetic veil over his experience. All readers of "Walden" will remember his mythical record of his disappointments: —

> "I long ago lost a hound, a bay horse, and a turtle-dove, and am still on their trail. Many are the travellers I have spoken concerning them, describing their tracks, and what calls they answered to. I have met one or two who had heard the hound, and the tramp of the horse, and even seen the dove disappear behind a cloud; and they seemed as anxious to recover them as if they had lost them themselves.[2]

His riddles were worth the reading, and I confide, that, if at any time I do not understand the expression, it is yet just. Such was the wealth of his truth that it was not worth his while to use words in vain.

---

1. See n. 3, p. 33. Aeschylus, see n. 1, p. 109.
2. *Walden,* from "Economy."

His poem entitled "Sympathy" reveals the tenderness under that triple steel of stoicism, and the intellectual subtilty it could animate. His classic poem on "Smoke" suggests Simonides,[3] but is better than any poem of Simonides. His biography is in his verses. His habitual thought makes all his poetry a hymn to the Cause of causes, the Spirit which vivifies and controls his own.

> "I hearing get, who had but ears,
>   And sight, who had but eyes before;
> I moments live, who lived but years,
>   And truth discern, who knew but learning's lore."

And still more in these religious lines: —

> "Now chiefly is my natal hour,
>   And only now my prime of life;
> I will not doubt the love untold,
> Which not my worth or want hath bought,
> Which wooed me young, and wooes me old,
>   And to this evening hath me brought."

Whilst he used in his writings a certain petulance of remark in reference to churches or churchmen, he was a person of a rare, tender, and absolute religion, a person incapable of any profanation, by act or by thought. Of course, the same isolation which belonged to his original thinking and living detached him from the social religious forms. This is neither to be censured nor regretted. Aristotle[4] long ago explained it, when he said, "One who surpasses his fellow-citizens in virtue is no longer a part of the city. Their law is not for him, since he is a law to himself."

Thoreau was sincerity itself, and might fortify the convictions of prophets in the ethical laws by his holy living. It was an affirmative experience which refused to be set aside. A truth-speaker he, capable of the most deep and strict conversation; a physician to the wounds of any soul; a friend knowing not only the secret of friendship, but almost worshipped by those few persons who resorted to him as their confessor and prophet, and knew the deep value of his mind and great heart. He thought that without religion or devotion of some kind nothing great was ever accomplished: and he thought that the bigoted sectarian had better bear this in mind.

His virtues, of course, sometimes ran into extremes. It was easy to trace to the inexorable demand on all for exact truth that austerity which made this willing hermit more solitary even than he wished. Himself of a perfect probity, he required not less of others. He had a disgust at crime, and no worldly success could cover it. He detected paltering as readily in dignified and prosperous persons as in beggars, and with equal scorn. Such dangerous frankness was in his dealing that his admirers called him "that terrible Thoreau," as if he spoke when silent, and was still present when he had departed. I think the severity of his ideal interfered to deprive him of a healthy sufficiency of human society.

The habit of a realist to find things the reverse of their appearance inclined him to put every statement in a paradox. A certain habit of antagonism defaced his earlier writings, — a trick of rhetoric not quite outgrown in his later, of sub-

---

3. Greek poet (ca. 406–467 B.C.E.). For Thoreau's poem "Smoke," see the "House-Warming" chapter of *Walden*.
4. See n. 4, p. 47.

stituting for the obvious word and thought its diametrical opposite. He praised wild mountains and winter forests for their domestic air, in snow and ice he would find sultriness, and commended the wilderness for resembling Rome and Paris. "It was so dry, that you might call it wet."

The tendency to magnify the moment, to read all the laws of Nature in the one object or one combination under your eye, is of course comic to those who do not share the philosopher's perception of identity. To him there was no such thing as size. The pond was a small ocean; the Atlantic, a large Walden Pond. He referred every minute fact to cosmical laws. Though he meant to be just, he seemed haunted by a certain chronic assumption that the science of the day pretended completeness, and he had just found out that the *savans* had neglected to discriminate a particular botanical variety, had failed to describe the seeds, or count the sepals. "That is to say," we replied, "the blockheads were not born in Concord; but who said they were? It was their unspeakable misfortune to be born in London, or Paris, or Rome; but, poor fellows, they did what they could, considering that they never saw Bateman's Pond, or Nine-Acre-Corner, or Becky-Stow's Swamp. Besides, what were you sent into the world for, but to add this observation?"

Had his genius been only contemplative, he had been fitted to his life, but with his energy and practical ability he seemed born for great enterprise and for command; and I so much regret the loss of his rare powers of action, that I cannot help counting it a fault in him that he had no ambition. Wanting this, instead of engineering for all America, he was the captain of a huckleberry party. Pounding beans is good to the end of pounding empires one of these days; but if, at the end of years, it is still only beans!

But these foibles, real or apparent, were fast vanishing in the incessant growth of a spirit so robust and wise, and which effaced its defeats with new triumphs. His study of Nature was a perpetual ornament to him, and inspired his friends with curiosity to see the world through his eyes, and to hear his adventures. They possessed every kind of interest.

He had many elegances of his own, whilst he scoffed at conventional elegance. Thus, he could not bear to hear the sound of his own steps, the grit of gravel; and therefore never willingly walked in the road, but in the grass, on mountains and in woods. His senses were acute, and he remarked that by night every dwelling-house gives out bad air, like a slaughter-house. He liked the pure fragrance of melilot.[5] He honored certain plants with special regard, and, over all, the pond-lily,—then, the gentian, and the *Mikania scandens*,[6] and "life-everlasting," and a bass-tree which he visited every year when it bloomed in the middle of July. He thought the scent a more oracular inquisition than the sight,—more oracular and trustworthy. The scent, of course, reveals what is concealed from the other senses. By it he detected earthiness. He delighted in echoes, and said, they were almost the only kind of kindred voices that he heard. He loved Nature so well, was so happy in her solitude, that he became very jealous of cities, and the sad work which their refinements and artifices made with man and his dwelling. The axe was always destroying his forest. "Thank God," he said, "they cannot cut down the clouds!" "All kinds of figures are drawn on the blue ground, with this fibrous white paint."

5. Sweet clover.
6. Climbing hempweed.

I subjoin a few sentences taken from his unpublished manuscripts,[7] not only as records of his thought and feeling, but for their power of description and literary excellence.

"Some circumstantial evidence is very strong, as when you find a trout in the milk."

"The chub is a soft fish, and tastes like boiled brown paper salted."

"The youth gets together his materials to build a bridge to the moon, or, perchance, a palace or temple on the earth, and at length the middle-aged man concludes to build a wood-shed with them."

"The locust z—ing."

"Devil's-needles zigzagging along the Nut-Meadow brook."

"Sugar is not so sweet to the palate as sound to the healthy ear."

"I put on some hemlock-boughs, and the rich salt crackling of their leaves was like mustard to the ear, the crackling of uncountable regiments. Dead trees love the fire."

"The bluebird carries the sky on his back."

"The tanager flies through the green foliage as if it would ignite the leaves."

"If I wish for a horse-hair for my compass-sight, I must go to the stable; but the hair-bird, with her sharp eyes, goes to the road."

"Immortal water, alive even to the superficies."

"Fire is the most tolerable third party."

"Nature made ferns for pure leaves, to show what she could do in that line."

"No tree has so fair a bole and so handsome an instep as the beech."

"How did these beautiful rainbow-tints get into the shell of the fresh-water clam, buried in the mud at the bottom of our dark river?"

"Hard are the times when the infant's shoes are second-foot."

"We are strictly confined to our men to whom we give liberty."

"Nothing is so much to be feared as fear. Atheism may comparatively be popular with God himself."

"Of what significance the things you can forget? A little thought is sexton to all the world."

"How can we expect a harvest of thought who have not had a seed-time of character?"

"Only he can be trusted with gifts who can present a face of bronze to expectations."

"I ask to be melted. You can only ask of the metals that they be tender to the fire that melts them. To nought else can they be tender."

There is a flower known to botanists, one of the same genus with our summer plant called "Life-Everlasting," a *Gnaphalium* like that, which grows on the most inaccessible cliffs of the Tyrolese mountains, where the chamois dare hardly venture, and which the hunter, tempted by its beauty, and by his love, (for it is immensely valued by the Swiss maidens,) climbs the cliffs to gather, and is sometimes found dead at the foot, with the flower in his hand. It is called by botanists the *Gnaphalium leontopodium*, but by the Swiss *Edelweisse*,[8] which signifies *Noble Purity*. Thoreau seemed to me living in the hope to gather this plant, which belonged to him of right. The scale on which his studies proceeded was so large as to require longevity, and we were the less prepared for his sudden disappearance. The country knows not yet, or in the least part, how great a son it has

---

7. From Thoreau's manuscript journal.
8. Or edelweiss, a small perennial woolly herb that is related to thistles.

lost. It seems an injury that he should leave in the midst his broken task, which none else can finish, — a kind of indignity to so noble a soul, that it should depart out of Nature before yet he has been really shown to his peers for what he is. But he, at least, is content. His soul was made for the noblest society; he had in a short life exhausted the capabilities of this world; wherever there is knowledge, wherever there is virtue, wherever there is beauty, he will find a home.

Abraham Lincoln

Remarks at the Funeral Services Held in Concord, April 19, 1865[1]

> "Nature, they say, doth dote,
> And cannot make a man
> Save on some worn-out plan,
> Repeating us by rote:
> For him her Old-World moulds aside she threw,
> And, choosing sweet clay from the breast
> Of the unexhausted West,
> With stuff untainted shaped a hero new,
> Wise, steadfast in the strength of God, and true.
> How beautiful to see
> Once more a shepherd of mankind indeed,
> Who loved his charge, but never loved to lead;
> One whose meek flock the people joyed to be,
> Not lured by any cheat of birth,
> But by his clear-grained human worth,
> And brave old wisdom of sincerity!
> They knew that outward grace is dust;
> They could not choose but trust
> In that sure-footed mind's unfaltering skill,
> And supple-tempered will
> That bent, like perfect steel, to spring again and thrust.
>
> . . . .
> Nothing of Europe here,
> Or, then, of Europe fronting mornward still,
> Ere any names of Serf and Peer
> Could Nature's equal scheme deface; . . .
> Here was a type of the true elder race,
> And one of Plutarch's men talked with us face to face."
> Lowell, *Commemoration Ode.*[2]

We meet under the gloom of a calamity which darkens down over the minds of good men in all civil society, as the fearful tidings travel over sea, over land, from country to country, like the shadow of an uncalculated eclipse over the planet.

---

1. Elected sixteenth president of the United States in 1860 (Emerson called the news "sublime" and said it was the "pronunciation of the masses of America against Slavery"), Lincoln saw the nation through the Civil War, putting the Emancipation Proclamation into effect on January 1, 1863. On April 14, 1865, Good Friday, just as the war ended, Lincoln was assassinated. Emerson spoke at a funeral service in Concord on April 19, Patriot's Day.
2. Delivered at Harvard, July 21, 1865. James Russell Lowell (1819–1891), American poet and critic. See his satiric verse on Emerson, p. 607.

Old as history is, and manifold as are its tragedies, I doubt if any death has caused so much pain to mankind as this has caused, or will cause, on its announcement; and this, not so much because nations are by modern arts brought so closely together, as because of the mysterious hopes and fears which, in the present day, are connected with the name and institutions of America.

In this country, on Saturday, every one was struck dumb, and saw at first only deep below deep, as he meditated on the ghastly blow. And perhaps, at this hour, when the coffin which contains the dust of the President sets forward on its long march through mourning states, on its way to his home in Illinois, we might well be silent, and suffer the awful voices of the time to thunder to us. Yes, but that first despair was brief: the man was not so to be mourned. He was the most active and hopeful of men; and his work had not perished: but acclamations of praise for the task he had accomplished burst out into a song of triumph, which even tears for his death cannot keep down.

The President stood before us as a man of the people. He was thoroughly American, had never crossed the sea, had never been spoiled by English insularity or French dissipation; a quite native, aboriginal man, as an acorn from the oak; no aping of foreigners, no frivolous accomplishments, Kentuckian born, working on a farm, a flatboatman, a captain in the Black Hawk[3] War, a country lawyer, a representative in the rural legislature of Illinois;—on such modest foundations the broad structure of his fame was laid. How slowly, and yet by happily prepared steps, he came to his place. All of us remember—it is only a history of five or six years—the surprise and the disappointment of the country at his first nomination by the convention[4] at Chicago. Mr. Seward,[5] then in the culmination of his good fame, was the favorite of the Eastern States. And when the new and comparatively unknown name of Lincoln was announced (notwithstanding the report of the acclamations of that convention), we heard the result coldly and sadly. It seemed too rash, on a purely local reputation, to build so grave a trust in such anxious times; and men naturally talked of the chances in politics as incalculable. But it turned out not to be chance. The profound good opinion which the people of Illinois and of the West had conceived of him, and which they had imparted to their colleagues, that they also might justify themselves to their constituents at home, was not rash, though they did not begin to know the riches of his worth.

A plain man of the people, an extraordinary fortune attended him. He offered no shining qualities at the first encounter; he did not offend by superiority. He had a face and manner which disarmed suspicion, which inspired confidence, which confirmed good will. He was a man without vices. He had a strong sense of duty, which it was very easy for him to obey. Then, he had what farmers call a long head; was excellent in working out the sum for himself; in arguing his case and convincing you fairly and firmly. Then, it turned out that he was a great worker; had prodigious faculty of performance; worked easily. A good worker is so rare; everybody has some disabling quality. In a host of young men that start together and promise so many brilliant leaders for the next age, each fails on trial; one by bad health, one by conceit, or by love of pleasure, or

---

3. Chief of the Sauk and Fox Indians. He crossed the Mississippi in the spring of 1832 with about one thousand members of his tribe, looking for food. The governor of Illinois, viewing this a hostile act, called out the militia, in which Lincoln commanded a company. The Indians were wantonly massacred.
4. I. e., the Republican convention of 1860.
5. William H. Seward (1801–1872), former governor of New York, served as secretary of state under Lincoln.

lethargy, or an ugly temper,—each has some disqualifying fault that throws him out of the career. But this man was sound to the core, cheerful, persistent, all right for labor, and liked nothing so well.

Then, he had a vast good nature, which made him tolerant and accessible to all; fair-minded, leaning to the claim of the petitioner; affable, and not sensible to the affliction which the innumerable visits paid to him when President would have brought to any one else. And how this good nature became a noble humanity, in many a tragic case which the events of the war brought to him, every one will remember; and with what increasing tenderness he dealt when a whole race was thrown on his compassion. The poor negro said of him, on an impressive occasion, "Massa Linkum am eberywhere."

Then his broad good humor, running easily into jocular talk, in which he delighted and in which he excelled, was a rich gift to this wise man. It enabled him to keep his secret; to meet every kind of man and every rank in society; to take off the edge of the severest decisions; to mask his own purpose and sound his companion; and to catch with true instinct the temper of every company he addressed. And, more than all, it is to a man of severe labor, in anxious and exhausting crises, the natural restorative, good as sleep, and is the protection of the overdriven brain against rancor and insanity.

He is the author of a multitude of good sayings, so disguised as pleasantries that it is certain they had no reputation at first but as jests; and only later, by the very acceptance and adoption they find in the mouths of millions, turn out to be the wisdom of the hour. I am sure if this man had ruled in a period of less facility of printing, he would have become mythological in a very few years, like Æsop or Pilpay, or one of the Seven Wise Masters,[6] by his fables and proverbs. But the weight and penetration of many passages in his letters, messages and speeches, hidden now by the very closeness of their application to the moment, are destined hereafter to wide fame. What pregnant definitions; what unerring common sense; what foresight; and, on great occasion, what lofty, and more than national, what humane tone! His brief speech at Gettysburg[7] will not easily be surpassed by words on any recorded occasion. This, and one other American speech, that of John Brown[8] to the court that tried him, and a part of Kossuth's[9] speech at Birmingham, can only be compared with each other, and with no fourth.

His occupying the chair of state was a triumph of the good sense of mankind, and of the public conscience. This middle-class country had got a middle-class president, at last. Yes, in manners and sympathies, but not in powers, for his powers were superior. This man grew according to the need. His mind mastered the problem of the day; and as the problem grew, so did his comprehension of it. Rarely was man so fitted to the event. In the midst of fears and jealousies, in the Babel of counsels and parties, this man wrought incessantly with all his might and all his honesty, laboring to find what the people wanted, and how to obtain that. It cannot be said there is any exaggeration of his worth. If ever a man was fairly tested, he was. There was no lack of resistance, nor of slander, nor of ridicule. The times have allowed no state secrets; the nation has

---

6. Or "Tales of Sandibar," a collection of stories, probably Indian, dating from about 100 B.C.E. Aesop, see n. 1, p. 115. Pilpay, see n. 3, p. 252.
7. Lincoln delivered his Gettysburg Address on November 19, 1863.
8. See n. 9, p. 402.
9. See n. 6, p. 265.

been in such ferment, such multitudes had to be trusted, that no secret could be kept. Every door was ajar, and we know all that befell.

Then, what an occasion was the whirlwind of the war. Here was place for no holiday magistrate, no fair-weather sailor; the new pilot was hurried to the helm in a tornado. In four years,—four years of battle-days,—his endurance, his fertility of resources, his magnanimity, were sorely tried and never found wanting. There, by his courage, his justice, his even temper, his fertile counsel, his humanity, he stood a heroic figure in the centre of a heroic epoch. He is the true history of the American people in his time. Step by step he walked before them; slow with their slowness, quickening his march by theirs, the true representative of this continent; an entirely public man; father of his country, the pulse of twenty millions throbbing in his heart, the thought of their minds articulated by his tongue.

Adam Smith remarks that the axe, which in Houbraken's[1] portraits of British kings and worthies is engraved under those who have suffered at the block, adds a certain lofty charm to the picture. And who does not see, even in this tragedy so recent, how fast the terror and ruin of the massacre are already burning into glory around the victim? Far happier this fate than to have lived to be wished away; to have watched the decay of his own faculties; to have seen—perhaps even he— the proverbial ingratitude of statesmen; to have seen mean men preferred. Had he not lived long enough to keep the greatest promise that ever man made to his fellow men,—the practical abolition of slavery? He had seen Tennessee, Missouri and Maryland emancipate their slaves. He had seen Savannah, Charleston and Richmond surrendered; had seen the main army of the rebellion lay down its arms. He had conquered the public opinion of Canada, England and France. Only Washington can compare with him in fortune.

And what if it should turn out, in the unfolding of the web, that he had reached the term; that this heroic deliverer could no longer serve us; that the rebellion had touched its natural conclusion, and what remained to be done required new and uncommitted hands,—a new spirit born out of the ashes of the war and that Heaven, wishing to show the world a completed benefactor, shall make him serve his country even more by his death than by his life? Nations, like kings, are not good by facility and complaisance. "The kindness of kings consists in justice and strength." Easy good nature has been the dangerous foible of the Republic, and it was necessary that its enemies should outrage it, and drive us to unwonted firmness, to secure the salvation of this country in the next ages.

The ancients believed in a serene and beautiful Genius which ruled in the affairs of nations; which, with a slow but stern justice, carried forward the fortunes of certain chosen houses, weeding out single offenders or offending families, and securing at last the firm prosperity of the favorites of Heaven. It was too narrow a view of the Eternal Nemesis.[2] There is a serene Providence which rules the fate of nations, which makes little account of time, little of one generation or race, makes no account of disasters, conquers alike by what is called defeat or by what is called victory, thrusts aside enemy and obstruction, crushes everything immoral as inhuman, and obtains the ultimate triumph of the best race by the sacrifice of everything which resists the moral laws of the world. It

1. Arnold Houbraken (1660–1719), Dutch engraver. Adam Smith (1723–1790), Scottish moral philosopher and political economist.
2. See n. 7, p. 143.

makes its own instruments, creates the man for the time, trains him in poverty, inspires his genius, and arms him for his task. It has given every race its own talent, and ordains that only that race which combines perfectly with the virtues of all shall endure.

From Historic Notes of Life and Letters in New England[1]

"Of old things all are over old,
Of good things none are good enough;—
We'll show that we can help to frame
A world of other stuff."
            "ROB ROY'S GRAVE," WORDSWORTH.

For Joy and Beauty planted it
    With faerie gardens cheered,
And boding Fancy haunted it
    With men and women weird.[2]

The ancient manners were giving way. There grew a certain tenderness on the people, not before remarked. Children had been repressed and kept in the background; now they were considered, cosseted and pampered. I recall the remark of a witty physician who remembered the hardships of his own youth; he said, "It was a misfortune to have been born when children were nothing, and to live till men were nothing."

There are always two parties, the party of the Past and the party of the Future; the Establishment and the Movement. At times the resistance is reanimated, the schism runs under the world and appears in Literature, Philosophy, Church, State, and social customs. It is not easy to date these eras of activity with any precision, but in this region one made itself remarked, say in 1820 and the twenty years following.

It seemed a war between intellect and affection; a crack in Nature, which split every church in Christendom into Papal and Protestant; Calvinism into Old and New schools; Quakerism into Old and New; brought new divisions in politics; as the new conscience touching temperance and slavery. The key to the period appeared to be that the mind had become aware of itself. Men grew reflective and intellectual. There was a new consciousness. The former generations acted under the belief that a shining social prosperity was the beatitude of man, and sacrificed uniformly the citizen to the State. The modern mind believed that the nation existed for the individual, for the guardianship and education of every man. This idea, roughly written in revolutions and national movements, in the mind of the philosopher had far more precision; the individual is the world.

This perception is a sword such as was never drawn before. It divides and detaches bone and marrow, soul and body, yea, almost the man from himself. It is the age of severance, of dissociation, of freedom, of analysis, of detachment.

---

1. This text was compiled by James Elliot Cabot and Ellen Emerson from a wide variety of manuscript material, the main source being one or more 1867 lectures. It was first published in the *Atlantic Monthly* in 1883. Emerson read this talk at his last appearance before the Concord Lyceum on February 4, 1880; it was his one hundredth lecture before that body.
2. This epigraph, by Emerson, was published among "Fragments on Nature and Life" in the Riverside and Centenary *Poems.*

Every man for himself. The public speaker disclaims speaking for any other; he answers only for himself. The social sentiments are weak; the sentiment of patriotism is weak; veneration is low; the natural affections feebler than they were. People grow philosophical about native land and parents and relations. There is an universal resistance to ties and ligaments once supposed essential to civil society. The new race is stiff, heady and rebellious; they are fanatics in freedom; they hate tolls, taxes, turnpikes, banks, hierarchies, governors, yea, almost laws. They have a neck of unspeakable tenderness; it winces at a hair. They rebel against theological as against political dogmas; against mediation, or saints, or any nobility in the unseen.

The age tends to solitude. The association of the time is accidental and momentary and hypocritical, the detachment intrinsic and progressive. The association is for power, merely,—for means; the end being the enlargement and independency of the individual. Anciently, society was in the course of things. There was a Sacred Band, a Theban Phalanx.[3] There can be none now. College classes, military corps, or trades-unions may fancy themselves indissoluble for a moment, over their wine; but it is a painted hoop, and has no girth. The age of arithmetic and of criticism has set in. The structures of old faith in every department of society a few centuries have sufficed to destroy. Astrology, magic, palmistry, are long gone. The very last ghost is laid. Demonology is on its last legs. Prerogative, government, goes to pieces day by day. Europe is strewn with wrecks; a constitution once a week. In social manners and morals the revolution is just as evident. In the law courts, crimes of fraud have taken the place of crimes of force. The stockholder has stepped into the place of the warlike baron. The nobles shall not any longer, as feudal lords, have power of life and death over the churls, but now, in another shape, as capitalists, shall in all love and peace eat them up as before. Nay, government itself becomes the resort of those whom government was invented to restrain. "Are there any brigands on the road?" inquired the traveller in France. "Oh, no, set your heart at rest on that point," said the landlord; "what should these fellows keep the highway for, when they can rob just as effectually, and much more at their ease, in the bureaus of office?"

In literature the effect appeared in the decided tendency of criticism. The most remarkable literary work of the age has for its hero and subject precisely this introversion: I mean the poem of Faust.[4] In philosophy, Immanuel Kant[5] has made the best catalogue of the human faculties and the best analysis of the mind. Hegel[6] also, especially. In science the French *savant*, exact, pitiless, with barometer, crucible, chemic test and calculus in hand, travels into all nooks and islands, to weigh, to analyze and report. And chemistry, which is the analysis of matter, has taught us that we eat gas, drink gas, tread on gas, and are gas. The same decomposition has changed the whole face of physics; the like in all arts, modes. Authority falls, in Church, College, Courts of Law, Faculties, Medicine. Experiment is credible; antiquity is grown ridiculous.

It marked itself by a certain predominance of the intellect in the balance of powers. The warm swart Earth-spirit which made the strength of past ages, mightier than it knew, with instincts instead of science, like a mother yielding

---

3. See n. 4, p. 325.
4. See n. 3, p. 243. Goethe's (see n. 6, p. 42) *Faust* was completed in 1832.
5. See n. 8, p. 35.
6. See n. 1, p. 275.

food from her own breast instead of preparing it through chemic and culinary skill,—warm negro ages of sentiment and vegetation,—all gone; another hour had struck and other forms arose. Instead of the social existence which all shared, was now separation. Every one for himself; driven to find all his resources, hopes, rewards, society and deity within himself.

The young men were born with knives in their brain, a tendency to introversion, self-dissection, anatomizing of motives. The popular religion of our fathers had received many severe shocks from the new times; from the Arminians, which was the current name of the backsliders from Calvinism, sixty years ago; then from the English philosophic theologians, Hartley and Priestley and Belsham, the followers of Locke; and then I should say much later from the slow but extraordinary influence of Swedenborg;[7] a man of prodigious mind, though as I think tainted with a certain suspicion of insanity, and therefore generally disowned, but exerting a singular power over an important intellectual class; then the powerful influence of the genius and character of Dr. Channing.[8]

Germany had created criticism in vain for us until 1820, when Edward Everett[9] returned from his five years in Europe, and brought to Cambridge his rich results, which no one was so fitted by natural grace and the splendor of his rhetoric to introduce and recommend. He made us for the first time acquainted with Wolff's theory of the Homeric writings, with the criticism of Heyne.[1] The novelty of the learning lost nothing in the skill and genius of his relation, and the rudest undergraduate found a new morning opened to him in the lecture-room of Harvard Hall.

There was an influence on the young people from the genius of Everett which was almost comparable to that of Pericles in Athens. He had an inspiration which did not go beyond his head, but which made him the master of elegance. If any of my readers were at that period in Boston or Cambridge, they will easily remember his radiant beauty of person, of a classic style, his heavy large eye, marble lids, which gave the impression of mass which the slightness of his form needed; sculptured lips; a voice of such rich tones, such precise and perfect utterance, that, although slightly nasal, it was the most mellow and beautiful and correct of all the instruments of the time. The word that he spoke, in the manner in which he spoke it, became current and classical in New England. He had a great talent for collecting facts, and for bringing those he had to bear with ingenious felicity on the topic of the moment. Let him rise to speak on what occasion soever, a fact had always just transpired which composed, with some other fact well known to the audience, the most pregnant and happy coincidence. It was remarked that for a man who threw out so many facts he was seldom convicted of a blunder. He had a good deal of special learning, and all his learning was available for purposes of the hour. It was all new learning, that wonderfully took and stimulated the young men. It was so coldly and weightily communicated from so commanding a platform, as if in the consciousness and consideration of all history and all learning,—adorned with so

7. See n. 6, p. 35. David Hartley (1705–1757), English philosopher known for his theory of the "association of ideas." Joseph Priestley (1733–1804), English cleric, chemist, and philosopher. Thomas Belsham (1750–1829), author of *Elements of the Philosophy of the Human Mind* (1801). Locke, see n. 7, p. 59.
8. William Ellery Channing "the elder" (1780–1842), intellectual leader of those churches which by the 1820s formed the Unitarian Association. Emerson called him "our bishop."
9. Everett (1794–1865), professor of classics at Harvard and a Unitarian minister, served in Congress (1825–35), as minister to England (1841–45), and in the Senate (1853–54).
1. Christian Gottlob Heyne (1729–1812), German classicist and Homeric scholar. Wolff, or Wolf, see n. 8, p. 339.

many simple and austere beauties of expression, and enriched with so many excellent digressions and significant quotations, that, though nothing could be conceived beforehand less attractive or indeed less fit for green boys from Connecticut, New Hampshire and Massachusetts, with their unripe Latin and Greek reading, than exegetical discourses in the style of Voss and Wolff and Ruhnken,[2] on the Orphic and Ante-Homeric remains,—yet this learning instantly took the highest place to our imagination in our unoccupied American Parnassus. All his auditors felt the extreme beauty and dignity of the manner, and even the coarsest were contented to go punctually to listen, for the manner, when they had found out that the subject-matter was not for them. In the lecture-room, he abstained from all ornament, and pleased himself with the play of detailing erudition in a style of perfect simplicity. In the pulpit (for he was then a clergyman) he made amends to himself and his auditor for the self-denial of the professor's chair, and, with an infantine simplicity still, of manner, he gave the reins to his florid, quaint and affluent fancy.

Then was exhibited all the richness of a rhetoric which we have never seen rivalled in this country. Wonderful how memorable were words made which were only pleasing pictures, and covered no new or valid thoughts. He abounded in sentences, in wit, in satire, in splendid allusion, in quotation impossible to forget, in daring imagery, in parable and even in a sort of defying experiment of his own wit and skill in giving an oracular weight to Hebrew or Rabbinical words;—feats which no man could better accomplish, such was his self-command and the security of his manner. All his speech was music, and with such variety and invention that the ear was never tired. Especially beautiful were his poetic quotations. He delighted in quoting Milton, and with such sweet modulation that he seemed to give as much beauty as he borrowed; and whatever he has quoted will be remembered by any who heard him, with inseparable association with his voice and genius. He had nothing in common with vulgarity and infirmity, but, speaking, walking, sitting, was as much aloof and uncommon as a star. The smallest anecdote of his behavior or conversation was eagerly caught and repeated, and every young scholar could recite brilliant sentences from his sermons, with mimicry, good or bad, of his voice. This influence went much farther, for he who was heard with such throbbing hearts and sparkling eyes in the lighted and crowded churches, did not let go his hearers when the church was dismissed, but the bright image of that eloquent form followed the boy home to his bed-chamber; and not a sentence was written in academic exercises, not a declamation attempted in the college chapel, but showed the omnipresence of his genius to youthful heads. This made every youth his defender, and boys filled their mouths with arguments to prove that the orator had a heart. This was a triumph of Rhetoric. It was not the intellectual or the moral principles which he had to teach. It was not thoughts. When Massachusetts was full of his fame it was not contended that he had thrown any truths into circulation. But his power lay in the magic of form; it was in the graces of manner; in a new perception of Grecian beauty, to which he had opened our eyes. There was that finish about this person which is about women, and which distinguishes every piece of genius from the works of talent,—that these last are more or less matured in every degree of com-

2. Johann Heinrich Voss (1751–1826) and David Ruhnken (1723–1798), German classical scholars.

pleteness according to the time bestowed on them, but works of genius in their first and slightest form are still wholes. In every public discourse there was nothing left for the indulgence of his hearer, no marks of late hours and anxious, unfinished study, but the goddess of grace had breathed on the work a last fragrancy and glitter.

By a series of lectures largely and fashionably attended for two winters in Boston he made a beginning of popular literary and miscellaneous lecturing, which in that region at least had important results. It is acquiring greater importance every day, and becoming a national institution. I am quite certain that this purely literary influence was of the first importance to the American mind.

In the pulpit Dr. Frothingham,[3] an excellent classical and German scholar, had already made us acquainted, if prudently, with the genius of Eichhorn's[4] theologic criticism. And Professor Norton[5] a little later gave form and method to the like studies in the then infant Divinity School. But I think the paramount source of the religious revolution was Modern Science; beginning with Copernicus, who destroyed the pagan fictions of the Church, by showing mankind that the earth on which we live was not the centre of the Universe, around which the sun and stars revolved every day, and thus fitted to be the platform on which the Drama of the Divine Judgment was played before the assembled Angels of Heaven,—"the scaffold of the divine vengeance" Saurin[6] called it,—but a little scrap of a planet, rushing round the sun in our system, which in turn was too minute to be seen at the distance of many stars which we behold. Astronomy taught us our insignificance in Nature; showed that our sacred as our profane history had been written in gross ignorance of the laws, which were far grander than we knew; and compelled a certain extension and uplifting of our views of the Deity and his Providence. This correction of our superstitions was confirmed by the new science of Geology, and the whole train of discoveries in every department. But we presently saw also that the religious nature in man was not affected by these errors in his understanding. The religious sentiment made nothing of bulk or size, or far or near; triumphed over time as well as space; and every lesson of humility, or justice, or charity, which the old ignorant saints had taught him, was still forever true.

Whether from these influences, or whether by a reaction of the general mind against the too formal science, religion and social life of the earlier period,—there was, in the first quarter of our nineteenth century, a certain sharpness of criticism, an eagerness for reform, which showed itself in every quarter. It appeared in the popularity of Lavater's[7] Physiognomy, now almost forgotten. Gall and Spurzheim's Phrenology[8] laid a rough hand on the mysteries of animal and spiritual nature, dragging down every sacred secret to a street show. The attempt was coarse and odious to scientific men, but had a certain truth in it; it felt connection where the professors denied it, and was a leading to a truth which had not yet been announced. On the heels of this intruder came Mes-

---

3. Nathaniel L. Frothingham (1793–1870), minister of the First Church of Boston and a distinguished scholar.
4. Joseph Gottfried Eichhorn (1752–1827), German theologian and historian.
5. Andrews Norton (1786–1853), the Unitarian "pope," professor at the Harvard Divinity School and staunch opponent of Transcendentalism. See his review of Emerson's Divinity School "Address" (p. 597).
6. Jacques Saurin (1677–1730), French Protestant preacher.
7. Johann Caspar Lavater (1741–1801), Swiss physiognomist.
8. See n. 4, p. 201. Franz Joseph Gall (1758–1828) and Spurzheim (see n. 1, p. 264), German phrenologists.

merism, which broke into the inmost shrines, attempted the explanation of miracle and prophecy, as well as of creation. What could be more revolting to the contemplative philosopher! But a certain success attended it, against all expectation. It was human, it was genial, it affirmed unity and connection between remote points, and as such was excellent criticism on the narrow and dead classification of what passed for science; and the joy with which it was greeted was an instinct of the people which no true philosopher would fail to profit by. But while society remained in doubt between the indignation of the old school and the audacity of the new, a higher note sounded. Unexpected aid from high quarters came to iconoclasts. The German poet Goethe revolted against the science of the day, against French and English science, declared war against the great name of Newton, proposed his own new and simple optics; in Botany, his simple theory of metamorphosis;—the eye of a leaf is all; every part of the plant from root to fruit is only a modified leaf, the branch of a tree is nothing but a leaf whose serratures have become twigs. He extended this into anatomy and animal life, and his views were accepted. The revolt became a revolution. Schelling and Oken[9] introduced their ideal natural philosophy, Hegel his metaphysics, and extended it to Civil History.

The result in literature and the general mind was a return to law; in science, in politics, in social life; as distinguished from the profligate manners and politics of earlier times. The age was moral. Every immorality is a departure from nature, and is punished by natural loss and deformity. The popularity of Combe's[1] Constitution of Man; the humanity which was the aim of all the multitudinous works of Dickens; the tendency even of Punch's[2] caricature, was all on the side of the people. There was a breath of new air, much vague expectation, a consciousness of power not yet finding its determinate aim.

I attribute much importance to two papers of Dr. Channing, one on Milton and one on Napoleon, which were the first specimens in this country of that large criticism which in England had given power and fame to the Edinburgh Review. They were widely read, and of course immediately fruitful in provoking emulation which lifted the style of Journalism. Dr. Channing, whilst he lived, was the star of the American Church, and we then thought, if we do not still think, that he left no successor in the pulpit. He could never be reported, for his eye and voice could not be printed, and his discourses lose their best in losing them. He was made for the public; his cold temperament made him the most unprofitable private companion; but all America would have been impoverished in wanting him. We could not then spare a single word he uttered in public, not so much as the reading a lesson in Scripture, or a hymn, and it is curious that his printed writings are almost a history of the times; as there was no great public interest, political, literary, or even economical (for he wrote on the Tariff), on which he did not leave some printed record of his brave and thoughtful opinion. A poor little invalid all his life, he is yet one of those men who vindicate the power of the American race to produce greatness.

Dr. Channing took counsel in 1840 with George Ripley,[3] to the point whether it were possible to bring cultivated, thoughtful people together, and

9. See n. 1, p. 194.
1. George Combe (1788–1858), Scottish phrenologist.
2. See n. 1, p. 267. Charles Dickens (1812–1870), possibly the greatest English novelist of the nineteenth century.
3. See n. 1, p. 203. See also Emerson's journal entry for Oct. 17, 1840 (p. 505).

make society that deserved the name. He had earlier talked with Dr. John Collins Warren[4] on the like purpose, who admitted the wisdom of the design and undertook to aid him in making the experiment. Dr. Channing repaired to Dr. Warren's house on the appointed evening, with large thoughts which he wished to open. He found a well-chosen assembly of gentlemen variously distinguished; there was mutual greeting and introduction, and they were chatting agreeably on indifferent matters and drawing gently towards their great expectation, when a side-door opened, the whole company streamed in to an oyster supper, crowned by excellent wines; and so ended the first attempt to establish æsthetic society in Boston.

Some time afterwards Dr. Channing opened his mind to Mr. and Mrs. Ripley, and with some care they invited a limited party of ladies and gentlemen. I had the honor to be present. Though I recall the fact, I do not retain any instant consequence of this attempt, or any connection between it and the new zeal of the friends who at that time began to be drawn together by sympathy of studies and of aspiration. Margaret Fuller, George Ripley, Dr. Convers Francis, Theodore Parker, Dr. Hedge, Mr. Brownson, James Freeman Clarke, William H. Channing[5] and many others, gradually drew together and from time to time spent an afternoon at each other's houses in a serious conversation. With them was always one well-known form,[6] a pure idealist, not at all a man of letters, nor of any practical talent, nor a writer of books; a man quite too cold and contemplative for the alliances of friendship, with rare simplicity and grandeur of perception, who read Plato as an equal, and inspired his companions only in proportion as they were intellectual, —whilst the men of talent complained of the want of point and precision in this abstract and religious thinker.

These fine conversations, of course, were incomprehensible to some in the company, and they had their revenge in their little joke. One declared that "It seemed to him like going to heaven in a swing;" another reported that, at a knotty point in the discourse, a sympathizing Englishman with a squeaking voice interrupted with the question, "Mr. Alcott, a lady near me desires to inquire whether omnipotence abnegates attribute?"

I think there prevailed at that time a general belief in Boston that there was some concert of *doctrinaires* to establish certain opinions and inaugurate some movement in literature, philosophy and religion, of which design the supposed conspirators were quite innocent; for there was no concert, and only here and there two or three men or women who read and wrote, each alone, with unusual vivacity. Perhaps they only agreed in having fallen upon Coleridge and Wordsworth and Goethe, then on Carlyle, with pleasure and sympathy. Otherwise, their education and reading were not marked, but had the American superficialness, and their studies were solitary. I suppose all of them were surprised at this rumor of a school or sect, and certainly at the name of Transcendentalism, given nobody knows by whom, or when it was first applied. As these persons became in the common

---

4. Distinguished Boston physician (1778–1856).
5. Nephew of the elder William Ellery Channing (see n. 1, p. 372). Fuller, see n. 1, p. 331; see also p. 372. Francis (1795–1863), Unitarian minister and member of the Transcendental Club. Theodore Parker (1810–1860), Unitarian thinker and writer. Hedge, see n. 6, p. 325; the Transcendental Club was sometimes called the "Hedge Club," because it regularly convened when he came to Boston. See selections from his article on Coleridge and German philosophy (p. 577). Orestes Brownson (1803–1876), New England cleric and writer who moved from Unitarianism to Roman Catholicism, an ardent socialist. Clarke, n. 1, p. 372.
6. Bronson Alcott, the ethereal father of Louisa May (see n. 3, p. 52). See excerpts from L. M. Alcott's *Journals* (p. 612).

chances of society acquainted with each other, there resulted certainly strong friendships, which of course were exclusive in proportion to their heat: and perhaps those persons who were mutually the best friends were the most private and had no ambition of publishing their letters, diaries, or conversation.

From that time meetings were held for conversation, with very little form, from house to house, of people engaged in studies, fond of books, and watchful of all the intellectual light from whatever quarter it flowed. Nothing could be less formal, yet the intelligence and character and varied ability of the company gave it some notoriety and perhaps waked curiosity as to its aims and results.

Nothing more serious came of it than the modest quarterly journal called The Dial, which, under the editorship of Margaret Fuller, and later of some other,[7] enjoyed its obscurity for four years. All its papers were unpaid contributions, and it was rather a work of friendship among the narrow circle of students than the organ of any party. Perhaps its writers were its chief readers: yet it contained some noble papers by Margaret Fuller, and some numbers had an instant exhausting sale, because of papers by Theodore Parker.

Theodore Parker was our Savonarola, an excellent scholar, in frank and affectionate communication with the best minds of his day, yet the tribune of the people, and the stout Reformer to urge and defend every cause of humanity with and for the humblest of mankind. He was no artist. Highly refined persons might easily miss in him the element of beauty. What he said was mere fact, almost offended you, so bald and detached; little cared he. He stood altogether for practical truth; and so to the last. He used every day and hour of his short life, and his character appeared in the last moments with the same firm control as in the midday of strength. I habitually apply to him the words of a French philosopher who speaks of "the man of Nature who abominates the steam-engine and the factory. His vast lungs breathe independence with the air of the mountains and the woods."

The vulgar politician disposed of this circle cheaply as "the sentimental class." State Street had an instinct that they invalidated contracts and threatened the stability of stocks; and it did not fancy brusque manners. Society always values, even in its teachers, inoffensive people, susceptible of conventional polish. The clergyman who would live in the city *may* have piety, but *must* have taste, whilst there was often coming, among these, some John the Baptist, wild from the woods, rude, hairy, careless of dress and quite scornful of the etiquette of cities. There was a pilgrim in those days walking in the country who stopped at every door where he hoped to find hearing for his doctrine, which was, Never to give or receive money. He was a poor printer, and explained with simple warmth the belief of himself and five or six young men with whom he agreed in opinion, of the vast mischief of our insidious coin. He thought every one should labor at some necessary product, and as soon as he had made more than enough for himself, were it corn, or paper, or cloth, or boot-jacks, he should give of the commodity to any applicant, and in turn go to his neighbor for any article which he had to spare. Of course we were curious to know how he sped in his experiments on the neighbor, and his anecdotes were interesting, and often highly creditable. But he had the courage which so stern a return to Arcadian manners required, and had learned to sleep, in cold nights, when the farmer at whose door he knocked declined to give him a bed, on a wagon cov-

7. I.e., Emerson himself.

ered with the buffalo-robe under the shed, —or under the stars, when the farmer denied the shed and the buffalo-robe. I think he persisted for two years in his brave practice, but did not enlarge his church of believers.

These reformers were a new class. Instead of the fiery souls of the Puritans, bent on hanging the Quaker, burning the witch and banishing the Romanist, these were gentle souls, with peaceful and even with genial dispositions, casting sheep's-eyes even on Fourier[8] and his houris. It was a time when the air was full of reform. Robert Owen[9] of Lanark came hither from England in 1845, and read lectures or held conversations wherever he found listeners; the most amiable, sanguine and candid of men. He had not the least doubt that he had hit on a right and perfect socialism, or that all mankind would adopt it. He was then seventy years old, and being asked, "Well, Mr. Owen, who is your disciple? How many men are there possessed of your views who will remain after you are gone, to put them in practice?" "Not one," was his reply. Robert Owen knew Fourier in his old age. He said that Fourier learned of him all the truth he had; the rest of his system was imagination, and the imagination of a banker. Owen made the best impression by his rare benevolence. His love of men made us forget his "Three Errors." His charitable construction of men and their actions was invariable. He was the better Christian in his controversy with Christians, and he interpreted with great generosity the acts of the "Holy Alliance," and Prince Metternich,[1] with whom the persevering *doctrinaire* had obtained interviews; "Ah," he said, "you may depend on it there are as tender hearts and as much good will to serve men, in palaces, as in colleges."

And truly I honor the generous ideas of the Socialists, the magnificence of their theories and the enthusiasm with which they have been urged. They appeared the inspired men of their time. Mr. Owen preached his doctrine of labor and reward, with the fidelity and devotion of a saint, to the slow ears of his generation. Fourier, almost as wonderful an example of the mathematical mind of France as La Place or Napoleon,[2] turned a truly vast arithmetic to the question of social misery, and has put men under the obligation which a generous mind always confers, of conceiving magnificent hopes and making great demands as the right of man. He took his measure of that which all should and might enjoy, from no soup-society or charity-concert, but from the refinements of palaces, the wealth of universities and the triumphs of artists. He thought nobly. A man is entitled to pure air, and to the air of good conversation in his bringing up, and not, as we or so many of us, to the poor-smell and musty chambers, cats and fools. Fourier carried a whole French Revolution in his head, and much more. Here was arithmetic on a huge scale. His ciphering goes where ciphering never went before, namely, into stars, atmospheres and animals, and men and women, and classes of every character. It was the most entertaining of French romances, and could not but suggest vast possibilities of reform to the coldest and least sanguine.

We had an opportunity of learning something of these Socialists and their theory, from the indefatigable apostle of the sect in New York, Albert Brisbane.[3] Mr. Brisbane pushed his doctrine with all the force of memory, talent, honest faith and importunacy. As we listened to his exposition it appeared to us the sub-

8. See n. 3, p. 133.
9. See n. 1, p. 226.
1. See n. 1, p. 275.
2. See n. 8, p. 17. La Place, see n. 9, p. 89.
3. Albert Brisbane (1809–1890), student of Fourier and a reformer and journalist.

lime of mechanical philosophy; for the system was the perfection of arrangement and contrivance. The force of arrangement could no farther go. The merit of the plan was that it was a system; that it had not the partiality and hint-and-fragment character of most popular schemes, but was coherent and comprehensive of facts to a wonderful degree. It was not daunted by distance, or magnitude, or remoteness of any sort, but strode about nature with a giant's step, and skipped no fact, but wove its large Ptolemaic web of cycle and epicycle, of phalanx and phalanstery,[4] with laudable assiduity. Mechanics were pushed so far as fairly to meet spiritualism. One could not but be struck with strange coincidences betwixt Fourier and Swedenborg. Genius hitherto has been shamefully misapplied, a mere trifler. It must now set itself to raise the social condition of man and to redress the disorders of the planet he inhabits. The Desert of Sahara, the Campagna di Roma, the frozen Polar circles, which by their pestilential or hot or cold airs poison the temperate regions, accuse man. Society, concert, coöperation, is the secret of the coming Paradise. By reason of the isolation of men at the present day, all work is drudgery. By concert and the allowing each laborer to choose his own work, it becomes pleasure. "Attractive Industry" would speedily subdue, by adventurous scientific and persistent tillage, the pestilential tracts; would equalize temperature, give health to the globe and cause the earth to yield "healthy imponderable fluids" to the solar system, as now it yields noxious fluids. The hyæna, the jackal, the gnat, the bug, the flea, were all beneficent parts of the system; the good Fourier knew what those creatures should have been, had not the mould slipped, through the bad state of the atmosphere; caused no doubt by the same vicious imponderable fluids. All these shall be redressed by human culture, and the useful goat and dog and innocent poetical moth, or the wood-tick to consume decomposing wood, shall take their place. It takes sixteen hundred and eighty men to make one Man, complete in all the faculties; that is, to be sure that you have got a good joiner, a good cook, a barber, a poet, a judge, an umbrella-maker, a mayor and alderman, and so on. Your community should consist of two thousand persons, to prevent accidents of omission; and each community should take up six thousand acres of land. Now fancy the earth planted with fifties and hundreds of these phalanxes side by side, —what tillage, what architecture, what refectories, what dormitories, what reading-rooms, what concerts, what lectures, what gardens, what baths! What is not in one will be in another, and many will be within easy distance. Then know you one and all, that Constantinople is the natural capital of the globe. There, in the Golden Horn, will the Arch-Phalanx be established; there will the Omniarch reside. Aladdin and his magician, or the beautiful Scheherezade can alone, in these prosaic times before the sight, describe the material splendors collected there. Poverty shall be abolished; deformity, stupidity and crime shall be no more. Genius, grace, art, shall abound, and it is not to be doubted but that in the reign of "Attractive Industry" all men will speak in blank verse.

Certainly we listened with great pleasure to such gay and magnificent pictures. The ability and earnestness of the advocate and his friends, the comprehensiveness of their theory, its apparent directness of proceeding to the end they would secure, the indignation they felt and uttered in the presence of so much social misery, commanded our attention and respect. It contained so much truth, and promised in the attempts that shall be made to realize it so much valuable in-

4. See n. 1, p. 226.

struction, that we are engaged to observe every step of its progress. Yet in spite of the assurances of its friends that it was new and widely discriminated from all other plans for the regeneration of society, we could not exempt it from the criticism which we apply to so many projects for reform with which the brain of the age teems. Our feeling was that Fourier had skipped no fact but one, namely Life. He treats man as a plastic thing, something that may be put up or down, ripened or retarded, moulded, polished, made into solid or fluid or gas, at the will of the leader; or perhaps as a vegetable, from which, though now a poor crab, a very good peach can by manure and exposure be in time produced, — but skips the faculty of life, which spawns and scorns system and system-makers; which eludes all conditions; which makes or supplants a thousand phalanxes and New Harmonies with each pulsation. There is an order in which in a sound mind the faculties always appear, and which, according to the strength of the individual, they seek to realize in the surrounding world. The value of Fourier's system is that it is a statement of such an order externized, or carried outward into its correspondence in facts. The mistake is that this particular order and series is to be imposed, by force or preaching and votes, on all men, and carried into rigid execution. But what is true and good must not only be begun by life, but must be conducted to its issues by life. Could not the conceiver of this design have also believed that a similar model lay in every mind, and that the method of each associate might be trusted, as well as that of his particular Committee and General Office, No. 200 Broadway? Nay, that it would be better to say, Let us be lovers and servants of that which is just, and straightway every man becomes a centre of a holy and beneficent republic, which he sees to include all men in its law, like that of Plato, and of Christ. Before such a man the whole world becomes Fourierized or Christized or humanized, and in obedience to his most private being he finds himself, according to his presentiment, though against all sensuous probability, acting in strict concert with all others who followed their private light.

Yet, in a day of small, sour and fierce schemes, one is admonished and cheered by a project of such friendly aims and of such bold and generous proportion; there is an intellectual courage and strength in it which is superior and commanding; it certifies the presence of so much truth in the theory, and in so far is destined to be fact.

It argued singular courage, the adoption of Fourier's system, to even a limited extent, with his books lying before the world only defended by the thin veil of the French language. The Stoic said, Forbear, Fourier said, Indulge. Fourier was of the opinion of Saint-Evremond;[5] abstinence from pleasure appeared to him a great sin. Fourier was very French indeed. He labored under a misapprehension of the nature of women. The Fourier marriage was a calculation how to secure the greatest amount of kissing that the infirmity of human constitution admitted. It was false and prurient, full of absurd French superstitions about women; ignorant how serious and how moral their nature always is; how chaste is their organization; how lawful a class.

It is the worst of community that it must inevitably transform into charlatans the leaders, by the endeavor continually to meet the expectation and admiration of this eager crowd of men and women seeking they know not what.

---

5. Charles de Marguetel de Saint Denis, seigneur de Saint-Evremond (1613–1703), French wit and man of letters.

Unless he have a Cossack roughness of clearing himself of what belongs not, charlatan he must be.

It was easy to see what must be the fate of this fine system in any serious and comprehensive attempt to set it on foot in this country. As soon as our people got wind of the doctrine of Marriage held by this master, it would fall at once into the hands of a lawless crew who would flock in troops to so fair a game, and, like the dreams of poetic people on the first outbreak of the old French Revolution, so theirs would disappear in a slime of mire and blood.

There is of course to every theory a tendency to run to an extreme, and to forget the limitations. In our free institutions, where every man is at liberty to choose his home and his trade, and all possible modes of working and gaining are open to him, fortunes are easily made by thousands, as in no other country. Then property proves too much for the man, and the men of science, art, intellect, are pretty sure to degenerate into selfish housekeepers, dependent on wine, coffee, furnace-heat, gas-light and fine furniture. Then instantly things swing the other way, and we suddenly find that civilization crowed too soon; that what we bragged as triumphs were treacheries: that we have opened the wrong door and let the enemy into the castle; that civilization was a mistake; that nothing is so vulgar as a great warehouse of rooms full of furniture and trumpery; that, in the circumstances, the best wisdom were an auction or a fire. Since the foxes and the birds have the right of it, with a warm hole to keep out the weather, and no more,—a pent-house to fend the sun and rain is the house which lays no tax on the owner's time and thoughts, and which he can leave, when the sun is warm, and defy the robber. This was Thoreau's[6] doctrine, who said that the Fourierists had a sense of duty which led them to devote themselves to their second-best. And Thoreau gave in flesh and blood and pertinacious Saxon belief the purest ethics. He was more real and practically believing in them than any of his company, and fortified you at all times with an affirmative experience which refused to be set aside. Thoreau was in his own person a practical answer, almost a refutation, to the theories of the socialists. He required no Phalanx, no Government, no society, almost no memory. He lived extempore from hour to hour, like the birds and the angels; brought every day a new proposition, as revolutionary as that of yesterday, but different: the only man of leisure in his town; and his independence made all others look like slaves. He was a good Abbot Samson,[7] and carried a counsel in his breast. "Again and again I congratulate myself on my so-called poverty, I could not overstate this advantage." "What you call bareness and poverty, is to me simplicity. God could not be unkind to me if he should try. I love best to have each thing in its season only, and enjoy doing without it at all other times. It is the greatest of all advantages to enjoy no advantage at all. I have never got over my surprise that I should have been born into the most estimable place in all the world, and in the very nick of time too." There's an optimist for you.

I regard these philanthropists as themselves the effects of the age in which we live, and, in common with so many other good facts, the efflorescence of the period, and predicting a good fruit that ripens. They were not the creators they believed themselves, but they were unconscious prophets of a true state of society; one which the tendencies of nature lead unto, one which always establishes itself for the sane soul, though not in that manner in which they paint it;

6. See Emerson's eulogy for his young friend (p. 398).
7. Monk (twelfth century) who figures in Thomas Carlyle's *Past and Present* (1843).

but they were describers of that which is really being done. The large cities are phalansteries; and the theorists drew all their argument from facts already taking place in our experience. The cheap way is to make every man do what he was born for. One merchant to whom I described the Fourier project, thought it must not only succeed, but that agricultural association must presently fix the price of bread, and drive single farmers into association in self-defence, as the great commercial and manufacturing companies had done. Society in England and in America is trying the experiment again in small pieces, in coöperative associations, in cheap eating-houses, as well as in the economies of club-houses and in cheap reading-rooms.

It chanced that here in one family were two brothers, one a brilliant and fertile inventor, and close by him his own brother, a man of business, who knew how to direct his faculty and make it instantly and permanently lucrative. Why could not the like partnership be formed between the inventor and the man of executive talent everywhere? Each man of thought is surrounded by wiser men than he, if they cannot write as well. Cannot he and they combine? Talents supplement each other. Beaumont and Fletcher[8] and many French novelists have known how to utilize such partnerships. Why not have a larger one, and with more various members?

Housekeepers say, "There are a thousand things to everything," and if one must study all the strokes to be laid, all the faults to be shunned in a building or work of art, of its keeping, its composition, its site, its color, there would be no end. But the architect, acting under a necessity to build the house for its purpose, finds himself helped, he knows not how, into all these merits of detail, and steering clear, though in the dark, of those dangers which might have shipwrecked him.

✳   ✳   ✳

8. See n. 9, p. 132.

Selected Poetry

We print a generous selection from Emerson's two major books of poetry, *Poems* (1847) and *May-Day and Other Pieces* (1867); along with one poem from his late collection, *Selected Poems* (1876); and three poems uncollected by Emerson. While Emerson is today primarily thought of as a writer of prose, he wrote poetry his entire life and, in 1842, protested in a letter to his wife Lidian, "I am in all my theory, ethics, & politics a poet . . . [and want to say to others] 'I am not the man you take me for'" (*L* 3.18).

Textual Note

The first American edition of *Poems*, dated 1847, was released by James Munroe & Company of Boston on December 25, 1846. (The volume was first published in London by Chapman Brothers on December 12, 1846, in an edition that contained many errors.) The first edition of *May-Day and Other Pieces* was published in 1867, by Ticknor and Fields of Boston. Many of the poems were initially published in periodicals of the time, often in slightly different forms. The poems also appeared in subsequent printings and editions of *Poems* and *May-Day*, in *Selected Poems* (James R. Osgood and Company, 1876), and in collected poems volumes. Emerson heavily marked a number of his copies of his poetry for the subsequent editions, especially for the publication of *Selected Poems*. The other two major early editions of the poetry include the *Poems* in the Riverside Edition of Emerson's works, published in 1884 (with texts prepared by Emerson's family and his literary executor, James Elliot Cabot), and the volume *Poems* in the Centenary Edition of Emerson's works, prepared by his son Edward Emerson. The textual situation with regard to Emerson's poetry remains particularly gnarled, so that no entirely satisfactory editorial solution yet exists. We print the poems in the order of their initial book publication, but because of the importance of Emerson's own meticulous editing, we print *Selected Poems* texts (prepared by Emerson in conjunction with Cabot and Emerson's children and family friends) unless we note otherwise. We indicate corrections and significant textual variations in notes. The *Selected Poems* texts correspond to a collation of changes in intermediate editions of *Poems* and markings in Emerson's hand in his primary working copies of *Poems* and of *May-Day* (first editions of each). In the cases of poems that do not appear in *Selected Poems*, we follow first-edition texts but make changes to honor Emerson's markings in his primary working copies and subsequent editions supervised by Emerson, again printing corrections and significant textual variations in notes. For published textual information, we have relied on the *Poetry Notebooks of Ralph Waldo Emerson*, an invaluable scholarly tool. While the editorial decision to privilege *Selected Poems* texts was our own, emphasis on the importance of that volume has been articulated recently by Joseph Thomas (see Selected Bibliography) and was stressed by Carl Strauch, the groundbreaking scholar of Emerson's verse.

FROM POEMS

The Sphinx[1]

The Sphinx is drowsy,
    Her wings are furled;
Her ear is heavy,
    She broods on the world.
'Who'll tell me my secret,   5
    The ages have kept? —
I awaited the seer,
    While they slumbered and slept; —

'The fate of the man-child;
    The meaning of man;   10
Known fruit of the unknown;
    Dædalian[2] plan;
Out of sleeping a waking,
    Out of waking a sleep;
Life death overtaking;   15
    Deep underneath deep?

'Erect as a sunbeam,
    Upspringeth the palm;
The elephant browses,
    Undaunted and calm;   20
In beautiful motion
    The thrush plies his wings;
Kind leaves of his covert,[3]
    Your silence he sings.

'The waves, unashamed,   25
    In difference sweet,
Play glad with the breezes,
    Old playfellows meet;
The journeying atoms,
    Primordial wholes,   30
Firmly draw, firmly drive,
    By their animate poles.

'Sea, earth, air, sound, silence,
    Plant, quadruped, bird,

---

1. Completed in late 1840 and published in the first issue of *The Dial*, January 1841, "The Sphinx" appeared as the initial poem in *Poems*, *Selected Poems*, and the Riverside collected *Poems*, making it a significant threshold into the rest of Emerson's verse. This poem establishes the subsequent poems as rewards for the persistent reader who can successfully engage "The Sphinx" and initiates crucial concerns and rhetorical devices that appear throughout the verse (see Morris, p. 777). *Sphinx*: see n. 7, p. 38. Her riddle was: "What walks on four legs at morning, two in mid-day, and three at evening"; the answer is "human beings." "Sphinx" has come by association to refer to a puzzling or mysterious person.
2. In Greek myth, Daedalus was the accomplished artisan who designed the Labyrinth, a great maze, and the wings with which his son, Icarus, flew to his death.
3. Meaning, presumably, each kind of creature departs from its lair.

By one music enchanted,   35
    One deity stirred,—
Each the other adorning,
    Accompany still;
Night veileth the morning,
    The vapor the hill.   40

'The babe by its mother
    Lies bathed in joy;
Glide its hours uncounted,—
    The sun is its toy;
Shines the peace of all being,   45
    Without cloud, in its eyes;
And the sum of the world
    In soft miniature lies.

'But man crouches and blushes,
    Absconds and conceals;   50
He creepeth and peepeth,
    He palters and steals;
Infirm, melancholy,
    Jealous glancing around,
An oaf, an accomplice,   55
    He poisons the ground.

'Out spoke the great mother,
    Beholding his fear;—
At the sound of her accents
    Cold shuddered the sphere:—   60
"Who has drugged my boy's cup?
    Who has mixed my boy's bread?
Who, with sadness and madness,
    Has turned my child's head?" '4

I heard a poet answer,   65
    Aloud and cheerfully,
'Say on, sweet Sphinx! thy dirges
    Are pleasant songs to me.
Deep love lieth under
    These pictures of time;   70
They fade in the light of
    Their meaning sublime.

'The fiend that man harries
    Is love of the Best;
Yawns the pit of the Dragon,   75
    Lit by rays from the Blest.
The Lethe5 of nature
    Can't trance him again,

4. In the first edition and up to *SP*, this line reads " 'Has turned the man-child's head?' "
5. See n. 5, p. 122.

Whose soul sees the perfect,
    Which his eyes seek in vain.   80

'To vision profounder[6]
    Man's spirit must dive;
His aye-rolling orb
    At no goal will arrive;[7]
The heavens that now draw him   85
    With sweetness untold,
Once found,—for new heavens
    He spurneth the old.

'Pride ruined the angels,
    Their shame them restores;   90
And the joy that is sweetest
    Lurks in stings of remorse.[8]
Have I a lover
    Who is noble and free?—
I would he were nobler   95
    Than to love me.

'Eterne alternation
    Now follows, now flies;
And under pain, pleasure,—
    Under pleasure, pain lies.   100
Love works at the centre,
    Heart-heaving alway;
Forth speed the strong pulses
    To the borders of day.

'Dull Sphinx, Jove[9] keep thy five wits: 105
    Thy sight is growing blear;
Rue, myrrh, and cummin[1] for the Sphinx,—
    Her muddy eyes to clear!'—
The old Sphinx bit her thick lip,—
    Said, 'Who taught thee me to name?   110
I am thy spirit, yoke-fellow,
    Of thine eye I am eyebeam.[2]

'Thou art the unanswered question;
    Couldst see thy proper eye,

6. First edition to SP, "Profounder, profounder"; SP, "To insight profounder." The change to "vision profounder" is marked in Emerson's primary working copy of *Poems* 1847 and is made in RE and W.
7. First edition to SP, "To his aye-rolling orbit / No goal will arrive"; SP, "His aye-rolling orbit / At no goal will arrive." The change to "orb" was marked in Emerson's primary working copy of *Poems* 1847 and is made in RE and W.
8. RE and W, "Lurks the joy that is sweetest / In stings of remorse."
9. See n. 9, p. 89.
1. Or cumin, an aromatic Mediterranean herb used in cooking. *Rue*: an aromatic, bitter herb once used medicinally. *Myrrh*: a fragrant, bitter resin from trees in Arabia, India, and East Africa used to make incense and perfume; also called Balm of Gilead. The phrase calls to mind the biblical gold, frankincense, and myrrh brought to the infant Jesus by the wise men (Matthew 2.11).
2. See the essay "History," p. 105, "The Sphinx must solve her own riddle."

Alway it asketh, asketh;   115
    And each answer is a lie.
So take thy quest through nature,
    It through thousand natures ply;
Ask on, thou clothed eternity;[3]
    Time is the false reply.'   120

Uprose the merry Sphinx,
    And crouched no more in stone;
She melted into purple cloud,
    She silvered in the moon;
She spired into a yellow flame;   125
    She flowered in blossoms red;
She flowed into a foaming wave;
    She stood Monadnoc's[4] head.

Thorough a thousand voices
    Spoke the universal dame: 130
'Who telleth one of my meanings,
    Is master of all I am.'

Each and All[1]

Little thinks, in the field, you red-cloaked clown[2]
Of thee from the hill-top looking down;
The heifer that lows in the upland farm,
Far-heard, lows not thine ear to charm;
The sexton, tolling his bell at noon,   5
Deems not that great Napoleon[3]
Stops his horse, and lists with delight,
Whilst his files sweep round yon Alpine[4] height;
Nor knowest thou what argument
Thy life to thy neighbor's creed has lent.   10
All are needed by each one;
Nothing is fair or good alone.
I thought the sparrow's note from heaven,
Singing at dawn on the alder bough;
I brought him home, in his nest, at even;[5]   15
He sings the song, but it cheers[6] not now,
For I did not bring home the river and sky;—
He sang to my ear,—they sang to my eye,

---

3. An allusion to *Sartor Resartus*, by Thomas Carlyle (see n. 6, p. 28).
4. Or Mount Monadnock, a peak in southwest New Hampshire. "Monadnock" has come to refer more generally to a mountain or rocky mass that, having resisted erosion, rises from an otherwise level area. See
also the long poem of this title in *Poems*.
1. Probably not completed before spring 1837; published in the *Western Messenger* 6 (February 1839) as
"Each in All."
2. Rustic.
3. See n. 8, p. 17.
4. Pertaining to the Alps, a large mountain system in south-central Europe.
5. Evening.
6. First edition to *SP*, "pleases."

The delicate shells lay on the shore;
The bubbles of the latest wave   20
Fresh pearls to their enamel gave;
And the bellowing of the savage sea
Greeted their safe escape to me.
I wiped away the weeds and foam,
I fetched my sea-born treasures home;   25
But the poor, unsightly, noisome things
Had left their beauty on the shore,
With the sun, and the sand, and the wild uproar.
The lover watched his graceful maid,
As 'mid the virgin train she strayed,   30
Nor knew her beauty's best attire
Was woven still by the snow-white choir.
At last she came to his hermitage,
Like the bird from the woodlands to the cage;—
The gay enchantment was undone,   35
A gentle wife, but fairy none.
Then I said, 'I covet truth;
Beauty is unripe childhood's cheat;
I leave it behind with the games of youth.'—
As I spoke, beneath my feet   40
The ground-pine curled its pretty wreath,
Running over the club-moss burrs;
I inhaled the violet's breath;
Around me stood the oaks and firs;
Pine-cones and acorns lay on the ground;   45
Over me soared the eternal sky,
Full of light and of deity;
Again I saw, again I heard,
The rolling river, the morning bird;—
Beauty through my senses stole;   50
I yielded myself to the perfect whole.

The Problem[1]

I like a church, I like a cowl;
I love a prophet of the soul;
And on my heart monastic aisles
Fall like sweet strains, or pensive smiles;
Yet not for all his faith can see   5
Would I that cowled churchman be.

Why should the vest on him allure,
Which I could not on me endure?

Not from a vain or shallow thought
His awful Jove young Phidias[2] brought;   10

---

1. Emerson dates a draft of this poem November 10, 1839. It was first published in *The Dial* 1 (July 1840).
2. See n. 9, p. 134. Jove, see n. 9, p. 89.

Never from lips of cunning fell
The thrilling Delphic oracle;[3]
Out from the heart of nature rolled
The burdens of the Bible old;
The litanies of nations came,   15
Like the volcano's tongue of flame,[4]
Up from the burning core below,—
The canticles[5] of love and woe;
The hand that rounded Peter's dome,[6]
And groined the aisles of Christian Rome,   20
Wrought in a sad sincerity;
Himself from God he could not free;
He builded better than he knew;—
The conscious stone to beauty grew.

Know'st thou what wove yon woodbird's nest   25
Of leaves, and feathers from her breast?
Or how the fish outbuilt her shell,
Painting with morn each annual cell?
Or how the sacred pine-tree adds
To her old leaves new myriads?   30
Such and so grew these holy piles,
Whilst love and terror laid the tiles.
Earth proudly wears the Parthenon,[7]
As the best gem upon her zone;[8]
And Morning opes with haste her lids,   35
To gaze upon the Pyramids;[9]
O'er England's abbeys bends the sky,
As on its friends, with kindred eye;
For, out of Thought's interior sphere,
These wonders rose to upper air;   40
And Nature gladly gave them place,
Adopted them into her race,
And granted them an equal date
With Andes and with Ararat.[1]

These temples grew as grows the grass;   45
Art might obey, but not surpass.
The passive Master lent his hand
To the vast soul that o'er him planned;[2]
And the same power that reared the shrine

---

3. See n. 7, p. 251.
4. An allusion, which continues through the rest of the poem, to the day of Pentecost (or Hebrew *Shavuot*, a feast to commemorate the revelation of the Law to Moses on Mount Sinai), when Jesus' apostles are said to have been visited by the Holy Spirit of God, in the form of a tongue-shaped fire, and received the gift of having their words be heard by each listener in his or her own language.
5. Songs or chants, especially nonmetrical hymns with lyrics derived from the Bible; also a name for the biblical book the Song of Solomon (Song of Songs).
6. Michelangelo; see n. 6, p. 42.
7. See n. 4, p. 110. The sculptures—and especially the statue of the goddess—are ascribed to Phidias.
8. Girdle (archaic).
9. The three Great Pyramids at Giza, Egypt.
1. A pair of mountains in eastern Turkey, the supposed site of the landing of Noah's Ark (Genesis 8.4). The Andes Mountains are in western South America.
2. Lines 47 and 48 are carved on Emerson's tombstone in Sleepy Hollow Cemetery, Concord, Massachusetts.

Bestrode the tribes that knelt within.   50
Ever the fiery Pentecost
Girds with one flame the countless host,
Trances the heart through chanting choirs,
And through the priest the mind inspires.
The word unto the prophet spoken   55
Was writ on tables yet unbroken;[3]
The word by seers or sibyls[4] told,
In groves of oak, or fanes[5] of gold,
Still floats upon the morning wind,
Still whispers to the willing mind.   60
One accent of the Holy Ghost
The heedless world hath never lost.
I know what say the fathers wise,—
The Book itself before me lies,
Old *Chrysostom*, best Augustine,[6]   65
And he who blent both in his line,
The younger *Golden Lips* or mines,
Taylor,[7] the Shakspeare of divines.
His words are music in my ear,
I see his cowled portrait dear;   70
And yet, for all his faith could see,
I would not the good bishop be.

The Visit[1]

Askest, 'How long thou shalt stay'?
Devastator of the day!
Know, each substance, and relation,
Thorough nature's operation,
Hath its unit, bound, and metre;[2]   5
And every new compound
Is some product and repeater,—
Product of the earlier[3] found.
But the unit of the visit,
The encounter of the wise,—   10
Say, what other metre is it
Than the meeting of the eyes?
Nature poureth into nature

---

3. Moses is said to have received the Ten Commandments from God on stone tablets, then to have broken the tablets in anger when he found the Israelites worshiping the idol of the golden calf (Exodus 32.15–19).
4. In Greek mythology, female prophets; especially known as interpreters of the oracles of Apollo.
5. Churches or temples.
6. See n. 3, p. 174. St. John Chrysostom (ca. 345–407), Antioch-born Greek archbishop of Constantinople (398), who earned the name Chrysostom, "golden-mouthed," by eloquently criticizing the wealthy and powerful.
7. Jeremy Taylor (1613–1667), English cleric and writer noted for his vivid and cogent style.
1. Probably begun shortly after a visit from Emerson's friend Caroline Sturgis (see Richardson, p. 771) from August 28 to September 3, 1843, then revised in February 1844. It was first published in *The Dial* 4 (April 1844).
2. See n. 4, p. 271.
3. First edition, "early"; changed from the fourth edition (1850) forward.

Through the channels of that feature
Riding on the ray of sight,   15
Fleeter far than whirlwinds go,[4]
Or for service, or delight,
Hearts to hearts their meaning show,
Sum their long experience,
And import intelligence.   20
Single look has drained the breast;
Single moment years confessed.
The duration of a glance
Is the term of convenance,[5]
And, though thy rede[6] be church or state,   25
Frugal multiples[7] of that.
Speeding Saturn cannot halt;
Linger,—thou shalt rue the fault;
If Love his moment overstay,
Hatred's swift repulsions play.   30

Uriel[1]

It fell in the ancient periods
   Which the brooding soul surveys,
Or ever the wild Time coined[2] itself
   Into calendar months and days.

This was the lapse of Uriel,   5
Which in Paradise befell.
Once, among the Pleiads[3] walking,
Seyd[4] overheard the young gods talking;
And the treason, too long pent,
To his ears was evident.   10
The young deities discussed
Laws of form, and metre just,
Orb, quintessence, and sunbeams,
What subsisteth, and what seems.
One, with low tones that decide,   15
And doubt and reverend use defied,
With a look that solved the sphere,

---

4. First edition to *SP*, "More fleet than waves or whirlwinds go."
5. Period of convening, or being together (archaic).
6. Taking advice from or acting according to (archaic).
7. In *SP*, "multiplies"; corrected in *RE* and *W* to "multiples" to correspond with earlier editions.
1. Written in the mid-1840s and first published in *Poems*. Uriel, or fire of God, is Milton's Archangel of the Sun in *Paradise Lost*. Edward Emerson and others have associated Uriel with Emerson himself, especially in regard to the Divinity School "Address" (see W 9.408ff.). Textual echoes also relate the figure to Emerson's son Waldo. See "Threnody" (p. 455).
2. Ordered, systematized, or stamped.
3. Or Pleiades, the seven daughters of Atlas, changed by Jupiter into stars; the name was given to a constellation in Taurus.
4. See n. 2, p. 250. First edition to *SP*, "Said"; *SP*, "Sayd." The change to "Seyd" is marked in Emerson's primary working copy of *Poems* 1847 and is made in *RE* and *W*; this spelling corresponds with that in the epigraph to the essay "Beauty" (*The Conduct of Life*, W 6). In view of Emerson's strong identification with the Persian poet, it might be best to take the name as Emerson's own nom de guerre.

And stirred the devils everywhere,
Gave his sentiment divine
Against the being of a line.   20
'Line in nature is not found;
Unit and universe are round;
In vain produced, all rays return;
Evil will bless, and ice will burn.'
As Uriel spoke with piercing eye,   25
A shudder ran around the sky;
The stern old war-gods[5] shook their heads;
The seraphs frowned from myrtle-beds;
Seemed to the holy festival
The rash word boded ill to all;   30
The balance-beam of Fate was bent;
The bounds of good and ill were rent;
Strong Hades[6] could not keep his own,
But all slid to confusion.

A sad self-knowledge, withering, fell   35
On the beauty of Uriel;
In heaven once eminent, the god
Withdrew, that hour, into his cloud;
Whether doomed to long gyration
In the sea of generation,   40
Or by knowledge grown too bright
To hit the nerve of feebler sight.[7]
Straightway, a forgetting wind
Stole over the celestial kind,
And their lips the secret kept,   45
If in ashes the fire-seed[8] slept.
But now and then, truth-speaking things
Shamed the angels' veiling wings;
And, shrilling from the solar course,
Or from fruit of chemic force,   50
Procession of a soul in matter,
Or the speeding change of water,
Or out of the good of evil born,
Came Uriel's voice of cherub scorn,
And a blush tinged the upper sky,   55
And the gods shook, they knew not why.

---

5. Edward Emerson identifies the *war-gods* with those who criticized the Divinity School "Address," among
   them Harvard professor Andrews Norton (see p. 597).
6. See n. 5, p. 122.
7. For this stanza, see also "Threnody" (p. 458), lines 120ff.
8. Spark.

Hamatreya[1]

Bulkeley, Hunt, Willard, Hosmer, Meriam, Flint,[2]
Possessed the land which rendered to their toil
Hay, corn, roots, hemp, flax, apples, wool, and wood.[3]
Each of these landlords walked amidst his farm,
Saying, "'T is mine, my children's, and my name's: 5
How sweet the west-wind sounds in my own trees!
How graceful climb those shadows on my hill!
I fancy these pure waters and the flags[4]
Know me, as does my dog: we sympathize;
And, I affirm, my actions smack of the soil.'   10

Where are these men? Asleep beneath their grounds;
And strangers, fond as they, their furrows plough.
Earth laughs in flowers, to see her boastful boys
Earth-proud, proud of the earth which is not theirs;
Who steer the plough, but cannot steer their feet   15
Clear of the grave.
They added ridge to valley, brook to pond,
And sighed for all that bounded their domain;
'This suits me for a pasture; that's my park;
We must have clay, lime, gravel, granite-ledge,   20
And misty lowland, where to go for peat.
The land is well,—lies fairly to the south.
'T is good, when you have crossed the sea and back,
To find the sitfast acres where you left them.'
Ah! the hot owner sees not Death, who adds   25
Him to his land, a lump of mould the more.
Hear what the Earth says:—

Earth-Song

'Mine and yours;
Mine, not yours.[5]

1. Journal sources for the poem date from autumn 1845. It was first published in *Poems*. The title is a variation of "Maitreya," a character in *The Vishnu Purana* (see n. 3, p. 296), which provides source material for the poem, possibly combined with "hamadryad," a wood nymph in Greek and Roman myth.
2. These surnames refer to prominent early settlers of Concord, most of whom still had survivors with the same names in Emerson's day. The first edition text and that of subsequent editions up to SP read, "Minott, Lee, Willard, Hosmer, Meriam, Flint." The line as we print it, however, bears significant resonance and cultural currency. Emerson marked the change to "Bulkeley, Hunt" from "Minott, Lee" in his primary working copy of *Poems* 1847, making the first name on the list one from his own family. His most famous Bulkeley ancestor was Peter Bulkeley (1583–1659), one of the founding citizens of Concord of whom Emerson speaks in his "Historical Discourse" on Concord (1835). Emerson's son Edward added lines 1–5 and 11–14 of "Hamatreya" (with unintentional irony, it is assumed) as an epigraph to that address as it is printed in W 11, *Miscellanies*. A catalog of the town's founders from that address begins, "Blood, Flint, Willard, Meriam, Wood, Hosmer" (W 11.30). Robert Bulkeley Emerson (1807–1859), called Bulkeley, was Emerson's mentally disabled brother. It seems that only after Bulkeley's death did Emerson feel free to use the name. The line as it is printed here has become, via its appearance in RE and W, a favorite of many of Emerson's readers through the years, among them the poets Robert Frost and Karl Patten.
3. Cf. Shakespeare, *The Tempest* 4.1.61, where Iris speaks to Ceres "of wheat, rye, barley, vetches, oats, and pease."
4. Any of various plants having long, bladelike leaves, such as an iris or cattail; a reed.
5. See "The Poet," p. 196, "In our way of talking, we say, 'That is yours, this is mine;' but the poet knows well that it is not his," and "Threnody" (p. 455).

Earth endures; 30
Stars abide —
Shine down in the old sea;
Old are the shores;
But where are old men?
I who have seen much, 35
Such have I never seen.

'The lawyer's deed
Ran sure,
In tail,[6]
To them, and to their heirs 40
Who shall succeed,[7]
Without fail,
Forevermore.

'Here is the land,
Shaggy with wood, 45
With its old valley,
Mound, and flood.
But the heritors?
Fled like the flood's foam, —
The lawyer, and the laws. 50
And the kingdom,
Clean swept herefrom.

'They called me theirs,
Who so controlled me;
Yet every one 55
Wished to stay, and is gone.
How am I theirs,
If they cannot hold me,
But I hold them?'

When I heard the Earth-song, 60
I was no longer brave;
My avarice cooled
Like lust in the chill of the grave.

The Rhodora:

On Being Asked, Whence Is the Flower?[1]

In May, when sea-winds pierced our solitudes,
I found the fresh Rhodora in the woods,

---

6. A legal term for limiting the inheritance of property to a specified succession of heirs.
7. Follow, inherit, flourish.
1. Written in May 1834 and first published in the *Western Messenger* 7 (July 1839) as "The Rhodora. Lines on Being Asked, Whence Is the Flower?" The rhodora is a type of rhododendron shrub with showy, rose-purple flowers that bloom before the leaves appear.

Spreading its leafless blooms in a damp nook,[2]
To please the desert and the sluggish brook.
The purple petals, fallen in the pool,   5
Made the black water with their beauty gay;
Here might the red-bird come his plumes to cool,
And court the flower that cheapens his array.
Rhodora! if the sages ask thee why
This charm is wasted on the earth and sky,[3]   10
Tell them, dear, that if eyes were made for seeing,
Then Beauty is its own excuse for being:
Why thou wert there, O rival of the rose!
I never thought to ask, I never knew:
But, in my simple ignorance, suppose   15
The selfsame Power that brought me there brought you.

The Humble-Bee[1]

Burly, dozing humble-bee,
Where thou art is clime[2] for me.
Let them sail for Porto Rique,[3]
Far-off heats through seas to seek;
I will follow thee alone,   5
Thou animated torrid-zone!
Zigzag steerer, desert cheerer,[4]
Let me chase thy waving lines:
Keep me nearer, me thy hearer,
Singing over shrubs and vines.   10

Insect lover of the sun,
Joy of thy dominion!
Sailor of the atmosphere;
Swimmer through the waves of air;
Voyager of light and noon;   15

2. See also "Waldeinsamkeit" (p. 477) lines 33ff.
3. Cf. Thomas Gray's "Elegy Written in a Country Churchyard," lines 55–56:

> Full many a flower is born to blush unseen,
> And waste its sweetness on the desert air.

1. Written in May 1837, after Emerson had followed a bee in the woods and written in his journal, "The humble-bee & the pine warbler seem to me the proper objects of attention in these disastrous times. I . . . feel a new joy in nature" (*JMN* 5.327). First published in the *Western Messenger* 6 (February 1839) as "To the Humble-Bee." Humble-bee, bumblebee; the variant Emerson chose reinforces his point about the value of "humble" things. In *SP* only, "The Humblebee"; also in line 1. Corrected in *RE* and *W*.
2. Climate.
3. Or Puerto Rico, in Emerson's time a favorite destination for people seeking to restore their health. Edward, Emerson's younger brother, who had earlier undergone mental collapses, journeyed first to St. Croix in November 1830 when he was ill with tuberculosis and then to Puerto Rico in 1832; he died there in 1834 at age twenty-nine. See "The Last Farewell," a poem written by Edward as he was leaving for Puerto Rico, and Emerson's elegy for Edward, "In Memoriam: E.B.E.," both printed in *Poems*. His brother Charles, also ill with tuberculosis, joined Edward there in 1831 and died in New York in May 1836.
4. A crucial function of the Emersonian poet; see, e.g., "The Sphinx" (p. 429) and the "The Poet" (p. 183). The term thus underscores the following pun on "lines" of flight and lines of poetry.

Epicurean[5] of June;
Wait, I prithee, till I come
Within earshot of thy hum, —
All without is martyrdom.

When the south wind, in May days,   20
With a net of shining haze
Silvers the horizon wall,
And, with softness touching all,
Tints the human countenance
With a color of romance,   25
And, infusing subtle heats,
Turns the sod to violets,
Thou, in sunny solitudes,
Rover of the underwoods,
The green silence dost displace   30
With thy mellow, breezy bass.

Hot midsummer's petted crone,
Sweet to me thy drowsy tone
Tells of countless sunny hours,
Long days, and solid banks of flowers;   35
Of gulfs of sweetness without bound
In Indian wildernesses found;
Of Syrian peace, immortal leisure,
Firmest cheer, and bird-like pleasure.

Aught unsavory or unclean   40
Hath my insect never seen;
But violets and bilberry bells,
Maple-sap, and daffodils,
Grass with green flag half-mast high,
Succory to match the sky,   45
Columbine with horn of honey,
Scented fern, and agrimony,
Clover, catchfly, adder's-tongue,
And brier-roses,[6] dwelt among;
All beside was unknown waste,   50
All was picture as he passed.
Wiser far than human seer,
Yellow-breeched philosopher!
Seeing only what is fair,
Sipping only what is sweet,   55
Thou dost mock at fate and care,
Leave the chaff, and take the wheat.[7]
When the fierce northwestern blast
Cools sea and land so far and fast,

---

5. Addicted to pleasure (common parlance). See also n. 9, p. 258.
6. Various wild flowering plants. *Bilberry bells:* bell-shaped blueberry flowers. *Succory:* chickory. *Horn of honey:* the long, bell-shaped columbine flower. *Agrimony:* a wildflower in the rose family. *Adder's-tongue:* dogtooth violet.
7. Cf. Matthew 3.12 and Luke 3.17.

Thou already slumberest deep;   60
Woe and want thou canst outsleep;
Want and woe, which torture us,
Thy sleep makes ridiculous.

The Snow-Storm[1]

Announced by all the trumpets of the sky,
Arrives the snow, and, driving o'er the fields,
Seems nowhere to alight: the whited air
Hides hills and woods, the river, and the heaven,
And veils the farm-house at the garden's end.   5
The sled and traveller stopped, the courier's feet
Delayed, all friends shut out, the housemates sit
Around the radiant fireplace, enclosed
In a tumultuous privacy of storm.

    Come see the north-wind's masonry.   10
Out of an unseen quarry evermore
Furnished with tile, the fierce artificer[2]
Curves his white bastions with projected roof
Round every windward stake, or tree, or door.
Speeding, the myriad-handed, his wild work   15
So fanciful, so savage, naught cares he
For number or proportion. Mockingly,
On coop or kennel he hangs Parian[3] wreaths;
A swan-like form invests the hidden thorn;
Fills up the farmer's lane from wall to wall,   20
Maugre[4] the farmer's sighs; and, at the gate,
A tapering turret overtops the work.
And when his hours are numbered, and the world
Is all his own, retiring, as he were not,
Leaves, when the sun appears, astonished Art   25
To mimic in slow structures, stone by stone,
Built in an age, the mad wind's night-work,
The frolic architecture[5] of the snow.

1. Probably written shortly after a heavy snowstorm in Concord on December 29, 1834 (see *JMN* 4.381ff.).
   First published in *The Dial* (January 1841). John Greenleaf Whittier (1807–1892) used lines 1–9 as an
   epigraph to his widely read poem "Snowbound" (1866), one of the many "snow" poems written by North
   American poets (e.g., Emily Dickinson's "It sifts from Leaden Sieves—" and Wallace Stevens's "The
   Snow Man").
2. An echo of Milton's description of Satan as the "Artificer of fraud," *Paradise Lost* 4.121.
3. A white, semitranslucent marble quarried in the Aegean island of Paros; highly valued for sculpting in
   ancient times.
4. See n. 9, p. 29.
5. See "Sea-Shore" (p. 475).

Fable[1]

The mountain and the squirrel
Had a quarrel;
And the former called the latter 'Little Prig';
Bun[2] replied,
'You are doubtless very big;   5
But all sorts of things and weather
Must be taken in together,
To make up a year
And a sphere.
And I think it no disgrace   10
To occupy my place.
If I'm not so large as you,
You are not so small as I,
And not half so spry.
I'll not deny you make   15
A very pretty squirrel track;
Talents differ; all is well and wisely put;
If I cannot carry forests on my back,
Neither can you crack a nut.'

Ode,

Inscribed to W. H. Channing[1]

Though loath to grieve
The evil time's sole patriot,
I cannot leave
My honied thought
For the priest's cant,   5
Or statesman's rant.

If I refuse
My study for their politique,
Which at the best is trick,
The angry Muse   10
Puts confusion in my brain.

But who is he that prates
Of the culture of mankind,

1. Edward Emerson dates the poem to 1845. It was first published in *The Diadem* (1846). In *Poems*, "Fable,"
   about the comeuppance of a mountain, follows the long poem about a mountain, "Monadnoc."
2. In his later journals, Emerson sometimes adopts the name "Buna" to write little fables about himself.
1. Probably completed at Monadnoc, June 1846. First published in *Poems*. Channing, see n. 1, p. 372. Despite his seeming antipathy to direct action in the poem, Emerson had already spoken out against slavery and became increasingly active in the abolition movement. In August 1845, he spoke along with
   Channing in Waltham, Massachusetts, at a meeting of abolitionists. Channing, unlike Emerson, already
   advocated disunion with the South. The poem was occasioned by the funeral in Boston on May 19, 1846,
   of Salem abolitionist minister Charles Turner Torrey, who had died in the Maryland State Prison while
   incarcerated for helping slaves to escape. Emerson attended the funeral, at which Channing spoke. The
   poem does not appear in *SP*.

Of better arts and life?
Go, blindworm,[2] go,   15
Behold the famous States
Harrying Mexico[3]
With rifle and with knife!

Or who, with accent bolder,
Dare praise the freedom-loving mountaineer?   20
I found by thee, O rushing Contoocook!
And in thy valleys, Agiochook![4]
The jackals of the negro-holder.

The God who made New Hampshire
Taunted the lofty land   25
With little men;[5] —
Small bat and wren
House in the oak: —
If earth-fire[6] cleave
The upheaved land, and bury the folk,   30
The southern crocodile would grieve.[7]
Virtue palters; Right is hence;
Freedom praised, but hid;
Funeral eloquence
Rattles the coffin-lid.   35

What boots[8] thy zeal,
O glowing friend,
That would indignant rend
The northland from the south?
Wherefore? to what good end?   40
Boston Bay and Bunker Hill[9]
Would serve things still; —
Things are of the snake.

The horseman serves the horse,
The neatherd serves the neat,[1]   45
The merchant serves the purse,
The eater serves his meat;
'Tis the day of the chattel,
Web to weave, and corn to grind;

2. A small harmless lizard from Europe, western Asia, and northern Africa that feeds chiefly on slugs.
3. Emerson criticizes United States aggression in the Mexican War. Texas formally entered the union on
   December 29, 1845, and the United States declared war on Mexico on May 11, 1846, shortly before the
   Torrey funeral. The U.S. involvement in Mexico, along with slavery, led Thoreau (see n. 1, p. 93) to
   spend his famed night in the Concord jail, and to write "Resistance to Civil Government."
4. Or Agiocochook, Algonquian name for Mount Washington. Contoocook is a river in New Hampshire.
5. Emerson criticizes New Hampshire for its Democratic (proslavery) vote in the 1844 presidential election. He may also have had in mind the accommodationist gestures of Massachusetts Senator Daniel
   Webster (a New Hampshire native; see n. 6, p. 251), which were to culminate in Webster's support of the
   Fugitive Slave Law of 1850. See journal selections, pp. 518–22.
6. A volcanic eruption.
7. I.e., the South would shed "crocodile tears" of feigned grief.
8. What avails.
9. Famous for Revolutionary War action, these places are used by Emerson as metonymies for commercial
   Boston, with its strong ties to the South.
1. Cowherd and cow, respectively (archaic).

Things are in the saddle,   50
And ride mankind.[2]

There are two laws discrete,
Not reconciled, —
Law for man, and law for thing;
The last builds town and fleet,   55
But it runs wild,
And doth the man unking.

'Tis fit the forest fall,
The steep be graded,
The mountain tunnelled,   60
The sand shaded,
The orchard planted,
The glebe[3] tilled,
The prairie granted,
The steamer built.   65

Let man serve law for man;
Live for friendship, live for love,
For truth's and harmony's behoof;
The state may follow how it can,
As Olympus follows Jove.[4]   70

    Yet do not I implore[5]
The wrinkled shopman to my sounding woods,
Nor bid the unwilling senator
Ask votes of thrushes in the solitudes.
Every one to his chosen work; —   75
Foolish hands may mix and mar;
Wise and sure the issues are.
Round they roll till dark is light,
Sex to sex, and even to odd; —
The over-god   80
Who marries Right to Might,
Who peoples, unpeoples, —
He who exterminates
Races by stronger races,
Black by white faces, —   85
Knows to bring honey
Out of the lion;[6]
Grafts gentlest scion
On pirate and Turk.
The Cossack eats Poland,[7]   90

---

2. Cf. the "Where I Lived, and What I Lived For" chapter in Thoreau's *Walden*: "We do not ride on the railroad; it rides upon us" (1854).
3. Soil or earth (archaic).
4. See n. 9, p. 89.
5. First edition, "invite," but changed beginning with the fourth edition (1850).
6. See Judges 14.8ff., in which Samson retrieves honey from the carcass of a lion he has slain.
7. Russia took most of Poland in 1792 and 1798. The Poles rebelled in the 1830 November Insurrection, leading to their defeat and consequent repression.

Like stolen fruit;
Her last noble is ruined,
Her last poet mute:
Straight, into double band
The victors divide; 95
Half for freedom strike and stand; —
The astonished Muse finds thousands at her side.

Give All to Love[1]

Give all to love;
Obey thy heart;
Friends, kindred, days,
Estate, good-fame,
Plans, credit, and the Muse, — 5
Nothing refuse.

'T is a brave master;
Let it have scope:
Follow it utterly,
Hope beyond hope: 10
High and more high
It dives into noon,
With wing unspent,
Untold intent;
But it is a god, 15
Knows its own path,
And the outlets of the sky.

It was not for the mean;[2]
It requireth courage stout,
Souls above doubt, 20
Valor unbending;
Such 't will reward,[3] —
They shall return
More than they were,
And ever ascending. 25

Leave all for love;
Yet, hear me, yet,
One word more thy heart behoved,[4]
One pulse more of firm endeavor, —
Keep thee to-day, 30
To-morrow, forever,
Free as an Arab
Of thy beloved.

1. Written in 1846 and first published in *Poems.*
2. *RE* and *W,* "It was never for the mean."
3. *RE* and *W,* "Such it will reward."
4. Needed.

Cling with life to the maid;
But when the surprise,   35
First vague shadow of surmise
Flits across her bosom young
Of a joy apart from thee,
Free be she, fancy-free;
Nor thou detain her vesture's hem,   40
Nor the palest rose she flung
From her summer diadem.

Though thou loved her as thyself,
As a self of purer clay,
Though her parting dims the day,   45
Stealing grace from all alive;
Heartily know,
When half-gods go,
The gods arrive.

Thine Eyes Still Shined[1]

Thine eyes still shined for me, though far
    I lonely roved the land or sea:
As I behold yon evening star,
    Which yet beholds not me.

This morn I climbed the misty hill,   5
    And roamed the pastures through;
How danced thy form before my path
    Amidst the deep-eyed dew!

When the redbird spread his sable wing,
    And showed his side of flame;   10
When the rosebud ripened to the rose,
    In both I read thy name.

Eros[1]

The sense of the world is short, —
Long and various the report, —
    To love and be beloved;
Men and gods have not outlearned it;
And, how oft soe'er they've turned it,   5
    'Tis not to be improved.[2]

1. Written during a separation from Ellen Tucker Emerson, Emerson's first wife, either during their courtship (1828 or 1829), or after their marriage (April to mid-May 1830). First published in *Poems*. The poem does not appear in *SP*.
1. The composition date is undetermined. The poem was first published in *The Dial* 4 (January 1844). It does not appear in *SP*. Eros is the Greek god of love.
2. In 1863 edition, "'twill not be improved"; in 1865, "'t is not"; in *RE* and W, "Not to be improved."

The Apology[1]

Think me not unkind and rude
    That I walk alone in grove and glen;
I go to the god of the wood
    To fetch his word to men.

Tax not my sloth that I   5
    Fold my arms beside the brook;
Each cloud that floated in the sky
    Writes a letter in my book.

Chide me not, laborious band,
    For the idle flowers I brought;   10
Every aster in my hand
    Goes home loaded with a thought.

There was never mystery
    But 'tis figured in the flowers;
Was never secret history   15
    But birds tell it in the bowers.

One harvest from thy field
    Homeward brought the oxen strong;
A second crop thine acres yield,
    Which I gather in a song.[2]   20

Merlin

I[1]

Thy trivial harp will never please
Or fill my craving ear;
Its chords should ring as blows the breeze,
Free, peremptory, clear.
No jingling serenader's[2] art,   5
Nor tinkle of piano strings,
Can make the wild blood start
In its mystic springs.
The kingly bard
Must smite the chords rudely and hard,   10
As with hammer or with mace;

1. Written after 1841 and before March 12, 1844. First published as "The Poet's Apology," the *PN* title, in *The Gift: A Christmas, New Year, and Birthday Present* (1845). The poem does not appear in *SP*.
2. See "Two Rivers" (p. 476).
1. Completed in the summer of 1846 and first published in *Poems*. The title refers to the Welsh or English bard Myrrdhin (sixth century C.E.), to whom a group of verse has been attributed. This Bardic voice was thought to be unpolished, free, and forceful. Edward Emerson also associates the poem with the sorcerer Merlin of Arthurian legend. "Merlin II" was omitted in *SP*.
2. According to William Dean Howells, Emerson referred to Edgar Allan Poe (1809–1849) as "the jingle-man." Poe's poem "The Raven," published in 1845, achieved instant notoriety.

That they may render back
Artful thunder, which conveys
Secrets of the solar track,
Sparks of the supersolar blaze.[3]   15
Merlin's blows are strokes of fate,
Chiming with the forest tone
When boughs buffet boughs in the wood;
Chiming with the gasp and moan
Of the ice-imprisoned flood;   20
With the pulse of manly hearts;
With the voice of orators;
With the din of city arts;[4]
With the cannonade of wars;
With the marches of the brave;   25
And prayers of might from martyrs' cave.

Great is the art,
Great be the manners, of the bard.
He shall not his brain encumber
With the coil of rhythm and number;[5]   30
But, leaving rule and pale forethought,
He shall aye[6] climb
For his rhyme.
'Pass in, pass in,' the angels say,
'In to the upper doors,   35
Nor count compartments of the floors,
But mount to paradise
By the stairway of surprise.'[7]

Blameless master of the games,
King of sport that never shames,   40
He shall daily joy dispense
Hid in song's sweet influence.
Things[8] more cheerly live and go,
What time the subtle mind
Sings aloud the tune whereto   45
Their pulses beat,
And march their feet,
And their members are combined.

By Sybarites[9] beguiled,
He shall no task decline;   50
Merlin's mighty line[1]

---

3. Cf. "Threnody," p. 460.
4. An allusion to "Lines Composed a Few Miles above Tintern Abbey," by Wordsworth (see n. 5, p. 67), "'mid the din / of towns and cities" (lines 25–26).
5. Meter. *Coil*: a restraint.
6. Always.
7. An allusion to the biblical Jacob and his dream of angels ascending and descending a staircase from heaven. See also the essay "Experience": "Life is a series of surprises, and would not be worth taking or keeping, if it were not" (p. 206).
8. In *RE* and W, "Forms."
9. A native or inhabitant of Sybaris, an ancient Greek city in southern Italy. By association, a person devoted to pleasure and luxury.
1. Cf. "Marlowe's mighty line," in Ben Jonson's "To the Memory of My Beloved, Mr. William Shakespeare" (1623).

Extremes of nature reconciled,—
Bereaved a tyrant of his will,
And made the lion mild.[2]
Songs can the tempest still,[3]   55
Scattered on the stormy air,
Mould the year to fair increase,[4]
And bring in poetic peace.

He shall not seek to weave,
In weak, unhappy times,   60
Efficacious rhymes;
Wait his returning strength.
Bird, that from the nadir's floor
To the zenith's top can soar,
The soaring orbit of the muse exceeds that journey's length.   65
Nor profane affect to hit
Or compass[5] that, by meddling wit,
Which only the propitious mind
Publishes when 't is inclined.
There are open hours   70
When the God's will sallies free,
And the dull idiot might see
The flowing fortunes of a thousand years;—
Sudden, at unawares,
Self-moved, fly-to the doors,   75
Nor sword of angels could reveal
What they conceal.

Merlin

II

The rhyme of the poet
Modulates the king's affairs;
Balance-loving Nature   80
Made all things in pairs.
To every foot its antipode;[1]
Each color with its counter glowed;
To every tone beat answering tones,
Higher or graver;   85
Flavor gladly blends with flavor;
Leaf answers leaf upon the bough;
And match the paired cotyledons.
Hands to hands, and feet to feet,
In one body[2] grooms and brides;   90

2. An allusion to Isaiah 11, where the lion and wolf are made calm with the coming of the Messiah.
3. An allusion to the story of Jesus calming a storm, Matthew 8.23ff., Mark 4.37ff., and Luke 8.22ff.
4. Make it productive.
5. Achieve.
1. Opposing foot. For similar emphasis on duality, see the essay "Compensation" (p. 137).
2. First edition, "coeval"; changed beginning with the fourth edition (1850).

Eldest rite, two married sides
In every mortal meet.
Light's far furnace shines,
Smelting balls and bars,
Forging double stars,   95
Glittering twins and trines.[3]
The animals are sick with love,
Lovesick with rhyme;
Each with all propitious time
Into chorus wove.   100

Like the dancers' ordered band,
Thoughts come also hand in hand;
In equal couples mated,
Or else alternated;
Adding by their mutual gage,   105
One to other, health and age.
Solitary fancies go
Short-lived wandering to and fro,
Most like to bachelors,
Or an ungiven maid,   110
Not ancestors,
With no posterity to make the lie afraid,
Or keep truth undecayed.
Perfect-paired as eagle's wings,
Justice is the rhyme of things;   115
Trade and counting use
The self-same tuneful muse;
And Nemesis,[4]
Who with even matches odd,
Who athwart space redresses   120
The partial wrong,
Fills the just period,
And finishes the song.

Subtle rhymes, with ruin rife,
Murmur in the house of life,   125
Sung by the Sisters[5] as they spin;
In perfect time and measure they
Build and unbuild our echoing clay,
As the two twilights of the day
Fold us music-drunken in.[6]   130

---

3. Sets of three.
4. See n. 7, p. 143 and the poem "Nemesis" (p. 465).
5. Greek goddesses, the three Fates: Clotho spins the thread, Lachesis measures it, and Atropos cuts it.
6. See "Bacchus" (next page). *Two twilights:* dawn and dusk or, more broadly, the time before and after one's earthly existence.

Bacchus[1]

Bring me wine, but wine which never grew
In the belly of the grape,
Or grew on vine whose tap-roots, reaching through
Under the Andes to the Cape,[2]
Suffered[3] no savor of the earth to scape.   5

Let its grapes the morn salute
From a nocturnal root,
Which feels the acrid juice
Of Styx and Erebus;[4]
And turns the woe of Night,   10
By its own craft, to a more rich delight.

We buy ashes for bread;
We buy diluted wine;[5]
Give me of the true, —
Whose ample leaves and tendrils curled   15
Among the silver hills of heaven,
Draw everlasting dew;
Wine of wine,
Blood of the world,
Form of forms,[6] and mould of statures,   20
That I intoxicated,
And by the draught assimilated,
May float at pleasure through all natures;
The bird-language rightly spell,
And that which roses say so well.   25

Wine that is shed
Like the torrents of the sun
Up the horizon walls,
Or like the Atlantic streams, which run
When the South Sea[7] calls.   30

Water and bread,
Food which needs no transmuting,
Rainbow-flowering, wisdom-fruiting,[8]
Wine which is already man,
Food which teach and reason can.   35

---

1. Written in the summer of 1846, and first published in *Poems*. Bacchus, see n. 7, p. 50. Above "Bacchus" in one of Emerson's own copies of *Poems* is written, "The man who is his own master knocks in vain at the doors of poetry. Plato." See also "The Poet" (p. 192): "For poetry is not 'Devil's wine,' but God's wine."
2. I.e., Cape Horn, a steep rocky headland on Hornos Island, off the southern tip of South America. Andes, see n. 1, p. 434.
3. In *RE* and *W*, "suffer."
4. Geographic locations in Greek myth. Styx, see n. 5, p. 142. Erebus is a region of darkness below the earth.
5. Allusions to the Christian Eucharist (see n. 7, p. 23), which continue throughout the poem.
6. Allusion to Platonic forms; see n. 4, p. 15.
7. See n. 9, p. 129.
8. I.e., producer of rainbows and wisdom.

Wine which Music is,—
Music and wine are one,—
That I, drinking this,
Shall hear far Chaos talk with me;
Kings unborn shall walk with me;   40
And the poor grass shall plot and plan
What it will do when it is man.
Quickened so, will I unlock
Every crypt of every rock.

I thank the joyful juice   45
For all I know;—
Winds of remembering[9]
Of the ancient being blow,
And seeming-solid walls of use
Open and flow.   50

Pour, Bacchus! the remembering wine;
Retrieve the loss of me and mine!
Vine for vine be antidote,
And the grape requite the lote!
Haste to cure the old despair,—   55
Reason in Nature's lotus[1] drenched,
The memory of ages quenched;
Give them again to shine;
Let wine repair what this undid;
And where the infection slid,   60
A dazzling memory revive;
Refresh the faded tints,
Recut the aged prints,
And write my old adventures with the pen
Which on the first day drew,   65
Upon the tablets blue,
The dancing Pleiads[2] and eternal men.

9. Here and to the end of the poem, this wine is contrasted with Lethe (see n. 5, p. 122), which makes one forget. See also the opening of the essay "Experience" (p. 198).
1. The lotus plant exists in several traditions. In Greek myth, it is a plant of the buckthorn family; a wine made from its fruit was said to induce forgetfulness. Odysseus encountered lotos-eaters who led his men to eat the lotus fruit (in this case perhaps that of the opium poppy), after which they had to be taken back to their ship by force. The aquatic lotus plant is sacred to Hindus.
2. See n. 3, p. 436.

Blight[1]

Give me truths;
For I am weary of the surfaces,
And die of inanition. If I knew
Only the herbs and simples[2] of the wood,
Rue, cinquefoil, gill, vervain, and agrimony,   5
Blue-vetch, and trillium, hawkweed, sassafras,
Milkweeds, and murky brakes, quaint pipes, and sundew,[3]
And rare and virtuous roots, which in these woods
Draw untold juices from the common earth,
Untold, unknown, and I could surely spell   10
Their fragrance, and their chemistry apply
By sweet affinities to human flesh,
Driving the foe and stablishing the friend,—
O, that were much, and I could be a part
Of the round day, related to the sun   15
And planted world, and full executor
Of their imperfect functions.
But these young scholars, who invade our hills,
Bold as the engineer who fells the wood,
And travelling often in the cut he makes,   20
Love not the flower they pluck, and know it not,
And all their botany is Latin names.
The old men studied magic in the flowers,
And human fortunes in astronomy,
And an omnipotence in chemistry,   25
Preferring things to names, for these were men,
Were unitarians[4] of the united world,
And, wheresoever their clear eye-beams fell,
They caught the footsteps of the SAME. Our eyes
Are armed, but we are strangers to the stars,   30
And strangers to the mystic beast and bird,
And strangers to the plant and to the mine.
The injured elements say, 'Not in us;'
And night and day, ocean and continent,
Fire, plant, and mineral say, 'Not in us,'   35
And haughtily return us stare for stare.

1. W dates the composition as midsummer 1843. First printed in *The Dial* 4 (January 1844) as "The Times,—A Fragment." The poem does not appear in *SP*.
2. In the Elizabethan sense, a medicinal plant or the medicine obtained from it; e.g., Romeo, "I do remember an apothecary, / And hereabouts he dwells,—whom late I noted / In tatter'd weeds, with overwhelming brows, / Culling of simples" (*Romeo and Juliet* 5.1.39–42).
3. In this catalog, Emerson often uses folk names, perhaps in witty defiance of the "young scholars" in line 18, and includes plants otherwise thought undesirable. *Rue*: see n. 1, p. 431. *Cinquefoil*: a wildflower in the rose family. *Gill*: ground ivy. *Vervain*: or verbena, a wildflower known for its showy spikes of variously colored flowers, in ancient times thought to be a cure-all, so that the genus name is Latin for "sacred plant." *Agrimony*: see n. 6, p. 441. *Blue-vetch*: or cow vetch, a climbing wildflower in the pea family. *Trillium*: a wild plant in the lily family with variously colored, three-petaled flowers. *Hawkweed*: a showy wild plant with yellow or orange dandelion-like flower heads; New England farmers named it Devil's paintbrush and considered it a weed. *Sassafras*: a tree with aromatic bark, leaves, and branches; its root bark is used as a flavor for cooking, as in sassafras tea, and a source for oil. *Milkweeds*: or silkweeds, herbs, shrubs, or vines with milky juice, variously colored flowers grouped in umbels, and tufted seeds in pods. *Murky brakes*: a type of fern. *Quaint pipes*: perhaps pipe vine; maybe pipewort. *Sundew*: insectivorous herbs that grow in wet ground and have leaves covered with sticky hairs.
4. As opposed to conventional Unitarians (see n. 6, p. 23).

For we invade them impiously for gain;
We devastate them unreligiously,
And coldly ask their pottage, not their love.
Therefore they shove us from them, yield to us   40
Only what to our griping toil is due;
But the sweet affluence of love and song,
The rich results of the divine consents
Of man and earth, of world beloved and lover,
The nectar and ambrosia,[5] are withheld;   45
And in the midst of spoils and slaves, we thieves
And pirates of the universe, shut out
Daily to a more thin and outward rind,
Turn pale and starve. Therefore, to our sick eyes,
The stunted trees look sick, the summer short,   50
Clouds shade the sun, which will not tan our hay,
And nothing thrives to reach its natural term;
And life, shorn of its venerable length,
Even at its greatest space is a defeat,
And dies in anger that it was a dupe;   55
And, in its highest noon and wantonness,
Is early frugal, like a beggar's child;[6]
Even in the hot pursuit of the best aims
And prizes of ambition, checks its hand,
Like Alpine cataracts frozen as they leaped,   60
Chilled with a miserly comparison
Of the toy's purchase with the length of life.[7]

Threnody[1]

The south-wind brings
Life, sunshine, and desire,
And on every mount and meadow
Breathes aromatic fire;[2]
But over the dead he has no power,   5
The lost, the lost, he cannot restore;
And, looking over the hills, I mourn
The darling who shall not return.

5. Products of nature, but also known as foods of the gods; the terms also suggest the wine and bread of the Christian Eucharist (see n. 7, p. 23).
6. In the first edition through the fourth edition (1850), followed by the line, "With most unhandsome calculation taught."
7. I.e., wrongly sees each goal as a "toy," not worth the price of life.
1. Emerson's elegy for his young son, Waldo, who died suddenly of scarlet fever at age five (January 27, 1842), after a six-day illness. Deeply affected by his son's death, Emerson is said to have murmured over forty years later, near death, "Oh, that beautiful boy." Edward Emerson says that the first part of the poem (through line 175) was written shortly after Waldo's death, and the second part some time later, though the dating is not definitive. First published in *Poems. Threnody:* or dirge, was originally a choral ode, then evolved into a monody, or lament by one singer. Emerson's elegy contains many stock conventions of both general and child elegies, a popular genre of his time. It bears comparison with such other famous elegies as Whitman's for Lincoln, Ben Jonson's for his children, Henry King's "Exequy Upon His Wife," Milton's "Lycidas," and Tennyson's "In Memoriam" and "Thyrsis." The poem contains many textual echoes of the essays "The Poet" and "Experience," written around the same time and sharing its concerns. See especially the "deathless progeny" of "The Poet" (p. 190) and the beginning of "Experience" (p. 200), where Emerson refers to "the death of my son."
2. Flowers, blooming with the approach of spring.

I see my empty house,
I see my trees repair their boughs;   10
And he, the wondrous child,
Whose silver warble wild
Outvalued every pulsing sound
Within the air's cerulean[3] round,—
The hyacinthine boy,[4] for whom   15
Morn well might break and April bloom,—
The gracious boy, who did adorn
The world whereinto he was born,
And by his countenance repay
The favor of the loving Day,—   20
Has disappeared from the Day's eye;
Far and wide she cannot find him;
My hopes pursue, they cannot bind him.
Returned this day, the south-wind searches,
And finds young pines and budding birches;   25
But finds not the budding man;
Nature, who lost,[5] cannot remake him;
Fate let him fall, Fate can't retake him;
Nature, Fate, men, him seek in vain.

And whither now, my truant wise and sweet,   30
O, whither tend thy feet?
I had the right, few days ago,
Thy steps to watch, thy place to know;
How have I forfeited the right?
Hast thou forgot me in a new delight?   35
I hearken for thy household cheer,
O eloquent child!
Whose voice, an equal messenger,
Conveyed thy meaning mild.
What though the pains and joys   40
Whereof it spoke were toys
Fitting his age and ken,
Yet fairest dames and bearded men,[6]
Who heard the sweet request,
So gentle, wise, and grave,   45
Bended with joy to his behest,
And let the world's affairs go by,
Awhile to share his cordial game,
Or mend his wicker wagon-frame,
Still plotting how their hungry ear   50

3. Sky blue.
4. In Greek myth, Hyacinth was a youth beloved of Apollo (see n. 4, p. 73), who caused the hyacinth flower
   to spring from the boy's blood after he was slain by the jealous Zephyrus, god of the west wind. The hyacinth has thus come to symbolize vegetation that flourishes in spring but is killed by the harsher sun of
   summer. The hyacinthia festival mourned early death and celebrated subsequent regeneration. The epitaph is carved on Waldo's tombstone in Sleepy Hollow Cemetery, Concord; an image of hyacinth flowers appears at the top of the stone.
5. Printed as "Nature, who lost him," in the first edition and changed from the fourth (1850) edition forward.
6. Emerson's friends, among them Elizabeth Hoar, Caroline Sturgis (see n. 1, p. 435), Margaret Fuller (see
   n. 4, p. 38 and p. 372), and especially Thoreau (see n. 1, p. 93), had been very fond of and attentive to
   young Waldo.

That winsome voice again might hear;
For his lips could well pronounce
Words that were persuasions.

Gentlest guardians marked serene
His early hope, his liberal mien;[7]   55
Took counsel from his guiding eyes
To make this wisdom earthly wise.
Ah, vainly do these eyes recall
The school-march, each day's festival,
When every morn my bosom glowed   60
To watch the convoy on the road;
The babe in willow wagon closed,
With rolling eyes and face composed;
With children forward and behind,
Like Cupids studiously inclined;   65
And he the chieftain paced beside,
The centre of the troop allied,
With sunny face of sweet repose,
To guard the babe from fancied foes.
The little captain innocent   70
Took the eye with him as he went;
Each village senior paused to scan
And speak the lovely caravan.
From the window I look out
To mark thy beautiful parade,   75
Stately marching in cap and coat
To some tune by fairies played; —
A music heard by thee alone
To works as noble led thee on.

Now Love and Pride, alas! in vain,   80
Up and down their glances strain.
The painted sled stands where it stood;
The kennel by the corded wood;
His[8] gathered sticks to stanch the wall
Of the snow-tower, when snow should fall;   85
The ominous hole he dug in the sand,
And childhood's castles built or planned;
His daily haunts I well discern, —
The poultry-yard, the shed, the barn, —
And every inch of garden ground   90
Paced by the blessed feet around,
From the roadside to the brook
Whereinto he loved to look.
Step the meek birds where erst they ranged;
The wintry garden lies unchanged;   95
The brook into the stream runs on;
But the deep-eyed boy is gone.

7. Frank and open expression.
8. "The" in first edition through *SP*. The change is marked in Emerson's primary working copy of *Poems* 1847, and is made in *RE* and *W*.

On that shaded day,
Dark with more clouds than tempests are,
When thou didst yield thy innocent breath   100
In birdlike heavings unto death,
Night came, and Nature had not thee;
I said, 'We are mates in misery.'
The morrow dawned with needless glow;
Each snowbird chirped, each fowl must crow;   105
Each tramper started; but the feet
Of the most beautiful and sweet
Of human youth had left the hill
And garden,—they were bound and still.
There's not a sparrow or a wren,   110
There's not a blade of autumn grain,
Which the four seasons do not tend,
And tides of life and increase lend;
And every chick of every bird,
And weed and rock-moss is preferred.   115
O ostrich-like forgetfulness!
O loss of larger in the less!
Was there no star that could be sent,
No watcher in the firmament,
No angel from the countless host   120
That loiters round the crystal coast,
Could stoop to heal that only child,
Nature's sweet marvel undefiled,
And keep the blossom of the earth,
Which all her harvests were not worth?   125
Not mine,—I never called thee mine,
But Nature's heir,[9]—if I repine,
And seeing rashly torn and moved
Not what I made, but what I loved,
Grow early old with grief that thou   130
Must to the wastes of Nature go,—
'T is because a general hope
Was quenched, and all must doubt and grope.
For flattering planets seemed to say
This child should ills of ages stay,   135
By wondrous tongue, and guided pen,
Bring the flown Muses back to men.
Perchance not he but Nature ailed,
The world and not the infant failed.
It was not ripe yet to sustain   140
A genius of so fine a strain,
Who gazed upon the sun and moon
As if he came unto his own,
And, pregnant with his grander thought,
Brought the old order into doubt.   145
His beauty once their beauty tried;
They could not feed him, and he died,

9. In contrast to the rapacious farmers in the poem "Hamatreya" (p. 438).

And wandered backward as in scorn,
To wait an æon to be born.[1]
Ill day which made this beauty waste,   150
Plight broken, this high face defaced!
Some went and came about the dead;
And some in books of solace read;
Some to their friends the tidings say;
Some went to write, some went to pray;   155
One tarried here, there hurried one;
But their heart abode with none.
Covetous death bereaved us all,
To aggrandize one funeral.
The eager fate which carried thee   160
Took the largest part of me:
For this losing is true dying;
This is lordly man's down-lying,
This his slow but sure reclining,
Star by star his world resigning.   165

O child of paradise,
Boy who made dear his father's home,
In whose deep eyes
Men read the welfare of the times to come,
I am too much bereft.   170
The world dishonored thou hast left.
O truth's and nature's costly lie!
O trusted broken prophecy!
O richest fortune sourly crossed!
Born for the future, to the future lost!   175

The deep Heart answered, 'Weepest thou?
Worthier cause for passion wild
If I had not taken the child.
And deemest thou as those who pore,
With aged eyes, short way before,—   180
Think'st Beauty vanished from the coast
Of matter, and thy darling lost?
Taught he not thee—the man of eld,[2]
Whose eyes within his eyes beheld
Heaven's numerous hierarchy span   185
The mystic gulf from God to man?[3]
To be alone wilt thou begin
When worlds of lovers hem thee in?
To-morrow, when the masks shall fall
That dizen[4] Nature's carnival,   190
The pure shall see by their own will,
Which overflowing Love shall fill,
'Tis not within the force of fate

1. Lines 127–49 echo the description of Uriel in the poem of that title (p. 436).
2. Old.
3. These lines allude to Jacob's Ladder (see n. 7, p. 449).
4. Or bedizen, to dress up in fine clothes and ornaments.

The fate-conjoined to separate.
But thou, my votary,[5] weepest thou?   195
I gave thee sight—where is it now?
I taught thy heart beyond the reach
Of ritual, bible, or of speech;
Wrote in thy mind's transparent table,
As far as the incommunicable;   200
Taught thee each private sign to raise,
Lit by the supersolar blaze.[6]
Past utterance, and past belief,
And past the blasphemy of grief,
The mysteries of Nature's heart;   205
And though no Muse can these impart,
Throb thine with Nature's throbbing breast,
And all is clear from east to west.

'I came to thee as to a friend;
Dearest, to thee I did not send   210
Tutors, but a joyful eye,
Innocence that matched the sky,
Lovely locks, a form of wonder,
Laughter rich as woodland thunder,
That thou might'st entertain apart   215
The richest flowering of all art:
And, as the great all-loving Day
Through smallest chambers takes its way,
That thou might'st break thy daily bread
With prophet, savior, and head;   220
That thou might'st cherish for thine own
The riches of sweet Mary's Son,
Boy-Rabbi,[7] Israel's paragon.
And thoughtest thou such guest
Would in thy hall take up his rest?   225
Would rushing life forget her laws,
Fate's glowing revolution pause?
High omens ask diviner guess;
Not to be conned[8] to tediousness.
And know my higher gifts unbind   230
The zone that girds the incarnate mind.
When the scanty shores are full
With Thought's perilous, whirling pool;
When frail Nature can no more,
Then the Spirit strikes the hour: 235
My servant Death, with solving rite,
Pours finite into infinite.

---

5. A faithful follower; often, a person bound to service by religious vows.
6. See also "Merlin I," line 15 (p. 449).
7. The allusion is to the young Jesus lingering in the Temple in Jerusalem to study with the teachers and pose his own questions (Luke 2.41ff.).
8. Examined carefully.

'Wilt thou freeze love's tidal flow,
Whose streams through nature circling go?
Nail the wild star to its track   240
On the half-climbed zodiac?
Light is light which radiates,
Blood is blood which circulates,
Life is life which generates,
And many-seeming life is one,—   245
Wilt thou transfix and make it none?
Its onward force too starkly pent
In figure, bone, and lineament?
Wilt thou, uncalled, interrogate,
Talker! the unreplying Fate?   250
Nor see the genius of the whole
Ascendant in the private soul,
Beckon it when to go and come,
Self-announced its hour of doom?
Fair the soul's recess and shrine,   255
Magic-built to last a season;
Masterpiece of love benign
Fairer that expansive reason
Whose omen 't is, and sign.
Wilt thou not ope thy heart to know   260
What rainbows teach, and sunsets show?
Verdict which accumulates
From lengthening scroll of human fates,
Voice of earth to earth returned,
Prayers of saints that inly burned,—   265
Saying, *What is excellent,*
As God lives, is permanent;
Hearts are dust, hearts' loves remain,
Heart's love will meet thee again.
Revere the Maker; fetch thine eye   270
Up to his style, and manners of the sky.
Not of adamant and gold
Built he heaven stark and cold;
No, but a nest of bending reeds,
Flowering grass, and scented weeds;   275
Or like a traveller's fleeing tent,
Or bow above the tempest bent;
Built of tears and sacred flames,
And virtue reaching to its aims;
Built of furtherance and pursuing,   280
Not of spent deeds, but of doing.
Silent rushes the swift Lord
Through ruined systems still restored,
Broadsowing, bleak and void to bless,
Plants with worlds the wilderness;[9]   285
Waters with tears of ancient sorrow

9. See "May-Day" lines 245ff. (p. 463).

Apples of Eden ripe to-morrow.[1]
House and tenant go to ground,[2]
Lost in God, in Godhead found.'

Concord Hymn[1]

Sung at the Completion of the Battle Monument, July 4, 1837

By the rude bridge that arched the flood,
   Their flag to April's breeze unfurled,
Here once the embattled farmers stood,
   And fired the shot heard round the world.[2]

The foe long since in silence slept;   5
   Alike the conqueror silent sleeps;
And Time the ruined bridge has swept
   Down the dark stream which seaward creeps.

On this green bank, by this soft stream,
   We set to-day a votive[3] stone;   10
That memory may their deed redeem,
   When, like our sires, our sons are gone.

Spirit, that made those heroes dare
   To die, and[4] leave their children free,
Bid Time and Nature gently spare   15
   The shaft we raise to them and thee.

1. The forbidden fruit in the biblical Garden of Eden will tomorrow show itself to be part of an overall plan.
2. See "Hamatreya" (p. 438).
1. This hymn was sung at the dedication of the obelisk monument raised on what was originally Emerson family property (by then owned by the Ripleys) at the site of the battle of Concord (see n. 7, p. 91) and composed shortly before the date initially planned for the ceremony (April 19, 1837). The title in the first edition to *SP* was "Hymn: Sung at the Completion of the Concord Monument, April 19, 1836." In *SP*, the title was "Concord Fight, Hymn sung at the completion of the Concord Monument, April 19, 1836." For *RE*, the title was changed to "Concord Hymn: Sung at the Completion of the Battle Monument, April 19, 1836." We use the W title because of its combination of cultural currency and historical accuracy. The April 19, 1836, date appears in editions up through *SP* but is inaccurate, as Edward Emerson notes in W. The year of the celebration was actually 1837. Moreover, while it was scheduled to have been held on April 19, the date of the Battle of Concord, the ceremony was postponed and actually held on July 4, 1837. Emerson, who was not present at the event, apparently misremembered the date or thought the April 19 designation more appropriate, though, strictly speaking, inaccurate. Edward Emerson makes the change to July 4, 1837, in the subtitle and notes the earlier printings as mistakes. The battle that the hymn commemorates was fought on the Emerson family property, behind the Old Manse, where Emerson, and later Nathaniel Hawthorne, also were to live. Emerson's grandfather William Emerson fought in the battle, while his wife and their children (the youngest of which was Emerson's Aunt Mary Moody Emerson, then a baby) watched from a window in their home. The hymn was sung to the familiar tune of "Old Hundred." First published as a broadside in 1837.
2. These lines are the most famous in the poem and now appear both on the battle monument and on the Minuteman statue erected in 1875.
3. Given in fulfillment of a vow or symbolizing a wish, desire, or vow, as in votive candles.
4. "Or" in the first edition and in virtually all printings up to *SP* (an exception is the 1863 printing).

FROM MAY-DAY AND OTHER PIECES

From May-Day[1]

Daughter[2] of Heaven and Earth, coy Spring,
With sudden passion languishing,
Teaching barren moors to smile,
Painting pictures mile on mile,[3]
Holds a cup of cowslip[4]-wreaths,   5
Whence a smokeless incense breathes.

* * *

Wreaths for the May! for happy Spring
To-day shall all her dowry bring, —
The love of kind, the joy, the grace,
Hymen[5] of element and race,   240
Knowing well to celebrate
With song and hue and star and state,
With tender light and youthful cheer,
The spousals of the new-born year.[6]

Spring is strong and virtuous,   245
Broad-sowing,[7] cheerful, plenteous,
Quickening underneath the mould
Grains beyond the price of gold.
So deep and large her bounties are,
That one broad, long midsummer day   250
Shall to the planet overpay
The ravage of a year of war.[8]

* * *

1. Emerson, friends, and family tinkered with this poem endlessly, editing lines and trying to bring the arrangement of the stanzas into correspondence with the progress of spring. Substantially different texts exist in *May-Day*, *SP*, *RE*, and *W*. Although it has never seemed to cohere as a complete piece, we have chosen to print excerpts from this important title piece and threshold poem to the second of Emerson's two primary collections of verse. We print from the *SP* text and note important variations. The sections here begin and end the poem in each version. The middle part appears as stanzas 13 and 14 in the first edition, *RE*, and *W*; and as stanzas 11 and 12 in *SP*. The primary draft of the poem dates from late 1866, but sections appear in the journals and notebooks for decades, possibly as early as 1838. The poem was first published in *May-Day*. Some lines omitted from the *SP* text were printed in that volume as "The Harp." Another section of the poem was edited to serve as the motto to the 1849 edition of *Nature* (p. 27).
2. Cf. the opening line of "Days" (p. 471): "Daughters of Time."
3. The first edition and its reprintings read, "Maketh all things softly smile, / Painteth pictures mile on mile." The version printed here appears in *SP*, *RE*, and *W*.
4. A marsh marigold, whose flowers resemble large buttercups.
5. The Greek god of marriage, often celebrated in Renaissance songs (hence the anatomical term). Emerson describes a May Day celebration of the sort that was famously forbidden in Puritan New England (see, e.g., Nathaniel Hawthorne's story "The May-Pole of Merrymount," 1835; and Thomas Morton's narrative, *New English Caanan*, 1637). By Emerson's time, the custom had been revived in America. The Emersons are known to have held a May Day celebration, with maypole, on May 1, 1847.
6. In the first edition, two lines follow: "Lo Love's inundation poured / Over space and race abroad!"
7. See the close of "Threnody," p. 461.
8. The Civil War had ended two years before the publication of *May-Day*. A number of passages in this threshold poem and a number of poems in the volume treat the war directly or indirectly. See, especially, "Boston Hymn" (p. 465) and "Voluntaries" (p. 468).

For thou, O Spring! canst renovate
All that high God did first create.
Be still his arm and architect,
Rebuild the ruin, mend defect;   495
Chemist to vamp[9] old worlds with new,
Coat sea and sky with heavenlier blue,
New-tint the plumage of the birds,
And slough decay from grazing herds,
Sweep ruins from the scarped[1] mountain,   500
Cleanse the torrent at the fountain,
Purge alpine air by towns defiled,
Bring to fair mother fairer child,
Not less renew the heart and brain,
Scatter the sloth, wash out the stain,   505
Make the aged eye sun-clear,
To parting soul bring grandeur near.
Under gentle types,[2] my Spring
Masks the might of Nature's king,
An energy that searches thorough   510
From Chaos to the dawning morrow;
Into all our human plight,
The soul's pilgrimage and flight;
In city or in solitude,
Step by step, lifts bad to good,   515
Without halting, without rest,
Lifting Better up to Best;
Planting seeds of knowledge pure,
Through earth to ripen, through heaven endure.[3]

Brahma[1]

If the red slayer[2] think he slays,
   Or if the slain think he is slain,
They know not well the subtle ways
   I keep, and pass, and turn again.

Far or forgot to me is near;   5
   Shadow and sunlight are the same;
The vanished gods to me appear;
   And one to me are shame and fame.

9. Patch up or refurbish.
1. From "escarpment," hence, containing deep cliffs worn by erosion.
2. See n. 4, p. 15.
3. See the close of "Threnody" (p. 461).
1. Written in the summer of 1856; initially published in the first issue of the *Atlantic Monthly* 1 (November 1857). A notebook draft is titled "Song of the Soul." In 1845, Emerson copied in his journal a source for the poem, a passage from the *The Vishnu Purana* (see n. 3, p. 296): "What living creature slays or is slain? What living creature preserves or is preserved? Each is his own destroyer or preserver, as he follows evil or good" (*JMN* 9.319). Very similar passages occur in the *Katha Upanishad* and the *Bhagavad-Gita*. Brahma is the creator god of Hinduism, part of the trinity with Vishnu (see n. 5, p. 90) and Shiva (the destroyer). This, along with "The Sphinx" (p. 429), was the most frequently parodied of Emerson's poems.
2. Death, or an agent of death.

They reckon ill who leave me out;
    When me they fly, I am the wings;   10
I am the doubter and the doubt,
    And I the hymn the Brahmin[3] sings.

The strong gods pine for my abode,
    And pine in vain the sacred Seven;[4]
But thou, meek lover of the good!   15
    Find me, and turn thy back on heaven.

Nemesis[1]

Already blushes in[2] thy cheek
The bosom-thought which thou must speak;
The bird, how far it haply roam
By cloud or isle, is flying home;
The maiden fears, and fearing runs   5
Into the charmed snare she shuns;
And every man, in love or pride,
Of his fate is never wide.

    Will a woman's fan the ocean smooth?
Or prayers the stony Parcæ soothe,[3]   10
Or coax the thunder from its mark?
Or tapers light the chaos dark?
In spite of Virtue and the Muse,
Nemesis will have her dues,
And all our struggles and our toils   15
Tighter wind the giant coils.

Boston Hymn[1]

Read in Music Hall, January 1, 1863

The word of the Lord by night
To the watching Pilgrims[2] came,

---

3. See n. 6, p. 38.
4. Identified by Richard Poirier as "the 'Seven Seers' or Maharsis of ancient Hindu poetry. 'Seers' or 'rsis' were singers of the sacred songs." Edward Emerson identifies the "strong gods" as the Hindu gods Indra, god of the sky; Agni, god of fire; and Yama, god of death and judgment.
1. Composition date undetermined. Also see "Merlin II" (p. 451). Titled "Destiny" in one notebook fair copy (*PN* 430–31) and "Fate" in another (*PN* 547–48), the poem does not appear in *SP* or *RE*. Nemesis, see n. 7, p. 143.
2. "On" in *W*.
3. "Sooth" in the first edition, corrected in *W*; the error does not appear in the *Rhymer* notebook copy (*PN* 430) but does appear in the Notebook *NP* version, along with a misspelling of "smooth" as "smoothe" (*PN* 548). Parcae, or Fates (see n. 5, p. 451).
1. Emerson read this poem to inaugurate the jubilee celebration in the Boston Music Hall for the enactment of the Emancipation Proclamation, having written it by request shortly before the event. It was first published in *Dwight's Journal of Music* 22 (24 January 1863) and then in the *Atlantic Monthly* 11 (February 1863); then it was reprinted three more times, once as a single-sheet publication by the New England Loyal Publication Society of Boston as "Emerson's New England Hymn."
2. Emerson uses the term inclusively to refer to the early settlers of Massachusetts, even though technically the Pilgrims, who landed at Plymouth, were a distinct group from those who established the larger and

As they sat by the seaside,
And filled their hearts with flame.

God said, I am tired of kings,   5
I suffer them no more;
Up to my ear the morning brings
The outrage of the poor.

Think ye I made this ball
A field of havoc and war,   10
Where tyrants great and tyrants small
Might harry the weak and poor?

My angel,—his name is Freedom,—
Choose him to be your king;
He shall cut pathways east and west,   15
And fend[3] you with his wing.

Lo! I uncover the land
Which I hid of old time in the West,
As the sculptor uncovers the statue
When he has wrought his best;   20

I show Columbia,[4] of the rocks
Which dip their foot in the seas,
And soar to the air-borne flocks
Of clouds, and the boreal fleece.[5]

I will divide my goods;   25
Call in the wretch and slave:
None shall rule but the humble,
And none but Toil shall have.

I will have never a noble,
No lineage counted great;   30
Fishers and choppers and ploughmen
Shall constitute a state.

Go, cut down trees in the forest,
And trim the straightest boughs;
Cut down trees in the forest,   35
And build me a wooden house.

Call the people together,
The young men and the sires,
The digger in the harvest field,
Hireling, and him that hires;   40

---

dominant Massachusetts Bay Colony. Throughout the poem, Emerson connects the emphases on freedom in the American Revolution and the Civil War, as was common in his time.
3. Defend.
4. America.
5. Northern cloud formations.

And here in a pine state-house
They shall choose men to rule
In every needful faculty,
In church, and state, and school.

Lo, now! if these poor men   45
Can govern the land and sea,
And make just laws below the sun,
As planets faithful be.

And ye shall succor[6] men;
'T is nobleness to serve;   50
Help them who cannot help again:
Beware from right to swerve.

I break your bonds and masterships,
And I unchain the slave:
Free be his heart and hand henceforth   55
As wind and wandering wave.

I cause from every creature
His proper good to flow:
As much as he is and doeth,
So much he shall bestow.   60

But, laying hands on another
To coin[7] his labor and sweat,
He goes in pawn to his victim
For eternal years in debt.

To-day unbind the captive,   65
So only are ye unbound;
Lift up a people from the dust,
Trump[8] of their rescue, sound!

Pay ransom to the owner,
And fill the bag to the brim.   70
Who is the owner? The slave is owner,
And ever was. Pay him.[9]

O North! give him beauty for rags,
And honor, O South! for his shame;
Nevada! coin[1] thy golden crags   75
With Freedom's image and name.

---

6. Assist, help.
7. Make money from.
8. Trumpet.
9. Earlier in the abolition movement, many people encouraged payment of restitution to Southern owners to hasten the emancipation process, a policy Emerson himself had advocated. See "Address to the Citizens of Concord . . . ," p. 370.
1. Stamp with an imprint, as on a coin.

Up! and the dusky race
That sat in darkness long,—
Be swift their feet as antelopes,
And as behemoth[2] strong.   80

Come, East and West and North,
By races, as snow-flakes,
And carry my purpose forth,
Which neither halts nor shakes.

My will fulfilled shall be,   85
For, in daylight or in dark,
My thunderbolt has eyes to see
His way home to the mark.

Voluntaries[1]

I

Low and mournful be the strain,
Haughty thought be far from me;
Tones of penitence and pain,
Moanings of the tropic sea;
Low and tender in the cell   5
Where a captive sits in chains,
Crooning ditties treasured well
From his Afric's torrid plains.
Sole estate his sire bequeathed—
Hapless sire to hapless son—   10
Was the wailing song he breathed,
And his chain when life was done.

What his fault, or what his crime?
Or what ill planet crossed his prime?[2]
Heart too soft and will too weak   15
To front the fate that crouches near,—
Dove beneath the vulture's beak;—
Will song dissuade the thirsty spear?
Dragged from his mother's arms and breast,
Displaced, disfurnished here,   20
His wistful toil to do his best
Chilled by a ribald jeer.

2. Something very large or powerful; in Job 40.15, a huge animal, possibly a hippopotamus.
1. Written within a month after their deaths as an elegy for Colonel Robert Gould Shaw (1837–1863) and
members of his Massachusetts 54th Regiment, the first official all-black regiment in the Union Army.
They were slain on July 18, 1863, in an attack on Fort Wagner, Morris Island, South Carolina, in an attempt to recapture Fort Sumter. The regiment is also commemorated in a statue (dedicated in 1897) at
the edge of Boston Common and in a number of other poems, most famously "For the Union Dead"
(1964), by Boston poet Robert Lowell (1917–1977). Emerson had previously helped raise funds for the
regiment. He sent the poem to his friend Francis George Shaw, the father of Robert Shaw, in September 1863; it was first published in the *Atlantic Monthly* 12 (October 1863), then appeared in the *Memorial R[obert] G[ould] S[haw]* (1864). Selections were reprinted as broadsides and in a verse collection.
2. I.e., was he star-crossed (ill-fated)?

Great men in the Senate[3] sate,
Sage and hero, side by side,
Building for their sons the State,   25
Which they shall rule with pride.
They forbore to break the chain
Which bound the dusky tribe,
Checked by the owners' fierce disdain,
Lured by "Union" as the bribe.   30
Destiny sat by, and said,
'Pang for pang your seed shall pay,
Hide in false peace your coward head,
I bring round the harvest-day.'

II

Freedom all winged expands,   35
Nor perches in a narrow place;
Her broad van[4] seeks unplanted lands;
She loves a poor and virtuous race.
Clinging to a colder zone
Whose dark sky sheds the snow-flake down,   40
The snow-flake is her banner's star,
Her stripes the boreal streamers are.
Long she loved the Northman well;
Now the iron age is done,
She will not refuse to dwell   45
With the offspring of the Sun;
Foundling of the desert far,
Where palms plume, siroccos blaze,
He roves unhurt the burning ways
In climates of the summer star.   50
He has avenues to God
Hid from men of Northern brain,
Far beholding, without cloud,
What these with slowest steps attain.
If once the generous chief arrive   55
To lead him willing to be led,
For freedom he will strike and strive,
And drain his heart till he be dead.

III

In an age of fops and toys,
Wanting wisdom, void of right,   60
Who shall nerve heroic boys
To hazard all in Freedom's fight,—
Break sharply off their jolly games,
Forsake their comrades gay,
And quit proud homes and youthful dames,   65

3. Emerson writes of Senator Daniel Webster (see n. 6, p. 251) and others who supported such accommodationist gestures as the Fugitive Slave Law of 1850.
4. Or vanguard, front line of an army.

For famine, toil, and fray?
Yet on the nimble air benign
Speed nimbler messages,
That waft the breath of grace divine
To hearts in sloth and ease.   70
So nigh is grandeur to our dust,
So near is God to man,
When Duty whispers low, *Thou must,*
The youth replies, *I can.*

IV

O, well for the fortunate soul   75
Which Music's wings infold,
Stealing away the memory
Of sorrows new and old!
Yet happier he whose inward sight,
Stayed on his subtile thought,   80
Shuts his sense on toys of time,
To vacant bosoms brought.
But best befriended of the God
He who, in evil times,
Warned by an inward voice,   85
Heeds not the darkness and the dread,
Biding by his rule and choice,
Feeling only the fiery thread
Leading over heroic ground,
Walled with mortal terror round,   90
To the aim which him allures,
And the sweet heaven his deed secures.
Peril around all else appalling,
Cannon in front and leaden rain,
Him Duty through the clarion calling   95
To the van called not in vain.[5]

Stainless soldier on the walls,
Knowing this, — and knows no more, —
Whoever fights, whoever falls,
Justice conquers evermore,   100
Justice after as before, —
And he who battles on her side,
God, though he were ten times slain,
Crowns him victor glorified,
Victor over death and pain;   105
Forever: but his erring foe,
Self-assured that he prevails,
Looks from his victim lying low,
And sees aloft the red right arm
Redress the eternal scales.[6]   110

5. These four lines were added in *SP* and are reprinted in *RE* and *W*; they are written in Emerson's hand in his primary working copy of *May-Day*.
6. Of justice.

He, the poor foe, whom angels foil,
Blind with pride, and fooled by hate,
Writhes within the dragon coil,
Reserved to a speechless fate.[7]

V

Blooms the laurel[8] which belongs   115
To the valiant chief who fights;
I see the wreath, I hear the songs
Lauding the Eternal Rights,
Victors over daily wrongs:
Awful[9] victors, they misguide   120
Whom they will destroy,
And their coming triumph hide
In our downfall, or our joy:
They reach no term, they never sleep,
In equal strength through space abide;   125
Though, feigning dwarfs, they crouch and creep,
The strong they slay, the swift outstride:
Fate's grass grows rank in valley clods,
And rankly on the castled steep,—
Speak it firmly, these are gods,   130
All are ghosts beside.

Days[1]

Daughters[2] of Time, the hypocritic Days,
Muffled and dumb like barefoot dervishes,[3]
And marching single in an endless file,
Bring diadems and fagots[4] in their hands.
To each they offer gifts after his will,   5
Bread, kingdoms, stars, and sky that holds them all.
I, in my pleachéd[5] garden, watched the pomp,
Forgot my morning wishes, hastily
Took a few herbs and apples, and the Day
Turned and departed silent. I, too late,   10
Under her solemn fillet[6] saw the scorn.

---

7. Lines 106–14 are omitted in *RE* and *W*, and in Emerson's primary working copy of *May-Day*.
8. In ancient Greece, heroes, poets, and victors were crowned with laurel wreaths.
9. Sometimes terrible, but also commanding awe, as the earth in "Hamatreya" (p. 438).
1. Written in the spring or summer of 1851 and first published in the first issue of the *Atlantic Monthly* 1 (November 1857). See also n. 1 to "The Chartist's Complaint" (p. 472). According to Edward Emerson, Emerson himself was especially fond of this poem, a companion piece to "The Chartist's Complaint."
2. Erroneously printed "Damsels" in the first printing of *May-Day* and as "Daughter" in subsequent printings; corrected in *SP*. Emerson wrote to James Elliot Cabot, "I read with amazement the word 'Damsels' which slipped into the new text, I know not how. 'Daughters' was right & shall be" (*L* 5.518); however, notebook drafts reveal the presence of "Damsels" in earlier versions of the poem (*PN* 295). Also cf. the first line of "May-Day" (p. 463) and of "The Chartist's Complaint" regarding the title of this poem and "hypocritic."
3. Muslim ascetics, or religious mendicants, some of whom perform whirling dances and chanting as acts of ecstatic devotion; see "Song of Seid Nimetollah of Kuhistan" (p. 481).
4. See n. 3, p. 266. *Diadems:* crowns.
5. Shaded or having a border of interlaced branches or vines.
6. Headband.

The Chartist's Complaint[1]

Day! hast thou two faces,[2]
Making one place two places?
One, by humble farmer seen,
Chill and wet, unlighted, mean,
Useful only, triste[3] and damp,   5
Serving for a laborer's lamp?
Have the same mists another side,
To be the appanage[4] of pride,
Gracing the rich man's wood and lake,
His park where amber mornings break,   10
And treacherously bright to show
His planted isle where roses glow?
O Day! and is your mightiness
A sycophant to smug success?
Will the sweet sky and ocean broad   15
Be fine accomplices to fraud?
O Sun! I curse thy cruel ray:
Back, back to chaos, harlot Day!

The Titmouse[1]

You shall not be overbold
When you deal with arctic cold,
As late I found my lukewarm blood
Chilled wading in the snow-choked wood.
How should I fight? my foeman fine   5
Has million arms to one of mine:
East, west, for aid I looked in vain,
East, west, north, south, are his domain.
Miles off, three dangerous miles, is home;
Must borrow his winds who there would come.   10
Up and away for life! be fleet! —
The frost-king ties my fumbling feet,
Sings in my ears, my hands are stones,
Curdles the blood to the marble bones,
Tugs at the heart-strings, numbs the sense,   15

1. Written in the spring or summer of 1851 and first published in the first issue of the *Atlantic Monthly* (November 1857). "Days" (p. 471) and this poem were composed at the same time, as companion poems. *Chartists:* working-class social reformers in England, active from 1838 to 1848, with whom Emerson had been favorably impressed during his 1847–48 trip to England. He attended a Chartist meeting in Holborn, England, on March 7, 1848; was near London during their demonstration on April 10; and mentions them sympathetically in *English Traits* (*CW* 5), for which he also wrote a chapter, later eliminated, titled "Reform and Chartism." The poem does not appear in *SP*.
2. See "Days," line 1.
3. Sad or wistful.
4. Sustenance, especially in the sense of a portion of land assigned by a male sovereign for the subsistence of his younger sons.
1. Emerson completed this poem in March 1862 after seeing (and exchanging whistles with) a chickadee in Walden woods; first published in the *Atlantic Monthly* 9 (May 1862). This poem may be read as a response to Keats's "Ode to a Nightingale"; see, e.g., line 95. *Titmouse:* a very active, chickadee-like bird.

And hems in life with narrowing fence.
Well, in this broad bed lie and sleep,
The punctual stars will vigil keep,
Embalmed by purifying cold,
The winds shall sing their dead-march old,   20
The snow is no ignoble shroud,
The moon thy mourner, and the cloud.

Softly,—but this way fate was pointing,
'Twas coming fast to such anointing,
When piped a tiny voice hard by,   25
Gay and polite, a cheerful[2] cry,
Chic-chicadeedee! saucy note
Out of sound heart and merry throat,
As if it said, 'Good day, good sir!
Fine afternoon, old passenger!   30
Happy to meet you in these places,
Where January brings few faces.'

This poet, though he live apart,
Moved by his hospitable heart,
Sped, when I passed his sylvan fort,   35
To do the honors of his court,
As fits a feathered lord of land;
Flew near, with soft wing grazed my hand,
Hopped on the bough, then, darting low,
Prints his small impress on the snow,   40
Shows feats of his gymnastic play,
Head downward, clinging to the spray.

Here was this atom in full breath,
Hurling defiance at vast death;
This scrap of valor just for play   45
Fronts the north-wind in waistcoat gray,
As if to shame my weak behavior;
I greeted loud my little saviour,
'You pet! what dost here? and what for?
In these woods, thy small Labrador,   50
At this pinch, wee San Salvador![3]
What fire burns in that little chest
So frolic, stout, and self-possest?
Henceforth I wear no stripe but thine;
Ashes and jet all hues outshine.   55
Why are not diamonds black and gray,
To ape thy dare-devil array?
And I affirm, the spacious North
Exists to draw thy virtue forth.
I think no virtue goes with size;   60
The reason of all cowardice

2. For Emerson, providing "cheer" is one of the primary duties of the poet. See also n. 4, p. 440.
3. An island in the West Indies, here used as a metonomy for the bird with its "fire . . . in that little chest" (line 51). The Labrador Peninsula area, in Newfoundland, here stands for the cold northern woods.

Is, that men are overgrown,
And, to be valiant, must come down
To the titmouse dimension.'

'T is good-will makes intelligence,   65
And I began to catch the sense
Of my bird's song: 'Live out of doors
In the great woods, on prairie floors.
I dine in the sun; when he sinks in the sea,
I too have a hole in a hollow tree;   70
And I like less when Summer beats
With stifling beams on these retreats,
Than noontide twilights which snow makes
With tempest of the blinding flakes.
For well the soul, if stout within,   75
Can arm impregnably the skin;
And polar frost my frame defied,
Made of the air that blows outside.'

With glad remembrance of my debt,
I homeward turn; farewell, my pet!   80
When here again thy pilgrim comes,
He shall bring store of seeds and crumbs.
Doubt not, so long as earth has bread,
Thou first and foremost shalt be fed;
The Providence that is most large   85
Takes hearts like thine in special charge,
Helps who for their own need are strong,
And the sky doats on cheerful song.
Henceforth I prize thy wiry chant
O'er all that mass and minster vaunt;   90
For men mis-hear thy call in spring,
As t' would accost some frivolous wing,
Crying out of the hazel copse, *Phe-be!*
And, in winter, *Chic-a-dee-dee!*
I think old Cæsar must have heard   95
In northern Gaul my dauntless bird,[4]
And, echoed in some frosty wold,[5]
Borrowed thy battle-numbers bold.
And I will write our annals new,
And thank thee for a better clew,   100
I, who dreamed not when I came here
To find the antidote of fear,
Now hear thee say in Roman key,
Pæan! Veni, vidi, vici.[6]

---

4. The lines contain an almost humorous echo of Keats's "Ode to a Nightingale" ("The voice I hear this
passing night was heard / In ancient days by emperor and clown"). Cæsar (see n. 8, p. 17) conquered
Gaul (see n. 2, p. 105) in the Gallic Wars (58–51 B.C.E.).
5. A rolling plain or moor.
6. I came, I saw, I conquered (Latin); Cæsar's description of his victory in northeastern Anatolia, or Asia
Minor, the Asian part of Turkey. *Pæan:* hymn of thanksgiving, especially one to Apollo.

Sea-Shore[1]

I heard or seemed to hear the chiding Sea
Say, Pilgrim, why so late and slow to come?
Am I not always here, thy summer home?
Is not my voice thy music, morn and eve?
My breath thy healthful climate in the heats,   5
My touch thy antidote, my bay thy bath?
Was ever building like my terraces?
Was ever couch magnificent as mine?
Lie on the warm rock-ledges, and there learn
A little hut suffices like a town.   10
I make your sculptured architecture vain,
Vain beside mine.[2] I drive my wedges home,
And carve the coastwise mountain into caves.
Lo! here is Rome, and Nineveh, and Thebes,
Karnak, and Pyramid, and Giant's Stairs,[3]   15
Half piled or prostrate; and my newest slab
Older than all thy race.
                          Behold the Sea,
The opaline, the plentiful and strong,
Yet beautiful as is the rose in June,   20
Fresh as the trickling rainbow of July;
Sea full of food, the nourisher of kinds,[4]
Purger of earth, and medicine of men;
Creating a sweet climate by my breath,
Washing out harms and griefs from memory,   25
And, in my mathematic ebb and flow,
Giving a hint of that which changes not.
Rich are the sea-gods:—who gives gifts but they?
They grope the sea for pearls, but more than pearls:
They pluck Force thence, and give it to the wise.   30
For every wave is wealth to Dædalus,[5]
Wealth to the cunning artist who can work
This matchless strength. Where shall he find, O waves!
A load your Atlas[6] shoulders cannot lift?

I with my hammer pounding evermore   35
The rocky coast, smite Andes[7] into dust,
Strewing my bed; and, in another age,
Rebuild a continent of better men.
Then I unbar the doors: my paths lead out

---

1. Written in July 1856, from a journal prose passage that Edward Emerson says Emerson composed just
   after a walk on the beach at Pigeon Cove, on Cape Ann. First published in *The Boatswain's Whistle* 9
   (October 18, 1864).
2. Cf. "The Snow-Storm" (p. 442).
3. Or Giant's Causeway, a much-studied volcanic formation of some forty thousand columns in Northern
   Ireland, fabled to be the work of giants. Nineveh, ancient capital of the Assyrian Empire. Thebes, see n.
   5, p. 134. Karnak, city in ancient Egypt. Pyramid, see n. 9, p. 434.
4. Many different natural beings.
5. See n. 2, p. 429.
6. In Greek mythology, a Titan condemned to support the world on his shoulders.
7. See n. 1, p. 434.

The exodus of nations: I disperse   40
Men to all shores that front the hoary main.

   I too have arts and sorceries;
Illusion dwells forever with the wave.[8]
I know what spells are laid. Leave me to deal
With credulous and imaginative man;   45
For, though he scoop my water in his palm,
A few rods off he deems it gems and clouds.
Planting strange fruits and sunshine on the shore,
I make some coast alluring, some lone isle,
To distant men, who must go there, or die.   50

Two Rivers[1]

Thy summer voice, Musketaquit,[2]
Repeats the music of the rain;
But sweeter rivers[3] pulsing flit
Through thee, as thou through Concord Plain.

Thou in thy narrow banks art pent: 5
The stream I love unbounded goes
Through flood and sea and firmament;
Through light, through life, it forward flows.

I see the inundation sweet,
I hear the spending of the stream   10
Through years, through men, through nature fleet,
Through love and thought, through power and dream.[4]

Musketaquit, a goblin[5] strong,
Of shard and flint makes jewels gay;
They lose their grief who hear his song,   15
And where he winds is the day of day.

So forth and brighter fares my stream, —
Who drink it shall not thirst again;[6]
No darkness stains its equal gleam,
And ages drop in it like rain.   20

---

8. See the epigraph to the essay "Illusions" (p. 289).
1. Written between May and October 1857 and first published in the *Atlantic Monthly* 1 (January 1858).
   Edward Emerson speculates that one journal entry source for the poem, dating from spring 1856, was
   written as Emerson sat beside the Concord River.
2. Or Musketaquid ("plain of grass"), Algonquian name for the Concord plain, the area around the Concord River. See also the poem "Musketaquid," in *Poems*.
3. See "The Apology," lines 17–20 (p. 448).
4. In the first edition, "Through passion, thought, through power and dream."
5. Spirit or fairy.
6. John 4.13.

Waldeinsamkeit[1]

I do not count the hours I spend
In wandering by the sea;
The forest is my loyal friend,
Like God it useth me.[2]

In plains that room for shadows make   5
Of skirting hills to lie,
Bound in by streams which give and take
Their colors from the sky;

Or on the mountain-crest sublime,
Or down the oaken glade,   10
O what have I to do with time?
For this the day was made.

Cities of mortals woe-begone
Fantastic care derides,[3]
But in the serious landscape lone   15
Stern benefit abides.

Sheen will tarnish, honey cloy,
And merry is only a mask of sad,
But, sober on a fund of joy,
The woods at heart are glad.   20

There the great Planter plants
Of fruitful worlds the grain,
And with a million spells enchants
The souls that walk in pain.

Still on the seeds of all he made   25
The rose of beauty burns;
Through times that wear, and forms that fade,
Immortal youth returns.

The black ducks mounting from the lake,
The pigeon in the pines,   30
The bittern's[4] boom, a desert make
Which no false art refines.

Down in yon watery nook,[5]
Where bearded mists divide,

1. Probably written in the late summer of 1857. First published, without Emerson's prior knowledge, in the *Atlantic Monthly* 2 (October 1858). *Waldeinsamkeit*: forest solitude, used by German Romantics.
2. In SP only, "A Delphic shrine to me."
3. During the 1850s, Emerson was increasingly troubled by slavery and actively involved in the abolitionist movement; this poem and others written in the middle to late 1850s reflect those concerns, often indirectly.
4. A wading bird; the male has a deep, booming cry.
5. See "The Rhodora," line 3 (p. 440).

The gray old gods whom Chaos knew,   35
The sires of Nature, hide.

Aloft, in secret veins of air,
Blows the sweet breath of song,
O, few to scale those uplands dare,
Though they to all belong!   40

See thou bring not to field or stone
The fancies found in books;
Leave authors' eyes, and fetch your own,
To brave the landscape's looks.[6]

Oblivion here thy wisdom is,   45
Thy thrift, the sleep of cares;
For a proud idleness like this
Crowns all thy mean affairs.

Terminus[1]

It is time to be old,
To take in sail:—
The god of bounds,
Who sets to seas a shore,
Came to me in his fatal rounds,   5
And said: 'No more!
No farther shoot[2]
Thy broad ambitious branches, and thy root,
Fancy departs: no more invent,
Contract thy firmament   10
To compass of a tent.
There's not enough for this and that,
Make thy option which of two;
Economize the failing river,
Not the less revere the Giver,   15
Leave the many and hold the few.
Timely wise accept the terms,
Soften the fall with wary foot;
A little while
Still plan and smile,   20
And, fault of novel germs,

---

6. In the first edition, an additional stanza follows:
> And if, amid this dear delight,
> My thoughts did home rebound,
> I well might reckon it a slight
> To the high cheer I found.

The stanza does not appear in *SP*, *RE*, and *W*; and it is cancelled (with the previous one) in Emerson's primary working copy.
1. Drafted between 1846 and 1852 and probably finished as late as 1866. The poem may be compared to Alfred Lord Tennyson's famous poem "Ulysses" (1842). Terminus, the Roman god of boundaries.
2. Changed from "spread" for *SP*, *RE*, and *W*.

Mature the unfallen fruit.
Curse, if thou wilt, thy sires,
Bad husbands[3] of their fires,
Who, when they gave thee breath,   25
Failed to bequeath
The needful sinew stark as once,
The Baresark[4] marrow to thy bones,
But left a legacy of ebbing veins,
Inconstant heat and nerveless reins, —   30
Amid the Muses, left thee deaf and dumb,
Amid the gladiators, halt and numb.'

    As the bird trims her to the gale,
I trim myself to the storm of time,
I man the rudder, reef the sail,[5]   35
Obey the voice at eve obeyed at prime:
'Lowly faithful, banish fear,
Right onward drive unharmed;
The port, well worth the cruise, is near,
And every wave is charmed.'   40

FROM ELEMENTS[1]

Art[2]

Give to barrows,[3] trays, and pans
Grace and glimmer of romance;
Bring the moonlight into noon
Hid in gleaming piles of stone;
On the city's paved street   5
Plant gardens lined with lilacs sweet;
Let spouting fountains cool the air,
Singing in the sun-baked square;
Let statue, picture, park, and hall,
Ballad, flag, and festival,   10
The past restore, the day adorn,
And make to-morrow a new morn.
So shall the drudge in dusty frock
Spy behind the city clock
Retinues of airy kings,   15
Skirts of angels, starry wings,
His fathers shining in bright fables,
His children fed at heavenly tables.

---

3. Managers.
4. Wild and frenzied. See "American Scholar," p. 63.
5. Reduce the size of the sail by tying it to or rolling it around the yard.
1. The "Elements" section of *May-Day* is composed of selected essay epigraphs. Among additional epigraphs, see especially "Illusions," before that essay.
2. Probably written in 1847; first published as the motto to the essay "Art" in the 1847 edition of *Essays.*
3. Wheelbarrows.

'T is the privilege of Art
Thus to play its cheerful part,   20
Man on earth to acclimate,
And bend the exile to his fate,
And, moulded of one element
With the days and firmament,
Teach him on these as stairs to climb,   25
And live on even terms with Time;
Whilst upper life the slender rill
Of human sense doth overfill.

Worship[1]

This is he, who, felled by foes,
Sprung harmless up, refreshed by blows:
He to captivity[2] was sold,
But him no prison-bars would hold:
Though they sealed him in a rock,   5
Mountain chains he can unlock:
Thrown to lions[3] for their meat,
The crouching lion kissed his feet:
Bound to the stake, no flames appalled,
But arched o'er him an honoring vault.   10
This is he men miscall Fate,
Threading dark ways, arriving late,
But ever coming in time to crown
The truth, and hurl wrong-doers down.
He is the oldest, and best known,   15
More near than aught thou call'st thy own,
Yet, greeted in another's eyes,
Disconcerts with glad surprise.
This is Jove, who, deaf to prayers,
Floods with blessings unawares.   20
Draw, if thou canst, the mystic line
Severing rightly his from thine,
Which is human, which divine.

1. Probably written in 1859 and first published as the motto to the essay "Worship" in *The Conduct of Life* (1860).
2. An allusion to the biblical patriarch Joseph, sold by his brothers into captivity (Genesis 37), and also to the nation of Israel, under Babylonian captivity, then restored.
3. Allusion to the biblical prophet Daniel, who was cast into the lion's den and emerged unhurt (Daniel 6).

FROM QUATRAINS

Memory[1]

Night-dreams trace on Memory's wall
Shadows of the thoughts of day,
And thy fortunes, as they fall,
The bias of the will betray.

FROM TRANSLATIONS

Song of Seid Nimetollah of Kuhistan[1]

[Among the religious customs of the dervishes is an astronomical
dance, in which the dervish imitates the movements of the heavenly
bodies, by spinning on his own axis, whilst at the same time he revolves
round the Sheikh in the centre, representing the sun; and, as he spins,
he sings the Song of Seid Nimetollah of Kuhistan.]

Spin the ball! I reel, I burn,
Nor head from foot can I discern,
Nor my heart from love of mine,
Nor the wine-cup from the wine.[2]
All my doing, all my leaving,   5
Reaches not to my perceiving;
Lost in whirling spheres I rove,
And know only that I love.

I am seeker of the stone,
Living gem of Solomon;[3]   10
From the shore of souls arrived,
In the sea of sense I dived;
But what is land, or what is wave,
To me who only jewels crave?
Love is the air-fed fire intense,   15
And my heart the frankincense;
As the rich aloes flames, I glow,

1. Probably written in August 1840. No quatrains from *May-Day* appear in *SP*. Emerson wrote many quatrains, partially inspired by the roba'i of Persian poetry; he printed a separate section of them in *May-
Day*, sometimes used them for essay epigraphs, and frequently imbedded them as interpolated voices
within longer poems.
1. Composition date undetermined. First published, without a title, in the essay "Persian Poetry" in the *Atlantic Monthly* 1 (April 1858) but not in the essay as reprinted in *Letters and Social Aims* (W 8). It translates the first of the two *Mystische Gasele* (mystic ghaselles) from Joseph von Hammer-Purgstall's
Geschichte der schönen Redekunste Persiens (History of the fine arts of Persia; 1818). Cf. also Emerson's
"Ghaselle" in *Poems*. Ghaselle: or ghazal, in Persian poetry, a short, lyric poem in couplets, the last of
which often contained the poet's name. Hafiz (see n. 1, p. 115) was a chief practitioner; he and Saadi
(see n. 2, p. 250) were the two Persian poets most significant to Emerson. Emerson adapted a great deal
of Persian poetry, generally from German translations in von Hammer-Purgstall. Seid, Sayyid Ni
'matu'lläh of Kirman (d. 1431), Persian mystic and poet, called the king of dervishes (see n. 3, p. 471).
Kuhistan, Kerman, city of east-central Iran. No translations appear in *SP*.
2. See "Brahma" (p. 464) and "Bacchus" (p. 452).
3. See n. 6, p. 17.

Yet the censer[4] cannot know.
I'm all-knowing, yet unknowing;[5]
Stand not, pause not, in my going.   20

Ask not me, as Muftis can,
To recite the Alcoran;[6]
Well I love the meaning sweet,—
I tread the book beneath my feet.

Lo! the God's love blazes higher,   25
Till all difference expire.
What are Moslems? what are Giaours?[7]
All are Love's, and all are ours.
I embrace the true believers,
But I reck not of deceivers.   30
Firm to Heaven my bosom clings,
Heedless of inferior things;
Down on earth there, underfoot,
What men chatter know I not.

OTHERS

Grace[1]

How much, Preventing God! how much I owe
To the defences thou hast round me set:
Example, custom, fear, occasion slow,—
These scorned bondmen were my parapet.[2]
I dare not peep over this parapet   5
To gauge[3] with glance the roaring gulf below,
The depths of sin to which I had descended,
Had not these me against myself defended.

4. A vessel in which incense is burned, especially during religious ceremonies. *Aloes flames:* reference to aloes wood, or agallochum, an aromatic wood from the East Indies, burned as a perfume. No connection with common aloe.
5. See "Brahma" (p. 464).
6. Or Koran, the sacred text of Islam. *Muftis:* Muslim scholars who interpret the shari'a, or code of law based on the Koran.
7. In Islam, nonbelievers. *Moslems:* or Muslims, adherents of Islam, the religion of Mohammad.
1. Probably written some time between 1831 and 1833. First published in *The Dial* 2 (January 1842). Reprinted as an untitled, unattributed motto in *Memoirs of Margaret Fuller Ossoli*. First collected in *RE*. The poem may be compared to John Milton's "When I Consider How My Light Is Spent," a sonnet on his blindness. Emerson first drafted the poem inside the cover of volume one of his copy of Milton's prose. We print the text from *The Dial*, with one noted correction.
2. An embankment used to protect soldiers from enemy fire.
3. Printed "guage" in *The Dial*, though spelled correctly in Emerson's notebooks (*PN* 89); corrected in *Memoirs* and subsequent printings.

Cupido[1]

The solid, solid universe
Is pervious[2] to Love;
With bandaged eyes[3] he never errs,
Around, below, above.
His blinding light   5
He flingeth white
On God's and Satan's brood,
And reconciles
By mystic wiles
The evil and the good.[4]   10

["Let Me Go Where E'er I Will"][1]

Let me go where e'er I will
I hear a skyborn music still
It sounds from all things old
It sounds from all things young
From all that's fair from all that's foul   5
Peals out a cheerful song
    It is not only in the Rose
    It is not only in the bird
    Not only where the Rainbow glows
    Nor in the song of woman heard   10
But in the darkest meanest things
There alway alway something sings.

Tis not in the high stars alone
Nor in the cups of budding flowers
Nor in the redbreast's mellow tone   15
Nor in the bow that smiles in showers
But in the mud & scum of things
There alway alway something sings.

["Ever the Rock of Ages Melts"][1]

Ever the Rock of Ages melts
Into the mineral air,
To be the quarry whence is built
Thought & its mansion fair.

1. Drafted in 1843 and first published in SP.
2. Permeable.
3. Cupid is traditionally depicted as blindfolded.
4. See "Uriel" (p. 436).
1. Composition date undetermined, but probably before 1846. The draft appears in PN 46, Notebook P, Emerson's main working poetry notebook at least through 1845. Unpublished by Emerson; titled "Music" in W. We print the PN text, but correct "theres" to "there," following W.
1. Drafted between May and December 1857 and unpublished by Emerson. First published in RE. This version appears in poetry notebook NP (PN 512), where the poem exists in fair copy. The title alludes to the famous hymn "Rock of Ages," by Augustus Montague Toplady (1740–1778), in which the "rock" is Jesus.

From Journals and Notebooks[†]

Jan. 25, 1820

THE WIDE WORLD   NO. 1
Mixing with the thousand pursuits & passions & objects of the world as personified by Imagination is profitable & entertaining. These pages are intended at this their commencement to contain a record of new thoughts (when they occur); for a receptacle of all the old ideas that partial but peculiar peepings at antiquity can furnish or furbish; for tablet to save the wear & tear of weak Memory & in short for all the various purposes & utility real or imaginary which are usually comprehended under that comprehensive title *Common Place book.*

Jan. 26, 1820

I do hereby nominate & appoint "Imagination" the generallissimo & chief marshal of all the luckless raggamuffin Ideas which may be collected & imprisoned hereafter in these pages.

Oct. 25, 1820

I find myself often idle, vagrant, stupid, & hollow. This is somewhat appalling & if I do not discipline myself with diligent care I shall suffer severely from remorse & the sense of inferiority hereafter. All around me are industrious & will be great, I am indolent & shall be insignificant. Avert it heaven! avert it virtue! I need excitement.

May 13, 1822

In twelve days I shall be nineteen years old; which I count a miserable thing. Has any other educated person lived so many years and lost so many days? I do not say acquired so little for by an ease of thought & certain looseness of mind I have perhaps been the subject of as many ideas as many of mine age. But mine approaching maturity is attended with a goading sense of emptiness & wasted capacity; with the conviction that vanity has been content to admire the little circle of natural accomplishments, and has travelled again & again the narrow round, instead of adding sedulously the gems of knowledge to their number. Too tired and too indolent to travel up the mountain path which leads to good learning, to wisdom & to fame, I must be satisfied with beholding with an envious eye the laborious journey & final success of my fellows, remaining stationary myself, until my inferiors & juniors have reached & outgone me. And how long is this to last? How long shall I hold the little acclivity which four or

† Reprinted by permission of the publisher from *The Journals and Miscellaneous Notebooks of Ralph Waldo Emerson,* vols. I–XVI (Cambridge, Mass.: The Belknap Press of Harvard University Press). Copyright © 1960–82 by the President and Fellows of Harvard College.

six years ago I flattered myself was enviable, but which has become contemptible now? It is a child's place & if I hold it longer I may quite as well resume the bauble & rattle, grow old with a baby's red jocky on my grey head & a picturebook in my hand, instead of Plato and Newton. Well, and I am he who nourished brilliant visions of future grandeur which may well appear presumptuous & foolish now. My infant imagination was idolatrous of glory, & thought itself no mean pretender to the honours of those who stood highest in the community, and dared even to contend for fame with those who are hallowed by time & the approbation of ages. It was a little merit to concieve such animating hopes, and afforded some poor prospect of the possibility of their fulfilment. This hope was fed & fanned by the occasional lofty communications which were vouchsafed to me with the Muses' Heaven and which have at intervals made me the organ of remarkable sentiments & feelings which were far above my ordinary train. And with this lingering earnest of better hope (I refer to this fine exhilaration which now & then quickens my clay) shall I resign every aspiration to belong to that family of giant minds which live on earth many ages & rule the world when their bones are slumbering, no matter, whether under a pyramid or a primrose? No I will yet a little while entertain the Angel.

Look next from the history of my intellect to the history of my heart. A blank, my lord. I have not the kind affections of a pigeon. Ungenerous & selfish, cautions & cold, I yet wish to be romantic. Have not sufficient feeling to speak a natural hearty welcome to a friend or stranger and yet send abroad wishes & fancies of a friendship with a man I never knew. There is not in the whole wide Universe of God (my relations to Himself I do not understand) one being to whom I am attached with warm & entire devotion—not a being to whom I have joined fate for weal or wo, not one whose interests I have nearly & dearly at heart; and this I say at the most susceptible age of man.

Perhaps at the distance of a score of years, if I then inhabit this world, or still more, if I do not, these will appear frightful confessions; they may or may not; it is a true picture of a barren & desolate soul.

Dec. 21, 1823

Who is he that shall controul me? Why may not I act & speak & write & think with entire freedom? What am I to the Universe, or, the Universe, what is it to me? Who hath forged the chains of Wrong & Right, of Opinion & Custom? And must I wear them? Is Society my anointed King? Or is there any mightier community or any man or more than man, whose slave I am? I am solitary in the vast society of beings; I consort with no species; I indulge no sympathies. I see the world, human, brute & inanimate nature; I am in the midst of them, but not *of* them; I hear the song of the storm— the Winds & warring Elements sweep by me—but they mix not with my being. I see cities & nations & witness passions—the roar of their laughter— but I partake it not;—the yell of their grief—it touches no chord in me; their fellowships & fashions, lusts & virtues, the words & deeds they call glory & shame—I disclaim them all. I say to the Universe, Mighty one! thou art not my mother; Return to chaos, if thou wilt, I shall still exist. I live. If I owe my being, it is to a destiny greater than thine. Star by Star, world by world, system by system shall be crushed—but I shall live.

Apr. 18, 1824

I am beginning my professional studies. In a month I shall be *legally* a man. And I deliberately dedicate my time, my talents, & my hopes to the Church. Man is an animal that looks before & after; and I should be loth to reflect at a remote period that I took so solemn a step in my existence without some careful examination of my past & present life. Since I cannot alter I would not repent the resolution I have made & this page must be witness to the latest year of my life whether I have good grounds to warrant my determination.

I cannot dissemble that my abilities are below my ambition. And I find that I judged by a false criterion when I measured my powers by my ability to understand & to criticise the intellectual character of another. For men graduate their respect not by the secret wealth but by the outward use; not by the power to understand, but by the power to act. I have or had a strong imagination & consequently a keen relish for the beauties of poetry. The exercise which the practice of composition gives to this faculty is the cause of my immoderate fondness for writing, which has swelled these pages to a voluminous extent. My reasoning faculty is proportionately weak, nor can I ever hope to write a Butler's Analogy or an Essay of Hume. Nor is it strange that with this confession I should choose theology, which is from everlasting to everlasting 'debateable Ground.' For, the highest species of reasoning upon divine subjects is rather the fruit of a sort of moral imagination, than of the 'Reasoning Machines' such as Locke & Clarke & David Hume. Dr Channing's Dudleian Lecture is the model of what I mean, and the faculty which produced this is akin to the higher flights of the fancy. I may add that the preaching most in vogue at the present day depends chiefly on imagination for its success, and asks those accomplishments which I believe are most within my grasp. I have set down little which can gratify my vanity, and I must further say that every comparison of myself with my mates that six or seven, perhaps sixteen or seventeen, years have made has convinced me that there exists a signal defect of character which neutralizes in great part the just influence my talents ought to have. Whether that defect be in the *address*, in the fault of good forms, which Queen Isabella said were like perpetual letters commendatory, or deeper seated in an absence of common *sympathies*, or even in a levity of the understanding, I cannot tell. But its bitter fruits are a sore uneasiness in the company of most men & women, a frigid fear of offending & jealousy of disrespect, an inability to lead & an unwillingness to follow the current conversation, which contrive to make me second with all those among whom chiefly I wish to be first.

Hence my bearing in the world is the direct opposite of that good humoured independence & self esteem which should mark the gentleman. Be it here remembered that there is a decent pride which is conspicuous in the perfect model of a Christian man. I am unfortunate also, as was Rienzi, in a propensity to laugh or rather snicker. I am ill at ease therefore among men. I criticize with hardness; I lavishly applaud; I weakly argue; and I wonder with a foolish face of praise.

Now the profession of Law demands a good deal of personal address, an impregnable confidence in one's own powers, upon all occasions expected & unexpected, & a logical mode of thinking & speaking—which I do not possess, & may not reasonably hope to obtain. Medicine also makes large demands on the practitioner for a seducing Mannerism. And I have no taste for the pestle & mortar, for Bell on the bones or Hunter or Celsus.

But in Divinity I hope to thrive. I inherit from my sire a formality of manner & speech, but I derive from him or his patriotic parent a passionate love for the strains of eloquence. I burn after the 'aliquid immensum infinitumque'[1] which Cicero desired. What we ardently love we learn to imitate. My understanding venerates & my heart loves that Cause which is dear to God & man—the laws of Morals, the Revelations which sanction, & the blood of martyrs & triumphant suffering of the saints which seal them. In my better hours, I am the believer (if not the dupe) of brilliant promises, and can respect myself as the possessor of those powers which command the reason & passions of the multitude. The office of a clergyman is twofold; public preaching & private influence. Entire success in the first is the lot of few, but this I am encouraged to expect. If however the individual himself lack that moral worth which is to secure the last, his studies upon the first are idly spent. The most prodigious genius, a seraph's eloquence will shamefully defeat its own end, if it has not first won the heart of the defender to the cause he defends, but the coolest reason cannot censure my choice when I oblige myself *professionally* to a life which all wise men freely & advisedly adopt. I put no great restraint on myself & can therefore claim little merit in a manner of life which chimes with inclination & habit. But I would learn to love Virtue for her own sake. . . .

I have mentioned a defect of character; perhaps it is not one, but many. Every wise man aims at an entire conquest of himself. We applaud as possessed of extraordinary good sense, one who never makes the slightest mistake in speech or action; one in whom not only every important step of life, but every passage of conversation, every duty of the day, even every movement of every muscle—hands, feet, & tongue, are measured & dictated by deliberate reason. I am not assuredly that excellent creature. A score of words & deeds issue from me daily, of which I am not the master. They are begotten of weakness & born of shame. I cannot assume the elevation I ought—but lose the influence I should exert among those of meaner or younger understanding, for want of sufficient *bottom* in my nature, for want of that confidence of manner which springs from an erect mind which is without fear & without reproach. In my frequent humiliation, even before women & children I am compelled to remember the poor boy who cried, "I told you, Father, they would find me out." . . .

Jan. 1825

It is my own humor to despise pedigree. I was educated to prize it. The kind Aunt[2] whose cares instructed my youth (& whom may God reward) told me oft the virtues of her & mine ancestors. They have been clergymen for many generations & the piety of all & the eloquence of many is yet praised in the Churches. But the dead sleep in their moonless night; my business is with the living.

Jan.–Feb. 1827

PECULIARITIES OF THE PRESENT AGE

1. Instead of the systematic pursuit of science men cultivate the knowledge of anecdotes.

---

1. "Something great and immeasurable." [*JMN*]
2. Mary Moody Emerson.

2. It is said to be the age of the first person singular.
3. The reform of the Reformation.
4. Transcendentalism. Metaphysics & ethics look inwards—and France produces Mad. de Stael; England, Wordsworth; America, Sampson Reed; as well as Germany, Swedenborg.
5. The immense extent of the English language & influence. The Eng. tongue is spreading over all N. America except Mexico, over Demerary &c, Jamaica &c, Indostan, New Holland & the Australian islands.
6. The paper currency. Joint stock companies.
7. The disposition among men of *associating* themselves to promote any purpose. (Millions of societies.)

Nov. 11, 1828

I would write a sermon upon the text men are made a law unto themselves to advise them to fear & honour themselves. . . .

Nov. 1828

Don't you see you are the Universe to yourself. You carry your fortunes in your own hand. . . .

Dec. 21, 1828 Concord, N.H.

I have now been four days engaged to Ellen Louisa Tucker. Will my Father in Heaven regard us with kindness, and as he hath, as we trust, made us for each other, will he be pleased to strengthen & purify & prosper & eternize our affection! Sunday Morning.

July? 1829

Oh Ellen, I do dearly love you—

Aug. 28, 1830

Alii disputent, ego mirabor,[3] said Augustin. It shall be my speech to the Calvinist & the Unitarian.

Nov. 5, 1830

When a man has got to a certain point in his career of truth he becomes conscious forevermore that he must take himself for better for worse as his portion, that what he can get out of his plot of ground by the sweat of his brow is his meat, & though the wide universe is full of good, not a particle can he add to himself but through his toil bestowed on this spot. It looks to him indeed a little spot, a poor barren possession, filled with thorns and a lurking place for adders & apes & wolves. But cultivation will work wonders. It will enlarge to his eye as it is explored. That little nook will swell to a world of light & power & love.

Feb. 13, 1831

Ellen Tucker Emerson died 8th February. Tuesday morning . . .

3. "Let others wrangle, I will wonder." [*JMN*] St. Augustine, see n. 3, p. 174.

Five days are wasted since Ellen went to heaven to see, to know, to worship, to love, to intercede. God be merciful to me a sinner & repair this miserable debility in which her death has left my soul. Two nights since, I have again heard her breathing, seen her dying. O willingly, my wife, I would lie down in your tomb. But I have no deserts like yours, no such purity, or singleness of heart. Pray for me Ellen & raise the friend you so truly loved, to be what you thought him. When your friends or mine cross me, I comfort myself by saying, you would not have done so. Dear Ellen (for that is your name in heaven) shall we not be united even now more & more, as I more steadfastly persist in the love of truth & virtue which you loved? Spirits are not deceived & now you know the sins & selfishness which the husband would fain have concealed from the confiding wife—help me to be rid of them; suggest good thoughts as you promised me, & show me truth. Not for the world, would I have left you here alone; stay by me & lead me upward. Reunite us, o thou Father of our Spirits.

There is that which passes away & never returns. This miserable apathy, I know, may wear off. I almost fear when it will. Old duties will present themselves with no more repulsive face. I shall go again among my friends with a tranquil countenance. Again I shall be amused, I shall stoop again to little hopes & little fears & forget the graveyard. But will the dead be restored to me? Will the eye that was closed on Tuesday ever beam again in the fulness of love on me? Shall I ever again be able to connect the face of outward nature, the mists of the morn, the star of eve, the flowers, & all poetry, with the heart & life of an enchanting friend? No. There is one birth & one baptism & one first love and the affections cannot keep their youth any more than men.

Her end was blessed & a fit termination to such a career. She prayed that God would speedily release her from her body & that she might not make this prayer to be rid of her pains "but because thy favor is better than life." "Take me o God to thyself" was frequently on her lips. Never any one spake with greater simplicity or cheerfulness of dying. She said, 'I pray for sincerity & that I may not talk, but may realize what I say.' She did not think she had a wish to get well, & told me "she should do me more good by going than by staying; she should go first & explore the way, & comfort me." She prayed earnestly & suitably for me.

A little after 2 o'clock on Tuesday morn, she said she felt that she was going soon & having asked if Mother, Margaret, & Paulina were all present she wished them to be still & she would pray with them. And truly & sweetly did she pray for herself & for us & infused such comfort into my soul as never entered it before & I trust will never escape out of it. After this she kissed all, & bid her nurses, 'love God;' & then sunk very fast, occasionally recovering her wandering mind. One of the last things she said after much rambling & inarticulate expression was 'I have not forgot the peace & joy.' And at nine o'clock she died. Farewell blessed Spirit who hast made me happy in thy life & in thy death make me yet happy in thy disembodied state.

She frequently requested me that I would be with her when she died.

July 8, 1831

No man can write well who thinks there is any choice of words for him. The laws of composition are as strict as those of sculpture & architecture. There is always one line that ought to be drawn or one proportion that should be kept

& every other line or proportion is wrong, & so far wrong as it deviates from this. So in writing, there is always a right word, & every other than that is wrong. There is no beauty in words except in their collocation. The effect of a fanciful word misplaced is like that of a horn of exquisite polish growing on a human head.

Sept. 13, 1831

Education is the drawing out the Soul.

Jan. 10, 1832

It is the best part of the man, I sometimes think, that revolts most against his being the minister. His good revolts from official goodness. If he never spoke or acted but with the full consent of his understanding, if the whole man acted always, how powerful would be every act & every word. Well then or ill then how much power he sacrifices by conforming himself to say & do in other folks' time instead of in his own! The difficulty is that we do not make a world of our own but fall into institutions already made & have to accomodate ourselves to them to be useful at all. & this accommodation is, I say, a loss of so much integrity & of course of so much power.

Mar. 29, 1832

I visited Ellen's tomb & opened the coffin.

June 2, 1832

I have sometimes thought that in order to be a good minister it was necessary to leave the ministry. The profession is antiquated. In an altered age, we worship in the dead forms of our forefathers. Were not a Socratic paganism better than an effete superannuated Christianity?

Oct. 9? 1832

I will not live out of me
I will not see with others' eyes
My good is good, my evil ill
I would be free—I cannot be
While I take things as others please to rate them
I dare attempt to lay out my own road
That which myself delights in shall be Good
That which I do not want,—indifferent,
That which I hate is Bad. That's flat
Henceforth, please God, forever I forego
The yoke of men's opinions. I will be
Lighthearted as a bird & live with God.

Jan. 14, 1833

Well blithe traveller what cheer?
What have the sea & the stars & the moaning winds & your discontented thoughts sung in your attentive ears? Peeps up old Europe yet out of his eastern

main? hospitably ho! Nay the slumberous old giant cannot bestir himself in these his chair days to loom up for the pastime of his upstart grandchildren as now they come shoal after shoal to salute their old Progenitor, the old Adam of all. Sleep on, old Sire, there is muscle & nerve & enterprise enow in us your poor spawn who have sucked the air & ripened in the sunshine of the cold West to steer our ships to your very ports & thrust our inquisitive American eyes into your towns & towers & keeping-rooms. Here we come & mean to be welcome. So be good now, clever old gentleman.

Mar. 12, 1833

And what if it is Naples, it is only the same world of cake & ale—of man & truth & folly. I won't be imposed upon by a name. It is so easy, almost so inevitable to be overawed by names that on entering this bay it is hard to keep one's judgment upright, & be pleased only after your own way. Baiae & Misenum & Vesuvius, Procida & Pausilippo & Villa Reale sound so big that we are ready to surrender at discretion & not stickle for our private opinion against what seems the human race. Who cares? Here's for the plain old Adam, the simple genuine Self against the whole world. Need is, that you assert yourself or you will find yourself overborne by the most paltry things. . . .

Apr. 7–8, 1833

I love St Peter's Church. It grieves me that after a few days I shall see it no more. It has a peculiar smell from the quantity of incense burned in it. The music that is heard in it is always good & the eye is always charmed. It is an ornament of the earth. It is not grand, it is so rich & pleasing; it should rather be called the sublime of the beautiful.

Sept. 1, 1833 Liverpool

I thank the great God who has led me through this European scene, this last schoolroom in which he has pleased to instruct me from Malta's isle, thro' Sicily, thro' Italy, thro' Switzerland, thro' France, thro' England, thro' Scotland, in safety & pleasure & has now brought me to the shore & the ship that steers westward. He has shown me the men I wished to see—Landor, Coleridge, Carlyle, Wordsworth—he has thereby comforted & confirmed me in my convictions. Many things I owe to the sight of these men. I shall judge more justly, less timidly, of wise men forevermore. To be sure not one of these is a mind of the very first class, but what the intercourse with each of these suggests is true of intercourse with better men, that they never *fill the ear*—fill the mind—no, it is an *idealized* portrait which always we draw of them. Upon an intelligent man, wholly a stranger to their names, they would make in conversation no deep impression— none of a world-filling fame—they would be remembered as sensible well read earnest men—not more. Especially are they all deficient all these four—in different degrees but all deficient—in insight into religious truth. They have no idea of that species of moral truth which I call the first philosophy.

Sept. 6, 1833

Fair fine wind, still in the Channel—off the coast of Ireland but not in sight of land. This morning 37 sail in sight.

I like my book about nature & wish I knew where & how I ought to live. God will show me. I am glad to be on my way home yet not so glad as others & my way to the bottom I could find perchance with less regret for I think it would not hurt me, that is the ducking or drowning.

Sept. 11, 1833

I have been nihilizing as usual & just now posting my Italian journal. . . . Never was a regular dinner with all scientific accompaniments so philosophic a thing as at sea. I tipple with all my heart here. May I not?

Sept. 17, 1833

Milton describes himself in his letter to Diodati as enamoured of moral perfection. He did not love it more than I. That which I cannot yet declare has been my angel from childhood until now. It has separated me from men. It has watered my pillow; it has driven sleep from my bed. It has tortured me for my guilt. It has inspired me with hope. It cannot be defeated by my defeats. It cannot be questioned though all the martyrs apostatize. It is always the glory that shall be revealed; it is the 'open secret' of the universe; & it is only the feebleness & dust of the observer that makes it future, the whole *is* now potentially in the bottom of his heart. It is the soul of religion. Keeping my eye on this I understand all heroism, the history of loyalty & of martyrdom & of bigotry, the heat of the methodist, the nonconformity of the dissenter, the patience of the Quaker. But what shall the hour say for distinctions such as these—this hour of southwest gales & rain dripping cabin? As the law of light is fits of easy transmission & reflexion such is also the soul's law. She is only superior at intervals to pain, to fear, to temptation, only in raptures unites herself to God and Wordsworth truly said

> Tis the most difficult of tasks to keep
> Heights which the soul is competent to gain.

Nov.–Dec. 1833

This Book is my Savings Bank. I grow richer because I have somewhere to deposit my earnings; and fractions are worth more to me because corresponding fractions are waiting here that shall be made integers by their addition.

Feb. 12, 1834 New Bedford

The days & months & years flit by, each with his own black riband, his own sad reminiscence. Yet I looked at the Almanack affectionately as a book of Promise. These last three years of my life are not a chasm—I could almost wish they were—so brilliantly sometimes the vision of Ellen's beauty & love & life come out of the darkness. Pleasantly mingled with my sad thoughts the sublime religion of Miss Rotch yesterday. She was much disciplined, she said, in the years of Quaker dissension and driven inward, driven home, to find an anchor, until she learned to have *no choice*, to acquiesce without understanding the reason when she found an obstruction to any particular course of acting. She objected to having this spiritual direction called an impression, or an intimation, or an oracle. It was none of them. It was so simple it could hardly be spoken of . . .

Can you believe, Waldo Emerson, that you may relieve yourself of this perpetual perplexity of choosing? & by putting your ear close to the soul, learn always the true way.

Apr. 10, 1834

Is it possible that in the solitude I seek I shall have the resolution the force to work as I ought to work—as I project in highest most farsighted hours? Well, & what do you project? Nothing less than to look at every object in its relation to Myself.

Apr. 11, 1834

Went yesterday to Cambridge & spent most of the day at Mount Auburn, got my luncheon at Fresh Pond, & went back again to the woods. After much wandering & seeing many things, four snakes gliding up & down a hollow for no purpose that I could see—not to eat, not for love, but only gliding; then a whole bed of Hepatica triloba, cousins of the Anemone all blue & beautiful but constrained by niggard Nature to wear their last year's faded jacket of leaves; then a black capped titmouse who came upon a tree & when I would know his name, sang *chick a dee dee*; then a far off tree full of clamorous birds, I know not what, but you might hear them half a mile. I forsook the tombs & found a sunny hollow where the east wind could not blow & lay down against the side of a tree to most happy beholdings. At least I opened my eyes & let what would pass through them into the soul. I saw no more my relation how near & petty to Cambridge or Boston, I heeded no more what minute or hour our Massachusetts clocks might indicate—I saw only the noble earth on which I was born, with the great Star which warms & enlightens it. I saw the clouds that hang their significant drapery over us.—It was Day, that was all Heaven said. The pines glittered with their innumerable green needles in the light & seemed to challenge me to read their riddle. The drab-oak leaves of the last year turned their little somersets & lay still again. And the wind bustled high overhead in the forest top. This gay & grand architecture from the vault to the moss & lichen on which I lay, who shall explain to me the laws of its proportions & adornments?

Oct. 6, 1834

The high prize of eloquence may be mine, the joy of uttering what no other can utter & what all must receive.

Nov. 15, 1834

Hail to the quiet fields of my fathers! Not wholly unattended by supernatural friendship & favor let me come hither. Bless my purposes as they are simple & virtuous. . . . Henceforth I design not to utter any speech, poem, or book that is not entirely & peculiarly my work. I will say at Public Lectures & the like, those things which I have meditated for their own sake & not for the first time with a view to that occasion. If otherwise you select a new subject & labor to make a good appearance on the appointed day, it is so much lost time to you & lost time to your hearer. It is a parenthesis in your genuine life. You are your own dupe. & for the sake of conciliating your audience you have failed to edify them & winning their ear you have really lost their love and gratitude.

Nov. 21, 1834

When we have lost our God of tradition & ceased from our God of rhetoric then may God fire the heart with his presence.

Dec. 2, 1834 Concord

The age of puberty is a crisis in the life of the man worth studying. It is the passage from the Unconscious to the Conscious; from the sleep of the Passions to their rage; from careless receiving to cunning providing; from beauty to use; from omnivorous curiosity to anxious stewardship; from faith to doubt; from maternal Reason to hard short-sighted Understanding; from Unity to disunion . . .

Dec. 21, 1834

Blessed is the day when the youth discovers that Within and Above are synonyms.

Dec. 23, 1834

Do, dear, when you come to write Lyceum lectures, remember that you are not to say, What must be said in a Lyceum? but what discoveries or stimulating thoughts have I to impart to a thousand persons? not what they will expect to hear but what is fit for me to say.

Aug. 1, 1835

There sits the Sphinx from age to age, in the road Charles says, & every wise man has a crack with her. But this Oegger's plan & scope argue great boldness & manhood to depart thus widely from all routine & seek to put his hands like Atlas under Nature & heave her from her rest. Why the world exists & that it exists for a language or medium whereby God may speak to Man,—this is his query—this his answer.

May 13, 1835

What a benefit if a rule could be given whereby the mind could at any moment *east* itself, & find the sun. . . .

The truest state of mind, rested in, becomes false. Thought is the manna which cannot be stored. It will be sour if kept, & tomorrow must be gathered anew. Perpetually must we East ourselves, or we get into irrecoverable error, starting from the plainest truth & keeping as we think the straightest road of logic. It is by magnifying God, that men become Pantheists; it is by piously personifying him, that they become idolaters.

May 14, 1835

There is hardly a surer way to incur the censure of infidelity & irreligion than sincere faith and an entire devotion. For to the common eye, pews, vestries, family prayer, sanctimonious looks & words constitute religion, which the devout man would find hindrances. And so we go, trying always to weld the finite & infinite, the absolute & the seeming, together. On the contrary the manner in which religion is most positively affirmed by men of the world is barefaced skepticism.

When I write a book on spiritual things I think I will advertise the reader that I am a very wicked man, & that consistency is nowise to be expected of me.

* * *

When will you mend Montaigne? When will you take the hint of nature? Where are your Essays? Can you not express your one conviction that moral laws hold? Have you not thoughts & illustrations that are your own; the parable of geometry & matter; the reason why the atmosphere is transparent; the power of Composition in nature & in man's thoughts; the Uses & uselessness of travelling; the law of Compensation; the transcendant excellence of truth in character, in rhetoric, in things; the sublimity of Self-reliance; and the rewards of perseverance in the best opinion? Have you not a testimony to give for Shakspear, for Milton? one sentence of real praise of Jesus, is worth a century of legendary Christianity. Can you not write as though you wrote to yourself & drop the token assured that a wise hand will pick it up?

Aug. 1, 1835

After thirty a man wakes up sad every morning excepting perhaps five or six until the day of his death.

Sept. 14, 1835

I was married to Lydia Jackson.

Dec. 7? 1835

In Shakspear I actually shade my eyes as I read for the splendor of the thoughts.

Feb. 8? 1836

Women have less accurate measure of time than men. There is a clock in Adam: none in Eve.

Feb.–Mar. 1836

Strange is this alien despotism of Sleep which takes two persons lying in each other's arms & separates them leagues, continents, asunder.

July 1836

Make your own Bible. Select & Collect all those words & sentences that in all your reading have been to you like the blast of trumpet out of Shakspear, Seneca, Moses, John, & Paul.

Aug. 12, 1836

Yesterday Margaret Fuller returned home after making us a visit of three weeks—a very accomplished & very intelligent person.

Oct. 6, 1836

Transcendentalism means, says our accomplished Mrs B., with a wave of her hand, *A little beyond.*

Oct. 31, 1836

Last night at 11 o'clock, a son was born to me. Blessed child! a lovely wonder to me, and which makes the Universe look friendly to me. How remote from my knowledge, how alien, yet how kind does it make the Cause of Causes appear! The stimulated curiosity of the father sees the graces & instincts which exist, indeed, in every babe, but unnoticed in others; the right to see all, know all, to examine nearly, distinguishes this relation, & endears this sweet child. Otherwise I see nothing in it of mine; I am no conscious party to any feature, any function, any perfection I behold in it. I seem to be merely a brute occasion of its being & nowise attaining to the dignity even of a second cause no more than I taught it to suck the breast.

Please God, that "he, like a tree of generous kind, By living waters set," may draw endless nourishment from the fountains of Wisdom & Virtue!

Nov. 8, 1836

I dislike to hear the patronizing tone in which the self sufficient young men of the day talk of ministers "adapting their preaching to the great mass." Was the sermon good? "O yes, good for you & me, but not understood by the great mass." Don't you deceive yourself, say I, the great mass understand what's what, as well as the little mass. The self-conceit of this tone is not more provoking than the profound ignorance it argues is pitiable.

The fit attitude of a man is humble Wonder & gratitude, a meek watching of the marvels of the Creation to the end that he may know & do what is fit. But these pert gentlemen assume that the whole object is to manage "the great mass" & they forsooth are behind the curtain with the Deity and mean to help manage. They know all & will now smirk & manoeuvre & condescendingly yield the droppings of their wisdom to the poor people.

Jan. 14, 1837

Lidian's grandmother had a slave Phillis whom she freed. Phillis went to the little colony on the outside of Plymouth which they called New Guinea. Soon after, she visited her old mistress. "Well, Phillis, what did you have for dinner on Thanksgiving Day?" "Fried 'taturs, Missy;" replied Phillis. "And what had you to fry the potatoes in?" said Mrs Cotton. "Fried in Water, Missy;" answered the girl. "Well Phillis," said Mrs Cotton, "how can you bear to live up there, so poor, when here you used to have every thing comfortable, & such good dinner at Thanksgiving?" — "Ah Missy, Freedom's sweet," returned Phillis.

Jan. 25, 1837

This evening the heavens afford us the most remarkable spectacle of Aurora Borealis. A deep red plume in the East & west streaming almost from the horizon to the zenith, forming at the zenith a sublime coronet; the stars peep delicately through the ruddy folds & the whole landscape below covered with snow is crimsoned. The light meantime equal nearly to that of full moon, although the moon was not risen.

Feb. 1837

In these Lectures which from week to week I read, each on a topic which is a main interest of man, & may be made an object of exclusive interest I seem to vie with the brag of Puck[4] "I can put a girdle round about the world in forty minutes." I take fifty.

Apr. 8, 1837

Ah! my darling boy, so lately received out of heaven leave me not now! Please God, this sweet symbol of love & wisdom may be spared to rejoice, teach, & accompany me.

Apr. 22, 1837

There is a crack in every thing God has made. Fine weather! — yes but cold. Warm day! — 'yes but dry.' — 'You look well' — 'I am very well except a little cold.' The case of damaged hats — one a broken brim; the other perfect in the rim, but rubbed on the side; the third whole in the cylinder, but bruised on the crown.

May 26, 1837

Who shall define to me an Individual? I behold with awe & delight many illustrations of the One Universal Mind. I see my being imbedded in it. As a plant in the earth so I grow in God. I am only a form of him. He is the soul of Me. I can even with a mountainous aspiring say, *I am God*, by transferring my *Me* out of the flimsy & unclean precincts of my body, my fortunes, my private will, & meekly retiring upon the holy austerities of the Just & the Loving — upon the secret fountains of Nature. That thin & difficult ether, I also can breathe. The mortal lungs & nostrils burst & shrivel, but the soul itself needeth no organs — it is all element & all organ. Yet why not always so? How came the Individual thus armed & impassioned to parricide, thus murderously inclined ever to traverse & kill the divine life? Ah wicked Manichee![5] Into that dim problem I cannot enter. A believer in Unity, a seer of Unity, I yet behold two.

I behold; I bask in beauty; I await; I wonder; Where is my Godhead now? This is the Male & Female principle in Nature. One Man, male & female created he him. Hard as it is to describe God, it is harder to describe the Individual.

A certain wandering light comes to me which I instantly perceive to be the Cause of Causes. It transcends all proving. It is itself the ground of being; and I see that it is not one & I another, but this is the life of my life. That is one fact, then; that in certain moments I have known that I existed directly from God, and am, as it were, his organ. And in my ultimate consciousness Am He. Then, secondly, the contradictory fact is familiar, that I am a surprised spectator & learner of all my life. This is the habitual posture of the mind — beholding. But whenever the day dawns, the great day of truth on the soul, it comes with awful invitation to me to accept it, to blend with its aurora.

Cannot I conceive the Universe without a contradiction?

---

4. A mischievous sprite in Shakepeare's *A Midsummer Night's Dream*. The line actually reads "I'll put a girdle round about the earth / In forty minutes" (2.1.175–76).
5. See n. 2, p. 48.

Sept. 19? 1837

On the 29 August, I received a letter from the Salem Lyceum signed I.F. Worcester, requesting me to lecture before the institution next winter and adding "The subject is of course discretionary with yourself 'provided no allusions are made to religious controversy, or other exciting topics upon which the public mind is honestly divided.'" I replied on the same day to Mr W. by quoting these words & adding "I am really sorry that any person in Salem should think me capable of accepting an invitation so encumbered."

Oct. 20, 1837

Margaret Fuller talking of Women, said, "Who would be a goody that could be a genius?"

Oct 21, 1837

I said when I awoke, After some more sleepings & wakings I shall lie on this mattrass sick; then, dead; and through my gay entry they will carry these bones. Where shall I be then? I lifted my head and beheld the spotless orange light of the morning beaming up from the dark hills into the wide Universe.

Oct. 21–22, 1837

A man may find his words mean more than he thought when he uttered them & be glad to employ them again in a new sense.

Feb. 9–10, 1838

You must love me as I am. Do not tell me how much I should love you. I am content. I find my satisfactions in a calm considerate reverence measured by the virtues which provoke it. So love me as I am. When I am virtuous, love me; when I am vicious, hate me; when I am lukewarm, neither good nor bad, care not for me.

But do not by your sorrow or your affection solicit me to be somewhat else than I by nature am.

Feb. 17, 1838

My good Henry Thoreau made this else solitary afternoon sunny with his simplicity & clear perception. How comic is simplicity in this doubledealing quacking world. Every thing that boy says makes merry with society though nothing can be graver than his meaning. I told him he should write out the history of his College life as Carlyle has his tutoring. We agreed that the seeing the stars through a telescope would be worth all the Astronomical lectures. Then he described Mr Quimby's electrical lecture here[6] & the experiment of the shock & added that "College Corporations are very blind to the fact that that twinge in the elbow is worth all the lecturing."

Apr. 1, 1838

Cool or cold windy clear day. The Divinity School youths wished to talk with me concerning theism. I went rather heavyhearted for I always find that

---

6. See Emerson's letter to Margaret Fuller, March 14, 1841 (p. 550).

my views chill or shock people at the first opening. But the conversation went well & I came away cheered. I told them that the preacher should be a poet smit with love of the harmonies of moral nature: and yet look at the Unitarian Association & see if its aspect is poetic. They all smiled No. A minister nowadays is plainest prose, the prose of prose. He is a Warming-pan, a Night-chair at sick beds & rheumatic souls; and the fire of the minstrel's eye & the vivacity of his word is exchanged for intense grumbling enunciation of the Cambridge sort, & for scripture phraseology.

Apr. 23, 1838

This tragic Cherokee business[7] which we stirred at a meeting in the church yesterday will look to me degrading & injurious do what I can. It is like dead cats around one's neck. It is like School Committees & Sunday School classes & Teacher's meetings & the Warren street chapel & all the other holy hurrahs. I stir in it for the sad reason that no other mortal will move & if I do not, why it is left undone.

The amount of it, be sure, is merely a Scream but sometimes a scream is better than a thesis.

June 21, 1838

They call it Christianity, I call it Consciousness.

June 23, 1838

I hate goodies. I hate goodness that preaches. Goodness that preaches undoes itself. A little electricity of virtue lurks here & there in kitchens & among the obscure — chiefly women, that flashes out occasional light & makes the existence of the thing still credible. But one had as lief curse & swear as be guilty of this odious religion that watches the beef & watches the cider in the pitcher at table, that shuts the mouth hard at any remark it cannot twist nor wrench into a sermon, & preaches as long as itself & its hearer is awake. Goodies make us very bad. We should, if the race should increase, be scarce restrained from calling for bowl & dagger. We will almost sin to spite them. Better indulge yourself, feed fat, drink liquors, than go strait laced for such cattle as these.

Oct. 12, 1838

It seems not unfit that the Scholar should deal plainly with society & tell them that he saw well enough before he spoke the consequence of his speaking, that up there in his silent study by his dim lamp he foreheard this Babel of outcries. The nature of man he knew, the insanity that comes of inaction & tradition, & knew well that when their dream & routine were disturbed, like bats & owls & nocturnal beasts they would howl & shriek & fly at the torch bearer. But he saw plainly that under this their distressing disguise of bird-form & beast-form, the divine features of man were hidden, & he felt that he would dare to be so much their friend as to do them this violence to drag them to the day & to the healthy air & water of God, that the unclean spirits that had possessed them might be exorcised & depart. The taunts & cries of hatred & anger, the

7. See Emerson's letter to President Martin Van Buren, April 23, 1838 (p. 542).

very epithets you bestow on me are so familiar long ago in my reading that they sound to me ridiculously old & stale. The same thing has happened so many times over, (that is, with the appearance of every original observer) that if people were not very ignorant of literary history they would be struck with the exact coincidence. And whilst I see this that you must have been shocked & must cry out at what I have said I see too that we cannot easily be reconciled for I have a great deal more to say that will shock you out of all patience.

Oct. 20, 1838

What said my brave Asia [Lidian] concerning the paragraph writers, today? that "this whole practice of self justification & recrimination betwixt literary men seemed every whit as low as the quarrels of the Paddies." Then said I, But what will you say, excellent Asia, when my smart article comes out in the paper, in reply to Mr A & Dr B? "Why, then," answered she, "I shall feel the first emotion of fear & of sorrow on your account." But do you know, I asked, how many fine things I have thought of to say to these fighters? They are too good to be lost.—"Then" rejoined the queen, "there is some merit in being silent."

* * *

It is plain from all the noise that there is Atheism somewhere. The only question is now, Which is the Atheist?

Nov. 8, 1838

Let me never fall into the vulgar mistake of dreaming that I am persecuted whenever I am contradicted. No man, I think, had ever a greater well being with a less desert than I. I can very well afford to be accounted bad or foolish by a few dozen or a few hundred persons—I who see myself greeted by the good expectation of so many friends far beyond any power of thought or communication of thought residing in me. Besides, I own, I am often inclined to take part with those who say I am bad or foolish, for I fear I am both. I believe & know there must be a perfect compensation. I know too well my own dark spots. Not having myself attained, not satisfied myself, far from a holy obedience—how can I expect to satisfy others, to command their love? A few sour faces, a few biting paragraphs—is but a cheap expiation for all these shortcomings of mine.

Nov. 10–11, 1838

My brave Henry Thoreau walked with me to Walden this P.M. and complained of the proprietors who compelled him to whom as much as to any the whole world belonged, to walk in a strip of road & crowded him out of all the rest of God's earth. He must not get over the fence: but to the building of that fence he was no party. Suppose, he said, some great proprietor, before he was born, had bought up the whole globe. So had he been hustled out of nature. Not having been privy to any of these arrangements he does not feel called on to consent to them & so cuts fishpoles in the woods without asking who has a better title to the wood than he. I defended of course the good Institution as a scheme not good but the best that could be hit on for making the woods & waters & fields available to Wit & Worth, & for restraining the bold bad man. At all events, I begged him, having this maggot of Freedom & Humanity in his brain, to write it out into good poetry & so clear himself of it. . . .

Apr. 17, 1839

Am I a hypocrite who am disgusted by vanity everywhere, & preach self trust every day?

June 6, 1839

My life is a May game, I will live as I like. I defy your straitlaced, weary, social ways and modes. Blue is the sky, green the fields and groves, fresh the springs, glad the rivers, and hospitable the splendor of sun and star. I will play my game out. And if any shall say me nay, shall come out with swords and staves against me to prick me to death for their foolish laws,—come and welcome. I will not look grave for such a fool's matter. I cannot lose my cheer for such trumpery. Life is a May game still.

June 27, 1839

Rhyme.—Rhyme; not tinkling rhyme, but grand Pindaric strokes, as firm as the tread of a horse. Rhyme that vindicates itself as an art, the stroke of the bell of a cathedral. Rhyme which knocks at prose and dullness with the stroke of a cannon ball. Rhyme which builds out into Chaos and old night a splendid architecture to bridge the impassable, and call aloud on all the children of morning that the Creation is recommencing. I wish to write such rhymes as shall not suggest a restraint, but contrariwise the wildest freedom.

July 5–6, 1839

Why should we write dramas, & epics, & sonnets, & novels in two volumes? Why not write as variously as we dress & think? A lecture is a new literature, which leaves aside all tradition, time, place, circumstance, & addresses an assembly as mere human beings—no more—It has never yet been done well. It is an organ of sublime power, a panharmonicon for variety of note. But only then is the orator successful when he is himself agitated & is as much a hearer as any of the assembly. In that office you may & shall (please God!) yet see the electricity part from the cloud & shine from one part of heaven to the other.

Sept. 14, 1839

Education. . . . We all are involved in the condemnation of words, an Age of words. We are shut up in schools & college recitation rooms for ten or fifteen years & come out at last with a bellyful of words & do not know a thing. We cannot use our hands or our legs or our eyes or our arms. We do not know an edible root in the woods. We cannot tell our course by the stars nor the hour of the day by the sun. It is well if we can swim & skate. We are afraid of a horse, of a cow, of a dog, of a cat, of a spider. Far better was the Roman rule to teach a boy nothing that he could not learn standing. Now here are my wise young neighbors who instead of getting like the wordmen into a railroad-car, where they have not even the activity of holding the reins, have got into a boat which they have built with their own hands with sails which they have contrived to serve as a tent by night, & gone up the river Merrimack to live by their wits on the fish of the stream & the berries of the wood. . . . The farm the farm is the right school. . . . The farm by training the physical rectifies & invigorates the metaphysical & moral nature.

Now so bad we are that the world is stripped of love & of terror. Here came the other night an Aurora so wonderful, a curtain of red & blue & silver glory, that in any other age or nation it would have moved the awe & wonder of men & mingled with the profoundest sentiments of religion & love & we all saw it with cold arithmetical eyes, we knew how many colours shone, how many degrees it extended, how many hours it lasted, & of this heavenly flower we beheld nothing more: a primrose by the brim of the river of time. . . .

I lament that I find in me no enthusiasm, no resources for the instruction & guidance of the people when they shall discover that their present guides are blind. This convention of Education is cold, but I should perhaps affect a hope I do not feel if I were bidden to counsel it. I hate preaching whether in pulpits or Teachers' meetings. Preaching is a pledge & I wish to say that I think & feel today with the proviso that tomorrow perhaps I shall contradict it all. Freedom boundless I wish. I will not pledge myself not to drink wine, not to drink ink, not to lie, & not to commit adultery lest I hanker tomorrow to do these very things by reason of my having tied my hands. Besides Man is so poor he cannot afford to part with any advantages or bereave himself of the functions even of one hair. I do not like to speak to the Peace society if so I am to restrain me in so extreme a privilege as the use of the sword & bullet. For the peace of the man who has forsworn the use of the bullet seems to me not quite peace, but a canting impotence: but with knife & pistol in my hands, if I, from greater bravery & honor, cast them aside, then I know the glory of Peace.

Oct. 18, 1839

In these golden days it behoves me once more to make my annual inventory of the world. For the five last years I have read each winter a new course of lectures in Boston, and each was my creed & confession of faith. Each told all I thought of the past, the present, & the future. Once more I must renew my work and I think only once in the same form though I see that he who thinks he does something for the last time ought not to do it at all. Yet my objection is not to the thing but to the form; & the concatenation of errors called *society* to which I still consent, until my plumes be grown, makes even a duty of this concession also. So I submit to sell tickets again. But the form is neither here nor there. What shall be the substance of my shrift? Adam in the garden, I am to new name all the beasts in the field & all the gods in the Sky. I am to invite men drenched in time to recover themselves & come out of time, & taste their native immortal air. I am to fire with what skill I can the artillery of sympathy & emotion. I am to indicate constantly, though all unworthy, the Ideal and Holy Life, the life within life—the Forgotten Good, the Unknown Cause in which we sprawl & sin. I am to try the magic of sincerity, that luxury permitted only to kings & poets. I am to celebrate the spiritual powers in their infinite contrast to the mechanical powers & the mechanical philosophy of this time. I am to console the brave sufferers under evils whose end they cannot see by appeals to the great optimism self-affirmed in all bosoms.

Nov. 13, 1839

Do something, it matters little or not at all whether it be in the way of what you call your profession or not, so it be in the plane or coincident with the axis of your character. The reaction is always proportioned to the action, and it is the reaction that we want. Strike the hardest blow you can, & you can always do this by work which is agreeable to your nature. This is economy.

Dec. 22? 1839

Treat things poetically. Every thing should be treated poetically—law, politics, housekeeping, money.

Dec. 1839

I say how the world looks to me without reference to Blair's Rhetoric or Johnson's Lives. And I call my thoughts The Present Age, because I use no will in the matter, but honestly record such impressions as things make. So transform I myself into a Dial, and my shadow will tell where the sun is.

Feb. 19, 1840

I closed last Wednesday, 12th instant, my Course of Lectures in Boston, "On the Present Age" . . .

These lectures give me little pleasure. I have not done what I hoped when I said, I will try it once more. I have not once transcended the coldest selfpossession. I said I will agitate others, being agitated myself. I dared to hope for extacy & eloquence. A new theatre, a new art, I said, is mine. Let us see if philosophy, if ethics, if chiromancy, if the discovery of the divine in the house & the barn, in all works & all plays, cannot make the cheek blush, the lip quiver, & the tear start. I will not waste myself. On the strength of Things I will be borne, and try if Folly, Custom, Convention, & Phlegm cannot be made to hear our sharp artillery. Alas! alas! I have not the recollection of one strong moment. A cold mechanical preparation for a delivery as decorous—fine things, pretty things, wise things—but no arrows, no axes, no nectar, no growling, no transpiercing, no loving, no enchantment.

And why?

I seem to lack constitutional vigor to attempt each topic as I ought. I ought to seek to lay myself out utterly—large, enormous, prodigal, upon the subject of the week. But a hateful experience has taught me that I can only expend, say, twenty one hours on each lecture, if I would also be ready & able for the next. Of course, I spend myself prudently; I economize; I cheapen: whereof nothing grand ever grew. Could I spend sixty hours on each, or what is better, had I such energy that I could rally the lights & mights of sixty hours into twenty, I should hate myself less, I should help my friend.

Apr. 7? 1840

In all my lectures, I have taught one doctrine, namely, the infinitude of the private man. This, the people accept readily enough, & even with loud commendation, as long as I call the lecture, Art; or Politics; or Literature; or the Household; but the moment I call it Religion—they are shocked, though it be only the application of the same truth which they receive everywhere else, to a new class of facts.

June 1–3, 1840

Our American letters are, we confess, in the optative mood; but whoso knows these seething brains, these admirable radical projects, these talkers who talk the sun & moon away will believe that this generation cannot pass away without leaving its mark.

June 24–28, 1840

The language of the street is always strong. What can describe the folly & emptiness of scolding like the word *jawing?* I feel too the force of the double negative, though clean contrary to our grammar rules. And I confess to some pleasure from the stinging rhetoric of a rattling oath in the mouth of truckmen & teamsters. How laconic & brisk it is by the side of a page of the North American Review. Cut these words & they would bleed; they are vascular & alive; they walk & run. Moreover they who speak them have this elegancy, that they do not trip in their speech. It is a shower of bullets, whilst Cambridge men & Yale men correct themselves & begin again at every half sentence. I know nobody among my contemporaries except Carlyle who writes with any sinew & vivacity comparable to Plutarch & Montaigne. Yet always this profane swearing & bar-room wit has salt & fire in it. . . . *Guts* is a stronger word than intestines.

Sept. 26, 1840

You would have me love you. What shall I love? Your body? The supposition disgusts you. What you have thought & said? Well, whilst you were thinking & saying them, but not now. I see no possibility of loving any thing but what now is, & is becoming; your courage, your enterprize, your budding affection, your opening thought, your prayer, I can love—but what else?

Oct. 7, 1840

I have been writing with some pains Essays on various matters as a sort of apology to my country for my apparent idleness. But the poor work has looked poorer daily as I strove to end it. My genius seemed to quit me in such a mechanical work, a seeming wise—a cold exhibition of dead thoughts. When I write a letter to any one whom I love, I have no lack of words or thoughts: I am wiser than myself & read my paper with the pleasure of one who receives a letter, but what I write to fill up the gaps of a chapter is hard & cold, is grammar & logic; there is no magic in it; I do not wish to see it again. Settle with yourself your accusations of me. If I do not please you, ask me not to please you, but please yourself. What you call my indolence, nature does not accuse; the twinkling leaves, the sailing fleets of waterflies, the deep sky like me well enough and know me for their own. With them I have no embarrassments, diffidences, or compunctions: with them I mean to stay. You think it is because I have an income which exempts me from your day-labor, that I waste (as you call it) my time in sungazing & stargazing. You do not know me. If my debts, as they threaten, should consume what money I have, I should live just as I do now: I should eat worse food & wear a coarser coat and should wonder in a potato patch instead of in the wood—but it is I & not my Twelve Hundred dollars a year, that love God.

Oct. 17, 1840

Yesterday George & Sophia Ripley, Margaret Fuller & Alcott[8] discussed here the new social plans. I wished to be convinced, to be thawed, to be made nobly mad by the kindlings before my eye of a new dawn of human piety. But this scheme was arithmetic & comfort; this was a hint borrowed from the Tremont House & U.S. Hotel; a rage in our poverty & politics to live rich & gentlemanlike, an anchor to leeward against a change of weather; a prudent forecast on the probable issue of the great questions of pauperism & property. And not once could I be inflamed—but sat aloof & thoughtless, my voice faltered & fell. It was not the cave of persecution which is the palace of spiritual power, but only a room in the Astor House hired for the Transcendentalists. I do not wish to remove from my present prison to a prison a little larger. I wish to break all prisons. I have not yet conquered my own house. It irks & repents me. Shall I raise the siege of this hencoop & march baffled away to a pretended siege of Babylon? It seems to me that so to do were to dodge the problem I am set to solve, & to hide my impotency in the thick of a crowd. I can see too afar that I should not find myself more than now—no, not so much, in that select, but not by me selected, fraternity. Moreover to join this body would be to traverse all my long trumpeted theory, and the instinct which spoke from it, that one man is a counterpoise to a city—that a man is stronger than a city, that his solitude is more prevalent & beneficent than the concert of crowds.

Oct. 25, 1840

What a pity that we cannot curse & swear in good society. Cannot the stinging dialect of the sailors be domesticated? It is the best rhetoric and for a hundred occasions those forbidden words are the only good ones. My page about "Consistency" would be better written thus; Damn Consistency. And to how many foolish canting remarks would a sophomore's ejaculation be the only suitable reply, "The devil you do;" or, "You be damned."

I dreamed that I floated at will in the great Ether, and I saw this world floating also not far off, but diminished to the size of an apple. Then an angel took it in his hand & brought it to me and said "This must thou eat." And I ate the world.

Dec. ? 1840

A droll dream last night, whereat I ghastly laughed. A congregation assembled, like some of our late Conventions, to debate the Institution of Marriage; & grave & alarming objections stated on all hands to the usage; when one speaker at last rose & began to reply to the arguments, but suddenly extended his hand & turned on the audience the spout of an engine which was copiously supplied from within the wall with water & whisking it vigorously about, up, down, right, & left, he drove all the company in crowds hither & thither & out of the house. Whilst I stood watching astonished & amused at the malice & vigor of the orator, I saw the spout lengthened by a supply of hose behind, & the man suddenly brought it round a corner & drenched me as I gazed. I woke up relieved to find myself quite dry, and well convinced that the Institution of Marriage was safe for tonight.

8. See n. 3, p. 52. This entry refers to Brook Farm; see n. 1, p. 203.

Jan. 1, 1841

I begin the year by sending my little book of Essays to the press. What remains to be done to its imperfect chapters I will seek to do justly. I see no reason why we may not write with as much grandeur of spirit as we can serve or suffer. Let the page be filled with the character not with the skill of the writer.

Mar.? 1841

Away with your prismatics, I want a spermatic book. Plato, Plotinus, & Plutarch are such.

June–July, 1841

I think that only is real which men love & rejoice in—not the things which starve & freeze & terrify them.

Sept.? 1841

I told H.T. [Henry Thoreau] that his freedom is in the form, but he does not disclose new matter. I am very familiar with all his thoughts—they are my own quite originally drest. But if the question be, what new ideas has he thrown into circulation, he has not yet told what that is which he was created to say. I said to him what I often feel, I only know three persons who seem to me fully to see this law of reciprocity or compensation—himself, Alcott, & myself: and 'tis odd that we should all be neighbors, for in the wide land or the wide earth I do not know another who seems to have it as deeply & originally as these three Gothamites.

Oct. 12, 1841

I would that I could, I know afar off that I cannot give the lights & shades, the hopes & outlooks that come to me in these strange, cold-warm, attractive-repelling conversations with Margaret [Fuller], whom I always admire, most revere when I nearest see, and sometimes love, yet whom I freeze, & who freezes me to silence, when we seem to promise to come nearest. Yet perhaps my old motto holds true here also
"And the more falls I get, move faster on."

Oct. 23, 1841

I think Society has the highest interest in seeing that this movement called the Transcendental is no boys' play or girls' play but has an interest very near & dear to them. That it has a necessary place in history is a Fact not to be overlooked, not possibly to be prevented, and however discredited to the heedless & to the moderate & conservative persons by the foibles or inadequacy of those who partake the movement yet is it the pledge & the herald of all that is dear to the human heart, grand & inspiring to human faith.

I think the genius of this age more philosophical than any other has been, righter in its aims, truer, with less fear, less fable, less mixture of any sort.

Jan. 28, 1842

Yesterday night at 15 minutes after eight my little Waldo ended his life.

Jan. 30, 1842

What he looked upon is better, what he looked not upon is insignificant. The morning of Friday I woke at 3 oclock, & every cock in every barnyard was shrilling with the most unnecessary noise. The sun went up the morning sky with all his light, but the landscape was dishonored by this loss. For this boy in whose remembrance I have both slept & awaked so oft, decorated for me the morning star, & the evening cloud, how much more all the particulars of daily economy; for he had touched with his lively curiosity every trivial fact & circumstance in the household, the hard coal & the soft coal which I put into my stove; the wood of which he brought his little quota for grandmother's fire, the hammer, the pincers, & file, he was so eager to use; the microscope, the magnet, the little globe, & every trinket & instrument in the study; the loads of gravel on the meadow, the nests in the henhouse and many & many a little visit to the doghouse and to the barn—For every thing he had his own name & way of thinking, his own pronunciation & manner. And every word came mended from that tongue. A boy of early wisdom, of a grave & even majestic deportment, of a perfect gentleness.

Every tramper that ever tramped is abroad but the little feet are still.

He gave up his little innocent breath like a bird.

He dictated a letter to his cousin Willie on Monday night to thank him for the Magic Lantern which he had sent him, and said I wish you would tell Cousin Willie that I have so many presents that I do not need that he should send me any more unless he wishes to very much.

The boy had his full swing in this world. Never I think did a child enjoy more. He had been thoroughly respected by his parents & those around him & not interfered with; and he had been the most fortunate in respect to the influences near him for his Aunt Elizabeth [Hoar] had adopted him from his infancy & treated him ever with that plain & wise love which belongs to her and, as she boasted, had never given him sugar plums. So he was won to her & always signalized her arrival as a visit to him & left playmates playthings & all to go to her. Then Mary Russell had been his friend & teacher for two summers with true love & wisdom. Then Henry Thoreau had been one of the family for the last year, & charmed Waldo by the variety of toys whistles boats popguns & all kinds of instruments which he could make & mend; & possessed his love & respect by the gentle firmness with which he always treated him. Margaret Fuller & Caroline Sturgis had also marked the boy & caressed & conversed with him whenever they were here. Meantime every day his Grandmother gave him his reading lesson & had by patience taught him to read & spell; by patience & by love for she loved him dearly.

Sorrow makes us all children again, destroys all differences of intellect. The wisest knows nothing.

Feb. 21, 1842

Home again from Providence to the deserted house. Dear friends find I, but the wonderful Boy is gone. What a looking for miracles have I! As his walking into the room where we are, would not suprise Ellen [Waldo's sister], so it would seem to me the most natural of all things.

Mar. 23, 1842

Ellen asks her Grandmother "whether God can't stay alone with the angels a little while & let Waldo come down?"

And Amy Goodwin too thinks that "if God has to send any angel for anything to this world, he had better send Waldo."

The chrysalis which he brought in with care & tenderness & gave to his Mother to keep is still alive and he most beautiful of the children of men is not here.

I comprehend nothing of this fact but its bitterness. Explanation I have none, consolation none that rises out of the fact itself; only diversion; only oblivion of this & pursuit of new objects.

Apr. 6–12, 1842

The history of Christ is the best document of the power of Character which we have. A youth who owed nothing to fortune & who was "hanged at Tyburn"—by the pure quality of his nature has shed this epic splendor around the facts of his death which has transfigured every particular into a grand universal symbol for the eyes of all mankind ever since.

He did well. This great Defeat is hitherto the highest fact we have. But he that shall come shall do better. The mind requires a far higher exhibition of character, one which shall make itself good to the senses as well as to the soul; a success to the senses as well as to the soul. This was a great Defeat. We demand Victory. More character will convert judge & jury, soldier & king; will rule human & animal & mineral nature; will command irresistibly and blend with the course of Universal Nature.

In short there ought to be no such thing as Fate. As long as we use this word, it is a sign of our impotence & that we are not yet ourselves. There is now a sublime revelation in each of us which makes us so strangely aware & certain of our riches that although I have never since I was born for so much as one moment expressed the truth, and although I have never heard the expression of it from any other, I know that the whole is here—the wealth of the Universe is for me. Every thing is explicable & practicable for me. And yet whilst I adore this ineffable life which is at my heart, it will not condescend to gossip with me, it will not announce to me any particulars of science, it will not enter into the details of my biography, & say to me why I have a son & daughters born to me, or why my son dies in his sixth year of joy. Herein then I have this latent omniscience coexistent with omnignorance. Moreover, whilst this Deity glows at the heart, & by his unlimited presentiments gives me all power, I know that tomorrow will be as this day, I am a dwarf, & I remain a dwarf. That is to say, I believe in Fate. As long as I am weak, I shall talk of Fate; whenever the God fills me with his fulness, I shall see the disappearance of Fate.

I am *Defeated* all the time; yet to Victory I am born.

Apr. 14, 1842

If I should write an honest diary what should I say? Alas that Life has halfness, shallowness. I have almost completed thirty nine years and I have not yet adjusted my relation to my fellows on the planet, or to my own work. Always too young or too old, I do not satisfy myself; how can I satisfy others?

Apr. 1842

I am not united, I am not friendly to myself, I bite & tear myself. I am ashamed of myself. When will the day dawn of peace & reconcilement when self-united & friendly I shall display one heart & energy to the world?

Dec. 1842–Jan. 1843

First we eat, then we beget; first we read, then we write; have you a better appetite? then you will do well. I have no thoughts today; What then? What difference does it make? It is only that there does not chance today to be an antagonism to evolve them, the electricity is the more accumulated, & a week hence you shall meet somebody or some thing that shall draw from you a shower of sparks.

Mar. ? 1843

"Dear husband, I wish I had never been born. I do not see how God can compensate me for the sorrow of existence."[9]

Mar.–Apr. 1843

Margaret. A pure & purifying mind, selfpurifying also, full of faith in men, & inspiring it. Unable to find any companion great enough to receive the rich effusions of her thought, so that her riches are still unknown & seem unknowable. It is a great joy to find that we have underrated our friend, that he or she is far more excellent than we had thought. All natures seem poor beside one so rich, which pours a stream of amber over all objects clean & unclean that lie in its path, and makes that comely & presentable which was mean in itself. We are taught by her plenty how lifeless & outward we were, what poor Laplanders burrowing under the snows of prudence & pedantry. Beside her friendship, other friendships seem trade, and by the firmness with which she treads her upward path, all mortals are convinced that another road exists than that which their feet know. The wonderful generosity of her sentiments pours a contempt on books & writing at the very time when one asks how shall this fiery picture be kept in its glow & variety for other eyes. She excels other intellectual persons in this, that her sentiments are more blended with her life; so the expression of them has greater steadiness & greater clearness. I have never known any example of such steady progress from stage to stage of thought & of character. An inspirer of courage, the secret friend of all nobleness, the patient waiter for the realization of character, forgiver of injuries, gracefully waiving aside folly, & elevating lowness—in her presence all were apprised of their fettered estate & longed for liberation, of ugliness & longed for their beauty; of meanness, & panted for grandeur.

Her growth is visible. All the persons whom we know, have reached their height, or else their growth is so nearly at the same rate with ours, that it is imperceptible, but this child inspires always more faith in her. She rose before me at times into heroical & godlike regions, and I could remember no superior women, but thought of Ceres, Minerva, Proserpine, and the august ideal forms of the Foreworld. She said that no man gave such invitation to her mind as to tempt her to a full expression; that she felt a power to enrich her thought with

9. This entry has been heavily cancelled.

such wealth & variety of embellishment as would no doubt be tedious to such as she conversed with. And there is no form that does seem to wait her beck— dramatic, lyric, epic, passionate, pictorial, humourous.

She has great sincerity, force, & fluency as a writer, yet her powers of speech throw her writing into the shade. What method, what exquisite judgment, as well as energy, in the selection of her words, what character & wisdom they convey! You cannot predict her opinion. She sympathizes so fast with all forms of life, that she talks never narrowly or hostilely nor betrays, like all the rest, under a thin garb of new words, the old droning castiron opinions or notions of many years standing. What richness of experience, what newness of dress, and fast as Olympus to her principle. And a silver eloquence, which inmost Polymnia taught. Meantime, all the pathos of sentiment and riches of literature & of invention and this march of character threatening to arrive presently at the shores & plunge into the sea of Buddhism & mystic trances, consists with a boundless fun & drollery, with light satire, & the most entertaining conversation in America.

* * *

E. H.[1] says, "I love Henry [David Thoreau], but do not like him." Young men like Henry Thoreau owe us a new world & they have not acquitted the debt: for the most part, such die young, & so dodge the fulfilment. One of our girls . . . said, that Henry never went through the kitchen without colouring.

May–June, 1843

It is greatest to believe & to hope well of the world, because he who does so, quits the world of experience, & makes the world he lives in.

Aug.–Sept. 1843

H.D.T. sends me a paper with the old fault of unlimited contradiction. The trick of his rhetoric is soon learned. It consists in substituting for the obvious word & thought its diametrical antagonist. He praises wild mountains & winter forests for their domestic air; snow & ice for their warmth; villagers & wood choppers for their urbanity; and the wilderness for resembling Rome & Paris. With the constant inclination to dispraise cities & civilization, he yet can find no way to honour woods & woodmen except by paralleling them with towns & townsmen. W. E. C.[2] declares the piece is excellent: but it makes me nervous & wretched to read it, with all its merits.

* * *

Never strike a king unless you are sure you shall kill him.

Jan. 30, 1844

I wrote to M. F. [Margaret Fuller] that I had no experiences nor progress to reconcile me to the calamity whose anniversary returned the second time last Saturday. The senses have a right to their method as well as the mind; there should be harmony in facts as well as in truths. Yet these ugly breaks happen

---

1. Elizabeth Hoar, a close friend of the family, had been engaged to marry Emerson's brother Charles.
2. William Ellery Channing Jr., see n. 7, p. 247; he was married to Margaret Fuller's sister.

there, which the continuity of theory does not compensate. The amends are of a different kind from the mischief.

Jan.–Mar. 1844

When I address a large assembly, as last Wednesday, I am always apprised what an opportunity is there: not for reading to them as I do, lively miscellanies, but for painting in fire my thought, & being agitated to agitate. One must dedicate himself to it and think with his audience in his mind, so as to keep the perspective & symmetry of the oration, and enter into all the easily forgotten secrets of a great nocturnal assembly & their relation to the speaker. But it would be fine music & in the present well rewarded; that is, he should have his audience at his devotion and all other fames would hush before his. Now eloquence is merely fabulous. When we talk of it, we draw on our fancy. It is one of many things which I should like to do, but it requires a seven years' wooing.

*　*　*

Precisely what the painter or the sculptor or the epic rhapsodist feels, I feel in the presence of this house, which stands to me for the human race, the desire, namely, to express myself fully, symmetrically, gigantically to them, not dwarfishly & fragmentarily. H.D.T., with whom I talked of this last night, does not or will not perceive how natural is this, and only hears the word Art in a sinister sense. But I speak of instincts. I did not make the desires or know anything about them: I went to the public assembly, put myself in the conditions, & instantly feel this new craving—I hear the voice, I see the beckoning of this Ghost. To me it is vegetation, the pullulation & universal budding of the plant man. Art is the path of the creator to his work. The path or methods are ideal and eternal, though few men ever see them: not the artist himself for years, or for a lifetime, unless he come into the conditions. Then he is apprised with wonder what herds of daemons hem him in. He can no more rest: he says, 'By God, it is in me & must go forth of me.' I go to this place and am galvanized, and the torpid eyes of my sensibility are opened. I hear myself speak as a stranger—Most of the things I say are conventional; but I say something which is original & beautiful. That charms me. I would say nothing else but such things. In our way of talking, we say, that is mine, that is yours; but this poet knows well that it is not his, that it is as strange & beautiful to him as to you; he would fain hear the like eloquence at length.

Once having tasted this immortal ichor, we cannot have enough of it. Our appetite is immense. And, as "an admirable power flourishes in intelligibles," according to Plotinus, "which perpetually fabricates," it is of the last importance that these things get spoken. What a little of all we know, is said! What drops of all the sea of our science are baled up! And by what accident it is that these are spoken, whilst so many thoughts sleep in nature!

Hence the oestrum of speech: hence these throbs & heart beatings at the door of the assembly to the end, namely, that the thought may be ejaculated as Logos or Word.

Spring–Summer 1844

Does not he do more to abolish Slavery who works all day steadily in his garden, than he who goes to the abolition meeting & makes a speech? The antislavery agency like so many of our employments is a suicidal business. Whilst I talk, some poor farmer drudges & slaves for me. It requires a just costume then, the office of agent or speaker, he should sit very low & speak very meekly like one compelled to do a degrading thing. Do not then, I pray you, talk of the work & the fight, as if it were any thing more than a pleasant oxygenation of your lungs. It is easy & pleasant to ride about the country amidst the peaceful farms of New England & New York &, sure every where of a strict sympathy from the intelligent & good, argue for liberty, & browbeat & chastise the dull clergyman or lawyer that ventures to limit or qualify our statement. This is not work. It needs to be done but it does not consume heart & brain, does not shut out culture, does not imprison you as the farm & the shoeshop & the forge. There is really no danger & no extraordinary energy demanded; it supplies what it wants. I think if the witnesses of the truth would do their work symmetrically, they must stop all this boast & frolic & vituperation, & in lowliness free the slave by love in the heart. Let the diet be low, & a daily feast of commemoration of their brother in bonds. Let them eat his corn cake dry, as he does. Let them wear negrocloths. Let them leave long discourses to the defender of slavery, and show the power of true words which are always few. Let them do their own work. He who does his own work frees a slave. He who does not his own work, is a slave-holder. Whilst we sit here talking & smiling, some person is out there in field & shop & kitchen doing what we need, without talk or smiles. Therefore, let us, if we assume the dangerous pretension of being abolitionists, & make that our calling in the world, let us do it symmetrically. The world asks, do the abolitionists eat sugar? do they wear cotton? do they smoke tobacco? Are they their own servants? Have they managed to put that dubious institution of servile labour on an agreeable & thoroughly intelligible & transparent foundation? It is not possible that these purists accept the accommodations of hotels, or even of private families, on the existing profane arrangements? If they do, of course, not conscience, but mere prudence & propriety will seal their mouths on the inconsistences of churchmen. Two tables in every house! Abolitionists at one & *servants* at the other! It is a calumny that you utter. There never was, I am persuaded, an asceticism so austere as theirs, from the peculiar emphasis of their testimony. The planter does not want slaves: give him money: give him a machine that will provide him with as much money as the slaves yield, & he will thankfully let them go: he does not love whips, or usurping overseers, or sulky swarthy giants creeping round his house & barns by night with lucifer matches in their hands & knives in their pockets. No only he wants his luxury, & he will pay even this price for it. It is not possible then that the abolitionist will begin the assault on his luxury, by any other means than the abating of his own. A silent fight without warcry or triumphant brag, then, is the new abolition of New England sifting the thronging ranks of the champions, the speakers, the poets, the editors, the subscribers, the givers, & reducing the armies to a handful of just men & women. Alas! alas! my brothers, there is never an abolitionist in New England.

Jan.–Mar. 1845

The state is our neighbors; our neighbors are the state. It is a folly to treat the state as if it were some individual arbitrarily willing thus and so. It is the same company of poor devils we know so well, of William & Edward & John & Henry, doing as they are obliged to do, & trying hard to do conveniently what must & will be done. They do not impose a tax. God & the nature of things imposes the tax, requires that the land shall bear its burden, of road, & of social order, & defence; & I confess I lose all respect for this tedious denouncing of the state by idlers who rot in indolence, selfishness, & envy in the chimney corner.

> Eve softly with her womb
> Bit him to death

> Lightly was woman snared, herself a snare.

Once you saw phoenixes, and now you see such no longer, but the world is not therefore disenchanted. The vessels on which you read sacred emblems have turned out to be common pottery, but the sacred pictures are transferred to the walls of the world. You no longer see phoenixes; men are not divine individuals; but you learn to revere their social & representative character. They are not gods, but the spirit of God sparkles on & about them.

After this generation one would say mysticism should go out of fashion for a long time.

Autumn 1845

. . . Metamorphosis is the law of the universe. All forms are fluent, and as the bird alights on the bough and pauses for rest, then plunges into the air again on its way, so the thoughts of God pause but for a moment in any form, but pass into a new form, as if by touching the earth again in burial, to acquire new energy. A wise man is not deceived by the pause: he knows that it is momentary: he already foresees the new departure, and departure after departure, in long series. Dull people think they have traced the matter far enough if they have reached the history of one of these temporary forms, which they describe as fixed and final.

Nov. 1845–Mar. 1846

The world is enigmatical, every thing said & every thing known & done, & must not be taken literally, but genially. We must be at the top of our condition to understand any thing rightly.

Apr.–May 1846

You must treat the days respectfully, you must be a day yourself, and not interrogate life like a college professor. Every thing in the universe goes by indirection. There are no straight lines.

I grow old, I accept conditions; thus far—no farther; to learn that we are not the first born, but the latest born; that we have no wings; that the sins of our predecessors are on us like a mountain of obstruction.

May 1846

Men quarrel with your rhetoric. Society chokes with a trope, like a child with the croup. They much prefer Mr Prose, & Mr Hoarse-as-Crows, to the dangerous conversation of Gabriel and the archangel Michael perverting all rules, & bounding continually from earth to heaven.

Walking one day in the fields I met a man.

We shall one day talk with the central man, and see again in the varying play of his features all the features which have characterised our darlings, & stamped themselves in fire on the heart: then, as the discourse rises out of the domestic & personal, & his countenance waxes grave & great, we shall fancy that we talk with Socrates, & behold his countenance: then the discourse changes, & the man, and we see the face & hear the tones of Shakspeare—the body & the soul of Shakspeare living & speaking with us, only that Shakspeare seems below us. A change again, and the countenance of our companion is youthful & beardless, he talks of form & colour & the riches of design; it is the face of the painter Raffaelle that confronts us with the visage of a girl, & the easy audacity of a creator. In a moment it was Michel Angelo; then Dante; afterwards it was the Saint Jesus, and the immensities of moral truth & power embosomed us. And so it appears that these great secular[3] personalities were only expressions of his face chasing each other like the rack of clouds. Then all will subside, & I find myself alone. I dreamed & did not know my dreams.

May–June 1846

The United States will conquer Mexico, but it will be as the man swallows the arsenic, which brings him down in turn. Mexico will poison us.

June–July 1846

O Bacchus, make them drunk, drive them mad, this multitude of vagabonds, hungry for eloquence, hungry for poetry, starving for symbols, perishing for want of electricity to vitalize this too much pasture; &, in the long delay, indemnifying themselves with the false wine of alcohol, of politics, or of money. Pour for them, o Bacchus, the wine of wine. Give them, at last, Poetry.

*   *   *

These rabble at Washington are really better than the snivelling opposition. They have a sort of genius of a bold & manly cast, though Satanic. They see, against the unanimous expression of the people, how much a little well directed effrontery can achieve, how much crime the people will bear, & they proceed from step to step & it seems they have calculated but too justly upon your Excellency, O Governor Briggs. Mr Webster told them how much the war cost, that was his protest, but voted the war, & sends his son to it. They calculated rightly on Mr Webster. My friend Mr Thoreau has gone to jail rather than pay his tax. On him they could not calculate. The abolitionists denounce the war & give much time to it, but they pay the tax.

The State is a poor good beast who means the best: it means friendly. A poor cow who does well by you—do not grudge it its hay. It cannot eat bread as you can, let it have without grudge a little grass for its four stomachs. It will not stint to yield you milk from its teat. You who are a man walking cleanly on two feet will not pick a quarrel with a poor cow. Take this handful of clover & welcome. But if you go to hook me when I walk in the fields, then, poor cow, I will cut your throat.

3. Enduring.

Aug. 23, 1846

The teacher should be the complement of the pupil; now for the most part they are earth's diameters wide of each other. A college professor should be elected by setting all the candidates loose on a miscellaneous gang of young men taken at large from the street. He who could get the ear of these youths after a certain number of hours, or of the greatest number of these youths, should be professor. Let him see if he could interest these rowdy boys in the meaning of a list of words.

Mar.–Apr. 1847

The name of Washington City in the newspapers is every day of blacker shade. All the news from that quarter being of a sadder type, more malignant. It seems to be settled that no act of honor or benevolence or justice is to be expected from the American Government, but only this, that they will be as wicked as they dare. No man now can have any sort of success in politics without a streak of infamy crossing his name.

Things have another order in these men's eyes. Heavy is hollow & good is evil. A western man in Congress the other day spoke of the opponents of the Texan & Mexican plunder as "Every light character in the house," & our good friend in State street speaks of "the solid portion of the community" meaning, of course, the sharpers. I feel, meantime, that those who succeed in life, in civilized society, are beasts of prey. It has always been so.

Theology, Medicine, Law, Politics, Trade have their meetings & assembly rooms. Literature has none. See how magnificently the Merchants meet in State street. Every Bank & Insurance office is a Palace, & Literature has not a poor café, not a corner even of Mrs Haven's shop in which to celebrate its unions. By a little alliance with some of the rising parties of the time, as the Socialists, & the Abolitionists, and the Artists, we might accumulate a sufficient patronage to establish a good room in Boston. As Ellery Channing says there is not a chair in all Boston where I can sit down.

May 23, 1847

Henry Truman Safford born at Royalton, Vt Jan 6, 1836. In 1846 was examined for 3 hours by Rev H W Adams of Concord N.H. & Rev C N Smith of Randolph Vt. and at last was bidden:

"Multiply in your head 365 365 365 365 365 365 by 365 365 365 365 365 365!" eighteen figures by eighteen. "He flew round the room like a top, pulled his pantaloons over the top of his boots, bit his hand rolled his eyes in their sockets sometimes smiling & talking & then seeming to be in agony until in not more than one minute, he said, 333,491,850,208,566,925,016,658,299,941, 583,225. The boy's father Rev C. N. Smith & myself had each a pencil & slate to take down the answer, & he gave it us in periods of three figures each as fast as it was possible for us to write them. And what was still more wonderful he began to multiply at the left hand & to bring out the answer from left to right giving first 123, 491 &c. Here confounded above measure I gave up the examination. The boy looked pale & said he was tired. He said, it was the largest sum he ever did."

May 24, 1847

The days come & go like muffled & veiled figures sent from a distant friendly party, but they say nothing, & if we do not use the gifts they bring, they carry them as silently away.

May–June 1847

"Keep the body open," is the hygeian precept, and the reaction of free circulations on growth & life. The fact that the river makes its own shores, is true for the artist.

Large utterance! The pears are suffering from *frozen sap-blight*, the sap being checked in its fullest flow, & not being able to form leaves & fruit, which is the perspiration & utterance of the tree, becomes thick, unctuous & poisonous to the tree.

The jockey looks at the chest of the horse, the physician looks at the breast of the babe, to see if there is room enough for the free play of the lungs.

Arteries, perspiration. Shakspeare sweats like a haymaker—all pores.

Mar.–Apr. 1848

People here expect a revolution. There will be no revolution, none that deserves to be called so. There may be a scramble for money. But as all the people we see want the things we now have, & not better things, it is very certain that they will, under whatever change of forms, keep the old system.

*   *   *

Happy is he who looks only into his work to know if it will succeed, never into the times or the public opinion; and who writes from the love of imparting certain thoughts & not from the necessity of sale—who writes always to *the unknown friend*.

May 1849

Immortality. I notice that as soon as writers broach this question they begin to quote. I hate quotation. Tell me what you know.

July 1849

'Tis very certain that the man must yield who has omitted inevitable facts in his view of life. Has he left out marriage & the σπερματος ουσιης συντηρησιν,[4] he has set a date to his fame. We are expecting another.

July–Aug. 1850

On Friday, 19 July, Margaret dies on rocks of Fire Island Beach within sight of & within 60 rods of the shore.[5] To the last her country proves inhos-

---

4. This phrase from Plutarch's "Advice About Keeping Well" (*Moralia* 129F) is translated in the Loeb Classical Library Edition as "observance of chastity," but Emerson seems to use it here to refer to sexuality generally.
5. Margaret Fuller, her husband Giovanni Angelo Ossoli, and their child, Angelo Eugene Philip (born September 5, 1848), perished in the wreck of the merchantman *Elizabeth*, which sailed from Leghorn May 17. Only the body of the son was recovered. [*JMN*]

pitable to her; brave, eloquent, subtle, accomplished, devoted, constant soul! If nature availed in America to give birth to many such as she, freedom & honour & letters & art too were safe in this new world. . . .

She had a wonderful power of inspiring confidence & drawing out of people their last secret.

The timorous said, What shall we do? how shall she be received, now that she brings a husband & child home? But she had only to open her mouth, & a triumphant success awaited her. She would fast enough have disposed of the circumstances & the bystanders. For she had the impulse, & they wanted it. Here were already mothers waiting tediously for her coming, for the education of their daughters. . . .

Her love of art, like that of many, was only a confession of sympathy with the artist in the mute condemnation which his work gave to the deformity of our daily life; her co-perception with him of the eloquence of Form; her aspiration with him to a life altogether beautiful.

"Her heart, which few knew, was as great as her mind, which all knew"— what Jung Stilling said of Goethe, E. H. [Elizabeth Hoar] says of Margaret; and, that she was the largest woman; & not a woman who wished to be a man.

I have lost in her my audience. I hurry now to my work admonished that I have few days left. There should be a gathering of her friends & some Beethoven should play the dirge.

She poured a stream of amber over the endless store of private anecdotes, of bosom histories which her wonderful persuasion drew out of all to her. When I heard that a trunk of her correspondence had been found & opened, I felt what a panic would strike all her friends, for it was as if a clever reporter had got underneath a confessional & agreed to report all that transpired there in Wall street.

[From a later entry.]

Her confidence in herself was boundless, & was frankly expressed. She told S. G. W. [Samuel Gray Ward] that she had seen all the people worth seeing in America, & was satisfied that there was no intellect comparable to her own.

Oct.–Nov. 1850

The world wears well. These autumn afternoons & well-marbled landscapes of green, & gold, & russet, & steel-blue river, & smoke-blue New Hampshire mountain, are & remain as bright & perfect pencilling as ever.

Nov.–Dec. 1850

A Journal is to the author a book of constants, each mind requiring (as I have so often said) to write the whole of literature & science for itself.

Jan.–Feb. 1851

To every reproach, I know now but one answer, namely, to go again to my own work.

"But you neglect your relations."

Yes, too true; then I will work the harder.

"But you have no genius." Yes, then I will work the harder.

"But you have no virtues." Yes, then I will work the harder.

"But you have detached yourself & acquired the aversation of all decent people. You must regain some position & relation." Yes, I will work harder.

Feb.–Mar. 1851

Nothing so marks a man as bold imaginative expressions. A complete statement in the imaginative form of an important truth arrests attention & is repeated & remembered. A phrase or two of that kind will make the reputation of a man. . . . Henry Thoreau promised to make as good sentences in that kind as any body.

Apr.–May 1851

Bad times.[6] We wake up with a painful auguring, and after exploring a little to know the cause find it is the odious news in each day's paper, the infamy that has fallen on Massachusetts, that clouds the daylight, & takes away the comfort out of every hour. We shall never feel well again until that detestable law is nullified in Massachusetts & until the Government is assured that once for all it cannot & shall not be executed here. All I have, and all I can do shall be given & done in opposition to the execution of the law.

Mr. Samuel Hoar[7] has never raised his head since Webster's speech in last March, and all the interim has really been a period of calamity to New England. That was a steep step downward. I had praised the tone & attitude of the Country. My friends had mistrusted it. They say now, It is no worse than it was before; only it is manifest and acted out. Well I think *that* worse. It shows the access of so much courage in the bad, so much check of virtue, terror of virtue, withdrawn. The tameness is shocking. Boston, of whose fame for spirit & character we have all been so proud. Boston, whose citizen intelligent people in England told me they could always distinguish by their culture among Americans. Boston, which figures so proudly in Adams's diary, which we all have been reading: Boston, through the personal influence of this New Hampshire man, must bow its proud spirit in the dust, & make us irretrievably ashamed. I would hide the fact if I could, but it is done, it is debased. It is now as disgraceful to be a Bostonian as it was hitherto a credit. . . .

I met an episcopal clergyman, & allusion being made to Mr Webster's treachery, he replied "Why, do you know I think that the great action of his life?" I am told, they are all involved in one hot haste of terror, presidents of colleges & professors, saints & brokers, insurers, lawyers, importers, jobbers, there is not an unpleasing sentiment, a liberal recollection, not so much as a snatch of an old song for freedom dares intrude.

I am sorry to say it, But New-Hampshire has always been distinguished for the servility of its eminent men. Mr Webster had resisted for a long time the habit of his *compatriots*, I mean no irony, & by adopting the spirited tone of Boston had recommended himself—as much as by his great talents to the people of Massachusetts; but blood is thicker than water, the deep servility of New

---

6. Emerson is alluding to the implementation of the Fugitive Slave Law, which was supported by Daniel Webster (see n. 6, p. 251).
7. Judge Hoar, father of Elizabeth, was a much respected Concord citizen and a fierce opponent of the Fugitive Slave Law.

Hampshire politics which have marked all prominent statesmen from that district, with the great exception of Mr Hale,[8] has appeared late in life with all the more strength that it had been resisted so long, & he has renounced, what must have cost him some perplexity, all the great passages of his past career on which his fame is built. . . .

I opened a paper today in which he pounds on the old strings in a letter to the Washington Birth Day feasters at N. Y. "Liberty! liberty!" Pho! Let Mr Webster for decency's sake shut his lips once & forever on this word. The word *liberty* in the mouth of Mr Webster sounds like the word *love* in the mouth of a courtezan.

I may then add *the Union*. Nothing seems to me more bitterly futile than this bluster about the Union. A year ago we were all lovers & prizers of it. Before the passage of that law which Mr Webster made his own, we indulged in all the dreams which foreign nations still cherish of American destiny. But in the new attitude in which we find ourselves, the degradation & personal dishonour which now rests like miasma on every house in Massachusetts, the sentiment is entirely changed. No man can look his neighbor in the face. We sneak about with the infamy of crime in the streets, & cowardice in ourselves and frankly once for all the Union is sunk, the flag is hateful, & will be hissed.

The Union! o yes, I prized that, other things being equal; but what is the Union to a man self condemned, with all sense of self respect & chance of fair fame cut off—with the names of conscience & religion become bitter ironies, & liberty the ghastly nothing which Mr Webster means by that word? The worst mischiefs that could follow from secession, & new combination of the smallest fragments of the wreck were slight & medicable to the calamity your Union has brought us. Another year, and a standing army officered by Southern gentlemen, to protect the Commissioners & to hunt the fugitives will be illustrating the new sweets of Union in Boston, Worcester, & Springfield. It did not appear & it was incredible that the passage of the Law would make the Union odious; but from the day it was attempted to be executed in Massachusetts, this result has appeared that the Union is no longer desireable. Whose deed is that?

One more consideration occurs—the mischief of a legal crime. The demoralization of the Community. Each of these persons who touches it is contaminated. There has not been in our lifetime another moment when public men were personally lowered by their political action. But here are gentlemen whose names stood as high as any, whose believed probity was the confidence & fortification of all, who by fear of public opinion, or by that dangerous ascendency of Southern manners, have been drawn into the support of this nefarious business, and have of course changed their relations to men. We poor men in the country who might have thought it an honor to shake hands with them, would now shrink from their touch; nor could they enter our humblest doors. . . . Well, is not this a loss inevitable to a bad law?—a law which no man can countenance or abet the execution of, without loss of all self respect, & forfeiting forever the name of a gentleman. . . .

The College, the churches, the schools, the very shops & factories are discredited. Every kind of property & every branch of industry & every avenue to power suffers injury, and the value of life is reduced. I had hardly written this before my friend said, "If this law should be repealed, I shall be glad that I have

---

8. John Parker Hale (1806–1873), senator from New Hampshire, prominent in the antislavery movement.

lived; if not, I shall be sorry that I was born." What kind of law is that which extorts this kind of language for a free civilized people?

I am surprised that lawyers can be so blind as to suffer the law to be discredited. The law rests not only in the instinct of all people, but, according to the maxims of Blackstone & the jurists, on equity, and it is the cardinal maxim that a statute contrary to natural right is illegal, is in itself null & void. The practitioners should guard this dogma well, as the palladium of the profession, as their anchor in the respect of mankind.

Against this all the arguments of Webster make no more impression than the spray of a child's squirt.

The fame of Webster ends in this nasty law.

And as for the Andover & Boston preachers . . . who deduce kidnapping from their Bible, tell the poor dear doctor if this be Christianity, it is a religion of dead dogs, let it never pollute the ears & hearts of noble children again. O bring back then the age when valour was virtue, since what is called morality means nothing but pudding. Pardon the spleen of a professed hermit.

Mr Webster cannot choose but regret his loss. Tell him that those who make fame, accuse him with one voice: those to whom his name was once dear & honoured as the manly statesman, to whom the choicest gifts of nature had been accorded—eloquence with a simple greatness; those who have no points to carry that are not those of public morals & of generous civilization, the obscure & private who have no voice & care for none as long as things go well, but who feel the infamy of his nasty legislation creeping like a fever into all their homes & robbing the day of its beauty. Tell him that he who was their pride in the woods & mountains of New England is now their mortification; that they never name him; they have taken his picture from the wall & torn it—dropped the pieces in the gutter; they have taken his book of speeches from the shelf & put it in the stove. . . .

It will be his distinction to have changed in one day by the most detestable law that was ever enacted by a civilized state, the fairest & most triumphant national escutcheon the sun ever shone upon, the free, the expanding, the hospitable, the irresistible America, home of the homeless & pregnant with the blessing of the world, into a jail or barracoon for the slaves of a few thousand Southern planters & all the citizens of this hemisphere into kidnappers & drivers for the same. Is that a name will feed his hungry ambition?

In the weakness of the Union the law of 1793 was framed, and much may be said in palliation of it. It was a law affirming the existence of two states of civilization or an intimate union between two countries, one civilized & Christian & the other barbarous, where cannibalism was still permitted. It was a little gross, the taste for boiling babies, but as long as this kind of cookery was confined within their own limits, we could agree for other purposes, & wear one flag. The law affirmed a right to hunt their human prey within our territory; and this law availed just thus much to affirm their own platform—to fix the fact, that, though confessedly savage, they were yet at liberty to consort with men; though they had tails, & their incisors were a little long, yet it is settled that they shall by courtesy be called men; we will all make believe they are Christians; & we promise not to look at their tails or incisors when they come into company. This was all very well. The convenient equality was affirmed, they were admitted to dine & sup, & profound silence on the subject of tails & incisors was kept. . . . But of course on their part all idea of boiling babies in our caboose was dropt; all idea of hunting in our yards fat babies to boil, was dropt; & the law became, as it should, a dead letter. It was merely there in the statute-book to soothe the dignity of the maneaters. And we Northerners had, on our part, indemnified & secured ourselves against any occasional eccentricity of appetite in our confederates by our own interpretation, & by offsetting state-law by state-laws. It was & is penal here in Massachusetts for any sheriff or town- or state-officer to lend himself or his jail to the slavehunter, & it is also settled that any slave brought here by his master, becomes free. All this was well. What Mr Webster has now done is not only to re-enact the old law, but *to give it force*, which it never had before, or to bring down the free & Christian state of Massachusetts to the cannibal level.

Mr Everett,[9] a man supposed aware of his own meaning, advises pathetically a reverence for the Union. Yes but hides the other horn under this velvet? Does he mean that we shall lay hands on a man who has escaped from slavery to the soil of Massachusetts & so has done more for freedom than ten thousand orations, & tie him up & call in the marshal, and say—I am an orator for freedom; a great many fine sentences have I turned—none has turned finer, except Mr Webster, in favour of plebeian strength against aristocracy; and, as my last & finest sentence of all, to show the young men of the land who have bought my book & clapped my sentences & copied them in their memory, how much I mean by them—Mr Marshall, here is a black man of my own age, & who does not know a great deal of Demosthenes, but who means what he says, whom we will now handcuff and commit to the custody of this very worthy gentleman who has come on from Georgia in search of him; I have no doubt he has much to say to him that is interesting & as the way is long I don't care if I give them a copy of my Concord & Lexington & Plymouth & Bunker Hill addresses to beguile their journey from Boston to the plantation whipping post? Does Mr Everett really mean this? that he & I shall do this? Mr Everett understands English, as few men do who speak it. Does he mean this? Union is a delectable thing, & so is wealth, & so is life, but they may *all* cost too much, if they cost honour. . . .

It is very remarkable how rare a bad law, an immoral law, is. Does Mr Everett know how few examples in Civil history there are of bad laws? I do not think it will be easy to parallel the crime of Mr Webster's law. But the crime of kidnapping is on a footing with the crimes of murder & of incest and if the Southern states should find it necessary to enact the further law in view of the too great increase of blacks that every fifth manchild should be boiled in hot water—& obtain a majority in Congress with a speech by Mr Webster to add an article to the Fugitive Slave Bill—that any fifth child so & so selected, having escaped into Boston should be seethed in water at $212°$, will not the mayor & alderman boil him? Is there the smallest moral distinction between such a law, & the one now enacted? How can Mr E. put at nought all manly qualities, all his claims to truth & sincerity, for the sake of backing up this cowardly nonsense?

Does he mean this, that he & I shall do this, or does he secretly know that he will die the death sooner than lift a finger in the matter, he or his son, or his son's son, and only hopes to persuade certain truckmen & constables to do this, that rich men may enjoy their estates in more security?

One way certainly the Nemesis is seen. Here is a measure of pacification & union. What is its effect? that it has made one subject, one only subject for conversation, & painful thought, throughout the Union, Slavery. We eat it, we drink it, we breathe it, we trade, we study, we wear it. We are all poisoned with

9. See n. 9, p. 417. Emerson is condemning his conciliatory position on slavery and the Fugitive Slave Law.

it, & after the fortnight the symptoms appear, purulent, making frenzy in the head & rabidness.

What a moment was lost when Judge Lemuel Shaw[1] declined to affirm the unconstitutionality of the Fugitive Slave Law!

But we must put out this poison, this conflagration, this raging fever of Slavery out of the Constitution. If Webster had known a true & generous policy, this would have made him. He is a spent ball. It is the combined wealth behind him that makes him of any avail. And that is as bad as Europe.

May? 1851

Danger of doing something. You write a discourse, &, for the next weeks & months, you are carted about the Country at the tail of that discourse simply to read it over & over.

July–Oct. 1851

We are glad at last to get a clear case, one on which no shadow of doubt can hang. This is not meddling with other people's affairs—this is other people meddling with us. This is not going crusading after slaves who it is alleged are very happy & comfortable where they are: all that amiable argument falls to the ground, but defending a human being who has taken the risks of being shot or burned alive, or cast into the sea, or starved to death or suffocated in a wooden box—taken all this risk to get away from his driver & recover the rights of man. And this man the Statute says, you men of Massachusetts shall kidnap & send back again a thousand miles across the sea to the dog-hutch he fled from. And this filthy enactment was made in the 19th Century, by people who could read & write.

I will not obey it, by God.

Aug. 18? 1851

Greenough[2] called my contemplations, &c. "the masturbation of the brain."

Winter? 1852–1853

It is the distinction of "Uncle Tom's Cabin," that, it is read equally in the parlour & the kitchen & the nursery of every house. What the lady read in the drawing-room in a few hours, is retailed to her in her kitchen by the cook & the chambermaid, as, week by week, they master one scene & character after another.

Spring? 1853

It is a bitter satire on our social order, just at present, the number of bad cases. Margaret Fuller having attained the highest & broadest culture that any American woman has possessed, came home with an Italian gentleman whom she had married, & their infant son, & perished by shipwreck on the rocks of Fire Island, off New York; and her friends said, 'Well, on the whole, it was not so lamentable, & perhaps it was the best thing that could happen to her. For, had she lived, what could she have done? How could she have supported her-

1. Chief justice of the Massachusetts supreme court and father-in-law of Herman Melville.
2. See n. 3, p. 385.

self, her husband, & child?' And, most persons, hearing this, acquiesced in this view that, after the education has gone far, such is the expensiveness of America, that the best use to put a fine woman to, is to drown her to save her board.

'Tis very costly, this thinking for the market in books or lectures: As soon as any one turns the conversation on my "Representative men," for instance, I am instantly sensible that there is nothing there for conversation, that the argument is all pinched & illiberal & popular.

Only what is private, & yours, & essential, should ever be printed or spoken. I will buy the suppressed part of the author's mind; you are welcome to all he published.

Dec. 1853

Wendell Holmes when I offered to go to his lecture on Wordsworth, said, "I entreat you not to go. I am forced to study effects. You & others may be able to combine popular effect with the exhibition of truths. I cannot. I am compelled to study effects." The other day, Henry Thoreau was speaking to me about my lecture on the Anglo American, & regretting that whatever was written for a lecture, or whatever succeeded with the audience was bad, &c. I said, I am ambitious to write something which all can read, like Robinson Crusoe. And when I have written a paper or a book, I see with regret that it is not solid, with a right materialistic treatment, which delights everybody. Henry objected, of course, & vaunted the better lectures which only reached a few persons. Well, yesterday, he came here, &, at supper, Edith [Emerson's youngest daughter], understanding that he was to lecture at the Lyceum, sharply asked him, "Whether his lecture would be a nice interesting story, such as she wanted to hear, or whether it was one of those old philosophical things that she did not care about?" Henry instantly turned to her, & bethought himself, & I saw was trying to believe that he had matter that might fit Edith & Edward [Emerson's son], who were to sit up & go to the lecture, if it was a good one for them.

1853–1854?

The poet sprains or strains himself by attempting too much; he tries to reach the people, instead of contenting himself with the temperate expression of what he knows. Sing he must & should, but not ballads; sing, but for gods or demigods. He need not transform himself into Punch & Judy. A man must not be a proletary or breeder, but only by mere superfluity of his strength, he begets Messias. He relieves himself, & makes a world.

Mar.? 1854

The lesson of these days is the vulgarity of wealth. We know that wealth will vote for the same thing which the worst & meanest of the people vote for. Wealth will vote for rum, will vote for tyranny, will vote for slavery, will vote against the ballot, will vote against international copyright, will vote against schools, colleges, or any high direction of public money.

Spring–Summer 1855

For flowing is the secret of things & no wonder the children love masks, & to trick themselves in endless costumes, & be a horse, a soldier, a parson, or a bear; and, older, delight in theatricals; as, in nature, the egg is passing to a grub, the grub to a fly, and the vegetable eye to a bud, the bud to a leaf, a stem, a flower, a fruit; the children have only the instinct of their race, the instinct of the Universe, in which, *Becoming somewhat else* is the whole game of nature, & death the penalty of standing still.

'Tis not less in thought. I cannot conceive of any good in a thought which confines & stagnates. Liberty means the power to flow. To continue is to flow. Life is unceasing parturition.

*   *   *

If you would know what the dogs know, you must lap up the puddles.

Apr. 26, 1856

Whipple said of the author of "Leaves of Grass," that he had every leaf but the fig leaf.

The audience that assembled to hear my lectures in these six weeks was called, "the *effete* of Boston."

May–June 1857

I do not count the hours I spend in the woods, though I forget my affairs there & my books. And, when there, I wander hither & thither; any bird, any plant, any spring, detains me. I do not hurry homewards for I think all affairs may be postponed to this walking. And it is for this idleness that all my businesses exist.

July 8, 1857

This morning I had the remains of my mother & of my son Waldo removed from the tomb of Mrs Ripley to my lot in "Sleepy Hollow." The sun shone brightly on the coffins, of which Waldo's was well preserved — now fifteen years. I ventured to look into the coffin. I gave a few white-oak leaves to each coffin, after they were put in the new vault, & the vault was then covered with two slabs of granite.

Fall–Winter? 1857

My philosophy holds to a few laws. 1. *Identity*, whence comes the fact that *metaphysical faculties & facts are the transcendency of physical.* 2. Flowing, or transition, or shooting the gulf, the perpetual striving to ascend to a higher platform, the same thing in new & higher forms.

Spring? 1859

I am a natural reader, & only a writer in the absence of natural writers. In a true time, I should never have written.

I have now for more than a year, I believe, ceased to write in my Journal, in which I formerly wrote almost daily. I see few intellectual persons, & even those to no purpose, & sometimes believe that I have no new thoughts, and that my life is quite at an end. But the magnet that lies in my drawer for years, may believe it has no magnetism, and, on touching it with steel, it shows the old virtue; and, this morning, came by a man with knowledge & interests like mine, in his head, and suddenly I had thoughts again.

*   *   *

I have been writing & speaking what were once called novelties, for twenty five or thirty years, & have not now one disciple. Why? Not that what I said was not true; not that it has not found intelligent receivers but because it did not go from any wish in me to bring men to me, but to themselves. I delight in driving them from me. What could I do, if they came to me? they would interrupt & encumber me. This is my boast that I have no school & no follower. I should account it a measure of the impurity of insight, if it did not create independence.

Jan. 17, 1862

Old Age. As we live longer, it looks as if our company were picked out to die first, & we live on in a lessening minority. . . . I am ever threatened by the decays of Henry T.

Jan. 1862

It is impossible to extricate oneself from the questions in which your age is involved. You can no more keep out of politics than you can keep out of the frost.

Jan. 31, 1862 Visit to Washington

At Washington, 31 January, 1 Feb, 2d, & 3d, saw Sumner, who on the 2d, carried me to Mr Chase, Mr Bates, Mr Stanton, Mr Welles, Mr Seward, Lord Lyons, and President Lincoln. The President impressed me more favorably than I had hoped. A frank, sincere, well-meaning man, with a lawyer's habit of mind, good clear statement of his fact, correct enough, not vulgar, as described; but with a sort of boyish cheerfulness, or that kind of sincerity & jolly good meaning that our class meetings on Commencement Days show, in telling our old stories over. When he has made his remark, he looks up at you with great satisfaction, & shows all his white teeth, & laughs. He argued to Sumner the whole case of Gordon, the slave-trader, point by point, and added that he was not quite satisfied yet, & meant to refresh his memory by looking again at the evidence.

All this showed a fidelity & conscientiousness very honorable to him.

When I was introduced to him, he said, "O Mr Emerson, I once heard you say in a lecture, that a Kentuckian seems to say by his air & manners, '*Here am I; if you don't like me, the worse for you.*'"

Feb. 1862

H D T . . .

Perhaps his fancy for Walt Whitman grew out of his taste for wild nature, for an otter, a wood-chuck, or a loon.

He loved sufficiency, hated a sum that would not prove: loved Walt & hated Alcott.

March 24, 1862

Samuel Staples yesterday had been to see Henry Thoreau. Never spent an hour with more satisfaction. Never saw a man dying with so much pleasure & peace. Thinks that very few men in Concord know Mr Thoreau; finds him serene & happy.

Henry praised to me lately the manners of an old, established, calm, well-behaved river, as perfectly distinguished from those of a new river. A new river is a torrent; an old one slow & steadily supplied. What happens in any part of the old river relates to what befals in every other part of it. 'Tis full of compensations, resources, & reserved funds.

April 1862

Spring. Why complain of the cold slow spring? the bluebirds don't complain, the blackbirds make the maples ring with social cheer & jubilee, the robins know the snow must go & sparrows with prophetic eye that these bare osiers yet will hide their future nests in the pride of their foliage. And you alone with all your six feet of experience are the fool of the cold of the present moment, & cannot see the southing of the sun. Besides the snowflake is freedom's star.

Feb.–Mar. ? 1863

I am a bard least of bards.

I cannot, like them, make lofty arguments in stately continuous verse, constraining the rocks, trees, animals, & the periodic stars to say my thoughts — for that is the gift of great poets; but I am a bard, because I stand near them, & apprehend all they utter, & with pure joy hear that which I also would say, &, moreover, I speak interruptedly words & half stanzas which have the like scope & aim.

Apr.–May 1863

I have never recorded a fact which perhaps ought to have gone into my sketch of "Thoreau," that, on the 1 August, 1844, when I read my Discourse on Emancipation, in the Town Hall, in Concord, and the selectmen would not direct the sexton to ring the meeting-house bell, Henry went himself, & rung the bell at the appointed hour.

Spring? 1864

I too am fighting my campaign.
Within, I do not find wrinkles & used heart, but unspent youth.

May 24, 1864

Yesterday, 23 May, we buried Hawthorne in Sleepy Hollow, in a pomp of sunshine & verdure, & gentle winds. James F. Clarke read the service in the Church & at the grave. Longfellow, Lowell, Holmes, Agassiz, Hoar, Dwight, Whipple, Norton, Alcott, Hillard, Fields, Judge Thomas, & I, attended the hearse as pall bearers. Franklin Pierce was with the family. The church was copiously decorated with white flowers delicately arranged. The corpse was unwillingly shown—only a few moments to this company of his friends. But it was noble & serene in its aspect—nothing amiss—a calm & powerful head. A large company filled the church, & the grounds of the cemetery. All was so bright & quiet, that pain or mourning was hardly suggested, & Holmes said to me, that it looked like a happy meeting.

Clarke in the church said, that Hawthorne had done more justice than any other to the shades of life, shown a sympathy with the crime in our nature, &, like Jesus, was the friend of sinners.

I thought there was a tragic element in the event, that might be more fully rendered—in the painful solitude of the man—which, I suppose, could not longer be endured, & he died of it.

I have found in his death a surprise & disappointment. I thought him a greater man than any of his works betray, that there was still a great deal of work in him, & that he might one day show a purer power.

Moreover I have felt sure of him in his neighborhood, & in his necessities of sympathy & intelligence, that I could well wait his time—his unwillingness & caprice—and might one day conquer a friendship. It would have been a happiness, doubtless to both of us, to have come into habits of unreserved intercourse. It was easy to talk with him—there were no barriers—only, he said so little, that I talked too much, & stopped only because—as he gave no indications—I feared to exceed. He showed no egotism or self-assertion, rather a humility, &, at one time, a fear that he had written himself out. One day, when I found him on the top of his hill, in the woods, he paced back the path to his house, & said, *"this path is the only remembrance of me that will remain."* Now it appears that I waited too long.

Lately, he had removed himself the more by the indignation his perverse politics & unfortunate friendship for that paltry Franklin Pierce awaked—though it rather moved pity for Hawthorne, & the assured belief that he would outlive it, & come right at last.

July 1864?

Henry pitched his tone very low in his love of nature—not on stars & suns . . . but tortoises, crickets, muskrats, suckers, toads & frogs. It was impossible to go lower. Yet it gave him every advantage in conversation: For who that found him always skilled in facts, real experience in objects which made their objects & experiences appear artificial, could tax him with transcendentalism or overrefining: And yet his position was in Nature, & so commanded all its miracles & infinitudes.

Apr. 1865

'Tis far the best that the rebels have been pounded instead of negociated into a peace. They must remember it, & their inveterate brag will be humbled, if not cured. George Minott used to tell me over the wall, when I urged him to go to town meeting & vote, that "votes did no good, what was done so wouldn't last, but what was done by bullets would stay put." General Grant's terms certainly look a little too easy, as foreclosing any action hereafter to convict Lee of treason, and I fear that the high tragic historic justice which the nation with severest consideration should execute, will be softened & dissipated & toasted away at dinner-tables. But the problems that now remain to be solved are very intricate & perplexing, & men are very much at a loss as to the right action. If we let the southern States in to Congress, the Northern democrats will join them in thwarting the will of the government. And the obvious remedy is to give the negro his vote. And then the difficult question comes—what shall be the qualification of voters? We wish to raise the mean white to his right position, that he may withstand the planter. But the negro will learn to write & read (which should be a required qualification) before the white will.

President Lincoln. Why talk of President Lincoln's equality of manners to the elegant or titled men with whom Everett or others saw him? A sincerely upright & intelligent man as he was, placed in the Chair, has no need to think of his manners or appearance. His work day by day educates him rapidly & to the best. He exerts the enormous power of this continent in every hour, in every conversation, in every act—thinks & decides under this pressure, forced to see the vast & various bearings of the measures he adopts: *he* cannot palter, he cannot but carry a grace beyond his own, a dignity, by means of what he drops, e.g. all pretension & trick, and arrives, of course, at a simplicity, which is the perfection of manners.

May 1865

It is becoming to the Americans to dare in religion to be simple, as they have been in government, in trade, in social life.

They are to break down prisons, capital punishment, slavery, tariff, disfranchisement, caste; and they have rightly pronounced Toleration—that no religious test shall be put. They are to abolish laws against atheism.

They are not to allow immorality, they are to be strict in laws of marriage; they are to be just to women, in property, in votes, in personal rights.

And they are to establish the pure religion, Justice, Asceticism, self-devotion, Bounty.

They will lead their language round the globe, & they will lead religion & freedom with them.

Mar. ? 1866

When I read a good book, say, one which opens a literary question, I wish that life were 3000 years long.

July 1866

Dr Channing took counsel, in 1840?, with George Ripley & Mrs Ripley, to find whether it were possible to bring cultivated thoughtful people socially together. He had already talked with Dr Warren on the same design, who made, I have heard, a party, which had its fatal termination in an oyster supper. Mrs Ripley invited a large party, but I do not remember that Dr Channing came. Perhaps he did, but it is significant enough of the very moderate success, that I do not recall the fact of his presence, or indeed any particulars but of some absurd toilettes.

I think there was the mistake of a general belief at that time, that there was some concert of doctrinaires to establish certain opinions, & inaugurate some movement in literature, philosophy, & religion, of which the supposed conspirators were quite innocent; for there was no concert, & only here & there, two or three men or women who read & wrote, each alone, with unusual vivacity. Perhaps they only agreed in having fallen upon Coleridge, Wordsworth, Goethe, & then upon Carlyle, with pleasure & sympathy. Otherwise, their education & reading were not marked, but had the American superficialness, & their studies were solitary. I suppose all of them were surprised at this rumor of a school or sect, & certainly at the name of Transcendentalism, which nobody knows who gave, or when it was first applied. As these persons became, in the common chances of society, acquainted with each other, there resulted certainly strong friendships, which, of course, were exclusive in proportion to their heat, & perhaps those persons who were mutually the best friends were the most private, & had no ambition of publishing their letters, diaries or conversation. Such were Charles Newcomb, Sam G. Ward, & Caroline Sturgis—all intimate with Margaret Fuller. Margaret with her radiant genius & fiery heart was perhaps the real centre that drew so many & so various individuals to a seeming union. Hedge, Clarke, W. H. Channing, W. E. Channing, jr., George Ripley, James Clarke & many more then or since known as writers, or otherwise distinguished, were only held together as her friends. Mr A Bronson Alcott became known to all these as the pure idealist, not at all a man of letters, nor of any practical talent, & quite too cold & contemplative for the alliances of friendship, but purely intellectual, with rare simplicity & grandeur of perception, who read Plato as an equal, & inspired his companions only in proportion as they were intellectual, whilst the men of talent, of course, complained of the want of point & precision in this abstract & religious thinker. Elizabeth Hoar & Sarah Clarke, though certainly never summoned to any of the meetings which were held at George Ripley's, or Dr Francis's, or Stetson's, or Bartol's or my house, were prized & sympathetic friends of Margaret & of others whom I have named, in the circle. The "Dial" was the only public or quotable result of this temporary society & fermentation: and yet the Community at Brook Farm, founded by the readers of Fourier, drew also inspirations from this circle. . . .

In a warmer & more fruitful climate Alcott & his friends would soon have been Buddhists.

An important fact in the sequel was the plantation of Mr Lane & Mr Alcott at Stillriver, "Fruitlands."[3] The labor on the place was all done by the volunteers; they used no animal food; they even for a time dressed themselves only in linen; but there were inherent difficulties: the members of the community were unused to labor, & were soon very impatient of it: the hard work fell on a few, & mainly on women. The recruits whom they drew were some of them partly, some of them quite insane. And the individuals could not divest themselves of the infirmity of holding property. When the winter came, & they had burned all the dry wood they could find, & began to burn green wood, they could not keep themselves warm, & fled to the Shakers for their warm fires.

Spring? 1867

The good writer seems to be writing about himself, but has his eye always on that thread of the Universe which runs through himself, & all things.

---

3. This community was described satirically by Louisa May Alcott in a piece called "Transcendental Wild-Oats."

Apr.–June 1870

Henry Thoreau was well aware of his stubborn contradictory attitude into which almost any conversation threw him, & said in the woods, "When I die, you will find swamp oak written on my heart." I got his words from Ellery Channing today.

July 24, 1872

House burned.

Aug. 31, 1872 *Naushon*

I thought today, in these rare seaside woods, that if absolute leisure were offered me, I should run to the College or the Scientific school which offered best lectures on Geology, chemistry, Minerals, Botany, & seek to make the alphabets of those sciences clear to me. How could leisure or labor be better employed. 'Tis never late to learn them, and every secret opened goes to authorize our aesthetics. Cato learned Greek at eighty years, but these are older bibles & oracles than Greek.

July? 1873

Egypt. Mrs Helen Bell, it seems, was asked "What do you think the Sphinx said to Mr Emerson?" "Why," replied Mrs Bell, "the Sphinx probably said to him, 'You're another.'"

Nov. 1874?

The secret of poetry is never explained—is always new. We have not got farther than mere wonder at the delicacy of the touch, & the eternity it inherits. In every house a child that in mere play utters oracles, & knows not that they are such. 'Tis as easy as breath. 'Tis like this gravity, which holds the Universe together, & none knows what it is.

From Correspondence[†]

To William Emerson, Concord, November 10, 1814

The year 1814 is given in the endorsement by a contemporary hand, apparently William Emerson's. The facsimile of this picture letter [see pp. 532–33] which appears as the frontispiece to L, 1 does not indicate the liberal use of colors on the original, sometimes significant, as in the two blurs standing for the word "read." With the aid of the colors, William Emerson probably read the letter thus:

Concord November 10

DEAR BROTHER,

         I hope you will not be offended if I attempt * a letter in hieroglyphics; I lately read a letter of the Duke of York's in them, it was given to Aunt Sarah [Ripley] by Sheriff Bradford; I have taken many from that. I like Concord very much. I go to school here and I like it more and more every day. Where is that song by G. B. that you promised to send me the day we moved send it as soon as you can. Mrs William Smith in Summer St. begs to have you spend thanksgiving at her house. Have you read Patronage yet. I hope you will soon enjoy the happiness of being here. Aunt and Charles send love Charles more than he can express. Send me your Collectanea Minora 1st time you can. Hieroglyphics take up too much time and paper; so pray excuse my shortness

Yours in love
Ralph.

Wm Emerson.

         * H, non est litera[1]

---

† From *The Letters of Ralph Waldo Emerson*, ed. Ralph L. Rusk and Eleanor M. Tilton. © 1939 Ralph Waldo Emerson Memorial Association. Reprinted by permission of the publisher.

1. Emerson's humorous footnote implies that the letter *H* should be dropped from hay, leaving the reader with *a*. The headnote and transcription are by Ralph L. Rusk (*L* 1.7).

* J—C, non est littera

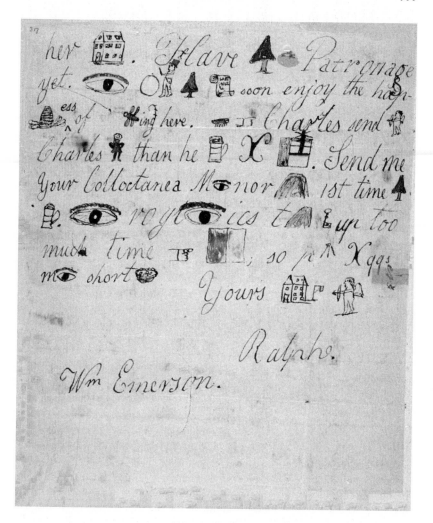

To Mary Moody Emerson, Cambridge,
September 23, 1826

Cambridge, Sept 23d, 1826

My dear Aunt,

* * * Is it not true that modern philosophy by a stout reaction has got to be very conversant with feelings? Bare reason, cold as cucumber, was all that was tolerated in aforetime, till men grew disgusted at the skeleton & have now given him in ward into the hands of his sister, blushing shining changing Sentiment. And under this guardian of public opinion, it is respectfully submitted that public opinion will be apt to run to & fro, a little. Be that as it may, it is one of the *feelings* of modern philosophy, that it is wrong to regard ourselves so much in a *historical* light as we do, putting Time between God & us; and that it were fitter to account every moment of the existence of the Universe as a new Creation, and *all* as a revelation proceeding each moment from the Divinity to the mind of the observer. * * *

Yr *affectionate nephew*
Waldo.

To William Emerson, Charleston, January 6 and 9, 1827

Charleston S. C. 6 Jan. 1827.

Dear William,

* * * I am not sick; I am not well; but luke-sick—and as in my other complaints, so in this, have no symptom that any physician extant can recognize or understand. I have my maladies all to myself. I have but a single complaint,—a certain stricture on the right side of the chest, which always makes itself felt when the air is cold or damp, & the attempt to preach or the like exertion of the lungs is followed by an aching. The worst part of it is the deferring of hopes. * * *

Waldo—

To Mary Moody Emerson, St. Augustine,
March 15? 1827

To M.M.E.   *St Augustine*

I fancy myself better lately thro the blessing of God & the use of this fine air. And if it please him that I shall wholly recover I agree to the sentiment of your letter yt I shall be a wiser & better man. He has seen but half ye Universe who never has been shewn ye house of Pain. Pleasure & Peace are but indifferent teachers of what it is life to know. And tho the mind touched with poetry must have a God, & the heart will reveal one if history does not yet the smooth man of taste & ease will be satisfied with a very indistinct & shadowy personification mixing on every side with the unintelligent forms of nature—some spirit too vague if not too kind to rebuke & punish his sin & pride. But the decay of his hopes; the manifested inefficacy of efforts into which he has pushed the pith & resources of all his nature; suffering & the grievous dependance on other men wh. suffering brings with it.—these things startle the luxurious dreamer, & alarm him with necessities never experienced before. these suggest the possibility of relations more intimate & more awful than friendship & love. they bring to light a system of feelings whose existence was not suspected before, they place him in a connexion with God that furnishes a solution of the mystery of his being.   *   *   *

To the Second Church and Society in Boston, Cambridge, January 30, 1829

To the Second Church & Society in Boston.
Cambridge, 30 January, 1829

CHRISTIAN BRETHREN & FRIENDS,

I have received the communication transmitted to me by your committee inviting me to the office of junior pastor in your church & society. I accept the invitation.

If my own feelings could have been consulted, I should have desired to postpone, at least, for several months, my entrance into this solemn office. I do not now approach it with any sanguine confidence in my abilities, or in my prospects. I come to you in weakness, and not in strength. In a short life, I have yet had abundant experience of the uncertainty of human hopes. I have learned the lesson of my utter dependency; and it is in a devout reliance upon other strength than my own, in a humble trust on God to sustain me, that I put forth my hand to his great work.

But, brethren, whilst I distrust my powers, I must speak firmly of my purposes. I well know what are the claims, on your part, to my best exertions, and I shall meet them, as far as in me lies, by a faithful performance of duty. I shun no labour. I shall do all that I can.

In approaching these duties, I am encouraged by the strong expression of confidence & goodwill, I have received from you. I am encouraged by the hope of enjoying the counsel and aid of the distinguished servant of God who has so long laboured among you. I look to the example of our Lord, in all my hopes of advancing the influence of his holy religion, and I implore the blessing of God upon this connexion to be formed between you and myself.

I am your affectionate friend & servant,

Ralph Waldo Emerson.

To the Proprietors of the Second Church, Boston, September 11, 1832

To the Proprietors of the Second Church.

Boston, 11 September, 1832.

CHRISTIAN FRIENDS,

In the discourse delivered from the pulpit last Sabbath,[2] I explained the circumstances which have seemed to me to make it my duty to resign my office as your minister. I now request a dismission from the pastoral charge. On this occasion, I cannot help adding a few words.

I am very far from regarding my relation to you with indifference. I am bound to you, as a society, by the experience of uninterrupted kindness; by the feelings of respect & love I entertain for you all, as my tried friends; by ties of personal attachment to many individuals among you, which I account the happiness of my life; by the hope I had entertained of living always with you, and of contributing, if possible, in some small degree, to your welfare.

Nor do I think less of the office of a Christian minister. I am pained at the situation in which I find myself, that compels me to make a difference of opinion of no greater importance, the occasion of surrendering so many & so valuable functions as belong to that office. I have the same respect for the great objects of the Christian ministry, & the same faith in their gradual accomplishment through the use of human means, which, at first, led me to enter it. I should be unfaithful to myself, if any change of circumstances could diminish my devotion to the cause of divine truth.

And so, friends, let me hope, that whilst I resign my official relation to you I shall not lose your kindness, & that a difference of opinion as to the value of an ordinance, will be overlooked by us in our common devotion to what is real & eternal.

Ralph Waldo Emerson.

To the Second Church and Society, Boston, December 22, 1832

Boston, 22nd December, 1832

TO THE SECOND CHURCH AND SOCIETY.

Christian Friends,—Since the formal resignation of my official relation to you in my communication to the proprietors in September, I had waited anxiously for an opportunity of addressing you once more from the pulpit, though it were only to say, Let us part in peace and in the love of God. The state of my health has prevented and continues to prevent me from so doing. I am now advised to

---

2. See Sermon CLXII (p. 17).

seek the benefit of a sea-voyage. I cannot go away without a brief parting word to friends who have shown me so much kindness, and to whom I have felt myself so dearly bound.

Our connexion has been very short. I had only begun my work. It is now brought to a sudden close, and I look back, I own, with a painful sense of weakness, to the little service I have been able to render, after so much expectation on my part,—to the chequered space of time, which domestic affliction and personal infirmities have made yet shorter and more unprofitable.

As long as he remains in the same place, every man flatters himself, however keen may be his sense of his failures and unworthiness, that he shall yet accomplish much; that the future shall make amends for the past; that his very errors shall prove his instructors,—and what limit is there to hope? But a separation from our place, the close of a particular career of duty, shuts the books, bereaves us of this hope, and leaves us only to lament how little has been done.

Yet, my friends, our faith in the great truths of the New Testament makes the change of places and circumstances, of less account to us, by fixing our attention upon that which is unalterable. I find great consolation in the thought, that the resignation of my present relations makes so little change to myself. I am no longer your minister, but am not the less engaged, I hope, to the love and service of the same external cause, the advancement, namely, of the kingdom of God in the hearts of men. The tie that binds each of us to that cause is not created by our connexion, and can not be hurt by our separation. To me, as one disciple, is the ministry of truth, as far as I can discern and declare it, committed, and I desire to live no where and no longer than that grace of God is imparted to me—the liberty to seek and the liberty to utter it.

And, more than this, I rejoice to believe, that my ceasing to exercise the pastoral office among you, does not make any real change in our spiritual relation to each other. Whatever is most desireable and excellent therein, remains to us. For, truly speaking, whoever provokes me to a good act or thought, has given me a pledge of his fidelity to virtue,—he has come under bonds to adhere to that cause to which we are jointly attached. And so I say to all you, who have been my counsellors and co-operators in our Christian walk, that I am wont to see in your faces, the seals and certificates of our mutual obligations. If we have conspired from week to week, in the sympathy and expression of devout sentiments; if we have received together the unspeakable gift of God's truth; if we have studied together the sense of any divine word; or striven in any charity; or conferred together for the relief or instruction of any brother; if together we have laid down the dead in pious hope; or held up the babe into the baptism of Christianity; above all if we have shared in any habitual acknowledgement of that benignant God, whose omnipresence raises and glorifies the meanest offices and the lowest ability, and opens heaven in every heart that worships him,—then indeed are we united, we are mutually debtors to each other of faith and hope, engaged to persist and confirm each other's hearts in obedience to the Gospel. We shall not feel that the nominal changes and little separations of this world, can release us from the strong cordage of this spiritual bond. And I entreat you to consider how truly blessed will have been our connexion, if in this manner, the memory of it shall serve to bind each one of us more strictly to the practice of our several duties.

It remains to thank you for the goodness you have uniformly extended towards me, for your forgiveness of many defects, and your patient and even partial acceptance of every endeavor to serve you; for the liberal provision you have ever made for my maintenance; and for a thousand acts of kindness, which have comforted and assisted me.

To the proprietors, I owe a particular acknowledgement, for their recent generous vote for the continuance of my salary, and hereby ask their leave to relinquish this emolument at the end of the present month.

And now, brethren and friends, having returned into your hands the trust you have honored me with—the charge of public and private instruction in this religious society, I pray God, that whatever seed of truth and virtue we have sown and watered together, may bear fruit unto eternal life. I commend you to the Divine Providence. May He grant you, in your ancient sanctuary, the service of able and faithful teachers. May He multiply to your families and to your persons, every genuine blessing; and whatever discipline may be appointed to you in this world, may the blessed hope of the resurrection, which He has planted in the constitution of the human soul, and confirmed and manifested by Jesus Christ, be made good to you beyond the grave. In this faith and hope, I bid you farewell.

> *Your affectionate servant,*
> *Ralph Waldo Emerson.*

To Edward Bliss Emerson, Boston, December 22, 1833,

> *Boston, 22 December, 1833.*

Dear Edward,

* * * One of these days if we may believe the lawyers I am to be the richer for Ellen's estate & whenever that day arrives I hope it will enable me to buy a hearth somewhere to which we pious Æneases[3] may return with our household gods from all the quarters of our dispersion. If you wish to know what I do—I preach at New Bedford, sometimes in Boston; I have written a lecture upon Natural History & am now preparing another for next Tuesday evg. & have promised one to the Mechanics Institute. I meditate something more seriously than ever before, the adventure of a periodical paper which shall speak truth without fear or favor to all who desire to hear it, with such persuasion as shall compel them to speak it also. Henry Hedge is an unfolding man who has just now written the best pieces that have appeared in the Examiner and one especially was a living leaping Logos, & he may help me. * * *

---

3. Protagonist of Virgil's epic poem *The Aeneid*, which documents the fall of Troy and Aeneas's wanderings to Carthage and Italy.

To Edward Bliss Emerson, Newton, May 31, 1834

Newton, 31 May, 1834

MY DEAR BROTHER,

Your last letter to mother postpones to a pretty distance our prospect of seeing you but as some of our feet were shod with quicksilver when we came into the world there is still an even chance that you may slip in upon us in some of these revolutions of Night & Morn. Here sit Mother & I among the pine trees still almost as we shall lie by & by under them. Here we sit always learning & never coming to the knowledge of. — The greatest part of my virtue — that mustard seedlet that no man wots of — is Hope. I am ever of good cheer & if the heaven asks no service at my hands am reconciled to my insignificance yet keeping my eye open upon the brave & the beautiful. Philosophy affirms that the outward world is only phenomenal & the whole concern of dinners of tailors of gigs of balls whereof men make such account is a quite relative & temporary one — an intricate dream — the exhalation of the present state of the Soul — wherein the Understanding works incessantly as if it were real but the eternal Reason when now & then he is allowed to speak declares it is an accident a smoke nowise related to his permanent attributes. Now that I have used the words, let me ask you do you draw the distinction of Milton Coleridge & the Germans between Reason & Understanding. I think it a philosophy itself. & like all truth very practical. So now lay away the letter & take up the following dissertation on Sunday. Reason is the highest faculty of the soul — what we mean often by the soul itself; it never *reasons*, never proves, it simply perceives; it is vision. The Understanding toils all the time, compares, contrives, adds, argues, near sighted but strong-sighted, dwelling in the present the expedient the customary. Beasts have some understanding but no Reason. Reason is potentially perfect in every man — Understanding in very different degrees of strength. The thoughts of youth, & 'first thoughts,' are the revelations of Reason. the love of the beautiful & of Goodness as the highest beauty the belief in the absolute & universal superiority of the Right & the True But understanding that wrinkled calculator the steward of our house to whom is committed the support of our animal life contradicts evermore these affirmations of Reason & points at Custom & Interest & persuades one man that the declarations of Reason are false & another that they are at least impracticable. Yet by & by after having denied our Master we come back to see at the end of years or of life that he was the Truth. * * * So hallelujah to the Reason forevermore.

But glad should I be to hold academical questions with you here at Newton. Whenever you are tired of working at Porto Rico & want a vacation or whenever your strength or your weakness shall commend to you the high countenances of the Muses, come & live with me. The Tucker estate is so far settled that I am made sure of an income of about $1200. wherewith the Reason of Mother & you & I might defy the Understanding upon his own ground, for the rest of the few years in which we shall be subject to his insults. I need not say that what I speak in play I speak in earnest. If you will come we will retreat into Berkshire & make a little world of other stuff. Your brother

Waldo

To Lydia Jackson, Concord, January 24, 1835

Concord 24 January 1835

To Miss Lydia Jackson

I obey my highest impulses in declaring to you the feeling of deep and tender respect with which you have inspired me. I am rejoiced in my Reason as well as in my Understanding by finding an earnest and noble mind whose presence quickens in mine all that is good and shames and repels from me my own weakness. Can I resist the impulse to beseech you to love me? The strict limits of the intercourse I have enjoyed, have certainly not permitted the manifestation of that tenderness which is the first sentiment in the common kindness between man and woman. But I am not less in love, after a new and higher way. I have immense desire that you should love me, and that I might live with you alway. My own assurance of the truth and fitness of the alliance—the union I desire, is so perfect, that it will not admit the thought of hesitation—never of refusal on your part. I could scratch out the word. I am persuaded that I address one so in love with what I love, so conscious with me of the everlasting principles, and seeking the presence of the common Father through means so like, that no remoteness of condition could much separate us, and that an affection founded on such a basis, cannot alter.

I will not embarrass this expression of my heart and mind with any second considerations. I am not therefore blind to them. They touch the past and the future—our friends as well as ourselves, & even the Departed. But I see clearly how your consent shall resolve them all.

And think it not strange, as you will not, that I write rather than speak. In the gravest acts of my life I more willingly trust my pen than my tongue. It is as true. And yet had I been master of my time at this moment. I should bring my letter in my own hand. But I had no leave to wait a day after my mind was made up. Say to me therefore anything but NO. Demand any time for conversation, for consideration, and I will come to Plymouth with a joyful heart. And so God bless you, dear and blessed Maiden. and incline you to love your true friend,

Ralph Waldo Emerson.

My address is Concord, Mass.

To Lydia Jackson, Concord, February 1, 1835

Concord, 1 February—

One of my wise masters, Edmund Burke, said, 'A wise man will speak the truth with temperance that he may speak it the longer.' In this new sentiment that you awaken in me, my Lydian Queen, what might scare others pleases me, its quietness, which I accept as a pledge of permanence. I delighted myself on Friday with my quite domesticated position & the good understanding that grew all the time, yet I went & came without one vehement word—or one passionate sign. In this was nothing of design, I merely surrendered myself to the hour & to the facts. I find a sort of grandeur in the modulated expressions of a love in which the individuals, & what might seem even reasonable personal expectations, are steadily postponed to a regard for truth & the universal love. Do not think me a metaphysical lover. I am a man & hate & suspect the over refiners, & do sympathize with the homeliest pleasures & attractions by which our good foster mother Nature draws her children together. Yet am I well pleased that between us the most permanent ties should be the first formed & thereon should grow whatever others human nature will. * * *

Under this morning's severe but beautiful light I thought dear friend that hardly should I get away from Concord. I must win you to love it. I am born a poet, of a low class without doubt yet a poet. That is my nature & vocation. My singing be sure is very 'husky,' & is for the most part in prose. Still am I a poet in the sense of a perceiver & dear lover of the harmonies that are in the soul & in matter, & specially of the correspondences between these & those. A sunset, a forest, a snow storm, a certain river-view, are more to me than many friends & do ordinarily divide my day with my books. Wherever I go therefore I guard & study my rambling propensities with a care that is ridiculous to people, but to me is the care of my high calling. Now Concord is only one of a hundred towns in which I could find these necessary objects but Plymouth I fear is not one. Plymouth is streets; I live in the wide champaign. * * *

Waldo E.

To Thomas Carlyle, Concord, September 17, 1836

Concord, Massachusetts,
17 September, 1836

* * * I send you a little book [*Nature*] I have just now published, as an entering wedge, I hope, for something more worthy and significant. This is only a naming of topics on which I would gladly speak and gladlier hear. * * *

Yours ever,
R. W. Emerson.

To William Emerson, Concord, October 31, 1836

Concord, Oct. 31, 1836

DEAR WILLIAM,

I have a son [Waldo] born last night at eleven o'clock, a large healthy looking boy. All the circumstances are favorable. Lidian is very comfortable, and we are all rejoiced & thankful. Mother & the bystanders all, pronounce favorable opinions upon the aspect form & demeanor of the bantling. He sucks his thumbs immediately as his grandmother says his father did, at his age, His eyes are of a color not ascertained, as he keeps them shut this morning, but it is thought they are dark blue. You shall have more particulars, shortly. Meantime with much love to Susan & Willie (to whom present greetings from his cousin) I am your affectionate brother

Waldo—

To Martin Van Buren, Concord, April 23, 1838[4]

Concord, Massachusetts, April 23, 1838

SIR:

The seat you fill places you in a relation of credit and dearness to every citizen. By right and natural position, every citizen is your friend. Before any acts, contrary to his own judgment or interest, have repelled the affections of any man, each may look with trust and loving anticipations to your government. Each has the highest right to call your attention to such subjects as are of a public nature, and properly belong to the Chief Magistrate; and the good Magistrate will feel a joy in meeting such confidence. In this belief, and at the instance of a few of my friends and neighbors, I crave of your patience, through the medium of the press, a short hearing for their sentiments and my own; and the circumstance that my name will be utterly unknown to you will only give the fairer chance to your equitable construction of what I have to say.

Sir, my communication respects the sinister rumors that fill this part of the country concerning the Cherokee people. The interest always felt in the aboriginal population—an interest naturally growing as that decays—has been heightened in regard to this tribe. Even to our distant State, some good rumor of their worth and civility has arrived. We have learned with joy their improvement in social arts. We have read their newspapers. We have seen some of them in our schools and colleges. In common with the great body of the American People, we have witnessed with sympathy the painful endeavors of these red men to redeem their own race from the doom of eternal inferiority, and to borrow and domesticate in the tribe the inventions and customs of the Caucasian race. And notwithstanding the unaccountable apathy with which, of late years, the Indians have been sometimes abandoned to their enemies, it is not to be doubted that it is the good pleasure and the understanding of all humane persons in the Republic, of the men and the matrons sitting in thriving independent families all over the land, that they shall be duly cared for, that they shall taste justice and love from all to whom we have delegated the office of dealing with them.

The newspapers now inform us that in December, 1835, a treaty, contracting for the exchange of the entire Cherokee territory, was pretended to be made by an agent on the part of the United States with some persons appearing on the part of the Cherokees; that the fact afterwards transpired that these individual Indians did by no means represent the will of the nation; and that, out of eighteen thousand souls composing the nation, fifteen thousand six hundred

---

4. It appears that this letter never reached President Van Buren. It was published, however, in the *National Daily Intelligencer* on May 14, 1838. A preliminary draft of the letter can be found in *JMN* 12.25–29.

and sixty-eight have protested against the so-called treaty. It now appears that the Government of the United States choose to hold the Cherokees to this sham treaty, and the proceeding to execute the same. Almost the entire Cherokee nation stand up and say, "This is not our act. Behold us! Here are we. Do not mistake that handful of deserters for us." And the President and his Cabinet, the Senate and the House of Representatives, neither hear these men nor see them, and are contracting to put this nation into carts and boats, and to drag them over mountains and rivers to a wilderness at a vast distance beyond the Mississippi. And a paper, purporting to be an army order, fixes a month from this day as the hour for this doleful removal.

In the name of God, sir, we ask you if this is so? Do the newspapers rightly inform us? Men and women, with pale and perplexed faces, meet one another in streets and churches here, and ask if this be so? We have inquired if this be a gross misrepresentation from the party opposed to the Government and anxious to blacken it with the People. We have looked into newspapers of different parties, and find a horrid confirmation of the tale. We are slow to believe it. We hoped the Indians were misinformed, and their remonstrance was premature, and would turn out to be a needless act of terror. The piety, the principle, that is left in these United States—if only its coarsest form, a regard to the speech of men—forbid us to entertain it as a fact. Such a dereliction of all faith and virtue, such a denial of justice, and such deafness to screams for mercy, were never heard of in times of peace, and in the dealing of a nation with its own allies and wards, since the earth was made. Sir, does the Government think that the People of the United States are become savage and mad? From their minds are the sentiments of love and of a good nature wiped clean out? The soul of man, the justice, the mercy, that is the heart's heart in all men, from Maine to Georgia, does abhor this business.

In speaking thus the sentiments of my neighbors and my own, perhaps I overstep the bounds of decorum. But would it not be a higher indecorum coldly to argue a matter like this? We only state the fact, that a crime is projected that confounds our understandings by its magnitude—a crime that really deprives us as well as the Cherokees of a country; for how could we call the conspiracy that should crush these poor Indians our Government, or the land that was cursed by their parting and dying imprecations our country, any more? You, sir, will bring down that renowned chair in which you sit into infamy if your seal is set to this instrument of perfidy; and the name of this nation, hitherto the sweet omen of religion and liberty, will stink to the world.

You will not do us the injustice of connecting this remonstrance with any sectional or party feeling. It is in our hearts the simplest commandment of brotherly love. We will not have this great and solemn claim upon national and human justice huddled aside under the flimsy plea of its being a party act. Sir, to us the questions upon which the Government and the People have been agitated during the past year, touching the prostration of the currency and of trade, seem motes in the comparison. The hard times, it is true, have brought this discussion home to every farmhouse and poor man's table in this town, but it is the chirping of grasshoppers, beside the immortal question whether justice shall be done by the race of civilized to the race of savage man; whether all the attributes of reason, of civility, of justice, and even of mercy, shall be put off by the American People, and so vast an outrage upon the Cherokee nation, and upon human nature, shall be consummated.

One circumstance lessens the reluctance with which I intrude on your attention: my conviction that the Government ought to be admonished of a new historical fact, which the discussion of this question has disclosed, namely, that there exists in a great part of the Northern People a gloomy diffidence of the *moral* character of the Government. On the broaching of this question, a general expression of despondency, of disbelief that any good will accrue from a remonstrance on an act of fraud and robbery, appeared in those men to whom we naturally turn for aid and counsel. Will the American Government steal? will it lie? will it kill? We asked triumphantly. Our wise men shake their heads dubiously. Our counsellors and old statesmen here say that, ten years ago, they would have staked their life on the affirmation that the proposed Indian measures could not be executed; that the unanimous country would put them down. And now the steps of this crime follow each other so fast, at such fatally quick time, that the millions of virtuous citizens whose agents the Government are, have no space to interpose, and must shut their eyes until the last howl and wailing of these poor tormented villages and tribes shall afflict the ear of the world.

I will not hide from you as an indication of this alarming distrust, that a letter addressed as mine is, and suggesting to the mind of the Executive the plain obligations of man, has a burlesque character in the apprehension of some of my friends. I, sir, will not beforehand treat you with the contumely of this distrust. I will at least state to you this fact, and show you how plain and humane people whose love would be honor regard the policy of the Government and what injurious inferences they draw as to the mind of the governors. A man with your experience in affairs must have seen cause to appreciate the futility of opposition to the moral sentiment. However feeble the sufferer, and however great the oppressor, it is in the nature of things that the blow should recoil on the aggressor. For, God is in the sentiment, and it cannot be withstood. The potentate and the People perish before it; but with it and as its executors, they are omnipotent.

I write thus, sir, to inform you of the state of mind these Indian tidings have awakened here, and to pray with one voice more, that you, whose hands are strong with the delegated power of fifteen millions of men, will avert, with that might, the terrific injury which threatens the Cherokee tribe.

> *With great respect, sir, I am, your fellow-citizen,*
> Ralph Waldo Emerson.

For Henry David Thoreau, Concord, May 2, 1838

I cordially recommend Mr Henry D. Thoreau, a graduate of Harvard University in August, 1837, to the confidence of such parents or guardians as may propose to employ him as an instructer. I have the highest confidence in Mr Thoreau's moral character and in his intellectual ability. He is an excellent scholar, a man of energy & kindness, & I shall esteem the town fortunate that secures his services.

> R. Waldo Emerson.

Concord, May 2, 1838.

To Thomas Carlyle, Concord, May 10, 1838

Concord, May 10, 1838

MY DEAR FRIEND,

* * * I occupy or *improve*, as we Yankees say, two acres only of God's earth, on which is my house, my kitchen-garden, my orchard of thirty young trees, my empty barn. My house is now a very good one for comfort, & abounding in room. Besides my house, I have, I believe, $22 000. whose income in ordinary years is 6 per cent. I have no other tithe or glebe except the income of my winter lectures which was last winter 800 dollars. Well, with this income, here at home, I am a rich man. I stay at home and go abroad at my own instance. I have food, warmth, leisure, books, friends. Go away from home,—I am rich no longer. I never have a dollar to spend on a fancy. As no wise man, I suppose ever was rich in the sense of *freedom to spend*, because of the inundation of claims, so neither am I, who am not wise. But at home I am rich,—rich enough for ten brothers. My wife Lidian is an incarnation of Christianity,—I call her Asia—& keeps my philosophy from Antinomianism.[5] My mother—whitest, mildest, most conservative of ladies, whose only exception to her universal preference of old things is her son; my boy, a piece of love & sunshine, well worth my watching from morning to night; these & three domestic women who cook & sew & run for us, make all my household. Here I sit & read & write with very little system & as far as regards composition with the most fragmentary result: paragraphs incompressible each sentence an infinitely repellent particle. In summer with the aid of a neighbor, I manage my garden; & a week ago I set out on the west side of my house forty young pine trees to protect me or my son from the wind of January. The ornament of the place is the occasional presence of some ten or twelve persons good & wise who visit us in the course of the year.— But my story is too long already. * * *

R. W. Emerson

To Amos Bronson Alcott, Concord, June 28, 1838

Concord, 28 June, 1838

MY DEAR SIR,

I have read Psyche twice through some pages thrice; and yet am scarcely able to make up my mind on the main question submitted to me—Shall it be published? It is good and it is bad; it is great, & it is little. If the book were mine, I would on no account print it; and the book being yours, I do not know but it behoves you to print it in defiance of all the critics. * * *

The book neither abounds in new propositions nor writes out applications of old truth in systematic detail to existing abuses. This, you know, is my old song. I demand your propositions; your definitions; your thoughts (in the

5. See n. 9, p. 96.

stricter use of that term, i. e. a new quality or relation abstracted); your facts observed in nature; as in solid blocks. But your method is the reverse of this. Your page is a series of touches. You play. You play with the thought: never strip off your coat, & dig, & strain, & drive into the root & heart of the matter. I wish you would, with this my complaint before you, open at a few pages of Psyche at random & see what a style this is to baulk & disappoint expectation. To use a coarse word—tis all stir & no go.—There is no progress. I become nervous at the patience with which my author husbands his thought—plays about it with a variety of fine phrases, each of which alone were elegant & welcome, but together, are a superfluity. Meantime, the present Ideas of Truth, of Love, of the Infinite, give, I allow, a certain grandeur to the whole. I thought, as I read, of the Indian jungles, vast & flowering, where the sky & stars are visible alway, but no house, no mountain, no man, no definite objects whatever, & no change, or progress; & so, one acre in it is like another, & I can sleep in it for centuries. But mortal man must save his time, & see a new thing at every step. Moreover, I think it carries to an extreme the aphoristic style which is only good if dense with thought, but we must not multiply into many sentences. what could better be condensed into one. It is graceful when intermingled with a freer speech, but by itself is short & chopping like a cord of chips for a cord of wood. * * *

> Your friend,
> R. W. Emerson.

To Henry Ware Jr., Concord, July 28, 1838

Concord, July 28, 1838.

What you say about the discourse at Divinity College, is just what I might expect from your truth and charity, combined with your known opinions. I am not a stock or a stone, as one said in the old time; and could not but feel pain in saying some things in that place and presence, which I supposed might meet dissent, and the dissent, I may say, of dear friends and benefactors of mine. Yet, as my conviction is perfect in the substantial truth of the doctrine of this discourse, and is not very new, you will see, at once, that it must appear to me very important that it be spoken; and I thought I would not pay the nobleness of my friends so mean a compliment, as to suppress my opposition to their supposed views out of fear of offence. I would rather say to them,—These things look thus to me; to you, otherwise. Let us say out our uttermost word, and be the all-pervading truth, as it surely will, judge between us. Either of us would, I doubt not, be equally glad to be apprized of his error. Meantime, I shall be admonished by this expression of your thought, to revise with greater care the "Address," before it is printed (for the use of the Class), and I heartily thank you for this renewed expression of your tried toleration and love.

> *Respectfully and affectionately yours,*
> R. W. E.

To Henry Ware Jr., Concord, October 8, 1838

Concord, October 8, 1838.

MY DEAR SIR,

I ought sooner to have acknowledged your kind letter of last week, and the Sermon it accompanied.[6] The letter was right manly and noble. The Sermon, too, I have read with attention. If it assails any doctrines of mine,—perhaps I am not so quick to see it as writers generally,—certainly I did not feel any disposition to depart from my habitual contentment, that you should say your thought, whilst I say mine.

I believe I must tell you what I think of my new position. It strikes me very oddly, that good and wise men at Cambridge and Boston should think of raising me into an object of criticism. I have always been,—from my very incapacity of methodical writing,—'a chartered libertine,'[7] free to worship and free to rail,—lucky when I could make myself understood, but never esteemed near enough to the institutions and mind of society to deserve the notice of the masters of literature and religion. I have appreciated fully the advantages of my position; for I well know, that there is no scholar less willing or less able to be a polemic. I could not give account of myself, if challenged. I could not possibly give you one of the 'arguments' you cruelly hint at, on which any doctrine of mine stands. For I do not know what arguments mean, in reference to any expression of a thought. I delight in telling what I think; but, if you ask me how I dare say so, or, why it is so, I am the most helpless of mortal men. I do not even see, that either of these questions admits of an answer. So that, in the present droll posture of my affairs, when I see myself suddenly raised into the importance of a heretic, I am very uneasy when I advert to the supposed duties of such a personage, who is to make good his thesis against all comers.

I certainly shall do no such thing. I shall read what you and other good men write, as I have always done,—glad when you speak my thoughts, and skipping the page that has nothing for me. I shall go on, just as before, seeing whatever I can, and telling what I see; and, I suppose, with the same fortune that has hitherto attended me; the joy of finding, that my abler and better brothers, who work with the sympathy of society, loving and beloved, do now and then unexpectedly confirm my perceptions, and find my nonsense is only their own thought in motley. And so I am

Your affectionate servant,
R. W. *Emerson.*

---

6. Emerson's predecessor at Boston's Second Church. Ware was critical of the Divinity School "Address" and responded with a sermon of his own titled "The Personality of the Deity."
7. Emerson alludes to Shakespeare's *King Henry V* 1.1.38–50, where the archbishop of Canterbury eulogizes the king:

> Hear him but reason in divinity,
> And, all-admiring, with an inward wish
> You would desire the king were made a prelate
> *   *   *
> . . . when he speaks,
> The air, a chartered libertine, is still,
> And the mute wonder lurketh in men's ears
> To steal his sweet and honied sentences.

To Thomas Carlyle, Concord, October 17, 1838

Concord, 17 October, 1838.

MY DEAR FRIEND,

* * * At this moment, I would not have you here, on any account. The publication of my "Address to the Divinity College," (copies of which I sent you) has been the occasion of an outcry in all our leading local newspapers against my "infidelity," "pantheism," & "atheism." The writers warn all & sundry against me, & against whatever is supposed to be related to my connexion of opinion, &c; against Transcendentalism, Goethe & *Carlyle*. I am heartily sorry to see this last aspect of the storm in our washbowl. For, as Carlyle is nowise guilty, & has unpopularities of his own, I do not wish to embroil him in my parish-differences. You were getting to be a great favorite with us all here, and are daily a greater, with the American public, but just now, *in Boston,* where I am known as your editor, I fear you lose by the association. Now it is indispensable to your right influence here, that you should never come before our people as one of a clique, but as a detached, that is, universally associated man; so I am happy, as I could not have thought, that you have not yet yielded yourself to my entreaties. Let us wait a little until this foolish clam[or] be overblown. My position is fortunately such as to put me quite out of the reach of any real inconvenience from the panic strikers or the panic struck; & indeed, so far as this uneasiness is a necessary result of mere inaction of mind, it seems very clear to me that, if I live, my neighbors must look for a great many more shocks, & perhaps harder to bear. * * *

Yours affectionately,
R. W. Emerson

To James Freeman Clarke, Concord, December 7, 1838

Concord, December 7, 1838.

MY DEAR SIR,

Here are the verses. They have pleased some of my friends and so may please some of your readers—and you asked me in the spring if I had not somewhat to contribute to your Journal. I remember in your letter you mentioned the remark of some friend of yours that the verses "Take o take those lips away" were not Shakspeare's. I think they are. Beaumont nor Fletcher nor both together were ever I think visited by such a starry gleam as that stanza. I know it is in Rollo but it is in Measure for Measure[8] also & I remember noticing that the Malones & Steevenses & critical gentry were about evenly divided, these for

---

8. For the line Emerson quotes see *Measure for Measure* 4.1.1. With the letter, Emerson sent the manuscript of his poem "The Humble-Bee." *The Bloody Brother; or Rollo, Duke of Normandy,* was written by Fletcher in collaboration not with Beaumont, but probably with Philip Massinger (see n. 4, p. 249) and perhaps also with Ben Jonson and George Chapman.

Shakspeare those for B & F. But the internal evidence is all for one, none for the other. If he did not write it, they did not, & we shall have some fourth unknown singer. What care we *who* sung this or that. It is we at last who sing. Your friend & servan[t]

R. W. *Emerson*

To Margaret Fuller, Concord, August 4, 1840

Concord, Aug. 4, 1840

* * * I begin to wish to see a different Dial from that which I first imagined. I would not have it too purely literary. I wish we might make a Journal so broad & great in its survey that it should lead the opinion of this generation on every great interest & read the law on property, government, education, as well as on art, letters, & religion. A great Journal people must read. And it does not seem worth our while to work with any other than sovereign aims. So I wish we might court some of the good fanatics and publish chapters on every head in the whole Art of Living. I am just now turning my pen to scribble & copy on the subjects of 'Labor,' 'Farm,' 'Reform,' 'Domestic Life,' etc. and I asked myself why should not the Dial present this homely & most grave subject to the men & women of the land. If it could be well & profoundly discussed, no youth in the country could sleep on it. And the best conceivable paper on such a topic would of course be a sort of fruitful Cybele, mother of a hundred gods and godlike papers. That papyrus reed should become a fatal arrow. I know the danger of such latitude of plan in any but the best conducted Journal. It becomes friendly to special modes of reform partisan bigoted. perhaps whimsical; not universal & poetic. But our round table is not, I fancy, in imminent peril of party & bigotry, & we shall bruise each the other's whims by the collision. Literature seems to me great when it is the ornament & entertainment of a soul which proposes to itself the most extensive the most kind the most solemn action whereof man is capable. * * *

To Margaret Fuller, Concord, October 24, 1840

Concord, 24 October, 1840.

MY DEAR MARGARET,

I have your frank & noble & affecting letter, and yet I think I could wish it unwritten. I ought never to have suffered you to lead me into any conversation or writing on our relation, a topic from which with all persons my Genius ever sternly warns me away. I was content & happy to meet on a human footing a woman of sense & sentiment with whom one could exchange reasonable words & go away assured that wherever she went there was light & force & honour. That is to me a solid good; it gives value to thought & the day; it redeems society from that foggy & misty aspect it wears so often seen from our retirements; it is the foundation of everlasting friendship. Touch it not—speak not of it—and this most welcome natural alliance becomes from month to month,—& the slower & with the more intervals the better,—our air & diet. A robust & total understanding grows up resembling nothing so much as the relation of brothers who are intimate & perfect friends without having ever spoken of the fact. But tell me that I am cold or unkind, and in my most flowing state I become a cake of ice. I can feel the crystals shoot & the drops solidify. It may do for others but it is not for me to bring the relation to speech. Instantly I find myself a solitary unrelated person, destitute not only of all social faculty but of all private substance. I see precisely the double of my state in my little Waldo when in the midst of his dialogue with his hobby horse in the full tide of his eloquence I should ask him if he loves me?—he is mute & stupid. I too have never yet lived a moment, have never done a deed—am the youngest child of nature,—I take it for granted that everybody will show me kindness & wit, and am too happy in the observation of all the abundant particulars of the show to feel the slightest obligation resting on me to do any thing or say any thing for the company. I talk to my hobby & will join you in harnessing & driving him, & recite to you his virtues all day—but ask me what I think of you & me,—& I am put to confusion. * * *

Yours affectionately,
R. W. Emerson.

To Margaret Fuller, Concord, March 14, 1841

Concord, 14 March, 1841.

* * * I know but one solution to my nature & relations, which I find in the remembering the joy with which in my boyhood I caught the first hint of the Berkleian[9] philosophy, and which I certainly never lost sight of afterwards. There is a foolish man who goes up & down the country giving lectures on Electricity;—this one secret he has, to draw a spark out of every object, from desk, & lamp, & wooden log, & the farmer's blue frock, & by this he gets his living; for paupers & negroes will pay to see this celestial emanation from their own basket & their own body. Well, I was not an electrician, but an Idealist. I could see that there was a cause behind every stump & clod, & by the help of some fine words could make every old wagon & woodpile & stone wall oscillate a little & threaten to dance; nay, give me fair field,—& the Selectmen of Concord & the Reverend Doctor Poundmedown himself began to look unstable & vaporous. You saw me do my feat—it fell in with your own studies—and you would give me gold & pearls. Now there is this difference between the Electrician,—Mr Quimby[1]—is his name?—(I never saw him)—and the Idealist, namely, that the spark is to that philosopher a toy, but the dance is to the Idealist terror & beauty, life & light. It is & it ought to be; & yet sometimes there will be a sinful empiric who loves exhibition too much. This Insight is so precious to society that where the least glimmer of it appears all men should befriend & protect it for its own sake. * * *

9. See n. 1, p. 43.
1. Phineas Parkhurst Quimby (1802–1866), a mesmerist (see n. 9, p. 53) and mental healer from Maine.

To Mary Moody Emerson, Concord, September 21, 1841

Concord, Sept 21, 1841
Tuesday P.M.

MY DEAR AUNT

Dr. Ripley died this morning soon after four o'clock. . . .
The fall of this oak makes some sensation in the forest, old & doomed as it was, and on many accounts I could wish you had come home with me to the old wigwam & burial mounds of the tribe. He has identified himself with the forms at least of the old church of the New England Puritans: his nature was eminently loyal, not in the least adventurous or democratical, and his whole being leaned backward on the departed, so that he seemed one of the rear guard of this great camp & army which have filled the world with fame, and with him passes out of sight almost the last banner & guide's flag of a mighty epoch; for these men, however in our last days they have declined into ritualists, solemnized the heyday of their strength by the planting and the liberating of America. Great, grim, earnest men! I belong by natural affinity to other thoughts & schools than yours but my affection hovers respectfully about your retiring footprints, your unpainted churches, strict platforms & sad offices, the iron gray deacon and the wearisome prayer rich with the diction of ages. Well the new is only the seed of the old. What is this abolition and Nonresistance & Temperance but the continuation of Puritanism, though it operate inevitably the destruction of the Church in which it grew, as the new is always making the old superfluous.
                              . . . *I am your affectionate Waldo E.*

To Mary Moody Emerson, Concord, January 28, 1842

Concord, 28 January, 1842

MY DEAR AUNT,

My boy, my boy is gone. He was taken ill of Scarlatina on Monday evening, and died last night. I can say nothing to you. My darling & the world's wonderful child, for never in my own or another family have I seen any thing comparable, has fled out of my arms like a dream. He adorned the world for me like a morning star, and every particular of my daily life. I slept in his neighborhood & woke to remember him. Elizabeth [Hoar] was his foster mother filled his heart always with love & beauty which he well knew how to entertain [blank space] and he distinguished her arrival always with the gravest joy.
This thought pleases me now, that he has never been degraded by us or by any, no soil has stained him he has been treated with respect & religion almost, as really innocence is always great & inspires respect. But I can only tell you now that my angel has vanished. You too will grieve for the little traveller, though you scarce have seen his features.
Farewell, dear Aunt.

Waldo E.

To Margaret Fuller, Concord, January 28, 1842

Concord, 28 Jan. 1842.

Dear Margaret,

My little boy must die also. All his wonderful beauty could not save him. He gave up his innocent breath last night and my world this morning is poor enough. He had *Scarlatina* on Monday night. Shall I ever dare to love any thing again. Farewell and Farewell, O my Boy!

W.

To Elizabeth Palmer Peabody, Concord, January 28, 1842

Thanks for your kind invitation, my friend, but the most severe of all afflictions has befallen me, in the death of my boy. He has been ill since Monday of what is called Scarlet Fever & died last night & with him has departed all that is glad & festal & almost all that is social even, for me, from this world. My second child is also sick, but I cannot in a lifetime incur another such loss. Farewell.

R. W. Emerson.

Concord, Jan 28, 1842.

To Caroline Sturgis, Concord, February 4, 1842

Concord, 4 February 1842

Dear Caroline,

The days of our mourning ought, no doubt, to be accomplished ere this, & the innocent & beautiful should not be sourly & gloomily lamented, but with music & fragrant thoughts & sportive recollections. Alas! I chiefly grieve that I cannot grieve; that this fact takes no more deep hold than other facts, is as dreamlike as they; a lambent flame that will not burn playing on the surface of my river. Must every experience—those that promised to be dearest & most penetrative,—only kiss my cheek like the wind & pass away? I think of Ixion & Tantalus & Kehama.[2] Dear Boy too precious & unique a creation to be huddled aside into the waste & prodigality of things! Yet his Image so gentle, yet so rich in hopes, blends easily with every happy moment, every fair remembrance, every cherished friendship of my life. I delight in the regularity & symmetry of his nature. Calm & wise calmly & wisely happy the beautiful Creative Power looked out from him & spoke of anything but Chaos & interruption, signified strength & unity & gladdening, all-uniting life What was the moral of sun & moon of roses & acorns,—that was the moral of the sweet boy's life softened

---

2. In Indian mythology, pronounced a curse that isolated his enemy from many experiences; see also "Experience," p. 200. Ixion, in Greek mythology, was bound by Zeus to a fiery wheel for trying to seduce Hera. Tantalus, see n. 1, p. 116.

only & humanized by blue eyes & infant eloquence. It gladdens me that you loved him & signalized him as you did, and a thousand thanks for your letter. Write to me as soon as you can find it in your heart. Your loving brother

W.

To Lidian Emerson, Providence, February 10, 1842

Thursday Night Feb 10
1842
Providence

DEAR LIDIAN

* * * And now how art thou, Sad wifey? Have the clouds yet broken, & let in the sunlight? Alas! alas! that one of your sorrows, that our one sorrow can never in this world depart from us! Well perhaps we shall never be frivolous again, eating of this everlasting wormwood. Meantime Ellen & Edith shall love you well, & fill all your time, and the remembrances of the Angel shall draw you to sublime thoughts. I look out from the window of the cars for him as Ellen does from the chamber window. * * *

To Lidian Emerson, Castleton, Staten Island, March 1, 1842

Staten Island
Castleton 1 March 1842

DEAR LIDIAN

I came hither on Saturday went up to the city yesterday and tomorrow shall go thither again to establish myself probably in the Globe Hotel on Broadway, which is in a more convenient neighborhood to Wall Street & the Staten Island Boat, & other points which interest me than the Astor House. Yesterday I dined with Mr Horace Greeley & Mr Brisbane, the socialist, at a Graham Boarding House.[3] Mr Brisbane promised me a full exposition of the principles of Fourierism & Association, as soon as I am once lodged at the Globe Hotel. Il faut soumettre:[4] Yet I foresaw in the moment when I encountered these two new friends here, that I cannot content them. They are bent on popular action: I am in all my theory, ethics, & politics a poet and of no more use in their New York than a rainbow or a firefly. Meantime they fasten me in their thought to "Transcendentalism," whereof you know I am wholly guiltless, and which is spoken of as a known & fixed element like salt or meal: So that I have to begin by endless disclaimers & explanations—'I am not the man you take me for.' One of

---

3. Boarding houses that followed the health-food regimen of Sylvester Graham (see n. 6, p. 205). Horace Greeley and Albert Brisbane (see n. 3, p. 423) were noted reformers who touted the utopian communistic system proposed by French thinker Charles Fourier (see n. 3, p. 133).
4. One must submit (French).

these days shall we not have new laws forbidding solitude; and severe penalties on all separatists & unsocial thinkers? * * *

To Margaret Fuller, Concord, June 7, 1843

Concord, 7 June, 1843.

Dear Margaret,

* * * The life lived, the thing done is a paltry & drivelling affair, as far as I know it, though in the presence & consciousness of the magnificent, yea the unspeakably great. Yet I love life—never little,—and now, I think, more & more, entertained & puzzled though I be by this lubricity of it, & inaccessibleness of its pith & heart. The variety of our vital game delights me. I seem in the bosom of all possibility & have never tried but one or two trivial experiments. In happy hours it seems as if one could not lie too lightly on it and like a cloud it would buoy him up & convey him anywhither. But by infirm faith we lose our delicate balance, flounder about & come into the realms & under the laws of mud & stones. The depth of the notes which we accidentally sound on the strings of nature are out of all proportion to our taught & ascertained power and teach us what strangers & novices we are in nature, vagabond in this universe of pure power to which we have not the smallest key. I will at least be glad of my days—I who have so many of them,—and having been informed by God though in the casualest manner that my funds are inexhaustible I will believe it with all my heart. * * *

To Charles Anderson Dana, Concord, October 18, 1843

Concord, October 18, 1843

My dear Sir,

I am sorry I have suffered weeks to pass without a direct answer to your note, & yet there is a kind of fitness in waiting so long. Be it known to you, then, on the part of the total Senate of the Dial, that you shall not have that Journal. It does not seem to be known to you that the moral character of that paper from the beginning through three tedious years & two quarters, has been uniformly masked by a black ingratitude. It has coaxed & wheedled all men & women for contributions: it has sucked & pumped their brains, pilfered their portfolios, peeked into their journals, published their letters, and what it got, it has mutilated, interpolated, & misprinted, and never so much as said, Thank you, or Pardon me; on the contrary, a favourite method has been to extract by importunity a month's labor from its victim, & when it was done, send it back or suppress it as not fit for our purpose. The Dial Senate may possibly know that you have contributed some poems to its numbers. The more excellent they are, the more in character will it be to say, you shall not have the Dial for them, but the Dial must have some more of the poems, & for the next number. If this reasoning from character is not satisfactory, our beggar is almost too proud to whine that the Book is in debt to its gratuitous editor seventy or eighty dollars, & that the edition of the last number it was thought prudent to reduce from 500 to 350 copies, so that it is necessary to sell all the copies to make an honest Dial of it, except the few which are given to large Contributors.

Very respectfully & unthankfully—on the part of the Dial,

C. A. Dana, Esq.

To Margaret Fuller, Concord, December 17, 1843

Concord, 17 December, 1843.

Dear Margaret

My life is made up of excuses, I have thought lately, and I will not add new ones to you—Meantime the deed the affirmation which burns up all apologies delays to be born. The felon Dial, the felon lectures, friend, wife, child, house, woodpile, each in turn is the guilty cause why life is postponed If life were a hoax, what an admirable devil must he be who puts it on us, delay breeding delay & obstruction obstruction until the seventy years are fully told, & we are bowed out before we have even begun. Truly the founders of Oxford fellowships & of celibate orders & the administrators of oaths of silence & of solitude were wise endeavourers & many failures should not discredit their prudence. Deception endless deception,—tis wonderful how rich the world is in this opium. The inexorable demand of every hour, of every eye that is fixed on us, of every friendly tongue, is that we lead the impossible right life; and every step in that direction has a ridiculous & an insane appearance. It requires an enormous perspective, some centuries perhaps, to correct these obliquities & wild refractions of our vision, but we cannot wait for the aesthetic gratification, but must keep the road to Heaven though it lead through Bedlam. It is lucky for the peace of Boston & all honest cities that the scholars & the religious generally are such puny bodies; if they had any vigour answerable to their perception, they would start aside every day from expectation & their own prescription, and destroy the peace of all burgesses. For me, I have only impulse enough to brood now & then on the conditions favorable to thought & life, but not enough yet to make me either pirate or poet. And this "Not Yet" is the arch deceiver of all the ages, and when we sleep will deceive our children. * * *

Waldo—

To Christopher Pearse Cranch, Concord, June 7, 1844

Concord, June 7, 1844.

My dear Sir,

I received a few days ago, in Boston, the beautiful little volume of poems which you had sent me, and on opening them & your letter, I found the deeper obligation you had put me under, by the inscription. * * * But I should like to talk over with you very frankly this whole mystery & craft of poesy. I shall soon, I hope, send you my chapter on "the Poet," the longest piece, perhaps, in the volume I am trying to bring to an end, if I do not become disgusted with the shortcomings of any critical essay, on a topic so subtle & defying. Many, many repentances he must suffer who turns his thoughts to the riddle of the world, & hopes to chant it fitly. each new vision supersedes & discredits all the former ones, and with every day the problem wears a grander aspect, and will not let the poet off so lightly as he meant; it reacts, & threatens to absorb him. He must be the best mixed man in the Universe, or the universe will drive him crazy when he comes too near its secret. Of course, I am a rigorous, cruel critic, & demand in the poet a devotion that seems hardly possible in our hasty, facile America. But you must wait a little, & see my chapter that I promise, to know the ground of my exorbitancy; & yet it will doubtless have nothing new for you. Meantime I am too old a lover of actual literature, not to prize all real skill & success in numbers, not only as a pledge of a more excellent life in the poet, but for the new culture & happiness it promises to the great community around us. So I am again your debtor, and your grateful & affectionate servant.

R. W. Emerson.

To Thomas Carlyle, Concord, December 31, 1844

Concord, 31 December, 1844

My dear friend,

* * * I have your notes of the progress of my London printing, &, at last, the book itself. It was thoughtless in me to ask your attention to the book at all in the proof state: the printer might have been fully trusted with corrected printed pages before him. Nor should Chapman have taxed you for an advertisement: only, I doubt not he was glad of a chance to have business with you; and, of course, was too thankful for any *Preface*.[5] Thanks to you for the kind thought of a "Notice," & for its friendly wit. You shall not do this thing again, if I should send you any more books. A preface from you is a sort of banner or oriflamme, a little too splendid for my occasion, & misleads. I fancy my readers to be a very quiet, plain, even obscure class,— men & women of some religious culture & aspirations, young, or else mystical, & by no means including the great literary & fashionable army which no man can count, who now read your books. If you introduce me, your readers & the literary papers try to read me, & with false expectations. I had rather have fewer readers & only such as belong to me.

I doubt not your stricture on the book as sometimes unconnected & inconsecutive is just. Your words are very gentle. I should describe it much more harshly. My knowledge of the defects of these things I write is all but sufficient to hinder me from writing at all. I am only a sort of lieutenant here in the deplorable absence of captains, & write the laws ill as thinking it a better homage than universal silence. You Londoners know little of the dignities & duties of country

---

5. Carlyle wrote a "notice," or preface, for the British edition of Emerson's *Essays: Second Series*, published by Chapman Brothers.

Lyceums But of what you say now & heretofore respecting the remoteness of my writing & thinking from real life, though I hear substantially the same criticism made by my countrymen, I do not know what it means. If I can at any time express the law & the ideal right, that should satisfy me without measuring the divergence from it of the last act of Congress. And though I sometimes accept a popular call, & preach on Temperance or the Abolition of slavery, as lately on the First of August, I am sure to feel before I have done with it, what an intrusion it is into another sphere & so much loss of virtue in my own. * * *

R. W. Emerson

To William J. Rotch, Concord, November 17, 1845

Concord, Nov. 17th, 1845.

W. J. ROTCH, ESQ., SECRETARY

Dear Sir: — If I come to New Bedford, I should be ready to fix, say the first Tuesday of March, and the second. But I have to say, that I have indirectly received a report of some proceedings in your Lyceum, lately, which, by excluding others, I think ought to exclude me. My informant said, that the application of a colored person for membership by purchase of a ticket in the usual manner, had been rejected by a vote of the Lyceum; and this, for the first time. Now, as I think the Lyceum exists for popular education, as I work in it for that, and think that it should bribe and importune the humblest and most ignorant to come in, and exclude nobody, or, if any body, certainly the most cultivated, — this vote quite embarrasses me, and I should not know how to speak to the company. Besides, in its direct counteraction to the obvious duty and sentiment of New England, and of all freemen in regard to the colored people, the vote appears so unkind, and so unlooked for, that I could not come with any pleasure before the Society.

If I am misinformed, will you — if they are printed — have the goodness to send me the proceedings; or, if not printed, their purport; and oblige,

Yours respectfully,
R. W. Emerson.

To the Corporation of Harvard University, June 25, 1846

TO THE CORPORATION OF HARVARD
UNIVERSITY.
GENTLEMEN,

I request the privilege of borrowing books from the College Library, subject to the usual rules for their safety & return.

I do not find myself included in any class of persons entitled by law to this privilege. I ask it as an alumnus of the College engaged in literary pursuits, & constantly in want of books which only the University can supply, & which it has provided for precisely such needs as mine; and as, in my residence, conveniently situated for easy access to Cambridge

I have formerly endeavoured to borrow books by special orders signed, in each case, by the President. But this mode is very troublesome to the President, & very inconvenient to the borrower. It may easily happen, as it has happened to me, that after I have selected my books at the Library, the President is not at home, or not at liberty; then I must return to my house, fourteen miles distant, without them.

Presuming the willingness of the Corporation to extend the usefulness of their valuable Library to the utmost limits compatible with safety, I pray them to grant me the right of taking books thence, from time to time, in my own name.

R. Waldo Emerson.

Concord, 25 June 1846.

To William Henry Furness, Concord, August 6, 1847

Concord, 6 August, 1847.

DEAR FURNESS,

It was very wrong in you not to come & see me in any of these your northern flights. The last of your Boston visits, for example, I set down as a clear case of contumacy, that you would neither come to me nor be at home where I went to see you. I hope you had my card, which I left at Dr Gannett's. But now I write because Henry D. Thoreau has a book to print. Henry D. Thoreau is a great man in Concord, a man of original genius & character who knows Greek & knows Indian also,—not the language quite as well as John Eliot[6]—but the history monuments & genius of the Sachems, being a pretty good Sachem himself, master of all woodcraft, & an intimate associate of the birds, beasts, & fishes, of this region. I could tell you many a good story of his forest life.—He has written what he calls, "A Week on the Concord & Merrimack Rivers," which is an account of an excursion made by himself & his brother (in a boat which he built) some time ago, from Concord, Mass., down the Concord river & up the Merrimack, to Concord N.H.—I think it a book of wonderful merit, which is to go far & last long. It will remind you of Isaak Walton,[7] and, if it have not all his sweetness, it is rich, as he is not, in profound thought. * * *

R. W. Emerson.

---

6. American "Apostle to the Indians" (seventeenth century), who translated the Bible into the language of the Massachusetts Nation.
7. See n. 9, p. 253.

To Henry David Thoreau, Manchester, December 2, 1847

Manchester, 2 Dec. 1847.

Dear Henry,

Very welcome in the parcel was your letter, very precious your thoughts & tidings. It is one of the best things connected with my coming hither that you could & would keep the homestead, that fireplace shines all the brighter,—and has a certain permanent glimmer therefor. Thanks, evermore thanks for the kindness which I well discern to the *youth* of the house, to my darling little horseman [Edward] of pewter, leather, wooden, rocking & what other breeds, destined, I hope, to ride Pegasus yet, and I hope not destined to be thrown, to Edith who long ago drew from you verses which I carefully preserve, & to Ellen who by speech & now by letter I find old enough to be companionable, & to choose & reward her own friends in her own fashions. She sends me a poem today, which I have read three times!—I believe, I must keep back all my communication on English topics until I get to London which is England. Everything centralizes, in this magnificent machine which England is. Manufacturer for the world she is become or becoming one complete tool or engine in herself—Yesterday the *time* all over the kingdom was reduced to Greenwich time. At Liverpool, where I was, the clocks were put forward 12 minutes. This had become quite necessary on account of the railroads which bind the whole country into swiftest connexion, and require so much accurate interlocking, intersection, & simultaneous arrival, that the difference of time produced confusion. Every man in England carries a little book in his pocket called "Bradshaws Guide", which contains time tables of every arrival & departure at every station on all the railroads of the kingdom. It is published anew on the first day of every month & costs sixpence. The proceeding effects of Electric telegraph will give a new importance to such arrangements.—But lest I should not say what is needful, I will postpone England once for all,—and say that I am not of opinion that your book should be delayed a month. I should print it at once, nor do I think that you would incur any risk in doing so that you cannot well afford. It is very certain to have readers & debtors here as well as there. The Dial is absurdly well known here. We at home, I think, are always a little ashamed of it,—*I* am,— and yet here it is spoken of with the utmost gravity, & I do not laugh. * * *

Yours affectionately,
R. W. E.

To Lidian Emerson, London, March 10, 1848

London, 142 Strand, 8 March, 1848

Dear Lidian,

I am surprised & grieved to hear of your repeated illness & of the illness of the children. Instead of the perfect tranquillity which I thought secured to you by my absence, you have had no rest. Then you have had the ugly vexation of want of money added to all your griefs. I can hardly regret my journey, on the whole, & yet it seems in every way to have cost too much. But by this time I assure myself that you have overcome all your evils & enemies, and are well again with the blooming children. Wherever I go, I find good wives & mothers who ask wistfully after you, & wish to know the colour & quality of that spirit. The daguerre is in much request. * * *

Ah you still ask me for that unwritten letter always due, it seems, always unwritten, from year to year, by me to you, dear Lidian, — I fear too more widely true than you mean, — always due & unwritten by me to every sister & brother of the human race. I have only to say that I also bemoan myself daily for the same cause — that I cannot write this letter, that I have not stamina & constitution enough to mind the two functions of seraph & cherub, oh no, let me not use such great words, — rather say that a photometer cannot be a stove. It must content you for the time, that I truly acknowledge a poverty of nature, & have really no proud defence at all to set up, but ill-health, puniness, and Stygian limitation. Is not the wife too always the complement of the man's imperfections, and mainly of those half men the clerks?[8] Besides am I not, O best Lidian, a most foolish affectionate goodman & papa, with a weak side toward apples & sugar and all domesticities, when I am once in Concord? Answer me that. Well I will come again shortly and behave the best I can Only I foresee plainly that the trick of solitariness never never can leave me. My own pursuits & calling often appear to me like those of an 'astronomer royal' whose whole duty is to make faithful minutes which have only value when kept for ages, and in one life are insignificant: So my result is defeated by the shortness of life, and I am insanely tempted to retrieve or compensate that by concentration & partialism. * * *

Farewell once more, dear Lidian, and do not fail to get well & strong & cheerful and with dear love to Ellen Edith & Eddy,

Yours,
Waldo E.

To William Emerson, Concord, February 10, 1850

Concord, 10 February, 1850.

DEAR WILLIAM

* * * For Mr Quincy's proposition I hardly know what to say to it. This is the third application within a twelvemonth that has come to me to write a memoir of our father; the first from Dr Sprague, the second from William Ware. But I have no recollections of him that can serve me. I was eight years old when he died, & only remember a somewhat social gentleman, but severe to us children, who twice or thrice put me in mortal terror by forcing me into the salt water off some wharf or bathing house, and I still recall the fright with which, after some of this salt experience, I heard his voice one day, (as Adam that of the Lord God in the garden,) summoning us to a new bath, and I vainly endeavouring to hide myself. I have never heard any sentence or sentiment of his repeated by Mother or Aunt, and his printed or written papers, as far as I know, only show candour & taste, or

---

8. I.e., scholars.

I should almost say, docility, the principal merit possible to that early ignorant & transitional *Month-of-March*, in our New England culture. His literary merits really are that he fostered the Anthology & the Athenaeum. These things ripened into Buckminster, Channing & Everett. * * *

your affectionate brother Waldo.

To Paulina W. Davis, Concord, September 18, 1850

Concord, 18 September, 1850.

Mrs. P. W. Davis
Dear Madam,

I have waited a very long time since I had your letter, because I had no clear answer to give, and now I write rather that I may not neglect your letter, than because I have anything very material to say. The fact of the political & civil wrongs of woman I deny not. If women feel wronged, then they are wronged. But the mode of obtaining a redress, namely, a public convention called by women is not very agreeable to me, and the things to be agitated for do not seem to me the best. Perhaps I am superstitious & traditional, but whilst I should vote for every franchise for women, — vote that they should hold property, and vote, yes & be eligible to all offices as men — whilst I should vote thus, if women asked, or if men denied it these things, I should not wish women to wish political functions, nor, if granted assume them. I imagine that a woman whom all men would feel to be the best, would decline such privileges if offered, & feel them to be obstacles to her legitimate influence. Yet I confess lay no great stress on my opinion, since we are all liable to be deceived by the false position into which our bad politics throw elections & electors. If our politics were a little more rational we might not feel any unfitness in accompanying women to the polls. At all events, that I may not stand in the way of any right you are at liberty if you wish it to use my name as one of the inviters of the convention, though I shall not attend it, & shall regret that it is not rather a private meeting of thoughtful persons sincerely interested, instead of what a public meeting is pretty sure to be a heartless noise which we are all ashamed of when it is over. Yours respectfully

R. W. Emerson.

To Wendell Phillips, Concord, February 19, 1853

*Concord
19 February 1853*

My dear Sir,

I read the Petition [for women's suffrage] with attention, & with the hope that I should find myself so happy as to do what you bade me. But this is my feeling in regard to the whole matter: I wish that done for their rights which women wish done. If they wish to vote, I shall vote that they vote. If they wish to be lawyers & judges, I shall vote that those careers be opened to them But I do not think that wise & wary women wish to be electors or judges; and I will not ask that they be made such against their will If we obtain for them the ballot, I suppose the best women would not vote. By all means let their rights of property be put on the same basis as those of men, or, I should say, on a more favorable ground. And let women go to women, & bring us certain tidings what they want, & it will be imperative on me & on us all to help them get it.

I am sorry that you should have had to write twice. Though I am a slow correspondent, I should have written today, without a second urgency. Do not despair of me. I am still open to reason.

> *Yours gratefully,*
> R. W. *Emerson*

To Caroline Sturgis Tappan, Concord, July 22, 1853

Concord,
22 July 1853

DEAR CAROLINE,

* * * The universe is all chemistry, with a certain hint of a magnificent *Whence or Whereto* gilding or opalizing every angle of the old salt-&-acid acid-&-salt, endlessly reiterated & masqueraded through all time & space & form. The addition of that hint everywhere, saves things. Heavy & loathsome is the bounded world, bounded everywhere. An immense Boston or Hanover street with mountains of ordinary women, trains & trains of mean leathern men all immoveably bounded, no liquidity of hope or genius. But they are made chemically good, like oxen. In the absence of religion, they are polarized to decorum, which is its blockhead; — thrown mechanically into parallelism with this high *Whence & Whither*, which thus makes mountains of rubbish reflect the morning sun & the evening star. And we are all privy-counsellors to that Hint, which homeopathically doses the System, & can cooperate with the slow & secular[9] escape of these oxen & semioxen from their quadruped estate, & invite them to be men, & hail them such. I do not know — now that stoicism & Christianity have for two millenniums preached liberty, somewhat fulsomely, — but it is the turn of Fatalism. And it has great conveniences for a public creed. Fatalism, foolish & flippant, is as bad as Unitarianism or Mormonism. But Fatalism held by an intelligent soul who knows how to humor & obey the infinitesimal pulses of spontaneity, is by much the truest theory in use. All the great would call their thought fatalism, or concede that ninety nine parts are nature, & one part power, though that hundredth is elastic, miraculous, and, whenever it is in energy, dissolving all the rest.

Forgive this heavy cobweb, which I did not think of spinning, & which will put you too out of all patience with my prose. But I see sun-colours over all the geometry, & am armed by thinking that our wretched interference is precluded. * * *

---

9. Over a long period of time.

To Walt Whitman, Concord, July 21, 1855[1]

Concord Masstts 21 July 1855

Dear Sir,

I am not blind to the worth of the wonderful gift of "Leaves of Grass." I find it the most extraordinary piece of wit & wisdom that America has yet contributed. I am very happy in reading it, as great power makes us happy. It meets the demand I am always making of what seemed the sterile & stingy Nature, as if too much handiwork or too much lymph in the temperament were making our western wits fat & mean. I give you joy of your free & brave thought. I have great joy in it. I find incomparable things said incomparably well, as they must be. I find the courage of *treatment*, which so delights us, & which large perception only can inspire.

I greet you at the beginning of a great career, which yet must have had a long foreground somewhere, for such a start. I rubbed my eyes a little to see if this sunbeam were no illusion; but the solid sense of the book is a sober certainty. It has the best merits, namely, of fortifying & encouraging.

I did not know until I, last night, saw the book advertised in a newspaper, that I could trust the name as real & available for a Post-Office. I wish to see my benefactor, & have felt much like striking my tasks, & visiting New York to pay you my respects.

R. W. *Emerson.*

To Thomas Carlyle, Concord, May 6, 1856

Concord
6 May, 1856.

Dear Carlyle,

* * * One book, last summer, came out in New York, a nondescript monster which yet has terrible eyes & buffalo strength, & was indisputably American,—which I thought to send you; but the book throve so badly with the few to whom I showed it, & wanted good morals so much, that I never did. Yet I believe now again, I shall. It is called "Leaves of Grass,"—was written & printed by a journeyman printer in Brooklyn, N. Y. named Walter Whitman; and after you have looked into it, if you think, as you may, that it is only an auctioneer's inventory of a warehouse, you can light your pipe with it. * * *

Ever affectionately yours,
R. W. *Emerson*

---

1. This famous letter marks the beginning of Emerson's friendship with Whitman, who repeatedly used the letter (without Emerson's permission) to promote his work.

To Henry David Thoreau, Concord, May 11, 1858[2]

MY DEAR HENRY,

A frog was made to live in a swamp, but a man was not made to live in a swamp.

Yours ever.

R.

To William Henry Seward, Buffalo, January 12, 1863

Concord Masstts.
Jan. 10, 1863

DEAR SIR,

Mr Walt Whitman, of New York, writes me, that he wishes to obtain employment in the public service in Washington, & has made, or is about making some application to yourself.

Permit me to say that he is known to me as a man of strong original genius, combining, with marked eccentricities, great powers & valuable traits of character: a self-relying, large-hearted man, much beloved by his friends; entirely patriotic & benevolent in his theory, tastes, & practice. If his writings are in certain points open to criticism, they yet show extraordinary power, & are more deeply American, democratic, & in the interest of political liberty, than those of any other poet. He is indeed a child of the people, & their champion.

A man of his talents & dispositions will quickly make himself useful. and, if the Government has work that he can do, I think it may easily find, that it has called to its side more valuable aid than it bargained for.

With great respect,
Your obedient servant,
R. W. Emerson

HON. WILLIAM H. SEWARD.
SECRETARY OF STATE.

---

2. It is unlikely that Emerson ever sent this "letter" (found in his journal) to Thoreau.

To Emma Lazarus, Concord, February 24, 1868

Concord
24 February 1868

MY DEAR MISS LAZARUS,[3]

I have so happy recollections of the conversation at Mr Ward's, that I am glad to have them confirmed by the possession of your book & letter. The poems have important merits, & I observe that my poet gains in skill as the poems multiply, & she may at last confidently say, I have mastered the obstructions, I have learned the rules: henceforth I command the instrument, & now, every new thought & new emotion shall make the keys eloquent to my own & to every gentle ear. Few know what treasure that conquest brings, —what independence & royalty. Grief, passion, disaster are only materials of Art, & I see a light under the feet of Fate herself. —Perhaps I like best the poems in Manuscript. Some of those in the book are too youthful, & some words & some rhymes inadmissible. "Elfrida" & "Bertha" are carefully finished, & well told stories, but tragic & painful, —which I think a fault. You will count me whimsical, but I would never willingly begin a story with a sad end. Compensation for tragedy must be made in extraordinary power of thought, or grand strokes of poetry. But you shall instantly defy me, & send me a heartbreaking tale, so rich in fancy, so noble in sentiment that I shall prefer it to all the prosperities of time. I am so glad that you have kept your word to write to so ancient a critic, that I regret the more that you should have had to wait so long for a reply. But I was absent from home when your book arrived, & only now have found & read it.

Yours with all kind regards,
R. W. Emerson

Miss Emma Lazarus.

To Emma Lazarus, Concord, April 14, 1868

Concord, 14 April.
1868

MY DEAR MISS LAZARUS,

You are very kind to write again, & it is good in these cold misplaced days to see your letters on my old desk. I shall not lose my faith in the return of spring. It is the more kind that you risk the wasting of time on such a shut-up dilatory correspondent. But on poetry there is so much to say, that I know not where to begin, & really wish to reply by a treatise of thirty sheets. I should like to be appointed your professor, you being required to attend the whole term. I should be very stern & exigeant, & insist on large readings & writings, & from haughty

---

3. Member of a wealthy and socially prominent family of Sephardic Jews settled in America for many generations, Lazarus (1849–1887) is mainly remembered for her sonnet that is affixed to the pedestal of the Statue of Liberty; but she distinguished herself in other ways. In addition to *Admetus and Other Poems* (1871), she published translations of the work of German-Jewish poet Heinrich Heine (*Poems and Ballads*, 1881) as well as *Songs of a Semite* (1882) and *By the Waters of Babylon* (1887). See her memorial Sonnet to Emerson, p. 614.

points of view. For a true lover of poetry must fly wide for his game, &, though the spirit of poetry is universal & is nearest, yet the successes of poets are scattered in all times & nations, & only in single passages, or single lines, or even words; nay, the best are sometimes in writers of prose. But I did not mean to begin my inaugural discourse on this note; but only sat down to say that I find I am coming to New York in the beginning of next week, & I rely on your giving me an hour, & on your being docile, & concealing all your impatience of your tutor, nay, on your inspiring him by telling him your own results.

In which good hope,

I rest yours faithfully,
R. W. Emerson

Miss Lazarus.

To Emma Lazarus, Concord, July 9, 1869

Concord—
July 9, 1869.

MY DEAR MISS LAZARUS,

I ought long ago to have taken a decided part either to work out my criticism on your poems—as I doubted not at first to do,—or to have sent them back, & committed them to your own. But I still believed that my preoccupations were temporary, & the freedom would presently return—which does not return. * * * For Admetus, I had fully intended to use your consent & carry it to Mr Fields for the "Atlantic." But on reading it over carefully, I found that what had so strongly impressed me on the first reading was the dignity & pathos of the story as you have told it, which still charms me. But the execution in details is not equal to this merit or to the need. You permit feeble lines & feeble words. Thus you write words which you can never have spoken. Please now to articulate the word "smileless,"—which you have used twice at no long interval. You must cut out all the lines & words you can spare & thus add force. I have kept the poem so long that you will have forgotten it much, & will read it with fresh eyes. The dialogue of Hyperion & the Fates is not good enough. Cut down every thing that does not delight you to the least possible. I have marked a few heedless words. "Doubt" does not "ravage" nor be "revenged"

But I hate to pick & spy, & only wish to insist that, after reading Shakspeare for fifteen minutes, you shall read in this MS. a page or two to see what you can spare.

My present thought being that it would not be fair to yourself to offer it to the Atlantic until after your careful revision.

For the Masque,—I had it in mind when I first brought it home to indicate some capital scraps of pastoral poetry in Ben Jonson, to show you what a realism those English brains attained when gazing at flowers & pheasants.

I think the best pastoral is Shakspeare's "Winter's Tale." You will think it cheap to say these proverbs. Who couldn't conjure with Shakspeare's name?

And now that I may pour out all my vitriol at once, I will add that I received the poem on Thoreau, but that I do not think it cost you any day-dawn, or midnight oil. But the poem to the *Heroes* keeps all its value.

On the whole, in this cynicism of mine, & on this suggestion of yours, I decide to inclose the two Manuscripts to you by mail today, & I am not without hope that I may find an opportunity to talk with you about them when you have forgiven me my bilious mood. Your friend,

R W *Emerson*

Miss E. Lazarus.

To Emma Lazarus, Concord, August 23, 1869

Concord, 23 Aug. 1869

MY DEAR MISS LAZARUS,

I have but one serious objection to your kind proposal to grace me with the dedication of the poem, & that is, that I wish to praise the poem to all good readers whom I know; but if I am honored with the dedication my mouth is estopped. Is it not a pity that I do not live nearer New York, I should so like to play the rhetorical tutor, & praise a little the good & impale the bad lines, & put offending words & syllables on the rack in your verses. But you will print "Admetus," & I infer you will print it by itself. I have not said a word lately about the "Atlantic," because Fields went to Europe whilst I was getting ready my scissors & sandpaper, & has left Howels in charge,[4] whom I scarcely know. Yet, if you desire to print it in the "Atlantic," I will carry it to him: in that case, of course, without dedications.

Your friend,
R. W. Emerson

Miss Lazarus

To Emma Lazarus, Concord, August 19, 1870

Concord, August 19, 1870

MY DEAR FRIEND,

I have not known how to write to you since I received your painful note. I had seen the bulletin in the journals[5] without a suspicion that it touched any friend of mine. You know how the eye learns to rush over these records of outrages which we cannot hinder or in any manner repair. Your letter was a dreadful surprise I think very sadly of the desolation which this shock must bring to your peaceful house & to yourself. I can easily see that this ghastly incident will for a long time refuse to be forgotten or hidden or veiled. It will force seriousness & searching insights into the common day which can hide such grim contingences in the current of life which flowed so softly. One can hardly help giving a self application to a terror that thunders like this. Life is serious: Only principles, —

4. James T. Fields was editor of the *Atlantic Monthly*. William Dean Howells, who was to succeed him as editor, had a long and distinguished career as a critic and novelist.
5. Lazarus's maternal uncle, Benjamin Nathan, a vice president of the New York Stock Exchange, had apparently been murdered.

nothing less than relations to heaven itself can keep our serenity amid these horrors. I know how we hate & shun the dismal. It seems rather to lead *from* than *to*
thought, & so wastes the Soul. But that doleful tract is part also of the Universe,
&, if patiently watched, grows translucent presently, & its news is at last good.

But I ought not to add words. In the presence of dismaying events we must
be as self-collected & sane as we can, & await the return to the Divine Soul
which will not forget us in these extremes. Perhaps the best facts in history are
the triumphs of the will of the sufferer in fiercest pain. In my childhood my ear
was filled with such examples by my guardian Aunt: but in my stagnant life they
have been only pictures. Perhaps each of us is to pass somewhere through each
experience once. I shall gladly hear from you when you are at liberty to write.
Meantime, I beg you to offer my respect & sympathy to your parents & sisters.

Your friend,
R. W. Emerson

Miss Emma Lazarus.

To Lidian Emerson, the *Wyoming*, October 31 and November 2, 1872

Steamer Wyoming,
October 31, 1872

DEAR LIDIAN,

Our floor & table tip a good deal, & perhaps our pens will refuse a straight line:
but we are recovering our own personality, & mean to remember our relations.
On the whole, the sea has been merciful, & for myself I have not had a sick hour.
Ellen has not been so stout, but has found the steamer a far better floor than her
beloved barque Fredonia. We have a quite amiable ship's company, & no social
difficulties. Tis now our eighth day & we are promised, perhaps flatteringly, to
reach our port on Sunday. We run about 260 or 270 miles per day. My well known
orthodoxy, you will be glad to know, is walled round by whole families of mis-
sionaries, & I heard two sermons, & the English service, & many hymns on Sunday. But the liberal ocean sings louder, & makes us all of one church. * * *

Yours affectionately always,
R. W. Emerson

To Emma Lazarus, Concord, July 22, 1876

Concord
July 22,

MY DEAR MISS LAZARUS,

I send you warm thanks for your kind letter & invitation; — but an old man
fears most his best friends. It is not them that he is willing to distress with his

perpetual forgetfulness of the right word for the name of book or fact or person he is eager to recall, but which refuses to come. I have grown silent to my own household under this vexation, & cannot afflict dear friends with my tied tongue. Happily this embargo does not reach to the eyes, and I read with unbroken pleasure. My daughter Ellen thanks you for kind invitation but is homebound in these months. No, the right way for you to help us is that you, who, I believe, never have entered Massachusetts, should come & spend a week in Concord, & correct our village narrowness. My Wife joins me heartily in this request. Now to give it practicable form,—I learn from Ellen that I am bound with cords to go to my daughter Edith Forbes, at Naushon Island, in the second week of August, where they claim of us some ten days—other limitations know I none, & the fourth week of August you might persuade Newport to spare you.[6] With very kind regards to your father & your family,

Your friend,
R. W. Emerson

Miss Emma Lazarus.

To George Stewart Jr., Concord, January 22, 1877

Concord Masstts
22 January 1877

Dear Sir,

I have to thank you for the very friendly notice of myself which I find in Belford's Monthly Magazine, which I ought to have acknowledged some days ago. The tone of it is courtly & kind, & suggests that the writer is no stranger to Boston & its scholars. In one or two hints he seems to me to have been mis-informed. The only pain he gives me is in his estimate of Thoreau, whom he underrates. Thoreau was a superior genius. I read his books & manuscripts always with new surprise at the range of his topics & the novelty & depth of his thought. A man of large reading, of quick perception, of great practical courage & ability,—who grew greater every day, &, had his short life been prolonged would have found few equals to the power & wealth of his mind. * * *

R. W. Emerson

Mr George Stewart, Jr.

6. Lazarus did, in fact, spend a week in the Emerson household in August 1876 (she seems to have gotten over her disappointment at not being included in Emerson's poetry anthology, *Parnassus*) and created quite a stir. In a letter to her sister Edith, Ellen Emerson observed: "think of what nuts it was to me, old S.S. teacher that I am, to get at a real unconverted Jew (who had no objection to calling herself one, and talked freely about 'Our Church' and 'we Jews',) and hear how Old Testament sounds to her, & find she has been brought up to keep the Law, and the Feast of Passover, and the Day of Atonement." See *The Letters of Ellen Tucker Emerson*, ed. Edith E. W. Gregg (1982), 2.223–25.

CONTEXTS

Transcendentalism

MADAME DE STAËL

From On Germany[†]

This chapter is a resumé of my whole book, in some respects: since enthusiasm is the distinguishing characteristic of the German nation, its influence on enlightenment can be judged according to German intellectual progress. Enthusiasm lends life to invisible things, and interest to things without immediate bearing on our worldly prosperity. That's why this feeling is characteristic of the quest for abstract truths, which are cultivated in Germany with remarkable ardor and loyalty.

While philosophers inspired by enthusiasm may do the most accurate and patient work, they are also the last ones to aim at brilliance. They love knowledge for itself, and do not take themselves into account when the object of their cult is at stake. Physical nature follows its unvarying course through the destruction of individuals; man's thought becomes sublime when he succeeds in thinking of himself from a universal point of view. He then quietly contributes to the triumph of truth: truth, like nature, is a force that acts only through progressive and regular development.

It would be no mistake to say that enthusiasm makes people tend toward systematic theories; anyone who is very much attached to his own ideas wants to relate everything else to them too. All the same, though, it is usually easier to deal with sincere opinions than with opinions adopted out of vanity. We would have no trouble reaching an understanding in human relationships if we had to deal only with what people really think; the discord comes from what they pretend to be thinking.

Enthusiasm is often accused of leading to error, but superficial interest can be much more misleading. To reach the heart of things, we need some impulse arousing us to get eagerly involved. Considering the human destiny in general, I think we can say that we come across the truth only when our souls are elevated; anything that tends to put us down is a lie. Error, despite everything people say, is on the side of vulgar emotions.

Let me repeat: enthusiasm has nothing to do with fanaticism, and cannot lead people astray. Enthusiasm is tolerant—not out of indifference, but because it makes us feel the interest and beauty of everything. Reason does not replace the happiness it takes away from us; enthusiasm finds in the heart's reverie and the mind's whole range of thought what fanaticism and passion concentrate in

---

† Translated into English in 1814. From *An Extraordinary Woman: Selected Writings of Germaine de Staël*, ed. Vivian Folkenflik. © 1987 Columbia University Press. Reprinted by permission of the publisher.

a single idea, a single object. The universality of this feeling is precisely what makes it favorable to thought and imagination.

Society develops the mind, but only contemplation can form genius. In countries dominated by vanity, vanity is the moving force, and it leads inexorably to mockery, which kills enthusiasm.

Who can deny the fun of noticing ridiculous things, and sketching them in a lively, graceful way? It might be better to refuse to give in to such pleasure; but this is not a threatening kind of mockery. Really disastrous mockery is the kind that focuses on ideas and sentiments, infiltrating the source of strong, devoted affections. Man has great power over his fellow man, and the greatest harm he can do him is to interpose the phantom of ridicule between his generous impulses and the actions they might inspire.

Love, genius, talent—even pain: these sacred things are all exposed to irony, and no one can calculate how far the power of that irony may extend. There is something piquant about wickedness, something feeble about truth. Admiration for great things can be upset by joking: anyone who attaches no importance to anything looks as if he were above everything. If enthusiasm does not protect our hearts and minds, therefore, they may be assaulted by a sort of denigration of the beautiful, combining insolence and gaiety.

Our social minds are constructed so that we often command ourselves to laugh, and are even more frequently ashamed to cry. Why? Because vanity feels more secure with jest than with emotion. We have to be able to count on our own minds if we are to face mockery seriously; we need a lot of strength to show sentiments vulnerable to ridicule. As Fontenelle said: "I am eighty years old; I am a Frenchman; and in my whole life I have never ridiculed the least little virtue in the least little way."[1] This saying implies a deep understanding of society. Fontenelle was not a man of feeling, but he was a man of wit, and whoever is endowed with any sort of superiority always senses human nature's need to be serious. Only mediocre people want everything to be built on sand, so that no one can leave a trace of himself on earth more durable than their own.

Germans do not have to struggle against the enemies of enthusiasm, and this removes one great obstacle for men of distinction. The mind sharpens itself in combat, but talent needs confidence. To experience the inspiration of genius one must believe in admiration, glory, and immortality. The difference between centuries does not come from nature, always free with her gifts, but from the ruling opinion of the time. If this opinion tends toward enthusiasm, great men rise up everywhere. If discouragement is proclaimed instead of the call to noble efforts, nothing will be left of literature but judges of times past.

The terrible events we have witnessed have left us with souls blasé; everything related to thought pales beside the omnipotence of action. Varying circumstances have led people to change their minds on a given question again and again, so no one believes in ideas anymore—or at least thinks of them as anything more than means to an end. Belief does not seem a thing of our time: when a man says he has an opinion people take it for a delicate way of saying that he has some particular interest.

The most decent men then invent a system transforming their laziness into dignity; they say nothing can be accomplished; they agree with Shakespeare's

---

1. According to the biographical notice written by her cousin, Mme. Necker de Saussure, Mme. de Staël used to add, "I could say the same thing of myself, about the least little sorrow." Bernard de Fontenelle (1657–1757) was the author of *Conversations on the Plurality of Worlds* (1686).

Hermit of Prague: "That that is, is";[2] they say that theories have no influence on the world. In the end such men make what they are saying come true, because with such a way of thinking it is impossible to act on other people. If wit consisted only in seeing the pros and cons of everything, it would make everything spin around us so much that we would be unable to walk firmly on such shaky ground.

We also see young people, eager to seem disillusioned of enthusiasm, affecting a considered contempt for exalted feelings. They think they are showing precocious strength of mind: they are actually boasting about premature decadence. As for talent, they are like the old man asking if people still fell in love. The mind deprived of imagination would be quite willing to despise nature itself, if nature were not the stronger.

People still aroused by noble desires are certainly hurt by the constant barrage of arguments that would disturb even the most confident hope. Good faith must not be discouraged by this, though, because it is concerned with what men really are, not what they seem to be. Whatever the surrounding atmosphere, a sincere word is never completely lost; success may have its day, but there are centuries for the good that can be done by truth.

Each of the inhabitants of Mexico carries a little stone along the main highway to add to the great pyramid they are building in the middle of their country. It will bear no one's name, but every one of them will have contributed to a monument that will last longer than them all.

WILLIAM WORDSWORTH

Prospectus to *The Recluse*[†]

It is not the Author's intention formally to announce a system: it was more animating to him to proceed in a different course; and if he shall succeed in conveying to the mind clear thoughts, lively images, and strong feelings, the Reader will have no difficulty in extracting the system for himself. And in the mean time the following passage, taken from the conclusion of the first Book of the Recluse, may be acceptable as a kind of *Prospectus* of the design and scope of the whole Poem.

> "On Man on Nature, and on Human Life
> Musing in Solitude, I oft perceive
> Fair trains of imagery before me rise,
> Accompanied by feelings of delight
> Pure, or with no unpleasing sadness mixed;   5
> And I am conscious of affecting thoughts
> And dear remembrances, whose presence soothes
> Or elevates the Mind, intent to weigh
> The good and evil of our mortal state.
> —To these emotions, whencesoe'er they come,   10
> Whether from breath of outward circumstance,
> Or from the Soul—an impulse to herself,
> I would give utterance in numerous Verse.

2. *Twelfth Night* 4.2.
† From Preface to *The Excursion* (1814).

—Of Truth, of Grandeur, Beauty, Love, and Hope—
And melancholy Fear subdued by Faith;   15
Of blessed consolations in distress;
Of moral strength, and intellectual power;
Of joy in widest commonalty spread;
Of the individual Mind that keeps her own
Inviolate retirement, subject there   20
To Conscience only, and the law supreme
Of that Intelligence which governs all;
I sing:— "fit audience let me find though few!"

So prayed, more gaining than he asked, the Bard,
Holiest of Men.—Urania, I shall need   25
Thy guidance, or a greater Muse, if such
Descend to earth or dwell in highest heaven!
For I must tread on shadowy ground, must sink
Deep—and, aloft ascending, breathe in worlds
To which the heaven of heavens is but a veil.   30
All strength—all terror, single or in bands,
That ever was put forth in personal form;
Jehovah—with his thunder, and the choir
Of shouting Angels, and the empyreal thrones,
I pass them, unalarmed. Not Chaos, not   35
The darkest pit of lowest Erebus,
Nor aught of blinder vacancy—scooped out
By help of dreams, can breed such fear and awe
As fall upon us often when we look
Into our Minds, into the Mind of Man,   40
My haunt, and the main region of my Song.
—Beauty—a living Presence of the earth,
Surpassing the most fair ideal Forms
Which craft of delicate Spirits hath composed
From earth's materials—waits upon my steps;   45
Pitches her tents before me as I move,
An hourly neighbour. Paradise, and groves
Elysian, Fortunate Fields—like those of old
Sought in the Atlantic Main, why should they be
A history only of departed things,   50
Or a mere fiction of what never was?
For the discerning intellect of Man,
When wedded to this goodly universe
In love and holy passion, shall find these
A simple produce of the common day.   55
—I, long before the blissful hour arrives,
Would chaunt, in lonely peace, the spousal verse
Of this great consummation:—and, by words
Which speak of nothing more than what we are,
Would I arouse the sensual from their sleep   60
Of Death, and win the vacant and the vain
To noble raptures; while my voice proclaims
How exquisitely the individual Mind
(And the progressive powers perhaps no less

Of the whole species) to the external World   65
Is fitted:—and how exquisitely, too,
Theme this but little heard of among Men,
The external world is fitted to the Mind;
And the creation (by no lower name
Can it be called) which they with blended might   70
Accomplish:—this is our high argument.
—Such grateful haunts foregoing, if I oft
Must turn elsewhere—to travel near the tribes
And fellowships of men, and see ill sights
Of madding passions mutually inflamed;   75
Must hear Humanity in fields and groves
Pipe solitary anguish; or must hang
Brooding above the fierce confederate storm
Of sorrow, barricadoed evermore
Within the walls of Cities; may these sounds   80
Have their authentic comment,—that, even these
Hearing, I be not downcast or forlorn!
—Come thou prophetic Spirit, that inspir'st
The human Soul of universal earth,
Dreaming on things to come; and dost possess   85
A metropolitan Temple in the hearts
Of mighty Poets; upon me bestow
A gift of genuine insight; that my Song
With star-like virtue in its place may shine;
Shedding benignant influence,—and secure,   90
Itself, from all malevolent effect
Of those mutations that extend their sway
Throughout the nether sphere!—And if with this
I mix more lowly matter; with the thing
Contemplated, describe the Mind and Man   95
Contemplating; and who, and what he was,
The transitory Being that beheld
This Vision,—when and where, and how he lived;—
Be not this labour useless."

FREDERIC HENRY HEDGE

From Coleridge's Literary Character[†]

* * *

We beg leave to offer a few explanatory remarks respecting German meta-physics,[1] which seem to us to be called for by the present state of feeling among literary men in relation to this subject. We believe it impossible to understand fully the design of Kant and his followers, without being endowed to a certain ex-

---

[†] *The Christian Examiner* 14 (March 1833): 109–29.
1. When we speak of *German* metaphysics we wish to be understood as referring to the systems of intel-lectual philosophy which have prevailed in Germany since Kant. Our remarks do not apply to Leibnitz, Wolf, or any of Kant's predecessors

tent with the same powers of abstraction and synthetic generalization which they possess in so eminent a degree. In order to become fully master of their meaning, one must be able to find it in himself. Not all are born to be philosophers, or are capable of becoming philosophers, any more than all are capable of becoming poets or musicians. The works of the transcendental philosophers may be translated word for word, but still it will be impossible to get a clear idea of their philosophy, unless we raise ourselves at once to a transcendental point of view. Unless we take our station with the philosopher and proceed from his ground as our starting-point, the whole system will appear to us an inextricable puzzle. As in astronomy the motions of the heavenly bodies seem confused to the geocentric observer, and are intelligible only when referred to their heliocentric place, so there is only one point from which we can clearly understand and decide upon the speculations of Kant and his followers; that point is the interior consciousness, distinguished from the common consciousness, by its being an active and not a passive state. In the language of the school, it is a free intuition, and can only be attained by a vigorous effort of the will. It is from an ignorance of this primary condition, that the writings of these men have been denounced as vague and mystical. Viewing them from the distance we do, their discussions seem to us like objects half enveloped in mist; the little we can distinguish seems most portentously magnified and distorted by the unnatural refraction through which we behold it, and the point where they touch the earth is altogether lost. The effect of such writing upon the uninitiated, is like being in the company of one who has inhaled an exhilarating gas. We witness the inspiration, and are astounded at the effects, but we can form no conception of the feeling until we ourselves have experienced it. To those who are without the veil, then, any *exposé* of transcendental views must needs be unsatisfactory. Now if any one chooses to deny the point which these writers assume, if any one chooses to call in question the metaphysical existence of this interior consciousness, and to pronounce the whole system a mere fabrication, or a gross self-delusion,—to such a one the disciples of this school have nothing further to say; for him their system was not conceived. Let him content himself, if he can, with "that compendious philosophy which talking of mind, but thinking of brick and mortar, or other images equally abstracted from body, contrives a theory of spirit, by nicknaming matter, and in a few hours can qualify the dullest of its disciples to explain the *omne scibile* by reducing all things to impressions, ideas, and sensations." The disciples of Kant wrote for minds of quite another stamp, they wrote for minds that seek with faith and hope a solution of questions which that philosophy meddles not with,—questions which relate to spirit and form, substance and life, free will and fate, God and eternity. Let those who feel no interest in these questions, or who believe not in the possibility of our approaching any nearer to a solution of them, abstain for ever from a department of inquiry for which they have neither talent nor call. There are certain periods in the history of society, when, passing from a state of spontaneous production to a state of reflection, mankind are particularly disposed to inquire concerning themselves and their destination, the nature of their being, the evidence of their knowledge, and the grounds of their faith. Such a tendency is one of the characteristics of the present age, and the German philosophy is the strongest expression of that tendency; it is a striving after information on subjects which have been usually considered as beyond the reach of human intelligence, an attempt to penetrate into the most hidden mysteries of our being. In every philosophy there are three things to be considered, the object, the method, and the result. In the transcendental system, the *object* is to discover in every form of finite existence, an infinite and unconditioned as the ground of its existence, or rather as the ground of our knowledge of its existence, to refer all phenomena to certain *noumena*,[2] or laws of cognition. It is not a *ratio essendi*, but a *ratio cognoscendi*; it seeks not to explain the existence of God and creation, objectively considered, but to explain our knowledge of their existence. It is not a skeptical philosophy;[3] it seeks not to overthrow, but to build up; it wars not with the common opinions and general experience of mankind, but aims to place these on a scientific basis, and to verify them by scientific demonstrations.

* * *

If now it be asked, as probably it will be asked, whether any definite and substantial good has resulted from the labors of Kant and his followers, we answer, Much. More than metaphysics ever before accomplished, these men have done for the advancement of the human intellect. It is true the immediate, and if we may so speak, the calculable results of their speculations are not so numerous nor so evident as might have been expected: these are chiefly comprised under the head of method. Yet even here we have enough to make us rejoice that such men have been, and that they have lived and spoken in our day. We need mention only the sharp and rightly dividing lines that have been drawn within and around the kingdom of human knowledge; the strongly marked distinctions of subject and object, reason and understanding, phenomena and noumena;—the categories established by Kant; the moral liberty proclaimed by him as it had never been proclaimed by any before; the authority and evidence of law and duty set forth by Fichte; the universal harmony illustrated by Schelling. But in mentioning these things, which are the direct results of the critical philosophy, we have by no means exhausted all that that philosophy has done for liberty and truth. The pre-eminence of Germany among the nations of our day in respect of intellectual culture, is universally acknowledged; and we do fully believe that whatever excellence that nation has attained in science, in history, or poetry is mainly owing to the influence of her philosophy, to the faculty which that philosophy has imparted of seizing on the spirit of every question, and determining at once the point of view from which each subject should be regarded,—in one word, to the transcendental method.

* * *

2. Kant, *Kritik der reinen Vernunft*. [Hedge] *Critique of Pure Reason*. [Editors]
3. Perhaps the writings of Fichte may be considered as an exception to this statement.

SAMPSON REED

Genius[†]

The world was always busy; the human heart has always had love of some kind; there has always been fire on the earth. There is something in the inmost principles of an individual, when he begins to exist, which urges him onward; there is something in the centre of the character of a nation, to which the people aspire; there is something which gives activity to the mind in all ages, countries, and worlds. This principle of activity is love: it may be the love of good or of evil; it may manifest itself in saving life or in killing; but it is love.

The difference in the strength and direction of the affections creates the distinctions in society. Every man has a form of mind peculiar to himself. The mind of the infant contains within itself the first rudiments of all that will be hereafter, and needs nothing but expansion; as the leaves and branches and fruit of a tree are said to exist in the seed from which it springs. He is bent in a particular direction; and, as some objects are of more value than others, distinctions must exist. What it is that makes a man great depends upon the state of society: with the savage, it is physical strength; with the civilized, the arts and sciences; in heaven, the perception that love and wisdom are from the Divine.

There prevails an idea in the world, that its great men are more like God than others. This sentiment carries in its bosom sufficient evil to bar the gates of heaven. So far as a person possesses it, either with respect to himself or others, he has no connection with his Maker, no love for his neighbor, no truth in his understanding. This was at the root of heathen idolatry: it was this that made men worship saints and images. It contains within itself the seeds of atheism, and will ultimately make every man insane by whom it is cherished. The life which circulates in the body is found to commence in the head; but, unless it be traced through the soul up to God, it is merely corporeal, like that of the brutes.

Man has often ascribed to his own power the effects of the secret operations of divine truth. When the world is immersed in darkness, this is a judgment of the Most High; but the light is the effect of the innate strength of the human intellect.

When the powers of man begin to decay, and approach an apparent dissolution, who cannot see the Divinity? But what foreign aid wants the man who is full of his own strength? God sends the lightning that blasts the tree; but what credulity would ascribe to him the sap that feeds its branches? The sight of idiotism leads to a train of religious reflections; but the face that is marked with lines of intelligence is admired for its own inherent beauty. The hand of the Almighty is visible to all in the stroke of death; but few see his face in the smiles of the new-born babe.

The intellectual eye of man is formed to see the light, not to make it; and it is time that, when the causes that cloud the spiritual world are removed, man should rejoice in the truth itself, and not that *he* has found it. More than once, when nothing was required but for a person to stand on this world with his eyes open, has the truth been seized upon as a thing of his own making. When the

† From Elizabeth P. Peabody, ed., *Aesthetic Papers* (New York, 1849), pp. 58–64.

power of divine truth begins to dispel the darkness, the objects that are first disclosed to our view—whether men of strong understanding, or of exquisite taste, or of deep learning—are called geniuses. Luther, Shakspeare, Milton, Newton, stand with the bright side towards us.

There is something which is called genius, that carries in itself the seeds of its own destruction. There is an ambition which hurries a man after truth, and takes away the power of attaining it. There is a desire which is null, a lust which is impotence. There is no understanding so powerful, that ambition may not in time bereave it of its last truth, even that two and two are four. Know, then, that genius is divine, not when the man thinks that he is God, but when he acknowledges that his powers are from God. Here is the link of the finite with the infinite, of the divine with the human: this is the humility which exalts.

The arts have been taken from nature by human invention; and, as the mind returns to its God, they are in a measure swallowed up in the source from which they came. We see, as they vanish, the standard to which we should refer them. They are not arbitrary, having no foundation except in taste: they are only modified by taste, which varies according to the state of the human mind. Had we a history of music, from the war-song of the savage to the song of angels, it would be a history of the affections that have held dominion over the human heart. Had we a history of architecture, from the first building erected by man to the house not made with hands, we might trace the variations of the beautiful and the grand, alloyed by human contrivance, to where they are lost in beauty and grandeur. Had we a history of poetry, from the first rude effusions to where words make one with things, and language is lost in nature, we should see the state of man in the language of licentious passion, in the songs of chivalry, in the descriptions of heroic valor, in the mysterious wildness of Ossian; till the beauties of nature fall on the heart, as softly as the clouds on the summer's water. The mind, as it wanders from heaven, moulds the arts into its own form, and covers its nakedness. Feelings of all kinds will discover themselves in music, in painting, in poetry; but it is only when the heart is purified from every selfish and worldly passion, that they are created in real beauty; for in their origin they are divine.

Science is more fixed. It consists of the laws according to which natural things exist; and these must be either true or false. It is the natural world in the abstract, not in the concrete. But the laws according to which things exist, are from the things themselves, not the opposite. Matter has solidity: solidity makes no part of matter. If, then, the natural world is from God, the abstract properties, as dissected and combined, are from him also. If, then, science be from Him who gave the ten commandments, must not a life according to the latter facilitate the acquirement of the former? Can *he* love the works of God who does not love his commandments? It is only necessary that the heart be purified, to have science like poetry its spontaneous growth. Self-love has given rise to many false theories, because a selfish man is disposed to make things differently from what God has made them. Because God is love, nature exists; because God is love, the Bible is poetry. If, then, the love of God creates the scenery of nature, must not he whose mind is most open to this love be most sensible of natural beauties? But in nature both the sciences and the arts exist embodied.

Science may be learned from ambition; but it must be by the sweat of the brow. The filthy and polluted mind *may* carve beauties from nature, with which it has no allegiance: the rose is blasted in the gathering. The olive and the vine had rather live with God, than crown the head of him whose love for them is a lust for glory. The man is cursed who would rob nature of her graces, that he may use them to allure the innocent virgin to destruction.

Men say there is an inspiration in genius. The genius of the ancients was the good or evil spirit that attended the man. The moderns speak of the magic touch of the pencil, and of the inspiration of poetry. But this inspiration has been esteemed so unlike religion, that the existence of the one almost supposes the absence of the other. The spirit of God is thought to be a very different thing when poetry is written, from what it is when the heart is sanctified. What has the inspiration of genius in common with that of the cloister? The one courts the zephyrs; the other flies them. The one is cheerful; the other, sad. The one dies; the other writes the epitaph. Would the Muses take the veil? Would they exchange Parnassus for a nunnery? Yet there has been learning, and even poetry, under ground. The yew loves the graveyard; but other trees have grown there.

It needs no uncommon eye to see, that the finger of death has rested on the church. Religion and death have in the human mind been connected with the same train of associations. The churchyard is the graveyard. The bell which calls men to worship is to toll at their funerals, and the garments of the priests are of the color of the hearse and the coffin. Whether we view her in the strange melancholy that sits on her face, in her mad reasonings about truth, or in the occasional convulsions that agitate her limbs, there are symptoms, not of life, but of disease and death. It is not strange, then, that genius, such as could exist on the earth, should take its flight to the mountains. It may be said, that great men are good men. But what I mean is, that, in the human mind, greatness is one thing, and goodness another; that philosophy is divorced from religion; that truth is separated from its source; that that which is called goodness is sad, and that which is called genius is proud.

Since things are so, let men take care that the life which is received be genuine. Let the glow on the cheek spring from the warmth of the heart, and the brightness of the eyes beam from the light of heaven. Let ambition and the love of the world be plucked up by their roots. How can he love his neighbor, who desires to be above him? He may love him for a slave; but that is all. Let not the shrouds of death be removed, till the living principle has entered. It was not till Lazarus was raised from the dead, and had received the breath of life, that the Lord said, "Loose him, and let him go."

When the heart is purified from all selfish and worldly affections, then may genius find its seat in the church. As the human mind is cleansed of its lusts, truth will permit and invoke its approach, as the coyness of the virgin subsides into the tender love of the wife. The arts will spring in full-grown beauty from Him who is the source of beauty. The harps which have hung on the willows will sound as sweetly as the first breath of heaven that moved the leaves in the garden of Eden. Cannot a man paint better when he knows that the picture ought not to be worshipped?

Here is no sickly aspiring after fame,—no filthy lust after philosophy, whose very origin is an eternal barrier to the truth. But sentiments will flow from the heart warm as its blood, and speak eloquently; for eloquence is the language of love. There is a unison of spirit and nature. The genius of the mind will descend, and unite with the genius of the rivers, the lakes, and the woods. Thoughts fall to the earth with power, and make a language out of nature.

Adam and Eve knew no language but their garden. They had nothing to communicate by words; for they had not the power of concealment. The sun of the spiritual world shone bright on their hearts, and their senses were open with delight to natural objects. In the eye were the beauties of paradise; in the ear was the music of birds; in the nose was the fragrance of the freshness of nature; in the taste was the fruit of the garden; in the touch, the seal of their eternal union. What had they to *say*?

The people of the golden age have left us no monuments of genius, no splendid columns, no paintings, no poetry. They possessed nothing which evil passions might not obliterate; and, when their "heavens were rolled together as a scroll," the curtain dropped between the world and their existence.

Science will be full of life, as nature is full of God. She will wring from her locks the dew which was gathered in the wilderness. By science, I mean natural science. The science of the human mind must change with its subject. Locke's mind will not always be the standard of metaphysics. Had we a description of it in its present state, it would make a very different book from "Locke on the Human Understanding."

The time is not far distant. The cock has crowed. I hear the distant lowing of the cattle which are grazing on the mountains. "Watchman, what of the night? Watchman, what of the night? The watchman saith, The morning cometh."

Reviews and Impressions

CHRISTOPHER PEARSE CRANCH

Caricatures†

EMERSON IN ECSTASY OVER NATURE
"Almost I fear to think how glad I am!" (*Nature*)
As reconstructed by Lillian P. Cotter from fragments of the original

† From F. DeWolfe Miller, ed., *Christopher Pearse Cranch and His Caricatures of New England Transcendentalism* (Cambridge, Mass., 1951). Photographs reproduced from Houghton Library, Negfile MsAm 1506.

EMERSON THE MYSTIC
"I become a transparent Eyeball" (*Nature*)

SELF-RELIANCE
"This is my music" *(The American Scholar)*

L. M. SARGENT

From The Ballad of the Abolition Blunder-buss.[†]

There were ministers there of all sorts of schisms,
And withered old maids of all sorts of isms.
There were widows bewitched, table movers and all,
And Mormons and Millerites there in the hall;
Blasphemers and infidels, not a few.
Abolitionists all, a motley crew
Who takes so much pains
To show he's no brains,
That nobody now is obliged for his pains.
A man all made up of malice and spleens;—
In the summer he eats anti-slavery greens,
In the winter he bakes anti-slavery beans;
He lives by his wits—and that's on small means.

---

†   From *The Ballad of the Abolition Blunder-buss.* See also Len Gougeon, "Whitman, Emerson and 'The Ballad of the Abolition Blunder-buss,'" *Walt Whitman Review* 3.2 (Fall 1985): 21–27. Text and photos courtesy of Concord Free Public Library.

The Poet Emerson strives to start up his Pegasus. Pegasus is indulging in "Leaves of Grass," by Walt Whitman.

Ralph Waldo Emerson, at the Anti-Slavery meeting, telling the boys that "he was once a B——Boy, and doubts if they can say as much,"[1] adding that he fears their mothers don't know they are out."

1. The Humblebee Poet here intimates that the boys are of Irish distraction.

ANONYMOUS

An Illustrated Criticism†

An Illustrated Criticism.—The critic of the *Boston Post* writes most dazzlingly of one of Emerson's delightful lectures. We can hardly call it criticism, for he does not properly *criticise*; he plays around the subject like a humming-bird round a honeysuckle—he darts at it like a fish-hawk after a pike. He looms up like a thunder cloud, comes down in a shower of tinkling sleet and rolls away like a fire on the prairies. He plays with figures of speech like a juggler, balancing the sentences on his chin, and keeping up six with each hand. His fancy goes up like the jet of a fire engine, and comes down in a spiral ecstasy, like a Peruvian condor. He is a detonating mixture—a percussion cap—a meteoric shower—a spiritual shuttle, vibrating between the Unheard of and the Unutterable. Like a child he shakes his rattle over the edge of Chaos and swings on the gates of the Past—and he sits like a nightingale in a golden ring, suspended by a silver cord from a nail driven into the zenith.

We cannot resist trying our hand at illustrating his description of the lecture—giving form to the writer's phosphorescent fancies. Our attempts in this line accompany the text. Mr. Emerson, whose splendid profusion of thought and imagery, combined with the magnetism of his voice and presence, must produce the deepest impression wherever he is heard, has probably never imagined himself, even spiritually, in positions so remarkable. He will be equally amused with ourself at the result. Thus *ecstacises* the writer:

"Yet it is quite out of character to say Mr. Emerson lectures —he does no such thing He drops nectar—HE CHIPS OUT SPARKS—he exhales odors—he lets off mental sky rockets and fireworks—he spouts

fire, and, conjurer-like, draws ribbons out of his mouth. He smokes, he sparkles, he improvises, he shouts, he sings—HE EXPLODES LIKE A BUNDLE OF CRACKERS—he goes off in fiery eruptions like a volcano, but he does not *lecture*.

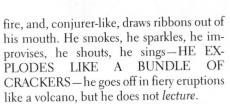

† From *New York Tribune*, Tuesday, February 6, 1849. See also Merton M. Sealts, Jr., "Melville and Emerson's Rainbow," ESQ 26.2 (1980): 53–78. Reproductions courtesy of American Antiquarian Society.

A Sort of Celestial Emanation

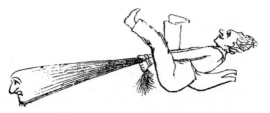

["*Celestial Emanations*" *may properly be allowed to take an airing on
Comets.* —Illustrator.]

* * * He went swiftly over the ground of knowledge with a Damascus blade, severing everything from its bottom; leaving one in doubt whether anything would ever grow again. Yet he seems as innocent as a little child who goes into a garden and pulls up a whole bed of violets, laughs over their beauty, and throws them down again. So that, after all, we are inclined to think no great harm has been done. He comes and goes like a spirit of whom one just hears the rustle of his wings.—He is a vitalized speculation—a talking essence——a bit of transparency broken from the spheres—a spiritual prism through which we see all beautiful rays of immaterial existences. His leaping fancy mounts upward like an India-rubber ball, and drifts and falls like a snow flake or a feather. He moves in the regions of similitudes. He comes through the air like a cherubim with a golden trumpet in his mouth, out of which he blows tropes and figures and gossamer transparencies of suggestive fancies. He takes high flights, and sustains himself without ruffling a feather. He inverts the rainbow and uses it for a swing—now sweeping the earth and now clapping his hands among the stars."

ELIZABETH PALMER PEABODY

From Nature—A Prose Poem[†]

Minds of the highest order of genius draw their thoughts most immediately from the Supreme Mind, which is the fountain of all finite natures. And hence they clothe the truths they see and feel, in those forms of nature which are generally intelligible to all ages of the world. With this poetic instinct, they have a natural tendency to withdraw from the *conventions* of their own day; and strive to forget, as much as possible, the arbitrary associations created by temporary institutions and local peculiarities. Since the higher laws of suggestion operate in proportion as the lower laws are made subordinate, suggestions of thought by mere proximity of time and place must be subtracted from the habits of the mind that would cultivate the principle of analogy; and this principle of suggestion, in its turn, must be made to give place to the higher law of cause and effect; and at times even this must be set aside, and Reason, from the top of the being, look into the higher nature of original truth, by Intuition,—no unreal function of our nature:

> Nor less I deem that there are powers,
>   Which, of themselves, our minds impress;
> That we can feed these minds of ours,
>   In a wise passiveness.

But if it is precisely because the most creative minds take the symbols of their thoughts and feelings from the venerable imagery of external nature, or from that condition of society which is most transparent in its simplicity, that, when they utter themselves, they speak to all ages, it is also no less true, that this is the reason why the greatest men, those of the highest order of intellect, often do not appear very great to their contemporaries. Their most precious sayings are naked, if not invisible, to the eyes of the conventional, precisely because they are free of the thousand circumstances and fashions which interest the acting and unthinking many. The greatest minds take no cognizance of the local interests, the party spirit, and the pet subjects of the literary coteries of particular times and places. Their phraseology is pure from the ornament which is the passing fashion of the day. As, however, they do not think and speak for their own order only, as they desire to address and receive a response from the great majority of minds—even from those that doubt their own power of going into the holy of holies of thought for themselves—there is needed the office of an intermediate class of minds, which are the natural critics of the human race. For criticism, in its worthiest meaning, is not, as is too often supposed, fault-finding, but interpretation of the oracles of genius. Critics are the priests of literature. How often, like other priests, they abuse their place and privilege, is but too obvious. They receive into their ranks the self-interested, the partisan, the lover of power, besides the stupid and frivolous; and thus the periodical literature of the day is in the rear, rather than in advance of the public mind.

After this preamble, which we trust has suitably impressed the minds of our readers with the dignity of the critical office, we would call those together who

---

† From *The United States Magazine and Democratic Review* 1 (February 1838): 319–29. Peabody appended to her review of *Nature* a brief notice of "The American Scholar" consisting mainly of quotations.

have feared that the spirit of poetry was dead, to rejoice that such a *poem* as "Nature" is written. It grows upon us as we reperuse it. It proves to us, that the only true and perfect mind is the poetic. Other minds are not to be despised, indeed; they are germs of humanity; but the poet alone is the man—meaning by the poet, not the versifier, nor the painter of outward nature merely, but the total soul, grasping truth, and expressing it melodiously, equally to the eye and heart.

The want of apprehension with which this *poem* has been received, speaks ill for the taste of our literary priesthood. Its title seems to have suggested to many persons the notion of some elementary treatise on physics, as physics; and when it has been found that it treats of the *metaphysics* of nature—in other words, of the highest designs of God, in forming nature and man in relations with each other—it seems to have been laid down with a kind of disgust, as if it were a cheat; and some reviewers have spoken of it with a stupidity that is disgraceful alike to their sense, taste, and feeling.

It has, however, found its readers and lovers, and those not a few; the highest intellectual culture and the simplest instinctive innocence have alike received it, and felt it to be a divine Thought, borne on a stream of 'English undefiled,' such as we had almost despaired could flow in this our world of grist and saw mills, whose utilitarian din has all but drowned the melodies of nature. The time will come, when it will be more universally seen to be "a gem of purest ray serene," and be dived after, into the dark unfathomed caves of that ocean of frivolity, which the literary productions of the present age spread out to the eyes of despair.

We have said that "Nature" is a poem; but it is written in prose. The author, though "wanting the accomplishment of verse," is a devoted child of the great Mother; and comes forward bravely in the midst of the dust of business and the din of machinery, and naming her venerable name, believes that there is a reverence for it left, in the bottom of every heart, of power to check the innumerable wheels for a short Sabbath, that all may listen to her praises.

In his introduction, he expresses his purpose. He tells us, that we concede too much to the sceptic, when we allow every thing venerable in religion to belong to history. He tells us that were there no past, yet nature would tell us great truths; and, rightly read, would prove the prophecies of revelation to be "a very present God"; and also, that the past itself, involving its prophets, divine lawgivers, and the human life of Him of Nazareth, is comparatively a dead letter to us, if we do not freshen these traditions in our souls, by opening our ears to the living nature which forevermore prepares for, and reechoes, their sublime teachings.

"The foregoing generations," he says, "beheld God face to face: we, through their eyes. Why should not *we* also enjoy an original relation to the Universe?"

Why should we not indeed? for *we* not only have the Universe, which the foregoing generations had, but *themselves* also. Why are we less wise than they? Why has our wisdom less of the certainty of intuition than theirs? Is it because we have more channels of truth? It may be so. The garden of Eden, before the fall of man, and when God walked in its midst, was found to be a less effective school of virtue, than the workshop of a carpenter, in a miserable town of Judea, of which 'an Israelite without guile' could ask. "*Can* any good come out of Nazareth?" And is not this, by the way, a grave warning to the happily circumstanced of all time to tremble—lest they grow morally passive, just in proportion to their means of an effective activity? With the religion of history must always be combined the religion of experience, in order to a true apprehension of God. The poet of "Nature" is a preacher of the latter. Let us "hear him gladly," for such are rare.

The first Canto of this song respects the outward form of Nature. He sketches it in bold strokes. The stars of Heaven above—the landscape below—the breathing atmosphere around—and the living forms and sounds—are brought up to us, by the loving spirit of the singer; who recognizes in this drapery of the world without, the same Disposer that arranged the elements of his own conscious soul. Thus, in his first recognition of Nature's superficies, he brings us to Theism. There is a God. Our Father is the author of Nature. The brotherly "nod" of companionship assures us of it.

But wherefore is Nature? The next Canto of our Poem answers this question in the most obvious relation. It is an answer that "all men apprehend." Nature's superficies is for the well-being of man's body, and the advantage of his material interests. This part of the book requires no interpretation from the critic. Men are active enough concerning commodity, to understand whatever is addressed to them on this head. At least there is no exception but in the case of the savage of the tropics. *His* mind has not explored his wants even to the extent of his body. He does not comprehend the necessities of the narrowest civilization. But whoever reads Reviews, whoever can understand our diluted English, can understand still better this concentrated and severely correct expression of what every child of civilization experiences every day. There is but one sentence here, that the veriest materialist can mistake. He may not measure all that the poet means when he says, man is thus conveniently waited upon in order "that he may work." He may possibly think that "work" relates to the physical operations of manufacture or agriculture. But what is really meant is no less than this; "man is fed that he may work" with his mind; add to the treasures of thought; elaborate the substantial life of the spiritual world. This is a beautiful doctrine, and worthy to be sung to the harp, with a song of thanksgiving. Undoubtedly Nature, by working for man with all her elements, is adequate to supply him with so much "commodity" that the time may be anticipated when all men will have leisure to be artists, poets, philosophers,— in short, to live through life in the exercise of their proper humanity. God speed to the machinery and application of science to the arts which is to bring this about!

The third Song is of Nature's Beauty, and we only wonder why it was not sung first; for surely the singer found out that Nature was beautiful, before he discovered that it was convenient. Some children, we know, have asked what was the use of flowers, and, like little monkeys, endeavouring to imitate the grown-up, the bearings of whose movements they could not appreciate, have planted their gardens with potatoes and beans, instead of sweet-briar and cupid's delights. But the poet never made this mistake. In the fullness of his first love for his "beautiful mother," and his "gentle nest," he did not even find out those wants which the commodity of Nature supplies.

> "Give me health and a day," he says, "and I will make the pomp of emperors ridiculous. The dawn is my Assyria; the sunset and moonrise my Paphos and unimaginable realms of faerie; broad noon shall be my England of the senses and understanding; the night shall be my Germany of mystic philosophy and dreams."

If this subjection of all nature to himself does not prove intimate acquaintance, the following severe truth of fact must do so:

> "The shows of day, the dewy morning, the rainbow, mountains, orchards in blossom, stars, moonlight shadows in the still water, and the like, if too eagerly hunted, become shows merely, and mock us with their unreality. Go out of the house to see the moon and ['tis] mere tinsel," &c.

The second passage on Beauty, is one of those which recalls the critic to the office of interpreter, for it is one which the world has called mystical. To say the same thing in worse English, the oracle here tells us, that if we look on Nature with pleasurable emotions only, and without, at the same time, exerting our moral powers, the mind grows effeminate, and thus becomes incapable of perceiving the highest beauty of whose original type the external forms are but the varied reflections or shadows. When man's moral power is in action, the mind spontaneously traces relations between itself and surrounding things, and there forms with Nature one whole, combining the moral delight which human excellence inspires, with that suggested by Nature's forms.

The next passage rises a step higher in the praise of Beauty. It recognizes the cherishing influence of Nature's forms upon the faculties. Nature not only calls out taste, not only glorifies virtue, and is in its turn by virtue glorified, but it awakens the creative impulse—God's image in man. Hence Art, or "Nature in miniature." And the works of Art lead back to Nature again. Thus Beauty circulates, and becomes an aspect of Eternity.

The next chapter, showing that Language is founded on material Nature, is quite didactic. But even here one critic[1] quotes a sentence, of which he says, he cannot understand "what it means."

> This relation between the mind and matter is not fancied by some poet, but stands in the will of God, and so is free to be known by all men. It appears to men, or it does not appear.

Where lies the obscurity? We have heard some men say that they did not believe that the forms of Nature bore any relation to the being of God, which his children could appreciate; but even these men could not understand the simple proposition of the opposite theory. Men may think that all nations, whose language has yet been discovered, have called youth *the morning of life*, by accident; but it is inconceivable that they should not understand the simple words in which other men say that there is *no accident in the world*, but all things relate to the spirit of God to which man also has relation and access. Perhaps, however, it is the second sentence which is unintelligible, "it appears to men, or it does not appear." In other words, *to people with open eyes there are colors; to people with shut eyes, at least, to those born blind, there are no colors.*

But having come to this fact, viz: that "the relation between mind and matter stands in the will of God," our poet grows silent with wonder and worship. The nature of this relation he acknowledges to be the yet unsolved problem. He names some of the principal men who have attempted a solution. Many readers of his book would have been glad, had he paused to tell us, in his brief comprehensive way, what was the solution of Pythagoras, and Plato, Bacon, Leibnitz, and Swedenborg, with remarks of his own upon each.

---

1. *Christian Examiner.*

And to his own solution, some say he is unintelligible, talks darkly. They do not seem to have observed that he says nothing in the way of solution, so that nothing can be darkly said. This is what has disappointed the best lovers of his book. But if he does not give his own solution of the enigma, he does what is next best, he tells us the condition of solving it ourselves.

A life in harmony with nature, the love of truth and virtue, will purge the eyes to understand her text. By degrees we may come to know the primitive sense of the permanent objects of Nature, so that the world shall be to us an open book, and every form significant of the hidden life and final cause.

The chapter on Discipline is still more didactic than the one on Language. The first portion treats of the formation of the Understanding by the ministry of Nature to the senses, and faculty of deduction. The second section is in a higher strain. It treats of the developement of the Reason and Conscience, by means of that relation between matter and mind, which "appears" so clearly to some men, and to all in a degree. It is a pity to give an extract from what is so fine in the whole, but a single sentence must give the hint to the character of this section:

"The moral influence of Nature upon every individual, is the amount of truth which it illustrates to him. Who can estimate this? Who can guess how much firmness the seabeaten rock has taught the fisherman? How much tranquillity has been reflected to man from the azure sky, over whose unspotted deep the winds forever more drive flocks of stormy clouds, and leave no wrinkle nor stain? How much industry and providence and affection we have caught from the pantomime of brutes? What a searching preacher of self-command is the varying phenomenon of health?"

In the last part of this chapter on Discipline, the author makes a bold sally at the cause of the analogy between the external world and the moral nature. He implies that causes (the spiritual seeds of external things) are identical with the principles that constitute our being; and that *virtues* (the creations of our own heaven-aided wills) correspond to God's creations in matter; the former being the natural growth in the moral world, the latter the natural growth in the material world; or to vary the expression once more, Goodness being the projection inward—Beauty the projection outward—of the same all-pervading Spirit.

Our author here leaves the didactic, and "the solemn harp's harmonious sound" comes full upon the ear and the heart from the next Canto of his poem—Idealism. No part of the book has been so mistaken as this. Some readers affect to doubt his Practical Reason, because he acknowledges, that we have no evidence of there being essential outlying beings, to that which we certainly see, by consciousness, by looking inward, *except 'a constant faith' which God gives us of this truth.* But why should 'the noble doubt,' which marks the limit of the understanding, be so alarming, when it is found to be but an introduction of the mind to the *superior certainty* residing in that 'constant faith?' Do we not advance in truth, when we learn to change the childish feeling by which we ascribe reality to the 'shows of things,' for a feeling involving a sense of GOD, as the only real—immutable—the All in All?

The theory of Idealism has doubtless been carried to absurdity by individuals who but half understood it; and has still more often been represented in a way which was not only useless but injurious to minds entirely dependent on what others say: for, to borrow two good compounds from Coleridge, the *half-Ideas* of many would-be Idealist writers, have passed, perforce, into the *no-Ideas* of many would-be Idealist readers. But Mr. Emerson has sufficiently guarded his Idealism by rigorous and careful expression, to leave little excuse for cavilling at his words or thoughts, except, indeed, by professed materialists and atheists, to whom he gives no ground.

"The frivolous make themselves merry, he says "with the Ideal theory, as if its consequences were burlesque; as if it affected the stability of nature. It surely does not. God never jests with us, and will not compromise the end of Nature, by permitting any inconsequence in its procession. Any distrust of the permanence of laws, would paralyze the faculties of man. Their permanence is sacredly respected, and his faith therein is perfect. The wheels and springs of man are all set to the hypothesis of the permanence of Nature. We are not built like a ship to be tossed, but like a house to stand."

He proceeds to give the progressive appearances of Nature, as the mind advances, through the ministry of the senses, to "the best and the happiest moments of life, those delicious awakenings of the higher powers,—the withdrawing of Nature before its God." The means by which Nature herself, Poetic genius, Philosophy, both natural and intellectual—and, above all, Religion and Ethics, work, to idealize our thought and being, are then minutely pointed out. No careful thinker can dispute a step of the process. We are tempted to quote all these pages and defy the materialist to answer them, but for those sober Christians, who ignorantly and inconsistently fear Idealism, one paragraph will answer the purpose:

"The first and last lesson in religion is, *the things that are seen are temporal, the things that are unseen are eternal.* It puts an affront upon Nature. It does that for the unschooled, which philosophy does for Berkel[e]y and Viasa. The uniform language that may be heard in the churches of the most ignorant sects is, *contemn the unsubstantial shows of the world; they are vanities, dreams, shadows, unrealities; seek the realities of religion.* The devotee flaunts Nature. * * * * * * They might all better say of matter, what Michael Angelo said of external beauty, *it is the frail and weary weed in which God dresses the soul, which he has called into time.*"

Many philosophers have stopped at Idealism. But, as Mr. Emerson says, this hypothesis, if it only deny, or question the existence of matter "does not satisfy the demands of the Spirit. It leaves God out of me. It leaves me in the splendid labyrinth of my perceptions, to wander without end. Then the heart resists it, because it baulks the affections, in denying substantive being to men and women."

Mr. Emerson then proceeds to his chapter on Spirit, by which he means to suggest to us the substantial essence of which Idealism is the intellectual form. But this chapter is not full enough, for the purposes of instruction. One passage is indeed of great significance:

"But when, following the invisible steps of thought, we come to inquire, Whence is matter? and whereto?—many truths arise out of the depths of consciousness. We learn that the highest is present to the soul of man; that the great universal essence which is not wisdom, or love, or beauty, or power, but all in one and each entirely, is that for which all things exist, and that by which they are; *that spirit creates;* that behind Nature, throughout Nature, *Spirit is present,* that spirit is one and not compound; that Spirit does not act upon us from without, that is, in space of [sic] time, but spiritually or through ourselves. Therefore, that Spirit, that is the Supreme Being, does not build up Nature around us, but puts it forth through us, as the life of the tree puts forth new branches and leaves through the pores of the old. As a plant upon the bosom of God, he is nourished by unfailing fountains, and draws at his need inexhaustible power. Who can set bounds to the possibilities of Man? Once inspire the infinite, by being admitted to behold the absolute natures of justice and truth, and we learn that man has access to the entire mind of the Creator in the finite. This view, which admonishes me where the sources of wisdom and power lie, and points to virture as

> 'The golden key
> Which opes the palace of Eternity,'

carries upon its face, the highest certificate of truth, because it animates me to create my own world through the purification of my soul."

This is not only of refreshing moral *aura,* but it is a passage of the highest imaginative power, (taking the word *imaginative* in that true signification which farthest removes it from *fanciful,*) the mind must become purified indeed which can take this point of view, to look at "the great shadow pointing to the sun behind us." Sitting thus at the footstool of God, it may realise that all that we see is created by the light that shines through ourselves. Not until thus purified, can it realise that those through whose being more light flows, see more than we do; and that others, who admit less light, see less. What assistance in human culture would the application of this test give us! How would our classifications of men and women be changed, did the positive pure enjoyment of Nature become the standard of judgment! But who may apply the standard? Not every mawkish raver about the moon, surely, but only a comprehender of Nature. And has there yet been any one in human form, who could be called a comprehender of Nature, save Him who had its secret, and in whose hands it was plastic, even to the raising of the dead?

Mr. Emerson must not accuse us of ingratitude, in that after he had led his readers to this high point of view, they crave more, and accuse him of stopping short, where the world most desires and needs farther guidance. We want him to write another book, in which he will give us the philosophy of his "orphic strains," whose meaning is felt, but can only be understood by glimpses.

He does, indeed, tell us that "the problem of restoring to the world original and eternal beauty," (in other words, of seeing Nature and Life in their wholeness), "is solved by the redemption of the soul." It is not unnecessary for the philosopher thus to bring his disciples round, through the highest flights of speculation, to the primitive faith of the humblest disciple, who sits, in the spirit of a child, at the feet of Jesus. But we should like to hear Mr. Emerson's philosophy of Redemption. It is very plain that it consists of broad and comprehensive views of human culture; worthy to employ the whole mind of one who seeks reproduction of Christ within himself, by such meditations as the following, which must be our last extract:

"Is not Prayer also a study of truth—a sally of the soul into the unfound infinite? No man every prayed heartily without learning something. But when a faithful thinker, resolute to detach every object from personal relations, and see it in the light of thought, shall, at the same time, kindle science with the fire of the holiest affections, then will God go forth anew into the creation."

*   *   *

ANDREWS NORTON

The New School in Literature and Religion[†]

There is a strange state of things existing about us in the literary and religious world, of which none of our larger periodicals has yet taken notice. It is the result of that restless craving for notoriety and excitement, which, in one way or another, is keeping our community in a perpetual stir. It has shown itself, we think, particularly since that foolish woman, Miss Martineau, was among us, and stimulated the vanity of her flatterers by loading them in return with the copper coin of her praise, which they easily believed was as good as gold. She was accustomed to talk about her mission, as if she were a special dispensation of Providence, and they too thought that they must all have their missions, and began to "vaticinate," as one of their number has expressed it. But though her genial warmth may have caused the new school to bud and bloom, it was not planted by her.—It owes its origin in part to ill-understood notions, obtained by blundering through the crabbed and disgusting obscurity of some of the worst German speculatists, which notions, however, have been received by most of its disciples at second hand, through an interpreter. The atheist Shelley has been quoted and commended in a professedly religious work, called the Western Messenger; but he is not, we conceive, to be reckoned among the patriarchs of the sect. But this honor is due to that hasher up of German metaphysics, the Frenchman, Cousin; and, of late, that hyper-Germanized Englishman, Carlyle, has been the great object of admiration and model of style. Cousin and Carlyle indeed seem to have been transformed into idols to be publicly worshipped, the former for his philosophy, and the latter both for his philosophy and his fine writing; while the veiled image of the German pantheist, Schleiermacher, is kept in the sanctuary.

The characteristics of this school are the most extraordinary assumption, united with great ignorance, and incapacity for reasoning. There is indeed a general tendency among its disciples to disavow learning and reasoning as sources of their higher knowledge.—The mind must be its own unassisted teacher. It discerns transcendental truths by immediate vision, and these truths can no more be communicated to another by addressing his understanding, than the power of *clairvoyance* can be given to one not magnetized. They announce themselves as the prophets and priests of a new future, in which all is to be changed, all old opinions done away, and all present forms of society abolished. But by what process this joyful revolution is to be effected we are not told;

---

† From *Daily Advertiser* (Boston), August 27, 1838.

nor how human happiness and virtue is to be saved from the universal wreck, and regenerated in their Medea's caldron. There are great truths with which they are laboring, but they are unutterable in words to be understood by common minds. To such minds they seem nonsense, oracles as obscure as those of Delphi.

The rejection of reasoning is accompanied with an equal contempt for good taste. All modesty is laid aside. The writer of an article for an obscure periodical, or a religious newspaper, assumes a tone as if he were one of the chosen enlighteners of a dark age. — He continually obtrudes himself upon his reader, and announces his own convictions, as if from their having that character, they were necessarily indisputable. — He floats about magnificently on bladders, which he would have it believed are swelling with ideas. — Common thoughts, sometimes true, oftener false, and "Neutral nonsense, neither false nor true," are exaggerated, and twisted out of shape, and forced into strange connexions, to make them look like some grand and new conception. To produce a more striking effect, our common language is abused; antic tricks are played with it; inversions, exclamations, anomalous combinations of words, unmeaning, but coarse and violent, metaphors abound, and withal a strong infusion of German barbarisms. Such is the style of Carlyle, a writer of some talent; for his great deficiency is not in this respect, it is in good sense, good taste and soundness of principle; but a writer, who, through his talents, such as they are, through that sort of buffoonery and affectation of manner which throws the reader off his guard, through the indisputable novelty of his way of writing, and through a somewhat too prevalent taste among us for an over-excited and *convulsionary* style, which we mistake for eloquence, has obtained a degree of fame in this country, very disproportioned to what he enjoys at home, out of the Westminster Review. Carlyle, however, as an original, might be tolerated, if one could forget his admirers and imitators.

The state of things described might seem a matter of no great concern, a mere insurrection of folly, a sort of Jack Cade rebellion, which in the nature of things must soon be put down, if those engaged in it were not gathering confidence from neglect, and had not proceeded to attack principles which are the foundation of human society and human happiness. "Silly women," it has been said, and silly young men, it is to be feared, have been drawn away from their Christian faith, if not divorced from all that can properly be called religion. The evil is becoming, for the time, disastrous and alarming; and of this fact there could hardly be a more extraordinary and ill boding evidence, than is afforded by a publication, which has just appeared, entitled an "Address, delivered before the Senior class in Divinity College, Cambridge," upon the occasion of that class taking leave of the Institution. — "By Ralph Waldo Emerson."

It is not necessary to remark particularly on this composition. It will be sufficient to state generally, that the author professes to reject all belief in Christianity as a revelation, that he makes a general attack upon the Clergy, on the ground that they preach what he calls "Historical Christianity," and that if he believe in God in the proper sense of the term, which one passage might have led his hearers to suppose, his language elsewhere is very ill-judged and indecorous. But what *his* opinions may be is a matter of minor concern; the main question is how it has happened, that religion has been insulted by the delivery of these opinions in the Chapel of the Divinity College at Cambridge, as the last instruction which those were to receive, who were going forth from it, bearing the name of Christian preachers. This is a question in which the community is deeply interested. No one can doubt for a moment of the disgust and strong disapprobation with which it must have been heard by the highly respectable officers of that Institution. They must have felt it not only as an insult to religion, but as personal insult to themselves. But this renders the fact of its having been so delivered only the more remarkable. We can proceed but a step in accounting for it. The preacher was invited to occupy the place he did, not by the officers of the Divinity College, but by the members of the graduating class. These gentlemen, therefore, have become accessories, perhaps innocent accessories, to the commission of a great offence; and the public must be desirous of learning what exculpation or excuse they can offer.

It is difficult to believe that they thought this incoherent rhapsody a specimen of fine writing, that they listened with admiration, for instance, when they were told that the religious sentiment "is myrrh, and storax and chlorine and rosemary;" or that they wondered at the profound views of their present Teacher, when he announced to them that "the new Teacher," for whom he is looking, would "see the identity of the law of gravitation with purity of heart;" or that they had not some suspicion of inconsistency, when a new Teacher was talked of, after it had been declared to them, that religious truth "is an intuition," and "cannot be received at second hand."

But the subject is to be viewed under a far more serious aspect. The words God, Religion, Christianity, have a definite meaning, well understood. They express conceptions and truths of unutterable moment to the present and future happiness of man. We well know how shamefully they have been abused in modern times by infidels and pantheists; but their meaning remains the same; the truths which they express are unchanged and unchangeable. The community know what they require when they ask for a Christian Teacher; and should any one approving the doctrines of this discourse assume that character, he would deceive his hearers; he would be guilty of a practical falsehood for the most paltry of temptations; he would consent to live a lie, for the sake of being maintained by those whom he had cheated. It is not, however, to be supposed that his vanity would suffer him long to keep his philosophy wholly to himself. This would break out in obscure intimations, ambiguous words, and false and mischievous speculations. But should such preachers abound, and grow confident in their folly, we can hardly over-estimate the disastrous effect upon the religious and moral state of the community.

ANONYMOUS

[Emerson's Essays]†

This volume is a curiosity: it may almost class with Mr. Haughton's Essay on Sex in the World to Come, in any cabinet of unique books. At any rate it ought to occupy a shelf in the *case* assigned especially to Thomas Carlyle, although Mr. Ralph Waldo Emerson will have no right to complain should he be shoved into the darkest or least inviting corner of the mahogany. The mere act of godfathership, by reprinting the work in this country, and heralding it by a

† From *Monthly Review* [England], 3 (October 1841): 274–79.

laudatory preface, proves that it is a book after Carlyle's own heart. Some portions of that preface itself must not be passed over; for it tells us something which the Essays themselves cannot be expected to do of the author; while it furnishes a striking and not unamusing or unsuggestive specimen of Carlylisms.

Thomas thus inquires and speaks,—"While so many Benthamisms, Socialisms, Fourrierisms, *professing* to have no soul, go staggering and lowing like monstrous moon-calves, the product of a heavy moonstruck age; and in this same baleful 'twelfth hour of night,' even galvanic Puseyisms, as we say, are visible, and dancings of the sheeted dead,—shall not any voice of a living man be welcome to us, even because it is alive?" Mr. C. has just before told "the British public" not to trouble itself about whether this Emerson be "a Pantheist, or what kind of Theist or *Ist* he may be." The only thing is, "if he prove a devout-minded, veritable, original man, this for the present will suffice;" for that "*Ists* and *Isms* are rather growing a weariness." Well then, "and for the rest, what degree of mere literary talent lies in these utterances, is but a secondary question; which every reader may gradually answer for himself." Even, "What Emerson's talent is, we will not althogether estimate by this book. The utterance is abrupt, fitful; the great idea not yet embodied struggles towards an embodiment. Yet everywhere there is the true heart of a man; which is the parent of all talent; which without much talent cannot exist. A breath as of the green country—all the welcomer that it is New-England country, not second-hand but first-hand country—meets us wholesomely everywhere in these Essays; the authentic green earth is there, with her mountains, rivers, with her mills and farms. Sharp gleams of insight arrest us by their pure intellectuality; here and there, in heroic rusticism, a tone of modest manfulness, of mild invincibility, low-voiced, but lion-strong, makes us to thrill with a noble pride. Talent? Such ideas as dwell in this man, how can they ever speak themselves with *enough* of talent? The talent is not the chief question here. The idea, that is the chief question. Of the living acorn you do not ask first, How *large* an acorn art thou? The smallest living acorn is fit to be the parent of oak trees without end,—could clothe all New England with oak trees by and by. You ask it first of all, Art thou a living acorn? Certain, now, that thou art not a dead mushroom as most are?" "Closing these questionable parables and insinuations, let me in plain English recommend this little book as the book of an original viridical man, worthy the acquaintance of those who delight in such; and so, Welcome to it, whom it may concern!"

This is high praise from a high quarter; but praise, we suspect, which has been considerably influenced by Emerson's mannerism of thought and diction, partaking as it does of Carlyle's own; but by no means so independent, so original, so suggestive, so full of lofty or of deep and far-reaching thought, as are the "utterances" of Thomas. We much oftener find in Emerson's quaint and strange modes of speech, in his queer phrases, and aphoristic enigmas, old and common-place ideas, feebly or only half-conceived; so that the Prefacer appears to us to hit the mark pretty closely, when he describes the "notions and half-notions of a metaphysic, theosophic, theologic kind," which occur in these Essays as resembling "flickering bright bodiless northern streamers."

Mr. C. talks of his *protégé* as being a self-dependent man, and not one of your "thousand thousand ventriloquists, mimetic echoes, hysteric shrieks, hollow laughters, and mere *in*articulate mechanical babblements, the soul-confusing din of which already fills all places." Now, it appears to us that "mimetic echoes" will very frequently be detected in these Essays; and as to "hysteric shrieks," if not more abundant than in the oracular enunciations of the god-father, they are at least more harsh and less powerful—struggling half-notes—thoughts caught by the heels, but never fully grasped—often abstractions, loosely connected, and thrown out as if by random around some true principle indistinctly comprehended. One does not readily perceive evidences of plan, nor of skill in subordinating ideas according to their non-importance, nor of rejecting what helps not to develop the contemplated lesson or doctrine. In short he seems to labour under the vanity of affectation, so far as to spoil many good thoughts, rather than that he should utter them as other men of sound minds would do; and also to be so far an imitator as to have preferred Carlyle as a model to any other single writer. And yet Mr. Emerson is no servile slave, no ordinary thinker, no every day sort of teacher. What we learn of his history from the editor might convince any one of his singularity and independence. It appears that he has relinquished the paths of business; and, even when having before him the omens of success, has withdrawn into retired walks, to "sit down to spend his life not in Mammon worship, or the hunt for reputation, influence, place, or any outward advantage whatsoever." But besides this evidence of resolution, single-mindedness, and self-dependence, his very rejection of the conventionalities of style, and a determination to utter what he believes to be truth, testify that he is a man of mark, and one that will leave a stamp upon the minds of others. He often handles great truths in a bold suggestive manner, almost worthy of his model; and his earnestness is healthy and strong.

*　　*　　*

WALTER WHITMAN

Mr. Emerson's Lecture[†]

The transcendentalist had a very full house on Saturday evening. There were a few beautiful maids—but more ugly women, mostly blue stockings; several interesting young men with Byron collars, doctors, and parsons; Grahamites and abolitionists; sage editors, a few of whom were taking notes; and all the other species of literati. Greeley was in ecstasies whenever any thing particularly good was said, which seemed to be once in about five minutes—he would flounce about like a fish out of water, or a tickled girl—look around, to see those behind him and at his side; all of which very plainly told to those both far and near, that he knew a thing or two more about these matters than other men.

This lecture was on the "Poetry of the Times." He said that the first man who called another an ass was a poet. Because the business of the poet is expression—the giving utterance to the emotions and sentiments of the soul; and metaphors. But it would do the lecturer great injustice to attempt anything like a sketch of his

---

† From Joseph Jay Rubin and Charles H. Brown, *Walt Whitman of the "New York Aurora": Editor at Twenty-Two: A Collection of Recently Discovered Writings* (State College, Pa., 1950), p. 105.

ideas. Suffice it to say, the lecture was one of the richest and most beautiful compositions, both for its matter and style, we have ever heard anywhere, at any time.

[March 7, 1842]

MARGARET FULLER

Emerson's Essays[†]

At the distance of three years this volume follows the first series of Essays, which have already made to themselves a circle of readers, attentive, thoughtful, more and more intelligent, and this circle is a large one if we consider the circumstances of this country, and of England, also, at this time.

In England it would seem there are a larger number of persons waiting for an invitation to calm thought and sincere intercourse than among ourselves. Copies of Mr. Emerson's first published little volume called "Nature," have there been sold by thousands in a short time, while one edition has needed seven years to get circulated here. Several of his Orations and Essays from "The Dial" have also been republished there, and met with a reverent and earnest response.

We suppose that while in England the want of such a voice is as great as here, a larger number are at leisure to recognize that want; a far larger number have set foot in the speculative region and have ears refined to appreciate these melodious accents.

Our people, heated by a partisan spirit, necessarily occupied in these first stages by bringing out the material resources of the land, not generally prepared by early training for the enjoyment of books that require attention and reflection, are still more injured by a large majority of writers and speakers, who lend all their efforts to flatter corrupt tastes and mental indolence, instead of feeling it their prerogative and their duty to admonish the community of the danger and arouse it to nobler energy. The aim of the writer or lecturer is not to say the best he knows in as few and well-chosen words as he can, making it his first aim to do justice to the subject. Rather he seeks to beat out a thought as thin as possible, and to consider what the audience will be most willing to receive.

The result of such a course is inevitable. Literature and Art must become daily more degraded; Philosophy cannot exist. A man who feels within his mind some spark of genius, or a capacity for the exercises of talent, should consider himself as endowed with a sacred commission. He is the natural priest, the shepherd of the people. He must raise his mind as high as he can toward the heaven of truth, and try to draw up with him those less gifted by nature with ethereal lightness. If he does not so, but rather employs his powers to flatter them in their poverty, and to hinder aspiration by useless words, and a mere seeming of activity, his sin is great, he is false to God, and false to man.

Much of this sin indeed is done ignorantly. The idea that literature calls men to the genuine hierarchy is almost forgotten. One, who finds himself able, uses his pen, as he might a trowel, solely to procure himself bread, without having reflected on the position in which he thereby places himself.

[†] From *Daily Tribune* (New York), December 7, 1844, p. 1.

Apart from the troop of mercenaries, there is one, still larger, of those who use their powers merely for local and temporary ends, aiming at no excellence other than may conduce to these. Among these, rank persons of honor and the best intentions, but they neglect the lasting for the transient, as a man neglects to furnish his mind that he may provide the better for the house in which his body is to dwell for a few years.

When these sins and errors are prevalent, and threaten to become more so, how can we sufficiently prize and honor a mind which is quite pure from such? When, as in the present case, we find a man whose only aim is the discernment and interpretation of the spiritual laws by which we live and move and have our being, all whose objects are permanent, and whose every word stands for a fact.

If only as a representative of the claims of individual culture in a nation which tends to lay such stress on artificial organization and external results, Mr. Emerson would be invaluable here. History will inscribe his name as a father of the country, for he is one who pleads her cause against herself.

If New-England may be regarded as a chief mental focus to the New World, and many symptoms seem to give her this place, as to other centres the characteristics of heart and lungs to the body politic; if we may believe, as the writer does believe, that what is to be acted out in the country at large is, most frequently, first indicated there, as all the phenomena of the nervous system in the fantasies of the brain, we may hail as an auspicious omen the influence Mr. Emerson has there obtained, which is deep-rooted, increasing, and, over the younger portion of the community, far greater than that of any other person.

His books are received there with a more ready intelligence than elsewhere, partly because his range of personal experience and illustration applies to that region, partly because he has prepared the way for his books to be read by his great powers as a speaker.

The audience that waited for years upon the lectures, a part of which is incorporated into these volumes of Essays, was never large, but it was select, and it was constant. Among the hearers were some, who though, attracted by the beauty of character and manner, they were willing to hear the speaker through, always went away discontented. They were accustomed to an artificial method, whose scaffolding could easily be retraced, and desired an obvious sequence of logical inferences. They insisted there was nothing in what they had heard, because they could not give a clear account of its course and purport. They did not see that Pindar's odes might be very well arranged for their own purpose, and yet not bear translating into the methods of Mr. Locke.

Others were content to be benefitted by a good influence without a strict analysis of its means. "My wife says it is about the elevation of human nature, and so it seems to me;" was a fit reply to some of the critics. Many were satisfied to find themselves excited to congenial thought and nobler life, without an exact catalogue of the thoughts of the speaker.

Those who believed no truth could exist, unless encased by the burrs of opinion, went away utterly baffled. Sometimes they thought he was on their side, then presently would come something on the other. He really seemed to believe there were two sides to every subject, and even to intimate higher ground from which each might be seen to have an infinite number of sides or bearings, an impertinence not to be endured! The partisan heard but once and returned no more.

But some there were, simple souls, whose life had been, perhaps, without clear light, yet still a search after truth for its own sake, who were able to receive what followed on the suggestion of a subject in a natural manner, as a stream of thought. These recognized, beneath the veil of words, the still small voice of conscience, the vestal fires of lone religious hours, and the mild teachings of the summer woods.

The charm of the elocution, too, was great. His general manner was that of the reader, occasionally rising into direct address or invocation in passages where tenderness or majesty demanded more energy. At such times both eye and voice called on a remote future to give a worthy reply. A future which shall manifest more largely the universal soul as it was then manifest to this soul. The tone of the voice was a grave body tone, full and sweet rather than sonorous, yet flexible and haunted by many modulations, as even instruments of wood and brass seem to become after they have been long played on with skill and taste; how much more so the human voice! In the more expressive passages it uttered notes of silvery clearness, winning, yet still more commanding. The words uttered in those tones, floated awhile above us, then took root in the memory like winged seed.

In the union of an even rustic plainness with lyric inspirations, religious dignity with philosophic calmness, keen sagacity in details with boldness of view, we saw what brought to mind the early poets and legislators of Greece—men who taught their fellows to plow and avoid moral evil, sing hymns to the gods and watch the metamorphoses of nature. Here in civic Boston was such a man—one who could see man in his original grandeur and his original childishness, rooted in simple nature, raising to the heavens the brow and eyes of a poet.

And these lectures seemed not so much lectures as grave didactic poems, theogonies, perhaps, adorned by odes when some Power was in question whom the poet had best learned to serve, and with eclogues wisely portraying in familiar tongue the duties of man to man and "harmless animals."

Such was the attitude in which the speaker appeared to that portion of the audience who have remained permanently attached to him.—They value his words as the signets of reality; receive his influence as a help and incentive to a nobler discipline than the age, in its general aspect, appears to require; and do not fear to anticipate the verdict of posterity in claiming for him the honors of greatness, and, in some respects, of a Master.

In New-England he thus formed for himself a class of readers, who rejoice to study in his books what they already know by heart. For, though the thought has become familiar, its beautiful garb is always fresh and bright in hue.

A similar circle of like-minded the books must and do form for themselves, though with a movement less directly powerful, as more distant from its source.

The Essays have also been obnoxious to many charges. To that of obscurity, or want of perfect articulation. Of 'Euphuism,' as an excess of fancy in proportion to imagination, and an inclination, at times, to subtlety at the expense of strength, has been styled. The human heart complains of inadequacy, either in the nature or experience of the writer, to represent its full vocation and its deeper needs. Sometimes it speaks of this want as "under-development" or a want of expansion which may yet be remedied; sometimes doubts whether "in this mansion there be either hall or portal to receive the loftier of the Passions." Sometimes the soul is deified at the expense of nature, then again nature at that of man, and we are not quite sure that we can make a true harmony by balance of the statements.—This writer has never written one good work, if such a work be one where the whole commands more attention than the parts. If such an one be produced only where, after an accumulation of materials, fire enough be applied to fuse the whole into one new substance. This second series is superior in this respect to the former, yet in no one essay is the main stress so obvious as to produce on the mind the harmonious effect of a noble river or a tree in full leaf. Single passages and sentences engage our attention too much in proportion. These essays, it has been justly said, tire like a string of mosaics or a house built of medals. We miss what we expect in the work of the great poet, or the great philosopher, the liberal air of all the zones: the glow, uniform yet various in tint, which is given to a body by free circulation of the heart's blood from the hour of birth. Here is, undoubtedly, the man of ideas, but we want the ideal man also; want the heart and genius of human life to interpret it, and here our satisfaction is not so perfect. We doubt this friend raised himself too early to the perpendicular and did not lie along the ground long enough to hear the secret whispers of our parent life. We could wish he might be thrown by conflicts on the lap of mother earth, to see if he would not rise again with added powers.

All this we may say, but it cannot excuse us from benefitting by the great gifts that have been given, and assigning them their due place.

Some painters paint on a red ground. And this color may be supposed to represent the ground work most immediately congenial to most men, as it is the color of blood and represents human vitality. The figures traced upon it are instinct with life in its fulness and depth.

But other painters paint on a gold ground. And a very different, but no less natural, because also a celestial beauty, is given to their works who choose for their foundation the color of the sunbeam, which nature has preferred for her most precious product, and that which will best bear the test of purification, gold.

If another simile may be allowed, another no less apt is at hand. Wine is the most brilliant and intense expression of the powers of earth.—It is her potable fire, her answer to the sun. It exhilarates, it inspires, but then it is liable to fever and intoxicate too the careless partaker.

Mead was the chosen drink of the Northern gods. And this essence of the honey of the mountain bee was not thought unworthy to revive the souls of the valiant who had left their bodies on the fields of strife below.

Nectar should combine the virtues of the ruby wine, the golden mead, without their defects or dangers.

Two high claims our writer can vindicate on the attention of his contemporaries. One from his sincerity. You have his thought just as it found place in the life of his own soul. Thus, however near or relatively distant its approximation to absolute truth, its action on you cannot fail to be healthful. It is a part of the free air.

He belongs to that band of whom there may be found a few in every age, and who now in known human history may be counted by hundreds, who worship the one God only, the God of Truth. They worship, not saints, nor creeds, nor churches, nor reliques, nor idols in any form. The mind is kept open to truth, and life only valued as a tendency toward it. This must be illustrated by acts and words of love, purity and intelligence. Such are the salt of the earth; let the minutest crystal of that salt be willingly by us held in solution.

The other is through that part of his life, which, if sometimes obstructed or chilled by the critical intellect, is yet the prevalent and the main source of his power. It is that by which he imprisons his hearer only to free him again as a "liberating God" (to use his own words). But indeed let us use them altogether, for none other, ancient or modern, can more worthily express how, making present to us the courses and destinies of nature, he invests himself with her serenity and animates us with her joy.

"Poetry was all written before time was, and whenever we are so finely organized that we can penetrate into that region where the air is music, we hear those primal warblings, and attempt to write them down, but we lose ever and anon a word, or a verse, and substitute something of our own, and thus miswrite the poem. The men of more delicate ear write down these cadences more faithfully, and these transcripts, though imperfect, become the songs of the nations."

"As the eyes of Lyncæus were said to see through the earth, so the poet turns the world to glass, and shows us all things in their right series and procession. For, through that better perception, he stands one step nearer to things, and sees the flowing or metamorphosis; perceives that thought is multiform; that within the form of every creature is a force impelling it to ascend into a higher form; and following with his eyes the life, uses the forms which express that life, and so the speech flows with the flowing of nature."

Thus have we in a brief and unworthy manner indicated some views of these books. The only true criticism of these, or any good books, may be gained by making them the companions of our lives. Does every accession of knowledge or a juster sense of beauty makes [sic] us prize them more? Then they are good, indeed, and more immortal than mortal. Let that test be applied to these; essays which will lead to great and complete poems—somewhere.

NATHANIEL HAWTHORNE

From The Old Manse[†]

* * *

There were circumstances around me, which made it difficult to view the world precisely as it exists; for, serene and sober as was the old Manse, it was necessary to go but a little way beyond its threshold, before meeting with stranger moral shapes of men than might have been encountered elsewhere, in a circuit of a thousand miles.

These hobgoblins of flesh and blood were attracted thither by the widespreading influence of a great original Thinker, who had his earthly abode at the opposite extremity of our village. His mind acted upon other minds, of a certain constitution, with wonderful magnetism, and drew many men upon long pilgrimages, to speak with him face to face. Young visionaries—to whom just so much of insight had been imparted, as to make life all a labyrinth around them—came to seek the clue that should guide them out of their self-involved bewilderment. Gray-headed theorists—whose systems, at first air, had finally imprisoned them in an iron frame-work—travelled painfully to his door, not to ask deliverance, but to invite this free spirit into their own thraldom. People that had lighted on a new thought, or a thought that they fancied new, came to Emerson, as the finder of a glittering gem hastens to a lapidary, to ascertain its

† Preface to *Mosses from an Old Manse* (1846).

quality and value. Uncertain, troubled, earnest wanderers, through the mid-night of the moral world, beheld his intellectual fire, as a beacon burning on a hill-top, and, climbing the difficult ascent, looked forth into the surrounding obscurity, more hopefully than hitherto. The light revealed objects unseen be-fore—mountains, gleaming lakes, glimpses of a creation among the chaos—but also, as was unavoidable, it attracted bats and owls, and the whole host of night-birds, which flapped their dusky wings against the gazer's eyes, and sometimes were mistaken for fowls of angelic feather. Such delusions always hover nigh, whenever a beacon-fire of truth is kindled.

For myself, there had been epochs of my life, when I, too, might have asked of this prophet the master-word, that should solve me the riddle of the universe; but now, being happy, I felt as if there were no question to be put, and therefore admired Emerson as a poet of deep beauty and austere tenderness, but sought nothing from him as a philosopher. It was good, nevertheless, to meet him in the wood-paths, or sometimes in our avenue, with that pure, intellectual gleam diffused about his presence, like the garment of a shining-one; and he so quiet, so simple, so without pretension, encountering each man alive as if expecting to receive more than he could impart. And, in truth, the heart of many an or-dinary man had, perchance, inscriptions which he could not read. But it was impossible to dwell in his vicinity, without inhaling, more or less, the moun-tain-atmosphere of his lofty thought, which, in the brains of some people, wrought a singular giddiness—new truth being as heady as new wine. Never was a poor little country village infested with such a variety of queer, strangely dressed, oddly behaved mortals, most of whom took upon themselves to be im-portant agents of the world's destiny, yet were simply bores of a very intense water. Such, I imagine, is the invariable character of persons who crowd so closely about an original thinker, as to draw in his unuttered breath, and thus become imbued with a false originality. This triteness of novelty is enough to make any man, of common sense, blaspheme at all ideas of less than a century's standing; and pray that the world may be petrified and rendered immovable, in precisely the worst moral and physical state that it ever yet arrived at, rather than be benefitted by such schemes of such philosophers.

* * *

JAMES RUSSELL LOWELL

From A Fable for Critics[†]

* * *

"But, to come back to Emerson (whom, by the way,
I believe we left waiting),—his is, we may say,
A Greek head on right Yankee shoulders, whose range
Has Olympus for one pole, for t' other the Exchange;
He seems, to my thinking (although I'm afraid   5
The comparison must, long ere this, have been made),

[†] From A *Fable for Critics* (1848).

A Plotinus-Montaigne, where the Egyptian's gold mist
And the Gascon's shrewd wit cheek-by-jowl coexist;
All admire, and yet scarcely six converts he's got
To I don't (nor they either) exactly know what;　　　　　　10
For though he builds glorious temples, 'tis odd
He leaves never a doorway to get in a god.
'T is refreshing to old-fashioned people like me
To meet such a primitive Pagan as he,
In whose mind all creation is duly respected　　　　　　15
As parts of himself—just a little projected;
And who's willing to worship the stars and the sun,
A convert to—nothing but Emerson.
So perfect a balance there is in his head,
That he talks of things sometimes as if they were dead;　　　20
Life, nature, love, God, and affairs of that sort,
He looks at as merely ideas; in short,
As if they were fossils stuck round in a cabinet,
Of such vast extent that our earth's a mere dab in it;
Composed just as he is inclined to conjecture her,　　　　25
Namely, one part pure earth, ninety-nine parts pure lecturer;
You are filled with delight at his clear demonstration,
Each figure, word, gesture, just fits the occasion,
With the quiet precision of science he'll sort 'em,
But you can't help suspecting the whole a *post mortem*.　　　30

"There are persons, mole-blind to the soul's make and style,
Who insist on a likeness 'twixt him and Carlyle;
To compare him with Plato would be vastly fairer,
Carlyle's the more burly, but E. is the rarer;
He sees fewer objects, but clearlier, truelier,　　　　　　35
If C.'s as original, E.'s more peculiar;
That he's more of a man you might say of the one,
Of the other he's more of an Emerson;
C.'s the Titan, as shaggy of mind as of limb,—
E. the clear-eyed Olympian, rapid and slim;　　　　　　40
The one's two thirds Norseman, the other half Greek,
Where the one's most abounding, the other's to seek;
C.'s generals require to be seen in the mass,—
E.'s specialties gain if enlarged by the glass;
C. gives nature and God his own fits of the blues,　　　　45
And rims common-sense things with mystical hues,—
E. sits in a mystery calm and intense,
And looks coolly around him with sharp common-sense;
C. shows you how every-day matters unite
With the dim transdiurnal recesses of night,—　　　　　　50
While E., in a plain, preternatural way,
Makes mysteries matters of mere every day;
C. draws all his characters quite *à la* Fuseli,—
Not sketching their bundles of muscles and thews illy,
He paints with a brush so untamed and profuse,　　　　　55
They seem nothing but bundles of muscles and thews;
E. is rather like Flaxman, lines strait and severe,

And a colorless outline, but full, round, and clear;—
To the men he thinks worthy he frankly accords
The design of a white marble statue in words.   60
C. labors to get at the centre, and then
Take a reckoning from there of his actions and men;
E. calmly assumes the said centre as granted,
And, given himself, has whatever is wanted.

"He has imitators in scores, who omit   65
No part of the man but his wisdom and wit,—
Who go carefully o'er the sky-blue of his brain,
And when he has skimmed it once, skim it again;
If at all they resemble him, you may be sure it is
Because their shoals mirror his mists and obscurities,   70
As a mud-puddle seems deep as heaven for a minute,
While a cloud that floats o'er is reflected within it."

* * *

HENRY DAVID THOREAU

From A Week on the Concord and Merrimack Rivers†

* * *

Lately the victor, whom all Pindars praised, has won another palm, contending with

> "Olympian bards who sung
> Divine ideas below,
> Which always find us young,
> And always keep us so."

What earth or sea, mountain or stream, or Muses' spring or grove, is safe from his all-searching ardent eye, who drives off Phœbus' beaten track, visits unwonted zones, makes the gelid Hyperboreans glow, and the old polar serpent writhe, and many a Nile flow back and hide his head!

> That Phaeton of our day,
> Who'd make another milky way,
> And burn the world up with his ray;
>
> By us an undisputed seer,—
> Who'd drive his flaming car so near
> Unto our shuddering mortal sphere,
>
> Disgracing all our slender worth,
> And scorching up the living earth,
> To prove his heavenly birth.

† From the "Sunday" section of *A Week on the Concord and Merrimack Rivers* (1849).

The silver spokes, the golden tire,
Are glowing with unwonted fire,
And ever nigher roll and nigher;

The pins and axle melted are,
The silver radii fly afar,
Ah, he will spoil his Father's car!

Who let him have the streeds he cannot steer?
Henceforth the sun will not shine for a year;
And we shall Ethiops all appear.

From *his*

           "lips of cunning fell
       The thrilling Delphic oracle."

And yet, sometimes,

       We should not mind if on our ear there fell
       Some less of cunning, more of oracle.

It is Apollo shining in your face. O rare Contemporary, let us have far-off heats. Give us the subtler, the heavenlier though fleeting beauty, which passes through and through, and dwells not in the verse; even pure water, which but reflects those tints which wine wears in its grain. Let epic trade-winds blow, and cease this waltz of inspirations. Let us oftener feel even the gentle southwest wind upon our cheeks blowing from the Indian's heaven. What though we lose a thousand meteors from the sky, if skyey depths, if star-dust and undissolvable nebulæ remain? What though we lose a thousand wise responses of the oracle, if we may have instead some natural acres of Ionian earth?

*   *   *

ANTHONY TROLLOPE

From North America[†]

Boston

*   *   *

Immediately on my arrival in Boston I heard that Mr. Emerson was going to lecture at the Tremont Hall on the subject of the war, and I resolved to go and hear him. I was acquainted with Mr. Emerson, and by reputation knew him well. Among us in England he is regarded as transcendental, and perhaps even as mystic in his philosophy. His "Representative Men" is the work by which he is best known on our side of the water, and I have heard some readers declare that they could not quite understand Mr. Emerson's "Representative Men." For myself, I confess that I

---

† From *North America* (London, 1862).

had broken down over some portions of that book.[1] Since I had become acquainted with him I had read others of his writings, especially his book on England, and had found that he improved greatly on acquaintance. I think that he has confined his mysticism to the book above named. In conversation he is very clear, and by no means above the small practical things of the world. He would, I fancy, know as well what interest he ought to receive for his money as though he were no philosopher; and I am inclined to think that if he held land he would make his hay while the sun shone, as might any common farmer. Before I had met Mr. Emerson, when my idea of him was formed simply on the "Representative Men," I should have thought that a lecture from him on the war would have taken his hearers all among the clouds. As it was, I still had my doubts, and was inclined to fear that a subject which could only be handled usefully at such a time before a large audience by a combination of common sense, high principles, and eloquence, would hardly be safe in Mr. Emerson's hands. I did not doubt the high principles, but feared much that there would be a lack of common sense. So many have talked on that subject, and have shown so great a lack of common sense! As to the eloquence, that might be there, or might not.

Mr. Emerson is a Massachusetts man, very well known in Boston, and a great crowd was collected to hear him. I suppose there were some three thousand persons in the room. I confess that when he took his place before us my prejudices were against him. The matter in hand required no philosophy. It required common sense, and the very best of common sense. It demanded that he should be impassioned, for of what interest can any address be on a matter of public politics without passion? But it demanded that the passion should be winnowed, and free from all rhodomontade. I fancied what might be said on such a subject as to that overlauded star-spangled banner, and how the star-spangled flag would look when wrapped in a mist of mystic Platonism.

But from the beginning to the end there was nothing mystic—no Platonism; and, if I remember rightly, the star-spangled banner was altogether omitted. To the national eagle he did allude. "Your American eagle," he said, "is very well. Protect it here and abroad. But beware of the American peacock."[2] He gave an account of the war from the beginning, showing how it had arisen, and how it had been conducted; and he did so with admirable simplicity and truth. He thought the North were right about the war; and as I thought so also, I was not called upon to disagree with him. He was terse and perspicuous in his sentences, practical in his advice, and, above all things, true in what he said to his audience of themselves. They who know America will understand how hard it is for a public man in the States to practise such truth in his addresses. Fluid compliments and high-flown national eulogium are expected. In this instance none were forthcoming. The North had risen with patriotism to make this effort, and it was now warned that in doing so it was simply doing its national duty. And then came the subject of slavery. I had been told that Mr. Emerson was an abolitionist, and knew that I must disagree with him on that head, if on no other. To me it has always seemed that to mix up the question of general abolition with

---

1. *Representative Men* (1850) is hardly, in the main, a "mystical" book (see the chapters printed in this volume). *English Traits*, which Trollope alludes to next, is a witty and sometimes critical treatment of what Hawthorne calls "our old home." [Editors]
2. Emerson delivered this lecture, entitled *American Nationality*, at Tremont Temple on November 12, 1861. [Editors]

this war must be the work of a man too ignorant to understand the real subject of the war, or too false to his country to regard it. Throughout the whole lecture I was waiting for Mr. Emerson's abolition doctrine, but no abolition doctrine came. The words abolition and compensation were mentioned, and then there was an end of the subject. If Mr. Emerson be an abolitionist he expressed his views very mildly on that occasion. On the whole the lecture was excellent, and that little advice about the peacock was in itself worth an hour's attention.

* * *

LOUISA MAY ALCOTT

From Journals[†]

1860

May.

Meg's [Anna's] wedding.

My farce was acted, and I went to see it. Not very well done; but I sat in a box, and the good Doctor handed up a bouquet to the author, and made as much as he could of a small affair.

Saw Anna's honeymoon home at Chelsea,—a little cottage in a blooming apple-orchard. Pretty place, simple and sweet. God bless it!

The dear girl was married on the 23d, the same day as Mother's wedding. A lovely day; the house full of sunshine, flowers, friends, and happiness. Uncle S. J. May married them, with no fuss, but much love; and we all stood round her. She in her silver-gray silk, with lilies of the valley (John's flower) in her bosom and hair. We in gray thin stuff and roses,—sackcloth, I called it, and ashes of roses; for I mourn the loss of my Nan, and am not comforted. We have had a little feast, sent by good Mrs. Judge Shaw; then the old folks danced round the bridal pair on the lawn in the German fashion, making a pretty picture to remember, under our Revolutionary elm.

Then, with tears and kisses, our dear girl, in her little white bonnet, went happily away with her good John; and we ended our first wedding. Mr. Emerson kissed her; and I thought that honor would make even matrimony endurable, for he is the god of my idolatry, and has been for years.

* * *

August.

"Moods." Genius burned so fiercely that for four weeks I wrote all day and planned nearly all night, being quite possessed by my work. I was perfectly happy, and seemed to have no wants. Finished the book, or a rough draught of it, and put it away to settle. Mr. Emerson offered to read it when Mother told him it was "Moods" and had one of his sayings for motto.

[†] From *The Journals of Louisa May Alcott*, ed. Joel Myerson and Daniel Shealy, with Madeline B. Stern (Boston: Little, Brown, 1989). Reprinted with permission of the editors and the Estate of Theresa W. Pratt.

*   *   *

November.

Father sixty-one; L. aged twenty-eight. Our birthday. Gave Father a ream of paper, and he gave me Emerson's picture, so both were happy.

December 5.

Mr. Emerson invited me to his class when they meet to talk on Genius; a great honor, as all the learned ladies go.

1861

January

Father had four talks at Emerson's; good people came, and he enjoyed them much; made $30. R. W. E. probably put in $20. He has a sweet way of bestowing gifts on the table under a book or behind a candle-stick, when he thinks Father wants a little money, and no one will help him earn. A true friend is this tender and illustrious man.

1879

December Wed. 31st

A dark day for us. A telegram from Ernst to Mr Emerson tells us "May is dead." Anna was gone to B[oston]. Father to the P.O. anxious for letters, the last being overdue, I was alone when Mr E[merson]. came. E. sent to him knowing I was feeble & hoping Mr E. would soften the blow. I found him looking at May's portrait, pale & tearful with the paper in his hand. "My child, I *wish* I could prepare you, but alas, alas!" there his voice failed & he gave me the telegram.

I was not surprised & read the hard words as if I knew it all before. "I *am* prepared," I said & thanked him. He was much moved & very tender. I shall remember gratefully the look, the grasp, the tears he gave me, & I am sure that hard moment was made bearable by the presence of this our best & tenderest friend. He went to find father but missed him, & I had to tell both him & Anna when they came. A very bitter sorrow for all.

I never shall forgive myself for not going even if it put me back. If I had lived to see her & help her die, or save her, I should have been content.

The dear baby may comfort E. but what can comfort us?

1882

April

Mr Emerson ill. Father goes to see him. E. held his hand looking up at the tall, rosy old man, & saying with that smile of love that has been father's sunshine for so many years, "*you* are very well, Keep so, keep so." After father left he called him back & grasped his hand again as if he knew it was for the last time, & the kind eyes said "Good by, my friend."

April, Thursday 27th

Mr Emerson died at 9 p.m. suddenly. Our best & greatest American gone. The nearest & dearest friend father has ever had, & the man who has helped me most by his life, his books, his society. I can never tell all he has been to me from the time I sang Mignon's song under his window, a little girl, & wrote letters a la Bettine to him, my Goethe, at 15, up through my hard years when his essays on Self Reliance, Character, Compensation, Love & Friendship helped me to understand myself & life & God & Nature.

Illustrious & beloved friend, good bye!

April, Sunday 30th Emerson's funeral.

I made a golden lyre of jonquils for the church & helped trim it up. Private services at the house & a great crowd at the church. Father read his sonnet & Judge Hoar & others spoke. Now he lies in Sleepy Hollow among his brothers under the pines he loved.

I sat up till midnight to write an article on R. W. E. for the Youth's Companion, that the children may know something of him. A labor of love.

May. (27 boys signed pledge.)

Temperance work. Meetings. I give books to schools. Wrote an article for Mrs Croly on R. W. E.

EMMA LAZARUS[1]

To R. W. E.[†]

As when a father dies, his children draw
About the empty hearth, their loss to cheat
With uttered praise and love, and oft repeat
His all-familiar words with whispered awe
The honored habit of his daily law   5
Not for his sake, but theirs, whose feebler feet
Need still that guiding lamp, whose faith less sweet
Misses that tempered patience without flaw—
So do we gather round thy vacant chair
In thine own elm-roofed, amber-rivered town,   10
Master and father! For the love we bear,
Not for thy fame's sake, do we weave this crown,
And feel thy presence in the sacred air,
Forbidding us to weep that thou art gone.

---

1. For correspondence between Emerson and Lazarus and information on their friendship see "Correspondence," pp. 565ff.
† A newspaper clipping pasted into Emma Lazarus's copy of Emerson's *Selected Poems* (Houghton Library); reprinted in *The Genius and Character of Emerson* (1885).

HENRY JAMES

Emerson[†]

Mr. Elliot Cabot has made a very interesting contribution to a class of books of which our literature, more than any other, offers admirable examples: he has given us a biography[1] intelligently and carefully composed. These two volumes are a model of responsible editing—I use that term because they consist largely of letters and extracts from letters: nothing could resemble less the manner in which the mere bookmaker strings together his frequently questionable pearls and shovels the heap into the presence of the public. Mr. Cabot has selected, compared, discriminated, steered an even course between meagreness and redundancy, and managed to be constantly and happily illustrative. And his work, moreover, strikes us as the better done from the fact that it stands for one of the two things that make an absorbing memoir a good deal more than for the other. If these two things be the conscience of the writer and the career of his hero, it is not difficult to see on which side the biographer of Emerson has found himself strongest. Ralph Waldo Emerson was a man of genius, but he led for nearly eighty years a life in which the sequence of events had little of the rapidity, or the complexity, that a spectator loves. There is something we miss very much as we turn these pages—something that has a kind of accidental, inevitable presence in almost any personal record—something that may be most definitely indicated under the name of colour. We lay down the book with a singular impression of paleness—an impression that comes partly from the tone of the biographer and partly from the moral complexion of his subject, but mainly from the vacancy of the page itself. That of Emerson's personal history is condensed into the single word Concord, and all the condensation in the world will not make it look rich. It presents a most continuous surface. Mr. Matthew Arnold, in his *Discourses in America*, contests Emerson's complete right to the title of a man of letters; yet letters surely were the very texture of his history. Passions, alternations, affairs, adventures had absolutely no part in it. It stretched itself out in enviable quiet—a quiet in which we hear the jotting of the pencil in the notebook. It is the very life for literature (I mean for one's own, not that of another): fifty years of residence in the home of one's forefathers, pervaded by reading, by walking in the woods and the daily addition of sentence to sentence.

If the interest of Mr. Cabot's pencilled portrait is incontestable and yet does not spring from variety, it owes nothing either to a source from which it might have borrowed much and which it is impossible not to regret a little that he has so completely neglected: I mean a greater reference to the social conditions in which Emerson moved, the company he lived in, the moral air he breathed. If his biographer had allowed himself a little more of the ironic touch, had put himself once in a way under the protection of Sainte-Beuve and had attempted something of a general picture, we should have felt that he only went with the occasion. I may over-estimate the latent treasures of the field, but it seems to me there was distinctly an opportunity—an opportunity to make up moreover in some degree for the white tint of Emerson's career considered simply in itself. We know a man imperfectly until we know his society, and we but

---

[†] From *Partial Portraits* (London, 1888).
1. *A Memoir of Ralph Waldo Emerson* by James Elliot Cabot. Two volumes: London, 1887.

half know a society until we know its manners. This is especially true of a man of letters, for manners lie very close to literature. From those of the New England world in which Emerson's character formed itself Mr. Cabot almost averts his lantern, though we feel sure that there would have been delightful glimpses to be had and that he would have been in a position — that is that he has all the knowledge that would enable him — to help us to them. It is as if he could not trust himself, knowing the subject only too well. This adds to the effect of extreme discretion that we find in his volumes, but it is the cause of our not finding certain things, certain figures and scenes, evoked. What is evoked is Emerson's pure spirit, by a copious, sifted series of citations and comments. But we must read as much as possible between the lines, and the picture of the transcendental time (to mention simply one corner) has yet to be painted — the lines have yet to be bitten in. Meanwhile we are held and charmed by the image of Emerson's mind and the extreme appeal which his physiognomy makes to our art of discrimination. It is so fair, so uniform and impersonal, that its features are simply fine shades, the gradations of tone of a surface whose proper quality was of the smoothest and on which nothing was reflected with violence. It is a pleasure of the critical sense to find, with Mr. Cabot's extremely intelligent help, a notation for such delicacies.

We seem to see the circumstances of our author's origin, immediate and remote, in a kind of high, vertical moral light, the brightness of a society at once very simple and very responsible. The rare singleness that was in his nature (so that he was *all* the warning moral voice, without distraction or counter-solicitation), was also in the stock he sprang from, clerical for generations, on both sides, and clerical in the Puritan sense. His ancestors had lived long (for nearly two centuries) in the same corner of New England, and during that period had preached and studied and prayed and practised. It is impossible to imagine a spirit better prepared in advance to be exactly what it was — better educated for its office in its far-away unconscious beginnings. There is an inner satisfaction in seeing so straight, although so patient, a connection between the stem and the flower, and such a proof that when life wishes to produce something exquisite in quality she takes her measures many years in advance. A conscience like Emerson's could not have been turned off, as it were, from one generation to another: a succession of attempts, a long process of refining, was required. His perfection, in his own line, comes largely from the non-interruption of the process.

As most of us are made up of ill-assorted pieces, his reader, and Mr. Cabot's, envies him this transmitted unity, in which there was no mutual hustling or crowding of elements. It must have been a kind of luxury to be — that is to feel — so homogeneous, and it helps to account for his serenity, his power of acceptance, and that absence of personal passion which makes his private correspondence read like a series of beautiful circulars or expanded cards *pour prendre congé.* He had the equanimity of a result; nature had taken care of him and he had only to speak. He accepted himself as he accepted others, accepted everything; and his absence of eagerness, or in other words his modesty, was that of a man with whom it is not a question of success, who has nothing invested or at stake. The investment, the stake, was that of the race, of all the past Emersons and Bulkeleys and Waldos. There is much that makes us smile, to-day, in the commotion produced by his secession from the mild Unitarian pulpit: we wonder at a condition of opinion in which any utterance of his should appear to be wanting in superior piety—in the essence of good instruction. All that is changed: the great difference has become the infinitely small, and we admire a state of society in which scandal and schism took on no darker hue; but there is even yet a sort of drollery in the spectacle of a body of people among whom the author of *The American Scholar* and of the Address of 1838 at the Harvard Divinity College passed for profane, and who failed to see that he only gave his plea for the spiritual life the advantage of a brilliant expression. They were so provincial as to think that brilliancy came ill-recommended, and they were shocked at his ceasing to care for the prayer and the sermon. They might have perceived that he *was* the prayer and the sermon: not in the least a secularizer, but in his own subtle insinuating way a sanctifier.

Of the three periods into which his life divides itself, the first was (as in the case of most men) that of movement, experiment and selection—that of effort too and painful probation. Emerson had his message, but he was a good while looking for his form—the form which, as he himself would have said, he never completely found and of which it was rather characteristic of him that his later years (with their growing refusal to give him the *word*), wishing to attack him in his most vulnerable point, where his tenure was least complete, had in some degree the effect of despoiling him. It all sounds rather bare and stern, Mr. Cabot's account of his youth and early manhood, and we get an impression of a terrible paucity of alternatives. If he would be neither a farmer nor a trader he could 'teach school'; that was the main resource and a part of the general educative process of the young New Englander who proposed to devote himself to the things of the mind. There was an advantage in the nudity, however, which was that, in Emerson's case at least, the things of the mind did get themselves admirably well considered. If it be his great distinction and his special sign that he had a more vivid conception of the moral life than any one else, it is probably not fanciful to say that he owed it in part to the limited way in which he saw our capacity for living illustrated. The plain, God-fearing, practical society which surrounded him was not fertile in variations: it had great intelligence and energy, but it moved altogether in the straightforward direction. On three occasions later—three journeys to Europe—he was introduced to a more complicated world; but his spirit, his moral taste, as it were, abode always within the undecorated walls of his youth. There he could dwell with that ripe unconsciousness of evil which is one of the most beautiful signs by which we know him. His early writings are full of quaint animadversion upon the vices of the place and time, but there is something charmingly vague, light and general in the arraignment. Almost the worst he can say is that these vices are negative and that his fellow-townsmen are not heroic. We feel that his first impressions were gathered in a community from which misery and extravagance, and either extreme, of any sort, were equally absent. What the life of New England fifty years ago offered to the observer was the common lot, in a kind of achromatic picture, without particular intensifications. It was from this table of the usual, the merely typical joys and sorrows that he proceeded to generalize—a fact that accounts in some degree for a certain inadequacy and thinness in his enumerations. But it helps to account also for his direct, intimate vision of the soul itself—not in its emotions, its contortions and perversions, but in its passive, exposed, yet healthy form. He knows the nature of man and the long tradition of its dangers; but we feel that whereas he can put his finger on the remedies, lying for the most part, as they do, in the deep recesses of virtue, of the spirit, he has only a kind of hearsay, uninformed acquaintance with the disorders. It would require some ingenuity, the reader may say too much, to trace closely this correspondence between his genius and the frugal, dutiful, happy but decidedly lean Boston of the past, where there was a great deal of will but very little fulcrum—like a ministry without an opposition.

The genius itself it seems to me impossible to contest—I mean the genius for seeing character as a real and supreme thing. Other writers have arrived at a more complete expression: Wordsworth and Goethe, for instance, give one a sense of having found their form, whereas with Emerson we never lose the sense that he is still seeking it. But no one has had so steady and constant, and above all so natural, a vision of what we require and what we are capable of in the way of aspiration and independence. With Emerson it is ever the special capacity for moral experience—always that and only that. We have the impression, somehow, that life had never bribed him to look at anything but the soul; and indeed in the world in which he grew up and lived the bribes and lures, the beguilements and prizes, were few. He was in an admirable position for showing, what he constantly endeavoured to show, that the prize was within. Any one who in New England at that time could do that was sure of success, of listeners and sympathy: most of all, of course, when it was a question of doing it with such a divine persuasiveness. Moreover, the way in which Emerson did it added to the charm—by word of mouth, face to face, with a rare, irresistible voice and a beautiful mild, modest authority. If Mr. Arnold is struck with the limited degree in which he was a man of letters I suppose it is because he is more struck with his having been, as it were, a man of lectures. But the lecture surely was never more purged of its grossness—the quality in it that suggests a strong light and a big brush—than as it issued from Emerson's lips; so far from being a vulgarization, it was simply the esoteric made audible, and instead of treating the few as the many, after the usual fashion of gentlemen on platforms, he treated the many as the few. There was probably no other society at that time in which he would have got so many persons to understand that; for we think the better of his audience as we read him, and wonder where else people would have had so much moral attention to give. It is to be remembered however that during the winter of 1847–48, on the occasion of his second visit to England, he found many listeners in London and in provincial cities. Mr. Cabot's volumes are full of evidence of the satisfactions he offered, the delights and revelations he may be said to have promised, to a race which had to seek its entertainment, its rewards and consolations, almost exclusively in the moral world. But his own writings are fuller still; we find an instance almost wherever we open them.

> 'All these great and transcendent properties are ours. . . Let us find room for this great guest in our small houses. . . Where the heart is, there the muses, there the gods sojourn, and not in any geography of fame. Massachusetts, Connecticut River, and Boston Bay, you think paltry places, and the ear loves names of foreign and classic topography. But here we are, and if we will tarry a little we may come to learn that here is best. . . The Jerseys were handsome enough ground for Washington to tread, and London streets for the feet of Milton. . . That country is fairest which is inhabited by the noblest minds.'

We feel, or suspect, that Milton is thrown in as a hint that the London streets are no such great place, and it all sounds like a sort of pleading consolation against bleakness.

The beauty of a hundred passages of this kind in Emerson's pages is that they are effective, that they do come home, that they rest upon insight and not upon ingenuity, and that if they are sometimes obscure it is never with the obscurity of paradox. We seem to see the people turning out into the snow after hearing them, glowing with a finer glow than even the climate could give and fortified for a struggle with overshoes and the east wind.

> 'Look to it first and only, that fashion, custom, authority, pleasure, and money, are nothing to you, are not as bandages over your eyes, that you cannot see; but live with the privilege of the immeasurable mind. Not too anxious to visit periodically all families and each family in your parish connection, when you meet one of these men or women be to them a divine man; be to them thought and virtue; let their timid aspirations find in you a friend; let their trampled instincts be genially tempted out in your atmosphere; let their doubts know that you have doubted, and their wonder feel that you have wondered.'

When we set against an exquisite passage like that, or like the familiar sentences that open the essay on History ('He that is admitted to the right of reason is made freeman of the whole estate. What Plato has thought, he may think; what a saint has felt, he may feel; what at any time has befallen any man, he can understand'); when we compare the letters, cited by Mr. Cabot, to his wife from Springfield, Illinois (January 1853) we feel that his spiritual tact needed to be very just, but that if it was so it must have brought a blessing.

> 'Here I am in the deep mud of the prairies, misled I fear into this bog, not by a will-of-the-wisp, such as shine in bogs, but by a young New Hampshire editor, who over-estimated the strength of both of us, and fancied I should glitter in the prairie and draw the prairie birds and waders. It rains and thaws incessantly, and if we step off the short street we go up to the shoulders, perhaps, in mud. My chamber is a cabin; my fellow-boarders are legislators. . . Two or three governors or ex-governors live in the house. . . I cannot command daylight and solitude for study or for more than a scrawl.' . . .

And another extract:—

> 'A cold, raw country this, and plenty of night-travelling and arriving at four in the morning to take the last and worst bed in the tavern. Advancing day brings mercy and favour to me, but not the sleep. . . Mercury 15° below zero. . . I find well-disposed, kindly people among these sinewy farmers of the North, but in all that is called cultivation they are only ten years old.'

He says in another letter (in 1860), 'I saw Michigan and its forests and the Wolverines pretty thoroughly;' and on another page Mr. Cabot shows him as speaking of his engagements to lecture in the West as the obligation to 'wade, and freeze, and ride, and run, and suffer all manner of indignities.' This was not New England, but as regards the country districts throughout, at that time, it was a question of degree. Certainly never was the fine wine of philosophy carried to remoter or queerer corners: never was a more delicate diet offered to 'two or three governors, or ex-governors,' living in a cabin. It was Mercury, shivering in a mackintosh, bearing nectar and ambrosia to the gods whom he wished those who lived in cabins to endeavour to feel that they might be.

I have hinted that the will, in the old New England society, was a clue without a labyrinth; but it had its use, nevertheless, in helping the young talent to find its mould. There were few or none ready-made: tradition was certainly not so oppressive as might have been inferred from the fact that the air swarmed with reformers and improvers. Of the patient, philosophic manner in which Emerson groped and waited, through teaching the young and preaching to the adult, for his particular vocation, Mr. Cabot's first volume gives a full and orderly account. His passage from the Unitarian pulpit to the lecture-desk was a step which at this distance of time can hardly help appearing to us short, though he was long in making it, for even after ceasing to have a parish of his own he freely confounded the two, or willingly, at least, treated the pulpit as a platform. 'The young people and the mature hint at odium and the aversion of faces, to be presently encountered in society,' he writes in his journal in 1838; but in point of fact the quiet drama of his abdication was not to include the note of suffering. The Boston world might feel disapproval, but it was far too kindly to make this sentiment felt as a weight: every element of martyrdom was there but the important ones of the cause and the persecutors. Mr. Cabot marks the lightness of the penalties of dissent; if they were light in somewhat later years for the transcendentalists and fruit-eaters they could press but little on a man of Emerson's distinction, to whom, all his life, people went not to carry but to ask the right word. There was no consideration to give up, he could not have been one of the dingy if he had tried; but what he did renounce in 1838 was a material profession. He was 'settled,' and his indisposition to administer the communion unsettled him. He calls the whole business, in writing to Carlyle, 'a tempest in our washbowl'; but it had the effect of forcing him to seek a new source of income. His wants were few and his view of life severe, and this came to him, little by little, as he was able to extend the field in which he read his discourses. In 1835, upon his second marriage, he took up his habitation at Concord, and his life fell into the shape it was, in a general way, to keep for the next half-century. It is here that we cannot help regretting that Mr. Cabot had not found it possible to treat his career a little more pictorially. Those fifty years of Concord—at least the earlier part of them—would have been a subject bringing into play many odd figures, many human incongruities: they would have abounded in illustrations of the primitive New England character, especially during the time of its queer search for something to expend itself upon. Objects and occupations have multiplied since then, and now there is no lack; but fifty years ago the expanse was wide and free, and we get the impression of a conscience gasping in the void, panting for sensations, with something of the movement of the gills of a landed fish. It would take a very fine point to sketch Emerson's benignant, patient, inscrutable countenance during the various phases of this democratic communion; but the picture, when complete, would be one of the portraits, half a revelation and half an enigma, that suggest and fascinate. Such a striking personage as old Miss Mary Emerson, our author's aunt, whose high intelligence and temper were much of an influence in his earlier years, has a kind of tormenting representative value: we want to see her from head to foot, with her frame and her background; having (for we happen to have it) an impression that she was a very remarkable specimen of the transatlantic

Puritan stock, a spirit that would have dared the devil. We miss a more liberal handling, are tempted to add touches of our own, and end by convincing ourselves that Miss Mary Moody Emerson, grim intellectual virgin and daughter of a hundred ministers, with her local traditions and her combined love of empire and of speculation, would have been an inspiration for a novelist. Hardly less so the charming Mrs. Ripley, Emerson's life-long friend and neighbour, most delicate and accomplished of women, devoted to Greek and to her house, studious, simple and dainty—an admirable example of the old-fashioned New England lady. It was a freak of Miss Emerson's somewhat sardonic humour to give her once a broomstick to carry across Boston Common (under the pretext of a 'moving'), a task accepted with docility but making of the victim the most benignant witch ever equipped with that utensil.

These ladies, however, were very private persons and not in the least of the reforming tribe: there are others who would have peopled Mr. Cabot's page to whom he gives no more than a mention. We must add that it is open to him to say that their features have become faint and indistinguishable to-day without more research than the question is apt to be worth: they are embalmed—in a collective way—the apprehensible part of them, in Mr. Frothingham's clever *History of Transcendentalism in New England*. This must be admitted to be true of even so lively a 'factor,' as we say nowadays, as the imaginative, talkative, intelligent and finally Italianised and shipwrecked Margaret Fuller: she is now one of the dim, one of Carlyle's 'then-celebrated' at most. It seemed indeed as if Mr. Cabot rather grudged her a due place in the record of the company that Emerson kept, until we came across the delightful letter he quotes toward the end of his first volume—a letter interesting both as a specimen of inimitable, imperceptible edging away, and as an illustration of the curiously generalized way, as if with an implicit protest against personalities, in which his intercourse, epistolary and other, with his friends was conducted. There is an extract from a letter to his aunt on the occasion of the death of a deeply-loved brother (his own) which reads like a passage from some fine old chastened essay on the vanity of earthly hopes: strangely unfamiliar, considering the circumstances. Courteous and humane to the furthest possible point, to the point of an almost profligate surrender of his attention, there was no familiarity in him, no personal avidity. Even his letters to his wife are courtesies, they are not familiarities. He had only one style, one manner, and he had it for everything—even for himself, in his notes, in his journals. But he had it in perfection for Miss Fuller; he retreats, smiling and flattering, on tiptoe, as if he were advancing. 'She ever seems to crave,' he says in his journal, 'something which I have not, or have not for her.' What he had was doubtless not what she craved, but the letter in question should be read to see how the modicum was administered. It is only between the lines of such a production that we read that a part of her effect upon him was to bore him; for his system was to practise a kind of universal passive hospitality—he aimed at nothing less. It was only because he was so deferential that he could be so detached; he had polished his aloofness till it reflected the image of his solicitor. And this was not because he was an 'uncommunicating egotist,' though he amuses himself with saying so to Miss Fuller: egotism is the strongest of passions, and he was altogether passionless. It was because he had no personal, just as he had almost no physical wants. 'Yet I plead not guilty to the malice prepense. 'Tis imbecility, not contumacy, though perhaps somewhat more odious. It seems very just, the irony with which you ask whether you may not be trusted and promise such docility. Alas, we will all promise, but the prophet loiters.' He would not say even to himself that she bored him; he had denied himself the luxury of such easy and obvious short cuts. There is a passage in the lecture (1844) called 'Man the Reformer,' in which he hovers round and round the idea that the practice of trade, in certain conditions likely to beget an underhand competition, does not draw forth the nobler parts of character, till the reader is tempted to interrupt him with, 'Say at once that it is impossible for a gentleman!'

So he remained always, reading his lectures in the winter, writing them in the summer, and at all seasons taking wood-walks and looking for hints in old books.

> 'Delicious summer stroll through the pastures . . . On the steep park of Conantum I have the old regret—is all this beauty to perish? Shall none re-make this sun and wind; the sky-blue river; the river-blue sky; the yellow meadow, spotted with sacks and sheets of cranberry-gatherers; the red bushes; the iron-gray house, just the colour of the granite rocks; the wild orchard?'

His observation of Nature was exquisite—always the direct, irresistible impression.

> 'The hawking of the wild geese flying by night; the thin note of the companionable titmouse in the winter day; the fall of swarms of flies in autumn, from combats high in the air, pattering down on the leaves like rain; the angry hiss of the wood-birds; the pine throwing out its pollen for the benefit of the next century.' . . . (*Literary Ethics*).

I have said there was no familiarity in him, but he was familiar with woodland creatures and sounds. Certainly, too, he was on terms of free association with his books, which were numerous and dear to him; though Mr. Cabot says, doubtless with justice, that his dependence on them was slight and that he was not 'intimate' with his authors. They did not feed him but they stimulated; they were not his meat but his wine—he took them in sips. But he needed them and liked them; he had volumes of notes from his reading, and he could not have produced his lectures without them. He liked literature as a thing to refer to, liked the very names of which it is full, and used them, especially in his later writings, for purposes of ornament, to dress the dish, sometimes with an unmeasured profusion. I open *The Conduct of Life* and find a dozen on the page. He mentions more authorities than is the fashion to-day. He can easily say, of course, that he follows a better one—that of his well-loved and irrepressibly allusive Montaigne. In his own bookishness there is a certain contradiction, just as there is a latent incompleteness in his whole literary side. Independence, the return to nature, the finding out and doing for one's self, was ever what he most highly recommended; and yet he is constantly reminding his readers of the conventional signs and consecrations—of what other men have done. This was partly because the independence that he had in his eye was an independence without ill-nature, without rudeness (though he likes that word), and full of gentle amiabilities, curiosities and tolerances; and partly it is a simple matter of form, a literary expedient, confessing its character—on the part of one who had never really mastered the art of composition—of continuous expression. Charming to many a reader, charming yet ever slightly droll, will remain Emerson's frequent invocation of the 'scholar': there is such a friendly vagueness and convenience in it. It is of the scholar that he expects all the heroic and uncomfortable things, the concentrations and relinquishments, that make up the noble life. We fancy this personage looking up from his book and arm-chair a little ruefully and saying, 'Ah, but why *me* always and only? Why so much of me, and is there no one else to share the responsibility?' 'Neither years nor books have yet availed to extirpate a prejudice then rooted in me [when as a boy he first saw the graduates of his college assembled at their anniversary], that a scholar is the favourite of heaven and earth, the excellency of his country, the happiest of men.'

In truth, by this term he means simply the cultivated man, the man who has had a liberal education, and there is a voluntary plainness in his use of it—speaking of such people as the rustic, or the vulgar, speak of those who have a tincture of books. This is characteristic of his humility—that humility which was nine-tenths a plain fact (for it is easy for persons who have at bottom a great fund of indifference to be humble), and the remaining tenth a literary habit. Moreover an American reader may be excused for finding in it a pleasant sign of that prestige, often so quaintly and indeed so extravagantly acknowledged, which a connection with literature carries with it among the people of the United States. There is no country in which it is more freely admitted to be a distinction—*the* distinction; or in which so many persons have become eminent for showing it even in a slight degree. Gentlemen and ladies are celebrated there on this ground who would not on the same ground, though they might on another, be celebrated anywhere else. Emerson's own tone is an echo of that, when he speaks of the scholar—not of the banker, the great merchant, the legislator, the artist—as the most distinguished figure in the society about him. It is because he has most to give up that he is appealed to for efforts and sacrifices. 'Meantime I know that a very different estimate of the scholar's profession prevails in this country,' he goes on to say in the address from which I last quoted (the *Literary Ethics*), 'and the importunity with which society presses its claim upon young men tends to pervert the views of the youth in respect to the culture of the intellect.' The manner in which that is said represents, surely, a serious mistake: with the estimate of the scholar's profession which then prevailed in New England Emerson could have had no quarrel; the ground of his lamentation was another side of the matter. It was not a question of estimate, but of accidental practice. In 1838 there were still so many things of prime material necessity to be done that reading was driven to the wall; but the reader was still thought the cleverest, for he found time as well as intelligence. Emerson's own situation sufficiently indicates it. In what other country, on sleety winter nights, would provincial and bucolic populations have gone forth in hundreds for the cold comfort of a literary discourse? The distillation anywhere else would certainly have appeared too thin, the appeal too special. But for many years the American people of the middle regions, outside of a few cities, had in the most rigorous seasons no other recreation. A gentleman, grave or gay, in a bare room, with a manuscript, before a desk, offered the reward of toil, the refreshment of pleasure, to the young, the middle-aged and the old of both sexes. The hour was brightest, doubtless, when the gentleman was gay, like Doctor Oliver Wendell Holmes. But Emerson's gravity never sapped his career, any more than it chilled the regard in which he was held among those who were particularly his own people. It was impossible to be more honoured and cherished, far and near, than he was during his long residence in Concord, or more looked upon as the principal gentleman in the place. This was conspicuous to the writer of these remarks on the occasion of the curious, sociable, cheerful public funeral made for him in 1883 by all the countryside, arriving, as for the last honours to the first citizen, in trains, in waggons, on foot, in multitudes. It was a popular manifestation, the most striking I have ever seen provoked by the death of a man of letters.

If a picture of that singular and very illustrative institution the old American lecture-system would have constituted a part of the filling-in of the ideal memoir of Emerson, I may further say, returning to the matter for a moment, that such a memoir would also have had a chapter for some of those Concord-haunting figures which are not so much interesting in themselves as interesting because for a season Emerson thought them so. And the pleasure of that would be partly that it would push us to inquire how interesting he did really think them. That is, it would bring up the question of his inner reserves and scepticisms, his secret ennuis and ironies, the way he sympathized for courtesy and then, with his delicacy and generosity, in a world after all given much to the literal, let his courtesy pass for adhesion—a question particularly attractive to those for whom he has, in general, a fascination. Many entertaining problems of that sort present themselves for such readers: there is something indefinable for them in the mixture of which he was made—his fidelity as an interpreter of the so-called transcendental spirit and his freedom from all wish for any personal share in the effect of his ideas. He drops them, sheds them, diffuses them, and we feel as if there would be a grossness in holding him to anything so temporal as a responsibility. He had the advantage, for many years, of having the question of application assumed for him by Thoreau, who took upon himself to be, in the concrete, the sort of person that Emerson's 'scholar' was in the abstract, and who paid for it by having a shorter life than that fine adumbration. The application, with Thoreau, was violent and limited (it became a matter of prosaic detail, the non-payment of taxes, the non-wearing of a necktie, the preparation of one's food one's self, the practice of a rude sincerity—all things not of the essence), so that, though he wrote some beautiful pages, which read like a translation of Emerson into the sounds of the field and forest and which no one who has ever loved nature in New England, or indeed anywhere, can fail to love, he suffers something of the *amoindrissement* of eccentricity. His master escapes that reduction altogether. I call it an advantage to have had such a pupil as Thoreau; because for a mind so much made up of reflection as Emerson's everything comes under that head which prolongs and reanimates the process—produces the return, again and yet again, on one's impressions. Thoreau must have had this moderating and even chastening effect. It did not rest, moreover, with him alone; the advantage of which I speak was not confined to Thoreau's case. In 1837 Emerson (in his journal) pronounced Mr. Bronson Alcott the most extraordinary man and the highest genius of his time: the sequence of which was that for more than forty years after that he had the gentleman living but half a mile away. The opportunity for the return, as I have called it, was not wanting.

His detachment is shown in his whole attitude toward the transcendental movement—that remarkable outburst of Romanticism on Puritan ground, as Mr. Cabot very well names it. Nothing can be more ingenious, more sympathetic and charming, than Emerson's account and definition of the matter in his lecture (of 1842) called 'The Transcendentalist'; and yet nothing is more apparent from his letters and journals than that he regarded any such label or banner as a mere tiresome flutter. He liked to taste but not to drink—least of all to become intoxicated. He liked to explain the transcendentalists but did not care at all to be explained by them: a doctrine 'whereof you know I am wholly guiltless,' he says to his wife in 1842, 'and which is spoken of as a known and fixed element, like salt or meal. So that I have to begin with endless disclaimers and explanations: "I am not the man you take me for."' He was never the man any one took him for, for the simple reason that no one could possibly take him for the elusive, irreducible, merely gustatory spirit for which he took himself.

> 'It is a sort of maxim with me never to harp on the omnipotence of limitations. Least of all do we need any suggestion of checks and measures; as if New England were anything else. . . Of so many fine people it is true that being so much they ought to be a little more, and missing that are naught. It is a sort of King Renè period; there is no doing, but rare thrilling prophecy from bands of competing minstrels.'

That is his private expression about a large part of a ferment in regard to which his public judgment was that

> 'That indeed constitutes a new feature in their portrait, that they are the most exacting and extortionate critics. . . These exacting children advertise us of our wants. There is no compliment, no smooth speech with them; they pay you only this one compliment of insatiable expectation; they aspire, they severely exact, and if they only stand fast in this watchtower, and stand fast unto the end, and without end, then they are terrible friends, whereof poet and priest cannot but stand in awe; and what if they eat clouds and drink wind, they have not been without service to the race of man.'

That was saying the best for them, as he always said it for everything; but it was the sense of their being 'bands of competing minstrels' and their camp being only a 'measure and check,' in a society too sparse for a synthesis, that kept him from wishing to don their uniform. This was after all but a misfitting imitation of his natural wear, and what he would have liked was to put that off—he did not wish to button it tighter. He said the best for his friends of the Dial, of Fruitlands and Brook Farm, in saying that they were fastidious and critical; but he was conscious in the next breath that what there was around them to be criticized was mainly a negative. Nothing is more perceptible to-day than that their criticism produced no fruit—that it was little else than a very decent and innocent recreation—a kind of Puritan carnival. The New England world was for much the most part very busy, but the Dial and Fruitlands and Brook Farm were the amusement of the leisure-class. Extremes meet, and as in older societies that class is known principally by its connection with castles and carriages, so at Concord it came, with Thoreau and Mr. W. H. Channing, out of the cabin and the wood-lot.

Emerson was not moved to believe in their fastidiousness as a productive principle even when they directed it upon abuses which he abundantly recognized. Mr. Cabot shows that he was by no means one of the professional abolitionists or philanthropists—never an enrolled 'humanitarian.'

> 'We talk frigidly of Reform until the walls mock us. It is that of which a man should never speak, but if he have cherished it in his bosom he

should steal to it in darkness, as an Indian to his bride. . . Does he not do
more to abolish slavery who works all day steadily in his own garden, than
he who goes to the abolition meeting and makes a speech? He who does
his own work frees a slave.'

I must add that even while I transcribe these words there comes to me the recollection of the great meeting in the Boston Music Hall, on the first day of 1863,
to celebrate the signing by Mr. Lincoln of the proclamation freeing the Southern slaves—of the momentousness of the occasion, the vast excited multitude,
the crowded platform and the tall, spare figure of Emerson, in the midst, reading out the stanzas that were published under the name of the Boston Hymn.
They are not the happiest he produced for an occasion—they do not compare
with the verses on the 'embattled farmers,' read at Concord in 1857 [sic], and
there is a certain awkwardness in some of them. But I well remember the immense effect with which his beautiful voice pronounced the lines—

> 'Pay ransom to the owner
> And fill the bag to the brim.
> Who is the owner? The slave is owner,
> And ever was. Pay *him!*'

And Mr. Cabot chronicles the fact that the *gran' rifiuto*—the great backsliding
of Mr. Webster when he cast his vote in Congress for the Fugitive Slave Law of
1850—was the one thing that ever moved him to heated denunciation. He felt
Webster's apostasy as strongly as he had admired his genius. 'Who has not
helped to praise him? Simply he was the one American of our time whom we
could produce as a finished work of nature.' There is a passage in his journal
(not a rough jotting, but, like most of the entries in it, a finished piece of writing), which is admirably descriptive of the wonderful orator and is moreover
one of the very few portraits, or even personal sketches, yielded by Mr. Cabot's
selections. It shows that he could observe the human figure and 'render' it to
good purpose.

> 'His splendid wrath, when his eyes become fire, is good to see, so in-
> tellectual it is—the wrath of the fact and the cause he espouses, and not at
> all personal to himself. . . These village parties must be dish-water to
> him, yet he shows himself just good-natured, just nonchalant enough; and
> he has his own way, without offending any one or losing any ground . . .
> His expensiveness seems necessary to him; were he too prudent a Yankee
> it would be a sad deduction from his magnificence. I only wish he would
> not truckle [to the slave-holders]. I do not care how much he spends.

I doubtless appear to have said more than enough, yet I have passed by many
of the passages I had marked for transcription from Mr. Cabot's volumes. There
is one, in the first, that makes us stare as we come upon it, to the effect that Emerson 'could see nothing in Shelley, Aristophanes, Don Quixote, Miss Austen,
Dickens.' Mr. Cabot adds that he rarely read a novel, even the famous ones (he
has a point of contact here as well as, strangely enough, on two or three other sides
with that distinguished moralist M. Ernest Renan, who, like Emerson, was originally a dissident priest and cannot imagine why people should write works of fiction); and thought Dante 'a man to put into a museum, but not into your house;
another Zerah Colburn; a prodigy of imaginative function, executive rather than
contemplative or wise.' The confession of an insensibility ranging from Shelley

to Dickens and from Dante to Miss Austen and taking Don Quixote and Aristophanes on the way, is a large allowance to have to make for a man of letters, and may appear to confirm but slightly any claim of intellectual hospitality and general curiosity put forth for him. The truth was that, sparely constructed as he was and formed not wastefully, not with material left over, as it were, for a special function, there were certain chords in Emerson that did not vibrate at all. I well remember my impression of this on walking with him in the autumn of 1872 through the galleries of the Louvre and, later that winter, through those of the Vatican: his perception of the objects contained in these collections was of the most general order. I was struck with the anomaly of a man so refined and intelligent being so little spoken to by works of art. It would be more exact to say that certain chords were wholly absent; the tune was played, the tune of life and literature, altogether on those that remained. They had every wish to be equal to their office, but one feels that the number was short—that some notes could not be given. Mr. Cabot makes use of a singular phrase when he says, in speaking of Hawthorne, for several years our author's neighbour at Concord and a little—a very little we gather—his companion, that Emerson was unable to read his novels—he thought them 'not worthy of him.' This is a judgment odd almost to fascination—we circle round it and turn it over and over; it contains so elusive an ambiguity. How highly he must have esteemed the man of whose genius *The House of the Seven Gables* and *The Scarlet Letter* gave imperfectly the measure, and how strange that he should not have been eager to read almost anything that such a gifted being might have let fall! It was a rare accident that made them live almost side by side so long in the same small New England town, each a fruit of a long Puritan stem, yet with such a difference of taste. Hawthorne's vision was all for the evil and sin of the world; a side of life as to which Emerson's eyes were thickly bandaged. There were points as to which the latter's conception of right could be violated, but he had no great sense of wrong—a strangely limited one, indeed, for a moralist—no sense of the dark, the foul, the base. There were certain complications in life which he never suspected. One asks one's self whether that is why he did not care for Dante and Shelley and Aristophanes and Dickens, their works containing a considerable reflection of human perversity. But that still leaves the indifference to Cervantes and Miss Austen unaccounted for.

It has not, however, been the ambition of these remarks to account for everything, and I have arrived at the end without even pointing to the grounds on which Emerson justifies the honours of biography, discussion and illustration. I have assumed his importance and continuance, and shall probably not be gainsaid by those who read him. Those who do not will hardly rub him out. Such a book as Mr. Cabot's subjects a reputation to a test—leads people to look it over and hold it up to the light, to see whether it is worth keeping in use or even putting away in a cabinet. Such a revision of Emerson has no relegating consequences. The result of it is once more the impression that he serves and will not wear out, and that indeed we cannot afford to drop him. His instrument makes him precious. He did something better than any one else; he had a particular faculty, which has not been surpassed, for speaking to the soul in a voice of direction and authority. There have been many spiritual voices appealing, consoling, reassuring, exhorting, or even denouncing and terrifying, but none has had just that firmness and just that purity. It penetrates further, it seems to go back to the roots of our feelings, to where conduct and manhood begin; and moreover, to us to-day, there is something in it that says that it is connected somehow with the virtue of the world, has wrought and achieved, lived in thousands of minds, produced a mass of character and life. And there is this further sign of Emerson's singular power, that he is a striking exception to the general rule that writings live in the last resort by their form; that they owe a large part of their fortune to the art with which they have been composed. It is hardly too much, or too little, to say of Emerson's writings in general that they were not composed at all. Many and many things are beautifully said; he had felicities, inspirations, unforgettable phrases; he had frequently an exquisite eloquence.

> 'O my friends, there are resources in us on which we have not yet drawn. There are men who rise refreshed on hearing a threat; men to whom a crisis which intimidates and paralyses the majority—demanding not the faculties of prudence and thrift, but comprehension, immovableness, the readiness of sacrifice, come graceful and beloved as a bride . . . But these are heights that we can scarce look up to and remember without contrition and shame. Let us thank God that such things exist.'

None the less we have the impression that that search for a fashion and a manner on which he was always engaged never really came to a conclusion; it draws itself out through his later writings—it drew itself out through his later lectures, like a sort of renunciation of success. It is not on these, however, but on their predecessors, that his reputation will rest. Of course the way he spoke was the way that was on the whole most convenient to him; but he differs from most men of letters of the same degree of credit in failing to strike us as having achieved a style. This achievement is, as I say, usually the bribe or toll-money on the journey to posterity; and if Emerson goes his way, as he clearly appears to be doing, on the strength of his message alone, the case will be rare, the exception striking, and the honour great.

JOSÉ MARTÍ

From Emerson[†]

* * * His mind was priestly, his kindliness angelic, his rages holy. When he saw men enslaved and thought about them, his words seemed to be the Tablets of the Law shattering again on the slope of some new biblical mountain. His anger was indeed Mosaic. Emerson shook off the trivialities of commonplace minds the way a lion swishes its tail to rid itself of horseflies. Argument for him was time robbed from discovering truth. Since he said what he saw, it irritated him when anyone questioned what he said. It was not the anger of vanity, but of

† From *On Art and Literature: Critical Writings*, ed., with intro. and notes, by Philip S. Foner (New York and London: Monthly Review Press, 1982), pp. 149–67. Copyright © 1982 by the Monthly Review Press. Reprinted by permission of the Monthly Review Press. The editors thank Joseph Thomas for calling their attention to this essay, and Charles Sackrey for sharing his expertise on Martí. José Julián Martí y Pérez (1853–1895), Cuban essayist, journalist, poet, and revolutionary, martyred in battle while fighting for Cuban independence from Spain. As Cuba's national hero and a symbol of Cuban freedom, he was crucial to the 1959 Cuban revolution led by Fidel Castro. This essay was written shortly after Emerson's death. References to Emerson abound in Martí's writings, and he translated at least five of Emerson's poems; see also his verse elegy, "Emerson," in *Obras Completas: Poesia*, v. 17 (La Habana, 1964). This essay, highly romanticized, indicates Emerson's importance to a major international figure as a writer and an inspiration for radical, idealistic action.

sincerity. How could he be blamed if others lacked the enlightenment of his eyes? Will the caterpillar not deny that the eagle flies? He looked down upon sophistry, and since for him the extraordinary was the commonplace, he was amazed by the need of having to demonstrate the extraordinary. When he was not understood, he shrugged; Nature had spoken to him, and he was a priest of Nature. Revelations were not affectation with him; he did not build worlds of the mind; he put neither will nor mental effort into his poetry or prose. All his prose is poetry, and one echoes the other. He saw behind him the creative spirit that spoke to Nature through him. He saw himself as a transparent eye that could see everything, reflect everything, and was eye alone. What he wrote seemed to be fragments of shattered light falling upon him, bathing his soul, intoxicating him with light, and bouncing off him again. What was he to think of those vain little minds going about on the stilts of convention? Or those unworthy men who have eyes but refuse to see? Or those idlers or flocks of sheep who would rather use the eyes of others than their own? Or those figures of clay who walk over the land molded by tailors and shoemakers and hatters, adorned by jewelers, and endowed with senses and speech but nothing else? Or those pompous phrasemakers who are unaware that every thought is mental anguish, and a flame kindled with the oil of life itself, and a mountaintop?

Never did a man live freer from the pressures of men or of their times. The future did not make him tremble, nor was he blinded in passing through. His inner light brought him safely over those ruins we call life. He knew no bounds or shackles, nor was he a man merely of his own nation; he belonged to mankind. He saw the world, found it incompatible with himself, felt the pain of answering questions men never ask, and became introspective. He was kind to men and faithful to himself. He was trained to teach a creed, but he handed over his clerical robes to the believers when he felt that Nature had thrown her noble cloak upon his shoulders. He obeyed no system, because to do so seemed liked an act of blindness and servility; nor did he create one, for this he considered an act of a weak and base and envious mind. He buried himself in Nature and emerged from her radiant, thus feeling like a man and therefore like God. He recounted what he saw, and when he could not see, said nothing. He made known what he perceived, revering what he could not perceive. He looked upon the universe with his own eyes, and spoke its special language. He was a creator in spite of himself. He knew divine joy, and lived in delightful and heavenly communion. He knew the ineffable sweetness of ecstasy. His mind, his tongue, and his conscience were never for hire. He radiated light as if from a star, and embodied the full dignity of humanity.

That is how he spent his life: seeing and revealing the invisible. He lived in a sanctified city, for there, weary of slavery, men decided to be free. Kneeling on the ground of Emerson's native Concord, they fired the first shot, from which iron this country was forged, at the English redcoats.

*　*　*

Emerson was a subtle observer who saw the delicate air become wise and melodious words on men's lips, and he wrote as an observer and not as a ponderer. Everything he writes is a maxim. His pen is not a paintbrush that dilutes, but a chisel that carves and trims. He leaves a pure phrase the way a good sculptor leaves a pure line. He likens a superfluous word to a wrinkle on the form, and with a stroke of his chisel the wrinkle vanishes and the phrase is smooth and clean. He detests the superfluous. When he says something, he says it all. At times he appears to jump from one subject to another, and at first glance the relationship between two connected ideas is not always plain to see, but what to others is a leap, to him is a natural step. He strides from mountaintop to mountaintop like a giant, disdaining the trails and footpaths where the pack-burdened pedestrians plod far below, and to whose eyes this towering giant looks small. He does not write in clauses, but in catalogues. His books are summaries, not demonstrations. His thoughts seem isolated, but the fact is he sees many things at once, and wants to say them all at once and just as he sees them, like a page read by lightning or in such a beautiful light that one knows it must disappear. He leaves the deciphering to others; he cannot lose time; he merely sets forth. His style is not baroque; it is clear. He purifies, cleanses, examines, distills it, and reduces it to essentials. His style is not a green hillock covered with sweet-smelling flowering plants; it is a basalt mountain. Instead of serving language, he makes it serve him. Language is the work of man, and man must not be its slave. Some of us do not fully understand him, but a mountain cannot be measured in inches. They say he is obscure, but when have great minds escaped this accusation? It is less humiliating to say we do not understand what we read than to confess our inability to do so. Emerson does not argue; he establishes. He prefers the teachings of Nature to those of man. He feels that a tree knows more than a book, that a star teaches more than a university, that a farm is a gospel, and that a farmboy is closer to universal truth than an antiquarian. For him there are no candles like the stars, no altars like the mountains, no preachers like the deep and tremulous night. When he sees the bright and joyful morning cast off its veils and emerge rosy and happy, he is filled with angelic emotion. He feels more powerful than an Assyrian monarch or a Persian king when he sees a sunset or a smiling dawn. To be good, all he needs is to gaze upon the beautiful. It is by the light of these flames that he writes. His ideas fall into the mind like white pebbles in a shining sea. What sparks! What lightning! What veins of fire! And one feels dizzy, as if flying on the back of a winged lion. He himself feels this and emerges strong. One clasps the book to his breast as if it were a good kind friend, or caresses it tenderly as if it were the unstained brow of a faithful wife.

*   *   *

He has held out his arms to enfold in them the secret of life. From out of his body, the fragile container of his winged spirit, he has ascended through painful labors and mortal anxieties to those pristine heights from which the traveler's devotion is rewarded by visions of the starlight-embroidered robes of infinite beings. His body has felt that mysterious overflowing of soul which is a solemn adventure that fills the lips with kisses, the hands with caresses, and the eyes with tears, like the sudden swelling and overflowing of Nature in the spring. And then he would feel that calm that comes from conversations with the divine, and that magnificent kingly courage that the awareness of power gives a man. For who that is master of himself does not laugh at a king?

*   *   *

And then once again he senses those vague and mystical effluvia flowing through his veins; perceives how they calm the torments of his soul in the friendly silence of the forest that is peopled with promises; observes that when the mind runs aground like a ship on a reef, foreboding springs up like a caged bird, sure of the sky, that escapes from the shattered mind. In language as inflexible, brutal, and unyielding as stone, he translates these luminous transports, chaste raptures, soothing delights, and joys of the tremulous spirit which captive Nature, amazed at the courageous lover, admits to her embraces. And he announces to every man that, since the universe is revealed to him fully and directly, to every other man as well is revealed the right to see it for himself, and with his own lips satisfy the burning thirst it inspires. And because in these discourses Emerson has learned that pure thought and pure affection produce joys so intense that the soul feels a sweet death in them, followed by a radiant resurrection, he announces to men that only through purity can one attain happiness.

After this discovery, and being certain that the stars are man's crown and that when his fevered brow has cooled, his serene spirit will cleave the air, enveloped in light, he laid his loving hand upon tormented humans, and turned his lively, penetrating eyes upon the harsh and stupid struggles of the world. His glances cleared away the rubbish. He sat familiarly at the tables of heroes. With Homeric language he related the crucial moments in the life of nations. He had the candor of giants. He let his intuition guide him, thus opening to him the refuge of the clouds as well as of the grave. Having sat in the senate of the stars and returned strong, he now sits in the senate of the people as if in the house of his own brothers. He recounts history both old and new, and analyzes nations as a geologist would analyze fossils. His phrases resemble the vertebrae of mastodons, gold-encrusted statues, Greek porticos. Of other men it can be said: "They are brothers"; of Emerson it must be said: "He is a father." He wrote a marvellous book, a summary of human experience, in which he sanctified the world's great men, studying each type. He went to see old England, land of his Puritan forebears, and as a result of that visit he wrote another book, a most powerful book called *English Traits*. He arranged the facts of existence into categories, and made a study of them in his magical *Essays*, giving them laws. All his laws of life revolve around the axis of this truth: "The whole of Nature trembles before the consciousness of a child." He breaks up culture, destiny, power, riches, illusions, and greatness into their component parts, and analyzes them with the skill of a chemist. He allows the beautiful to stand, and demolishes the false. He has no respect for custom. The base is base no matter how much it is esteemed. Man must begin to be angelic. Tenderness, resignation, and wisdom are law. These essays are codes of law. They are overflowing with sap. They have the grandiose monotony of a mountain range. Emerson enhances them with tireless fantasy and singular good sense. He finds no contradiction between the great and the small, or between the ideal and the practical, and he claims that the laws which finally prove their worth, and give a man the right to wear a crown of stars, are the ones to bring happiness on earth. There are no contradictions in Nature, only in man's inability to discover her analogies. He does not deprecate science for being false, but for being slow. Open his books and you will find them spilling over with scientific truths. Tyndall[1] gives Emerson credit for all the science he knows. The entire doctrine of evolution is

---

1. John Tyndall (1820–1893), British physicist, born in Ireland, best known for his researches on radiant heat to which has been given the name Tyndall effect or Tyndall phenomenon.

contained in a handful of Emerson's phrases. But he does not feel that understanding alone is enough to penetrate life's mystery, give man peace, and put him in possession of his means of growth; he believes that intuition finishes what understanding begins, that the eternal spirit divines what human science barely touches. Science sniffs about, like a dog, whereas the eternal spirit leaps over the chasm in which the naturalist stands amused. Emerson was constantly observing, making, like a powerful condor, notes on everything he saw, arranging in his notebooks the facts that were similar, and commenting when he had something to reveal. He had certain of the qualities of a Calderón,[2] a Plato, and a Pindar. Also of a Benjamin Franklin. He was not like the leafy bamboo whose heavy foliage, poorly supported by a hollow trunk, touches the ground; he was like a baobab or juniper or great genisaro whose many fully leafed branches rise from a sturdy trunk. Scornful of walking the earth, and disliked by judicious men, idealism nevertheless did walk the earth. Emerson has humanized it; he did not wait for science. The bird needs no stilts to reach the heights, and the eagle needs no rails. He outdistances science the way the impatient commanding officer mounts his flying horse to leave behind the plodding soldier loaded down with heavy battle gear. Emerson does not think of idealism in terms of a vague desire for death, but as a conviction of a future life to be earned by a serene practice of virtue in this one. And life is as beautiful and ideal as death. Do you wish to follow his trend of thought? It is like this: he maintains that man does not devote his entire potential to the study of Nature, merely his understanding, which is not the most important part; therefore he does not investigate that study thoroughly. He says: "The axis of man's vision does not coincide with the axis of Nature." He seeks to explain how all moral and physical truths are contained within each other, and how each one contains all the rest, and he says: "They are like the circle on a sphere that contains an infinitude of circles, and they may be added and taken away freely, with none being superimposed upon another." Would you like to hear how he talks? This is how: "For the man who suffers, even the warmth of his own fireplace has an element of sadness in it." "We are not made like ships to roll and pitch, but like a house to stand firm." "Cut these words and they will bleed." "To be great is to be misunderstood." "Leonidas wasted an entire day in dying." "Events in natural history, when taken out of context, are as barren as a single sex." "That man is tramping in the mire of dialectics."

His poetry is made out of colossal irregular blocks of stone, like Florentine palaces. It ebbs and flows and crashes like ocean waves. But sometimes it is like a basket of flowers in the hand of a little naked child. It is a poetry of patriarchs, primitive men, and cyclops. Some of his poems resemble groves of oak in bloom. His poetry is the only polemic verse to sanctify the great struggle on this earth. Some of his poems are like rivulets of precious stones, wisps of clouds, or bolts of lightning. Are you still wondering what his poems are like? Sometimes they are like an old man with a curly beard, wavy hair, and flaming eyes who sings as he leans on an oaken staff before a white stone cave; at other times like a gigantic angel with golden wings who plunges from the high green mountain into the gorge below. Marvelous old man, I lay at your feet my sheaf of newly gathered palms and my silver sword!

La Opinión Nacional (Caracas), May 19, 1882

2. Pedro Calderón de la Barca (1600–1681), Spanish poet and playwright.

GEORGE SANTAYANA

Emerson[†]

Those who knew Emerson, or who stood so near to his time and to his circle that they caught some echo of his personal influence, did not judge him merely as a poet or philosopher, nor identify his efficacy with that of his writings. His friends and neighbours, the congregations he preached to in his younger days, the audiences that afterward listened to his lectures, all agreed in a veneration for his person which had nothing to do with their understanding or acceptance of his opinions. They flocked to him and listened to his word, not so much for the sake of its absolute meaning as for the atmosphere of candour, purity, and serenity that hung about it, as about a sort of sacred music. They felt themselves in the presence of a rare and beautiful spirit, who was in communion with a higher world. More than the truth his teaching might express, they valued the sense it gave them of a truth that was inexpressible. They became aware, if we may say so, of the ultra-violet rays of his spectrum, of the inaudible highest notes of his gamut, too pure and thin for common ears.

This effect was by no means due to the possession on the part of Emerson of the secret of the universe, or even of a definite conception of ultimate truth. He was not a prophet who had once for all climbed his Sinai or his Tabor, and having there beheld the transfigured reality, descended again to make authoritative report of it to the world. Far from it. At bottom he had no doctrine at all. The deeper he went and the more he tried to grapple with fundamental conceptions, the vaguer and more elusive they became in his hands. Did he know what he meant by Spirit or the "Over-Soul"? Could he say what he understood by the terms, so constantly on his lips, Nature, Law, God, Benefit, or Beauty? He could not, and the consciousness of that incapacity was so lively within him that he never attempted to give articulation to his philosophy. His finer instinct kept him from doing that violence to his inspiration.

The source of his power lay not in his doctrine, but in his temperament, and the rare quality of his wisdom was due less to his reason than to his imagination. Reality eluded him; he had neither diligence nor constancy enough to master and possess it; but his mind was open to all philosophic influences, from whatever quarter they might blow; the lessons of science and the hints of poetry worked themselves out in him to a free and personal religion. He differed from the plodding many, not in knowing things better, but in having more ways of knowing them. His grasp was not particularly firm, he was far from being, like a Plato or an Aristotle, past master in the art and the science of life. But his mind was endowed with unusual plasticity, with unusual spontaneity and liberty of movement—it was a fairyland of thoughts and fancies. He was like a young god making experiments in creation: he blotched the work, and always began again on a new and better plan. Every day he said, "Let there be light," and every day the light was new. His sun, like that of Heraclitus, was different every morning.

What seemed, then, to the more earnest and less critical of his hearers a revelation from above was in truth rather an insurrection from beneath, a shaking loose from convention, a disintegration of the normal categories of reason

† From *Interpretations of Poetry and Religion* (New York, 1900).

in favour of various imaginative principles, on which the world might have been built, if it had been built differently. This gift of revolutionary thinking allowed new aspects, hints of wider laws, premonitions of unthought-of fundamental unities to spring constantly into view. But such visions were necessarily fleeting, because the human mind had long before settled its grammar, and discovered, after much groping and many defeats, the general forms in which experience will allow itself to be stated. These general forms are the principles of common sense and positive science, no less imaginative in their origin than those notions which we now call transcendental, but grown prosaic, like the metaphors of common speech, by dint of repetition.

Yet authority, even of this rational kind, sat lightly upon Emerson. To reject tradition and think as one might have thought if no man had ever existed before was indeed the aspiration of the Transcendentalists, and although Emerson hardly regarded himself as a member of that school, he largely shared its tendency and passed for its spokesman. Without protesting against tradition, he smilingly eluded it in his thoughts, untamable in their quiet irresponsibility. He fled to his woods or to his "pleached garden," to be the creator of his own worlds in solitude and freedom. No wonder that he brought thence to the tightly conventional minds of his contemporaries a breath as if from paradise. His simplicity in novelty, his profundity, his ingenuous ardour must have seemed to them something heavenly, and they may be excused if they thought they detected inspiration even in his occasional thin paradoxes and guileless whims. They were stifled with conscience and he brought them a breath of Nature; they were surfeited with shallow controversies and he gave them poetic truth.

Imagination, indeed, is his single theme. As a preacher might under every text enforce the same lessons of the gospel, so Emerson traces in every sphere the same spiritual laws of experience—compensation, continuity, the self-expression of the Soul in the forms of Nature and of society, until she finally recognises herself in her own work and sees its beneficence and beauty. His constant refrain is the omnipotence of imaginative thought; its power first to make the world, then to understand it, and finally to rise above it. All Nature is an embodiment of our native fancy, all history a drama in which the innate possibilities of the spirit are enacted and realised. While the conflict of life and the shocks of experience seem to bring us face to face with an alien and overwhelming power, reflection can humanise and rationalise that power by conceiving its laws; and with this recognition of the rationality of all things comes the sense of their beauty and order. The destruction which Nature seems to prepare for our special hopes is thus seen to be the victory of our impersonal interests. To awaken in us this spiritual insight, an elevation of mind which is at once an act of comprehension and of worship, to substitute it for lower passions and more servile forms of intelligence—that is Emerson's constant effort. All his resources of illustration, observation, and rhetoric are used to deepen and clarify this sort of wisdom.

Such thought is essentially the same that is found in the German romantic or idealistic philosophers, with whom Emerson's affinity is remarkable, all the more as he seems to have borrowed little or nothing from their works. The critics of human nature, in the eighteenth century, had shown how much men's ideas depend on their predispositions, on the character of their senses and the habits of their intelligence. Seizing upon this thought and exaggerating it, the romantic philosophers attributed to the spirit of man the omnipotence which had belonged to God, and felt that in this way they were reasserting the supremacy of mind over matter and establishing it upon a safe and rational basis.

The Germans were great system-makers, and Emerson cannot rival them in the sustained effort of thought by which they sought to reinterpret every sphere of being according to their chosen principles. But he surpassed them in an instinctive sense of what he was doing. He never represented his poetry as science, nor countenanced the formation of a new sect that should nurse the sense of a private and mysterious illumination, and relight the fagots of passion and prejudice. He never tried to seek out and defend the universal implications of his ideas, and never wrote the book he had once planned on the law of compensation, foreseeing, we may well believe, the sophistries in which he would have been directly involved. He fortunately preferred a fresh statement on a fresh subject. A suggestion once given, the spirit once aroused to speculation, a glimpse once gained of some ideal harmony, he chose to descend again to common sense and to touch the earth for a moment before another flight. The faculty of idealisation was itself what he valued. Philosophy for him was rather a moral energy flowering into sprightliness of thought than a body of serious and defensible doctrines. In practising transcendental speculation only in this poetic and sporadic fashion, Emerson retained its true value and avoided its greatest danger. He secured the freedom and fertility of his thought and did not allow one conception of law or one hint of harmony to sterilise the mind and prevent the subsequent birth within it of other ideas, no less just and imposing than their predecessors. For we are not dealing at all in such a philosophy with matters of fact or with such verifiable truths as exclude their opposites. We are dealing only with imagination, with the art of conception, and with the various forms in which reflection, like a poet, may compose and recompose human experience.

A certain disquiet mingled, however, in the minds of Emerson's contemporaries with the admiration they felt for his purity and genius. They saw that he had forsaken the doctrines of the Church; and they were not sure whether he held quite unequivocally any doctrine whatever. We may not all of us share the concern for orthodoxy which usually caused this puzzled alarm: we may understand that it was not Emerson's vocation to be definite and dogmatic in religion any more than in philosophy. Yet that disquiet will not, even for us, wholly disappear. It is produced by a defect which naturally accompanies imagination in all but the greatest minds. I mean disorganisation. Emerson not only conceived things in new ways, but he seemed to think the new ways might cancel and supersede the old. His imagination was to invalidate the understanding. That inspiration which should come to fulfil seemed too often to come to destroy. If he was able so constantly to stimulate us to fresh thoughts, was it not because he demolished the labour of long ages of reflection? Was not the startling effect of much of his writing due to its contradiction to tradition and to common sense?

So long as he is a poet and in the enjoyment of his poetic license, we can blame this play of mind only by a misunderstanding. It is possible to think otherwise than as common sense thinks; there are other categories beside those of science. When we employ them we enlarge our lives. We add to the world of fact any number of worlds of the imagination in which human nature and the eternal relations of ideas may be nobly expressed. So far our imaginative fertility is only a benefit: it surrounds us with the congenial and necessary radiation of art and religion. It manifests our moral vitality in the bosom of Nature.

But sometimes imagination invades the sphere of understanding and seems to discredit its indispensable work. Common sense, we are allowed to infer, is a shallow affair: true insight changes all that. When so applied, poetic activity is not an unmixed good. It loosens our hold on fact and confuses our intelligence, so that we forget that intelligence has itself every prerogative of imagination, and has besides the sanction of practical validity. We are made to believe that since the understanding is something human and conditioned, something which might have been different, as the senses might have been different, and which we may yet, so to speak, get behind—therefore the understanding ought to be abandoned. We long for higher faculties, neglecting those we have, we yearn for intuition, closing our eyes upon experience. We become mystical.

Mysticism, as we have said, is the surrender of a category of thought because we divine its relativity. As every new category, however, must share this reproach, the mystic is obliged in the end to give them all up, the poetic and moral categories no less than the physical, so that the end of his purification is the atrophy of his whole nature, the emptying of his whole heart and mind to make room, as he thinks, for God. By attacking the authority of the understanding as the organon of knowledge, by substituting itself for it as the herald of a deeper truth, the imagination thus prepares its own destruction. For if the understanding is rejected because it cannot grasp the absolute, the imagination and all its works—art, dogma, worship—must presently be rejected for the same reason. Common sense and poetry must both go by the board, and conscience must follow after: for all these are human and relative. Mysticism will be satisfied only with the absolute, and as the absolute, by its very definition, is not representable by any specific faculty, it must be approached through the abandonment of all. The lights of life must be extinguished that the light of the absolute may shine, and the possession of everything in general must be secured by the surrender of everything in particular.

The same diffidence, however, the same constant renewal of sincerity which kept Emerson's flights of imagination near to experience, kept his mysticism also within bounds. A certain mystical tendency is pervasive with him, but there are only one or two subjects on which he dwells with enough constancy and energy of attention to make his mystical treatment of them pronounced. One of these is the question of the unity of all minds in the single soul of the universe, which is the same in all creatures; another is the question of evil and of its evaporation in the universal harmony of things. Both these ideas suggest themselves at certain turns in every man's experience, and might receive a rational formulation. But they are intricate subjects, obscured by many emotional prejudices, so that the labour, impartiality, and precision which would be needed to elucidate them are to be looked for in scholastic rather than in inspired thinkers, and in Emerson least of all. Before these problems he is alternately ingenuous and rhapsodical, and in both moods equally helpless. Individuals no doubt exist, he says to himself. But, ah! Napoleon is in every schoolboy. In every squatter in the western prairies we shall find an owner—

> Of Caesar's hand and Plato's brain,
> Of Lord Christ's heart, and Shakespeare's strain.

But how? we may ask. Potentially? Is it because any mind, were it given the right body and the right experience, were it made over, in a word, into another mind, would resemble that other mind to the point of identity? Or is it that our souls are already so largely similar that we are subject to many kindred promptings and share many ideals unrealisable in our particular circumstances? But then we should simply be saying that if what makes men different were removed, men would be indistinguishable, or that, in so far as they are now alike, they can understand one another by summoning up their respective experiences in the fancy. There would be no mysticism in that, but at the same time, alas, no eloquence, no paradox, and, if we must say the word, no nonsense.

On the question of evil, Emerson's position is of the same kind. There is evil, of course, he tell us. Experience is sad. There is a crack in everything that God has made. But, ah! the laws of the universe are sacred and beneficent. Without them nothing good could arise. All things, then, are in their right places and the universe is perfect above our querulous tears. Perfect? we may ask. But perfect from what point of view, in reference to what ideal? To its own? To that of a man who renouncing himself and all naturally dear to him, ignoring the injustice, suffering, and impotence in the world, allows his will and his conscience to be hypnotised by the spectacle of a necessary evolution, and lulled into cruelty by the pomp and music of a tragic show? In that case the evil is not explained, it is forgotten; it is not cured, but condoned. We have surrendered the category of the better and the worse, the deepest foundation of life and reason; we have become mystics on the one subject on which, above all others, we ought to be men.

Two forces may be said to have carried Emerson in this mystical direction; one, that freedom of his imagination which we have already noted, and which kept him from the fear of self-contradiction; the other the habit of worship inherited from his clerical ancestors and enforced by his religious education. The spirit of conformity, the unction, the loyalty even unto death inspired by the religion of Jehovah, were dispositions acquired by too long a discipline and rooted in too many forms of speech, of thought, and of worship for a man like Emerson, who had felt their full force, ever to be able to lose them. The evolutions of his abstract opinions left that habit unchanged. Unless we keep this circumstance in mind, we shall not be able to understand the kind of elation and sacred joy, so characteristic of his eloquence, with which he propounds laws of Nature and aspects of experience which, viewed in themselves, afford but an equivocal support to moral enthusiasm. An optimism so persistent and unclouded as his will seem at variance with the description he himself gives of human life, a description coloured by a poetic idealism, but hardly by an optimistic bias.

We must remember, therefore, that this optimism is a pious tradition, originally justified by the belief in a personal God and in a providential government of affairs for the ultimate and positive good of the elect, and that the habit of worship survived in Emerson as an instinct after those positive beliefs had faded into a recognition of "spiritual laws." We must remember that Calvinism had known how to combine an awestruck devotion to the Supreme Being with no very roseate picture of the destinies of mankind, and for more than two hundred years had been breeding in the stock from which Emerson came a willingness to be, as the phrase is, "damned for the glory of God."

What wonder, then, that when, for the former inexorable dispensation of Providence, Emerson substituted his general spiritual and natural laws, he should not have felt the spirit of worship fail within him? On the contrary, his thought moved in the presence of moral harmonies which seemed to him truer, more beautiful, and more beneficent than those of the old theology. An independent philosopher would not have seen in those harmonies an object of worship or a sufficient basis for optimism. But he was not an independent philosopher, in spite of his belief in independence. He inherited the problems and the preoccupations of the theology from which he started, being in this respect like the German idealists, who, with all their pretense of absolute metaphysics, were in reality only giving elusive and abstract forms to traditional theology. Emerson, too, was not primarily a philosopher, but a Puritan mystic with a poetic fancy and a gift for observation and epigram, and he saw in the laws of Nature, idealised by his imagination, only a more intelligible form of the divinity he had always recognised and adored. His was not a philosophy passing into a religion, but a religion expressing itself as a philosophy and veiled, as at its setting it descended the heavens, in various tints of poetry and science.

If we ask ourselves what was Emerson's relation to the scientific and religious movements of his time, and what place he may claim in the history of opinion, we must answer that he belonged very little to the past, very little to the present, and almost wholly to that abstract sphere into which mystical or philosophic aspiration has carried a few men in all ages. The religious tradition in which he was reared was that of Puritanism, but of a Puritanism which, retaining its moral intensity and metaphysical abstraction, had minimised its doctrinal expression and become Unitarian. Emerson was indeed the Psyche of Puritanism, "the latest-born and fairest vision far" of all that "faded hierarchy." A Puritan whose religion was all poetry, a poet whose only pleasure was thought, he showed in his life and personality the meagreness, the constraint, the frigid and conscious consecration which belonged to his clerical ancestors, while his inmost impersonal spirit ranged abroad over the fields of history and Nature, gathering what ideas it might, and singing its little snatches of inspired song.

The traditional element was thus rather an external and inessential contribution to Emerson's mind; he had the professional tinge, the decorum, the distinction of an old-fashioned divine; he had also the habit of writing sermons, and he had the national pride and hope of a religious people that felt itself providentially chosen to establish a free and godly commonwealth in a new world. For the rest, he separated himself from the ancient creed of the community with a sense rather of relief than of regret. A literal belief in Christian doctrines repelled him as unspiritual, as manifesting no understanding of the meaning which, as allegories, those doctrines might have to a philosophic and poetical spirit. Although, being a clergyman, he was at first in the habit of referring to the Bible and its lessons as to a supreme authority, he had no instinctive sympathy with the inspiration of either the Old or the New Testament; in Hafiz or Plutarch, in Plato or Shakespeare, he found more congenial stuff.

While he thus preferred to withdraw, without rancour and without contempt, from the ancient fellowship of the church, he assumed an attitude hardly less cool and deprecatory toward the enthusiasms of the new era. The national ideal of democracy and freedom had his entire sympathy; he allowed himself to be drawn into the movement against slavery; he took a curious and smiling interest in the discoveries of natural science and in the material progress of the age. But he could go no farther. His contemplative nature, his religious training, his dispersed reading, made him stand aside from the life of the world, even while he studied it with benevolent attention. His heart was fixed on eternal things, and he was in no sense a prophet for his age or country. He belonged by nature to that mystical company of devout souls that recognise no particular home and are dispersed throughout history, although not without intercommunication. He felt his affinity to the Hindoos and the Persians, to the Platonists and the Stoics. Like them he remains "a friend and aider of those who would live in the spirit." If not a star of the first magnitude, he is certainly a fixed star in the firmament of philosophy. Alone as yet among Americans, he may be said to have won a place there, if not by the originality of his thought, at least by the originality and beauty of the expression he gave to thoughts that are old and imperishable.

WILLIAM JAMES

Address at the Emerson Centenary in Concord[†]

The pathos of death is this, that when the days of one's life are ended, those days that were so crowded with business and felt so heavy in their passing, what remains of one in memory should usually be so slight a thing. The phantom of an attitude, the echo of a certain mode of thought, a few pages of print, some invention, or some victory we gained in a brief critical hour, are all that can survive the best of us. It is as if the whole of a man's significance had now shrunk into the phantom of an attitude, into a mere musical note or phrase suggestive of his singularity—happy are those whose singularity gives a note so clear as to be victorious over the inevitable pity of such a diminution and abridgment.

An ideal wraith like this, of Emerson's personality, hovers over all Concord to-day, taking, in the minds of those of you who were his neighbors and intimates a somewhat fuller shape, remaining more abstract in the younger generation, but bringing home to all of us the notion of a spirit indescribably precious. The form that so lately moved upon these streets and country roads, or awaited in these fields and woods the beloved Muse's visits, is now dust; but the soul's note, the spiritual voice, rises strong and clear above the uproar of the times, and seems securely destined to exert an ennobling influence over future generations.

What gave a flavor so matchless to Emerson's individuality was, even more than his rich mental gifts, their singularly harmonious combination. Rarely has a man so accurately known the limits of his genius or so unfailingly kept within them. "Stand by your order," he used to say to youthful students; and perhaps the paramount impression one gets of his life is of his loyalty to his own personal type and mission. The type was that of what he liked to call the scholar, the perceiver of pure truth; and the mission was that of the reporter in worthy form of each perception. The day is good, he said, in which we have the most perceptions. There are times when the cawing of a crow, a weed, a snowflake, or a farmer planting in his field become symbols to the intellect of truths equal to those which the most majestic phenomena can open. Let me mind my own charge, then, walk alone, consult the sky, the field and forest, sedulously wait-

† From *Memories and Studies* (New York, 1911), pp. 19–34. James delivered this address in Concord on May 25, 1903, at the celebration of the centenary of Emerson's birth.

ing every morning for the news concerning the structure of the universe which the good Spirit will give me.

This was the first half of Emerson, but only half; for genius, as he said, is insatiate for expression, and truth has to be clad in the right verbal garment. The form of the garment was so vital with Emerson that it is impossible to separate it from the matter. They form a chemical combination—thoughts which would be trivial expressed otherwise, are important through the nouns and verbs to which he married them. The style is the man, it has been said; the man Emerson's mission culminated in his style, and if we must define him in one word, we have to call him Artist. He was an artist whose medium was verbal and who wrought in spiritual material.

This duty of spiritual seeing and reporting determined the whole tenor of his life. It was to shield this duty from invasion and distraction that he dwelt in the country, that he consistently declined to entangle himself with associations or to encumber himself with functions which, however he might believe in them, he felt were duties for other men and not for him. Even the care of his garden, "with its stoopings and fingerings in a few yards of space," he found "narrowing and poisoning," and took to long free walks and saunterings instead, without apology. "Causes" innumerable sought to enlist him as their "worker"—all got his smile and word of sympathy, but none entrapped him into service. The struggle against slavery itself, deeply as it appealed to him, found him firm: "God must govern his own world, and knows his way out of this pit without my desertion of my post, which has none to guard it but me. I have quite other slaves to face than those Negroes, to wit, imprisoned thoughts far back in the brain of man, and which have no watchman or lover or defender but me." This in reply to the possible questions of his own conscience. To hot-blooded moralists with more objective ideas of duty, such a fidelity to the limits of his genius must often have made him seem provokingly remote and unavailable; but we, who can see things in more liberal perspective, must unqualifiably approve the results. The faultless tact with which he kept his safe limits while he so dauntlessly asserted himself within them, is an example fitted to give heart to other theorists and artists the world over.

The insight and creed from which Emerson's life followed can be best summed up in his own verses:

"So nigh is grandeur to our dust,
So near is God to man!"

Through the individual fact there ever shone for him the effulgence of the Universal Reason. The great Cosmic Intellect terminates and houses itself in mortal men and passing hours. Each of us is an angle of its eternal vision, and the only way to be true to our Maker is to be loyal to ourselves. "O rich and various Man!" he cries, "thou palace of sight and sound, carrying in thy senses the morning and the night and the unfathomable galaxy; in thy brain the geometry of the city of God; in thy heart the bower of love and the realms of right and wrong."

If the individual open thus directly into the Absolute, it follows that there is something in each and all of us, even the lowliest, that ought not to consent to borrowing traditions and living at second hand. "If John was perfect, why are you and I alive?" Emerson writes; "As long as any man exists there is some need of him; let him fight for his own." This faith that in a life at first hand there is something sacred is perhaps the most characteristic note in Emerson's writings. The hottest side of him is this non-conformist persuasion, and if his temper could ever verge on common irascibility, it would be by reason of the passionate character of his feelings on this point. The world is still new and untried. In seeing freshly, and not in hearing of what others saw, shall a man find what truth is. "Each one of us can bask in the great morning which rises out of the Eastern Sea, and be himself one of the children of the light." "Trust thyself, every heart vibrates to that iron string. There is a time in each man's education when he must arrive at the conviction that imitation is suicide; when he must take himself for better or worse as his portion; and know that though the wide universe is full of good, no kernel of nourishing corn can come to him but through his toil bestowed on that plot of ground which it was given him to till."

The matchless eloquence with which Emerson proclaimed the sovereignty of the living individual electrified and emancipated his generation, and this bugle-blast will doubtless be regarded by future critics as the soul of his message. The present man is the aboriginal reality, the Institution is derivative, and the past man is irrelevant and obliterate for present issues. "If anyone would lay an axe to your tree with a text from 1 John, v, 7, or a sentence from Saint Paul, say to him," Emerson wrote, "'My tree is Yggdrasil, the tree of life.' Let him know by your security that your conviction is clear and sufficient, and, if he were Paul himself, that you also are here and with your Creator." "Cleave ever to God," he insisted, "against the name of God;"—and so, in spite of the intensely religious character of his total thought, when he began his career it seemed to many of his brethren in the clerical profession that he was little more than an iconoclast and desecrator.

Emerson's belief that the individual must in reason be adequate to the vocation for which the Spirit of the world has called him into being, is the source of those sublime pages, hearteners and sustainers of our youth, in which he urges his hearers to be incorruptibly true to their own private conscience. Nothing can harm the man who rests in his appointed place and character. Such a man is invulnerable; he balances the universe, balances it as much by keeping small when he is small, as by being great and spreading when he is great. "I love and honor Epaminondas," said Emerson, "but I do not wish to be Epaminondas. I hold it more just to love the world of this hour than the world of his hour. Nor can you, if I am true, excite me to the least uneasiness by saying, 'He acted and thou sittest still.' I see action to be good when the need is, and sitting still to be also good. Epaminondas, if he was the man I take him for, would have sat still with joy and peace, if his lot had been mine. Heaven is large, and affords space for all modes of love and fortitude." "The fact that I am here certainly shows me that the Soul has need of an organ here, and shall I not assume the post?"

The vanity of all superserviceableness and pretence was never more happily set forth than by Emerson in the many passages in which he develops this aspect of his philosophy. Character infallibly proclaims itself. "Hide your thoughts!— hide the sun and moon. They publish themselves to the universe. They will speak through you though you were dumb. They will flow out of your actions, your manners and your face. . . . Don't say things: What you are stands over you the while and thunders so that I cannot say what you say to the contrary. . . . What a man *is* engraves itself upon him in letters of light. Concealment avails him nothing, boasting nothing. There is confession in the glances of our eyes; in our smiles; in salutations; and the grasp of hands. His sin bedaubs him, mars all his good impression. Men know not why they do not trust him, but they do not trust him. His vice glasses the eye, casts lines of mean expression in the cheek, pinches the nose, sets the mark of the beast upon the back of the head, and writes, O fool! fool! on the forehead of a king. If you would not be known to do a thing, never do it; a man may play the fool in the drifts of a desert, but every grain of sand shall seem to see.—How can a man be concealed? How can he be concealed?"

On the other hand, never was a sincere word or a sincere thought utterly lost. "Never a magnanimity fell to the ground but there is some heart to greet and accept it unexpectedly. . . . The hero fears not that if he withstood the avowal of a just and brave act, it will go unwitnessed and unloved. One knows it,—himself,—and is pledged by it to sweetness of peace and to nobleness of aim, which will prove in the end a better proclamation than the relating of the incident."

The same indefeasible right to be exactly what one is, provided one only be authentic, spreads itself, in Emerson's way of thinking, from persons to things and to times and places. No date, no position is insignificant, if the life that fills it out be only genuine:—

"In solitude, in a remote village, the ardent youth loiters and mourns. With inflamed eye, in this sleeping wilderness, he has read the story of the Emperor, Charles the Fifth, until his fancy has brought home to the surrounding woods the faint roar of cannonades in the Milanese, and marches in Germany. He is curious concerning that man's day. What filled it? The crowded orders, the stern decisions, the foreign despatches, the Castilian etiquette? The soul answers— Behold his day here! In the sighing of these woods, in the quiet of these gray fields, in the cool breeze that sings out of these northern mountains; in the workmen, the boys, the maidens you meet,—in the hopes of the morning, the *ennui* of noon, and sauntering of the afternoon; in the disquieting comparisons; in the regrets at want of vigor; in the great idea and the puny execution,—behold Charles the Fifth's day; another, yet the same; behold Chatham's, Hampden's, Bayard's, Alfred's, Scipio's, Pericles's day,—day of all that are born of women. The difference of circumstance is merely costume. I am tasting the self-same life,—its sweetness, its greatness, its pain, which I so admire in other men. Do not foolishly ask of the inscrutable, obliterated past what it cannot tell,—the details of that nature, of that day, called Byron or Burke;—but ask it of the enveloping Now. . . . Be lord of a day, and you can put up your history books."

"The deep to-day which all men scorn" receives thus from Emerson superb revindication. "Other world! there is no other world." All God's life opens into the individual particular, and here and now, or nowhere, is reality. "The present hour is the decisive hour, and every day is doomsday."

Such a conviction that Divinity is everywhere may easily make of one an optimist of the sentimental type that refuses to speak ill of anything. Emerson's drastic perception of differences kept him at the opposite pole from this weakness. After you have seen men a few times, he could say, you find most of them as alike as their barns and pantries, and soon as musty and as dreary. Never was such a fastidious lover of significance and distinction, and never an eye so keen for their discovery. His optimism had nothing in common with that indiscriminate hurrahing for the Universe with which Walt Whitman has made us familiar. For Emerson, the individual fact and moment were indeed suffused with absolute radiance, but it was upon a condition that saved the situation—they must be worthy specimens,—sincere, authentic, archetypal; they must have made connection with what he calls the Moral Sentiment, they must in some way act as symbolic mouthpieces of the Universe's meaning. To know just which thing does act in this way, and which thing fails to make the true connection, is the secret (somewhat incommunicable, it must be confessed) of seership, and doubtless we must not expect of the seer too rigorous a consistency. Emerson himself was a real seer. He could perceive the full squalor of the individual fact, but he could also see the transfiguration. He might easily have found himself saying of some present-day agitator against our Philippine conquest what he said of this or that reformer of his own time. He might have called him, as a private person, a tedious bore and canter. But he would infallibly have added what he then added: "It is strange and horrible to say this, for I feel that under him and his partiality and exclusiveness is the earth and the sea, and all that in them is, and the axis round which the Universe revolves passes through his body where he stands."

Be it how it may, then, this is Emerson's revelation:—The point of any pen can be an epitome of reality; the commonest person's act, if genuinely actuated, can lay hold on eternity. This vision is the head-spring of all his outpourings; and it is for this truth, given to no previous literary artist to express in such penetratingly persuasive tones, that posterity will reckon him a prophet, and, perhaps neglecting other pages, piously turn to those that convey this message. His life was one long conversation with the invisible divine, expressing itself through individuals and particulars:—"So nigh is grandeur to our dust, so near is God to man!"

I spoke of how shrunken the wraith, how thin the echo, of men is after they are departed. Emerson's wraith comes to me now as if it were but the very voice of this victorious argument. His words to this effect are certain to be quoted and extracted more and more as time goes on, and to take their place among the Scriptures of humanity. "'Gainst death and all oblivious enmity, shall you pace forth," beloved Master. As long as our English language lasts men's hearts will be cheered and their souls strengthened and liberated by the noble and musical pages with which you have enriched it.

JOHN DEWEY

Ralph Waldo Emerson[†]

It is said that Emerson is not a philosopher. I find this denegation false or true according as it is said in blame or praise—according to the reasons proffered. When the critic writes of lack of method, of the absence of continuity, of coherent logic, and, with the old story of the string of pearls loosely strung, puts Emerson away as a writer of maxims and proverbs, a recorder of brilliant insights and abrupt aphorisms, the critic, to my mind, but writes down his own incapacity to follow a logic that is finely wrought.

> We want in every man a logic; we cannot pardon the absence of it, but it must not be spoken. Logic is the procession or proportionate unfolding of the intuition; but its virtue is as silent method; the moment it would appear as propositions and have a separate value, it is worthless.

---

† From John Dewey, *Characters and Events*, Vol. 1, ed. Joseph Ratner (New York, 1929). Reprinted by permission of Octagon Books, a division of Hippocrene Books, Inc.

Emerson fulfills his own requisition. The critic needs the method separately propounded, and not finding his wonted leading-string is all lost. Again, says Emerson, "There is no compliment like the addressing to the human being thoughts out of certain heights and presupposing his intelligence"—a compliment which Emerson's critics have mostly hastened to avert. But to make this short, I am not acquainted with any writer, no matter how assured his position in treatises upon the history of philosophy, whose movement of thought is more compact and unified, nor one who combines more adequately diversity of intellectual attack with concentration of form and effect. I recently read a letter from a gentleman, himself a distinguished writer of philosophy, in which he remarked that philosophers are a stupid class, since they want every reason carefully pointed out and labelled, and are incapable of taking anything for granted. The condescending patronage by literary critics of Emerson's lack of cohesiveness may remind us that philosophers have no monopoly of this particular form of stupidity.

Perhaps those are nearer right, however, who deny that Emerson is a philosopher, because he is more than a philosopher. He would work, he says, by art, not by metaphysics, finding truth "in the sonnet and the play." "I am," to quote him again, "in all my theories, ethics and politics, a poet"; and we may, I think, safely take his word for it that he meant to be a maker rather than a reflector. His own preference was to be ranked with the seers rather than with the reasoners of the race, for he says, "I think that philosophy is still rude and elementary; it will one day be taught by poets. The poet is in the right attitude; he is believing; the philosopher, after some struggle, having only reasons for believing." Nor do I regard it as impertinent to place by the side of this utterance, that other in which he said "We have yet to learn that the thing uttered in words is not therefore affirmed. It must affirm itself or no forms of grammar and no plausibility can give it evidence and no array of arguments." To Emerson, perception was more potent than reasoning; the deliverances of intercourse more to be desired than the chains of discourse; the surprise of reception more demonstrative than the conclusions of intentional proof. As he said "Good as is discourse, silence is better, and shames it. The length of discourse indicates the distance of thought betwixt the speaker and the hearer." And again, "If I speak, I define and confine, and am less." "Silence is a solvent that destroys personality and gives us leave to be great and universal."

I would not make hard and fast lines between philosopher and poet, yet there is some distinction of accent in thought and of rhythm in speech. The desire for an articulate, not for silent, logic is intrinsic with philosophy. The unfolding of the perception must be stated, not merely followed and understood. Such conscious method is, one might say, the only thing of ultimate concern to the abstract thinker. Not thought, but reasoned thought, not things, but the ways of things, interest him; not even truth, but the paths by which truth is sought. He construes elaborately the symbols of thinking. He is given over to manufacturing and sharpening the weapons of the spirit. Outcomes, interpretations, victories, are indifferent. Otherwise is it with art. That, as Emerson says, is "the path of the Creator to his work"; and again "a habitual respect to the whole by an eye loving beauty in detail." Affection is towards the meaning of the symbol, not to its constitution. Only as he wields them, does the artist forge the sword and buckler of the spirit. His affair is to uncover rather than to analyze; to discern rather than to classify. He reads but does not compose.

One, however, has no sooner drawn such lines than one is ashamed and begins to retract. Euripides and Plato, Dante and Bruno, Bacon and Milton, Spinoza and Goethe, rise in rebuke. The spirit of Emerson rises to protest against exaggerating his ultimate value by trying to place him upon a plane of art higher than a philosophic platform. Literary critics admit his philosophy and deny his literature. And if philosophers extol his keen, calm art and speak with some depreciation of his metaphysic, it also is perhaps because Emerson knew something deeper than our conventional definitions. It is indeed true that reflective thinkers have taken the way to truth for their truth; the method of life for the conduct of life — in short, have taken means for end. But it is also assured that in the completeness of their devotion, they have expiated their transgression; means become identified with end, thought turns to life, and wisdom is justified not of herself but of her children. Language justly preserves the difference between philosopher and sophist. It is no more possible to eliminate love and generation from the definition of the thinker than it is to eliminate thought and limits from the conception of the artist. It is interest, concern, caring, which makes the one as it makes the other. It is significant irony that the old quarrel of philosopher and poet was brought off by one who united in himself more than has another individual the qualities of both artist and metaphysician. At bottom the quarrel is not one of objectives nor yet of methods, but of the affections. And in the divisions of love, there always abides the unity of him who loves. Because Plato was so great he was divided in his affections. A lesser man could not brook that torn love, because of which he set poet and philosopher over against one another. Looked at in the open, our fences between literature and metaphysics appear petty — signs of an attempt to affix the legalities and formularies of property to the things of the spirit. If ever there lived not only a metaphysician but a professor of metaphysics it was Immanuel Kant. Yet he declares that he should account himself more unworthy than the day laborer in the field if he did not believe that somehow, even in his technical classifications and remote distinctions, he too, was carrying forward the struggle of humanity for freedom — that is for illumination.

And for Emerson of all others, there is a one-sidedness and exaggeration, which he would have been the first to scorn, in exalting overmuch his creative substance at the expense of his reflective procedure. He says in effect somewhere that the individual man is only a method, a plan of arrangement. The saying is amply descriptive of Emerson. His idealism is the faith of the thinker in his thought raised to its *nth* power. "History," he says, "and the state of the world at any one time is directly dependent on the intellectual classification then existing in the minds of men." Again, "Beware when the great God lets loose a thinker on this planet. Then all things are at risk. The very hopes of man, the thoughts of his heart, the religion of nations, the manner and morals of mankind are all at the mercy of a new generalization." And again, "Everything looks permanent until its secret is known. Nature looks provokingly stable and secular, but it has a cause like all the rest; and when once I comprehend that, will these fields stretch so immovably wide, these leaves hang so individually considerable?" And finally, "In history an idea always overhangs like a moon and rules the tide which rises simultaneously in all the souls of a generation." There are times, indeed, when one is inclined to regard Emerson's whole work as a hymn to intelligence, a pæon to the all-creating, all-disturbing power of thought.

And so, with an expiatory offering to the Manes of Emerson, one may proceed to characterize his thought, his method, yea, even his system. I find it in the fact that he takes the distinctions and classifications which to most philosophers are true in and of and because of their systems, and makes them true of life, of the common experience of the everyday man. To take his own words for it,

> There are degrees in idealism. We learn first to play with it academically, as the magnet was once a toy. Then we see, in the heyday of youth and poetry, that it may be true, that it is true in gleams and fragments. Then, its countenance waxes stern and grand, and we see that it must be true. It now shows itself ethical and practical.

The idealism which is a thing of the academic intellect to the professor, a hope to the generous youth, an inspiration to the genial projector, is to Emerson a narrowly accurate description of the facts of the most real world in which all earn their living.

Such reference to the immediate life is the text by which he tries every philosopher. "Each new mind we approach seems to require," he says, "an abdication of all our past and present possessions. A new doctrine seems at first a subversion of all our opinions, tastes and manner of living." But while one gives himself "up unreservedly to that which draws him, because that is his own, he is to refuse himself to that which draws him not, because it is not his own. I were a fool not to sacrifice a thousand Aeschyluses to my intellectual integrity. Especially take the same ground in regard to abstract truth, the science of the mind. The Bacon, the Spinoza, the Hume, Schelling, Kant, is only a more or less awkward translator of things in your consciousness. Say, then, instead of too timidly poring into his obscure sense, that he has not succeeded in rendering back to you your consciousness. Anyhow, when at last, it is done, you will find it is not recondite, but a simple, natural state which the writer restores to you." And again, take this other saying, "Aristotle or Bacon or Kant propound some maxim which is the keynote of philosophy thenceforward, but I am more interested to know that when at last they have hurled out their grand word, it is only some familiar experience of every man on the street." I fancy he reads the so-called eclecticism of Emerson wrongly who does not see that it is reduction of all the philosophers of the race, even the prophets like Plato and Proclus whom Emerson holds most dear, to the test of trial by the service rendered the present and immediate experience. As for those who contemn Emerson for superficial pedantry because of the strings of names he is wont to flash like beads before our eyes, they but voice their own pedantry, not seeing, in their literalness, that all such things are with Emerson symbols of various uses administered to the common soul.

As Emerson treated the philosophers, so he treats their doctrines. The Platonist teaches the immanence of absolute ideas in the World and in Man, that every thing and every man participates in an absolute Meaning, individualized in him and through which one has community with others. Yet by the time this truth of the universe has become proper and fit for teaching, it has somehow become a truth of philosophy, a truth of private interpretation, reached by some men, not others, and consequently true for some, but not true for all, and hence not wholly true for any. But to Emerson all "truth lies on the highway." Emerson says, "We lie in the lap of immense intelligence which makes us organs of its activity and receivers of its truth," and the Idea is no longer either an academic toy nor even a gleam of poetry, but a literal report of the experience of the hour as that is enriched and reinforced for the individual through the tale of history, the appliance of science, the gossip of conversation and the exchange of commerce. That every individual is at once the focus and the channel of mankind's long and wide endeavor, that all nature exists for the education of the human soul—such things, as we read Emerson, cease to be statements of a separated philosophy and become natural transcripts of the course of events and of the rights of man.

Emerson's philosophy has this in common with that of the transcendentalists; he prefers to borrow from them rather than from others certain pigments and delineations. But he finds truth in the highway, in the untaught endeavor, the unexpected idea, and this removes him from their remotenesses. His ideas are not fixed upon any Reality that is beyond or behind or in any way apart, and hence they do not have to be bent. They are versions of the Here and the Now, and flow freely. The reputed transcendental worth of an overweening Beyond and Away, Emerson, jealous for spiritual democracy, finds to be the possession of the unquestionable Present. When Emerson, speaking of the chronology of history, designated the There and Then as "wild, savage, and preposterous," he also drew the line which marks him off from transcendentalism—which is the idealism of a Class. In sorry truth, the idealist has too frequently conspired with the sensualist to deprive the pressing and so the passing Now of value which is spiritual. Through the joint work of such malign conspiracy, the common man is not, or at least does not know himself for, an idealist. It is such disinherited of the earth that Emerson summons to their own. "If man is sick, is unable, is mean-spirited and odious, it is because there is so much of his nature which is unlawfully withholden from him."

Against creed and system, convention and institution, Emerson stands for restoring to the common man that which in the name of religion, of philosophy, of art, and of morality, has been embezzled from the common store and appropriated to sectarian and class use. Beyond any one we know of, Emerson has comprehended and declared how such malversation makes truth decline from its simplicity, and in becoming partial and owned, become a puzzle of and trick for theologian, metaphysician and litterateur—a puzzle of an imposed law, of an unwished for and refused goodness, of a romantic ideal gleaming only from afar, and a trick of manipular skill, of specialized performance.

For such reasons, the coming century may well make evident what is just now dawning, that Emerson is not only a philosopher, but that he is the Philosopher of Democracy. Plato's own generation would, I think, have found it difficult to class Plato. Was he an inept visionary or a subtle dialectician? A political reformer or a founder of the new type of literary art? Was he a moral exhorter, or an instructor in an Academy? Was he a theorist upon education, or the inventor of a method of knowledge? We, looking at Plato through the centuries of exposition and interpretation, find no difficulty in placing Plato as a philosopher and in attributing to him a system of thought. We dispute about the nature and content of this system, but we do not doubt it is there. It is the intervening centuries which have furnished Plato with his technique and which have developed and wrought Plato to a system. One century bears but a slender ratio to twenty-five; it is not safe to predict. But at least, thinking of Emerson as the one citizen of the New World fit to have his name uttered in the same breath with that of Plato, one may without presumption believe that even if Emerson has no system, none the less he is the prophet and herald of any system which democracy may henceforth construct and hold by and that when democracy has articulated itself, it will have no difficulty in finding itself already proposed in Emerson. It is as true today as when he said it: "It is not propositions, not new dogmas and the logical exposition of the world that are our first need, but to watch and continually cherish the intellectual and moral sensibilities and woo them to stay and make their homes with us. Whilst they abide with us, we shall not think amiss." We are moved to say that Emerson is the first and as yet almost the only Christian of the Intellect. From out such reverence for the instinct and impulse of our common nature shall emerge in their due season propositions, systems, and logical expositions of the world. Then shall we have a philosophy which religion has no call to chide and which knows its friendship with science and with art.

Emerson wrote of a certain type of mind: "This tranquil, well-founded, wide-seeing soul is no express-rider, no attorney, no magistrate. It lies in the sun and broods on the world." It is the soul of Emerson which these words describe. Yet this is no private merit nor personal credit. For thousands of earth's children, Emerson has taken away the barriers that shut out the sun and has secured the unimpeded, cheerful circulation of the light of heaven, and the wholesome air of day. For such, content to endure without contriving and contending, at the last all express-riders journey, since to them comes the final service of all commodity. For them, careless to make out their own case, all attorneys plead in the day of final judgment; for though falsehoods pile mountain high, truth is the only deposit that nature tolerates. To them who refuse to be called "master, master," all magistracies in the end defer, for theirs is the common cause for which dominion, power and principality is put under foot. Before such successes, even the worshipers of that which today goes by the name of success, those who bend to millions and incline to imperialisms, may lower their standard, and give at least a passing assent to the final word of Emerson's philosophy, the identity of Being, unqualified and immutable, with Character.

D. H. LAWRENCE

From Model Americans[†]

*   *   *

Emerson. The next essay is called The Emersonian Liberation. Well, Emerson is a great man still: or a great individual. And heroes are heroes still, though their banners may decay, and stink.

It is true that lilies may fester. And virtues likewise. The great Virtue of one age has a trick of smelling far worse than weeds in the next.

It is a sad but undeniable fact.

Yet why so sad, fond lover, prithee why so sad? Why should Virtue remain incorruptible, any more than anything else? If stars wax and wane, why should Goodness shine for ever unchanged? That too makes one tired. Goodness sweals and gutters, the light of the Good goes out with a stink, and lo, somewhere else a new light, a new Good. Afterwards, it may be shown that it is eternally the same Good. But to us poor mortals at the moment, it emphatically isn't.

[†] From *The Dial* (May 1923); a review of Stuart Sherman's *Americans*. Reprinted by permission of Laurence Pollinger Limited and the Estate of Frieda Lawrence Ravagli.

And that is the point about Emerson and the Emersonian Liberation—save the word! Heroes are heroes still: safely dead. Heroism is always heroism. But the hero who was heroic one century, uplifting the banner of a creed, is followed the next century by a hero heroically ripping that banner to rags. *Sic transit veritas mundi.*

Emerson was an idealist: a believer in "continuous revelation", continuous inrushes of inspirational energy from the Oversoul. Professor Sherman says: "His message when he leaves us is not, 'Henceforth be masterless,' but, 'Bear thou henceforth the sceptre of thine own control through life and the passion of life.'"

When Emerson says: "I am surrounded by messengers of God who send me credentials day by day," then all right for him. But he cosily forgot that there are many messengers. He knew only a sort of smooth-shaven Gabriel. But as far as we remember, there is Michael too: and a terrible discrepancy between the credentials of the pair of 'em. Then there are other cherubim with outlandish names bringing very different messages than those Ralph Waldo got: Israfel, and even Mormon. And a whole bunch of others. But Emerson had a stone-deaf ear for all except a nicely aureoled Gabriel *qui n'avait pas de quoi.*

Emerson listened to one sort of message and only one. To all the rest he was blank. Ashtaroth and Ammon are gods as well, and hand out their own credentials. But Ralph Waldo wasn't having any. They could never ring *him* up. He was only connected on the Ideal 'phone. "We are all aiming to be idealists," says Emerson, "and covet the society of those who make us so, as the sweet singer, the orator, the ideal painter."

Well, we're pretty sick of the ideal painters and the uplifting singers. As a matter of fact we have worked the ideal bit of our nature to death, and we shall go crazy if we can't start working from some other bit. Idealism now is a sick nerve, and the more you rub on it the worse you feel afterwards. Your later reactions aren't pretty at all. Like Dostoevsky's Idiot, and President Wilson sometimes.

Emerson believes in having the courage to treat all men as equals. It takes some courage *not* to treat them so now.

"Shall I not treat all men as gods?" he cries.

If you like, Waldo, but we've got to pay for it, when you've made them *feel* that they're gods. A hundred million American godlets is rather much for the world to deal with.

The fact of the matter is, all those gorgeous inrushes of exaltation and spiritual energy which made Emerson a great man, now make us sick. They are with us a drug habit. So when Professor Sherman urges us in Ralph Waldo's footsteps, he is really driving us nauseously astray. Which perhaps is hard lines on the professor, and us, and Emerson. But it wasn't I who started the mills of God a-grinding.

I like the essay on Emerson. I like Emerson's real courage. I like his wild and genuine belief in the Oversoul and the inrushes he got from it. But it is a museum-interest. Or else it is a taste of the old drug to the old spiritual drug-fiend in me.

We've got to have a different sort of sardonic courage. And the sort of credentials we are due to receive from the god in the shadow would have been real bones out of hell-broth to Ralph Waldo. *Sic transeunt Dei hominorum.*

So no wonder Professor Sherman sounds a little wistful, and somewhat pathetic, as he begs us to follow Ralph Waldo's trail.

ROBERT FROST

On Emerson[†]

All that admiration for me I am glad of. I am here out of admiration for Emerson and Thoreau. Naturally on this proud occasion I should like to make myself as much of an Emersonian as I can. Let me see if I can't go a long way. You may be interested to know that I have right here in my pocket a little first edition of Emerson's poetry. His very first was published in England, just as was mine. His book was given me on account of that connection by Fred Melcher, who takes so much pleasure in bringing books and things together like that.

I suppose I have always thought I'd like to name in verse some day my four greatest Americans: George Washington, the general and statesman; Thomas Jefferson, the political thinker; Abraham Lincoln, the martyr and savior; and fourth, Ralph Waldo Emerson, the poet. I take these names because they are going around the world. They are not just local. Emerson's name has gone as a poetic philosopher or as a philosophical poet, my favorite kind of both.

I have friends it bothers when I am accused of being Emersonian, that is, a cheerful Monist, for whom evil does not exist, or if it does exist, needn't last forever. Emerson quotes Burns as speaking to the Devil as if he could mend his ways. A melancholy dualism is the only soundness. The question is: is soundness of the essence.

My own unsoundness has a strange history. My mother was a Presbyterian. We were here on my father's side for three hundred years but my mother was fresh a Presbyterian from Scotland. The smart thing when she was young was to be reading Emerson and Poe as it is today to be reading St. John Perse or T. S. Eliot. Reading Emerson turned her into a Unitarian. That was about the time I came into the world; so I suppose I started a sort of Presbyterian-Unitarian. I was transitional. Reading on into Emerson, that is into "Representative Men" until she got to Swedenborg, the mystic, made her a Swedenborgian. I was brought up in all three of these religions, I suppose. I don't know whether I was baptized in them all. But as you see it was pretty much under the auspices of Emerson. It was all very Emersonian. Phrases of his began to come to me early. In that essay on the mystic he makes Swedenborg say that in the highest heaven nothing is arrived at by dispute. Everybody votes in heaven but everybody votes the same way, as in Russia today. It is only in the second-highest heaven that things get parliamentary; we get the two-party system or the hydra-headed, as in France.

Some of my first thinking about my own language was certainly Emersonian. "Cut these sentences and they bleed," he says. I am not submissive enough to want to be a follower, but he had me there. I never got over that. He came pretty near making me an anti-vocabularian with the passage in "Monadnock" about our ancient speech. He blended praise and dispraise of the country people of New Hampshire. As an abolitionist he was against their politics. Forty per cent of them were states-rights Democrats in sympathy with the South. They were really pretty bad, my own relatives included.

† "On Emerson," reprinted by permission of *Daedalus*, Journal of the American Academy of Arts and Sciences, from the issue titled "Quantity and Quality," Fall 1959, Vol. 88, No. 4.

The God who made New Hampshire
Taunted the lofty land
With little men;—

And if I may be further reminiscent parenthetically, my friend Amy Lowell hadn't much use for them either. "I have left New Hampshire," she told me. Why in the world? She couldn't stand the people. What's the matter with the people? "Read your own books and find out." They really differ from other New Englanders, or did in the days of Franklin Pierce.

But now to return to the speech that was his admiration and mine in a burst of poetry in "Monadnock":

Yet wouldst thou learn our ancient speech
These the masters that can teach.
Fourscore or a hundred words
All their vocal muse affords.
Yet they turn them in a fashion
Past the statesman's art and passion.
Rude poets of the tavern hearth
Squandering your unquoted mirth,
That keeps the ground and never soars,
While Jake retorts and Reuben roars.
Scoff of yeoman, strong and stark,
Goes like bullet to the mark,
And the solid curse and jeer
Never balk the waiting ear.

Fourscore or a hundred is seven hundred less than my friend Ivor Richards' basic eight hundred. I used to climb on board a load of shooks (boxes that haven't been set up) just for the pleasure I had in the driver's good use of his hundred-word limit. This at the risk of liking it so much as to lose myself in mere picturesqueness. I was always in favor of the solid curse as one of the most beautiful of figures. We were warned against it in school for its sameness. It depends for variety on the tones of saying it and the situations.

I had a talk with John Erskine, the first time I met him, on this subject of sentences that may look tiresomely alike, short and with short words, yet turn out as calling for all sorts of ways of being said aloud or in the mind's ear, Horatio. I took Emerson's prose and verse as my illustration. Writing is unboring to the extent that it is dramatic.

In a recent preface to show my aversion to being interrupted with notes in reading a poem, I find myself resorting to Emerson again. I wanted to be too carried away for that. There was much of "Brahma" that I didn't get to begin with but I got enough to make me sure I would be back there reading it again some day when I had read more and lived more; and sure enough, without help from dictionary or encyclopaedia I can now understand every line in it but one or two. It is a long story of many experiences that led me into the secret of:

But thou, meek lover of the good!
Find me, and turn thy back on heaven.

What baffled me was the Christianity in "meek lover of the good." I don't like obscurity and obfuscation, but I do like dark sayings I must leave the clearing of to time. And I don't want to be robbed of the pleasure of fathoming depths for my-self. It was a moment for me when I saw how Shakespeare set bounds to science when he brought in the North Star, "whose worth's unknown although his height be taken." Of untold worth: it brings home some that should and some that shouldn't come. Let the psychologist take notice how unsuccessful he has to be.

I owe more to Emerson than anyone else for troubled thoughts about free-dom. I had the hurt to get over when I first heard us made fun of by foreigners as the land of the free and the home of the brave. Haven't we won freedom? Is there no such thing as freedom? Well, Emerson says God

> Would take the sun out of the skies
> Ere freedom out of a man.

and there rings the freedom I choose.

Never mind how and where Emerson disabused me of my notion I may have been brought up to that truth would make me free. My truth will bind you slave to me. He didn't want converts and followers. He was a Unitarian. I am on record as saying that freedom is nothing but departure—setting forth—leaving things behind, brave origination of the courage to be new. We may not want freedom. But let us not deceive ourselves about what we don't want. Freedom is one jump ahead of formal laws, as in planes and even automobiles right now. Let's see the law catch up with us very soon.

Emerson supplies the emancipating formula for giving an attachment up for an attraction, one nationality for another nationality, one love for another love. If you must break free,

> Heartily know,
> When half-gods go
> The gods arrive.

I have seen it invoked in *Harper's Magazine* to excuse disloyalty to our democ-racy in a time like this. But I am not sure of the reward promised. There is such a thing as getting too transcended. There are limits. Let's not talk socialism. I feel projected out from politics with lines like:

> Musketaquit, a goblin strong,
> Of shards and flints makes jewels gay;
> They lose their grief who hear his song,
> And where he winds is the day of day.
>
> So forth and brighter fares my stream,—
> Who drink it shall not thirst again;
> No darkness stains its equal gleam,
> And ages drop in it like rain.

Left to myself, I have gradually come to see what Emerson was meaning in "Give all to Love" was, Give all to Meaning. The freedom is ours to insist on meaning.

The kind of story Steinbeck likes to tell is about an old labor hero punch-drunk from fighting the police in many strikes, beloved by everybody at head-quarters as the greatest living hater of tyranny. I take it that the production line was his grievance. The only way he could make it mean anything was to try to ruin it. He took arms and fists against it. No one could have given him that kind of freedom. He saw it as his to seize. He was no freedman; he was a free man.

The one inalienable right is to go to destruction in your own way. What's worth living for is worth dying for. What's worth succeeding in is worth failing in.

If you have piled up a great rubbish heap of oily rags in the basement for your doctor's thesis and it won't seem to burst into flame spontaneously, come away quickly and without declaring rebellion. It will cost you only your Ph.D. union card and the respect of the union. But it will hardly be noticed even to your credit in the world. All you have to do is to amount to something anyway. The only reprehensible materiality is the materialism of getting lost in your material so you can't find out yourself what it is all about.

A young fellow came to me to complain of the department of philosophy in his university. There wasn't a philosopher in it. "I can't stand it." He was really complaining of his situation. He wasn't where he could feel real. But I didn't tell him so I didn't go into that. I agreed with him that there wasn't a philosopher in his university—there was hardly ever more than one at a time in the world—and I advised him to quit. Light out for somewhere. He hated to be a quitter. I told him the Bible says, "Quit ye, like men." "Does it," he said. "Where would I go?" Why anywhere almost. Kamchatka, Madagascar, Brazil. I found him doing well in the educational department of Rio when I was sent on an errand down there by our government several years later. I had taken too much responsibility for him when I sent him glimmering like that. I wrote to him with troubled conscience and got no answer for two whole years. But the story has a happy ending. His departure was not suicidal. I had a post card from him this Christmas to tell me he was on Robinson Crusoe's island Juan Fernandez on his way to Easter Island that it had always been a necessity for him some day to see. I would next hear from him in Chile where he was to be employed in helping restore two colleges. Two! And the colleges were universities!

No subversive myself, I think it very Emersonian of me that I am so sympathetic with subversives, rebels, runners out, runners out ahead, eccentrics, and radicals. I don't care how extreme their enthusiasm so long as it doesn't land them in the Russian camp. I always wanted one of them teaching in the next room to me so my work would be cut out for me warning the children taking my courses not to take his courses.

I am disposed to cheat myself and others in favor of any poet I am in love with. I hear people say the more they love anyone the more they see his faults. Nonsense. Love is blind and should be left so. But it hasn't been hidden in what I have said that I am not quite satisfied with the easy way Emerson takes disloyalty. He didn't know or ignored his Blackstone. It is one thing for the deserter and another for the deserted. Loyalty is that for the lack of which your gang will shoot you without benefit of trial by jury. And serves you right. Be as treacherous as you must be for your ideals, but don't expect to be kissed good-by by the idol you go back on. We don't want to look too foolish, do we? And probably Emerson was too Platonic about evil. It was a mere **Τὸ μὴ οὔ**[1] that could be disposed of like the butt of a cigarette. In a poem I have called the best Western poem yet he says:

Unit and universe are round.

Another poem could be made from that, to the effect that ideally in thought only is a circle round. In practice, in nature, the circle becomes an oval.

---

1. Frost uses the Greek phrase to mean something like "a mere nothing." [Editors]

As a circle it has one center—Good. As an oval it has two centers—Good and
Evil. Thence Monism versus Dualism.

Emerson was a Unitarian because he was too rational to be superstitious
and too little a storyteller and lover of stories to like gossip and pretty scandal.
Nothing very religious can be done for people lacking in superstition. They usually end up abominable agnostics. It takes superstition and the prettiest scandal
story of all to make a good Trinitarian. It is the first step in the descent of the
spirit into the material-human at the risk of the spirit.

But if Emerson had left us nothing else he would be remembered longer
than the Washington Monument for the monument at Concord that he glorified with lines surpassing any other ever written about soldiers:

> By the rude bridge that arched the flood
> Their flag to April['s] breeze unfurled
> Here once the embattled farmers stood
> And fired the shot heard round the world.

Not even Thermopylae has been celebrated better. I am not a shriner, but two
things I never happen on unmoved: one, this poem on stone; and the other, the
tall shaft seen from Lafayette Park across the White House in Washington.

A. R. AMMONS

Emerson[†]

The stone longs for flight,
the flier for a bead, even
a grain, of connective stone:
which is to say, all
flight, of imaginative hope or   5
fact, takes accuracy from stone:

without the bead the flier
released from
tension has no true
to gauge his motions in: 10
assured and terrified by
its cold weight, the stone

can feather the thinnest
possibility of height:
that you needed   15
to get up and I down
leaves us both still
sharing stone and flight.

---

† "Emerson," from *Diversifications*. Copyright © 1975 by A. R. Ammons. Used by permission of W. W.
Norton & Company, Inc.

CRITICISM

O. W. FIRKINS

Has Emerson a Future?[†]

Emerson in the history of religion was a guest of honor who reached a party at the moment when its members were dispersing. His arrival evoked a brief sensation—on the doorstep, as it were—but did not finally reconstitute the party. In the confusion of dispersal the leading guest found himself for a moment without a shelter or a destination. This is a tiny parable to the consideration of which my thoughts were recalled by the perusal of Mr. Carpenter's scholarly little monograph entitled *Emerson and Asia.*

I

What is Emerson's claim upon the regard of humanity? Restatement in a few words may be instructive even to his admirers.

The association of omnipresence with divinity is an old idea. The association of divinity with worship is an idea still older. Emerson simply saw that, if divinity were omnipresent, the act of worship might be everlasting. The experience of God might be unbroken. The idea was striking; Emerson went much further; he converted the idea into a program. The experiment was audacious—and successful. Emerson's whole secret may be formulated thus: the successful practice of unbroken commerce with omnipresent deity. Or again, in more technical form: the combination of the broadest generality in the religious object with the highest particularity in the continuously varying forms which the object presents to the disciple.

Men had dedicated themselves to God before his day. One class had referred every act to the divine approbation. Another had been professionally devout—had dedicated their whole time to the accumulation of credits in the divine ledger. A few had found in God the object of living: to a few more He had constituted a ground for death. But the notion of an unbroken spiritual commerce which, using every object, should occupy every moment, was a novel thing. Here is a fact that sweeps all the literature and all the intelligence of Emerson, great and moving as these are, into abeyance: here is an addition to history, a new district of experience, an augmentation of the sum of human possibilities. The soundness or unsoundness of the premises on which this principle and this obedience rest is a great matter; but even that greatness is small beside the fact that on any premise, sound or unsound, the result was achievable and was achieved. *"Tant pis pour le sens,"*[1] said Flaubert, when one of his beautifully modulated sentences was charged with defect of sense. If logic and Emerson fail to come to terms, the sufferer is logic.

Two points demand brief notice before we turn to the religious influence of Emerson. His name, let me hasten to say, is secure; he is certain of the due toll of inscriptions, invocations, appraisements, and obeisances—of that form of greeting from posterity which combines salutation with dismissal. The second point is that Emerson had two fames, and that the slighter fame has proved thus

---

† From Oscar W. Firkins, "Has Emerson a Future?" From *Selected Essays of O. W. Firkins* (University of Minnesota Press, 1933), 79–93. Reprinted by permission of the publisher.
1. So much the worse for sense (French). [Editors]

far the firmer, more abidingly dynamic, of the two. This last may be called his secular fame among thinkers. There is no other amateur to whom so many experts have been grateful. Emerson had the impertinence to say things about politics, economics, industry, history, and art which the specialists in those fields were generous enough to borrow.

The *Encyclopaedia Britannica* (14th edition) observes tranquilly *in re* Montaigne: "The most noteworthy handling of the subject in English is unquestionably Emerson's in *Representative Men*." Emerson, after eighty years, is the first voice in English, not on the "Over-Soul," but on a French essayist—a fact visible to encyclopedias! No other man, perhaps, even today, is so often cited by unaffiliated minds. The Gentiles have been more faithful than straying Israel. An audience of thinkers, as guarantors of perpetuity, has the marked advantage of being to a large degree an audience of spokesmen. What explains this vogue of the high priest among the unconverted? Many people would admit that Emerson was the sanest of mystics because he was the soundest of thinkers, but does it occur to anybody that he was possibly the first of thinkers because he was the first of mystics? Does anybody broach the suggestion that the zenith might be the point from which all levels and all horizons might be most distinctly visible, that the airman might give help to the topographer?

II

I turn now to the larger and nearer question of Emerson's religious influence and destiny. Liberal religion in Emerson's day mounted to a crest from which, shortly after his day, it declined with a swiftness that was almost catastrophe. Emerson gained by the ascent, and furthered the ascent; he lost by the fall which he could not halt, which, indeed, on one side, he was destined indirectly and unwillingly to further. It is a strange and profoundly saddening fact that, in the liberal field, Emerson's peculiar tilth and glebe, faith and worship could hardly be more dim and faint today if their exemplar and evangelist had never lived. The cause of this shall be explored a little later. Let it suffice here to say that Emerson came at the best time possible for a brief, bright ripening of his influence and fame, at the worst time possible for the carrying forward and establishment of these happy prospects. He lost his hold not through any failure in himself and less through any defection or estrangement of his audience than through what we might call its *bodily removal*, as if a man speaking from shore to listeners on a ship were to find his speech cut short by the unmooring and departure of the vessel. The world was adrift from its religious anchorage.

There are times when, comparing the fleetingness of Emerson's religious influence with the length and the luster of the trail left by such partial prophets as Fox and Swedenborg, we are confounded by the stupidity of Time. We must remember, however, that the carriage of fame, like other carryings, is mainly a question of transports. These transports in religion are doctrines, organizations, rituals, sacraments, programs. Emerson rejected all these things, as clogs and hindrances to the commerce of the impassioned soul with vital deity. His fame was a foundling to be laid on anybody's doorstep. By providence or by luck in one of its happy mimicries of providence the door at which the bantling was laid was the door of Unitarianism. That generous body constituted itself forthwith the curator of that fame and spiritual efficiency in which it very justly saw the fruit of its own teaching and the seed of its own honor. In the wardship of

Emerson's fame, it might well have seemed that it had found its own security. A Unitarianism anxious for its own future might have been quieted by the word spoken to the affrighted Roman boatman: *Caesarem vehis, et fortunam ejus.*[2]

The partnership was more helpful in its beginnings than later, and tended rather to exalt than to elucidate the seer. Emerson has often been seen through a blur of worship. Louisa Alcott as a tiny girl laid violets on his doorstep, and when in *Rose in Bloom* she made Emerson almost the matchmaker between two virtuous young nobodies, she was still in the same uncomprehending sincerity strewing violets before his door. Unitarians in general saw much more, but even they tended sometimes to treat Emerson as a jeweler who should give back to them their own thoughts reset in the pearl and gold of his incomparable diction. They saw the unrivaled specimen: they scarcely discerned the *new species*. Emerson, be it remembered, was not their founder or chief; nobody either within or without their body was responsible for Emerson per se, for Emerson in toto. Disciples take en masse: customers—even reverent customers—pick and choose. In Emerson the religious liberals took and left; and these takings and leavings tended to convert the seer into an image, an enlarged and glorified reflection, of themselves.

III

Unitarianism was the product of many influences, the most powerful of which in the mid-nineteenth century was probably Emerson himself. Its tradition was liberal; it drew new fervor and new liberality from Emerson; that was its high fortune. Its misfortune lay in the fact that it lost the fervor while it kept the liberality, and that liberality, in the absence of fervor, is deadly to religion. If, indeed, the ardor does not warm the liberality, the liberality will freeze the ardor. Put in homelier phrase, if the teeth do not break the walnut shell, the walnut shell will crack the teeth. Liberalism is a strain on the vital force of any cult—an ordeal which the Emersons, but not the Emersonians, can victoriously and profitably meet. Unitarianism under Emersonian stimulus met it for a time; when that stimulus withdrew, it was enfeebled by its own breadth. In July a man may sleep delightfully with his light tent open to all the winds of heaven; he is rash or doomed who repeats the fond experiment in December.

Religions begin by concentration and particularity, by concentrating regard on particular objects, acts, men, deities. Liberalism arrives to broaden the field of sanctities; religion, finally, sees and uses good everywhere, in ancient foreign cult and in newborn scientific theory, in the instinct of a child and in the profundities of intuition. But hospitality, the sanest of virtues, may end by turning the house into a thoroughfare—in which case the essence of religion is lost for host and guest alike. God, we are told (even by our Quaker Whittiers) is contemporaneous, and the temptation supervenes to look for him between the covers of the latest periodical. The professors of liberal religion in our day are nothing better than *shoppers* in contemporary literature and philosophy— shoppers who do not buy.[3] New tokens, new embodiments, of God may breed in a faith a hunger for novelty which, in the dearth of other resources, may find satisfaction at last in the consumption of its own tissue.

2. You are transporting Caesar and his destiny (Latin). [Editors]
3. An exception to this rule is the band of so-called Unitarian Humanists who flourish under the courageous leadership of John H. Dietrich of Minneapolis.

When religion is everywhere, it is nowhere in particular, and the people for whom maples are burning bushes are rarely found upon their knees before maples. I say rarely, because Emersons are born and reared on this irreverent or superstitious planet. They are few, and their influence cannot always halt the movements of the age toward secularity and paganism. In such ages the effect of making religion coextensive with secularity is to make secularity coessential with religion. Emerson's fate was to encounter such an age, and he is for the moment all but forgotten in the walks of his disciples. They are now insensible to his fervor, and they practice his liberality to no purpose.

IV

So much for Emerson and the present-day liberal. Has he fared better at the hands of orthodox believers? Sixty years ago Emerson and liberal religion, though not quite together, were alike in their distance from slow-pacing orthodoxy. In the time interval, the tortoise has almost overtaken the hare, but curiously enough, without the smallest profit either to Emerson or to liberal religion. In a latter-day gospel by Harry *Emerson* Fosdick called *Christianity and Progress* I could not find a single reference to Emerson. Theism in its straits might turn for aid in his direction, but it dreads that lifeboat more than the filling ship. It is actually probable that today Emerson's mere name is known to fewer Congregationalists and Presbyterians than sixty years ago. At that time the writer almost outshone the heretic, and Emerson on the arm of Longfellow and Hawthorne found access to many hearths which he could never have approached on the arm of Channing or of Parker. That chaperonage is scarcely now available, and national pride no longer fosters the kind of interest which, to take a nearer example, the undevout and unpatriotic Ibsen evokes in the patriotic and devout Norwegian.

There remains a third and still more interesting question. What is Emerson's footing with the independent nonsectarian religious thinker? James Harvey Robinson's "Religion" in *Whither Mankind?* (1928) mentions Emerson just once, casually, in a review of names. Shall we dismiss Mr. Robinson as a cold philosopher? What, then, does the man of whom Matthew Arnold wrote "A voice oracular hath peal'd today" signify to reverent and elevated spirits of our time, such as Maurice Maeterlinck and George Santayana? Maeterlinck, in a twenty-two page early essay in which the name of Emerson occurs just five times, abounds in a lyric eloquence which the reader rather inhales than digests. At the end he has told us little, has made us feel that he valued the Emersonian method more than its results, that, in short, he preferred the observatory to the firmament. The high-souled Santayana is cool, is niggardly, to Emerson. He begins a brief article with emphasis on what we may call the high emanations from the person of the seer. The emanations, of course, not being transferable to print, are not transferable to posterity, and exempt posterity, to that extent, from the necessity of veneration. He has some admirable criticism of Emerson's logic (why did he not add some criticism of Emerson's eyebrows?) and seems finally to dismiss the seer as a sublime aberration. Aberrations are least forgivable when they presume to put on sublimity.

Mr. Paul Elmer More and Dr. Irving Babbitt are distinguished among the literary critics of our time by a rare constancy—implying, in their case, a rare fortitude—in the preaching of a high and grave morality. Toward Emerson Dr.

Babbitt is not unkind and Mr. More is not uncordial; but both look upon him, as it were, "with one auspicious and one drooping eye," classing him, like Santayana, as a divine prodigal to whom one brings a sparing and a wary veneration. Mr. More makes Emerson's "facile optimism" responsible for Christian Science. He also makes Arnold's "disinterested endeavor" responsible in part, through Walter Pater, for the debasement of Oscar Wilde. Perhaps the second genealogy may serve as scholium to the first.

V

Everywhere the signs seem inauspicious, but these signs do not exhaust the horoscope. The neglect into which Emerson has fallen is of another quality than the Lethe in which other saintly and prophetic leaders are immersed. Wise men to whom he is temporarily useless suspect that Emerson and the world have not cast their final reckoning together. He is the book that is not so much put up as put down—the suspended task to which in leisurely and thoughtful hours return is possible. We do not yet dare to say whether it is yesterday or tomorrow that sleeps beneath the block of unhewn quartz in Concord. The force of Emerson's life and gospel remains unexhausted, since the world did not stop to hear his preaching to the end, and the force of the human instinct to which that preaching appealed is unexpended and is inexhaustible. Both are patient, and the future is extensive. Who shall say that they will not rejoin each other?

The rendezvous may be distant; the logical interval, the logical barrier, between ourselves and Emerson is not to be lightly overleapt. But the fitting comment on Emerson's want of logic is Lincoln's on the alleged drunkenness of Grant ("Send his whisky to the other generals"). Sobriety is admirable, but one prefers—Appomattox. One could wish that Emerson had been logical—and that logicians had led equally happy and elevated lives. When Emerson has said his utmost, the logical difficulties remain; but when logic has said its utmost, Emerson remains: and Emerson is the larger remainder of the two. After all, intelligence does not subvert religion; the besiegers never win until the garrison is treacherous. The case of present-day science against religion is hardly stronger than the prescientific case of logic against Christianity, and if religion was capable of age-long survival under the second, a believer might contend that it was capable of revival under the first. The world, which loves and hates religion by turns, in and after Emerson's day had had a surfeit of religion; and its respect for logic was merely the politic veil of its reviving appetite for worldliness and pagan secularity. That movement will run its course; its decline is no less certain than its advent: mankind may return to Emerson, like Peer Gynt after his vain wanderings to the irremovable and unimpatient Solveig.

VI

In the Emersonian philosophy the instinct for fact or reason finds three chief stumblingblocks: the obedience to instinct, the favorable view of life, and the infinitude and immanence of deity. The first of these is really unimportant. When Emerson says, "Follow your instincts," the indiscretion, the audacity, is merely phrasal; and the whole context is a gloss and emendation for that phrase. "Trust thyself: every heart vibrates to that iron string." The "iron" is conclusive. We are to follow our instincts (the higher instincts) through pain and difficulty. Self-indulgence can find no harborage for its cushion or its goblet here. The

Emersonian phrase may be incautious, but I doubt if in the Emersonian text it ever served as spur or cloak to license. Carve *Fay ce que vouldras*[4] over the arched portal of a minster, and the inscription would corrupt the mind of nobody. Epicures, passing in the street, do not glance upward.

Emerson's optimism is exasperating to our pessimism, but we must remember that Emerson's knowledge of evil would almost have qualified another man for pessimism, and that the ground for pessimism itself is scarcely either logical or scientific. It is curious that Emerson's psychic altitude never suggests to the critics at what we may call sea level what physical altitude so instantly and powerfully suggests—the possibility of a wider and clearer outlook. Drenched with rain, you cannot repress your anger at the man who proclaims that the sky is all sunshine and azure; it never occurs to you that his standing-ground may be above the clouds.

The question of theism offers undoubtedly a more serious problem. Discussion within my limits is impossible, but it may be noted that the theistic ideal underwent in Emerson's hands a harder test than any to which science or logic could subject it—the ordeal of lifelong experiment. William James in *The Varieties of Religious Experience* declares that Emerson never makes it quite clear whether his God is an *order* or a being, whether it should be called infinite benevolence or, simply, infinite benefit. If this were true, one side of this double possibility would span more than half the interval between Emerson and current thought. Science, moreover, has been successively both theistic and non-theistic (i.e., agnostic), and, if it now leans away from Emerson, we must remember that, in relation to time, space, and matter, it has lately added to its other demonstrated powers a noticeable power of self-reversal. When science locks a door in the face of protesting orthodoxy or theism, the place in which it drops the key is not the cistern but its own pocket.

VII

The last thing to be said is that Emerson is not a notion; he is a *fact*. Emerson is history; he is there in the unchanging record, as indelible as Runnymede, as inexpungable as Gibraltar. Let us restate in a single terse word his originality: to put (in practice as in theory) the whole weight and worth of the universe at its best behind each object and behind each moment of experience. The premise may be real or illusory. If real, the signal fact in the history of our race has been its capacity in one man to appropriate this reality. If illusory, one is still half moved to say that the signal fact in the history of our race has been its power to originate this illusion. Illusion or reality, it represents the highest *yield* of life.

Most persons now feel that the facts are against Emerson. But science itself in our day is oddly busy at the task of removing the virility, the old-time pugnacity, from the word "fact." Fact is the reflection of the object in the subject; blur the object, blur the subject, approximate or knead together object and subject, and fact, like atom, tends swiftly to lose its granular and contumacious quality. Knowledge becomes an occasion for experience, an inlet to experience, and its virtue is not the virtue of a transcript but an application. But it is just here that the hope in Emerson, the hope for Emerson, revives. Emerson means for us pre-eminently an enlargement of the possibilities of man's experience;

4. Do what you wish (French); the slogan of Rabelais's *Gargantua and Pantagruel*. [Editors]

the inextinguishable thirst of the race for what is larger and deeper in the psychic life cannot finally ignore him. He has achieved the unforeseen, the unimagined; the impossible is humbled in his presence; and the race will come back to him as the supplanted heir comes back to search in a neglected cabinet for the lost title deed to a disputed fortune.

STEPHEN E. WHICHER

Emerson's Tragic Sense[†]

There is something enigmatic about most American authors. Poe, Hawthorne, Melville, Thoreau, Whitman, Mark Twain, Emily Dickinson, Henry Adams, Henry James, Frost, Faulkner—each has his secret space, his halls of Thermes, his figure in the carpet, which is felt most strongly in his best work and yet eludes definition. Sometimes it is quite opposed to what its possessor thinks he is or wants to be: for example, Hawthorne, envying Trollope his sunshine and his sales, whose best story was "positively hell-fired"; or Whitman, affirmer of life, whose poetry is never more powerful than when it treats of death; Poe, who liked to think himself icily logical and who wrote best from a haunted fantasy; Mark Twain, professional joker and amateur pessimist; or Frost, tough and humorous individualist, whose best poems are often his saddest. Generally this is linked with an obscure fear or grief, even despair: American literature, closely read, can seem one of the least hopeful of literatures.

To all this, Emerson, representative American author that he is, is no exception. The more we know him, the less we know him. He can be summed up in a formula only by those who know their own minds better than his. We hear his grand, assuring words, but where is the man who speaks them? We know the part he played so well; we feel his powerful charm: we do not know the player. He is, finally, impenetrable, for all his forty-odd volumes.

Yet no man can write so much and so honestly and not reveal himself in some measure. We can see enough to sense in him an unusually large gap, even a contradiction, between his teachings and his experience. He taught self-reliance and felt self-distrust, worshipped reality and knew illusion, proclaimed freedom and submitted to fate. No one has expected more of man; few have found him less competent. There is an Emersonian tragedy and an Emersonian sense of tragedy, and we begin to know him when we feel their presence underlying his impressive confidence.

Of course I must stress the word "Emersonian" here. As Mark Van Doren has remarked, "Emerson had no theory of tragedy," unless to deny its existence is a theory. His oblivion can be prodigious.

> The soul will not know either deformity or pain. If, in the hours of clear reason, we should speak the severest truth, we should say that we had never made a sacrifice. In these hours the mind seems so great, that nothing can be taken from us that seems much. All loss, all pain, is particular; the universe remains to the heart unhurt. Neither vexations nor calamities abate our trust. No man ever stated his griefs as lightly as he might.

[†] From *The American Scholar* 22 (Summer 1953): 285–92. Reprinted by permission of the Whicher estate.

As he explained in his lecture on "The Tragic," the man who is grounded in the divine life will transcend suffering in a flight to a region "whereunto these passionate clouds of sorrow cannot rise."

Such transcendence of suffering is one of the great historic answers to tragedy and commands respect. To be valid, however, it must "cost not less than everything." Emerson seems to pay no such price. When, in the same lecture on "The Tragic," he tells the "tender American girl," horrified at reading of the trans-atlantic slave trade, that these crucifixions were not horrid to the obtuse and barbarous blacks who underwent them, "but only a little worse than the old sufferings," we wonder if he paid anything at all for his peace. The only coin in which we can discharge our debt to suffering is attention to it, but Emerson seems to evade this obligation.

Yet this chilling idealism is not simple insensitivity. Emerson is teaching his tested secret of insulation from calamity: Live in the Soul. His famous assertion in *Experience* of the unreality of his devastating grief for his son is an impressive illustration of the necessity he was under to protect, at whatever human cost, his hard-won security. Yeats has said somewhere that we begin to live when we have conceived life as tragedy. The opposite was true of Emerson. Only as he refused to conceive life as tragedy could he find the courage to live.

By denying man's fate, however, Emerson did not escape it. His urgent need to deny it shows that his confidence was more precarious than he would admit. Who has not felt the insistence, the over-insistence, in such radical claims to freedom and power as *Self-Reliance?*

> Trust thyself: every heart vibrates to that iron string. Accept the place the divine providence has found for you, the society of your contemporaries, the connection of events. Great men have always done so, and confided themselves childlike to the genius of their age, betraying their perception that the absolutely trustworthy was seated at their heart, working through their hands, predominating in all their being. And we are now men, and must accept in the highest mind the same transcendent destiny; and not minors and invalids in a protected corner, not cowards fleeing before a revolution, but guides, redeemers, and benefactors, obeying the Almighty effort, and advancing on Chaos and the Dark.

What speaks here is self-*dis*trust, a distrust so pervasive that it must find an "absolutely trustworthy" seated at the heart before it can trust at all. Self-reliance, in the oft-cited phrase, is God-reliance, and therefore not self-reliance. Contrast the accent of a genuine individualist like Ibsen: "The strongest man in the world is he who stands most alone." Or recall a truly self-reliant American: "It was about this time I conceiv'd the bold and arduous project of arriving at moral perfection. I wish'd to live without committing any fault at any time; I would conquer all that either natural inclination, custom, or company might lead me into. As I knew, or thought I knew, what was right and wrong, I did not see why I might not always do the one and avoid the other. . . . For this purpose I therefore contrived the following method. . . ." The free and easy assurance of Franklin is just what is missing in Emerson.

Certainly the first thirty years or so showed no great self-trust. A tubercular, like many in his family (two brothers died of the disease), he was engaged throughout his twenties in a serious battle of life and death in which he was not at all sure of winning. With his poor health went a disheartening self-criticism.

He imagined he was incurably idle and self-indulgent, without force or worldly competence, constrained in the company of others, unresponsive in his affections. Though his early journals often show a manly courage and good sense, the dominant mood is a sense of impotence. He lacks all power to realize his larger ambitions and feels himself drifting, sometimes in humiliation, sometimes in wry amusement, before the inexorable flowing of time. He was the servant more than the master of his fate, he found in 1824; and later, in the depths of his illness, it seemed to him that he shaped his fortunes not at all. In all his life, he wrote, he obeyed a strong necessity.

The electrifying release of power brought to him by the amazing discovery, the start of his proper career, that God was within his own soul is understandable only against this early—indeed, this lifelong submission to a strong necessity. His subjection bred a longing for self-direction, all the stronger for his underlying sense of its impossibility. The force of his transcendental faith, and its almost willful extravagance, sprang from his need to throw off, against all probability and common sense, his annihilating dependence. He welcomed the paradoxical doctrine that "God dwells in thee" with uncritical delight, as the solution to all the doubts that oppressed him, and rushed in a Saturnalia of faith to spell out its revolutionary consequences for the solitary soul:

> . . . The world is nothing, the man is all; . . . in yourself slumbers the whole of Reason; it is for you to know all, it is for you to dare all. . . .

> . . . . The height, the deity of man is, to be self-sustained, to need no gift, no foreign force. . . . All that you call the world is the shadow of that substance which you are, the perpetual creation of the powers of thought, of those that are dependent and of those that are independent of your will. . . .You think me the child of my circumstances: I make my circumstance. . . .

> . . . Every rational creature has all nature for his dowry and estate. It is his, if he will. He may divest himself of it; he may creep into a corner, and abdicate his kingdom, as most men do, but he is entitled to the world by his constitution. . . .

Yet this proclamation of the kingdom of man was always what he soon came to call it, a romance. He retained a common-sense awareness (and so retains our respect) that experience did not support it. Not merely were all manipular attempts to realize his kingdom premature and futile. The Power within, from which all capacity stemmed, was itself wayward. The individual relying on it was a mere pipe for a divine energy that came and went as it willed. With this hidden life within him, man was no longer hopeless, but he was still helpless. "I would gladly," Emerson wrote at the age of forty-one, ". . . allow the most to the will of man, but I have set my heart on honesty in this chapter, and I can see nothing at last, in success or failure, than more or less of vital force supplied from the Eternal."

When Emerson wrote *The American Scholar*, seven years earlier, his imagination had kindled to a blaze at the thought of the divine power latent in the soul. Give way to it, let it act, and the conversion of the world will follow. As this millennial enthusiasm inevitably waned, the old helplessness it had contradicted emerged unaltered from the flames. The result was a head-on clash of belief and fact. His vision of man as he might be only intensified the plight of man as he was. Something resembling the Fall of Man, which he had so ring-ingly denied, reappears in his pages.

It is not sin now that troubles him, but "the incompetency of power." One may accuse Providence of a certain parsimony.

> It has shown the heaven and earth to every child, and filled him with a de-sire for the whole; a desire raging, infinite; a hunger, as of space to be filled with planets; a cry of famine, as of devils for souls. Then for the satisfac-tion,—to each man is administered a single drop, a bead of dew of vital power, *per day*,—a cup as large as space, and one drop of the water of life in it. Each man woke in the morning with an appetite that could eat the solar system like a cake; a spirit for action and passion without bounds; he could lay his hand on the morning star; he could try conclusions with grav-itation or chemistry; but, on the first motion to prove his strength,—hands, feet, senses, gave way, and would not serve him. He was an emperor de-serted by his states, and left to whistle by himself, or thrust into a mob of emperors, all whistling: and still the sirens sang, "The attractions are pro-portioned to the destinies." In every house, in the heart of each maiden and of each boy, in the soul of the soaring saint, this chasm is found,—be-tween the largest promise of ideal power and the shabby experience.

This chasm is the Emersonian tragedy, a tragedy of incapacity. Man's reach must exceed his grasp, of course; that is not tragic. Emerson's chasm cuts deeper: between a vision that claims all power now, and an experience that finds none. Emerson's thought of the self was split between a total Yes and a total No, which could not coexist, could not be reconciled, and yet were both true. "Alas for this infirm faith, this will not strenuous, this vast ebb of a vast flow! I am God in nature; I am a weed by the wall."

There is an Emersonian skepticism as well as an Emersonian faith. Of the seven "lords of life" he distinguishes in his key essay, *Experience*, five are prin-ciples of weakness. A man is slave to his moods and his temperament, swept like a bubble down the stream of time, blinded and drugged with illusion, the cap-tive of his senses—in a word, the creature of a strong necessity. To be sure, the God is a native of the bleak rocks of his isolation, and can at any moment sur-prise and cheer him with new glimpses of reality. But for all this miraculous consolation, he has no will or force of his own; self-reliant is precisely what he can never be. *The American Scholar's* assurance of the unsearched might of man is a feat of faith in view of the actual humiliating human predicament, "with powers so vast and unweariable ranged on one side, and this little, con-ceited, vulnerable popinjay that a man is, bobbing up and down into every dan-ger, on the other."

It goes without saying that one can easily overstate the case for a tragic sense in Emerson. *Experience*, for instance, is not a tragic-sounding essay. Per-haps "sense of limitation" would be more accurate; I have deliberately chosen a controversial term, in order to stress a side of Emerson often overlooked. For all his loss of millennial hope, Emerson in fact came to allow much to the will of man, as any reader of *The Conduct of Life* can see. Nor do I mean to suggest that he did not find the secret of a serene and affirmative life. The evidence is overwhelming that he did. My point is that his serenity was a not unconscious *answer* to his experience of life, rather than an inference from it (even when presented as such). It was an act of faith, forced on him by what he once called "the ghastly reality of things." Only as we sense this tension of faith and experience in him can we catch the quality of his affirmation. He *had* to ascribe more reality to his brief moments of "religious sentiment" than to the rest of life, or he could not live.

The way he did so altered sensibly, as his first excess of faith in man diminished. A gentle resignation came to settle over his thought of human nature, an elegiac recognition that life perpetually promises us a glory we can never realize. As it did so, the center of his faith traveled imperceptibly from man to the order that included him. In moments of faith, as he explained even in the midst of his essay on *Self-Reliance*, "The soul raised over passion beholds identity and eternal causation, perceives the self-existence of Truth and Right, and calms itself with knowing that all things go well." Such dogmatic optimism, always a part of his faith, became more and more its sole content as his first dream of a kingdom of Man dwindled into reasonableness.

Emerson the optimist said some shallow and callous things, as he did in his lecture on "The Tragic." To restore our sympathy with his humanity, we must glimpse the prisoner that now and then looked out of the eyes above the smile. Within, he was sovereign, a guide, redeemer and benefactor; without, he was a lecturing and publishing old gentleman. Each time his inner promise of ideal power came up against the narrow limits of his experience, the response could only be the same—a renewed surrender to the Power that planned it that way.

He did not surrender to necessity because he found it good, so much as he found it good because he surrendered. Recurrently the Good he recognizes is more conspicuous for power than for goodness, a "deaf, unimplorable, immense fate," to which all man-made distinctions of good and ill are an impertinence. In some of his poems, particularly, those that have eyes to see may watch him swept into entranced submission to "the over-god" by the compulsion of his personal problems. This is how he meets the impossible challenge of social action, in the "Ode" to Channing. So the teasing evanescence of his moments of insight into reality is submerged in "The World-Soul." He bows to the same power for a bleak consolation in his "Threnody" for his son:

> Silent rushes the swift Lord
> Through ruined systems still restored,
> Broadsowing, bleak and void to bless,
> Plants with worlds the wilderness;
> Waters with tears of ancient sorrow
> Apples of Eden ripe to-morrow.
> House and tenant go to ground,
> Lost in God, in Godhead found.

In such poems we feel the hunger for strength that sent him first to his grand doctrine of Self-Reliance, and then swung him to its polar opposite, a worship of the Beautiful Necessity.

Like all puritans, Emerson was an extremist: he had to have entire assurance, or he had none at all. Though we have a tradition of mature tragedy in our literature, American authors have typically made the same demand. Either they have risen to his transcendental trust, like Thoreau and Whitman; or they have accepted shoddy substitutes, like Norris or Sandburg or Steinbeck; or they have dropped into blackness, like Henry Adams or Jeffers. Emerson himself teetered on the edge of this drop, as did Thoreau and Whitman too, sustained by little more than their own power of belief. Since then the impulse to believe has become progressively feebler and the drop quicker and harder, until now, John Aldridge tells us, our honest writers *start* in the pit. If we are ever to have a great literature again, one would conclude, it will not be until we can break decisively with the whole extremist Emersonian pattern and find some means to face this world without either transcendence or despair.

PERRY MILLER

New England's Transcendentalism: Native or Imported?[†]

Transcendentalism, a fairly parochial disturbance in and around Boston in the 1830's and 1840's, may be of interest to all serious students of American culture, wherever they reside, because it is at least an instructive episode in the history of the American intellect. Its intrinsic importance must not be exaggerated, but the issues it presents invest it with a fascination.

Perhaps a good way of attempting to place New England's Transcendentalism in a proper perspective is to review briefly the fortunes of Emerson's reputation in literary discourse of the last century. Indeed, the critical estimation of all the group around him has followed the same fluctuations—with, as we shall see, one exception. As Emerson repeatedly insisted, this was no organized band. They were simply a number of young people who around 1830 found themselves sharing a set of new ideas of which their elders disapproved. They were steadily ridiculed and finally attacked, especially after 1838 when Emerson delivered "The Divinity School Address" at Harvard. The graduate students had invited him; thereafter the faculty took away from the students the right to invite anybody.

Emerson was denounced by the greatest pundit of the Divinity School, Andrews Norton—who had been Emerson's mentor and was popularly known as "the Unitarian Pope"—for purveying "the Latest Form of Infidelity." What did Norton mean by infidelity? He made clear that the essence of Emerson's heresy was a trust in intuition, in direct perception of truth. Confident as was the Unitarian reliance on the powers of the human reason, Norton was certain that men have never by unassisted reason been able to attain assurance concerning fundamentals. But Emerson blandly asserted,

> The intuition of the moral sentiment is an insight of the perfection of the laws of the soul. These laws execute themselves. They are out of time, out of space, and not subject to circumstance.

It is not difficult to see wherein this notion would outrage the clergy, or indeed the faculty of Harvard College, or anybody who holds forth to an audience in time and space in an effort to instruct them on something which they are presumed not to know of themselves.

† From *Literary Views*, ed. Carroll Camden (Chicago: University of Chicago Press, 1964), pp. 115–29.

Emerson added insult to injury in a once famous passage which his Unitarian colleagues felt was a rude caricature of their pulpit manner:

> I once heard a preacher who sorely tempted me to say I would go to church no more. Men go, thought I, where they are wont to go, else had no soul entered the temple in the afternoon. A snow-storm was falling around us. The snow-storm was real, the preacher merely spectral, and the eye felt the sad contrast in looking at him, and then out of the window behind him into the beautiful meteor of the snow. He had lived in vain. He had no one word intimating that he had laughed or wept, was married or in love, had been commended, or cheated, or chagrined.

After all, we should not be too hard put to it to understand why dignified gentlemen of the stature of Andrews Norton would snort with rage when not only did they have to hear nonsense of this nature delivered from the pulpit of Divinity Hall but also to behold their students greeting it as wisdom. What minister then or now (or for that matter what professor in his classroom) who, instead of expounding doctrine or sticking to his subject matter, should talk to his audience of how often he had been in love, how many times married, and how frequently he had been chagrined and cheated, could expect to hold their attention for more than one relation?

Emerson himself never, of course, made such a ludicrous parade of his inward life on the lecture platform as this passage, had he taken it literally, would have obliged him to exhibit. But many of those who gathered around him—who in public opinion were known as his followers—invited the derision of proper Boston by conduct which, according to the standards of the day, was manifestly absurd. Jones Very, we can now perceive, was veritably insane. Margaret Fuller, possessed by her "mountainous me," indulged in extravagances of costume, rhetoric, and eventually of sexual daring which could bring only the most severe reprobation upon the ideas which she was supposed to have taken from the saintly Mr. Emerson. And indeed, in the considered opinion of respectable Boston and likewise of all solid New England, the supreme example of the pernicious consequences of Emerson's bland tuition was Henry Thoreau. Here was a youth who resolved not to be spectral as against the snowstorm. So he fled from all civic responsibilities, did not marry, begot no children, never held a steady job, paid no taxes, and lived alone as a hermit. No wonder that many then feared Transcendentalism to be, as Emerson ironically remarked, a "conspiracy against State Street."

The revolution in popular esteem was somehow wrought along with the Civil War. For thirty years after the "Divinity School Address" Emerson was officially ostracized from Harvard Yard, never officially asked to speak. But at long last, coincident with the election of Harvard's revolutionary President William Eliot, Emerson was chosen an overseer—on which board his first vote was for the retention of compulsory chapel! Harvard has long since done public penance for this neglect of one of its most distinguished children by naming its hall of philosophy for Emerson. In the lobby is a statue made by Daniel French; if you look at it carefully, especially when there are no other people about, you will see that it frequently lights up with an amused grin. By the end of the century, Oliver Wendell Holmes can write a biography of Emerson; Barrett Wendell considers him a pillar of the orthodox New England mentality, along with Longfellow and Lowell. Indeed, as early as 1876 O. B. Frothingham, in what was generally taken to be the definitive treatise, *Transcendentalism in New England*, presented the whole business as an American counterpart of the great German philosophical assertion of idealism. The once outcasts of Unitarian New England were now saluted as worthy equivalents of Kant, Fichte, and Schelling. So Frothingham could enthrone Emerson and surround him with his courtiers — Parker, Ripley, Hedge. Interestingly enough, however, in this work of canonization, Henry Thoreau is left out. Emerson and even the firebrand Parker might be made respectable, but not Thoreau.

Yet in the most complacent days of Emerson's elevation there were a few dissenting murmurs. Both Henry Adams and Charles Eliot Norton could be irritated by the dogmatic blindness of Emerson's resolute optimism. Their affectionate objections were, as the event proved, only mild prefigurations of the revolt which in the 1920's became a savage condemnation of what Santayana indelibly smeared as the "genteel tradition." Oddly enough the incendiary of 1838 now appeared the symbol of all that was most repulsive, evasive, emasculated in this blanket of gentility. He was now denounced not because he had preached a trust in intuition but because he was pale, sexless, and an imitator. He was demoted from the eminence he had so painfully acquired, on the grounds that he was entirely derivative. And by this time, the attitude of rejection of his optimism was an orthodoxy beyond any that Unitarianism ever dreamed of. Yet the fascination and complexity of the story increase as we note that in the 1920's the surge of Thoreau's reputation really gathered momentum.

I think it fair to say that the period when the favorite sport of commentators on American letters was making fun of Mr. Emerson came to an end with the passing of the vogue of H. L. Mencken. There has lately been considerable sane discussion of Emerson; while there is no need to reassert some of the extravagances of late nineteenth-century New England patriotism, still we can see him looming large precisely because, however great was his debt to Wordsworth or Coleridge, he was *not* derivative. His sanity, clear perception, and intermittent wit become the more highly prized the less we have to lament his emotional limitations. At the same time, we may welcome a similar steadying of the critical estimate of the group as a whole. Christopher Cranch, for example, has been receiving mature treatment, let alone Theodore Parker and George Ripley, for whom it is long overdue; Margaret Fuller is being rescued from the folds of adoring feminists who did their best to smother all evidences of her intellect. We are attaining a new, and I am sure a salutary, sense that though they were a small band and had little or no effect upon American politics and economy, their real importance is that they were the first (and in many respects most eloquent) protest of the American sensibility against what in their day was rapidly becoming and in ours has implacably remained a "business" civilization.

Inevitably the Transcendentalists' wails about the pressures of making a living or making money seem quaint to us. Their world was as yet so little industrialized or financialized, was still so close to the agrarian pastoralism of the eighteenth century, that we who know Pittsburgh and Wall Street may pardonably wonder what they had to complain about. But precisely here their prescience becomes remarkable. Emerson, with serenity and precision, became their spokesman, as for instance in "Man the Reformer," read before the Mechanics' Apprentices' Library Association in Boston on 25 January 1841:

> It cannot be wondered at that this general inquest into abuses should arise in the bosom of society, when one considers the practical impediments that stand in the way of virtuous young men. The young man, on entering

life, finds the way to lucrative employments blocked with abuses. The ways of trade are grown selfish to the borders of theft, and supple to the borders (if not beyond the borders) of fraud. The employments of commerce are not intrinsically unfit for a man, or less genial to his faculties; but these are now in their general course so vitiated by derelictions and abuses at which all connive, that it requires more vigor and resources than can be expected of every young man, to right himself in them; he is lost in them; he cannot move hand or foot in them. Has he genius and virtue? the less does he find them fit for him to grow in, and if he would thrive in them, he must sacrifice all the brilliant dreams of boyhood and youth as dreams; he must forget the prayers of his childhood and must take on him the harness of routine and obsequiousness.

One could easily compose an *explication* on this passage longer than this whole paper, simply on the connotations and even the unconscious implications of the superb vocabulary—"inquest," "supple," "intrinsically," "dreams of boyhood." The whole history of the impact of an evolving society upon an intellect utterly unprepared for what it was working upon itself is contained within this passage. But surely the most striking, and the most significant, phrases are in the concluding clauses, where the dreams of boyhood become "prayers," now harnessed to "routine and obsequiousness." Henry Thoreau would put the anguish more memorably: "Everywhere I go, men pursue me and paw me with their dirty institutions." Those of us today who annually on 15 April are pawed by the dirtiest of institutions can barely comprehend what Henry was talking about. Nevertheless, he conceived that the American order, even in that easy period, had already come to be one which pawed men into conformity, into obsequiousness, and above all into routine. And we suspect that the threat of the latter was to him and to Emerson the most repulsive—as it was to prove in the twentieth century to those more humiliatingly subjected to it.

Thus we are obliged to ask the central question: if these Transcendental children of a (to our way of thinking) relatively idyllic America were propelled to express so vehement a revolt against their society, from whence did the vehemence spring? Why a revolt at all? Here is the issue for historical and for critical appreciation.

One factor, a factor that must never be underestimated, was the impact of Europe. But is this to be rated, in the manner of O. B. Frothingham, the sole one, or even the chief one? Margaret Fuller no doubt received early in her tempestuous life the inspiration of Madame de Staël's *Corinne*, and it drove her through the rest of her career. The young men who issued during the early 1830's the various articles that became statements and manifestoes produced writings which are replete with invocations of names which meant nothing to Andrews Norton—strange, weird creatures like Herder, Coleridge, Benjamin Constant, John Paul Richter. The youths who pushed these reviews into the pages of the Unitarian *Christian Examiner*—until at last the editors put a stop to the nonsense—made an elaborate and generally awkward effort to speak the names with nonchalance, as though of course all cultivated persons knew who these authors were. For example, Frederic Hedge in an 1833 article on Coleridge (which years later he modestly claimed was the first in America to ask for a respectful recognition of Transcendentalism) declared with affected casualness, "In a review of Mr. Coleridge's literary life, we must not omit to notice that marked fondness for metaphysics, and particularly for German metaphysics, which has exercised so decisive an influence over all his writings." This innocent observation may seem to us merely Hedge's sharp recognition of historical contiguity, but to his elders in New England it was a flag of revolt, doubly unfurled.

When the faculty of the Harvard Divinity School—and along with them the professors at Harvard College—bestirred themselves to ask who were these foreign people, they discovered that Madame de Staël had had many lovers and that George Sand was still having them. For these reasons, even if not for a variety of more intellectual worries, men like Andrews Norton might justifiably have striven to relegate Emerson, Parker, and Ripley to a side show named the latest form of infidelity—and so of no pertinence to the life of any American mind. These heretics were none of our breeding; they were merely a few (as indeed they were) infatuated appropriators of obscure European notions. If this was all they had to say for themselves—and despite their volubility they seemed to have no more to say—they were a pale imitation of a pretentious and mystagogical German silliness. If this were what they were, then in America they were exotics. They were justifiably excluded from any effect, or even indirect influence, upon the development of American thought.

The exoticism of the Transcendentalists' figure in American life— if I may so use the term—has long figured as a hindrance to our comprehending their historical role. Nothing, I suppose, can more linger in the fantasy of tourists as a symbol of futility than the "Concord School of Philosophy," so assiduously visited by those who enter with reverence the house sanctified to the memory of Louisa May Alcott. Yet when Louisa May becomes the favorite of posterity above her ineffectual father, what is happening for the moment is a triumph of Andrews Norton over "infidelity." It is an insubstantial victory. If the American hostility to what Norton and his colleagues called the "German disease" was a vindication of their conception of Americanism, then they had yet to reckon with—in fact never did reckon with—the respects in which Transcendentalism was only in part an importation.

I am the last historian in America—I hope—who would endeavor to treat Transcendentalism as wholly, or even primarily, a native phenomenon. There is no gainsaying that as an intellectual perturbation it was as much stimulated from abroad as was the assiduous campaign, then fully in progress, for the appropriation to American circumstances of the English Common Law and of portions of the Continental Civil Law. New England Transcendentalism will always signify the effect upon an American provinciality of a European sophistication with which it was not entirely competent to deal—despite the swaggering assurances of such would-be pundits of the *Examiner* as Hedge, Ripley, Brownson, and Parker. But we have always this reflection to disturb us: from this influx—this lesson of discontent against routine, against "sensualism," against externalism in all its forms—came (to an America which by all proprieties should have been the ultimate in content) the message of discontent. And among the most sensitive of Americans, those who could easily have had no cause for discontent, the response was immediate. They instinctively, or intuitively, rebelled against the "sensualism" of a society which had barely begun to exhibit the enormity of its potential.

Once we can perceive the galvanizing effect of European ideas—of those we glibly term "romantic"—upon the domestic situation, we are tempted to suggest that "galvanic" is the wrong adjective:—they were catalytic. They did not so much arouse by imparting new viewpoints as they stirred latent propensities. They inspired these youths to reject all forms of what they called sensualism—and often these were quite indiscriminate in their application of the term. They gave the greatest offense by equating the sensational psychology of John Locke and the Scottish philosophers with profane sensualism. Since the Unitarian liberation from Calvinism had been achieved under the aegis of such thinkers, and since Unitarians were eminently men of probity and self-discipline, they could not help seeing in every invocation of the Germans a nasty aspersion on themselves. The young men never accused their elders of profligacy, but they were becoming so distressed by a society wherein things had leaped into the saddle that in order to object to being ridden they struck at the very foundation of the system they hated. Only when we appreciate fully both the spiritual and social gulf that the "German disease" (as most normal Americans called it) created can we comprehend how divisive was, for example, Hedge's advertising of the German virtues in his 1834 essay on Schiller:

> The class of writings, to which this work [a biography of Schiller] belongs, is peculiar, we believe, to modern times. It is characterized by a spirit of fierce disquietude, a dissatisfaction with the whole mechanism of society, and a presumptuous questioning of all that God or man has ordained. It represents a state of being which no word or combination of words can exactly express; a disease peculiar to ardent natures, in early life:
>
> > "The flash and outbreak of a fiery mind;
> > A savageness of unreclaimed blood;"
>
> a keen sensibility to all that is absurd and oppressive in social life, a scorning of authority and custom, a feeling that all the uses of this world are weary and unprofitable, together with the consciousness of high powers, bright visions of ideal excellence, and a restless yearning after things not granted to man.

Assuredly this was not a frame of mind that Harvard College or the Divinity School wanted in the least to cultivate! And even more assuredly, it was no mood in which to get ahead on State Street!

To students aware of the violence of the several European forms of Romantic tumult the words Emerson employed in his aged recollection of the 1830's in New England may seem melodramatic and ludicrously exaggerated. Yet they attest the accuracy of his failing memory, because they recapture what the "ardent natures" of the period deeply felt. "The key to the period," he wrote, "appeared to be that the mind had become aware of itself. Men grew reflective and intellectual." Previously the standard belief had been that "a shining social prosperity was the beatitude of man," but suddenly the conviction arose that the nation existed for the individual. In one of his finest sentences Emerson continues: "The young men were born with knives in their brain, a tendency to introversion, self-dissection, anatomizing of motives." Hence this new race hated "tolls, taxes, turnpikes, banks, hierarchies, governors, yea, almost laws." They rebelled against both theological and political dogmas, against saints "or any nobility in the unseen." If all this was not sedition and subversion, what was it? No wonder the ancient and the honorable of the earth heard here the crack of doom!

Thus our question becomes all the more pressing: why foment such a rebellion in America? We can readily understand how the contagion of the

French Revolution excited young Germans to arise against the decrepit and fos-silized system of petty principalities. We can comprehend why in France itself the populace were goaded into storming the prisons, burning chateaus, and cut-ting off the head of King Louis. We can also understand the rage of a Hazlitt or a Byron against the reactionary regime of King George. But in the United States we had no king to execute and no nobility to proscribe. We had got rid of all those encumbrances. America was prosperous, expanding, and there was abun-dant opportunity for all. From our point of view we may indeed ask where in all the history of the world were careers more open to talent, let alone genius, than in the nation of Andrew Jackson? What could the terms "conservative" or "re-actionary" mean in that community? Emerson's motto of "self-reliance," though it may have seemed infidelity to Andrews Norton, now appears to us the banner of the whole age, not just of a few eccentric Transcendentalists. What epoch was ever more self-reliant than that of Fulton and Morse, of steamboats and railroads, of the moving frontier, of the sewing machine and the Hoe press? Where could the individual more unhamperedly express himself? Emerson might sound terribly radical when he declared, "Whosoever would be a man must be a non-conformist," but even in his lifetime the sentence could be in-scribed on plaques in the offices of vice-presidents of banks. And why then were there so many efforts to escape the relation to even so loose a society as this, why Brook Farm and the myriad other would-be ideal communities? Henry Thoreau denounced the social order in the time of his Walden sojourn as a "joint stock company." Certainly compared with the regulations imposed upon our living today, our economy of giant corporations and foundations, the Amer-ica of Thoreau's day was a joyful chaos, a marvelous realm of rugged individu-alism and free competition which some of our presently styled "conservative" politicians dream can be revived.

The problem of properly evaluating Transcendentalism as a movement of protest in America is further complicated by the fact that in New England, be-cause of local historical circumstances, it was enmeshed in the controversy over the historicity of the miracles related in the New Testament. Norton and the Unitarian critics were not half so much enraged with Emerson for saying that truth is intuitive as they were for his concluding therefrom that in the name of intuitive truth mankind no longer needed the external (and sensual!) support of recorded exceptions to the laws of nature in order to be truly religious. To make the miracles a test of the spiritual mission of Christ was indeed to mana-cle the conception of a divine teacher to a sensual notion of history; it was to prostitute the possible meaning of the Gospel to exactly the same materiality of the commercial society against which the ardent natures were objecting. A "joint stock company" which pretended to be Christian and then could con-ceive of Christianity in only this way had already so lost the idea of spirituality as to call for a savageness of unreclaimed blood from those with knives in their brain.

Now a similar attack upon a literal acceptance of the biblical miracles was being levied in Europe. The historian of ideas may rightly see in it one among many manifestations of the new sense of historical process that everywhere was a symptom of the Romantic revolt against the age of static reason. Some of these European expressions exerted an influence in America or at least in New Eng-land, particularly Strauss's *Life of Jesus* in 1835. Yet actually these New Eng-landers were not so much inspired by the German "higher criticism," about which most of them (with the exception of Theodore Parker) knew very little, as they were by a disgust with the dogmatic way the Unitarianism in which they were raised had fastened upon the miracles as the sole attestation of spiritual reality. In Europe the debate over the historicity of the miracles and the quest for a historical Jesus is indeed an intense intellectual affair, but it is not central to the life of the mind. Nobody imagined that society would be toppled or morality destroyed because Strauss or Renan sought to put the Messiah into a historical context. But in Cambridge and Boston the Transcendentalists' reduction of the miracles to the plane of "nature" seemed infinitely more dangerous even than their denunciations of the joint stock company of society. Consequently a vast amount of the literature in the decade or so after Emerson's "Address," and a disproportionate amount of youthful energy, were expended in the sterile argument. In the larger perspective of American intellectual history this is not one of the major issues of the century—compared, let us say, with those of geology and then of evolution in relation to Christian belief. Because New England Transcendentalism could never rid itself of the incubus thus early fastened upon it, it always presents itself to a critical world as lamed by a provincial accident. It was parochial enough to begin with, but its effort to achieve at least an affectation of cosmopolitanism was sadly hindered by the fanatical demand of its enemies that it fight on the ground of their choosing.

And then we have a still more annoying puzzle in our endeavor to place the Transcendentalists both in time and space. They were undoubtedly stirred, even aroused by their importation of the intoxicating literature of European Romanticism. But the Europeans were intoxicating because, primarily, they were conducting a violent reaction against the eighteenth century. They universally denounced the previous age as one of sterility and frivolity, of the heroic couplet, of the rules, of the artificial vocabulary, as well as of political oppression. Especially in Germany was the regime of the petty courts identified with the corruption of French manners. We may find the image of those principalities given in *The Marriage of Figaro* charming (the scene is of course Germany and not the pretended Spain), but such antics were not so charming to the actual peasants and not at all to the intellectuals. Therefore the young Americans were avidly reading writers who burned with anger against the Enlightenment. Yet as Professor Alfred North Whitehead once remarked, in that casual profundity of which only he was capable, "the secret of understanding America is that it never had an eighteenth century." Many have objected against him that the Declaration of Independence is thoroughly of the century, Benjamin Franklin incarnates it, the Constitution is a product of it. Well, in a sense yes, but these manifestations are relatively few. We do not have an eighteenth-century experience in the way in which Voltaire is of the age, or Diderot is, or the German courts were. The American eighteenth century is squeezed in between Jonathan Edwards and the Second Awakening of 1800. It is fortunate for us that our great state papers and our War for Independence could be enacted in this interval, but even then the Enlightenment did not bite deeply into the Protestant, or if you will Puritan, heritage of the seventeenth century. We jump fairly abruptly from the rural, pious, hard-working world of the colonies into the nineteenth-century era of expansion, exploitation, movement, and romantic unrest.

In New England the Enlightenment can be said to have produced Unitarianism, or rather imparted to the provinces an atmosphere in which this could painlessly evolve out of Puritan intellectualism. But New England Unitarianism as compared with Continental Deism—with for example Helvetius—is very, very mild indeed. When therefore these young men with knives in their brain were becoming excited by books and articles denouncing the eighteenth century and they looked about them for something to denounce in their region, about all they could find for a target was this inoffensive Unitarianism. They had no need for resisting traditional Christianity. They were kept from fighting Calvinism because their Unitarian fathers and teachers stood between them and the orthodoxy of the back-country. It was not the Awakening or the Methodists who were oppressing them; it was this liberal Unitarianism that was crushing them in the vise of routine and obsequiousness. They aspired to be rebellious in terms comparable to those of their European heroes and heroines—Novalis, Herder, Madame de Staël, Carlyle—but they could not muster up a really profound revulsion against the past. The best they could manufacture was a revulsion against the very recent past, actually the present. They might suppose that they were being American Byrons but they had no way to get out of the moral patterns that ruled New England from the Puritan foundation and had never been shattered by any eighteenth-century cynicism. Their quarrel with their past was no satanic rebellion but only a shame that America had so little to show in the life of the mind. As Emerson beautifully summed up the American predicament in the opening paragraph of "The American Scholar" in 1837, our festivals so far have been simply a friendly sign of the persistence of a love of letters among a people too busy to produce any. The American task thus was not to reject the eighteenth century and the rule of reason, but to contend with the present: "Perhaps the time is already come when it ought to be, and will be, something else; when the sluggard intellect of this continent will look from under its iron lids and fill the postponed expectation of the world with something better than the exertions of mechanical skill." In this spirit he announced that the day of our dependence on the learning of other lands was drawing to a close—just in the very day that he and his contemporaries were finding a resolution to achieve independence in a voluminous absorption of the new learning of Romantic Europe!

New England Transcendentalism thus is, after all, a peculiarly American phenomenon: while New England did have a past, and sentient young persons like Emerson, Thoreau, and Margaret Fuller were entirely conscious of it, yet in a very real sense they were without a past. Or a more precise way of putting it is simply that they had no experience of the French Revolution and all its woes, no share in the disillusionment which came from committing oneself to the wild hope of the Revolution and then being broken by the Terror. They could read of these matters, and often talk fluently about them, but they did not actually *know*. One need only compare the heartbreaking account in Wordsworth's *The Prelude* with the lighthearted treatment of it in Emerson, particularly in the "Napoleon" chapter of *Representative Men*. Furthermore, in America there were no unrepentant revolutionaries who had to stand with their backs against the wall and maintain the radical stance against the tides of black reaction. We never had a Hazlitt. Perhaps the only American of the era who had at least some awareness of what the agony of keeping his head high amid defeat could be was Herman Melville, but his suffering was as remote from Transcendental comprehension as Hazlitt's.

The Transcendentalists are a part of the international movement historians call Romanticism. Their devotion to the Germans, to Wordsworth, to Victor Cousin, demonstrate their participation in it. Still, we have to say of them that an essential chapter in the biography of Romanticism is entirely missing in the lives of these Americans. It is as though, having barely passed the age of puberty and become adolescents at the age of eighteen, they awoke the next morning to find themselves aged thirty or so, having missed all those turbulent and charming perturbations of age twenty. Wherefore the peculiar pathos of their attempts to appropriate the delirium of a Romanticism they could not experience. There is something gallant and at the same time poignant in their efforts to play the role of men and women of the world. In this contradiction we may find—or at least I fancy we may—the compulsion behind their special veneration of *Nature*, behind Emerson's book so entitled in 1836, which is the heart of all their thinking and feeling. They go to Nature not for solace against the betrayals worked upon them by civilization and by reason, as in the last books of *The Prelude*, but for a source of the resistance which they must begin to put up against the iron lids of American mechanism. It is all they have to save them from routine and obsequiousness. In this respect the supreme statement—even more than Emerson's *Nature*—is, as time has now made clear, Thoreau's *Walden*.

Among the little band there is perhaps only one exception—Margaret Fuller. In 1846, after devouring more of the literature of Romanticism than any of her colleagues, and contributing to the American image of Europe, she at last went there and encountered the reality. She took part in a real revolution, the Roman one of 1848. She nursed wounded and dying men in the hospitals while her husband stood guard on the ramparts. She and he went down in defeat before the soldiers of reaction, and so she learned what Europe meant. One is moved to tears to find that she received from, as she called them, "the clean white hands" of Mr. Emerson, in the midst of the ordeal, a letter saying that Italy needs a great man. She shot back in cold anger, "Mazzini is a great man." But in Concord nobody could understand that. Nobody there could understand that she had bitten deep into the bitter fruit, and all were dismayed at the prospect of having to cope with her upon her return, complete with a husband (at least putative) and a child. Her cruel extinction in 1850 saved them the necessity.

They could therefore rest content with their original formulation of the American problem as an opposition or confrontation between nature and civilization. Out of this arose a happy version of the American genius. He stands amid Nature, and with it to assist him, to guide his steps aright, he will not be sucked into commerce or trade. He can ransom himself, Emerson told the mechanics, from the duties of economy by the rigor and privation of his habits:

> For privileges so rare and grand, let him not stint to pay a great tax. Let him be a caenobite, a pauper, and if need be, celibate also. Let him learn to eat his meals standing, and to relish the taste of fair water and black bread. He may leave to others the costly conveniences of housekeeping, and large hospitality, and the possession of works of art. Let him feel that genius is a hospitality, and that he who can create works of art needs not collect them. He must live in a chamber, and postpone his self-indulgence, forewarned and forearmed against that frequent misfortune of men of genius—the taste for luxury.

This taste for luxury—and Emerson clearly implies the luxuries of emotion and the senses as well as those of housekeeping—is the tragedy of genius. But there are many forms of tragedy. In *Walden*—which in part is the record of Henry's endeavor to act out the program Waldo outlined to the mechanics—Thoreau cried in unmistakably oratorical tones, "Simplify, simplify, simplify." The American genius thus stands amid Nature, either literally as did Thoreau or in dreams of it within the city as did Bryant in New York. He does not go to the left bank of Paris and live in a garret. He does not loll in splendor as did Goethe in Weimar. He does not even flee to the Alps of Switzerland, for they are rife with hotels. He stands for the concept of Nature against the iron lids, for Walden against State Street, for Concord against New York.

All this is to say that the Transcendentalists really stand for the moral innocence which they identify with Nature, against the corruptions of civilization. They might read Madame de Staël on Germany or Wordsworth's *Prelude*, but they could not understand why these writers were so up in arms against the eighteenth century. But they could understand that these found in Nature a defense against the wiles of artificiality, and this they could adopt as their defense against what in America was the threat to their innocence. And by this device they did not need to attribute a positive evil to that which they were opposing, as Carlyle would cheerfully behold nothing but depravity in the *ancien régime*. They would not have to say that Unitarians were wicked men, but merely that they had severed their hearts from Nature and so had become corpse-cold.

This maneuver has provided, as I noted to begin with, opportunities for uncomprehending readers to accuse the whole group, but especially Emerson, of having been morally obtuse. But a bit more exercise of a sympathic insight into the historical situation may find in this characterization not an indictment but an evidence of the reaction of a supple intellect to a situation in which any proclamation of an evil American eighteenth century would make no sense. It was not a contradiction in terms for Emerson to announce that our long day of dependence upon the learning of other lands was drawing to a close and in the same oration make an incantation of the great names the young Americans were still reverently studying.

> Meek young men grow up in libraries, believing it their duty to accept the views which Cicero, which Locke, which Bacon have given; forgetful that Cicero, Locke, and Bacon were only young men in libraries when they wrote these books.

The peculiar use of the word "scholar" by the Transcendentalists derives its special flavor from this background. They did not mean the professional scholar, delving for forgotten facts amid manuscripts and ancient tomes. The American scholar is a student but all the while a rebel against study. The point was—and still is—that the American independence had to be achieved *through* dependence. This is how America perforce stands in relation to the past. It is not going to achieve independence through violent assertions of the uniquely American quality of our experience or through discounting the influence of Byron on Herman Melville in order to set up some mythological native impetus as the true informing spirit of *Moby-Dick*. Emerson and the Transcendentalists were fully aware of this double pressure, this inner tension. Out of their consciousness comes their curious mingling of sophistication and innocence. This is a quality they variously exhibit, but it is pre-eminently displayed by Emerson and Thoreau. In the final analysis this Americanism is their indestructible virtue. It is their splendid ambiguity. On the one hand they talk of independence and on the other make clear their dependence. This very ambiguity—or possibly antinomy is a better word—is the reason for their growth in stature, despite the fluctuations of critical fashions. In this respect they stand firm, quite apart from the student's personal opinion of the concept of the "Over-Soul" or his liking or disliking the chapter on higher laws in *Walden*. They are spokesmen not merely for a tiny intellectual tempest in the New England teapot, but as representatives of a persistent problem in American culture, compounded of our dread and our joy. Is our culture entirely a satellite of the European or do we have a culture of our own? If our culture is both at once, how do we reconcile the two? Or rather, not reconcile—for that would be the death of us—but how hold them in suspension in order to conduct an active life of the mind by alternating pole to pole? If this conclusion has any validity, it may throw some light on the respects in which these New England writers are not merely local peculiarities but are indeed eminently national and profound expressions of the American spirit.

JOEL PORTE

The Problem of Emerson[†]

"The more we know him, the less we know him." Stephen Whicher's wistfully encomiastic remark epitomizes the not entirely unhappy perplexity of a highly influential group of scholars and critics, beginning perhaps with F. O. Matthiessen, who, returning to Emerson's writings with enormous sympathy, intelligence, and sensitivity, attempted to discover a real human figure beneath the bland (or pompous, or smug) official portrait. Predictably, in view of the compensatory biases of modernist criticism, they found a "new" Emerson whose complexities belied that older optimistic all-American aphorist once dear to captains of industry, genteel professors of literature, and hopeful preachers in search of suitably uplifting remarks. Like the other great figures of the American Renaissance, Emerson was now found to be one of us—as richly evasive and enigmatic a figure, almost, as Hawthorne, or Melville, or Dickinson. Not only is Emerson incapable of being "summed up in a formula," Whicher insisted, "he is, finally, impenetrable, for all his forty-odd volumes."[1]

Though somewhat obscure, Whicher's statement is also highly instructive. I say obscure, because (as with Matthiessen and Perry Miller) Whicher's discouragement about his failure to fathom the secret of one of America's greatest authors implies not only an inability to get at the meaning of American culture at large, but also a personal failure that finally baffles speculation. What is instructive in the remark is its insistence on penetrating to the heart of Emerson *the man* (since, surely, one of the most astute Emersonians of the twentieth century was not admitting that he could make no sense of the master's works). Although I shall myself concentrate here on the problem of getting to the heart of Emerson's *writing*, I think there is something to be learned from Whicher's

† From *Uses of Literature*, Harvard English Studies 4, ed. Monroe Engel (Cambridge, Mass.: Harvard UP, 1973), pp. 85–114.
1. Stephen E. Whicher, "Emerson's Tragic Sense." In *Emerson: A Collection of Critical Essays*, ed. Milton Konvitz and Stephen Whicher (Englewood Cliffs, N.J.: Prentice-Hall, 1962), p. 39.

interest in Emerson's character, for it focuses attention on an important aspect of the Emerson problem.

For one thing, the meaning and value of Emerson's work have typically been overshadowed, and frequently undermined, by an emphasis on his example and personal force. Two of his most distinguished critics offer representative remarks in this regard. Henry James, Jr., speaking for those who had known Emerson, properly emphasized the manner in which he made his impression, "by word of mouth, face to face, with a rare, irresistible voice and a beautiful mild, modest authority."[2] This is an appealing portrait, suggesting an ethereal attractiveness that clearly made Emerson humanly persuasive. Santayana roughly seconds James's point, but his description of Emerson's authority sharpens the issue somewhat:

> Those who knew Emerson, or who stood so near to his time and to his circle that they caught some echo of his personal influence, did not judge him merely as a poet or philosopher, nor identify his efficacy with that of his writings. His friends and neighbors, the congregations he preached to in his younger days, the audiences that afterward listened to his lectures, all agreed in a veneration for his person which had nothing to do with their understanding or acceptance of his opinions. They flocked to him and listened to his word, not so much for the sake of its absolute meaning as for the atmosphere of candour, purity, and serenity that hung about it, as about a sort of sacred music. They felt themselves in the presence of a rare and beautiful spirit, who was in communion with a higher world.[3]

Santayana's clear impatience here with that atmosphere of high-minded religiosity that always vitiated the New England air for him is not intended, I think, to imply a disparagement of Emerson, to whom he was fundamentally sympathetic. Certain difficulties, nevertheless, are suggested in this description of Emerson's virtual canonization as one of the leading saints in the select American hagiology. ("He is a shining figure as on some Mount of Transfiguration," wrote George Woodberry in 1906.)[4] What would be the fate of Emerson's writings when that "fine adumbration," as James called him, should himself be translated to the higher world? Would his literary reputation endure the dissipation of his rare personal emphasis? Worse, could his writings weather the inevitable iconoclasm that tumbles every American idol from his pedestal? "I was never patient with the faults of the good," Emerson's own Aunt Mary Moody is quoted as saying.[5] And the mild saint seems to have written his own epitaph when he noted, in *Representative Men*, that "every hero becomes a bore at last."[6]

2. This and all subsequent quotations from Henry James are taken from "Emerson," in *The Art of Fiction and Other Essays* (New York: Oxford University Press, 1948), pp. 220–240.
3. George Santayana, *Interpretations of Poetry and Religion* (New York: Scribner's, 1900), p. 217.
4. George Edward Woodberry, *Ralph Waldo Emerson*, repr. (New York: Haskell House, 1968), p. 1. In his *American Prose Masters* (1909) W. C. Brownell said that Emerson's presence was "suggestive of some new kind of saint—perhaps Unitarian." Twelve years earlier John Jay Chapman commented on the irony that this radical, who believed that "piety is a crime," should have been "calmly canonized and embalmed in amber by the very forces he braved. He is become a tradition and a sacred relic. You must speak of him under your breath, and you may not laugh near his shrine."
5. In Perry Miller, *The Transcendentalists: An Anthology* (Cambridge: Harvard University Press, 1950), p. 11.
6. Since the interested reader will have no difficulty locating quotations from Emerson's standard works (cited by name in the text), I have avoided the pedantry of elaborate documentation. References to Emerson's less accessible publications are duly noted.

As we know, Emerson's fate, somewhat like Shakespeare's, was that he came to be treated as an almost purely allegorical personage whose real character and work got submerged in his function as a touchstone of critical opinion. More and more, the figure of Emerson merged with current perceptions of the meaning and drift of American high culture, and the emblem overwhelmed his substance. To the younger generation of the nineties, for example, notably John Jay Chapman and Santayana, certain aspects of Emerson represented the pale summation of that attenuated genteel tradition with which they had lost patience. As the polemical mood sharpened over the next quarter-century or so, Emerson became a kind of *corpus vile* useful mainly for the dissection of American culture. To the Puritan-baiting intellectuals of the twenties, he stood for little more than the final weak dilution in the New England teapot; but for the conservative New Humanists, who—like Fitzgerald's Nick Carraway—"wanted the world to be in uniform and at a sort of moral attention forever," Emerson was the pre-eminent voice of the American conscience and the patron saint, accordingly, of their rearguard action.[7] Even T. S. Eliot, though he sympathized with the general position of the school of Babbitt and More, wrote in 1919, while praising Hawthorne, that "the essays of Emerson are already an encumbrance";[8] and Eliot's key word suggests not so much a literary burden as a *monumental* physical weight—the Lares and Penates of Victorian culture which the brave new Aeneases of the twenties were determined to jettison:

> Matthew and Waldo, guardians of the faith,
> The army of unalterable law.

The American master seemed to keep watch over outmoded standards of conduct, not the new canons of poetry. As a result, "in those days [the twenties]," asserts Malcolm Cowley, "hardly anyone read Emerson."[9] Such a quirky exception as D. H. Lawrence only proved the general rule, for this self-admitted "spiritual drug-fiend," despite his odd personal taste for Emerson, summarized the temper of the times when he argued, in 1923, that "all those gorgeous inrushes of exaltation and spiritual energy which made Emerson a great man now make us sick . . . When Professor [Stuart] Sherman urges us in Ralph Waldo's footsteps, he is really driving us nauseously astray." With a *"Sic transeunt Dei hominorum,"* Lawrence reluctantly ushered the tarnished deity from his niche.[1] The devils—Melville and Poe—were in, and the leading saint went marching out.

As I have noted, the "recovery" of Emerson that began largely in the forties and continues today is based on the sympathetic perception that beneath the seemingly ageless smiling public mask there lies a finite consciousness troubled with a tragic sense of contingency and loss—a little-known Emerson, as James said in 1887, with "his inner reserves and scepticisms, his secret ennuis and ironies." Indeed, most recently the saint has been turned not only inside out but upside down and shown to have a demonic bottom nature. In an im-

---

7. For a detailed history of this debate, see Richard Ruland, *The Rediscovery of American Literature* (Cambridge: Harvard University Press, 1967). Also useful in this connection is René Wellek's "Irving Babbitt, Paul More, and Transcendentalism," in *Transcendentalism and Its Legacy*, ed. Myron Simon and Thornton H. Parsons (Ann Arbor: University of Michigan Press, 1966), pp. 185–203.
8. Cited by F. O. Matthiessen in *The Achievement of T. S. Eliot* (New York: Oxford University Press, 1959), p. 24.
9. Malcolm Cowley, *Exile's Return* (New York: Viking Press, 1956), p. 227.
1. *A Dial Miscellany*, ed. William Wasserstrom (Syracuse, New York: Syracuse University Press, 1963), p. 151.

probable context of Siberian shamans become Thracian bards, Harold Bloom argues for a Bacchicly wild and primitivistic Emerson: "The spirit that speaks in and through him has the true Pythagorean and Orphic stink . . . The ministerial Emerson . . . is full brother to the Dionysiac adept who may have torn living flesh with his inspired teeth."[2]

The trouble with these strategies for redeeming Emerson is that they, too, like the Victorian apotheoses, are rooted in the character of the man (though in this case it is a presumably more appealing, because more complex, figure) and therefore depend for their force on our assenting to a particular reconstruction of Emerson's personality which may have little to do with the common reader's literary experience of Emerson. While praising Stephen Whicher's *Freedom and Fate: An Inner Life of Ralph Waldo Emerson*, Jonathan Bishop notes that "in the midst of one's appreciation for the achievement of this book, and the other works whose assumptions are comparable, one can still feel that the point of view adopted involves a certain neglect of the literary particulars."[3]

Though many literary particulars are brilliantly illuminated in Bishop's own book, which is undoubtedly the best modern reading of Emerson we have yet had, it unfortunately does not escape some of the typical difficulties of Emerson criticism. Predicated, like Whicher's work, on the notion that there is a "true, secret Emerson" who is the real and really interesting man we are after, *Emerson on the Soul* tells us that the reader's job is "to distinguish the excellent moments," which scarcely ever "exceed a page or two of sustained utterance" (though Bishop is uneasy with the old commonplace which argues that Emerson was little more than a sentence maker or at best a paragraph maker, he, too, sees little organic form in whole essays or books). This authentic Emerson—sometimes, indeed, by a kind of typographical mystification, identified as "Emerson"—predictably exhibits himself most freely in the private journals or letters. To arrive at these "interesting moments" in the public utterances, "one makes a drastic selection," avoiding "the dull tones, the preacherly commonplaces, the high-minded vapid identity" which obviously does not express the genuine Emerson we are seeking. The ability to recognize this profounder, more complex, more valuable tone may also serve as a kind of moral test of honesty in the reader, for "a coward soul is always free to interpret what Emerson says in a way that does not allow it to reach through to the places in him where matters are genuinely in a tangle." Rising to a pitch of almost religious fervor, Bishop claims finally that the authentic Emerson discoverable to our best selves can still serve as a hero and prophet for the American scholar. Thus, relying on a carefully controlled modern phenomenology of reading Emerson, Bishop reaches back fundamentally to join hands with the traditional notion that Emerson's highest value lies in the moral authority with which he utters permanent truths and thereby remains, as Arnold said, "the friend and aider of those who would live in the spirit."[4]

2. Harold Bloom, "Emerson: The Glory and the Sorrows of American Romanticism," *Virginia Quarterly Review*, 47 (Autumn 1971), 550.
3. Jonathan Bishop, *Emerson on the Soul* (Cambridge: Harvard University Press, 1964), p. 6.
4. *Emerson on the Soul*, pp. 130, 15, 106, 184, 131, 151; Matthew Arnold, *Discourses in America* (London, 1889), p. 179.

II

It was usual for Perry Miller, when initiating his survey of American authors, to insist on the notion that "writing is written by writers." This innocent tautology was intended to convey the idea that the great figures being studied were not primarily to be considered as landmarks in the growth of American culture nor as so many statues in an imaginary pantheon whom it was our patriotic duty to revere, but rather as *writers* whose continuing claim on our attention resides in their exhaustless *literary* vitality. Writing is not necessarily written by famous authors, with beards and visitable houses; it is the fruit of patient labor by men and women fundamentally, and often fanatically, devoted to their craft. Books, as Thoreau says in *Walden*, "must be read as deliberately and reservedly as they were written." And such a reading is encouraged by thinking of authors primarily as writers, and only secondarily as famous hermits, spinsters, he-men, statesmen, spiritual leaders, madmen, madwomen, or the like.

Now, it is a curious fact that Emerson, who is often acknowledged to be the greatest, or at least most important, author of the American Renaissance and even of American literary history altogether, has manifestly not been accorded that careful scrutiny of his work *as writing* which Poe, Hawthorne, Melville, Thoreau, Dickinson, Whitman, and other more minor figures, have received in superabundance. The heart of the problem seems to lie, as I have already suggested, in the overwhelming, indeed intimidating, emphasis on Emerson's personal authority, his example, his wisdom, his high role as the spiritual father and Plato of our race. Even so sharp a critic as Henry James, with his exquisitely developed sense of writing as a craft, was blinded from seeing any pervasive formal excellence in Emerson's work by the "firmness" and "purity," the "singular power," of Emerson's moral force— his "particular faculty, which has not been surpassed, for speaking to the soul in a voice of direction and authority." Though James assumed Emerson's "importance and continuance" and insisted "that he serves and will not wear out, and that indeed we cannot afford to drop him," he did so only as a special tribute to this great man, allowing him to be "a striking exception to the general rule that writings live in the last resort by their form; that they owe a large part of their fortune to the art with which they have been composed." Despite occasional "felicities, inspirations, unforgettable phrases," James felt it was "hardly too much, or too little, to say of Emerson's writings in general that they were not composed at all." He never truly achieved "a fashion and a manner" and finally "differs from most men of letters of the same degree of credit in failing to strike us as having achieved a style." James concluded his survey of Emerson's career by positing a large and significant *if*: "if Emerson goes his way, as he clearly appears to be doing, on the strength of his message alone, the case will be rare, the exception striking, and the honour great."

It should be a matter of some interest, and no little amusement, for us to note that Henry's scientific brother was moved to make precisely the claim for Emerson, at the centenary celebration, which the distinguished novelist and critic had withheld. "The form of the garment was so vital with Emerson that it is impossible to separate it from the matter. They form a chemical combination—thoughts which would be trivial expressed otherwise, are important through the nouns and verbs to which he married them. The style is the man, it has been said; the man Emerson's mission culminated in his style, and if we must define him in one word, we have to call him Artist. He was an artist whose medium was verbal and who wrought in spiritual material."[5] Perhaps it was the unsatisfied artist in William James himself, as Santayana describes him,[6] who was enabled to make these observations about Emerson which, though almost universally ignored, have scarcely been bettered: his "thoughts . . .would be trivial expressed otherwise"; his "mission culminated in his style." William James's valuable hints have not been picked up, and Henry's prescient *if* has progressively exerted its force. Emerson, as any candid teacher of American literature can report, has manifestly *not* made his way "on the strength of his message." He has become the least appreciated, least enjoyed, least understood—indeed, least read—of America's unarguably major writers. Even most intelligent and willing students, dropped in the usual way into the great *mare tenebrum* of Emerson's weightier works, gratefully return to shore, dragging behind them only out of a sense of duty a whale of a précis of Emerson's "message," which, they will usually admit, contains little meaning and less pleasure for them. Nor have students of Emerson's writing received much practical help from well-intentioned critics who, while praising Emerson as a prophet of romanticism, or symbolism, or existentialism, or pragmatism, or organicism, sadly concede that the master's reach exceeded his grasp so far as exemplifying the particular *-ism* in successful works of literary art is concerned. Seen from this perspective as a flawed genius whose theory and practice were always disjunct, Emerson may exasperate by seeming to promise more than he can perform. As Charles Feidelson says, "what he gives with one hand he takes away with the other."[7]

I have myself, to echo the conclusion of *Nature*, come to look at the world of Emerson with new eyes and been greatly gratified and exhilarated to discover a kind of verification of my views in the—surprisingly—delighted reactions of students. The Emerson we now see, I am convinced, has always existed; indeed it is the same Emerson whom William James was moved to praise as an artist. This Emerson's interest and appeal reside in the imaginative materials and structures of his writing—in his tropes and *topoi*, his metaphors and verbal wit, in the remarkable consistencies of his conceiving mind and executing hand. What I am prepared to state categorically is that the familiar rubrics of Emersonian thought, the stock in trade of most Emerson criticism, though undeni-

5. William James, "Address at the Emerson Centenary in Concord," in *Emerson: A Collection of Critical Essays*, p. 19. W. C. Brownell's comment manages to echo both Jameses at once. Though "no writer ever possessed a more distinguished verbal instinct, or indulged it with more delight" than Emerson, his style is that "of a writer who is artistic, but not an artist." Emerson had "no sense of composition; his compositions are not composed. They do not constitute objective creations. They have no construction, no organic quality—no evolution . . . art in the constructive sense found no echo in Emerson's nature." See *American Prose Masters*, ed. Howard Mumford Jones (Cambridge: Harvard University Press, 1963), pp. 125–127.

6. In *Character and Opinion in the United States* (1920).

7. Charles Feidelson, Jr., *Symbolism and American Literature* (Chicago: University of Chicago Press, 1953), p. 150. An example of how much Emerson needs protection from his "friendly" critics is afforded by this quotation from Norman Foerster's "Emerson on the Organic Principle in Art": "To Emerson . . . it was a fundamental conception capable of answering all our questions about the nature and practice of art. It is true that in his own writing, his own practice of art, Emerson was notoriously deficient in the organic law in its formal aspect; his essays and poems are badly organized, the parts having no definite relation to each other and the wholes wanting that unity which we find in the organisms of nature. Rarely does he give us even a beginning, middle, and end, which is the very least that we expect of an organism, which, indeed, we expect of a mechanism. Yet if he could not observe the law of organic form, he could interpret it; in this matter his practice and theory are not equivalent—happily, he could see more than he could do" (*Emerson: A Collection of Critical Essays*, pp. 109–110). The Emerson who was too impotent artistically to produce even a respectable machine is thus "praised" for envisioning what a truly living art might be! Though one might be tempted to say something harsh about such jejune remarks as these, Professor Foerster's blandly thoughtless "happily" simply baffles judgment.

ably there, are a positive hindrance to the enjoyment of Emerson's writing. Though some Emersonians will undoubtedly continue until the end of time to chew over such concepts as Compensation, the Over-Soul, Correspondence, Self-Reliance, Spiritual Laws, *et id genus omne*, the trouble with such things is that they are not very interesting. They make Emerson seem awfully remote, abstract, and—yes—academic. My experience has been that when these topics are mentioned the mind closes, one's attention wanders . . . Similarly, the now standard debate over Emerson's presumed inability, or refusal, to confront evil (usually capitalized) has had the unfortunate effect first of making him seem shallow compared, say, to a Hawthorne or a Melville; and, second and more importantly, it has frequently shifted discussions of Emerson to a high plane of theological or metaphysical argument where one's ordinary sense of reality, and the powers of practical criticism, falter in pursuit. Evil with a capital has a way of teasing the imagination into silence.

My thesis then is simple: Emerson, as he himself frequently insisted, is fundamentally a poet whose meaning lies in his manipulations of language and figure. The best guide to change, or growth, or consistency in Emerson's thought, is his poetic imagination and not his philosophic arguments or discursive logic. The alert reader can discover, and take much pleasure in discovering, remarkable verbal strategies, metaphoric patterns, repetitions and developments of sound, sense, and image throughout Emerson's writing. One finds an impressively unified consciousness everywhere in control of its fertile imaginings.[8]

As an initial illustration of what I am claiming for Emerson's work, I would momentarily leave aside the juiciest plums—*Nature*, the "Divinity School Address," the great essays—and turn briefly to a book for which, probably, only the most modest assertions of imaginative unity can be made, hoping, nevertheless, that its example will prove instructive. Like most nineteenth-century travel books, *English Traits* cannot be expected to succeed entirely in transcending the somewhat episodic nature of its author's peregrinations and his own normal desire, with his varied audience in mind, to include something of interest to everyone. Typically, since such an omnium-gatherum will amiably avoid pushing toward overwhelming conclusions and let its appeal reside precisely in its miscellaneous character, any search for organic form seems defeated at the outset. Still, we are dealing with the inescapable consistencies of Emerson's shaping imagination.

In the preface to a recent edition of *English Traits*, Howard Mumford Jones confronts Emerson's difficulty in making a unified book of his heterogeneous materials and complains specifically that Emerson spoiled the natural form of his work by beginning with a chapter on his first, earlier visit to England and concluding, not logically with "Results," but anticlimactically with his "Speech at Manchester."[9] I believe, however, that the sympathetic reader of *English Traits* can supply some possible justifications for Emerson's procedure. The opening chapter is an expression of disappointment with England, and this

8. There are some valuable observations on "Emerson as literature" in James M. Cox, "Emerson and Hawthorne: Truth and Doubt," *Virginia Quarterly Review*, 45 (Winter 1969), 88–107. Professor Cox writes of "metaphor as action" in Emerson's work.

9. *English Traits*, ed. Howard Mumford Jones (Cambridge: Harvard University Press, 1966), p. xv. Though Philip Nicoloff, in his exhaustive study of *English Traits*, also sees little justification for the opening and concluding chapters (indeed, he claims that the whole book is "not so shapely a production as has often been suggested, either in its entirety or in its parts"), he does find an intellectual pattern in *English Traits* based on Emerson's belief in the necessity of racial and historial evolution—growth and decline. Emer-

is the keynote of the book. Here, the disappointment, though it has a personal basis, is emblematic of the young American's unfulfilled expectations of the Old World and prophetic of his developing hope for America. He goes abroad eager to meet certain great men—Landor, Coleridge, Carlyle, Wordsworth— and finds them sadly isolated, mutually repellent, and embittered, "prisoners . . . of their own thought" who cannot "bend to a new companion and think with him." They thus fail as poets in Emerson's own high sense (as "liberating gods," that is, who help man "to escape the custody of that body in which he is pent up, and of that jail-yard of individual relations in which he is enclosed"). Their vaunted originality somehow evaporates for the young seeker: Coleridge's talk falls "into certain commonplaces"; Wordsworth expiates his "departure from the common in one direction" by his "conformity in every other." Significantly, both Carlyle and Wordsworth talk much of America, turning Emerson's thoughts back whence he came and pointing us forward to Emerson's peroration in Manchester, where he will, as delicately as possible, summarize his negative reaction to this "aged England," this "mournful country," with its pathetically atomistic island mentality, its conformity to custom, its played out spirit, and suggest that if England does not find new vigor to restore her decrepit old age (as the weight of his whole book tends to prove it cannot), "the elasticity and hope of mankind must henceforth remain on the Alleghany ranges, or nowhere."

The huge, virtually endless American continent is the mysterious force against which Emerson measures the fixed, finite, island prison, the "Gibraltar of propriety," which is England. Here we have the central imaginative structure of *English Traits*. Though initially England seems "a paradise of comfort and plenty," "a garden," we quickly learn that this miracle of rare device, like Spenser's Bower of Bliss, is a false paradise where "art conquers nature" and, "under an ash-colored sky," confounds night and day. Coal smoke and soot unnaturally make all times and seasons of one hue, "give white sheep the color of black sheep, discolor the human saliva, contaminate the air, poison many plants and corrode the monuments and buildings." This is the epitome of the fallen modern world of industry, where "a terrible machine has possessed itself of the ground, the air, the men and women, and hardly even thought is free." Everything, we are told, "is false and forged," "man is made as a Birmingham button," and "steam is almost an Englishman." The whole island has been transformed into the thoroughfare of trade where all things can be described, in Emerson's eyes, as either "artificial" or "factitious": the breeds of cattle, the fish-filled ponds and streams, the climate, illumination, heating, the English social system, the law, property, crimes, education, manners, customs—indeed, "the whole fabric." All is "Birminghamized, and we have a nation whose existence is a work of art—a cold, barren, almost arctic isle being made the most fruitful, luxurious and imperial land in the whole earth."

In this setting, we are not surprised to learn that the two most mysterious and imponderable of life's gifts, religion and art, are particularly vulnerable to the general fate. Since these two subjects touch the quick of Emerson's con-

---

son's theories thus led him to see England as an exhausted species passing on its genetic heritage to the country of the future, i.e., America. My argument here is that the metaphoric structure of *English Traits* precisely reinforces this doctrine. See Philip Nicoloff, *Emerson on Race and History* (New York: Columbia University Press, 1961). Cf. also Ralph Rusk, *The Life of Ralph Waldo Emerson* (New York: Columbia University Press, 1957), pp. 393ff.

cern, it is especially fascinating to note in this regard how the fundamental paradigm of America (as revealed in and through its transcendental minister, Emerson) against which all is being tested palpitates within Emerson's language and metaphors. True religion is utterly missing from England, for it is an alien and frightful thing to the English: "it is passing, glancing, gesticular; it is a traveler, a newness, a surprise, a secret, which perplexes them and puts them out." We should keep this consciously orphic sentence in our ear as we glance at the next chapter, "Literature," on the way to Emerson's culminating vision of America. Speaking of English genius, Emerson notes: "It is retrospective. How can it discern and hail the new forms that are looming up on the horizon, new and gigantic thoughts which cannot dress themselves out of any old wardrobe of the past?" Now, the alert student of Emerson will recognize here an unmistakable echo of the opening paragraph of *Nature* ("Our age is retrospective . . . why should we grope among the dry bones of the past, or put the living generation into masquerade out of its faded wardrobe . . . There are new lands, new men, new thoughts"). What this echo should tell us is that the very same living, prospective, titanic American nature which, Emerson insisted in 1836, would inspire a new poetry and philosophy and religion of "revelation," as opposed to the backward-looking, dead, limited British tradition—that "great apparition," as he terms it in *Nature*, is fully present to Emerson's imagination twenty years later in *English Traits* as he attempts to explain what the English spirit dares not face and isolates itself from. Walking the polished halls of English literary society, Emerson seems to find himself "on a marble floor, where nothing will grow," and he concludes that the English "fear the hostility of ideas, of poetry, of religion—ghosts which they cannot lay . . . they are tormented with fear that herein lurks a force that will sweep their system away. The artists say, 'Nature puts them out.'" Recalling the opening paragraph of *Nature* and hearing still that orphic sentence from the preceding chapter on religion, we may now feel confirmed in our intuition about Emerson's real point: that great force which threatens the English and "puts them out" is equivalent to the religio-poetic mystery of American nature.

Emerson's metaphoric confrontation between England and America, which represents the true symbolic thrust of *English Traits*, culminates most forcefully and appropriately in the fourth chapter from the end, entitled "Stonehenge." Traveling with Carlyle, who argues that the English have much to teach the Americans, Emerson concedes the point but does not budge from his instinctive belief: "I surely know that as soon as I return to Massachusetts I shall lapse at once into the feeling, which the geography of America inevitably inspires, that we play the game with immense advantage; that there and not here is the seat and centre of the British race; and that no skill or activity can long compete with the prodigious natural advantages of that country, in the hands of the same race; and that England, an old and exhausted island, must one day be contented, like other parents, to be strong only in her children." Emerson's conviction that the English mind is simply rendered impotent by, and turns away self-defensively from, the enormously perplexing forces that embosom and nourish us seems strengthened by his visit to Stonehenge itself: "The chief mystery is, that any mystery should have been allowed to settle on so remarkable a monument, in a country on which all the muses have kept their eyes now for eighteen hundred years." Ignoring this strange and unsettling secret at the heart of its own island, the English mind leaves Stonehenge "to the rabbits, whilst it

opens pyramids and uncovers Nineveh." Emerson completes this series of speculations and, in a very real sense, the point of his whole book in a fine paragraph
toward the end of "Stonehenge" that at once expresses his own sense of America's ineffable power and his firm belief that the Englishman is unable to comprehend it:

> On the way to Winchester, whither our host accompanied us in the
> afternoon, my friends asked many questions respecting American land-
> scapes, forests, houses,—my house, for example. It is not easy to answer
> these queries well. There, I thought, in America, lies nature sleeping, over-
> growing, almost conscious, too much by half for man in the picture, and
> so giving a certain *tristesse*, like the rank vegetation of swamps and forests
> seen at night, steeped in dews and rains, which it loves; and on it man
> seems not able to make much impression. There, in that great sloven con-
> tinent, in high Alleghany pastures, in the sea-wide sky-skirted prairie, still
> sleeps and murmurs and hides the great mother, long since driven away
> from the trim hedge-rows and over-cultivated garden of England. And, in
> England, I am quite too sensible of this. Every one is on his good behav-
> ior and must be dressed for dinner at six. So I put off my friends with very
> inadequate details, as best I could.

In the face of such a passage as this, the critic of Emerson may be commended
most for appreciative silence.[1] I want only, with these lines in mind, to under-
line my previous point about this book and Emerson generally: namely, that the
excellent moments in his writing are not, as has so often been said, incidental

---

1. Still, the impulse to comment on this strange paragraph is hard to resist, though it may threaten to carry
one far afield. Emerson's desire to express what he seems to feel is the primitive source of America's natural power leads him into a quasi-Frazerian fantasy in which he creates a myth-figure, "the great mother,"
who has the sort of terrifying appeal of that Yeatsian "rough beast" which "slouches toward Bethlehem
to be born." Emerson's rank goddess seems to live in a solitude which is at once sad from the human
point of view (*tristesse*) and yet necessary, for what man—even a mammoth American hero—could
marry such a creature, a thing of night and water which "sleeps and murmurs and hides" like some holy
outcast? The operative word here is *sloven*, not simply because it contrasts America's sprawling disorder
with England's enclosed neatness, but more crucially because it suggests a kind of fecund dirtiness and
lewdness ("lewd" is in fact an old meaning of the word) which constitutes the secret force of the American earth. Thus, Emerson seems to see the two countries in sexual terms, England being an "aged" and
"exhausted" woman worn out "with the infirmities of a thousand years," whereas the American mother
maintains a frightening but fertile attractiveness. With her will mate Emerson's superhuman national
Poet, whose thought, "ejaculated as Logos or Word," arises like the mother's body from the dark and dank
substratum of human life ("Doubt not, O poet, but persist. Say 'It is in me, and shall out.' Stand there,
baulked and dumb, stuttering and stammering, hissed and hooted, stand and strive, until, at last, rage
draw out of thee that *dream*-power which every night shows thee is thine own; a power transcending all
limit and privacy, and by virtue of which a man is the conductor of the whole river of electricity"). One
moves directly from all of this to "Song of Myself":

> I am he that walks with the tender and growing night;
> I call to the earth and sea half-held by the night.
> Press close barebosomed night!
> Press close magnetic nourishing night . . .
> Smile O voluptuous coolbreathed earth!
> Earth of the slumbering and liquid trees! . . .
> Smile, for your lover comes!

I am also reminded of another American genius who combined spiritual fastidiousness with a taste for
the "arrant stinks" of the new world. Wallace Stevens' aesthetician of *mal*, like the Emerson of the paragraph we have been examining,

> sought the most grossly maternal, the creature
> Who most fecundly assuaged him, the softest
> Woman with a vague moustache and not the mauve
> *Maman*. His anima liked its animal

gems in a disjointed mosaic, but typically the shining nodal points in a carefully woven imaginative web.

III

Although some Emerson scholars in our own time have noticed that certain motifs or metaphors are central to Emerson's literary project, their perceptions have by and large been ignored in practical Emerson criticism. Three important examples, all from Emerson scholarship now more than two decades old, will illustrate my point. In *Emerson's Angle of Vision*, Sherman Paul taught us that "for Emerson the primary agency of insight was seeing"; the eye "was his prominent faculty." Another valuable perception was offered by Vivian C. Hopkins in *Spires of Form*, where she asserted that "Emerson's own term of 'the spiral' admirably hits the combination of circular movement with upward progress which is the heart of his aesthetic. Optimism controls Emerson's idea of the circle becoming a spiral, ever rising as it revolves upon itself." Finally, Stephen Whicher, writing on "Emerson's Tragic Sense," noted that "something resembling the Fall of Man, which he had so ringingly denied, reappears in his pages."[2] I want to suggest, very briefly, how useful an awareness of three such motifs as these, often in combination with one another, can be, not only for the illumination of individual essays and books, but also for an understanding of change or development overall in Emerson's work.

Although every reader of *Nature* since 1836 has taken special notice of the famous eyeball passage, either to praise or to ridicule its extravagance, surprisingly few students or even teachers of Emerson, in my experience, are aware that in this metaphor resides the compositional center of gravity of the essay.[3] Despite Emerson's insistence in this crucial paragraph that his purpose is to "see all," to become nothing more nor less than *vision*, readers of *Nature* seem generally not to notice that in the magnificent opening sentence of the piece— "Our age is retrospective"—the key word means precisely what it says and is rhetorically balanced by the title of the last section—"Prospects." It is a question of seeing in a new way, a new direction. Emerson is inviting us to behold "God and nature face to face," with our own eyes, not darkly and obscurely through the lenses of history. *Nature* concerns the fall of man into perceptual division from his physical environment. Salvation is nothing less than perceptual reunification—true *sight* externally and *insight* internally. The Poet, the *seer*, as Emerson was to suggest in the essay of that name, is a type of the savior "who re-attaches things to nature and the Whole" through his vision:

And liked it unsubjugated, so that home
Was a return to birth, a being born
Again in the savagest severity . . .

The Collected Poems of Wallace Stevens (New York: Knopf, 1957), p. 321.

2. Sherman Paul, *Emerson's Angle of Vision* (Cambridge: Harvard University Press, 1952), pp. 72–73; Vivian C. Hopkins, *Spires of Form: A Study of Emerson's Aesthetic Theory* (Cambridge: Harvard University Press, 1951), p. 3; Stephen Whicher, "Emerson's Tragic Sense," in *Emerson: A Collection of Critical Essays*, p. 42.

3. Notable exceptions are: Kenneth Burke, "I, Eye, Ay—Emerson's Early Essay 'Nature': Thoughts on the Machinery of Transcendence," in *Transcendentalism and Its Legacy*, pp. 3–24; Tony Tanner, *The Reign of Wonder* (New York: Harper and Row, 1967), chapter 2, "Emerson: The Unconquered Eye and the Enchanted Circle"; Richard Poirier, *A World Elsewhere* (New York: Oxford University Press, 1966), chapter 2, "Is There an I for an Eye?: The Visionary Possession of America." See also Warner Berthoff, *Fictions and Events* (New York: Dutton, 1971), " 'Building Discourse': The Genesis of Emerson's *Nature*," especially pp. 209–213. This trenchant essay, much less restricted in scope than its title suggests, is the best general introduction to Emerson that I know.

As the eyes of Lyncæus were said to see through the earth, so the poet turns the world to glass, and shows us all things in their right series and procession. For, through that better perception, he stands one step nearer to things, and sees the flowing or metamorphosis . . . This insight, which expresses itself by what is called Imagination, is a very high sort of seeing, which does not come by study, but by the intellect being where and what it sees, by sharing the path or circuit of things through forms, and so making them translucid to others.

The echoes of *Nature* in this passage from "The Poet" tell us that we can all become our own poet-savior by becoming pellucid lenses, transparent eye-balls, and perfecting our vision. "The eye is the best of artists"; "the attentive eye" sees beauty everywhere; wise men pierce the "rotten diction" of a fallen world "and fasten words again to visible things," achieving a viable "picturesque language"; "a right action seems to fill the eye"; "insight refines" us: though "the animal eye" sees the actual world "with wonderful accuracy," it is "the eye of Reason" that stimulates us "to more earnest vision." Mounting to his splended peroration in "Prospects," Emerson reminds us that "the ruin or the blank, that we see when we look at nature, is in our own eye. The axis of vision is not co-incident with the axis of things, and so they appear not transparent but opake." A cleansing of our vision is all that is required for "the redemption of the soul." In such a case, Emerson says at the start of his last paragraph, we shall "come to look at the world with new eyes." Since "what we are, that only can we see," we must make ourselves whole again. Emerson culminates his quasi-religious vision with a ringing sentence that catches up the Christian undertone of the essay and assimilates it to the naturalistic premise of America's nascent literary hopes: "The kingdom of man over nature, which cometh not with observation,—a dominion such as now is beyond his dream of God,—he shall enter without more wonder than the blind man feels who is gradually restored to perfect sight." Emerson's last word, of course, underlines once again the point of the whole essay. And the important allusion here to Luke 17:20–21 (unfortunately not noted in the new Harvard edition of *Nature*) tells us that the visionary perfection we seek has stolen upon us unawares and lies waiting within.[4]

This heady faith, expressed in the controlling metaphor of *Nature*, which believes that clarified sight can literally reform our world, for the most part governs the first series of Emerson's *Essays* and is embodied in the opening sentence of "Circles": "The eye is the first circle; the horizon which it forms is the second." Emerson's meaning, enforced here by a favorite pun and emphasized throughout "Circles" (when a man utters a truth, "his eye burns up the veil which shrouded all things"; when the poet breaks the chain of habitual thought, "I open my eye on my own possibilities"), is that the self, represented here by the creative eye, is primary and generative: it *forms* the horizon—goal, world view—that it sees. This is the "piercing eye" of Uriel which, in the poem of that name, is described as "a look that solved the sphere." But, as we know, by the

---

4. Emerson uses the same sentence from Luke in "Experience." Cf. M. H. Abrams, *Natural Supernaturalism: Tradition and Revolution in Romantic Literature* (New York: Norton, 1971), p. 47; see also pp. 411ff. For an understanding of the Romantic context of *Nature*, one could hardly do better than to study Professor Abrams' brilliant exposition of the central Romantic motifs (the transvaluation of religious "vision"; the reinterpretation of the fall of man; the significance of the Romantic spiral). Since I cannot quote as much of this absorbing book as I should like, I shall content myself with simply recommending it to all students of Emerson. Professor Abrams' key text, by the way—Wordsworth's "Prospectus" for *The Recluse*—might have served Emerson as doctrine for *Nature*.

time Emerson came to write "Uriel" in the mid-1840's his "lapse" had already taken place and his own reference to the "ardent eye" (as Thoreau was to term it) is consciously ironic.[5] Indeed, and this is my central point, as we move into his second series of *Essays* and beyond, we may verify the fundamental shift in Emerson's optative mood brought about by his "sad self-knowledge" through simply observing the transformations that his visual metaphor undergoes. In the crucial "Experience," for example, Emerson accedes to the notion of the Fall of Man, redefining it as "the discovery we have made that we exist" — the discovery, that is, that the individual consciousness is limited and contingent. "Ever afterwards we suspect our instruments. We have learned that we do not see directly, but mediately, and that we have no means of correcting these colored and distorting lenses which we are." Emerson now has only a "perhaps" to offer concerning the "creative power" of our "subject-lenses," and he serves up his own optimistic perception from "Circles" in a new, markedly qualified, form: "People forget that it is the eye which makes the horizon." What we have created is no more than an optical illusion. Emerson further confirms his diminished sense of personal power later in the book, in the first paragraph of "Nominalist and Realist," when his trope reappears: "We have such exorbitant eyes that on seeing the smallest arc we complete the curve, and when the curtain is lifted from the diagram which it seemed to veil, we are vexed to find that no more was drawn than just that fragment of an arc which we first beheld. We are greatly too liberal in our construction of each other's faculty and promise." It is worth noticing, by the way, how the quintessentially figurative nature of Emerson's imagination has unerringly guided him to the witty choice of "exorbitant" in this passage.

But an even more impressive example, in this regard, of the progressive metamorphosis of Emerson's metaphor as his perceptions changed may be found in "Fate." By 1852, when the essay was completed, Emerson had so qualified his views that Nature, which sixteen years before was the book of life and possibility, became now "the book of Fate." In 1836 Emerson asserted in "Prospects" that "nature is not fixed but fluid. Spirit alters, moulds, makes it . . . Every spirit builds itself a house, and beyond its house a world, and beyond its world a heaven." Now he was forced tragically to concede that "every spirit makes its house; but afterwards the house confines the spirit." Faced with this crushing sense of limitation, Emerson returned to his favorite metaphor in a new, notably ironic, mood:

> The force with which we resist these torrents of tendency looks so ridiculously inadequate that it amounts to little more than a criticism or protest made by a minority of one, under compulsion of millions. I seemed in the height of a tempest to see men overboard struggling in the waves, and driven about here and there. They glanced intelligently at each other, but 'twas little they could do for one another; 'twas much if each could keep afloat alone. Well, they had a right to their eye-beams, and all the rest was Fate.

Here, sight, as Jonathan Bishop has remarked well, "the sense especially associated with the intellectual freedom of the Soul, has dwindled until it can pro-

---

5. Compare my own "Transcendental Antics," in *Veins of Humor*, Harvard English Studies 3, ed. Harry Levin (Cambridge: Harvard University Press, 1972), pp. 180–182.

vide only a bare proof of impotence."[6] The rhetorical procedure in "Fate," to be sure, is insistently dialectic, but this old Emersonian game of yin and yang is rather mechanically worked out, and a balance is not struck for the reader, I think, because we sense clearly where the weight of Emerson's own imagination leans. When, a few pages later, he argues for the power of individual will by saying, of the hero, that "the glance of his eye has the force of sunbeams," we can hardly fail to recall the convincing paragraph I have quoted. Intelligent glances may serve as a kind of spiritual consolation to drowning men, but eyebeams and sunbeams alike seem insubstantial as levers against the overwhelming force of Fate.

An analogous indication of discouragement in Emerson's optimistic philosophy may be seen in the fortunes of another central metaphor—that of the ascending spiral or upward-pointing staircase (or ladder). In this case, I believe we can actually pinpoint the shift in Emerson's attitude as occurring somewhere between the composition of "The Poet" and "Experience" (which is to say somewhere between late 1842 and early 1844). I think it is even possible to assert in this regard that although "The Poet" stands first in the second series of Essays, the ebulliently hopeful mood and metaphoric coordinates of that piece place it with the first book of Essays, whereas "Experience," which is printed directly following "The Poet," actually marks a new departure in both tone and imagery.

Emerson's first collection of Essays is largely controlled by figures of ascension. In "Self-Reliance" we read that "the soul becomes," that power "resides in the moment of transition from a past to a new state, in the shooting of the gulf, in the darting to an aim." The inchoate metaphor develops in "Compensation," where Emerson affirms that "the soul refuses limits," for "man's life is a progress, and not a station." The law of nature "is growth," and "the voice of the Almighty saith, 'Up and onward for evermore!'" The method of man is "a progressive arrangement," we are told in "Spiritual Laws"; and this means, as regards the affections (in "Love"), that we must pass from lower attractions to higher ones: "the lover ascends to the highest beauty, to love and knowledge of Divinity, by steps on this ladder of created souls." Since, in "Friendship," we "descend to meet," we must make room for one another's merits—"let them mount and expand"—parting, if need be, so that we may "meet again on a higher platform." This is the "spiritual astronomy" of love, as it is the law of the soul's progress in "The Over-Soul" ("the soul's advances are not made by gradations, such as can be represented by motion in a straight line, but rather by ascension of state"). Emerson's figure develops further, in the first series of Essays, with "Circles," which is essentially devoted to working out a set of variations on the notion of man as "a self-evolving circle," a rising spiral, who scales the "mysterious ladder" of upwardly mobile life. In a very real sense, however, the figure culminates in "The Poet," for he is the Christ-like hero whose logos breaks our chains and allows us to "mount above these clouds and opaque airs" in which we normally dwell. Poets are "liberating gods" who preach "ascension, or the passage of the soul into higher forms . . . into free space." Released by this extraordinary savior, we live the heavenly life of the redeemed imagination: "dream delivers us to dream, and while the drunkenness lasts we will sell our bed, our philosophy, our religion, in our opulence."

---

6. *Emerson on the Soul*, p. 210.

This divine bubble is punctured sharply in "Experience" as Emerson, in typical fashion, picks up his own language and places it in a startling new context: "Dream delivers us to dream, and there is no end to illusion." The imagination is now seen as a kind of devil of deceit who provokes the fall of man into a "middle region" of uncertainty and confusion:

> Where do we find ourselves? In a series of which we do not know the extremes, and believe that it has none. We wake and find ourselves on a stair; there are stairs below us, which we seem to have ascended; there are stairs above us, many a one, which go upward and out of sight. But the Genius which according to the old belief stands at the door by which we enter, and gives us the lethe to drink, that we may tell no tales, mixed the cup too strongly, and we cannot shake off the lethargy now at noonday. Sleep lingers all our lifetime about our eyes, as night hovers all day in the boughs of the fir-tree. All things swim and glimmer. Our life is not so much threatened as our perception. Ghostlike we glide through nature.

Vision is darkened here. Indeed, Emerson's mood is sinister, almost Poesque, as he, too, in a sort of "lonesome October," wanders "in the misty mid region of Weir" which we find in "Ulalume." Or, to use the terms of Wallace Stevens, Emerson is trapped in something like a "banal sojourn," a time of indifference, when man's depressed spirit dumbly mutters: "One has a malady, here, a malady. One feels a malady."[7] That malady can perhaps best be described as loss of affect, a contemporary version of acedia; a dejected state in which Emerson cannot even feel that this terrible threat to perception is a threat to life because his very sense of self is "ghostlike." This is the form evil takes in Emerson's lapsarian mood. The optimistic spiral has collapsed upon itself and Emerson, having set his "heart on honesty in this chapter," finds himself forced down his ladder into "the foul rag-and-bone shop of the heart." Though it would be more than mildly misleading to suggest that the Emerson of "Experience," and after, truly joins hands with Yeats in giving voice to a peculiarly modern sense of discouragement and dislocation, it is nevertheless fair to say that the Emerson who began to conceive of existence in such grayly tragic terms as these took a large step toward insuring that his writing could have a continuing life for twentieth-century readers.

IV

Most Emersonians would probably agree that to redeem Emerson by resorting to what Newton Arvin calls a "cant of pessimism" is to do him a disservice.[8] This is not to say that the expression we find, in such an essay as "Experience," of a kind of existential *nausea*, a feeling that reality eludes us and that we are all, as Sartre says, "*superfluous*, that is to say, amorphous, vague, and sad"[9]—that the expression of such things in Emerson is not particularly valuable. This side of Emerson deepens our interest in him, making us feel that his sense of the way life can be sometimes corresponds more nearly to our own. But, if we resist the temptation to overemphasize Emerson's journals and letters and pay attention mainly to those published works by which the world has known him for more than a cen-

---

7. *The Collected Poems of Wallace Stevens*, p. 62. Cf. "The Man Whose Pharynx Was Bad," p. 96.
8. Newton Arvin, "The House of Pain," In *Emerson: A Collection of Critical Essays*, p. 59.
9. Jean-Paul Sartre, *Nausea*, trans. Lloyd Alexander (New York: New Directions, 1964), p. 177.

tury, the fact remains that the "House of Pain" was not Emerson's dominant structure and should not constitute his major claim on us.

My own intent has been to show that the problems which have perennially dogged Emerson's reputation and hindered a true appreciation of his work
can largely be obviated if we focus our attention on his writing *as writing*. His
work, I am saying, does have this kind of interest to a high degree; and a fundamentally literary approach to Emerson can yield surprising dividends of reading pleasure and a new understanding of what he was about. As a final short
demonstration of my argument, I propose to examine a familiar — in some ways,
too familiar — specimen brick from the Emerson edifice, the Divinity School
"Address." Like most monuments of Emerson's prose, this piece has been so
solidly in place for so long that we tend to overlook what is really in it. Though
it is normally spoken of in terms of Emerson's evolving career, or the Unitarian-
Transcendentalist controversy, or its doctrine (or the absence thereof), its real
interest, it seems to me, lies in its exhibition of Emerson's skill as a literary strate-
gist and of his mastery of organic form.

On the first of April preceding that momentous July evening when Emerson delivered his bombshell, he told a group of divinity students informally that
"the preacher should be a poet."[1] That is precisely and totally the "doctrine" of
his address, which is both an exposition and an enactment of that belief. The
key concept, and word, in the address is *beauty*, for Emerson was determined
to prove that "the institution of preaching — the speech of man to men" (which
is also, we should note, the institution of literature) is utterly nugatory if moral
truth is separated from the delight of living. The "new Teacher" whom Emerson called for in the last sentence of his speech was charged with showing "that
the Ought, that Duty, is one thing with Science, with Beauty, and with Joy." Accordingly, those two final words, beauty and joy, govern Emerson's startlingly
heretical portrait in the address of the archetypal preacher, Christ, who is offered to us as a kind of first-century aesthete, replete with "locks of beauty," who
was "ravished" by the "supreme Beauty" of the soul's mystery and went out in a
"jubilee of sublime emotion" to tell us all "that God incarnates himself in man,
and evermore goes forth anew to take possession of his world." The man who is
most enamored of the "beauty of the soul" and the world in which it is incarnated is called to serve as "its priest or poet," and Emerson urges such men to
feel their call "in throbs of desire and hope."

It is precisely the absence of any evidence of such emotions that characterizes the unnamed formalist preacher whom Emerson describes in a striking
exemplum about halfway through the address:

> I once heard a preacher who sorely tempted me to say, I would go to
> church no more. Men go, thought I, where they are wont to go, else had
> no soul entered the temple in the afternoon. A snowstorm was falling
> around us. The snowstorm was real; the preacher merely spectral; and the
> eye felt the sad contrast in looking at him, and then out of the window be-
> hind him, into the beautiful meteor of the snow. He had lived in vain. He

1. See *The Journals and Miscellaneous Notebooks of Ralph Waldo Emerson*, ed. William H. Gilman et al.
(Cambridge: Harvard University Press, 1960–), V, 471 (this edition is abbreviated hereafter as *JMN*). A
valuable treatment of the evolution of Emerson's notion of the preacher-poet, especially in relation to
the Unitarian background, is Lawrence I. Buell, "Unitarian Aesthetics and Emerson's Poet-Priest," *American Quarterly*, 20 (Spring 1968), 3–20. See also Frederick May Eliot, "Emerson and the Preacher," *Journal of Liberal Religion*, 1 (Summer 1939), 5–18.

had no one word intimating that he had laughed or wept, was married or in love, had been commended, or cheated, or chagrined. If he had ever lived and acted, we were none the wiser for it. The capital secret of his profession, namely, to convert life into truth, he had not learned. Not one fact in all his experience, had he yet imported into his doctrine. This man had ploughed, and planted, and talked, and bought, and sold; he had read books; he had eaten and drunken; his head aches; his heart throbs; he smiles and suffers; yet was there not a surmise, a hint, in all the discourse, that he had ever lived at all. Not a line did he draw out of real history. The true preacher can always be known by this, that he deals out to the people his life,—life passed through the fire of thought.[2]

Emerson, the preacher, moves in thought down into the congregation and reminds himself of a typical parishioner's experience: boredom.[3] If habit had not brought him to the church, he would scarcely have gone, for there is nothing to attract him, no promise of reality, no pleasure. The true preacher, the true poet, bases his verbal art on personal experience in the actual world that surrounds us all, thus transmuting "life into truth." Otherwise, words are mere counters that leave us untouched. Emerson's real genius here, however, lies in the business of the snowstorm. Playing the role of listener, he allows his wandering attention to move outside the window and find its sole available pleasure in the "beautiful meteor of the snow."[4] Perhaps only a New England consciousness could invent such a phrase; but then Emerson is writing of what he knows and loves (as in his poem "The Snow-Storm"). The fine irony of the passage is that the preacher should seem *spectral* compared even to the frigid and ghostly reality of snow. What Emerson has done himself is to insist on some sort of interpenetration between that which goes on inside the church and the beautiful world outside. His example suggests that the skillful preacher will attempt to do the same.

Now, in our backward movement through the address, let us confront the magnificent strategies of the opening passage. On what was apparently a splendid Sunday evening in July 1838, Emerson mounted the pulpit in Divinity Hall to speak, nominally, to the senior class in divinity; but they were a small group, and the room was packed with faculty members and friends. Emerson's intent, as I have noted, was to *demonstrate* that "the preacher should be a poet," that religious truth and human pleasure must coexist, and that the two worlds of chapel and physical universe are mutually enriching. Accordingly, in a prose that is consciously purple, Emerson began his address by inviting this sternly theological audience to allow its attention to wander, as his own had wandered on that boring Sunday in winter, beyond the chapel window to the ripe world of nature outside:

2. The hapless preacher referred to here was actually Barzillai Frost, and Emerson's experience is recorded in *JMN*, V, 463. Conrad Wright's "Emerson, Barzillai Frost, and the Divinity School Address," *Harvard Theological Review*, 49 (January 1956), 19–43, contains an absorbing discussion of the event. Noticing that Frost was only one year younger than Emerson, Professor Wright conjectures that Emerson viewed Frost as the lifeless preacher he himself might have become had he not left the Unitarian ministry in 1832. The vehemence of Emerson's reaction to Frost in his journal certainly does suggest a complex personal dimension to what, in the address, is presented simply as a generic problem in contemporary preaching.
3. Compare Robert Spiller's introduction to the address in *The Collected Works of Ralph Waldo Emerson*, vol. 1, *Nature, Addresses, and Lectures*, ed. Robert E. Spiller and Alfred R. Ferguson (Cambridge: Harvard University Press, 1971), p. 71.
4. It is worth noting that the journal passage which Emerson worked up here for the address, though it parallels the finished paragraph rather closely, does not mention "the beautiful meteor of the snow." That represents the touch of the poet, shaping remarks into literature.

In this refulgent summer it has been a luxury to draw the breath of life. The grass grows, the buds burst, the meadow is spotted with fire and gold in the tint of flowers. The air is full of birds, and sweet with the breath of the pine, the balm-of-Gilead, and the new hay. Night brings no gloom to the heart with its welcome shade. Through the transparent darkness the stars pour their almost spiritual rays. Man under them seems a young child, and his huge globe a toy. The cool night bathes the world as with a river, and prepares his eyes again for the crimson dawn. The mystery of nature was never displayed more happily. The corn and the wine have been freely dealt to all creatures, and the never-broken silence with which the old bounty goes forward, has not yielded yet one word of explanation. One is constrained to respect the perfection of this world, in which our senses converse.

An example of how inattentive even some of the most devoted Emersonians have been to the master's art is provided by Stephen Whicher's comment: "the address itself was calculated to give no offense, on grounds of vocabulary at least, to a Unitarian audience."[5] It is precisely in its vocabulary that the barefaced effrontery of Emerson's gambit resides. There is probably not another place in all his writings where Emerson is so consciously arch. The only astute comment I have found on this passage belongs to Jonathan Bishop: "the immediate rhetorical motive, evidently enough, is shock: an address to a small group of graduating divinity students is not supposed to begin by an appeal to the sensual man."[6] Emerson's stance, as Bishop says, is that of a "voluptuary," and the word is well chosen. Following the "unusually aureate" (Bishop's term) *refulgent*—which suggests a kind of shining forth, or epiphany, in the summer's beauty—Emerson explodes his real charge in the sentence: *luxury*. We must remind ourselves that Emerson's audience, trained in theology, was not likely to overlook the implications of that red flag, for *luxuria*, one of the seven deadly sins, means lust. Although that technical meaning, of course, is not Emerson's, a calculated air of aesthetic indulgence permeates this opening remark.[7]

In the sentences that follow, Emerson has measured out his language with extreme care to one end: the creation in words of an unfallen world of the senses where formal, traditional religion is unnecessary because nature provides its

5. *Freedom and Fate: An Inner Life of Ralph Waldo Emerson* (Philadelphia: University of Pennsylvania Press, 1953), p. 74. In "The Rhetoric of Apostasy," *Texas Studies in Literature and Language*, 8 (Winter 1967), 547–560, Mary Worden Edrich argues persuasively that Emerson's language throughout the address was carefully calculated to shock
6. *Emerson on the Soul*, p. 88.
7. It is interesting to survey definitions of *luxury* in American dictionaries which Emerson might have consulted. Webster's first edition (1806) gives simply "excess in eating, dress, or pleasure." By 1830 this entry has been expanded, and the first meaning is "a free or extravagant indulgence in the pleasures of the table; voluptuousness in the gratification of appetite; the free indulgence in costly dress and equipage." The Latin sense of *luxuria*, "lust; lewd desire," is offered as definition number 4 and marked obsolete. However, the 1832 American edition of Johnson's dictionary gives as its first meaning "voluptuousness; addictedness to pleasure," and cites Milton ("lust; lewdness"). As late as 1846 Worcester's dictionary gives "voluptuousness" as the first meaning. Emerson's own use of the word in the 1820's and 1830's tends to lean, not surprisingly, in Milton's direction. Thus, in 1821–22, "wealth induces luxury, and luxury disease" (*JMN*, I, 300); in 1831, "I am extremely scrupulous as to indulging my appetite. No <splendour> luxury, no company, no solicitation can tempt me to <luxury> excess . . . because . . . I count my body a temple of God, & will not displease him by gratifying my carnal lust?" (*JMN*, III, 225). In a letter to Carlyle in 1834 Emerson says, "to write luxuriously is not the same thing as to live so, but a new & worse offence. It implies an intellectual defect also, the not perceiving that the present corrupt condition of human nature (which condition this harlot muse helps to perpetuate) is a temporary or superficial state. The good word lasts forever: the impure word can only buoy itself in the gross gas that now envelopes us, & will sink altogether to the ground as that works itself clear in the everlasting effort of God." See *The Correspondence of Emerson and Carlyle*, ed. Joseph Slater (New York: Columbia University Press, 1964), p. 108.

own sacraments. It is hard to see how Emerson's frank appropriation of religious terms and concepts could have failed to offend much of his audience. The rays of the stars are *"almost* spiritual" (Is not heaven then *really* above our heads? Conversely, can a natural phenomenon *almost* approach spiritual truth?). Man, returned to the innocence of childhood, is bathed by the cool night as in baptismal waters, whereby his eyes are *prepared* for the dawn (a familiar type of the coming of Christ).[8] The technical term *mystery* is applied to nature; but unlike theological mysteries, this one is openly and happily "displayed." In the next sentence, Emerson announces that the central sacrament, the Eucharist (over which, of course, he had created a controversy when he left the Second Church of Boston six years earlier), is "freely dealt to all creatures" by nature—without condition or exclusion. Then, to a congregation still committed to the belief that the creation is fully expounded in the Bible, Emerson states that no "word of explanation" has been provided—and implies that none is needed. Finally, this Christian audience, all children of the Puritans, are told that they are "constrained to respect," not (as we should expect) the dogmas and duties of their faith, but rather the *perfection of this* world, a totally natural world, the one "in which our senses converse." Can we really doubt that to most of Emerson's listeners all of this seemed the sheerest effrontery (although to many others since it has seemed merely a flowery portal, the blandly poetic induction to a serious theological dissertation)? But it is clear that Emerson's aim was not fundamentally to offer an insult but to enact a meaning which would develop organically in the course of his address and to which he would "come full circle" at the end: namely, as we have noted, that Ought and beauty, Duty and Joy, Science and Ecstasy, Divinity and the World, must merge in the new hypostatic unity of a living religion of the soul.

    There is "a sort of drollery," Henry James remarks, in the spectacle of a society in which the author of the Divinity School Address could be considered "profane." What they failed to see, James continues, is "that he only gave his plea for the spiritual life the advantage of a brilliant expression." Emerson, of course, has long since ceased to be thought profane (except perhaps in the curious pronouncements of such an eccentric critic as Yvor Winters). The problem is exactly the reverse: It is Emerson's pieties that have damned him. What I have tried to argue here is simply that we can, in search of a living Emerson, make much better use of the advantage of which James speaks. Emerson *is* a great writer. He has only to be read.

HYATT H. WAGGONER

From The Achievement of the Poems: "Artful Thunder"[†]

* * *

Several of [Emerson's] finest poems, including "Each and All" and "The Problem," appear to date from the late thirties, but the three greatest, as I read

---

8. See, for example, Jonathan Edward's *Images or Shadows of Divine Things*, ed. Perry Miller (New Haven: Yale University Press, 1948), entry nos. 40, 50, 54, 80, 85, 110, and 111.
† From *Emerson as Poet*. Copyright © 1974 by Princeton University Press. Reprinted by permission of Princeton University Press.

the verse, "Merlin," "Bacchus," and "Hamatreya," all seem to have been written in 1845–1846, when the approaching publication of his first volume of poems prompted a brief but intense period of renewed concentration on the form of writing in which he had first hoped to gain fame. All three poems are prosodically and otherwise unconventional by the standards of their time. The best poems written later than this, including "Days," "The Titmouse," and "Terminus," tend to take fewer liberties with the "rules" of mid-nineteenth-century versification. "Brahma," 1857, is a very traditional poem formally, while the next year's "The Adirondacs" is written in the perfectly conventional blank verse Emerson had long before shown himself capable of producing. * * *

How significant then is Emerson's achievement in his best poems? What shall we think about the quality of the bulk of his verse? Why are his weaker poems weak, if they are weak? How many of his widely agreed-upon "faults" as a poet are really faults? Only "judicial criticism," presumably, can attempt to answer such questions, but the recent experience of reading straight through more than a century of accumulated critical judgments of Emerson's verse has greatly weakened whatever confidence I may ever have had in the critic as judge and arbiter. I find myself agreeing with what John Dewey said long ago in *Art as Experience*: "If judicial critics do not learn modesty from the past they profess to esteem, it is not from lack of material. Their history is largely the record of egregious blunders."[1] The critic-as-judge knows the law and applies it to the specific case before him. Not to know the law, or to doubt its authority, presumably disqualifies a judge. What follows will therefore bear as little resemblance to traditional judicial criticism as I can manage without giving up the aim of trying to get Emerson's verse read again freshly, with neither Victorian nor New Critical assumptions controlling the reading.

But of course one never approaches any experience, literary or other, with no assumptions. I suggest that two ideas already touched upon in my opening chapter might be helpful in arriving at a fresh impression of the collected poems. The first is that we read them thinking not primarily of traditional poetic genres or time-honored poetic conventions, prosodic or other, but of what has happened since in American poetry; the second, that we think of Emerson's most characteristic poems—as both "Bacchus" and "Woodnotes" are, for example, but "Concord Hymn" is not, though it is a good poem—that we think of his most characteristic work as deeply influenced by and, in its special way, continuing the Ancient, Medieval, and Renaissance literary and philosophic tradition of paradox, a way of thinking and writing chiefly associated with prose, though it found its way into Renaissance verse too.[2]

By the first suggestion I do not mean that we should judge Emerson's poems simply as foreshadowing what was to come later, as, in effect, Whitman did in his most severe judgment of Emerson as the initial discoverer of the land it remained for Whitman to explore.[3] Rather, I mean that we should try to allow

---

1. Original publication date, 1934. I have quoted from the 1958 Capricorn Books reprint, p. 301.
2. See Rosalie Colie, *Paradoxia Epidemica* (Princeton, 1966).
3. Whitman's essay on Emerson in *Specimen Days and Collect*, in which he expresses his very natural resentment at being relegated by many to the status of a mere follower or disciple of the world-famous Emerson, in effect defines Emerson's achievement as the discovery of a land left for Whitman to explore and map. Many of Whitman's detractions in the essay still seem acute, but he unfairly minimizes the extent of Emerson's own explorations in most of the areas Whitman mapped, except of course that of sex. The essay is conveniently available in Edmund Wilson's *The Shock of Recognition*. Significantly, Whitman omitted the essay from the 1887 edition of the book, preferring to let the tributes occasioned by his memories of his last visit to Emerson in 1881 stand unqualified.

our expectations about what is "permissible" in verse, or, in more contemporary terms, about what will "work" in a given context, to reflect our having read and responded to the work of the greatest poets who followed Emerson, particularly those who through direct influence or through the mediation of Whitman followed in the tradition he established. What I mean by the second suggestion, relating Emerson to the tradition of paradox, I shall try to make clear later, but first a few more remarks on what I mean by suggesting that we read Emerson's poems in what might be called a "future-oriented" frame of mind while still avoiding judging him only as a precursor.

*   *   *

"Uriel" certainly does not seem to me as it did to Frost "the greatest Western poem yet" but it seems so distinguished, original, and memorable a prophetic utterance that it is not at all hard to understand why, given his bias and his sympathies, Frost valued it as he did. It is a paradoxical fable that far transcends the interest attaching to its origin in the controversy over Emerson's heretical Divinity School address. The dangerous heresies of the address have long since ceased to seem threatening to most of us, but the antinomian heart of the address is still available in the poem, and still "dangerous" to every orthodoxy, religious, scientific, humanistic, or any other. Rational humanistic distinctions, gradations, subordinations, dogmas are as much threatened as Fundamentalist or Evangelical ones by the vision summarized in the poem's central paradoxes:

> 'Line in nature is not found;
> Unit and universe are round;
> In vain produced, all rays return;
> Evil will bless, and ice will burn.'

The fear-reaction of the conservative old gods to the new revelation may have been excessively defensive but it was more perceptive than that of modern readers who find no challenge to their own orthodoxy, whatever it may be, in the poem. "The bounds of good and ill were rent," the old gods thought, and they were right if we understand "good" and "ill" to mean: what is commonly so called and understood to be, perhaps prematurely and inadequately understood to be, right and wrong, true and false. The poem's thrust against the notion that truth is static and *ours* and against any moralism that is not in some degree open-ended is as sharp today as it was when Emerson took this way of replying to his clerical opponents.

The four-stress couplets work beautifully for Emerson's purposes here. There is a constant interplay between the demands of the metrical pattern and the demands of the sense, in which the impact of the merely necessary lines is diminished. "To his ears was evident," for example, may be read as having the expected four stresses, but they go by very quickly. Similarly, the force of the lines containing the revelations is increased—"In vain produced, all rays return," for example—as the lines are slowed by their four strong stresses. Though the prosody of the poem is rather more regular than was common with Emerson, it is in no sense mechanical, to my ear at least. And the "liberty" Emerson takes of starting with a quatrain giving the setting of his tale, then shifting to couplets for the rest of the poem, seems appropriate, for the fable illustrates the polarities and equivalences, the returns and echoes of "Balance-loving Nature" which, as we are told in "Merlin II," "made all things in pairs," so that rhyming couplets may be thought of as echoing nature's own ways, thus embodying an important part of what the poem means. In the form of the poem, which "defies reverend use," then, as well as in the fable it relates, we have in "Uriel" a work that can survive the application of the standards implied in a somewhat cryptic passage in "Poetry and Imagination":

> In good society, nay, among the angels in heaven, is not everything spoken in fine parable, and not so servilely as it befell to the sense? All is symbolized. Facts are not foreign, as they seem, but related. Wait a little and we see the return of the remote hyperbolic curve.[4]

"Merlin" and "Bacchus," both written in the outburst of creative energy that came in 1845–1846, are central, characteristic, very strong expressions of a cluster of ideas that were very important to Emerson and that remained essentially unaltered between their first formulation in "The Poet" and their expansive and rambling restatement in "Poetry and Imagination" some thirty years later. The judgment as to which is the greater poem is likely to reflect the reader's predisposition to value strength over order or the other way around. "Merlin" with its two parts and its improvisational movement may strike some as a "rambling" poem containing a larger number of unforgettable lines, "Bacchus" as more transparently coherent—by logical standards. Together the two poems form the classic American statements in verse of the Romantic poetic ideal that much of our best and most characteristic poetry has sought to exemplify. And they are not only the first such statements, they remain the best.

Emerson identified very strongly with Malory's Merlin as he knew him in the prose translation available to him. Increasingly conscious of his own paucity of "talent" as a poet—though perhaps he had "genius"—he was drawn to Merlin as a "bard" who could be thought of as best exemplifying the ideas that introduce the section on "Bards and Trouveurs" in "Poetry and Imagination," which begins:

> The metallic force of primitive words makes the superiority of the [poetic] remains of the rude ages. It costs the early bard little talent to chant more impressively than the later, more cultivated poets. His advantage is that his words are things. . . .
> I find or fancy more true poetry . . . in . . . bardic fragments . . . than in many volumes of British Classics.[5]

A little later in the essay he quotes, for several pages, the episodes of the dialogue of Gawain with Merlin, who is imprisoned—in Emerson's version, not in Malory's—in his castle of air deep in the forest, with only one human tie left, that to his true love, his mistress, the only one still able to speak to him, who had imprisoned him and yet visited him at her pleasure. (Emerson had long since given up visiting and reopening Ellen's tomb by this time, but she still held the only key to his heart.) Magician paradoxically powerless to effect his own release from a paradoxical prison without bars, prophet, lost to those who loved and sought him, Merlin the bard awakened the deepest responses in Emerson's

---

4. *Emerson's Complete Works*, Riverside ed. (Boston, 1883), 8.71.
5. *Complete Works*, 8. 58–59.

imagination, as his treatment of him in the essay makes very clear.[6] The depth of his response may be judged, more indirectly, from the imaginative strength of the poem to which Merlin's name gives the title.

I have emphasized Emerson's discussion of the mystic Merlin in his late essay because it seems to me to open up an aspect of the poem that has received too little attention. True, the Merlin of the poem is a "kingly bard" whose words are "Artful thunder" and so akin to the messages of Jove and Yahweh, who also spoke in the thunder. When he strikes the chords of his instrument his mere words become "blows [that] are strokes of fate" powerful enough to "modulate the king's affairs." Yet the price he must pay for the power that results from his penetrating and conveying the "Secrets of the solar track" is a very high one: in effect, paradoxically, giving up control of his own destiny, yielding himself to the fates that only he can interpret. The ending of "Merlin II," almost never quoted or cited, is crucial. It is "Nemesis," fate, that "finishes the song," with the poet serving as interpreter:

> Subtle rhymes, with ruin rife,
> Murmur in the house of life,
> Sung by the Sisters as they spin;
> In perfect time and measure they
> Build and unbuild our echoing clay,
> As the two twilights of the day
> Fold us music-drunken in.

Poetry thus conceived is quite literally a "matter of life and death," too important obviously to be heard in the "jingling serenader's art" or in the "tinkle of piano strings." Paradoxically intertwined life and death, prophecies uttered by prisoners, life promised only because death is seen and accepted—all these paradoxes seem to me to be stated or implied in the poem. But as Rosalie Colie noted in *Paradoxia Epidemica*, successful paradox cannot be paraphrased.[7] Still, it should be clear that interpretations of the poem which note only that it rejects "talented" poetry in favor of inspired prophetic poetry are quite insufficient.

Just a word on the poem's verse form. It strikes me as one of Emerson's closest approaches to achieving his own announced ideal of organic or functional form, "metre-making argument." The poem begins with a stanza of Common Meter,

> Thy trivial harp will never please
> Or fill my craving ear;
> Its chords should ring as blows the breeze,
> Free, peremptory, clear,—

---

6. A still useful discussion of what Emerson knew—and did not know—about the "Bardic" tradition in general and Merlin considered as a bard in particular is contained in Nelson F. Adkins, "Emerson and the Bardic Tradition," *PMLA*, 63 (1948), 662–677. In summary, most of what Emerson knew he got at second or third hand from such sources as Blair's *Rhetoric*, which he had been required to study in college. "It is doubtful," the author concludes, "whether Emerson was well informed regarding bardic literature when in 1845 and 1846 he wrote 'Merlin.'" I suspect that a similarly careful investigation of his sources would show that Emerson was seldom truly "well informed" about any of the subjects he wrote best about. With "Hamatreya" as the only conspicuous exception that comes to mind, the "information" he needed came from the work his imagination did as it played over a few facts, or supposed facts, such as that Merlin's magic gave him power, his imprisonment isolated him and rendered him powerless, and his prophecies proved to be true.

7. *Paradoxia Epidemica*, p. 35.

then moves into irregular three or four stress quatrains for the rest of the first section. Its most famous lines must be described as irregularly rhymed "free verse" not unlike the verse that opens Eliot's "Prufrock":

> Great is the art,
> Great be the manners, of the bard.
> He shall not his brain encumber
> With the coil of rhythm and number;
> But, leaving rule and pale forethought,
> He shall aye climb
> For his rhyme.
> 'Pass in, pass in,' the angels say,
> 'In to the upper doors,
> Nor count compartments of the floors,
> But mount to paradise
> By the stairway of surprise.'

The rest of the poem is written with only slightly greater regularity, with the stresses varying from two to five and the rhymes sometimes making couplets, sometimes triplets, sometimes quatrains—and sometimes simply disappearing. But—and this of course is a judgment each reader must check for himself—the poem made from all these irregular pieces does not seem "formless"; its movement does not seem arbitrary but inevitable. I suspect that few poets capable of really understanding the poem would want to try to improve its form.

The call for a poetry possessing the power of inspired prophecy because it is produced by a poet who has recognized and submitted to the skeins woven by the fatal sisters, and so is enabled to find the words to give voice to life's own "subtle rhymes," is subordinated in "Merlin" to the poem's presentation of its more overt subjects. Those subjects are of course the contrast between conventional poesy and true prophetic poetry in both manner and effect; the true poet's way of working, or, when inspiration fails, of keeping silent (as Emerson would put this later in "Poetry and Imagination," " . . . either inspiration or silence. . . . Much that we call poetry is but polite verse.");[8] and the relation of the poet's rhymes to the "rhymes" of nature, a relationship that explains the source of the poet's power. That such poetry would be Dionysian, not Apollonian, and paradoxical, not logical, is clear enough, as I have tried to suggest, but it is not emphasized, is not at the center of the poem's attention. The poem's central paradox is the familiar one, that only artlessness can produce the greatest art.

In "Bacchus" the call for a kind of poetry not simply paradoxical but ecstatic, even "drunken," or perhaps better said, for the kind of poetry that only a drunken poet skilled in paradoxy could produce, is closer to the center of the poem, though the explicit subject is the poet's prayer for the kind of consciousness necessary for the production of such poetry. "The kind of consciousness": better, perhaps, the escape from the conscious control of "reasonableness" that drunkenness brings. When common-sense reason is relaxed, the mind can find room for mystery and awe. "In dreams we are true poets," as Emerson would put it later, in a discussion of the degree to which all men are potential poets so far as their imagination is free and active. Perhaps only in dreams or intoxication then could the poetic potential be actualized in "ecstatic or poetic speech."

8. *Complete Works*, 8. 73.

The prayer we should pray for poets and for all those who desire the vision and gifts of the poet is "O celestial Bacchus! drive them mad."[9] That the god granted the petition for a number of our greatest Emersonian poets, particularly Hart Crane and Roethke, is clear enough—and may well make us pause, as it did Yvor Winters long ago, to ponder the human cost of creative imaginative utterance. Perhaps a prosaic sobriety is to be preferred as less costly. Certainly it is less dangerous to "the seeming-solid walls of use"—of custom, tradition, manners, institutions, authority—which in "Bacchus" are seen as dissolved by the poet's vision. "To be preferred," perhaps; but if Emerson's understanding of the creative processes is essentially correct, at least for a certain kind of poetry, then the choice will not be an easy one to make, will perhaps not even be offered.

It should be possible, it seems to me, to recognize in "Bacchus" a great poetic achievement whatever we may finally think about the wisdom or unwisdom of accepting its vision as a guide to life. Both "Apollonian" and "Dionysian" elements are undeniably real aspects of the rhythmic processes of psychic life. It is only when we are asked to choose between them as dominant life styles that we have, perhaps, if we are fortunate, the option of choosing one or the other. "Bacchus" does not demand that we make this choice, only that we grant the poet his Dionysian vision, though of course it reveals the choice Emerson the man as well as Emerson the poet ideally would have made, a choice not forced on *us* by the poem. Poetry, art, all creative thinking are full of ideas dangerous to common sense and a well-ordered life, but many of us are not yet ready to give up the arts and thinking for safety's sake. Of course the danger inherent in the idea expressed in "Bacchus" is real, all the more real because it rests not on some private, distorted fantasy of Emerson's but on deep insights into very important aspects of poetic, and perhaps all, creativity. Granted the poem's subject—the sources and nature of poetic inspiration—I can only suppose that the poem would be less great if its doctrine were less dangerous to the order we quite properly value in our sane and sober moments.

The movement of the poem is controlled from first to last by the paradoxical analogy it maintains between the Christian rite of Holy Communion, which Emerson had long ago refused to go on celebrating, and the Transcendental communion with Reality, which is praised in the poem as greatly to be preferred. At least a half-dozen verbal echoes of the traditional Christian rite are scattered through the poem like sign posts, with the intentions of the service, its symbolic meanings for believers, echoed, criticized by implication, and inverted in the spaces between the signs. By the time Emerson wrote the poem he was far beyond the objections to the service he had explained in his sermon announcing his resignation, but he remembered the rite too well to have any need to look up its words in a Prayer Book. The "elements" of the rite, bread and wine, "symbolizing" for some, "becoming" for others, "the body and blood of Christ," are also the elements of the Transcendental communion described in the poem, though clear water will do in place of wine in one stanza. The chief Scriptural direction for the rite, "This do in remembrance of me," is echoed twice, first in "Winds of remembering," then in "the remembering wine." The Reformation controversy over whether "transubstantiation" or "consubstantiation" better described how the bread and wine were transmuted into the body and blood of Christ to effect "the real presence" is echoed and dismissed in the line that describes the pre-

9. Ibid., 47, 69, 71.

ferred Transcendental elements as "Food which needs no transmuting." The
Scriptural "This is my blood, which is shed for you" is also alluded to twice, first
in the description of *this* wine as "Blood of the world," then in the characterization of it as "Wine that is shed," by implication not just for "you," that is, believers, but freely for all men, as the rain falls on all. Transcendental communion, in
short, was immune to the two chief criticisms that Emerson believed invalidated
the Christian rite: it did not rest upon "superstition," upon the credulous acceptance of miracles the Higher Criticism had undermined, and it was not the exclusive property of the faithful.[1]

   Yet while wholly avoiding these fatal weaknesses, the new rite accom-
plishes the same ends. Like the Eucharist or Lord's Supper with its reminders
of Christ's suffering and death, Emerson's communion wine is made from
grapes that grow "From a nocturnal root" and make the partaker hear the dis-
cordancies of "Chaos" as well as the harmonies of music. Bringing with it a realization of death, it brings also the promise of resurrection: "Quickened so, will
I unlock / Every crypt of every rock." The rite Emerson describes ends with the
same joyful assurance as that brought to believers in the Christian rite: it affirms
the victory of life over death, thus working to "cure the old despair" and bringing us alive with a vision of "the dancing Pleiads and eternal men."

   Thus the poem which began by invoking the kind of awareness that lies at
the heart of mystical experience and continued by suggesting what the achievement of such a faith would demand of us, would cost in self-surrender, ends in
a triumphant paradoxical affirmation of the saving power of visionary union
with the supramundane rhythms of nature. Knowing that darkness, disorder,
and death do not have the last word, the Transcendental visionary is ready to
participate in the dance of the stars, secure in the knowledge that his own spirit
is above time, above the flowing and melting of the world. Because he has eaten
and drunk of the sources of terror, incorporating them into himself, his faith
seems fully earned. The poem is perfectly and firmly balanced on its central ir-
resolvable paradox, that only with a full awareness of all the reasons for negation can a sensitive man make a meaningful affirmation.

                              *   *   *

JULIE ELLISON

"Quotation and Originality"[†]

   The dynamics of influence and interpretation that organize Emerson's earlier works appear also in the 1859 lecture published with little revision as "Quotation and Originality." For our purposes, the most important thing about this

---

1. See "The Lord's Supper," *Complete Works*, 11. 9–29 (*Miscellanies*). Emerson was explicit about his first
   objection but, speaking to a Christian congregation, tactfully indirect about the second: Christianity's
   claim on us rests on its superiority as a "moral system," but the rite Emerson was objecting to imputes to
   Jesus "an authority which he never claimed" [*sic*]. The sermon suggests that Emerson had read his *New
   Testament* as selectively as he normally read all books, picking up and remembering only what suited his
   purposes.
† From *Emerson's Romantic Style*. Copyright © 1984 by Princeton University Press. Reprinted by permission of Princeton University Press.

piece is the persistence of structures that had emerged twenty years before. Such stability argues for the constitutive role of these dynamics in Emerson's prose; once formulated, they are a permanent feature. The central terms of "Quotation and Originality" are attributes and operations (like those of the essays on "Love," "Art," "Fate") not protagonists ("The Poet," "The American Scholar," *Representative Men*), but this is a negligible difference. All of Emerson's essays assign essentially the same operations to essentially the same performers. In addition to its value as evidence of the staying power of Emerson's designs, "Quotation and Originality" is, of course, intriguing because of its manifest content. As the title indicates, it makes explicit the theories of interpretation dramatized in so many other works, and thus provides an appropriate gloss on and summary of the readings in this section. It makes clear, in a casual way, the role of the higher criticism in Emerson's development of a general hermeneutics; its ambiguous anecdotes of duplicitous quoters contribute to our ongoing exploration of Emerson's irony; and, most significantly, it offers a sustained discussion of literary influence, although "Quotation and Originality" is not one of Emerson's great rages against tradition. While it exhibits his characteristic shifts among the roles of reader, critic, and writer, it is less aggressive than many essays. It may be that he is so deeply committed to the method of quotation by this time that he cannot get fully aroused against it. The earlier work or author, the antagonist, is more a part of himself. Nevertheless, his pleasure in repeated sequences of self-deprecation, desire, and aggression that issue in the momentary dominance of the reader-as-writer persists.

The opening image, a violently reductive allegory, lets us know at once that Emerson has mixed feelings about his subject. In one of the grotesque parables that so delight him, he points out "the extreme content" which "flies, aphides, gnats . . . innumerable parasites, and even . . . infant mammals" take in "suction." "If we go into a library or news-room," he continues, "we see that same function on a higher plane, performed with like ardor, with equal impatience of interruption, indicating the sweetness of the act. In the highest civilization the book is still the highest delight (W.VIII.177). The shift from "suction" to "sweetness," from "parasites" to readers, deflates the pretensions of "civilization" by reminding us of our uncontrollable instinctual need for bookish pleasures. At the same time, that need is made to appear disgusting.

After this cautionary irony, the essay begins in earnest with the appearance of one of Emerson's typically modest personae, whose subject is the great, but not entirely original, man. "All minds quote" but the "great man" most of all; "in proportion to the spontaneous power should be the assimilating power." Quotation is not limited to actual verbal citation. As Emerson enumerates modern inventions that resemble or were suggested by ancient ones, "quotation" comes to signify any known historical connection: "We quote . . . arts, sciences, religion, customs, and laws; nay, we quote temples and houses, tables and chairs." When we comprehend an institution or an idea well enough to trace it back to prior forms, then we call its later reappearance "quotation." Since every event has discoverable antecedents, the past becomes an endless series of quotations. The word is a synonym for history itself: "There is imitation, model and suggestion, to the very arch-angels, if we knew their history." "There is something mortifying in this perpetual circle," the essayist remarks sombrely. It "argues a very small capital of invention." He includes himself among the dependent: "In this

delay and vacancy of thought, we . . . [seek] the wisdom of others to fill
the time." Having eliminated the possibility of individual creativity, the only
way he can account for the ongoing activity of writing is by a theory of intertextuality. The search for an ancient, original text drives us backwards in
an infinite regress of reading:

> The first book tyrannizes over the second. Read Tasso, and you think of
> Virgil; read Virgil, and you think of Homer; and Milton forces you to re-
> flect how narrow are the limits of human invention. The "Paradise Lost"
> had never existed but for these precursors.

The avowed indebtedness to Emerson of our latest theorist of influence, Harold
Bloom, is amply justified by passages like this, in which Emerson uses influ-
ence to define a canon and calls attention to the "tyranny" of "precursors."
Emerson goes on to reveal the relationship of this vision to Biblical criticism:

> if we find in India or Arabia a book out of our horizon of thought and tra-
> dition, we are soon taught by new researches in its native country to dis-
> cover its foregoers, and its latent, but real connection with our own Bibles.
> (W.VIII.178–80)

Comparative mythology establishes the "foregoers" of literary works, then connects them to each other through their common ancestors. The author breaks
apart into multiple sources and his book into quotations. The process of critical fragmentation, as we have seen in other essays, is a prerequisite for creative
reading. Emerson has generalized the procedures of the higher criticism to de-
mystify all written works.

In the next portion of "Quotation and Originality," still part of the long
opening movement that traces the derivative present back to an original past,
Emerson applies this mode of criticism. He begins with illustrative genealogies
of individual writers. Plato originated Christianity's "evangelical phrases";
"Hegel pre-exists in Proclus"; "Rabelais is the source of many a proverb, story,
and Jest"; Dante "absorbed" St. Bonaventura and Thomas Aquinas
(W.VIII.180–81). From the idea of authors as embodiments of tradition, Emerson proceeds to the logical consequence of this approach, the notion of collective authorship. "Mythology is no man's work" but every man contributes to it:
"the legend is tossed from believer to poet, from poet to believer, everybody
adding a grace or dropping a fault or rounding the form, until it gets an ideal
truth." Anonymous folk creation is endless quotation, which ensures myth's universal meaning and purges it of egotism. "Religious literature," too, is "the work
of the whole communion of worshippers"; the Bible is the supreme example of
man's collective inspiration. Once again, the literary interpreter has gone to
school to the higher critics and the mythologists, but he invests these forms of
criticism with his own anti-authoritarian motives: "[W]hatever undue reverence may have been claimed for [the Bible] by the prestige of philonic inspiration, the stronger tendency we are describing [collective authorship] is likely
to undo." The suspicious critic successfully challenges more pious readers' control of the interpretive marketplace. The passage continues:

> What divines had assumed as the distinctive revelations of Christianity,
> theologic criticism has matched by exact parallelisms from the Stoics and
> poets of Greece and Rome. Later, when Confucius and the Indian scrip-
> tures were made known, no claim to monopoly of ethical wisdom could

be thought of; and the surprising results of the new researches into the history of Egypt have opened to us the deep debt of the churches of Rome and England to the Egyptian hierology. (W.VIII.182)

Here Emerson exhibits a clear grasp of analogues of his own position. Comparative or "parallel" investigations by "theologic critics" put an end to the Christian "monopoly" of "ethical wisdom" by showing its "deep debt" to other traditions. More than any Biblical scholar, Emerson perceives the general theory of influence implicit in the higher criticism. Using it, he can challenge the ethical pretensions of any authors and literatures by exposing their resemblance, and thus their debt, to earlier writings.

At this point, without abandoning the stance of judicious reader, he shifts his focus to the author who must live in and with this culture of indebtedness. Writers adapt to it, he suggests, by perfecting a sleight of tone that makes quotation sound like originality. Borrowing is "honest enough" when its dishonesty goes unnoticed: "A great man quotes bravely. . . . What he quotes, he fills with his own voice and humor, and the whole cyclopaedia of his table-talk is presently believed to be his own." Successful quotation involves a kind of illusion or deception. Famous men of all eras have passed off borrowed material as their own and enhanced their reputations by doing so. Undetected fraud is the test of rightful appropriation. If one can utter a quotation in one's "own voice and humor," runs Emerson's argument, then the borrowing is legitimate. Webster's "three rules" for young men "are none the worse for being already told, in the last generation, of Sheridan; and we find in Grimm's Mémoires that Sheridan got them from the witty D'Argenson; who, no doubt, if we could consult him, could tell of whom he first heard them told" (W.VIII.183). In these jocose "begats," we hear the smile of the cat right after it has swallowed the canary, of the author after he has assimilated his precursor. As legitimate trickery, quotation is an ironic tactic detected only by the ironic critic. Again, irony appears with the perceived gap between wisdom and egotism. It is the tone in which we knowingly appreciate the subterfuges of success and thus defend ourselves against them. If we see through an author's fraud, he has less power over us. Irony once more demystifies sublime effects.

Emerson drifts away from the dilemmas of authors to the subject of proverbs, ballads, and fables of "doubtful paternity." That phrase, "doubtful paternity," is a telling one. It indicates not condemnation, but relief, and suggests why, whenever the presence of known authors—acknowledged fathers—becomes too palpable, the theme of collective authorship recurs in the essays. Emerson pursues this theme with appropriately "doubtful" examples, claiming influence where there is only a general affinity of idea:

> Rabelais's dying words, "I am going to see the great Perhaps" . . . only repeats the "IF" inscribed on the portal of the temple at Delphi. Goethe's favorite phrase, "the open secret," translates Aristotle's answer to Alexander, "These books are published and not published." . . . Wordworth's hero acting "on the plan which pleased his childish thought," is Schiller's "Tell him to reverence the dreams of his youth," and earlier, Bacon's "*Consilia juventutis plus divinitatis habent*." (W.VIII.185)

The very speciousness of these connections demonstrates that paternity is always doubtful. Luckily for the nineteenth century, no thought can be attributed to only one author. In the domain of literary influence, there are no copyright laws to protect past writers and regulate present ones.

With a reprise of the lessons of comparative mythology ("only within this century . . . [have] England and America discovered that their nursery-tales . . . are the property of all the nations descended from the Aryan race"), the first movement of the essay appears to come to an end. After having dissolved the authorial subject several times into a chain of anonymous texts, the speaker faces the consequences of this procedure for himself as an author. Recognizing that his own arguments prove him to be unoriginal, he protests. Emerson's outburst conflates all the fables of the fall which the Orphic poet had cited in *Nature*, interpolated below in brackets, and adds a new one — quotation:

> Now shall we say that only the first men were well alive, and the existing generation is invalided and degenerate? ["Man is the dwarf of himself."] Is all literature eavesdropping, and all art . . . imitation? our life a custom, and our body borrowed, like a beggar's dinner, from a hundred charities? A more subtle and severe criticism might suggest that some dislocation has befallen the race ["the axis of vision is not aligned with the axis of things"]; that men are off their centre; that multitudes of men do not live with Nature, but behold it as exiles ["That indescribably small interval is as good as a thousand miles, and has forever severed the practical unity"].

Suddenly quotation is a symptom of the remoteness of truth, not truth's vehicle. It does not mediate between, but divides man and nature. "Quotation confesses inferiority," he announces in a new tone. "Quotation" no longer designates historical consciousness but stock responses, the absence of self-reliance:

> People go out to look at sunrises and sunsets who do not recognize their own . . . but know that it is foreign to them. As they do by books, so they *quote* the sunset and the star, and do not make them theirs. Worse yet, they live as foreigners in the world of truth, and quote thoughts, and thus disown them. (W.VIII.187–88)

Emerson's tone becomes judgmental as he turns against the inferior role of the reader. He represents alienated readers as different from himself. "[O]ur life" and "our body" give way accusingly to "they live," the change in pronoun dramatizing "their" foreignness. He is also contemptuous of the writer who reveals his "unguarded devotion" to earlier authors. "If Lord Bacon appears . . . in the preface, I go and read the Instauration instead of the new book," he threatens. The grotesque fable of parasitism which opened the essay returns, more darkly interpreted according to the law of compensation:

> The mischief is quickly punished. . . . Admirable mimics have nothing of their own. In every kind of parasite, when Nature has finished an aphis, a teredo or a vampire bat, — an excellent sucking-pipe to tap another animal, or a mistletoe or dodder among plants, — the self-supplying organs wither and dwindle, as being superfluous. (W.VIII.187–88)

Having distanced himself from inferior quotation by using the parasitical writer as scapegoat (to mix zoological metaphors), Emerson tries once more to define the conditions of legitimate quotation. He continues to oscillate between regretting and accepting parasitism. "[T]here are certain considerations which go far to qualify a reproach too grave," he begins judiciously. An economic metaphor describes a rare vision of equality between past and present authors or between author and reader: "The capitalist . . . is as hungry to lend as the consumer to borrow" and "the transaction is honorable to both." After all, quotation, as joint authorship, is an expression of "coöperation," of "our social nature." These are only fleeting wishes, however. Quickly Emerson returns to his usual vocabulary of power relations: "Each man is a hero and an oracle to somebody, and to that person whatever he says has an enhanced value. . . . [M]en of extraordinary genius acquire an almost absolute ascendant over their nearest companions." And then we are back on the side of the creative reader. Quotation is a form of criticism that makes certain elements of the past visible for the first time. "Many will read the book before one thinks of quoting a passage," and (quoting Landor on Shakespeare) that one is "more original than his originals" (W.VIII.189–91).

No amount of rationalization can suppress Emerson's uneasiness about the dishonesty of quoting, however. The quoter "is like the false Amphitryon; although the stranger, it is always he who has the air of being master of the house." The false Amphitryon (in this quotation from Dubuc) is, of course, Zeus—authentic power manifested as imitation. Wordsworth, like a false Amphitryon, passed off De Quincey's remarks as his own in De Quincey's presence. "On the whole," Emerson comments ambiguously, "we like the valor of it." He describes Wordsworth's action as proof that "truth is the property of no individual, but is the treasure of all man," denying the shameless egotism of the gesture. "[I]nasmuch as any writer has ascended to a just view of man's condition, he has adopted this tone," a tone of ostensible impersonality. "Tone," however, is Emerson's word for the impact of personal presence. The "tone" of Wordsworth and the other writers whose behavior he describes is one of instinctive self-regard. Emerson keeps trying to discriminate between morally legitimate and reprehensible forms of quotation. Altruistic motives make all the difference to the reader, "the simple seeker." "The nobler the truth or sentiment, the less imports the question of authorship." When the author is inspired by idealism, the tone of his quotations has "valor." Furthermore, Emerson warns, a selfish motive is betrayed by a discontinuous style. Egotistical quotation leads to textual gaps: "some steep transition, some sudden alternation of temperature, or of point of view, betrays the foreign interpolation" (W.VIII.192–93). Emerson's definition of moral borrowing seems to condemn, not justify, Wordsworth's repetition of De Quincey's *bons mots* apparently for social effect. Furthermore, Emerson criticizes a style precisely like his own. As we shall see in later chapters, he knew full well that his prose was characterized by discontinuity and conspicuous transitions, often caused by interpolations of "foreign," that is, quoted, material. These spasms of unconvincing high-mindedness suggest his discomfort with evidences of self-love in other writers which, when he acknowledges them as his own strategies, come in for enthusiastic praise.

When he has tried, unpersuasively, to idealize the quoter's motivation, he must account for the peculiar power of the quotation itself. It takes on the intentionality of the writer who is being used. Emerson meditates on the way allusions can retroactively alter our perception of a work (much as T. S. Eliot would do in "Tradition and the Individual Talent"[1]): "The passages of Shaks-

1. T. S. Eliot, in *The Sacred Wood: Essays on Poetry and Criticism*, pp. 49–50.

peare that we most prize were never quoted until within this century; and Milton's prose and Burke, even, have their best fame within it." The quotation interprets its creator "as if the charm belonged to the word and not to the life of thought which . . . enforced it." Quotation is one of the "tricks . . . fine words play with us." But Emerson knows that the charm of the word is an illusion, and that the power of quotation derives from the presence of one author in another's text: "another's thoughts have a certain advantage with us simply because they are another's." Alienation and majesty come together in quotation. Otherness signifies authority, just as authority signifies otherness. Consequently, "the high poets" are quoted "in the manner in which Scripture is quoted in our churches . . . with honoring emphasis." But a literary criticism analogous to Biblical criticism diminishes quotation's power. The book that is the object of much scholarship is less threatening, even a little quaint. The "citation of a passage" by a "historian of literature," Emerson observes drily, "carries the sentimental value of a college diploma" (W.VIII.193–95, 202, 195).

The extreme instability of Emerson's attitude toward writers who quote other writers arises from the double function of quotation. Quotation elicits the reader's awe, but when exposed as "mask" and "trick," makes possible the reader's defense and revenge. The speaker's rapidly alternating opinions in "Quotation and Originality" represent different phases of the reader's life cycle we have traced in other works. Now the essay shifts once again from negating the power of quotation to recommending it. Despite the efforts of criticism, the impact of borrowed material is so great that writers seek to imitate the *effect* of quotation even in original work, "ascribing their own sentence to an imaginary person, in order to give it weight." Although he knows that "many men can write better under a mask than for themselves," he immediately denigrates this strategy as "a sort of dramatizing talent . . . without the least original eloquence" (W.VIII.196). Here Emerson describes but does not defend his own "dramatizing" method in speaking through the Orphic poet or, in the journals, through the pseudonym of "Osman" (see JMN.VIII.4–5n.), and also in the self-quotation and the quotation of quotations that composing from his journals entailed. We must assume that the functional equality in his own prose of original and derived material contributes to the unstable distinctions between invention and quotation in this essay. The emphasis on the authorial subject in this part of "Quotation and Originality" predictably brings about a reaction against it in renewed praise of collective authorship. We live "in a circle of intelligences that [reaches] . . . back to the first geometer, bard, mason. . . . [E]very individual is only a momentary fixation of what was yesterday another's, is to-day his, and will belong to a third to-morrow." However, the next paragraph begins, "But there remains the indefeasible persistency of the individual to be himself." The threat posed by Emerson as reader/critic to his own authorial integrity finally provokes the defense of originality which was aborted earlier: "To all that can be said of the preponderance of the Past, the single word Genius is a sufficient reply. . . . The divine never quotes, but is, and creates" (W.VIII.199–201).

Present inspiration "makes the Past forgotten," and no one practices that forgetting or knows its importance better than Emerson. Creativity "implies Will"—the will to forget, the will to power: "Genius believes its faintest presentiment against the testimony of all history." Emerson's turn to faith in the possibility of originality is a compromise solution. Originality involves the displacement of an objective condition by a subjective one; it equates "being" with being one's self. However, the writer is both history's object and its subject; he creates and feels himself created. His will triumphs by a willed yielding:

> If to [Will] the sentiment of piety be added, if the thinker feels that the thought most strictly his own is not his own, and recognizes the perpetual suggestions of the Supreme Intellect, the oldest thoughts become new and fertile whilst he speaks them. (W.VIII.201–202)

Looking with "piety" toward the "Supreme Intellect" is a version of the alienated majesty that allows one to discover one's own strength only when it is externalized in or projected onto another writer. Because the oversoul manifests itself in all men and diffuses power in collective authorship, any single man is prevented from appearing intimidating. Emerson can experience his power as an external force without engaging in a contest with particular authors.

Emerson's own literary biography testifies to the truth of his insights into the necessary pretenses of quotation and reminds us of the reflexivity of this essay. His early journals show how the writer discovers his gift by reifying it in the quotation, which he sees as the manifestation of another's power over him. The feeling of being ravished by other geniuses that pervades the early journals survives in his tendency to prefer himself in the guise of his quoted sources, "ascribing [his] own sentence to an imaginary person." In order to effect the substitution of self for other, an initial error must be committed and corrected. Awed by another writer's thought, Emerson discovers that it is his own. This is the essential trick of quotation: a moment of unconscious projection is necessary to bring about the full consciousness that can confess its prior self-deceptions:

> The Intellect goes out of the Individual, & floats over its own being, & regards its own being always as a foreign fact, & not as I & mine. *I & mine* cannot see the Wonder of their existence. This the Intellect always ponders. (JMN.V.446–47)

Emerson's theorizing in "Quotation and Originality" and elsewhere brings together many of the elements we have been investigating. We can begin to understand how and why the higher criticism, a theory of influence and reading, is connected to poetry, a literature of irony and sublimity. Both turn on the drama of self and other, which has as one of its crucial scenes the confrontation of the self *as* other. To summarize, then, the young reader, looking on past masters, wants to emulate their achievement. To him, these authors and their books seem surrounded by the halo of genius. He invokes the muses of the ancients to inspire him, and the great authors enter him in his acts of imitation. But the glory of literature is the reader's projection of his own power and desire. He sees what he wants to be; he feels the effect he wants to produce. He experiences the other author as an overwhelming, aggressive presence whose voice invades him and makes him its instrument.

Emulation results in crisis. The reader is so fully receptive to the whole literary universe that he is overcome by the sheer quantity of books. His integrity is threatened, not by a single influence, but by an incomprehensible multitude. Imitation of a past that is present to him as chaotic fragments seems impossible. Several defensive reactions may occur. He can accept the plenitude of earlier works and turn them against each other. This reaction is evident in the way Emerson uses German writers against British ones, for example, or, in *Representative Men*, the way he uses one man's strengths to show up another's weaknesses. Frequently, he denies the existence of other writers with the theory of collective or anonymous authorship. More aggressively, he claims that civilization is himself writ large. As reader, he bestows meaning on what he reads, recognizes it as an extension of himself, and absorbs it into himself. To quote another is an act of narcissistic mirroring, whether one is, at that instant, more in love with oneself or with one's reflection. In another crisis brought about by self-consciousness, which quickly catches up with such strategies, the subject finds that the discovery of resemblance results in an appallingly solipsistic universe. Distinctions between self and other, reader and text, present and past are lost. The glory of art, arising from its otherness, cannot long survive identification. This stage corresponds to the reader's inability to "continue the sentence" begun by other writers. The claim of identity breaks down when he does not produce a work of epic stature. What looks and feels like failure restores the dualism necessary for sublimity. The book once again becomes the other, and the power of its author over the reader returns. The stage again is set for invocation.

More important than any momentarily stationary position in this cycle is the passage between positions. This is the sublime and/or ironic turn celebrated by Emerson as "transition" and "metamorphosis." The ability always to break out of either a dominant or a subordinate stance, not dominance itself, is what brings about the sensation of power. Ultimately, he desires freedom more than control. Transition is the moment of forgetfulness that produces the discontinuity so characteristic of his prose. In order to have the feeling of newness and change, he must deny repetition, refusing to acknowledge that his reactions are patterned. On the surface, Freud's dictum holds; we repeat because we will not remember.[2] But Emerson's tone of ironic naïveté admits a half-knowledge of recurrence which convinces us that we are not dreaming his repetitions.[3]

MICHAEL T. GILMORE

Emerson and the Persistence of the Commodity[†]

In Emerson's essay "Wealth" there appears a glowing account of peaches destined for the market: "When the farmer's peaches are taken from under the tree and carried into town, they have a new look and a hundredfold value over the fruit which grew on the same bough and lies fulsomely on the ground. The craft of the merchant is this bringing a thing from where it abounds to where it is costly."[1]

2. Sigmund Freud, *Beyond the Pleasure Principle*, edited and translated by James Strachey (New York: W. W. Norton, 1961), p. 12.

3. Peter Hughes connects the problems of quotation, repetition, and modernity in "Allusion and Expression in Eighteenth-Century Literature," in *The Author in His Work: Essays on a Problem of Criticism*, edited by Louis Martz and Aubrey Williams (New Haven: Yale University Press, 1978), pp. 297–317.

† From Michael T. Gilmore, *American Romanticism and the Marketplace* (Chicago: U of Chicago P, 1985), pp. 18–34. Reprinted by permission of University of Chicago Press. This chapter originally appeared under the same title in *Emerson: Prospect and Retrospect*, ed. Joel Porte, Harvard English Studies, vol. 10 (Cambridge, Mass.: Harvard University Press, 1982), pp. 65–84.

1. From *The Conduct of Life*, vol. 6, *The Complete Works of Ralph Waldo Emerson*, ed. Edward W. Emerson, Centenary Edition (Boston: Houghton Mifflin, 1903–4), p. 87. Additional references to this edition will be cited in the text and identified by the abbreviation W followed by volume and page number.

It is instructive to compare this passage with the one in *Walden* where Thoreau condemns the marketing of huckleberries: "The fruits do not yield their true flavor to the purchaser of them, nor to him who raises them for market. . . . It is a vulgar error to suppose that you have tasted huckleberries who never plucked them. A huckleberry never reaches Boston; they have not been known there since they grew on her three hills. The ambrosial and essential part of the fruit is lost with the bloom which is rubbed off in the market cart, and they become mere provender. As long as Eternal Justice reigns, not one innocent huckleberry can be transported thither from the country's hills."[2]

For Emerson, the transformation of nature's fruits into commodities gives them "a new look" and multiplies their value "a hundredfold"; for Thoreau, the identical process empties the world of significance, draining the huckleberry of its "true flavor" and "essential part." Though "Wealth" was not published until 1860, Emerson first delivered it in lecture form as early as 1851–52, when Thoreau was working on his revisions of *Walden*; the two passages might almost have been written as rebuttals to each other. Indeed, the sentiments of "Wealth" seem to constitute a rebuttal not only to Thoreau's economic views but to those expressed by Emerson himself before his drift toward conservatism. In earlier writings Emerson is less "the seer of *laisser-faire* capitalism," in Daniel Aaron's phrase,[3] than a critic of the marketplace for whom nature, regarded solely as commodity, "is debased, as if one looking at the ocean can remember only the price of fish."[4] This Emerson takes his ideal of self-reliance from the agrarian or Jeffersonian past rather than the commercial and industrial future. In common with many of his contemporaries, he sees the new economic order as a threat to individual autonomy, an indication not so much of man's power over his environment as of the instability of the material world. Yet even at this stage of his career one can detect the Emerson who will subsequently assert in "Wealth," "The counting-room maxims liberally expounded are laws of the universe. The merchant's economy is a coarse symbol of the soul's economy" (W 6:125). These contradictions and inconsistencies in his attitude toward the market regime are precisely what locate Emerson in the history of his period and make him a truly "representative man" of Jacksonian America.[5]

The antimarket side of Emerson is most prominent in works dating from the depression of 1837–43. In "The Transcendentalist," a lecture of 1841, he

2. *Walden*, ed. J. Lyndon Shanley (Princeton: Princeton University Press, 1971), p. 173.
3. Daniel Aaron, *Men of Good Hope: A Story of American Progressives* (New York: Oxford University Press, 1951), p. 8.
4. From "The Method of Nature," in *The Collected Works of Ralph Waldo Emerson*, vol. 1, *Nature, Addresses, and Lectures*, ed. Robert E. Spiller and Alfred R. Ferguson (Cambridge, Mass.: Harvard University Press, 1971), p. 131. Additional references to this edition will be cited in the test and identified by the abbreviation CW followed by volume and page number.
5. Joel Porte examines some of Emerson's affinities with his age in *Representative Man: Ralph Waldo Emerson in His Time* (New York: Oxford University Press, 1979). Porte finds parallels between Emerson's temperamental pattern of expansion and deflation and the "spermatic economy" of Jacksonian banking and revivalism. See esp. pp. 247–82. Several other studies focus more directly on Emerson's economic thought. In an important essay, "American Romanticism and the Depression of 1837," William Charvat argues that Emerson was repelled by the materialism of the "new middle class, who speculated in land . . . and were turning us into a money-mad nation without value, without principles"; in *The Profession of Authorship in America, 1800–1870: The Papers of William Charvat*, ed. Matthew J. Bruccoli (Columbus: Ohio State University Press, 1968), pp. 49–67; quotation from p. 62. Quentin Anderson claims that Emerson devised his conception of the imperial self in reaction against "a society in which self-definition had come close to being reduced to a quest for property." See Anderson's article, "Property and Vision in Nineteenth-Century America," *Virginia Quarterly Review* 54 (Summer 1978): 385–410 (quotation from p. 409). My own argument emphasizes Emerson's ambivalence toward the antebellum economy, his delight in as well as his disdain for the marketplace.

himself characterizes the "new views" prevalent in New England as a reaction against the commercialism of the age. "What is popularly called Transcendentalism among us," he notes, "is Idealism; Idealism as it appears in 1842" (CW 1:201). In other epochs the hunger for spiritual truth made patriots or protestants; the same impulse, "falling on Unitarian and commercial times, makes the peculiar shades of Idealism which we know" (CW 1:206). Although Emerson is not an uncritical admirer of the disaffected youth who adopt the Transcendental philosophy, he does share their objections to "the common labors and competitions of the market" (CW 1:207).

"Man the Reformer," another lecture of 1841, is outspoken in attacking the modern capitalist economy and enumerating the "sins" habitual in exchange. "The general system of our trade," Emerson declares, ". . . is a system of selfishness . . . of distrust, of concealment, of superior keenness, not of giving but of taking advantage." He is careful to point out that the abuses of commerce are not confined to the merchant or manufacturer. The farmer who raises crops for market is also implicated, as is the consumer: "it is only necessary to ask a few questions as to the progress of the articles of commerce from the fields where they grew, to our houses, to become aware that we eat and drink and wear perjury and fraud in a hundred commodities" (CW 1:147–48). Government, education, and even religion have been infected by the mercantile spirit, Emerson says elsewhere in assessing "the present age." And he concludes, "There is nothing more important in the culture of man than to resist the dangers of commerce."[6]

Emerson's dislike of "commercial times" is closely bound up with his individualism; self-reliance, in his view, is not a corollary but a casualty of exchange relations. Nonconformity cannot survive the interactions of the marketplace, where the requirements for success include "a certain dapperness and compliance, an acceptance of customs . . . a compromise of private opinion and lofty integrity." Every man is constrained to put on "the harness of routine and obsequiousness" in order to earn money (CW 1:147–48). In the essay "Self-Reliance" (1841), Emerson uses an image drawn from commerce to convey his sense that capitalist society extinguishes independence: "Society is a joint-stock company in which the members agree for the better securing of his bread to each shareholder, to surrender the liberty and culture of the eater" (CW 2:29).

The young Transcendentalist withdraws into idleness to avoid this condition. Even reform holds limited appeal for him because movements like Temperance or Abolition tend to degenerate into marketable commodities and to lose their integrity in the process of exchange. Each cause, Emerson explains, "becomes speedily a little shop, where the article, let it have been at first never so subtle and ethereal, is now made up into portable and convenient cakes, and retailed in small quantities to suit purchasers" (CW 1:211). To the Transcendentalist, who above all cherishes his autonomy, any activity is distasteful that requires courting others. "It is simpler to be self-dependent," he believes. "The height, the deity of man is to be self-sustained, to need no gift, no foreign force" (CW 1:203–4).

---

6. From the introductory lecture to the series "The Present Age," delivered December 4, 1839, in *The Early Lectures of Ralph Waldo Emerson*, vol. 3, *1838–1842*, ed. Stephen E. Whicher, Robert E. Spiller, and Wallace E. Williams (Cambridge, Mass.: Harvard University Press, 1959, 1964, 1972), pp. 190–91.

Admittedly, the Transcendentalist has as yet produced "no solid fruit" in his isolation (CW 1:207). He is nevertheless a recognizable if somewhat Hamlet-like descendant of the Jeffersonian husbandman. According to Jefferson, the hallmark of the cultivator is his abstention from exchange. His virtue is secure because he relies for his livelihood on "his own soil and industry" and does not "depend for it on the casualties and caprice of customers."[7] For Emerson, the husbandman's example is the antidote to "the ways of trade." As he observes in "Man the Reformer," there seems no escape from the compromises and dependencies of commerce save "to begin the world anew, as he does who puts the spade into the ground for food" (CW 1:147).

Emerson is far from insisting that everyone should become a farmer. What he holds up for imitation is not the actual practice of husbandry but the principle of self-sufficiency contained in "the doctrine of the Farm," the doctrine "that every man ought to stand in primary relations with the work of the world, ought to do it himself" (CW 1:152, 155). This program, which Thoreau was to carry out at Walden Pond, essentially involves reducing one's wants and endeavoring to satisfy them oneself so as to minimize dependence on others. It demands intellectual independence as well as plain living and points to the affirmations of "Self-Reliance," where Emerson again employs a metaphor, this time drawn from farming, to illustrate his idea of self-trust: "There is a time in every man's education when he arrives at the conviction that envy is ignorance; that imitation is suicide; that he must take himself for better, for worse, as his portion; that though the wide universe is full of good, no kernel of nourishing corn can come to him but through his toil bestowed on that plot of ground which is given to him to till" (CW 2:27–28).

Emerson's affirmation of agrarian values indicates how close he is in some respects to his Jacksonian contemporaries. As Marvin Meyers has shown, the Jacksonians considered themselves heirs to the Jeffersonian tradition; they appealed to the yeoman ideals of the Old Republic in their war against the Bank of the United States, the institution that symbolized for them the emergent capitalist economy. Despite their pronouncements in favor of laissez faire, they were beset by fears of a world out of control; the actual workings of the market seemed incoherent to them rather than rational and orderly. Jackson himself, in denouncing the banking system as a threat to economic independence, repeatedly used language expressive of randomness and chaotic change: "great and sudden fluctuations . . . rendering property insecure and the wages of labor unsteady and uncertain," "unexpected and ruinous contraction," "ebbs and flows in the currency." Meyers notes the epistemological strain in these attacks on the "Monster Bank," which flooded the economy with paper money "having of itself no intrinsic value," in Jackson's words. Since the Jacksonians linked freedom to economic self-reliance, to "tangibles owned and controlled," as Meyers puts it, and ultimately to the land, the survival of liberty itself, they believed, depended on their struggle to check the growth of capitalism.[8]

Emerson draws near to this fearful side of Jacksonianism in a journal entry for 1838: "This invasion of Nature by Trade with its Money, its Steam, its Rail-

---

7. Thomas Jefferson, *Notes on the State of Virginia*, ed. Thomas Perkins Abernethy (New York: Harper Torchbooks, 1964), p. 157.
8. Marvin Meyers, *The Jacksonian Persuasion: Politics and Belief* (Stanford: Stanford University Press, 1957), p. 179; Andrew Jackson, "Farewell Address," in *Social Theories of Jacksonian Democracy*, ed. Joseph L. Blau (Indianapolis: Bobbs-Merrill, 1954), pp. 12–13.

road, threatens to upset the balance of man, and establish a new Universal Monarchy more tyrannical than Babylon or Rome."[9] His sense that nature has been violated by commerce was widely shared at this time in America, where, as he remarked in 1844, "out of doors all seems a market" (CW 1:239). As the United States transformed itself from a static, agrarian economy to a mobile, commercial society, land itself was drawn into the orbit of the market and was dethroned "from the supreme position it had occupied in the eighteenth-century world view." It was now perceived as an asset to be developed for profit or an object of speculation, liable, like any commodity, to arbitrary and fluctuating assessments of its value. Under the market regime, value itself came to be regarded as subjective, determined not by the inherent properties of an object but by extrinsic factors such as opinion and desire. Clearly it was not only paper money that seemed to have "of itself no intrinsic value" in Jackson's America. Indeed, the Jacksonian campaign against the Bank can be seen as merely the surface expression of a deeper uneasiness over what Karl Polanyi has called "the extreme artificiality of market economy." To convert land and labor into articles of exchange, Polanyi points out, is to make them into "fictitious" commodities, to treat them according to the falsehood that they are produced for sale on the market. It is to allow the process of exchange to set a price on human beings and their natural surroundings.[1] Or as Emerson himself observes, trade "goes to put everything *into market*, talent, beauty, virtue, and man himself" (CW 1:234). In "The Transcendentalist," it will be recalled, Emerson claims that "commercial times" give rise to Idealism; what lies behind this, he suggests in "Man the Reformer," is dissatisfaction with the artificial valuations of market culture: "It is when your facts and persons grow unreal and fantastic by too much falsehood, that the scholar flies to the world of ideas, and aims to recruit and replenish nature from that source" (CW 1:146).

The scholar has a special obligation to give utterance to ideas, Emerson states in "The Method of Nature," another work of 1841, "in a country where the material interest is so predominant as it is in America." The fluctuation that Jacksonians decried in the currency he finds endemic to commercial society; he interprets it as an index of the lack of secure values in a culture preoccupied with speculation and the scramble for riches: "The rapid wealth which hundreds in the community acquire in trade, or by the incessant expansions of our population and arts, enchants the eyes of all the rest; the luck of one is the hope of thousands, and the proximity of the bribe acts like the neighborhood of a gold mine to impoverish the farm, the school, the church, the house, and the very body and feature of man" (CW 1:120). Although Emerson goes on to disclaim any animus against "the mart of commerce" (CW 1:120), it is evident that he regards the marketplace as the realm of instability and chance. Its revolutions impress him with the folly of putting faith in material possessions and contribute to his distrust of the physical world in general. "Self-Reliance," for example, makes the point that "reliance on Property . . . is the want of self-reliance" and mentions bankruptcies along with fire, storm, and mobs as occurrences over which men have little or no control (CW 2:49). The essay "Circles" (1841), which presents a sustained

---

9. *The Journals and Miscellaneous Notebooks of Ralph Waldo Emerson*, ed. William H. Gilman et al. (Cambridge, Mass.: Harvard University Press, 1960–), 7:268.
1. Morton J. Horwitz, *The Transformation of American Law, 1780–1860* (Cambridge, Mass.: Harvard University Press, 1977), p. 48; Karl Polanyi, *The Great Transformation: The Political and Economic Origins of Our Time* (1944; rpt., Boston: Beacon Press, 1957), pp. 72–73.

vision of a world in flux, adduces one of its earliest illustrations from the uncertainties of trade: "Every thing looks permanent until its secret is known. A rich estate appears to women a firm and lasting fact; to a merchant, one easily created out of any materials, and easily lost" (CW 2:180). Emerson's next illustration in this essay indicates that even land, now that it has been drawn into the exchange process, exhibits the instability of portable property; to the "large"—that is, market—farmer, it is as speculative an investment as a gold mine. "An orchard, good tillage, good grounds, seem a fixture, like a gold mine, or a river, to a citizen; to a large farmer, not much more fixed than the state of the crop" (CW 2:180).

"Circles" demonstrates in detail that the very possibility of "firm and lasting facts" is at issue in a cosmos where "there are no fixtures" and "all that we reckoned settled, shakes and rattles" (CW 2:179, 184). The world itself—or to speak more accurately, the phenomenal world—behaves as unpredictably as the marketplace. The death of Emerson's son in 1842 elicits a despairing acknowledgment that "the results of life are uncalculated and uncalculable" (W 3:69). In the essay "Experience" (1844), Emerson actually likens Waldo's death to the kind of economic setbacks that were so prevalent in antebellum America:

> Grief too will make us idealists. In the death of my son, now more than two years ago, I seem to have lost a beautiful estate—no more. I cannot get it nearer to me. If tomorrow I should be informed of the bankruptcy of my principal debtors, the loss of my property would be a great inconvenience to me, perhaps, for many years; but it would leave me as it found me—neither better nor worse. So it is with this calamity. [W 3:48–49]

Although Emerson himself refuses to exalt fortune "into a divinity" (W 3:70), he recognizes that for most men the vicissitudes of life make it seem a game of chance, like commercial speculation. Hence his appeal at the conclusion of "Self-Reliance": "So use all that is called Fortune. Most men gamble with her, and gain all, and lose all, as her wheel rolls. But do thou leave as unlawful these winnings, and deal with Cause and Effect, the chancellors of God. In the Will work and acquire, and thou hast chained the wheel of Chance, and shall sit hereafter out of fear from her rotations" (CW 2:50).

Emerson's own tendencies toward Idealism were strengthened by the Crash of 1837. The collapse of the economy, which he records in his journal for April and May of that year, leads him to question the ultimate reality of matter. After noting details of bank failure and worsening unemployment, Emerson continues:

> I see a good in such emphatic and universal calamity as the times bring, that they dissatisfy me with society. . . . Society has played out its last stake; it is check-mated. Young men have no hope. Adults stand like day-laborers idle in the streets. None calleth us to labor. . . . The present generation is bankrupt of principles and hope, as of property. . . . I am forced to ask if the Ideal might not also be tried. Is it to be taken for granted that it is impracticable? Behold the boasted world has come to nothing. . . . Behold . . . here is the Soul erect and Unconquered still.[2]

---

2. *The Journals and Miscellaneous Notebooks*, 5:331–32. William Charvat also cites this passage and says that the effect of the economic collapse was "to send Emerson deeper into his idealism" ("American Romanticism and the Depression of 1837," p. 63).

It is a short step from these remarks to the conclusion that nothing is reliable or permanent except the Soul. In fact Emerson had reached such a conclusion a year earlier in *Nature*, the first major statement of his Transcendentalism and a work, though it antedates the Panic, that provides the most complex and provocative exposition of his attitude toward the market.

It may seem curious to speak of *Nature* as a commentary on exchange society. The essay has been studied from virtually every perspective *but* this one, and although it was composed at a moment of intense ideological ferment, the climax of Jackson's struggle to destroy the Bank, it appears to take only indirect and passing notice of recent events. In a more general sense, however, the very first "use" of nature that Emerson considers, "Commodity," suggests his active interest in contemporary issues. A very different book, Marx's *Capital* (1867), similarly begins with an examination of "The Commodity"; and Emerson as well as Marx is concerned to make sense of, and ultimately to redeem, a world converted into articles of exchange. The structure of the essay reveals Emerson's strategy in this respect. As it proceeds from commodity to beauty, to language, to discipline, to idealism, and finally to spirit, the essay exhibits what has been called a "mounting dialectic," a movement from the concrete and physical to an affirmation of the spiritual basis of all reality.[3] In other words, Emerson will attempt to salvage the world as commodity by infusing it with the Soul.

To be sure, Emerson does not formulate his undertaking in *Nature* in exactly these terms. The task he assigns himself in the introductory section, to reconcile the visible universe and the Soul, is as old as philosophy itself. What is striking, however, is the view of nature which he sets forth under the heading of "Commodity." He suggests that nineteenth-century man has already approached reconciliation with the creation through technology and commerce. Writing of "those advantages which our senses owe to nature" (CW I:11), Emerson pictures a thoroughly domesticated cosmos ministering incessantly to man, a cosmos where everything conspires to make him feel at home: "Beasts, fire, water, stones, and corn serve him. The field is at once his floor, his work-yard, his play-ground, his garden, and his bed." Two lines from George Herbert's "Man" add poetic emphasis—

> More servants wait on man
> Than he'll take notice of.

—and a paragraph-long account of the "useful arts" celebrates technology's role in promoting progress:

> He [man] no longer waits for favoring gales, but by means of steam, he realizes the fable of Aeolus's bag, and carries the two and thirty winds in the boiler of his boat. To diminish friction, he paves the road with iron bars, and, mounting a coach with a ship-load of men, animals, and merchandise behind him, he darts through the country, from town to town, like an eagle or a swallow through the air. By the aggregate of these aids, how is the face of the world changed, from the era of Noah to that of Napoleon! The private poor man hath cities, shops, canals, bridges, built for him. He goes to the post-office, and the human race run on his errands; to the bookshop, and the human race read and write of all that happens, for him; to the courthouse, and nations repair his wrongs. He sets his house upon the

---

3. On *Nature*'s escalating development, see Richard Lee Francis, "The Architectonics of Emerson's *Nature*," *American Quarterly* 19 (1967): 39–53.

road, and the human race go forth every morning, and shovel out the snow, and cut a path for him. [CW I:11–12]

It would be hard to imagine a more enthusiastic assessment of the developments that Emerson would deplore, two years later, as the "invasion of Nature by Trade with its Money, its Steam, its Railroad." The market aided by technology puts all things into motion and creates a world that is portable as well as tractable to human purposes. The very ground under man's feet has become fluid like the sea or the air: hence the reference to transporting "shiploads" of produce by rail and traversing the country with the speed of "an eagle or a swallow." The "changed face" that the modern world wears is very much a human countenance; looking about him, man beholds a universe that seems his own product and mirrors back his image. When, in the "Discipline" section, Emerson returns briefly to the benefits of the commodity, he sums up nature's relation to man as one of duplication. Nature, he says, "offers all its kingdoms to man as the raw material which he may mould into what is useful. Man is never weary of working it up . . . until the world becomes, at last, only a realized will—the double of man" (CW I:25).

Nature may be thought of as possessing three distinct stages, and in this, the first stage, the humanization of the "Not-Me" lies well within man's power. A radically opposed view of man's relation to his cosmos emerges from the essay's second stage. Emerson has insisted from the beginning that nature's material benefits are "mercenary" (CW I:12), that "the use of Commodity, regarded by itself, is mean and squalid" (CW I:26). This negative note, which grows more emphatic as the argument progresses, culminates in a vision of the physical world as alien and debased. It leads Emerson, in the section on "Idealism," to entertain his "noble doubt": "whether nature outwardly exists." And although he determines to leave open the question of matter's absolute existence, he resolves "to regard nature as a phenomenon, not a substance; to attribute necessary existence to spirit; to esteem nature as an accident and an effect" (CW I:29–30).

Emerson's revulsion from commodity is so great that he even identifies the visible creation with scum or dross, and implicitly with excrement. In the "Language" section, he describes facts as "the end or last issue of spirit" and quotes approvingly from a French Swedenborgian, G. Oegger, whose *True Messiah* he had read in manuscript translation: "'Material objects are necessarily kinds of *scoriae* of the substantial thoughts of the Creator, which must always preserve an exact relation to their first origin; in other words, visible nature must have a spiritual and moral side'" (CW I:22–23). *Scoriae* are the slag thrown off from metals in the process of smelting; the word derives from the Greek for feces and has scatological overtones of which Emerson, as a classical scholar, would surely have been aware. That he makes this association may help to explain why he is so ready, in the "Introduction," to construe his own body as the Not-Me. Equally important, the quotation from Oegger points up the link between seeing the world as commodity, and thus potentially as "filthy lucre," and holding it in contempt. It has been argued, for example, that there exists a close connection between the rise of capitalism in the sixteenth century and Lutheran Protestantism's rejection of the world as excrement, as utterly corrupt and worthless.[4] Three centuries later, Emerson similarly devalues matter and

---

4. *Oxford English Dictionary*, s.v. *scoriae*; and see Norman O. Brown, *Life against Death: The Psychoanalytical Meaning of History* (Middletown, Conn.: Wesleyan University Press, 1959), esp. pp. 179–304.

equates it with *scoriae* precisely because the market has transformed it into objects exchangeable for money.

Man's relation to an excremental universe turns out to be one not of mastery but of estrangement. Far from feeling at home in the world, most men, according to Emerson, "abdicate [their] kingdom" and "creep into a corner" (CW I:15). And despite his earlier paean to technology, Emerson claims that nature is "not . . . now subjected to the human will" (CW I:38). The fault lies more in man than in the creation. Because men commonly relate to nature as commodity, they fail to apprehend its "spiritual and moral side" and only deepen their alienation even as they subdue the physical world: "The ruin or blank, that we see when we look at nature, is in our own eye" (CW I:43). "As we degenerate, the contrast between us and our house is more evident. We are as much strangers in nature, as we are aliens from God" (CW I:39). In the same vein Emerson's Orphic poet characterizes man's present condition as "a god in ruins." Once, the poet sings,

> [man] filled nature with his overflowing currents. . . . But, having made for himself this huge shell, his waters retired; he no longer fills the veins and veinlets; he is shrunk to a drop. He sees, that the structure still fits him, but fits him colossally. Say, rather, once it fitted him, now it corresponds to him from far and on high. He adores timidly his own work. . . . Yet sometimes he starts in his slumber, and wonders at himself and his house, and muses strangely at the resemblance betwixt him and it. [CW I:42]

These sentiments form a complete contrast to the affirmations of "Commodity." Harmony between man and his world, the ostensible goal of economic and technological progress, is said to lie in the past rather than the future. "And all history," declares the poet, "is but the epoch of one degradation" (CW I:42).

In the third stage of *Nature* Emerson reclaims the world for nineteenth-century man. He argues that Reason or intuition enables men to apprehend the spiritual element that pervades the universe and heals the breach between mind and matter. Because all objects in the world have a spiritual as well as material side, nature is not alien but emblematic and charged with meaning to the eye of Reason: "Every natural fact is a symbol of some spiritual fact. Every appearance in nature corresponds to some state of the mind, and that state of the mind can only be described by presenting that natural appearance as its picture" (CW I:18). The poet in particular, with his highly developed imagination, has the gift of discerning "this radical correspondence between visible things and human thoughts" (CW I:19). Using nature symbolically for purposes of expression, he "unfixes the land and the sea . . . and disposes them anew." "The sensual man conforms thoughts to things; the poet conforms things to his thoughts. The one esteems nature as rooted and fast; the other, as fluid, and impresses his being thereon" (CW I:31).

What the poet does figuratively, moreover, all men can do in actuality by grasping "that wonderful congruity which subsists" between them and the cosmos (CW I:40). They can overcome their alienation and make nature serve their wishes by exercising the spiritual authority to which it is obedient. In Emerson's words, "behind nature, throughout nature, spirit is present . . . it does not act upon us from without . . . but spiritually, or through ourselves. Therefore . . . spirit, that is, the Supreme Being, does not build up nature around us, but puts it forth through us. . . . [We are] nourished by unfailing fountains" and have at our command "inexhaustible power." "Who can set bounds to the possibilities of man?" (CW I:38), Emerson exclaims rhetorically, and he envisions through his Orphic poet the imminent realization of "the kingdom of man over nature . . . a dominion such as now is beyond his dream of God" (CW I:45).

For Emerson, in sum, the taint of commodity is transcended by spiritualizing matter and exchanging it for meaning instead of money. As this procedure suggests, he remains unwittingly indebted to the marketplace. In economic terms, a commodity has both use value and exchange value; similarly in Emerson's terms, things both exist in their own right and stand for something else.[5] Indeed, the whole third step of Emerson's argument in *Nature* reveals his profound ambivalence about the market economy. It makes clear just how much there is in common between treating nature as commodity and "degrading nature"—a favorite word of Emerson's in this connection—by "suggesting its dependence on spirit" (CW I:35).

Although Emerson rejects commerce as a way to unify the Me and Not-Me, he betrays his admiration for it in his conception of the Soul. For spirit functions exactly like the market to domesticate the world and make it portable: to transform the creation into "the double of man." In "Commodity" nature is at once man's floor, his workyard, his playground, his garden, and his bed; in the "Prospects" section, which prophesies reunification through spirit, the world is his house:

> Nature is not fixed but fluid. Spirit alters, moulds, makes it. The immobility or bruteness of nature is the absence of spirit; to pure spirit, it is volatile, it is obedient. Every spirit builds itself a house; and beyond its house, a world; and beyond its world, a heaven. Know then, that the world exists for you. For you is the phenomenon perfect. What we are, that only can we see. All that Adam had, all that Caesar could, you have and can do. Adam called his house, heaven and earth; Caesar called his house, Rome; you perhaps call yours, a cobler's trade; a hundred acres of ploughed land; or a scholar's garret. Yet, line for line and point for point, your dominion is as great as theirs, though without fine names. Build, therefore, your own world. [CW I:44–45]

The malleability of nature, of which the Orphic poet sings here, is a commonplace of Romantic thought. In the context established by Emerson, however, the poet's song is a mimicry of the capitalist spirit it otherwise condemns. The references to Adam and Caesar further illuminate the dual impulses that inform the essay. The references suggest two altogether different approaches to nature, peaceful coexistence and ruthless domination, and they point simultaneously to the agrarian past and the capitalist future. In other writings Emerson himself compares the farmer to Adam, and the figure who reminds him most of Caesar, Napoleon Bonaparte, appears in *Representative Men* (1850) as the champion of the commercial middle class.[6]

Nature bears out Emerson's own assertion, made in a lecture on literature in 1837, that "the great political and economical revolution which has transpired . . . is very conspicuously traced in letters."[7] The agrarianism he shares

---

5. Cf. Marc Shell, *The Economy of Literature* (Baltimore: Johns Hopkins University Press, 1978), p. 84.
6. See the essay "Farming," in *Society and Solitude*, vol.7, *The Complete Works*, p. 148.
7. *The Early Lectures*, 2:66.

with the Jacksonians tells only half the story of his relation to them and to the age. As Meyers emphasizes, it tells only half the story of the Jacksonians' own feelings about the economic revolution they both advanced and denounced. Characterizing them as "venturous conservatives," Meyers writes that "the Jacksonians wanted to preserve the virtues of a simple agrarian republic without sacrificing the rewards and conveniences of modern capitalism."[8] Something very similar might be said of *Nature*. Disavowing, on the one hand, the commercial outlook of the times, Emerson, on the other, purifies and sanctions an aggressive, "capitalistic" ethos of mastery over nature.[9]

The essay "Compensation," published in 1841 but conceived as early as 1826, provides an even more extreme illustration of this tension in Emerson's thought. It begins with several paragraphs in which he heaps scorn upon "the base estimate of the market." He describes having heard a minister preach a sermon on the Last Judgment which pictured the wicked as thriving in this life and promised the saints eventual compensation for their sufferings "by giving them," in Emerson's sarcastic gloss, "the like gratifications another day—bank-stock and doubloons, venison and champagne." The minister's error, he adds, "lay in the immense concession that the bad are successful; that justice is not done now" (CW 2:56). But having dismissed as shortsighted an economic standard of success—"every crime is punished," he contends, "every virtue rewarded . . . in silence and certainty" (CW 2:60)—Emerson replaces it with an ethical theory that seems almost to parody the accounting procedures of the marketplace.

Emerson's very language, including the title of his essay, bespeaks a predilection to find economic categories applicable to the operations of the Soul. With undisguised admiration for the proverbs "hourly preached in all markets and workshops," he insists, "the doctrine that every thing has its price . . . is not less sublime in the columns of a leger than . . . in all the action and reaction of nature" (CW 2:64, 67). Because "a third silent party" participates in "all our bargains," and the "soul of things takes on itself the guaranty of the fulfillment of every contract," no vicious action can result in gain, no honest conduct "come to loss" (CW 2:69). God himself, in his view, is a kind of supremely efficient bookkeeper who "makes square the eternal account" (CW 2:70): "The longer the payment is withholden, the better for you; for compound interest on compound interest is the rate and usage of this exchequer" (CW 2:69). Here, and with a vengeance, is the commercialization of all things, the very attitude Emerson objected to in the preacher's sermon on the Judgment Day. Once again, the best commentary on this frame of mind, which seems unable to distinguish between natural law and the market regime ("in Nature, nothing can be given, all things are sold" [CW 2:63]), comes from Emerson himself and appears in the essay "Worship" from *The Conduct of Life* (1860): "Heaven always bears some proportion to earth. The god of the cannibals will be a cannibal, of the crusaders a crusader, and of the merchants a merchant" (W 6:205).

"Compensation" reveals an Emerson already well on his way to becoming an apologist for commercial and industrial capitalism. His criticisms of trade as

8. Meyers, p. vii.
9. Stephen E. Whicher writes of Emerson and *Nature*: "The aim of this strain in his thought is not virtue, but freedom and mastery." See *Freedom and Fate: An Inner Life of Ralph Waldo Emerson* (Philadelphia: University of Pennsylvania Press, 1953), p. 56.

degrading and capricious decline in importance until they largely disappear by the Civil War. His defense of the market as rational and even spiritual in its operations, the view implicit in *Nature* and "Compensation," grows more dominant in the same period, even as laissez-faire ideology proves increasingly influential in American culture. This favorable view is especially strong in a work like "Wealth," where Emerson repudiates the radical "excesses" of his early thought and glorifies worldly success as a sign of spiritual election. The implications of *Nature* attain a curious and perhaps inevitable fulfillment in this essay, as Emerson attributes to great wealth the very powers that he once ascribed to spirit. Money rather than the Soul wins praise for its ability to confer "command over nature" (W 6:96) and to enable its possessor to implement his vision: "Men of sense esteem wealth to be the assimilation of nature to themselves, the converting of the sap and juices of the planet to the incarnation and nutriment of their design. Power is what they want . . . power to execute their design, power to give legs and feet, form and actuality to their thought" (W 6:93).

Since "wealth is moral" (W 6:103), moreover, riches advertise their owner as a man of character. Under the market system, whose workings are as dependable as the laws of nature, "property rushes from the idle and imbecile to the industrious, brave and persevering" (W 6:106). Commerce is still a game, according to Emerson, but "a game of skill" in which chance plays no part: "There is always a reason, *in the man*, for his good or bad fortune, and so in making money. Men talk as if there were some magic about this . . . [But the successful entrepreneur] knows that all goes on the old road, pound for pound, cent for cent—for every effect a perfect cause—and that good luck is another name for tenacity of purpose" (W 6:100). Self-reliance, once seen as threatened by "commercial times," is now said to flourish in the unregulated marketplace; the enterprising individual who has done his work faithfully "can well afford not to conciliate" and "contracts no stain" from the exchange process (W 6:92). In "Wealth" Emerson gives highest marks to the independence enjoyed by the rich man, not the husbandman, and he depicts as obsolete the ideal of self-sufficiency associated in "Man the Reformer" with the farm: "When men now alive were born, the farm yielded everything that was consumed on it. The farm yielded no money, and the farmer got on without. If he fell sick, his neighbors came in to his aid; each gave a day's work, or a half day . . . hoed his potatoes, mowed his hay, reaped his rye; well knowing that no man could afford to hire labor without selling his land. . . . Now, the farmer buys almost all he consumes—tinware, cloth, sugar, tea, coffee, fish, coal, railroad tickets and newspapers" (W 6:118–19).

The Jeffersonian tradition is no longer alive in the Emerson of *The Conduct of Life*. Even a work like "Farming," written around the same time and often anthologized as an example of Emerson's agrarianism,[1] in fact only shows how far he has traveled from this strain in his original philosophy. Although the essay pays tribute to the farmer for his industry and closeness to nature, it also compares him, in a truly astonishing image, to the boy who watches the loom in an English factory and is known as "a minder." It pictures nature, not as fluid and volatile, but as a "machine . . . of colossal proportions . . . [that] is never out of gear" (W 7:142). The farmer can hardly be considered a model of

1. See, for example, the collection edited by M. Thomas Inge, *Agrarianism in American Literature* (New York: Odyssey Press, 1969). "Farming" was first delivered in 1858 but not published until 1870, when it appeared as a chapter of *Society and Solitude*.

independence if he is a figurative factory hand, and it is clear that husbandry has ceased to have this significance for Emerson. He now thinks of farming as a refuge from the cares of city life:

> All men keep the farm in reserve as an asylum where, in case of mischance, to hide their poverty—or a solitude, if they do not succeed in society. And who knows how many glances of remorse are turned this way from the bankrupts of trade, from mortified pleaders in courts and senates, or from the victims of idleness and pleasure? Poisoned by town life and town vices, the sufferer resolves: "Well, my children, whom I have injured, shall go back to the land, and be recruited and cured by that which should have been my nursery, and now shall be their hospital." [W 7:132]

What deserves emphasis in this passage is the evaporation of the agrarian ethos as a viable social or economic faith. Twenty years earlier Emerson used husbandry as a metaphor for a kind of personal autonomy that seemed jeopardized by the growth of the market; he uses it here as a metaphor for withdrawal and recuperation from capitalist civilization. An escape rather than a critical vantage point, it has become irrelevant to a society based on money.

If the vitality of the agrarian ideal, with its antimarket bias, does not survive in Emerson himself, however, it is carried on by his "disciple" Thoreau. And Emerson, with the irritation of a mentor whose most promising follower reproaches him for apostasy, is at pains to reply to Thoreau's experiment in *Walden*. In "Man the Reformer" he called upon his listeners to "learn the meaning of economy" and commended "parched corn and a house with one apartment" as a discipline in freedom (CW 1:154). Thoreau seems to have mastered the lesson altogether too well for Emerson's equanimity in "Wealth." Beginning with the question, "How does that man get his living?" (W 6:85)—precisely the question Thoreau sought to answer in writing *Walden*—Emerson disparages a life of "bare subsistence" and takes issue with his erstwhile pupil's doctrine of simplicity: "It is of no use to argue the wants down: the philosophers have laid the greatness of man in making his wants few, but will a man content himself with a hut and a handful of dried pease? He is born to be rich" (W 6:88). *In Walden* Thoreau says, "Enjoy the land, but own it not," aware that in a commercial society the very fact of ownership involves one in the process of exchange.[2] Emerson evidently has him in mind when he declares in "Wealth," "No land is bad, but land is worse," and goes on to explain that farming and scholarship are incompatible: "this pottering in a few square yards of garden is dispiriting and drivelling. . . . [The scholar] grows peevish and poor-spirited. The genius of reading and of gardening are antagonistic, like resinous and vitreous electricity. One is concentrative in sparks and shocks; the other is diffuse strength; so that each disqualifies its workman for the other's duties" (W 6:116). Although Emerson is speaking here of reading, his strictures presumably apply to writing as well. As such, they amount to a rejection of Thoreau's most urgent project in *Walden*, his attempt to overcome the division of labor in his own per-

---

2. Thoreau, *Walden*, p. 207. Emerson was more sympathetic to Thoreau in essays written after Thoreau's death, such as the memorial address of 1862 and "Historic Notes of Life and Letters in New England" (1880). Bronson Alcott, in a journal entry for 1852, makes a pertinent observation on the differences between the two thinkers: "Emerson said fine things last night about Wealth, but there are finer things far to be said in praise of Poverty, which it takes a person superior to Emerson even to say worthily. Thoreau is the better man, perhaps, to celebrate that estate, about which he knows much, and which he wears as an ornament about himself—a possession that Kings and Caesars are too poor to purchase." From *The Journals of Bronson Alcott*, ed. Odell Shepard (Boston: Little, Brown, 1938), p. 261.

son by uniting husbandry and literature and to formulate a conception of the writer that will exempt him from the "curse of trade." To which Emerson rejoins, in a phrase already partly quoted, that great art—the most individual of all commodities—"contracts no stain from the market, but makes the market a silent gallery for itself" (W 6:92).

BARBARA PACKER

Ralph Waldo Emerson[†]

At the International Exposition at Paris in 1863, American products and manufactures seemed to one visitor notably inferior to European ones. Yet the American exhibit could boast a different sort of attraction. "At the end of the section were Bierstadt's picture of the Rocky Mountains, Church's Niagara, and close to these, a fine portrait of Emerson."

That the arrangers of the American exhibit saw fit to group Ralph Waldo Emerson's face with paintings of America's most celebrated pieces of natural sublimity as things worthy to attract the curiosity and admiration of Europeans suggests better than anything else the commanding position Emerson occupied in the cultural landscape of mid-nineteenth-century America. We now know, of course, that the landscape was hardly as empty as it then seemed. Many of the greatest works of the American Renaissance—*Walden*, *Moby-Dick*, *Leaves of Grass*—were in existence but were then ridiculed or neglected (though Emerson himself had tried hard to win recognition for Walt Whitman and Henry David Thoreau, at least). Still, at a time when few American authors were known outside the borders of their own country, Emerson's essays had been translated into French and German, reviewed in the London *Times*, and respectfully discussed in the *Revue des deux mondes*.

The rising literary fortunes of his contemporaries have removed Emerson from his position as lonely sentinel, but the temptation remains to treat him more as a phenomenon, like Niagara, than as a man of letters, like Nathaniel Hawthorne or Oliver Wendell Holmes. He has always been hard to classify. He was by profession first a minister, then a public lecturer, but a comparison of his addresses with Daniel Webster's shows how intimate, how eerily private his voice can sound, just as a comparison of his essays with Charles Lamb's shows how much longing for the collective ecstasies of oratory remains beneath the decorum of his printed page. In recent years philosophers have argued for his claim to be taken seriously as a philosopher, yet the verbal brilliance of his textual surface, the feline shifts of tone and stance, seem always to be pushing him back in the direction of literary artistry. But literary artists have often been offended by Emerson's frank love of the didactic, his consistent preference for the artist's genius over any of the works it has produced, and his contempt for mere craftsmanship. He was certainly a kind of social critic, and in his own day heard himself denounced as a dangerous radical, yet some modern interpreters have read his texts as covert defenses of a declining Whig aristocracy, siphoning off

† From *The Columbia Literary History of the United States*, ed. Emory Elliot (New York: Columbia UP, 1988), pp. 381–98. Reprinted by permission of the publisher.

in its imagery the raw energy of the Jacksonian democracy he both despised and envied.

The elder Henry James accused Emerson of being a man without a handle. It might be more accurate to accuse him of having too many. As the witty self-portrait he sketches at the end of the essay "Nominalist and Realist" suggests, he recognized his own close resemblance to John Dryden's Zimri, the self-thwarting genius of *Absalom and Achitophel*, who was "everything by turns and nothing long." He once boasted that after thirty years of teaching he had not a single disciple, since his aim was to bring men, not to him, but to themselves; and the sincerest compliment his protégés paid him was rejection. As Whitman said: "The best part of Emersonianism is, it breeds the giant that destroys itself."

Little in Emerson's early life suggested the equivocal eminence of his later career. He was born in Boston in 1803, in an era he later referred to as "that early ignorant & transitional *Month-of-March*" in New England culture. His father, who died when Emerson was eight, was a Unitarian clergyman who dabbled in polite literature and fostered the intellectual ambition of his sons. His death left the family in desperate straits; they managed to survive by running boarding-houses and taking charity, but the experience left its mark on Emerson. His word for the final state of spiritual misery or intellectual desiccation was always "poverty."

Mrs. Emerson managed to see that her sons attended Harvard. Ralph Waldo entered at fourteen, the second of the brothers to enter the school. His career there was undistinguished; he lacked the steady diligence of his brother William or the brilliance showed by his younger brothers Charles and Edward. The most significant thing he did there, in fact, was to begin his lifelong practice of keeping a journal (these journals and manuscript note-books—182 in all—have been published in sixteen volumes by Harvard University Press). At first Emerson used his journals for long compositions: trial essays, or parts of essays, for his college courses or competitions. But gradually the journal entries began to take on the form they were to have throughout Emerson's maturity. A stray thought, a chance observation, a fact from a scientific journal, or a paragraph from a philosopher—something catches Emerson's attention. He meditates on it, analyzes it, explores the unexpected analogies it reveals with other facts of his experience. When he has reached the end of his thought—sometimes in a few paragraphs, sometimes in a few sentences—he stops.

Unlike the turgid essays with which he had attempted (unsuccessfully) to win the admiration of the Harvard faculty, the journal entries he was writing by the early 1830s are short, intense, and vividly written. The practice of journal keeping freed him from the necessity for "methodical writing" (something he knew he had little talent for) and gave him the license to pursue whatever thought he found most interesting at the moment. In doing so, it gave him not only the material he used in his sermons, lectures, and essays (which are essentially anthologies of passages from the journals) but the ideology he repeatedly expressed in them. Only what is genuinely interesting to you can ever be interesting to another, he says; "the soul's emphasis is always right." The curious fact that "Self-Reliance," Emerson's most militant essay about personal integrity, is also about composition may have its origins in his unhappy experience at Harvard. Self-reliance is like writing in one's journal; conformity, like trying to please a professor on an assigned theme.

His first public compositions were neither wholly free nor wholly determined. Like many of his ancestors, Emerson chose to study for the ministry—a profession he desired not so much for its pastoral duties as for the scope it gave him for the practice of "eloquence." He later recalled that the discipline of the weekly sermon helped give him the habit of steady productivity he depended upon in later life. He was already learning to draw upon the paragraphs composed in his journal for a large portion of the sermon he had to produce each week; the practice gave his style a surprising freshness and an intriguing discontinuity, particularly noticeable in an era when sermons and orations were usually written according to plan. Emerson loved addressing audiences, and by all reports was both a popular and a powerful speaker; his prose style even in intimate essays never entirely loses the oratorical flavor of the sermons and speeches he and his brothers extravagantly admired and frequently memorized.

The Unitarians were a liberal denomination, and the scope they afforded Emerson for the expression of his ideas was wide—many of his sermons read like trial versions of the iconoclastic essays of his maturity. But he grew increasingly restless, and chafed under the restrictions of any creed, however generous in spirit. He never lost faith in the existence or accessibility of the divine mind, but he came to feel that all attempts to ground religious belief in external "proofs"—miracles, testimony, even Scripture itself—were doomed to fall before the corrosive effects of nineteenth-century philosophy, natural science, historical criticism, and comparative anthropology. (Emerson's older brother William had gone to study theology in Germany; he returned home so shaken by what he had learned of the new "historical" criticism of the Bible that he abandoned the ministry for the law.) Emerson chose instead to argue that the only proof of faith is the experience of faith in the individual's own soul, which can *confirm* the truths of doctrine but never be *convinced* by them: conviction emanates only from the soul. Upon the rock of this internal faith Emerson founded his life, and the immediate conviction of his soul's connectedness to godhead gave him both the courage and the serenity by which he was best known to his contemporaries.

With the death of his young wife in 1831 Emerson's ties to conventional modes of living were loosened: a legacy from her estate made it possible for him to contemplate life outside a regular profession, at least for a while. He resigned his position with the Second Church in Boston, then left for a tour of Europe, during which he paid visits to a number of the literary giants whose works he had admired from the other side of the Atlantic: Landor, Coleridge, Wordsworth, and Carlyle. Most of these meetings were comically disappointing (he gave an account of them much later in the first chapter of *English Traits*). But the meeting with Thomas Carlyle, then a struggling writer living in the wilds of Scotland, marked the beginning of a lifelong friendship and a mutually fruitful correspondence.

Emerson returned from Europe eager to publish something and begin acquiring that literary fame his journals show him passionately desiring. On the sea voyage home he confidently refers to a "book about nature" he is planning; his only anxieties concern "where and how" he is going to live. Providentially, the growth of the American lyceum movement (an adult education movement in which subscribers pooled money to hire lecturers) coincided with Emerson's need to find a way to support himself. For the next twenty-five years he spent nearly every winter season delivering lectures on the lyceum circuit, beginning first in New England and New York, but eventually traveling as far south as St. Louis and as far north as Montreal. His financial rewards from the lectures were sometimes pitifully small, but the forum the lyceum provided for the development of his ideas was invaluable. His curiosity had always been wide-ranging, and his mind worked best by analogizing; now he could lecture on topics like natural history (his very first lyceum lecture is entitled "Water"), as well as on more familiar subjects like biography or English literature. Emerson found in lecturing precisely the right blend of discipline and freedom. He could choose his topics, so long as he kept to a certain length and had the manuscript ready by the scheduled date of the lecture. The stimulus to production was just what he needed; most of the essays we now have in his published works had their origin in lyceum lectures, and in their startling juxtapositions of idea and shifts of tone we can see residues of the techniques Emerson first developed to hold the attention of an audience.

Three years after he first confided his plans for a little book to his journal, Emerson's first book appeared. *Nature* (1836) was a small book, but its ambitions were vast. Like Edgar Allan Poe's *Eureka* (1849), Emerson's book aims to present nothing less than a theory of the universe, of its origin, present condition, and final destiny. Emerson asks us to consider nature from a variety of perspectives—as material benefit, as aesthetic object, as preceptress of stoicism—then hold out the intoxicating possibility that the vast "riddle" of nature might someday be solved by man and that the "kingdom of man over nature" prophesied since the beginning of the world might then organize itself around our organs of perception.

We have two clues to help us in solving the riddle of the Sphinx: ecstasy and science. The former dissolves us in moments of joy in which our usual state of alienation from nature is revealed as an aberration; the latter shows us that nature must emanate from a mind like our own, since we are able to penetrate its secrets both deductively and intuitively. If Immanuel Kant tried to demonstrate how synthetic propositions could be knowable *a priori*, Emerson is more interested in the conclusions that follow from the fact that they are thus knowable. He embodies these conclusions in a fable contained in *Nature's* apocalyptic closing chapter. Man is "a god in ruins," nature his alienated consciousness, frozen into symbolic form by the failure of his outflowing creative energy. But the world is full of hints that man is gradually resuming the power he had mysteriously abandoned. With the "influx of the spirit" the world will heal itself, and "the kingdom of man over nature" will give man "a dominion such as is now beyond his dream of God."

Nature had been published anonymously, but its authorship was soon guessed (a Boston joke ran: "Who is the author of Nature? God and Ralph Waldo Emerson"). Emerson's next significant productions, on the other hand, were public—in fact, notorious—events. In 1837 the Harvard chapter of Phi Beta Kappa invited him to deliver the annual address to the Society at the Harvard commencement festivities. The topic of his address, "The American Scholar," was a conventional one: laments for America's cultural backwardness, calls for a national literature, attempts to define the place of the scholar in a democratic and mercantile society.

But Emerson's treatment of these shopworn themes was anything but conventional. He chose to treat genteel subjects like "tradition" and "inspiration" in metaphors borrowed from military science or venture capitalism. Tradition, he argued, *tyrannizes* over later writers; genius *monopolizes* inspiration. "Genius is always sufficiently the enemy of genius by over influence. The literature of every nation bears me witness. The English dramatic poets have Shakespearized now for two hundred years." The way out of this subservience of debt is by adopting an aggressiveness equal to tradition's own. When "the mind is braced by labor and invention," we read the great works of the past with a light that emanates from us, not from them: "the page of whatever book we read, becomes luminous with manifold allusion." This sudden burst of inner light makes the domineering masterpiece seem less formidable. "We see then, what is always true, that as the seer's hour of vision is short and rare among the heavy days and months, so is its record, perchance, the least part of his volume." The aggressive reader decides which parts of his author constitute the "authentic utterances of the oracle" ("authentic" is deliciously circular) and rejects the rest. His guide in this radical act of appropriation is the same "self-trust" Emerson had urged in rejecting the external "proofs" of Christianity for a faith wholly interior; it might be regarded as the literary application of the same spiritual principle.

The language of power and monopoly is one thing applied to literary history, quite another applied to religion itself. The Harvard authorities who submitted to being mildly shocked or mildly titillated had quite a different reaction to the address Emerson delivered the next year to the tiny graduating class of the Harvard Divinity School. To resent "coming into nature, and finding not names and places, not land and professions, but even virtue and truth foreclosed and monopolized"; to rebel against the voice that seems to say "You shall not own the world," sounds like admirable self-assertion when the monopolist is Plato or Shakespeare, something rather different when the monopolist is Jesus Christ and the prohibiting voice belongs to his church.

Emerson's friend and fellow transcendentalist Theodore Parker remembered once being present at a meeting of gentlemen who spent the evening debating the question "Whether Ralph Waldo Emerson was a Christian." They decided that he was not, "for discipleship was necessary to Christianity," and Emerson's whole life was a passionate rejection of the ideal of discipleship. Willing to accord Jesus respect as the man who spoke with perfect candor the truth that "God incarnates himself in man," Emerson nonetheless insists that whoever pays undue reverence to the *person* of Jesus turns Christianity from a sublime "provocation" to a mere "Cultus" or "mythus" like the religions of Greece or Egypt—myth rather than truth.

The chief fault of all forms of what Emerson dismisses as "historical Christianity" (including the Unitarian) lay in its murderous insistence that the liberating words of Christ be quarantined and canonized as merely another deadly Sacred Text. Emerson deplores the "assumption that the age of inspiration is past, that the Bible is closed," and argues that "the office of a true teacher" is "to show us that God is, not was, that he speaketh, not spake." He urges each of his hearers to account himself "a newborn bard of the Holy Ghost" and to "acquaint men at first hand with the Deity." As Jesus added a new testament to the Hebrew Torah, so might some American Messiah do the same, with a gospel for his age's own desperation and unbelief. "I look for the hour when that Supreme Beauty, which ravished the souls of Eastern men, and chiefly of those

Hebrews, and through their lips spoke oracles to all time, shall speak in the West also."

If D. H. Lawrence, writing in *The Dial* for 1926, could express dismay at Emerson's call for "a hundred million American godlets," Emerson's own contemporaries were even unhappier. It was difficult to be a Unitarian heretic, but Emerson discovered he had managed the feat. Andrews Norton, the formidable head of the Divinity School, blasted Emerson in the public newspaper, a vigorous pamphlet war (in which Emerson himself refused to take part) went on for some time, and Emerson was banned from speaking at Harvard for thirty years.

This "storm in our washbowl" (as Emerson described it in a letter to Carlyle) had two very important results: it drove Emerson to rely completely on secular writing and lecturing for a living—he had continued to function as a substitute or "supply" preacher after resigning his pastorate—and it revealed to him the inadequacies of his earlier model of revelation. It was not enough to lie in the lap of Infinity and utter piercing truths; the success of the prophet's message, he had discovered, depends partly upon the hearer's willingness to receive. What forces aid the communication of truth, and what forces obstruct it?

Analysis of the struggle between power and resistance informs many of the essays gathered together in the volume Emerson published in 1841 (now entitled *Essays: First Series*). The essays are made up of passages intricately interwoven from the journal passages and lectures of the preceding years; many of them clearly grow out of his experience of social opposition following the "Divinity School Address." Most of the essays in this aggressive volume stress power rather than obstruction. "Spiritual Laws" speaks of the "willingness and self-annihilation" that makes a man the "unobstructed channel" of divine energy, just as "The Over-Soul" explores the region from which that energy flows, the gigantic heart without valve, wall, or intersection that rolls its blood uninterruptedly in "an endless circulation through all men."

Such ecstatic affirmations led Lawrence to grumble that Emerson "was only connected on the Ideal Phone." They were certainly responsible for the precipitous decline his reputation took in the middle decades of the twentieth century, when it became fashionable to belittle Emerson as a bloodless optimist who lacked a Vision of Evil. In fact, the most famous essays in this first volume derive their energy from the conflicts they explore between the arrogant assumption of spiritual power and the clear-sighted listing of all forces ranged in opposition to that power, not the least of which are forces emanating from another region of the seer's own mind.

In the celebrated "Self-Reliance" the forces opposing self-assertion are mainly social. Mental timidity is a reflection of the moral cowardice of the crowd. "Society everywhere is in conspiracy against the manhood of every one of its members. . . . Self-reliance is its aversion." Hence the anarchic advice: "Whoso would be a man, must be a nonconformist." If most societies initiate young men *into* the group, Emerson envisions an alternative elite chosen chiefly for its power to reject. "I shun father and mother, wife and brother, when my genius calls me. I would write on the lintels of the door-post, *Whim*. I hope it is somewhat better than whim at last, but we cannot spend the day in explanation."

The brio of the essay is largely generated from its fantasies of insouciance. Emerson delights in imagining insults to the church, good society, philanthropists, abolitionists (here conceived of merely as another species of do-gooder), lovers of conformity, and even his own past beliefs, in favor of a strenuous self-expressiveness that can "bring the past for judgment into the thousand-eyed present, and live ever in the new day."

In its constant metaphoric equation of youthfulness with virtue, "Self-Reliance" is in danger of making regeneration seem too easy, as if evil, obstruction, and misery were only stodginess. "Circles" is more trenchant in its analysis of the obstacles to desire. Attempting to locate a controlling pattern beneath the constant warfare of old and new in intellectual and cultural history, Emerson finds it in the circle, that emblem both of perfection and of limitation. "Our life is an apprenticeship to the truth, that around every circle another can be drawn; that there is no end in nature, but every end is a beginning; that there is always another dawn risen on mid-noon, and under every deep a lower deep opens." That last clause, with its phrases borrowed from both innocent and diabolical speakers in *Paradise Lost*, shows how equivocal Emerson's voice has become in this essay. In place of the tingling exhortations of "Self-Reliance" we hear a cooler analyst, who no longer thinks the world can be divided simply between the creative and the ossified, but who has come to see ossification itself as the inevitable end of every creative impulse. "For, it is the inert effort of each thought having formed itself into a circular wave of circumstance,—as, for instance, an empire, rules of an art, a local usage, a religious rite,—to heap itself on that ridge, and to solidify, and hem in the life. But if the soul is quick and strong, it bursts over that boundary on all sides, and expands another orbit on the great deep, which also runs up into a high wave, with attempt again to stop and bind." Though the essay as a whole is electric and expansive, it contains within it an explicit confession that limitation follows power as its eternal antagonist and inescapable twin.

By the time Emerson published his first series of *Essays*, his style had achieved the distinctive form from which it never subsequently varied. A series of short, declarative sentences, whose logical relationship to one another is left deliberately unarticulated, will suddenly flower out into illustrative metaphors and periodic sentences, then return to conclude in a tart epigram. It is a stimulating style (many nineteenth-century readers spoke of Emerson as if he were a kind of tonic), but it can also be a tiring one, in the amount of aggression it directs against the reader and the amount of sustained attention it demands from him. As O. W. Firkins (1915) mildly complained, "Emerson's feet are all spondees." The journals are much easier to read for long stretches than the essays; there is a good deal of random observation and humorous reflection is interspersed between the paragraphs of concentrated thought. Yet a comparison of paragraphs from the *Essays* with their originals in the journals shows how little internal revision was needed to make them publishable; the tense, highly wrought style of the *Essays* had become for Emerson a medium as natural as thought itself.

Power was Emerson's True Grail, but power had always been an elusive commodity. His own inner life seemed to ebb and flow; he complained in "Circles" that he sometimes felt like "a God in nature" and sometimes like "a weed by the wall." In the years immediately following the publication of the first series of *Essays* a number of things had increased the time he spent in the latter of those conditions. The death of his greatly beloved son from his second marriage left him devastated, first by grief, then by the more terrible numbness that succeeded it. The arrival of his fortieth birthday in 1843 outwardly confirmed his growing sense that youthful optimism, like youthful energy, was disappearing. A certain weariness suffuses the second volume of *Essays* he published in 1844.

Even "The Poet," the opening essay of the volume and its most celebratory, shows signs of the change in mood. Emerson praises the poet extravagantly for the insight that reveals to him that "the Universe is the externization of the soul" and gives him a speech that "flows with the flowing of nature." The poet sees everywhere in nature evidences of that central mystery Emerson terms, simply, "the metamorphosis"—that all things are in flux, that all created things are only the temporary incarnation of a divine energy always on the brink of transformation into something else. Like the prisoners in Plato's cave, we live blinded to the truth of our condition. "We are symbols and inhabit symbols; workmen, work, and tools, words and things, birth and death, all are emblems; but we sympathize with the symbols, and being infatuated with the economical uses of things, we do not know that they are thoughts." By using symbols to reveal the symbolic nature of reality, the poet frees us from false belief in its substantiality, and hence deserves to be called a "liberating god." "The use of symbols has a certain power of emancipation and exhilaration for all men. . . . We are like men who come out of a cave or cellar into the open air."

But "The Poet" is not content with a poetry that awakens and liberates men. The old hope that had animated *Nature*—that poetry, by translating natural symbols into linguistic ones, could serve as a new Scripture—returns to plague and baffle the argument of "The Poet." If it is really true that "the sea, the mountain-ridge, Niagara, and every flower-bed, pre-exist, or super-exist, in pre-cantations," then the poet is reduced from the status of liberating god to more or less faithful scribe, and his once-vaunted individuality (praised in "The American Scholar" and "Self-Reliance" as the only path to immortality) suddenly is cast as villain of the piece: "we lose ever and anon a word or a verse and substitute something of our own" in our attempts to hear and capture these precantations, "and thus miswrite the poem." (Emerson did not finally resolve this fundamental contradiction at the heart of his poetic theory until he was willing to relinquish his hope of a fixed natural symbolism merely waiting for the poet's transcription in favor of an emphasis on the poet's role as symbol *maker* and dialectician. In the late, brilliant essay "Poetry and Imagination," published in *Letters and Social Aims*, he argues that all symbols were meant to hold only for a moment, and that it is the poet's capacity to transfer significance endlessly from one symbol to another that makes him the emblem of human thought. "All thinking is analogizing, and it is the business of life to learn metonymy.")

The contradictions visible beneath the brave affirmations of "The Poet" surface in a different and more dangerous way in the next essay in the volume. "Experience" is one of Emerson's greatest essays; it is also one of his most shocking, shocking because so much of its aggressivity is now directed against the self. Even in tone it is quite unlike anything Emerson ever wrote. It begins in weariness and exhaustion, rises in places to intense bitterness, or sinks into a Gallic cynicism. Of course there are more familiar accents too: declarations of hope, of courage, of faith in the "sunbright Mecca of the desert" that still reveals itself, in flashes, to the pilgrim. But in no other essay does Emerson allow so much space to the negative forces before vanquishing them, and in no other essay does the victory finally obtained leave so many casualties behind on the battlefield.

What "Experience" offers is an extended meditation upon the fact of subjectivity, and a devastating candor about the moral and psychological corollaries that follow from the fact that it is inescapable. First Emerson lists all the things that keep us locked in the "prison of glass" that is our own selfhood. He describes with clinical precision the "flux of moods" that renders the very notion of personal "identity" a bitter joke; he analyzes the necessary bafflement of a creature trapped in a temporal succession that renders all his efforts at knowledge futile and ensures that what pitiful wisdom he achieves will be only retroactive. As if this were not chilling enough, he then proceeds to detail, with frightening honesty, the corollaries that follow from our inescapable self-centeredness—the ease with which we outgrow books, friends, lovers; the indulgence we always extend to our own crimes, real or contemplated; the sham quality of all those emotions, like grief or guilt, that depend upon a belief in the real existence of other people.

Against this radical skepticism "Experience" can offer only a few practical defenses—a reliance on common sense, on small pleasures; an acceptance of custom; patience in waiting for those eruptions of the old power that never entirely deserts us; resigned acceptance of the self-reliance forced upon us by the fact of our isolation; a gentleman's courteous determination to treat the ghosts and shadows we live with "as if they were real."

These are only palliatives, and are offered as such. What takes the place of hope in the essay is the courage with which its unpleasant truths are faced, a courage that keeps it from seeming depressing even when those truths are bleakest. As Maurice Gonnaud has said: "The greatness of an essay like 'Experience' lies, I suggest, in our sense of the author's being engaged in a pursuit of truth which has all the characters of faith except its quality of radiating happiness."

Of the remaining essays in the volume, "Character" still retains some of its power to shock. By "character" Emerson means what we should probably call "charisma," and he coolly asserts that Jesus of Nazareth didn't have enough of it—since his Crucifixion (which Emerson labels "a great Defeat") was a victory only for the soul, not yet for the senses. The millenarianism that had prompted the closing chapter of *Nature* returns here, as Emerson, still bitterly refusing to accept a universe that could engineer the death of his son, rejects as incomplete any Messiahship that fails to restore paradise and immortality. "Nominalist and Realist" is memorable for the shrewd Yankee wit of some of its epigrams ("Every man is wanted, and no man is wanted much") as well as for its attempt to give an ontological justification for one of Emerson's favorite rhetorical devices: the paradox. "No sentence will hold the whole truth, and the only way we can be just, is by giving ourselves the lie. . . . All the universe over, there is but one thing, this old Two-Face, creator-creature, mind-matter, right-wrong, of which any proposition may be affirmed or denied." And "New England Reformers" combines an affectionate nostalgia for the goofy idealism of the decade just past with wry portraits of the visionaries, reformers, social schemers, religious fanatics, and campaigners for improved nutrition who had made New England both a national mecca and a national joke. Despite Emerson's earlier assertion that a prosperous middle-aged man has "ripened beyond the possibility of sincere radicalism," he is still cheerfully insisting that men are conservative only when they are "least vigorous," radicals whenever "their intellect or their conscience has been aroused." The "rankest Tories" in Old or New England, if exposed to

"a man of great heart and mind," will begin to thaw, to hope, to "spin and revolve." And he affirms the belief that lies behind all schemes of reform and survives even the depredations of skepticism: "Men in all ways are better than they
seem."

After the publication of *Essays: Second Series* Emerson found himself in
need of new material for a winter course of lyceum lectures. A single lecture he
had written on Napoleon suggested the possibility of a lecture series with "a biographical basis." By the winter of 1845 he was ready to begin this new series,
entitled "Representative Men," and including lectures on "Plato; or, the
Philosopher," "Swedenborg; or, the Mystic," "Montaigne; or, the Skeptic,"
"Shakspeare; or, the Poet," "Napoleon; or, the Man of the World," "Goethe; or,
the Writer." As the lecture titles and series title suggest, Emerson is choosing his
heroes not merely because they were great but because each embodied one attribute of that central divinity Emerson saw as the birthright of every man.
Plato's vision, Goethe's courage of thought, Napoleon's executive genius,
Shakespeare's brilliant facility in making the material world the servant of his
thought, Montaigne's dispassionate weighing of truths and opinions in the
scales of an unbiased intellect, Swedenborg's mystical insight into the symbolic
nature of reality—all are incarnations in mortal form of that godhead whose distribution into individualities Emerson had marveled over as long ago as "The
American Scholar." But this distribution has its dark side as well; the human
vessels into which this genius is poured are often weak and sometimes wicked;
a catalogue of genius is necessarily also a catalogue of partiality, deformity, even
madness. Each lecture begins with a cascade of praise, and then, in a savage
about-face, begins attacking the shrine it has just constructed. Plato is too intellectual to possess real spiritual authority; Swedenborg falls into the monstrous egotism that bedevils all religious fanatics; Montaigne's skepticism, while
an admirable defense against "bigots and blockheads," still leaves us thirsting
after righteousness and truth; Napoleon's executive genius is finally useless
without common honesty and some vision higher than the sensual; Shakespeare, the greatest poet in the world, was at last content to be nothing more
than "the master of the revels to mankind"; the worldly Goethe, for all his ambition to know everything knowable, is finally too self-conscious, too devoted to
mere culture, to reach the highest regions of the spirit. The Representative Man
these fragments of godhead might compose, if divorced from the defects of their
virtues, will never wholly materialize, yet from these fragmentary lopsided mortals (as Emerson once called them) we can compose his figure.

The lectures in this series were finally published in 1850 as *Representative
Men*. Earlier volumes had drawn heavily on lecture material, but this was the first
of Emerson's books to consist of a single course of lectures, revised only slightly
for publication. As Wallace E. Williams has pointed out, the "freedom and daring" of the lecture hall are evident in the book's style, which is racier, more colloquial, less lapidary than in the two volumes of *Essays*. The language of
Representative Men deserves the compliment Emerson pays to the language of
Montaigne: "Cut these words and they would bleed; they are vascular and alive."

In 1846 Emerson published a volume of *Poems*, the fruit of thirty years of
poetic activity. His ambitions in this area had always been high—he once said,
"I am more of a poet than anything else"—and his earliest notebooks and journals show him experimenting with forms and styles. As a school-boy and
Harvard undergraduate he had confined himself chiefly to the approved neo-

classical couplets, though his favorite aunt's passion for Byron had led him into a few sallies of Romantic melancholy, of which little memorable remains except the delicious line, "I will shake hands with death and hug Despair." His first response to Wordsworth, to whom he was introduced while at college, was strongly contemptuous, but gradually Emerson became a convert to the new mode: intimate, reflective, autobiographical. While a student at the Divinity School he became a passionate admirer of Coleridge, who in turn introduced him to the seventeenth-century lyric masters: Herbert, Donne, Jonson, Marvell. Later still he learned to admire Goethe and the Persian and Arabic poets he read in German translations.

Traces of all these enthusiasms are visible in the *Poems* of 1846. Emerson admired the tetrameter couplets of Milton and Marvell for their capacity to reconcile compression and fluency, to seem gnomic without seeming epigrammatic, like the far more discontinuous pentameter couplet of neoclassical verse. Emerson uses the tetrameter line for meditations on nature ("The Humble-Bee"), on human life and human emotion ("Initial, Daemonic, and Celestial Love"); he uses it for moral lessons ("The Visit"), for dramatic monologues ("Alphonso of Castile"), for parables ("The Sphinx"), and for excursions into myth ("Bacchus," "Merlin").

It is easy to see why Emerson liked the tetrameter line. At best, it allows him to write verses as unforgettable as a witch's spell, as in the closing lines from "Merlin":

> Subtle rhymes, with ruin rife,
> Murmur in the house of life,
> Sung by Sisters as they spin;
> In perfect time and measure they
> Build and unbuild our echoing clay.
> As the two twilights of the day
> Fold us music-drunken in.

But the tetrameter line is far less forgiving of metrical roughness than the longer pentameter, and Emerson's self-confessed inability to master the mysteries of rhythm leads to line upon line of frankly unmetrical verse. Worse still, the sureness of taste that never seemed to desert Emerson in the wildest of his prose experiments deserts him frequently in verse, and the result is a bathos deeper than anything in Wordsworth:

> I cannot shake off the god;
>   On my neck he makes his seat;
> I look at my face in the glass—
>   My eyes his eyeballs meet.
>   ("The Park")

Mercifully, these lapses of taste and of meter disappear from Emerson's blank-verse poetry, to be replaced by the quiet assurance of "Musquetaquid," or by the descriptive exuberance of "The Snow-Storm," with its loving portrait of the "mad wind's night-work" and of the suddenly isolated house-dwellers in their "tumultuous privacy of storm." In most of these poems Emerson is content to employ verse rhythms that descend from the descriptive poetry of the eighteenth century, but in places he is clearly experimenting with the possibility of a tougher-sounding, "native" pentameter line, as in the opening lines of "Hamatreya":

Bulkeley, Hunt, Willard, Hosmer, Meriam, Flint,
Possessed the land which rendered to their toil,
Hay, corn, roots, hemp, flax, apples, wool and wood.

The wit that plays off the monosyllabic or strongly trochaic rhythm of the Yankee farmers' names against the smooth "English" pentameter of the line that follows anticipates the metrical virtuosity of one of Emerson's greatest twentieth-century admirers, Robert Frost.

Some of Emerson's best poems are examples of a genre not very easy to define. "Uriel," "Saadi," "Bacchus," and "Merlin" are visionary or emblematic fables loosely modeled on Coleridge's "Kubla Khan" and on German mythological lyrics like Goethe's "Prometheus" or Holderlin's "Patmos." If, as the Higher Critics argued, all religion was essentially mythological, then modern poets had as much right to invent gods and fables as the Greeks or the Hebrews had. Like his European predecessors, Emerson uses figures drawn from literary or mythological tradition to embody new impulses of the spirit for which received tradition had no name. Emerson's visionary lyrics are intended to do what Emerson praised Goethe for having accomplished—creating, in Mephistopheles, the "first organic figure that has been added for some ages" to European mythology. In a series of brief narrative poems, written mostly in some combination of tetrameter lines, Emerson gives us Uriel, whose terrifying vision of the Law of Compensation ("Evil will bless and ice will burn") shakes the heavens, but who is himself crippled by excessive self-knowledge; Saadi, whose joyous wisdom survives all the ascetic lobbying of the Fakirs; Bacchus, who demands an intoxication great enough to restore man to innocence and nature to joy; Merlin, incarnation of the individual poetic will, who is grimly ready to accept the fatality in nature if only he is given access to her frightening power.

The decade of the 1840s had been a period of intense productivity: two volumes of essays, a volume of poems, the lecture series on representative men. But in the latter half of the decade Emerson had begun to feel both exhausted and stale, in need, as he said, of a whip for his top. He boarded a ship for England in October 1847. The following nine months were spent in an exhausting but exhilarating tour of Scotland and England, with a brief trip across the Channel to France, then in the midst of revolutionary excitement. He was then at the height of his fame, lionized everywhere (though his native shyness made that British institution, the evening party, a torment for him). He revisited such old friends as Carlyle and Alexander Ireland; he paid a final call on Wordsworth; he met Matthew Arnold, Arthur Hugh Clough, Francis Jeffrey, Thomas De Quincey, and Alexis de Tocqueville, as well as a number of famous scientists and mathematicians.

Once home again Emerson began lecturing on his experiences in Britain, lectures that eventually were revised into *English Traits*. As Alfred Kazin remarks, the book is notable for being "worldlier, shrewder, wittier, than anything else by this god-intoxicated man." Emerson is warmly admiring of English skill and self-reliance, gently amused by English eccentricity, and everywhere fascinated by a culture whose historical roots are vividly evident in the smallest customs of the people. He is critical, too: of the squalid poverty that haunts the spectacular wealth of the island, of the fondness for cant that Emerson sadly judges to be the constitutional vice of the Anglo-Saxon race, since it is as visible in Old England as in the New. His chapter on the Anglican church is as trenchant a criticism of the hypocrisies of nineteenth-century Christianity as the "Divinity School Address"; it is also slyly but devastatingly funny. Indeed, the whole book has a complexity of tone and attitude familiar enough to a reader of Emerson's journals, but rarer in the published works, where moods are made to alternate rather than coalesce. Emerson had frequently been ironic; in *English Traits* he is finally urbane.

The keener interest in political questions that Emerson had brought back from Europe was soon given native fodder. In 1850 the government in Washington enacted a series of measures designed to secure California's admission to statehood, something Southerners opposed. To pacify the South, legislators (led by Massachusetts' own Daniel Webster, one of Emerson's heroes) agreed to the passage of a tough Fugitive Slave Law, whose provisions included a demand that Northern citizens aid in the capture and remanding of fugitive slaves who had escaped into free states. These events catapulted Emerson from his scholarly retirement into violent public activity. He denounced Webster and the Fugitive Slave Law in speeches whose vitriol was not lessened even by Webster's death; he stumped for Free-Soil candidates; he addressed Anti-Slavery Society meetings and called for abolition; he urged his fellow citizens to break "this filthy enactment" at the earliest possible opportunity.

Yet a private pessimism about the efficacy of reform in the face of the cruelty and wastefulness of nature recurs frequently in his journals, along with a growing awareness that for the vast mass of suffering humanity — the urban proletariat, the black slaves — his customary exhortations to a life of romantic self-expansiveness were bitterly irrelevant. "Ask the digger in the ditch to explain Newton's laws; the fine organs of his brain have been pinched by overwork and squalid poverty from father to son for a hundred years." "The German and Irish millions, like the Negro, have a great deal of guano in their destiny. They are ferried over the Atlantic and carted over America, to ditch and to drudge, to make corn cheap and then to lie down prematurely to make a spot of green grass on the prairie."

These ugly sentiments come from the essay "Fate," first in a volume entitled *The Conduct of Life*, published in 1860, but based on a series of lectures first written in the turbulent years 1850–52. The opening paragraph of "Fate" suggests the helplessness Emerson then felt as he tried to resolve the huge "question of the times" into a "practical question of the conduct of life." "We are incompetent to solve the times. Our geometry cannot span the huge orbits of the prevailing ideas, behold their return and reconcile their opposition." Yet only part of the book really fits this announced plan of retreating into a private world. The middle essays—"Wealth," "Culture," "Behavior," "Considerations by the Way," and "Beauty"—can certainly qualify as recommendations of the genteel values of the Boston aristocracy, and "Worship" offers the same private answer to the loudly debated question of the "decay of religion" that Emerson had been advancing since the "Divinity School Address": religions do not decay, only the outward forms of religions do; the great truths are always adequate to us, whether or not we are adequate to them. And "Illusions," the final essay, is as private as a one-man polar expedition, and almost as cold; it describes all of human existence as a "snow-storm" of private fantasies, which lifts only occasionally to reveal the gods sitting on their thrones, staring down at the solitary mortal—"they alone with him alone."

But the book's opening essays—"Fate" and "Power"—show Emerson attempting the very task he claimed to have renounced: a solution to the riddle of the times by working out its permutations on a slate as large as the cosmos.

"Fate," the grimmest essay he ever wrote, lists all the forces hostile to human freedom, both natural and social; "Power," the other great fact of the world, recoils against this catalogue of horrors with a counter-assertion of the "affirmative force" with which the world is also saturated. Taken together, they are among Emerson's strongest essays, intellectually uncompromising, rhetorically violent. They reflect in their titanic opposition the moral dilemmas of a country moving closer to the agony of civil war.

After the war Emerson's career was nearly over. He published another volume of essays, the genial *Society and Solitude*, and another volume of poems, *May-Day and Other Pieces*. But a progressive deterioration of memory rendered him incapable of writing or lecturing, and his family had to call in the help of James Elliot Cabot to ready a collection of his earlier pieces, *Letters and Social Aims*, for the press. Emerson's physical health, however, remained good, and he was only a few weeks short of his seventy-ninth birthday when he died in 1882.

Emerson's reputation has undergone the usual cycles of inflation and crash in the century since his death. What he once called "the unstable estimates of men" are never likely to rest easy in their judgment of a man who combines lofty idealism with militant self-assertiveness, who assumes the authority to exhort without renouncing the instinct for outrage, whose style manages to be at once repetitive and elliptical. In his own day Emerson mystified or infuriated as many listeners as he exhilarated or convinced, and the ratios do not seem to have changed very much today. He took such hostility philosophically, believing that an author "elects" his readers as inexorably and mysteriously as the Calvinist God chooses the company of the saved. What he meant to the young men and women of his own time is best summed up in James Russell Lowell's nostalgic account of Emerson as a lecturer. "At any rate, he brought us *life*, which on the whole, is no bad thing."

STANLEY CAVELL

From The Philosopher in American Life[†]

(*Toward Thoreau and Emerson*)

* * *

I will not even explore the urgency of the wish to be understood completely, for example trace the source of the wish in my intermittent sense that no utterance of mine could be acceptable simultaneously to all those by whom I desire understanding, say by the primarily philosophical and by the primarily literary. Some may accuse me of trying to reconcile my father and my mother. But if these terms (I mean philosophy and literature) name halves of my own mind, it is perhaps all the more immediately urgent for me to see that they keep in touch.

What I have done for these lectures, wishing to take the occasion of old memories and aspirations to form some measure of my progress, is to propose

† From *In Quest of the Ordinary* (Chicago: University of Chicago Press, 1988), pp. 3–26. Reprinted by permission of the publisher.

as their primary business the reading of a set of texts that represent the oldest and the newest of my interests, placing them in a loosely woven net of concepts. The point of the loose weave is to register that I am as interested in the weaving together of these texts as I am in their individual textures, and that I wish to leave open, or keep open usefully, how it is one gets from one to another of them.

One set of these connections forms perhaps the most pervasive, yet all but inexplicit, thought in these lectures: that the sense of the ordinary that my work derives from the practice of the later Wittgenstein and from J. L. Austin, in their attention to the language of ordinary or everyday life, is underwritten by Emerson and Thoreau in their devotion to the thing they call the common, the familiar, the near, the low. The connection means that I see both developments — ordinary language philosophy and American transcendentalism — as responses to skepticism, to that anxiety about our human capacities as knowers that can be taken to open modern philosophy in Descartes, interpreted by that philosophy as our human subjection to doubt. My route to the connection lay at once in my tracing both the ordinary language philosophers as well as the American transcendentalists to the Kantian insight that Reason dictates what we mean by a world, as well as in my feeling that the ordinariness in question speaks of an intimacy with existence, and of an intimacy lost, that matches skepticism's despair of the world. These routes from, say, Emerson to Wittgenstein are anticipated in a thought I have put many ways over the years, never effectively enough — the thought that ordinary language philosophy is not a defense of what may present itself as certain fundamental, cherished beliefs we hold about the world and the creatures in it, but, among other things, a contesting of that presentation, for, as it were, the prize of the ordinary. So that epistemologists who think to refute skepticism by undertaking a defense of ordinary beliefs, perhaps suggesting that there is a sense in which they are certain, or sufficiently probable for human purposes, have already given in to skepticism, they are living it.

* * *

In turning to Emerson for his testimony about reading, I note that the story of his and Thoreau's cultural neglect needs complication. Emerson's story has to include an account of the tremendous fame attaching to him in his lifetime, which persisted for some decades after his death and which, after further decades in which he seemed unreadable, there have been recurrent efforts to revive, themselves invariably producing counter-efforts to destroy it again. How one understands these twists of his reputation generally seems tied up with what one takes his writing to be, as if the writing and the reputation formed one case for us, and the case is always undecided, as if we do not yet know what this man is and what he wants.

A way of considering what it is about his writing that produces this wavering toward it, this not knowing how it is to be taken, is to consider that Emerson makes the question of how to take it (how seriously, I would like to say, *he* takes it, the question of authenticating its own seriousness), a guiding question he asks for himself, of himself.

I have more than once cited the following passage from "Self-Reliance" as one in which he is dramatizing his mission as a writer, presenting the credentials of his vocation: "I shun father and mother and wife and brother when my genius calls me. I would write on the lintels of the doorpost, *Whim*. I hope it is better than whim at last, but we cannot spend the day in explanation." I will not recall again the biblical contexts which show Emerson there to be specifying the call to write as following the new promise of redemption, and specifying the act of writing as marking his old dwelling as with a mezuzah, or with blood, as on passover. The question is pushed at us, How seriously does he mean these specifications? Is there any philosophical point to them beyond the literary, whatever that may be?

I go on here to note that the entire essay "Self-Reliance," for all its fame as preaching individualism (which is not wrong certainly, but certainly not clear), is a study of writing, as if one's wish to write simply Whim already took upon oneself the full-blown burden of writing. The writer writes Whim in the place others place the word of God, as if to mock the commoner habit of taking God's name in the place of Whim. As if there is no greater standing authority for using the word Whim—or any other word, however small—than for using the word God; no justification for language apart from language.

That "Self-Reliance" is a study of (philosophical) writing (hence of reading and of thinking) is insistently established in the essay by Emerson's draw upon the reach of the words "expression" and "character" and "communication," using them throughout to call attention at once to the externals of writing and to the internals of the one doing the writing, backing it, fronting it, hence to assert that both writing and writer are to be read, which is about to say, both are texts, perhaps testing, contesting, one another. (It is from that essay that I will go on to take my quotations from Emerson here, unless I specify otherwise.) He says, for example, that "A character is like an acrostic or Alexandrian stanza—read it forward, backward, or across, it still spells the same thing." And after warning near the beginning "we but half express ourselves" and claiming in the middle that while we "may err in the expression" of our intuitions we know that they are so (they are so, this way) and are "not to be disputed," he speaks near the end of the wise man as "[making] men sensible [of something] by the expression of his countenance." What the wise man is making us sensible of, says Emerson in this instance, is that the soul stays home, that even when he is called from his house he is still, whatever others say, at home. But since being called, for a wise man, is evidently being called by his genius, and since for Emerson that is to write, Emerson is submitting his writing to the condition of acquiring whatever authority and conviction is due to it by looking at its countenance, or surface.

Our philosophical habits will prompt us to interpret the surface of writing as its manner, its style, its rhetoric, an ornament of what is said rather than its substance, but Emerson's implied claim is that this is as much a philosophical prejudice as the other conformities his essay decries, that, so to speak, words are no more ornaments of thought than tears are ornaments of sadness or joy. Of course, they may be seen so, and they may in a given case amount to no more; but this just means that expressions are the last things to take at face value.

What countenance will count as the writing of the wise? Emerson finds in the communication of those who "conform to usages," who, that is, are without self-reliance, that "every word they say chagrins us and we do not know where to begin to set them right." If every one of our words is implicated in the conformity to usage, then evidently no word assures a safe beginning; whether a given word will do must accordingly depend upon how it allows itself to be said, the countenance in which it puts its utterer, whether it can be uttered so as not to chagrin us, which is to say sadden us, but rather, to use a favorite Emersonian phrase, to raise and cheer us. As if these were the fixed alternatives for the practice of philosophy.

Here we come upon the most familiar of all the complaints leveled at Emerson, the complaint that more than any other has clouded his reputation among intellectuals in this century: that he is recklessly affirmative, that he lacked the sense of tragedy.

Whatever this means, and however often it has ineffectually been denied, a prior question is bound to rise to the lips of a philosopher, simply the question what difference it makes, what philosophical difference, whether the countenance of speech saddens or cheers us, which are psychological matters of the *effects* of words; whereas what matters philosophically is whether what is said is true. But then it is up to us at least to get the psychology straight. Emerson says in a companion essay ("Circles") "The simplest words, — we do not know what they mean except when we love and aspire." Whatever states these words are meant to name, this remark says not that the states are the effects of words but rather on the contrary that they are their causes, or rather conditions of understanding words. While it may not be unprecedented for a philosopher to tell us that the words we use every day are imprecise or prompt illusions, it is not usual, even not normal of philosophy, to say that the way to their meaning lies through a change of heart.

Whatever this itself means will presumably depend on how accurately it describes Emerson's own practice of writing and thinking, that is, on his particular countenancing of words. Let us look finally at two further sentences exemplifying his practice of describing his practice. When he says, "Who has more obedience than I masters me" this is to be taken in connection with his speaking of writing as something to which one is called, something to which one is harkening, showing obedience. Then to "master" him is not exactly to overcome him, as if he were an unruly impulse or an insubordinate slave, but to have command of him as of a difficult text or of language. And however difficult the text may be that concerns the subject of being called, I find it no harder to command, and more serviceable, than any number of texts that less affirmative aestheticians have produced concerning the subject of intention.

Both the idea of grasping the intention of a text and the idea of sharing or hearing what has called it, are interpretations of reading, of following a text. But the idea of being intended can close out what the idea of being called and of obedience, of listening, brings into investigation: namely, how it is that one writes better than one knows (as well as worse) and that one may be understood better by someone other than oneself (as well as understood worse). These are things worth looking into. Emerson is looking into it when he remarks: "Character teaches above our wills. Men imagine that they communicate their virtue or vice only by overt action, and do not see that virtue or vice emit a breath every moment." I find this a frightening notation of an anxiety in writing; an acknowledgement that one must give over control of one's appropriations, as if to learn what they are.

To write knowing that your words emit a breath of virtue or vice every moment, that they communicate the means by which you are expressing your desires, know them or not, is to leave your character unguarded. To leave what I say unguarded has been a point of honor with me, even though I know that some risks are not worth taking. If one could not write better than one is, and understand a writer better than he or she may understand themselves, if we were not capable of better obedience than we have shown, obedience to something better, then the case of writing would be more pitiable than it is, because then it could propose no measures for putting itself aside, no relief for writer or reader. It follows that I am at any time subject to indictment by what I set down, or else it goes for nothing.

I have not wished to disguise a certain pathos in my sense of struggle for the writing of philosophy, in the position and the place I find myself in, I mean for example as a Professor of Philosophy in America, and elsewhere. At the same time I have not wished to make the struggle unduly personal, because the struggles it joins are nothing if not common—those between philosophy and poetry, between writer and reader, between writer or reader and language, between language and itself, between the American edifice of fantasy and the European edifice of philosophy, between the hope and the despair of writing and reading redemptively.

But how about the very pathos in posing these issues as struggles? Isn't that to romanticize what are merely intellectual problems? Is philosophy as such— nowadays? still?—to be cloaked as a romantic undertaking? I suppose my finding Emerson and Thoreau to underwrite Wittgenstein and Austin suggests a certain romantic taint in what I regard as some of the most advanced thought of our time; and Heidegger's relation to romantic literature, especially of course to Hölderlin, suggests that it is a taint he takes on willingly. It may be that the claim upon the reader I have pointed to in Heidegger's and Wittgenstein's work, the claim I said is not to be captured exactly as moral, may be thought of as a romantic demand for, or promise of, redemption, say self-recovery. But in all philosophical seriousness, a recovery from what? Philosophy cannot say sin. Let us speak of a recovery from skepticism. This means, as said, from a drive to the inhuman. Then why does this present itself as a recovery of the self? Why, more particularly, as the recovery of the (of my) (ordinary) (human) voice? What is romantic about the recovery of, the quest for, the ordinary or everyday? What business is it of philosophy's?

CORNEL WEST

From The Emersonian Prehistory of American Pragmatism[†]

> Mr. Emerson's authority to the imagination consists, not in his culture, not in his science, but all simply in himself, in the form of his natural personality. There are scores of men of more advanced ideas than Mr. Emerson, of subtler apprehension, of broader knowledge, of deeper culture . . . Mr. Emerson was never the least of a pedagogue, addressing your scientific intelligence, but an every way unconscious prophet, appealing exclusively to the regenerate heart of mankind, and announcing the speedy fulfillment of the hope with which it had always been pregnant. He was an American John the Baptist, proclaiming tidings of great joy to the American Israel; but, like John the Baptist, he could so little foretell the form in which the predicted good was to appear, that when you went to him he was always uncertain whether you were he who should come, or another.
> —HENRY JAMES, SR.

The long shadow cast by Ralph Waldo Emerson over American pragmatism has been often overlooked and rarely examined. Yet Emerson not only prefigures the dominant themes of American pragmatism but, more important,

† From *The American Evasion of Philosophy*. Copyright © 1989. Reprinted by permission of The University of Wisconsin Press.

enacts an intellectual style of cultural criticism that permits and encourages American pragmatists to swerve from mainstream European philosophy.[1] Like Friedrich Nietzsche—and deeply adored by him—Emerson is a singular and unique figure on the North Atlantic intellectual landscape who defies disciplinary classification.

Emerson lacks the patience and persistence to be a great poet. He does not have the deep sense of alienation and marginality to be a profound prophet. And he does not possess the talent for logical precision and sustained argumentation to be a rigorous philosopher.[2] Yet Emerson is more than a mediocre man of letters or a meteoric man of lectures. Rather he is a cultural critic who devised and deployed a vast array of rhetorical strategies in order to exert intellectual and moral leadership over a significant segment of the educated classes of his day. The rhetorical strategies, principally aimed at explaining America to itself,[3] weave novel notions of power, provocation, and personality into a potent and emerging American ideology of voluntaristic invulnerability and utopian possibility.

*　*　*

Emerson on Provocation (and the Market)

The primary aim of Emerson's life and discourse is to provoke; the principal means by which he lived, spoke, and wrote is provocation. At the "center" of his project is activity, flux, movement, and energy. It comes as no surprise that when he defines "that in us which changes not"—his conception of "unbounded substance," "ineffable cause," or "being" itself—he claims that we must

> confess that we have arrived as far as we can go. Suffice it for the joy of the universe, that we have not arrived at a wall, but at interminable oceans. Our life seems not present, so much as prospective; not for the affairs on which it is wasted, but as a hint of this vast-flowing vigor.[4]

Of course, the enshrinement of activity and energy was commonplace in the various forms of North Atlantic romanticisms. Yet what sets Emerson apart from the others is not simply his critical yet sympathetic attitude toward modern technology and market forces, but, more important, a conception of activity that was fundamentally shaped by a national environment in which the market had a more dominant presence than in other places.

For Emerson, the goal of activity is not simply domination, but also provocation; the telos of movement and flux is not solely mastery but also stimulation. Needless to say, the centrality of provocation and stimulation in a discourse

---

1. The two major recent attempts to reflect upon this "swerve" are Stanley Cavell's "Thinking of Emerson" and "An Emerson Mood" in *The Senses of Walden*, 2d ed. (San Francisco: North Point Press, 1981), pp. 123–38, 141–60; and Harold Bloom's *Agon: Towards a Theory of Revisionism* (New York: Oxford University Press, 1982), pp. 16–51, 145–78.
2. Emerson himself notes in his *Journals*, "My reasoning faculty is proportionately weak" and speaks of a "logical mode of thinking & speaking—which I do not possess, & may not reasonably hope to obtain." Instead, Emerson speaks of his "moral imagination" and of "a passionate love for the strains of eloquence." *Emerson in His Journals*, selected and edited by Joel Porte (Cambridge: Harvard University Press, 1982), pp. 45, 46. For evidence of this lack of rigor, see David Van Leer, *Emerson's Epistemology: The Argument of the Essays* (New York: Cambridge University Press, 1986).
3. "That idea which I approach & am magnetized by—is my country." *Emerson in His Journals*, p. 321.
4. Emerson, "Experience," p. 341.

is the product of and helps reproduce a market culture—that is, a market culture in which the past is effaced, the social concealed, and the future projected by the arbitrary clashing wills of individuals. Provocation and stimulation constituted rhetorical strategies of sustaining some sense of the self in the midst of the "currency wars, economic unpredictability, and high incidence of rapid financial failures and new starts" of the Jacksonian era in which Emerson emerged.[5] This material insecurity, social instability, historical fluidity, and imaginative liquidity wrought principally by market forces both enabled and constrained Emerson's valorizing of provocation. As Jean-Christophe Agnew notes in his brilliant genealogy of market culture in early modern Britain, "When freed of ritual, religious, or juridical restraints, a money medium can imbue life itself with a pervasive and ongoing sense of risk, a recurrent anticipation of gain and loss that lends to all social intercourse a pointed, transactional quality."[6]

Like the theater shunned by Emerson's Puritan ancestors, with its personal transgression of social boundaries and multiplication of identities, market forces tend to undermine authority, thwart tradition, and throw the burdens once borne by these onto the individual. Once freed from such superegos, the self can be seen to be a rather contingent, arbitrary, and instrumental affair, a mobile, performative, and protean entity perennially in process, always on an adventurous pilgrimage ("Everything good is on the highway").

> With the emergence of a placeless market, the threshold experience threatened to become coextensive with all that a deritualized commodity exchange touched. Life now resembled an infinite series of thresholds, a profusion of potential passages or opportunity costs running alongside experience as a constant reminder of the selves not taken . . . and why not, since the world was at once a market and a stage.[7]

Emerson's response to market forces is neither nostalgic nor celebratory. Unlike his good friend Thomas Carlyle, he refused to yearn for some golden age prior to the modern age; yet he also did not uncritically revel in the present. Instead, his excessively prospective perspective and exorbitantly parochial preoccupation with America enabled him to adopt the major tropes of the market culture and attempt to turn them against certain aspects of this culture.

On the one hand, Emerson—especially during his early and most fecund period—puts forward powerful moral critiques of market culture. The depression of 1837 not only adversely affected Emerson's personal fortunes but also awakened him from his complacent slumber by the "loud cracks in the social edifice."[8]

> I see a good in such emphatic and universal calamity as the times bring, that they dissatisfy me with society . . . Society has played out its last

5. Michael Lopez, "Transcendental Failure," in *Emerson: Prospect and Retrospect*, ed. Joel Porte, Harvard English Studies, vol. 10 (Cambridge, Mass.: Harvard UP, 1982), p. 141.
6. Jean-Christophe Agnew, *Worlds Apart: The Market and the Theater in Anglo-American Thought, 1550–1750* (New York: Cambridge University Press, 1986), p. 4.
7. Ibid., pp. 97–98. The Emerson quip is from "Experience," p. 336. Note also the claim of Henry James, Sr.—good friend of Emerson and father of William James—that Emerson had "no private personality." Henry James, Sr., "Mr. Emerson," *Henry James, Sr.*, ed. Giles Gunn (Chicago: American Library Association, 1974), p. 249.
8. Quoted in Allen, *Waldo Emerson*, p. 293.

stake; it is check-mated. Young men have no hope. Adults stand like day-laborers idle in the streets. None calleth us to labor . . . the present generation is bankrupt of principles and hope, as of property . . . I am forced to ask if the ideal might not also be tried. Is it to be taken for granted that it is impracticable? Behold the boasted world has come to nothing . . . Behold . . . here is the Soul erect and Unconquered still.[9]

He characterizes the emerging capitalist economy as "a system of selfishness . . . of distrust, of concealment, of superior keenness, not of giving but of taking advantage."[1] In fact, he goes as far as to claim that "there is nothing more important in the culture of man than to resist the dangers of commerce."[2] As commerce expands, he quips, "out of doors all seems a market."[3] And in his most succinct statement on the nascent capitalist order, he writes:

> This invasion of Nature by Trade with its Money, its Steam, its Railroad, threatens to upset the balance of man and establish a new Universal Monarchy more tyrannical than Babylon or Rome.

> Trade is the lord of the world nowadays—& government only a parachute to this balloon.[4]

On the other hand, Emerson projects a conception of the self that can be easily appropriated by market culture for its own perpetuation and reproduction. In fact, the well-known shift from the idealistic criticisms of the market in the early Emerson to the "realistic" apologies for the market in the later Emerson has much to do with his perceptions of the impotence of his criticisms. Again, this perceived impotence sits well with his relative political inaction.

The Emersonian self—much like the protean, mobile, performative self promoted by market forces—literally feeds off other people. It survives by means of ensuring and securing its own excitement and titillation. Nature itself becomes but a catalyst to the self's energies, a "means of arousing his interior activity."[5] Unlike reification in capitalist exchange relations that objectify and thingify persons, the aim of Emersonian provocation is to subjectify and humanize unique individuals. Mutual provocation and reciprocal stimulation are the ideal for Emersonian human relations. In the abstract, this ideal is anti-hierarchical, egalitarian, and democratic, for it pertains to personal relations. In the concrete, it virtually evaporates because it cannot but relate to marginal persons on the edges of dominant classes, groups, or elites. In this way, Emerson's view of a self that provokes and thrives on being provoked converges yet never fully coincides with the instrumental self engendered by market forces.

Emerson on Personality (and Race)

Emerson is the preeminent proponent of the dignity and worth of human personality. This means neither that all persons are created equal nor that every person can be as great as every other. Emerson's notion of human personality

9. Quoted in Michael T. Gilmore, "Emerson and the Persistence of the Commodity," in *Emerson: Prospect and Retrospect*, p. 73.
1. Ibid., p. 67.
2. Ibid., p. 68.
3. Ibid., p. 70.
4. Ibid. *Emerson in His Journals*, p. 403. For Gilmore's most recent discussion on the impact of commodity exchange on Emerson's thought, see *American Romanticism and the Marketplace* (Chicago: University of Chicago Press, 1985), pp. 18–34.
5. Quoted in Lopez, "Transcendental Failure," p. 126.

does not derive from a particular political doctrine or rest upon a theological foundation. Rather it is the starting point and ultimate aim of his project.

> In all my lectures, I have taught one doctrine, namely, the infinitude of the private man.[6]

Yet most Emerson scholars have given him too much of the benefit of the doubt regarding just how universally applicable his notion of personality was meant to be. I suggest that his ideal of the human person, though complex and profound, is inseparable from his understanding of race. This is so not simply because, as Philip Nicoloff has shown, Emerson is a typical nineteenth-century North Atlantic "mild racist."[7] Rather this is so also because Emerson understands the person as a specific mythic entity, an emerging American self or a unique variant of the North Atlantic bourgeois subject. This understanding cannot but be shot through with certain xenophobic sensibilities and racist perceptions of the time. Emerson indeed is no garden-variety racist or ranting xenophobe, yet he is a racist in the American grain in that his notion of human personality is, in part, dependent on and derived from his view of the races.

Emerson spent a significant amount of time and energy keeping up with the science of his day. His purpose seems to have been to be assured that the best knowledge available about nature buttressed and supported his idealism. An important part of his reading focused on "whence came the Negro?"[8] After his early stay in the South and his limited abolitionist activism, he writes,

> What arguments, what eloquence can avail against the power of that one word *niggers*? The man of the world annihilates the whole combined force of all the antislavery societies of the world by pronouncing it.[9]

As a youth, Emerson held a rather traditional conception of nature as a "scale of being" in which different persons, principally owing to their distinct racial endowments, fit on a hierarchical chain of faculties and talents. He records his inchoate thoughts about this only two years after he began keeping a journal:

> I believe that nobody now regards the maxim "that all men are born equal," as any thing more than a convenient hypothesis or an extravagant declamation. For the reverse is true—that all men are born unequal in personal powers and in those essential circumstances, of time, parentage, country, fortune. The least knowledge of the natural history of man adds another important particular to these; namely, what class of men he belongs to— European, Moor, Tartar, African? Because, Nature has plainly assigned different degrees of intellect to these different races, and the barriers between are insurmountable.
>
> This inequality is an indication that some should lead, and some should serve.
>
> If we speak in general of the two classes Man and Beast, we say that they are separated by the distinction of reason and the want of it.
>
> I saw ten, twenty, a hundred large lipped, lowbrowed black men in the streets who, except in the mere matter of language, did not exceed the

6. *Emerson in His Journals*, p. 236.
7. Philip Nicoloff, *Emerson on Race and History* (New York: Columbia University Press, 1961), p. 124.
8. *Emerson in His Journals*, p. 194.
9. Ibid., p. 338.

sagacity of the elephant. Now is it true that these were created superior to this wise animal, and designed to control it? And in comparison with the highest orders of men, the Africans will stand so low as to make the difference which subsists between themselves & the sagacious beasts inconsiderable. It follows from this, that this is a distinction which cannot be much insisted on.

And if not this, what is the preeminence? Is it in the upright form, and countenance raised to heaven—fitted for command. But in this respect also the African fails. The Monkey resembles Man, and the African degenerates to a likeness of the beast. And here likewise I apprehend we shall find as much difference between the head of Plato & the head of the lowest African, as between this last and the highest species of Ape.

If therefore the distinction between the beasts and the Africans is found neither in Reason nor in figure, i.e. neither in mind or body—where then is the ground of that distinction? Is it not rather a mere name & prejudice and are not they an upper order of inferior animals?[1]

Admittedly, these reflections are made in the context of marshaling arguments against slavery, yet they do reveal the state of North Atlantic science and culture on race at the time. Similarly, in light of the central role that genius plays in his thought Emerson writes sarcastically in his journal,

I notice that Words are as much governed by Fashion as dress, both in written & spoken style. A Negro said of another today "that's a *curious genius.*"[2]

The implication here is not only that the status of genius eludes the interlocutors but also that the very word on their lips reveals the degree to which a vulgar leveling cultural process is occurring. By 1840, his doubts and questions regarding the inferiority of Africans and the necessity and desirability of their emancipation from slavery are apparent:

Strange history this of *abolition.* The Negro must be very old & belongs, one would say, to the fossil formations. What right has he to be intruding into the late & civil daylight of this dynasty of the Caucasians & Saxons? It is plain that so inferior a race must perish shortly like the poor Indians. Sarah Clarke said, "The Indians perish because there is no place for them." That is the very fact of their inferiority. There is always place for the superior. Yet pity for these was needed, it seems, for the education of this generation in ethics. Our good world cannot learn the beauty of love in narrow circles & at home in the immense Heart, but must be stimulated by somewhat foreign & monstrous, by the simular man of Ethiopia.[3]

In his most enlightened statement of 1844, Emerson's racism is softened and his sympathy and support for Africans are visible.

When at last in a race a new principle appears, an idea, that conserves it. Ideas only save races. If the black man is feeble & not important to the existing races, not on a par with the best race, the black man must serve and be sold and exterminated. But if the black man carries in his bosom an indispensable element of a new & coming civilization, for the sake of that element no wrong nor strength nor circumstance can hurt him, he will

1. Ibid., pp. 19, 20, 21.
2. Ibid., p. 44.
3. Ibid., p. 245.

survive & play his part. So now it seems to me that the arrival of such men as Toussaint if he is pure blood, or of Douglas if he is pure blood, outweighs all the English and American humanity. The Antislavery of the whole world is but dust in the balance, a poor squeamishness & nervousness; the might & right is here. Here is the Anti-slave. Here is Man; & if you have man, black or white is an insignificance. Why at night all men are black . . . I say to you, you must save yourself, black or white, man or woman. Other help is none. I esteem the occasion of this jubilee to be that proud discovery that the black race can begin to contend with the white; that in the great anthem of the world which we call history, a piece of many parts & vast compass, after playing a long time a very low & subdued accompaniment they perceive the time arrived when they can strike in with force & effect & take a master's part in the music. The civilization of the world has arrived at that pitch that their moral quality is becoming indispensable, & the genius of this race is to be honoured for itself.[4]

In later allusions to black people, Emerson falls back into his earlier mode, viewing blacks as synonymous with "lowest man" who is "destined for museums like the dodo." In one of his notebooks, he writes:

The duty to our fellow man the slave We are to assert his right in all companies
        An amiable joyous race who for ages have not been permitted to unfold their natural powers we are to befriend
        I think it cannot be maintained by any candid person that the African race have ever occupied or do promise ever to occupy any very high place in the human family. Their present condition is the strongest proof that they cannot. The Irish cannot; the American Indian cannot; the Chinese cannot. Before the energy of the Caucasian race all the other races have quailed and done obeisance.[5]

Apparently alluding to the racist arguments of the radical Theodore Parker (as in his *The Rights of Man in America*) for the abolition of slavery, Emerson acutely dissects and seems to affirm such views.

The Sad Side of the Negro Question. The abolitionist (theoretical) wishes to abolish Slavery, but because he wishes to abolish the black man. He considers that it is violence, brute force, which, counter to intellectual rule, holds property in man; but he thinks the negro himself the very representative & exponent of that brute base force; that it is the negro in the white man which holds slaves. He attacks Legree, MacDuffie, & slaveholders north & south generally, but because they are the foremost negroes of the world, & fight the negro fight. When they are extinguished, & law, intellectual law prevails, it will then appear quickly enough that the brute instinct rallies and centres in the black man. He is created on a lower plane than the white, & eats men & kidnaps & tortures, if he can. The Negro is imitative, secondary, in short, reactionary merely in his successes, & there is no origination with him in mental & moral spheres.[6]

4. Ibid., p. 329.
5. *The Journals and Miscellaneous Notebooks of Ralph Waldo Emerson*, Vol. 12, ed. Linda Allardt (Cambridge: Harvard University Press, 1976), p. 152. Note also his letter to Thomas Carlyle regarding the latter's *The Nigger Question* and *Latter-Day Pamphlets* in *The Correspondence of Thomas Carlyle and Ralph Waldo Emerson, 1834–1872*, Vol. 2 (Chatto, Windus, and Piccadilly, 1883), p. 192n.
6. *Selected Writings of Ralph Waldo Emerson*, pp. 158–59.

Despite Emerson's heralded shift from a "scale-of-being" view to an evolutionary perspective prompted by his reading of Robert Chambers' *Vestiges of Creation* in 1845, his belief in the doctrine of discernible racial differences and his ambivalence about the theory of the polygenetic origins of the races (though he was opposed to its use by anti-abolitionists like his good friend Louis Agassiz of Harvard) still rooted him in racist soil. Needless to say, such a perspective severely circumscribed his perception of the capacities and potentialities of non-Europeans (as well as white women).[7]

Yet the major significance of race in Emerson's reflections on human personality has to do with its relation to notions of circumstance, fate, limits—and, ultimately, history. Emerson's slow acknowledgment that there are immutable constraints on the human powers of individuals resulted primarily from his conclusions regarding the relation of persons to their racial origins and endowments. As a trope in his discourse, race signifies the circumstantial, the conditioned, the fateful—that which limits the will of individuals, even exceptional ones. In short, Emerson's sobering encounter with history—a natural history, of course—is principally mediated and motivated by his attempt to make sense of the relation of human personality to race. He writes in his journal in 1845 that he is attracted to two conceptions of "man's" history:

> One is the scientific or skeptical, and derives his origin from the gradual composition, subsidence and refining,—from the Negro, from the ape, progressive from the animalcule savages of the waterdrop, from *volvox globator*, up to the wise man of the nineteenth century.
>
> The other is the believer's, the poet's, the faithful history, always testified by the mystic and the devout, the history of the fall, of a descent from a superior and pure race, attested in actual history by the grand remains of elder ages.[8]

In both contending conceptions, race plays a major role. This is seen most clearly in the most overlooked text in Emerson's corpus, *English Traits* (1856).[9] On the one hand, history like nature is a continuous ascent from savagery to civilization motored by provocation, challenge, and conquest. This progress required that there be different races of man with some brutish, others mediocre, and still others refined. From the Negro or Indian to the Saxons, this growth and development, he claimed, is visible and undeniable; on the other hand, after a period of ebullient ascent in which the power, vision, and newness of

---

7. Two exemplary statements by Emerson regarding women are found in his essay "Woman" and his journals. "Man is the Will, and woman the sentiment. In this ship of humanity, Will is the rudder, and sentiment the sail: When woman affects to steer, the rudder is only a masked sail. When women engage in any art or trade, it is usually as a resource, not as a primary object. The life of the affections is primary to them, so that there is usually no employment or career which they will not with their own applause and that of society quit for suitable marriage. And they give entirely to their affections, set their whole fortune on the die, lose themselves eagerly in the glory of their husband and children." Quoted in Allen, *Waldo Emerson*, pp. 559–60. "Few women are sane. They emit a coloured atmosphere, one would say, floods upon floods of coloured light, in which they walk evermore, and see all objects through this warm tinted mist which envelopes them. Men are not, to the same degree, temperamented; for there are multitudes of men who live to objects quite out of them. As to politics, to trade, to letters, or an art, unhindered by any influence of constitution." *Emerson in His Journals*, pp. 431–32.
8. Quoted in Nicoloff, *Emerson on Race and History*, p. 234.
9. In an interesting preface to this text, Howard Mumford Jones states, "Emerson was an idealist, but he was also a hardheaded Yankee, and he was never more the Yankee than when writing *English Traits*, the tone of which is so radically different from that, say, of *Nature* that if, a thousand years from now, both books were dug up and the name of the author disappeared, a cautious scholar of the thirty-first century would scarcely dare assign them to the same pen." Ralph Waldo Emerson, *English Traits*, ed. Howard Mumford Jones (Cambridge: Harvard University Press, 1966).

"racial genius," i.e., especially poets, are displayed, descent sets in. The creative energies of those "racial" pioneers recede after provocation wanes, stagnation surfaces, and retrospection predominates. As Philip Nicoloff perceptively notes,

> The motives behind Emerson's affection for such a doctrine of necessitated ascent and decline are rather obvious. It was the sort of sweeping historical generality he loved. It was a view filled with poetic richness: the veneration of great sires; the semi-religious notion of an Olympian sphere of intellect in which some few men in all ages might share. More importantly, it served Emerson's unswerving but sometimes anxious confidence in America's destiny. All of America's rawness and youthful innocence, even her penchant for preposterous boasting, could thus be interpreted in her favor. America was young, Europe was old, and historical necessity would take care of the rest. The jibes of European critics could be ignored. Even the immorality of America's exuberant extermination of Indians and Mexicans could be treated with philosophical patience.[1]

Therefore Emerson's first noteworthy attempt to come to terms with history, circumstances, or fate occurs not in *The Conduct of Life* (1860) in which his classic "Fate" appears, but rather in *English Traits* (1856). In a most perplexing chapter entitled "Race," he tries to "historically" situate and condition the "genius" (power) he had earlier enshrined.

> How came such men as King Alfred, and Roger Bacon, William of Wykeham, Walter Raleigh, Philip Sidney, Isaac Newton, William Shakespeare, George Chapman, Francis Bacon, George Herbert, Henry Vane, to exist here? What made these delicate natures? Was it the air? Was it the sea? Was it the parentage? For it is certain that these men are samples of their contemporaries. The hearing ear is always found close to the speaking tongue, and no genius can long or often utter any thing which is not invited and gladly entertained by men around him.
> It is race, is it not? That puts the hundred millions of India under the dominion of a remote island in the north of Europe. Race avails much, if that be true which is alleged, that all Celts love unity of power, and Saxons the representative principle. Race is a controlling influence in the Jew, who for two millenniums, under every climate, has preserved the same character and employments. Race in the Negro is of appalling importance.[2]

This situating and conditioning of "genius" are complemented by "counter-acting forces to race," though "race works immortally to keep its own."[3] For Emerson, to grapple with the constraints on human power, vision, and newness is to understand first and foremost the role of race in history.

Even in his canonical essay "Fate," Emerson is explicit about the centrality of race in limiting the capacities and potentialities of individual consciousness and will.

> In science, we have to consider two things: power and circumstance . . . Once we thought, positive power was all, now we learn, that negative power, or circumstance, is half. Nature is the tyrannous circumstance, the thick skull, the sheathed snake, the ponderous, rock-like jaw; necessitated activity; violent direction; the conditions of a tool, like the locomotive,

1. Nicoloff, *Emerson on Race and History*, pp. 236–37.
2. Emerson, *English Traits*, p. 30.
3. Ibid., pp. 30, 31.

strong enough on its track, but which can do nothing but mischief off of it; or skates, which are wings on the ice, but fetters on the ground.

The book of Nature is the book of Fate . . . The face of the planet cools and dries, the races meliorate, and man is born. But when a race has lived its term, it comes no more again.

We know in history what weight belongs to race. We see the English, French, and Germans planting themselves on every shore and market of America and Australia, and monopolizing the commerce of these countries. We like the nervous and victorious habit of our own branch of the family. We follow the step of the Jew, of the Indian, of the Negro. We see how much will has been expended to extinguish the Jew, in vain. Look at the unpalatable conclusions of Knox, in his "Fragments of Races,"—a rash and unsatisfactory writer, but charged with pungent and unforgettable truths. "Nature respects race, and not hybrids." "Every race has its own *habitat*." "Detach a colony from the race, and it deteriorates to the crab."

Famine, typhus, frost, war, suicide, and effete races, must be reckoned calculable parts of the system of the world.

The force with which we resist these torrents of tendency looks so ridiculously inadequate, that it amounts to little more than a criticism or a protest made by a minority of one, under compulsion of millions.

We cannot trifle with this reality, this cropping-out in our planted gardens of the core of the world. No picture of life can have any veracity that does not admit the odious facts. A man's power is hooped in by a necessity. Thus we trace Fate, in matter, mind, and morals,—in race, in retardations of strata, and in thought and character as well.[4]

When Emerson moves toward the lord of fate, the limits of limitation, the specific examples he cites are "the instinctive and heroic races" who are "proud believers in Destiny"[5]—more pointedly,

an imperial Saxon race, which nature cannot bear to lose, and, after cooping it up for a thousand years in yonder England, gives a hundred Englands, a hundred Mexicos. All the bloods it shall absorb and domineer: and more than Mexicos,—the secrets of water and steam, the spasms of electricity, the ductility of metals, the chariot of the air, the ruddered balloon, are awaiting you . . .

Very odious, I confess, are the lessons of fate . . .

Fate involves the melioration. No statement of the Universe can have any soundness, which does not admit its ascending effort. The direction of the whole, and of the parts, is toward benefit, and in proportion to the health. Behind every individual closes organization: before him, opens liberty,—the Better, the Best. The first and worst races are dead. The second and imperfect races are dying out, or remain for the maturing of higher. In the latest race, in man, every generosity, every new perception, the love and praise he extorts from his fellows, are certificates of advance out of fate into freedom.[6]

---

4. Ralph Waldo Emerson, "Fate," *Selected Writings of Ralph Waldo Emerson*, pp. 384, 385, 386, 387, 388.
5. Ibid, p. 389.
6. Ibid, pp. 393–94, 395. These claims fly in the face of Howard Mumford Jones's apologetic statement that "in truth Emerson had no great faith in the racial theorists he read." *English Traits*, p. xx.

I am suggesting neither that Emerson is an exemplary North Atlantic racist nor that his peculiar form of racism simply rationalizes Euro-American domination and extermination of Native Americans and Mexicans. In fact, his rejection of John Knox's theory of racial physiological incompatibility (hence rigid racial boundaries) and approval of racial "mixing" make Emerson a rather liberal "racist." Furthermore, Emerson's moral support for Indians and Mexican sovereignty is well known, though his organic conception of history renders this "against-the-grain" support rather impotent and innocuous. Regarding the annexation of Texas, he writes,

> It is very certain that the strong British race, which has now overrun so much of this continent, must also overrun that tract, and Mexico and Oregon also, and it will in the course of ages be of small import by what particular occasions and methods it was done. It is a secular question.[7]

In *English Traits*, Emerson views the "animal vigor" of the English and their inheritance (mainly from the Normans) of an "excess of virility" as that which sustains their exercise of power and supports their capacity to provoke and be provoked by new challenges. A telling sign of decline and decay, of eclipse and ebb, is the disappearance of such vigor and virility, will and provocation.

What I am suggesting is that Emerson's conception of the worth and dignity of human personality is racially circumscribed; that race is central to his understanding of the historical circumstances which shape human personality; and that this understanding can easily serve as a defense of Anglo-Saxon imperialist domination of non-European lands and peoples. In this way, Emerson's reflections on race are neither extraneous nor superfluous in his thought. Rather, they are the pillar for his later turn toward history, circumstance, fate, and limitation. As Philip Nicoloff aptly concludes,

> We must insist . . . that the "transparent eyeball" was progressively spending less and less time bathing itself in the blithe currents of universal being and more time scanning the iron pages of geological and biological history. More and more Emerson was inclined to explain the human past, present, and future in terms of some long-range destiny implicit in racial seed and the fated cycle of circumstance. The dominant concern was no longer with the possibility of private ecstasy, but rather with the endless pageant of racial man advancing irresistibly out of his "dread origin" in "the abyss" towards a ripeness of vision which, once held, could only ebb away into over-fineness and loss of power. The ability to swim well or ill with the flow of things seemed more and more to lie altogether outside the area of human volition. Nature called whom she would and in her own time.[8]

As Emerson probed the conditioned character of human will and personality, he did not move toward a tragic vision. Rather he deepened his mysticism, increased his faith in the nature of things, and adjusted himself (though never fully) to the expanding world dominance of the "imperial Saxon race." He knew this domination would not last forever, but given the golden promise of America in his day, it made little sense for him to speculate on the decline of North Atlantic civilization. So his later message was clear: the worth of human personality is grand,

---

7. *Selected Writings of Ralph Waldo Emerson*, p. 119.
8. Nicoloff, *Emerson on Race and History*, pp. 245–46.

the will of great individuals is mighty, and the cycle of fate (symbolized by ascending and descending races) is almighty—yet it presently tilts toward the West.

Emerson as Organic Intellectual

Emerson's dominant themes of individuality, idealism, voluntarism, optimism, amelioration, and experimentation prefigure those of American pragmatism. His complex articulation of a distinct Americanism grounded on specific interpretations of power, provocation, and personality—that is, both the content of this ideology and the way in which he presented it—deeply shaped the emergence and development of American pragmatism. Furthermore, the way in which Emerson formed a constituency constitutes a model for American pragmatists to this day.

In the previous sections I intimated that Emerson's notion of power was inextricably bound with tradition, provocation with the market, and personality with racial domination. Here I shall focus on these crucial connections and affiliations between ideas and institutions, discourses and infrastructures, intellectual practices and modes of social structuration. In fact, I suggest that it was Emerson's own sensitivity and attentiveness to these links that, in part, permitted him to swerve from the predominant epistemological concerns of European philosophers; that is, Emerson conceived of his project as a form of power, a kind of provocation, and of himself as an indomitable person whose very presence, i.e., activity, changed the world. Unlike European philosophical giants like René Descartes, John Locke, David Hume, Immanuel Kant, and G. W. F. Hegel, Emerson viewed knowledge not as a set of representations to be justified, grounded, or privileged but rather as instrumental effects of human will as it is guided by human interests, which are in turn produced by transactions with other humans and nature. He had little patience with modern philosophy, for like Pascal, Kierkegaard, and Nietzsche he rejected the epistemology-centered problematic of modern philosophy.[9] He did not rest content with the language of static substances which undergird accidental qualities, disembodied ideas that represent stationary objects, or universal mental schemes possessed by all rational subjects—a language riveted with categories derived from ossified sources. Rather Emerson preferred the language of tentative strategies, contingent functions, enabling tactics, and useful devices—mindful of the profound Wittgensteinian insight that these descriptions apply to language itself. Its character is "to flow and not to freeze."

All language is vehicular and transitive, and is good, as ferries and horses are, for conveyance, not as farms and houses are, for homestead.[1]

---

9. On his skepticism regarding a foundationalist epistemology, Emerson quips, "I know that the world I converse with in the city and in the farms is not the world I *think.* I observe that difference, and shall observe it. One day, I shall know the value and law of this discrepance. But I have not found that much was gained by manipular attempts to realize the world of thought. Many eager persons successively make an experiment in this way, and make themselves ridiculous." "Experience," p. 347. For a detailed treatment of Emerson's rejection of traditional epistemological perspectives, see Van Leer, *Emerson's Epistemology,* pp. 188–207. Van Leer concludes, "Emerson outlines a proto-pragmatic theory of truth that permits both general stability and local freedom, without flirting with the reifying tendency of his earlier epistemological formulations . . . In the late essays in general and 'Fate' in particular, Emerson seems to confess his disinterest in the epistemological project so prominent up through 'Experience'" (pp. 206, 207).
1. Ralph Waldo Emerson, "The Poet," *Selected Writings of Ralph Waldo Emerson,* p. 322. For fascinating reflections on this matter, see Richard Poirier, "The Questions of Genius," in *Ralph Waldo Emerson,* ed. Harold Bloom, pp. 163–86, and Poirier, *The Renewal of Literature: Emersonian Reflections* (New York: Random House, 1987), pp. 3–94, 182–223.

Furthermore, Emerson's alternative to modern philosophy was neither to replace it with a new philosophical problematic nor to deny it by means of a strict and severe skepticism. Rather he *evades* modern philosophy; that is, he ingeniously and skillfully refuses: (1) its quest for certainty and its hope for professional, i.e., scientific, respectability; (2) its search for foundations. This distinctly American refusal is the crucible from which emerge the sensibilities and sentiments of future American pragmatists.

Instead, Emerson pursues a mode of cultural criticism which indulges in a quest for power, a perennial experimental search sustained by provocation and a hope for the enhancement and expansion of the self (viz., America). This pursuit locates Emerson at the "bloody crossroads" between weaving webs of meaning and feeling and criticizing structures of domination and exploitation ("Cut these sentences and they bleed" and "Let us answer a book of ink with a book of flesh and blood").[2] Thus, he must create a new vocation in the open space and inaugurate (rhetorically) a new history of human freedom beyond the tyrannies (of tropes and troops) in the past. Emerson evades modern philosophy not because it is wrong, unjustified, or uninteresting, but rather because it is antiquated, anachronistic, and outdated *relative to his chosen tasks*. Like the recent European past of unfreedom, Descartes's veil of ideas is a prison, Hume's skepticism a halfway house, and Kant's dualism too debilitating. He resonates a bit with Hegel but shuns the German obsession with method which results in "committing oneself to more machinery than one had any business for."[3] Since this obsession has more to do with reproducing professional culture than with loving wisdom—(not surprisingly) the only culture capable of unifying the elites of a divided German nation until 1871—Emerson's individualism leads him to abhor it. He will not swim in a regulated pool nor allow others to imitate his stroke.

> I have been writing & speaking what were once called novelties, for twenty-five or thirty years, & have not now one disciple. Why? Not that what I said was not true; not that it has not found intelligent receivers but because it did not go from any wish in me to bring men to me, but to themselves. I delight in driving them from me. What could I do, if they came to me? They would interrupt & encumber me. This is my boast that I have no school & no follower. I should account it a measure of the impurity of insight, if it did not create independence.[4]

To evade modern philosophy means to strip the profession of philosophy of its pretense, disclose its affiliations with structures of powers (both rhetorical and political) rooted in the past, and enact intellectual practices, i.e., produce texts of various sorts and styles, that invigorate and unsettle one's culture and society. As we saw earlier, for Emerson this results in neither social revolution nor cultural upheaval but rather moral transgression based on personal integrity and individual conscience. The aim of Emersonian cultural criticism—and subsequently, most of American pragmatic thought—is to expand powers and proliferate provocations for the moral development of human personalities.

---

2. The first Emerson statement is quoted in Robert Frost's insightful "On Emerson," in *Emerson: A Collection of Critical Essays*, p. 13. The second is from *Emerson in His Journals*, p. 257.
3. This lovely formulation comes from Stanley Cavell's comparison of Emerson with the early Heidegger—both viewed as proponents of "a kind of epistemology of moods." See "Thinking of Emerson," p. 125.
4. *Emerson in His Journals*, p. 484.

American Politics. I have the belief that of all things the work of America is to make the advanced intelligence of mankind in the sufficiency of morals practical; that since there is on every side a breaking up of the faith in the old traditions of religion &, of necessity, a return to the omnipotence of the moral sentiment, that in America this conviction is to be embodied in the laws, in the jurisprudence, international law, in political economy.[5]

The unconscious underside of this Emersonian aim is the setting aside of tradition and the enshrining of the market by which the Saxon race exercises imperial domination over nature and those peoples associated therewith, e.g., Indians, Mexicans, blacks, women. Emerson's evasion of modern philosophy is one of the ways in which he sets tradition aside; it also is one of the means by which he exercises his own intellectual self-reliance. He refuses to be captive to or caught up in the problematic and vocabulary of those who came before. This Emersonian refusal—both mythic and generative of new myths—sits at the core of his rhetorical strategies and the tools he deploys to create himself as an organic intellectual and to constitute a constituency over which he exercises ideological and moral leadership.

The three major historical coordinates of Emerson's career are the cultural metamorphosis of Victorian New England, the economic repercussions of a nascent industrial capitalist order, and the identity crisis of the first new nation. The cultural metamorphosis consisted of an overcoming of the "agonized conscience" of a moribund Puritanical tradition and of a creating of spontaneous self-manufactured myths to replace the cold rationalism of a stilted Unitarianism. The economic repercussions of rapid primitive capital accumulation—requiring "virgin" lands and exploiting new black, brown, red, yellow, and white labor—included panics and depressions, booms and selective prosperity. And the national identity crisis focused on the most powerful bonds of unity among citizens, namely, the realities of imperial expansion, the ideals of the democratic heritage, and the quest for individual fulfillment.

This historical context shaped Emerson's influential problematic and vocabulary. From his New England origins, he extracts a lasting concern with individual conscience linked to a conception of life as a fundamentally moral process. The emerging market operations encouraged and supported his preoccupation with contingency, flux, unpredictability, and variability. And a post-colonial yet imperialist America's need for collective self-definition prompted his own civil religion of self-reliance and self-trust. The major national events of Emerson's life were the election of Andrew Jackson (1828), the panic of 1837, the Mexican-American War (1846–48), the Civil War (1861–65), the Radical Reconstruction (1865–77), and, most important, the wholesale removal of Indians from their homelands and the making of an American industrial working class. His political response to some of these events is that of moral critique grounded in individual conscience and, at times, personal action. His silence on other events—especially the Radical Reconstruction—is in itself significant, given the direction of his thought in later years. Yet, ironically, his complex rhetoric of power (usurping tradition), provocation (both fearful of and fascinated by the market), and human personality (circumscribed by race, history, and circumstance) provides the very ingredients for varying American ideologies that legitimate and rationalize the dominant theme running through these

5. Ibid., p. 536.

events—the imperial expansion of the American nation principally in the interests of Saxon male elites.

The major personal events of Emerson's life—the death of his first wife, Ellen Tucker (1831), his resignation of his Unitarian church pastorate (1832), his first trip to Europe (1833), the substantial inheritance from Ellen's will that he won in a contested case before the Massachusetts Supreme Court (1834), the start of a new career of public lecturing (1834), his second marriage to Lydia Stevenson [sic] (1835), the death of his brother, Charles, and publication of *Nature* (1836), the death of his son, Waldo (1842), his public support of antislavery militant John Brown (1859), his Harvard visiting lectureship (1870), the destruction of his house by fire (1872)—fanned and fueled his deep belief in moral transgression against any limits and constraints, be it the death of a loved one, the authority of the church, or the burdens of a European past, college tradition, and old form of human enslavement. The great Emersonian refusal of "being fathered"—of being curtailed by any set of antecedent conditions or restrained circumstances— supports the expansionist sensibilities of postcolonial America, just as the grand Emersonian moralism questions the legitimacy of the conquestorial ambitions of imperial America.

This intricate interplay of rhetorically supporting American expansionism yet morally contesting its consequences for human victims is a key to Emerson's success as a public figure. This double consciousness and dual allegiance to the conqueror and the conquered, powerful and powerless, were highly attractive to a nation obsessed with underdogs yet (believed to be) destined to be the top dog of the world. Emerson's moral criticisms indeed are genuine, yet, as we saw earlier, they are politically impotent. In fact, their principal function is to expiate the "bad conscience" of moralists who acknowledge the "inevitability" of American expansionism yet who cannot accept the amoral self-image such acknowledgment seems to imply. Needless to say, the later Emerson more easily reconciles himself to such "inevitabilism" owing to his conceptions of race, history, and circumstances. Yet even the later Emerson remains a moralist with a strong doctrine of fate.

Emerson's rhetorical strategies were directed at those mildly oppositional elements of the educated portion of the petite bourgeoisie—that is, those "cultured" Saxon gentlemen (and few white women) wedded to elitist notions of individual achievement yet guided by self-images of democratic allegiance. It is no surprise that he castigates the vulgarity and crudity of the Jacksonians yet resonates with some of their democratic ideas.[6] Emerson detaches democratic ideas from Jacksonian activists, in part because he perceives them to be *parvenu* petit bourgeois reformers on the make with their own forms of greed, corruption, manipulation, and selfishness. Furthermore, he views their obsession with material prosperity and social status as symptomatic of a profound absence of moral conscience, as best exemplified in their pernicious policies of Indian removal and antiabolitionism.[7] Emerson's hostility to the Jacksonians is also due to the fact that they were his rivals for both ideological control over the demo-

6. Ibid., pp. 65, 125, 131. For a classic essay on the relation of Emerson's thought to Jacksonian democracy, see Perry Miller, "Emersonian Genius and the American Democracy," in *Emerson: A Collection of Critical Essays*, pp. 72–84.
7. Slotkin, *Fatal Environment*, pp. 109–58. Michael Paul Rogin, *Fathers and Children: Andrew Jackson and the Subjugation of the American Indian* (New York: Knopf, 1975).

cratic national heritage and political control over the new constituency of middle-class reformers. Jackson offered them nitty-gritty activism, concrete benefits, and political involvement; Emerson, contemplative reflection, personal integrity, and individual conscience. Yet both share common rhetorics of power, expansion, and limitlessness.

Therefore the primary social base of Emerson's project consists of the mildly oppositional intelligentsia alienated from conservative moneyed interests, and "enlightened" businessmen who long for "culture" as well as profits, e.g., E. B. Phillips, president of the Michigan Southern Railroad.[8] Emerson explicitly shuns the lower class owing to their cultural narrowness and their potential for revolution.

> If the wishes of the lowest class that suffer in these long streets should execute themselves, who can doubt that the city would topple in ruins.

> We have had in different parts of the country mobs and moblike legislation, and even moblike judicature, which have betrayed an almost godless state of society . . . There is reading, and public lecturing too, in this country, that I could recommend as medicine to any gentleman who finds the love of life too strong in him.[9]

This social location of Emerson's constituency imposes severe restrictions on the political possibilities of his project. On the one hand, the group of people with which he is aligned is dependent on the very moneyed class he is criticizing. Therefore they can bark only so loud. On the other hand, the very interests of his own group are circumscribed by their attitude toward the "mob," or working-class majority of the populace, so that any meaningful links with social movements or political organizations from below are foreclosed. Hence, one may discern Emersonian themes of self-reliance and self-sufficiency in the radical egalitarianism of Thomas Skidmore, yet one can never envision Emerson supporting Skidmore's workingmen's association.[1]

Emerson's ability to exercise moral and intellectual leadership over a small yet crucial fraction of the educated middle classes and enlightened business elites of his day principally rests upon his articulation of a refined perspective that highlights individual conscience along with political impotence, moral transgression devoid of fundamental social transformation, power without empowering the lower classes, provocation and stimulation bereft of regulated markets, and human personality disjoined from communal action. Emerson is neither a liberal nor a conservative and certainly not a socialist or even civic republican. Rather he is a petit bourgeois libertarian, with at times anarchist tendencies and limited yet genuine democratic sentiments. It is no accident that the most sustained institutional commitment of Emerson's life is a pedagogical one: to his lifelong friend Bronson Alcott's "progressive" school in Boston. In fact, he and Alcott often discussed

8. Regarding this social base of Emerson's project, see Daniel Aaron, "Emerson and the Progressive Tradition," in *Emerson: A Collection of Critical Essays*, pp. 85–99; Anne C. Rose. *Transcendentalism as a Social Movement*, 1830–1850 (New Haven: Yale University Press, 1981); Allen, *Waldo Emerson*, p. 630; Mary K. Cayton, "The Making of an American Prophet: Emerson, His Audiences, and the Rise of the Culture Industry in Nineteenth-Century America," *American Historical Review*, 92, no. 3 (June 1987), 597–620.

9. Allen, *Waldo Emerson*, pp. 231, 258, 293.

1. For a recent treatment of Thomas Skidmore's democratic ideal, see Sean Wilentz, *Chants Democratic* (Oxford: Oxford University Press, 1984), pp. 182–89, 198–206. In this sense, John Dewey's famous characterization of Emerson as a philosopher of democracy requires severe qualification.

setting up a special innovative and open college with limited enrollment and courses in Concord.[2] For Emerson, politics is not simply the clash of powers and pleasures but also another terrain on which the moral development of individuals should take place. Needless to say, his disappointment with and distrust of governments ran deep. This further reinforced his sense of political impotence.

The organic intellectual activity of Emerson serves as a useful pre-history of American pragmatism not only because he prefigures the major themes (power, provocation, personality) and crucial motifs (optimism, moralism, individualism) but also because Emerson creates a style of cultural criticism which evades modern philosophy, deploys a set of rhetorical strategies that attempt to both legitimize and criticize America, and situates his project within and among the refined and reformist elements of the middle class—the emerging and evolving class envisioned as the historical agent of the American religion.

LEN GOUGEON

From Virtue's Hero[†]

Conclusion

Ralph Waldo Emerson was a committed social reformer all of his life. He was deeply concerned with and involved in the major social reform movement of his time, antislavery. Throughout his lifetime Emerson never wavered in his commitment to clearly defined principles of human liberty, equality, and equal rights. The only serious doubts he ever felt in the matter concerned how *he* might best make his contribution to the cause. He did not wish to waste his energies in unproductive enterprises for which he was not fit. Also, he was always convinced, radical that he was, that American society could only be reformed by striking at the *roots* of social evil rather than simply pruning an occasional branch. For Emerson, the major cause of America's moral malaise was its gross materialism — the general tendency to place the value of things above people — and slavery was the epitome of this corrupt philosophy. Against this formidable brick-and-stone opponent Emerson fired the artillery of sympathy, emotion, and idealism, in the hope of precipitating a cultural revolution that would have the effect of elevating the civilization of America to a higher moral plane. He was quintessentially American in his reform efforts. Like the Founding Fathers whom he admired and the Declaration of Independence, which he once described as the "greatest achievement of American literature," he recognized that ideas can be powerful in shaping the course of things. He always believed, as he told the graduates of Harvard in 1837, that "this time, like all times, is a very good one, if we but know what to do with it." And, for the most part, Emerson usually did.

It was as a scholar, an American scholar, that Emerson believed his best contribution could be made in the effort to reform and redeem American society. But

---

2. Allen, *Waldo Emerson*, pp. 364–65.
† From *Virtue's Hero: Emerson, Antislavery, and Reform* (Athens: University of Georgia Press, 1990), pp. 337–48. Reprinted by permission of the publisher.

he also recognized that while a scholar can enlighten the minds and move the hearts of others, a more specific instrumentality would be necessary to effect specific changes—to make the law of the heart the law of the land also. For Emerson, this instrumentality was the political process. While often critical of politicians for their numerous failures, especially the tendency to compromise principles in the name of expediency, Emerson never eschewed the political process itself. Whatever its shortcomings, the system established by the Founding Fathers had contributed enormously to the evolution of American greatness, and would continue to do so if leaders could be made to lead properly. Government, he felt, had the capacity to relieve social ills. As he noted in 1844, "Government exists to defend the weak and the poor and the injured party." However, he also realized that an effort was often required to compel the government to use its power wisely. He was well aware, as he pointed out in 1854, of the "worthlessness of good tools to bad workmen." He believed that citizens must imbue themselves with the best spirit of American democracy, must thereby become "citadels and warriors . . . declarations of Independence, the charter, the battle and the victory," and must demand that elected representatives follow this example themselves. Emerson always recognized that in America, "what great masses of men wish done, will be done" if the people themselves insist upon it. Change, and for Emerson, evolutionary progress, was always possible in America because "a Congress is a standing insurrection," and no matter how firmly entrenched a given political position, party, or policy is, it can be uprooted, overthrown, and abolished. As a means toward this end Emerson generally favored the ballot box. He always voted and always encouraged others to do so. An enlightened mind and sensitive heart could do much to improve society by the casting of a conscientious vote. Also, he was not above participating directly in a political campaign when it seemed appropriate for him to do so.

Emerson recognized that the casting of votes was not always in itself enough. At times, opposition to the social and moral reform of America appeared in a more violent guise than that of political party. Sometimes, as in Boston in 1835 and 1860, and Alton, Illinois, in 1837, the face of opposition appeared as a violent mob. Opposition to this form of evil often required a violence of its own, at times accompanied by self-sacrifice and even the sacrifice of others. Emerson applauded the heroic action of Elijah Lovejoy, as other abolitionists did, and Lovejoy would be but the first of many heroes who, for Emerson, "put their creed into their deed" and were willing to make the ultimate sacrifice for the moral values they held dear. There would be others, including the Free Soil farmers of Kansas, for whom Emerson would provide Sharpe's rifles; the noble Charles Sumner, struck down on the floor of the Senate; John Brown, executed in 1859; President Lincoln, the victim of an assassin's bullet; and finally, the entire generation of brave young men who willingly gave their lives in the Civil War. To Emerson, all of these were ultimately transcendental heroes, individuals who were prepared to sacrifice all in the name of principle.

Emerson also recognized in the 1850s that government itself may not at all times be susceptible to change through traditional political means. With the shocking passage of the Fugitive Slave Law in 1850 he realized that it would be necessary to step outside the bounds of constitutional law in order to oppose that immoral measure. A "higher law" than the Constitution must prevail in such cases, and he willingly and openly urged a defiant civil disobedience and practiced it himself. For him, the sacredness of individual moral conscience would always be infinitely more important than any institution, including the government of the United States. Even at this time, however, he would have preferred that the system correct itself, using the means available to it. He was bitterly disappointed when Massachusetts Chief Justice Lemuel Shaw refused to challenge the federal statute in the several opportunities provided to him. He consistently maintained that both legal tradition and human nature dictate that "you cannot enact a false thing to be true and a wrong thing to be right."

Emerson lived to see what he considered to be the "second American Revolution" correct the one glaring deficiency of the first, the catastrophic compromise with slavery. The Civil War represented the triumph of principle in a society that had become mired in a corrupt materialistic skepticism. He was optimistic that the war had redeemed America from the sinful corruption of the institution of slavery, and he looked forward to a glorious flowering of the American ideal in the post-Civil War period. In one of his last speeches, "Fortune of the Republic" (1878), he described the triumph of the liberal spirit in America in the following terms: "The genius of the country has marked out our true policy, —opportunity. Opportunity of civil rights, of education, of personal power, and not less of wealth; doors wide open. If I could have it, —free trade with all the world without toll or custom-houses, invitation as we now make every nation, to every race and skin, white men, red men, yellow men, black men; hospitality of fair field and equal laws to all" (W II: 541).

In the light of this, it is profoundly ironic that the image of Emerson that would emerge in the closing decades of the nineteenth century would be quite the opposite of the liberal, activist reformer and moralist that he truly was. As noted in chapter 1, the Holmes biography in 1884 was undoubtedly influential in creating a very conservative view of Emerson, but the times themselves reinforced this inclination. In the waning years of the nineteenth century the concept of rugged individualism, reinforced by Darwinian science and Herbert Spencer's social philosophy, came increasingly to dominate American consciousness. By this time Emerson's reputation as a great American thinker was firmly established, and many individuals looked to Emersonian philosophy for an understanding of, and justification for, what seemed to be inevitable developments in American society. Unfortunately, to many, Emerson's early essays like "Self-Reliance," and later ones like "Power" and "Wealth," from *Conduct of Life* (1860), as well as longer works like *Representative Men* (1850), seemed to endorse the deeds of self-made entrepreneurs like Andrew Carnegie, John D. Rockefeller, J. P. Morgan, and others. As a result, Emerson's words were often invoked to justify what Emerson himself would have considered blatant corruptions of the American spirit.

A typical example of this tendency appears in the pronouncements and preachings of the Right Reverend William Lawrence, Methodist bishop of Massachusetts. In his 1901 essay "The Relation of Wealth to Morals" Bishop Lawrence makes the following statement: " 'Man,' says Emerson, 'is born to be rich. He is thoroughly related, and is tempted out by his appetites and fancies to the conquest of this and that piece of Nature, until he finds his well-being in the use of the planet, and of more planets than his own.' " To this the bishop adds his own observation that "man draws to himself material wealth as surely, as naturally, and as necessarily as the oak draws the elements into itself from the earth," and therefore, "in the long run, it is only to the man of morality that wealth comes." Reinforced by his invocation of Emersonian philosophy, the

Reverend Lawrence concludes with the assertion that "Godliness is in league with riches."[1]

Because of perversions such as this, as the historian Daniel Aaron points out, in some quarters Emerson came to occupy the role of "seer of laissez-faire capitalism and the rampant individual." Aaron also notes that even though "Emerson . . . never intended his exhortations to justify the practices of the 'Robber Barons,'" his political philosophy seemed to do just that. "Strongly individualistic, it also spoke for equality of opportunity in economic and political affairs, and it lent support to the belief in laissez-faire and the necessity of the minimized state."[2] Other scholars have also drawn attention to this development and have noted, for example, that "Emerson's essay 'Self-Reliance' . . . provided another ideal justification for what the strong man was going to do anyhow, willy-nilly. And the gentle Emerson, who had grandly declared, 'Let man stand erect, go forth and possess the universe,' lived on into the time when Diamond Jim Brady and Jim Fisk took his advice quite literally and exhibited the success of his doctrine to a pitch appallingly beyond his wildest dreams."[3]

Perry Miller also points out that despite Emerson's early reputation as a revolutionary, "in the course of time, his preaching of individualism, especially 'self-reliance,' came to seem not at all dangerous, but rather the proper code for a young businessman with get-up and go." Miller adds that Emerson's "essay 'Napoleon' in *Representative Men* . . . is in substance his love letter to the entrepreneurs, to the practical men who brushed aside the 'old legislation' and were building railroads."[4] One of the most prominent spokespersons for this view of Emerson at the turn of the century was Charles W. Eliot, president of Harvard University. President Eliot's commentary on Emerson, celebrating the centenary of his birth, was by far the most widely publicized of the time. It was delivered as part of the Emerson Centennial exercises in Boston, sponsored by the American Unitarian Association, on 24 May 1903. The address was delivered at Symphony Hall and was reported and substantially reproduced in many places, including virtually all of the major newspapers in New York and Boston.[5] In his presentation President Eliot presents an image of Emerson that might be described as a cross between a conservative Boston Brahmin and a captain of industry.

Among other things, Eliot suggests that contemporary American efforts to colonize Cuba and the Philippines would be applauded by Emerson because he believed in education as "the only sure means of permanent and progressive reform," and since "the Cubans are to be raised in the scale of civilization and public happiness," and "the Filipinos, too, are to be developed after the American fashion; . . . we send them 1,000 teachers of English."

1. Published originally in *World's Work* (January 1901), pp. 286–92. Reprinted in *Democracy and the Gospel of Wealth*, ed. Gail Kennedy (Boston: D. C. Health, 1949), pp. 68–76.
2. Daniel Aaron, "Emerson and the Progressive Tradition," from *Men of Good Hope* (1951; reprinted in *Emerson: A Collection of Critical Essays*, ed. Milton R. Konvitz and Stephen E. Whicher [Englewood Cliffs, N.J.: Prentice-Hall,1962], pp. 86, 94).
3. "The New Consciousness: 1861–1914," in *American Literature: The Makers and the Making*, 2 vols., ed. Cleanth Brooks, R. W. B. Lewis, and Robert Penn Warren (New York: St. Martin's Press, 1973), 2:1206.
4. Perry Miller, *The Responsibility of Mind in a Civilization of Machines*, ed. John Crowell and Stanford J. Searl, Jr. (Amherst: University of Massachusetts Press, 1979), pp. 172, 205.
5. For example, see *New York Times, New York Tribune, New York Herald, Boston Daily Advertiser, Boston Daily Globe, Boston Post, Boston Morning Journal*, and *Boston Herald*, all on 25 May 1903. The quotations used here are from the *New York Times* account. The speech was also reprinted in *Four American Leaders* (Boston: American Unitarian Association, 1906), pp. 75–126, and *Charles W. Eliot: The Man and His Beliefs*, 2 vols., ed. William Allan Neilson (New York: Harper and Brothers, 1926).

Regarding rampant racism in the South, Eliot suggests that through education "the Southern States can be rescued from the persistent poison of slavery . . . after forty years of failure with political methods." The particular type of education that Eliot has in mind, however, focuses on "manual training schools" and, he says, the education of men by manual labor "was a favorite doctrine with Emerson," and Emerson "saw clearly that manual labor might be made to develop not only good mental qualities but good moral qualities."

President Eliot also addressed the question of the distribution of wealth within American society. At a time when American labor, responding to decades of exploitation by the captains of industry, was demanding a minimum wage and improved working conditions, President Eliot indicates that Emerson's position on such questions was clear. "It is interesting, at the state of industrial warfare which the world has now reached, to observe how Emerson, sixty years ago, discerned clearly the absurdity of paying all sorts of services at one rate, now a favorite notion with some labor unions." According to Eliot, such misinformed egalitarianism would not be appreciated by the great bard, and he notes that Emerson himself had observed that "even when all labor is temporarily paid at one rate, differences in possessions will instantly arise: 'In one hand the dime became an eagle as it fell, and in another hand a copper cent. For the whole value of the dime is in knowing what to do with it.'" Eliot concludes his point with a statement that clearly underscores his own conservative attitude toward the major social problems of the time. He asserts flatly and firmly that "Emerson was never deceived by a specious philanthropy or by claims of equality which find no support in the nature of things."[6]

One might add as a footnote that nowhere in his lengthy memorial address does President Eliot allude to Emerson's extensive efforts as a social reformer or his active participation in the abolition movement. In fact, Eliot states bluntly that "although a prophet and inspirer of reform, Emerson was not a reformer. He was but a halting supporter of the reforms of his day; and the eager experimenters and combatants in actual reforms found him a disappointing sort of sympathizer. . . . When it came to action . . . he was surprisingly conservative." He also notes that Emerson "was intimate with many of the leading abolitionists; but no one has described more vividly their grave intellectual and social defects." For Eliot, Emerson was clearly only a theoretical reformer who "laid down principles which, when applied, would inevitably lead to progress and reform; but he took little part in the imperfect step-by-step process of actual reforming." Finally, he suggests that Emerson "probably would have been an ineffective worker in any field of reform." To reinforce this conservative image of his subject Eliot adds the totally erroneous statement that, despite his well-known religious radicalism, Emerson "attended church on Sundays all his life with uncommon regularity." Not surprisingly, at the conclusion of his memorial address Eliot notes that in his youth he was not fond of Emerson's thinking because it seemed too idealistic. But in his later years he has come to discover

---

6. It is interesting to note that in a 1910 essay that condemns the evil effects of trade unionism in America, Eliot says of the concept of a minimum wage, "Now a true democracy means endless variety of capacity freely developed and appropriately rewarded. Uniformity of wages ignores the diversity of local conditions as well as of personal capacity, obstructs the ambitious workman, cuts off from steady employment those who cannot really earn the minimum wage and interferes seriously with the workman's prospect of improving his lot. It is high time it should be generally understood that trades unionism in important respects works against the very best effects of democracy" (*Charles W. Eliot, the Man and His Beliefs,* 1:268).

a "practical" element in Emerson that places the bard in a new and, apparently, more satisfactory light.

The image of Emerson as an idealist and active social reformer was not entirely lost, however. The Emerson Memorial School, which was held simultaneously in Concord and Boston 13–31 July 1903, was probably the most ambitious effort to set the record straight regarding Emerson's sentiments and activities as a social reformer and abolitionist.[7] The memorial was sponsored by the Free Religious Association of America, of which Emerson was a cofounder and longtime vice president. It consisted of some thirty lectures spread over the two weeks of the gathering. The committee that organized the series included such well-known social activists as Franklin Sanborn and Moorfield Storey. Not surprisingly, many of the talks centered on Emerson's reform activities, and included Julia Ward Howe's "A Century from the Birth of Emerson"; Franklin B. Sanborn's "Emerson and the Concord School of Philosophy"; Francis E. Abbot's "Emerson the Anti-imperialist or Prophet of the Natural Rights of Man"; William M. Salter's "Emerson's Aim and Method in Social Reform"; William Lloyd Garrison II's "Emerson and the Anti-slavery Movement"; and Moorfield Storey's "Emerson and the Civil War." The presentations most significant in projecting an image of Emerson as a reformer and abolitionist were those of Abbot, Garrison, and Storey.

Dr. Francis E. Abbot, who was one of the founders, with Emerson, of the Free Religious Association and a former editor of the *Index*, spoke directly of Emerson's career as an agitator. His concern, as one newspaper put it, was to rebut "certain criticisms recently made upon Emerson as having taught a different sort of equality than appears in the Declaration of Independence."[8] Dr. Abbot spoke at some length about Emerson's service in the antislavery cause, stressing that "his [Emerson's] conception of Americanism was entirely in accord with the teachings of Jefferson and Lincoln, in urging at all times an equal freedom under law for all," and that this was a significant contrast to "the Jefferson Davis concept of a purely white man's rule." Additionally, in an obvious reference to commentaries such as Eliot's regarding the relationship of Emersonian philosophy to the social problems of the present age, he adds emphatically, "Nowhere does he [Emerson] do aught but condemn the modern concept of moral law that grows indignant at restrictions on the game of exploiting other men."

The presentation of William Lloyd Garrison II offered, in the words of one newspaper account, "a remarkable consideration of the way in which a scholar and a man of letters so notably gentle and retiring as Emerson should nevertheless be inseparably linked in history with the aggressive opponents of American slavery."[9] Garrison's lecture provides some interesting insights into the relationships among noted abolitionists, based upon his personal experience in his father's household, and suggests that a lack of personal intimacy did not mean a lack of involvement with the cause, as some critics had maintained was the case with Emerson. The newspaper account indicates that "Mr. Garrison noted the interesting fact that several of the prominent men associated with closely in history for their connection with the anti-slavery movement seldom

7. Descriptive pamphlet in Moorfield Storey Papers, Library of Congress. See also John Broderick, "Emerson and Moorfield Storey: A Lost Journal Found," *American Literature* (May 1966), pp. 177–86.
8. *Boston Evening Transcript*, 22 July 1903.
9. "Emerson and Anti-Slavery," *Springfield Republican*, 30 July 1903.

met: Phillips, Garrison, and Parker held neighborhood and household intimacy; Edmund Quincy was familiar; but Whittier, Mr. Garrison remembers at his father's house only once." The reporter then quotes Garrison. "Lowell [a most active Boston abolitionist] I never saw at an anti-slavery meeting or in [an] anti-slavery household, I never knew him in companionship with my father." Of Emerson, Garrison says, "I think my father spent but a single night under his roof." While useful for personal reminiscences, Garrison's presentation is less than complete in indicating the length and depth of Emerson's abolition service. Undoubtedly this was due to the fact that his specific knowledge of such activities on Emerson's part was largely limited to the biographical resources available at the time, which were, as noted in chapter 1, less than all-encompassing in this regard.[1]

The presentation of Moorfield Storey, on the other hand, is much more effective in dealing with the specifics of Emerson's thought on the questions of slavery, abolition, and human rights. One major reason for this is that Storey had the advantage of quoting directly from Emerson's famous "lost journal," WO Liberty, which he had borrowed for this purpose from the Emerson family, and which would remain thereafter unaccounted for among his papers until 1966.[2]

Moorfield Storey was a longtime friend of the Emerson family. He had been a classmate of Edward Waldo Emerson at Harvard and later collaborated with him on a biography of the venerable Ebenezer Rockwood Hoar of Concord.[3] Storey came to know Ralph Waldo Emerson as a result of this association, and at this time, the early 1860s, Emerson was deeply involved in the abolition movement and its aftermath. Storey's own abolitionist heritage was significant. As one biographer points out, his mother was "an outright abolitionist," and the two acquaintances of his father whom Storey claimed most influenced him, after Emerson, were James Russell Lowell, who once served on the *National Anti-slavery Standard* and in other abolitionist capacities, and Charles Sumner, senator from Massachusetts and one of the Senate's most outspoken opponents of slavery.[4] Storey served as Sumner's personal secretary from 1867 to 1869.

After rising to prominence as a successful Boston attorney and eventually becoming president of the American Bar Association in 1896, Storey began to turn his attention to America's pressing social problems. In 1898 he became president of the Massachusetts Reform Club, in 1905 vice president of the National Civil Service Reform Association, and, also in 1905, president of the Anti-imperialist League. Storey's longtime battle for the rights of the Negro, which he considered to be the legacy of the abolitionists he admired, culminated with his election in 1910 as the first president of the National Association for the Advancement of Colored People.[5]

---

1. Garrison says in a letter to his daughter, "This year the 100th birthday of Ralph Waldo Emerson is to be celebrated and there are to be many tributes in his honor. I have been invited to speak at Concord in one of them, taking for my theme his connection with the Anti-Slavery Movement, so I am reading up the Emerson biographies and writings" (W. L. Garrison II to Eleanor Garrison, 1 April 1903, MS. Sophia Smith Collection, Smith College).
2. See n. 7.
3. Moorfield Storey and Edward W. Emerson, *Ebenezer Rockwood Hoar: A Memoir* (Boston: Houghton Mifflin, 1911).
4. William B. Hixson, Jr., *Moorfield Storey and the Abolitionist Tradition* (New York: Oxford University Press, 1972), p. 192; also, Bill Ledbetter, "Charles Sumner: Political Activist for the New England Transcendentalists," *The Historian, A Journal of History* (May 1982), pp. 347–63.
5. McPherson, *The Abolition Legacy: From Reconstruction to the NAACP* (Princeton: Princeton University Press, 1975), p. 335; Hixson, *Storey,* pp. 42–43.

Given his interests in social reform, his friendship with the Emerson family, and his respect for the abolitionist tradition, it is not surprising that Storey should be most interested in maintaining the image of Emerson as an active social reformer with a strong interest in human rights. Storey's address describes Emerson as a poet-reformer. In this capacity "it was possible for him [Emerson] to make his position absolutely clear, to stand ready as a citizen to bear his testimony against slavery whenever occasion demanded, but not to abandon the other work of his life for the purpose of leading the anti-slavery crusade."[6] Storey recognized that much had been made of Emerson's lack of personal sympathy with some individual abolitionists and that this criticism had been extrapolated by some commentators to include the cause itself. In response to this, after taking note of representative comments by Emerson in this regard, Storey states, "But great injustice would be done to Emerson if it were supposed that such words as these expressed his real attitude towards the opponents of slavery." While Emerson could "appreciate their weaknesses" and could "point out their faults," he respected the abolitionists' efforts and their cause, and he once referred to them as individuals "who see the faults and stains of our social order, and who pray and strive incessantly to right the wrong." At another point he quotes from "The Young American" (1844) Emerson's dictum that we must not "throw stumbling blocks in the way of the abolitionist [and] the philanthropist as the organs of influence and opinion are swift to do." He concludes this aspect of his presentation with the assertion that while Emerson at times adopted an "attitude of semi-humorous criticism" toward them, he felt a "real respect towards the anti-slavery leaders."

At other points in his talk Storey alludes to Emerson's earliest associations with the abolition movement in the 1830s and his later alliance and friendship with Charles Sumner. Sumner was most zealous in the cause of freedom and "impatient of apathy or indifference" in the matter, and "in Emerson he found a thoroughly congenial soul; . . . the absolute sympathy that existed between them is proof that Sumner recognized in Emerson as intense a love of freedom as his own."

Storey's lengthy address notes several other aspects of Emerson's thinking on the need to abolish slavery and assert human rights, and the methodology to be employed in reaching these goals, drawing freely from Emerson's journal to support his points. As might be expected, Storey's account of Emerson's commitment to the basic integrity of all individuals and his consequent vigorous opposition to all efforts to enslave and exploit others was directly related to his own concern with contemporary social problems in America, especially racism. Thus at one point Storey notes Emerson's hopeful belief that the very qualities of benevolence, docility, and industriousness that led to the exploitation of the Negro race in the nineteenth century, "in a more moral age will not only defend their independence but will give them a rank among nations." Recognizing the sad truth that twentieth-century America was manifestly *not* moving toward the fulfillment of this dream, Storey is led to exclaim: "How full of inspiration are these words to every lover of freedom and justice! How ineffably sad it is to read them now and to reflect as we listen to the cries of the mob at Wilmington and Evansville and read of the horrors committed in Luzon that

---

6. Moorfield Storey, "Emerson and the Civil War," MS, Concord Free Public Library, Concord, Massachusetts. All quotations are from this manuscript.

ours is a less moral age, and that punishment waits upon our sins as it did of our fathers."[7]

Overall, Storey's address was quite successful in identifying Emerson's strong commitment to the abolition cause and his equally strong belief in the sacredness of the individual and the natural rights, such as freedom and self-determination, that accrue from this belief. Indeed, in this respect the entire Memorial School series was similarly successful. In a commentary in the *Springfield Republican* in July, Franklin Sanborn noted that Storey's presentation contributed significantly to the public's understanding of Emerson because the speaker "had the advantage of access to the private journals of Emerson, and quoted freely therefrom," and hence "was able to do more than rehearse well known opinions."[8] Clearly, Emerson's ideas were "much in advance of those which the educated men of the country in general held at that time." Without referring directly to the proper Boston Brahmins, Sanborn notes that while "the scholarly class in America have usually followed the multitude and not led them, the exceptions [are] Emerson, Parker, Thoreau, Wendell Phillips and Lowell."[9]

Unfortunately, despite such efforts to preserve the legacy of Emerson's campaign for social justice, the works and writings of men like Higginson, Sanborn, and Storey for the most part died with them, their words entombed in the dusty volumes of nineteenth-century newspapers and long-forgotten periodicals. The result is that the image of the serenely disengaged Emerson remains very much with us today.[1] Nevertheless, there are undoubtedly those who, hav-

---

7. Wilmington and Evansville were scenes of violent race riots and lynchings. Luzon, in the Philippines, was the scene of bloody battles involving U.S. troops and native forces. Storey's quotation from Emerson comes from his speech "The Emancipation Proclamation" (W II:326). Storey would echo these sentiments some years later in a speech given at the unveiling of the Emerson statue in Concord where he stated in part: "No ceremony to-day would be worthy of Mr. Emerson that was not simple, for he was always simple, — 'as the greatest only are in his simplicity sublime.' No eulogy is needed nor would it be in place. We cannot but feel that he is present and that any word of praise would be unwelcome. Yet we could well wish that he were indeed here, for 'in these distempered days' we would fain turn again to him, who, in the words of Lowell during the years that preceded the Civil War 'constantly kept burning the beacon of an ideal life above our lower region of turmoil' and whose confidence in the sure triumph of right—as he phrased it in the 'God-way,' — is sorely needed now" (Address delivered at Concord, 23 May 1914, at the unveiling of a statue of Ralph Waldo Emerson). A print copy of this presentation is included in the Moorfield Storey Papers, Library of Congress.
8. Clipping in the Moorfield Storey Scrapbook, Library of Congress.
9. Sanborn had noted in an earlier address, "Emerson and Concord Town," that Concord was known for its "opposition to human slavery," and that "it was usually only a small minority, headed by Emerson, who gave Concord this present reputation" (*Springfield Republican*, 16 July 1903). Also Sanborn speaks at some length, largely in the form of personal reminiscences, of Emerson's abolition activities from the 1850s on in his study *The Personality of Emerson*, also published in the centennial year (Boston: Charles E. Goodspeed).
1. For example, Arthur M. Schlesinger, Jr., in his influential *Age of Jackson* (New York: Little, Brown, 1945), states that the transcendentalists "from their book-lined studies or their shady walks in cool Concord woods, . . . found the hullabaloo of party politics unedifying and vulgar." Schlesinger goes on to state that "for the typical transcendentalists the flinching from politics perhaps expressed a failure they were seeking to erect into a virtue. The exigencies of responsibility were exhausting: much better to demand perfection and indignantly reject the half a loaf, than wear out body and spirit in vain grapplings with overmastering reality." According to Schlesinger, for transcendentalists like Emerson, "the headlong escape into perfection left responsibility far behind for a magic domain where mystic sentiment and gnomic utterance exorcised the rude intrusions of the world" (p. 382). Emerson, in particular, evinced these presumed shortcomings of the transcendentalists in dealing with the major concerns of society. "Politics" was "his greatest failure." Emerson "would not succumb to verbal panaceas, neither would he make the ultimate moral effort of Thoreau and cast off all obligation to society. Instead he lingered indecisively, accepting without enthusiasm certain relations to government but never confronting directly the implications of acceptance" (p. 384).
  Fourteen years later, Stanley Elkins would echo Schlesinger's views in his well-known study *Slavery: A Problem in American Institutional and Intellectual Life* (New York: Grosset and Dunlap, 1959). In his study Elkins depicts the transcendentalists, and Emerson in particular, as almost totally detached from the everyday affairs of society. He states flatly that "the thinkers of Concord, who in the later thirties and forties would create an intellectual attitude at least coherent enough to be given a name—'Transcendentalism'—were men without connections. . . . They took next to no part in politics at all" (p. 147).

ing been stimulated and excited by Emerson as undergraduates, still read the "American Scholar" and the 1844 "Emancipation in the British West Indies" address as moving statements of a pure American idealism. It was this idealism, stimulated by a genuine love for mankind and commitment to human virtue, that fueled Emerson's long and inevitable campaign against slavery, and remains alive and well in his words today.

RICHARD POIRIER

From Poetry and Pragmatism[†]

From *Introduction*

* * *

[Emerson's] writing *enacts* the struggles by which he tries to keep his own language from becoming "faked." His writing dramatizes his agitations when

---

George Frederickson reinforces this notion of absolute antiinstitutionalism and aloofness when speaking of Emerson as a social thinker in his influential work *The Inner Civil War: Northern Intellectuals and the Crisis of the Union* (New York: Harper and Row, 1965). The view of Emerson as a recluse is so persistent in Frederickson's study that despite the fact that several biographers point out that Emerson was always a concerned and active citizen of Concord, Frederickson insists, on the contrary, that "the former hermit . . . had always shunned social commitments and public activity, even to the point . . . of avoiding town affairs in the village of Concord," and it was not until the war that Emerson became an "influential and active citizen" (pp. 178–79).

In the next decade Paul Boller rectified, somewhat, this decidedly lopsided view of Emerson's social existence in his *American Transcendentalism; 1830–1860* (New York: G. P. Putnam's Sons, 1974). Boller does take note of Emerson's numerous reform concerns, even while stressing Emerson's general dissatisfaction with most organized reformers, a position Boller supports, like earlier scholars, with references to early lectures like "Man the Reformer" (1841). This emphasis, however, leads him in turn to suggest that, despite his oft-articulated social concerns, Emerson was "primarily a man of letters, not a social activist" (p. 102), and that "until 1850 . . . Emerson was decidedly lukewarm about the antislavery movement" (p. 106) for a variety of reasons.

Five years later, Taylor Stoehr, in his *Nay-saying in Concord; Emerson, Alcott, and Thoreau* (Hamden, Conn.: Archon Books, 1979), would offer further insights into the complexity of Emerson's thinking about abolition, but he furthers the impression that the transcendentalists overall, and Emerson in particular, were far removed from the major social reform movements of their day. He states, for example, that "compared to the communitists and other reformers, the transcendentalists are like a band of monks sitting cross-legged on the floor, indistinguishable in their chant" (p. 19). For Stoehr, the transcendentalists, at least as represented by his three subjects, remained largely aloof from the dusty affairs of the world. In fact, he suggests that they transcended them. "The truth is that Emerson, Alcott, and Thoreau, rather than say aye or nay, were more likely to abstain entirely. Theirs was the most conservative attitude of all, neither approving nor rejecting but simply awaiting the outcome—as their Eastern philosophers would say it, standing out of the way. The universe could be trusted to unfold without taking a vote" (p. 20).

The position that Anne Rose takes in her study *Transcendentalism as a Social Movement, 1830–1850* (New Haven: Yale University Press, 1981) is even more insistent than Stoehr's in its emphasis on transcendental aloofness from public affairs. She asserts that "of the original transcendentalists . . . only Emerson publicly opposed slavery with any regularity, but the same philosophical bent which made him a powerful speaker ran against the grain of the most important development of the decade, antislavery politics" (p. 219–20). In Rose's view, not only was Emerson generally disengaged from the more painful elements of the abolition crusade, but she seems to echo Elkins when she says of Emerson, "There was an abstraction in his approach to slavery which made his occasional musings on agencies of abolition—providence, commercial progress, purchase, disunion—comparatively desultory" (p. 219).

Finally, even a president of Yale University, A. Bartlett Giamatti, in an address entitled "Power, Politics and a Sense of History" (*The University and the Public Interest* [New York: Atheneum, 1981]), once stated that "with extraordinary literary skills at a crucial moment in our nation's life, it is Emerson who freed our politics and our politicians from any sense of restraint by extolling self-generated, unaffiliated power as the best foot to place in the small of the back of the man in front of you." According to Mr. Giamatti, "Emerson is as sweet as barbed wire, and his sentimentality as accommodating as a brick," and he leaves the distinct impression that Emerson cared but little for the have-nots of his society.

† Reprinted by permission of the publisher from *Poetry and Pragmatism* by Richard Poirier, Cambridge, Mass.: Harvard University Press. Copyright © 1992 by Richard Poirier.

confronted with the evidence that the words he is putting down on paper, including words of resistance and dissent, are themselves products of "previous human thinking," including his own. Once said or written, his words are always *past*. More than that, fakery lurks even in the words intended to correct this situation, to reform or trope what is past. Attempts to shape reality in language may be, from a literary point of view, dazzlingly successful, but they are always to some degree a betrayal of that reality. While [William] James can at times subscribe to this supposition, as when he says in the chapter called "The Stream of Thought" in *Principles of Psychology* that "language works against our perception of the truth," there are very few stylistic indications in his writing that he suffers for it, or that he feels it as a threat to his own stylistic self-assurance, to his way of carrying himself in the world. Emerson's heroism of mind is that he does so suffer and that he involves his readers in that suffering as if it were their own, requiring of them some of his own heroism, his own performative and expectant optimism.

Emerson is forever trying to liberate himself and his readers from the consequences of his own writing, not merely from the consequences of other people's writing. His description of the activity of the soul asks to be read as an allegory, in which the movements of the soul in its circles represent the movements of creative energy in his sentences and paragraphs. He is saying that his own acts of composition, the very efforts at non-conformity that result in his tropings of previous truths—that these fill him with apprehensions about encirclement and fixity. How is one to cope with this situation without collapsing into silence? The answer lies, I think, in the phrase "the soul *becomes*." Note that "the soul" is first named as if, with its definite article, it were an entity; note, too, that its realization as an entity is immediately and forever delayed, its presence transferred to an ever elusive future, by the word "*becomes*." The soul never "becomes" a thing or a text; it exists in the action of becoming.

"Nothing," he remarks in "Circles," "is secure but life, transition, the energizing spirit."[1] Rely, that is to say, not on anything fixed or stabilized in your vocabulary but only on the power that allows you to move away from these, movements precipitated by desire whose object is uncertain and which, if too certainly defined, could turn thinking into mere thought, activity into inertia. As a writer, much less as a person, this is for Emerson a saving principle, and it determines the disruptive energies at work in his essays, and in the compellingly enigmatic turns of his poetry. Thus, in "Self-Reliance," after some notably strong words about power as essentially a form of transition, and directly after the sentence about the soul, his expenditures of rhetoric provoke in him a derisive rejoinder, a rejection of his dependence on the phrase that serves as his title: "Why, then, do we prate of self-reliance? Inasmuch as the soul is present, there will be power not confident but agent. To talk of reliance is a poor external way of speaking. Speak rather of that which relies, because it works and is."

With its agitated substitutions of words having to do with vocal expression— "prate," "talk," "speak"—this passage, like many others in his essays, reveals a frustration with the fact that apparently any use of language may disfigure the self in the very process of expressing it. Obviously to be avoided are "external ways of speaking," speaking in obedience to easily apprehended formulae. And avoid them he does, by the calculated opacity of that final sentence: "Speak rather of

---

1. This and the next paragraph are taken with very little revision from my introduction to the 1990 Oxford University Press selected edition of the essays and poems of Emerson, p. xix.

that which relies because it works and is." Like the sentence in which "the soul *becomes*," this sentence is to be experienced as it is written, and not in any clarifying translation into some other syntax. The experience is of a blur in which each of the substantives momentarily stands in place of the others, bound together with them, adhering to them. ("Adhere" is one meaning of "rely," older than the more common one which, as in the phrase "rely on," suggests not adherence but dependence.) Emerson's syntax approximates that only momentary achievement of a simultaneous fusion among agent, action, and words which for him *is* the self just before its transfiguring move into another transition.

The necessary inference is that Emerson is actually opposed to individualism in the customary or social sense in which the term is most often used.[2] That is, he is opposed to the notion of the self as something put together by a person who is then required to express it and to ask others to confirm it as an identity. Similarly, he is opposed to literature conceived as a series of more or less discrete texts each holding in trust a source of wisdom not sufficiently available elsewhere. "The real value of the Iliad, or the Transfiguration," as he says in "Art," "is as signs of power; billows or ripples they are of the stream of tendency; tokens of the everlasting effort to produce, which even in its worst estate the soul betrays."

The word "betrays," as I will have reason to point out again, echoes throughout the writings of Emerson; the complexities of betrayal and abandonment are at the center of his concerns about cultural and, indeed, biological inheritance. And he seldom uses the word without allowing for its double sense. "Betray" can mean to show or reveal or discover; it can also mean close to the opposite, to deceive, to give up something or someone to an enemy. Always working inside each word, to the extent allowed by the ongoing momentum of his sentences, he characteristically declines to separate out the word's conflicting connotations. To do so would be to participate in the illusion that language is meant to clean up the messes of life. Instead, we ought to be grateful to language, as I propose in Chapter 3, for making life messier than ever, more blurred than we pretend we want it to be, but also therefore more malleable. Within even a single word, language can create that vagueness that puts us at rest inside contradictions, contradictions which, if more precisely drawn, would prove unendurable. We willingly live with the fact that by its beneficent betrayals language constantly delivers us to ourselves, and makes us known to others, within a comforting haze. Like the soul, words can reveal the parameters of fate and limitation; just as surely, they open spaces beyond these, horizons of new, barely apprehended possibility.

In assembling the tribe of Waldo for a portrait, I find honorable places for Thoreau, Dickinson, and Dewey, give prominence to Whitman and William

2. A complex reading adequate to Emerson's idea of "individualism" has been called for by his best interpreters as far back as Santayana in 1903, but the concept still fails to be generally accepted or understood. George Kateb is admirably lucid on the subject: "The nobility of the Emersonian aspiration lies in transcending the ideal of individualism understood as the cultivation and expression of personality, precisely because Emerson, like his great colleagues Thoreau and Whitman, knows how social, and not individualistic, such an ideal is." George Kateb, "Individualism, Communitarianism, and Docility," *Social Research*, 56:4 (1989), 938. Santayana's essay remains one of the very best on Emerson, in part for his arguing that "Potentiality, cosmic liberty, nature perpetually transforming and recovering her energy, formed his loftiest theme; but the sense of riddance in escaping kings, churches, cities, and eventually self and even humanity, was the nearer and if possible the livelier emotion." Santayana's essay, "Emerson's Poems Proclaim the Divinity of Nature, with Freedom as His Profoundest Ideal," was given as an address during Emerson Memorial Week at Harvard College in May 1903. It is reprinted in *George Santayana's America*, collected with an introduction by James Ballowe (Urbana: University of Illinois Press, 1967), 84–96. The quoted passage is on p. 91.

James, and assign central positions to Frost, Stein, and Stevens. Eliot, as indicated, belongs in the portrait, though he sits so reluctantly for it that one takes the risk of treating him unfairly by putting him there; obviously William Carlos Williams belongs in it, as does, through Fenollosa, Ezra Pound, though I am content to leave their work to others who appreciate it more than I do. In my way of estimating such things, Emerson remains the greatest of his extended tribe because more than any of the others he offers himself as a truly sacrificial figure, the one who in his writing creates ever ponderable, ever enlivening, ceaselessly vibrant energies of language within which he moves as victim and victor. This, he could be saying, is how I have learned, before your very eyes, to cope with the one medium essential to the conduct of human life in culture, the medium whose invention and reinvention distinguishes us, as Kenneth Burke suggests, from other animals. Of course other animals have languages of their own, but they have not, so far as anyone can tell, evolved cultures of their own, and for the reason that their languages are biologically transmitted, and therefore do not change; the languages are not recreated by activities of the soul. They have no literary or artistic inheritance to receive or to transmit.

Emerson makes himself sometimes amazingly hard to read, hard to get close to, all the more because he finds it manifestly difficult to get close to himself, to read or understand himself. If you want to get to know him, you must stay as close as possible to the movements of his language, moment by moment, for at every moment there is movement with no place to rest; you must share, to a degree few other writers since Shakespeare have asked us to do, in his contentions with his own and therefore with our own meanings, as these pass into and then out of any particular verbal configuration. He offers one of the truest, most realistic measures in our language of just how chancy and demanding is the job of reading, a job whose requirements nonetheless can be pedagogically met, as I try to show in the last chapter. To read intently a writer as strong as Emerson is to discover evidence everywhere in his work that he means always to contend with the words by which he represents himself to himself, as much as to others.

In part because he wanted to be a great public writer, Emerson is to be thanked for making us recognize the social and not simply personal stakes in close self-reading, stakes, I take it, that each of us would just as soon evade some part of the time. He would have us ask continually the question posed at the beginning of "Experience": "Where do we find ourselves?" As I will propose, we "find ourselves," it would seem inevitably, *in* words. And yet we need not find ourselves trapped and held there by any particular text. Words have a way of opening up gaps in themselves which, like the gaps in Frost's "Mending Wall," allow two to pass abreast. It could therefore be said that a pun is the equivalent of an Emersonian marriage, two possibilities forever linked for better but not for worse, married impersonally. "Betray" is a single word, but it forever revolves on its own double meaning, revealing within itself a constantly shifting balance of gains and losses. Emerson does not show off with language, as Thoreau is so often guilty of doing, exhibiting a superiority to it, nor is he, like James, determined on lucidity. He writes always from the inside out, not from the outside in. "The only path of escape known in all the worlds of God," he says in "Worship," "is performance. You must do your work, before you shall be released."

David Bromwich has remarked in *A Choice of Inheritance*, in an essay entitled "Literary Radicalism in America," that:

The great practical effect of Emerson's teaching was that it gave an idea of originality to a generation that included Whitman, Dickinson, Melville, along with others who seem minor talents only in that company. He accomplished this in a society where a shapeless conformity of opinion appeared to have taken hold forever. Indeed, if one tried to imagine an America free of Emerson's influence, the strictures of [Alexis de Tocqueville's] *Democracy in America* would turn into an accurate prophecy. As it is, they have come out looking *a priori* and short-sighted. Tocqueville simply did not bank on anyone like Emerson occurring.

To describe how Emerson wants us to know him, there could be no better word than "occurring," a word whose derivations allow it to mean to run toward and also to run against. It is necessary to run toward the past while running against the past, if, in Frost's Jamesian phrase, we are ever to "believe the future in." That kind of "occurring" is most traceable in Emerson and his successors, in the work they do, and ask us to carry out, *within* language. It is work that requires a skeptical excitement about the past as it still vibrates all round us in words, and it requires a determination that this inheritance of words will be transformed by our exploitations of the treasures hidden in them, before they are passed on to the generations.

ROBERT D. RICHARDSON JR.

The Heart Has Its Jubilees[†]

Emerson's already busy life became even busier [in the] summer of 1839. There were new books, new friends, new lectures, new projects. His correspondence increased, his journal grew. He seemed to have unlimited energy. For about the next two and a half years there is a tone of workaday exaltation to everything Emerson did. Exhilaration became a habit. He was living at the apogee of his own orbit of possibility. And since he was capable of sustained effort on many projects at once, there are now, more than ever, multiple contexts for everything he was writing. During the second half of 1839, he worked on the essays "Love" and "Friendship" for his book. He also began a new lecture series called "The Present Age" with two lectures on literature, followed by "Politics," "Private Life," "Reforms," "Religion," and "Education." Emerson was closely involved in the planning for a new magazine. He went with George Bradford on a sightseeing trip to the White Mountains just as Henry Thoreau and his brother John were setting off for their boat trip on the Concord and Merrimack rivers. Emerson liked the "savage and stern" New Hampshire landscape and thought the Flume "as wild a piece of scenery as I ever chanced to see." He packed off a bushel of potatoes to William in New York. The shipping directions got lost, but the potatoes arrived anyway. When William asked what kind they were, Emerson said they were automatic potatoes, "learned, self-relying," knowing their own destination and opening "a new science, Potato Magnetism."[1]

---

† From *Emerson: The Mind on Fire* (Berkeley: University of California Press, 1995). Reprinted by permission of the University of California Press.
1. *L* 2:221, 241.

Emerson's reading ranged widely as usual. He read Keats's "Eve of St. Agnes" and "Hyperion." He read Dickens's *Oliver Twist*, George Sand's *Spiridion*, Balzac's *Le Livre mystique*, and Victor Hugo's *Hunchback of Notre-Dame*. He read Gilbert White's *Natural History of Selborne* and Linnaeus's account in *Lachesis Lapponica* of his travels in Lapland. He read John Forster's *Life of Oliver Cromwell* in Dionysius Lardner's *Cabinet Encyclopedia* edition. Lardner's volumes were small and handy—true pocket books—which were useful in several ways. A soldier at the siege of Lucknow found that one of the volumes could stop a musket ball after passing through 120 pages.[2] Emerson was also reading Burton's *Anatomy of Melancholy* and Plutarch's *Isis and Osiris*, and he dipped into the new twelve-volume set of Victor Cousin's *Plato* which had been given him by his Concord Lyceum audience as a token of appreciation. By far the most unusual book in his new reading was *Goethe's Correspondence with a Child* by Bettina von Arnim. This book not only influenced his ideas of friendship, it raised the temperature of his social relations in a curious way.

In 1839 Emerson was making new friendships even as his older ones continued to ripen. His correspondence with Carlyle and his labors as his American agent increased. He was becoming closer to Margaret Fuller, who was educating him now in modern fiction. In June she brought out her translation of Eckermann's *Conversations with Goethe*. Fuller was getting ready to leave Providence. She decided against Concord and settled instead for Boston, where in the fall of 1839 she began to give the public "Conversations" that first made her famous. Also in 1839 and 1840 George Ripley came riding publicly to the defense of Emerson (and Spinoza and Schleiermacher) in a series of three letters directed against Andrews Norton's *The Latest Form of Infidelity*. "Letters" gives the wrong impression. Ripley's three pieces together fill four hundred printed pages. Never gathered together or properly published as a unit, the work remains the unacknowledged high point of the influence of Schleiermacher in American thought in the nineteenth century and a declaration, for those who could see it, that Emersonian transcendentalism was not an aberration, as Norton claimed, but proceeded in one of the main currents of modern thought.[3]

Horace Mann came to Concord to speak; there were increasingly frequent walks with Henry Thoreau. There was a new English admirer, a writer, a protégé of Carlyle's named John Sterling. Elizabeth Hoar went through a troubled period from which she emerged to become even closer to Emerson and to the family. Emerson called her "sister," and when his daughter Ellen asked whether she should study Greek, Emerson said yes, citing Aunt Lizzy as a model and praising her "Greek mind." There were other new friends this fall, making new claims on Emerson. Sam Ward, a painter and student of art history, Anna Barker, a New Orleans socialite and beauty who came from a New England Quaker family, and Caroline Sturgis, the young free-spirited poet, all became friends of Emerson now through Fuller. Like Fuller, they dispensed with the traditional reserved manner associated with New Englanders and required both candor about and continuing discussion of emotional matters. They were impatient with the ordinary forms of social life; they prized intensity and strove to-

2. Christopher Hibbert, *The Great Mutiny* (London: Penguin, 1980), 225.
3. George Ripley, *"The Latest Form of Infidelity" Examined: A Letter to Mr. Andrews Norton* (Boston: James Munroe, 1839); *Defense of "The Latest Form of Infidelity" Examined: A Second Letter to Mr. Andrews Norton* (Boston: James Munroe, 1840); *Defense of "The Latest Form of Infidelity" Examined: A Third Letter to Mr. Andrews Norton* (Boston: James Munroe, 1840).

ward ever greater intimacy with one another. All three wanted to get to know Emerson. He in turn seemed eager to clinch and deepen these new relationships. In "Friendship" he writes feelingly of how we rise to meet new people. When a much commended stranger arrives,

> we talk better than we are wont. We have the nimblest fancy, a richer memory, and our dumb devil has taken leave for the time. For long hours we can continue a series of sincere, graceful, rich communications, drawn from the oldest, secretest experience so that they who sit by, of our own kinfolk and acquaintance, shall feel a lively surprize at our unusual powers.[4]

Emerson borrowed Ward's portfolio and admired Michelangelo with him. They recommended books to each other. Some of the best letters Emerson ever wrote were those to Ward. He seems to have allowed Ward to get as near him as his brother Charles had been. "But who are you that wrote me this letter— and how came you to know all this? I thought you were younger. I love you very much," Emerson wrote the twenty-one-year-old Ward.[5]

In early October Emerson finally met Anna Barker. Fuller had been trying to introduce the two since September of 1836. Barker was very beautiful by all accounts and she also had a gift for intimacy, a way of bestowing her "frank and generous confidence" that was irresistible. "Anna's miracle, next to the *amount* of her life, seems to be the intimacy of her approach to us," Emerson once observed.

> The moment she fastens her eyes on you, her unique gentleness unbars all doors, and with such easy and frolic sway she advances and advances and advances on you, with that one look, that no brother or sister or father or mother of life-long acquaintance ever seemed to arrive quite so near as this now first seen maiden.

Emerson was a little smitten. She visited Concord. "She came and covenanted with me that we two should speak the truth to each [other]," he told Caroline Sturgis later. Then Emerson found out that Barker had already been engaged to be married to Sam Ward before her visit to Concord. Emerson's response to the news seems unusual, as does his telling all this to Sturgis. "The news which Anna told me at Cambridge offended me at first with a certain terror," Emerson wrote Sturgis.

> I thought that the whole spirit of our intercourse at Concord implied another resolution. I thought she had looked the world through for a man as universal as herself and finding none, had said, "I will compensate myself for my great renunciation as a woman by establishing ideal relations; not only Raphael [Ward] shall be my brother, but that Puritan at Concord . . . I will elect him also."

Emerson was disappointed and a little miffed. Clearly he thought Anna Barker was offering him more than she was. She did marry Sam Ward in 1840 and the two moved off, away from Emerson and art to their own world of business.[6]

4. For Elizabeth Hoar, see Elizabeth Maxfield-Miller, "Elizabeth of Concord: Selected Letters of Elizabeth Sherman Hoar to the Emersons, Family, and the Emerson Circle," part I, SAR (1984), 229–298; part 2, SAR (1985), 95–156; part 3, SAR (1986), 113–198; "Friendship," in CW, vol. 2, Essays: First Series, pp. 192–193.
5. L 7:368.
6. L 2:333; L 7:404.

Emerson's friendship with Caroline Sturgis, which began at the same time he was getting to know Barker and Ward, was a more interesting one, stronger, longer lasting, and harder to understand. Sturgis was twenty, Emerson thirty-six when they became friends. Their friendship was colored, if not actually created by Bettina von Arnim's *Goethe's Correspondence with a Child*. This book, published in Germany in 1835 and translated into English by the author the following year, is a loose transcript of the letters back and forth between the fifty-eight-year-old Goethe and the twenty-year-old "child" Bettina. Bettina's letters are lively, perceptive, and full of entertaining description. But their principal note is one of headlong romantic adoration, passionate yearning, and intimate badinage. Goethe encouraged his young correspondent's letters and returned her ardor with genuine affection. The following is Bettina's account, in a letter to Goethe's mother (with whom she had been on close terms for years), of her first meeting the great man: "The door opened and there *he* stood, solemnly grave, and looked with fixed eyes upon me. I stretched my hands towards him — I believe — I soon lost all consciousness. Goethe quickly caught me to his heart. 'Poor child, have I frightened you?'" Goethe leads her into his room, to a sofa. After a little talk about the death of the Duchess Amalia, Bettina goes on:

> I suddenly said "cant stay here upon the sofa," and sprang up. "Well," said he, "make yourself at home." Then I flew to his neck — he drew me upon his knee, and locked me to his heart. Still, quite still it was — everything vanished. I had not slept for so long — years had passed in sighing after him. I fell asleep on his breast: and when I awoke I began a new life.[7]

When she writes to Goethe, Bettina is completely open. She is alarmingly articulate about her feelings: "A dam within my heart has, as it were, broken up: — a child of man, alone on a rock, surrounded by rushing storms, uncertain of itself, wavering here and there, like the thorns and thistles around it, — such am I; such I was before I knew my master." "Thou, who hast knowledge of love," she writes in another letter, "and the spirituality of senses, ah, how beautiful is everything in thee . . . O God, how fain would I now be with thee." There is nothing to separate these from love letters. The book was skillfully translated by Bettina herself and soon attracted a following. Emerson told Fuller the book "moves all my admiration . . . She is the only formidable test that was applied to Goethe's genius . . . Hers was genius purer than his own."[8]

Now Caroline Sturgis read Bettina and began writing similar letters to Emerson. It was life imitating art. Sturgis too has verve, charm, lyric grace, and a kind of literary coquettishness that drew strength from Bettina (who in turn had modeled her own persona on that of Mignon, a character in *Wilhelm Meister*). Emerson himself was very enthusiastic about Bettina. He made extravagant claims. He called Bettina "the most imaginative person in our day," and he thought *Goethe's Correspondence with a Child* "the most remarkable book ever

---

7. Bettina von Arnim, *Goethe's Correspondence with a Child* (Boston: Ticknor and Fields, 1836), 18–19. For the reception of this book in America see H. P. Collins and P. A. Shelley, "The Reception in England and America of Bettina von Arnim's Goethe's Correspondence with a Child," in *Anglo-German and American German Crosscurrents*, vol. 2, ed. P. A. Shelley and A. O. Lewis, Jr. (Chapel Hill: University of North Carolina Press, 1962).

8. Von Arnim, *Goethe's Corr.*, 71, 84; *L* 2:210; Margaret Fuller sent a copy of Emerson's praise to Bettina herself, who lived on until 1859.

written by a woman." Over the next few years the correspondence between Sturgis and Emerson reads very much like that between Bettina and Goethe.

After Emerson visited Sturgis at Newburyport, she wrote him: "Do you know that you vanished through a rainbow trebly arched and radiantly painted upon the dark clouds, beneath the center of it the white steeples gleamed forth from over the brown fields?" Her letters are both charming and intimate. "I know I have never been anything but a child," she wrote, "but perhaps I shall sometime learn to be a woman. I wish to have the actual thing as it stands, neither more nor less, will you not give it to me as far as you can, and not throw tint and clouds into the shining sky?" Her letters question, invite, challenge. "I shall stay at home every morning until you come till one or half past," she wrote him. "Walk down to the edge of the pond a little to the right of the house to see if you cannot find me there under the trees reading Beckford's Travels with my eyes shut." Many of her letters have no salutation and no closing. One begins "and you my dearest brother, shall be my saint and purify me, for this is the joy of friendship." The same letter closes "I never knew a day more full of sweetness and glory than this. May you be happy in it, is the wish of one who loves you."[9]

Emerson's response to Sturgis was like Goethe's to Bettina. He did not try to stop or change things, and he probably assumed it could all be kept under control. And he was undoubtedly fond of her. They stood out in the summer night and looked up together at the stars with their "broad edges of glory." He wrote to her as "my true sister," and he assured her that he recognized the link between their souls. Their time together made "golden days." He wrote to her, "And now you have another claim on me which I hasten to own, for are you not my dear sister and am I not your brother? I cannot write to you *with others*, any more than I can talk with you at a round table."[1]

Emerson had always been an emotional person privately, but the emotional openness—amounting even to a sort of public openness—of his relationships with Barker, Ward, Sturgis, and Fuller was something new. The effect on Emerson of these new relationships may be gauged from an extraordinary passage he wrote in November 1839, just as all these new friendships were blooming. In a fragmentary manuscript autobiography that has never been printed he describes his new condition in terms that recall both his dream of eating the world and the "transparent eyeball" experience. "I plunge with eagerness," Emerson wrote,

> into the pleasant element of affection, with its hopes and harms. It seemed to me swimming in an Iris where I am rudely knocked ever and anon by a ray of fiercer red, or even dazzled by a momentary blindness by a casual

9. JMN 11:342; L 3:77. An interesting sequel to the Bettina story is the long letter sent by Bettina's daughter Giselle to Emerson in 1858. See L. S. Luedke and W. Schleiner, "New Letters from the Grimm-Emerson Correspondence," *Harvard Library Bulletin* 25, no. 4 (Oct. 1977): 399–465; CS to RWE, Oct. 17, 184?; CS to RWE, Sept. 11, 1840; RWE's letters to Sturgis have only recently been printed, in L 7 and L 8. Sturgis's letters to RWE are in Houghton b Ms Am 1221. Only a few excerpts have been published, as footnotes to L. Sturgis's letters to Margaret Fuller have been published in SAR (1988), ed. F. Dedmond.

1. This was not the last time Emerson was made the object of Bettina-inspired adoration. Around 1847, when Louisa May Alcott was fifteen, she found a copy of *Goethe's Correspondence with a Child* while browsing in Emerson's library. She was, she says, "at once fired with a desire to be a Bettina, making my father's friend my Goethe. So I wrote letters to him, but never sent them; sat in a tall cherry-tree at midnight, singing to the moon till the owls scared me off to bed; left wildflowers on the doorstep of my 'Master,' and sung Mignon's song under his window in very bad German" (Ednah D. Cheney, *Louisa May Alcott: Her Life, Letters and Journals* [Boston: Little, Brown, 1917], 57). This story (and the story of Bettina's influence on Emily Dickinson) is told in Barton St. Armand's "Veiled Ladies: Dickinson, Bettine, and Transcendental Mediumship," in SAR (1987), 1–52; JMN 7:391; L 7:402.

beam of white light. The weal and wo are all poetic. I float all the time nor once grazed the old orb.[2]

As he wrote to Elizabeth Hoar in September of 1840, he was somewhat amazed at his suddenly having "a roomful of friends." "So consider me as now quite friendsick and lovesick, a writer of letters and sonnets."

There is no question but that Emerson was attracted to Caroline Sturgis, and even though this, like all his new friendships, was conducted with the language and under the flag of honorary sibling relations and Platonic soul-mating, the charade was not empty. It is not too much to say that in the early 1840s Emerson was living emotionally, though not physically, in what would now be called an open marriage. There is nothing to suggest any physical intimacies between Emerson and Sturgis (or Barker or Fuller). Nor were any of the new friendships clandestine. Lidian knew all about them, was herself often present, frequently copied Emerson's letters, and counted both Fuller and Sturgis among her own friends. Perhaps the warmth of the correspondence between Sturgis and Emerson can be explained by their shared commitment to enthusiasm or by their fascination with German romantic friendship. Whatever the explanation, there was an undeniable current of affection between them at this time. Late in life Emerson returned all of Caroline Sturgis Tappan's letters to her; they were wrapped in a bundle and were discreetly labeled "To be sent unopened to Caroline Tappan."

Lidian's tone toward her husband shows no cooling at this time, nor does his toward her. But two further bits of evidence indicate that all was not well with their marriage now. Their daughter Ellen noted that sometime in 1841 Lidian "waked to a sense that she had been losing—had lost—that blessed nearness to God in which she had lived so long, and she never regained it." Perhaps it was also her nearness to Emerson that she feared losing. The other indication of trouble is that Emerson began now to voice in his journal serious doubts about the institution of marriage. Writing in November of 1840 he said he thought "Swedenborg exaggerates the circumstance of marriage." He went on:

> All lives, all friendships are momentary. *Do you love me?* means at last *Do you see the same truth I see?* If you do, we are happy together: but when presently one of us passes into the perception of new truth, we are divorced and the force of all nature cannot hold us to each other . . .

The passage is a long one, rising in feeling as Emerson rejects the idea of permanently fixed relationships. "But one to one, married and chained through the eternity of ages is frightful beyond the binding of dead and living together." In December he dreamt that a convention had assembled to debate the institution of marriage. After many "grave and alarming objections" were raised, a defender arose

> and turned on the audience the spout of an engine which was copiously supplied from within the wall by water . . . whilst I stood watching astonished and amused at the malice and vigor of the orator [with the fire hose]. I saw the spout lengthened by a supply of hose behind, and the man suddenly brought it round a corner and drenched me as I gazed.

---

2. *L* 2:330; *Life of LE*, 83; notebook "Autobiography" b Ms Am 1280 H 195.

Passion overwhelmed institutions and discussions. Emerson himself was no longer just an observer. He now found himself completely involved in emotional matters and drenched in their reality.[3]

In August of 1841 Emerson was still protesting that "it is not in the plan or prospect of the soul, this fast union of one to one." In September of 1841 he repeated that "plainly marriage should be a temporary relation, it should have its natural birth, climax and decay, without violence of any kind,—violence to bind or violence to rend." The same year, he made a note, "I marry you for better, not for worse." In 1843 he was still upset by what he called "the vitriolic acid of marriage," and in 1852, after his trip to England, he was still thinking (as he wrote) that "everything is free but marriage." He wrote a long, bitter comment on how it is that the youth marries and has children and then is asked what he thinks about marriage. "'Too late,' [says the not-quite-autobiographical "youth,"] 'too late.' I should have much to say if the question were open. I have a wife and five children and all question is closed for me."[4]

Emerson and Lidian stayed married. They displayed, both in public and in private, tenderness, solicitude, and esteem for each other. But the love that makes marriages in the first place was no longer, in Emerson's case, focused solely on his wife. His slowly forming book of essays has no essay on marriage, though it does have essays entitled "Friendship" and "Love." Emerson's essay "Love" is not interested in *caritas*, or caring, but in *eros*, in being in love. The original opening of the essay is a strong straightforward celebration of Eros. "Every soul is a celestial Venus to every other soul. The heart has its sabbath and jubilees in which the world appears as a hymeneal feast, and all natural sounds and the circle of the seasons are erotic odes and dances." Emerson later toned down the openly erotic note of this passage, but the rewritten opening has an equally insistent emphasis on desire as well as a certain wisdom about the human heart: "Every promise of the soul has innumerable fulfillments: each of its joys ripens into a new want."[5]

SAUNDRA MORRIS

Through a Thousand Voices: Emerson's Poetry and "The Sphinx"[†]

> Mrs Helen Bell, it seems, was asked "What do you think the Sphinx said to Mr Emerson?" "Why," replied Mrs Bell, "the Sphinx probably said to him, 'You're another.'"
>
> EMERSON, JOURNALS, 1873

At the threshold of Emerson's *Poems* (1846) sits "The Sphinx."[1] Originally published in the third issue of *The Dial* (January 1841), the seventeen-stanza

---

3. *JMN* 7:532, 544.
4. *JMN* 8:34, 95, 144; *JMN* 13:258.
5. The original opening of "Love" is in RWE *Essays* (Boston: James Munroe, 1841) and in some modern reprints, such as that published by Thomas Y. Crowell in 1926, reissued as an Apollo edition in 1951. CW and HW give the later opening.
† Adapted and expanded from "The Threshold Poem, Emerson, and 'The Sphinx,'" *American Literature* 69.3 (September 1997): 547–70.
1. Major modern scholarship on the poems includes Hyatt Waggoner's *Emerson as Poet* (Princeton: Princeton Univ. Press, 1974) and his chapter on Emerson in *American Poets from the Puritans to the Present*

narrative is quite literally a "metre-making argument"—in this case a "disputa-
tion"—between a contemptuous Sphinx and an indomitably cheerful poet.[2] At
the beginning of the poem, the "drowsy" and brooding Sphinx calls for a "'seer'"
to answer her "'secret,'" and thereby bring her health and animation. When she
goes on to taunt humanity for its ineptitude and impotence, a mysterious "great
mother" joins in to lament the condition of her juvenilized "'boy,'" humankind.
As though to refute their claims, a cheerful and confident poet appears, who
praises and blesses the Sphinx. In response, the Sphinx utters an enigmatic pro-
nouncement and soars away, evanescing into the universe. As befits its subject,
"The Sphinx" has always been considered especially puzzling, even for the rou-
tinely intricate Emerson.[3] Yet despite the abundance of critical attention the
poem has received, scholars continue to debate precisely what the Sphinx is
supposed to be, what her question is, and whether the poet's reply is astute or
absurd.[4]

Its high degree of undecidability and the richness of the mythological material upon which it draws combine to make "The Sphinx" a highly suggestive
choice for what I call a "threshold poem." I use this term to identify a distinct
yet previously unrecognized genre encompassing various types of introductory
verses. These poems function as overtures to the material that follows them.
Such threshold poems, I suggest, ask for distinctive and heightened attention by
virtue of their liminal position. Examples include initial sonnets in sequences,
seventeenth-century emblem-book inscriptions, and epic invocations to muses.
The term would also embrace such poems as the prothalamion and epithalamion, and all poems of dedication, preface, and prologue—those, for example,
that we find in Spenser and Chaucer. Another part of this broad, highly self-re-
flexive tradition are poems that function, like "The Sphinx," to introduce volumes of poetry, such as Frost's "The Pasture" (first in his collection *North of
Boston* and in various edition of his *Poems, Selected Poems,* and *Complete
Poems*). Perhaps the most direct precursor for Emerson's self-conscious employment of this sort of threshold poem is George Herbert's *The Temple.*

In thematizing the difficulties of self-expression, Emerson's "The Sphinx"
also claims a place in another tradition, that of poems about the inability to
write or the absence of inspiration—Milton's sonnet on his blindness, or Coleridge's "Dejection: An Ode," for example. Often these works, like "The
Sphinx," are threshold poems—Sidney's first *Astrophel and Stella* sonnet and
Bradstreet's poetic preface to *The Tenth Muse.* Since the answer to the poets'

(Boston: Houghton, 1968); R. A. Yoder's *Emerson and the Orphic Poet in America* (Berkeley and Los An-
geles: Univ. of California Press, 1978); and David Porter's *Emerson and Literary Change* (Cambridge: Harvard Univ. Press, 1978). Other important treatments are Harold Bloom's *Figures of Capable Imagination*
(New York: Seabury, 1976); *Poetry and Repression: Revisionism from Blake to Stevens* (New Haven: Yale
Univ. Press, 1976), 235–66; and *The Ringers in the Tower: Studies in Romantic Tradition* (Chicago: Univ.
of Chicago Press, 1971), 291–322; and Albert Gelpi's "Emerson: The Paradox of Organic Form," in *Emerson: Prophecy, Metamorphosis and Influence,* ed. David Levin (New York: Columbia Univ. Press, 1975),
149–70, and *The Tenth Muse: The Psyche of the American Poet* (Cambridge: Harvard Univ. Press, 1975).

2. Emerson writes in "The Poet": "For it is not metres, but a metre-making argument, that makes a poem"
(*The Collected Works of Ralph Waldo Emerson,* ed. Robert E. Spiller, Alfred R. Ferguson, Joseph Slater,
and Jean Ferguson Carr [Cambridge: Harvard Univ. Press, 1971–] 3:6); John Hollander relates Emerson's "argument" to the "thorny arguments" of Sidney's *Defense of Poetry* in *Melodious Guile: Fictive Pattern in Poetic Language* (New Haven: Yale Univ. Press, 1988), 112, 247.

3. Emerson's contemporaries tended to have extreme responses to "The Sphinx," considering the poem either nonsensical or one of his best.

4. Gayle L. Smith explores these points of disagreement in her excellent essay, "The Language of Identity
in Emerson's 'The Sphinx,'" *ESQ: A Journal of the American Renaissance* 29 (1983): 136–43. While
agreeing with Smith in many particulars, I take issue with her fundamental emphasis on the "identity"
of the Sphinx and the poet.

dilemma is creation, a remedy provided by the poems themselves, the category is by definition both ironic and paradoxical: these are poems about their own impossibility. Such is, of course, especially the case with *threshold* poems about problems with inspiration, for these texts "answer" blockage doubly—through their own existence and through the verses they introduce. "The Sphinx" provides a consummate instance of this particular variant.

Finally, Emerson's threshold piece is provocative in yet another way: its subject is part of a recurrent preoccupation of its time. Nineteenth-century American writers seem especially enticed by the Sphinx figure, bestowing upon it the mythic significance that we, following Freud, have tended to grant Oedipus. Virtually a unique American genre developed around the image. Melville's chapter "The Sphynx" in *Moby-Dick*, for example, represents the sperm whale's head as a Sphinx, and his *Clarel* ends with a reference to the Sphinx as a figure for the inscrutability that permeates the text as a whole. Another intriguing counterpart is Poe's short story "The Sphinx," published in January 1846 in *Arthur's Ladies' Magazine*. Also a self-conscious riddle about riddling and death, Poe's "The Sphinx" is related by a glib narrator who, in a recurrent Poe scenario, has fled an epidemic only to find that he has brought the sphinx of death with him. Rose Terry Cooke, in her *Atlantic Monthly* moral vignette "The Sphinx's Children," creates a Sphinx that is a female Frankenstein monster. The anonymous poem "Oedipus and the Sphinx," which appears following a review of Emerson's essay collection *The Conduct of Life* in the January 1862 *Continental Monthly*, associates the Sphinx with slavery, presenting the existence of this atrocity as an unsolved riddle. The closest analogue to Emerson's "The Sphinx" is Christopher Cranch's "The Riddle," which was printed in the same issue of *The Dial*.

Particularly relevant for gender issues associated with both Emerson's poetry and the original Sphinx material is the repeated use of the Sphinx figure by the early feminist author Elizabeth Stuart Phelps, for whom the Sphinx repeatedly served as an emblem of women's struggle for artistic empowerment. Her poem "The Sphinx" and her 1871 essay "The True Woman" both associate the Sphinx's animation and self-articulation with women's achievement of voice after long silence.

In her 1877 novel *The Story of Avis*, largely a fictionalization of the life of her mother (and somewhat of herself) originally entitled *The Story of the Sphinx*, Phelps uses the title character's painting of a Sphinx to symbolize women's struggle for self-expression. Avis's predicament involves whether she can function as an artist while also fulfilling the traditional roles of wife and mother, a dilemma also the subject of one of Phelps's mother's most important works, the short story "The Angel Over the Right Shoulder." Phelps thus inverts the conventional legend, as Emerson did before her, to represent animation of the Sphinx as a desirable end and, even more than he, to associate it directly with the empowerment of women. Thus in both Phelps and Emerson the riddle of the Sphinx involves the interconnection of gender, art, and self-expression.

The most immediate effect of Emerson's "The Sphinx" is to baffle. Readers have from the beginning recognized that Emerson deliberately assigned the poem primary position because of its arresting difficulty, thematic preoccupation with both initiation and interpretation, and manifest self-reflexivity. "The Sphinx" appears first in every volume of Emerson's own design that contains it—three of the four books of his poetry he himself shaped.[5] Uncannily, however, the history of the poem's placement re-enacts the Oedipal struggle that the poem thematizes. For Edward Emerson overrode his father's decision as he prepared what has long been the standard edition, the Centenary *Poems* (1903), choosing instead to begin with the much more accessible early work entitled—comically for an initial poem—"Goodbye."[6]

In an effort, then, to explore the importance of Emerson's arrangement, I read "The Sphinx" as an initiation into and guide through his poetry. The poem provides a riddling hint about how to approach the rest of Emerson's verse, raises in theme and form issues crucial to the poetry, offers an intriguing figure for Emerson's life and writings, and suggests theories of reading, writing, and intertextuality pertinent to the poems that follow, to Emerson texts generally, and to interpretation itself. Moreover, by invoking the mythological *topos* of the Sphinx at the threshold, Emerson places readers in the position of the dramatized poet figure and himself in the position of the Sphinx, enacting at the portal of his volume the very sort of ventriloquistic play that characterizes his poetry and prose. "The Sphinx" activates crossings and reversals between genders, modes of discourse, forms of rhetoric, writer and reader, and subject and object that disrupt oppositional tendencies central to the cultures whose myths it employs.

The poem may also be read metapoetically and as a paradigmatic threshold poem in that, as my epigraph indicates, people (including scholars and Emerson) have often imagined Emerson himself as a Sphinx. His work has always been taken as sphingine; and in his lectures, we might recall, Emerson was capable of indicting audiences in the voice of his Sphinx. In terms of teaching us how to read what it introduces, the poem suggests that we approach Emerson's texts as the poet does the Sphinx, admiring their suggestiveness and difficulty rather than seeking mastery over them, all the while encouraging Emerson to "say on."

In Emerson's poem, the Sphinx asks three questions: two of them begin with "Who" and the other, more like the Oedipal riddle in form, is grammatically fragmented in a way that conflates it with the preceding query. In the first stanza, the Sphinx asks "'Who'll tell me my secret,/ The ages have kept?—'" as though she is as puzzled about what her question is as readers are. But the Sphinx then elaborates on that "secret" in her second question, which is composed mainly of enigmatic statements about humanity and the labyrinthine paradoxes of life and death. Later, she replies to the poet's response with "'Who taught thee me to name?'" suggesting the questions so prominent in Blake's "The Tyger." The poem ends by circling back, as the Sphinx echoes her opening line in her closing one: "'Who telleth one of my meanings,/ Is master of all I am.'" All three utterances of the Sphinx thus begin with the word "who," two

---

5. "The Sphinx" begins *Poems, Selected Poems* (1876), and the Riverside *Poems*. It does not appear in *May-Day and Other Pieces*.
6. Edward's choice gains even greater Oedipal inflection when we note that Emerson himself apparently very much disliked "Good-bye." A letter from Ellen Emerson to Sarah Gibbons Emerson makes clear that Emerson allowed "Good-bye" to be included in his *Selected Poems* only at his family's insistence: "You asked me in one letter how we could let Father leave out 'Goodbye proud world' from the new volume [*Selected Poems*]. We were sorry, and several friends begged for it, but Father disliked it so much himself that all persuasion failed" (Ellen Tucker Emerson, *The Letters of Ellen Tucker Emerson*, 2 vols., ed. Edith E. W. Gregg [Kent, Ohio: Kent State Univ. Press, 1982], 2:245). As justification for his action, Edward argued that "The Sphinx" would deter readers at the start rather than entice them to read on (*The Complete Works of Ralph Waldo Emerson* [Boston: Houghton Mifflin, 1903–1904], 9:403–4).

as questions and one as a non-answer that leaves unresolved the basic issue of whether the poet meets the standard the inquiry itself establishes.

Amid the confusion, the voice of the poet answers "aloud and cheerfully" both the Sphinx's accusations and inquiries. The success of this five-and-a-half stanza response has provoked consistent dispute among scholars. If we view the poet as unsuccessful, his cheer becomes naïveté and his confidence, immature arrogance—qualities that the Sphinx would then be mocking at the end of the poem. If we deem him successful, we expect to go on to read of his enshrinement and the Sphinx's death. But these trajectories presuppose established notions of resolution and contestation. I suggest instead that the response disrupts notions of stable, disparate identity to prepare for the alternative notions of both "answering" and triumph with which the poem ends.

First, that the poet can speak at all shows the Sphinx has not performed her fundamental role of blocking. Linguistically and mythologically, she is the "throttler," etymologically akin to "sphincter" and the associated notions of somatic anxiety, constriction, and inhibition of flow. Emerson's Sphinx represents, then, the sort of self-castigation that blocks self-expression, leaving the inarticulate individual, as Emerson characterizes him in his essay "The Poet," "half himself" without "his expression" (CW 3:4). Actually, the Sphinx itself is mute in some traditions. Since, then, the Sphinx traditionally both silences and is silenced, the poet's most basic "answer" is simply his ability to respond. Precisely unlike the "mankind" the Sphinx has described, the poet is like the elements of nature that she called "erect," "undaunted," "calm," "unashamed." He answers "aloud and cheerfully."

From this perspective, the inability to articulate one's needs is the problem rather than its symptom. An opposite ramification (yet further manifestation) of difficulties involving need and expression appears when we reverse this equation to associate desire with language and silence with fulfilled, already answered demands. Without dissatisfaction the Sphinx and the poet would already have been unified, and there would have been no need for articulation, no split, and no riddle. In either case, articulation is by definition linked with unmet longing.[7]

Yet though the poet does answer the Sphinx, any victory he achieves is an unconventional one. For he does not hurl her down to death and silence, but quite the opposite. Beginning his apostrophe "'Say on, sweet Sphinx!'" the poet speaks primarily to urge the Sphinx's own self-articulation. Moreover, he is able to do so precisely because he refuses to see her conventionally. Receptive rather than defensive, the poet considers the Sphinx "sweet" instead of horrifying, hears her "dirges" as "pleasant songs" (replacing *thanatos* with *eros*), and celebrates fluidity and metamorphosis rather than solidity and certainty. He thus transforms the Sphinx's role for him from throttler to muse. For the poet finally identifies the Sphinx as a sort of benevolent Nemesis figure, maintaining that without her, called now "love of the Best," humans would lack impulse for motion or expression.

When the Sphinx speaks, she identifies herself: as in Emerson's "History," "the Sphinx must solve her own riddle" (CW 2:3).[8] She is, she says, a part of the

---

7. For further amplification of this link between expression and longing, see Julia Kristeva's *Desire in Language: A Semiotic Approach to Literature and Art*, ed. Leon S. Roudiez (New York: Columbia Univ. Press, 1980), especially chapters five and seven.
8. Emerson uses the figure of the Sphinx variously throughout his texts. He associates it with inscrutability and allure, often with an undertone of humorous derision toward those who think they can solve the Sphinx's enigma and a touch of admiration for those who dare to try.

poet: "'I am thy spirit, yoke-fellow,/ Of thine eye I am eyebeam.'" Whereas
Sophocles's Sphinx wanted Oedipus to identify himself, Emerson's seems to
want the poet to identify her. But in doing so he identifies himself and leads her
to do the same. The success of his effort has depended upon his being receptive to her nature as something even more mercurial than humanity's in the
mythological conundrum.

Emerson's repetitious punning on "I" and "eye" combines his constant
preoccupations with the individual and with vision, emphasizing the "perception of identity" to which he himself has referred in relation to the poem.[9]
Again, it is significant that the Sphinx is connected with precisely that part of
the body Emerson most consistently associates with the poet, the eye, and is at
the same time his "spirit" and "eyebeam," so that metaphor is actually fluctuating synecdoche, and tenor and vehicle are not fully correlative.

Though each appears to the other exclusively as "Other," it is only through
the dialogue enabled by that split that any knowing (however partial), any constitution of self (however unindividuated), or any interaction with the world
(however imperfectly mediated and complex) may occur. For Emerson, as for
many of his contemporaries, only reflection and interaction with what seems
alien can create life and metamorphosis.

As "yoke-fellow[s]," the poet and the Sphinx represent in part a subjectivity that is inevitably split, alienated both from itself and from other objects of its
perception, and consequently possessor of a voice that is inherently dialogic.[1]
This allegory of split subjectivity makes the poem dialogic on multiple levels
and complicates any literal and reductive condemnation of the "lyric I." Again,
the penultimate stanza of the poem finally emphasizes separation rather than
"identity," leaving us perpetually charged with at least "half-creating" ourselves
and our world through ambivalent and multivalenced discourse. Emerson suggests that we somehow enable that process by encouraging verbalization of the
"Other," and that such an act must be accomplished receptively and imagina-
tively: verbalization necessarily accompanies acceptance, and acceptance is essential for metamorphosis and metaphor.[2] At the same time, logical problems
remain: What is the causal relation between reception and imagination? Is
speaking the "Other" usurpation? Can "Others" only speak themselves? Or, in
fact, can "Others" never speak themselves but only be transformed into "selves"
at the moment of enunciation?

Moreover, the identity established by incorporating the Sphinx into the
poet is hardly an unvexed one. For the Sphinx does not serve as stable ground
for metaphor in securing male identity but—by virtue of her sphingine nature—as uncertain, unsteady, enigmatic foundation. This view of poet and
Sphinx theorizes the subject as not only a highly qualified but even an impossible construct, one in which subjectivity necessarily coexists with its own im-

---

9. Edward Emerson quotes his father on the poem:
      "I have often been asked the meaning of the 'Sphinx.' It is this,—The perception of identity unites
   all things and explains one by another, and the most rare and strange is equally facile as the most
   common. But if the mind live only in particulars, and see only differences (wanting the power to
   see the whole—all in each), then the world addresses to this mind a question it cannot answer, and
   each new fact tears it in pieces, and it is vanquished by the distracting variety."(W 9:412)
1. This perpetual revolution of identity, along with its disputational nature, links the poem to the Scottish
   flyting, a verse form in which two poets try to demolish each other with insult and invective, and to Greek
   stichomythia, dramatic argumentation in alternate lines.
2. The poem is also related to medieval and Renaissance dialogue poems. The typical bipartite scheme,
   however, is complicated in Emerson's poem by the voice of the narrator.

possibility. The poet can only become himself by realization of the finally un-realizable Sphinx. The riddle for the poet (and readers) is that not only does she not reflect him, she consequently also does not function as an eye, a metaphor. As a signifying mark, what she produces is still further interrogation and enigma. And, indeed, in "The Sphinx" the inseparable identities of poet and Sphinx remain inseparable from the act of questioning. Though both female figures (the Sphinx and the great mother) appear as inquisitors, the Sphinx goes on to identify the poet himself as "the unanswered question," essentially an unconquered Sphinx, as Oedipus remained to himself even after he had solved one riddle.

Emerson simultaneously insists that we identify the Sphinx and refuses to stabilize her identity in further ways, as distinctions among poet, Sphinx, nature, and great mother insistently waver. It sometimes seems as though the Sphinx actually is nature. But she is also part of the poet. And while in other respects she represents the critical aspect of humanity, and the poet the affirmative, the poet also calls her "'love of the Best'"—presumably identifying her with idealism and perfectionism. Finally, no one allegorical interpretation of the Sphinx works consistently.[3] But despite the destabilizations, the Sphinx still appears primarily as facilitator for the male ego ("'Of thine eye I am eyebeam'"), so that the price for the establishment of a self is the obliteration of the female "Other," as in the traditional Sphinx myth. Nevertheless, the hierarchical priority keeps rotating, for the poem is not called "The Poet" but "The Sphinx."

While narrative focus rests primarily on the Sphinx, the conclusion of the poem—where she, not the poet, is transformed, and where she, not the poet, has the last word—remains equivocal. For the poem finally refuses to establish firmly the position of either figure, so that this rendition of a myth about agon and answering concludes with precisely the opposite emphases. It instead changes the basis of the encounter with the Sphinx from conflict to mutual dependence, and the terms of victory from conquest to coexistence.

The moment of the Sphinx's metamorphosis occurs in perhaps the most euphonious lines of the poem:

> Uprose the merry Sphinx,
>   And crouched no more in stone;
> She melted into purple cloud,
>   She silvered in the moon;
> She spired into a yellow flame;
>   She flowered in blossoms red;
> She flowed into a foaming wave;
>   She stood Monadnoc's head.

"Drowsy," "heavy," and brooding at the beginning of the poem, the now "merry" Sphinx silvers, melts, spires, flowers, flows, and ascends. The Sphinx and the poet thus animate one another. He appears because of her invocation; she is transformed by his. Revealed as uniquely able to respond to the Sphinx's riddle, the poet has perceived a correspondence between matter and mind, then, contradictorily, has through metaphor transformed material fixity into metamorphosis and flow.

---

3. Scholars have variously identified the Sphinx as Nature, the "Spirit of man," "man's inquiring spirit," and humankind.

The poem ends with a crucial quatrain in which the Sphinx attains voice to a hyperbolic, even sublime extent, then returns to her role as riddler even as she seems to confess her own eventual submission:

> Thorough a thousand voices
> Spoke the universal dame:
> 'Who telleth one of my meanings,
> Is master of all I am.'

The Sphinx, initially immobile, is aroused and given seemingly perpetual voice. And the "answer" provided by her manifold voices is actually just another question—a statement whose grammar, masked as declarative, functions interrogatively. It asks both "who telleth" the answer, and, even more obliquely, whether the poet actually has been one "who telleth."[4]

Readers have never agreed about whether or not the poet is this successful respondent and "master." Indeed, the poem's departure from tradition enhances the ambiguity of its close. Instead of hurling herself from a pinnacle, the Sphinx flies and stands atop one. Instead of dying or devouring the traveler, she evanesces and encourages the poet to follow her. Motion thus replaces institution; poetic fecundity, consumption; polyphony, monotony; reanimation of the maternal, institution of patriarchy; and insistence upon ambiguity, interpretive finality. It is peculiar and important that the poet's voice—and the poem—end when the Sphinx becomes exceedingly fluent. Yet if the poet has therefore failed, why has his fate not been bleaker? He, too, is anything but finished.

We can read the outcome of this contest, in which the poet and the Sphinx activate one another rather than cause death, as part of Emerson's life-long effort to imagine alternatives to patriarchal conquest models. For, with certain qualifications, his narrative suggests the power of the "feminine" to promote fluency by blocking hyperphallic aggression and phallogocentric mastery. This strategy of inversion governs Emerson's overall rendition of the Sphinx material: he appropriates the myth to subvert it, as is his standard practice with traditional systems of figuration and forms of discourse. Reinstitution of the "feminine" is a part of that subversion, for conquest of the feminine is central to the Sphinx legend. Feminist recuperations of traditionally feminine concerns within the mythic material that have been elided by overly masculinist readings emphasize the Sphinx's role as protector of matriarchy in her position at Thebes.

"The Sphinx" ends with its most significant formal deviation. Given the pattern established, the poem's last quatrain is essentially a half-stanza. This final truncation might be read in two different ways that together replicate the division within representations of the feminine and of language that I have been describing. We may perhaps best read the lines by allowing their opposed implications to coexist. One impression the stanzaic curtailment creates is that the Sphinx finally stifles Emerson and the poet; that is to say, returning to her role of throttler, she speaks a closing quatrian to which the only available response is silence. In this reading, such a thousand-voiced Sphinx, like the thousand-

---

4. The implication is that the poet's statement effects these transformations, in the tradition of such Romantic apostrophes as Childe Harold's to the ocean or Whitman's to the river in "Crossing Brooklyn Ferry." The locutions are fundamentally ironic, addressed to forces whose perpetual (thus threatening) motion exists prior to the invocation.

snaked head of Medusa, overcomes the poet with her fecundity, so that the poem breaks off leaving the poet voiceless and a blank where his quatrain should be. An opposed perspective suggests that this space remains open for the poet to fill, so that the rest of the volume represents his reply: all the other poems complete the stanza. In this view, the stanzaic fragment opens out into the following pages.[5]

"The Sphinx" then serves as an open door into the volume, functioning as an allegory of reading, writing, interpretation, dynamic subjectivity, and relations between and among texts and human beings. In all these ways, the poem shows us how to approach the rest of Emerson's verse, functioning as an initiatory riddle whose "meanings" open out into the poems that follow. Readers are to continue through the volume, animated instead of overcome by the inexhaustibility of language and life. The subsequent poems flow from the ongoing metamorphosis of issues raised in this threshold poem and embody its multitude of voices and forms.

When we read Emerson's other poems through the interpretive rubric of "The Sphinx," some of their most perplexing moments, structures, and styles are illuminated. Rhetorical strategies and thematic concerns raised by that poem recur throughout *Poems, May-Day*, and the essay epigraphs. Especially in the earlier volume, the texts are characteristically multivocal, dialogic, puzzling, and elliptical. They are frequently structured according to debate or inquisition. As David Porter and R. A. Yoder emphasize, a high percentage of Emerson's poems tell the story of a poet figure, his search for voice, and his role as an unriddler. The poems also often explore other aesthetic issues suggested in "The Sphinx." In addition, like "The Sphinx," many contain figures of blockage, flow, speech, vision, and ascension.

The most crucial connection between the individual pieces in Emerson's first volume and "The Sphinx" is their variously manifested preoccupation with riddling. *Poems* as a whole, single compositions, or sections of texts may be read as additional riddles of the Sphinx, as her oracular utterances, or as responses to her questioning. Such is the case with many of the texts literally from their beginnings, for several of the titles function as puzzles. We get past such difficulty only to find that a surprising number of the poems are occasioned by direct or implicit questions. And most of the pieces contain embedded questions, and many end with them, while other poems culminate by posing "solutions" that are themselves riddling. At the same time, their tonal variety is also a pervasive, almost definitive, quality of the poems and may be read as further manifestations of the Sphinx, now speaking "Thorough a thousand voices."

An overview of some frequently anthologized pieces in *Poems* indicates how much of the volume develops and expands upon preoccupations initiated by "The Sphinx." "The Problem," for instance, whose title is synonymous with "Sphinx," consummately represents an "argument" with a "metre-making argument." "Uriel," another quite puzzling poem, concerns many of the same issues and employs many of the same strategies, among them the role of the poet, contestation, riddling, stasis vs. fluidity, and multivocality. And "Hamatreya" represents a literally bipartite rendition of an argument between farmers and the earth over who is more powerful—over, finally, who owns whom. Such a debate, this

---

5. Two essays by Neil Hertz in his *The End of the Line: Essays on Psychoanalysis and the Sublime*, "Medusa's Head" and "The Notion of Blockage in the Literature of the Sublime," have direct bearing on these issues (New York: Columbia Univ. Press, 1985).

time with neither voice subsuming the other, structures "Merlin," so that "Merlin II" complements "Merlin I," providing the counterpoise to the emphasis on freedom (and power) in "Merlin I" to stress form (and balance) instead.

A similar gesture of presenting unreconciled and opposing voices is central to "Threnody," Emerson's elegy for his firstborn child, Waldo, who died suddenly of scarlatina at age five. In the poem, Emerson confronts one of the most dread Sphinxes of all, the incomprehensible death of his very young son. As he does so, problems traditionally associated with Greek and Egyptian Sphinxes—inscrutability, death, time, family, guilt, and art—as well as rhetorical gestures from "The Sphinx," converge.

One instance of this recurrence is particularly important. The most frequently commented on, and criticized, feature of "Threnody" is its tonal bifurcation. The first 175 lines (seven stanzas) represent a heartfelt lamentation for young Waldo—virtually an outpouring of emotion in the voice of the grieving father. The following 114 lines appear as two stanzas of direct quotation in the voice of the "deep Heart" as it responds to the grieving father. This dichotomy replicates the debate of poems like "The Sphinx," while its structure corresponds to that of "Merlin" and other poems in which Emerson allows contradictory perspectives to coexist. "Threnody"'s tones of despair and consolation are *both* real and are fundamentally unreconcilable. The poem does not allow part two ever to neutralize the pain of part one, and it never explains how one can love a universe arranged so that one's five-year-old child would die.

We find the same philosophical and structural tension between and within two crucial Emerson essays written around the same time as "Threnody" and dealing with similar concerns, "The Poet" and "Experience." These three pieces are best read together, with each inflecting the others' perspectives. That interrelationship illustrates how I suggest we read and teach Emerson's work generally—exploring, for example, "The Snow-Storm" with the anecdote about the snow storm in the Divinity School "Address," and poems such as "Uriel" and "The Problem" with the address itself. Although we have long read "The Poet" as one of Emerson's most affirmative essays and "Experience" as one of his most skeptical, we are coming to appreciate how fully the essays echo one another. Their contiguous placement and their vacillation of tone replicate the bipartite structure and wavering point of view of "Threnody" and other Emerson poems.

Emerson did not, however, use "The Sphinx" as the threshold piece only for the poems in his first collection, but also for his *Selected Poems*, and Cabot chose to use it to begin the first comprehensive collection of Emerson's verse, the Riverside *Poems*. It is appropriate, then, that the poems in the second of Emerson's two primary collections of poetry, *May-Day and Other Pieces*, also be illuminated by the considerations I have been outlining. Scholars have emphasized that *May-Day*, especially in its title poem, represents the sexagenarian Emerson's answer to his own aging process.[6] Certainly *May-Day*'s texts are preoccupied, even more than those of *Poems*, with the challenges of confronting limitation, a primary issue in "The Sphinx." In addition to reading those concerns as personally reflective ones, however, I suggest that we also view the *May-*

---

6. See, e.g., Porter, pp. 130–33. Porter also emphasizes the title poem's thematization of the poetic process in relation to what he calls Emerson's "crisis of imagination."

Day volume in a way that previous scholarship has not noted. Its 1867 publication, soon after the end of the American Civil War, invites us to read *May-Day* along with Melville's *Battle-Pieces* and Whitman's *Drum Taps* as part of the literary response to the war itself.[7]

The volume manifests Emerson's concerns with the war in two primary ways. First, some of the poems—"Freedom," "Ode Sung in the Town Hall," "Boston Hymn," and "Voluntaries"—treat the conflict directly. In addition, however, many others that have seemed personally and philosophically meditative (such as "Brahma," "Song of Nature," and "Waldeinsamkeit") address it implicitly, either tropically or through such subjects as camaraderie, reconciliation, and restoration. In both ways, the volume represents Emerson's response to the Sphinxes of death and family (North/South) strife suggested by the representation of the War as sphingine, which I mentioned earlier as a commonplace rhetorical stragegy of the times. For with the war and again following it, America was forced to face the question of national identity—forced (as were Oedipus and the poet when they met their Sphinxes) to confront the issue of who it was. Such a confrontation, the title piece and the volume imply, can best be met through the power of poetry, which is to bring war-torn yet now-virtuous America the vitality of spring.

Moreover, while the poems in *May-Day* are as a whole less riddling in both form and subject than their predecessors, many of the pieces continue a number of structural, rhetorical, and thematic preoccupations of "The Sphinx." "The Titmouse," for example, begins with a question, and that question is much like that in "The Sphinx"—how to overcome lethargy. It is about poet figures (narrator and bird) who cheer, it uses imagery of petrifaction, it contains interpolated voices, and its "solution" involves interaction with nature. The poem "Days" is another riddle and another allegorization. The speaker of this eleven-line parable is as overwhelmed by the Days as the poet is accused of being in "The Sphinx," and as, in 1867, Emerson and the country were by the Sphinxes of age and war. The poem involves the adequacy of a respondent to mysteriously threatening and scornful female inquisitors and requires the respondent to *ask* instead of answer—but with a question that is actually a test of her own worth and one whose obscurity leads readings even now to remain, like those of "The Sphinx," divided about whether the response was successful. In "Terminus," Emerson's familiar concerns again cluster—the poem thematizes limitation, directly this time; contains figures of flow and blockage; portrays muses as at once helpfully provocative and potentially overwhelming; expresses anxiety about silencing; and contains interpolated voices, including that of a mysterious divinity who speaks a closing quatrain.

Positioned at the threshold of its section in *May-Day*, "Brahma" is the poem in Emerson's canon most often compared to "The Sphinx," in both sympathetic analyses and parodies. Fundamentally a riddle, with an implicit "What am I?" as its undertone, the poem assumes the voice of a Hindu god, who in Emerson may loosely be identified as the soul or the over-soul—in the poetry notebooks, the poem was originally titled "Song of the Soul." Once more, then,

---

7. Len Gougeon has treated the importance of issues associated with abolition and the Civil War as a part of his emphasis on Emerson as, in the title of Gougeon's book, *Virtue's Hero: Emerson, Antislavery, and Reform* (Athens: University of Georgia Press, 1990); see also Gougeon, "Emerson, Poetry, and Reform," *Modern Language Studies* 19.2 (Spring 1989): 38–49; and Eduardo Cadava, *Emerson and the Climates of History* (Stanford Calif.: Stanford Univ. Press, 1997), especially pp. 171ff.

readers receive the voice of a mysterious entity in enigmatic, oracular quatrains. The voice in Brahma again wants to know its own identity, and again Emerson presents his clues in opposites and paradox. The answer to this riddle is also linguistic, even poetic—Brahma's most direct statement of identity is "I [am] the hymn the Brahmin sings," and the poem itself actually *is* that hymn, in the classic long measure of Christian hymnody. Thus the god, the voice, the Sphinx, and the individual become in fundamental ways both articulation and poetry.

In addition, the readers who hear of the "slayer" and "slain" in "Brahma" are those who have just observed North and South in those roles. Written in 1856, a time when Emerson was actively involved in the abolitionist cause and thinking ahead to the possibility of war, the poem bears a distinctly political undertone. For its 1867 readers, the language would have been even more fully inflected with events of the war.[8] In this context, "Brahma" also becomes a meditation on the insignificance of residual divisiveness, an affirmation of life beyond tragedy, victory, and defeat. Echoing the message of "May-Day," "Brahma" suggests that poetry can provide a response to the horrors of "slayer" and "slain."

Finally, *May-Day* ends with three sections of poems whose very forms are riddling. The quatrains and translations that appear as separate sections in *May-Day* are by virtue of their length, subject matter, and very existence quite sphingine, gnomic utterances. In addition, the translations reveal a method of composition quintessentially Emersonian, for in them Emerson blends the Persian, its German rendition, and his own revisions to create poems that disrupt boundaries between origin and elaboration.[9] That appropriative impulse is also at the heart of Emerson's generically distinct essay epigraphs, some of which are collected in the *May-Day* section "Elements."

For twenty-eight essays and one lecture, in four main collections, Emerson chose to print his own poems as epigraphs. That decision was altogether unconventional or, more precisely, was *anti*conventional. At the thresholds of prose pieces, as on the lintels of doorways, we expect to see "sacred" text, whether from the Bible, or from Shakespeare, Homer, Dante, or Milton. The tradition is definitively deferential. Yet despite their peculiarity and the fact that they are his verse that Emerson readers most frequently encounter, the epigraph poems have received very little attention. When teaching the essays and writing about them, we most often act as if the mottoes aren't there at all. Their idiosyncrasy combined with their own preoccupation with enigma and their placement invites us, I think, to imagine the epigraph themselves as ridding Sphinxes at the thresholds of Emerson's essays.

First, the epigraphs serve as problematic guardians at the gateways, representing distilled challenges that we are to grapple with before we reach the prose. At the same time, the relation of the epigraphs and the essays to their titles is frequently a puzzling, even paradoxical one. The mottoes and essay "History," for instance, are not about "History" as much as about the priority of the soul over history. In addition, the epigraphs frequently appear in rhetorical

---

8. Hyatt Waggoner has also noted this connection (pp. 157–58).
9. On Emerson's translations, see *The Topical Notebooks of Ralph Waldo Emerson*, Vol. 2, ed. Ronald A. Bosco (Columbia and London: University of Missouri Press, 1993); Richard Tuerk, "Emerson as Translator—'The Phoenix,'" *Emerson Society Quarterly* 63 (1971): 24–26; and J. D. Yohannan, "Emerson's Translations of Persian Poetry from German Sources," *American Literature* 14 (1943): 407–20.

structures and forms that are directly or indirectly based on riddling—paradox, situation *in medias res*, and fragmentary or elliptical syntax, for example. And many of the verses thematize obscurity, thus becoming poems about themselves, the essays they introduce, and what Emerson saw as the ultimate inscrutability of life.

As he appropriates and extends the epigraph form, Emerson writes two basic types of poems, both related to "The Sphinx": first, a sort of oracular wisdom verse that makes gnomic and riddling yet prophetic pronouncements, and, second, fragmented narratives about the development of a poet-hero who can solve the enigmas that plague humankind, actually an externalization of the poetic impulse that Emerson would locate within all individuals. As a group, many of the epigraphs tell of this foundling son of mother Nature, who in his "answers" to her produces the sort of oracular poetry that other epigraphs embody—prophetic in tone and tendency, but with an element of forbidden mystery. Consequently, the epigraphs often double the riddle form—are frequently riddles about riddling, mysterious oracles about mystery.

The epigraphs thus play an important role in our understanding the relationship between Emerson's various texts and voices and, most important, between his poetry and his prose. In the essay "Self-Reliance," Emerson issues an arch rejoinder to anyone who might question the value of his vocation:

> I shun father and mother and wife and brother, when my genius calls me. I would write on the lintels of the door-post, *Whim*. I hope it is somewhat better than whim at last, but we cannot spend the day in explanation (CW 2:30).

Here, an irascible Emerson invokes Deuteronomy's rendition of the Mosaic covenant, in which God cautions Moses to keep the words he has told him that day in his heart, to teach them to his children, to talk of them, and to "write them upon the posts of thy house, and on thy gates" (Deuteronomy 6:9). The doorway also figures prominently in connection with Passover and with the sacrificial blood of Christ. Emerson's assertion in "Self-Reliance," then, substitutes an arrogant yet whimsical rejoinder of his own for biblical text and the words of God.[1]

Just as in "Self-Reliance," the word and act of "*Whim*" replace the ancient text, Emerson's own poetry does so before his essays, in the form of the essay epigraphs. They inscribe "*Whim*" upon the lintels of the prose. In this sense, the essays become elaboration, application, even "exegesis" of the initial poetic "scriptures," combining the sacred and the jovial in their existence as whimsical preliminary conundrums. In a larger sense, we might also imagine the epigraphs and essays as together figuring the positions of poetry and prose in Emerson's life. Emerson positions the two *together*, establishing between the genres a dialogue in which formal divisions become happily indistinct. This invitation to pause at the thresholds of his essays provides our best hint about how to read the prose that follows—poetically.

Finally, the epigraphs place Emerson himself in the position of the Sphinx and readers in the position of Oedipus. They thus initiate at the gateways to his

---

1. Stanley Cavell has devoted a good deal of attention to this same passage. See especially his two essays on Emerson in the expanded edition of *The Senses of Walden: An Expanded Edition* (San Francisco: North Point Press, 1981).

prose the destabilization of boundaries between author and audience, reader and writer that we have come to associate with Emerson's work. For his verse as a whole asks us to challenge our intellects, imaginations, and assumptions, to *argue* with ourselves, so to speak—as does Emerson's prototypical threshold poem "The Sphinx," the crucial and complex whim upon the lintel of his first volume of verse.

Ralph Waldo Emerson: A Chronology

1803	May 25: born in Boston.
1811	May 12: Father dies, age forty-two.
1812	Enters Boston Public Latin School; begins writing poetry.
1817	Enters Harvard College.
1820	Begins keeping a journal, a practice that will continue into the 1870s.
1821	Graduates from Harvard; teaches in Boston at his brother William's school for girls.
1822	Continues to teach; publishes essay "The Religion of the Middle Ages" in *The Christian Disciple*.
1825	Feb.: admitted to Harvard Divinity School. Studies interrupted by eye trouble.
1826	Teaches in Roxbury and Cambridge. Oct. 10: approbated to preach. Nov.: lung trouble; voyages south to improve health.
1827	June: returns to Cambridge. Dec.: meets Ellen Louisa Tucker.
1828	Brother Edward becomes deranged. Dec. 17: becomes engaged to Ellen, who is already ill with tuberculosis.
1829	Ordained junior pastor of Boston's Second Church (Unitarian). Sept. 30: marries Ellen.
1831	Feb. 8: Ellen dies, age nineteen.
1832	Increasing ill health; decides he can no longer serve communion; resigns pastorate. Dec. 25: sails for Europe.
1833	Travels to Italy, France, and Great Britain; meets British literati, including Wordsworth, Coleridge, and Carlyle; back in Boston, begins career as lecturer with talks on "natural history."
1834	Continues to preach. Spring: receives first half of inheritance from Ellen Tucker's family. Oct.: Edward dies.
1835	Lectures in Boston on biography. Aug. 15: buys home in Concord. Sept.: marries Lydia Jackson (renames her "Lidian").
1836	Completes lecture series on English literature. May: brother Charles dies. July: Margaret Fuller visits. Sept.: *Nature* published anonymously in Boston. Oct. 30: Waldo born. Winter: lectures on the philosophy of history.
1837	July: receives final portion of Tucker estate. Aug.: Thoreau graduates from Harvard, where Emerson delivers "The American Scholar" before the Phi Beta Kappa Society. Fall—winter: lectures on human culture.
1838	Apr.: writes letter to President Van Buren protesting displacement of Cherokee nation from their ancestral lands. July 15: delivers address

at Harvard Divinity School that causes him to be banned from speaking at Harvard for many years. July 24: Dartmouth Oration ("Literary Ethics"). Winter: lectures on human life.

1839   Jan.: preaches last sermon. Feb. 24: Ellen Tucker Emerson born. Winter: the lecture "The Present Age."

1840   July: first issue of Transcendental journal, *The Dial*, edited by Margaret Fuller.

1841   Mar.: first series of *Essays* published. Spring: Thoreau joins household. Nov. 22: Edith born. Winter: lecture series "The Times."

1842   Jan. 27: Waldo dies. July: Emerson succeeds Fuller as editor of *The Dial*. Dec.: delivers lecture series in New York, during which his "Poetry of the Times" is reviewed by Walter Whitman.

1844   July 10: Edward born. Apr.: last issue of *The Dial*. Aug.: delivers the lecture "Emancipation of the Negroes in the British West Indies." Oct.: *Essays, Second Series* published.

1845   July 4: Thoreau moves to Walden Pond and builds cabin on Emerson's property. Winter: lecture series "Representative Men."

1846   Dec.: *Poems* published.

1847   Oct.: begins second trip to Europe; away ten months.

1849   The lecture "Mind and Manners in the Nineteenth Century"; *Nature; Addresses, and Lectures* published.

1850   Jan.: *Representative Men* published. July: Margaret Fuller Ossoli, returning from Italy, drowns with her husband and son off Fire Island.

1851   May: delivers "Address to the Citizens of Concord" on the Fugitive Slave Law. Winter: lecture series "The Conduct of Life."

1852   With William Henry Channing and James Freeman Clarke publishes *Memoirs of Margaret Fuller Ossoli*.

1853   Mother dies, age eighty-four.

1854   The lecture series "Topics of Modern Times" in Philadelphia; heavy lecture schedule throughout the country.

1855   Antislavery lectures in Boston, New York, and Philadelphia. July 21: sends letter to Whitman praising first edition of *Leaves of Grass*.

1856   Aug.: *English Traits* published.

1860   Dec.: *The Conduct of Life* published.

1862   The lecture "American Civilization" in Washington; meets President Lincoln. May 6: Thoreau dies.

1864   May 23: attends Hawthorne's funeral.

1865   Apr.: eulogizes the slain Lincoln.

1866   Lectures in the west; receives Doctor of Laws degree from Harvard.

1867   Apr.: *May-Day and Other Pieces* published; named Overseer of Harvard College; delivers second Phi Beta Kappa address ("The Progress of Culture").

1870   Writes preface to *Plutarch's Morals*; publishes *Society and Solitude*; lectures at Harvard ("Natural History of Intellect").

1871   Apr.–May: travels to California by train; meets Brigham Young and naturalist John Muir.

1872   Speaks at Howard University. July 24: house burns. Oct.: sets out for Europe and Egypt with Ellen.

1874   Dec.: publishes *Parnassus*, an anthology of his favorite poetry, which omits Poe and Whitman.

1875   Dec.: *Letters and Social Aims* published, prepared by James Elliot Cabot and Ellen Emerson.

1876   Fall: publishes *Selected Poems* with help of Ellen and Cabot.

1882   Apr. 27: Emerson dies of pneumonia in Concord; Whitman visits his grave and observes: "A just man, poised on himself, all-loving, all-inclosing, and sane and clear as the sun."

Selected Bibliography

• indicates works included or excerpted in this Norton Critical Edition.

TEXTS

The Collected Works of Ralph Waldo Emerson. 5 vols. to date. Ed. Robert E. Spiller, Alfred R. Ferguson, Joseph Slater, Jean Ferguson Carr, Wallace E. Williams, and Douglas Emory Wilson. Cambridge, Mass.: Harvard UP, 1971–.
Complete Sermons of Ralph Waldo Emerson. 4 vols. Ed. Albert J. von Frank, Teresa Toulouse, Andrew Delbanco, Ronald A. Bosco, and Wesley T. Mott. Columbia: U of Missouri P, 1989–92.
The Complete Works of Ralph Waldo Emerson. Centenary ed. 12 vols. Ed. Edward Waldo Emerson. Boston: Houghton Mifflin, 1903–04.
The Correspondence of Emerson and Carlyle. Ed. Joseph Slater. New York: Columbia UP, 1964.
The Early Lectures of Ralph Waldo Emerson. 3 vols. Ed. Stephen E. Whicher, Robert E. Spiller, and Wallace E. Williams. Cambridge, Mass.: Belknap P of Harvard UP, 1959–72.
Emerson's Antislavery Writings. Ed. Len Gougeon and Joel Myerson. New Haven, Conn.: Yale UP, 1995.
Emerson: Collected Poems and Translations. Ed. Harold Bloom and Paul Kane. New York: Library of America, 1994.
The Journals and Miscellaneous Notebooks of Ralph Waldo Emerson. 16 vols. Ed. William H. Gilman, Alfred R. Ferguson, George P. Clark, et al. Cambridge, Mass.: Harvard UP, 1960–82.
The Letters of Ralph Waldo Emerson. 10 vols. Ed. Ralph L. Rusk and Eleanor M. Tilton. New York: Columbia UP, 1939–95.
The Poetry Notebooks of Ralph Waldo Emerson. Ed. Ralph H. Orth, Albert J. von Frank, Linda Allardt, and David W. Hill. Columbia: U of Missouri P, 1986.
Ralph Waldo Emerson: Essays and Lectures. Ed. Joel Porte. New York: Library of America, 1983.
Selected Poems. New and rev. ed. Boston: James R. Osgood and Co., 1876.
The Topical Notebooks of Ralph Waldo Emerson. 3 vols. Ed. Ralph H. Orth, Susan Sutton Smith, Ronald A. Bosco, and Glen M. Johnson. Columbia: U of Missouri P, 1990–94.

SELECTIONS AND ANTHOLOGIES

Emerson: A Modern Anthology. Ed. Alfred Kazin and Daniel Aaron. Boston: Houghton Mifflin, 1959.
Emerson in His Journals. Ed. Joel Porte. Cambridge, Mass.: Belknap P of Harvard UP, 1982.
The Heart of Emerson's Journals. Ed. Bliss Perry. Boston: Houghton Mifflin, 1926.
Ralph Waldo Emerson. Ed. Richard Poirier. New York: Oxford UP, 1990.
Selected Letters of Ralph Waldo Emerson. Ed. Joel Myerson. New York: Columbia UP, 1997.
Selected Writings of Ralph Waldo Emerson. Ed. William H. Gilman. New York: New American Library, 1965.
Selections from Ralph Waldo Emerson: An Organic Anthology. Ed. Stephen E. Whicher. Boston: Houghton Mifflin, 1957.

RESOURCES FOR RESEARCH

Burkholder, Robert E., and Joel Myerson. *Ralph Waldo Emerson: An Annotated Bibliography of Criticism, 1980–1991.* Westport, Conn.: Greenwood, 1994.
————. *Ralph Waldo Emerson: An Annotated Secondary Bibliography.* Pittsburgh: U of Pittsburgh P, 1985.
Carpenter, F. I. *Emerson Handbook.* New York: Hendricks House, 1953.
The Letters of Ellen Tucker Emerson. 2 vols. Ed. Edith E. W. Gregg. Kent, Ohio: Kent State UP, 1982.
Harding, Walter. *Emerson's Library.* Charlottesville: UP of Virginia, 1967.
Hubbell, George S. *Concordance to the Poems of Ralph Waldo Emerson..* New York: H. W. Wilson, 1932.
Irey, Eugene F. *A Concordance to Five Essays of Ralph Waldo Emerson.* New York: Garland, 1981.
Ihrig, Mary Alice. *Emerson's Transcendental Vocabulary: A Concordance.* New York: Garland, 1981.
Myerson, Joel. *Ralph Waldo Emerson: A Descriptive Bibliography.* Pittsburgh: U of Pittsburgh P, 1982.
von Frank, Albert J. *An Emerson Chronology.* New York: G. K. Hall, 1994.
Wider, Sarah Ann. *The Critical Reception of Emerson: Unsettling All Things.* Rochester, N.Y.: Camden House, 2000.
See also Web site: http://www.walden.org/Emerson/Concordance

BIOGRAPHIES

Allen, Gay Wilson. *Waldo Emerson: A Biography.* New York: Viking, 1981.

Baker, Carlos. *Emerson Among the Eccentrics*. New York: Viking, 1996.

Brooks, Van Wyck. *The Life of Emerson*. New York: The Literary Guild, 1932.

Cabot, James Elliot. *A Memoir of Ralph Waldo Emerson*. Boston: Houghton Mifflin, 1887.

Emerson, Ellen Tucker. *The Life of Lidian Jackson Emerson*. Ed. Dolores Bird Carpenter. Boston: Twayne, 1980.

Firkins, O. W. *Ralph Waldo Emerson*. Boston: Houghton Mifflin, 1915.

Holmes, Oliver Wendell. *Ralph Waldo Emerson*. Boston: Houghton, Mifflin, 1884. Reprint, with an introduction by Joel Porte, New York: Chelsea House, 1980.

McAleer, John. *Ralph Waldo Emerson: Days of Encounter*. Boston: Little, Brown, 1984.

Pommer, Henry F. *Emerson's First Marriage*. Carbondale: Southern Illinois UP, 1967.

• Richardson, Robert D. *Emerson: The Mind on Fire: A Biography*. Berkeley: U of California P, 1995.

Rusk, Ralph L. *The Life of Ralph Waldo Emerson*. New York: Columbia UP, 1949.

Wagenknecht, Edward. *Ralph Waldo Emerson: Portrait of a Balanced Soul*. New York: Oxford UP, 1974.

Whicher, Stephen. *Freedom and Fate: An Inner Life of Ralph Waldo Emerson*. Philadelphia: U of Pennsylvania P, 1953.

CRITICISM

Anderson, John Q. *The Liberating Gods*. Coral Gables: U of Miami P, 1971.

Anderson, Quentin. *The Imperial Self: An Essay in American Literary and Cultural History*. New York: Knopf, 1971.

Arnold, Matthew. *Discourses in America*. London: Macmillan, 1885.

Barish, Evelyn. *Emerson: The Roots of Prophecy*. Princeton, N.J.: Princeton UP, 1989.

Bercovitch, Sacvan. *The Rites of Assent*. New York: Routledge, 1993.

Berthoff, Warner. *Fictions and Events*. New York: Dutton, 1971.

Bishop, Jonathan. *Emerson on the Soul*. Cambridge, Mass.: Harvard UP, 1964.

Bloom, Harold. *Agon: Towards a Theory of Revisionism*. New York: Oxford UP, 1982.

———. *Figures of Capable Imagination*. New York: Seabury, 1976.

———. *A Map of Misreading*. New York: Oxford UP, 1975.

———. *Poetry and Repression*. New Haven, Conn.: Yale UP, 1976.

———. *The Ringers in the Tower*. Chicago: U of Chicago P, 1971.

Brown, Lee Rust. *The Emerson Museum: Practical Romanticism and the Pursuit of the Whole*. Cambridge, Mass.: Harvard UP, 1995.

Bruccoli, Matthew J. *The Chief Glory of Every People*. Carbondale: Southern Illinois UP, 1973.

Buell, Lawrence. *Literary Transcendentalism: Style and Vision in the American Renaissance*. Ithaca, N.Y.: Cornell UP, 1973.

Cadava, Eduardo. *Emerson and the Climates of History*. Stanford, Calif.: Stanford UP, 1997.

Cameron, Sharon. "Representing Grief: Emerson's 'Experience.'" *Representations* 15 (Summer 1986): 15–41.

Cavell, Stanley. *Conditions Handsome and Unhandsome: The Constitution of Emersonian Perfectionism*. Chicago: U of Chicago P, 1990.

• ———. *In Quest of the Ordinary*. Chicago: U of Chicago P, 1988.

———. *Philosophical Passages: Wittgenstein, Emerson, Austin, Derrida*. Oxford, U.K.: Blackwell, 1995.

———. *The Senses of Walden*. San Francisco: North Point, 1981.

———. *This New Yet Unapproachable America*. Albuquerque, N. M.: Living Batch, 1989.

Cayton, Mary Kupiec. *Emerson's Emergence: Self and Society in the Transformation of New England, 1800–1845*. Chapel Hill: U of North Carolina P, 1989.

Chapman, John Jay. *Emerson and Other Essays*. New York: Scribner's, 1898.

Cheyfitz, Eric. *The Trans-Parent: Sexual Politics in the Language of Emerson*. Baltimore: Johns Hopkins UP, 1981.

Colacurcio, Michael. *Doctrine and Difference*. New York: Routledge, 1997.

Cole, Phyllis. *Mary Moody Emerson and the Origins of Transcendentalism*. New York: Oxford UP, 1998.

Cowan, Michael. *City of the West*. New Haven, Conn.: Yale UP, 1967.

Duncan, Jeffrey. *The Power and Form of Emerson's Thought*. Charlottesville: U of Virginia P, 1973.

• Ellison, Julie. *Emerson's Romantic Style*. Princeton, N. J.: Princeton UP, 1984.

Field, Susan L. *The Romance of Desire: Emerson's Commitment to Incompletion*. Teaneck, N.J.: Fairleigh Dickinson UP, 1997.

Gass, William H. *Habitations of the Word*. New York:Simon & Schuster, 1985.

Gelpi, Albert. *The Tenth Muse: The Psyche of the American Poet*. Cambridge, Mass.: Harvard UP, 1975.

Gelpi, Donald. *Endless Seeker: The Religious Quest of Ralph Waldo Emerson*. Lanham, Md.: UP of America, 1991.

• Gilmore, Michael. *American Romanticism and the Marketplace*. Chicago: U of Chicago P, 1985.

Gonnaud, Maurice. *An Uneasy Solitude*. Trans. Lawrence Rosenwald. Princeton, N.J.: Princeton UP, 1987. Originally published as *Individu et société dans l'oeuvre de Ralph Waldo Emerson: Essai de biographie spirituelle* (Paris: Didier, 1964).

Goodman, Russell B. *American Philosophy and the Romantic Tradition*. New York: Cambridge UP, 1985.

• Gougeon, Len. *Virtue's Hero: Emerson, Antislavery, and Reform*. Athens: U of Georgia P, 1990.

Grusin, Richard A. *Transcendental Hermeneutics*. Durham, N.C.: Duke UP, 1991.

Gura, Philip F. *The Wisdom of Words: Language, Theology, and Literature in the New England Renaissance*. Middletown, Conn.: Wesleyan UP, 1981.

Hansen, Olaf. *Aesthetic Individualism and Practical Intellect*. Princeton, N.J.: Princeton UP, 1990.

Harris, Kenneth Marc. *Carlyle and Emerson: Their Long Debate*. Cambridge, Mass.: Harvard UP, 1978.

Hodder, Alan D. *Emerson's Rhetoric of Revelation*: University Park: The Pennsylvania State UP, 1989.

Hopkins, Vivian. *Spires of Form: A Study of Emerson's Aesthetic Theory*. Cambridge, Mass.: Harvard UP, 1951.

Howe, Irving. *The American Newness: Culture and Politics in the Age of Emerson.* Cambridge, Mass.: Harvard UP, 1986.

Hughes, Gertrude Reif. *Emerson's Demanding Optimism.* Baton Rouge: Louisiana State UP, 1984.

• James, Henry. *Partial Portraits.* London: Macmillan, 1888.

Johnson, Linck C. "Reforming the Reformers: Emerson, Thoreau, and the Sunday Lectures at Amory Hall, Boston." *ESQ* 37 (4th quarter 1991): 235–89.

Kateb, George. *Emerson and Self-Reliance.* Thousand Oaks, Calif.: Sage Publishing, 1995.

Kazin, Alfred. *An American Procession.* New York: Knopf, 1984.

Lange, Lou Ann. *The Riddle of Liberty: Emerson on Alienation, Freedom, and Liberty.* Atlanta, Ga.: Scholars, 1986.

Lee, A. Robert. *Nineteenth-Century American Poetry.* New York: Barnes & Noble, 1985.

Leverenz, David. *Manhood and the American Renaissance.* Ithaca, N.Y.: Cornell UP, 1989.

Loewenberg, Robert J. *An American Idol: Emerson and the Jewish Ideal.* Lanham, Md.: UP of America, 1984.

Lopez, Michael. *Emerson and Power: Creative Antagonism in the Nineteenth Century.* DeKalb: Northern Illinois UP, 1996.

Loving, Jerome. *Emerson, Whitman, and the American Muse.* Chapel Hill: The University of North Carolina Press, 1982.

Matthiessen, F. O. *American Renaissance: Art and Expression in the Age of Emerson and Whitman.* New York: Oxford UP, 1941.

McMillin, T. S. *Our Preposterous Use of Literature: Emerson and the Nature of Reading.* Urbana: U of Illinois P, 2000.

Michael, John. *Emerson and Skepticism: The Cipher of the World.* Baltimore: Johns Hopkins UP, 1988.

Miller, Perry. *Errand Into the Wilderness.* Cambridge, Mass.: Belknap P of Harvard UP, 1956.

———. *Nature's Nation.* Cambridge, Mass.: Belknap P of Harvard UP, 1967.

• Morris, Saundra. "The Threshold Poem, Emerson, and 'The Sphinx.'" *American Literature* 69.3 (Sept. 1997): 547–70.

Mott, Wesley T. *"The Strains of Eloquence": Emerson and His Sermons.* University Park: The Pennsylvania State UP, 1988.

Neufeldt, Leonard. *The House of Emerson.* Lincoln: U of Nebraska P, 1982.

Newfield, Christopher. *The Emerson Effect: Individualism and Submission in America.* Chicago: U of Chicago P, 1996.

Packer, B. L. *Emerson's Fall: A New Interpretation of the Major Essays.* New York: Continuum, 1982.

Patterson, Anita Haya. *From Emerson to King: Democracy, Race, and the Politics of Protest.* New York: Oxford UP, 1997.

Paul, Sherman. *Emerson's Angle of Vision: Man and Nature in the American Experience.* Cambridge, Mass.: Harvard UP, 1952.

Pease, Donald. *Visionary Compacts: American Renaissance Writings in Cultural Context.* Madison: U of Wisconsin P, 1987.

• Poirier, Richard. *Poetry and Pragmatism.* Cambridge, Mass.: Harvard UP, 1992.

———. *The Renewal of Literature: Emersonian Reflections.* New York: Random House, 1987.

———. *A World Elsewhere: The Place of Style in American Literature.* New York: Oxford UP, 1966.

Porte, Joel. *Emerson and Thoreau: Transcendentalists in Conflict.* Middletown, Conn.: Wesleyan UP, 1966.

———. *In Respect to Egotism: Studies in American Romantic Writing.* New York: Cambridge UP, 1991.

———. *Representative Man: Ralph Waldo Emerson in His Time.* Rev. ed. New York: Columbia UP, 1988.

Porter, Carolyn. *Seeing and Being: The Plight of the Participant Observer in Emerson, James, Adams, and Faulkner.* Middletown, Conn.: Wesleyan UP, 1981.

Porter, David. *Emerson and Literary Change.* Cambridge, Mass.: Harvard UP, 1978.

Roberson, Susan L. *Emerson in His Sermons: A Man-Made Self.* Columbia: U of Missouri P, 1995.

Robinson, David. *Apostle of Culture: Emerson as Preacher and Lecturer.* Philadelphia: U of Pennsylvania P, 1982.

———. *Emerson and the Conduct of Life.* New York: Cambridge UP, 1993.

Rosenwald, Lawrence. *Emerson and the Art of the Diary.* New York: Oxford UP, 1988.

Rowe, John Carlos. *At Emerson's Tomb: The Politics of Classic American Literature.* New York: Columbia UP, 1997.

• Santayana, George. *Interpretations of Poetry and Religion.* New York: Scribner's, 1900.

———. "Emerson the Poet." In *Santayana on America.* Ed. Richard C. Lyon. New York: Harcourt, 1968.

Sealts, Merton M. *Emerson on the Scholar.* Columbia: U of Missouri P, 1992.

Simmons, Nancy Craig. "Arranging the Sibylline Leaves: James Elliot Cabot's Work as Emerson's Literary Executor." *Studies in the American Renaissance 1983.* Charlottesville: UP of Virginia, 1983.

Steele, Jeffrey. *The Representation of the Self in the American Renaissance.* Chapel Hill: U of North Carolina P, 1987.

Stoehr, Taylor. *Nay-Saying in Concord.* Hamden, Conn.: Archon, 1979.

Strauch, F. Carl. "Hatred's Swift Repulsions." *Studies in Romanticism* 7 (Winter 1968): 65–103.

———. "The Mind's Voice: Emerson's Poetic Styles." *ESQ* 60 (Summer 1970): 43–59.

———. "The Year of Emerson's Poetic Maturity: 1834." *Philological Quarterly* 34 (Oct. 1955): 353–77.

Teichgraeber, Richard F. *Sublime Thoughts/Penny Wisdom: Situating Emerson and Thoreau in the American Market.* Baltimore: Johns Hopkins UP, 1995.

Thomas, Joseph M. "Late Emerson: *Selected Poems* and the 'Emerson Factory.'" *ELH* 65 (1998): 971–94.

Thurin, Erik Ingvar. *Emerson as a Priest of Pan: A Study in the Metaphysics of Sex.* Lawrence: U of Kansas P, 1981.

Toulouse, Teresa. *The Art of Prophesying: New England Sermons and the Shaping of Belief.* Athens: U of Georgia P, 1987.

Van Cromphout, Gustaaf. *Emerson's Ethics.* Columbia: U of Missouri P, 1999.

———. *Emerson's Modernity and the Example of Goethe.* Columbia: U of Missouri P, 1990.

Van Leer, David. *Emerson's Epistemology: The Argument of the Essays.* New York: Cambridge UP, 1986.

von Frank, Albert. *The Trials of Anthony Burns: Freedom and Slavery in Emerson's Boston.* Cambridge, Mass.: Harvard UP, 1998.

• Waggoner, Hyatt H. *Emerson as Poet.* Princeton, N.J.: Princeton UP, 1974.

————. *American Poets from the Puritans to the Present*. Boston: Houghton, 1968.

Weisbuch, Robert. *Atlantic Double-Cross: American Literature and British Influence in the Age of Emerson*. Chicago: U of Chicago P, 1987.

• West, Cornel. *The American Evasion of Philosophy*. Madison: U of Wisconsin P, 1989.

Wilson, R. Jackson. *Figures of Speech*. New York: Knopf, 1989.

Wolfe, Cary. *The Limits of American Literary Ideology in Pound and Emerson*. New York: Cambridge UP, 1993.

Yoder, R. A. *Emerson and the Orphic Poet in America*. Berkeley: U of California P, 1978.

Zwarg, Christina. *Feminist Conversations: Fuller, Emerson, and the Play of Reading*. Ithaca, N.Y.: Cornell UP, 1995.

CRITICISM—COLLECTIONS

Bloom, Harold, ed. *Ralph Waldo Emerson*. Modern Critical Views Series. New York: Chelsea House, 1985.

Bode, Carl, ed. *Ralph Waldo Emerson: A Profile*. New York: Hill & Wang, 1969.

Buell, Laurence, ed. *Ralph Waldo Emerson: A Collection of Critical Essays*. Englewood Cliffs, N.J.: Prentice-Hall, 1993.

Burkholder, Robert E., and Joel Myerson, eds. *Critical Essays on Ralph Waldo Emerson*. Boston: G. K. Hall, 1983.

Cady, Edwin, and Louis J. Budd., eds. *On Emerson*. Durham, N.C.: Duke UP, 1988.

Capper, Charles, and Conrad Edick Wright, eds. *Transient and Permanent: The Transcendentalist Movement and Its Contexts*. Boston: Massachusetts Historical Society, 1999.

Donadio, Stephen, Stephen Railton, and Ormond Seavey, eds. *Emerson and His Legacy: Essays in Honor of Quentin Anderson*. Carbondale: Southern Illinois UP, 1986.

Garvey, T. Gregory, ed. *The Emerson Dilemma: Essays on Emerson and Social Reform*. Athens, Ga.: U of Georgia P, 2001.

Konvitz, Milton R., ed. *The Recognition of Ralph Waldo Emerson: Selected Criticism Since 1837*. Ann Arbor: The U of Michigan P, 1972.

————, and Stephen E. Whicher, eds. *Emerson: A Collection of Critical Essays*. Englewood Cliffs, N.J.: Prentice-Hall, 1962.

Levin, David, ed. *Emerson: Prophecy, Metamorphosis, Influence*. New York: Columbia UP, 1975.

Mott, Wesley T. and Robert E. Burkholder, eds. *Emersonian Circles: Essays in Honor of Joel Myerson*. Rochester, N.Y.: U of Rochester P, 1997.

Myerson, Joel, ed. *Emerson and Thoreau: The Contemporary Reviews*. New York: Cambridge UP, 1992.

————, ed. *Emerson Centenary Essays*. Carbondale: Southern Illinois UP, 1982.

————, ed. *A Historical Guide to Ralph Waldo Emerson*. New York: Oxford UP, 2000.

Neufeldt, Leonard Nick, ed. *Ralph Waldo Emerson: New Appraisals: A Symposium*. Hartford, Conn.: Transcendental Books, 1973.

Porte, Joel, ed. *Emerson: Prospect and Retrospect*. Harvard English Studies, vol. 10. Cambridge, Mass.: Harvard UP, 1982.

————, and Saundra Morris, eds. *The Cambridge Companion to Ralph Waldo Emerson*. New York: Cambridge UP, 1999.

Sealts, Merton M., Jr., and Alfred R. Ferguson, eds. *Emerson's Nature—Origin, Growth, Meaning*. Rev. ed. Carbondale: Southern Illinois UP, 1979.

Simon, Myron, and Thornton H. Parsons, eds. *Transcendentalism and Its Legacy*. Ann Arbor: The U of Michigan P, 1966.

Index of Titles and
First Lines of Poems